Introduction to

The M & E Handbook Series

Introduction to Business Law

P W D Redmond LLM
Barrister, formerly Senior Lecturer
in Commercial Law, City of London Polytechnic

Revised by
R G Lawson PhD
Consultant, formerly Senior Lecturer
in Law, University of Southampton

Sixth Edition

Pitman Publishing
128 Long Acre, London WC2E 9AN

A Division of Longman Group UK Limited

First published as *Mercantile Law* 1964
Second edition 1968
Third edition 1972
Fourth edition 1974
Fifth edition 1979
Sixth edition published as *Introduction to Business Law* 1990
Reprinted 1990
Reprinted in this format 1991

© Macdonald & Evans Ltd 1964, 1968, 1972, 1979
© Longman Group UK Ltd 1990

British Library Cataloguing in Publication Data
Redmond, P.W.D. (Peter William Dawson)
 Introduction to business law. – 6th ed.
 – (M & E handbook series).
 1. Great Britain. Commercial Law
 I. Title II. Lawson, R.G. (Richard Grenville), *1943–*
 III. Redmond, P.W.D. (Peter William Dawson).
 Mercantile laws
 344.106'7

ISBN 0 7121 1034 8

All rights reserved; no part of this publication may be reproduced, stored in a retrieval system, or transmitted in any form or by any other means, electronic, mechanical, photocopying, recording, or otherwise without either the prior written permission of the Publishers or a licence permitting restricted copying in the United Kingdom issued by the Copyright Licensing Agency,
90 Tottenham Court Road, London W1P OBR. This book may not be lent, resold, hired out or otherwise disposed of by way of trade in any form of binding or cover other than that in which it is published, without the prior consent of the Publishers.

Founding Editor: P.W.D. Redmond

Printed and bound in Singapore

Contents

Preface vi
Table of Cases vii
Table of Statutes xviii

Part one: The law of contracts

1 Nature and classification of contracts 3
   Nature of contracts; Classification of contracts; Void, voidable, and unenforceable contracts; Quasi-contracts

2 Formation of contracts 12
   Rules governing offers; Rules governing acceptance; Standard form contracts; Exemption clauses; Certainty of terms; Terms of a contract; Conflict of laws

3 Form, consideration and capacity 31
   Formal requirements; Valuable consideration; Rules relating to consideration; Contractual capacity; Capacity of minors

4 Void, voidable and illegal contracts 47
   Mistake; Misrepresentation and fraud; Duress and undue influence; Illegality; Contracts subject to a disabiltiy; Contracts illegal at common law; Contracts in restraint of trade

5 Discharge of contracts 72
   Discharge by performance; Discharge by agreement; Discharge by operation of law; Frustration of contracts; Breach of contract and remedies

Contents

6 Privity, assignment and negotiability 89
Privity of contract; Transfer and assignment of contracts

7 Fair trading 94
Freedom to contract; Fair Trading Act 1973; Monopolies and Mergers Commission; Restrictive trade practices; Trade Descriptions Act 1968; Miscellaneous matters

Part two: Agency and partnership

8 Agency 113
Formation of agency; Termination of agency; Duties of principal and agent; The authority of the agent; Special classes of agent

9 Partnerships 130
Nature and formation of partnerships; Dealings with outsiders; Rights and duties of partners; Dissolution of partnership; Limited partnership

Part three: Mercantile agreements

10 Sale of goods, supply of goods and services, hire and hire-purchase 151
The contract for the sale of goods; Terms implied by the Sale of Goods Act; Passing of ownership and risk; *Nemo dat quod non habet;* Performance of the contract; Rights of an unpaid seller against the goods; Actions for breach of contract; Auction sales; Contract for the supply of goods and services; Contracts of hire, hire purchase and conditional sale

11 Carriage of goods 188
Common carriers; Carriage by land; Carriage by air; Carriage by sea; Bills of lading; Charterparties

12 Insurance 203
Nature of insurance; Life insurance; Fire insurance; Accident, burglary and other forms of insurance; Marine insurance; State supervision

13 Bailment   216
   Nature and kinds of bailment

14 Arbitration and awards   224
   Arbitration; Conduct of proceedings

Part four: Negotiable instruments

15 Negotiable instruments   237
   Negotiability; Bills of exchange; Signature, delivery and indorsement; Liability of parties; Acceptance, payment and dishonour; Cheques; Promissory notes and miscellaneous instruments

Part five: Securities

16 Securities   281
   Summary of property law; Securities generally; Pledges and mortgages of personalty; Liens

17 Guarantees and indemnities   292
   Nature of guarantee; Position of the guarantor; Discharge of guarantor

Part six: Bankruptcy

18 Bankruptcy   307
   Commencement of proceedings; Proceedings after receiving order; The trustee in bankruptcy; Distribution of property; Payment of debts; Deeds of arrangement

   Appendix: 321
   Examination technique

   Index   326

Preface

Introduction to Business Law replaces the fifth edition of the classic *Mercantile Law*. This new edition has been necessitated by the many pieces of legislation that have been enacted, or implemented, since the fifth edition in 1979. The Consumer Credit Act, which had been on the statute book since 1974 with little of substance in force, was finally implemented in 1983. Since the previous edition of this book there have been two major upheavals in the law of bankruptcy, first by the Insolvency Act 1985 and second by the Insolvency Act 1986 which replaced the 1985 Act.

The Minors' Contracts Act 1987 is also, albeit over a smaller compass, an Act of major significance. At the same time, particularly in the field of sale of goods, case law has continued to make its vital presence felt. M & E Handbooks do not pretend to be works of profound scholarship, but they continue to provide the reader with a quick and easy way to grasp the fundamentals of our law.

Dr. R. G. Lawson: September 1989.

Table of cases

Akerheim v. De Mare [1959]
A.C. 789; [1959] 3 All E.R. 485   *57*
Alexander v. Railway Executive [1951]
2 K.B. 882; [1951] 2 All E.R. 442
217, 220
Alexander v. Rayson [1936] 1 K.B. 169
23, 63
Allcard v. Skinner [1887] 36 Ch. D. 145
61
Aluminium Industrie BV v. Romalpa
Aluminium Ltd [1976] 1 W.L.R. 676
170
Amalgamated Investment and Property
Co. Ltd v. Walker (John) & Sons Ltd
[1977] 1 W.L.R. 164; [1976] 3 All E.R.
509   *47, 81*
Amber Size & Chemical Co. v. Menzel
[1913] 2 Ch. 239   *69*
Andrabell, Re [1984] 3 All ER 407   *170*
Andrews v. Hopkinson [1957] 1 Q.B.
229; [1956] 3 All E.R. 422   *29, 182*
Anglia Television v. Reed [1972] 1 Q.B.
60; [1971] 3 All E.R. 690   *85*
Applegate v. Moss [1971] 1 Q.B. 406
[1971] 1 All E.R. 747   *78*
Appleson v. Littlewoods Ltd. [1939] 1
All E.R. 464   *4*
Arenson v. Casson Beckman [1977]
A.C. 405; [1975] 3 All E.R. 901   *227*
Armstrong v. Jackson [1917] 2 K.B.822
118
Ascherson v. Tredegar Dry Dock Co
[1909] 2 Ch. 401; [1908] 2 All E.R.
510   *297*
Ashbury Carriage Co. v. Riche (1875)
L.R. 7 H.L. 653   *43*

Ashington Piggeries Ltd v. Christopher
Hill Ltd [1972]   *156*
Associated Japanese Bank
(International) Ltd v. Credit du
Nord SA [1988] 3 All ER 902   *49*
Astley Industrial Trust v. Miller [1968]
2 All E.R. 36   *125*
Attorney General of Australia v.
Adelaide SS. Co. (1913) 15 C.L.R. 65
68
Attwood. v. Lamont[1920] 3K.B. 571   *70*
Attwood v. Maude (1868) 3 Ch. 369
140
Avery v. Bowden (1856) 5 E. & B. 714
79, 80, 83
Avon County Council v. Howlett [1983]
1 All ER 1073   *10*

Bainbridge v. Firmstone (1838) 8 A. &
E. 743   *37*
Balfour v. Balfour [1919] 2 K.B. 571;
[1918–1919] All E.R. 860   *3, 13*
Ballett v. Mingay [1943] 1 K.B. 281;
[1943] 1 All E.R. 143   *45*
Banbury v. Bank of Montreal [1917]
1 K.B. 409   *126*
Bank of England v. Vagliano Bros.
[1891] A.C. 107   *242, 253*
Banque Financière v. Westgate
Insurance, Financial Times, 12
August 1988   *56, 58*
Behn v. Burness (1863) 3 B. & S. 751
25, 200
Belfast Ropework Co. Ltd v. Bushell
[1918] 1 K.B. 210   *189*

Table of cases

Bell v. Lever Bros. [1932] A.C. 161 *49*

Benton v. Campbell, Parker & Co. Ltd [1925] 2 K.B. 410 *175*

Beresford v. Royal Insurance Co. [1938] A.C. 586 *205*

Bernstein v. Pamson Motors [1987] 2 All E.R. 220 *157, 167*

Berry v. Berry [1929] 2 K.B. 316 *75*

Beswick v. Beswick [1968] A.C. 58; [1967] 2 All E.R. 1197 *90, 91*

Bettini v. Gye (1876) 1 Q.B.D. 183 *26*

Bigg v. Boyd Gibbons Ltd [1971] 1 W.L.R. 913; [1971] 2 All E.R. 183 *14*

Birkham v. Drake (1841) 8 M. & W. 846 *133*

Birkmyr v. Darnell (1704) 1 Salk. 27 *294*

Blisset v. Daniels (1853) 10 Hare 493 *137*

Bolton v. Mahadeva [1972] 1 W.L.R. 1009; [1972] 2 All E.R. 1322 *73*

Bolton Partners v. Lambert (1889) 41 Ch. D. 295 *116*

Bond v. Gibson (1808) 170 E.R. 923 *133*

Bond Worth, Re [1980] Ch. 228 *170*

Boorne v. Wicker [1927] 1 Ch. 667 *142*

Borden (UK) Ltd v. Scottish Timber Products [1981] Ch 25 *170*

Boulton v. Jones (1857) 2 H. & N. 564 *12*

Bourgeois v. Weddell & Co. [1924] 1 K.B. 539 *228*

Brace v. Calder [1895] 2 Q.B. 253 *84*

Bradbury v. Morgan (1862) 1 H. & C. 249 *14*

Bradford Old Bank v. Sutcliffe [1918] 2 K.B. 833 *300*

Brandao v. Barnett (1846) 3 C.B. 519 *291*

Brewster v. Drennan [1945] 2 All E.R. 705 *221*

Brinkibon v. Stahag Stahl & Stahlwarenhandelsgesellschaft [1983] 2 A.C. 34 *17*

British Airways Board v. Taylor [1976] 1 W.L.R. 13; [1976] 1 All E.R. 65 *101*

British Concrete Co. v. Schelff [1921] 2 Ch. 563; [1921] All E.R. 696 *71*

British Movietonews Ltd v. London, etc., Cinemas Ltd [1952] A.C. 166; [1951] 2 All E.R. 617 *81*

British Westinghouse Electric & Manufacturing Co. Ltd v. Underground Electric Rail Co. Ltd [1912] A.C. 673. *84*

Brown v. Raphael [1958] Ch. 636; [1958] 2 All E.R. 79 *54*

Brown & Davis Ltd v. Galbraith [1972] 1 W.L.R. 997; [1972] 3 All E.R. 31 *27*

Browne v. Brandt [1902] 1 K.B. 696 *221*

Buckpitt v. Oates [1968] 1 All E.R. 1145 *5*

Burchell v. Wilde [1900] 1 Ch. 551 *142*

Burge v. Ashley & Smith Ltd. [1900] 1 Q.B. 744 *65*

Burnett v. Westminster Bank Ltd [1966] 1 Q.B. 742; [1965] 3 All E.R. 81 *266*

Bute (Marquess) v. Barclays Bank [1955] 1 Q.B. 202; [1954] 3 All E.R. 365 *266*

Byrne v. Van Tienhoven (1880) 5 C.P.D. 344 *15*

Campbell . Edwards [1976] 1 W.L.R. 403; [1976] 1 All E.R. 785 *227*

Candler v. Crane Christmas [1951] 2 K.B. 164; [1951] 1 All E.R. 426 *55*

Car & Universal Finance Co. v. Caldwell (1965) 1 Q.B. 525; [1964] 1 All E.R. 290 *164*

Carlill v. Carbolic Smoke Ball Co. [1893] 1 Q.B. 256 *13, 16, 17*

Carter (John) Ltd v. Hanson (H) Haulage (Leeds) Ltd [1965] 2 Q.B. 495; [1965] 1 All E.R. 113 *190*

Castellain v. Preston (1883) 11 Q.B.D. 380 *207*

Table of cases ix

Cehave N.V. v. Bremer [1976] Q.B. 44; [1975] 3 All E.R. 739 *83, 154*

Central Asbestos Co. Ltd. v. Dodds [1973] A.C. 578; [1972] 2 All E.R. 1135 *78*

Central London Property Trust v. High Trees, etc. [1947] K.B. 130; [1946] 1 All E.R. 256 *41*

Central Newbury Car Auctions v. Unity Finance [1957] 1 Q.B. 371 [1956] 3 All E.R. 905 *165*

Chandler v. Webster [1904] 1 K.B. 493 *81*

Chapelton v. Barry U.D.C. [1940] 1 K.B. 532 *20*

Chaplin v. Leslie Frewin (Publishers) Ltd. [1966] Ch.71; [1975] 3 All E.R. 764 *44*

Chapman v. Oakleigh Animal Products Ltd. (1970) 114 S.J. 432 *121*

Chappell v. Poles (1837) 2 M. & W. 867 *8, 61*

Charge Card Services, Re [1988] 3 All E.R. 702 *75, 169*

Charnock v. Liverpool Corporation [1968] 1 W.L.R. 1498; [1968] 3 All E.R. 473 *27*

Charrington Fuel Oil v. Parvant, *The Times*, 28 December 1988 *123*

Chaudhry v. Prabhakar [1988] 3 All E.R. 718 *118*

Chelmsford Auctions Ltd. v. Poole [1973] 1 Q.B. 542; [1973] 1 All E.R. 810 *113*

Chesworth v. Farrar [1967] 1 Q.B. 407; [1966] 2 All E.R. 107 *217*

Christoforides v. Terry (1924) A.C. 566 *121*

Churton v. Douglas (1859) Joh. 174 *143*

City Centre Properties Ltd v. Tersons Ltd [1969] 1 W.L.R. 772; [1969] 2 All E.R. 1121 *227*

Clayton's Case (1816) 1 Mer. 572 *75, 292*

Clough Mill v. Martin [1985] 1 W.L.R 111; [1984] 3 All E.R. 982 *170*

Clutton v. Attenborough [1897] A.C. 90 *253*

Cohen v. Roche [1927] 1 K.B. 169 *175*

Coldman v. Hill [1919] 1 K.B. 443 *217*

Coldunell v. Gallon [1986] Q.B. 1184 *61*

Coliseum (Barrow) Ltd, Re [1930] 2 Ch. 44 *78*

Collen v. Wright (1857) 8 E. & B. 647 *123, 324*

Colley v. Overseas Exporters [1921] A.E.R. 596 *168*

Combe v. Combe [1951] 2 K.B. 215; [1951] 11 All E.R. 767 *41*

Commissioners of Taxation v. English, Scottish & Australian Bank Ltd [1920] A.C. 683 *265*

Consolidated Tea & Lands Co v. Oliver's Wharf [1910] 2 K.B. 395 *188*

Cooper v. Phibbs (1867) L.R. 2 H.L. 149 *48*

Couchman v. Hill [1947] K.B. 554 [1947] 1 All E.R. 103 *323*

Coughlin v. Gillison [1899] 1 Q.B. 145 *218*

Courtney v. Tolaini [1975] 1 W.L.R. 297; [1975] 1 All E.R. 716 *24*

Coutts & Co. v. Browne-Lecky [1947] K.B. 104; [1947] 2 All E.R. 207 *45*

Couturier v. Hastie (1856) 5 H.L.C. 673 *49, 161*

Cowern & Nield [1912] K.B. 419 *46*

Craddock Bros. v. Hunt [1923] 2 Ch. 136 *63*

Craig, Re [1971] Ch. 95; [1970] 2 All E.R. 390 *60*

Craven-Ellis v. Canons Ltd [1936] 2 K.B. 403 *86*

Cricklewood Property Co. v. Leighton's Investment Trust [1945] A.C. 221 *79*

Cullinane v. British 'Rema' Mfg. Co. [1954] 1 Q.B. 292; [1953] 2 All E.R. 1257 *85*

Cummings v. Ince (1847) 11 QB. 112 *59*

Currie v. Misa (1875) L.R. 10 Ex. 153 *36*

x Table of cases

Curtis v. Chemical Cleaning & Dyeing Co. Ltd. [1951] 1 K.B. 805; [1951] 1 All E.R. 631   *19, 219*
Cutter v. Powell (1795) 6 Term. Rep. 320   *72*
Czarnikov v. Roth, Schmidt & Co. [1922] 2 K.B. 478   *228*

D. & C. Builders Ltd v. Rees [1966] 2 Q.B. 617; [1965] 3 All E.R. 837   *40*
Daily Office Cleaning Contractors Ltd v. Shefford [1977] R.T.R. 361   *85*
Dakin v. Lee [1916] 1 K.B. 566   *86*
Daulia Ltd v. Four Millbank Nominees (1978) 2 W.L.R. 621   *16*
David & Mathews, *Re* [1899] 1 Ch. 378   *142*
Davies v. Beynon-Harris (1931) 47 T.L.R. 424   *45*
Davies v. Collins [1945] 1 All E.R. 247   *219*
Davies & Co. v. William Old (1969) 113 S.T. 262   *14*
Davis (Clifford) Management v. W.E.A. Records Ltd. [1975] 1 W.L.R. 61; [1975] 1 All E.R. 237   *22*
Davis Contractors Ltd v. Fareham U.D.C. [1956] A.C. 696; [1956] 2 All E.R. 145   *80*
De Bussche v. Alt (1878) 8 Ch. D. 286   *119*
De Mattos v. Benjamin (1894) 63 L.J.Q.B.   *65*
Dearle v. Hall (1828) 3 Russ 1   *93, 237*
Decouvreur v. Jordan, *The Times*, 25 May 1987   *34*
Derry v. Peek (1889) 14 App. Cas. 337   *57*
Dickinson v. Dodds (1876) 2 Ch. D. 463   *15*
Discount Kitchens v. Crawford, *The Times*, 5 December 1988   *122*
Dodson v. Downey [1901] 2 Ch. 620   *138*
Dore v. Wilkinson (1817) 171 E.R. 648   *133*

Doyle v. White City Stadium [1935] 1 K.B. 110   *44*
Dunlop Pneumatic Tyre Co. v. New Garage Co. [1915] A.C. 79   *85*
Dunlop Pneumatic Tyre Co. v. Selfridges Ltd. [1915] A.V. 847   *38*

Eaglehill Ltd v. Neeham Builders Ltd [1973] A.C. 992; [1972] 1 All E.R. 895   *259*
Eastwood v. Kenyon (1840) 11 A. & E. 438   *33*
Eccles v. Bryant [1948] Ch. 93; [1947] 2 All E.R. 865   *16*
Edmunds v. Wallingford (1885) 14 Q.B.D. 811   *9*
Elder Dempster v. Zochonis & Co. [1924] A.C. 522   *196*
Eliason v. Henshaw (1819) 1 Wheaton 225   *14, 16*
Elkington v. Amery [1936] 2 All E.R. 86   *43*
English v. Dedham Vale Properties Ltd (1978) 1 W.L.R. 93   *120*
Entores v. Miles Far East Corpn. [1955] 2 Q.B. 327; [1955] 2 All E.R. 493   *17*
Esso Petroleum Co. v. Commissioners of Customs and Excise [1976] 1 W.L.R. 1; [1976] 1 All E.R. 117   *13*
Evans v. Merzario [1976] 1 W.L.R. 1078; [1976] 2 All E.R. 930   *19, 29*

Faccenda Chicken Ltd v. Fowler [1986] 3 WLR 288   *69*
Falkingham v. Victoria Rly. Commissioners [1900] A.C. 452   *228*
Felthouse v. Bindley (1862) 6 L.T. 157   *17*
Fibrosa Case [1943] A.C. 32   *81*
First National Securities v. Jones (1978) 2 W.L.R. 475   *7*
Fisher v. Bell [1961] 1 Q.B. 394; [1960] 3 All E.R. 731   *13*
Fisher & Sons, *Re* [1912] 2 K.B. 491   *132*

Table of cases xi

Fitch v. Dewes [1921] 2 A.C. 158 70
Fletcher v. Sledmore [1973] R.T.R. 371 101
Foakes v. Beer (1884) 9 App. Cas 605 74, 75
Foley v. Classique Coaches Ltd. [1934] 2 K.B. 1 24
Footman Bower & Co. Ltd., Re [1961] Ch. 443; [1961] 2 All E.R. 161 79
Foster v. Driscoll [1929] 1 K.B. 470 66
Foster v. Mackinnon (1869) L.R. 4 C.P. 704 19, 52
Frost v. Aylesbury Dairies Ltd. [1905] 1 K.B. 608; [1904–1907] All E.R. 132 158

Gadd v. Houghton (1876) 1 Ex. D. 357 124
Garner v. Murray [1904] 1 Ch. 57 142
Garnham, Harris & Elton Ltd. v. Ellis (Alfred W.) Transport Ltd [1967] 1 W.L.R. 940; [1967] 2 All E.R. 940 190
Geier v. Kujawa [1970] 1 Lloyd's Rep. 364 20
General Billposting Co. v. Atkinson [1909] A.C. 118 69
Gibson v. Manchester City Council [1979] 1 All E.R. 972 12
Goode v. Harrison [1871] 1861–73 All E.R. (Reprint) 813 130
Goodyear Tyre & Rubber Co. Ltd. v. Lancashire Batteries Ltd. [1958] 1 W.L.R. 857; [1958] 3 All E.R. 7 90
Griffiths v. Arch Engineering [1968] 3 All ER 217 218
Grist v. Bailey [1967] Ch. 532; [1966] 2 All E.R. 875 53
Guthing v. Lynn (1831) 2 B. & Ad. 232 13

Hadley v. Baxendale (1854) 9 Ex. 341 83, 84, 190
Haigh v. Brooks (1839) 10 A. & E. 309 39

Halfdan Grieg & Co. AS v. Sterling Coal & Navigation Corp. [1973] Q.B. 843; [1973] 2 All E.R. 1073 228
Hampstead Guardians v. Barclays Bank (1923) 39 T.L.R. 229 265
Harbutt's Plasticine Ltd. v. Wayne Tank and Pump Co. Ltd. [1970] 1 Q.B. 447; [1970] 1 All E.R. 225 23
Harris v. Nickerson (1873) L.R. 8 Q.B. 286 14
Harvey v. Facey [1893] A.C. 552 14
Hawkins v. Smith [1978] R.T.R. 49, D.C. 101
Heald v. Kenworthy (1855) 10 Ex. 739 125
Hedley Byrne & Co. v. Heller [1964] A.C.465; [1963] 2 All E.R. 575 55, 57
Helby v. Matthews [1895] A.C. 471 220
Helstan Securities Ltd. v. Hertfordshire County Council [1978] 3 All E.R. 262 91
Hendon v. Adelman, The Times, June 16, 1973 246
Hendy Lennox (Industrial Engines) Ltd v. Puttick Ltd [1984] 2 All ER 152 170
Herman v. Jeuchner (1885) 15 Q.B.D. 561 67
Hermann v. Charlesworth [1905] 2 K.B. 123 67
Herne Bay S.S. Co. v. Hutton [1903] 2 K.B. 603 79
Hibernian Bank v. Gysin & Hanson [1939] 1 K.B. 483 245
Hill v. Hill (William) Ltd [1949] A.C. 530; [1949] 2 All E.R. 452 65
Hitchman v. CBS Services, The Times, 10 June 1983 137
Hochster v. De La Tour (1853) 2 E.& B. 678 81
Hodgson v. Marks [1971] Ch. 892; [1971] 2 All E.R. 684 61
Hoenig v. Isaacs [1952] 2 All E.R. 176 73

Hollingworth v. Southern Ferries [1977] 2 Lloyd's Rep. 70 *20*
Holwell Securities v. Hughes [1974] 1 W.L.R. 155; [1974] 1 All E.R. 161 *18*
Home Counties Dairies Ltd. v. Skilton [1970] 1 W.L.R. 526; [1970] 1 All E.R. 1227 *70*
Hong Kong Fir Shipping Co. Ltd. v. Kawasaki Kishen Kaisha Ltd [1962] 2 Q.B. 26; [1962] 1 All E.R. 474 *83*
Horn v. Minister of Food [1948] 2 All E.R. 1036 *161*
Horsfall v. Thomas (1862) 1 H. & C. 90 *55*
Houghland v. Low (R.R.) (Luxury Coaches) Ltd [1962] 1 Q.B. 694; [1962] 2 All E.R. 159 *216, 217*
Household Fire Insurance Co. v. Grant (1879) 4 Ex. D. 216 *17*
Howard Marine v. Ogden (1978) 2 W.L.R. 515 *56*
Howatson v. Webb [1907] 1 Ch. 537 *52*
Hudgell Yeates & Co. v. Watson (1978) 2 W.L.R. 661 *139*
Hyde v. Wrench (1840) 3 Beav. 334 *16*

Imperial Loan Co. v. Stone [1892] 1 Q.B. 599 *42*
Inche Noriah v. Shaik Allie Bin Omar [1929] A.C. 127 *61*
Ingram v. Little [1961] 1 Q.B. 31; [1960] All E.R. 332 *51*
Interfoto Picture Library v. Stiletto Visual Programmes [1988] 1 All ER 348 *21*
Iqbal v. London Transport Executive, *The Times*, June 7, 1973 *122*

Jackson v. Horizon Holidays [1975] 1 W.L.R. 1468; [1975] 3 All E.R. 92 *90*
James, *Ex p.* [1874] L.R. 9 Ch. 609 *10*
Joachimsson v. Swiss Bank Corporation [1921] 3 K.B. 110 *126*

Johnson v. Agnew [1980] A.C. 367; [1979] 1 All E.R. 883 *87*
Jones (R.E.) Ltd v. Waring & Gillow Ltd [1926] A.C. 670 *255*

Karsales Ltd v. Wallis [1956] 1 W.L.R. 936; [1956] 2 All E.R. 866 *323*
Keever, *Re* [1967] Ch 182; [1966] 3 All E.R. 631 *267*
Keighley Maxsted v. Durant [1901] A.C. 240 *115*
Kelner v. Baxter (1886) L.R. 2. C.P. 174 *116*
Kemble v. Farren (1829) 6 Bing. 141 *85*
Kendall v. Hamilton (1879) 4 App. Cas. 504 *74, 133, 135, 295, 296*
Kennedy v. Thomassen (1929) 1 Ch. 426 *14*
Keppel v. Wheeler [1927] 1 K.B. 577 *118*
Kier v. Whitehead Iron Co. [1938] 1 All E.R. 591 *19*
Kleinwort Benson Ltd v. Malaysia Mining Corporation [1989] 1 All ER 785 *4*
Kores Ltd. v. Kolok Ltd. [1959] Ch. 108; [1958] 2 All E.R. 65 *70*
Krell v. Henry [1903] 2 K.B. 740; [1900–1903] All E.R. 20 *79*

Lacey (William) Ltd. v. Davis [1957] 1 W.L.R. 932; [1957] 2 All E.R. 712 *11*
Lampleigh v. Braithwaite (1615) Hob. 105 *40*
Lancashire Loans Ltd. v. Black [1934] 1 K.B. 380 *60*
Lane v. Williams (1692) 1 Eq. 1100 *133*
Lazenby Garages v. Wright [1976] 1 W.L.R. 459 *174*
Leaf v. International Galleries [1950] 2 K.B. 86; [1950] 1 All E.R. 693 *47, 49, 57*

Table of cases xiii

Leesh River Tea Co. Ltd v. British India S.N. Co. Ltd [1967] 2 Q.B. 250; [1966] 3 All E.R. 593 *199*
Lener v. L.C.C. (1949) 2 K.B. 683 *10*
Leng v. Andrews (1909) 78 L.J. Ch.80. *70*
Leslie v. Sheill [1914] 3K.B. 607; [1914–1915] All E.R. 511 *45*
L'Estrange v. Graucob [1934] 2 K.B. 394 *19, 51*
Levison v. Patent Steam Carpet Cleaning Co. [1978] Q.B. 69; [1977] 3 All E.R. 498 *23, 217, 218*
Lewis v. Averay [1973] 1 W.L.R. 510; [1973] 2 All E.R. 229 *51, 53*
Lilley v. Doubleday (1881) 7 Q.B.D. 510 *23, 219*
Lilly v. Smales [1892] 1 Q.B. 456 *123*
Limpus v. London General Omnibus Co. (1862) 1 H. & C. 526 *122*
Lloyd v. Grace, Smith & Co. [1912] A.C. 176 *121*
Lloyds Bank v. Bundy [1975] Q.B. 326; [1974] 3 All E.R. 757 *22, 60*
Loftus v. Roberts (1902) 18 T.L.R. 532 *23*
Logicrose v. Southend United Football Club [1988] 1 WLR 1256 *120*
Lombard North Central v. Butterworth [1987] QB 527; [1987] 1 All ER 267 *85*
London General Omnibus Co. v. Holloway [1912] 2 K.B. 72 *294*
London Joint Stock Bank v. Macmillan and Arthur [1918] A.C. 777 *127, 267*
Long v. Lloyd [1958] 1 W.L.R. 753; [1958] 2 All E.R. 402 *167*
Long v. Millar (1879) 4 C.P.D. 450 *34*
Lumsden & Co. v. London Trustee Savings Bank [1971] 1 Lloyd's Rep 114 *266*
Luxor Ltd v. Cooper [1941] A.C. 108 *121*

Macdonald v. Green [1951] K.B. 594; [1950] 2 All E.R. 1240 *65*

Mackenzie Mills v. Buono [1986] BTLC 399 *254*
Marsh v. Joseph [1897] 1 Ch. 213 *116*
Marshall (Thomas) (Exports) Ltd v. Guinle [1973] 3 W.L.R. 116 *69*
Martell v. Consett Iron Co. Ltd [1955] Ch. 363; [1955] 1 All E.R. 481 *67*
Maschi v. Lep Air Services [1972] 2 W.L.R. 1175 *300*
Mason v. Provident Clothing Co. [1913] A.C. 724 *70*
Mendelsohn v. Normand Ltd. [1970] 1 Q.B. 177; [1969] 2 All E.R. 1215 *19*
Merrit v. Merrit [1970] 1 W.L.R. 1211; [1970] 2 All E.R. 760 *4*
Mersey Docks and Harbour Board v. Coggins and Griffith (Liverpool) [1947] A.C.1; [1946] 2 All E.R. 345 *121*
Metropolitan Water Board v. Dick, Kerr & Co. Ltd [1918] A.C. 119 *80*
Microbeads AC v. Vinhurst Road Markings Ltd [1975] 1 All ER 529 *155*
Midland Bank v. Shephard [1988] BTLC 395 *61*
Miller (James) & Partners Ltd. v. Whitworth Street Estates Ltd. [1970] A.C. 583; [1970] 1 All E.R. 796 *29*
Mitchell v. London Borough of Ealing [1978] 2 W.L.R. 999 *217*
Monickendam v. Leanse (1923) 39 T.L.R. 445 *9, 35*
Montefiore v. Menday Motor Components Ltd [1918] 2 K.B. 241 *67*
Moorcock, The (1889) 14 P.D. 64 *24, 27*
Morris v. Baron [1918] A.C. 1 *75*
Morris v. Martin (C.W.) & Sons Ltd [1966] 1 Q.B. 716; [1965] 2 All E.R. 725 *218*
Morris v. Saxelby [1916] 1 A.C 688 *68*
Mount v. Oldham Corporation [1973] Q.B. 309; [1973] 1 All E.R. 26 *80*

xiv Table of cases

Napier v. National Business Agency [1951] W.N. 392; [1951] 2 All E.R. 264 *62*
Nash v. Inman [1908] 2 K.B. 1 *44*
National Bank of Nigeria Ltd v. Awolesi [1964] 1 W.L.R. 1311 *298*
National Carriers Ltd v. Panalpina (Northern) Ltd [1981] AC 675; [1981] All ER 161 *81*
National Provincial Bank v. Glanusk [1913] 3 K.B. 335 *294*
National Westminster Bank v. Morgan [1985] 1 All ER 821 *61*
New Zealand Shipping Co. v. Satterthwaite [1975] A.C 154; [1974] 1 All E.R. 1015 *90*
Nicolene Ltd v. Simmonds [1953] 1 Q.B. 543; [1953] 1 All E.R. 822 *24*
Nordenfeldt v. Maxim-Nordenfeldt Co. [1894] A.C. 535 *71*
Norman v. Bennett [1974] 1 W.L.R. 1229; [1974] 3 All E.R. 351 *101*
Norman v. Ricketts (1886) 3 T.L.R. 182 *74*
North & South Trust Co. v. Berkeley [1971] 1 W.L.R. 471; [1971] 1 All E.R. 980 *119*
North Ocean Shipping Co. v. Hyundai Construction Co. [1979] Q.B. 705; [1979] 3 WLR 419 *59*
Nowell v. Nowell (1869) 7 Eq. 538 *142*

Olley v. Marlborough Court Ltd [1949] K.B. 532; [1949] 1 All E.R. 127 *20, 221*
Orbit Mining & Trading Co. Ltd v. Westminster Bank Ltd [1963] 1 Q.B. 794; [1962] 3 All E.R. 565 *240*
O'Shea, Re [1911] 2 K.B. 981 *65*
Owen v. Tate [1976] Q.B. 402; [1975] 2 All E.R. 129 *297*

Parker v. Clarke [1960] 1 W.L.R. 286; [1960] 1 All E.R. 93 *5, 36*
Parker v. S.E. Railway (1877) 2 C.P.D. 416 *20, 22*

Parkinson v. College of Ambulance Ltd. [1925] 2 K.B. 1 *66*
Parsons v. Uttley Ingham [1978] Q.B. 791; [1977] 2 Lloyd's Rep. 522 *84*
Payne v. Cave (1789) 3 T.R. 148 *13*
Peachdart, Re [1984] Ch 131; [1983] 3 WLR 878 *170*
Pearce v. Brooks (1866) L.R. 1 Ex. 213 *66*
Pennington v. Crossley & Son (1897) 77 L.T. 43 *74, 262*
Percival Ltd v. L.C.C. (1918) 87 L.J.K.B. 677 *18*
Perry v. Stopher [1959] 1 W.L.R. 415 *229*
Pharmaceutical Soc. v. Boots etc.[1953] 1 Q.B. 401; [1953] 1 All E.R. 482 *13*
Phillips v. Brooks [1919] 2 K.B. 243 *51, 164*
Phoenix Assurance Co. v. Spooner [1905] 2 K.B. 753 *208*
Photo Production Ltd v. Securicor Transport Ltd [1980] AC 827 *25*
Pickard v. Sears (1837) 6 A. & E. 469 *162*
Pickering v. Ilfracombe Rail Co (1868) L.R. 3 C.P. 235 *61*
Pinnel's Case (1602) 5 Co. Rep. 117a *40, 74*
Planché v. Colburn (1831) 8 Bing. 14 *86*
Port Swettenham Authority v. Wu (T.W.) & Co. [1978] 3 All E.R. 337 *217*
Porter v. Freudenberg [1915] 1 K.B. 857 *41*
Porter v. Taylor (1817) 6 M. & S. 156 *133*
Prenn v. Simmonds [1971] 1 W.L.R. 1381; [1971] 3 All E.R. 237 *28*
Price v. Easton (1833) 4 B. & Ad. 433 *90*
Priest v. Last [1903] 2 K.B. 148 *158*
Printing & Numerical Co. v. Sampson (1875) L.R. 19 Eq. 462 *62*

R. v. Clarksons Holidays (1972) 57 Cr.
App. R. 38   *101*
R. v. Haesler [1973] R.T.R. 486   *101*
R. v. Hammerton Cars Ltd. [1976] 1
W.L.R. 1243; [1976] 3 All E.R. 758
101
R. v. Kylsant [1932] 1 K.B. 442   *55*
R. v. Pentonville Prison Governor, *ex p.*
Teja [1971] 2 Q.B. 274; [1971] 2 All
E.R. 11   *42*
R. v. Sunair Holidays [1973] 1 W.L.R.
1105; [1973] 2 All E.R. 1233   *101*
Rae v. Yorkshire Bank, *The Times*, 12
October 1987; [1988] BTLC 35   *266*
Raffles v. Wichelhaus (1864) 2 H. & C.
906   *3, 50*
Ramsgate Hotel v. Montefiore (1866)
L.R. 1 Exch. 109   *14*
Rann v. Hughes (1778) 7 Term. Rep.
350n   *31*
Rasnoimport v/o v. Guthrie & Co. Ltd
[1966] 1 Lloyd's Rep. 1   *199*
Read v. Price [1909] 1 K.B. 577   *78*
Reading v. Attorney General [1951]
A.C. 507; [1951] 1 All E.R. 617   *10*
Reid v. Metropolitan Police
Commissioners [1973] 1 Q.B. 551;
[1973] 2 All E.R. 97   *164*
Regent OHG v. Francesco of Jermyn
Street [1981] 3 All ER 327   *166*
Rhodes v. Forwood (1876) 1 App. Cas.
256   *121*
Rickards v. Oppenheim [1950] 1 K.B.
616; [1950] All E.R. 420   *74*
Ricketts v. Tilling [1915] 1 K.B. 644
122
Robb v. Green [1895] 2 Q.B. 315   *69*
Robertson v. Dicicco [1972] R.T.R. 431
101
Robinson v. Cook (1815) 6 Taunt. 336
73
Robinson v. Davison (1871) L.R. 6 Ex.
269   *80*
Robinson v. Graves [1935] 1 K.B. 579
152
Rogers v. Parish (Scarborough) [1987]
Q.B. 933; [1987] 2 All ER 232   *158*

Roscorla v. Thomas (1842) 3 Q.B. 234
39
Rose v. Plenty [1976] 1 W.L.R. 141;
[1976] 1 All E.R. 97   *122*
Rose & Frank v. Crompton Bros. [1923]
2 K.B. 261   *4*
Roselodge v. Castle [1966] 2 Lloyd's
Rep. 105   *204, 209*
Ross v. London County Bank [1919] 1
K.B. 678   *266*
Routledge v. Grant (1828) 4 Bing. 653
15
Rowland v. Divall [1923] 2 KB 500   *155*
Rowlandson v. National Westminster
Bank Ltd (1978) 1 W.L.R. 798   *267*
Salford Corporation v. Lever [1891] 1
Q.B. 168   *119*
Saunders v. Anglia Building Society
[1971] A.C. 1004; [1970] 3 All E.R.
961   *52*
Savills v. Scott [1988] 12 E.G. 115
124
Scammell v. Ouston [1941] A.C. 251
24
Scarf v. Jardine (1882) 7 App. Cas. 345
115
Scholfield v. Londesborough [1896]
A.C. 514   *266*
Scorer v. Seymour-Johns [1966] 3 All
E.R. 347   *71*
Scott v. Avery (1856) 5 H.L.C. 811   *225*
Scott v. Coulson [1903] 2 Ch. 240
48–49
Scriven v. Hindley [1913] 2 K.B. 564
50
Scruttons Ltd v. Midland Silicones Ltd
[1962] A.C. 446; [1962] 1 All E.R. 1
38, 90
Seddon v. N.E. Salt Co. [1905] 1 Ch.
326   *58*
Seymour v. Bridge (1885) 14 Q.B.D.
460   *117*
Seymour v. Pickett [1905] 1 K.B 715
75
Shadwell v. Shadwell (1860) 30 L.J.C.P.
145   *39*

xvi Table of cases

Shaw & Co. v. Symmons & Sons Ltd [1917] 1 K.B. 799 *216*
Shayler v. Woolf [1946] Ch. 320; [1946] 2 All E.R. 54 *226*
Shelley v. Paddock [1978] 2 W.L.R. 877; [1978] 3 All E.R. 129 *63*
Simkins v. Pays [1955] 3 All E.R. 10 *3*
Sims v. Midland Rly. [1913] 1 K.B. 103 *189*
Sky Petroleum Ltd. v. V.I.P. Petroleum Ltd. [1974] 1 W.L.R. 576; [1974] 1 All E.R. 954 *86*
Smart v. Saunders [1848] All E.R. (Reprint) 758 *117*
Smith v. Cox [1940] 3 All E.R. 546 *74*
Smith v. Wood [1929] 1 Ch. 14 *299*
Solle v. Butcher [1950] 1 K.B. 671; [1949] 2 All E.R. 1107 *53*
Sorrell v. Finch [1977] A.C 728; [1976] 2 All E.R. 371 *127*
Spiro v. Lintern [1973] 1 W.L.R. 1002; [1973] 3 All E.R. 319 *115*
Springer v. G.W. Railway [1921] 1 K.B. 257 *116*
State of Norway's Application, Re [1989] 1 All ER 745 *126*
Steinberg v. Scala Ltd [1923] 2 Ch. 452 *45*
Stekel v. Ellice [1973] 1 W.L.R. 191; [1973] 1 All E.R. 465 *132*
Sterns Ltd v. Vickers Ltd [1923] 1 K.B. 78 *162*
Stewart v. Casey [1892] 1 Ch. 104 *40*
Stilk v. Myrick (1809) 2 Camp. 317 *39*
Stocks v. Wilson [1913] 2 K.B. 235 *45*
Stockton v. Mason [1978] 2 Lloyd's Rep. 26 C.A. *203*
Strathcona S.S. Case [1926] A.C. 108 *91*
Suisse Atlantique etc. v. N.V. Rotterdamsche Kolen Centrale [1967] 1 A.C. 361; [1966] 2 All E.R. 61 *22, 25, 94*
Sumpter v. Hedges [1898] 1 Q.B 673 *73, 86*
Sutcliffe v. Thackrah [1974] A.C. 727; [1974] 1 All E.R. 859 *227*

Sykes (F. & G.) (Wessex) Ltd v. Fine Fare Ltd. [1967] 1 Lloyd's Rep. 24 *53*

Tai Hing Cotton Mill Ltd v. Liu Chong Hing Bank Ltd [1985] 2 All ER 847 *268*
Tarleton Engineering Co. v. Nattrass [1973] 1 W.L.R. 1261; [1973] 3 All E.R. 699 *101*
Taylor v. Caldwell (1863) 32 L.J.Q.B. 164 *79*
Taylor v. Laird (1863) 25 L.J. Ex. 329 *13*
Teheran-Europe Ltd v. Belton (S.T.) Ltd [1968] 2 Q.B. 545; [1968] 2 All E.R. 886 *124*
Thompson v. L.M.S. Railway [1930] 1 K.B. 41 *20*
Thompson v. Robinson [1955] Ch. 177; [1955] 1 All E.R. 154 *174*
Thornton v. Shoe Lane Parking Ltd [1971] 2 Q.B. 163; [1971] 1 All E.R. 686 *20*
Tiney Engineering Ltd v. Amods Knitting Machinery Ltd [1986] BTLC 324 *40*
Tomlinson v. Broadsmith [1896] 1 Q.B. 386 *134*
Torkington v. Magee [1903] 1 K.B. 644 *92*
Trade & Transport Incorporated v. Iino Kaiun Paisha (The Angelica) [1973] 1 W.L.R. 210; [1973] 2 All E.R. 144 *25*
Trego v. Hunt [1896] A.C. 7 *142, 143*
Tritonia Shipping Inc. v. South Nelson Forest Products Corpn. [1966] 1 Lloyd's Rep. 114 *226*
Trollope & Colls v. N.W. Metropolitan Regional Hospital Board [1973] 1 W.L.R. 601; [1973] 2 All E.R. 260 *27*
Tweddle v. Atkinson (1861) 1 B. & S. 393 *90*

UDT v. Taylor [1980] S.L.T. 28 *183*

Underwood Ltd v. Martins Bank [1924] All E.R. 230 *266*
Unigate v. Bentley (25 November 1986) *298*
United Dominions Trust v. Western [1976] Q.B. 513; [1975] 3 All E..R 1017 *52*
United Overseas Bank v. Jiwani 1977] 1 All ER 733 *266*
Universal Cargo Carriers Corpn. v.Citati [1958] 2 Q.B. 254; [1958] 2 All E.R. 563 *228*
Victoria Laundry v. Newman Industries [1949] 2 K.B. 528; [1949] 1 All E.R. 997 *84*
Vinden v. Hughes [1905] 1 K.B. 795 *253*

Wakeham v. McKenzie [1968] 1 W.L.R. 1175; [1968] 2 All E.R. 783 *36*
Walker v. Hirsch (1884) 27 Ch. D. 460 *131*
Walker v. Mottram (1881) 19 Ch. D. 355 *143*
Ward v. Bignall [1967] 1 Q.B. 534;[1967] 2 All E.R. 449 *173*
Ward v. Hobbs (1878) 3 Q.B.D. 150 4 App. Cas. 13 *54*
Warner Bros. v. Nelson [1937] 1 K.B. 209 *88*
Wathes (Western) Ltd v. Austins (Menswear) Ltd [1976] 1 Lloyd's Rep. 14 *23*
Watteau v. Fenwick [1893] 1 Q.B. 346 *114, 122*
Webster v. Cecil (1861) 30 Beav. 62 *53, 86*
Wheeler v. Young (1897) 13 T.L.R. 486 *261*

Table of cases xvii

White v. Bluett (1853) 23 L.J. Ex. 36 *39*
White & Carter Ltd v. McGregor [1962] A.C. 413; [1961] 3 All E.R. 1178 *82*
Williams v. Carwardine (1833) 4. B. & Ad. 621 *17, 18*
Williams v. Curzon Syndicate Ltd (1919) 35 T.L.R. 475 *217*
Williams v. Linnitt (1951) 1 K.B. 565; [1951] 1 All E.R. 278 *221*
Williams & Thomas, Re [1909] 1 Ch. 713; (1877) 7 Ch. D. 138 *209*
Wilson v. Brett (1843) 11 M. & W. 113 *217*
Wilson v. Carnley [1908] 1 K.B. 729 *66*
Wilson & Meeson v. Pickering [1946] K.B. 422; [1946] 1 All E.R. 394 *263*
Wings Ltd v. Ellis [1985] AC 272 *102*
With v. O'Flanagan [1936] 1 Ch. 575 *55*
Woods v. Martins Bank [1959] 1 Q.B. 55; [1958] 3 All E.R. 166 *127*
Woolcott v. Sun Alliance and London Assurance Co. (1978) 1 W.L.R. 493 *204*
Worcester Works Finance v. Cooden Engineering Co. Ltd [1972] 1 Q.B. 210; [1971] 3 All E.R. 708 *163*
Wormell v. RHM Agriculture (East) Ltd [1987] 3 All ER 75 *158*
Wythes v. Labouchere (1859) 3 De G. & J. 593 *293*

Yenidje Tobacco Co. Ltd., Re [1916] 2 Ch. 426 *140*
Yonge v. Toynbee [1910] K.B. 215 *118, 123*

Table of statutes

Administration of Justice Act 1970 *227*
Administration of Justice Act 1982 *229*
Arbitration Act 1950 *224*
Arbitration Act 1975 *224, 225*
Arbitration Act 1979 *224, 228*
Auctioneers Act 1845 *175*
Auctions (Bidding Agreements) Act 1969 *176*

Bail Act 1976 *6*
Banking and Financial Dealings Act 1971 *259*
Bankruptcy Act 1914 (repealed) *305*
Betting and Loans (Infants) Act 1892 (repealed) *46*
Betting, Gaming and Lotteries Act 1963 *65*
Bills of Exchange Act 1882 *32, 39, 45, 134, 239–69, 291*
Bills of Exchange Act (1882) Amendment Act 1932 *270*
Bills of Sale Acts 1878–1882 *153, 286–7*
Business Names Act 1985 *64, 132*

Carriage by Air and Road Act 1979 *194*
Carriage of Goods by Road Act 1965 *194*
Carriage of Goods by Sea Act 1971 *195, 196, 198, 200*
Carriers Act 1830 *191, 192*

Cheques Act 1957 *75, 260, 262, 264, 265, 270*
Civil Liability (Contribution) Act 1978 *133, 295*
Coinage Act 1971 *73*
Coinage Act 1983 *73*
Companies Act 1948 *15, 59*
Companies Act 1985 *32, 43, 56, 116, 131, 132, 144, 170*
Competition Act 1980 *95, 99*
Consumer Arbitration Agreements Act 1988 *230*
Consumer Credit Act 1974 *22, 29, 32, 62, 63, 64, 75, 76, 114, 151, 179–84, 220, 255, 271, 283–4, 288, 293, 294, 319*
Consumer Protection Act 1987 *77, 100, 174*
Copyright, Patents and Designs Act 1988 *32*
Corporate Bodies Contracts Act 1960 *32*
Criminal Law Act 1967 *67*
Currency and Bank Notes Act 1954 *73*

Diplomatic Privileges Act 1964 *41*

Enduring Powers of Attorney Act 1985 *114, 117, 118*
Estate Agents Act 1979 *128*

Factors Act 1889 *163, 322*
Fair Trading Act 1973 *94–7, 102*
Family Law Reform Act 1969 *43*

Table of statutes xix

Financial Services Act 1986 *64, 213*
Fire Prevention (Metropolis) Act 1774 *207*
Forgery and Counterfeiting Act 1981 *247*

Gaming Act 1835 *65*
Gaming Act 1892 *65*
Gaming Act 1968 *65*
Gaming and Wagering Acts 1835–1960 *65*

Honours (Prevention of Abuses) Act 1925 *66*
Hotel Proprietors Act 1956 *221*

Infants Relief Act 1874 (repealed) *44, 46*
Innkeepers Act 1878 *219, 222*
Innkeepers Liability Act 1878 *290*
Insolvency Act 1986 *300, 305–17*
Insurance Brokers (Registration) Act 1975 *214*
Insurance Companies Act 1982 *213, 214*

Judgments Act 1838 *229*
Judicature Acts 1873–1875 *52*

Latent Damage Act 1986 *78*
Land Charges Act 1972 *91*
Law of Property Act 1925 *9, 31, 32, 34, 91, 92, 93, 237, 271, 281, 286*
Law Reform (Contributory Negligence) Act 1945 *266*
Law Reform (Enforcement of Contracts) Act 1954 *33*
Law Reform (Frustrated Contracts) Act 1943 *81*
Law Reform (Married Women and Tortfeasors) Act 1935 *42*
Law Reform (Miscellaneous Provisions) Act 1934 *84*
Law Reform (Miscellaneous Provisions) Act 1970 *66*
Life Assurance Act 1774 *205, 207*

Limitation Act 1980 *7, 32, 39, 77, 78, 230, 261, 262, 300*
Limited Partnership Act 1907 *143–5*
Lloyd's Acts 1871–1982 *241*

Marine Insurance Act 1906 *32, 210, 211–13*
Married Women's Property Act 1882 *205*
Matrimonial Homes Act 1983 *316*
Matrimonial Proceedings and Property Act 1970 *42*
Mental Health Act 1983 *139*
Mercantile Law Amendment Act 1856 *34, 293*
Merchant Shipping Acts 1894–1988 *41, 196*
Minors' Contracts Act 1987 *46, 296*
Misrepresentation Act 1967 *28, 54, 56, 58, 141, 155*
Mock Auctions Act 1961 *176*
Monopolies Act 1948 *97*
Monopolies and Mergers Act 1965 *95*

Partnership Act 1890 *130, 131, 133, 134–8, 139–42, 295, 300*
Perjury Act 1911 *228*
Policies of Assurance Act 1867 *206*
Policyholders' Protection Act 1975 *214*
Powers of Attorney Act 1971 *114, 117*
Powers of Criminal Courts Act 1973 *308*
Prevention of Corruption Act 1916 *119*

Resale Prices Act 1976 *69, 90, 91, 95, 100*
Restrictive Trade Practices Act 1956 *99*
Restrictive Trade Practices Act 1976 *69, 95, 99–100*
Road Traffic Act 1960 *194*
Road Traffic Act 1988 *90, 91, 210*

Sale of Goods Act 1979 *24, 25, 26, 27, 42, 43, 49, 74, 151–76, 181, 290*

Table of statutes

Shops Act 1950   *63*
State Immunity Act 1978   *42*
Statute Law (Repeals) Act 1969   *63*
Statute of Frauds 1677   *32, 33, 34, 292, 293*
Statute of Frauds Amendment Act 1828   *293*
Suicide Act 1961   *205*
Sunday Observance Act 1677   *63*
Supply of Goods and Services Act 1982   *151, 177–8, 218*
Supply of Goods (Implied Terms) Act 1973   *22, 27, 154, 180*
Supreme Court Act 1981   *163*

Third Parties (Rights against Insurers) Act 1930   *209*
Torts (Interference with Goods) Act 1977   *163, 174, 219, 290*
Trade Descriptions Act 1968   *95, 100–2*

Trading with the Enemy Act 1939   *67*
Transport Act 1962   *188, 191, 192, 194*
Transport Act 1968   *188, 191*
Transport Act (London) 1969   *188*
Transport Act 1978   *5*
Transport Act 1985   *191*

Unfair Contract Terms Act 1977   *5–6, 21, 22, 23, 33, 56, 94, 156, 157, 158, 159, 177, 178, 190, 194, 198, 218, 224, 230*
Uniform Laws on International Sales Act 1967   *18*
Unsolicited Goods and Services Act 1971   *17, 33, 216, 217*
Unsolicited Goods and Services Act 1975   *17, 33, 216, 217*

Part one
The law of contracts

1
Nature and classification of contracts

Nature of contracts

1. Definition of contract. A contract is a legally binding agreement: that is, an agreement which will be enforced by the courts. Sir William Anson, in his *Principles of the Law of Contract*, defined a contract as 'a legally binding agreement made between two or more persons, by which rights are acquired by one or more acts or forbearances on the part of the other or others.'

2. Consensus ad idem. An agreement occurs when two minds meet upon a common purpose. This meeting of minds is called *consensus ad idem*, i.e. consent to the matter.

Absence of consensus may make a contract null and void, e.g. where the parties are fundamentally mistaken as to each other's intentions: *Raffles v. Wichelhaus* (1864), *see* 4: **5**.

3. Agreements which are not contracts. Mere domestic or social agreements are not usually intended to be binding, and therefore are not contracts.

EXAMPLES: (1) Three friends joined to enter a newspaper competition and agreed to share any winnings. HELD: They intended to create legal relations and their agreement was therefore a binding contract: *Simpkins v. Pays* (1955). (2) A husband promised to pay a housekeeping allowance to his wife. HELD: A mere domestic arrangement, with no intention to create legally binding relations, therefore no contract: *Balfour v. Balfour*

(1919). (However, where the spouses are legally separated it will be presumed that they did intend to create a legally binding contract: *Merrit* v. *Merrit* (1970).)

4. Intention to create legal relations. A binding contract is usually in the nature of a commercial bargain, involving some exchange of goods or services for a price (called the consideration).

But even such bargains will not be legally binding if the parties intend otherwise, i.e. do not intend to create legal relations.

In considering whether sufficient intention to create a binding contract is present, two situations are possible.

(*a*) Where the parties expressly deny the intention. Here the courts will almost invariably hold that there is no contract:

EXAMPLES: (1) A written commercial agreement described itself merely as an 'honourable pledge' and stated expressly that it was not 'to be subject to the jurisdiction of any court.' HELD: The parties did not intend to create legal relations, and the agreement was not a contract: *Rose & Frank Co.* v. *Crompton Bros.* (1923). (2) A condition imposed by a football pool laid down that the relationship should not be legally binding. HELD: No intention to create legal relations: *Appleson v. Littlewoods Ltd* (1939). (This is a common condition of entrance in football pools etc.) (3) In *Kleinwort Benson Ltd* v. *Malaysia Mining Corporation* (1989), the plaintiff bank agreed with the defendants to make a loan facility of up to £10m available to the defendants' wholly owned subsidiary which traded in tin. The defendants provided the plaintiffs with two 'letters of comfort' which stated that 'it is our policy to ensure that the business of [the subsidiary] is at all times in a position to meet its liabilities to you' under the loan facility arrangement. The subsidiary later went into liquidation and the plaintiffs sought the whole amount owing from the defendants. When the defendants refused to pay, the plaintiffs brought an action against them to recover the amount owing. The Court of Appeal ruled that a 'letter of comfort' stating that it was the policy of a company to ensure that its subsidiary was 'at all times in a position to meet its liabilities' in respect of a loan made by the lender to the subsidiary

1. Nature and classification of contracts 5

did not have contractual effect if it was merely a statement of present fact regarding the parent company's future conduct. On the facts, the comfort letters were in terms a statement of present fact and not a promise as to future conduct, and in the context in which the letters were written were not meant to be anything other than a representation of fact giving rise to no more than a moral responsibility on the part of the defendants to meet the subsidiary's debt.

(*b*) Where the parties do not expressly deny intention to create legal relations. Here it is in each case a question of construction for the Court to decide as to whether a contract is intended.

Thus: (*i*) in commercial agreements there is a rebuttable presumption that a contract is intended; but (*ii*) in social and domestic or family agreements there is a rebuttable presumption that no contract is intended. (But note that in each case the presumption is rebuttable by evidence to the contrary.)

EXAMPLES: (1) C persuaded her niece, P, to sell her own house and come and live in C's on condition that C would leave her house to P by will. After some time C ejected P from the house, and refused to leave it to her by will. P claimed damages for breach of contract. HELD: Although a family agreement, there was consideration for C's promise and evidence of intention to create legal relations. P was therefore entitled to damages: *Parker* v. *Clarke* (1960). (2) B and O habitually rode in each other's cars. Neither had insurance to cover injury to passengers. While in O's car, B was injured through O's negligence and sued for damages in contract or in tort. B had contributed to petrol costs and claimed this gave rise to a contract. O claimed: (*i*) there was no intention to create a binding contract; and (*ii*) B had consented to the risk of injury, since there was a notice in the car disclaiming liability to passengers. HELD: There was no contract, and B could not get damages (either in contract or in tort): *Buckpitt* v. *Oates* (1968).

If the car owner had advertised for someone to share petrol costs as he can do under the Transport Act 1978, it is more likely to be presumed that a contract exists. Note that under the Unfair Contract

Terms Act 1977, liability for negligence causing death or personal injury cannot be excluded: *see* 2: **18**.

Classification of contracts.

5. Contracts of record. These are obligations whose terms are recorded by a court of record, e.g. the Supreme Court or a county court.

They are not true contracts, since the obligations of the parties arise independently of any agreement and solely by reason of entry upon the court records. Two types are as follows.

(*a*) *Judgments*: by which a court imposes on some person a legal obligation, e.g. to pay damages. This judgment, when enrolled on the court records, constitutes a contract of record between the parties to the action in which the judgment was pronounced.

(*b*) *Recognisances:* written acknowledgment of a debt due to the Crown, made before a judge or authorised officer, and enrolled on the court records, e.g. a promise to 'keep the peace' or to attend court when called (an accused person in a criminal case was sometimes released on bail pending trial, on his own recognisance, i.e. a promise to attend when called, or to forfeit a stated sum of money); but *see* the Bail Act 1976, s. 8(3).

6. Contracts by deed (specialty contracts). A contract by deed is a promise written on paper or parchment, signed, sealed, and delivered (either actually or constructively) by the promisor to the promisee or his agent.

(*a*) *Execution of deed:* when a deed has been 'signed, sealed, and delivered' it is said to be executed, and it becomes legally binding immediately (unless it is directed to be held by the recipient in escrow).

(*b*) *Escrows:* an escrow is a deed executed subject to a condition that it is not to become effective until the condition is satisfied, e.g. the occurrence of a certain event, or the expiry of a period of time. Escrows are usually delivered to a neutral intermediary, with instructions not to complete delivery to the promisee until further instructions from the promisor.

1. Nature and classification of contracts 7

(c) *Sealing and delivery:* sealing a deed is usually done by affixing a disc or wafer of red paper to the bottom of the deed (next to the signature of the person signing). Delivery is largely a matter of intention; thus it may be by actually handing over the deed to the promisee, or by giving him the keys to a box in which the deed is kept (constructive delivery). It has been held by the Court of Appeal that, as a matter of law, it is not necessary for the due execution of a deed that there should be any physical seal attached to, or impression on, the paper. A document purporting to be a deed was capable in law of being such, even though it bore nothing more than an indication of where the seal should be. This particular document had a circle in which there were letters showing that this was where the seal should go. The signature had been placed across the circle and a witness had signed a clause saying that the document had been signed, sealed and delivered in his presence. The court said that this was enough evidence that the document had been executed by the party as his deed: *First National Securities Ltd v. Jones* (1978).

(d) *Indentures and deeds poll:* a deed to which there is only one party is called a deed poll, e.g. a deed of gift. A deed to which there are two or more parties is called an indenture, e.g. any contract by deed.

7. Characteristics of contracts by deed.

(a) *Consideration:* a deed does not require to be supported by valuable consideration, like simple contracts: *see below.*

(b) *Merger:* a special contract absorbs, or merges into itself, any earlier simple contract made between the same parties and on the same terms.

(c) *Limitation of actions:* an action for breach of a specialty contract can be commenced at any time within twelve years of the breach occurring; but an action for breach of a simple contract must generally be commenced within six years: Limitation Act 1980 and *see* 5: 15.

NOTE: Formerly a person who had signed a deed could not thereafter deny the accuracy of statements made therein, i.e he was estopped from denying the accuracy of the deed. This was called estoppel by deed. The rule is now obsolete and evidence is admissible to show that the deed in inaccurate, like any other contract.

8. Simple contracts. Simple or 'parol' contracts are by far the most common and important variety. They are informal contracts and may be made in any way — orally, in writing, or by implication from conduct. A person who takes a seat in a bus is entering into an implied contract to pay his fare.

A simple contract must possess the following essentials:

(a) An offer and unqualified acceptance thereof: see 2: **1–15**
(b) Intention to create legal relations: see 4 above.
(c) Valuable consideration: see 3: **10–12**
(d) Genuineness of consent (*consensus ad idem*), e.g. the agreement must not have been induced by fraud or coercion: see 4.
(e) Capacity of parties: see 3: **20–29**.
(f) Legality of objects: see 4: **25**.
(g) Possibility of performance: see 4.
(h) Certainty of terms: see 2: **21–23**.

Void, voidable and unenforceable contracts.

9. Void contracts. A void contract is one which is destitute of legal effect, i.e. of which the court will take no notice, for example, contracts void on the grounds of fundamental mistake: see 4: **1–7**.

Property transferred under a void contract can usually be recovered as the transferee can have no legal right to it: *Chappell* v. *Poles* (1837). But if the contract is void on the grounds that its object is illegal or contrary to public policy property transferred is generally irrecoverable; see 4.

10. Voidable contracts. A voidable contract is one which can be made void by one party, at his option. Thus a contract induced by fraud can be avoided by the party misled whenever he chooses: see 4.

11. Unenforceable contracts. An unenforceable contract is one which, though perfectly valid in all other respects, lacks some technical requirement needed to make it enforceable, e.g. some necessary written evidence. Such a contract will not be enforced by the courts unless and until the defect is rectified.

Thus contracts for the sale of land or any interest therein must be evidenced in writing, signed by the defendant, before they can be the subject of a successful action at law: Law of Property Act 1925, s. 40.

But such unenforceable contracts are not void, and therefore if they have been performed and property has been transferred the court will not intervene to set the agreement aside. Thus if A orally agrees to buy B's house and pays a deposit to B, then later changes his mind and refuses to sign a written contract to purchase the house, B will be unable to sue A for damages or performance of the contract but will be able to keep A's deposit, and the court will not assist A to recover it: *Monickendam* v. *Leanse* (1923).

Quasi-contracts

Sometimes the law imposes obligations of a contractual nature even where no true agreement exists between the parties. The object of such imposition is to prevent a person obtaining 'unjust enrichment' merely because there is no contract between himself and the person seeking the court's aid. The chief examples of such artificial or *quasi-contracts* are given below.

12. Money paid to the use of another. If A, at the express or implied request of B, pays to X a sum of money legally owed by B to X, the law implies a quasi-contract between A and B under which B must compensate A for the sum paid, e.g. where A pays rent owed by B to prevent the landlord seizing A's goods, which are stored at B's premises: *Edmunds* v. *Wallingford* (1885).

13. Accounts stated. Where there has been a series of transactions between A and B and they agree a balance, showing a sum payable by A to B, the agreed balance constitutes an 'account stated.' If B now has occasion to sue A for the amount so stated, he does not need to prove the details of the transactions between them but can rely entirely on the account stated as an admission of indebtedness.

14. Total failure of consideration. Where a valid contract has been made between A and B (supported by consideration) but subsequently B fails to provide any of the promised consideration, there is said to be a total failure of consideration and A can sue for the recovery of any money he has paid.

(Contrast the situation where the consideration has only partially failed, e.g. where A pays money for goods to B, who later delivers some but not all the good ordered. If A decides to accept this partial delivery, which he is not obliged to do, A can sue for damages for breach of contract, and the damages will be measured as the amount needed to compensate him for his loss, i.e. he is unlikely to recover all the money he has paid. If A decided that he will not accept partial delivery, which he is entitled to do, he can recover all the money paid.)

15. Money had and received. If A wrongfully obtains money to which B is legally entitled, B can sue A for recovery of the money in a quasi-contractual action for money had and receives, e.g where an employee receives money on behalf of his master and refuses to pass it on to the proper recipient.

Thus where B used the authority of his army uniform to assist him in smuggling activities, it was held that the army, as his employer, was entitled to the profits he had made out of the smuggling: *Reading* v. *Attorney-General* (1951).

16. Money paid under mistake of fact. Where money is paid under a mistake of fact it is generally recoverable by the payer, e.g. where an employer overpays wages under a mistake as to the employee's entitlement: *Lener* v. *LCC* (1949). Where a local authority had overpaid an employee it was estopped from recovering amounts where the employee had, in good faith and without notice of the claim and also in reliance on the representation, so changed his position that it would be inequitable to ask him to repay the money: *Avon County Council* v. *Howlett* (1981).

NOTE: Money paid under mistake of law is generally irrecoverable, since ignorance of the law is no excuse (*ignorantia juris neminem excusat*). But to this rule there are the following exceptions: (1) where the payee knew of or induced the payer's mistake; (2) where the money was paid to an officer of the court, e.g. a trustee in bankruptcy: *Ex parte James* (1874); (3) where money was paid under unjustified threat of legal proceedings against the payer; (4) where the payee was under a fiduciary duty to the payer, e.g. where paid by a client to his solicitor; (5) where the mistake of law is treated as one of fact, e.g. (i) mistake of foreign law; (ii) mistake as to private proprietary rights.

17. Quantum meruit. Where there is a breach of an essential condition in a contract, the injured party may either (*a*) seek to enforce the contract and sue for damages by way of compensation or (*b*) treat the contract as discharged, in which case he cannot sue for damages for its breach.

However, where he treats the contract as discharged, and has incurred expenses under it, he is entitled to bring a quasi-contractual action for compensation for work done. This is called a *quantum meruit* action (literally 'how much is it worth?'): *see* 5: **30**

In addition to providing a remedy in certain cases of breach of contract like those above, *quantum meruit* may also be used by the court to impose quasi-contractual liability where there is no contract between the parties but justice requires that some remuneration should be paid for work done.

EXAMPLE: L, a builder, did certain work for D on the understanding that D would give him a contract later for some major building work. D did not give L the expected contract and L sued for (1) damages for breach of contract or (2) *quantum meruit* relief. HELD: There was no contract between L and D and therefore L could not get damages, but he was entitled to reasonable remuneration on a quasi-contract: *William Lacey Ltd* v. *Davis* (1957).

2
Formation of contracts

In order to constitute a contract there must be an offer, express or implied by one person (the 'offeror'), and unqualified acceptance, express or implied, by the person to whom the offer is made (the 'offeree'). The House of Lords has emphasised that save in exceptional circumstances, a binding contract requires an offer and an acceptance: *Gibson* v. *Manchester City Council* (1979).

Rules governing offers

1. **How made.** An offer may be oral, written, or implied from conduct. Thus an implied offer is made by a bus company when it sends its buses along the street and stops them at fixed places to let people get on (the people who then get on a bus are thus accepting the offer by implication).

2. **To whom.** An offer may be specific, i.e. to a particular person or group of persons, or general, i.e. to the world at large.

   (*a*) *A specific offer* can usually be accepted only by the person or persons to whom it was made: *Boulton* v. *Jones* (1857).

   (*b*) *A general offer* can be accepted by anyone (and usually without prior notification of intention to accept).

   Thus a newspaper advertisement offering £100 to anyone who contracted influenza despite using a patent medicine in a specified way was held to be (*i*) a general offer, (*ii*) which could be accepted

2. Formation of contracts   13

by conduct, (*iii*) without previously notifying the offeror of the acceptance: *Carlill* v. *Carbolic Smoke Ball Co.* (1893).

3. Communication to offeree. The offer must be communicated to the offeree before it can be accepted.

EXAMPLE: A seaman helped to navigate a ship home, and before sailing wrote to the owners telling them of his intention and asking a particular wage for his services. The owners did not receive the letter of offer until the ship was nearly home. HELD: The owners had no reasonable opportunity to accept or reject the offer, therefore the seaman could not compel them to pay him wages for navigating the ship: *Taylor* v. *Laird* (1856).

4. Certainty of offer. The offer must be definite, not vague or illusory. Thus a promise to pay an increased price for a horse 'if it proves lucky to me' is too vague: *Guthing* v. *Lynn* (1831).

5. Intention to create legal relations. The offeror must intend the creation of legal relations, i.e. must intend that if his offer is accepted a legally binding agreement shall result: *see Balfour* v. *Balfour*, 1: **3**. The House of Lords had indicated that there is an intention to create legal relations where 'free' medallions are given away with so many gallons of petrol purchased: *Esso* v. *Commissioners of Customs and Excise* (1976).

6. An offer must be distinguished from the following.

(*a*) *An invitation to treat* (invitation to make offers), e.g. an auctioneer's request for bids (which will themselves be offers): *Payne* v. *Cave* (1789); or the display of goods in a shop window with prices marked upon them: *Fisher* v. *Bell* (1961); or the display of priced goods in a self-service store: *Pharmaceutical Soc.* v. *Boots, etc.* (1953). But indicating that medallions are given away with the purchase of petrol is probably not an invitation to treat, but is an offer: *Esso* v. *Commissioners of Customs and Excise* (1976).

(*b*) *A mere statement of intention*, e.g. an announcement of a forthcoming auction sale. Thus a person who attends the advertised place of auction could not sue for breach of contract if the sale were cancelled: *Harris* v. *Nickerson* (1873).

(c) *A mere communication of information* in the course of negotiations, e.g. a statement of the price at which one is prepared to consider negotiating the sale of a piece of land: *Harvey* v. *Facey* (1893).

> EXAMPLE: In discussing a possible sale of land, A wrote offering £20,000 and B replied: 'As you are aware that I paid £25,000 for this property, your offer of £20,000 would appear to be at least a little optimistic. For a quick sale I would accept £26,000 . . .' A replied accepting this offer. HELD: B's letter was an offer which A had accepted, so making a contract: *Bigg* v. *Boyd Gibbins Ltd* (1971) C.A.

7. An offer lapses under the following circumstances.

(*a*) *If either offeror or offeree dies before acceptance*: *Kennedy* v. *Thomassen* (1929). But the death of the offeror may not invalidate subsequent acceptance provided: (*i*) the offeree did not know of the death when he accepted, and (*ii*) the personalty of the offeror is not vital to the contract: *Bradbury* v. *Morgan* (1862).

(*b*) *If it is not accepted within* (*i*) the specified time (if any), or (*ii*) a reasonable time, if none is specified. What is a reasonable time depends on the circumstances. Five months has been held to be an unreasonable delay in accepting an offer to take shares in a company: *Ramsgate Hotel* v. *Montefiore* (1866).

(*c*) *If the offeree does not make a valid acceptance*, e.g. makes a counter-offer or conditional acceptance; or, if a particular manner of acceptance has been requested, he accepts in some other manner, e.g. by sending a letter by mail when a reply by hand was requested: *Eliason* v. *Henshaw* (1819), USA case.

> NOTE: Where a counter-offer is accepted the terms of the counter-offer then form the basis of the resulting contract (and not the terms of the original offer): *Davies & Co.* v. *William Old* (1969).

2. Formation of contracts 15

8. An offer may be revoked any time before acceptance.

(a) *Revocation must be communicated.* Until the offeree actually received the revocation, he is entitled to accept and so create a binding contract.

EXAMPLE: A sent an offer by cable to B on the 1st October requesting acceptance by the same method. B received the offer on 11th October and immediately cabled acceptance. On 8th October A had posted a letter revoking the offer, which did not reach B till after he had cabled his acceptance. HELD: B had accepted before receiving the revocation therefore a contract was made and the revocation was ineffective: *Byrne* v. *Van Tienhoven* (1880).

(b) *Indirect communication.* If the offeree learns of the revocation, he cannot later accept, even though he learns indirectly, e.g. where a prospective purchaser of land learns through a reliable third party that the offeror has sold the land to someone else. He cannot then accept the offer and sue the offeror for damages: *Dickinson* v. *Dodds* (1876).

NOTE: An offer for shares or debentures in a public company made as a result of an advertisement or prospectus cannot be revoked until the 3rd day after the opening of the subscription lists: Companies Act 1948, ss. 82, 86.

9. Options. An offer to keep an offer open for a specified time (an option) is not binding unless (a) made under seal, or (b) supported by valuable consideration, like any other simple contract: *Routledge* v. *Grant* (1828).

PROBLEMS: (1) A wrote offering to sell a car to B and to keep the offer open 'till Wednesday noon.' On Tuesday B learned through overhearing a conversation that A had sold the car to C on Monday. Can B now accept A's offer and sue A for damages for breach of contract? (*See* **8** above.) Would it make any difference to your answer if B had paid A 25p to keep the offer open till Wednesday? (*See* **9** above.) (2) A published an advert saying that he would pay £100 to the first person to swim a particular lake on 1st April. B swims the lake and claims the reward. A now says the advert was a joke. Can B compel payment of the reward? (*See* **2** and **5** above.)

NOTE: In a unilateral contract, which is where A promises to give B something if B first does something for A (see the example in (2) above), it has been said that 'although the offeror (A in our example) is entitled to require full performance of the condition which he has imposed and although short of that he is not bound, once the offeree (B in our example) has embarked on performance of the condition (as by starting to swim across the lake) there is an implied obligation on the part of the offeror not to prevent performance and he cannot revoke his offer': *Daulia Ltd* v. *Four Millbank Nominees Ltd* (1978).

Rules governing acceptance

10. **How made.** Acceptance may be oral, written or implied from conduct: *Carlill* v. *Carbolic Smoke Ball Co.* (1893).

But if a particular method of acceptance is required the offeree must accept in the prescribed manner: *Eliason* v. *Henshaw* (1819).

11. **Unqualified acceptance.** Acceptance must be unqualified and must correspond with all the terms of the offer.

A counter-offer or conditional acceptance operates as a rejection of the offer, and causes it to lapse. Thus where a house is offered for sale at £1000 and the offeree counter-offers £950, the offer lapses: *Hyde* v. *Wrench* (1840).

Similarly a conditional acceptance 'subject to a proper contract being drawn up' causes lapse of offer: *Eccles* v. *Bryant* (1948) (but an agreement 'subject to contract' would be binding if the phrase simply meant the agreement was to be subject to the terms of a contract already existing).

12. **Positive conduct.** There must be active acceptance: mere passive intention to accept is ineffective.

Thus an offer by letter containing the words, 'If I hear no more, I shall consider the horse is mine,' is incapable on its own of

2. Formation of contracts 17

constituting its own acceptance. There must be some positive communication of acceptance by the offeree; it would not be enough to show that the offeree intended to accept but died before writing a letter of acceptance: *Felthouse* v. *Bindley* (1862). Furthermore, where goods are sent unrequested to a private individual, they can become his after six months without him having to do anything: Unsolicited Goods and Services Acts 1971 and 1975.

13. Communication of acceptance. Normally an acceptance is ineffective unless and until communicated to the offeror.

EXCEPTIONS: (1) Where the offeror expressly or impliedly waives communication, e.g. where a general offer requires merely conduct as its acceptance: *Carlill* v. *Carbolic Smoke Ball Co.* (1893). Similarly an offer of a reward is accepted by doing what is required, without any previous communication: *Williams* v. *Carwardine* (1833). (2) Where the contract is made by post, or the post is envisaged as the means of communication, e.g. in most commercial contracts today. Here acceptance is complete as soon as it is posted, provided it is properly stamped and addressed: *Household Fire Insurance Co.* v. *Grant* (1879).

In postal cases therefore it does not matter if the letter of acceptance is lost in the post and never reaches the offeror: the contract is complete as soon as the letter of acceptance is posted. As a matter of commercial expediency the Post Office is treated as agent for the offeror, and communication to the agent is treated as communication to the principal.

The same rule applies to telegrams (but where the method of communication is instantaneous, e.g. telex or telephone, acceptance is not complete until it actually reaches its destination. *Entores* v. *Miles Far East Corpn.* (1955)). This point was confirmed by the House of Lords in *Brinkibon* v. *Stahag Stahl und Stahlwarenhandelsgesellschaft* (1983) where an offer was made by telex in Vienna and accepted by a telex message from London to Vienna. The House of Lords held that the contract was made in Vienna. The telex machines were in the offices of the respective parties, and the telexes were sent during business hours. The House of Lords left open the position where telexes are transmitted through agencies or outside office hours.

Where acceptance is to be 'by notice in writing to the offeree,'mere posting of acceptance does not constitute notice — actual delivery must be proved: *Holwell Securities* v. *Hughes* (1974).

NOTE: Mere posting is not sufficient in contracts governed by the Uniform Laws on International Sales Act 1967.

14. Motive for acceptance. No one can accept an offer in ignorance of its existence, but provided he knows of the offer his motive for accepting is usually irrelevant.

EXAMPLE: C offered a reward for information leading to the arrest of a criminal. W provided the information (knowing of the offer) but saying that she did so simply 'to ease her conscience.' Therefore C refused to pay the reward. HELD: Since W knew of the offer and accepted it, her motive for doing so was irrelevant and she was entitled to the money: *Williams* v. *Carwardine* (1833).

15. Tenders. A tender is a form of offer for the supply of goods or services, usually made in response to a request for tenders. Tenders take the following forms.

(a) *Single offer*, e.g. a tender to build a factory. Acceptance of such a tender constitutes a contract.

(b) *Standing offer*, e.g. a tender to supply goods as and when required. Here the tenderer must supply as and when agreed, whenever an order is made. But he cannot insist on any orders being made at all.

EXAMPLE: P tendered to supply goods up to a certain amount to the LCC over a certain period. The LCC's orders did not come up to the amount expected and P sued for breach of contract. HELD: Each order made a separate contract and P was bound to fulfil the orders made, but there was no obligation to make any orders at all: *Percival Ltd* v. *LCC* (1918).

2. Formation of contracts 19

(c) *Sole supplier*. The person seeking the tender may agree to take all his requirements for certain goods from the tenderer. This agreement does not oblige him to make any orders at all but if he does require goods within the category agreed he must take them from the tenderer: *Kier* v. *Whitehead Iron Co.* (1938).

Standard form contracts

There is an increasing tendency for an offeror to write out the contract entirely himself, and then demand that the offeree shall accept the detailed terms of the offer without modification.

The offeror may state all his terms in one document or, as in the case of railway tickets, may simply incorporate by reference certain standard conditions contained in another document. These 'offers with terms annexed' are subject to special rules. They include most forms of transport ticket, by air, sea, or rail, many printed leases, and most contracts for the supply of gas, electricity, etc.

16. If the contract is signed by the offeree, he is bound by all the conditions contained in the document signed even if he has not read them: *L'Estrange* v. *Graucob* (1934).

> EXCEPTIONS: (1) Where he can prove he signed the document under a fundamental mistake as to its nature (not merely as to its contents). This is the Common Law defence of *non est factum*. It covers, for example, cases where a person is induced to sign a cheque on the mistaken assumption that it is merely a guarantee: *Foster* v. *Mackinnon* (1869), and *see* 4: **7**. (2) Where he can prove that he was induced to sign as a result of a misrepresentation by the offeror, or the offeror's agent, whether innocent or fraudulent: *Curtis* v. *Chemical Cleaning & Dyeing Co. Ltd* (1951); *Mendelsohn* v. *Normand Ltd* (1970); *Evans & Son* v. *Merzario* (1976). (3) Where, in a hire purchase contract, the hirer signed the contract at a place other than the trader's place of business, the hirer can cancel his signature within four days of signing: *see* 10: **81**.

17. If the contract is unsigned, e.g. railway tickets, the offeree is bound by all the terms in the document or annexed to it if:

(a) a reasonable man would assume the document to be contractual, e.g. not merely a receipt for money: *Chapelton* v. *Barry UDC* (1940);

(b) reasonable care was taken by the offeror to bring the terms of the offer to his attention, e.g. by a notice 'for conditions see Company's rules and regulations' clearly displayed on the face of the ticket.

If the notice given is reasonable the contract is binding whether the offeree reads the conditions or not: *Parker* v. *S.E. Railway* (1877), or even whether the offeree is illiterate and unable to read them: *Thompson* v. *L.M.S. Railway* (1930); but if it is known that the person cannot read the clause because he is not English he is not bound by it: *Geier* v. *Kujawa* (1970);

(c) notice of annexed conditions must be contemporaneous with the making of the contract: *Olley* v. *Marlborough Court Ltd* (1949) and *Thornton* v. *Shoe Lane Parking Ltd* (1971).

NOTE: An oral contract could also contain exemption clauses, but they would clearly be harder to prove.

EXAMPLES: (1) C took a deck chair from a pile under a notice 'Hire of chairs—3d.' Later an attendant came round to collect the money and C paid him, receiving in return a ticket which said on it, 'The Council will not be liable for any accident or damage arising from hire of chair.' C put the ticket in his pocket without reading it, thinking it was merely a receipt. The chair collapsed and he was injured and sued the Council. HELD: The Council could not rely on the exclusionary notice since none of rules (a), (b), or (c) above was satisfied: *Chapelton* v. *Barry U.D.C.* (1940). (2) O registered at a hotel by signing the visitor's book, and then went to his room where was displayed a notice excluding the hotel's liability for articles lost. HELD: He made his contract when he signed the book, and the hotel could not rely on the exclusionary notice since it was not brought to his attention contemporaneously with the making of the contract: *Olley* v. *Marlborough Court Ltd* (1949). (3) B booked a passage for P and himself on D's vessel. He later received tickets containing an exlusion clause. It was held that the contract was made before the tickets were received, so the exclusion clause had no effect: *Hollingworth* v. *Southern Ferries* (1977).

2. Formation of contracts

(*d*) in *Interfoto Picture Library Ltd* v. *Stiletto Visual Programmes Ltd* (1988) a photographic library provided transparencies to an advertising agency on terms which specified that, if the transparencies were held for longer than 14 days, then a charge of £7.50 per day would be made until their return. The transparencies were held for more than 14 days and the library sought to rely on the above term. The Court of Appeal ruled that this term was particularly onerous since the usual rate at the time was £3.50 per week. Where a clause was unreasonable and extortionate in this way, then it would not be held to be part of the contract unless the party seeking to enforce it could show that it had been fairly and reasonably brought to the attention of the other party. This had not been done in this case, and so the term was not part of the contract.

Exemption clauses

18. Nature of exemption clauses. Annexed conditions are usually aimed at exempting the offeror from some legal liability to which he would otherwise be subject, e.g. liability for negligence in carrying out the contract. Exemption clauses are viewed with increasing disfavour by the courts, and both statutory and judicial restrictions have been imposed on their employment.

(*a*) *Statutory restrictions*. Examples are as follows.

(*i*) The Unfair Contract Terms Act 1977 limits the effectiveness of exclusion clauses in contracts of sale and hire-purchase. In contracts made by businesses with consumers, clauses excluding the implied terms as to description, quality and fitness for purpose are void. The use of such clauses is also unlawful by virtue of the Consumer Transactions (Restrictions on Statements) Orders 1976 No. 1813 and 1978 No. 127. In contracts made between businesses, clauses excluding these terms are valid if they can be shown to be reasonable.

(*ii*) The same Act also imposes restrictions on some exclusion clauses in contracts made on written standard terms or between a business and a consumer (i.e. whether or not on written standard terms). Clauses covered by this part of the Act, s. 3, are only valid if proved to be reasonable. The clauses which are covered by the Act are the following: (1) those which seek to exclude or restrict liability for breach of contract; (2) those which claim to allow a contractual performance 'substantially different' from that expected; (3) those which claim to allow no performance at all.

(*iii*) The Act states that no exclusion clause can restrict or exclude liability for negligence resulting in death or personal injury. Where negligence results in any other type of loss, such as damage to property, the clause is valid if it can be proved to be reasonable.

(*iv*) The Unfair Contract Terms Act, s. 8 makes void any term in a contract seeking to exempt a party from legal liability for any misrepresentation made by him before the contract was entered into (unless it is shown that the clause was reasonable).

(*v*) The Consumer Credit Act 1974, s. 173, makes void a term in a contract which excludes the protection afforded by the Act.

(*vi*) The Supply of Goods (Implied Terms) Act 1973 makes void clauses seeking to avoid the warranties as to title and merchantable quality implied into redemptions of trading stamps for goods.

(*b*) *Judicial restrictions.* The attitude of the courts can be summarised as follows.

(*i*) An exclusion clause will never be enforced unless adequate advance notice of it has been given to the other party: *Parker* v. *S.E. Railway* (1877).

(*ii*) Under the *contra proferentem* rule exclusion clauses are narrowly construed, against the person who inserted them.

(*iii*) Where the parties are on unequal footing, the court will more readily reject an exclusion clause designed to protect the stronger party. In one case, a young songwriter made an agreement with a publishing company for a five-year period. It was a particularly stringent standard form contract, for example, there was no obligation on the publishers to publish any of the songs produced. It was said, in finding that the contract could not be enforced, that the courts intervene to protect those 'whose power is weak against being forced by those whose bargaining power is stronger to enter into bargains which are unconscionable': *Schroeder (A) Music Publishing Co. Ltd* v. *Macaulay* (1974). See also *Clifford Davis Management* v. *W.E.A. Records Ltd* (1975) and *Lloyds Bank* v. *Bundy* (1975).

(*iv*) Where the exclusion clause seeks to evade liability for breach of a fundamental term of the contract the courts will be particularly reluctant to enforce it: *Suisse Atlantique etc.* v. *N.V.*

2. Formation of contracts 23

Rotterdamsche Kolen Centrale (1966); *Harbutt's Plasticine Ltd* v. *Wayne Tank and Pump Co. Ltd* (1970) and *Wathes (Western) Ltd* v. *Austins (Menswear) Ltd* (1976).

> EXAMPLES: Exemption clauses were thus held void where (1) a bailee for safe custody handed the goods deposited to a stranger instead of returning them to the bailor: *Alexander* v. *Railway Executive* (1951); (2) a bailee stored goods in a warehouse other than that agreed with the bailor and the goods were destroyed by fire: *Lilley* v. *Doubleday* (1881). Where a bailee loses goods, the onus is on him to show he was not in fundamental breach: *Levison* v. *Patent Steam Carpet Cleaning Co.* (1977).

19. Indemnity clauses. The Unfair Contract Terms Act 1977, s. 4, controls clauses which require a consumer to indemnify another party for liability which the latter might incur through negligence or breach of contract. Such clauses are now only valid if they are proved to be reasonable.

20. Guarantees. Where a guarantee is provided by a manufacturer that he will make good loss arising from negligence in the distribution or manufacture of the goods, this guarantee cannot exclude liability for the loss or damage: s. 5 of the 1977 Act.

> NOTE: The Consumer Transactions (Restrictions on Statements) Order 1976 requires all guarantees (whether given by the manufacturer or the retailer) to be accompanied by a statement to the effect that the consumer's rights against the retailer are unaffected.

Certainty of terms

21. Terms must be certain. It is for the parties to make their intentions clear in their contract. The court will not enforce a contract the terms of which are uncertain.

Thus an agreement to agree in the future ('a contract to make a contract') will not consititute a binding contract, e.g. a promise to pay an actress 'a West End salary to be mutually agreed between us' is not a contract, since the salary is not yet agreed: *Loftus* v. *Roberts*

(1902). Similarly an agreement providing that the price will be subject to later negotiations is not a contract, since contracts to negotiate are not known to the law: *Courtney* v. *Tolaini* (1975).

Similarly, where the terms of a final agreement are too vague, the contract will fail for uncertainty, e.g. sale of a van 'on hire-purchase terms' is too vague, since there are several types of hire-purchase agreement: *Scammell* v. *Ouston* (1941).

22. Id certum est quod certum reddi potest (*that is certain which can be reduced to certainty*).

An agreement which at first sight appears to be too vague may be enforced under the following conditions.

(*a*) If the parties themselves have provided machinery in the contract for resolving the uncertainty, e.g. where no price was fixed for the sale of petrol, but the agreement stated that all disputes should be referred to arbitration, it was held that the arbitrator could fix the prices and so resolve the uncertainty: *Foley* v. *Classique Coaches Ltd* (1934). Also where a five-year contract for the supply of chickens failed to state the number of chickens, but contained an arbitration clause, it was held that the numbers could be fixed by arbitration: *F. & G. Sykes (Wessex) Ltd* v. *Fine Fare Ltd* (1966).

(*b*) The deficiency can be remedied by the court implying a term, either (*i*) from the course of dealing between the parties in the past (if any), or (*ii*) from trade usages in the particular trade (if any), or (*iii*) where certain terms are implied by statute in similar contracts, e.g. the Sale of Goods Act 1979. The court may always imply a term into a contract to save it from collapse, but will do so only where it is clearly necessary and equitable: *The Moorcock* (1889).

23. Meaningless clauses. An agreement which is definite on the whole will be enforced, notwithstanding the presence of some meaningless or unnecessary words or phrases. The court in such a case will ignore the meaningless words and enforce the contract without them (unless the parties have given such a phrase a common meaning): *Nicolene Ltd* v. *Simmonds* (1953).

Terms of a contract

24. Express or implied terms. The parties may expressly state every term of their contract with varying degrees of precision; or they may simply agree the basic purpose of the contract and leave the detailed terms to be deduced from the surrounding circumstances.

Contractual terms are of two kinds: (*a*) conditions (main terms); or (*b*) warranties (subordinate terms). Whether a term is a condition or a warranty is a question of intention to be deduced by the court in the light of the surrounding circumstances. Mistaken use of the words 'condition' or 'warranty' by the parties will not be regarded as conclusive. And *see* 5: **25**.

25. Conditions. A condition is an essential term, which goes to the root of the contract, i.e. it may constitute the main purpose of the agreement, or one of several main purposes.

Breach of condition entitles the injured party to treat the contract as at an end: *Behn* v. *Burness* (1863), and *see* 5: **23–29**. (Alternatively he may treat the breach as a mere breach of warranty, claim damages and insist on the contract being performed.) The Sale of Goods Act 1979 declares, ss. 13 and 14, that the implied terms as to description, quality and fitness for purpose are conditions, as is the sellers's duty to have a right to sell: s. 12(1).

> NOTE: Fundamental term. This is a condition so important that it constitutes the fundamental purpose of the contract, in the view of the court. Where there is breach of such a term (fundamental breach) the courts will not allow the contract-breaker to escape liability by relying on even an express exemption clause unless the clause clearly covers the particular breach: *Suisse Atlantique etc.* v. *N.V. Rotterdamsche Kolen Centrale* (1966) H.L. (*the Suisse Atlantique* case); *Photo Production Ltd* v. *Securicor Transport Ltd* (1980).
>
> There is no fundamental breach where breach is caused by circumstances beyond the control of the non-performing party and an exemption covers the situation: *Trade & Transport Incorporated* v. *Iino Kaiun Paisha (The Angelica)* (1973).

26 The law of contracts

26. Kinds of condition.

(*a*) *Condition precedent*: a condition that the contract shall not bind one or both of the parties until such condition is fulfilled, e.g .'this contract is not to be binding until the war ends.'

(*b*) *Condition subsequent:* a condition under which the contract shall cease to be binding at the option of one party on the happening of a certain event, e.g. 'this contract shall cease to be binding if war breaks out.' This is called a determinable contract and remains binding until the condition subsequent is fulfilled; contrast a voidable contract, which can be made completely void at the option of one party.

(*c*) *Condition concurrent*: a condition under which performance by one party is made dependent on performance by the others at the same time, e.g. payment of price upon delivery of goods ordered.

27. Warranties.
A warranty is a subordinate term, subsidiary to the main purpose of the contract: Sale of Goods Act (S.G.A.) 1979, s. 61(1).

Breach of warranty entitles the injured party to sue for damages, but he cannot regard the contract as at and end and must perform his part of it.

> EXAMPLE: B promised to attend rehearsals for six days before a concert, but arrived in London only in time for two days' rehearsals, whereat G claimed the contract was discharged by breach of condition. HELD: Attendance at rehearsals was a warranty only and therefore the contract was not discharged, though G was entitled to damages: *Bettini* v. *Gye* (1876). The obligation on the seller that the goods are free from any encumbrance and that the buyer will enjoy quiet possession are *warranties:* Sale of Goods Act 1979, s. 12(2)

28. Ex post facto warranties.
Where a breach of condition occurs the injured party can (*a*) treat the contract as discharged, or (*b*) if he prefers he may treat the breach as breach of a warranty, go on with the contract and sue for damages.

In some cases he must adopt the second alternative, e.g. where in a contract for sale of goods the purchaser has accepted a substantial part of the goods, before discovering a breach of condition, he must treat the breach as a breach of warranty: S.G.A. 1979, s. 11(1).

This treating a breach of condition after it has occurred as though it were a breach of warranty is called treating it as breach of an *ex post facto* warranty, i.e. a warranty after the event.

29. Implied terms. The general rule is that the parties are presumed to have expressed their intentions fully.

The courts will only imply additional terms where it is strictly necessary to give effect to the clear intentions of the parties, or where custom or statute requires the implication: *The Moorcock* (1889), and *see* **22** *above*.

When express terms are clear and unambiguous, the court will only imply a term if it is clear that the parties must have intended it to form part of the contract: *Trollope & Colls* v. *N.W. Metropolitan Regional Hospital Board* (1973).

EXAMPLE: C's insurance company employed the X garage to repair C's car, damaged in an accident. The court found that there was an implied contract between C and X (contrary to X's claim that its only contract was with the insurance company). There was no term in this implied contract fixing the time to be taken for the repairs: X took eight weeks and C claimed damages for unreasonable delay. HELD: In the interests of business efficacy the court implied that repairs must be completed in a reasonable time (in this case five weeks) and awarded damages to C: *Charnock* v. *Liverpool Corporation* (1968); *see* also *Brown & Davis Ltd.* v. *Galbraith* (1972).

Occasionally, terms are implied by statute: e.g. Sale of Goods Act (contracts of sale); Supply of Goods (Implied Terms) Act (hire-purchase): *see* **25** and **27** above.

30. Terms and representations. Frequently during preliminary negotiations one of the parties (e.g. the seller of goods) may make a series of statements, or representations, to help persuade the other party to enter the contract. Whether such representations become terms in the contract (and so binding the maker) depends on the construction which the court puts upon them.

The test is: Did the plaintiff accept the representations as mere inducements, or did he insist that he would not enter into the contract unless the representations could be regarded as binding conditions or warranties?

The following rules apply.

(*a*) A representation will not be regarded as a term of the contract unless the parties so agree, expressly or by implication.

(*b*) If a representation is treated as a mere inducement, the plaintiff cannot sue for breach of contract if it proves untrue. (Though he may be able to avoid the contract and obtain damages on the grounds of misrepresentation: Misrepresentation Act 1967, *see* **4:11**).

(*c*) If a representation is agreed by the parties to be a term of the contract, the plaintiff's remedies will depend on whether it is regarded by the court as a condition or as a warranty: *see* **25** and **27** above and **5: 25**.

31. Construction of terms. In construing the terms of a contract the courts apply the following rules.

(*a*) Language used must be construed as far as possible in such a way as to give effect to the intentions of the parties.

(*b*) Words used must be presumed to have their normal literal meaning, unless the contrary is proved.

(*c*) Where there are two possible meanings, one legal and the other illegal, the legal meaning is to be preferred so as to render the contract enforceable (Illegal contracts are void: *see* **4: 25**.)

(*d*) The contract is to be construed most strongly against the party who drew it up (the *contra proferentem* rule: *see* **18**).

(*e*) Contracts are to be construed according to their proper law, i.e. usually the law of the country in which they were made: *see* **33**.

(*f*) If the contract fails to express the undoubted intentions of the parties, the court will rectify it so as to make it express such intentions: *see* **4:9** below.

NOTE: In construing the terms of a written contract the court cannot admit evidence of (1) the negotiations preceding contract, or (2) the parties' intentions during negotiations. *Prenn* v. *Simmonds* (1971) H.L.

2. Formation of contracts 29

32. Collateral contracts. Where A and B enter into a contract the rights and duties arising will normally affect only A and B: *see Privity of Contract*, 6: **1–4**. But sometimes if A was induced to enter into this contract by the representations of X, the court may imply a collateral contract between X and A, the consideration for which is A's agreement to enter into the contract with B.

EXAMPLE: X induced A to buy a car from B on hire-purchase. The hire-purchase contract was between A and B and X was not a party to it. The car was defective and injured A. X's statements as to the condition of the car were found to be false. HELD: A had no remedy against B, by reason of an exemption clause. But there was an implied collateral contract between X and A, under which A promised to buy the car from B; X was liable in damages for his false statements: *Andrews* v. *Hopkinson* (1956). *See also Evans* v. *Merzario* (1976).

NOTE: Under the Consumer Credit Act 1974, B would now be liable in contract for misrepresentations by his agent, X: *see* **10:84.**

Conflict of laws

33. Conflict of laws. There is an increasing tendency for mercantile contracts to be made between people in different countries and the question may then arise: which of several possible systems of law should the English court apply to resolve a dispute upon the contract?

The general rule is that the 'proper law' of a commercial contract is that which the parties have expressly or impliedly chosen. This will usually be the *lex loci contractus* – 'the law of the place of contracting,' but the court will not be restricted to the *lex loci* and will make an objective assessment as to which system of law is most closely and intimately connected: *James Miller & Partners Ltd* v. *Whitworth Street Estates Ltd* (1970).

34. Rules applicable to commercial contracts.

(*a*) Contractual capacity of a party is generally governed by the law of his domicil (the *lex domicilii*).

A person's domicil is the country in which he resides with intention to remain there permanently.

(*b*) Whether the contract itself is valid or not depends on the proper law of the contract, i.e. whether it is void, voidable, or enforceable.

(*c*) Questions relating to the form of the contract are decided by reference to the *lex loci contractus*.

(*d*) Procedural matters and questions relating to the evidence required to prove the contract are governed by English law.

(*e*) Questions relating to construction and discharge of the contract are governed by its proper law.

(*f*) The legality of the contract is assessed by the following rules:

(*i*) If the contract is illegal by the *lex loci contractus* it will not be enforced in Britain.

(*ii*) If the contract is legal where made, but would be illegal in the country in which it is to be performed, it will not be enforced in Britain.

(*iii*) A contract valid by its proper law but illegal by English law will not be enforced in Britain.

3
Form, consideration and capacity

Generally a contract can be made in any form, but in exceptional cases the law lays down a particular requirement, e.g. that the contract shall be by deed.

All simple contracts must be supported by consideration, that is by some element of exchange which is measurable in money or money's worth, e.g. goods in return for cash, or services in return for wages or goods.

Generally any person can make any sort of contract, i.e. has full capacity to contract. But certain special classes of person suffer from contractual incapacities of various kinds, e.g. minors.

Formal requirements

1. Generally no formality. Most contracts can be made in any form, i.e. orally, by writing, by telephone, telegram, or by deed.

But in the following special cases the law requires that a particular form shall be adopted, usually to provide better evidence of the terms and so prevent disputes.

2. Contracts void unless made by deed.

   (*a*) Promises of gifts: *Rann* v. *Hughes* (1778).
   (*b*) Transfers of British ships or shares therein.
   (*c*) Conditional bills of sale: *see* 16: **13**.
   (*d*) Certain documents creating or transferring estates or interests in land, e.g. conveyances of land, legal mortgages, and leases for more than three years: Law of Property Act 1925.

32 The law of contracts

Note that corporations' contracts formerly had to be made by deed if the contract was other than of day-to-day or trivial importance. This rule has been abolished and corporations can now make their contracts in whatever form would be appropriate to private individuals: Corporate Bodies Contracts Act 1960.

3. Contracts void unless fully written. These include the following.

(*a*) Bills of exchange: Bills of Exchange Act 1882, s. 3(1)
(*b*) Assignments of copyrights: Copyright, Patents and Designs Act 1988, s. 90(3).
(*c*) Contracts of marine insurance: Marine Insurance Act 1906.
(*d*) Transfers of shares in registered companies: Companies Act 1985.
(*e*) Acknowledgements of statute-barred debts: Limitation Act 1980.
(*f*) Articles of association of registered companies.
(*g*) Moneylending contracts.
(*h*) Contracts of employment.

NOTE: Hire-purchase contracts, credit sales and conditional sales are unenforceable unless written in proper form and signed by the hirer (or purchaser): Consumer Credit Act 1974, and *see* 10.

4. Contracts unenforceable unless 'evidenced' in writing. Note that these contracts are merely unenforceable unless in the required form, while those in **2** and **3** above are void: *see* 1: **9** (meaning of void, etc.).

Contracts in this class are as follows.

(*a*) *Contracts of guarantee* (*see* below): Statute of Frauds 1677, s. 4.
(*b*) *Contracts for the sale or other disposition of land* or any interest therein. This includes contracts to grant mortgages, leases, etc.: L.P.A., s. 40. (Notice that the contract to dispose of land must be evidenced in writing, while the conveyance which effects the actual transfer must by deed: *see* **2** above.)

3. Form, consideration and capacity 33

NOTE: Section 4, Statute of Frauds, originally applied to several types of contract besides guarantees, e.g. contracts for sale of goods worth more than £10, contracts not to be performed within one year of their making, executor's promises to pay a deceased's debts out of his own pocket, etc. But the L.R. (Enforcement of Contracts) Act 1954 reduced this list to guarantees only; the other contracts formerly covered by the Statute of Frauds can now be made in any form.

(c) *Contracts for directory entries*: Unsolicited Goods and Services Acts 1971 and 1975.

5. Contracts of guarantee. A guarantee is a contract 'to answer for the debt, default or miscarriage of another': s. 4, Statute of Frauds; that is, a contract to discharge another's obligations if that other fails to do so himself, sometimes called a contract of secondary liability (for guarantees generally, *see* 17).

Contrast contracts of indemnity: promises to discharge another's obligation or to ensure that it is discharged, i.e. a contract in which the indemnifier accepts primary liability (indemnities do not need to be evidenced in writing).

NOTE: Guarantees do not need to be evidenced in writing if they are merely part of larger transactions, e.g. where, on his appointment, an agent guarantees to make good losses incurred by his employer if any of the clients introduced by the agent fail to pay their debts. Here the guarantee is merely part of the contract of agency and therefore the whole contract can be oral if so desired: *Eastwood* v. *Kenyon* (1840).

The Unfair Contract Terms Act 1977, s. 5, makes special provision for the guarantee or consumer goods. Where loss or damage arises from a defect in the goods, and results from negligence in the manufacture or distribution of goods, no contract term or notice can exclude or restrict liability by referring to a guarantee. This rule only applies to 'third party' guarantees, such as those provided by manufacturers.

The same Act, s. 4, controls indemnity clauses. A consumer

34 The law of contracts

cannot be made to indemnify another for that other's negligence or breach of contract, unless the clause is reasonable (*see* 10).

6. Meaning of 'evidenced in writing.' The minimum of necessary written evidence suffices provided it contains all the material terms of the contract, i.e. any signed note or memorandum of material terms on any scrap of paper. The note or memorandum must contain the following.

(*a*) *The signature of the 'party to be charged'* or of his agent, i.e. the signature of the defendant in any action brought upon the contract. It need not be signed by the plaintiff in the action. Any writing by which the guarantor of a debt can be identified in a memorandum of the guarantee, and which shows an intention to adopt the guarantee, suffices as a signature for the purposes of s. 4 of the Statute of Frauds: *Decouvreur* v. *Jordan* (1987).

(*b*) *All material terms* of the contract, i.e. (*i*) names of the parties or sufficient identification; (*ii*) description of the subject matter, e.g. the address of a house being sold; (*iii*) the price or other consideration.

NOTE: Although, like other simple contracts, guarantees must be supported by consideration, the consideration does not need to be expressly stated in the memorandum of guarantee: Mercantile Law Amendment Act 1856.

7. When and how made. The note or memorandum can be made at any time after the contract is agreed, providing it is made (and signed by the defendant) before the contract is disputed in court.

It may consist of several documents, provided there is sufficient evidence to connect them beyond reasonable doubt, e.g. a letter headed 'Dear Sir' might be linked to the envelope which contained it, so identifying the recipient: *Long* v. *Millar* (1879).

PROBLEM: A contracted to buy a house from B, vacant possession to be given on completion. A paid a 10 per cent deposit and B gave him a signed receipt which identified the parties, stated the purpose of the deposit, but contained no mention of vacant possession. Would this receipt be a sufficient memorandum?

3. Form, consideration and capacity 35

Would it be sufficient if it mentioned the requirement as to vacant possession?

8. Effect of non-compliance. If a contract required to be evidenced in writing is not so evidenced it is unenforceable. Therefore, although it may be perfectly lawful, if one party breaks the contract the other cannot sue him for damages for breach of contract in the normal way (but he would be entitled to keep any deposit he had obtained: *see* 1: **11**).

NOTE: (1) The parties retain all other rights, except action in the courts. Thus, in an oral contract for the sale of land which fails through the fault of the purchaser, the vendor would be entitled to retain a deposit the purchaser had put down (normally 10 per cent) and the court would not assist the purchaser to recover it: *Monickendam* v. *Leanse* (1923) and *see* **1:11**. (2) If one party has fully performed his part of the contract the court may give him an order for specific performance, commanding the defendant to perform his side of the bargain despite the absence of written evidence (this is the equitable doctrine of part performance, and it applies only to contracts for the transfer of some interest in land).

9. The doctrine of part performance. An oral contract for the transfer of any estate or interest in land is unenforceable by action: L.P.A., s. 40. (Breach of such contract does not give rise to any action for damages.)

But if A has performed his part of the contract and B then refuses to perform his part, the court will intervene to save A from hardship by ordering B to perform his side of the bargain. Such an order for specific performance is discretionary and will only be granted under the following conditions.

(*a*) Where the contract is one of which specific performance can be ordered, i.e. where damages would be inadequate to compensate the plaintiff, and performance can be compelled without requiring constant supervision by the court: *see* specific performance, 5: **31**.

36 The law of contracts

(*b*) The act of part performance relied on is referable to the contract alleged: *Wakeham* v. *McKenzie* (1968)

(*c*) The act of part performance relied on is such that it would amount to fraud on the part of the defendant to take advantage of the absence of writing.

(*d*) There is sufficient oral evidence of the material terms of the contract.

EXAMPLES: (1) X orally promised a woman to leave her his house in his will if she gave up her own house and came to keep house and care for him until his death. She did so, but paid for her own board. When he died his will made no mention of the bargain. She sued the executors. HELD: Her actions were sufficiently clear part performance of the oral contract: *Wakeham* v. *McKenzie* (1968).
(2) P wrote asking C to come and live with him, and promised to leave his house to C. C sold his own home and went to live with P. Later P ejected C, who sued for specific performance. HELD: C's sale of his own home taken in conjunction with P's request and promise constituted a binding contract, under which C was entitled to live in O's house and to inherit it on O's death: *Parker* v. *Clarke* (1960).

Valuable consideration

10. Importance of consideration. The courts will not enforce a simple contract unless it is supported by valuable consideration, which is therefore an essential element in most contracts. (Consideration is not necessary in specialty contracts or contracts of record: *see* 1. **5–8.**)

11. Meaning of 'valuable consideration.' It has been defined as the price for which a promise is bought (Sir Frederick Pollock).

Consideration itself means 'some right, interest, profit, or benefit accruing to one party or some forbearance, detriment, loss of responsibility given, suffered or undertaken by the other': *per* Lush J., *Currie* v. *Misa* (1875).

Consideration therefore means the element of exchange in a bargain, and in order to satisfy the requirements of English law it must be valuable consideration, i.e. something which is capable of

3. Form, consideration and capacity

being valued in terms of money or money's worth, however slight. It may take the form of money, goods, services, a promise to marry, a promise to forbear from suing the promisee, etc.

12. Kinds of consideration.

(*a*) *Executory consideration,* i.e. where the consideration consists of a promise to do something in the future (such as to render a service at a future date).
(*b*) *Executed consideration,* i.e. where the act constituting the consideration is wholly performed.

Thus if X pays a shopkeeper now for goods which are promised to be delivered later, X has executed his consideration, but the shopkeeper is giving executory consideration, i.e. a promise to be executed in the future.

Rules relating to consideration

These require to be fully learned and understood, and are set out in detail below.

13. Necessity for consideration. Every simple contract must be supported by valuable consideration, otherwise it is normally void.

EXCEPTIONS: (1) *Gratuitous bailments.* A bailment is the delivery of a chattel to a hirer or borrower for some limited purpose or period. Most bailments are for reward, i.e. are supported by some payment, but even where the bailment is gratuitous it is still recognised as an enforceable contract: *Bainbridge* v. *Firmstone* (1838). (In such cases the courts tend to regard the owner's parting with possession of his chattel as sufficient notional consideration, so that this is not a real exception to the doctrine of consideration.)
(2) *Gratuitous services when performance commenced.* If A gratuitously promises to dig B's garden, and fails to do so, B cannot sue A for breach of contract since there is no consideration for A's promise. But it has been suggested that if A once commenced the digging, he would be under an obligation to exercise reasonable care in the work and could be sued for damages if he were negligent.

14. Legality of consideration. The consideration must be legal, e.g. not some illegal act, such as paying someone to commit a crime. If the consideration is illegal, the contract is void: *see* 4: **25–29**.

15. Consideration must move from the promisee. That is, a person seeking to enforce a simple contract in court must prove that he himself has given consideration in return for the promise he is seeking to enforce.

> EXAMPLE: D had supplied goods to a wholesaler, X, on condition that any retailer to whom X resupplied the goods should promise X not to sell them to the public without fulfilling stated conditions. X supplied goods to S upon this condition, but nevertheless S sold them in breach of stated conditions. HELD: There was a contract between D and X, and a contract between X and S, but none between D and S. Therefore D could not obtain damages from S. The main reason for this decision was the fact that D could not show that he himself had given any consideration for S's promise to X: *Dunlop Pneumatic Tyre Co.* v. *Selfridges Ltd* (1915) (affirmed in *Scruttons Ltd* v. *Midland Silicones Ltd* (1962), H.L.).

> NOTE: Compare this rule with the doctrine of privity of contract, *see* 6: **1**. In effect, in any contractual action, the court asks two implied questions which must be satisfied before the plaintiff can succeed in his action: (1) Is the plaintiff a party to the contract he seeks to enforce? (privity of contract) and (2) if so, has he given consideration for the promise he seeks to enforce? In *Dunlop Pneumatic Tyre Co.* v. *Selfridges Ltd* (1915) the plaintiff failed to supply satisfactory answers to both questions.

16. It must be something more than the promisee is already bound to do for the promisor. That is, the person seeking to enforce the promise must show that he himself has undertaken some obligation to the promisor beyond what he has already bound to do either (*a*) as part of his legal duty as a citizen, or (*b*) as part of a private contractual duty owed to the promisor.

> EXAMPLE: If a seaman deserts his ship — so breaking his contract — and is induced to return to his duty by the promise of extra

wages, he cannot later sue for the extra wages since he has only done what he was already contracted for: *Stilk* v. *Myrick* (1809). BUT NOTE: Performance by A of an existing duty owed to B will suffice to support a promise by C to A. Thus where A was engaged to marry B, and C promised A a sum of money to carry out this promise to B, it was HELD that A could sue C for the money as soon as he had performed his promise and married B: *Shadwell* v. *Shadwell* (1860).

17. Consideration must be real. That is, it must not be vague, indefinite, or illusory, e.g. a son's vague promise to 'stop being a nuisance' to his father: *White* v. *Bluett* (1853).

Although the consideration must be real, it need not be adequate, i.e. it is up to the parties to fix their own prices, and providing there is some definite valuable consideration the court will not set a contract aside merely because the price is inadequate: *Haigh* v. *Brooks* (1839).

But a ridiculously inadequate consideration may be prima facie evidence of misrepresentation or coercion: *see* 4.

EXAMPLE: A bought a guarantee contract from B which later turned out to be unenforceable. HELD: A had got what he wanted and could not later rescind the contract merely because it turned out to be worth less than he thought: *Haigh* v. *Brooks* (1839).

18. Consideration must not be past. That is, a promise made in return for some past service is unenforceable, e.g. where, having bought a horse, the purchaser promised to give the seller an extra sum because of his satisfaction with the purchase, it was HELD that the promise was unenforceable since it related to a past sale, and the purchaser was therefore receiving no new benefit as consideration for his new promise: *Roscorla* v. *Thomas* (1842).

EXCEPTIONS: Past consideration is sufficient in the following cases: (1) *To revive a statute barred claim,* a mere written acknowledgement is enough without any fresh consideration: Limitation Act 1980 (for limitation of actions, *see* 5: **15**). (2) *A bill of exchange can be supported* by any antecedent debt or liability: B.E.A. 1882, s. 27. (3) Where the past consideration was

40 The law of contracts

rendered in response to an earlier request by the person who subsequently promises to pay for the service rendered: the rule in *Lampleigh* v. *Braithwait* (1615). Here the promisor's request is held to imply a promise to pay a reasonable sum later and the subsequent promise to pay merely fixes the sum: *Stewart* v. *Casey* (1892).

EXAMPLE: A asked B to use his influence to obtain a royal pardon for A, who had committed a crime. B did as he was asked, and later (in consideration of this past service) A promised to pay B £100. HELD: B could enforce payment: *Lampleigh* v. *Braithwait* (1615).

19. Payment of a smaller sum will not discharge a liability to pay a larger: the rule in *Foakes* v. *Beer* (1884). This if A owes B £100 and B agrees to accept £50 in complete discharge of the debt there is nothing to stop B later changing his mind and suing for the remaining £50. In *Tiney Engineering Ltd* v. *Amods Knitting Machinery Ltd* (1986) the plaintiff and defendant were engaged in a transaction involving the sale of a knitting machine. The parties met and agreed that a commission should be paid. They later disagreed whether the commission should be 10% as the plaintiff claimed, or 5% as the defendant claimed. The parties met again, and the plaintiff accepted 5% in 'full and final settlement'. The court of appeal ruled that, since there was no consideration for the plaintiff's agreement to accept only 5% commission, and since there was no accord between the parties when the reduced commission was negotiated, it would not be inequitable to allow the plaintiff to receive the remaining 5%.

EXCEPTIONS: (1) *Where the smaller sum is paid in a form or manner different* from that originally intended, e.g. where the smaller sum is paid earlier than the debt was due, or where a money debt is settled in goods, or is paid by handing over 'a horse, hawk, or robe': *Pinnel's Case* (1602). But it is important to note that the creditor's acceptance of the smaller sum must be voluntary. Thus where a debtor put pressure on his creditor to accept a smaller sum, it was held that the acceptance was not binding: *D. & C. Builders Ltd* v. *Rees* (1966). (2) Where (*i*) the creditor promises to accept a smaller sum (*ii*) intending his

3. Form, consideration and capacity

position to be relied upon and (*iii*) the debtor alters his financial position in reliance on the promise, the creditor may be estopped from going back on his promise, even though it was unsupported by consideration.

EXAMPLE: A leased property to B at a rent of £2,500 p.a. but promised to accept half this sum during the war years, and B relied on this promise, making no attempt to earn the money necessary to pay the full rent. If later A went back on his promise and sued for the full rental the court would exercise its equitable discretion and estop A from retracting his promise: The High Trees Case (*Central London Property Trust v. High Trees House* (1947)).

This is an application of the principle of equitable estoppel, whereby a man may be prevented from denying any promise unconscionably even though it was unsupported by consideration. But the High Trees rule can only be raised as a defence, and not as a cause of action by the debtor, e.g. where a creditor has retracted his promise to accept a smaller sum and has forced the debtor to pay him the full amount, the debtor could not use the High Trees rule as the basis of an action to recover the extra money paid: *Combe v. Combe* (1951).

Contractual capacity

The general rule is that all persons have full capacity to make binding contracts, but the following exceptional cases exist: *see also* Minors, **25**, *below*.

20. Aliens. They have full capacity, save that they cannot own or hold shares in British ships: Merchant Shipping Act 1894, s. 1.

Aliens residing in countries at war with Britain are classed as enemy aliens (whatever their nationality). They cannot sue in British courts during war-time, but can be sued; and if sued they can defend the action, appeal, and lodge counter-claims in the normal way, either personally or through agents: *Porter v. Freudenberg* (1915).

21. Foreign sovereigns and diplomats. They have diplomatic immunity and cannot be sued in British courts, unless they voluntarily submit to the jurisdiction: Diplomatic Privileges Act 1964. *See also* the State Immunity Act 1978 (no immunity in respect of commercial contracts; or contracts to be performed wholly or partly in the United Kingdom).

NOTE: Diplomatic immunity does not arise until the diplomat's appointment is accepted by the British Government: *R. v. Pentonville Prison Governor, ex parte Teja* (1971).

22. Married women. They now have full contractual capacity, can sue or be sued in their own names, can be bankrupted for their debts, etc.: L.R. (Married Women & Tortfeasors) Act 1935.

The common law doctrine of a wife's agency of necessity was abolished under s. 41 of the Matrimonial Proceedings and Property Act 1970.

23. Mental patients and drunkards. Their contracts are voidable, if (*a*) they were so drunk or mentally unbalanced as not to understand what the contract was about, and (*b*) the other party was aware of this: *Imperial Loan Co. v. Stone* (1892). Such voidable contracts can be ratified during lucid or sober intervals.

The Sale of Goods Act 1979, s. 2, lays down that lunatics drunkards, and minors are bound to pay a reasonable price for necessaries (*see* Minors, **25**, *below*).

24. Corporations. A corporation is an artificial personality recognised by the law. Consequently it can only contract through human agents.

Under the *ultra vires doctrine* a statutory or registered corporation can only contract validly within the powers conferred upon it. Any contract which is *ultra vires* ('beyond the powers') is void. (Corporations created by royal charter are not subject to the doctrine, though if they exceed their authority their charter may be revoked.)

NOTE: (1) *Statutory companies,* i.e. those created by special Act of Parliament: the statute will define the company's powers, and any contract beyond those powers is void absolutely. (2) *Registered companies*, i.e. those incorporated by registration under the Companies Acts: their powers are not usually expressly

3. Form, consideration and capacity

stated, but such companies must register a memorandum of association in which the objects of the company must be stated. The powers of the company will then be such powers as are necessary to the achievement of its objects. Any contract which exceeds such powers is void and cannot be ratified even by the unanimous vote of all the members: *Ashbury Carriage Co.* v. *Riche* (1875).

Registered companies must also have articles of association which govern the internal regulations of the company, e.g. the rights of members and the powers of directors. If the directors exceed the powers delegated to them by the articles, the contract is voidable by the company and is said to be '*ultra vires* the directors' (but if the contract in question is within the powers of the company itself, it can ratify such contract if it wishes). But by the Companies Act 1985, s. 36(4), in favour of any person dealing in good faith with a company, any contract made by directors on behalf of the company is deemed to be *intra vires* and valid.

Capacity of minors

25. Minor's contracts. A minor attains his majority at the first instant of his eighteenth birthday: Family Law Reform Act 1969. (Formerly the age of majority was twenty-one.)

Minors' contracts are roughly divisible into three classes: binding, voidable, and void.

26. Contracts binding on minors.

(*a*) *Contracts for 'necessaries'*, i.e. goods and services necessary to maintain the minor, having regard to his social position.

Goods: A minor must pay (*i*) a reasonable price for goods (*ii*) suitable for his condition in life and (*iii*) to his actual requirements, at the time of (*iv*) sale and (*v*) delivery: S.G.A. 1979, s. 2 (before he can be made to pay for goods, the supplier must prove all five points).

Goods may be classed as necessaries even if they are luxuries, provided they have some actual utility and fit the actual requirements of the minor, e.g. an engagement ring: *Elkington* v. *Amery* (1936).

EXAMPLE: A minor ordered eleven fancy waistcoats, which could have been considered necessaries having regard to his financial position. HELD: He could not be made to pay for them, as he was already sufficiently supplied with articles of this kind: *Nash* v. *Inman* (1908).

NOTE: Goods necessary when ordered might have ceased to be necessary by the time they were delivered, e.g. where a minor orders a suit from a tailor but buys other suits before that ordered is actually delivered. Here the minor could not be made to pay the tailor.

(b) Beneficial contracts relating to education or training, e.g. contracts intended to assist the minor in training for adult life or for a career (non-educational contracts would not be binding even if beneficial).

These contracts are binding even if they contain one or two burdensome terms, providing they are on the whole beneficial to the minor.

EXAMPLES: (1) A contract signed by a young boxer, which was intended to protect him from exploitation during his minority, contained a clause by which he was to forfeit his pay for a fight if disqualified for fouling. HELD: This clause was burdensome but was binding since the contract as a whole was beneficial: *Doyle* v. *White City Stadium* (1935). (2) C contracted with a publisher to publish his autobiography, since his wife and child needed money. Later C tried to avoid the contract. HELD: It was binding, as beneficial in earning C a livelihood: *Chaplin* v. *Leslie Frewin (Publishers) Ltd.* (1966).

27. Contracts void against minors. The following are absolutely void against a minor:

(*a*) Contracts to repay money lent or to be lent.

(*b*) Contracts for goods supplied or to be supplied, other than necessaries.

(*c*) All accounts stated, e.g. IOUs: Infants Relief Act 1874, s. 1. But *see* now **29**, *below*.

3. Form, consideration and capacity 45

NOTE ALSO: (1) A minor incurs no liability by signing a bill of exchange (such as a cheque) whether as drawer, indorser, or acceptor: B.E.A. 1882. s. 22. (2) If a minor fraudulently misrepresents his age in order to obtain a loan of money, he cannot be made to repay the loan; nor can he be sued for damages for fraudulent misrepresentation, since this would amount to indirect enforcement of the void contract of loan: *Leslie* v. *Sheill* (1914). (3) If a minor obtains unnecessary goods under a void contract, he must return them if possible. If it is impossible (perhaps because the goods have been consumed), he cannot be made to pay any compensation for them: *Stocks* v. *Wilson* (1913). But if he has sold such goods to another person, he is liable for damages for the tort of conversion since he had no right to the goods and has dealt with them in a manner inconsistent with the rights of the true owner: *Ballet* v. *Mingay* (1943). (4) A minor can only recover money he has transferred under a void contract if he has received no benefit under the contract: *Steinberg* v. *Scala Ltd* (1923). (5) If an adult guarantees a loan made to a minor, the guarantee is void as well as the contracted loan: *Coutts & Co.* v. *Browne-Lecky* (1947). (6) If a minor borrows money to buy necessaries he must repay the loan, as the lender is placed in the position of the seller of the necessaries, i.e. subbrogated into the position of the seller.

28. Contracts voidable by a minor.

(*a*) *Contracts requiring express repudiation* before or within a reasonable time after reaching eighteen, e.g. contracts involving a continuing interest in property of a permanent nature, such as leases of land or contracts to take shares in a company

Such contracts will become binding unless repudiated by the minor within a reasonable time after his eighteenth birthday. Thus if a minor leases a flat, he must pay rent while he is in occupation but can repudiate the lease and escape liability for future rent any time until a few weeks after his eighteenth birthday; if he fails so to repudiate he will become liable for all the rent up to his majority and for the whole of the lease thereafter: *Davies* v. *Beynon-Harris* (1931).

(*b*) *Contracts not requiring express repudiation,* e.g. trading contracts and promises to marry. These remain voidable, even after the eighteenth birthday and even if confirmed by a fresh promise

46 The law of contracts

after eighteen, unless such promise was supported by fresh and additional consideration (otherwise any purported ratification by the minor after eighteen is ineffective: Infants Relief Act 1874, s. 2). But *see* now **29**, *below*.

Thus a trading contract is not binding on a minor even if beneficial to him. And if a minor in business received payment for goods sold by him, but refuses to deliver them, he cannot usually be sued for their value: *Cowern* v. *Nield* (1912).

29. Effect of Minors' Contracts Act 1987. Section 1 of this Act repeals the Infants Relief Act 1874. This applies to contracts made after 9 June 1987. Section 2 makes a guarantee of a minor's contractual obligations enforceable against the guarantor even though the main contractual obligation is not enforceable against the minor. This section ensures that the guarantee of a minor's unenforceable contract is as effective as if the minor had been an adult. Section 3 provides that where a minor has acquired property under a contract that is unenforceable against him, or which he has repudiated on the grounds of his minority, then he may be required by the court, where it considers it 'just and equitable' to do so, to return the property, or property which represents that which he has acquired. The Betting and Loans (Infants) Act 1891, which invalidated contracts to repay loans advanced during minority, has also been repealed.

4
Void, voidable and illegal contracts

These include contracts invalidated because they rest upon some fundamental mistake of fact (void), contracts induced by misrepresentation or coercion (voidable), and contracts which are contrary to some statute or to common law (void and illegal).

Mistake

1. Effect of mistake. The general common law rule is that mistake made by one or both parties in making a contract has no effect on the validity of the contract, e.g. where a person pays an excessive price for goods under a mistake as to their true value: *Leaf* v. *International Galleries* (1950).

However, where the parties contracted under a fundamental mistake of fact, the contract may be void if:

(*a*) the mistake is one of fact, and not of law or opinion; and
(*b*) the mistake is so fundamental as to negative the agreement.

For a mistake to be 'operative', it must exist at or before the time when the contract was made. Thus, there is no mistake where parties to a contract for the sale of a building believe it is not listed, if the listing occurs after they have made their contract: *Amalgamated Investment and Property Co. Ltd* v. *John Walker & Sons Ltd* (1976).

Mistake which thus renders a contract void is called 'operative mistake.'

2. Mistakes of law and of fact. Mistakes of law generally have no effect, since 'ignorance of the law is no excuse' (*ignorantia juris neminem excusat*).

In two exceptional cases, however, mistakes of law are treated as though they were mistakes of fact.

(a) *Mistake of foreign law*, since the laws of a foreign country require to be proved in British courts as ordinary facts.

(b) *Mistake as to private rights*, e.g. a right of property, as where a purchaser buys property which already belongs to him: *Cooper* v. *Phibbs* (1867) (*see* NOTE, '*Money paid under mistake of law,*' 1: **16**).

3. Operative mistakes of fact. It is difficult to deduce consistent principles from the numerous cases on the subject, but it is fairly well established that in the following cases a fundamental mistake of fact will avoid a contract.

(*a*) Common mistake as to the existence of the subject-matter of the contract.

(*b*) Mutual mistake as to the terms of an offer, or the identity of the subject-matter.

(*c*) Unilateral mistake as to the identity of the person contracted with.

(*d*) Unilateral mistake as to the nature of a contract signed.

NOTE: *Common mistake* is where both parties make the same mistake. *Mutual mistake* is where each makes a different mistake, i.e. they misunderstand one another. *Unilateral mistake* is where only one party is mistaken. Unilateral mistake is generally of no effect, unless (1) it concerns some fundamental fact, and (2) the other party is aware of the mistake. Thus unilateral mistake has no effect where it relates merely to an error of judgement by one of the parties.

4. Common mistake as to existence of subject-matter, i.e. where, unknown to both parties, the subject-matter has been destroyed before the contract was made.

EXAMPLES: (1) The sale of a life insurance policy on the life of a person who, unknown to purchaser or seller, is already dead: *Scott*

4. Void, voidable and illegal contracts 49

v. *Coulson* (1903). (2) The sale of goods which, unknown to the contractors, have already been destroyed: *Couturier* v. *Hastie* (1856), and Sale of Goods Act 1979, s. 6 (*see* 10: **28**).
NOTE: Mistakes as to the quality of the subject-matter generally have no effect. The general maxim of English law is *caveat emptor* ('let the buyer beware') and if a man mistakenly pays an unduly high price for something he has only himself to blame for the bad bargain.

EXAMPLES: (1) L paid a senior employee £50,000 compensation for loss of office when dismissing him before his contract had expired. Later L discovered that the employee had committed breaches of duty which would have entitled L to dismiss him without compensation. HELD: L could not recover the money on discovering the truth, since the House of Lords considered that the mistake related only to the quality of what was purchased, namely release from the contract of employment: *Bell* v. *Lever Bros.*(1932). (2) L bought from G a painting which both mistakenly believed to be by Constable and of great value. Later L discovered it was by an unknown artist and comparatively worthless. HELD: L could not avoid the contract, as his mistake related only to the quality of the subject-matter: *Leaf* v. *International Galleries* (1950). (3) In *Associated Japanese Bank (International) Ltd* v. *Credit du Nord SA* (1988), a party concluded a sale and leaseback transaction with the plaintiff in respect of four machines which were described by serial numbers. The obligations assumed by him as lessee of the machines were subsequently guaranteed by the defendant bank. The lessee paid the first quarterly rental but subsequently defaulted. It was then discovered that the machines did not exist. The plaintiff then sued on the contract of guarantee. The defendant contended that it was not liable on the guarantee, either because it was an express or implied condition precedent to the guarantee that the machines existed, or because the guarantee was void because of common mistake. The Commercial Court held that, given that the terms of the guarantee referred to the leasing of four identified machines and stipulated that any substitution of those machines could only be done with the consent of the guarantor, the only sensible construction was that the guarantee was subject to an express condition precedent that there was a lease in respect of existing machines. Alternatively, there was an implied condition precedent to the guarantee that the machines existed, having regard both to the fact that both parties were informed that the machines existed and to the express terms of the guarantee. The plaintiff's claim was dismissed. The court said that, except where a party seeking to rely on a mistake has no reasonable ground for his belief, a contract will be void for common mistake where both parties share the same mistake as to facts existing at the time the contract is made and the mistake renders the subject matter of the contract essentially and radically different from the subject matter which the parties believed to exist.

5. Mutual mistake.

(*a*) *As to the terms of the offer.* Where the parties misunderstand each other as to the terms of the offer, the contract will be void if the mistake is sufficiently fundamental.

Here there is no real concurrence of offer and acceptance, since the offeree is accepting on a mistaken understanding of what the offeror intended.

> EXAMPLE: A and B contracted to ship a cargo on the Peerless from Bombay. Unknown to either party there were two ships of the same name, and both were at Bombay and were due to sail on different dates. A had in mind one of the two ships, and B had in mind the other. HELD: The contract was void: *Raffles* v. *Wichelhaus* (1864).

(*b*) *As to the identity of the subject-matter*, i.e. the parties misunderstand each other as to what is to constitute the subject matter of the contract.

> EXAMPLE: At an auction X, misled by the catalogue, bid an absurdly high price for some tow (thinking it was hemp) and the auctioneer accepted the bid thinking that X was merely mistaken as to the value of tow. HELD: Contract void: *Scriven* v. *Hindley* (1913).

4. Void, voidable and illegal contracts 51

6. Unilateral mistake as to the identity of the person contracted with. Such mistake will only operate to avoid the contract where:

(a) the identity of the person contracted with is of fundamental importance; and
(b) this is made clear by the party mistaken before or at the time of contracting (so that the other party knows of the mistake).

NOTE: Where the parties contracted 'face to face' the presumption is that there can be no mistake as to identity: *Lewis* v. *Averay* (1973). (But this presumption may be rebutted by clear evidence to the contrary: *Ingram* v. *Little* (1960).)

EXAMPLES: (1) A rogue, X, entered a jeweller's and offered to buy goods. His offer was accepted, and he then offered to pay by cheque. The jeweller accepted the cheque, but said delivery would be delayed until the cheque was cleared. The rogue then said he was a well-known person and asked to take some of the jewels immediately. Deceived as to his identity, the jeweller let him take some of the jewels. X took the goods and sold them to a pawnbroker, and the cheque proved worthless. HELD: The contract was made before the identity became important, therefore it was not void on the ground of mistake: *Phillips* v. *Brooks* (1919) (the contract was probably voidable on the ground of misrepresentation). (2) L advertised his car for sale and B, a rogue, answered, describing himself as a well-known film-star. L was impressed and accepted B's cheque after B had produced a film-studio admission card as proof of identity. B then took the car and sold it to A, a *bona fide* purchaser. When L discovered the fraud he sued A to recover the car. HELD: L intended to contract with the man he met 'face to face' and the contract was therefore not void for mistake, but merely voidable for misrepresentation: *Lewis* v. *Averay* (1973) C.A.

7. Unilateral mistake as to nature of a contract signed. Generally a person who signs a contract is bound by it, even if he has not read it: *L'Estrange* v. *Graucob, see* 2: **16**.

52 The law of contracts

But a person who signs a document under a fundamental mistake as to its nature may have it avoided, e.g. where A is induced to sign a negotiable instrument believing it is merely a guarantee: *Foster* v. *Mackinnon* (1869). Notice that the mistake must be as to the fundamental legal nature of the document — not merely as to its contents.

> EXAMPLES: (1) A, who was senile, was persuaded to sign a bill of exchange under the misapprehension that it was a guarantee. HELD: The bill was void for mistake: *Foster* v. *Mackinnon* (1869). (2) A executed a transfer of land under a misapprehension as to its contents and effect. HELD: Contract not void. The mistake was not sufficiently fundamental: *Howatson* v. *Webb* (1907). (3) G an elderly lady, signed without reading a document which L informed her was a gift transferring her house to her nephew P. In fact it was a transfer on sale (for £3000) to L. G. sought to have the sale annulled. HELD: She failed on the facts of the case because: (*a*) the document was not radically different in type from what she thought she was signing; (*b*) she was careless and (*c*) she had failed in her evidence to show that she would not have signed had she known the true facts: *Saunders* v. *Anglia Building Society* (1971) H.L. (4) In another case, a person signed a form in blank addressed to a finance house, believing it to be a hire-purchase agreement. It was, in fact, a loan agreement. It was held that a binding contract existed between the signatory and the finance house. The signatory was under a duty of care to ensure that the completed document represented his true intention. He had not shown he had acted carefully, so he was bound by his signature: *U.D.T.* v. *Western* (1975).

8. Mistake in equity. The common law rules relating to mistake stated above render the contract either completely void or completely valid, even though neither conclusion may be completely just.

But since the Judicature Acts (1873–75) allow equity to be administered in all courts to modify the common law in the interests of justice, the courts have used equitable principles to achieve a

4. Void, voidable and illegal contracts

compromise result where it would be unjust to one or both of the parties to apply the common law doctrine rigidly in cases of mistake. Equity will thus intervene for the following purposes.

(*a*) *To rectify* (amend) a written instrument containing patent errors of expression.

(*b*) *To refuse to order specific performance* of a contract against a defendant who is labouring under a mistake such that it would be grossly unjust to compel him to perform his contract, e.g. where A, by a slip of the pen, writes offering to sell land to B for '£1,250' when he meant to write '2,250.' Here if B tries to enforce a contract at the lower price equity will refuse to help him and will protect A against the consequence of his mistake: *Webster* v. *Cecil* (1861).

(*c*) *To set aside an agreement on terms* fair to all parties, where common law will not declare it void: *Solle* v. *Butcher* (1950). *See also Grist* v. *Bailey* (1966) where a sale of a house was held voidable on grounds of common mistake as to value, which was not sufficient to render the contract void at law. This discretionary power to rescind the contract operates only if:

(*i*) the contract is not void at common law (but merely voidable in equity): see *Lewis* v. *Averay* (1973);

(*ii*) there is a fundamental mistake common to both parties; and

(*iii*) the party seeking rescission is not at fault. (The maxim is: 'He who comes to Equity must come with clean hands.')

9. **Rectification.** Where a written contract does not accurately express the intentions of the parties, the court will amend (rectify) the contract to make it express the true intentions. The party seeking rectification must prove the following.

(*a*) The mistake to be rectified lies only in the words used.
(*b*) There is a complete and final contract between the parties.
(*c*) There is clear oral or written evidence of the true intention of the parties.
(*d*) The mistake is common to both parties: *Craddock Bros* v. *Hunt* (1923).

Misrepresentation and fraud

10. Caveat emptor. In English law a person is generally under no duty to disclose all facts in his possession to the other contracting party. Each must protect his own interests unaided. The rule is 'buyer beware' (*caveat emptor*). Keeping silent therefore is generally not actionable, even though it causes damage to the other party.

> EXAMPLE: H sold pigs 'with all faults' to W, knowing that they had swine fever and that W was unaware of this. HELD: W could not have the contract set aside: *Ward* v. *Hobbs* (1878).

11. Misrepresentation. But where one party makes a positive false statement which deceives the other, this may amount to misrepresentation rendering the contract voidable at the option of the party misled.

The deceived party may also be entitled to damages: (*a*) for deceit, if he can prove fraud, or (*b*) for negligent misrepresentation, unless the defendant can show that he had reasonable grounds for believing that what he said was true: Misrepresentation Act 1967, s. 2(1).

12. What is misrepresentation? A misrepresentation is (*a*) a false statement (*b*) of material fact, (*c*) made by a party to the contract or his agent, (*d*) which induces the other party to enter into the contract.

Misleading conduct may also amount to misrepresentation, if it presents a misleading picture about material facts and satisfies (*c*) and (*d*) above.

> NOTE: (1) *The statement must be of fact*, not of law or opinion (but an opinion expressed by a person who might be expected to know the facts, e.g. by a technical expert on his own subject, may amount to a statement of fact: *Brown* v. *Raphael* (1958)). (2) *It must be of material importance* in the transaction, e.g. in the sale of a car a statement that the car is in good working order. But representations relating to trivial matters, such as the condition of the windscreen wipers, would not amount to actionable misrepresentation. (3) *It must be made by a party to the contract* or his agent, i.e. not by a mere bystander. Thus where A invests

money in a company in reliance on a false statement by the company's auditor in the company's balance sheet, A cannot sue the company for misrepresentation because the contract is between him and the company and the auditor is not an agent for the company for the purpose of making statements to lure investors: *Candler* v. *Crane Christmas* (1951) (but an action might be possible against the auditor for the tort of negligence: *Hedley Byrne & Co.* v. *Hellers, etc.* (1964), H.L.). (4) *It must be relied upon,* i.e it must succeeded in inducing the offeree to enter into the contract. Thus, A sold a broken gun to B and patched the barrel with clay to conceal the crack. B did not examine the gun and therefore was not deceived by the patch. HELD: The misrepresentation was not actionable, since it had no effect on B: *Horsfall* v. *Thomas* (1862) (5) *It must be by positive words or conduct,* not by mere silence unless the silence amounts to active concealment of facts, or silence about some facts puts those revealed into a false and deceptive light. Thus where a company's prospectus showed that it had paid dividends for several years, without disclosing that these had been paid out of reserves as the company was trading at a loss, it was HELD that the omission was deceptive and amounted to misrepresentation: *R.* v. *Kylsant* (1932). (6) *Statements true when made but becoming false before the contract is made must be corrected.* Thus R arranged to sell a business to Y and estimated profits at £2000 p.a. By the time the sale was completed the profits had fallen considerably. HELD: A's failure to disclose the change amounted to misrepresentation: *With* v. *O'Flanagan* (1936).

Thus an exceptional duty of disclosure is imposed in (5) above where silence is actually deceptive, and in (6) where facts true when stated subsequently become untrue before negotiations are completed. A further duty of disclosure is imposed in *uberrimae fidei* contracts: *see* **19** *below.*

13. Innocent misrepresentation. If a person makes a misrepresentation believing what he says is true he commits innocent misrepresentation, providing he had reasonable grounds for his belief.

The party misled may:

(*a*) affirm the contract and treat it as binding or may rescind the contract by notifying the other party and — where necessary — obtaining the court's assistance to secure restitution;
(*b*) sue for damages under the Misrepresentation Act 1967, s. 2. If he obtains damages, he cannot also rescind the agreement. *See also* 14(*b*).

14. Damages for innocent misrepresentation. Formerly a plaintiff could not secure damages for innocent misrepresentation, but the Misrepresentation Act 1967 gives a right to damages in certain cases.

(*a*) Where the misrepresentation was made negligently. Note that negligence is presumed; the defendant can only escape liability for damages if he can show that he had reasonable grounds for believing what he said was true at the time the contract was made: s. 2(1). In *Banque Financiere* v. *Westgate Insurance* (1989), the Court of Appeal pointed out that s. 2(1) uses the words 'where a misrepresentation has been made. . . .' It therefore held that where a failure to disclose had been made in breach of the rule of *uberrimae fidei* (*see* **19** *infra*), no action could lie under the Misrepresentation Act 1967 since no represtation had been 'made': if it had been the intention of the legislature that a mere failure to discharge the duty in the case of a contract *uberrimae fidei* would fall to be treated as the 'making' of a representation within the meaning of the 1967 Act, we are of the opinion that the legislature would have said so'.
(*b*) Where the plaintiff has sought rescission, the court has power to award damages in lieu of rescision: s. 2(2)

NOTE: Any exemption clause seeking to exclude liability for misrepresentation is void unless it satisfies the requirement of reasonableness: s. 3, as substituted by the Unfair Contract Terms Act 1977: *Howard Marine* v. *Ogden* (1978).

Damages are also obtainable against the makers of innocent misrepresentation made in a company prospectus: Companies Act 1985, s. 67.

4. Void, voidable and illegal contracts 57

15. Fraudulent misrepresentation. 'An untrue statement made knowingly, or without belief in its truth, or recklessly, careless whether it be true or false': per Lord Herschel, *Derry* v. *Peek* (1889). Thus if the maker believes that his representation is true, he cannot be guilty of fraud, even if he was negligent or unreasonable in saying what he did: *Akerheim* v. *De Mare* (1959). (But in such cases he may be liable for damages for the tort of negligence: *Hedley Byrne & Co.* v. *Hellers, etc.* (1964).)

16. Remedies for fraudulent misrepresentation.

(*a*) The plaintiff may sue for damages for the tort of deceit (fraud).

(*b*) The plaintiff may repudiate the contract or have it rescinded by the court (with or without claiming damages for deceit).

(*c*) The plaintiff may affirm the contract and still claim damages for deceit.

17. Limits to the right of rescission. Although the misled party can generally get the contract rescinded (set aside by the court) this right is lost in the following cases:

(*a*) *Affirmation*: where the injured party has expressly or impliedly affirmed the contract after learning of the misrepresentation.

(*b*) *Restitution impossible:* where the parties cannot be restored to their original position, i.e. *restitutio in integrum* (total restitution) is impossible.

(*c*) *Prejudice of third parties*: where an innocent third party has obatined an interest in the subject-matter of the contract in good faith and for value: *see Phillips* v. *Brooks* at **6,** *supra*. (In that case the innocent purchaser of the jewels from the rogue was held entitled to them since he had bought them from a person with a voidable title to them before that title was avoided and without notice of the fraud: *see* 10: **35**).

(*d*) *Undue delay:* where in a case of innocent misrepresentation the plaintiff delays unreasonably in seeking rescission, the court may refuse to grant him the discretionary remedy of rescission: *Leaf* v. *International Galleries* (1950).

NOTE: Formerly rescission was unobtainable where a contract had been performed under the Rule in *Seddon* v. *N.E. Salt Co.* (1905). This rule was abrogated by the 1967 Act, s. 1.

18. Representation as terms of a contract. If a representation is made during negotiations and is later incorporated as a term of the contract, the remedies of the injured party will be basically those for breach of contract. The remedies available will then depend on whether the term concerned is a condition or a warranty: *see* 2: **24**.

NOTE: Formerly rescission was unobtainable in such circumstances. But the injured party may now rescind for misrepresentation: 1967 Act, s. 1. If, however, the innocent party would have been entitled to rescind the contract without alleging fraud, he will still be entitled to do so even though the misrepresentation has become a term of the contract: Misrepresentation Act 1967, s. 1(*b*).

19. Contracts uberrimae fidei ('of the utmost good faith'). Although there is no general duty of disclosure, in some exceptional contracts the law imposes a special duty to act with the utmost good faith, i.e. to disclose all material information. In *Banque Financiere* v. *Westgate Insurance Co* (1988), the Court of Appeal ruled that the duty of full disclosure was neither contractual, tortious, fiduciary nor statutory in character, but was founded on the jurisdiction originally exercised by the courts of equity to prevent imposition and did not give rise to a claim in damages.

Failure to disclose renders the contract voidable at the option of the other party (and note the duty of disclosure imposed in ordinary contracts in certain circumstances: *see* **12**(5) and (6) *above*).

EXAMPLES: (1) *Contracts of insurance.* The insured must disclose all facts which might influence the judgement of a prudent insurer, whether to decline the risk or increase the premium. In the *Banque Financiere* case, the court stated that the obligation to disclose material facts was a mutual and absolute obligation imposing reciprocal duties on both insurer and insured, and in the case of the insurer required him to disclose all facts known to him which were material either to the nature of the risk sought to be covered

4. Void, voidable and illegal contracts 59

or the recoverability of a claim under the policy which a prudent insured party would take into account when deciding whether to place with that insurer the risk for which he was seeking cover. (2) *Contracts of family arrangement,* for the settlement of family property, etc. Each member of the family must disclose any portions he or she has already received without the knowledge of other members of the family. (3) *Company prospectuses.* Directors, promoters, etc., must make full disclosure of material facts in any prospectus inviting the public to subscribe for shares in the company: Companies Act 1948, ss. 67–69. Failure to do so renders the contract voidable and makes the directors, etc., liable for damages. (4) *Contracts for sale of land.* The vendor must disclose any defects in his title to the land, of which he knows. The duty does not extend to other matters, e.g. there is no obligation to disclose physical defects in the property sold. (5) *Suretyship and partnership contracts.* These contracts are not *uberrimae fidei* at their formation, but since made they impose a duty of utmost good faith on the parties to disclose to each other all material facts coming to light after the making of the contract (*see Partnership,* 9: **13**, and *Guarantees,* 4: **17**).

Duress and undue influence

20. Duress. This means actual or threatened violence to the person (not the property) of the party coerced or to his wife, children, or parents, and its effect is to render the contract voidable at the option of the party coerced.

Threats of imprisonment are included under this head, e.g. where A was induced to part with valuable documents by threats of continued confinement: *Cummings* v. *Ince* (1847).

Contracts made under economic duress may also be void: *North Ocean Shipping Co.* v. *Hyundai Construction Co.* (1978).

21. Undue influence. This means any pressure or coercion not amounting to duress, which prevents the party coerced from exercising free judgement, and it makes the contract voidable by him at the discretion of the court (thus a plaintiff who proves duress is entitled to rescission, while one who can only prove undue influence is dependent on the discretion of the court).

Undue influence covers all types of pressure not amounting to duress, e.g. moral pressure, threats of violence to property, playing on victim's superstitions, etc.

To be actionable the undue influence need not have been exercised by a party to the contract (cf. misrepresentation).

EXAMPLE: A mother coerced her daughter into making a money lending contract with X, a moneylender, who knew of the mother's actions. HELD: The contract was voidable by the daughter: *Lancashire Loans Ltd v. Black* (1934).

22. Undue influence may be presumed. The court presumes that undue influence has been available to one party (and exerted) in contracts between persons in a fiduciary relationship, i.e. where one party is in a position to influence the other unfairly. Wherever undue influence is thus presumed, the burden of proof will lie on the defendant to disprove its exercise if he wishes to preserve the contract.

Undue influence is presumed in contracts between parent and child, trustee and beneficiary, solicitor and client, doctor and patient, priest and communicant, teacher and pupil, etc.

The defendant can disprove undue influence by showing that:

(*a*) full disclosure of all material facts was made;
(*b*) the consideration was adequate; and
(*c*) the weaker party was in receipt of independent legal advice.

EXAMPLE: The age and health of the person influenced may be relevant. Thus undue influence was presumed between a woman secretary of strong personality and an aged and infirm employer who had been persuaded to make valuable gifts to her: *Re Craig* (1970). Where an elderly farmer mortgages his property to help a company run by his son, the bank must ensure that he has independent advice: *Lloyds Bank v. Bundy* (1975).

23. Other cases of undue influence. Even where it is not presumed,

4. Void, voidable and illegal contracts   61

undue influence may still be alleged. In such cases the burden of proof lies on the plaintiff to show that such influence existed and was exerted.

EXAMPLE: A nephew managing the affairs of an elderly aunt persuaded her to give him some shares, for the purpose of getting control of the company. HELD: The contract was voidable, despite the fact that she had received independent legal advice, since the lawyer who advised her to make the contract was not informed that the shares were virtually all the property the woman possessed: *Inche Noriah* v. *Shaik Allie Bin Omar* (1929), *see also Hodgson* v. *Marks* (1971); *National Westminster Bank plc* v. *Morgan* (1985); *Coldunell Ltd* v. *Gallon* (1986) and *Midland Bank* v. *Shephard* (1988).

24. Right to relief lost. Since remedies for undue influence are discretionary, they will only be awarded where the plaintiff's own conduct is equitable. A claim for relief may be disallowed where:

(*a*) the plaintiff's conduct has been tricky or unfair; or
(*b*) the plaintiff has delayed unreasonably in seeking rescission of the contract: *Allcard* v. *Skinner* (1887).

Illegality

25. Meaning of 'illegality.' An illegal contract is one which is void because (*a*) it is for an illegal purpose, or (*b*) it is contrary to some rule of public policy.

The courts will generally give the parties to such contracts no protection at all, even to prevent hardship (except as stated in **29** *below*). Contrast contracts which are void for some other reason than illegality, e.g. mistake, *see* **2** above; in these cases the court will assist the parties to the extent of ordering the return of property transferred under the contract: *Chappell* v. *Poles* (1837).

26. The doctrine of severance. Where a contract is for several independent purposes, some of which are legal and others illegal, the court may sever the illegal terms from the contract and enforce the remaining legal terms: *Pickering* v. *Ilfracombe Rail Co.* (1868), and *see* **49** *below*.

62 The law of contracts

But this is only possible where the legal and illegal terms are clearly independent. The court will not re-write the main terms of the contract so as to make it legal: *Napier* v. *National Business Agency* (1951).

27. Presumption in favour of validity. The courts are reluctant to declare any contract void on the grounds of illegality and will do so only where:

(*a*) a statute clearly prohibits the contract; or

(*b*) a well-established rule of common law makes such contract illegal on grounds of public policy. Otherwise the general attitude of the courts has been stated thus: 'You have this paramount policy to consider — that you are not lightly to interfere with the freedom of contract': *per* Sir George Jessel, in *Printing & Numerical Co.* v. *Sampson* (1875).

28. Consequences of illegality.

(*a*) The contract is entirely void, unless the doctrine of severance can be applied to save part of it.

(*b*) Money paid or property transferred under an illegal contract cannot be recovered (subject to the exceptions in **29** *below*). The maxim is in *pari delicto potior est conditio defendentis* ('in cases of equal guilt, more powerful is the condition of the defendant'). Thus where the parties are equally guilty, if the plaintiff is suing for the return of money paid under the illegal contract, the court will usually allow the defendant to keep it. (For the rules applicable where the parties are not equally guilty *see* **29** *below*.)

(*c*) Negotiable securities, such as cheques and other bills of exchange, transferred between the parties to the contract are void as between them. But an innocent third party who acquires such securities in good faith and for value can usually enforce them: *see Bills of Exchange*, 15: **2**. Thus where A pays a gambling debt to B by cheque, B cannot enforce payment against A; but if B sells the cheque to C, who buys in good faith and without notice of any irregularity, C will be able to enforce the cheque. *See also* Consumer Credit Act 1974, ss. 123–125.

(*d*) *Ex turpi causa non oritur actio* ('from an evil cause, no action

4. Void, voidable and illegal contracts 63

arises'). Where a plaintiff seeking the court's assistance has to base his claim on his own illegal or immoral act, his claim will fail.

> EXAMPLE: A rented a flat to R at £1,200 p.a. To avoid tax they agreed to describe the money as £450 for rent and £750 for 'services.' Later R attempted to bilk A by refusing to pay the £750 on the grounds that he had received no services, and A sued for the money. HELD: The contract was illegal as an attempt to defraud the Revenue, and A could not recover the money since he could only get it by admitting that it was really rent and this involved admitting his own guilt. But to prevent R benefiting from this situation the court terminated his tenancy on the grounds that it was illegal, and offfered him a new one at the full rent: *Alexander v. Rayson* (1936).

29. Recovery of property transferred. Money paid or property transferred under an illegal contract is normally irrecoverable.

> EXCEPTIONS: (1) Where the transferor repents of making the contract before any part of the illegal purpose is carried out, or (2) Where: (i) He is not *in pari delicto* (equally guilty) with the defendant, e.g. where he was induced to make the contract by the fraud of the defendant (*Shelley* v. *Paddock* (1978)); or (ii) The transferee was under a fiduciary duty to protect the plaintiff's interest, and has abused this duty by making the illegal contract, e.g. where he is the plaintiff's solicitor or trustee; or (iii) The contract is made illegal by a statute intended to protect a class of which the plaintiff is a member, e.g. a borrower suing to recover excessive interest from a moneylender under a contract illegal under the Consumer Credit Act (which is intended to protect borrowers).

Contracts subject to a disability

30. Contracts for trading or selling on a Sunday. Such contracts were formerly prohibited under the Sunday Observance Act 1677, but this was repealed by the Statute Law (Repeals) Act 1969. In many cases, the Shops Act 1950 makes it a criminal offence for a shop to be open on Sunday but this does not appear to affect the validity of any contract, though it will probably be the case that the courts would refuse to enforce an action on the contract by either party.

31. Registration of business names. Under the Business Names Act 1985, all orders, invoices, business letters etc., must disclose the true surname of all owners of the business (whether individuals or companies) and also the addresses within Great Britain at which they can be contacted. In addition, such information must be displayed on a notice in a prominent position at the business premises. A customer is entitled to ask for a written list of the required information which must be supplied to him immediately. These requirements are relaxed in the case of a partnerhsip of more than 20 persons provided the following conditions are satisfied: the document must not contain the names of any partners except as signatories; and it must state an address at which a full list of partners can be inspected. Actions in contract by a person who has failed to comply with the requirements of the Act can be dismissed if the defendant can show that he has a claim against that person because of his failure to comply, or if he has suffered financial loss because of such failure. The court can, however, allow the action if it considers it to be just and equitable.

32. Consumer Credit Act 1974. Under the Consumer Credit Act 1974, all those who extend credit or hire out goods in the course of a business must be licensed by the Office of Fair Trading. An unlicensed business cannot enforce contracts except with the consent of the Director General of Fair Trading. The Act also requires contracts to be in a specific form; if they are not, they can only be enforced on a court order.

33. Financial Services Act 1986. Investment businesses can only carry on business if they are authorised under the Act or are exempt from the need for authorisation. A contract made in breach of this requirement can be enforced only on a court order. The Act also provides for restrictions on the issue of investment advertisements. Investment contracts made following an unlawful advertisement can be enforced only on a court order.

34. Gaming and wagering contracts. A wager is a promise to give or

4. Void, voidable and illegal contracts 65

pay something on the ascertainment of an uncertain future event, e.g. a horse race. A bet is a wager on the result of a game. Such contracts are void under the Gaming and Wagering Acts 1835–1960. The position is complex, but the following basic rules apply.

(*a*) Money earned as commission on bets and wagers is irrecoverable: Gaming Act 1892. An agent cannot therefore recover his commission from his principal. But the principal can recover any winnings received on his behalf by the agent: *De Mattos* v. *Benjamin* (1894).

(*b*) Negotiable instruments given for a bet are given for an illegal consideration and are void as between the parties: Gaming Act 1835. But an innocent third party who becomes a holder in due course of such an instrument may be able to enforce it fully: *see Bills of Exchange*, 15: **38**.

(*c*) Money lent to a loser to pay his bets is recoverable: *Re O'Shea* (1911); but not if the lender himself pays the winner, since he is then participating in the forbidden transaction: *Macdonald* v. *Green* (1951).

(*d*) The winner of a wager cannot sue the loser for his winnings even though the loser later makes a fresh promise to pay supported by fresh consideration: *Hill* v. *William Hill Ltd* (1949).

This rule still applies, even though the Betting, Gaming and Lotteries Act 1963 legalised gambling in certain circumstances, i.e. the contracts resulting from such legalised gambling were void. *See now* the Gaming Act 1968.

(*e*) Money paid to a stakeholder to retain pending the result of a wager can be recovered from the stakeholder by the payer at any time before he has handed it over to the other party to the wager: *Burge* v. *Ashley & Smith Ltd* (1900).

(*f*) The essence of a wager is that neither party has any legitimate interest in the uncertain event wagered upon, except the money staked. Where a party has something to gain or lose apart from the money staked, the agreement is not a wager, e.g. insurance contracts. Thus if A insures his life, his ship, or his house against death, loss or damage, he stands to lose the value of his ship or house (or his life) quite apart from the wager. Although an insurance contract is similar in its other characteristics to a wager, it is valid and enforceable: *see* 12.

Contracts illegal at common law

35. Contracts tainted with sexual immorality. A contract superficially lawful will be void if, to the knowledge of the parties, its ultimate purpose was immoral, e.g. an ordinary lease of a house would be void if the house was to be used as a brothel.

> EXAMPLE: A hired a carriage to a woman knowing that she was a prostitute and would use the carriage for the purpose of soliciting. HELD: The contract was void and he could not recover unpaid hiring charges: *Pearce* v. *Brooks* (1866). This is an example of the working of the maxim *in pari delicto potior est conditio defendentis*: *see* **28** above.

36. Contracts tending to interfere with the sanctity of marriage, e.g. a promise by a married man to marry another woman as soon as his wife is dead: *Wilson* v. *Carnley* (1908).

Were a married man to promise to marry another woman, the other woman could not sue him for breach of promise if she knew he was married when he made the promise. The right to sue for breach of promise to marry has, however, been abolished by the Law Reform (Miscellaneous Provisions) Act 1970, s. 1.

37. Contracts for the sale of public offices or titles of honour, e.g. a promise to use influence to obtain a title or commission for the promisee in return for money: *Parkinson* v. *College of Ambulance Ltd* (1925). The Honours (Prevention of Abuses) Act 1925 makes parties to such a contract guilty of an offence.

38. Contracts to commit crimes or torts, whether in Britain or any foreign friendly nation, e.g. a contract to smuggle goods into the United States of America: *Foster* v. *Driscoll* (1929).

39. Contracts to obtain an unfair benefit from the government, e.g. a promise to use influence to obtain exemption from a legal duty,

4. Void, voidable and illegal contracts 67

such as military service: *Montefiore* v. *Menday Motor Components Ltd* (1918).

40. Contracts involving trade with an enemy nation are illegal at common law and also under the Trading with the Enemy Act 1939.

41. Contracts to defraud the Revenue, see *Alexander* v. *Rayson,* **28**, above.

42. Contracts tending to impede the administration of justice, e.g. a promise by an accused person to indemnify someone who has stood bail for him: *Herman* v. *Jeuchner* (1885).

43. Contracts prejudical to the freedom of marriage, e.g. imposing a general restraint upon a person to prevent marriage, though a particular restraint might be valid if not unreasonable, e.g. a contract forbidding a girl from marrying a particular man.

Marriage brokage contracts are also in this category and are void, i.e. contracts to arrange marriages for a reward: *Hermann* v. *Charlesworth* (1905).

44. Contracts involving champerty or maintenance. Maintenance means giving financial or other assistance to a party to a law suit, where the maintainer has no sufficient legal or moral interest in the case. Champerty means maintenance with a view of sharing the profits of the action. The Criminal Law Act 1967 states that maintenance and champerty can no longer be punished as a crime or tort, but provides that a contract may still be treated as contrary to public policy or otherwise illegal.

NOTE: A shared commercial interest is sufficient to negative maintenance: *Martell* v. *Consett Iron Co. Ltd* (1955).

Contracts in restraint of trade

These are contracts which seek to restrict a person from freely exercising his trade or profession. For students of Mercantile Law this is the most important category of illegal contracts.

68 The law of contracts

45. Restraints prima facie void. All restraints on trade are prima facie void, though they may be enforceable if they seek merely to protect some legitimate commercial interest. By contrast, a restraint which seeks merely to prevent competition is always void: *Morris* v. *Saxelby* (1916).

A restraint may be (*a*) general, i.e. forbidding trading throughout a large area, such as throughout the United Kingdom, or Europe, or (*b*) particular, i.e. forbidding trade in some localised area such as a particular town and its environs. General restraints are more disfavoured than particular restraints.

46. When restraints are valid. A restraint will be held void unless the party seeking to enforce it can prove:

(*a*) that is is reasonable in the public interest;
(*b*) that is reasonable as between the parties, i.e. seeks to provide reasonable protection for some legitimate interest of the plaintiff, such as trade secrets or business goodwill;
(*c*) that the plaintiff has given valuable consideration for the promise he seeks to enforce. In this type of contract consideration is necessary even if the contract is under seal.

Whether a restraint is reasonable or not is a question of law to be decided by the judge; whether the individual restraint under dispute is in fact reasonable is a question of fact in each case.

A restraint which is reasonable between the parties is presumed to be reasonable in the public interest, unless there is some rule of law to the contrary: *Attorney-General of Australia* v. *Adelaide S.S. Co.* (1913).

47. Kinds of restraint. Restraints can be grouped roughly into three categories.

(*a*) Between employer and employee, to prevent the employee competing with his employer after leaving his job: *see* **48** *below*.
(*b*) Between the vendor and the purchaser of a business, to prevent the seller harming the goodwill of the business sold, *see* **50** *below*.

4. Void, voidable and illegal contracts

(c) Between traders, to regulate conditions of trade. These are now largely governed by statute, e.g. the Restrictive Trade Practices Act 1976 and the Resale Prices Act 1976.

48. Restraints upon employees. An employer may compel an employee to sign a covenant promising not to injure the employer's interests either (*a*) during the continuance of the employment (e.g. by passing confidential information to outsiders) or (*b*) after leaving the employment (e.g. by luring away his former employer's customers).

Such agreements are viewed with disfavour by the courts because of the element of coercion: *see undue influence*, **21**, *above*. They will only be enforced if they satisfy the tests set out in **49** *below*.

NOTE: Apart from any express covenant, an employer is entitled to prevent an employee from disclosing trade secrets during the employment or after leaving: *Amber Size & Chemical Co.* v. *Menzel* (1913); or from making a list of the employer's clients with a view to competition after leaving: *Robb* v. *Green* (1895). *See also Thomas Marshall (Exports) Ltd* v. *Guinle* (1978). But even if an express covenant exists and is enforceable the employer loses the right to enforce it if he himself breaks the contract of employment, e.g. by wrongfully dismissing the employee: *General Billposting Co.* v. *Atkinson* (1909). In *Faccenda Chicken Ltd* v. *Fowler* (1986), the Court of Appeal ruled that an employer could not restrict the use or disclosure of confidential information by a restrictive covenant in the employee's contract of employment unless the information sought to be protected was a trade secret or equivalent to a trade secret. In order to determine whether information fell into this category, it was necessary to have regard to the nature of the employment, the nature of the information itself, whether the employer had stressed the confidentiality of the information to the employee; whether the information could easily be isolated from other non-confidential information which was part of the same package of information. In the case itself, the court ruled that sales information and prices charged did not come in to the category of information which could not be used or disclosed once the contract of employment had ceased.

49. Restraints upon emplyees: when enforeable. Restraints upon employees will only be enforced if they satisfy the following tests.

(*a*) The restraint is void unless supported by valuable consideration. The payment of wages is the usual consideration given by the employeer. If therefore the covenant is only imposed when the employee is leaving, there may be no consideration for it (unless some special payment is made to bind the contract).

(*b*) The restraint is void unless the employee has some real capacity to damage the employer and the covenant seeks to guard against such damage.

Thus a master is entitled to protection of trade secrets, or to a covenant that an employee in an influential position will not use his influence to seduce the master's clients.

Therefore the employee must generally be in some confidential capacity, e.g. a solicitor's managing clerk: *Fitch* v. *Dewes* (1921); but not a mere door-to-door salesman: *Mason* v. *Provident Clothing Co.* (1913); nor a newspasper correspondent: *Leng* v. *Andrews* (1909) (though a newspaper editor might be in a sufficiently confidential capacity).

(*c*) The restraint is void if it seeks merely to restrict or prevent competition.

(*d*) The restraint must be reasonable, having regard to:

    (*i*)   the type of employment: *Mason* v. *Provident Clothing Co.* (1913).

    (*ii*) the period of restraint: *Kores Ltd* v. *Kolok Ltd* (1959).

    (*iii*) the area of restraint, e.g. a solicitor's managing clerk covenanted not to open a competing practice within seven miles of his former employers. HELD: Reasonable and enforceable: *Fitch* v. *Dewes* (1921).

EXAMPLES: (1) A tailor's assistant covenanted not to open a competing business within ten miles of his former employer's. HELD: Void, because in this particular case the assistant had no confidential relationship with customers and the covenant was therefore aimed merely at preventing ordinary competition: *Attwood* v. *Lamont* (1920), *see also*: *Home Counties Dairies Ltd* v. *Skilton* (1970) − milk roundsman. (2) S was an estate agent with offices in Dartmouth and Kingsbridge. J was employed at the

4. Void, voidable and illegal contracts 71

Kingsbridge office and covenanted not to open a competing business within five miles of Dartmouth or Kingsbridge within three years of leaving the employ. HELD: The restraint was too wide, since J had never worked at Dartmouth, but was valid insofar as it related to Kingsbridge. (This was an application of the doctrine of severance: *see* **26** *above.*) *Scorer* v. *Seymour-Jones* (1966).

50. Restraints on sale of a business. Restraints imposed by the purchaser of a business on the seller, preventing the latter from opening another business in such a way as to damage the goodwill of the business sold, are enforced if reasonable in the circumstances.

Restraints of this kind are more readily enforced than those between employer and employee, because they lack the element of coercion which may be present between the parties in contracts of emloyment.

A restraint of this kind will be reasonable if (*a*) it satisfies the tests set out in **46** *above* and (*b*) it is intended merely to protect the purchaser's investment in the goodwill of the business bought, i.e. not intended to protect other businesses the purchaser already owned, or merely to prevent ordinary competition.

EXAMPLES: (1) N, an inventor of guns, sold his world-wide business to M and promised not to manufacture guns anywhere in the world for twenty-five years. HELD: Reasonable and binding: *Nordenfeldt* v. *Maxim-Nordenfeldt Co.* (1894) H.L. (2) S sold his localised business to C (who already had branches all over Britain) and promised not to open a competing business anywhere within ten miles of any of C's branches. HELD: Void. The restraint was more than was necessary to protect the goodwill of the small local business purchased from S: *British Concrete Co.* v. *Schelff* (1921).

5
Discharge of contracts

Discharge by performance

1. Complete performance. In order to effect discharge, performance must be complete and exactly in accord with the terms of the contract.

Partial performance, even if substantial, will not discharge the contract (except in the special cases stated below).

> EXAMPLE: A sailor, having signed on to receive a lump sum payment for a complete voyage, died before he completed the journey. HELD: His widow could not claim any part of his wages since he was entitled to payment only if he completed his contracted obligations: *Cutter* v. *Powell* (1795). (NOTE: On the facts this case would now be decided differently, but the general rule it lays down is still valid.)

2. Exceptional cases.

(a) Performance prevented by the promisee. Here the promisor can obtain compensation for work actually done in pursuance of the contract by suing on a *quantum meruit* claim: *see* **30**, *below*.

(b) Partial performance accepted. If the promisee voluntarily accepts less than complete performance where he had genuine freedom of choice, the promisor is entitled to claim payment on *quantum meruit*, e.g. A contracted to erect a building for B, and when the work was half done A abandoned the job. B had to complete the building himself, but A sued him for work done. HELD: B need pay

5. Discharge of contracts

nothing under the contract, as he had not freely chosen to complete the building himself, but had been compelled to do so by A's breach: *Sumpter v. Hedges* (1898).

(c) *Divisible contracts.* If performance is to be by instalments payment can be recovered for instalments actually completed (unless the intention of the parties appears to be to the contrary).

(d) *Substantial performance*, i.e. where performance is as complete as a reasonable man could expect, even though not strictly in accord with every detail of the contract. This is a question of fact.

EXAMPLES: (1) A decorated B's flat for £750, but because of faulty worksmanship B had to pay an extra £290 to complete the job. B. refused to pay any money at all to A. HELD: A was entitled to recover the £750, less the £290 paid to make good his defective workmanship: *Hoenig v. Isaacs* (1952). (2) A installed a defective central heating system for B at a charge of £560. B had to spend £174 to get C to put the system into working order. HELD: There had not been substantial performance of the contract and B need not pay A anything − not even the £385 that A claimed: *Bolton v. Mahadeva.* (1972).

3. Tender of performance and payment.

(a) *Tender of performance.* It is sometimes sufficient if the promisor attempts to perform his side of the contract. Then, if performance is rejected, the promisor is discharged from further liability and may sue for breach of contract if he so wishes.

(b) *Tender of payment.* This relieves the promisor from future liability to make further tenders, but does not discharge him from liability to pay.

Under the Currency and Bank Notes Act 1954, and the Coinage Acts 1971 and 1983, Bank of England notes (and gold coins issued by the Mint) are legal tender for any amount, silver (or cupro-nickel) coins of more than 10p denomination are legal tender up to £10, silver (or cupro nickel) coins of 10p or less are legal tender up to £5, and bronze coins for any amount up to 20p. (But the debtor should produce the correct amount: the creditor is not obliged to give change: *Robinson v. Cook* (1815).)

74 The law of contracts

4. Time for performance or payment. Failure to perform or pay on time may be a breach of warranty but is rarely a breach of condition, i.e. is rarely 'of the essence' of the contract.

(*a*) *Time of payment* is not of the essence unless otherwise agreed expressly or impliedly. (This rule is statutorily applied to contracts for the sale of goods: S.G.A. 1979, s. 10.)

(*b*) *Time of performance* is not usually of the essence but may be made so by agreement, and this is usually done in mercantile contracts.

EXAMPLE: O waived the original delivery date but stipulated a later date as final. HELD: This made the later date of the essence, i.e. a condition, of the contract and failure to deliver on the new date entitled O to rescind the contract: *Rickards* v. *Oppenheim* (1950).

5. Rules re payment of money.

(*a*) Payment of a smaller sum will not usually discharge liability to pay a larger: *Foakes* v. *Beer* (1884)), except where the rules in *Pinnel's Case* or the *High Trees Case* apply; *see* 3: **19**.

(*b*) Payment to an agent is usually a good discharge, if the agent is held out by the creditor as having authority to receive money.

(*c*) Payment by a third party is not a good discharge unless he pays as agent for the debtor: *Smith* v. *Cox* (1940).

(*d*) Payment to one joint creditor discharges liability to the others: *Kendall* v. *Hamilton* (1879).

(*e*) Payment by negotiable instrument is conditional payment only, until the negotiable instrument is cashed (or as otherwise agreed).

The creditor can always refuse to take a negotiable instrument such as a cheque and can insist on cash.

(*f*) Payment by post is ineffective if the letter is lost in the post unless the creditor requested this method of payment: *Pennington* v. *Crossley & Son* (1897).

But if the creditor did request payment by post, payment is effective once posted, even if the letter is lost in the post: *Norman* v. *Ricketts* (1886).

5. Discharge of contracts

(g) Payment by cheque is prima facie evidence of receipt (once the cheque has been cashed) but a formal receipt can also be demanded: Cheques Act 1957, s. 3.

(h) Payment by cheque or bill of exchange is conditional, so that the debtor remains liable to pay if the cheque or bill is for whatever reason dishonoured. However, if a person pays a debt by credit card, and the credit card company goes into liquidation before the supplier is reimbursed, the supplier cannot seek further payment from the debtor. However, the credit card company, or any third party to whom it had factored accounts due, could seek payment from the debtor: *Re Charge Card Services* (1988).

6. Appropriation of payments. Where there are several debts outstanding between the parties, it is sometimes important to ascertain what payment has discharged what debt. The following legal rules apply:

(a) The debtor can appropriate any payment to any debt, no matter which is the longest outstanding.

(b) If the debtor makes no appropriation, the creditor can appropriate in any way he chooses, e.g. applying the money to pay off a statute-barred debt: *Seymour* v. *Pickett* (1905).

(c) The Rule in *Clayton's Case* (1816). If there is a current account between the parties, subject to constant incomings and outgoings, then if neither party makes any express appropriation the law presumes that the first payment in discharges the earliest outstanding debt.

(d) Certain rules prescribed for credit agreements by the Consumer Credit Act 1974, s. 81.

Discharge by agreement

7. Executory contracts, i.e. those wholly unperformed by either side, can be discharged by simple waiver. Consideration for the waiver lies in the exchange of promises not to sue to enforce the contract.

8. Executed contracts, i.e. those wholly or partly performed by one party. Discharge of such contracts must be supported by consideration or must be under seal.

(a) *Deed of release,* for which no consideration is necessary.

(b) *Accord and satisfaction,* i.e. a simple contract agreement (the accord) + valuable consideration (the satisfaction) other than performance of the actual obligations under the original contract. The consideration may take the form of some alternative method of performance, or mere executory promises. But some consideration is necessary to prevent the Rule in *Foakes* v. *Beer* coming into operation: *see* 3: 19.

9. Substituted agreement. A contract can also be discharged by the parties making a fresh contract in substitution for the old. But this method is available only where the contract is not yet wholly performed on either side, i.e. is still partly executory on both sides.

A new contract substituted for an earlier in this way is called a novation.

10. Variation of contracts. Discharge by agreement may be total or partial.

Variation (which may amount to partial discharge) can generally take any form, except that contracts unenforceable unless evidenced in writing can only be varied in writing: *Morris* v. *Baron* (1918). In the case of credit agreements, certain variations are ineffective unless in a prescribed form: Consumer Credit Act 1974, s. 82.

(Total rescission can always be made in any form, e.g. a specialty contract can be rescinded orally: *Berry* v. *Berry* (1929).

11. Unauthorised alteration. If one party makes a material alteration to a contract without the consent of the other, the contract is automatically discharged.

A material alteration is one which alters the effect of the contract, e.g. altering the crossing or the amount payable on a cheque.

Discharge by operation of law

12. By merger. A contract is discharged if it is merged in a higher obligation, e.g. a deed swallows or merges into itself a simple contract on the same terms and between the same parties.

13. Contracts for personal services. These are automatically discharged by death in most cases. Contracts of a non-personal nature may survive for the benefit of the deceased's estate.

14. Discharge in bankruptcy. Where a bankrupt obtains his discharge the order automatically cancels liability on all provable debts existing at that date.

15. Lapses of time: Limitation Act 1980. The Act lays down that actions for breach of contract must be commenced within a certain time after the breach occurs, otherwise the right of action lapses, i.e. is statute-barred. (The right of action is not destroyed by lapse of time, it simply cannot be enforced: *see* **17**, *below*.)

The more important periods of time laid down by the Act are as follows.

(*a*) Six years for actions for breach of simple contracts.

(*b*) Twelve years for actions for breach of specialty contracts.

(*c*) Thirty years in actions of land where the Crown is the plaintiff; twelve years in other cases.

(*d*) Three years where the claim is for damages for personal injury: Limitation Act 1980. But this period can be extended by the court where the plaintiff did not realise he had suffered until more than three years after the breach of contract.

(*e*) Actions under Part I of the Consumer Protection Act 1987 (which allows for claims to be brought for damage to person or property against the producer of defective goods whether negligent or not) expire 10 years after the product was supplied: LA, s. 11A.

(*f*) In cases of negligence, except personal injury or death, the limitation period is 6 years: LA, s. 14A.

16. When time runs. The limitation period under the Act is generally calculated from the moment the breach occurs, except where:

(*a*) the plaintiff was under a legal disability at the date of the breach, e.g. minority or mental incapacity. Here time runs from the date when the disability ceases, or the plaintiff dies while still disabled: s. 28;

(*b*) the action is based on fraud, mistake, etc. Here time begins to run from the date when the fraud or mistake is discovered by the plaintiff, and not from the date when the cause of action arose: L.A., s. 32.

EXAMPLES: (1) Eight years after his house was built A discovered that in breach of contract the builder had laid defective foundations. HELD: He could not have discovered the truth as the builder had concealed the facts, and consequently his right of action was not barred: *Applegate* v. *Moss* (1971). (2) In order to prevent the L.A. operating, the plaintiff's mistake must be as to facts, e.g. not merely ignorance or mistake as to his rights in law: *Central Asbestos Co. Ltd* v. *Dodds* (1972).

(*c*) A major change was made to the period from which time runs by the Latent Damage Act 1986 which amends the LA. The change in the law applies to all cases of latent damage caused by negligence except personal injuries. The effect of the new s. 14A of the Limitation Act is that the basic six year limitation period is overridden by allowing a further three years from the date when the damage was discoverable. The new s. 14B of the Limitation Act provides, however, that no action can be brought once 15 years has elapsed from the date when any act or omission alleged to constitute negligence occurred.

17. Acknowledgements and part payments. When a right of action has lapsed it may be revived by the following:

(*a*) A written acknowledgement constituting an express or implied admission of liability. Thus a letter admitting liability but refusing to pay and relying on the Limitation Act has been held to be a sufficient acknowledgment for this purpose: *Re Coliseum (Barrow) Ltd* (1930). (If the written acknowledgement is lost, its contents can be proved by oral evidence: *Read* v. *Price* (1909).)

(*b*) A part payment of a statute-barred debt.

Where there is an acknowledgement or part payment, it starts time running again, i.e. the plaintiff has a further six years (or twelve if a specialty contract is involved) in which to commence action: L.A., ss. 29–31.

5. Discharge of contracts

NOTE: a part payment into a bank current account which is overdrawn operates to revive the right of action for the whole account, including debts incurred more than six years previously: *Re Footman Bower & Co. Ltd.* (1961).

Frustration of contracts

18. Supervening impossibility of performance. Where at the outset it is clearly impossible to perform a contract, such contract lacks an essential element and is void, e.g. contracts to walk across the Atlantic.

But sometimes a contract possible when made subsequently becomes impossible to perform, e.g. a lawful contract involving trade between Britain and Russia became impossible to perform when the Crimean War broke out between the two countries: *Avery v. Bowden* (1856).

The general rule is that supervening impossibility of performance does not discharge the contract, except where the doctrine of frustration applies.

19. Doctrine of frustration. This has been developed to mitigate hardship which might be caused by the supervening impossibility rule stated above.

Under the doctrine of frustration the courts will imply a term into a contract providing for the discharge of the contract if certain types of impossibility arise after the contract is made: *Cricklewood Property Co. v. Leighton's Investment Trust* (1945).

20. Frustration occurs in the following cases.

(*a*) Where the basis is destroyed. If the contract depends on the continued existence of something, and that thing is destroyed, e.g. hire of a theatre frustrated by the theatre being burned down: *Taylor v. Caldwell* (1863).

(*b*) Where there is non-occurrrence of an essential event. If the contract depends on the occurrence of an event which does not in fact happen, e.g. hire of rooms to watch the coronation procession of Edward VII, frustrated by cancellation of the procession: *Krell v. Henry* (1903); contrast *Herne Bay S.S. Co. v. Hutton* (1903).

(c) Where there is death or illness. A contract for personal services may be frustrated by death or unduly prolonged illness of the employee. What amounts to unduly prolonged illness is a question of fact in each case, e.g. if a concert pianist hired for three performances is ill when due to play at the first, this might amount to frustration: *Robinson* v. *Davison* (1871).

(d) Where there is government interference. Where the government prohibits performance for such a period that it would be unreasonable to expect performance after the prohibition ceases: *Metropolitan Water Board* v. *Dick, Kerr & Co. Ltd.* (1918).

(e) Where there is a change in law. Where a contract legal when made subsequently becomes unlawful through a change in the legal situation: *Avery* v. *Bowden* (1856).

(f) Where the method of performance is impossible. If a particular manner of performance is essential, and when the time comes for performance this particular method has become impossible.

EXAMPLES: (1) A contracted to build for B seventy-eight houses in eight months for £92,000. It was impossible to meet the contract date, and rises in costs added £17,000 to A's bill. There was no clause in the contract to cover this eventuality. The time ultimately taken by A was twenty-two months. A claimed that the original contract was frustrated by impossibility, and sued for £109,000 on *quantum meruit*. HELD: Contract was not frustrated, and therefore A had no *quantum meruit* claim. He should have foreseen his troubles and written a clause into the contract to cover them: *Davis Contractors Ltd* v. *Fareham U.D.C.* (1956). (2) Headmaster of school was suspended by his employers after a criminal charge had been made against him, of which he was acquitted six months later. HELD: His enforced absence from his work did not frustrate his contract of employment, since his presence as headmaster was not vital to the continued running of the school: *Mount* v. *Oldham Corporation* (1973). (3) Property was advertised as being suitable for redevelopment. On the date when the parties entered the contract, they did not know that the Department of the Environment proposed to list the building as being of architectural or historical significance. This happened the following day. This brought the development value of the property down to £200,000 from £1.7m. The court said listing was an inherent risk which the purchaser of property had to bear. Listing did not make the contract radically different and so it was not frustrated: *Amalgamated Investment and Property Co. Ltd v. John Walker & Sons Ltd* (1976).

21. Limits of the doctrine. Frustration does not occur in the following cases.

(*a*) Express terms may cover the contingency complained of. The court will refuse to treat the contract as frustrated where to do so would be contrary to the express terms of the contract: *British Movietonews Ltd v. London, etc. Cinemas Ltd* (1952), H.L.

(*b*) Self-induced frustration cannot be pleaded as grounds for discharge, as it may amount to breach of contract. Although it used to be thought that the doctrine did not apply to leases, the House of Lords ruled to the contrary in *National Carriers Ltd v. Panalpina (Northern) Ltd* (1981).

22. Effect of frustration. The contract is discharged for the future (from the date of the frustrating event), but it is not void *ab initio*. Therefore it may be important to ascertain who should bear the loss and who should pay for any services rendered up to the time of frustration.

(*a*) Before 1943. At common law the loss lay where it fell, i.e. money which had become payable before frustration remained payable, and money paid before frustration was irrecoverable, but money not due until after frustration ceased to be payable: *Chandler v. Webster* (1904).

This harsh rule was later modified to allow apportionment of loss where there had been total failure of consideration: *Fibrosa Case* (1943).

(*b*) L.R. (Frustrated Contracts) Act 1943 reformed the above position by providing the following.

(*i*) Money paid before frustration is prima facie recoverable (unless its retention can be justified by expenses incurred by the recipient before frustration).

(*ii*) Money due before frustration ceases to be payable (unless needed to cover expenses as in (*i*) above).

(*iii*) Benefits received before frustration must be paid for, and a party who has incurred expense before frustration is entitled to compensation therefore.

NOTE: The Act can be excluded by express agreement, and in any case it does not apply to (1) charter parties, (2) carriage of goods by sea, (3) sales of specific goods, (4) insurance contracts.

Breach of contract and remedies

23. Breach of contract occurs where one party:

(*a*) repudiates his obligations;
(*b*) disables himself from performing his part of the contract;
(*c*) fails to perform his part of the contract as and when agreed.

24. Anticipatory breach. In (*a*) and (*b*) above the breach may occur before the date fixed for performance, e.g. where A hired B to act as a courier commencing employment 1st June but wrote to B in May repudiating the agreement, it was held that B was immediately entitled to sue, and need not wait till 1st June for his right of action to accrue: *Hochster* v. *De La Tour* (1853). But a party can ignore such a breach, perform his own side, and later claim damages for breach: *White & Carter Ltd* v. *McGregor* (1962).

25. Effect of breach. The effect depends largely on whether the breach is of a condition or of a warranty: *see* 2: **25–27**.

(*a*) *Breach of warranty:* the injured party can only sue for damages and must go on with the contract, i.e. the breach does not operate to discharge the contract.

(*b*) *Breach of condition:* the injured party can choose whether: (*i*) to treat the breach as a breach of ex post facto warranty (and sue for damages while going on with the contract); or (*ii*) to treat the breach of condition as automatically discharging the contract.

NOTE: If he chooses alternative (*ii*) he cannot also sue for damages for breach, since he has indicated a willingness to regard the contract as dead and has therefore waived his right of action for

5. Discharge of contracts   83

damages (but if he has incurred expense under the contract he can bring a quasi-contractual *quantum meruit* action for compensation.) If he chooses alternative (*i*) he keeps the contract alive, and should immediately commence action to enforce it, i.e. should sue for damages or specific performance. If he delays suing he takes the risk that some unforeseen event may occur to discharge the contract by frustration thus depriving him of his right of action.

EXAMPLE: A hired B's ship to carry a cargo from Russia. Later B repudiated the contract, thus entitling A either to treat the contract as discharged or to sue for damages. A delayed a decision hoping B would change his mind before the performance date. War broke out between Russia and Britain before the performance date, frustrating the contract. HELD: A had lost his right to sue for damages by his delay: *Avery* v. *Bowden* (1856).

NOTE: In recent times, a somewhat different approach has been adopted. It has been said that many contractual undertakings cannot readily be called 'conditions' or 'warranties'. Instead, the proper approach, it is said, is to examine the consequences of the breach. If the breach is disastrous, the contract may be taken as terminated: if not disastrous only damages may be claimed: *Hong Kong Fir Shipping Co. Ltd* v. *Kawasaki Kishen Kaisha Ltd* (1962); *Cehave N.V.* v. *Bremer* (1975).

26. Remedies for breach. The common law remedy is damages by way of compensation. In addition there are the discretionary equitable remedies of specific performance and injunction, which are usually available where damages are inadequate to compensate the plaintiff for the breach.

27. Damages for breach of contract. The plaintiff can recover financial compensation for his actual loss, provided it is not too remote.
   Under the Rule in *Hadley* v. *Baxendale* (1854) damage is not too remote if:

(a) it is the natural consequence of the breach, e.g. B unduly delayed delivery of a mill-shaft to A's mill, whereby the mill was out of action for a considerable time. A had informed B that the lack of the shaft would necessitate closure of the mill. HELD: A could recover damages for the delay in delivery, but not for loss of profits occasioned by closure of the mill, since there was no way B could have foreseen that his delay would cause the closure: *Hadley* v. *Baxendale*;

(b) although not arising naturally from the breach, the damage caused was something which was within the contemplation of the parties when making the contract. (Thus in *Hadley* v. *Baxendale* the mill-owner could have recovered damages for loss of profits if he had informed the carrier of the likely result of delayed delivery.)

EXAMPLE: A contracted to supply a boiler to B's laundry and was five months late in delivery. HELD: B could recover damages for loss of ordinary profits occasioned by the delay since A knew the laundry would be closed pending delivery of the boiler (but B could not recover damages for loss of exceptional profits expected to arise under a valuable contract of which A was not informed): *Victoria Laundry* v. *Newman Industries* (1949); *Parsons* v. *Uttley Ingham* (1978).

28. The measure of damages. Damages for breach of contract are intended to compensate the plaintiff, not to punish the defendant.

NOTE: (1) The plaintiff must mitigate or minimise his loss as far as he reasonably can, he cannot recover additional damages for loss occasioned by his failure to do so: *British Westinghouse Electric & Manufacturing Co. Ltd* v. *Underground Electric Rail Co. Ltd* (1912). Thus if an employee is wrongfully dismissed he can recover damages for loss of wages, but must reduce his loss as much as he can by seeking new employment. He will not recover extra heavy damages if he is out of work for a long time, by reason of his own failure to seek work: *Brace* v. *Calder* (1895). (2) Interest on any sum claimed is not allowed unless: (*i*) the parties have previously so agreed, or (*ii*) the claim is on a bill of exchange or promissory note, or (*iii*) the court exercises it statutory discretion to award interest under the L.R. (Miscellaneous Provisions) Act 1934.

5. Discharge of contracts

(3) The plaintiff must quantify his loss of profit in financial terms. If he cannot do so, he may recover wasted expenditure, even though the expenditure was incurred before the contract was made (provided it was within the contemplation of the parties at the time of contracting): *Anglia Television* v. *Reed* (1971). See also *Cullinane* v. *British 'Rema' Mfg. Co.* (1954). (4) The plaintiff can claim his loss even where his acts of mitigation have made matters worse. It is only necessary that he does what seems reasonable at the time: *Daily Office Cleaning Contractors Ltd* v. *Shefford* (1977).

29. Penalties and liquidated damages. Where the amount of compensation claimed is left to be assessed by the court, damages claimed are called unliquidated damages.

But sometimes the parties agree in advance the amounts payable in the event of breach. Such an amount is called liquidated damages, and in any action for breach of such contract the court will award the pre-assessed sum unless it has been fixed in such a way as to break the rules against penalties.

Liquidated damages are a genuine pre-estimate of the measure of loss which a breach of the contract is likely to cause. A penalty on the other hand is a sum fixed at random to frighten a party into performing his contract: *Dunlop Pneumatic Tyre Co.* v. *New Garage Co.* (1915). In *Lombard North Central* v. *Butterworth* (1987), a lease for a computer provided that in the event of default in payment, the lessors were entitled to all arrears of instalments and to all future instalments which would have been due had the agreement not been terminated. The Court of Appeal ruled that this was an unenforceable penalty clause, since, in the absence of repudiation by the lessee, it obliged him regardless of the seriousness or triviality of the breach to make payment in respect of future instalments.

A sum is a penalty if:

(*a*) it is extravagant having regard to the maximum possible loss which could result from the breach;

(*b*) failure to pay a sum of money results in liability to pay a larger sum;

(*c*) a single sum is payable on the occurrence of any of several events of differing degrees of importance: *Kemble* v. *Farren* (1829).

If a sum is held to be a penalty the court will not award it, but will make its own assessment of damages. The fact that the parties describe a sum as a penalty or a clause as a 'penalty clause' is not decisive. The court will apply the above tests in each case, and if satisfied that the sum is a genuine pre-estimate of loss the court will award it to the plaintiff as liquidated damages.

30. Quantum meruit. Where there has been a breach of condition and the injured party has elected to treat the contract as at an end, he cannot later sue for damages for breach of contract since he has already accepted breach as terminating the contract's existence. However, in such cases, if he has incurred loss, he can bring a quasi-contractual *quantum meruit* action for compensation for work done, expense incurred, etc.. see 1: **17**.

A *quantum meruit* (literally 'how much is it worth?') claim can thus arise where:

(*a*) the defendant has abandoned or repudiated the contract, e.g. where after commissioning a writer to do a series of articles, a magazine closes down before the series is completely written: *Planché* v. *Colburn* (1831). The writer could not sue for breach of contract here because he had not completed his own side of the bargain;

(*b*) under a void contract one party has done work and the defendant has received the benefit of it: *Craven-Ellis* v. *Canons Ltd* (1936). Here again the plaintiff could not have sued on the contract since it was void;

(*c*) the parties have agreed to terminate the contract but the plaintiff has performed a substantial part of his own side of the bargain. Here he can sue on a *quantum meruit* claim, but not on the contract since he has accepted termination: *Dakin* v. *Lee* (1916);

(*d*) one party has obtained a benefit which he could not reasonably expect to get without paying for it, e.g. where a builder leaves building materials on X's land and X uses the materials, the builder can sue for the value of the materials: *Sumpter* v. *Hedges* (1898) and *see* **2**, *above*.

Similarly if a grocer by mistake leaves goods at the wrong house and the occupant uses the goods, the grocer could sue for their value.

5. Discharge of contracts 87

31. Specific performance. This is a discretionary remedy for breach of contract and consists of a court order compelling the defendant to perform his side of the bargain. It may be awarded in addition to or instead of damages.

Specific performance will only be awarded where:

(*a*) damages would be inadequate to compensate the plaintiff, e.g. in contracts to sell or lease land, or for the sale of valuable and unique chattels such as rare paintings. It will not be awarded in ordinary contracts for sale of goods where the plaintiff could easily obtain replacement articles with the money received as damages, e.g. in sales of ordinary cars, books, furniture.

Under a contract made in March 1970, the plaintiff agreed to buy all its petrol and diesel fuel from the defendant for at least ten years. The defendant company attempted to terminate the agreement when the market for oil was in an unusual state. The court granted an interlocutory injunction restraining the threatened breach because the court could order specific performance of a contract to sell and purchase chattels which were not specific, or ascertained where, as the evidence showed here, damages would not be an effective remedy: *Sky Petroleum Ltd.* v. *V.I.P. Petroleum Ltd* (1974);

(*b*) the enforcement of the order would not require constant supervision by the court, e.g. not in building contracts or contracts of employment;

(*c*) the contract is equally enforceable by both parties. Thus a minor plaintiff cannot obtain specific performance of a contract which would not be enforceable against him, since it would be impossible for the adult defendant party to claim specific performance against the minor (in such cases the minor can of course obtain damages): *Johnson* v. *Agnew* (1980) (CA);

(*d*) the plaintiff himself has acted fairly and equitably. He cannot obtain specific performance if his own conduct has been tricky or unfair: *Webster* v. *Cecil* (1861), *see* 4: **8.**

32. Injunctions. An injunction is a discretionary court order and is either:

(*a*) *prohibitory:* forbidding a person to do something; or
(*b*) *mandatory:* commanding a person to do something.

88 The law of contracts

Mandatory injunctions are rarely granted since they might call for supervision by the court, which may not have the resources to enforce the injunction adequately.

Injunctions may take the following forms.

(*a*) *Quia timet injunctions:* issued to prevent an apprehended injury before it has occurred, but where there is reasonable ground for fearing a breach of contract may occur.

(*b*) *Interim or interlocutory injunctions:* usually granted pending the decision of a case, e.g. prohibiting the defendant from taking disputed property overseas until the dispute as to its ownership has been settled in court.

(*c*) *Perpetual:* issued when a dispute has been finally settled, e.g. where an interim injunction is made perpetual when the dispute has been finally settled in court.

33. Injunctions to restrain breaches of contract. An injunction is a suitable additional or alternative remedy to damages where the plaintiff wants to prevent the defendant breaking the contract, or continuing to break it.

Injunctions may be available where specific performance is not. Thus a contract of personal services cannot be enforced by an order for specific performance, since this would necessitate constant supervision by the court. But the court might in such a case grant a prohibitory injunction, forbidding the defendant from breaking the contract (and threatening him with imprisonment if he disobeys).

An injunction will only be granted to restrain a breach of contract if the clause the plaintiff seeks to enforce is negative in substance, though it may be positive in form. Thus a contract under which a film star is to work exclusively for a plaintiff company appears positive in form, but has a negative meaning, i.e. that the film star must not work for anyone else. An injunction could be granted therefore to prevent the film star working for anyone else: *Warner Bros.v. Nelson* (1937).

6
Privity, assignment, and negotiability

Privity of contract

1. Doctrine of privity. A contract is a private relationship between the parties who make it, and no other person can acquire rights or incur liabilities under it.

Compare this rule with the separate rule that 'consideration must move from the promisee.' The two rules together means that a person seeking to sue upon a contract must satisfy the court: (*a*) that he is a party to the contract he seeks to enforce, and (*b*) that he has given consideration for the promise he seeks to enforce (or that the contract is under seal): *see* 3: **10–12**.

Contrast a legal duty with a contractual duty. A legal duty is one which, if not performed, can be sued upon by any person injured by the breach of duty; actions for tort are actions for breach of this sort of duty. A contractual duty is one which is owed only to the other party to the contract, and only that party can sue to enforce it. (Also contractual duties arise by agreement, while legal duties are imposed by the law independently of any agreement between the parties.)

2. Scope of doctrine. The doctrine of privity has two aspects.

(*a*) No one can acquire rights under a contract to which he is not a party.

(*b*) No one can incur liabilities under a contract to which he is not a party.

EXAMPLE: B sold his business to C on condition that C should pay (1) £6.50 per week to B for life, and (2) £5 per week for life to Mrs B after B's death. B died and C refused to pay Mrs B, since she was not a party to the contract. HELD: (1) Mrs B was not a party to the contract and therefore could not personally enforce it, but (2) as administratrix of her late husband's estate (which was a party to the contract) she could enforce the contract: *Beswick* v. *Beswick* (1968); *Scruttons Ltd* v. *Midland Silicones Ltd* (1962); *N.Z. Shipping Co.* v. *Satterthwaite* (1975).

3. Acquisition of rights. If A and B make a contract whereby B is to pay A to do something for X, X cannot sue A if he fails to do what he promised. It makes no difference if X has given consideration for the promise — he cannot sue unless he is a party to the contract: *Price* v. *Easton* (1833) nor that B and X – are closely related: *Tweddle* v. *Atkinson* (1861).

EXCEPTIONS: (1) *Constructive trust.* Where B is regarded as a trustee for X, X may sue A (and join B as co-defendant) if the contract between B and A is broken. (A constructive trust is one imposed by the courts to prevent injustice, and arises independently of any agreement between the parties.) (2) *Resale Prices Act 1976, s. 26.* A retailer who obtains goods from a wholesaler with notice of restrictive conditions imposed on resale of the goods by the original supplier may be bound by such conditions, even though they arose from the contract between the wholesaler and the supplier (to which the retailer was not a party: *Goodyear Tyre & Rubber Co. Ltd* v. *Lancashire Batteries Ltd* (1958). (3) *Negotiable instruments.* If X is the holder for value of a bill of exchange he may sue the drawer (A) upon the bill: *see* 15: **37, 38**. (4) *Agency.* Where B is secretly acting as agent for X, X can intervene to enforce the contract between A and B, in which case B drops out and the contract subsists directly between A and X. This is called the doctrine of the undisclosed principal: *see* 8: **17**. But it has also been held that where a person makes a contract for a holiday for himself and his family, he can recover damages for everyone for the disappointment suffered when the holiday is a disaster: *Jackson* v. *Horizon Holidays* (1975). (5) *Road Traffic Act 1988, ss. 151, 152.* Persons specified in a third party car insurance

6. Privity, assignment, and negotiability 91

policy can sue the insurance company to enforce the policy for their own benefit. (6) *Law of Property Act* 1925, s. 56, states that a person may take 'an immediate or other interest' under a contract, providing it is in writing. But the House of Lords has refused to regard this provision as creating a general exception to the doctrine of privity: *Beswick* v. *Beswick* (1968). (7) *Road Traffic Act* 1988, s. 148. This provides that insurance covers any person driving a motor vehicle with the consent of the owner.

4. Acquisition of liabilities. A contract between A and B cannot impose liabilities on X, save in the following exceptional cases.

(*a*) Resale Prices Act 1976, s. 26: *see* **3**, *above.*
(*b*) Commercial usage or trade customs may so provide.
(*c*) Sale of ships. If X buys a ship from B which has previously been chartered by A, he may be bound by the terms of the charterparty if he has notice of its terms: *Strathcona S.S. Case* (1926).
(*d*) Restrictive covenants affecting land. These may run with the land, i.e. if X buys land he may be bound by a covenant between A and B, the seller of the land, provided (*i*) X accepts the covenant when buying the land, or (*ii*) the covenant is registered at the Land Charges Registry under the Land Charges Act 1972.

Transfer and assignment of contracts

5. Transfer of contracts. Rights and liabilities under a contract can be transferred in some cases. In this situation, in accordance with the doctrine of privity, if in a contract between A and B, B transfers the contract to X, B drops out of the contract which now subsists between A and X. B thereafter generally has no further rights or obligations under the contract.

6. Transfer of liabilities. This is only possible where:

(*a*) the contract so provides; or
(*b*) the parties later so agree. If the parties to a contract agree that it cannot be assigned, any purported assignment is therefore invalid and the intended assignee has no rights under the original contract: *Helstan Securities Ltd* v. *Hertfordshire County Council* (1978).

Transfer is effected by cancellation of the existing contract between A and B and substitution of a new agreement between B an X, i.e. a novation.

NOTE: In a contract between A and B, if performance is not a personal matter, B can always delegate performance to some other person, e.g. his employee. This does not involve transfer of the contract, and privity still exists between A and B who remain fully liable on the contract.

7. Assignment of rights: choses in action. A right or benefit arising under a contract is called a *chose* (or 'thing') *in action*, i.e. a personal right of property which can usually be enforced only by suing (by action) and not by taking physical possession: *Torkington* v. *Magee* (1902). Contrast a *chose in possession,* which is a piece of property capable of actual physical possession, e.g. goods, ships.

Whether the benefit of a contract can be assigned depends on the intention of the parties. Thus a contract of employment cannot usually be assigned, unless otherwise agreed.

Choses in action can be assigned in two ways: (*a*) in accordance with s. 136, Law of Property Act 1925, and (*b*) in accordance with the rules of equity (i.e. any assignment not complying with s. 136, L.P.A.).

8. Statutory assignments: L.P.A. 1925, s. 136. Such an assignment operates to transfer (*a*) the full legal obligation, (*b*) the right to enforce the obligation, and (*c*) power to give a valid discharge.

REQUIREMENTS: (1) The assignment must be absolute, i.e. of the whole debt or other obligation. (2) The assignment must not be by way of charge only. (3) It must be in writing, signed by the assignor. (4) It need not be supported by valuable consideration. (5) Express notice in writing must be given to the obligee by the assignee, to avoid the obligee performing the contract for the benefit of the assignor.

Thus if A owes B £100, B can sell his right to collect payment to X (in the form set out above), and this will entitle X to enforce the debt

6. Privity, assignment, and negotiability

against A. But X should notify A of the assignment to avoid A paying B.

9. Effect of statutory assignments.

(a) The assignee (X) can sue in his own name to enforce the chose in action, e.g. by suing A for debt.

(b) The assignee (X) takes subject to equities having priority over his assignment, e.g. if A has paid part of his debt to B before receiving notice of the assignment X cannot compel A to pay the full amount (but must try to recover the money from B).

10. Equitable assignments. This means any assignment which though valid fails to comply with the requirements of s. 136 L.P.A., e.g. an oral assignment.

In an equitable assignment the assignee (X) cannot sue in his own name, but must join the assignor (B) as co-plaintiff in any action against the debtor or other obligee (A), or as co-defendant if he refuses. Thus the action will be either X and B. v. A, or X. v. B. and A.

ESSENTIALS: (1) Intention to assign (no particular form is necessary). (2) Notice is necessary to the obligee to prevent him paying assignor: the Rule in *Dearle v. Hall* (1828). (3) Value is necessary only in assignments of future rights, e.g. the assignor's expectations under a will.

11. Negotiable instruments. Some choses in action possess the quality of negotiability, e.g. cheques and other bills of exchange. These negotiable instruments are freely transferable by mere delivery (with or without indorsement by the transferor), and the transferee usually obtains an indefeasible title free of equities, etc.

Negotiability must therefore be distinguished from assignability. If a chose is merely assignable, the assignee obtains no better rights to the chose than were possessed by the assignor; but if the chose is negotiable, the transferee may obtain a better right than that possessed by the transferor: *see Negotiable Instruments*, 15: **2**.

7
Fair trading

Freedom to contract

1. Freedom to contract. It is traditionally a basic principle of English law that a man should be free to make whatever contract he chooses, provided it is not illegal. However, this presupposes that both parties to a contract have equal freedom. In practice however, over the last fifty years, the courts have increasingly recognised that too often 'the freedom is all on one side' (Lord Denning).

Thus where a person buys a railway or bus ticket he has little real choice as to whether he agrees or does not agree to the terms imposed on the contract by the carrier: *see* 2: **16-18** *above*. If the carrier imposes exemption clauses restricting his common law liability, the passenger either accepts them or is debarred from travelling.

As explained in 2, the courts have attacked this situation by applying the *contra proferentem* rule, i.e. construing the contract stringently against the person who lays down the terms in it. Also in recent years the courts have shown themselves hostile to any exemption clause which would, if enforced, eliminate the true or fundamental purpose of the contract: see the *Suisse Atlantique Case*, 2:**25** *above*.

In the same way the legislature has increasingly shown hostility to the imposition of one-sided terms in contracts, or to situations which in a more general sense involve unfair trading. This hostility has culminated in the Fair Trading Act 1973, and the Unfair Contract Terms Act 1977 (2: **18**) which set out to establish machinery for the protection of the consumer of goods or services and also co-ordinate

7. Fair trading 95

and reform earlier statutory regulations relating to monopolies and restrictive trade practices.

2. Earlier restrictions on freedom to contract. These can roughly be summarised as follows.

(a) *Judical restrictions.*
  (i) The contra proferentem rule; *see* 2: **18**.
  (ii) The fundamental term doctrine: *see* 2: **18**.
(b) *Statutory restrictions.*
  (i) The Restrictive Trade Practices Act 1976: *see* **11–12** *below*.
  (ii) The Monopolies and Mergers Act 1965: *see* **7–10** *below*.
  (iii) The Resale Prices Act 1976: *see* **13** *below*.
  (iv) The Trade Descriptions Act 1968: *see* **14** *below*.
  (v) The Competition Act 1980: *see* **10** *below*.

Fair Trading Act 1973

3. Objects. The main objects of the Act are as follows.

(a) The appointment of a Director-General of Fair Trading and of a Consumer Protection Advisory Committee (to advise the Director and the Secretary of State for Trade on the protection of consumers).

(b) To confer on the Director and the Committee and on the Restrictive Practices Court and on certain other courts new functions for the protection of consumers.

(c) To reform the law relating to monopolies and restrictive practices, and extend the law relating thereto.

(d) To regulate pyramid selling and similar trading schemes.

(e) To amend the provisions regarding trade descriptions, and certain other matters.

4. The Director-General. He is appointed (for a period not exceeding five years) by the Secretary of State for Trade: s. 1.

(a) *Chief functions.* These are:
  (i) to review the supply of goods and services to consumers in the UK for their better protection;
  (ii) to review commercial activities in the UK with regard to monopoly situations;
  (iii) to advise the Secretary of State of matters appearing to him to be detrimental to the interests of consumers in the UK: s. 2.
(b) *Reference to Restrictive Practices Court.* The Director has power to refer cases of unfair trading to the R.P. Court, where the persons at fault refuse or fail to amend their conduct: ss. 34, 35.
(c) *Monopolies.* The Director is empowered to ascertain whether a monopoly situation exists in the supply of goods or services to the public; he may refer the case to the Monopolies and Mergers Commission for investigation and possible prosecution of the offenders: ss. 44, 50.

5. Consumer Protection Advisory Committee. This consists of not fewer than ten and not more than fifteen members appointed by the Secretary of State for Trade, either full- or part-time: s. 3. The Committee acts as watch-dog for the public in all matters relating to 'consumer trade practices'.

(a) Consumer trade practices mean practices relating to the supply of goods or services to consumers, and affecting (i) terms and conditions of supply and the method of communication of such terms etc., (ii) promotion, advertising and methods of selling, (iii) packaging and delivery, (iv) methods of securing payment from the customer: s. 13. Any Minister or the Director may refer a case to the Committee if the interests of consumers in the UK are affected: s. 14. The Committee may require the Director to use his powers to carry out any necessary investigations: s. 14.
(b) Action by Secretary of State may follow a recommendation of the Committee (s. 22), and on prosecution an offender may be fined up to £2,000 or sentenced to imprisonment: s. 23.
(c) Defences include honest and reasonable mistake, and that the defendant took all reasonable precautions to avoid commission of an offence: s. 25.

6. Other provisions of the Act. These relate mainly to monopolies

7. Fair trading

and restrictive practices, and are dealt with separately in the following notes.

Monopolies And Mergers Commission

7. Monopolies And Mergers Commission. This was originally set up by the Monopolies Act 1948, and its powers and functions have been gradually extended. Under its new name the Commission consists of not fewer than ten and not more than twenty-five members appointed by the Secretary of State: s. 4.

(*a*) *Functions*. The Commission investigates any question referred to it:
 (*i*) with respect to the existence of a monopoly situation;
 (*ii*) with respect to a transfer of a newspaper;
 (*iii*) with respect to certain commercial mergers: s. 5.

(*b*) *Monopoly references*. These may be made by the Director where they relate to supply of goods or services: s. 50. In addition any Minister or the Secretary of State may make such references to the Commission, over a wider field. The Commission has wide powers to investigate and report to the appropriate Minister, and recommend appropriate action: s. 54. In its report the Commission specifies the ways in which a monopoly appears to be detrimental to the public interest: s. 56.

8. Monopoly situations. The Fair Trading Act 1973 sets out specific types of situation to be dealt with by the Commission.

(*a*) A monopoly situation in relation to the supply of goods shall be deemed to exist if:
 (*i*) at least one quarter of such goods as are supplied in the UK are supplied by or to one person or inter-connected group of persons or bodies corporate, or
 (*ii*) agreements are in operation as a result of which such goods are not supplied in the UK at all: s. 6.

(*b*) A monopoly situation in relation to the supply of services shall be deemed to exist if one person (or inter-connected group) controls one quarter of the supply in the UK, or is in a position to prevent any supply at all: s. 7.

(c) A monopoly situation in relation to exports shall be deemed to exist if at least one quarter of the goods in question (produced in the UK) are produced by one person or inter-connected group, or if any agreements exist which prevent or distort competition in relation to the export of such goods: s. 8.

9. Mergers. The Commission has jurisdiction to supervise, investigate and — where necessary — stop commercial mergers of such a nature that they affect the public interest, in particular mergers of newspapers.

(a) *Newspaper merger references.* Where newspapers owned by a newspaper proprietor, when taken with the circulation of the paper to be acquired, have a circulation of 500,000 copies or more per issue, any merger is void unless made with express permission of the Secretary of State: s. 58. Where application for permission is made to the Secretary, he will refer the case to the Commission for investigation, and the Commission will report within three months giving reasons for its decisions: ss. 59, 60.

(b) *Other merger references.* Where it appears to the Secretary of State that two or more enterprises (of which one at least is carried on in the UK) have lost their distinct independence (i.e. have 'merged'), and (i) supply at least one quarter of the goods or services in their field in the UK, or (ii) the value of the assets taken over exceeds £15 million, he may refer the case to the Commission for investigation: s. 64. Businesses cease to be distinct enterprises if they (i) come under common ownership or control, or (ii) cease to trade as a result of an agreement between them to prevent competition: s. 65. The Commission must report within six months, stating reasons for its conclusions: ss. 70, 72.

10. References other than monopoly and merger references. The Secretary of State or any other Minister may require the Commission to report on the general effect on the public interest of (a) practices of a specified class of persons adopted for the purpose of achieving a monopoly situation, or (b) any practices appearing to be uncompetitive practices: s. 78. In this way restrictive labour practices may be referred to the Commission to ascertain whether they operate adversely to the public interest: s. 79. (Restrictive labour practices mean those designed to restrict competition unnecessarily, and which do not relate merely to rates of remuneration: s. 79.)

Under the Competition Act 1980 the Director General of Fair Trading may ask the Commission to decide if an anti-competitive practice is contrary to the public interest. The Commission can also under this Act be asked to carry out efficiency audits into public and quasi-public bodies, and the Act gives the government the power to ask the Director General to enquire into prices of 'major public concern'.

Restrictive Trade Practices

11. Restrictive trade practices. The Restrictive Trade Practices Act 1956 lays down regulations under which the Restrictive Practices Court may invalidate agreements between groups of persons which interfere with freedom of competition, e.g. by fixing prices throughout a particular industry. The Fair Trading Act 1973 repeals parts of these Acts and introduces many amendments, e.g. in particular the former office of Registrar of R.T. Practices is abolished and his functions are handed over to the Director-General of Fair Trading. The 1956 Act was repealed and consolidated in the Restrictive Trade Practices Act 1976.

The Restrictive Practices Court is staffed by High Court judges and specially appointed industrial experts and has itself High Court status, and wide powers. Appeal on questions of law lies to the Court of Appeal, but on questions of fact the R.P. Court's decision is final.

12. Registration of agreements. Agreements are registrable if:

(*a*) they are between two or more persons or bodies in the UK carrying on business in the production or supply of goods or services, or

(*b*) they involve the acceptance by two or more parties of restrictions on pricing of goods or services, conditions of supply, etc.

The Director has power to demand registration (or cause to be shown why an agreement should not be registered) wherever he thinks an agreement of the kind noted is in existence.

It is presumed that any registrable agreement is contrary to the public interest, and the onus of proving that it is not is on the persons seeking to uphold it.

The Restrictive Practices Court will only uphold an agreement if it is satisfied that:

(a) it is reasonably necessary to protect the public;
(b) removal of the restrictions would not be beneficial to the public;
(c) it is reasonably necessary to protect the legitimate interest of the parties to it;
(d) removal of the restrictions would adversely affect employment in the industry in question;
(e) it does not unduly restrict or discourage competition: R.T.P. Act 1976.

13. Resale Prices Act 1976. This renders void any agreement purporting to fix resale prices of goods (only net books and medicaments are exempt), unless approved by the R.P. Court. Agreements must be registered with the Director, and the court will only declare such agreements valid if they appear in the public interest, e.g.:

(a) by preserving quality or variety of goods;
(b) by preserving the number of retail outlets;
(c) by preserving the level of prices against undue increase:
(d) by preventing sale in such a way as to damage health;
(e) by preserving standards of sales service or after-sales service.

Trade Descriptions Act 1968

14. Trade Descriptions Act 1968. This makes it a criminal offence for anyone in course of trade to apply a false description to goods, or to supply goods to which one has been applied: s. 1.

The description complained of must be false to a material degree: s. 3. It may relate to quantity, quality, size, composition, fitness for any particular purpose, testing of goods, place or type of manufacture, name of manufacturer, identity of previous owner (of used goods) etc: s. 2. The Consumer Protection Act 1987 replaces the provisions of the 1968 Act as to misleading prices.

With regard to provision of services (as distinct from goods) it is an offence in the course of trade to make a statement which the maker 'knows to be false,' or 'recklessly': s. 14.

EXAMPLES: (1) Omission of words 'ex Channel Islands' from log-book of car when sold has been held to be an offence: *R.v. Haesler* (1973) CA. (2) To describe an unroadworthy car as 'beautiful' or as in 'showroom condition' is a false trade description: *Robertson v. Dicicco* (1973); *Hawkins v. Smith* (1978). (3) D was repairing a car for X, a dealer, to whom D had sold the car. X brought a prospective purchaser to look at the car, and D falsely described it as having a 'good little engine.' HELD: D committed an offence, even though he was not a party to the sale: *Fletcher v. Sledmore* (1973). (4) Tour agency's brochure praised a hotel which did not yet exist. HELD: An offence: *R. v. Clarksons Holidays* (1972). (5) The Act does not cover mere predictions for the future as distinct from statements as to existing fact. Tour agent who predicted high quality for a future hotel was held not liable under the Act: *R. v. Sunair Holidays* (1973); *British Airways Board v. Taylor* (1976). (6) Falsification of distance shown on car's odometer is capable of being a false trade description, if used to assist in persuading the purchaser to buy: *Tarleton Engineering Co. v. Nattrass* (1973). (7) Disclaimers are often used to avoid offences under the Trade Descriptions Act, particularly with regard to odometer readings. But these disclaimers will only be effective if they are as 'bold, precise and compelling' as the trade description they are seeking to disclaim: *Norman v. Bennett* (1974); *R. v. Hammerton Cars Ltd* (1976). (8) Where a holiday brochure is published with a false statement that a particular room is air-conditioned, and the tour operator who published it advises all outlets that this is an error, an offence is still committed by the operator if, in the normal course of business, a holidaymaker is given the brochure without the error in it being pointed out to him: *Wings Ltd v. Ellis* (1984).

Miscellaneous matters

15. Pyramid selling. This is a trading tactic whereby a supplier or manufacturer of goods engages participants (who may likewise be

102 The law of contracts

encouraged to engage others) to help him sell his wares to the public in return for a commission (and sometimes requiring the participants to invest money in the project). Thus A manufactures goods and supplies them to B as agent for sale on commission, and B in turn involves C and D, who in turn involve E, F, G, etc.

The Fair Trading Act brings such trading schemes under the surveillance and control of the Secretary of State for Trade: s. 118. The Secretary of State is empowered to make regulations generally for schemes of this kind, and also to prohibit individual suppliers from operating particular schemes: s. 119. The regulations are the Pyramid Selling Schemes Regulations 1973 No. 1740. Persons who operate such a scheme contrary to the regulations commit a criminal offence and on conviction can be fined up to £2,000 or imprisoned for up to two years: ss. 120, 122.

16. Creation of new offences. The Fair Trading Act effectively grants the Secretary of State power to create new offences relating to unfair trading. Procedure is for the Director to refer a practice he considers reprehensible to the Consumer Protection Advisory Committee on the ground that:

(*a*) it may mislead or confuse consumers as to quality or quantity of goods or services; or
(*b*) it may mislead consumers as to their rights or obligations, or subject them to undue pressure; or
(*c*) it may impose inequitable terms on consumers.

If the Committee then (within three months of the reference to it) advises such action, the Secretary of State may then prohibit the particular practice, or nullify exemption clauses in contracts complained of, or demand that contracts complained of shall embody certain clauses for the protection of the consumers, etc. Breach of the Secretary of State's prohibition will constitute an offence under the Act. To date, three statutory instruments have followed upon recommendations by the Committee:

(*a*) The Mail Order Transactions (Information) Order 1976 No. 1812.

(b) The Consumer Transactions (Restrictions on Statements) Order 1976 No. 1813, as amended by the Consumer Transactions (Restrictions on Statements) (Amendment) Order 1978 No. 127.

(c) The Business Advertisements (Disclosure) Order 1977 No 1918.

Progress test 1

Law of contracts

1. How does a binding contract differ from other agreements? What kinds of contract are there, and what are their characteristics? (1: **1–4, 5–8**)

2. What is a quasi-contract? When if ever can money be recovered on the grounds of mistake in payment? (1: **12–17**)

3. Distinguish an offer from: (*a*) an invitation to treat, and (*b*) a statement of intention. (2: **1–6**)

Apply the rules of offer and acceptance to the following situations.
    (*i*)   Bidding at an auction
    (*ii*)   Putting a coin in a slot machine.
    (*iii*) Display of goods in a shop or self-service store.
    (*iv*) Boarding a bus.

4. Comment on the statement that there cannot be a contract to make a contract. (2: **21**)

A agreed orally to sell his house to B for £110,000 'subject to contract.' The next day C offered A £110,500 for the house and A accepted this offer and sold the house to C. Can B sue A for breach of contract?

Would it make any difference to your answer if the agreement between A and B was in writing? (2: **11, 13**; 3: **4**)

5. In what circumstance may an offer: (*a*) lapse, and (*b*) be revoked? (2: **7, 8**)

6. A wrote to B offering to sell his house for £110,000, the offer to remain open 'until Wednesday noon.' On Tuesday A sells his house to C. What remedies, if any, has B against A? Would it make any difference to your answer if B had paid A 5p to keep the offer open till Wednesday? (2: **9**)

7. When if ever may communication of acceptance be dispensed with? (2: **13**)

8. What is a tender, and what forms may a tender take? (2: **15**)

9. In what circumstances may an offeree be bound by the terms or a written offer which he has not read? Where such terms are designed to limit the liability of the offeror, what is meant by saying that they are interpreted *contra proferentem?* (2: **17, 18**)

10. In what circumstances may the court imply a term in a contract? (2: **22**)

11. Distinguish between conditions and warranties in a contract, and explain what is meant by *ex post facto* warranties. (2: **24–28**) Why is it important to distinguish between a term of a contract and a mere representation made during negotiations? (2: **30**)

12. What is meant by the proper law of a contract, and why is it important? (2: **33, 34**)

13. What contracts are void unless made (*a*) by deed, or (*b*) in writing? What contracts are merely unenforceable unless supported by written evidence? What is the distinction between void and unenforceable contracts? (3: **1–4**)

14. Define 'consideration'. When if ever is a simple contract enforceable when unsupported by valuable consideration? (3: **10–12**)

15. What is a guarantee, and how does it differ from an indemnity? Is it true to say that a guarantee does not need to be supported by consideration? (3: **4, 5**)

16. What is meant by evidence in writing, in contracts covered by s. 40, Law of Property Act? How does the doctrine of part performance modify the application of this section? (3: **6–9**)

17. Explain the difference between executory, executed, and past consideration. Why is the distinction between executed and past consideration important?

A fell into a river and shouted for help. B hearing the cry rescued him, and in gratitude A promised B £10,000. A now refuses to pay the money. Can B recover it by an action for breach of contract? (3: **12, 18**)

18. Explain briefly the Rule in *Foakes* v. *Beer* (1884) and any exceptions of which you know. (3: **19**)

19. What contracts are (*a*) binding on a minor, (*b*) voidable at the minor's option? What must be proved by a shopkeeper suing a minor for the price of goods supplied? (3: **26–28**)

7. Fair trading 105

20. When, if ever, may a contract be avoided at common law on the grounds of mistake (*a*) of law, or (*b*) of fact? What relief is available in equity in cases of mistake? (4: **1–3, 8**)

21. When if ever may a person who has signed a written acceptance of an offer evade the consequences of his signature? (2: **16**; 4. **7**)

22. 'Mistakes in the formation of contracts may be common, mutual or unilateral.' Discuss this statement, and explain the cases where such mistakes may avoid a contract. (4: **1–8**)

23. What is 'misrepresentation' ? When, if ever, is there a positive duty of disclosure imposed on a party to a contract? (4: **12, 19**)

24. Distinguish between innocent, negligent and fraudulent misrepresentation and explain the remedies available for each (4: **13, 17**)

25. Explain the importance of the distinction between a mere misrepresentation, and a misrepresentation which has become a term of a contract. (4: **18**; 2: **22–28**)

26. 'Adequacy of consideration is of itself no grounds for avoiding a contract, but it may be evidence of undue influence.' Explain this statement. (3: **13**; 4: **20–22**)

27. What is meant by an 'illegal' contract, and what are the consequences of illegality? (4: **25–29**)

28. Explain briefly the main provisions of the Consumer Credit Act 1974 in regard to loans by professional moneylenders. (4: **32**)

29. Summarise briefly the rules relating to gaming and wagering contracts and their effects. (4: **33**)

30. 'Restraints of trade are prima facie void.' How far is this true? (4: **45–47**)

31. Explain briefly the cases in which the courts will enforce covenants by an employee not to compete with his former employer. (4: **48–49**)

32. State briefly the five ways in which a contract may be discharged. (5)

33. 'To effect discharge, performance must be complete.' What exceptions are there to this rule? (5: **1–2**)

34. Explain briefly the rules relating to the appropriation of payments by a debtor, or creditor. How does the Rule in *Clayton's Case* affect the position? (5: **6**)

35. Explain what is meant by: (*a*) Deed of Release; (*b*)

106 The law of contracts

Accord and satisfaction; (c) Novation; (d) The Rule in *Morris* v. *Baron*. (5: **8–10**)

36. When are rights of action arising under a contract liable to lapse? How may such lapsed rights be revived? (5: **15–17**)

37. 'Supervening impossibility of performance has no effect on contracts.' Discuss this statement. (5: **18–22**)

38. A, in Whiteland, and B, in Redland, made a contract for the supply of machines by A, for which B paid in advance. The contract contained a clause stating: 'This contract shall be avoided and the loss shall lie where it falls if war breaks out between Whiteland and Redland.' War does break out, when A has supplied only half the machines. The contract was made in England, and B wants to know whether he can recover any of his money under the L.R. (Frustrated Contracts) Act 1943. Advise him. (5: **25, 26**)

39. What is meant by 'anticipatory breach of contract'? A was due to perform a contract on 1st May, but in April repudiated his obligations. On 29th April the contract became illegal through a change in the law. B, the other party to the contract, commenced an action for breach of contract on 30th April. Discuss. (5: **20–24**)

40. Explain briefly the rule in *Hadley* v. *Baxendale* (1854). What is meant by saying that the plaintiff must mitigate his loss? (5: **27, 28**)

41. Distinguish between penalties and liquidated damages in the law of contracts, and explain when interest may be allowed on sums claimed by way of unliquidated damages. (5: **28, 29**)

42. 'You cannot both treat a breach of condition as discharging a contract and also sue for damages for the breach.' Discuss this statement. Explain how the plaintiff might have a right of action on a *quantum meruit* claim in these circumstances. (5: **25, 30**)

43. Explain when the court may award the discretionary remedies of specific performance or injunctions in actions upon contracts. (5: **31, 32**)

44. The rule that an outsider cannot claim benefits or incur liabilities under a contract is not invariably applicable. Discuss. (6: **1–4**)

45. Why is it easier to transfer the benefit than the burden of a contract? Distinguish between legal and equitable assignments of choses in action, and explain how the effects differ. (6: **5–10**)

46. Summarise the main purposes of the Fair Trading Act 1973,

and outline the functions of the Director-General of Fair Trading. (7: **3, 4**)

47. Explain the functions and powers of the Monopolies and Mergers Commission and state what is meant by a 'monopoly situation.' (7: **7–9**)

48. What agreements must be registered under the Restrictive Trade Practices Act, and in what circumstances will they be enforced? (7: **12**)

49. What constitutes a 'false description' under the Trade Descriptions Act 1968. Give examples from recent cases. (7: **14**)

Specimen questions

1. (*a*) 'In the formation of a contract consideration must be real but need not be adequate.' Explain the meaning of this statement.

Does a promise made without consideration ever affect the promisor's position?

(*b*) Oris, a greengrocer, wished to go to Italy for his annual holiday. He requested Robert, a friend and a neighbour, to look after his children for two weeks. Robert looked after the children while Oris was away. On his return Oris told Robert 'I am grateful for your help and promise to pay you £500 as a reward at the end of this month.'

Oris has now changed his mind and refuses to pay £500 to Robert. Advise Robert.

2. (*a*) What is a penalty and how does it differ from liquidated damages?

(*b*) Distinguish between a *quantum meruit* claim and a claim for damages. In what circumstances is a *quantum meruit* claim appropriate?

3. (*a*) What is generally the purpose of exemption clauses in contracts? In what circumstances are such clauses enforced by the courts?

(*b*) A bought an electric blanket manufactured by X Ltd from B, a dealer in electrical goods, and gave it to C as a birthday present. Owing to defective manufacture the blanket caught fire the first time it was used and C was badly burned. C wishes to recover compensation. Advise him.

4. C went to D's circus, and bought a ticket at the entrance. On the back of this ticket there was a printed notice: 'The management accept no responsibility for the safety of their audiences.' Just before the circus was due to start an announcement was made to a similar effect. During the performance the stand upon which C was seated collapsed due to the fact that D's workmen had erected it carelessly, and C was injured.
Advise C.

5. On 1st January D wrote to C offering to sell him his motor car for £3,500. On 1st June C replied saying, 'I accept your offer, but I consider that £3,450 is enough.' D had in fact sold the car to X on 1st May.
C consults you as to his rights: advise him.

6. What are the requirements for establishing a defence of *non est factum* to a contractual claim?

7. J bought a ticket for a world cruise from the agents of K & Co, a shipping line. J was allergic to a certain type of deodorant; so, after he had paid the agent for the ticket and put it away in his wallet, he asked the agents' clerk whether this deodorant was in use on the ship. The clerk said that it was not. There was a statement on the ticket that 'The company accept no responsibility for any illness or other physical loss occasioned to passengers as a result of the state of the ship or of the use of any preparations or appliances theron.'
The deodorant in question was in fact in use on the ship. J went on the cruise and became ill as a direct consequence of inhaling it.
Advise J.

8. (*a*) 'An offer and an invitation to treat must be carefully distinguished, but a tender may be either.' Discuss.
(*b*) In the course of a conversation, A offered to sell his caravan to B for £1,000. B replied that he would like time to think it over, and A said 'I will give you three days.' That same day B posted a letter to A enclosing a cheque for £1,000 and agreeing to buy the caravan. On the same evening A and B chanced to meet and A informed B that he had just sold the caravan to C for £1,200. Advise B.

9. 'No one can claim the benefit of a contract unless he is a party to it.'
Consider this statement.

10. (*a*) Explain the rules the courts will apply in the assessment of unliquidated damages in an action for breach of contract.

(*b*) Golden Films Ltd decided to make a film and engaged Sir Austin, a famous actor, as the leading man. Before engaging Sir Austin, Golden Films Ltd had already incurred expenses in employing a script editor and a director. Sir Austin's engagements abroad were such that he could not perform the contract. So he repudiated the contract. Golden Films Ltd accepted the repudiation but were unsuccessful in finding a suitable replacement.

Advise Golden Films Ltd whether they can:

(*i*) sue Sir Austin for specific performance,

(*ii*) recover the expenses incurred before the contract in the form of salaries.

11. (*a*) Explain the equitable remedies for a mistake which is not recognised as an operative mistake at common law.

(*b*) Justin, an accountancy student, advertised his Mini for sale for £2,400. A rogue, posing as 'Sir Richard' the famous film producer, offered to buy the car. Justin accepted 'Sir Richard's' offer and received a cheque signed 'Sir Richard.' He was worried that the cheque might be worthless and was reluctant to let the rogue remove the car. Noticing Justin's hesitation the rogue produced a special identity card authorising 'Sir Richard' to enter the famous Brightwood Studios. Justin, being satisfied about 'Sir Richard's' identity, handed over the log book and allowed him to remove the car. The rogue, now posing as Justin, sold the car to David. David bought the car in good faith. Justin has received a letter from his bank that the cheque signed 'Sir Richard' has been dishonoured.

Advise Justin as to whether he can sue David and recover the car.

12. (*a*) 'The mere fact that one of the parties to a contract acted under a mistake does not, as a general rule, affect the validity of the contract.' When will a mistake by one of the parties affect the validity of the contract?

(*b*) B, a builder, submits an estimate to H, a householder, for the erection of a garage. H, who is satisfied with the price quoted, asks B to do the work. While building is still in progress B discovers that he made a mistake in his calculations on which the estimate was based and he asks your advice as to whether he is bound by his estimate which formed the basis of the contract with H.

13. (*a*) Distinguish carefully between conditions and warranties as terms of a contract. How will the court decide whether a contractual term is a condition or a warranty?

(b) A, who wished to take his family on a holiday, rents from B a villa for the month of August at an agreed rent. The agreement signed by A and B states *inter alia* that the villa is two hundred yards from the beach and that it has been recently redecorated.

What action may A take if he discovers in July that the villa is a good mile from the beach? Would your answer differ if the villa was in fact only two hundred yards from the beach but had not been decorated for five years? Give reasons for your answer.

14. (a) What rules do the courts apply in determining whether or not a covenant in restraint of trade is valid?

(b) D sold his newspaper shop to a large company which operated newspaper shops all over Britain. In the contract of sale D convenanted not to open a competing business within five miles of any of the purchaser's branches within five years. Three years later, D, who had become bored with retirement, opened a small newspaper shop three miles from one of the branches of the company that had purchased his business, but over a hundred miles from the shop he had sold. The company now seek an injunction to stop D from trading. Will their application be successful?

Part two
Agency and partnership

8
Agency

Formation of agency

1. Definition of agency. An agent is a person who is employed to bring his principal into contractual relations with third parties.

Since the agent does not contract on his own behalf, he does not need to possess full contractual capacity, e.g. he may be a minor. But the principal must have full capacity to make the contract in question.

NOTE: Under the doctrine of privity of contract, the agent is an outsider to the contract between principal and third party. Therefore he can only enforce the contract on his own behalf against the third party if he has a personal interest in it, e.g. a lien on proceeds of sale, such as is possessed by an auctioneer: *Chelmsford Auctions Ltd* v. *Poole* (1972).

2. Kinds of agency.

(*a*) *Universal:* an agent appointed to handle all the affairs of his principal. This kind of agency is very rare: it has to be created by deed, and is a form of general power of attorney.

(*b*) *General:* an agent who has authority to represent his principal in all business of a certain kind, e.g. to manage a branch bank.

Such an agent has implied authority to represent his principal in all matters incidental to the business in question. And a third party dealing with the agent is not affected by any secret restrictions on the agent's authority: *Watteau* v. *Fenwick* (1893), *see* **13** *below*.

(*c*) *Special:* an agent appointed for a particular purpose, not part of his normal business activities, and who is therefore given only limited powers, e.g. where a bank manager is asked by a friend to act as agent in the sale of the friend's house.

(*d*) *Del credere:* an agent employed to sell goods, who promises to make sure that clients introduced by him to his principal will pay for the goods sold. (Note: this is not a contract of guarantee and does not need to be evidenced in writing.)

3. Express appointment. Where the agent is employed to execute a deed on behalf of his principal his appointment must be by deed, and the agency is called a Power of Attorney, e.g. where A is appointed to execute a conveyance of land: *see* the Powers of Attorney Act 1971. Under the Enduring Powers of Attorney Act 1985 powers of attorney may be created which will survive any mental incapacity of the donor and may make provision regarding such powers.

In most other cases the agent's appointment can be in any form.

4. Implied agency. An agency may be implied from certain relationships, e.g. partnership. Thus where a dealer acts as middleman between a hire-purchase finance company and the hirer of goods, there is now an implied agency between the company and the dealer to the extent that the company must accept liability for representations made by the dealer: Consumer Credit Act 1974, *see* 10.

This can be extremely important, particularly in relation to buying an item, such as a motor car, with money made available by a hire-purchase company. Suppose that money is loaned to a customer of a car dealer because the finance house has an agreement with that dealer by which it provides finance to customers of that dealer. Under the Consumer Credit Act, the dealer is the agent of the finance house. This means that the latter has to take the responsibility for anything said by the dealer, his agent, in negotiating the supply of the car. The effect is that if, for instance, the dealer (the agent) has made a misrepresentation, the customer will be able to take action against the finance house (as principal). The customer will be entitled therefore to rescind the credit agreement and the agreement for the supply of the car.

5. Agency by estoppel. Where P allows third parties to believe that A is acting as his authorised agent, he will be estopped from denying the agency (even if in fact he had no authority at all) if such third parties rely on it to their detriment.

This rule applies even where no agency was ever intended by the principal.

Similarly a husband, partner or master, who allows his wife, co-partner or servant to act as his agent cannot evade liability on the agent's contracts even after revocation of the agency unless he has expressly notified third parties with whom the agent has habitually been dealing: *Scarf* v. *Jardine* (1882).

> EXAMPLE: L owned a house and allowed his wife to induce S to buy it, though he did not give her authority to sell it. S commenced doing repairs to the house and L then decided he did not wish to sell it. S claimed specific performance and L denied that his wife had authority to sell. HELD: L had allowed S to believe Mrs L was a properly authorised agent and was therefore estopped from denying her authority to contract on his behalf: *Spiro* v. *Lintern* (1973).

6. Agency by ratification. Where (*a*) a duly appointed agent exceeds his authority, or (*b*) a person having no authority purports to act as agent, the principal incurs no liability on the contract supposedly made on his behalf. *See* **14** *below*.

But in such cases the principal may expressly or impliedly ratify the agent's transaction and so accept liability.

Ratification is only possible where:

(*a*) the agent claimed expressly to be contracting as agent, and named his principal: *Keighley Maxsted* v. *Durant* (1901);
(*b*) the principal had full contractual capacity both (*i*) at the time of ratification, and (*ii*) at the time the agent made the contract. Thus a company after its incorporation cannot ratify a contract supposedly made on its behalf before incorporation, since it did not exist and therefore had no contractual capacity when the

contract was made: *Kelner* v. *Baxter* (1866). But where a person purports to contract as agent for a nonexisting company, he will be liable personally on the contract: Companies Act 1985, s. 36(4);

(c) at the time of ratification the principal had full knowledge of all material facts, or had agreed to dispense with it: *Marsh* v. *Joseph* (1897).

> NOTE: Where ratification takes place it is retrospective, i.e. it dates back to the time when the contract was made by the agent. Thus ratification might defeat an attempted repudiation by the third party, made after the date of contracting and on the discovery by the third party of the agent's lack of authority: *Bolton Partners* v. *Lambert* (1889).

7. Agency of necessity. Commercial agency of necessity may arise in favour of a carrier, shipmaster, etc., providing the person claiming it can prove the following:

(*a*) That it was impossible to get instructions from the principal, e.g. because communication was impossible: *Springer* v. *G.W. Railway* (1921).

(*b*) That there was a real and definite commercial necessity, e.g. where the master of a ship sells a cargo to prevent it rotting.

(*c*) That he acted honestly in the interests of his principal while lacking any instructions.

(These rules probably mean that a commercial agency of necessity will only be implied in favour of a person who is already a duly appointed agent for the principal, and who must exceed his instructions in an emergency. It is doubtful whether a person not already an agent could claim an agency of necessity.)

Termination of agency

8. By act of parties. An agency may be terminated by mutual agreement like any other contract, but in addition the principal may at any time revoke the agent's authority and so prevent him making binding contracts with third parties (though revocation, if unjustified, may leave the agent with a right of action for breach of contract against the principal).

Revocation is not possible in these circumstances:

(*a*) Where the authority is 'coupled with interest,' i.e. where the agent was appointed to enable him to secure some benefit already owed to him by the principal: *Smart* v. *Saunders* (1848).

(*b*) A power of attorney (agency granted under a seal) cannot be revoked where it is granted to secure (*i*) a proprietary interest of the grantee, or (*ii*) performance of an obligation owed to the grantee.

The power remains irrevocable so long as (*i*) the grantee continues to possess the proprietary interest, or (*ii*) the obligation remains undischarged, unless the grantor discharges the obligation, dies, becomes bankrupt or incapacitated, or (if a body corporate) is dissolved: Powers of Attorney Act 1971, s. 4.

The Enduring Powers of Attorney Act 1985 makes provision for powers of attorney executed in a prescribed form and expressed to continue in spite of the donor's supervening mental incapacity. Such an enduring power is not revoked by such incapacity but when such incapacity occurs, the power is in effect suspended until registered by the court. Once an enduring power has been registered, it can no longer be revoked by the donor, but only with the consent of the court.

(*c*) Where revocation would involve personal loss to the agent, the principal may be estopped from revoking without the consent of the agent: *Seymour* v. *Bridge* (1885).

(*d*) The principal cannot revoke in such a way as to damage the interests of innocent third parties, e.g. by breaking contracts the agent has already made with them.

9. By operation of law. Agency is automatically terminated in the following cases.

(*a*) By death of principal or agent, save in some exceptional cases.

(*b*) By bankruptcy or insanity of principal or agent, save in exceptional cases:

EXAMPLE: X employed T as solicitor to sue Y. T commenced the action and brought the case to court. Unknown to T, X had gone insane in the meanwhile. HELD: T's agency was automatically terminated, and he was therefore liable to Y for damages for breach of warranty of authority: *Yonge* v. *Toynbee* (1910).

(c) By frustration: *see* 5: **18**.
(d) By intervening illegality.
(e) By the agent accomplishing his mission.
(f) By effluxion of time, where the agency was created for a limited time.
(g) By the principal becoming an alien enemy.
(h) *See* Enduring Powers of Attorney Act 1985 and **8**, *above*.

Duties of principal and agent

10. Duties of agent. Apart from the obvious duty to obey the principal's instructions, these are as follows:

(a) To exercise due care and diligence on the principal's behalf, plus any special skill he professes to have: *Keppel* v. *Wheeler* (1927). In *Chaudhry* v. *Prabhakar* (1988), the plaintiff asked a close friend, who had some knowledge of motor cars, but who was not a mechanic, to find her a suitable second-hand car to buy. She stipulated that it should not have been involved in any accident. He found one but noticed that the bonnet had been crumpled and straightened or replaced, yet thought the car to be in good condition. He recommended the plaintiff to buy it, which she did. A few months later it became apparent that the car had been in a very bad accident, was poorly repaired and unroadworthy. The court held that a gratuitous agent who offered to buy a second-hand car for another owed that other a duty of care to exercise the degree of care and skill which could be reasonably expected of him in all the circumstances of the case, that degree of skill and care being measured objectively and not subjectively. Since the friend knew that the plaintiff was relying on him, and since he ought to have been put on enquiry by the crumpled bonnet as to whether the car had been in any accident, he was in breach of his duty to take reasonable care.

(*b*) To disclose promptly to the principal any material information he may receive in execution of his task.

(*c*) Not to disclose confidential information entrusted to him by his principal.

(*d*) Not to delegate performance of his duties (*delegatus non potest delegare:* 'a delegate cannot delegate'). But this prohibition is not strictly applied, and the agent may usually delegate performance where required by (*i*) commercial usage or (*ii*) necessity, or (*iii*) where expressly or impliedly authorised by the principal: *De Bussche* v. *Alt* (1878).

(*e*) Not to let his interest conflict with his duty, e.g. not to compete with his principal. An agent must maintain a high standard of good faith. Thus it is wrong for a broker employed to buy goods to sell his own goods to his principal without full disclosure: *Armstrong* v. *Jackson* (1917). Similarly an agent should not accept a commission from both parties without his principal's knowledge and consent: *North & South Trust Co.* v. *Berkeley* (1971).

(*f*) Not to make any secret profit. If, beyond his commission, he receives any extra profit in the course of his duties he must disclose this to the principal.

If he fails to do so: (*i*) the principal can sue him for the amount kept secret; (*ii*) the principal can refuse to pay the agent his commission, and can terminate the agency without notice; (*iii*) the principal can sue the agent and the third party for damages to compensate him for any loss he has sustained; (*iv*) the principal can repudiate the contract (whether or not the bribe was effective); (*v*) the agent and the briber are criminally liable: *Salford Corporation* v. *Lever* (1891): *see* the Prevention of Corruption Act 1916.

EXAMPLES: (1) E owned property which D offered to purchase. Before contracts had been exchanged, the defendants made an application for planning permission in the name of E and signed as 'agent' for E. Planning permission was given before completion, but unknown to E. It was held that E was entitled to the profits which had accrued to D from the granting of planning permission. D had acted as self-appointed agents and had placed themselves in a fiduciary relationship to E with the result that they were obliged to disclose the application for planning permission: *English* v. *Dedham Vale Properties Ltd* (1978). (2) In *Logicrose* v. *Southend United Football Club* (1988), M had a controlling shareholding in the defendants as nominee for J who was the defendants' chairman. He negotiated the grant of a licence to the plaintiffs to operate a market on the defendants' land. M, in reaching that agreement, failed to disclose to the defendants' board that their solicitors had strongly advised against that agreement or that, acting on J's instructions, he had required the plaintiffs to pay £70,000 to an offshore company controlled by him. Subsequently M disclosed the payment and accounted for most of that sum. The defendants served a notice to determine the licence. The plaintiffs claimed the return of £70,000 or damages, and the defendants counterclaimed for rescission. The court gave judgement for the defendants and said that a principal who discovered that his agent had either obtained or arranged to obtain a bribe from the other party to the transaction was entitled to treat it as void *ab initio*. He was also entitled to rescind where, to the knowledge of the other party, the agent had placed himself in a position where his interests and duties conflicted so that he could no longer give disinterested advice; but that in these circumstances, the other party had to have actual knowledge or be blind wilfully to the fact that the agent intended to conceal his dealings from his principal. Since the plaintiffs knew that M was concealing his dealings from his principal, the defendants were entitled to rescind the contract and it was immaterial that the plaintiffs, who had the requisite knowledge, did not know whether M's concealment of his dealings was for his personal interest or not. Where an agent received a bribe, the principal was entitled to recover it from the agent whether the principal elected to affirm or rescind the contract. In recovering the money, there was no implication that he adopted the transaction.

11. Duties of principal.

(*a*) To pay any agreed commission or remuneration and not to prevent or hinder the agent from earning this: *Rhodes* v. *Forwood* (1876).

The agent has a lien over goods belonging to the principal enabling him to retain such goods until his commission is paid.

When commission becomes payable depends on the contract between principal and agent, e.g. when the agent is employed to sell goods or land, his commission may become payable:

(*i*) when he introduces a client (whether sale results or not); or

(*ii*) on completion of the sale, and payment of the price. (The signing of an agreement 'subject to contract' does not amount to completion: *Luxor Ltd* v. *Cooper* (1941).)

(*b*) To indemnify the agent against liabilities properly incurred in the discharge of his duties: *Christoforides* v. *Terry* (1924).

12. Vicarious liability. A master may be liable for wrongs (torts) committed by his agent. The extent of this indirect or vicarious liability depends on whether the agent is:

(*a*) an independent contractor, i.e. an outsider employed to do certain work and told what to do but left free to decide how he will do it. The principal is only liable for his torts if (*i*) he expressly or impliedly commissioned the tort, or (*ii*) he delegated to the contractor performance of a legal duty and the contractor is negligent;

(*b*) a servant, i.e. a person employed as an integral part of the principal's business, who is told both what to do and how to do it: *Mersey Docks etc.* v. *Coggins* (1947).

The principal is liable for all torts committed by a servant *in the course of his employment*, i.e. where the servant does improperly what he is employed to do properly.

NOTE: (*i*) *Course of employment*. What acts are part of the course of employment, or reasonably incidental thereto, is a question of fact in each case: *Chapman* v. *Oakleigh Animal Products Ltd* (1970). Thus a solicitor was held liable where one of his staff gave fraudulent advice to a client of the firm, despite the solicitor's claim that giving fraudulent advice could not be regarded as part of the course of employment: *Lloyd* v. *Grace,*

Smith & Co. (1912). But a bus company was held not liable for the negligent driving of a bus conductor who had temporarily taken over the wheel, since this was not what he was employed to do: *Ricketts* v. *Tilling* (1915). *(ii) Express prohibition.* The master is vicariously liable if the servant is doing improperly what he is employed to do properly, even if the master has expressly forbidden the particular wrongful act. Thus a bus company was held liable for an accident caused by bus drivers racing to bus stops, despite the fact that the company had expressly prohibited such racing: *Limpus* v. *L.G.O.C.* (1862). A dairy company was liable when a passenger in a milkfloat was injured through the driver's negligence, even though giving lifts was expressly prohibited: *Rose* v. *Plenty* (1976).

> EXAMPLE: Bus conductor (contrary to orders) drove a bus at the depot to enable his own bus to be driven out of the depot, and injured fellow-employees. HELD: He was acting outside the course of his employment and his employers were not vicariously liable for his negligent driving: *Iqbal* v. *L.T.E.* (1973).

The authority of the agent

13. Real and ostensible authority. Extent of the agent's authority depends (*a*) on his contract with his principal, or (*b*) on the law, where this implies a particular authority for particular kinds of agency.

This implied, or ostensible authority, may exceed the agent's actual authority from his principal, and may therefore render the principal liable on contracts made by the agent beyond the limits of his actual authority.

> EXAMPLES: (1) The manager of a public house was forbidden to order tobaccos by his principal but did so. HELD: The principal was liable to pay the seller, since a manager of a public house would usually have authority to make orders of this kind, and the seller could therefore rely on the agent's ostensible authority in the absence of express knowledge of the limitation imposed by the principal: *Watteau* v. *Fenwick* (1893). (2) In *Discount Kitchens* v. *Crawford* (1988), it was held that where an employee

of company A had had discussions with a potential purchaser, and had then left to join company B but continued negotiations and entered into a contract with the purchaser of goods and services to be provided by company B, the employee could not be said to have fixed company A with any liability since he had not only no actual authority, but he had no apparent authority.

(3) In *Charrington Fuel Oil* v. *Parvant* (1988), it was held that where property changes hands, a request by the owners to previous suppliers of goods (who have no notice of the change) to deliver further goods to the same address, does not amount to a representation that would form the basis of an estoppel on which the ostensible authority concept could be founded, and under which the former owner could be held liable for payment.

14. Breach of warranty of authority. Every person professing to act as agent for another impliedly warrants that he has authority to make binding contracts on behalf of his principal.

If therefore an agent lacks the authority he professes to have he is liable to an action for damages for breach of the implied warranty of authority, brought by the person with whom he has been dealing: *Collen* v. *Wright* (1857).

The agent is still liable for damages, even if he was acting in good faith, genuinely believing he had the authority he claimed, e.g. where his authority has been terminated without his knowledge by the death of his principal: *Yonge* v. *Toynbee* (1910).

But he is not liable if his lack of authority was known to the third party at the time of making the contract, or if the third party agreed to exclude the liability for breach of warranty: *Lilly* v. *Smales* (1892).

(Where a dishonest agent deliberately claims authority he knows he does not possess, he is also liable to an action for fraud by the third party whom he has deceived.)

15. Relations between principal and third parties. Generally, once he has made a contract on behalf of his principal the agent drops out of the transaction and privity of contract exists between the principal and the third party: *see* 6: 1–3.

But the results of an agent's contract differ slightly depending on whether (*a*) he has disclosed the fact of his agency, or (*b*) he has concealed the fact that he is merely an agent for another person.

Each of these possibilities is dealt with separately below.

16. Agent acting for named principal. Here the agent generally incurs neither rights nor liabilities under the contract, and drops out as soon as it is made: *Gadd* v. *Houghton* (1876). Where a person holds himself out as an agent for a named person, but is in fact the agent of an unnamed person, the agent is personally liable: *Savills* v. *Scott* (1988).

> EXCEPTIONS: (1) Where the agent agrees to accept personal liability. (2) Where the agent signs a deed he is personally liable thereon and the principal incurs no liability unless the agent was himself appointed by deed (a power of attorney) — in which case the agent drops out and the principal is liable in the ordinary way. (3) Where the agent signs a bill of exchange in his own name, he is personally liable thereon. (To avoid this he should make it perfectly clear that he is signing merely as agent, e.g. by signing 'for and on behalf of' a named principal. A director signing a cheque on behalf of his company should always take this precaution.) (4) Where trade custom makes the agent personally liable, e.g. formerly where an agent acted for an overseas principal, there was a presumption that he accepted personal responsibility; this presumption no longer exists, and the agent is not personally liable in such a case unless it can be shown that he volunteered to accept personal liability: *Teheran-Europe Ltd* v. *S.T. Belton Ltd* (1968). (5) Where the supposed agent is in fact the principal, but purports to contract merely as an agent.

17. Agent acting for undisclosed principal. This covers two possible situations: (*a*) where the agent discloses the fact that he is merely an agent, but conceals the identity of his principal, and (*b*) where he conceals the agency altogether, and appears to be acting on his own behalf.

(*a*) *Agency revealed: principal concealed.* Here the agent drops out in the normal way, providing he makes it clear when contracting that he does so merely as agent. If he fails to do so he is personally liable on the contract. (The exceptions stated under **16** *above* apply to this situation.)

(*b*) *Agency concealed altogether: the doctrine of the undisclosed principal.* Here the third party can enforce the contract against the agent or, when he discovers his identity and existence, against the principal.

The third party thus has an option whether to compel the agent to accept personal liability, or to shift liability to the principal as soon as his identity is revealed.

BUT NOTE: (1) He cannot enforce the contract against both agent and principal. If he sues one he cannot later sue the other. (2) He may be estopped from suing the principal at all if he allows the principal to think he has settled matters satisfactorily with the agent, e.g. by unreasonable delay in taking action against the principal after his identity is revealed: *Heald* v. *Kenworthy* (1855).

Special classes of agent

18. Factors. A factor is a mercantile agent employed to sell goods for a commission 'in the ordinary course of his business,' i.e. a professional buying and selling agent: Factors Act 1889. (A factor differs from a broker in that he has possession of the goods to be sold, while a broker usually does not.)

If a factor has possession of goods with the consent of the owner for some purpose other than sale but contrary to his instructions does sell the goods, the purchaser obtains a good title (providing he did not know of the limitation on the factor's authority). In such cases the principal is legally estopped from denying that the purpose of the factor's possession was sale: Factors Act 1889, s. 2. Such an agent cannot pass good title under the Act, unless he has had continuous physical possession of the goods as factor: *Astley Industrial Trust* v. *Miller* (1968).

A factor has a lien over goods in his possession and power to pledge them for security.

19. Brokers. A broker is a commercial agent employed to make contracts between his principal and others for a commission usually called brokerage. (An agent employed to make non-commercial contracts is therefore not a broker, e.g. a contract to hire a singer for a charity concert.)

Unlike factors brokers do not have possession of goods for sale, and cannot therefore sell in their own name. They have no lien over goods and no power to lodge them for security.

A broker is primarily agent for the seller of goods, but on making a contract with a purchaser he becomes agent for the purchaser also.

20. Auctioneers: *see* 10: **63–67.**

21. Position of banks. The relationship between bank and customer is primarily that of debtor and creditor, with the bank usually the debtor (as long as the customer's account is in credit).

In addition there is a complex implied contract between a bank and its customers, which imposes many duties on the bank similar to those of an ordinary agent: *Joachimsson* v. *Swiss Bank Corporation* (1921).

'The limits of a banker's business cannot be laid down as a matter of law': *Banbury* v. *Bank of Montreal* (1918), but the following general rules apply.

(*a*) The bank is legally bound to honour its customer's cheques up to the limit of his credit (or agreed loan facilities) but not beyond. Thus if the account is £100 in credit and the customer draws a cheque for £100.50, the bank is theoretically entitled to refuse payment (it cannot legally pay part of a cheque).

(*b*) The bank has an implied right to charge reasonable commission for its services (and interest on loans).

(*c*) The bank must not disclose its customer's affairs, save under compulsion of law, e.g. under a court order. In *Re State of Norway's Application (No 1)* (1989), the State of Norway issued letters of request to the High Court in England requesting certain bankers to give evidence in proceedings before a Norwegian court. The witnesses appealed to the Court of Appeal against an order granting the application on the ground that the giving of the testimony would be a breach of their duty of confidence as bankers. The Court of Appeal ruled that in order to determine whether witnesses should be ordered to break their duty of confidence by answering the questions in the letter of request, the court had to consider whether the interest in protecting the confidence was outweighed by the public interest in assisting a foreign court. In the circumstances the balance was against compelling the witnesses to violate their duty of confidence.

(*d*) Unlike most agents, the bank has a general lien over any of the customer's securities in its possession, e.g. shares, title deeds, insurance policies.

(*e*) Advice on investment is a service offered expressly by most banks. Where offered, there is an implied duty to exercise care in providing advice, and the bank could be liable in negligence if one of its managers gave negligent advice and so caused damage to the customer: *Woods* v. *Martins Bank* (1958).

(*f*) A bank is entitled to dispose as it pleases of money deposited by a customer provided it pays his cheques on demand (during business hours) or through a clearing house.

(*g*) A bank must abide by an express mandate of the customer, and by any express agreement made with him.

(*h*) The bank is entitled to require that the customer shall exercise reasonable care in drawing cheques. If the bank pays a forged cheque and the forgery was facilitated by the customer's carelessness, the loss falls on the customer and not on the bank: *London Joint Stock Bank* v. *Macmillan & Arthur* (1918).

22. Estate agents. These are agents employed to manage property, and also to buy or sell land or houses for a commission (usually paid by the seller).

The scope of their authority as seller's agent varies, but mere engagement of an estate agent does not confer any authority to receive as agent of the vendor a pre-contract deposit. Where a deposit is paid to the agent in such circumstances, the purchaser is at all times until contract the only person with any claim or right to the deposit and his was a right on demand. The vendor has no such claim or right and no control over the deposit. Accordingly, where a vendor has not authorised an agent to receive a deposit on his behalf, he is not liable to repay it on the agent's default: *Sorrell* v. *Finch* (1976).

With regard to commission, if that commission is payable 'on introducing a person ready, willing and able to purchase', commission will be payable only if the person introduced shows his willingness and ability to buy (not necessarily by a binding contract) and remains so willing and able up to the time of completion. If the purchaser does not complete, no commission is payable even if the purchaser's deposit is forfeited by the vendor. Nor is the vendor bound to claim specific performance of any binding contract. Once there is a binding contract of sale, however, the vendor cannot withdraw except at the risk of having to pay his agent commission, because it is his own fault that the sale has not been completed. In order to give business efficacy to an agency contract under which commission is payable on the agent introducing a buyer, there is an implied term that once a sale contract is concluded with a buyer introduced by an agent, the principal (vendor) will not commit a breach of contract with the buyer which would deprive the agent of his commission. Moreover, if a person who is able to purchase is introduced and expresses readiness and willingness, by an unqualified offer, to purchase, though such offer has not been accepted by the vendor and could be withdrawn, if it is not the vendor but the purchaser who withdraws, the case is entirely different and no commission is payable. Where commission was payable on introducing someone 'willing and able to purchase' leasehold property, and after contract the landlord refused consent to the assignment, it was held that the agent was not entitled to commission because, although the person introduced was financially able to effect the purchase, he was not suitable and acceptable on other grounds, and was therefore not 'able' to purchase.

Estate agents are also subject to the provisions of the Estate Agents Act 1979. Section 3 of the Act empowers the Director General of Fair Trading to ban persons who are unfit to carry on estate agency work. The Act also provides for minimum standards of competence, though the relevant section is not yet in force. Further provisions of the Act include the following: (*a*) the duty to give certain information about charges and the time when such charges become payable. Failure to comply with this obligation means that the contract can be enforced only on a court order. (*b*) The duty to declare any conflict of interest, actual or potential, or any personal interest with respect to the transaction. (*c*) No estate agent may seek from a purchaser a pre-contract deposit in excess of a prescribed limit (this section is not yet in force). (*d*) Where a deposit is taken from a purchaser, either as a pre-contractual deposit or as a deposit on exchange of contracts, there are duties relating to the keeping of such money in separate client accounts.

9
Partnerships

Nature and formation of partnerships

1. Definition of partnership. 'Partnership is the relation which subsists between persons carrying on a business in common with a view of profit': Partnership Act 1890, s. 1.

Registered, statutory and chartered companies are specifically excluded from this definition (note also that a non-profit-making association cannot be a partnership).

Capacity to form a partnership is governed by the ordinary rules of contractual capacity: *see* 3. A minor who remains a partner after becoming eighteen becomes liable for the firm's debts incurred after his eighteenth birthday: *Goode* v. *Harrison* (1871).

The general rule is that a partnership must not consist of more than 20 persons. This does not, however, prohibit the formation of: a partnership carrying on practice as solicitors and consisting of persons each of whom is a solicitor; a partnership carrying on practice as accountants and consisting of persons each of whom is a member of a body of accountants established in the United Kingdom and for the time being recognised by the Secretary of State, or is a person for the time being authorised by the Secretary of State to be appointed as an auditor either as having similar qualifications obtained outside the United Kingdom or as having obtained adequate knowledge and experience in the course of his employment by a member of a body of accountants recognised by the Secretary of State, or as having, before 6 August 1947, practised in Great Britain as an accountant; a partnership carrying on business as a member of a recognised stock exchange and consisting of persons each of whom is a member of that stock exchange; and a partnership carrying on business of a description specified in regulations made by the Secretary of State: Companies Act 1985, s. 716. Statutory instruments have been made in relation to partnerships consisting of: patent agents, surveyors, auctioneers, valuers, estate agents, land agents and those engaged in land management, actuaries, consulting engineers, building designers and loss adjusters: *see* the Partnership (Unrestricted Size) Regulations, Nos. 1–5, 1968, 1970 and 1982.

2. Tests for establishing partnerships: P.A., s. 2.

(*a*) *Co-ownership* of property does not of itself create a partnership in the property, even though the co-owners share profits.

(*b*) *Sharing of gross returns* of a business does not of itself indicate a partnership, even if coupled with co-ownership of the property or business.

(*c*) *Share of profits* is presumptive evidence of partnership, but the presumption can be rebutted by showing that the purpose of sharing was for some other reason, e.g.:

(*i*) payment of a debt by instalments out of profits;

(*ii*) remuneration to a servant or agent of the business;

(*iii*) payment of an annuity or portion to a widow or child of a deceased partner in the business;

(*iv*) payment of interest (varying with profits) on a loan advanced for use in the business;

(*v*) payment to the seller of the goodwill of a business (where the consideration is a share of profits).

However, if the business goes bankrupt, the recipient of moneys under (*iv*) and (*v*) above is a deferred creditor in the bankruptcy: 18.

NOTE: Whether a partnership exists therefore depends on the circumstances in each case and the intention of the parties. Sharing losses is stronger evidence of partnership than sharing profits, but is still not conclusive: *Walker* v. *Hirsch* (1884). If executors of a will carry on the testator's business as instructed in the will, they do not automatically become partners: *Re Fisher & Sons* (1912). Even where a partnership exists, a salaried partner on termination of the partnership cannot ask for a winding-up order. He does not share in the equity of the firm, being only entitled to his salary: *Stekel* v. *Ellice* (1973).

3. The firm name. Under the provisions of the Business Names Act 1985, all orders, invoices, business letters etc. must disclose the true names of all owners of the business (whether individuals or companies) and also the addresses within Great Britain at which they can be contacted. In addition, such information must be displayed on a notice in a prominent position at the business premises. A customer is entitled to ask for a written list of the required information which must be supplied to him immediately. These requirements are relaxed in the case of a partnership which consists of more than 20 members, provided two conditions are satisfied. First, the document must not contain the names of any partners except as signatories; and second, it must state an address at which a full list of partners can be inspected. Actions in contract by a person who has failed to comply with the Act can be dismissed if the defendant can show that he has a claim against that person because of his failure to comply or if he has suffered loss because of such failure. The court can allow the action to proceed if it considers it just and equitable. Failure to satisfy the requirements of the Act is also a criminal offence.

4. Illegal associations. An association may be illegal because of the following.

(*a*) Its objects are illegal;
(*b*) Its membership exceeds the statutory limits (i.e. twenty in banking and most other partnerships, or more in some firms of solicitors, accountants and stockbrokers): Companies Act 1985;
(*c*) It is an association forbidden by law, e.g. a professional partnership between a solicitor and an unqualified person.

The effects of illegality are that (*i*) the members cannot enforce any rights or obligations among themselves, (*ii*) the members cannot enforce any contract against any innocent outsider, and (*iii*) the illegality cannot be raised as a defence in any action brought against them by an innocent outsider.

Dealings with outsiders

5. Agency of partners. Each general partner is an implied agent for the firm, and can make his co-partners liable on debts incurred by him on behalf of the firm: P.A., s. 5. But he has no implied authority to bind the firm in any matter outside the scope of the firm's business: s. 7.

A person dealing with a partner is not affected by any secret restriction on the partner's agency, unless he knows of it or does not believe him to be a partner: s. 8.

Liability of partners for debts and other contractual obligations is joint: s. 9 (contrast liability in tort). Thus a creditor can sue all the partners jointly, or any one of them for the whole debt. But he has only one right of action, and if he obtains judgement for the whole debt against one (even if the judgement is unsatisfied) he cannot later launch proceedings against the others, since he is taken to have waived his rights against them: Rule in *Kendall* v. *Hamilton* (1879). The Rule in *Kendall's* case has been modified by s. 3 of the Civil Liability (Contribution) Act 1978 as follows: 'Judgement recovered against one person in respect of any debt or damage shall not be a bar to an action, or to the continuance of an action, against any other person who is (apart from such bar) jointly liable with him in respect of the same debt or damage'.

6. Extent of implied agency.

(*a*) A partner can bind the firm by the following transactions.
    (*i*)   By selling the firm's goods: *Dore* v. *Wilkinson* (1817).
    (*ii*) By purchasing goods for the firm: *Bond* v. *Gibson* (1808).
    (*iii*) By accepting payment of debts due to the firm: *Porter* v. *Taylor* (1817).
    (*iv*) By engaging or discharging employees: *Birkham* v. *Drake* (1841).

(*b*) In a trading partnership, he has the following additional powers:
    (*i*)   To borrow money on the firm's credit: *Lane* v. *Williams* (1692).

(*ii*) To sign bills of exchange on behalf of the firm; Bills of Exchange Act 1882.

(*iii*) To employ a solicitor on behalf of the firm: *Tomlinson* v. *Broadsmith* (1896).

NOTE: There is no implied authority (1) to execute deeds — this requires express authorisation by power of attorney: *see* 8: 1–7; (2) to submit disputes to arbitration; and (3) to give a guarantee in the firm's name, unless the giving of guarantees is within the usual business of the firm.

7. Liability of incoming and outgoing partners.

(*a*) *Incoming partners.* A new partner is not liable (unless otherwise agreed) for debts incurred before he joined the firm: P.A., s. 17(1).

(*b*) *Outgoing partners.* A retiring partner is not liable for debts incurred after he retired, but is liable for debts incurred before his retirement: s. 17(2). (Release from this liability is by means of a novation under which the remaining partners are substituted for the retiring partner in respect of his liability to the creditors, with the latters' consent.)

But an outgoing partner remains liable if he has allowed creditors to believe him to be continuing in the firm: s. 36. To protect himself from this liability, he must (*i*) give express notice of his retirement to persons who were dealing with the firm before his retirement, (*ii*) notify persons who trade with the firm in the future by advertising his retirement in the *London Gazette*: s. 36(2).

(*c*) *Death or bankruptcy.* The estate of a deceased or bankrupt partner is not liable for partnership debts incurred after death or bankruptcy: s. 36(3).

(*d*) *Dormant partners.* A general partner not known to be a member of the firm to creditors seeking to enforce a partnership debt is not liable for debts contracted after his retirement from active participation.

(*e*) *Holding out.* A person not a partner who holds himself out, or allows others to hold him out, as being a partner in a firm is liable to persons who rely on such representations as though he were in fact a partner, i.e. he becomes a partner by estoppel: s. 14.

(*f*) *A continuing guarantee* given to a firm is terminated as to future transactions by any change in the membership of the firm: s. 18. This section does not apply where (*i*) there is an agreement to the contrary, (*ii*) the guarantee relates to past transactions, or (*iii*) the guarantee is given by the firm: *see Guarantees*, 17.

8. Nature of firm's liability.

(*a*) Partners are jointly liable for the firm's contracts, unless otherwise agreed: P.A., s. 9. (The liability may be joint and several if the partners expressly so agree.)

(*b*) Partners are jointly and severally liable for torts committed on behalf of the firm: s. 12.

(*c*) The estate of a deceased partner is severally liable for the firm's debts incurred during his lifetime, subject to the prior payment of his own separate debts: s. 9.

> NOTE: Difference between joint and several liability. (1) In joint liability, the plaintiff has only one right of action and he may use this either in suing the firm jointly, or in suing any individual partner separately. But if he sues one alone he waives his right of action against the others, and cannot later sue them even though he obtains judgement against the one sued but is unable to get his money because of that partner's insolvency: *Kendall* v. *Hamilton* (1879). But *see* the modification of this judgement as explained in 5, *above*. (2) In joint and several liability, the plaintiff has several causes of action. He can sue all partners together, or can sue them separately (in successive actions if necessary). (3) As between the partners themselves, whether the liability is joint or joint and several, they must contribute equally to the damages paid.

9. Notices and admissions.

(*a*) Any admissions or representation by a partner in the course of business and about the firm's affairs are evidence against the firm: P.A., s. 15.

(*b*) Notice given bona fide to any active partner concerning business matters operates as notice to the firm: s. 16.

Rights and duties of partners

10. Partnership articles. A partnership may arise by express agreement, or by implication, i.e. where persons conduct a business in common with a view of profit: P.A., s. 1. Where a partnership is formed by express agreement (the 'partnership articles'), the rights and duties of the partners among themselves are regulated by that agreement. Where a partnership arises by implication, or wherever the articles (if any) are silent, the rights and duties of the partners are governed by the Partnership Act 1890.

NOTE: Once formed, a partnership is a relationship requiring the utmost good faith and each partner must disclose to his colleagues all material information coming to his notice: *see* 4: **19**.

11. Rights and duties: P.A., s. 24. Unless otherwise agreed, the following rules apply.

(*a*) *Equal shares.* Partners are entitled to share equally in capital and profits, and must contribute equally towards losses (agreement to the contrary may be inferred from past dealings).

(*b*) *Indemnity.* The firm must indemnify a partner against liabilities properly incurred (*i*) in the ordinary course of business, or (*ii*) in anything necessarily done for the preservation of the business.

(*c*) *Interest on advances.* A partner is entitled to interest at 5 per cent on money (other than capital) advanced to the business (but he is not entitled, before the ascertainment of profits, to interest on capital).

(*d*) *Management.* Every partner is entitled to participate in management of the business.

(*e*) *No remuneration.* A partner is not entitled to any remuneration for his services (unless expressly agreed).

(*f*) *New partners* can only be introduced with the consent of all existing partners. (Notice that there is no implied power to expel partners: *see* **12**, *below*.)

(g) *Disputes as to ordinary matters* may be settled by majority (but change of business requires unanimous agreement).

(h) *Partnership books* are to be kept at the firm's principal place of business and every partner is entitled to inspect them and copy them whenever he thinks fit.

12. Expulsion of partners. A partner can only be expelled from the firm if a power to do so has been conferred by express agreement between the partners: P.A., s. 25. Such power must be executed in good faith and in the interests of the firm, otherwise the expulsion is void: *Blisset* v. *Daniels* (1853). It was held in *Hitchman* v. *CBAS Services* (1983) that a clause in a partnership deed which required a particular partner to be a signatory to any notice expelling a partner did not apply when that partner was being expelled.

13. Duties of partners. Apart from any duties imposed by the partnership articles, the following statutory duties are implied.

(a) *Uberrima fides.* Partners must render true accounts and full information on partnership matters to their colleagues: s. 28.

(b) *To account* for any benefits derived from the partnership business without the consent of the other partners, i.e. a partner must not make 'secret profits' (c.f. agents: *see* 8: **10**).

(c) *Not to compete* with the firm, without the consent of the other partners. Any profits made by such unauthorised competition can be claimed by the firm: s. 30.

14. Partnership property. All partnership property must be held and applied exclusively for the purposes of the firm and in accordance with the partnership articles (if any): s. 20(1).

Whether property is partnership property or not is a question of fact in each case. 'Partnership property' includes the following:

(a) Property originally brought into the partnership stock: s. 20(1).

(b) Property acquired on account of the firm, for the purpose of and in the course of the partnership business: s. 20(1).

(c) Property purchased with the firm's money (unless otherwise agreed): s. 21.

(Thus the mere fact that partners are co-owners of land and share its profits does not make it automatically partnership property, unless it falls into one of the above categories: s. 20(3).)

As between partners, partnership land is treated as personal property: s. 22. Land is conveyed to the partners (or to four of them, if there are more than four) as trustees for sale.

15. Execution against a partner. A creditor who obtains judgement against an individual partner cannot seize partnership property in execution of the judgement: s. 23. His remedy is to appoint a receiver of the debtor partner's share of profits.

By s. 33(2) if a receiver is so appointed, or a partner's share is otherwise charged with payment of his private debts, this entitles the other partners to dissolve the partnership.

16. Assignment of a partner's share. A partner's share in the business is the proportion of the existing assets to which he would be entitled if all the firm's assets were sold and proceeds distributed after discharge of all the firm's debts.

A partner may assign his share (by way of sale, gift, mortgage, etc.) but the assignee does not thereby become a member of the firm, can take no part in management or inspect books, etc., unless the other partners agree: s. 31.

Thus the assignor remains a partner, though his assignee becomes entitled to his share of profits and of the assets in the event of any distribution. The firm's creditors can therefore sue the assignor for the firm's debts, but he can (unless otherwise agreed) claim indemnity from the assignee: *Dodson* v. *Downey* (1901).

Dissolution of partnership

The effect of dissolution is to terminate the partnership relation and to entitle the partners (unless otherwise agreed) to share the assets after payment of the firm's debts. Dissolution may occur in the ways listed below.

17. By agreement.

(*a*) Under the partnership articles, if they provide a method.

(*b*) By express and unanimous agreement at any time (overriding the articles).

18. By operation of law.

(*a*) *Expiration*. If entered into for a fixed term or for a single venture, the firm is dissolved on expiration of the fixed term or termination of the venture. (If, however, the partnership is continued beyond the term originally agreed, the rights and duties of the partners remain the same: s. 26.)

(*b*) *Notice*. If entered into for an undefined term, any partner may determine the partnership at any time by notice to the others: s. 26. (If the partnership was originally constituted by deed, the notice must be in writing: s. 26(2).)

The partnership is then dissolved (*i*) from the date stated in the notice or (*ii*) if not stated, then from the date of communication of the notice to the other partners: s. 32.

19. By death or bankruptcy (unless otherwise agreed): s. 33(1).
Also if a partner allows his share to be charged with payment of his debts this entitles the others to dissolve the partnership if they wish: s. 33(2).

20. By supervening illegality,
i.e. if some event occurs which makes it unlawful for the business to be carried on: s. 34. The partnership in a firm of solicitors is automatically dissolved when one of the partners forgets to renew his practising certificate: *Hudgell Yeates & Co.* v. *Watson* (1978).

21. By court order: s. 35.
The court may order dissolution on the application of any partner in the following cases.

(*a*) *Mental incapacity* of any partner: Mental Health Act 1983, s. 96.

(*b*) *Permanent incapacity* of a partner (other than the applicant).

(*c*) *Conduct prejudicial* to the business (by any partner other than the applicant).

(*d*) *Breach of the partnership agreement* (by any other than the applicant). This includes conduct which makes it impracticable for the other partners to carry on.

(*e*) Where the business can only be carried on at a loss.

140 Agency and partnership

(*f*) Where, in the opinion of the court, it is just and equitable, e.g. where there are only two partners and they are at loggerheads: *Re Yenidje Tobacco Co. Ltd* (1916).

22. Notice of dissolution. To avoid incurring liability after dissolution (e.g. by estoppel) a partner may publish notice of dissolution and can compel his co-partners to join him: s. 37.

23. Effect of dissolution. The authority of partners to bind the firm continues so long as is necessary to wind up the business, provided that the firm is in no case bound by the acts of a partner who has been bankrupted: s. 38.

Also each partner has an equitable lien (*see* 16: 19) over the firm's assets entitling him to have them applied in payment of the firm's debts, and in payment of whatever is due to partners; this lien can be enforced by injunction forbidding unfair distribution: s. 39.

24. Return of premium: s. 40. To buy entry into an existing firm, a new member sometimes has to pay a premium (in consideration of existing goodwill) in addition to any investment of capital.

On dissolution, he is entitled to demand the return of a proportion of the premium if the partnership was for a fixed term and was dissolved before the expiry of that term, unless dissolution was caused by (*a*) agreement, or (*b*) misconduct by the party seeking return of the premium, or (*c*) death of a partner: s. 40.

The portion returned will usually be in the same ratio to the whole premium as the unexpired term bears to the whole term: *Attwood* v. *Maude* (1868).

25. Dissolution through misrepresentation: s. 41. Where a partnership agreement is rescinded on the grounds of fraud or misrepresentation by any partner, the partner entitled to rescission can also demand the following.

(*a*) *A lien* on the firm's assets (after payment of debts) for any money he had invested.

(b) *Subrogation*, i.e. a right to stand in the place of any of the firm's creditors for any payment made by him to discharge the firm's debts.

(c) *To be indemnified* by the person guilty of the fraud or misrepresentation against all the firm's debts and liabilities.

(d) *Damages* may also be claimed under the Misrepresentation Act 1967, s. 2, since here rights are without prejudice to other rights.

26. Profits made after dissolution: s. 42. If a partner dies or retires and the other partners carry on the business after the dissolution, without any final settlement of accounts, the outgoing partner or his estate can (unless otherwise agreed) claim:

(a) *such share of profits* after dissolution as is attributable to the use of his share of the assets (after due allowance for the labour and skill of the continuing partners); or

(b) *interest* at 5 per cent on the share of the assets. This claim is not exercisable where the articles give continuing partners an option to purchase a deceased or retiring partner's share, and they duly exercise that option.

27. Settling accounts: s. 44. Unless otherwise agreed, the following rules apply.

(a) *Losses* (including deficiencies of capital) are paid first out of profits, next out of capital and lastly (if necessary) by the partners individually in the proportion in which they are entitled to share profits.

(b) *The assets* (including sums contributed to make up losses or deficiencies of capital) are then applied in the following manner.

(*i*) In paying outside creditors.

(*ii*) In repaying advances made by partners (distinct from investment of capital).

(*iii*) In repaying capital to partners.

(*iv*) The residue, if any, is divided among the partners in the proportions in which profits are divisible.

NOTE: Where after paying (*i*) and (*ii*) above there is insufficient to repay capital to all the partners in full, deficiencies are shared in the same way as profits: *Nowell* v. *Nowell* (1869). But under the Rule in *Garner* v. *Murray* (1904), if such deficiency is attributable to the insolvency of one of the partners, it must (unless otherwise agreed) be borne by the other partners in the proportion of their last agreed capitals (and not in the proportion in which they share profits or losses).

Thus G, M, & W were partners investing unequal capitals. On dissolution (after paying outside creditors) their balance sheet showed:

Liabilities		Assets		
G. (capital)	£2,500	Cash		£1,891
M. (capital)	£ 314	W. (indebted)	£263	
		Deficiency	£660	
				£ 923
	£2,814			£2,814

HELD: (*a*) The firm's loss of £660 must be shared by the partners equally, and (*b*) W's total deficit (£263 + one third of £660 = £483) must be shared between G and M in proportion to their last agreed capitals, i.e. £2,500 and £314 respectively: *Garner* v. *Murray* (1904).

28. Goodwill. This is a partnership asset and means the good reputation and business connections of a firm developed over the years: *Trego* v. *Hunt* (1896).

Unless otherwise agreed in the articles, upon dissolution the goodwill must be sold and the proceeds of sale distributed as capital. Where dissolution is caused by death, the estate of the deceased partner is entitled to share in the proceeds of sale: *Re David & Mathews* (1899).

If the goodwill is not sold and there is no agreement as to its disposal, any partner can carry on the business (even using the firm's name), providing that by so doing he does not expose former partners to liability: *Burchell* v. *Wilde* (1900).

But if by agreement the goodwill is assigned to any person, he can restrain partners from (*a*) soliciting old customers of the firm, or (*b*) using the firm's name (but not from setting up a merely competing business): *Boorne* v. *Wicker* (1927).

29. Sale of goodwill. Where goodwill is sold (either to a partner or to an outsider) the value is divisible among the partners in the same manner as they share profits and losses (unless otherwise agreed).

(*a*) *Purchaser's rights* (unless otherwise agreed). (*i*) He may represent himself as continuing the former business of the vendors. (*ii*) He has exclusive rights to the firm's name: *Churton* v. *Douglas* (1859). He has the sole right to solicit former customers of the business bought: *Trego* v. *Hunt* (1896), except where the vendor did not sell voluntarily, e.g. where a bankrupt's trustee sells his business, the bankrupt can recommence business after his discharge and can then solicit any former customers: *Walker* v. *Mottram* (1881).

(*b*) *Vendor's rights.* He is entitled to open a competing business, unless restrained by a covenant in the contract of sale: *see Restraints of Trade*, 4: **45–50.**

Limited partnerships

30. Limited Partnership Act 1907. This allows a partnership to claim limited liability for some of its members. Limited partnerships are not common, since it is easier and more advantageous to operate a limited registered company.

31. Characteristics of limited partnerships.

(*a*) *Number of partners.* A limited partnership shall not consist of more than 20 partners, of whom at least one must be a general partner: Limited Partnership Act 1907, s. 4(2). This does not apply, however, to a partnership carrying on business as solicitors and consisting of persons each of whom is a solicitor; a partnership carrying on a practice as accountants and consisting of persons who belong to a member of a body of accountants established in the United Kingdom and for the time being recognised by the Secretary of State, or a person for the time being authorised by the Secretary of State to be appointed as an auditor either as having similar qualifications obtained outside the United Kingdom, or as having obtained adequate knowledge and experience in the course of his employment by a member of a body of accountants recognised by the Secretary of State, or as having before 6 August 1947 practised in Great Britain as an accountant; a partnership carrying on business as a member of a recognised stock exchange and consisting of persons each of whom is a member of that stock exchange. The limit of 20 partners is inapplicable in the case of a limited partnership carrying on one or more of the following activities: surveying, auctioneering, valuing, estate agency, land agency and estate management. Not less than three-quarters of the total number of partners must be members of either the Royal Institution of Chartered Surveyors, and not more than one-quarter of the total number of partners can be limited partners: Companies Act 1985, s. 717; Limited Partnerships (Unrestricted Size) Regulations 1971.

(b) *General and limited partners:* a general partner is fully liable for all debts and obligations of the firm as in an ordinary partnership, and is entitled to participate in management.

A limited partner (*i*) contributes a stipulated amount to the firm's capital, and is not liable for the firm's debts beyond that amount (which cannot be withdrawn from the business, except on dissolution), (*ii*) cannot participate in management (and if he does so he loses his limitation of liability), (*iii*) has no agency for the firm, and (*iv*) is entitled to inspect accounts, etc.: Limited Partnership Act 1907, ss. 4, 6.

(c) *Registration:* a limited partnership must register (*i*) the firm's name, (*ii*) the nature of the business, (*iii*) the principal place of business, (*iv*) the full names of each partner, (*v*) any fixed term for which the partnership is created, (*vi*) a statement that the liability of some of the partners is limited, (*vii*) the sum contributed by each limited partner (in default of registration the firm cannot claim limited liability: s. 5).

(d) *Majority decisions:* in any ordinary partnership the votes of all partners count, but in a limited partnership only the votes of general (unlimited) partners count, unless otherwise agreed.

(e) *New partners:* in an ordinary firm admission of new members generally requires consent of existing partners: P.A., s. 24. In a limited partnership, unless otherwise agreed (*i*) a new partner can be admitted without consent of any limited partner, and (*ii*) a limited partner may assign his share to another person (with consent of the general partners, but without the consent of other limited partners): s. 6.

(*f*) *No dissolution by notice:* a limited partner cannot dissolve the firm by notice: s. 6(5).

(*g*) *Death, bankruptcy, or lunacy* of a limited partner does not automatically dissolve the partnership: s. 6(2).

(*h*) *Winding-up:* if a limited partnership is dissolved, the firm's affairs are wound up by the general partners alone, unless the court orders to the contrary: s. 6(3).

(*i*) *General partner becoming limited partner:* if by agreement a general partner becomes a limited partner, such change in status must be notified in the *London Gazette* and the change confers no limitation of liability until notified: s. 10(1).

Progress test 2

Agency and partnership

1. Explain how an agency may arise (*a*) by implication, (*b*) by estoppel, (*c*) by necessity. (8: **4, 5, 7**)
2. In what circumstances may a person ratify a contract made on his behalf but without his authority? (8: **6**)
3. A, a minor, hires X as his agent to buy a house. X contracts to buy the house before discovering that A is a minor. A few days later A reaches his 18th birthday and purports to ratify the contract made by X. Is the ratification effective? (8: **6**)
4. 'Generally a principal can revoke his agent's appointment at any time.' Discuss. (8: **8**)
5. What are the chief rights and duties of an agent, in regard to his principal? (8: **10, 11**)
6. Explain briefly: (*a*) ostensible authority of an agent, (*b*) breach of implied warranty of authority by an agent, (*c*) the doctrine of the undisclosed principal. (8: **13–17**)
7. In what circumstances may an agent be personally liable on a contract he has made on behalf of his principal? (8: **16**)
8. Distinguish between factors and brokers, and explain the normal limits of their authority. (8: **18, 19**)
9. 'The limits of a banker's business cannot be laid down as a matter of law.' Discuss. (8: **21**)

10. Define a partnership and state the tests outlined by the Partnership Act 1890 for deciding whether a partnership exists or not. (9: **1, 2**)

11. Explain what is meant by an illegal association. In what circumstances must a business association register a trade name? (9: **3, 4**)

12. To what extent can a partner be regarded as having implied authority to act as agent for his firm? (9: **5, 6**)

13. In what circumstances may a retired partner continue liable for the firm's debts after his retirement? (9: **7**)

14. Explain what is meant by saying that the liability of partners is generally either joint, or joint and several. (9: **8**)

15. 'The rights and duties of partners depend on agreement, express or implied, between themselves.' How far do you agree? What are the usual rights and duties of partners? (9: **10–13**)

16. Explain what is meant by: (*a*) partnership property, (*b*) execution against a partner's share, and (*c*) goodwill. (9: **14, 15, 28**)

17. In what circumstances may a partner assign his share in a firm, and what is the effect of such assignment? (9: **16**)

18. Explain briefly the circumstances in which a partnership may be dissolved. What is the effect of dissolution? (9: **17–23**)

19. On dissolution of a partnership how, in the absence of contrary agreement, are accounts settled? (9: **27**)

20. Distinguish between, and explain briefly, the rules in (*a*) *Nowell* v. *Nowell* (1869), and (*b*) *Garner* v. *Murray* (1904). (9: **27**)

21. A and B, partners, sold their business to X two years ago, for an inclusive price to cover goodwill. X now learns that A, trading under his own name, has opened a competing business and is writing to old customers of the A & B firm, saying: 'Please note that A, formerly of A & B, has now opened new premises at 333 New Street.' Explain the legal position. (9: **28, 29**)

22. What is a limited partnership? How is such a partnership formed, and how does it differ from an ordinary partnership? (9: **30, 31**)

Specimen questions

1. In relation to the law of agency discuss:
    (*a*) the nature of the duties owed by agent to principal;

(*b*) the legal effect of ratification.

2. (*a*) Describe with examples what is meant by an 'agency by necessity.'

(*b*) P, a university professor at a South American University, has asked A, a London bookseller, to acquire for him a library of scientific books due to be sold by public auction and has made funds available for this purpose. A secures the books but is unable to ship them to P because a revolution has broken out in P's country and all shipping is stopped. A finds that he has difficulties in storing the books and he sells them to C, a *bona fide* buyer, at a price 10 per cent higher than paid for them at the auction sale. P now seeks your advice concerning his legal rights against A and C.

3. (*a*) When, if ever, is an agent personally liable upon contracts made by him on behalf of his principal?

(*b*) P appointed A his agent to sell radios on his behalf. A sold the radios to X, without disclosing that he was negotiating the contract as an agent. X paid the agreed price but the radios were not delivered to him, so he wishes to sue for the recovery of the purchase price.

In the meantime A has sold the radios to Y, who offered him the gift of a car in return for arranging the deal.

What are the respective rights of X and P in these circumstances?

4. (*a*) State and explain the duties owed by an agent to his principal.

(*b*) E, an estate agent, agreed to find a buyer for S's house. E introduced P, who agreed to buy the house, subject to contract, and left £5000 with E as a deposit. P subsequently withdrew from the sale. P was unable to recover the deposit from E, who had gone into liquidation.

Advise P as to his rights against S.

What would your answer be if E had accepted the deposit as a 'stake holder'?

5. What rights have (*a*) a retiring partner and (*b*) a purchaser of a firm's business in respect of the goodwill of the business?

6. (*a*) Explain the distinction between joint and several liability. Why is the distinction important in partnership law?

(*b*) A and B are in partnership as greengrocers. While negligently driving the firm's van on business, A injures X. X is now suing the firm for damages and it is found that A is insolvent. Advise B on the extent of his own liability and that of the firm.

7. (a) 'The duties of a partner to his firm are fundamentally the same as those of an agent to his principal.' Discuss this statement.

(b) L, M and N are partners. Having reached the age of 70, L wishes to retire from the business and to assign his share to his son, who has worked in the business for 10 years. M and N object to the assignment and wish to purchase L's share themselves. Advise M and N.

8. What is the essential nature of a partnership?

F and G were in process of forming a company to vend garden equipment. G without F's knowledge, and in his own name, ordered from E six mowing machines and put them in a shed at the site which had been selected for the company's garden centre. As G is unable to pay the agreed price for the machines, E wishes to claim the money from F.

Advise E.

9. (a) Explain the way partnership property would be applied on its dissolution.

(b) John has been a partner in a trading firm of repute. He wishes to retire and has agreed to sell his share of the goodwill to Charles and Peter, the continuing partners.

Advise John as to the steps he must take to protect himself against liability in respect of the debts of the partnership incurred while he was a partner and in respect of the firm's future debts.

10. (a) 'There is normally a right in the principal unilaterally to revoke the agency at any time before the agency has been completely performed by giving notice.' Explain the rule and indicate whether there are any exceptions to it.

(b) Shaw owes Lamb £700. Shaw has appointed Lamb as his agent to collect certain debts owing to Shaw and to deduct 20 per cent of each amount collected until his loan to Lamb is fully repaid. The agreement also provides that Lamb should receive a commission of 5 per cent of all gross amounts collected.

Lamp has collected £3,000 and thus recovered £600 of his loan. Now Shaw wishes to cancel the arrangement. Advise Lamb as to his rights in the matter both in respect of the unrecovered balance of the loan and of the commission.

Part three
Mercantile agreements

10
Sale of goods, supply of goods and services, hire and hire purchase

The law relating to the sale of goods is laid down by the Sale of Goods Act 1979 which consolidated existing law. The law relating to the supply of goods and services is laid down in the Supply of Goods and Services Act 1982 which also consolidated existing law. The law relating to hire and hire purchase is now contained in the Consumer Credit Act 1974.

The contract for the sale of goods

1. Sale of Goods Act 1979, s. 1. This defines a contract of sale as one 'whereby the seller (*a*) transfers, or (*b*) agrees to transfer the property in the goods to a buyer for a money consideration called the price'. Section 61 of the Act says that 'property' means 'general property' and not merely a 'special property'. In effect, the reference to 'general property' is a reference to the full rights of ownership.

2. Meaning of 'goods', s. 61. Goods means all chattels and tangible things in possession, but not things in action or money (unless the money is traded as goods and not as money, such as an antique coin). 'Goods' also means the following:

(*a*) *Industrial growing crops*, once they have been severed from the land. Until severance, they are classed as part of the land and are not goods.

(b) *Future goods*, i.e. goods to be made or acquired after the contract has been made.

3. Sale and agreement to sell. When the property in goods is to be transferred immediately, the contract is known as a 'sale'. If property is to be transferred at some future time, the contract is known as 'an agreement to sell': s. 2. All contracts relating to future goods (*see* **2** *above*) are agreements to sell: s. 5(3). A common form of an agreement to sell is the conditional sale under which a buyer agrees to buy goods with the price payable in instalments.

4. Contracts for work and materials. The Sale of Goods Act does not apply to contracts in which the purchaser is buying the skills of a craftsman and not merely the goods produced by him. Instead, they are governed by the Supply of Goods and Services Act 1982 (*see* **68–74** *below*). The test usually applied is: is the essential object of the agreement the provision of goods or the exercise of skill?

> EXAMPLE: The employment of an artist to paint a portrait is a contract for the supply of work and materials, since the artist's skill is the main constituent of the contract: *Robinson* v. *Graves* (1935).

5. Contracts of barter. The 1979 Act lays down that a contract for the sale of goods is one where money is exchanged for goods, so it does not apply to contracts of barter. Here too the transaction is governed instead by the Supply of Goods and Services Act (*see* **68–74** *below*). Where a contract is one of part-exchange (a typical example being an old car plus cash in exchange for a new car), that is probably a contract for the sale of goods, certainly where a specific sum is allocated to the trade-in. If a contract of part-exchange is not a contract for the sale of goods, it will be covered by the Supply of Goods and Services Act (*see* **68–74** *below*).

6. Sale and loan on security. The Sale of Goods Act does not apply

10. Sale and supply of goods, services, hire and HP

to any transaction in the form of a contract of sale which is intended to operate by way of mortgage, pledge, charge or other security. These are governed by the Bills of Sale Acts 1878–1882 (*see* **16**).

7. Capacity to contact. Capacity to contract is governed by the ordinary rules as to making a contract: s. 3. The Act provides that where necessaries are supplied to someone under the age of 18, to a drunkard or someone lacking full mental capacity, that person must pay a 'reasonable price' for them. *See*, too, *Minors*, 3.

8. Form of contract. Any form suffices, written or oral, and a contract may be implied from conduct: s. 4.

9. Price.

(*a*) *Fixed by parties.* The price (*i*) may be fixed at the time of contracting by the parties themselves, or (*ii*) may be left to be determined in the course of dealings between the parties, or (*iii*) may be left to be fixed by some third party: s. 8.

(*b*) *Fixed by a third party.* Where the contract states that the price is to be fixed by a third party, and he fails to do so, the contract is void: s. 9. But if the purchaser has by then taken the benefit of the goods, he must pay a reasonable price for them. If the third party's failure to fix the price is due to the fault of one of the parties, that party is liable in an action for damages, s. 9(2).

(*c*) *Where no price is fixed* in any of the ways listed above, the purchaser must pay a reasonable price.

Terms implied by the Sale of Goods Act

10. Conditions and warranties. The terms implied by the Sale of Goods Act are described in the Act as being either 'conditions' or 'warranties'. The former is not defined in the Act, but a warranty is defined as something 'collateral' to the main purpose of the Act, for breach of which the injured party may claim only damages but cannot repudiate the contract: s. 61. In effect, these terms bear their conventional meaning so that a 'condition' is a major term of a contract, while a 'warranty' is a minor term (*see* 2: **24–32**). The importance of the distinction lies in the remedies available on breach. Where a warranty is broken the position is as stated above. Where the breach is of a condition, the injured party may both claim damages and elect to terminate the contract.

11. Assessment of terms. If the Act states specifically that a particular term is a condition or a warranty, that of course concludes the matter (*see* **14** *below*). There will be many cases, however, where nothing is said specifically in the Act. In such cases, the courts will look to other relevant Acts, case law and the intentions of the parties. In recent years, the courts have also developed the theory of the 'innominate term'. If there is no clear guidance as to whether a term is a condition or a warranty, then the effects of a breach of this 'innominate term' will depend on whether or not it goes to the root of the contract: *Cehave N.V.* v. *Bremer* (1975).

12. Ex post facto warranties. The buyer is always entitled to treat any breach of condition as a breach of warranty: s. 11(2). This means that he will be able to claim damages but will lose his right to terminate the agreement. In some cases (unless otherwise agreed in the contract), the buyer has to treat a breach of condition as a breach of warranty. This arises where the contract is non-severable and the buyer has accepted any part of the goods: s. 11(4). This does not apply where the buyer is not a trade buyer and the agreement is a conditional sale agreement (*see* **3** *above*): Supply of Goods (Implied Terms) Act 1973, s. 14(1). In such cases, a condition is to be treated as a warranty when it would have been treated in such a way in a hire purchase agreement: SG (IT) A, s. 14(2).

13. Terms and mere representations. It used to be of considerable importance to determine whether some statement made in the course of contractual negotiations was a term of the contract or a mere representation inducing the other party to make the contract. The difference could affect the remedies available if the statement was false. If it was a representation, and was made innocently, then the contract could be terminated, but damages were unavailable. If, on the other hand, the same statement were a term of the

10. Sale and supply of goods, services, hire and HP

contract, the victim would always be able to claim damages and could also, if the term were a condition, terminate the contract. Now, however, the Misrepresentation Act 1967 has considerably reduced the relevance of the distinction because (*a*) it no longer matters that a representation has become a term of the contract: s. 1 MA, and (*b*) damages and termination are allowed for a negligent misrepresentation and damages can be awarded at the court's discretion for an innocent misrepresentation as an alternative to termination of the contract: s. 2 MA.

Terms implied by the Sale of Goods Act

14. Implied terms as to title. Section 12, SGA, provides as follows:

Subsections 1 and 2: In every contract of sale, other than one to which subsection 3 applies (*see immediately below*), there is:

(*a*) *an implied condition* that the seller has the right to sell the goods, or, in an agreement to sell (*see* 3 *above*), the right to sell at the time when the property is to pass and

(*b*) *an implied warranty* that the goods shall be free of any undisclosed charge or encumbrance and that the buyer shall enjoy quiet possession (subject to any encumbrance or charge disclosed or known to him).

> EXAMPLES: (1) A purchased a car for £334 from B and resold it to C for £400. A then discovered that the car had never belonged to B who had bought it in good faith from someone with no title. The car was reclaimed by the original owner and A paid off C by refunding him the £400. He sued B for the return of the £334 and was upheld in the Court of Appeal: *Rowland* v. *Divall* (1923). (2) In another case, the buyer was entitled to claim for disturbance of quiet possession when a third party validly claimed that he had patent rights over the machine sold by the seller: *Microbeads AC* v. *Vinhurst Road Markings Ltd* (1975).

Subsection 3: Where it appears from the contract, or can be inferred from the circumstances, that the seller is transferring only such title as he or a third person may have, there is:

(*a*) *an implied warranty* that all known charges or encumbrances have been disclosed to the buyer, and

(*b*) *an implied warranty* that neither (*i*) the seller, nor (*ii*) any third person to whose claims the sale is subject, nor (*iii*) any person claiming under the seller or such third person, will disturb the buyer's quiet possession (subject to any encumbrance or charge disclosed or known to him).

15. Exclusion clauses. The terms as to title cannot be excluded: Unfair Contract Terms Act, s. 6. If such an exclusion clause is incorporated into a consumer contract, a criminal offence is committed: Consumer Transactions (Restrictions on Statements) Order 1976.

16. Correspondence with description: s. 13. In every sale of goods by description, there is an implied condition that the goods shall correspond with their description.

NOTE: (1) Sale by description means that the buyer relies for his information on the description of the goods given by the seller, e.g. in the contract or in preliminary negotiations. Thus, where he buys goods which he has not seen, this must be a sale by description. (2) The question whether goods correspond to their description is 'a test of mercantile character. The question whether that is what the buyer bargained for has to be answered according to such tests as men in the market would apply, leaving more delicate questions of condition, or quality, to be determined under other clauses of the contract or sections of the Act': *Ashington Piggeries Ltd* v. *Christopher Hill Ltd* (1972). In this case, herring meal contaminated with a substance which made it unsuitable for feeding to mink was sold to buyers for use as mink food. It was held by the House of Lords that the goods were still properly described as 'herring meal'. (3) A discrepancy between description and actuality such as could not have been seen on reasonable examination is a breach of this condition, e.g. the buyer examined lace described as seventeenth century and after purchase discovered it was actually eighteenth century. HELD: the discrepancy was not discernible on examination and he was entitled to rescind the contract. (4) A

10. Sale and supply of goods, services, hire and HP

seller is liable for breach of s. 13 however free of blame he might be for not providing goods of the contract description.

17. Exclusion clauses. The Unfair Contract Terms Act 1977 states that where the buyer is a consumer, the seller cannot exclude s. 13 SGA. If the buyer is a business buyer, s. 13 can be excluded only if the seller can prove that the exclusion is a reasonable one: s. 6 UCTA. In addition, it is a criminal offence to include in a consumer contract a clause excluding s. 13: Consumer Transactions (Restrictions on Statements) Order 1976.

18. Merchantable quality: s. 14 (2). Where the seller sells goods in the course of a business, there is an implied condition that the goods shall be of merchantable quality, except that there is no such condition:

(*a*) as regards defects specifically drawn to the buyer's attention before the contract is made; or
(*b*) if the buyer examines the goods before the contract is made, as regards defects which that examination ought to reveal: s. 14(2)(*a*), (*b*).

NOTE: (1) Goods are of merchantable quality if they are as fit for the purpose or purposes for which goods of that kind are commonly bought as it is reasonable to expect, having regard to any description applied to them, the price (if relevant) and all other relevant circumstances: s. 14(6). (2) A seller is liable for a breach of s. 14(2) however free of blame he might be in not providing goods which are of merchantable quality.

EXAMPLES: (1) A car is not of merchantable quality if an oil pipe is blocked. This renders the car potentially unsafe since the blockage might lead to the steering seizing up while the car is in the fast lane of a motorway: *Bernstein v. Pamson Motors (Golders Green) Ltd* (1987). (2) A new Range Rover had to be returned several times for repair, but problems remained. It was held that the vehicle was not of merchantable quality even though the defects could be repaired and even though the defects had not destroyed the workable character of the car.

The Court of Appeal ruled that when considering if a car was of merchantable quality, there had to be considered not just the owner's purpose of driving the car from one place to another, but his doing so with the appropriate degree of comfort, ease of handling and pride in the vehicle's appearance: *Rogers* v. *Parish (Scarborough) Ltd* (1986).

19. Exclusion clauses. The Unfair Contract Terms Act 1977 states that where the buyer is a consumer, the seller cannot exclude, s. 14(2) SGA. If the buyer is a business buyer, s. 14 (2) can be excluded only if the seller can prove that the exclusion clause is a reasonable one: s. 6 UCTA. In addition, it is a criminal offence to include in a consumer contract a clause excluding s. 14(2): Consumer Transactions (Restrictions on Statements) Order 1976.

20. Fitness for particular purpose: s. 14(3). Where the seller sells goods in the course of a business and the buyer, expressly or by implication, makes known to the seller any particular purpose for which the goods are being bought, there is an implied condition that the goods are reasonably fit for that purpose, whether or not it is a purpose for which such goods are commonly supplied, except where the circumstances show that the buyer did not rely or that it was unreasonable for him to rely on the seller's skill or judgement.

By s. 14(4) an implied condition or warranty as to fitness for a particular purpose may be annexed to a contract of sale by usage, e.g. trade custom.

NOTE: (1) Where the goods have only one normal purpose, the seller is assumed to know what they are wanted for. The buyer of a bottle of milk does not have to tell the seller that he wants to drink it, nor does the buyer of a hot water bottle have to explain what he wants it for: *Frost* v. *Aylesbury Dairies Ltd* (1905); *Priest* v. *Last* (1903). (2) A seller is liable for a breach of s. 14(3) even if he is completely free of blame for the goods not being reasonably fit for their purpose. (3) The instructions accompanying goods are part of the goods themselves. So if the instructions are misleading the goods will not be reasonably fit for their purpose, nor will they be of merchantable quality: *Wormell* v. *RHM Agriculture (East) Ltd* (1987).

21. Exclusion clauses. The Unfair Contract Terms Act 1977 states that where the buyer is a consumer, the seller cannot exclude s. 14(3) SGA. If the buyer is a business buyer, s. 14(3) can be excluded only if the seller can prove that the exclusion clause is a reasonable one: s. 6 UCTA. In addition, it is a criminal offence to include in a consumer contract a clause excluding s. 14(3): Consumer Transactions (Restrictions on Statements) Order 1976.

22. Sale by sample: s. 15. In a sale by sample, there is an implied condition that:

(a) the bulk shall correspond with sample in quality, and
(b) the buyer shall have a reasonable opportunity to compare the bulk with the sample; and
(c) the goods shall be free of any defect rendering them unmerchantable, and which would not be apparent on reasonable examination of the sample.

NOTE: (1) Where part only of the goods are not up to sample, the buyer must still accept or reject all of the goods, unless the contract is severable, i.e. in instalments, in which case each instalment must be treated separately. (2) Mere display of a sample during negotiations does not make the contract a sale by sample. There must be an agreement, express or implied, to that effect. (3) The seller is liable for a breach of s. 15 even if he is completely free of any blame.

23. Exclusion clauses. The Unfair Contract Terms Act 1977 states that where the buyer is a consumer, the seller cannot exclude s. 15 SGA. If the buyer is a business buyer, s. 15 can be excluded only if the seller can prove that the exclusion clause is a reasonable one: s. 6 UCTA. In addition, it is a criminal offence to include in a consumer contract a clause excluding s. 15: Consumer Transactions (Restrictions on Statements) Order 1976.

Passing of ownership and risk

24. Passing of ownership. The transfer of the legal property in the goods is important for assessing who bears the risk of loss or deterioration, etc.

The position depends (*a*) on whether the contract is a sale or an agreement to sell, and (*b*) on whether the goods are specific and ascertained, or unascertained: *see below*.

25. Specific and ascertained goods.

(*a*) *Specific goods* means goods identified and agreed upon at the time of making the contract: s. 61(1).

Goods are not specific merely because the source of supply has been agreed, e.g. '500 tonnes of coal from stack no. 2'.

(*b*) *Ascertained goods* means goods identified and agreed upon after the making of the contract.

(*c*) *Unascertained goods* means goods not yet identified and agreed upon, but merely described, e.g. the coal in (*a*) above.

26. When the property passes.

(*a*) *Specific and ascertained goods:* The property in them passes whenever the parties intend it to pass. The intention of the parties may be (*i*) stated in the contract or (*ii*) left to be ascertained by the court from the circumstances: *see* **27,** *below*.

(*b*) *Unascertained goods:* The property passes only when they become ascertained, i.e. no property can pass in unascertained goods.

27. Tests of intention. Where the contract does not state when the property is to pass, the court will apply the following tests to ascertain the intentions of the parties:

(*a*) *Unconditional contract* for sale of specific goods in a deliverable condition: the property passes when the contract is made (even if delivery is postponed): s. 18(1).

The risk then passes to the buyer, even though the seller retains a lien for unpaid purchase money: s. 20.

(*b*) *Sale of specific goods not in a deliverable state:* the property does not pass until (*i*) the seller puts them into a deliverable state, and (*ii*) the buyer is notified thereof: s. 18(2).

(c) *Sale of specific goods in a deliverable state*, but requiring some additional act such as weighing, measuring, testing, etc., to fix the price: the property does not pass until (*i*) the seller has done the required act, and (*ii*) the buyer is notified thereof: s. 18(3).

(d) *Goods delivered on approval or on sale or return, etc.:* the property does not pass until (*i*) the buyer signifies acceptance, or adopts the goods (e.g. by using them), or (*ii*) the buyer retains the goods for an unreasonable time or beyond any agreed time limit. What is a reasonable time is a question of fact in each case: s. 18(4).

(e) *Contract for sale of unascertained or future goods:* the property passes when (*i*) the seller unconditionally appropriates goods of the required description to the contract, (*ii*) puts them in a deliverable state, and (*iii*) notifies the buyer: s. 18(5).

(Appropriation by the seller includes delivery to the buyer or to a carrier on behalf of the buyer, provided the seller has not reserved a right of disposal: s. 18(5). If a right of disposal is reserved, property does not pass until the seller's conditions are satisfied: s. 19(1). Where the goods are shipped on a bill of lading to the order of the seller or his agent, it is presumed that a right of disposal is reserved: s. 19(2).)

28. Perishing of specific goods.

(a) *If before the contract is made*, the contract is void: s. 6 (and see *Couturier* v. *Hastie* (1857), 4: **4**). This is a simple case of common mistake as to the existence of the subject-matter of the contract.

(b) *If after the contract is made*, and before the property passes to the buyer; the contract is void: s. 7. (But if the destruction was due to the fault of either party, the contract would not be void: instead the innocent party could sue for breach of contract.)

(c) *If after the contract is made*, and after the property has passed to the buyer: the buyer bears the loss and must pay for the goods.

'Perished' means destroyed or so changed or deteriorated as to defeat the purpose of the contract. But mere deterioration does not amount to perishing unless it causes the goods to become valueless: *Horn* v. *Minister of Food* (1948).

162 Mercantile agreements

29. Passing of risk. Unless otherwise agreed, the risk will pass to the buyer only when the property in the goods passes to him.

Note that passing of risk is independent of possession, e.g. if the property in the goods has passed to the buyer, the risk falls on him even though the seller has not yet delivered the goods.

> NOTE: (1) Where performance of the contract is delayed by the fault of one party, the risk of loss or damage falls on that party: *Sterns Ltd* v. *Vickers Ltd* (1923). (2) Where delivery involves a sea journey, the goods remain at the seller's risk unless he gives the buyer reasonable notice (so that he can insure the goods): s. 32(3). (3) Where delivery is to a distant place, and the seller agrees to deliver at his own risk, the buyer must nevertheless accept the risk of any necessary deterioration incidental to the long journey: s. 33.

Nemo dat quod non habet

There is a general rule of law that *nemo dat quod non habet* ('No one can give what he has not got'). As applied to the sale of goods, the rule means that a seller of goods cannot give a better title to the purchaser than he himself possesses. Thus a purchaser who buys stolen goods from a thief can get no valid title to them, since the thief has no title: *see* **14**, *above*.

The Sale of Goods Act 1979 lays down important exceptions to this general rule and these are stated below.

30. Estoppel. Where the true owner is estopped from denying the actual seller's right to sell the purchaser will get a good title.

> EXAMPLE: A allowed some of his property wrongfully to be detained by S, and also allowed B to think that S was entitled to the property. S sold the goods to B. HELD: B got a good title, as A was estopped from denying S's right to sell: *Pickard* v. *Sears* (1837).

31. Orders for sale. Where a person not the owner sells goods (*a*) under a court order, or (*b*) under a legal power of sale, e.g. the

10. Sale and supply of goods, services, hire and HP 163

power of sale given to a legal mortgagee the purchaser gets a good title.

EXAMPLE: A deposits goods with B for B to repair them, and then fails to collect and pay for the repaired goods. B has a statutory power to sell the goods: Torts (Interference with Goods) Act 1977, and *see* 13: **6**.

32. Factors Act 1889, s. 2. The purchaser will get a good title if he buys in good faith from a factor, with whom the owner deposited the goods (even though the factor may have no actual authority to sell).

A factor is a mercantile agent whose ordinary business is the buying and selling of goods in his possession: Factors Act 1889, s. 1, *see* 8: **18** *above*.

33. Sale of Goods Act 1979, ss. 24 and 25.

(*a*) *Seller in possession after sale.* If the buyer of goods allows the seller to remain in possession of them (or in possession of documents of title thereto) the seller can resell the goods to a second purchaser who will get a good title. The seller can then be sued in damages by the first buyer: s. 24. It is irrelevant whether the buyer has consented to the seller's retention of possession or not: *Worcester Works Finance* v. *Cooden Engineering Co. Ltd* (1971).

(*b*) *Buyer in possession after sale.* If the seller allows the buyer to get possession of goods (or documents of title thereto) before paying for them the buyer can sell the goods and pass a good title: s. 25(1). (The seller can then only sue the original buyer for damages.)

34. Writs of execution. If a person fails to pay a debt when ordered by the court, a writ may be issued empowering the sheriff to seize his chattels and to sell them in satisfaction of the debt. The sheriff then has power to give a good title, although he is not the owner of the goods sold: Supreme Court Act 1981, s. 138.

35. Sale under voidable title. The purchaser from a seller whose own title is voidable will get a good title, provided (*a*) he had no knowledge of any defect in the seller's title and (*b*) the seller's title had not been avoided at the time of the sale.

> EXAMPLE: A rogue obtained jewels on credit from P by fraud and sold them to B before P discovered the fraud. HELD: P could avoid the rogue's title to the jewels on the grounds of fraud, but since he had not done so before B bought the jewels B got a good title: *Phillips* v. *Brooks* (1919), *see* 4: **6.**

It appears that where the other party cannot be found, avoidance is effective as soon as the victim exhibits clear intention to avoid, e.g. by reporting the fraud to the police: *Car & Universal Finance Co.* v. *Caldwell* (1964).

36. Market overt. The purchaser normally gets a good title if he buys in a market overt (open market).

The term 'market overt' covers (*a*) all shops in the City of London, and (*b*) elsewhere, all markets established by statute, charter or custom as open markets.

A bona fide purchaser for value without notice of any defect in the seller's title will get a good title, provided:

(*a*) the sale is in accordance with the customs of the particular market;

(*b*) the sale took place in public, e.g. in the public part of a shop;

(*c*) the market dealer was the seller, not the purchaser;

(*d*) the goods were openly displayed, and were of a class the seller normally deals in;

(*e*) the sale took place in the normal opening hours of the market, e.g. between sunrise and sunset: *Reid* v. *Metropolitan Police Commissioner* (1973).

> NOTE: The market overt provisions do not protect a purchaser where: (1) the transaction took place in Scotland; (2) the goods sold belong to the Crown; (3) the sale took place in a private part of the shop or stall, e.g. behind a curtain.

10. Sale and supply of goods, services, hire and HP

Performance of the contract

37. Delivery. It is the duty of the seller to deliver the goods, and of the buyer to accept and pay for them: s. 27. Unless otherwise agreed payment and delivery are normally concurrent: s. 28.

Delivery means voluntary transfer of possession from one person to another. It may be actual or constructive, e.g. by handing over documents of title, or authority for the buyer to obtain the goods from some person in whose possession they are: *Central Newbury Car Auctions* v. *Unity Finance* (1957).

Delivery may also be by the seller agreeing to hold the goods as agent for the buyer: this is known as attornment.

38. Time and place of delivery.

(*a*) *Time for delivery.* Where the seller is to send the goods to the buyer but no time is fixed, they must be sent within a reasonable time and delivery must be at a reasonable hour: s. 29(3).

The seller usually bears the expense of putting the goods into a deliverable condition, and he must take reasonable care to see that they reach the right person: s. 29(6).

(*b*) *Place of delivery* (unless otherwise agreed) is the seller's place of business, or if he has none then his residence: s. 29(2).

If the sale is of specific goods known by both parties to be lodged at some other place, then delivery is to be made at that place: s. 29(2).

39. Delivery to a carrier. Where the seller is to send the goods, delivery to a carrier (as agent for the buyer) whether named by the buyer or not, is prima facie proper delivery to the buyer: s. 32(1).

In such cases the seller must make a reasonable contract with the carrier, otherwise the buyer is entitled to refuse to be bound: s. 32(2).

40. Delivery of wrong quantities: s. 30.

(*a*) *If less than ordered* the buyer may reject the lot; if he accepts the lesser quantity he must pay a proportionately reduced price.

(b) *If more than ordered*, the buyer may reject the lot, or may accept the agreed quantity only (if this is possible). He must then pay a proportionate price.

(c) *If goods ordered are mixed* with goods not ordered, the buyer may accept those ordered and reject the others (if it is possible to separate them, otherwise he must accept or reject the lot).

41. Delivery by instalments. Delivery is presumed to be in one transaction, unless it was expressly agreed that it should be by instalments.

If instalments are to be paid for separately on delivery, it is a question of fact whether failure to deliver one instalment justifies repudiation of the whole contract: s. 31.

The test is: Is the breach regarding one instalment sufficiently fundamental to injure the contract as a whole? It is relevant to consider the likelihood of the breach being repeated. In *Regent OHG* v. *Francesco of Jermyn Street* (1981), the plaintiffs were manufacturers of menswear. They agreed to sell 62 suits to the defendants who owned a retail shop. Delivery was to be by instalments. The number and size of the instalments was to be left to the plaintiffs' discretion. The defendants later informed the plaintiffs that they wished to cancel the order but the plaintiffs insisted on delivery of the suits which were in production. Because of shortage of cloth, one consignment was delivered one suit short, the plaintiffs having previously informed the defendants of the fact. The defendants, consistent with their wish to cancel the entire order, rejected delivery of all the consignments. The plaintiffs were forced to sell the suits elsewhere at a much lower price and brought an action against the defendants for non-acceptance. The defendants contended short delivery of one instalment amounted to short delivery on the whole contract, and the plaintiffs having delivered a quantity of goods less than they contracted to sell, they were entitled under s. 30 SGA to reject all the goods even though the parties had agreed on delivery in instalments. The plaintiffs contended that the contract was divisible into separate instalments and that under s. 31, whether the short delivery was a repudiation of the whole contract or merely a severable breach depended on the terms of the contract and the relevant circumstances. The court held that the plaintiffs were entitled to damages for the following reasons. First, on its true construction, the contract was divisible even though the number and size of the individual deliveries were not fixed in advance but were left to the plaintiffs' discretion. It followed that s. 30 SGA (*see* **40** *above*) did not apply to the contract and that the defendants were not entitled to cancel the contract under s. 30 because of short delivery of one suit. Second, in any event, where the nature of the delivery of goods was short delivery in one instalment, the more flexible provisions of s. 31 were to apply in preference to those of s. 30. Applying s. 31, the short delivery of one suit, in all the circumstances, could not be said to go to the root of the whole contract and did not entitle the defendants to repudiate the whole contract.

42. Acceptance by the buyer.

(*a*) The buyer is entitled to examine goods not previously seen, before accepting them: s. 34. Generally the place of delivery is the place of examination, unless otherwise agreed.

(*b*) The buyer accepts: (*i*) when he so informs the seller, or (*ii*) except where the buyer was unable to exercise his right under s. 34 to examine the goods, when he does some act of ownership, e.g. sells the goods, or (*iii*) keeps the goods an unreasonable time without notifying the seller that he wishes to reject them: s. 35. In *Bernstein* v. *Pamson Motors* (1987), a buyer of a new car had it for approximately 3 weeks during which time he drove some 140 miles. The High Court ruled that enough time had run against him with the result that he was unable to reject the car.

(*c*) If the buyer rejects the goods, when entitled to do so, he is not bound to return them to the seller, but only to notify the seller of rejection so as to enable the latter to collect them: s. 36.

(*d*) If the buyer's rejection amounts to repudiation of the contract the seller has an immediate right of action. The same applies when the buyer keeps the goods for an unreasonable length of time without making up his mind.

In such a case the seller's damages will be measured as the amount of loss caused by the wrongful retention: *Long* v. *Lloyd* (1958).

168　Mercantile agreements

43. Delivery by sea. In contracts for the carriage of goods sold by sea, various special terms are usual. These may be expressly agreed between the parties, but more often they rely on one of the established customary agreements with the implied terms that these contain.

The most common of these standard agreements are f.o.b., c.i.f., and ex-ship contracts: *see* below.

44. F.O.B. (free on board). Under such a contract, the seller's duties (unless otherwise agreed) are as follows.

(*a*) To deliver the goods to a named port of shipment.

(*b*) To put the goods on board ship at his own expense.

(*c*) To negotiate a reasonable bill of lading or other contract of carriage, and forward it to the buyer (who pays the freight).

(*d*) To notify the buyer of shipment, so as to enable him to insure the goods at sea. (If the seller fails to do this the goods will travel at his risk; otherwise the goods will be at the buyer's risk.)

Once the goods are shipped the property in them (and usually the risk) passes to the buyer. If the seller is prevented from putting the goods on board, e.g. by a strike, the property and risk remain with him: *Colley* v. *Overseas Exporters* (1921).

45. C.I.F. (cost, insurance, freight). Here the seller's duties go further than in an f.o.b. contract, and are as follows.

(*a*) To deliver the goods to the port of shipment at his own expense, and to see them safely on board.

(*b*) To insure the goods during transit.

(*c*) To negotiate a suitable bill of lading or other contract of carriage and to forward this to the buyer to enable him to claim the goods on arrival at the port of destination. (Purchase money is not normally paid until the documents of title reach the buyer.)

Once the goods are delivered to the ship the risk passes to the buyer (and should be covered by his insurance). The property in the goods passes to the buyer when the goods are shipped, unless the seller reserves a right of disposal in which case property does not pass until the price is paid.

10. Sale and supply of goods, services, hire and HP

The buyer is entitled to reject (*a*) the documents of title, and/or (*b*) the goods. Acceptance of one does not bind him to accept the other. But the buyer must pay the price when he receives the documents of title, even though he has not yet examined the goods. (It is also the buyer's responsibility to pay unloading charges, and transport from the port of destination to any further inland destination.)

46. Ex-ship. Here the seller is bound to arrange the shipment of the goods to the port of destination, and to such further inland destination as the buyer may stipulate. The buyer is not bound to pay for the goods until they are unloaded from the ship and all freightage charges paid. The goods travel at the seller's risk, but he is not bound to insure them (though of course he usually does).

Rights of an unpaid seller against the goods

47. Unpaid seller. The term includes any person who is in the position of seller, though not himself the owner, e.g. a factor.

The seller is unpaid as long as any part of the purchase price is outstanding.

Payment by a negotiable instrument is conditional only, i.e. is not effective until the negotiable instrument has been honoured. However, payment by means of a credit card is unconditional. If the credit card company goes into liquidation before it has paid the suppliers who took the particular card, the suppliers have no right of recourse against the customers. The company can, however, pursue the debts as can any third party to whom the company may have sold its receivables: *Re Charge Card Services* (1988).

48. Differing situations. The seller may have to contend with two different legal situations, (*a*) where the property has not passed to the buyer, and (*b*) where the property has passed to the buyer. His rights differ in these two cases.

49. Property not passed to buyer. Here the seller may (*a*) withhold delivery if the price is unpaid or not tendered, or if the buyer is insolvent, or (b) if part of the goods have been delivered, he may withhold the remainder: s. 39.

It has become increasingly common in recent years for sellers to incorporate into their contracts a 'retention of title' clause. These have many forms but they usually stipulate that the seller retains the property in the contract goods until such time as the buyer has paid off all amounts under the contract. Sometimes this is extended to all amounts owing under the particular contract and any other contract outstanding between the same parties. The validity of these clauses was first upheld in *Aluminium Industrie* v. *Romalpa* (1976). The position would appear to be that since the goods supplied by the seller start off as his property, and since the clause allows him to retain his title, no charge is conferred over the property within the Companies Act 1985 and it does not need to be registered to be valid: *Clough Mill* v. *Martin* (1984). It was also said in that case that if a seller exercises his rights under a retention clause and repossesses the goods and resells them while the contract still subsists, he is only entitled to resell the amount needed to discharge the balance of the outstanding price and if he sells more he is accountable to the buyer for the surplus. However, if the contract had been terminated, as by an accepted repudiation, the seller can resell the goods as owner uninhibited by any contractual restrictions and therefore while he would have to refund any part of the purchase price paid by the buyer, which would be recoverable on the ground of failure of consideration, he is entitled to retain any profit on the resale. It was also said that if goods which are subject to a retention clause are incorporated in or used as material for other goods, it is to be assumed that the newly manufactured goods are owned by the buyer of the original goods, subject to a charge created in favour of the seller by the retention clause unless the use of the original goods leaves them in a separate and identifiable state, in which case it is possible for the seller to retain ownership of them. *See also*: *Re Bond Worth* (1980); *Borden (UK) Ltd* v. *Scottish Timber Products* (1981); *Re Peachdart* (1983); *Hendy Lennox (Industrial Engines) Ltd* v. *Puttick Ltd* (1984) and *Re Andrabell* (1984). It should be added that a buyer against whom a retention clause is incorporated can still make a valid resale of the goods as a person who has agreed to buy goods: *see* **33**(b) *above*.

10. Sale and supply of goods, services, hire and HP

50. Property passed to buyer. Here the seller has the following rights.

(*a*) Lien *see* **51** *below*.
(*b*) Stoppage in transit: *see* **54** *below*.
(*c*) Re-sale *see* **58** *below*.

51. Lien: s. 41. The seller's lien is a right to retain possession of goods until payment or tender of payment.

A lien arises when:

(*a*) goods have been sold without any agreement as to credit; or
(*b*) goods have been sold on credit, but the period of credit has expired; or
(*c*) goods have been sold on credit and the buyer has become insolvent (whether the period of credit has expired or not).

52. Lien is lost when:

(*a*) goods have been delivered to a carrier for transmission to the buyer, without the seller reserving a right of disposal; or
(*b*) the buyer or his agent lawfully obtains possession of the goods; or
(*c*) the seller waives his lien: s. 43.

53. The seller may exercise a lien:

(*a*) when in possession merely as agent for the buyer;
(*b*) where part delivery has taken place (the lien extends over the remainder of the goods);
(*c*) if the seller breaks his contract while the buyer is solvent, he will still be entitled to claim a lien if the buyer subsequently becomes insolvent.

54. Stoppage in transit: s. 44. This means a right to stop the goods when they are on their way to the buyer (and after they have left the possession of the seller).

The right arises when:

(*a*) the goods are in transit (*see* **55** *below*); and
(*b*) the buyer becomes insolvent. (The buyer is insolvent if he

has ceased to pay his debts as they fall due or in the ordinary course of business: s. 62.)

55. Meaning of transit. Goods are in transit until the buyer accepts them, i.e. if in the hands of a carrier prior to delivery, or if rejected by the buyer when delivered: s. 45.

> NOTE: Where goods are in the possession of a carrier, the position depends on whether he is agent for the seller or for the buyer (a question of fact in each case). If he is agent for the seller, then the goods are still in the possession of the seller and his right is one of lien, not stoppage. If he is agent for the buyer transit is over, and the seller has no right of stoppage. (The carrier may become agent for the buyer either by appointment as such, or by notifying the buyer that he holds the goods on his behalf, i.e. that they await collection.)

Transit ceases when the goods reach their ultimate destination, but not some intermediate destination (unless further instructions are conveyed to the carrier to send them on, in which case transit has ceased).

56. How stoppage is effected. This is done by the seller (*a*) taking possession of the goods or documents of title thereto, or (*b*) giving notice to the carrier of his exercise of the right of stoppage.

If the seller wrongfully stops the goods, e.g. where the buyer is solvent, he is liable for damages for the tort of conversion if the property has passed to the buyer, or for damages for breach of contract if the property has not yet passed to the buyer.

If a carrier wrongfully delivers stopped goods to the buyer, he is liable for damages to the seller. And if he wrongfully obeys the seller's instructions to stop transit, he is liable for damages to the buyer.

57. Transit ceases when:

(*a*) goods reach their destination and possession is delivered to the buyer or his agent;

10. Sale and supply of goods, services, hire and HP

(*b*) the buyer or his agent obtains delivery before they reach their destination;

(*c*) a carrier wrongfully refuses to deliver the goods to the buyer or his agent;

(*d*) the goods have reached their destination and the carrier has notified the buyer that he holds them as his agent;

(*e*) goods are delivered to the master of the buyer's ship, or of a ship which the buyer has chartered.

NOTE: Sale by the buyer does not affect the seller's right of stoppage, unless the seller has assented thereto.

58. Resale: s. 48. The contract is not necessarily rescinded by the exercise by the seller of his rights of lien or stoppage, nor does the seller automatically thereby acquire a right to resell the goods to another purchaser.

The seller has a right of resale after exercise of his rights of lien or stoppage in transit where:

(*a*) the goods are perishable; or

(*b*) the price has not been paid within a reasonable time after notice given by the seller of his intention to resell; or

(*c*) such right was expressly reserved by him in the contract.

In addition to the above, the seller may also have a right of action for damages for breach of contract: *Ward* v. *Bignall* (1967).

Actions for breach of contract

59. By the seller: s. 49. He has the following rights of action.

(*a*) For the price.

(*i*) Where the property in the goods has passed to the buyer and he has failed to pay for them.

(*ii*) Where the price is payable on a certain day and has not been paid, the seller can sue for the price notwithstanding that the property has not passed to the buyer or the goods have not yet been appropriated to the contract.

(*b*) Damages for non-acceptance. This action lies where the buyer has refused to accept the goods and the property has not passed to him: s. 50(1).

The measure of damages is the estimated loss directly and naturally resulting to the seller: s. 50(2). Where there is an available market for the goods, the measure of damages will therefore normally be the difference between the contract price and the market price at the date of breach: s. 50(3). Where there is no available market, the seller is entitled to damages for loss of his bargain: *Thompson* v. *Robinson* (1955) and *Lazenby Garages Ltd* v. *Wright* (1976).

60. By the buyer.

(*a*) *For non-delivery.* The buyer can recover damages calculated in the same manner as in **59** *above*: s. 51(1).

(*b*) *For recovery of price*, where this has been paid and the goods have not been delivered.

(*c*) *For specific performance*, where the contract is for sale of specific or ascertained goods. But such an order is discretionary, and the court may award damages instead: s. 52.

(*d*) *For tort* (conversion) if the property has passed to the buyer and the seller has wrongfully detained or disposed of the goods. The action for detinue was abolished by the Torts (Interference with Goods) Act 1977.

(*e*) *For breach of condition* the buyer can reject the goods, or, if he chooses, accept them and sue for damages for breach of an *ex post facto* warranty: *see* 2: **28**.

(*f*) *For breach of warranty*, the buyer can only sue for damages; he cannot reject the goods.

NOTE: The Consumer Protection Act 1987 gives the government power to lay down standards of safety in manufacture of goods to protect consumers. Any person injured by defects in such goods (whether he is the actual buyer or not) can sue the seller, the manufacturer or any importer — whoever is more appropriate. (Exemption clauses cannot remove this liability.)

10. Sale and supply of goods, services, hire and HP

Auction sales

61. Auction sales. An auction is a sale at which the auctioneer (as agent for the seller) invites persons present to bid (offer) for goods sold.

The bidder is the offeror, and can withdraw his bid at any time before the auctioneer accepts it, usually by knocking with a hammer.

The general rules laid down by the Sale of Goods Act apply to sales of goods by auction; therefore if the sale is of specific goods the property in them will pass to the buyer as soon as the hammer falls, i.e. as soon as the contract is made: s. 57(2).

Each lot put up for sale becomes the subject of a separate contract.

62. Position of auctioneer. Auctioneers require to be licensed annually: the Auctioneers Act 1845.

(*a*) *Agent for the seller.* He is primarily agent for the seller, but on accepting a bid he becomes also agent for the buyer. Thus his signature on a memorandum of sale would be binding on both seller and buyer: *Cohen* v. *Roche* (1927).

NOTE: He has a lien on the goods for his charges and has a right of action for the price against a buyer who has taken delivery and has failed to pay. He has implied authority to receive payment in cash, but no implied authority to sell on credit.

(*b*) *Auctioneer's warranties.* Independently of any liability as agent, he impliedly warrants on his own behalf:
    (*i*)   that he has authority to sell the goods;
    (*ii*) that he knows of no defect in the seller's title;
    (*iii*) that he will give possession upon payment of the price, and that the purchaser's possession will not be disturbed by the seller or by himself.

(He does not warrant the seller's title in a sale of specific goods, unless he fails to make it clear he is merely acting as agent: *Benton* v. *Campbell, Parker & Co. Ltd* (1925).)

176 Mercantile agreements

63. Auctions with and without reserve.
(*a*) *Auctions with reserve.* This means any auction which is announced as being (*i*) subject to a reserve price being reached, and/or (*ii*) subject to the seller himself reserving a right to bid. If a reserve price has been announced and the auctioneer inadvertently accepts a bid at a lower price, the buyer cannot enforce the sale.

(*b*) *Auctions without reserve.* These are the normal auctions, and in such sales the seller cannot legally bid, either personally or through an agent. If he does so, the buyer can treat the sale as fraudulent.

64. Bidding rings. It is a criminal offence for any dealer to make an agreement supported by consideration to abstain from bidding at any sale which he attends: Auctions (Bidding Agreements) Act 1969. (A 'dealer' is any person who makes it his business to attend auctions for the purpose of buying goods for resale.)

If a dealer is convicted under this enactment, the buyer can claim damages for fraud against any person who is a party to the agreement (and providing the buyer is innocent of any complicity). Also the seller can avoid the sale, unless the goods were bought by an innocent purchaser.

NOTE: The Auctions (Bidding Agreements) Act 1969 attempted to prevent operation of 'rings', by enabling the courts to ban participants from auction for from one to three years and to order restoration to the seller of the property sold. (The Act must be displayed at auctions, but is of doubtful value.)

65. Mock Auctions Act 1961. It is a criminal offence to promote or conduct a 'mock auction', i.e. an auction at which:
(*a*) articles are sold to a bidder (*i*) for a sum lower than his highest bid, or (*ii*) where part of the price is refunded; or
(*b*) the right to bid is restricted to persons who have already agreed to buy one or more other articles; or
(*c*) an article is offered as a gift by way of inducement.

10. Sale and supply of goods, services, hire and HP 177

Contracts for the supply of goods and services

66. The Supply of Goods and Services Act 1982. This Act, which deals only with implied terms, applies to many contracts where ownership or possession of goods passes but where the contract is not a contract of sale, *see* 1, 4 and 5 *above*. It does not apply to contracts of hire purchase, *see below*. A typical case covered by the 1982 Act is a contract for work and materials, *see* 4 *above*. If a plumber is employed to install a tap, the contract is for work and materials and is governed by the 1982 Act.

67. Implied terms. Where ownership of goods passes, the supplier of the goods is under identical obligations as to title, description, merchantable quality, fitness for purpose and sample as the seller of goods under a contract of sale, *see* 14, 16, 18, 20 and 22 *above* and *see* SGSA Act, ss. 2–5.

68. Exclusion clauses. The implied terms as to title cannot be excluded: Unfair Contract Terms Act 1977, s. 7(3A). In relation to the other implied terms, these cannot be excluded in contracts with consumers, but in business to business contracts the terms can be excluded provided the particular exclusion clause is reasonable: UCTA, s. 7(2),(3).

69. Contracts of hire. The Act provides that the owner of goods which are hired out is subject to a condition that he has a right to transfer possession, or will have that right where possession is to be transferred at a date later than the contract itself: SGSA, s. 7(1). There is also an implied warranty that the person taking the goods on hire will have quiet possession except insofar as that possession is disturbed by the owner of the goods or some other person entitled to the benefit of a charge or encumbrance disclosed or known to the hirer before the contract was made. In addition, there are conditions as to description, sample, merchantable quality and fitness for purpose identical to those in contracts for the sale of goods, *see* 14, 16, 18, 20 and 22 *above* and *see* SGSA, ss. 8–10.

70. Exclusion clauses. The terms as to description, sample, merchantable quality and fitness for purpose cannot be excluded in contracts with a consumer: Unfair Contract Terms Act 1977, s. 7(2). In contracts between businesses, those terms can be excluded if the exclusion clause is a reasonable one: UCTA, s. 7(3). The terms as to transferring possession and the assurance of quiet possession can be excluded in consumer and business contracts if the exclusion clause is reasonable: UCTA, s. 7(4).

71. Supply of services. Where services are supplied under a contract, whether or not the ownership or possession of goods is also transferred.

(*a*) The supplier must provide his services with reasonable care and skill: SGSA, s. 13;

(*b*) Where the time for carrying out the service is not fixed by the contract, left to be determined in a way agreed in the contract or determined by the course of dealing between the parties, the supplier must carry out the service in a reasonable time: SGSA, s. 14.

(*c*) Where no charge is agreed in advance, left to be determined in a way agreed in the contract, or determined by the course of dealing, only a reasonable charge can be made: SGSA, s. 15.

72. Exclusion clauses. Liability for any act of negligence resulting in death or personal injury cannot be excluded: Unfair Contract Terms Act 1977, s. 2(1). Where the negligence results in any other kind of loss, liability can be excluded only if the exclusion clause is reasonable: UCTA, s. 2(2). In so far as breach of contract is concerned, the duty to exercise reasonable care and skill can only be excluded if the exclusion clause is reasonable. In business to business contracts, however, this is only the case if the contract is on written standard terms: UCTA, s. 3.

Contracts of hire, hire purchase and conditional sale

73. A contract of hire. Such a contract arises where a person agrees to hire goods for a particular or indeterminate period. Such contracts are sometimes called contracts of bailment. A contract of

hire purchase is one where a person hires goods for a specified period and has an option to purchase the goods hired, often at the end of the period of hire. During the period of hire, he is a mere bailee of the goods: see Bailment, 13 below. Such a contract must be distinguished from contracts of conditional sale (*see* 3 *above*) where the buyer agrees to pay off the price in instalments, but commits himself at the outset to making the purchase.

74. Regulating hire and hire purchase businesses. The Consumer Credit Act 1974 creates a system for controlling regulated consumer hire and consumer credit agreements. These are defined as follows:

(*a*) *a regulated consumer hire agreement* is an agreement with a non-corporate hirer where the agreement must run for at least 3 months and the rental does not exceed £15,000: s. 15.

NOTE: Goods hired from the public utilities such as British Gas or British Telecom are not covered by the definition: s. 16(6).

(*b*) *a regulated consumer credit agreement* is an agreement with a non-corporate borrower for any kind of financial accom- modation (and includes hire purchase agreements) providing the accommodation does not exceed £15,000: s. 8.

NOTE: An agreement is not regulated if it is exempt. Generally agreements are exempt if they cover mortgage loans made by local authorities, friendly societies and insurance companies: s. 16(1),(2). There are also exemptions for agreements where the number of payments does not exceed a specified number or the rate of interest does not exceed a particular percentage: s. 16(5); Consumer Credit (Exempt Agreements) Order 1989.

75. Licensing of businesses. A business providing any kind of regulated agreement must be licensed by the Office of Fair

Trading: s. 21(1). A local authority, however, does not need to apply for a licence nor does a body corporate empowered by a public general Act naming it to carry on a business: s. 21(2),(3).

76. Type of licence. A licence issued by the OFT is either standard or group: s. 22(1). Standard licences cover individual applications and last for ten years. Group licences cover a particular group where the OFT feels that this would be better than having members of the group apply individually for a licence: s. 22(1)(*b*). The Law Society has a licence covering solicitors in practice. Where a licence is refused, an appeal may be made to the Secretary of State for Trade and Industry, and from him to the High Court: ss. 41, 42.

77. Unlicensed trading. An offence is committed by a business which needs a licence but which does not have one: s. 39. In addition, agreements made by an unlicensed trader cannot be enforced by him unless he has been granted an order by the OFT: s. 40. Appeals against refusals of an order are as in **76** *above*.

78. Form and content of agreements. Agreements which are regulated consumer hire and regulated consumer credit agreements have to be in the specified form: ss. 60, 61; Consumer Credit (Agreements) Regulations 1983. If the prescribed formalities are not observed, then the agreement is 'improperly executed' and it can only be enforced on a court order: ss. 61, 65.

79. Copy requirements. The customer under a regulated consumer hire or consumer credit agreement is entitled to copies of the agreement within strictly controlled time limits: ss. 62–64; Consumer Credit (Cancellation Notices and Copies of Documents) Regulations 1983. If these requirements are not observed, then the agreement is improperly executed with the consequences referred to in **78** *above*: ss. 62(3), 64(5), 65.

80. Terms implied into agreements. As regards hire purchase agreements, the Supply of Goods (Implied Terms) Act 1973 implies conditions and warranties which are identical to those implied in contracts for the sale of goods (*see* **14, 16, 18, 20** and **22**

10. Sale and supply of goods, services, hire and HP

above). The position with regard to exclusion clauses is also identical (*see* **15, 17, 19, 21** and **23** *above*). With regard to conditional sales, these are contracts of sale covered by the Sale of Goods Act.

81. Statutory right of cancellation. If the negotiations leading up to a regulated consumer hire or consumer credit agreement included oral representations made in the presence of the customer, the agreement may be cancelled by the customer for any reason. His right to cancel lasts in most cases for 5 days from the day following his receipt of his copy of the agreement (*see* **79** *above*).

> NOTE: An agreement cannot be cancelled if (*i*) the credit extended is a mortgage loan or a bridging loan, or (*ii*) the agreement was signed by the customer on the other party's business premises, or (*iii*) the agreement is secured on land.

82. Statutory right to withdraw. The customer has a right to withdraw from any regulated consumer credit or consumer hire agreement before it is made: s. 57(2). In addition, where the agreement is to be secured on land, certain formalities must be followed: ss. 58(1), 61(2); Consumer Credit (Cancellation Notices and Copies of Documents) Regulations 1983. If these requirements are not observed, then the agreement is improperly executed with the consequences referred to in **78** *above*: s. 61(2), 65.

83. Statutory right of termination. The customer under a hire purchase or conditional sale agreement can, if the agreement is regulated (*see* **74**) terminate it any time. His liability is to bring his payments up to at the most one half of the total price and any installation charges: ss. 99, 100. If the agreement is a regulated consumer hire agreement (*see* **74**), the customer can terminate the agreement at any time when it has lasted 18 months: s. 101(1), (3).

> NOTE: (1) A conditional sale agreement for the purchase of land cannot be terminated after the property has passed to the customers: s. 99(3), and a conditional sale agreement for the purchase of goods cannot be terminated if the property has

passed to the customer who has transferred it to a third party: s. 99(4). (2) A hire agreement cannot be terminated if (*i*) the goods are hired out for business purposes, or (*ii*) if the goods are selected by the customer and then acquired by the other party from a third party, or (*iii*) if the rental payments exceed £900 a year: s. 101(7).

84. Liability. In many hire purchase or conditional sale transactions, there are in fact three parties involved. Thus, A wishes to buy a car and arranges to take one stocked by B, a dealer, who offers to arrange terms through C, a finance company. B then sells the car to C who lets it out to the customer, A. A therefore has no direct contract with B. However, it has been ruled that A has a right to sue B for any misrepresentation or breach of the 'collateral' contract between himself and B (i.e. a contract whereby A agrees to hire or buy the car from C in return for B arranging a hire purchase or conditional sale): *Andrews* v. *Hopkinson* (1956). Furthermore, anything said by the dealer in the negotiations preceding the contract with the finance company is said by him as agent of the finance company who must therefore take responsibility for what is said: CCA, s. 56. The foregoing provisions apply to all goods, not just cars, but the CCA only applies to regulated consumer hire or regulated consumer credit agreements (*see* **74** *above*).

85. Joint and several liability. In certain circumstances, a customer will buy goods direct from a dealer with credit extended to him by a third party. In such cases his contract for the supply of the goods, unlike the position discussed in **84** *above*, will be directly with the dealer. If the customer has any claim against the dealer for misrepresentation or breach of contract under a regulated consumer credit agreement, he has the same claim against the party who extended the credit who is therefore 'jointly and severally' liable with the dealer so long as there was some kind of business tie-up between the dealer and the party providing the credit: CCA, s. 75(1). This means that each is responsible to the customer for the full amount of his loss.

NOTE: (1) These provisions do not apply if the credit was not provided in the course of a business: CCA, s. 75(3)(*a*). (2) These provisions do not apply if the cost of the particular item was £100 or less or was more than £30,000: s. 75(3)(*b*). (3) If the creditor is sued by the customer, he will be able to seek compensation from the dealer, subject to any agreement made between them: s. 75(2). (4) If the breach or misrepresentation entitles the customer to rescind the agreement, he will also be entitled to rescind the credit agreement: *UDT* v. *Taylor* (1980).

86. Supply of information. Customers under regulated agreements are entitled, on payment of 50p, to a copy of the agreement and to a statement of account. This information must be supplied within 12 working days of receiving a request in writing. If this is not done, the agreement cannot be enforced while the default continues. If default in supplying the information extends for a month, a criminal offence is committed: CCA, ss. 77, 78 and 79; Consumer Credit (Prescribed Period for Giving Information) Regulations 1983. Customers who have 'running account' credit agreements (whereby they have a credit limit and can keep borrowing up to that limit) are also entitled to regular information without having to make a separate request: s. 78(4).

87. Default notices. No action can be taken to enforce or terminate a regulated agreement unless due notice has been given in the prescribed form giving a minimum of 7 days' notice: CCA, ss. 76, 87, 88 and 98; Consumer Credit (Enforcement, Default and Termination Notices) Regulations 1983.

88. Statutory rebate. The customer under a regulated consumer credit agreement (*see* **74**) has a right to pay off the agreement early. If he does so, he is entitled to a rebate of credit charges: ss. 94, 95; Consumer Credit (Rebate on Early Settlement) Regulations 1983.

89. Protected goods. When the customer under a regulated hire purchase or conditional sale agreement has paid all the installation charges and at least one third of the total price, the other party cannot recover the goods in the event of a breach of contract without a court order. If he does recover the goods without a court order, the agreement is terminated and all sums paid in the past can be recovered: ss. 90, 91.

90. Extortionate credit bargains. The rules relating to extortionate credit bargains apply to all agreements for the provision of credit, whether or not regulated. If the court finds that the bargain is extortionate, it can reopen matters to do justice between the parties: s. 137. A bargain is extortionate if:

(*a*) it requires the customer or a relative to make payments which are grossly exorbitant; or it

(*b*) otherwise grossly contravenes ordinary principles of fair dealing: s. 138.

> NOTE: These provisions do not apply to hire agreements. However, where goods hired out under a regulated consumer hire agreement are repossessed, the customer can apply to the court for relief from sums paid or to be paid: s. 132.

91. Ancillary credit businesses. The Consumer Credit Act also lists five 'ancillary credit businesses'. These are: credit-brokerage, debt-adjusting, debt-counselling, debt-collecting and the operation of a credit reference agency. The provisions of **75–77** *above* apply in such cases.

92. Powers of the court. On application the court has the power to issue time orders (time to pay or remedy a breach); protection orders (for protecting property subject to the particular agreement); return orders (for the handing over by customer of goods to which a regulated consumer hire purchase or conditional sale agreement relates) and transfer orders (passing of title to customer under regulated hire purchase or conditional sale agreement of some of the goods, return to other party of balance): ss. 129, 313, 133.

Specimen questions

1. (*a*) What terms as to quality or fitness for purpose are

10. Sale and supply of goods, services, hire and HP

implied by law in a contract for the sale of goods? To what extent, if at all, is it possible for a seller to exclude liability for the breach of such terms?

(b) In the course of his employment with the Radon Company, Watkins was sent to take delivery of a machine which the company was buying from the Metalwork Company. Watkins examined the machine superficially and failed to notice that an important working part was defective. He took delivery and, due to the faulty part, the machine did not work. The Radon Company wish to know their rights (if any) against the Metalwork Company.

2. (a) Describe in outline the principal exceptions to the rule 'nemo dat quod non habet' whereby a person cannot pass a better title to goods than he himself possesses.

(b) Robin is an absentminded person. One day he goes off to work without locking up his house. Sly, a thief, lets himself in and steals a valuable clock which he sells to Tom, a private collector. Tom buys in good faith, paying Sly £1000. Robin now wishes to know whether he can recover the clock from Tom.

3. (a) What remedies has the buyer of goods against the seller where the latter has been guilty of a breach of contract?

(b) Some months before the investiture of the Prince of Wales, W, a Welsh shopkeeper, orders from M, a manufacturer, a large quantity of commemorative drinking mugs for delivery one week before the investiture. In fact, the mugs are delivered to him one week after the investiture. State with reasons whether W will be legally entitled: (i) to refuse to accept delivery of the mugs, (ii) to claim damages.

4. (a) When does the property in goods sold 'on sale or return' pass to the buyer?

(b) Jack has been supplied with a colour television set by Televisions Galore Ltd on two weeks' approval. After a week, Jack sold the set to Jim and went abroad. Jim bought the set in good faith and was not aware of the circumstances. Advise Television Galore Ltd whether they can recover the set from Jim. What is Jack's legal position?

5. (a) James, a client of yours, wishes to introduce credit facilities in his shop. Explain to him the nature of a hire purchase and conditional sale contract, and explain to him the formalities which are necessary for the creation of a valid hire purchase or

conditional sale contract under the Consumer Credit Act 1974 and explain to him the legal consequences of the failure to comply with these formalities.

6. What remedies has an unpaid seller of goods against the goods themselves?

A, whose business was in London, had agreed to send a consignment of diamonds to B in Newcastle. A hired a car from an independent firm and gave the diamonds to the driver with the instructions to deliver them at B's address. No sooner had the car left London than A heard that B was insolvent and this was in fact the case. A then telephoned X, a friend in Newcastle, and asked X to get the diamonds back for him. X met the car outside B's office and told the driver to give them to him, but at that moment B came out and persuaded the driver to give them to him instead. The diamonds are now in the hands of B's trustee in bankruptcy from whom A claims them.

7. (*a*) Define a contract for the sale of goods and explain what is meant by goods in this context.

(*b*) A agreed in writing to sell a yacht to B, but when the agreement was signed they had not yet fixed a price. What would be the legal position if:

(*i*) the agreement stated that 'the price shall be mutually agreed at a later date'; or

(*ii*) the agreement stated that 'the price shall be fixed by C'; or

(*iii*) no price was mentioned in the agreement at all.

8. (*a*) The Fruitex Co. Ltd contracted to sell to the Supplies Co. Ltd a consignment of canned fruit at an exceptionally low price. By written notice they stated that they gave 'no guarantee as to the merchantability of the contents of any item included in the consignment'. The goods having been delivered, the Supplies Co. Ltd discovered that all the contents of the cans were defective and unsaleable. The Fruitex Co. Ltd now threaten to sue the Supplies Co. Ltd for the price.

9. The Computer Co. Ltd contracted to deliver 144 electronic devices to the Communications Co. Ltd in a year. Delivery to be made at the rate of 12 devices a month. After 3 months, the Communications Co. Ltd discover that all the devices were

seriously defective. They have now indicated that they wish to repudiate the contract.

10. On 1 January, Higgs agreed to sell his lawnmower to Watts 'on 1 February'. On 8 January, there was a freak storm and the shed in which Higgs kept the mower was struck by lightning and was entirely destroyed together with the mower. On 1 February Higgs claimed the price of the mower from Watts. Is Higgs entitled to do so, or could Watts claim that he no longer has to pay because the goods have been destroyed?

11
Carriage of goods

Carriage of goods, whether by land, sea or air, is usually conducted by persons who make carrying their business and who fall within the category of 'common carriers.'

Common carriers

1. Common carriers. A common carrier is one who offers for hire to transport from place to place, either by land, air or water, the goods of anyone wishing to employ him.

The law traditionally imposes special duties on common carriers, above and beyond those imposed on people who casually, for hire or otherwise, carry goods.

> NOTE: A private carrier is a person who carries goods for another in pursuance of some special agreement, e.g. a warehouse company delivering goods to a ship: *Consolidated Tea & Lands Co.* v. *Oliver's Wharf* (1910). A private carrier's responsibility is that of an ordinary bailee: *see* 13: **2**.

Common carriers are rare today. The Transport Act 1962 expressly states that British Rail is not a common carrier. The Transport Act 1968 makes a similar provision regarding the National Freight Corporation, and the Transport (London) Act 1969 also states that the London Transport Executive is not a common carrier.

2. Position of common carriers. The carrier is bound to carry all goods offered to him at a fair price (which may be demanded in advance), unless (*a*) he has no space, (*b*) the goods are of a kind he does not profess to carry, or (*c*) the destination is not on his normal route, or (*d*) the goods are dangerous or are inadequately packed.

If he unjustifiably refuses to carry goods he may be prosecuted and/or sued for damages.

(Many carriers evade classification as common carriers by reserving in advance the right to refuse to carry any goods at will. Thus A offered to carry various types of goods, while reserving the right to reject any, and to charge varying rates according to the kinds of goods carried, the destination etc. HELD: He was not a common carrier: *Belfast Ropework Co. Ltd* v. *Bushell* (1918).)

3. Duties of carriers. It is the duty of any carrier (whether common or not):

(*a*) to deliver at the place directed. This is discharged by delivery at the right place, not necessarily to any particular person;
(*b*) to deliver within a reasonable time, allowing extension of time for unforeseeable delays such as unexpected strikes: *Sims* v. *Midland Rly.* (1913);
(*c*) to obey the instructions of the consignor as to alterations of delivery, etc.;
(*d*) not to deviate unnecessarily from his agreed route.

The carrier's rights are: (*i*) to demand reasonable payment (in advance, if desired), (*ii*) to refuse goods not properly packed, and (*iii*) to claim a lien on the goods carried for his charges.

NOTE: A common carrier has at common law a particular lien allowing him to retain the particular goods until his charges are paid. He has no right to use or otherwise dispose of the goods in the absence of express agreement.

4. Liability of common carrier. He is an insurer for the safety of the goods he carries, from the moment they are received by him until they are delivered. He is therefore liable for all damage to the goods, whether occasioned by negligence or not, except where the damage is caused by the following.

(a) *Act of God:* an act of nature of such extraordinary description or degree that no reasonable person could be expected to guard against or foresee it, e.g. lightning, freak winds, earthquake, etc.

(b) *Queen's enemies:* the forces of a state with which this country is at war, e.g. capture of the carrier's ship by an enemy warship, but not damage by rioters, rebels, etc., since they are not the forces of an enemy state.

(c) *Inherent vice in the goods carried:* some latent defect in the goods themselves, over which no one has control and against which the carrier cannot guard, e.g. in animals, disease not visible when consigned, but not mere normal unruliness or stupidity.

(d) *Fault or fraud of the consignor:* although the carrier is bound to insure the safety of the goods, he is not liable for harm caused directly by the negligence of the consignor, e.g. through bad packing.

5. Measure of damages. This will be (a) the value of the goods, assessed at destination on the date of scheduled delivery, or (b) loss attributable to delay or depreciation, etc.

Provided that the carrier must not be made liable for damage other than that which: (a) flows naturally and directly from his breach of duty; plus (b) such additional damage as he should reasonably have foreseen at the time of making the contract: *Hadley* v. *Baxendale* (1854), and *see* 5: **27**.

6. Modification of carrier's liability. Save where prohibited by statute, common carriers may vary their legal liability by contract; but the courts interpret exemption clauses strictly, and as far as possible to the disadvantage of the carrier. Exemption clauses by private carriers are less strictly interpreted and may even protect the carrier against liability for theft by his servants: *John Carter Ltd* v. *H. Hanson Haulage (Leeds) Ltd* (1965). But no exemption clause will protect any carrier against a fundamental breach (*see* 2: **18** above), e.g. where he consigns a valuable cargo to another carrier without the owner's consent: *Garnham, Harris & Elton Ltd* v. *Alfred W. Ellis (Transport) Ltd* (1967).

NOTE: The Unfair Contract Terms Act 1977 controls and invalidates the use of certain exclusion clauses, except where these are authorised by statute. Clauses excluding or limiting liability arising from negligence causing death or personal injury are void. Where negligence results in some other kind of damage, such as damage to personal property, clauses of this kind are only valid if proved to be reasonable. Other clauses valid only if reasonable are (providing the contract is with a consumer or on the other party's written standard terms): those excluding or restricting liability for breach of contract and those which purport to allow no performance of the contract or one which is substantially different from the performance which was reasonably expected. The first Schedule to the Act states, however, that the provisions on negligence resulting in death or personal injury apply to contracts for the carriage of goods by ship or hovercraft, but that the other provisions only apply in favour of a person dealing as a consumer. Furthermore, the same Schedule makes special provision for the carriage of goods by ship or hovercraft in pursuance of a contract which either specifies that as the means of carriage over part of the journey to be covered, or makes no provision as to the means of carriage and does not exclude that means. The position here is that the above provisions concerning negligence resulting in death or personal injury apply. The other provisions do not extend to the contract as it operates for and in relation to the carriage of the goods by that means, except in favour of a person dealing as a consumer.

7. Liability of consignor. The consignor must notify the carrier if goods are dangerous, e.g. explosives or combustibles. He is also deemed to warrant the fitness of goods to be carried, and is liable for damages for breach of warranty even if ignorant of an unfitness which causes harm to the carrier.

Carriage by land

8. The principal statutes. The Carriers Act 1830, the Transport Act 1962, the Transport Act 1968 and the Transport Act 1985 are the principal statutes governing carriage by land. Otherwise, the applicable rules are those of common law, stated in the preceding section.

192 Mercantile agreements

9. Carriers Act 1830. This applies only to common carriers (but not to carriage of goods by sea). The main provisions of the Act are:

(*a*) The carrier is under no liability for loss or damage to packages containing certain articles, worth all told more than £10, unless at the time of consignment the consignor notified the carrier of the true value and contents of the package. (The carrier may then charge a higher fee for the increased risk. The carrier must post notice of such extra charges at his office; otherwise he is not allowed to charge them. When such higher fee is charged, the consignor may demand a receipt for any payment made.)

Articles covered include: gold, silver, gems, watches, bills and securities, paintings and engravings, title deeds and some other documents, glass, china, furs, etc.

(*b*) A notice alone cannot limit or reduce the carrier's liability: there must be express agreement to that effect.

(*c*) The Act gives no protection to the carrier for loss or damage caused by the crime of the carrier's servants, or the carrier's own negligence. (But the burden of proof is on the consignor.)

(*d*) A carrier is only liable for the real value (of which he may require proof), i.e. he need not accept the consignor's assessment.

10. Carriage by rail. This is governed by the various Transport Acts, and the Act of 1962 stipulates that British Rail is not to be regarded as a common carrier (and is therefore not subject to the Carriers Act 1830). Contracts for carriage of goods by rail are governed by the BR Rules, which envisage two main types of agreement:

(*a*) *Board's risk conditions.* The Board is liable for any loss, misdelivery or damage, unless it can prove Act of God, seizure under legal process, default of consignor (e.g. bad packing, or inherent vice in goods), or wastage through normal conditions.

It may also evade liability for casualty if it can prove it has exercised reasonable care, or there has been fraud by the consignor.

The Board is also usually liable for loss caused by deviation from the scheduled route causing delay unless it can prove that the deviation was not caused by any negligence.

The Board has a general lien for carriage charges and expenses, and other charges outstanding against the owners. Goods may be sold if not claimed within a reasonable time.

(b) *Owner's risk conditions.* The Board's liability is lower, so are the carriage charges. The Board is not liable for loss, damage, deviation, misdelivery, delay or detention, save where such is proved to have been caused by wilful misconduct of the Board's servants, including gross negligence.

Negligence is presumed where loss arises through non-delivery of the whole consignment.

> NOTE: Damageable goods improperly packed. The Board may refuse such goods, and where it agrees to carry them it is only liable if (*a*) there is wilful misconduct, or (*b*) damage would have occurred even though the goods have been properly packed, and (*c*) the Board would have been liable under Board's risk conditions.

11. Termination of rail transit. Transit ceases when (*a*) the goods are delivered, or (*b*) the sender exercises his right of stoppage in transit, *see* 10: **54**, or (*c*) where it is agreed to take goods to a particular depot to await collection — here transit ceases one day after notice of arrival.

12. Notice of claims must be served on the Board within three days of termination of transit, and any claim must be made within seven days. (If the claim is for non-delivery, the times are extended to twenty-eight days and forty-two days from commencement of transit.)

13. Passengers' luggage. To make the Board liable, the passenger must prove (*a*) that BR assumed control of the luggage, and (*b*) that the luggage was 'personal luggage,' i.e. for the personal use of the passenger.

Assumption of control is a question of fact in each case. Putting luggage in the guard's van is indicative of assumption of control, but the fact that the passenger took the luggage into the compartment with him does not of itself rule out the possibility that BR has assumed control.

14. Railway passengers. The Board is not a common carrier of passengers and therefore (*a*) may refuse any passenger, and (*b*) does not insure passengers' safety.

The Board can lay down any limitation on contractual or other liability for the safety of passengers, save that it cannot impose conditions which (*i*) negative liability for death or injury, or (*ii*) prescribe a time limit for the enforcement of claims therefore. This was laid down in the Transport Act 1962, s. 43(7). This was repealed and replaced with identical provisions by the Unfair Contract Terms Act 1977.

15. Carriage by road. Where a passenger is carried by road transport, in public service vehicles, the contract cannot negative in any way claims for bodily injury or death of the passenger: Road Traffic Act 1960, s. 151.

Ordinary common carriers are under the usual liabilities of common carriers. Private carriers are liable only for negligence, or as otherwise agreed.

Carriage of goods by road within Britain is largely free of statutory restrictions, save those laid down by the Carriers Act 1830, and the various Road Traffic Acts. Where goods are to be transported internationally within the EEC and some other countries, carriage is governed by the detailed provisions of the Carriage of Goods by Road Act 1965. Reference should also be made to the Carriage by Air and Road Act 1979.

Carriage by air

16. Carriage by air. The Carriage by Air and Road Act 1979 governs international carriage between the United Kingdom and countries which are parties to the various international conventions dealing with carriage by air.

Under the Act the carrier is liable for loss of goods or injury to passengers, unless he can establish one of the specified defences, e.g.:

(*a*) that all reasonable precautions were taken for safety of goods;

(*b*) that loss or injury was due to negligent pilotage or navigation.

Maximum liability (*i*) for death or injury is 250,000 francs, and (*ii*) for loss or damage to goods is 250 francs per kilo (unless agreed otherwise). The maximum liability for goods may be increased by Order in Council, up to 25,000 francs per kilo.

The Carriage by Air Acts (Application of Provisions) Order 1967 applies similar rules to carriage by air within the United Kingdom, i.e. 'non-international' carriage.

Carriage by sea

17. Carriage by sea. The owner of a ship may be a common carrier, and as such (if not protected by contract) is an insurer of goods carried, subject to the usual general defences, e.g. Act of God.

Carriage by sea is arranged under a contract called a contract of affreightment, either in the form of a charterparty or a bill of lading.

NOTE: Carriage by sea is governed by the normal common law rules relating to common carriers, save as amended by the Hague Rules as enacted for Britain by the Carriage of Goods by Sea Act 1971.

18. Contracts of affreightment. These are normally of two kinds.

(*a*) *Bills of lading.* Usually the shipper arranges with the owner or master of the ship the amount of freight (the carriage charge) and the terms of carriage. He gets a receipt for the goods consigned (the mate's receipt) on delivery to the ship, and a bill of lading signed by the master when the goods are actually put on board.

The bill of lading contains the terms of the contract, and must be stamped. The bill usually states that the goods were received in good order and condition (if such was the case), the weights and measures of the goods (if known) and the conditions of carriage.

(*b*) *Charterparties.* Sometimes a shipper hires a ship for his own sole purposes, i.e. charters it. Under such a charterparty he may take over control of the ship and crew, in which case master and crew become his servants. Such a contract is not really a contract of carriage so much as a lease of the ship.

More usually the shipper charters the ship for a definite voyage, agreeing to take all its freightage space for the voyage or series of voyages, and the master and crew remain the servants of the owners.

19. Implied undertakings by shipowners.

(*a*) *That the ship is seaworthy*, i.e. is fit for the particular voyage contemplated. This is an absolute warranty, and breach of it renders the owners liable irrespective of any question of fault or negligence on their part, unless liability is modified by the contract.

Bad stowage may amount to unseaworthiness if it endangers the safety of the ship (not merely the safety of the cargo): *Elder Dempster* v. *Zochonis & Co.* (1924).

If the shipper discovers unseaworthiness before the voyage commences, he may repudiate the contract.

(NOTE: The warranty is not absolute in bills of lading governed by the Carriage of Goods by Sea Act 1971.)

(*b*) *That the ship will be ready* (*i*) to load cargo and (*ii*) to sail, on the agreed date. (If delay is fundamental, the shipper may repudiate the contract; otherwise he can only sue for damages.)

(*c*) *That the ship will not deviate unnecessarily.* Deviation to save life is permissible, but deviation to save property is not (except in bills of lading governed by the Carriage of Goods by Sea Act 1971).

Most contracts contain a deviation clause allowing the ship to call at agreed ports in any order, and to make other necessary and pre-agreed deviations. But such clauses are strictly construed.

20. Liability of shipowners. The Merchant Shipping Acts 1894–1988 provide that, regarding British ships, no owner, charterer, manager, or operator, etc., shall be liable for damage for which he is not personally or jointly responsible in the following cases:

(*a*) *Loss or damage by fire* (even though caused by unseaworthiness).

(*b*) *Loss caused by robbery* of such articles as jewels, watches, gold, silver, etc., unless the true value was declared by the consignor at the time of contracting.

(c) *Where loss of life or bodily injury* is caused to passengers, or damage to goods (or to persons other than passengers), by negligence or default in navigation, the damages payable by the owners are limited to (*i*) 3,100 gold francs per ton of the ship's weight for injury to persons, and (*ii*) 1,000 gold francs for injury to goods. *See* the Merchant Shipping (Sterling Equivalents) (Various Enactments) (Amendment) Order 1986.

(d) *The dangerous nature of any goods* must be notified to the shipowner, who may refuse to carry dangerous goods, or charge additional sums, etc.

21. Freight. The shipowner's carriage charges are called freight and usually become payable only when (*a*) he has delivered the goods, or (*b*) he is prevented from delivering them by some fault of the consignor. Unless otherwise agreed, the person responsible for paying freight is the consignor.

Freight may take the following forms.

(*a*) *Advance freight*, payable before the goods will be delivered. If through no fault of the shipowner the goods are lost (e.g. through one of the excepted perils), liability to pay freight remains.

(*b*) *Lump sum freight*, i.e. a sum payable by a charterer for the use of the ship. If the ship is ready on the agreed date but no cargo is loaded, the charterer still becomes liable to pay the freight.

(*c*) *Pro rata freight*, i.e. a reduced sum payable where (by agreement) the cargo is delivered at some port other than that originally agreed.

(*d*) *Dead freight*, i.e. a sum payable by way of compensation for loss of revenue where a charterer fails in a promise to provide a full and complete cargo.

22. General and particular average. three types of proprietary interest are risked in sea voyages: the ship (owner's interest), the freight (charterer's interest), and the cargo (cargo owner's interest). Loss sustained by any one interest must usually be borne by that interest alone, and is called a particular average loss, e.g. cost of damage to the ship, falling on the owner alone.

But if one interest suffers loss by reason of damage or expense incurred on behalf of the whole venture (i.e. on behalf of all three interests), such loss must be averaged out over all three interests, and the other two must contribute compensations to the interest which has sustained loss, i.e. a general average assessment is made. (*See also Marine Insurance*: 12: **26**.)

General average contributions can only be claimed where:

(*a*) the danger was common to all, and was real danger, e.g. not a false alarm;

(*b*) the party claiming contribution must not have caused the danger;

(*c*) the interest against which contribution is claimed must have been saved.

23. The Athens Convention 1974. This Convention has been effectively brought into force by the Unfair Contract Terms Act 1977, s. 28. A shipowner may limit liability to such amounts as are prescribed in the Merchant Shipping (Sterling Equivalents) (Various Enactments) (Amendment) Order 1986.

Bills of lading

24. Bill of lading. This is a document signed by the master, the shipowner, or his agent, specifying the goods shipped and setting out the terms of carriage.

Such a document is a receipt, evidence of contract, and a document of title to the goods. A bill of lading is not a negotiable instrument, but does entitle the holder to delivery of the goods; and property in the goods passes to the transferee of a bill on indorsement of the bill to him.

25. Carriage of Goods by Sea Act 1971. This Act (based on the international Hague Rules) governs all bills of lading for the carriage of goods from any port in Great Britain or Northern Ireland.

The 1971 Act provides the following:

(*a*) There is no absolute warranty as to seaworthiness: s. 3.

(*b*) Bills governed by the Act must contain (*i*) particulars of identification of the goods (by 'leading marks' stamped upon them), (*ii*) the number of pieces shipped, (*iii*) the condition of the goods as they appear on inspection. This statement is evidence of their receipt in the stated condition.

The shipper is deemed to guarantee the accuracy of particulars furnished by him to the carrier.

(*c*) Statements as to apparent condition of goods refer only to external appearance, i.e. defects apparent on reasonable inspection.

(*d*) A bill of lading is prima facie evidence of receipt by the carrier of the stated goods, but the master's signature does not estop the owner from proving (*i*) that the goods were not in fact shipped, or (*ii*) that the owner's agent acted without authority — where this happens the agent himself may be liable to breach of warranty of authority: *V/o Rasnoimport* v. *Guthrie and Co. Ltd* (1966).

(*e*) The Act implies that the shipowner will (*i*) use reasonable diligence to make the ship seaworthy, (*ii*) properly man and equip it, (*iii*) provide adequate hold storage, refrigeration plant, etc., and (*iv*) use reasonable care in loading and unloading, or that his agents will do so. (The burden of proving compliance with these requirements is on the shipowner.)

(*f*) Excepted perils. The shipowner is not liable for damage due to (*i*) negligence or default by the master, crew, etc., in navigating or managing the ship at sea (not in dock), (*ii*) fire, (*iii*) accidents of navigation, (*iv*) Act of God, (*v*) war, (*vi*) strikes and lock-outs, (*vii*) riots and civil commotion, (*viii*) saving life or property at sea, (*ix*) wastage due to inherent vice in the goods, (*x*) inadequate packing, or other fault of the consignor, (*xi*) latent defects not discoverable by careful inspection.

These exemptions only apply provided that loss is not occasioned by the negligence or default of the carrier or his servants or agents, including stevedores: *Leesh River Tea Co. Ltd* v. *British India S.N. Co. Ltd* (1966).

(*g*) The carrier cannot contract out of or reduce his liability under the Act. However, when the value of the goods is declared beforehand the carrier may limit his liability to 10,000 gold francs per kilo or whichever is the higher. There are special provisions for containers. *See* the Merchant Shipping (Sterling Equivalents) (Various Enactments) (Amendment) Order 1986.

The defences given to the carrier are extended to his servants or agents. Neither he nor they are entitled to limit the damage if it resulted from acts *or* omissions done with intent to cause damage, or recklessly, and knowing damage would probably result.

Charterparties

26. Charterparties. A charterparty is a contract whereby a charterer hires a ship for the carriage of cargo on a particular voyage (a voyage charter) or for a period of time (a time charter). Possession of the ship and control of the crew usually remain with the owner, but occasionally the ship is completely leased to the charterer (a charter by demise), and he may provide his own crew.

A charterparty differs from a bill of lading in that it deals with the whole ship, while a bill does not.

27. Form of charterparty. It must be in writing and usually contains the following.

(*a*) A statement of the ship's tonnage (so that its cargo capacity can be assessed). A substantial inaccuracy in tonnage gives rise to a right of action for breach of warranty.

(*b*) A statement of the ship's whereabouts, which is a condition of the contract and if untrue entitles the charterer to repudiate the contract: *Behn* v. *Burness* (1863).

A charterparty may also contain a paramount clause, i.e. one which stipulates that the liability of the shipowner shall be limited in the manner provided by bills of lading covered by the Carriage of Goods by Sea Act 1971.

28. Usual terms. In a voyage charter the following terms are usually included:

(*a*) An undertaking by the owner that on the agreed date the ship will be seaworthy, fully provisioned and ready to sail when loaded to the agreed port of destination.

(*b*) An 'excepted perils' clause, protecting the owner from liability for loss caused by Act of God or the Queen's enemies, restraint of princes (interference by a foreign state), barratry (wilful default by the master, mutiny by the crew, etc.) and perils of the sea, e.g. natural disasters, storms, icebergs.

(*c*) An undertaking by the charterer to complete loading and unloading within a certain number of days (called lay days) and to pay compensation (called demurrage) for undue delay.

Sometimes the charterparty also provides that if the charterer completes loading and unloading more quickly than agreed, the freight charge shall be reduced; the reduction is called dispatch money.

29. Shipowner's implied undertakings. The following undertakings by shipowners are implied by law in all charterparties.

(*a*) That the ship will be seaworthy.

(*b*) That it will be ready to load and sail on the agreed dates (substantial delay may amount to breach of condition; trifling delay is merely breach of warranty).

(*c*) That the ship will not deviate from its route except for good cause, or as agreed in the contract.

Good cause usually means where necessitated by (*i*) the safety of the ship, or (*ii*) for the purpose of saving life (not merely property).

30. Full and complete cargo. A charterparty sometimes binds the charterer to provide the ship with a full and complete cargo, i.e. as much as the ship can safely carry (excluding deck loading, unless otherwise agreed). If a particular quantity of cargo is agreed (usually measured in tons), the charterer discharges his obligation if he provides approximately that quantity, even though he fails to take all available space.

If the charterer fails to provide the agreed full and complete cargo, the shipowner (unless otherwise agreed) can:

(*a*) charge the charterer dead freight, i.e. damages for loss of revenue for the unoccupied space; or

(*b*) deviate from his route to collect supplementary cargo.

31. Cesser and lien clauses. These are usually inserted and provide the following.

(*a*) *Cesser clause*: the charterer's liability under the charterparty is to cease as soon as the agreed cargo is loaded.

(*b*) *Lien clause*: the master and owners are given a lien on the cargo for the unpaid freight and for demurrage charges.

Specimen questions

1. State the forms which a contract of affreightment may take, and mention what undertakings by the shipowner or carrier are implied in every contract of affreightment.
Explain what is meant by 'deviation' and state the effect thereof. In what circumstances is deviation allowable by statute or otherwise?

2. (a) Who is a 'common carrier' and how does his position in law differ from that of a 'private carrier'?

(b) Miss E contracted with G, a local removal man, that he move her furniture from London to Brighton. One of the conditions of the contract was that G would not be responsible for loss or damage by fire. During transit one of the removal men carelessly dropped a cigarette in the van. The van caught fire and Miss E's furniture was lost. Consider with reasons whether Miss E will be able to recover damages from G.

3. (a) What is a bill of lading and what are its functions? What is the legal effect of a statement in a bill of lading that the goods are 'in apparent good order and condition'?

(b) What provisions are implied in a bill of lading to which the Carriage of Goods by Sea Act 1971 applies?

4. The K Shipping Co. agreed to carry a cargo of pig iron for the J Co. from the United Kingdom to Australia. It was within the terms of the charterparty that the ship should call at a port in the Island of Rebellia. Upon approaching that island the ship's captain was warned by a radio message from Rebellia that there was a revolution in progress, and that shipping should avoid the port. The captain, nevertheless, entered the harbour whereupon the vessel was seized by the rebels. When it was released six months later the voyage was continued. At the time of delivery of the cargo at Sydney, the price of pig iron having fallen heavily, J Co. made much less profit on the sale of it there than they would have made but for the delay.
Consider the rights of J Co.

12
Insurance

Nature of insurance

1. Nature of insurance. A contract of insurance is one which has as its object indemnification of the insured against loss, or the payment of a sum of money to the insured or nominees on the happening of a stated event.

The document of contract is usually called a policy, and the person seeking to be insured is the proposer.

NOTE: The insurance broker in the field of non-marine insurance is the agent of the insurer: *Stockton* v. *Mason* (1978).

2. Insurance not a wager. Distinguish carefully between an insurance contract (which is valid and enforceable) and a wager (which is void: *see* 2: **34**).

(*a*) A wager is a contract to pay money on the ascertainment of some uncertain future event. What renders this void is that the parties have nothing to lose, apart from the money staked on the wager, e.g. a wager on the outcome of a horse race.

(*b*) An insurance contract is a contract to provide compensation to the insured in the event of him suffering some apprehended harm to some insurable interest, e.g. his property, or his health. Here the insured would suffer harm (to property or health) irrespective of the contract, and the contract is simply an attempt to provide him with compensation if the apprehended danger materialises.

(If the insured had no 'insurable interest,' the contract would be a wager and therefore void.)

3. Insurance is uberrimae fidei. The parties to any insurance contract must make full disclosure of all material facts at the time of contracting, otherwise the contract will be voidable by the other party.

This duty falls primarily on the proposer, who must disclose to the insurer all facts which might influence a prudent insurer whether to accept the risk or not, or whether to charge a higher premium. Thus a motorist proposing an accident insurance must disclose any previous motor accidents, and a householder proposing burglary insurance must disclose the true value of the property to be insured.

Failure to disclose such material facts (and any alterations in them subsequent to the making of the contract) entitles the insurer to avoid the contract. The insurer may even require the proposer to warrant the truth of immaterial matters, and breach of such warranty will then also render the contract voidable: *Roselodge Ltd* v. *Castle* (1966), *see* **13** *below*.

EXAMPLE: In a mortgage application form, one of the clauses asked whether the applicant requested insurance cover. There was no separate proposal form; but one of the questions was: 'Are there any other matters which you wish to be taken into account?' The applicant answered in the negative. He did not disclose that he had several convictions including one for robbery, for which he had received twelve years' imprisonment. It was held that the applicant was obliged to disclose such facts as a reasonable or prudent insurer might have treated as material, and therefore to disclose his record for this could affect the moral hazard which the insurers had to assess. The absence of a proposal form did not modify that duty in any way. This meant that the insurance company could avoid the policy so far as it affected the applicant's interest: *Woolcott* v. *Sun Alliance and London Insurance Co.* (1978).

4. Double insurance. If the insured takes out simultaneous policies against the same risk, so providing insurance beyond the extent of his potential loss, he can still recover only the amount of his actual loss.

Thus if X's house is worth £100,000 and he takes out two fire policies (each for £100,000) with two different insurers, he still cannot recover more than the amount of his real loss if the house is destroyed by fire, i.e. a maximum of £100,000. But he can choose which insurer to call upon, and the insurer who pays out on the policy is then entitled to contribution from the other.

Life insurance

5. The contract of life insurance. This is a contract under which the insurer promises to pay a stated sum upon the death of the person whose life is insured.

The consideration for the insurer's promise is the payment by, or on behalf of, the insured of certain sums called premiums.

> NOTE: (1) *Insurable interest.* The contract is void unless the proposer has an insurable interest in the life insured: Life Assurance Act 1774, s. 1. A person has an insurable interest in his own life, and the following have insurable interests in each other's lives: (*i*) husband and wife, (*ii*) employer and employee, (*iii*) creditor and debtor (and guarantor). But there is no insurable interest between parents and children, brothers and sisters, etc., unless the person seeking the insurance is financially dependent on the person whose life is insured. (2) The name of the person who is to receive the moneys payable under the policy must be inserted in it: L.A.A., s. 2. A policy taken out by a husband or wife, and designated as being for the benefit of his or her spouse, creates a trust of the moneys payable, so that the moneys payable are not liable to death duties on the death of the insured: Married Women's Property Act 1882, s. 11. (3) Suicide of insured. If the insured commits suicide while sane the sum assured by the policy is irrecoverable: *Beresford* v. *Royal Insurance* (1938). But since the Suicide Act 1961, suicide is no longer a crime and so no question of public policy arises. Insurers may still reject a claim since the risk does not cover loss due to the wilful act of the insured, unless the policy expressly so provides. So insurers may still reject a sane suicide, unless the policy otherwise provides. If the insured

commits suicide while of unsound mind, the policy moneys are recoverable (unless the contract provides otherwise).

6. Assignment of life policies. A life policy may be assigned either by (*a*) delivery and endorsement of the policy, or by (*b*) delivery with an accompanying instrument of assignment.

Written notice of the assignment must be given to the insurer, who must acknowledge receipt thereof: Policies of Assurance Act 1867, s. 3. Where there are competing claims, the date of receipt by the insurer of the notice of assignment regulates all questions of priority of the competing claims: P.A.A. 1867, s. 6.

As with other assignments of choses in action, the assignee takes his assignment subject to equities arising before receipt of notice by the insurer. The assignee can sue in his own name to enforce the policy.

> NOTE: It appears that a person may take out a policy on his own life, and then assign it to another who has no insurable interest, without invalidating the policy. Thus the assignee of a policy, who has no insurable interest, may still be able to enforce it: for this reason life policies can be assigned as securities — *see* below.

7. Assignment by way of mortgage. A life policy can be used as security for a loan (e.g. by a bank). The methods by which this can be achieved are as follows.

(*a*) Legal assignment to the creditor (who must then give the notice to the insurer required by the P.A.A. 1867).

> NOTE: (1) The assignment must be under seal; (2) the assignee can sue in his own name; (3) the insurer holds the policy moneys for the benefit of the assignee; and (4) the assignee gains priority from the date of registration.

(*b*) Equitable assignment to the creditor, by deposit of the policy plus a memorandum of the reasons for deposit.

On redemption of a legal mortgage of a policy, the mortgagee reassigns the policy to the mortgagor. When an equitable mortgage is redeemed, no formal reassignment is necessary: the lender merely cancels the memorandum of deposit and returns the policy.

8. Life policies as securities. They have several advantages and disadvantages as securities.

(*a*) *Advantages*: (*i*) methods of mortgaging are simple; (*ii*) the surrender value of the policy is increased by each payment of premium, so that the value of the security will appreciate as long as premiums are paid; (*iii*) the policy can be realised immediately (if, for instance, the insured fails to pay his premiums when due) by surrender to the insurer; (*iv*) death of the insured makes the moneys assured immediately available.

(*b*) *Disadvantages*: (*i*) the mortgagee is to some extent at the mercy of the person paying the premiums, and his default may invalidate the policy; (*ii*) the insurer may be able to avoid the policy if the proposer failed to disclose all material facts; (*iii*) suicide of the insured may invalidate the policy; (*iv*) the policy may contain provision for avoidance by the insurer on breach of various covenants by the insured.

Fire insurance

9. The contract. A contract of fire insurance is one providing for indemnification of the insured up to a certain amount in the event of injury or loss by fire, caused to a specified property during a specified time.

The insured can only recover for actual loss: *Castellain* v. *Preston* (1883).

The proposer must have an insurable interest in the property insured: Life Assurance Act 1774, s. 1. Owners, tenants, trustees, and mortgagees have insurable interests, but a shareholder in a company has no insurable interest in the property of the company.

NOTE: To discourage people setting fire to their own property in order to get insurance money, the Fire Prevention (Metropolis) Act 1774, s. 83, provides that any person interested in the property (such as a tenant, mortgagee, etc.) can compel the insured to use the money in repairing and reinstating the damaged premises.

10. Average clauses. A fire policy often contains an average clause which provides that the insured can only recover such proportion of the loss caused by fire as the value of the policy bears to the value of the property insured.

Thus, if property worth £150,000 is insured for only £75,000 and fire damage is caused to the extent of £75,000, the insurer can refuse to pay more than half this amount.

11. Subrogation. On payment of all moneys due under the policy, the insurer is entitled to be subrogated to the rights of the insured, i.e. to pursue any remedies available in the insured in contract or tort in respect of the loss. Thus if the fire was caused by the negligence of X, the insurer (after paying out on the policy) could sue X for his negligence.

If the insured forestalls this right of subrogation by discharging or waiving any claim against such third parties, the insurer is likewise discharged from liability under the policy to the same extent: *Phoenix Assurance Co.* v. *Spooner* (1905).

Subrogation is only available where the insurer has paid the whole claim of the insured, and any action can only be brought in the name of the insured.

12. Excepted perils. Risks covered include loss by fire (even though caused by the insured's own negligence, but not if caused by his wilful default), and loss occasioned by a fire brigade in putting out the fire.

Excepted perils include riot, civil commotion, war, explosion, and sometimes Act of God.

A policy will not cover consequential loss (such as loss of profits of a business), unless expressly so agreed.

Accident, burglary, and other forms of insurance

13. The contract. The same general rules apply as with life and fire insurance. Note that burglary insurance is a form of indemnity insurance (i.e. compensation for actual loss), while accident insurance is often lump sum insurance (i.e. stipulating for the payment of a lump sum on the occurrence of a specified event).

Policies in this class usually provide that notice of the burglary, accident, etc., must be given to the insurer within a specified time, failing which the insurer may be discharged from liability: *Re Williams & Thomas* (1909). The Unfair Contract Terms Act 1977 does not apply to contracts of insurance: Schedule 1.

EXAMPLE: Diamond merchants insured their wares but failed to disclose a fact they considered immaterial, i.e. that their sale manager had been convicted of smuggling diamonds in the U.S.A. eight years previously. Later they were robbed of diamonds and claimed under the policy. HELD: Even though the manager was not involved in the robbery, his conviction was a material fact and should have been disclosed in the proposal — the claim was dismissed: *Roselodge Ltd v. Castle* (1966).

14. Burglary insurance. The policy usually provides cover against house-breaking and theft from the premises insured. Cover is restricted to the premises agreed.

15. Accident policies. These usually provide for the payment of a lump sum in the event of death by accident, and of smaller sums in other eventualities. Provision may also be made for payment of weekly sums during disability, sickness, etc.

The policy usually covers only accidents (or sickness) to the insured alone, though other persons may be included if so desired.

(*a*) *Accidents to the insured.* Cover is for personal injury or death, caused by chance or by the negligent or intentional act of any third person, e.g. assault. It will not cover injuries deliberately self-inflicted.

(*b*) *Accidents to third parties*, e.g. to passengers in the insured person's car, or a visitor to his premises, etc. Such cover gives the injured person a right to sue the insurer for the sum assured if (*i*) the insured becomes bankrupt, or makes any composition with his creditors, or (*ii*) is a company which goes into liquidation. Otherwise only the insured can sue: Third Parties (Rights against Insurers) Act 1930.

NOTE: All motorists must be insured against injury to third parties and in addition passengers must be covered by the driver's insurance (even if they have agreed to travel at their 'own risk'): Road Traffic Act 1988. A person injured by a car who obtains judgment against the motorist can recover the damages awarded in that action from the motorist's insurer: Road Traffic Act 1988, ss. 151–153. In such policies, restrictions on the insurer's liability because of the age or condition of the assured or of the car (provided the car is roadworthy), or of the load carried, are void.

Marine insurance

16. The contract. This is a contract whereby the insurer (underwriter) promises to indemnify the insured against loss caused by maritime perils: Marine Insurance Act 1906, s. 1.

Maritime perils means perils at sea, but the policy may be extended to cover inland navigation: M.I.A. 1906, s. 2.

17. Insurable interest. The insured must have an insurable interest in the vessel, or in the maritime venture at the time of the loss: s. 5.

Persons having insurable interests include mortgagees of a ship, lenders of money on security of the ship and/or freight ('bottomry'), or on the security of the cargo ('respondentia'), the master and crew to the extent of their wages, the owners of the ship, cargo, etc.; the underwriter himself (who can thus re-insure against his own risk as insurer).

18. Duty of disclosure. The contract, like all insurance contracts, is *uberrimae fidei* and full disclosure must be made of facts which materially affect the risk.

Matters need not be disclosed if: (*a*) they diminish the risk, or (*b*) are waived, or (*c*) may be deemed to be known in the ordinary course of trade.

Where the contract is made by an agent, he must disclose all facts which are known (or should be known) to his principal.

19. Kinds of policy.

(*a*) *Voyage policies*, to insure for a voyage from one place to another, i.e. a particular voyage.

(*b*) *Time policies*, which provide cover for a stated period. (This must not be longer than twelve months, subject to any renewals at the end of the twelve months.)

(*c*) *Mixed policies*, i.e. a combination of voyage and time cover.

(*d*) *Valued policies*, where the value insured is specified.

(*e*) *Unvalued policies*, where the value insured is not specified but is left open for assessment in accordance with customary usage if the occasion arises.

(*f*) *Floating policies*, where the name of the ship is left blank so that the policy is available for any ship owned by the insurer.

(*g*) *Open cover.* This is not an actual insurance policy, but a contract to issue a policy at a given time or on the occurrence of a particular event.

(*h*) *Re-insurance*, where the underwriter himself insures against his own liability under a marine insurance policy.

20. Measure of indemnity.
The assured can only recover for actual loss. If the loss is total, he is entitled to the maximum sum assured by the policy whatever that may be.

In the case of partial loss the position is as follows.

(*a*) *Partial loss to ship*. The insured can recover the cost of repairs, or the amount of depreciation if the ship is not repaired.

(*b*) *Partial loss of goods.* The insured can recover the value of goods lost, or if the policy is a valued policy the loss calculated as a proportion of the total amount assured.

21. Warranties.
In marine insurance the word warranty is largely used in the same sense as the word condition in ordinary contracts, and means that the assured undertakes absolutely that something shall be done or some requirement fulfilled, or affirms or denies the existence of particular facts.

Such a warranty must be exactly complied with, otherwise the policy will be avoided: M.I.A. 1906, s. 33.

212 Mercantile agreements

Warranties may be expressed or implied by the Marine Insurance Act 1906.

22. Implied warranties.

(*a*) In a voyage policy (*i*) that the ship shall be seaworthy at the start of the voyage: s. 39, (*ii*) that the ship is normally fit to carry any goods insured: s. 40.

(*b*) Generally, (*i*) that the adventure is legal: s. 41, (*ii*) if cover is granted for the ship in port, that she shall be reasonably fit to meet the hazards of the port: s. 39.

(There are no implied warranties covering (*i*) the nationality of the ship, or the seaworthiness of a ship covered by a time policy, or (*ii*) that goods insured are seaworthy.)

23. Premiums. These must normally be paid before the policy is issued, and are returnable as and when agreed, or where the policy is void for any reason, or where in an unvalued policy the venture has been over-insured: s. 84.

24. Risks covered. These include all the normal risks of sea journeys, loss from fire, pirates or thieves, barratry (wilful misconduct by master or crew), and collision (up to three-quarters of the damage sustained).

The insurers are only bound to compensate for direct loss, and consequential loss (e.g. loss of profits) requires express cover.

25. Loss may be total or partial. Total loss may be either actual or constructive.

(*a*) *Actual.* The property covered is destroyed or is so changed as to have changed its character entirely, or where the assured is deprived of its use. (Actual loss may be presumed if a ship is missing for an unreasonable time, and no information can be obtained as to its whereabouts).

(*b*) *Constructive.* The property covered is reasonably abandoned in circumstances which make it appear that total loss is inevitable, e.g. where the crew leaves a sinking ship, of which no more is heard. (Where there is constructive total loss, the insured may treat it as partial loss if he wishes, or may relinquish his property to the insurer who may salvage it if possible. In the latter case he must give notice of abandonment to the insurer, and acceptance of such notice is conclusive evidence that the insurer admits liability.)

26. General average loss. Where a general average loss has occurred, the assured may recover the total value assured from the insurer who may then (by subrogation) recover his due contribution from the other parties' liability.

(For meaning of general average, see *Carriage of Goods*, 11: **22**.)

27. Assignment of policy. Unless prohibited by the contract, a marine policy can be assigned by indorsement: s. 50. The assignment is subject to equities in the normal way. It may be made either before or after loss.

28. Discharge of insurer. In a voyage policy the insurer is automatically discharged if the ship (*a*) sails from a port other than specified in the policy, or (*b*) deviates unreasonably from the scheduled route (in which case discharge dates from the time of deviation).

Deviation is excused (*i*) where authorised by the policy, or (*ii*) where for the purpose of saving life (not property), or (*iii*) where necessary to obtain medical aid for any person aboard the ship, or (*iv*) where necessary for the safety of the ship, or (*v*) otherwise where caused by circumstances beyond the control of the master or his employer.

State supervision

29. Insurance Companies Act. A company is not able to start an insurance business unless authorised by the Secretary of State for Trade and Industry under the Insurance Companies Act 1982 or unless exempted under the Act. A person authorised under that Act is also counted as an authorised investment business under the terms of the Financial Services Act 1986. An insurance company with its head office in the United Kingdom must possess the standard solvency margin. The 1982 Act lays down detailed regulations for companies to deposit accounts and statements of their business with

214 Mercantile agreements

the Secretary of State, to apply assets relating to long term business alone thereto, and a number of other matters designed to prevent or give warning of insolvency. The Act also provides for a cooling-off period in relation to long term policies. Those who work as Lloyd's brokers are subject to the regime provided by the Lloyd's Acts 1871 to 1982.

30. Policyholders' protection. If an insurance company fails, the Policyholders' Protection Board, appointed under the Policyholders' Protection Act 1975, takes over. The Board is financed by levies on insurance companies authorised to conduct business in the United Kingdom under the Insurance Companies Act 1982. The Board ensures that insured persons are not left without cover.

31. Brokers. These are required to be registered under the Insurance Brokers (Registration) Act 1975. If not registered, a business commits an offence if it describes itself as an 'insurance broker', or if it indicates in any way that it is registered.

Specimen questions

1. Explain the expression 'insurable interest' in connection with a contract of marine insurance; and state what persons possess an insurable interest in such a contract.

2. (*a*) What is the nature of a contract created by a fire insurance policy?

(*b*) A is insured with several companies in respect of the same property to an amount exceeding the value of the property. In the event of a loss through fire what are the rights of A and the insurance companies?

3. Adam made a proposal to an insurance company for an insurance on his life for £50,000. On the proposal form he answered various questions truthfully and disclosed all relevant facts. A few days later, but before the proposal was definitely accepted, Adam was taken ill with pneumonia. Subsequently the company accepted the proposal and the first premium was paid. Two days later Adam died of pneumonia and the company learned for the first time of his illness. Is the company liable to pay the £50,000?

4. (a) What is meant by a warranty in a contract of marine insurance? How does it differ from a warranty in a contract for the sale of goods?

(b) What warranties are implied in a contract of marine insurance?

5. In respect of a contract of insurance explain what is meant by

(a) an insurable interest;

(b) subrogation.

Give examples of the former and illustrate the operation of the latter by reference to a set of facts which you may devise for this purpose.

13
Bailment

Nature and kinds of bailment

1. Definition of bailment. A bailment is a delivery of goods by one person to another for some limited purpose, on condition that when the purpose has been accomplished the goods shall be returned.

The bailment may be simple or exclusive. In an exclusive bailment the bailee (the person to whom the goods are bailed) can during the continuance of the bailment retain the goods against anyone, including the bailor, e.g. a pledge or pawn of goods: *see* 16: **9**. In a simple bailment the bailee can defend his possession against anyone, except the bailor.

2. Duties of bailee. These are defined by common law, though the duties of an 'involuntary bailee' are now regulated by the Unsolicited Goods & Services Acts 1971 and 1975: *see* **3** *below*.

(*a*) *To take reasonable care of the goods* bailed to him. If goods are lost or damaged the onus is on the bailee to prove that he did exercise reasonable care, irrespective of whether the bailment was for reward or was gratuitous: *Houghland* v. *R. R. Low (Luxury Coaches) Ltd* (1962).

(*b*) *To return the goods* in accordance with the contract. If he fails to do so, he is liable for loss or damage notwithstanding the exercise of reasonable care. If he entrusts goods to a servant who steals them, the bailee is liable in conversion to the bailor: *Shaw & Co.* v. *Symmons & Sons Ltd* (1917).

(Contracts of bailment frequently contain a clause restricting the duty of care or excluding it, but if the bailee returns the goods to the wrong person he has no protection from such a clause: *Alexander* v. *Rly. Executive* (1951), and *see* **5** *below*.)

NOTE: (*i*) The burden of proving exercise of reasonable care is on the bailee. Therefore if he has lost the goods or they are damaged when returned, it is for the bailee to prove that loss or damage was not due to his negligence.
(*ii*) If goods are lost or damaged while in his custody, and the bailee cannot show how this happened, he is liable: *Houghland* v. *R. R. Low Ltd* (1962): *Levison* v. *Patent Steam Carpet Cleaning Co. Ltd* (1977); *Port Swettenham Authority* v. *T. W. Wu & Co.* (1978); *Mitchell* v. *London Borough of Ealing* (1978).
(*iii*) If goods are lost while in his custody it is not enough for the bailee to show that he was reasonably careful to protect them; he must show also that he made reasonable efforts to recover them: *Coldman* v. *Hill* (1919).
(*iv*) The bailee is liable for the negligence or dishonesty of his servants, if he did not use reasonable care in selecting them, e.g. where he entrusts goods bailed to a known thief: *Williams* v. *Curzon Syndicate Ltd* (1919). But he is not generally liable for wrongs committed by his independent contractors, or by servants if he can show he was reasonably careful in his selection of them.
(*v*) If the bailee professes a particular skill, he is liable if he fails to exercise that skill, even if the bailment is gratuitous: *Wilson* v. *Brett* (1843).
(*vi*) The bailee is not liable for loss or damage occasioned by Act of God (inevitable and unforeseeable accident), robbery with violence, or war.
(*vii*) Where there is no express contract between the parties, the duties of the bailee arise from the law of tort: *Chesworth* v. *Farrar* (1966).

3. Involuntary bailees. By the Unsolicited Goods & Services Acts 1971 and 1975, where a person becomes an involuntary bailee, e.g. has unsolicited goods delivered to him by post, so that he cannot easily refuse to take delivery, the following rules apply.

(*a*) The goods become the property of the recipient:

(i) after thirty days, if he has served notice on the sender with a demand for removal of the goods, or

(ii) after six months, if no notice has been given to the sender.

(b) These rules do not apply if the goods were sent for the purposes of the recipient's trade or business.

4. Duty of bailor. In the case of a gratuitous bailment, a bailor is under a duty to disclose any defect in the goods of which he is aware: *Coughlin* v. *Gillison* (1899). It may be that he is also under a duty to take reasonable steps to ensure that the goods are safe and must disclose defects of which he ought reasonably to be aware: *Griffiths* v. *Arch Engineering* (1968).

In the case of a contract for hire, the Supply of Goods and Services Act 1982 implies terms as to merchantable quality and fitness for purpose which apply to contracts for the sale of goods, as well as identical provisions as to description and sample: *see* 10. The 1982 Act also implies a condition on the part of the bailor that he has a right to transfer possession, and also implies a warranty as to quiet possession. Under the Unfair Contract Terms Act 1977, none of these implied terms can be excluded or restricted, except that, in business to business contracts, the terms relating to merchantable quality, fitness for purpose, description and sample can be excluded or restricted subject to the requirement of reasonableness.

5. Particular contracts. The bailee may by express terms seek to exclude liability for negligence, particularly in bailments for reward. Such terms must be clear and unambiguous and are generally construed against the bailee as far as possible, under the *contra proferentem* rule: *Morris* v. *C. W. Martin & Sons Ltd* (1965): *Levison* v. *Patent Steam Carpet Cleaning Co. Ltd* (1977).

Thus the bailee loses the protection of such exemption clauses if he breaks the contract in some other way, e.g. by delivering goods to the wrong person: *Alexander* v. *Rly. Executive* (1951).

EXAMPLES: (a) If the bailment is a contract for personal service, the bailee loses the protection of exemption clauses if he breaks his contract by delegating performance to another, e.g. where a laundry accepted articles 'at owner's risk entirely' and then delivered them for cleaning to another firm which lost them:

Davies v. *Collins* (1945). (*b*) The bailee is liable if he deviates from the contract, and cannot then rely on exemption clauses, e.g. where he undertakes to store goods at a certain warehouse but in fact warehouses them elsewhere and they are lost: *Lilley* v. *Doubleday* (1881). (*c*) The bailee also loses the benefit of exemption clauses if he or his agent misrepresents the effect of the clauses: *Curtis* v. *Chemical Cleaning & Dyeing Co.* (1951).

NOTE: *See* further **11** *below*.

6. Bailee's power of sale. A bailee cannot sell or otherwise dispose of goods bailed unless:

(*a*) the contract so provides; or
(*b*) a right of sale is conferred by statute.

Otherwise if he sells goods bailed he is liable for damages for the tort of conversion, i.e. converting to his own use and disposition goods to which another is entitled.

A statutory power of sale of uncollected goods is given by the Innkeepers Act 1878, and the Torts (Interference with Goods) Act 1977.

For the 1977 Act to apply, the goods must be in the control or possession of the bailee, where:

(*a*) the bailor is obliged to take delivery or could give directions as to their delivery; or
(*b*) the bailee could impose such an obligation, but cannot trace or communicate with the bailor; or
(*c*) the bailee can reasonably expect to be relieved of any duty to safeguard the goods on giving notice, but cannot trace or communicate with the bailor.

The Act makes special provision for goods accepted for repair or other treatment, goods accepted for valuation or appraisal, and the storage, warehousing and the like, of goods.

If the bailor fails to collect his goods after the prescribed notice has been given (or after the bailee has made reasonable attempts, but failed, to give such notice) the bailee may sell the goods. He must account over to the bailor less the costs of sale and sums outstanding.

220 Mercantile agreements

7. Types of bailment.

(a) *Deposit (depositum)* means goods are deposited for safe custody, e.g. in a cloakroom. The bailee cannot use the goods and must (subject to any terms of the contract) exercise reasonable care of them while in his possession. He must return them to the bailor, and no exemptionary clause will protect him if he delivers them to the wrong person: *Alexander v. Rly. Exec.* (1951).

(b) *Loan for use (commodatum)*. The bailee is entitled to use the goods loaned and is not liable for fair wear and tear unless he deviates from the conditions of the loan.

(c) *Hire (locatio rei)*. Here the bailor impliedly warrants the fitness of the goods bailed for the purpose hired. The bailee must take reasonable care of the goods and use them in accordance with the terms of the contract. He is not liable for loss by robbery, accidental fire occasioned without negligence, etc. In a hire for reward the owner cannot usually reclaim the goods save in accordance with the terms of the contract, i.e. the bailment is exclusive.

Hiring is automatically determined (even in hire-purchase contracts) if the hirer attempts to sell the goods: *Helby v. Matthews* (1895).

(d) *Innkeepers.* They are bailees of their guests' luggage in certain circumstances: *see* **8, 9** *below*.

(e) *Deposit for work to be done (locatio operis faciendi)*, e.g. deposit for repair or alteration. The bailee must take care of the goods and hand them to the true owner or his agent when requested, but he has a lien over the goods for his charges and need not return them until his charges are paid.

(f) *Pawn or pledge (vadium)* of chattels as security for a loan: *see* **16: 9**.

(g) *A consumer hire agreement.* This is an agreement capable of lasting for more than three months and where the rental does not exceed £15,000: Consumer Credit Act 1974, s. 15. Various formalities attach to such agreements. The hirer (the bailee) also has the right to terminate most agreements after eighteen months: s. 101.

NOTE: A hire-purchase agreement is *not* a consumer hire agreement.

8. Innkeepers and guests. A hotel or innkeeper is one who holds himself out as ready to receive all travellers who: (*a*) are willing to pay a reasonable price for accommodation offered, and (*b*) come in a condition fit to be received: Hotel Proprietors Act 1956, s. 1.

An innkeeper must accept all travellers provided he has enough room and they are willing to pay and are in a reasonably fit condition to be received. Failure to accept *bona fide* travellers renders him liable to an action for damages: *Browne* v. *Brandt* (1902), and possibly to prosecution.

Any person is a traveller who calls for a meal or a drink: *Williams* v. *Linnitt* (1951). But he is only entitled to protection for his luggage if he stays to take sleeping accommodation.

9. Innkeeper's liability. The inn or hotel keeper is an insurer of his guests' luggage (but not of their pet animals, cars, etc.), and can only evade liability for loss or damage by showing that it was caused by: (*a*) Act of God, (*b*) war, (*c*) guest's own negligence (though leaving luggage in an unlocked room is not usually such negligence: *Brewster* v. *Drennan* (1945)), or (*d*) inherent vice in the goods themselves.

By the Hotel Proprietors Act 1956, the innkeeper's liability is restricted to £50 for any one article or a total of £100 for any one guest, unless:

(*a*) loss or damage was caused by the wilful default or negligence of the innkeeper or his servants; or
(*b*) the goods were expressly deposited with the innkeeper for safe custody in some place specially provided, e.g. the hotel safe.

A notice of these restrictions on liability must be given to the guest before or at the time of registering (when the contract is made), and a notice place in the room is therefore inadequate: *Olley* v. *Marlborough Court Hotel* (1949).

Such notice must be prominently displayed at or near the reception office and/or in the main hall of the hotel. If not so displayed the innkeeper loses the protection of the Act.

10. Innkeeper's lien. The innkeeper has a right to retain all a guest's luggage for non-payment of his charges. The lien does not extend to

222 Mercantile agreements

things over which the innkeeper owes no duty of care, e.g. the guest's car or pet animals.

The lien is lost if the guest is allowed to remove the goods; there is no power to detain the guest himself.

By the Innkeepers Act 1878, the hotelier is given a statutory right to sell such goods as are subject to his lien, and reimburse himself for his charges out of the proceeds of sale. The right to sell becomes exercisable when the goods have been retained for six weeks; and one month's notice of the sale must be given to the guest to give him a final chance to pay the bill.

Specimen questions

1. To what extent is the borrower of goods loaned to him for use under a duty to take care of the goods?

B deposited a motor van with a firm of garage proprietors for sale on commission upon the terms of a printed document which stated that 'customers' vehicles are driven by our staff at customers' sole risk.' While the van was being demonstrated to a prospective buyer, it was damaged through the negligence of one of the staff. Discuss the legal position.

2. Explain the nature of a bailment. Mention three forms which bailment may take, and explain the nature of the consideration which will support a contract of bailment.

B contracted to warehouse D's furniture at B's depository in Chelsea, but B warehoused a part of the furniture at a depository in Fulham. The furniture warehouse at Fulham was destroyed by fire. Discuss the legal position.

3. (*a*) Define the term 'bailee.' What are the duties of a bailee of goods?

(*b*) Fred has received an unsolicited parcel of goods from Inertia Sales Ltd. Fred has written to Inertia Sales Ltd informing them that he does not wish to buy the goods sent and that he wishes them to be removed from his premises as soon as possible.

For six weeks Fred did not hear from Inertia Sales Ltd and eventually decided to sell the goods.

Now Fred has received a letter from Inertia Sales Ltd demanding payment and threatening legal proceedings if the payment is not made by return of post.

Advise Fred.

Would your answer be different if Fred had not written to Inertia Sales Ltd requiring them to remove the goods?

14
Arbitration and awards

Arbitration

1. **Reference to arbitration.** Arbitration in mercantile disputes is now mainly governed by the Arbitration Act 1950, the Arbitration Act 1975 and the Arbitration Act 1979. A dispute may be referred to arbitration in the following ways:

(*a*) *By order of the court.* The Rules of the Supreme Court provide that the court may refer settlement of disputes to official referees, Masters of the Court, registrars, district registrars, etc. The reference may relate to a specified issue (e.g. the costs in an action before the court), or to the whole dispute.

Reference by the court usually occurs in cases where some special technical or local knowledge is required, and all the parties consent to the dispute going before a specially qualified arbitrator.

(*b*) *By certain statutes* which may provide that disputes arising under the statute are to be settled by arbitration. The statute may then lay down special rules for the conduct of the arbitration (otherwise the Arbitration Act 1950 will normally apply).

(*c*) *By consent of the parties*, out of court, e.g. under an arbitration clause in a contract. An arbitration agreement is 'a *written* agreement to submit present or future differences to arbitration, whether an arbitrator is named therein or not': A.A., 1950, s. 32. An agreement to submit to arbitration is not an exclusion clause: Unfair Contract Terms Act 1977, s. 13. Oral agreements are valid but are not covered by the Arbitration Act.

14. Arbitration and awards

(Contrast a valuation, which is made before any dispute arises and in order to forestall disagreement.)

(d) *The Arbitration Act 1975* provides for the recognition of arbitration agreements with an international element, and the consequent staying of court proceedings concerning disputes which should be arbitrated, and the recognition and enforcement in the United Kingdom of arbitral awards made in other countries party to the New York Convention on the Recognition of Foreign Arbitral Awards.

2. Arbitration agreements. If in a contract there is an arbitration clause, the court may stay any proceedings respecting the agreement and refer the dispute to arbitration: A.A., s. 4 and 1975 Act, s. 1.

The court may stay proceedings if:

(a) The dispute is within the scope of the arbitration clause.

(b) The applicant has not in any way consented to proceedings being brought before the court, e.g. by filing a defence.

(c) The applicant is willing to do anything necessary to assist arbitration.

(d) The contract stipulates that no right of action is to accrue under the contract until the arbitration procedure described therein has been resorted to: *Scott* v. *Avery* (1856).

(e) There is no reason in the interests of justice to refuse the application.

NOTE: Reasons for refusing the application (A.A., s. 24) include (i) suspected bias of the arbitrator, e.g. where he is an associate or relative of one of the parties to the dispute, (ii) the fact that allegations of fraud are being made against one of the parties to the dispute, (iii) the fact that the dispute involves a point of law and is therefore best left to the court.

Refusal to enforce Convention awards is permissible, e.g. where the party to the arbitration agreement is under some incapacity: Arbitration Act 1975, s. 5.

3. Construction of arbitration agreements. The Act of 1950 implies the following clauses in arbitration agreements, unless expressly excluded by the parties:

(*a*) Reference is to a single arbitrator, unless otherwise stated. (If reference is to two arbitrators, they must appoint an umpire to decide between them, by a casting vote.)

(*b*) Parties to arbitration must submit to examination on oath, must produce necessary documents if ordered, etc. Witnesses may also have to submit to examination on oath.

(*c*) The arbitrator's award is final and binding, but he can always make an interim award, pending final decision.

(*d*) Arbitrators can apportion costs, and any provision in the agreement that any party must pay his own costs however the arbitration is decided is void.

(*e*) Arbitrators can order specific performance, except in contracts relating to land.

(*f*) The parties may alter the arbitration agreement by mutual consent, but the arbitrator cannot. (The court may rectify the agreement at any time, but not so as to introduce new matter; as to rectification, *see* 4: **9**.)

(*g*) The time for making the awards may be fixed by the agreement; if not, then a reasonable time is implied, and can be extended by the courts.

(*h*) If the contract itself is assignable and is assigned, any arbitration clause in it is also assigned: *Shayler* v. *Woolf* (1946).

(*i*) Death or bankruptcy of any party to the agreement does not affect the validity of the agreement or the arbitrator's appointment.

(*j*) An arbitration agreement may be revoked by the court if (*i*) the arbitrator shows bias, or (*ii*) there is any question of fraud involved in the dispute.

Conduct of proceedings

4. The arbitrator. Any person can be an arbitrator, even though personally interested in the subject-matter of the dispute.

Reference to an arbitrator is presumed to mean a single arbitrator, unless otherwise stated. If a dispute is referred to a single arbitrator and none is appointed (or the one appointed refuses to act), and the parties fail to agree on a replacement, any party can serve seven days notice demanding appointment. If then no appointment is made, he can appeal to the court: A.A., 1950 s. 10; *Tritonia Shipping Inc.* v. *South Nelson Forest Products Corpn.* (1966).

14. Arbitration and awards 227

If reference is to two arbitrators and one is not appointed, the appointor of the other arbitrator can serve similar seven days notice and on expiry of the notice can make his own appointment (subject to the court's power to invalidate such appointment).

If reference is to three arbitrators, an award by two of them is binding.

An arbitrator's authority is irrevocable (unless otherwise agreed). But the court may revoke his appointment, or remove him, or nullify the arbitration agreement entirely. Grounds for removal would include misconduct, bias, fraud, or failure to act with reasonable speed: s. 23. When removing an arbitrator, the court may appoint a replacement: s. 25. Only exceptional circumstances (such as misconduct) will justify the court allowing revocation of the appointment: *City Centre Properties Ltd* v. *Tersons Ltd* (1969).

An arbitrator or valuer in a commercial dispute is presumed to be entitled to reasonable remuneration, unless otherwise agreed, and he has a lien for his fees on the subject-matter of the award. An arbitrator (unlike a valuer) is not liable for negligence in making his award: *Sutcliffe* v. *Thackrah* (1974); *Arenson* v. *Casson Beckman* (1975); *Campbell* v. *Edwards* (1976).

NOTE: A judge of the Commercial Court may act as a sole arbitrator (or as an umpire) with permission of the Lord Chief Justice. Appeals from such judge/arbitrator are to the Court of Appeal, not to the High Court: Administration of Justice Act 1970, s. 4.

5. Conduct of proceedings.

(*a*) The arbitration agreement may provide rules for governing proceedings, e.g. the customs of a particular trade.

(*b*) The arbitrator is entitled to call for examination on oath, discovery of documents, presentation of pleadings in writing, etc., unless otherwise agreed.

(*c*) At the hearing the arbitrator may exclude persons other than the parties.

(*d*) The arbitrator fixes the time and place of the hearing and must notify the parties. If any party fails to attend, the arbitrator can

228 Mercantile agreements

proceed in his absence but must first give reasonable notice of his intention to do so.

(e) The arbitrator must hear both sides, and obey the ordinary rules of evidence. Improper rejection of evidence is grounds for setting the award aside, but not if it was caused by mere honest mistake as to its value: *Falkingham* v. *Victorian Rly. Commissioners* (1900).

(f) Attendance of witnesses can be compelled by writ of *sub poena* issued by the High Court, at the arbitrator's request. Any witness giving false evidence on oath is guilty of the crime of perjury: Perjury Act 1911, s. 1.

(g) In commercial cases where an umpire is appointed, arbitrators may appear before him and give evidence as witnesses: *Bourgeois* v. *Weddell & Co.* (1924).

(h) The arbitrator can state his award in the form of a 'special case' for the opinion of the court, and can be ordered to do so if the court thinks fit: s. 9. The special case may state a question of law for the court's decision, or may relate to the award itself. A clause in the arbitration agreement prohibiting the stating of a special case is void: *Czarnikov* v. *Roth, Schmidt & Co.* (1922). The court does not construe special cases rigidly, and may draw inferences from the facts: *Universal Cargo Carriers Corpn.* v. *Citati* (1958). Statement of the special case renders the arbitrator *functus officio* and terminates his jurisdiction.

NOTE: Where there is a clear-cut point of law involved arbitrators must 'state a case' on request by a party to the arbitration: *Halfdan Grieg & Co.* v. *Sterling Coal & Navigation Corp.* (1973).

(i) The Arbitration Act 1979 places strict limits on the judicial review of arbitration awards.

6. The award.

(a) The arbitrator can make his award at any time, unless otherwise stated in the agreement. If a time is fixed by the Arbitration Act 1950 or any other statute, the court generally has power to extend the time limit.

(b) The award may be verbal or in writing, or in such form as the agreement expressly requires.

(c) The Administration of Justice Act 1982 inserts a provision into the Arbitration Act 1950 which allows an arbitrator to award interest on awards or any sums paid before the award, unless the arbitration agreement contains a term to the contrary. The rate of interest payable varies in conjunction with that payable under the scheme for judgment debts in the Supreme Court (see the Judgments Act 1838, s. 17). Under the Judgment Debts (Rate of Interest) Order, the rate of 15% has been fixed in relation to judgment debts.

(d) Costs are generally in the discretion of the arbitrator, which must be fairly exercised but need not be supported by reasons: *Perry v. Stopher* (1959).

7. Requisites of a valid award.

(a) It must be certain in meaning (though the court may assist interpretation where necessary, and may rectify mistakes in expression).

(b) It must be final (though this does not prohibit the making of interim awards, pending final decision of the dispute).

(c) It must be possible and reasonable.

(d) It must settle all the points referred to arbitration, but must not deal with matters outside the reference.

(If part of the award is valid and part void, the court may apply the doctrine of severance to separate the good from the bad and enforce the valid parts.)

8. Remission to arbitrator.

The award is final, but the court has power to remit any matter back to the arbitrator for re-consideration any time within three months of the award being made: s. 22.

Grounds for remission are (a) defect in the award, sufficient to justify setting it aside, (b) serious omission through inadvertence, (c) formal defect, (d) mistake by the arbitrator, (e) technical misconduct by the arbitrator, (f) discovery of new and material evidence.

9. Setting awards aside.

An award may be set aside because of (a) misconduct of the arbitrator, (b) uncertainty or lack of finality in the award, (c) illegality of the contract on which the award was made.

230 Mercantile agreements

(In a reference by consent of the parties, mistake is rarely grounds for setting aside the award unless it is a mistake of law.)

10. Enforcement of awards. Enforcement is as follows: (*a*) in the same manner as a judgment of a court, (*b*) by action in the court to enforce the award, (*c*) by court order for specific performance.

Arbitration agreements are subject to the Limitation Act 1980, and rights of reference or enforcement of any award may lapse thereunder.

11. Consumer Arbitration Agreements. The Consumer Arbitration Agreements Act 1988 was enacted to cover the growing trend for contracts made with consumers to contain clauses requiring disputes to be referred to arbitration. Section 1 of the Act provides that such a clause is unenforceable unless the consumer gave his written consent after the differences in question had arisen or where he has submitted to arbitration in respect of those or other differences. These provisions only apply if the proceedings would be within the jurisdiction of the county court (i.e. within the £5000 limit). The provisions of s. 1 do not apply to an arbitration agreement which is other than a domestic arbitration agreement, nor does the section apply to contracts within Sch. 1 of the Unfair Contract Terms Act 1977. This relates to insurance contracts; contracts relating to land; contracts relating to intellectual property rights; contracts relating to companies; contracts relating to carriage; contracts of employment; and contracts relating to certain diseases resulting from employment in the coal industry. The courts are also empowered by s. 4 of the CAA Act not to apply s. 1 where there is no detriment to the consumer. The court can only make such an order if proceedings would fall outside the small claims limit (presently £500), or if the consumer has submitted to arbitration in pursuance of the agreement.

Specimen questions

1. (*a*) In what ways may a reference to arbitration be made? What is the effect of an oral submission?

(*b*) What are the main advantages and disadvantages of arbitration?

2. Define an arbitration agreement, and state to what arbitration agreements the Arbitration Acts 1950 and 1979 apply.

Where one party to an arbitration agreement commences legal proceedings concerning the subject-matter of the agreement, mention the circumstances in which the court may stay the proceedings.

R rendered services to a sanitary authority under an agreement whereby disputes were to be referred to the authority's surveyor. Disputes arose which would probably lead to a conflict of interest between R and the surveyor. If R commences proceedings against the authority, ought the court in your opinion to stay the proceedings?

3. A contract provided for any dispute between the parties to it to be referred to arbitration. A dispute has arisen and been properly referred to a single arbitrator, who has made a valid award.

(*a*) Can either party appeal against the award?
(*b*) How can the award be enforced?

4. State FIVE of the provisions which, unless a contrary intention is expressed, are included in every arbitration agreement.

5. State the conditions upon which an award obtained in an arbitration conducted in a foreign country may be enforced in England.

6. A contract between a British subject and a French company provided that disputes arising under it should be determined by arbitration in France. An arbitration held in France has resulted in an award being made in favour of the British party to the contract, and he desires to enforce the award in England. Can he do so, and if so, subject to what conditions?

7. Explain the difference between an arbitrator and an umpire.

In what circumstances may an arbitration award be set aside?

8. State the main requisites of a valid arbitration award and examine the grounds upon which an award may be set aside.

9. In what circumstances is a consumer bound to refer a dispute to arbitration?

Progress test 3

Mercantile agreements

1. Distinguish between an agreement to sell, and a contract for the sale of goods. How do such contracts differ from contracts for the supply of work and materials? (10: **1, 3, 4**)
2. In what circumstances must the injured party treat a breach of condition in a contract for the sale of goods as though it were a breach of warranty? (10: **12**)
3. Summarise briefly the conditions and warranties implied by the Sale of Goods Act and explain how such terms can be excluded from contracts covered by the Act. (10: **14–23**)
4. Explain the meaning of the following phrases in connection with the sale of goods: (*a*) sale by sample; (*b*) sale by description; (*c*) merchantable quality. (10: **16–23**)
5. 'Generally in a sale of goods there is no term implied that goods shall be of any particular quality or that they shall be fit for any particular purpose.' How far do you agree? (10: **16–23**)
6. A enters B's shop and asks for soap. B, who runs a general store, sells him soap intended for washing poodles. A uses the soap to wash his own hair and as a result goes bald. Has A any remedy under the Sale of Goods Act? (10: **20–21**)
7. A buys a car from B in reliance on B's assertion that the car has not done more than 20,000 miles. At the time of purchase A signs a contract which states: 'This contract overrides and excludes all conditions and warranties implied by the Sale of Goods Act, and all representations made by the seller.' A now finds that the car has done 100,000 miles. What is his legal position? (10: **14–23**)
8. Distinguish between specific, ascertained and unascertained goods and explain why the distinction is important. (10: **24–29**)
9. When, if ever, may a purchaser of goods get a better title than was possessed by the person from whom he bought the goods? (10: **30–36**)
10. Explain briefly the rules laid down by the Sale of Goods Act regarding: (*a*) delivery of wrong quantities, (*b*) delivery by instalments, and (*c*) time and place of delivery. (10: **38, 40–41**)
11. Summarise the duties of the seller in f.o.b., c.i.f. and ex-

ship contracts and explain the meaning of these technical terms. (10: 44–46)

12. What are the rights of an unpaid seller, and what does this term mean? (10: 47–58)

13. What is the position of an auctioneer as agent for the seller and the buyer of property? (10: 62)

14. 'Hire-purchase is much more hire than purchase.' Discuss. (10: 73)

15. What conditions and warranties are implied by the Supply of Goods (Implied Terms) Act 1973 and to what contracts does this Act apply? (10: 80)

16. A is persuaded to take a car on hire-purchase through the misrepresentation of B, the dealer. The car is sold by B to a finance company, which then lets the car to A on hire-purchase. Later A discovers the misrepresentation, and wishes to know whether he can sue B for damages. Explain the legal position. (10: 70)

17. What is a common carrier, and what are his duties and liabilities at common law? How far can such duties and liabilities be modified by contract? (11: 1–6)

18. Explain briefly the main provisions of: (*a*) The Carriers Act 1830, and (*b*) The Transport Act 1962. (11: 9, 10)

19. How far is a railway company liable for the safety of (*a*) passengers, and (*b*) passengers' luggage? (11: 13, 14)

20. Explain briefly the meaning and significance of the following: (*a*) bill of lading, (*b*) charterparty, (*c*) freight, (*d*) demurrage, (*e*) general average. (11: 18–22)

21. State briefly the main provisions of the Carriage of Goods by Sea Act 1971, with regard to bills of lading. (11: 24)

22. Write short explanatory notes on the following: (*a*) voyage charter, (*b*) paramount clause in charterparty, (*c*) full and complete cargo. (11: 27, 30)

23. How does an insurance contract differ from a wager? What is meant by 'insurable interest' (*a*) in life insurance, and (*b*) marine insurance? (12: 2, 5, 17)

24. State the main provisions of the Policies of Assurance Act 1867, with regard to the assignment of life insurance policies. Explain how such a policy can be used as security for a loan. (12: 6, 7)

25. Explain the significance of the average clause in a fire insurance

policy. In what circumstances can the insurer claim subrogation to the rights of the insured? (12: **10, 11**)

26. What is meant by a warranty in a marine insurance contract, and what warranties are implied under the Marine Insurance Act 1906? (12: **21, 22**)

27. In connection with marine insurance, explain the following terms: (*a*) bottomry, (*b*) respondentia, (*c*) constructive total loss, (*d*) general average loss. (12: **17, 25, 26**)

28. Explain how the state supervises insurance business. (12: **29, 30**)

29. Explain briefly the following: (*a*) *depositum*, (*b*) *locatio rei*, (*c*) Torts (Interference with Goods) Act 1977, (*d*) innkeepers' lien. (13: **6, 7, 10**)

30. What are the duties of a bailee? How far is a bailee liable for loss occasioned by the negligence of his employees? (13: **2**)

31. Explain the main provisions of the Hotel Proprietors Act 1956. (13: **8, 9**)

32. How may reference to an arbitrator occur? (14: **1**)

33. In what circumstances may the court stay proceedings, and refer a dispute to arbitration under an arbitration agreement? (14: **2**)

34. What are the principal powers of an arbitrator under the Arbitration Act 1950 as amended by the Arbitration Act 1979? How may an arbitration award be enforced? (14: **3, 4–6, 10**)

Part four
Negotiable instruments

15
Negotiable instruments

Negotiability

1. Meaning of negotiability. Certain classes of chose in action, called 'negotiable instruments,' can be transferred (or negotiated) without the formalities necessary in assignments of choses in action under s. 136 the Law of Property Act or the rules of equity.

A negotiable instrument is a document evidencing an obligation, which (*a*) is transferable by mere delivery (or by delivery plus indorsement), (*b*) such delivery operating to transfer all legal rights to the obligation evidenced, (*c*) free of any defects in the transferor's title.

(A negotiable instrument payable to bearer, such as a bank note, is transferable by delivery alone. One payable to the order of a specified person, such as most cheques, is transferred by delivery of the instrument indorsed (signed) on the back by the payee or other transferor.)

2. Characteristics of negotiable instruments.

(*a*) Title passes by delivery (or by delivery + indorsement); whereas a legal assignment of an ordinary chose in action must be in writing under s. 136, LPA, and any assignment not in writing is merely equitable: *see* 6: **8**.

(*b*) No notice is necessary to the debtor or other obligee; whereas ordinary assignments must be notified under s. 136, LPA or the Rule in *Dearle* v. *Hall*: *see* 6: **8, 10**.

(c) The holder can sue in his own name; whereas an equitable assignee of an ordinary chose in action cannot.

(d) A bona fide transferee for value takes free of any defects in the transferor's title; whereas an assignee of an ordinary chose gets no better title than his assignor had.

(e) A transferee in due course (*see* **38** *below*) takes free of any defences which could have been raised by the debtor against the transferor; whereas any defence available against an assignor of an ordinary chose in action can be raised against the assignee.

3. Examples of negotiable instruments. A chose in action may become negotiable either (a) by statute, or (b) by mercantile custom judicially recognised.

Instruments negotiable by statute include bills of exchange and promissory notes. Instruments negotiable by custom include bank notes, share warrants, bearer debentures, and exchequer bills.

> NOTE: The following are not negotiable instruments, though they are freely transferable: bills of lading, Post Office orders, share certificates, IOUs and receipts.
>
> EXAMPLE: A postal order and a £5 note are stolen from X. The thief sells both to Z. (*i*) The bank note is a negotiable instrument payable to bearer and Z becomes the legal owner of it: X cannot recover it from Z and can only sue the thief. (*ii*) The postal order is transferable, but not negotiable; therefore the seller of it cannot give a better title than he has himself. The thief has no title, therefore Z can get no title; X can recover the postal order or its value from Z (who can only sue the thief for damages).

4. Who can sue on a negotiable instrument? If a negotiable instrument is dishonoured (i.e. not paid when due), a holder for value can sue any person who signed the bill before it came into his possession.

The persons who may be liable are: (a) the drawer, i.e. the person who first issued the instrument, (b) the acceptor, i.e. the person (if any) who has accepted liability on the instrument, and (c) any indorser, i.e. any person who has transferred the instrument to another and indorsed it to effect the transfer (he will also have a right of action against accommodation parties, i.e. persons who have signed an instrument merely to lend the credit of their names to the instrument).

EXCEPTIONS: A signatory may avoid liability in the following cases: (*i*) where he signed under a fundamental mistake as to the nature of the document: *see* 4: 1–7; (*ii*) where his signature was forged (since, then, he has not signed it himself), unless he is estopped from denying the genuineness of the signature, e.g. where he facilitated the forgery; (*iii*) where he signed *sans recours* ('without recourse'), indicating that he accepted no liability on the instrument; (*iv*) where for some reason the law will not allow him to be sued, e.g. minors, bankrupts, enemy aliens.

Bills of exchange

5. Bills of Exchange Act 1882. This Act codified the law relating to cheques and other bills of exchange, the most important kinds of negotiable instruments.

(Most of the rules laid down by the Act as applying to bills of exchange generally apply also to cheques, which are bills of exchange drawn on a banker. But since cheques are bills payable on demand, the rules relating to presentation for acceptance do not apply to them.)

6. Bills of exchange defined. A bill of exchange is 'An unconditional order in writing, addressed by one person to another, signed by the person giving it, requiring the person to whom it is addressed to pay on demand, or at a fixed or determinable future time a sum certain in money to or to the order of a specified person or to bearer': Bills of Exchange Act 1882, s. 3(1).

The person issuing the order is called the drawer, and the person to whom it is addressed is the drawee. If the bill is made payable to a named person, or to his order, it is an order bill and he is the payee. Otherwise a bill may be payable to bearer, and such a bearer bill is transferable by mere delivery (without any indorsement). An order bill, however, requires to be indorsed by the payee to effect transfer.

(The definition of bills of exchange should be memorised, and the comments on the definition (below) studied carefully.)

7. **'Unconditional order.'** It must be a positive order to pay, not a mere request or authorisation. The usual wording is 'Pay X . . .', though 'Please pay X . . .' is also regarded as unconditional.

An order is not unconditional if:

(*a*) it gives the drawee a discretion whether to pay or not, e.g. 'Pay X, if satisfied with goods consigned';

(*b*) it orders payment from a particular fund, e.g. 'Pay X out of my current account.' (But where an unconditional order to pay is merely coupled with mention of a particular fund, for the guidance of the drawee, this is sufficiently unconditional);

(*c*) it requires the drawee to do something more than to pay money, e.g. 'Pay X and notify me in writing'.

8. Parties to a bill. The three necessary parties are the drawer, the drawee, and the payee (or bearer). One person may fulfil two different capacities, e.g. where he draws a bill payable to himself, or payable to the drawee (such as a cheque on X Bank and payable to the bank in payment of a debt). In such cases the bill is fully valid and can be negotiated in the normal way.

But where the drawer and drawee are the same legal person (e.g. where a branch of a company draws a bill on its head office), the order is not strictly a bill of exchange, but a promissory note in favour of the payee: BEA, s. 5(2).

A bill is also treated as a promissory note if the payee is a fictitious person or lacks contractual capacity: BEA, s. 5(2).

9. Addressed to drawee. He must be identified with reasonable certainty (depending on the circumstances).

A bill can be addressed to joint drawees (e.g. to X, Y, and Z), but not to alternate drawees (e.g. to X, Y, or Z).

> NOTE: An instrument made payable to 'cash' is not payable 'to the order of a specified person or to bearer' and therefore is not a bill of exchange: *Orbit Mining & Trading Co. Ltd* v. *Westminster Bank Ltd* (1963).

10. Dating a bill. If a bill is undated the holder may insert what he believes to be the correct date of issue (which may be necessary for calculating time for payment).

If an incorrect date is inserted the bill is nevertheless enforceable by a holder in due course as though the date were correct: BEA, s. 12.

A bill should bear the correct weekday date, but is not invalid merely because it is post-dated, ante-dated, or Sunday dated.

Any date appearing on a bill is presumed to be the correct one unless the contrary is proved: BEA, s. 13.

(NOTE: By BEA, s. 45, the drawer and indorsers are discharged from liability if the bill is not presented for payment on the due date. BEA, s. 12 (above) therefore protects a holder in due course against s. 45, where he has in good faith relied on an incorrect date.)

11. Consideration and capacity.

(*a*) *Consideration.* Bills of exchange require to be supported by consideration like other simple contracts, but note the following.
    (*i*) *Consideration is presumed, in favour of a holder.* Thus the normal burden of proof is reversed; in other contracts the person seeking to enforce the contract must prove that he has given consideration, in bills of exchange it is for the defendant to show that no consideration has been given.
    (*ii*) *Past consideration suffices*, i.e. any antecedent debt or other obligation: BEA, s. 27.

(*b*) *Capacity to contract* by bill of exchange is generally co-extensive with ordinary contractual capacity: *see* 3. Thus a minor incurs no liability by signing a bill, but adult signatories to the same bill would be fully liable.

12. Sum payable. A bill must order the payment of a 'sum certain in money,' i.e. not in goods or services, etc. (Note also that the words used are 'sum certain,' not 'a certain sum' which could mean an unspecified sum.)

(*a*) A sum may be certain within the meaning of the Act even though it is to be paid:
    (*i*) with interest (usually calculated from the date of the bill);

(*ii*) by instalments; or

(*iii*) according to some indicated rate of exchange, e.g. where a bill drawn in pounds in Britain is payable in dollars in the USA: BEA, s. 9(1).

(*b*) Where the sum payable is stated in both words and figures (though this is not legally necessary) which do not agree, the sum denoted by the words is the amount payable: BEA, s. 9(2).

13. Order and bearer bills. A bill may be drawn payable to bearer, or to the order of the drawer, payee, or (sometimes) drawee: BEA, s. 3(1).

(*a*) *Order bills* are those payable to a named payee or some person designated by him.

A bill is an order bill if:

(*i*) the bill itself so states; or

(*ii*) it is payable to a specified person without further words prohibiting transfer e.g. 'Pay X' or 'Pay X or order.' (But a bill payable to 'X only' is not an order bill and in fact is not really a negotiable instrument at all, but an ordinary chose in action. Such a bill is enforceable by X, but if X sells it to Y, Y cannot enforce it against the drawer or drawee except through the agency of X.)

(*b*) *Bearer bills* are those transferable by mere delivery.

A bill is a bearer bill if:

(*i*) the bill itself so states;

(*ii*) the last or only indorsement is in blank (*see* **27**,(*g*) *below*); or

(*iii*) the bill is payable to a fictitious or non-existent person: BEA, ss. 7(3) and 8.

(A non-existent person is one of whose existence the drawer is unaware, or who does not exist at all. A fictitious person is one of whose existence the drawer is aware, but who was not intended by the drawer to receive payment: *Bank of England* v. *Vagliano Bros.* (1891).)

14. Inland and foreign bills.

(*a*) *An inland bill* is one which is or purports to be (*i*) both drawn and payable within the British Isles, or (*ii*) drawn within the British Isles upon some person resident therein: BEA, s. 4(1).

(*b*) *Foreign bills* are all other bills. But unless the contrary appears on the face of the bill the holder may treat it as an inland bill.

15. Bills in a set. A set of bills means a bill executed in duplicate, triplicate, etc. The payment of one part of a bill in a set discharges the other parts also: BEA, s. 71.

But if the drawee mistakenly accepts two or more parts of the same bill he will be liable on each part accepted as if it were a separate bill. Similarly a holder who indorses several parts is liable on each.

16. Inchoate instruments. Where a person signs a blank piece of paper and (*a*) delivers it to another, (*b*) intending it to be converted into a bill, it operates as authority to fill it up as a complete bill for any amount, using the signature already upon it as that of drawer, acceptor, or indorser: BEA, s. 20(1).

Such a bill can only be enforced against the original signer if it is:

(*a*) filled up within a reasonable time of delivery, and
(*b*) completed strictly within the limits of the authority given: s. 20(2).

But after completion the bill is fully enforceable in the usual way. Thus where S signs an inchoate instrument and delivers it to X with authority to complete it for not more than £100, if X fills it up for £1,000 he cannot force S to accept liability for that amount. But if X sells (negotiates) the bill to H, who takes it in good faith and without notice of the £100 limit, H as a holder in due course could enforce the bill for the full £1,000 against S. (As to the meaning of 'holder in due course,' *see* **38** *below*.)

17. Material alterations: s. 64.

(*a*) What alterations are material: amount, date, payee's name, terms of acceptance, place for payment, crossings on a cheque, altering order to bearer. (Alteration of the place where drawn is material if it changes an inland bill into a foreign bill, or vice versa.)

(*b*) Effect. An unauthorised alteration discharges from liability all persons who became party to the bill before the alteration, unless they expressly or impliedly assent to the alteration: BEA, s. 64.

(*c*) *Apparent and non-apparent alterations.* The effect of s. 64 differs slightly where the alteration is not apparent.

(*i*) *Alteration is not apparent*: a holder in due course can enforce as if it had not been altered, i.e. with the alteration deleted: s. 64.

(*ii*) *Alteration apparent*: all parties prior to the alteration are discharged from liability (even against a subsequent holder in due course). But the bill will be valid and enforceable as between persons who became parties subsequent to the alteration.

> EXAMPLE: S draws a cheque for £100 in favour of X, who fraudulently alters the amount to £1,000 and sells (negotiates) it to Y who negotiates it to Z. Here: Z can enforce it against Y and X, even if the alteration is apparent; but he has no remedy against S unless he is a holder in due course and the alteration was not apparent (when he can make S liable for the unaltered amount).

(*d*) *Cheques.* The provisions of s. 64 apply to cheques, but note if a cheque is altered and the drawer later authorised the alteration (usually by initialling it) the effect is (*i*) the drawer is bound by the cheque as altered, (*ii*) other parties are protected by s. 64 unless they too have assented to the alteration.

18. Overdue bills. A bill is deemed to be overdue in the following circumstances.

(*a*) Bills payable on demand are overdue when they have been in circulation for an unreasonable time.

(*b*) Other bills are overdue when the date fixed for payment has passed without the bill being presented: BEA, s. 36.

Effect of a bill being overdue is (*i*) that it can still be negotiated, but (*ii*) a transferee can get no better title to it than his transferor had, i.e. he cannot be a holder in due course.

(A holder in due course is one who takes a bill in good faith and for value before it is overdue, and he gets a perfect legal title to the bill irrespective of any defects in his transferor's title.)

19. Lost bills. If a bill is lost before it is overdue, the holder can compel the drawer to issue a replacement (though he cannot compel any other parties to sign the copy): s. 69.

Where this happens the drawer can demand security from the holder, to guard against the possibility of having to pay twice over, i.e. on the original bill and on the replacement.

20. Bills as conditional payment. A creditor who receives a cheque or other bill in settlement of his debt is not regarded as finally paid, since he has not received cash but merely a contractual right to obtain cash under the terms of the bill.

Payment by bill of exchange therefore is conditional, i.e. subject to a condition that if the bill is dishonoured the creditor shall have a right of action for the debt against the debtor.

Signature, delivery and indorsement

21. Meaning of negotiation. A bill is negotiated when it is transferred in such a way as to constitute the transferee the holder of the bill, i.e. by delivery of a bearer bill, or by delivery plus indorsement of an order bill: BEA, s. 31.

Negotiation may be prohibited by clear words written on the face of the bill, e.g. by marking the bill 'not negotiable.'

> NOTE: The addition of the words 'not negotiable' has differing effects in cheques and other bills. (*i*) A cheque crossed 'not negotiable' remains transferable, but the transferee gets no better title than his transferor possessed, i.e. the instrument descends to the status of an ordinary assignable chose in action: *see* **52** *below*. (*ii*) Any other bill marked 'not negotiable' ceases to be transferable altogether: *Hibernian Bank* v. *Gysin & Hanson* (1939). (*iii*) A cheque or other bill marked 'not transferable' ceases to be transferable altogether (and therefore is not really a bill of exchange).

22. No liability without signature. Liability on a bill is incurred only by a person who has signed it, either as drawer, acceptor or indorser: s. 23.

(*a*) *Signature in an assumed name,* or on behalf of a firm, confers full liability: s. 23.

(*b*) *Transfer by delivery.* A person who transfers a bill by delivery without indorsement (i.e. a bearer bill) is not liable upon it (except to his immediate transferee): s. 58.

(*c*) *Indorsement by a stranger.* A person who is not a party to a bill but who signs it for any reason is fully liable on the bill, by reason of his signature, to a holder in due course: s. 56.

(*d*) *Agent's signature.* Any agent signing a bill incurs full personal liability unless he makes it clear that he signs merely on behalf of someone else e.g. by signing '*per pro*' or 'for and on behalf of' his principal: s. 26. Thus a company director who signs a cheque merely as 'director' or 'manager' will be personally liable on the cheque: he should sign 'J. Jones, directors, *per pro* X Co. Ltd.'

> EXAMPLE: Directors of a company signed a cheque on which the ampersand was omitted from the name 'X. & Co. Ltd.' HELD: The company was not properly named and the directors were personally liable on the cheque: *Hendon* v. *Adelman* (1973).

23. Signature sans recours. The drawer or any indorser can negative or limit his liability by clear words accompanying his signature on the bill: s. 16.

(*a*) Signature *sans recours* ('without recourse') negatives all liability of the signer on the bill.

(*b*) Signature *sans frais* ('without expenses') limits the signer's liability to the actual value of the bill, i.e. excludes liability for any expenses arising through dishonour and subsequent action for enforcement.

24. Forged signatures: s. 24. 'Where a signature on a bill is forged or placed thereon without the authority of the person whose signature it purports to be, the forged or unauthorised signature is wholly inoperative' and no rights can be acquired by reason of such signature (unless the party against whom enforcement is sought is for some reason estopped from denying the genuineness of the signature).

NOTE: (*a*) Forged or unauthorised. A forged signature is one which is false or altered, e.g. where X signs S's name to a cheque, or alters a signature to that of another person. An unauthorised signature is where X signs his own name, but without authority to do so, e.g. where an agent without authority to do so signs a cheque on behalf of his principal. (*b*) Ratification of unauthorised signatures. An unauthorised signature can be ratified by the person by whose authority it purports to be made, thus validating it. (A forgery cannot be ratified in any circumstances since falsely making or altering any document is a criminal offence, and as such can never by validated: Forgery and Counterfeiting Act 1981. (*c*) Estoppel. If a person knows that his signature to a bill has been forged, but leads others to believe that the signature is genuine he will be estopped from denying the genuineness of the signature and will be fully liable on the bill, e.g. where S habitually lets his wife forge his signature to cheques and obtain cash thereon, he may be estopped from denying the genuineness of such signature if a dispute later arises.

25. Effect of forged signatures.

(*a*) *Forgery of drawer's signature*: the bill is void since it fails to satisfy the definition in BEA, s. 3(1) of an order 'addressed by one person to another, signed by the person giving it'.

(But the bill will remain valid as between subsequent parties to it, e.g. X draws a cheque in favour of himself on S's bank and forges S's signature as drawer. He then negotiates the cheque for value to Y. Here S incurs no liability on the bill (unless estoppel applies), but Y has full rights of action against X.)

(*b*) *Forgery of the acceptor's signature*: the acceptor incurs no liability, but a holder has full rights against other persons whose signatures are genuine, i.e. the drawer and indorsers.

(*c*) *Forgery of indorsement*: If the bill is an order bill indorsement is vitally necessary to effect legal transfer; therefore any forgery of such in- dorsement nullifies transfer. Thus the transferee gets no title to the bill, and has no claims against persons who became parties to it before the forgery. (But by s. 55 the bill will be valid and enforceable as between parties subsequent to the forgery.)

EXAMPLE: S draws a cheque in favour of A, who negotiates it to B. X steals it from B and negotiates it (by forging B's indorsement) to Y who negotiates it to Z. Z can enforce the bill against Y (and X) and Y can claim compensation from X. But neither Y nor Z have any claims against S, A, or B. (But B could compel S to issue another cheque, on giving adequate security.)

NOTE: In cases (a) and (c) above no person who takes the bill subsequent to the forgery can be a holder in due course (though by ss. 54, 55 he may have the legal rights of such a holder against persons who became parties subsequent to the forgery).

26. Delivery of bills. No person is liable upon a bill unless he has (a) signed it, and (b) delivered it. An order bill must have the signature of the transferor on it in order to effect a valid transfer; but a bearer bill is transferable by delivery without indorsement.

NOTE: (a) Importance of delivery. No person is liable on a bill even if he has signed it, if he can prove positively that he did not deliver it, either actually or constructively. Delivery means deliberately and unconditionally transferring possession to another: BEA, s. 21(1). Thus if a bill is stolen from X, he has not delivered it and he (and prior parties) incur no liability except under (b) below. (b) Delivery presumed, (i) Delivery is conclusively presumed in favour of a holder in due course, who can thus enforce a bill even against a person who can show that he did not deliver it: s. 21(2). (ii) Delivery is also rebuttably presumed in favour of any holder (though here it can be disproved so as to avoid liability): s. 21(3). (c) When delivery is rebuttably presumed. Delivery is not presumed conclusively where (i) the bill was not complete or was irregular when it left the possession of the party to be charged, e.g. an inchoate instrument, or (ii) where the person seeking to enforce it is not a holder in due course. (d) Conditional delivery. Where a bill is delivered subject to the fulfilment of some condition, delivery is incomplete until the condition is satisfied, and the bill is not enforceable between the parties to the conditional delivery. (But such bill is fully enforceable by a holder in due course: see (b) above.) (e) When deliverer liable. Although a person who delivers a bill without signing it is not generally liable on the bill, he impliedly warrants (*i*) that he will indemnify his immediate transferee (but no one else), (*ii*) that the bill is genuine, and (*iii*) that he is entitled to transfer it. (This warranty does not apply if the transferee has not given value for the bill.)

27. Valid indorsements. An order bill requires the indorsement (signature) of the transferor in order for the transfer to be effective.

Requirements of valid indorsements:

(*a*) It must be written (on the back of the bill). The signature of the indorser is sufficient, without further words indicating transfer: s. 32(1).

Indorsement may be in ink, print, pencil, etc. (but banks discourage indorsements in pencil, since they are easily obliterated; and indorsement by rubber stamp on a cheque will not usually be accepted by a bank).

(*b*) Partial indorsement is ineffective. The indorsement must relate to the full value of the bill: s. 32(2).

(*c*) Where there are several payees, all should indorse (unless one has authority to indorse on behalf of the others, e.g. in a partnership): s. 32(3).

(*d*) Manner of indorsement should correspond exactly with the drawing, e.g. if the payee's name is misspelt he should indorse in the misspelt version (adding the correct spelling if he wishes): s. 32(4).

(*e*) Allonge. Where there is insufficient space on the bill for further indorsements, an additional piece of paper (called an allonge) may be glued to the bill to receive further indorsements.

(*f*) Indorsement by agent. An agent is personally liable as indorser unless he makes it clear that he indorses only on behalf of another, e.g. by indorsing 'per pro' his principal.

(*g*) Blank and special indorsements. If the indorser merely signs his own name (without adding that of the transferee), the indorsement is said to be in blank and the bill becomes payable to bearer (so that it can be further negotiated by mere delivery).

If the indorser adds the name of the transferee the bill is specially indorsed, and is payable to order, i.e. if the transferor wishes to negotiate it further he must himself indorse the bill.

(Thus by means of its indorsement, an order bill may be converted into a bearer bill at any time, and vice versa.)

28. Restrictive and conditional indorsements.

(*a*) A restrictive indorsement is one which prohibits further transfer or limits transferability, e.g. 'Pay X only, signed J. Smith,' or an indorsement indicating that the indorsee is to receive payments only as agent for the indorser: s. 35(1).

By this means an indorser can deprive the bill of its negotiability. This will not affect the rights of the transferee as against the indorser, but will prevent him passing a full title to any further transferee: s. 35(2).

(*b*) Conditional indorsement is one which makes payment or transfer subject to some condition, e.g. 'Pay X, after his marriage to Z.'

Such a condition can be ignored by the payer: s. 33.

(*c*) Indorsement *sans recours*. If the indorser seeks to restrict his liability to the transferee by indorsing *sans recours*, or *sans frais* (*see* 23 *above*), the transferee can refuse to accept the bill with this indorsement. If he does take the bill so indorsed, he is bound by the restriction.

(*d*) Falculative indorsement is one in which the indorser waives some of his legal rights in favour of the transferee, e.g. indorsement with 'notice of dishonour waived': s. 16(2). In such a case the transferee and subsequent transferees can enforce the bill against the indorser without giving notice of dishonour, etc.

Liability of parties

29. **Parties to a bill.** A party means a person who is liable on the bill, i.e. the drawer, acceptor, and indorsers.

However, the payee (before he indorses the bill) has rights under it, and can also be described as a party.

30. Order of liability.

(*a*) *Before acceptance* the drawer is the principal debtor and primarily liable.

(b) *After acceptance*, the drawee takes over primary liability (and the drawer and indorsers are merely sureties for him).

(c) *After indorsement*, the indorser becomes liable as a surety for the value of the bill.

The holder can thus enforce the bill against the drawer, the acceptor (primarily) and any indorsers. He can sue any one or he can sue any combination of them, and each is liable for the full value of the bill.

(As between themselves the parties have no right of contribution: contrast guarantors, *see* 17: **9–10**. But any party who has been made to pay the full amount on the bill has a right of action for that amount against his immediate transferor.)

31. The drawer: s. 55.

(a) *Liability*. He engages that (i) on due presentment it will be paid according to its tenor, and (ii) if dishonoured, he will compensate the holder or any indorser who has suffered loss thereby (provided necessary proceedings on dishonour are taken).

(b) *Estoppel*. He is precluded from denying to a holder in due course the existence and capacity of the payee.

32. The drawee/acceptor.

He is the person to whom the order is addressed. He is under no liability on the bill unless and until he accepts it, after which he assumes primary liability (and is called the acceptor).

Where a bill is not payable on demand it must be presented to the drawee for him to signify his acceptance of liability (or to reject it), and later presented to him again for payment. A bill payable on demand, such as a cheque, is merely presented for payment without any prior presentation for acceptance.

(a) *Acceptor's liability*. He engages that he will pay the bill on due presentment for payment according to its tenor.

(b) *Estoppel*. He is precluded from denying (i) the existence, capacity and signature of the drawer, (ii) the existence and capacity of the payee of an order bill (though he may deny the validity or genuineness of the payee's indorsement): s. 24.

33. Indorsers.
They are people (including the payee) who indorse an order bill in order to transfer it.

(a) Liability. They engage *(i)* that on due presentment the bill will be accepted and paid according to its tenor, and *(ii)* that if it is dishonoured they will compensate the holder (or any indorser who is compelled to pay it) providing necessary proceedings for dishonour are taken: s. 66.

(b) Estoppel. An indorser is precluded from denying *(i)* to a holder in due course — the genuineness of the drawer's signature and of all indorsements prior to his own, *(ii)* to a later indorser — the validity of the bill or his own title when he indorsed it.

(Remember that any person signing a bill otherwise than as drawer or acceptor incurs the full liability of an indorser.)

34. Accommodation party.
This means a person who has signed a bill as drawer, acceptor or indorser without receiving value therefore.

An accommodation party is liable on the bill to any holder for value, but not to the person whom he has accommodated, i.e. the person to whom he lent the credit of his name.

An accommodation bill is one of which the acceptor is an accommodation party: s. 59(3), i.e. a person who accepts for the honour of the drawer or some other party. (When a bill is not accepted by the original drawee, some other person may step in to accept the bill to save the drawer or any indorser from being sued for dishonour. This is called 'acceptance for honour.')

35. Referee in case of need.
The drawer or any indorser who fears that a bill may not be accepted by the drawee may designate some other person in addition to the drawee as 'referee in case of need,' to whom the holder may apply for payment (if he wishes) in the event of dishonour by the drawee: s. 15.

If the referee accepts liability, the bill becomes an accommodation bill and he is said to be accepting for honour of the drawer or any indorser on whose behalf he intervenes: ss. 65–68.

36. Fictitious and non-existing payees: s. 7. Where the payee of a bill is a fictitious or non-existing person, the bill may be treated as payable to bearer (and can be negotiated without the indorsement of such payee): s. 7(3).

(*a*) Fictitious payee means someone whom the drawer did not intend to receive payment, though he may be an existing person and may be named by the drawer as payee.

EXAMPLES: (*i*) V's clerk G obtained V's acceptance of bills G had forged, and apparently drawn by a customer of V in favour of X, a person known to V. G then forged X's indorsement to the bills and obtained their value. HELD: The clerk was the real drawer of the bills, and he knew of X's existence but did not intend him to obtain payment, therefore X was a fictitious payee and the bills were payable to bearer: *Bank of England* v. *Vagliano Bros.* (1891). (*ii*) A clerk induced his employer to draw cheques payable to X, to whom the employer owed money. The employer intended X to be the payee, but the amounts of the cheques were forged by the clerk, who later forged X's indorsements and obtained payment. HELD: The cheques were not payable to a fictitious payee since the drawer intended X to receive payment, though not of the amounts stated. Thus the cheques were order bills, needing a valid indorsement by X to effect transfer, therefore the forged indorsements by the clerk were ineffective and the transferee obtained no title: *Vinden* v. *Hughes* (1905).

(*b*) Non-existing payee means someone (living or not) of whose existence the drawer is unaware, even though he may have intended him to receive payment.

EXAMPLE: A clerk induced his employer to draw cheques in favour of X (an actual person), by pretending that the money was owing to X. The clerk then forged X's indorsements and obtained the value of the cheques. HELD: X was a non-existing payee, and these cheques were therefore bearer bills. Consequently transfer would have been effective without indorsement at all: *Clutton* v. *Attenborough* (1897).

37. Position of holder.

(a) *Meaning of holder.* He is the payee or indorsee of a bill, who is in possession of it, or the bearer of a bearer bill: s. 2.

Thus a person who takes an order bill by means of a forged indorsement is not a holder, since he is neither the indorsee of it, nor the bearer of a bearer bill.

(b) *Position of holder.* He can enforce the bill (*i*) against any person who has signed it, and (*ii*) against the transferor from whom he obtained it, whether that person signed it or not.

To have full rights of enforcement he should (*i*) have given value himself (in which case he is probably a holder in due course: *see below*), or (*ii*) have obtained it from a person who has given value for it (in which case he is a holder for value: *see* **39** *below*).

But in any case the law presumes in favour of any holder that his possession is supported by valuable consideration, and in any action brought by the holder it will be for the defendant to disprove this presumption (not for the holder to prove the existence of consideration): *see* **11** *above*.

38. Holder in due course: s. 29.

(a) *Meaning.* He is a holder who has taken a bill (*i*) complete and regular on the face of it, (*ii*) before it was overdue and without notice that it had been dishonoured (if such was the case), (*iii*) in good faith and for value and (*iv*) without notice of any defect in the transferor's title: s. 29(1): *see* **66** *below*. In *Mackenzie Mills* v. *Buono* (1986), the defendant imported furniture from suppliers in Italy. Following discussions between the defendant and the suppliers as to the quality of the furniture, payment was made by a post-dated cheque in exchange for a promise that the suppliers would replace certain defective items. A number of the cheques were dishonoured. A further cheque was endorsed by the suppliers and handed over to the plaintiffs, a firm of solicitors who were acting for the suppliers in their dispute with the defendant. At that time the suppliers owed the plaintiffs some £500 in respect of costs already incurred in respect of the dispute. That cheque too was dishonoured on being countermanded by the defendant. In an action on the cheque, the plaintiffs obtained judgment for the full amount of the cheque with interests and costs. The defendant appealed, contending that the plaintiffs were not holders in due course of the cheque, not having given any value for it. The court held that, the cheque having been given in payment for the furniture in anticipation of the defective items being replaced, it was clear that as between the defendant and suppliers value had been given for it, notwithstanding that in proceedings between them the defendant could be in a position to contend that the consideration originally given for it had wholly failed. It followed that the plaintiffs were deemed to be holders of the cheque for value and therefore were holders in due course.

> NOTE: (*i*) That the payee cannot be a holder in due course, since he did not take the bill by the process of negotiation, i.e. he was one of the original parties to the issue of the bill: *R. E. Jones Ltd v. Waring & Gillow Ltd* (1926). (*ii*) A person who derives his title through a forged indorsement cannot be a holder in due course, since a holder is a person who derives his title through a valid indorsement (s. 2) and a forgery is an invalid and inoperative indorsement (s. 24). The Consumer Credit Act 1974 has imposed certain restrictions on the holder in due course in relation to negotiable instruments taken under regulated agreements. These are explained in **66** *below*.

(*b*) *Rights.* A holder in due course can (*i*) sue on the bill in his own name, and (*ii*) defeat any defences arising from defects of title or arising from the relations of the parties before he took the bill.

Thus the only defences that can be raised against his claims are (*i*) that he does not satisfy the definition given in s. 29(1), e.g. that the bill was overdue when he took it, or had some patent defect (such as disagreement of words and figures of the amount), (*ii*) that a forged indorsement vitiates his title, (*iii*) that issue, acceptance or negotiation of the bill were produced by fraud, coercion or illegality (in which case the holder in due course can still enforce the bill but only if he can prove positively that, subsequent to the alleged fraud, coercion or illegality, value has in good faith been given for the bill, i.e. the burden of proof shifts to the holder): s. 30(2).

(*c*) *Presumption in favour of holder.* Every holder of a bill is presumed to be a holder in due course until the contrary is proved.

(d) *Good faith*. Negligence of the holder (e.g. failure to make reasonable enquiries) does not preclude him from being a holder in due course, i.e. does not necessarily amount to bad faith.

39. Holder for value.

(a) *Meaning.* He is a holder of a bill for which value has at some time been given; he need not have given value himself.

(b) *Rights.* He can enforce the bill against all persons who became parties prior to the giving of such value. (Remember also the presumption in favour of all holders that value has been given for the bill.)

He can sue on the bill in his own name, but he obtained no better title than his transferor possessed. Thus if a holder in due course gives the bill as a present to V, V is a holder for value (since value has been given by the holder in due course) and has as good a title as his transferor, i.e. in this case a perfect title.

> EXAMPLE: S draws a cheque in favour of A, who indorses it for value to B, who gives it gratuitously to C who gives it gratuitously to D. Presuming all indorsements are valid, D is a holder for value (even though he did not himself give value) and can enforce the cheque against all persons who became parties prior to value being given, i.e. against S and A, but not against B or C.

Acceptance, payment and dishonour

40. Acceptance of bills of exchange. Bills not payable on demand must be accepted by the drawee as a prerequisite to payment. (Bills payable on demand, including cheques, bypass this intervening stage and proceed straight to payment.)

(a) *Drawee's liability.* The drawee is under no liability to holders of the bill until he accepts liability, by signing across the face of the bill. (Though he may be liable to damages for breach of contract to the drawer if he improperly refuses to accept a bill which he was contractually bound to accept.)

Acceptance is signified by the drawee signing across the face of the bill, with or without addition of the date or such words as 'accepted': s. 17.

(*b*) *When made.* Acceptance may be made at any time, even before the drawer's signature of the bill (though usually after). A bill may be accepted when overdue or when previously dishonoured: s. 18.

If a bill payable after sight is dishonoured by non-acceptance but the drawee later changes his mind and accepts it, the holder is entitled to have the acceptance back-dated to the date when it was first presented for acceptance: s. 18(3). This may be important, e.g. where a bill is payable 3 months after sight by the drawee.

(*c*) *Kinds of acceptance.* Acceptance may be either general (unqualified acceptance of the bill as drawn) or qualified. The holder is entitled to general acceptance, and may treat the bill as dishonoured if only a qualified acceptance is offered: s. 44(1). If he takes a qualified acceptance he loses his right of recourse against prior parties to the bill (except such of them as authorised him to do so): s. 44(2).

(*d*) *Kinds of qualified acceptance.*

  (*i*) Conditional, e.g. 'Accepted subject to deduction for expenses.'

  (*ii*) Partial, e.g. for part only of the sum specified.

  (*iii*) Local, i.e. payable only at a particular place. (Merely naming a place for payment is general acceptance, unless it is to be made only at the place named.)

  (*iv*) Qualified as to time, e.g. 'accepted payable in six months' where the bill specified three months.

  (*v*) Acceptance by some only of several joint drawees.

41. Presentment for acceptance.

A bill payable after sight must be presented for acceptance within a reasonable time and if not so presented the drawer and all indorsers prior to presentation are discharged from liability: s. 40(1).

Presentment is only necessary where:

(*a*) The bill is payable after sight or after demand (since presentation will enable calculation of the period after which the bill shall be payable).

(*b*) There is an express stipulation for presentment.

(c) The bill is payable elsewhere than at the residence or place of business of the drawee, e.g. at a bank. (But the drawee for his own convenience may nominate his bank or some other place as the place for payment, in which case the bill is said to be domiciled. Domiciling a bill is not qualified acceptance, unless it is done in such a way as to prohibit the holder from seeking payment anywhere else.)

42. Presentment for acceptance is excused, and the bill may be treated as dishonoured where:

(a) The drawee is dead, bankrupt, lacks capacity or is a fictitious person.

(b) Presentment is impossible, e.g. because the drawee cannot be found.

(c) Acceptance is refused: s. 42(2).

43. Presentment for payment. A bill not payable on demand must be presented for payment on the due date (as fixed by the bill, e.g. three months after acceptance, or 'after sight').

(a) Presentment must be at a reasonable hour on a business day, and at the proper place: s. 45(3).

(b) Delay in presentment is excused if due to circumstances beyond the holder's control: s. 46(1).

(c) A bill not presented within due time is not invalidated, but it cannot be enforced against persons who drew or indorsed it unless such person's signature was added within a reasonable time. (Compare the position of the drawer of a cheque, who is discharged by delay only to the extent he has suffered damage: s. 74 and *see* **48**.)

(d) Presentment for payment may be excused where: (i) after reasonable diligence it cannot be effected, e.g. because the acceptor cannot be found; (ii) the drawee is a fictitious person; or (iii) presentment has been waived: s. 45(2).

(e) A bill is dishonoured by non-payment when (i) it is properly presented but payment is refused or cannot be obtained, or (ii) presentment is excused: s. 47(1). An offer of partial payment can be treated as dishonoured, or it can be accepted and the bill treated as dishonoured for the balance.

NOTE: Formerly three 'days of grace' were added to the due date for the benefit of the drawee but to bring English law into line with international usage these were abolished by the Banking and Financial Dealings Act 1971.

44. Procedure on dishonour. The holder of a dishonoured bill must notify the fact of dishonour to all prior parties against whom he reserves a right of action; persons not so notified are discharged.

Similarly any indorser must reserve his rights of action by notifying parties prior to himself.

But even where it is known that a bill will be dishonoured on presentation on maturity (because, e.g., of the drawer's insolvency) notice of dishonour must not be given until dishonour has actually occurred: *Eaglehill Ltd* v. *Needham Builders Ltd* (1972).

(*a*) *Inland bills*: Notice of dishonour can be in any form, oral or written, providing it clearly identifies the bill: s. 49(5). Return of a dishonoured bill is sufficient notice to the drawer: s. 49(6). Notice must be given within a reasonable time of dishonour: s. 49(12).

(*b*) *Foreign bills: Noting and Protesting.* Formal notice of dishonour is required in the case of foreign bills (and is optional in the case of inland bills).

Formal notice is achieved by getting the bill re-presented by a notary public (or, if none can be found, by a householder in the presence of witnesses), who notes on the bill the answer obtained, if any.

The notary or householder then issues a formal certificate of dishonour (called the Protest), setting out the circumstances of dishonour. The Protest and a copy of the noted bill are then sent by the holder to the person or persons he intends to make liable.

45. Circumstances under which notice of dishonour is dispensed with.

(*a*) When after exercise of reasonable diligence it cannot be given, e.g. where the address cannot be found.

(*b*) When waived, expressly or by implication, by the person entitled to notice.

(c) As regards the drawer: (i) where drawer and drawee are the same person, (ii) where the drawee is a fictitious person or lacks capacity, (iii) where the drawer is the person to whom presentment for payment was made, (iv) where the drawee was under no obligation to the drawer to accept the bill, or (v) where the drawer has countermanded payment.

(d) As regards the indorser: (i) where the drawee is a fictitious person or has no capacity, and the indorser was aware of this when he indorsed, (ii) where the indorser is the person to whom the presentment was made, or (iii) where the bill was accepted or made only for the indorser's accommodation.

46. Discharge of bills. This occurs by the following means.

(a) By payment in due course, i.e. to a bona fide holder without the payer having notice of any defect in the holder's title: s. 59.

Note that by s. 60 where a banker, in reliance on a forged indorsement, pays a bill drawn on him (i) in good faith and (ii) in the ordinary course of business, the bill is effectively discharged and the bank incurs no liability. (The Cheques Act 1957, s. 1, reduces the importance of this rule by providing that indorsements are no longer necessary in most cases.)

(b) By an acceptor becoming the holder of all rights on the bill at or after its maturity: s. 61.

(c) By renunciation by the holder of all rights against the acceptor: s. 62. (Renunciation must be in writing, or the bill must be delivered up to the acceptor.)

(d) By intentional cancellation by the holder or his agent: s. 63. (Unintentional cancellation is ineffective.)

(e) By material alteration of the bill or its acceptance, without the consent of all parties liable upon it, e.g. by alteration of date, amount, etc.: s. 64.

Cheques

47. Definition. A cheque is a bill of exchange drawn on a banker and payable on demand: BEA, s. 73.

It is not necessary that the words 'on demand' should appear on a cheque, since all bills are treated as payable on demand where no time is specified for payment: s. 10.

48. Stale and overdue cheques.

(*a*) A stale cheque is one which has been in circulation for a considerable period of time. Banks generally refuse to honour a cheque more than six months old.

(*b*) An overdue cheque is one which has been in circulation for an unreasonable time: s. 36. (A person who takes an overdue cheque cannot be a holder in due course.)

NOTE: (*i*) What is a reasonable time? This depends on all the circumstances of each case. Thus where a cheque is intended by the drawer to be presented within two or three days, failure to present within that time might amount to unreasonable delay: *Wheeler* v. *Young* (1897). By contrast, if a cheque was issued overseas for payment in Britain time would have to be allowed for its transmission to Britain in computing what is a reasonable time. (*ii*) Discharge of drawer. If not presented within a reasonable time the drawer is discharged to the extent of any damage he suffers from the delay. In the absence of such damage he remains fully liable for 6 years, after which his liability is statute-barred: Limitation Act 1980. (*iii*) Summary on delay in presentation. (*a*) Bills other than cheques — drawer and indorsers completely discharged: BEA, s. 45; (*b*) Delay re cheques: indorsers discharged under s. 45; drawer discharged only to extent of damage suffered: s. 74. (*iv*) Damage suffered by drawer. Example: A drew a cheque for £100 in favour of B, who failed to present it for some time. When drawn, A's account had funds to meet the cheque, but during the intervening time the bank went into liquidation. HELD: B could claim for the money as a creditor of the *bank*, but A was under no liability and B had no claim against him: *Wheeler* v. *Young* (1897).

49. Undated and post-dated cheques.

(*a*) *Undated cheques.* A banker is not bound to honour such a cheque, but it must be remembered that any holder is entitled to fill

262 Negotiable instruments

in the correct date: s. 20(1). Any date appearing on a bill is presumed to be the correct date.

(b) *Post-dated cheques.* These are not really cheques, since they are not payable on demand. However, a banker is entitled to pay a post-dated cheque when it falls due. If he pays it before its date he cannot debit the customer's account, and must bear the loss if the customer stops the cheque before its due date.

(Post-dated cheques are frequently used today instead of bills of exchange payable at some time after sight, e.g. where a purchaser of goods issues a post-dated cheque for goods to be delivered later, thus being entitled to stop the cheque if the goods are not delivered when agreed.)

50. Payment by cheque.

(a) *Conditional payment.* Payment by any bill is conditional only. A creditor is entitled therefore to refuse payment by cheque, and in any case payment is not effective until the cheque is honoured. (But a creditor who takes a cheque in payment may be estopped from action against the debtor if the cheque is dishonoured because he negligently failed to demand payment himself. But the cheque will remain enforceable by other parties against the drawer for six years: Limitation Act 1980.)

(b) *Cheques through the post.* If a cheque is sent through the post and is lost, the loss falls on the sender, unless the creditor requested this method of payment. Such a request will not be implied; it must be express: *Pennington* v. *Crossley & Son* (1897).

(c) *Cheques as evidence of payment.* An unindorsed cheque which appears to have been paid by the banker on whom it was drawn is prima facie evidence of receipt by the payee of the sum stated on the cheque, even without the payee's indorsement: Cheques Act 1957, s. 3.

51. Crossings on cheques.

The object of crossing a cheque is to convey instructions that it is not to be paid otherwise than through a bank, or to make some other stipulation as to the manner of payment: s. 76.

A crossing is a material part of a cheque and any unauthorised alteration of a crossing is unlawful (s. 78) and discharges the cheque: s. 64.

The drawer or any holder may cross a cheque, or add to an existing crossing, e.g. where the holder of a cheque crossed generally adds the words 'not negotiable.'

Crossings are usually intended as instructions to the paying banker, but a crossing 'account payee' is an instruction to the collecting banker.

52. Types of crossing.

(*a*) *General crossing:* indicated by drawing two transverse lines across the face of the cheque, thus //, with or without the addition of the words '& Co.' between the lines (or such other words as 'not negotiable': *see below*).

The effect of such a crossing is to make the cheque payable only to a collecting banker, i.e. it precludes the paying banker from paying cash for the cheque across the counter.

(*b*) *Special crossing:* indicating the name of a particular banker, with or without the addition of two transverse lines. The effect is that the paying banker must pay the cheque only to the collecting banker named on the crossing, and to no other.

(*c*) *'Not negotiable':* this general crossing deprives the cheque of its negotiability, and it becomes an ordinary transferable chose in action, i.e. it can be assigned, but the assignee obtains no better title than was possessed by his assignor: s. 81.

Thus where a clerk took a blank cheque from his employer, which was already crossed 'not negotiable,' and fraudulently made it payable to P, it was HELD that the employer could recover the value from P (who had obtained cash), since the clerk had no title to the cheque and P could get no better title than the clerk had: *Wilson & Meeson* v. *Pickering* (1946).

(*d*) *'Account payee'* (*or 'Account payee only'*): this is not a statutory crossing but is recognised and obeyed by banker's custom. A collecting bank which collects for some person other than the payee named may therefore be liable for negligence. (A paying banker is not generally affected by this crossing.)

53. Alterations on a cheque. Any material alteration of a cheque or

other bill discharges from liability any party to the bill who did not assent to the alteration. On a cheque, alterations of date, amount, name of payee, or of any crossing would be material.

Bankers therefore should not pay a cheque unless any alteration is initialled by the drawer, and where the words 'or order' have been altered to 'bearer' the normal practice is to insist on the drawer's full signature by way of assent.

(Note the distinction between apparent and non-apparent alterations: *see* **17** *above*.)

54. Indorsements. The general rule about indorsements apply to cheques.

Note that the Cheques Act 1957, s. 1, dispenses with the need for an indorsement where the apparent payee or indorsee of a cheque is paying it into his own account. But the Committee of the London Clearing Banks has decided that though these provisions dispense in law with the necessity of a banker requiring to see a payee's indorsement in all cases, bankers will in practice insist upon the payee's indorsement except where a cheque is paid into a bank for the credit of the payee's account or for the credit of a joint or partnership account where the payee is one of the account holders. Therefore indorsement will be required in the following situations: (*a*) if the payee, or his transferee, presents the cheque to the drawee bank for payment over the counter (only possible in the case of an open cheque). A banker disregarding the requirement as to indorsement would not be acting in the ordinary course of business and would as a result be outside the protection afforded by s. 1. No indorsement is, however, required where the customer presents his own cheque for payment; (*b*) order cheques which are to be paid into an account other than that of the original payee, i.e. order cheques which have been negotiated; (*c*) if the payee combines cheques and receipt forms marked 'R'.

55. Duty of bankers as to crossed cheques. The banker is liable to the true owner for any loss occasioned where:

(*a*) he pays a cheque which is crossed specially to more than one banker (unless the additional special crossing merely indicates that one of the bankers named is to collect merely as agent for the other);

(b) he pays a cheque crossed generally otherwise than to a bank, i.e. treats it as an open cheque;

(c) he pays a cheque crossed specially otherwise than to the banker named in the crossing or his agent: s. 79.

56. Protection of paying banker. The drawee bank is statutorily protected against liability if it pays in the following circumstances.

(a) *Cheques with forged indorsements:* provided they are paid (i) in good faith and (ii) in the ordinary course of business: BEA, s. 60.

(b) *Crossed cheques:* provided the bank pays a cheque drawn upon it (i) in accordance with the crossing, (ii) in good faith, and (iii) without negligence: BEA, s. 80.

(c) *Cheques not indorsed or irregularly indorsed:* provided the cheque is drawn on the bank and is paid (i) in good faith, (ii) in the ordinary course of business: Cheques Act 1957, s. 1.

57. Protection of collecting banker. A collecting banker, that is one who presents a cheque to the drawee bank on behalf of a customer, is protected from liability where he receives payment for a customer who has no title or defective title, provided he does so (i) in good faith and (ii) without negligence (whether or not the cheque is crossed): Cheques Act 1957, s. 4.

NOTE: (a) The section applies only to customers. A person becomes a customer as soon as he opens an account, i.e. where the bank obliges someone, not having an account, by cashing his cheques from time to time, this does not make such person a customer: *Commissioners of Taxation* v. *English, Scottish & Australian Bank Ltd* (1920). (b) The following have been held to amount to negligence by a collecting bank:

(i) Opening an account for someone without making adequate enquiries about him: *Hampstead Guardians* v. *Barclays Bank* (1923).

(ii) Collecting payment for a customer of a cheque made out

to the customer's employer without making enquiries: *Underwood Ltd* v. *Martins Bank* (1924).

(*iii*) Paying into a customer's private account a cheque payable to him in an official capacity: *Ross* v. *London County Bank* (1919).

(*iv*) Receiving payment for a customer of cheques clearly indicating they are payable to him only as agent for someone else: *Bute (Marquess)* v. *Barclays Bank* (1955).

(*v*) Where a bank uses a computer to identify the branch on which a cheque is drawn and a customer with accounts at two branches alters a cheque from branch A to draw it on branch B and the computer fails to recognise the change, if the computer directs the cheque to branch A which pays the cheque, the bank may be liable for negligence: *Burnett* v. *Westminster Bank Ltd* (1966).

(*c*) Where a collecting banker is negligent he may be sued for damages for the tort of conversion by the true owner of the cheque.

(*d*) Where the customer's own negligence in drawing cheques contributes to the loss the amount recoverable from the banker is reduced under the Law Reform (Contributory Negligence) Act 1945: *Lumsden & Co.* v. *London Trustee Savings Bank* (1971).

NOTE: There is no corresponding duty of care imposed on the drawer or acceptor of any bill: *Scholfield* v. *Londesborough* (1896). In an action for breach of contract for failing to honour a cheque, the customer is not entitled to claim damages for vexation and disappointment: *Rae* v. *Yorkshire Bank* (1987).

(*e*) If a bank has credited the customer's account with more than it should have done, the customer is not generally entitled to retain the extra sum. However, if the customer has relied on the misleading statement and altered his position in reliance on it, the bank cannot reclaim the money. In *United Overseas Bank* v. *Jiwani* (1977), the bank was able to reclaim the money, even though part had been used to buy a hotel, since it was established that the customer would have made the purchase anyway and did not rely on the bank.

58. Termination of banker's authority: s. 75. A banker's authority to pay a cheque drawn by his customer is terminated by the following.

15. Negotiable instruments 267

(*a*) *Countermand of payment*, written or oral, though if oral countermand is made, it is the practice to insist on written confirmation and merely to postpone payment pending receipt of confirmation.

(*b*) *Notice of the customer's death.* Observe that it is not the death which terminates the authority, but notice of the death.

(*c*) *Notice of the mental incapacity* of the customer.

(*d*) *Notice of the presentation of a bankruptcy petition against* the customer.

Note that if the bank receives notice of an act of bankruptcy committed by the customer, it can still pay out to the customer himself but should not pay out cheques drawn by him in favour of third parties (otherwise it may be liable to make good such payments to the trustee in bankruptcy): *Re Keever* (1966).

(*e*) *The making of a receiving order* in bankruptcy against the customer.

(*f*) *The service of a garnishee order* attaching the balance of the customer's account, i.e. a court order addressed to a debtor commanding him not to pay the stated debt to his creditor but to hold the money pending further orders from the court (which may eventually direct that the money shall be paid to some other person).

(*g*) *Notice of a breach of trust*, i.e. when a customer is about to use trust funds for his own purposes.

(*h*) *Notice of a defect in the presenter's title.*

(*i*) *Insufficient credit* in the customer's account, or where payment would increase the customer's indebtedness beyond some agreed limit.

The bank is entitled to refuse to pay a cheque if it exceeds the customer's entitlement by as little as a penny, and it cannot pay part of a cheque. If it wrongly refuses to honour a cheque properly drawn it is liable to the customer for damages for breach of contract, but is not liable to the holder. A bank may also be liable for damages for libel if it makes a defamatory comment unjustifiably on a cheque, e.g. where it wrongly marks a cheque 'No funds.'

(*j*) *Where money is paid into a trust account*, a bank is liable if it knowingly assists in a dishonest and fraudulent design on the part of the trustees: *Rowlandson* v. *National Westminster Bank Ltd* (1978).

59. Duties of the customer. It is the duty of the customer, in drawing a cheque, to take usual and reasonable precautions to prevent forgery and fraud.

> EXAMPLES: (1) M's clerk was entrusted with the task of filling in M's cheques for signature. The clerk prepared a bearer cheque on which the sum payable was not mentioned in words and which bore the figures £2.0s.0d. M signed it. The clerk then added the words 'one hundred and twenty pounds' and placed a '1' and a '0' either side of the '2' in the spaces which he had left. The clerk obtained payment of the cheque. It was held that the bank could debit the client's account to the full amount of the cheque since the loss was caused by M's failure to ensure that the cheque could not be altered in the way it was: *London Joint Stock Bank* v. *Macmillan* (1918). (2) A dishonest employee forged cheques on his employer's account over more than 6 years, taking around HK$5.5m. The company did not check thoroughly its monthly statements and did not detect the loss. The court required the bank to make good the loss, ruling that the company was not required to check its bank statements nor to operate a system of control which would aid the bank in detecting fraud. A bank could impose such a duty, but it would have to do so expressly in the terms of its contract with the customer: *Tai Hing Cotton Mill Ltd* v. *Liu Chong Hing Bank Ltd* (1985).

Promissory notes and miscellaneous instruments

60. Promissory note: s. 83. This is an unconditional promise in writing by one person to another, signed by the maker, and engaging to pay on demand or at a fixed or determinable future time a sum certain in money to, or to the order of a specified person or to bearer.

A promissory note is inchoate and incomplete until delivery to the payee or bearer: s. 83.

61. Difference from bills of exchange.

(*a*) Acceptance of a note is never necessary, since there is no drawee.

(*b*) A promissory note (unlike a bill) cannot be drawn in a set.

15. Negotiable instruments

(*c*) The maker is the person liable to pay. (In a bill, the drawer is only liable until the drawee accepts.)

(*d*) A promissory note must contain an unconditional promise to pay. (The acceptor of a bill may make a conditional promise to pay.)

(*e*) A promissory note is a promise to pay; a bill is an order to pay.

(*f*) A bill may be treated as a promissory note where (*i*) drawer and drawee are the same person; (*ii*) the drawee is fictitious or lacks capacity: s. 5(2).

62. Bank notes. These are promissory notes payable to bearer. When presenting a note for payment it is not necessary for the bearer to reveal how he came by the note, but if the circumstances arouse suspicion the bank would be entitled to refuse payment until satisfied of good faith; if, however, the bearer sued the bank for its refusal, the burden of proving bad faith would rest on the bank.

63. Joint, and joint and several notes. Where a note is issued by two or more persons, their liability may be joint or joint and several, depending on the circumstances.

(*a*) *On a joint note*, each maker is fully liable for the whole amount, but a person suing to enforce the note has only one cause of action and can sue all, or one or any combination, but cannot later bring a second action against parties not sued in the first.

If the maker of a joint note dies, his estate ceases to be liable on the note.

(*b*) *On a joint and several note*, each maker is fully liable but a holder has several rights of action, e.g. he may sue all, or any one, or bring successive actions against the makers. And the death of a maker does not relieve his estate from liability on the note.

NOTE: Where a note runs 'I promise to pay' and is signed by two or more makers, it is deemed to be a joint and several note: s. 85.

64. Miscellaneous banking instruments.

(*a*) *Banker's drafts*. These are drafts to order payable on demand, drawn by an office of a bank upon itself or upon some other office of the same bank: Bills of Exchange Act (1882) Amendment Act 1932.

Drafts may be crossed, and the crossing has the same effect as the crossing on a cheque. The Cheques Act 1957 extends the protection given bankers by the BEA to cover bankers' drafts.

(b) *Conditional orders.* These are documents ordering payment of money subject to the fulfilment of some stated condition. They may be crossed like cheques, and the Cheques Act 1957 extends the provisions of the BEA protecting bankers to conditional orders.

Note that a document apparently a cheque may in fact be a conditional order, e.g. a cheque stating on it that payment is not to be made unless an attached receipt form is signed. But the mere fact that a cheque contains a receipt form does not make it a conditional order, unless payment is made conditional on the signing of the receipt.

(c) *Dividends and interest warrants.* These are drafts issued by a company and ordering its bank to pay the stated sum to a named person. They can be crossed like cheques, and are covered by the protections given by the Cheques Act 1957.

(d) *Deposit receipts.* These are acknowledgments by a banker that he holds funds to a certain amount for the depositor. They are not negotiable instruments.

65. Quasi-negotiable instruments. The following documents have some of the qualities of negotiability, but not all, and are therefore not negotiable instruments.

(a) *Bills of lading*: receipts for goods shipped, signed by the carrier or his agent. A bill of lading is a document of title to the goods specified therein, and possession of the bill entitles the holder to delivery of the goods. But it is not a negotiable instrument, so that a transferee gets no better title than was possessed by his transferor.

(b) *Dock warrants*: documents issued by a dock or warehouse company acknowledging that it holds certain goods on behalf of the person named, or his indorsee. They are documents of title assignable by delivery plus indorsement, but they are not negotiable instruments and the indorsee gets no better title than his transferor.

(c) *American share certificates* usually have a transfer form printed on the back, and the owner can sign this form leaving the name of the transferee blank. This then operates as a power of attorney to a subsequent transferee to fill in his own name or the name of another, the person named being entitled to apply to the company for registration as a shareholder. Such transferee gets no better title than his transferor.

(d) *I.O.U.s*. These are merely written admission of the existence of a debt (with an implied promise to pay at some future date). They are not negotiable but can be assigned under s. 136, LPA, 1925.

Note that if the document contained an express promise to pay, it would be a promissory note.

66. Negotiable instruments under the Consumer Credit Act 1974. Sections 123–125 of the CCA impose the following restrictions on the use of negotiable instruments taken under regulated agreements. A creditor or owner is not able to take a negotiable instrument in payment other than a bank note or cheque. Where a cheque is taken, it must be negotiated direct to a bank. The Act further provides that a negotiable instrument cannot be taken as any kind of security for a regulated agreement. If any of the foregoing provisions is not complied with, the agreement under which the relevant sum is payable is enforceable on a court order. Where a negotiable instrument is taken in contravention of the Act, the person taking it is not a holder in due course (*see* **38**). If that person further negotiates the instrument, the holder can enforce the instrument but the creditor or owner under the regulated agreement must indemnify the consumer who gave him the instrument. If a cheque is taken, which it can be, but it is not negotiated as it should be directly to a bank, that constitutes a defect in title. This means that any subsequent holder who knew or ought to have known of the defect in the cheque cannot enforce it. If he neither knew nor ought to have known, and enforces the cheque, the consumer has the same right of indemnity as in the case of an improperly taken negotiable instrument.

Progress test 4

Negotiable instruments

1. How would you define a negotiable instrument? What are the

characteristics of such an instrument, and how does it differ from other choses in action? (15: **1–3**)

2. What persons are liable on a negotiable instrument and to whom? (15: **4**)

3. Define a bill of exchange. Explain what is meant by saying that a bill must be unconditional. What is a conditional order and what is its effect? (15: **6, 7, 64**)

4. What is meant by saying that there must be three parties to a bill of exchange? What is the effect where the drawer and drawee are one and the same person? (15: **8, 61**)

5. X is the holder of an undated cheque, and when he presents it to his bank the bank refuses to take it. Explain why the bank refused it and what X can do to remedy the situation. (15: **10, 49**)

6. 'A cheque is an exception to the rule that past consideration is no consideration.' Discuss. (3: **18**; 15: **11**)

7. What is meant by saying that a bill must order the payment of a 'sum certain' and not a 'certain sum' of money? (15: **12**)

8. Distinguish between order and bearer bills, and explain how each can be negotiated. Distinguish also between non-existing and fictitious payees. (15: **13, 36**)

9. Explain briefly the meaning of: (*a*) Inland and foreign bills; (*b*) Bills in a set; (*c*) Inchoate instruments. (15: **14–16**)

10. What is, and what is the effect of, a material alteration of a bill? Why is it important to distinguish between apparent and non-apparent alterations? (15: **17, 53**)

11. What is meant by an overdue bill? How does an overdue cheque differ from a stale cheque? (15: **18, 48**)

12. X owes Y £100 and draws a cheque for that amount in favour of Y. The cheque is lost or stolen before Y is able to present it to his bank. Y now maintains that he has not been paid. What is the legal position? (15: **19, 20, 50**)

13. What is meant by the negotiation of a bill? Explain the effect of marking a bill or a cheque 'not negotiable.' (15: **21**)

14. X negotiates a bearer bill to Y for value and later, when the bill is dishonoured, X maintains that he is under no liability (*a*) to Y, or (*b*) to any person to whom Y has negotiated the bill. What is the legal position? Would it make any difference to Y's position if he had not given value? (15: **11, 22**)

15. Explain the effect of the following signatures on a bill of

15. Negotiable instruments

exchange: (*a*) signature of a stranger; (*b*) agent's signature; (*c*) signature *sans recours*; (*d*) signature *sans frais*. (15: **22, 23**)

16. 'A forged or unauthorised signature is wholly inoperative on a bill of exchange.' Discuss this statement, distinguishing between forged and unauthorised signatures and explaining how estoppel may operate to prevent a person whose signature has been forged from denying that he signed the bill. (15: **24**)

17. Distinguish carefully between the effect of forgery of the signature on a bill of: (*a*) the drawer; (*b*) the drawee; (*c*) an indorser. (15: **25**)

18. What is meant by the delivery of a bill? What is conditional delivery and what is its effect? (15: **26**)

19. 'Delivery is presumed in favour of any holder of a bill of exchange.' Explain this statement, and state the cases where delivery is not presumed conclusively. (15: **26**)

20. 'An order bill is transferable by delivery plus indorsement.' Explain this statement, and explain also what is meant by a valid indorsement.' (15: **26, 27**)

21. Explain the following terms: (*a*) Blank and special indorsements; (*b*) Restrictive indorsements; (*c*) Conditional indorsement; (*d*) Indorsement *sans recours*. (15: **27, 28**)

22. In what order are the parties to a bill liable upon it? Explain carefully the liability of: (*a*) the drawer; (*b*) the drawee; (*c*) an indorser. (15: **30–33**)

23. Explain the significance of the following terms: (*a*) Referee in case of need; (*b*) Accommodation party; (*c*) Accommodation bill; (*d*) Fictitious payee; (*e*) Non-existing payee. (15: **34–36**)

24. Distinguish carefully between the following terms in relation to bills of exchange: (*a*) holder, (*b*) holder for value, (*c*) holder in due course. (15: **37–39**)

25. What are the rights of a holder in due course and of a holder for value? (15: **38, 39**)

26. What is meant by saying that neither a payee of a cheque nor the paying banker can be a holder in due course? (15: **38, 56**)

27. When does a bill of exchange require acceptance by the drawee in order to render it payable? What is, and what is the effect of, qualified acceptance? (15: **40, 41**)

28. When is presentment for acceptance (*a*) necessary, (*b*) unnecessary? (15: **41, 42**)

274 Negotiable instruments

29. Explain the following: (*a*) days of grace, (*b*) Noting and Protesting, (*c*) Presentment for payment. (15: **43, 44**)

30. When is presentment for payment excused? (15: **43**)

31. When is a bill dishonoured (*a*) by non-acceptance, and (*b*) by non-payment? (15: **40, 44**)

32. When is notice of dishonour necessary and when is it unnecessary? What form should such notice take (*a*) in the case of Inland Bills, and (*b*) in the case of Foreign Bills? (15: **44, 45**)

33. What is a promissory note and how does it differ from a bill of exchange? What is the distinction between (*a*) joint notes and (*b*) joint and several notes? (15: **60, 61, 63**)

34. Define the following, and explain how far they are subject to the provisions of the Cheques Act 1957: (*a*) Bankers' draft, (*b*) Conditional order, (*c*) Dividend warrant, (*d*) Deposit receipt. (15: **64**)

35. Some instruments are negotiable by statute, and others are negotiable by custom; others again have some of the characteristics of negotiable instruments, but not all. Explain this statement. (15: **3, 65**)

36. Define a cheque. How does a cheque differ from an ordinary bill of exchange? (15: **6, 47**)

37. An overdue cheque is one which has been in circulation for an unreasonable time. What is meant by 'unreasonable time' in this context? (15: **48**)

38. The effect of delay in presenting a cheque differs from the effect of delay in presenting other bills. How? (15: **48**)

39. 'A banker is not bound to honour an undated or post-dated cheque.' Do you agree? (15: **49**)

40. On 1st June X sent to his insurance company a cheque to cover the insurance on his car. The cheque arrived on 2nd June. On 2nd June X was charged by the police with driving an uninsured vehicle, since his insurance expired in May. Explain why the prosecution would succeed. (15: **50**)

41. What is the object of crossing a cheque, and what types of crossing are legally recognised? (15: **51, 52**)

42. When does a banker's authority to pay a cheque drawn upon him cease? (15: **58**)

43. State and explain briefly the protections given to paying bankers by statute. (15: **56**)

44. A collecting banker who collects a cheque for the wrong person may be liable in tort to the true owner. What form does this liability take, and when does it arise? (15: **57**)

45. Explain the significance of the Consumer Credit Act 1974. (15: **66**)

Specimen questions

1. As a general rule, a bill of exchange must be presented for payment in order to retain the liability of the drawer and of the indorsers.

You are required to state:

(*a*) those circumstances which excuse delay in presentment for payment; and

(*b*) those circumstances which make it unnecessary to present the bill at all.

2. (*a*) How does the Bills of Exchange Act 1882 define the following terms:

    (*i*)   a general acceptance;
    (*ii*) a partial acceptance;
    (*iii*) a local acceptance?

(*b*) The holder of a bill for £1,000 drawn at one month after date presents it to the drawee for acceptance. The drawee accepts the bill payable two months after date. What type of acceptance has been given, and what steps should the holder take?

3. (*a*) What condition must be fulfilled before a person may be regarded as a 'holder in due course'? How does his legal position differ from that of the 'holder'?

(*b*) Ivor has received the following cheques, in good faith and for value, from John:

    (*i*) A cheque crossed 'A/c payee only' payable to Stephen Cole and indorsed by him;

    (*ii*) A cheque crossed 'Not negotiable' payable to and indorsed by P. Offerman, who had obtained it by fraud;

    (*iii*) A crossed cheque payable to 'Christine Dickens or order,' on which Christine Dickens' indorsement had been forged.

Ivor had no knowledge of the history of these cheques when he received them. Advise him as to whether he has a good title to them.

4. L drew a cheque for £1300 payable to M in payment for a motor cycle. M specially indorsed the cheque to N in payment for a picture, and N specially indorsed it to O, telling him that the money was to be used for O to have a holiday. Instead of using the cheque as directed O specially indorsed it to P as a gift.

As the cheque has been dishonoured, P wishes to know his rights against all the parties concerned. Advise him.

5. L drew a cheque for £100 in favour of X and gave the cheque to Y (L's secretary) to remit to X. Y indorsed the cheque by forging X's signature, and negotiated it to M in return for goods.

Advise L as to his rights.

6. Jones transferred the following cheques to Brown:

(*a*) An uncrossed cheque payable to Smith whose indorsement had been forged by Jones.

(*b*) A cheque crossed 'not negotiable' payable to Jones and indorsed by him, which Jones had obtained by fraud.

(*c*) A cheque crossed 'account payee' payable to Jones and indorsed by him.

Brown had no knowledge of the history of the cheques and gave value to Jones for them. Advise Brown whether he has a good title to any of these cheques.

7. (*a*) What is meant in the law relating to bills of exchange by a holder in due course? Why is it important to ascertain whether the holder of a bill is a holder in due course?

(*b*) D owed £100 to C for goods supplied. When payment fell due, D drew a cheque for £100 in C's favour and sent it to him. Subsequently, however, D stopped payment of the cheque before C had cashed it. Will C have a right of action on the cheque against D? Would your answer be the same if the cheque had been drawn in C's favour by D's friend, F, acting at D's request and F had stopped payment? Would, in this case, C have a right of action against F? Give reasons.

8. Williams sells goods to Thomas at the price of £100 and Thomas gives Williams a cheque for the amount, payable to Williams or order. What are Williams' rights and liabilities in each of the following situations:

(*a*) Williams loses the cheque and asks Thomas for another, but Thomas declines to give one.

(*b*) Williams indorses the cheque to Rees to satisfy a debt of £85 which he owes to Rees. The cheque is subsequently dishonoured and Thomas cannot be traced. Rees claims the sum of £100 from Williams.

9. A buys goods from B and asks B to accept C's cheque for part of the money and the balance in cash. He explains that he has no banking account of his own and that C's cheque is crossed. B agrees to this and the goods are given to A and he hands B the cheque and cash as arranged. The cheque is payable to 'A or order,' but B omits to obtain A's indorsement. He subsequently discovers his mistake.

(*a*) Is B entitled to ask for A's indorsement?

(*b*) Will B's rights against C be affected if he finds A obtained the cheque by fraud?

10. (*a*) Allen sells a typewritter to Baker, an infant, who pays for it by his cheque. Allen indorses the cheque to Cook who takes it in good faith and for value. The cheque is dishonoured on presentation. Can Cook enforce payment of the cheque against A or B?

(*b*) Davis, by mistake, draws a cheque payable to Evans, who does not exist. The cheque is negotiated by Franks by a forged indorsement to Green, who takes it in good faith and for value. Can Green enforce payment of the cheque?

11. (*a*) Explain the rights and duties of a paying banker and a collecting banker in relation to cheques.

(*b*) How is a banker's authority to pay a cheque drawn on him by his customer terminated?

12. (*a*) What is a bill of exchange? How does a cheque differ from other bills of exchange?

(*b*) What is meant by the 'negotiation' of a bill of exchange? How does the addition of the words 'not negotiable' affect the transferability of (*i*) bills of exchange generally, and (*ii*) cheques?

Part five
Securities

16
Securities

Summary of property law

1. Understanding of property law. Students who are required to study the subject of securities need at least a background knowledge of the law of property. This section is intended to provide a superficial outline to facilitate understanding of the law relating to securities, but students who have no prior knowledge of the subject would be well advised to make a more detailed study of property law.

2. Ownership and possession. The owner of property is the person who has the maximum legal rights over the property (including the right to actual possession). He may however part with possession, without surrendering ownership, e.g. where the owner lends property to another.

Ownership is a legal concept; possession is a state of fact, and involves actual control over the property. When the owner of land leases it to a tenant, the tenant acquires legal possession and can assert his right of control against anyone (even against the owner, if the owner in breach of the lease attempts to regain possession).

3. Transfer of ownership.

(*a*) *Personal property.*
  (*i*) Chattels can be transferred by mere delivery, with intention to pass ownership (and not merely possession).
  (*ii*) Choses in action require to be assigned either in accordance with the method laid down by s. 136 LPA or equity or

in accordance with some particular method laid down for particular choses, e.g. share transfers.

(*b*) *Real property*. Freehold land (and also leasehold) should be transferred by deed if legal ownership is intended to pass. Any attempted conveyance which is not by deed operates to transfer only an equitable interest in the property.

A deed is not necessary in the following cases.

(*i*) Leases for a term not exceeding three years.

(*ii*) Assents by personal representatives. A deceased person's land vests in his personal representatives and they can transfer it to the beneficiaries under the deceased's will (or upon his intestacy) by a mere written assent.

(*iii*) Disclaimers by a trustee in bankruptcy need only be in writing.

(*iv*) On redemption of a mortgage of land, the land revests in the mortgagor as soon as the mortgagee signs a receipt for the mortgage moneys.

Securities generally

4. Meaning of 'security.' A security is some right or interest in property given to a creditor so that, in the event of the debtor failing to pay his debt as and when due, the creditor may reimburse himself for the debt out of the property charged.

Both real and personal property may be charged with repayment of a debt in this way. (Real property means freehold land, and personal property includes leasehold land and all movable property, such as chattels and choses in action.)

5. Forms of security.

(*a*) *Mortgages*. A mortgage is an assurance to the creditor of the legal or equitable interest in property as security for the discharge of debt, subject to a proviso that on repayment of the debt the property shall revert to the borrower.

The characteristic of a mortgage is that possession of the property remains vested in the mortgagor (the borrower), while the mortgagee (the lender) obtains some or all of the rights of ownership, or the right to obtain ownership if the debtor defaults.

Land is the form of property most usually mortgaged, but chattels can be mortgaged by conditional bill of sale (*see* **10** *below*), and choses in action (such as insurance policies) can be mortgaged by assignment subject to a condition that on repayment the chose shall revert to the borrower.

(*b*) *Pledges or pawns.* A pledge is a deposit of chattels with a lender as security for a debt. If the pledgee is a professional lender upon this type of security (a pawnbroker) the pledge is called a pawn.

A pledge differs from a mortgage in that the lender obtains possession of the chattel, while the borrower retains ownership.

(*c*) *Liens.* A lien is a right to retain property until a debt is paid (a possessory lien) or to seek a court order for sale of the property (equitable lien).

A lien differs from mortgages and pledges in that it arises by implication of law from certain situations, while mortgages and pledges are the result of express agreement between a borrower and a lender.

6. Appropriate formalities. The Consumer Credit Act 1974 lays down various requirements concerning formalities for securities provided in relation to regulated agreements:

(*a*) Any security must be in writing and must conform to requirements laid down in regulations yet to be made as to form and content: s. 105.

(*b*) A security instrument must be properly executed (i.e. signed in the prescribed manner; embodying all the terms of the security; its terms are readily legible; and a copy is provided at the proper time): s. 105.

(*c*) Failure to observe the requirements of (*a*) or (*b*) means that the security is enforceable against the surety on an order of the court only: s. 105.

(*d*) If an application for an order is dismissed other than on technical grounds, the security is to be treated as ineffective: ss. 105 and 106.

(*e*) Regulations yet to be made may provide for any matters relating to the sale or other realisation of securities: s. 112.

(*f*) The Consumer Credit Act cannot be avoided by the use of a security: s. 113. For example, where a hire-purchase agreement is terminated under s. 100 CCA, the hirer is not liable for more than 50 per cent of the total purchase price. The CCA, s. 113, would make it impossible for a security to be used so as to obtain more than 50 per cent.

7. Land mortgages. Where a prospective regulated agreement is to be secured on land, the prospective mortgagor must receive a copy of the unexecuted agreement which contains a prescribed notice indicating his right to withdraw from the prospective agreement: CCA, s. 58. This agreement must be sent by post to the mortgagor for signature not less than seven days after the copy was given. During the 'consideration period', the mortgagee must not communicate in any way with the mortgagor except at the mortgagor's specific request. The 'consideration period' runs from the date when the copy of the unexecuted agreement is first given and expires seven days after the day the unexecuted agreement is sent for signature; or its return, with signature, by the mortgagor, whichever comes first: s. 61. A land mortgage securing a regulated agreement is enforceable on an order of the court only: s. 126.

8. Legal and equitable interests. In English property law a distinction is drawn between legal interests in property (which are enforceable in any court and against any person), and equitable interests (which are personal rights against a particular individual and are not enforceable against other persons, save in certain exceptional circumstances: *see below*). Both legal and equitable interests in property can be used as security for loans, but the limited enforceability of equitable interests makes them less acceptable securities.

Differences between legal and equitable interests:

(*a*) *Creation.* A legal interest is one created in the correct form for the particular type of property, e.g. a deed of conveyance to create a legal interest or estate in land. An equitable interest is either (*i*) the result of an informal creation, e.g. a conveyance of land not under seal, or (*ii*) the result of a transfer of an existing equitable interest, since these cannot be converted into legal interests (even by conveyance under seal).

(*b*) *Enforceability.* If a person has a legal interest in property his claims are enforceable against all comers, and are indefeasible. But the holder of an equitable interest in property can (*i*) enforce his interest only against the person through whom he derives it, i.e. the owner of the parallel legal interest in the property, and (*ii*) can have his interest in the property destroyed if the legal owner sells the property to a purchaser for value without notice of the equitable interest attaching to the property.

(*c*) *Parallel interests.* In any one piece of property there may be parallel legal and equitable interests, vested in different persons. Thus, in a trust, the legal owner of property is compelled to hold the property as trustee for the benefit of the beneficiary, that is the owner of the equitable interest. (And the beneficiary's claims are enforceable only against the trustee, and can be extinguished if the trustee sells the property to a purchaser who buys without knowing of the beneficiary's interest.)

9. Legal and equitable mortgages. Just as there can be parallel legal and equitable ownership of property, mortgages can also be either legal or equitable. And where there are several mortgages of a piece of land some may be legal and others equitable.

Where the mortgagee obtains a legal interest in the property charged his mortgage is a legal mortgage; if he obtains merely an equitable interest, his mortgage is equitable (and is a weaker security).

Pledges and mortgages of personalty

10. Mortgages of personalty. The method of mortgaging personalty is to transfer legal ownership to the mortgagee, subject to a condition for re-transfer on repayment of the loan.

The method of mortgaging therefore depends on the method of transfer of legal title appropriate to the particular form of personalty.

(*a*) Chattels are transferable by delivery without the need for any accompanying document, but in order to provide the mortgagee with documentary evidence (while leaving possession in the hands of the mortgagor) a conditional bill of sale is normally used: *see* **12** *below*.

(b) Choses in action are transferable by assignment, either legal (under LPA, s. 136) or equitable: *see* 6: 7.

In some cases particular statutes lay down special requirements for the assignment of particular choses in action, e.g. insurance policies, copyrights, etc., and these requirements would have to be observed in a mortgage of such a chose.

11. Pledge or mortgage. Where chattels are to be mortgaged, a conditional bill of sale must be used. But this procedure is not popular: *see* **12** *below*.

An easier method of using small chattels as security is to pledge them, i.e. to deliver possession to the lender subject to a condition that he shall return the chattels on repayment of the loan. But pledging is only appropriate in connection with smaller chattels, which can be easily moved or stored. Larger chattels, such as pianos, motor cars, collections of furniture or paintings, etc., must normally be mortgaged by bill of sale.

12. Conditional bills of sale. An absolute bill of sale is a documentary assignment of chattels, giving title with or without delivery of the chattels comprised. Since chattels can pass by delivery, without documentation, and since most sales take effect in actual or constructive delivery, absolute bills of sale are rarely used. Their only use today is where the purchaser requires for some reason documentary evidence of his purchase, e.g. where he is buying goods for export and may have to prove to the customs authorities that he is the owner of the goods.

A conditional bill of sale is one used as documentary evidence of a mortgage of chattels, i.e. it transfers ownership to the mortgagee (while leaving the mortgagor in possession as bailee for the lender), subject to a condition that the chattels shall be re-assigned to the borrower on repayment of the loan.

13. Form of conditional bills of sale. These must comply with the requirements of the Bills of Sale Acts 1878 and 1882, as follows.

(*a*) The bill must be by deed, attested by at least one witness; otherwise it is void.

(b) The bill must be registered at the Central Office of the Supreme Court within seven days of creation; otherwise it is void.

(c) Consideration for the bill must be truly stated therein.

(d) Interest payable and date for repayment must be stated in the bill, together with any other conditions.

(e) The chattels comprised in the bill must be inventoried, and the inventory must be attached to the bill on registration.

(f) The lender's remedy under a conditional bill of sale which has been properly registered and drawn is seizure of the chattels. The right to seizure arises (i) on failure to repay the loan as agreed, (ii) on bankruptcy of the borrower, or (iii) on any fraudulent dealing by the debtor with the chattels with the intention of removing them from the lender's power, e.g. an attempted sale to another person.

NOTE: A conditional bill of sale takes its priority from the date of registration. Therefore a bill created earlier than a rival may rank after the rival if registered later. Because of the technicalities and publicity involved, bills of sale are not popular forms of security. They are sometimes taken by professional moneylenders, but very rarely by non-professional moneylenders such as bankers. From a borrower's point of view a pledge offers an easier way of raising money on security of chattels; the difficulty here is that a pawnbroker will not usually take a pledge of large and cumbersome chattels, which may then only be useful as security if someone can be found who is willing to take a conditional bill of sale, e.g. pianos, cars, collections of paintings, etc.

14. Pledges. A pledge of chattels involves actual or constructive delivery of chattels to the lenders. Constructive delivery might be by giving the pledgee the key to a warehouse in which the goods are stored.

The pledgor remains the legal owner of the goods, and the pledgee becomes a bailee who must return the goods on repayment as agreed. The pledgor is entitled to demand a receipt for deposit of the goods.

The pledgee owes a duty of care for the goods while in his possession, and if they are lost or damaged through his negligence he must make good the loss. (But if the goods were taken from him by robbery with violence, he is generally excused liability.) The pledgee generally has no right to use the goods deposited unless otherwise agreed.

The pledgee has a possessory lien over the goods entitling him to retain them until repayment, even if there is no written agreement stating the purpose of deposit.

15. Pawnbrokers. The Consumer Credit Act 1974 replaces the controls which were formerly imposed on pawnbrokers by the now-repealed Pawnbrokers Acts 1872–1960. Pawnbrokers must be licensed as creditors under the Act by the Office of Fair Trading. The person who takes an article in pawn must provide a receipt. This must be in the form prescribed by the Consumer Credit (Pawn-Receipts) Regulations 1983. If the receipt is lost, the borrower may provide a statutory declaration which must be in the form prescribed by the Consumer Credit (Loss of Pawn-Receipt) Regulations 1983, or, if the lender agrees, give him a written statement in the form prescribed by those Regulations. The latter alternative is possible only where the amount of the loan exceeds £25. Copies of the pawn agreement must be provided, and the agreement must be drawn up in the manner specified by the Consumer Credit (Agreements) Regulations 1983 and the Consumer Credit (Cancellation Notices and Copies of Documents) Regulations 1983. Breach of these provisions means that the agreement can be enforced against the debtor only on a court order. Breach of the provisions relating to copies is an offence.

(*a*) *Redemption.* The article given in pawn can be redeemed during the period for which credit is extended. There is, however, a guaranteed minimum redemption period of 6 months. If the pawn-receipt is tendered while the redemption period lasts, the goods must be handed over if payment is made of the money owing. The lender need not redeem the goods, however, if he knows or ought reasonably to suspect that the person taking the goods is unauthorised to receive them or owns the article in question. If the goods are handed over to an unauthorised party, and the lender has no reason to suspect that the person taking the goods is unauthorised, then the lender incurs no liability in tort to the real owner. It is a criminal offence, however, to refuse redemption of the article without reasonable cause. If the pawn is not redeemed by the end of the redemption period, it remains redeemable to the time when it is realised, unless the article has already become the lender's property. If the credit limit under the agreement was not more than £25, and if the redemption period was 6 months, the goods in question become the property of the lender if the redemption period has passed without redemption. If the application has been made to the court for a time order, the goods instead become the lender's property within the 5 days following the end of the redemption period. If the credit limit is more than £25, or if the redemption period is not 6 months, the goods become realisable by the lender.

(*b*) *Realisation.* The lender may not sell the article unless he has given the period of notice in the form, giving the details, required by the Consumer Credit (Realisation of Pawn) Regulations 1983. Once the goods have been sold, the lender must provide the debtor with a statement of the amount realised and the expenses. If the net proceeds cover the cost of redemption, the debt is discharged and any surplus must be handed over. If the proceeds are insufficient, the balance remains payable. The debtor can challenge the amount realised, the expenses charged, or both.

Liens

16. Definition. A lien is a right over the property of another arising by operation of law (independently of any agreement), and gives the lienor a right (*a*) to retain the property until the owner has settled some debt owed to the lienor (a common law or possessory lien), or (*b*) to sell the property in satisfaction of the debt (an equitable lien).

A lien must be distinguished from a deposit of chattels by way of pledge. A pledge is security derived from express agreement; a lien generally arises independently of agreement.

17. Common law or possessory liens. These arise where the creditor has actual possession of some of the debtor's property, and obtains a right to retain such property until an outstanding debt is paid.

> NOTE: (1) A common law lien cannot arise independently of possession, i.e. the creditor is not entitled to obtain possession solely for the purpose of claiming such a lien. (Cf. equitable liens:

see **19** *below*.) (2) A common law lien is exercisable only by detaining the goods until the debt is paid, i.e. there is no right of sale, save in some exceptional cases where a right of sale is given by statute. A statutory right of sale is given to innkeepers (Innkeepers Liability Act 1878), unpaid sellers of goods (Sale of Goods Act 1979), and repairers (Torts (Interference with Goods) Act 1977). (3) A common law lien is extinguished by (*i*) agreement, express or implied, (*ii*) payment of the debt, (*iii*) loss of possession, or (*iv*) taking security for the debt. (4) A common law lien may be general or particular, i.e. may be available against any goods of the debtor coming into possession of the creditor, or only against the particular goods in connection with which the debt was incurred. Thus a carrier has a particular lien for his freight charges, while stockbrokers and factors have general liens. A banker's lien is also a general lien: *see* **20** *below*.

18. Maritime liens. A maritime lien is one attaching to a ship, in favour of the shipmaster (for disbursements and wages), seamen (for their wages), salvors (for charges in connection with salvage), etc.

The lien is exercised against the ship itself, not against the owners, and it arises independently of possession. A notice of lien is affixed to the ship, and proceedings may be taken in the Admiralty court to arrest the ship. If the lien is not discharged, the ship will not be allowed to leave harbour, and a court order for sale may be given to the lienor.

If the owner of a ship subject to a lien sells the ship, the purchaser takes it subject to the lien, i.e. becomes responsible for discharging the lien.

19. Equitable liens. Unlike common law liens these are not founded on possession, and can be exercised by a court order for sale of the property subject to the lien. But like all equitable rights they can be extinguished by the owner selling the property to a bona fide purchaser for value without notice of the lien.

They arise mainly in connection with the sale of land, e.g. a vendor of land who has given possession to the purchaser has a lien over the land for unpaid purchase money, and a purchaser who hands over a deposit before obtaining possession has a lien for his deposit.

20. Banker's lien. This is a general possessory lien arising at common law, but unlike other common law liens it gives the banker a right of sale of securities subject to the lien.

> NOTE: (1) The lien arises out of a general course of dealing, and covers 'All securities deposited with them as bankers, by a customer, unless there be an express contract, or circumstances that show an implied contract, inconsistent with the lien': *Brandao v. Barnett* (1846). (The lien therefore usually arises by implication from the relationship, but it appears that it may also be granted expressly unlike other liens.) (2) Property subject to the lien includes all securities coming into the banker's possession in the ordinary course of dealing, e.g. promissory notes, bills of exchange, foreign bonds, etc. It does not cover securities deposited merely for safe custody, unless at some time the customer agrees to allow the banker to hold these as security for an advance (in which case they are subject to an equitable mortgage, rather than a lien). (3) The banker's lien has been called an 'implied pledge' (*Brandao v. Barnett*) which appears to confer a power of sale, at least in so far as it affects negotiable securities. The Bills of Exchange Act 1882, s. 27, provides that any person having a possessory lien over a bill is deemed to be a holder for value to the extent of his lien, and can therefore sell and transfer the bill.

17
Guarantees and indemnities

Nature of guarantee

1. Definition of guarantee. A guarantee, or surety contract, is an undertaking 'to be answerable for the debt, default, or miscarriage of another': Statute of Frauds 1677, s. 4.

Guarantees may be either specific or continuing.

(a) A specific guarantee relates to one isolated debt only. (Where a bank accepts a specific guarantee of a single loan, a separate account should be opened for that loan, otherwise the guarantee may be cancelled out by operation of the Rule in *Clayton's Case*, see 5.6.)

(b) A continuing guarantee is one covering a series of transactions, e.g. a guarantee of an overdraft on a current account at a bank. (A bank, in order to enforce such a guarantee of an overdraft, should stipulate expressly in the guarantee form that the guarantee shall cover the final balance. Otherwise it will be interpreted as covering only the overdraft as it existed at the date of the agreement, and payments in after that date would thus reduce the guarantor's liability.)

2. Characteristics of guarantees.

(a) *Three parties*: principal creditor, principal debtor and guarantor (or surety).

(b) *Primary liability to pay* must attach to the principal debtor. The surety only becomes liable to pay if the debtor defaults.

(c) *The guarantor has no interest in the contract* between the principal debtor and the principal creditor, except in so far as he agrees to accept liability if the debtor fails to pay.

3. Form of guarantees. The Statute of Frauds, s. 4, requires any contract of guarantee to be evidenced in writing, by some sufficient note or memorandum; *see* 3: **4–6**. (This requirement does not apply where the guarantee is part of some larger transaction, e.g. a contract of agency.)

Guarantees require to be supported by consideration, but the consideration does not need to be stated in the written memorandum: Mercantile Law Amendment Act 1856. (Thus the consideration may be proved by independent oral evidence if necessary.) Guarantee bonds do not require consideration.

NOTE: (a) Representations made in order to assist someone to obtain credit must be in writing, personally signed by the party making the representation. Otherwise the representation is not actionable: Statute of Frauds Amendment Act 1828. (b) Guarantees can also be securities within the Consumer Credit Act 1974: *see* 16: **6**.

4. Guarantees not uberrimae fidei. Neither the principal creditor nor the principal debtor is under any legal duty to disclose to the guarantor facts which might influence him against entering into the contract. Thus if A offers to guarantee B's bank account, the bank is under no obligation to reveal matters which show that B is a bad risk: *Wythes v. Labouchere* (1859).

NOTE: (a) Active misrepresentation by the creditor (or by the debtor with the creditor's knowledge) will be grounds for rescission. (b) Active concealment of material facts may amount to misrepresentation, e.g. keeping silent about some facts so as to put facts disclosed into a deceptive light. (c) Once the contract of guarantee is made, the creditor owes a duty of the utmost good faith to the guarantor, who is entitled to be discharged if this duty is not observed. Thus the creditor must disclose material facts coming to his knowledge and affecting the guarantor's risk, but need not disclose mere suspicions, e.g. A guaranteed B's bank account, and B overdrew on the guaranteed account to pay off debts to another creditor. The bank suspected that A was being defrauded, but did not disclose this. HELD: They were under no duty to do so: *National Provincial Bank* v. *Glanusk* (1913). (*d*) Guarantees in the nature of insurance are *uberrimae fidei*, e.g. 'fidelity guarantees' (of the character and good faith of some third person). Thus A gave a fidelity guarantee in respect of L to L's employer, B. B omitted to disclose that L had misappropriated some of B's money and was only being retained in employment in reliance on A's guarantee bond. HELD: L's former dishonesty should have been disclosed, and A was not liable on his guarantee: *London General Omnibus Co.* v. *Holloway* (1912).

5. Indemnity contracts. An indemnity contract is one in which the indemnifier promises to preserve the other party from loss. Unlike a guarantee (*a*) it is a contract of primary liability, and (*b*) it does not require written evidence, and (*c*) there are only two parties, i.e. the indemnifier and the person he promises to indemnify.

In *Birkmyr* v. *Darnell* (1704) guarantees and indemnities were distinguished thus:

A and B enter a shop and B asks X for goods on credit. Then (*i*) if A says to X, 'Give B the goods, and if he does not pay for them I will,' this is a contract of guarantee (since A will only become liable if B defaults, i.e. A's liability is secondary to B's); (*ii*) if A says to X, 'Give B the goods and I will see that you get paid,' this is an indemnity since A accepts the principal or primary liability for the debt.

NOTE: An indemnity may be a security within the Consumer Credit Act 1974: *see* 16: **6**.

6. Capacity to contract. Capacity to guarantee is generally co-extensive with normal contractual capacity, but note:

(*a*) A partner as guarantor has no power to bind his firm unless (*i*) so authorised by his co-partners, or (*ii*) giving guarantees is part of the firm's normal business. Even where he has authority, he cannot bind the firm in a guarantee under seal unless (*i*) he is so authorised

17. Guarantees and indemnities   295

by deed (power of attorney), or (*ii*) all the partners sign the guarantee deed.

(*b*) Guarantees by married women are enforceable only against their separate estates. (Thus a bank considering a guarantee from a married women cannot take her husband's status into account in assessing the value of her guarantee.)

(*c*) Trading companies have implied power to borrow money, but there is probably no implied power to give guarantees. (Thus a bank before accepting a guarantee from a company must examine the memorandum and articles of the company to make sure there is power to give guarantees.)

7. Position of creditor. His rights against the guarantor are dependent on the terms of the contract. But a continuing guarantee by or to a partnership is revoked as to future transactions by any change in the constitution of the firm: Partnership Act 1890, s. 18.

8. Joint and several guarantees. Sometimes several persons join in giving a guarantee, and the liability of such co-guarantors may then (depending on the agreement) be joint, or several, or joint and several.

(*a*) *Joint guarantors:* Each guarantor is personally liable for the full amount, but the creditor has only one cause of action against them and should therefore sue all in one action. If he elects to sue just one of the guarantors, he cannot later sue the others since he has exhausted his one cause of action, and is taken as having waived his claims against the others: the Rule in *Kendall* v. *Hamilton* (1879). The Rule in *Kendall's* case has been modified by the Civil Liability (Contribution) Act 1978, s. 3 of which states that: 'Judgment recovered against any person liable in respect of any debt or damage shall not be a bar to an action, or to the continuance of an action, against any other person who is (apart from any such bar) jointly liable with him in respect of the same debt or damage'.

Also on the death or bankruptcy of a joint guarantor, his estate is discharged from all liability. (As between themselves joint guarantors have a right of contribution for any sums paid beyond their fair share of liability.)

296 Securities

(b) *Several guarantors.* Each is fully liable for the whole debt, and can be sued separately and successively, i.e. the creditor has several rights of action and the rule in *Kendall* v. *Hamilton* does not apply. Further, the death or bankruptcy of a several guarantor does not release his estate from liability for claims arising before the death or bankruptcy.

(c) *Joint and several guarantors.* Here the creditor can either sue them jointly or separately and successively, and death or bankruptcy has the same effect as in (b) above. (From the creditor's point of view therefore a several, or joint and several guarantee is preferable, e.g. bank guarantees are nearly always drafted on the basis of joint and several liability.)

Position of the guarantor

9. Liability of the guarantor. This arises only when the principal debtor has defaulted, and not until then.

The surety's liability depends partly on the terms of the contract and partly on the following rules of law:

(a) If the transaction between the creditor and the principal debtor is void, the surety is not bound by his guarantee. With regard to guarantees of contracts made by minors, s. 2 of the Minors' Contracts Act 1987 makes such a guarantee enforceable against the guarantor, even though the main contractual obligation may not be enforceable against the minor.

(b) The creditor may be entitled to treat the guarantor as a principal debtor, unless he makes it clear that he is a surety only and only secondarily liable.

(c) The creditor is under a legal duty not to prejudice the guarantor in any way, e.g. by increasing his liability by allowing release of any co-guarantor. (In such a case the guarantor can demand release also: *see* **11–17** *below*.)

(d) If the surety goes bankrupt, the creditor can prove in the bankruptcy for the amount guaranteed. (Bank guarantees usually provide expressly for this contingency, and for the bankruptcy of the debtor.)

(*e*) When he has accepted liability to the creditor, the guarantor immediately acquires a right of action against the debtor for the value of the guarantee. But this right does not arise until he has accepted liability himself (even though he has not yet actually paid the creditor): *Ascherson* v. *Tredegar Dry Dock Co.* (1909).

10. Rights of the guarantor.

(*a*) *Indemnification by debtor.* The surety can sue the debtor for all sums properly paid under the guarantee plus damages for any additional loss. But he cannot recover the whole value of the guarantee if he was only made to pay a smaller sum. (This right to compensation arises as soon as he actually accepts liability to the creditor; but he cannot sue the debtor until he has actually paid the creditor himself.) However, a person who without being asked to do so guarantees payment of another's debt is not entitled on paying the debt to be indemnified by the principal debtor: *Owen* v. *Tate* (1975).

(*b*) *Set-offs and counter-claims.* If sued by the creditor, the surety can avail himself of any set-offs or counter-claims which the debtor has against the creditor, e.g. where he is sued on a £1,000 guarantee and finds that the creditor owes the debtor £200 for goods or services, he is entitled to set-off the £200 against the guarantee and so reduce his own liability to £800.

(*c*) *Delivery of securities held by the creditor.* On paying his guarantee to the creditor, the surety is entitled to possession of any securities the debtor may have earlier deposited with the creditor in respect of the same debt, even if the surety did not know of them when he made his guarantee.

(*d*) *Hotchpot.* A co-guarantor who has received securities from the principal debtor (or creditor) must share the benefit of them with other co-guarantors, even though they may have been unaware of their existence when they became guarantors.

(*e*) *Contribution from co-guarantors.* If one surety pays the whole debt, he is entitled to compensation from co-sureties (in a joint, or joint and several guarantee), even if (*i*) their guarantees are contained in different instruments, or (*ii*) he did not know of the existence of the co-sureties when he signed his own guarantee.

This right is implied by equity, and is independent of contract. (It may however be modified by contract.)

Discharge of guarantor

Unless otherwise agreed, a guarantor is automatically discharged in the following circumstances.

11. Unauthorised variation of terms. The guarantor is automatically released if the debtor and creditor vary the contract between them, without the guarantor's knowledge and approval (even though the variation is not prejudicial to the guarantor).

> EXAMPLE: A guaranteed D's overdraft. Without A's knowledge the bank allowed D to open a second account into which he paid substantial sums, while leaving his existing overdraft undiminished. HELD: This amounted to an unauthorised variation of the guarantee and A was discharged: *Nat. Bank of Nigeria Ltd* v. *Awolesi* (1964).

12. Creditor relinquishes securities. If the creditor relinquishes securities of the debtor held by him in respect of the debt guaranteed, this automatically releases the guarantor (unless otherwise agreed).

13. Creditor omitting to do something to protect the surety. If the creditor omits to do something he reasonably should do for the protection of the guarantor, this operates as automatic release, e.g. where he fails to register an equitable mortgage granted to him by the debtor, since such a mortgage may be void if not registered (and the surety would be entitled to a transfer of such mortgage on payment of the guarantee).

14. Unauthorised extension of time to the debtor. If the creditor makes a binding agreement to grant the debtor an extension of time for payment of the debt, this automatically releases the surety. In *Unigate* v. *Bentley* (1986), D gave a guarantee in consideration of a payment of £325,000 by P to a particular company. The guarantee related to performance by BV, the company in question, of its obligations under an agreement between P and BV. The money was to be repaid to P in the event of certain circumstances specified in the agreement. D contended that the final date for completing certain tests specified in the agreement had been extended by mutual agreement between P and BV and that as a consequence it had been prejudiced because the date on which he could pay the money and exercise his right of indemnity had been postponed without his consent and that he was accordingly discharged from liability under the guarantee. The court dismissed D's argument, saying that the type of prejudice contended for was strictly confined to cases where the surety had guaranteed the payment of a debt on a fixed time and that date was postponed by agreement between the parties. This was not such a case.

> EXCEPTIONS: (1) Where the extension was expressly or impliedly sanctioned by the original guarantee agreement (as in bank guarantees in some cases). (2) Where judgment has already been obtained against the surety and the principal debtor together. (3) Where there are several distinct debts, extensions of time in respect of one debt will only discharge the surety in respect of that debt alone.

15. Release of co-surety, i.e. where the creditor discharges any co-surety, thus depriving the remainder of their rights of contribution against the surety discharged: *Smith* v. *Wood* (1929).

16. Revocation. This is only possible where the consideration for the guarantee is divisible, i.e. in continuing guarantees, which can always be revoked as to future liabilities (unless otherwise agreed).

Specific guarantees cannot generally be revoked, and revocation of a continuing guarantee does not affect liability for debts already incurred.

Also if the consideration for any guarantee is a forbearance to sue (i.e. a promise by the creditor not to sue the debtor for the debt, in reliance on the guarantee), it appears that the guarantee is irrevocable.

17. Release of debtor. Release of the debtor automatically releases the surety, unless the creditor expressly or impliedly reserves his rights against the surety in the original contract (as is usually done in bank guarantees). However, a creditor's acceptance of a debtor's wrongful repudiation of a contract does not discharge a guarantor from liability under his guarantee, though the action against him is not to repay the debt but to pay damages for breach of contract: *Maschi* v. *Lep Air Services* (1972).

18. Death of guarantor. It depends on the terms of the contract whether his death will discharge his estate from liability under his guarantee. Thus bank guarantee forms usually stipulate that the guarantee shall remain operative until the bank receives notice of the guarantor's death.

Death of joint guarantor discharges his estate from liability, but surviving joint guarantors remain liable.

19. Bankruptcy of guarantor. The creditor can prove for the debt in the guarantor's bankruptcy: Insolvency Act 1986, s. 322. If the surety obtains his discharge from bankruptcy, this operates in most cases to release him from his guarantee: IA, s. 281. In addition, under the 1986 Act, s. 345, the court can discharge a contract between the bankrupt and another party, on the latter's application and on such terms as the court thinks equitable.

20. Change in constitution of firm. A continuing guarantee given to a firm, or to a third party regarding transactions by a firm, is automatically revoked as to future liabilities by any change in the constitution of the firm, e.g. on the death or retirement of any partner: Partnership Act 1890, s. 18.

21. Limitation Act 1980. The creditor's rights against the guarantor are statute-barred after six years (twelve years if the guarantee was under seal), but time begins to run only when the debt becomes due from the principal debtor.

Thus bank guarantee forms usually stipulate that the guarantor shall not become liable until the bank formally notifies him that it proposes to call in his guarantee. Time then begins to run only after the bank makes this formal demand, even though the debtor may have become liable considerably earlier: *Bradford Old Bank* v. *Sutcliffe* (1918).

17. Guarantees and indemnities

The Act also bars the guarantor's claim for indemnification against the debtor, and for contribution from co-sureties, after the limitation period has elapsed.

Progress test 5

Securities

1. What is a security, and what forms may it take? (16: **4, 5**)
2. Distinguish between legal and equitable interest in property, and explain how ownership of the various forms of property can be transferred at law. (16: **3, 8**)
3. How can personalty be (*a*) mortgaged, and (*b*) pledged? What sort of chattels are suitable for pledging? (16: **10–14**)
4. Explain briefly the main provisions of (*a*) The Bills of Sale Acts, and (*b*) those provisions of the Consumer Credit Act dealing with pawnbroking. (16: **13, 15**)
5. What is a lien? Distinguish between possessory, equitable and maritime liens. (16: **16–19**)
6. When, if ever, does a lien confer a power of sale? (16: **16–20**)
7. Define a guarantee. How does it differ from an indemnity contract, and what form must it take? (17: **1, 3, 5**)
8. Guarantees are not *uberrimae fidei* contracts, but once formed a guarantee imposes similar duties upon the creditor. Explain. (17: **4**)
9. Distinguish between joint, and joint and several guarantees. (17: **8**)
10. What are the rights and liabilities of a guarantor under a contract of guarantee? (17: **9, 10**)
11. In what circumstances is a guarantor discharged from liability? (17: **11–15**)
12. In what circumstances may a guarantor revoke his guarantee? (17: **16**)
13. G guaranteed D's overdraft to the amount of £1,000. Later the bank allowed D to increase his overdraft to £1,200. What effect, if any, has this on G's liability? (17: **11**)
14. In what ways, if any, does capacity to act as a guarantor differ from normal contractual capacity? (17: **6**)

Specimen questions

1. 'Guarantees are subject to the ordinary rule of English law that all contracts, except those under seal, must be supported by consideration.'

(*a*) Explain the meaning of the term 'consideration' in this quotation.

(*b*) Is there any provision in English law which requires that a contract of guarantee shall be in any particular form?

(*c*) In relation to a contract of guarantee, is there any provision in English law which *either* requires that the consideration must be stated in the written agreement, *or*, on the other hand, provides that the consideration need not be stated there?

2. E and F were partners in a furriers' business. G asked E whether the firm would guarantee G's overdraft with the H Bank up to £1,000. Without consulting F, E agreed and he gave the H Bank a written guarantee in the name of 'E and F, furriers.'

G has now failed to settle his overdraft and F consults you as to his legal position.

Advise him.

3. What special rules govern a contract of suretyship?

X, who was employed in A's shop, stole some money from the till. When A discovered the theft he told X that he would overlook it but, nevertheless, though it wise to obtain a guarantee of X's fidelity. This A asked B to do, and B signed a document to that effect. A did not tell B about the theft. Later X stole £50 from the till and absconded.

Advise A.

4. (*a*) How far is it true to say that a creditor is not bound to disclose to a prospective guarantor facts about the debtor which might influence him against becoming guarantor?

(*b*) In what circumstances is a contract of guarantee automatically discharged?

5. (*a*) Distinguish between a possessory lien, a maritime lien and an equitable lien.

(*b*) Eddy, a solicitor, acted for Roy and had possession of the title deeds to Roy's land. Roy mortgaged his land to Allan and the deeds remained with the solicitor who acted for both parties. Roy fails to pay Eddy the legal fees and Eddy claims a lien over the title deeds.

Advise Allan.

17. Guarantees and indemnities

6. State the essentials of a contract of guarantee.

A and Co. were stockbrokers who agreed with B that he should have half the commission earned as a result of his introductions and that he should pay half of any losses which might be sustained from them. Explain whether or not this is a contract of guarantee.

7. (*a*) An executor finds that the deceased had, during his life-time, given a continuing guarantee.

  (*i*) In what circumstances would the guarantee be revoked by death?

  (*ii*) If it is revoked, what action should the executor take?

(*b*) Jones gives Brown a continuing guarantee for the due fulfilment by a partnership firm, Robinson & Co., of its business transactions with Brown. A partner in the firm retires and another partner is taken in. What effect, if any, has the change in the partnership on Jones' guarantee?

8. When one of two sureties has paid the debt to the creditor what remedies are available to such surety against:

(*a*) the debtor,

(*b*) the creditor, and

(*c*) the co-surety?

9. G signed a guarantee in respect of the banking account of C. The latter is unable to repay his overdraft, and the bank has demanded payment from G under his guarantee. G wishes to deny liability on the ground that the bank failed to disclose to him: (*i*) that C's wife had served a prison sentence and (*ii*) that C's wife had authority to draw on C's account. Advise G whether or not he is liable to the bank.

10. A customer has applied to his bank for an overdraft of £1,000, and he has offered as security a life policy on his own life for £5,000 with profits, the surrender value being £990.

Explain what is meant by 'surrender value,' and describe the steps which should be followed to enable the bank to obtain a legal mortgage of this policy.

11. (*a*) Define a guarantee and explain how it differs from an indemnity contract.

(*b*) P orally hired A as his agent for the sale of some valuable paintings, and as part of the contract A guaranteed P against failure of any of A's clients to pay for the paintings they bought. State with reasons whether the guarantee is enforceable.

Part six
Bankruptcy

Part six
Bankruptcy

18
Bankruptcy

The whole of the law of bankruptcy has been substantially rewritten by the Insolvency Act 1986 which came into force in December 1987.

1. Introduction. While the Act legislates also for corporate insolvency (receiverships and liquidations), personal bankruptcy is dealt with in ss. 252–358 and in Schedules 5, 6 and 9.

The Bankruptcy Act 1914 is repealed, but the general intentions of the new law remain much the same:

(*a*) to identify cases of individuals' insolvency;
(*b*) to ascertain if the debtor's own proposals for a voluntary arrangement with his creditors are workable and acceptable; and/or
(*c*) to freeze debtor assets, and control them by the appointment of an even-handed caretaker;
(*d*) to pay to creditors what reasonably and realistically can be paid; and
(*e*) to rehabilitate the bankrupt.

2. Insolvency practitioners. The Act introduces a licensing procedure to ensure the professional competence, integrity and independence of practitioners in view of their considerable responsibilities to their parties. A person who holds office as: trustee in bankruptcy, liquidator, administrator or administrative receiver, or supervisor under the new voluntary arrangement procedures is required to be authorised.

3. Voluntary arrangements. The new voluntary arrangement procedure is available to any debtor whether or not he is bankrupt. The purpose of the interim order is to allow time for the formulation of proposals. The main effects of the order are that during the period for which it is in force, no bankruptcy petition relating to the debtor may be presented or proceeded with, and no other proceedings or execution or other legal process may be commenced or continued against the debtor's person or property except with the leave of the court. The individual concerned must intend to make a proposal to a 'nominee' for a satisfaction of his debts or a scheme of arrangement of his affairs.

4. Report by nominee. The nominee must form a professional judgment of the terms of the proposal which the debtor is intending to put to his creditors. Only if the nominee concludes that it would be worthwhile to put the debtor's proposals to a meeting of creditors, and if he duly reports to the court in those terms, will the court give the necessary direction which has the effect of prolonging the duration of the interim order pending the convening of a creditors' meeting. Unless the nominee applies successfully for an extension to the order, it lapses at the end of fourteen days, from the date when it was made, or at the end of the period which may be expressly given in the order.

5. Creditor's meeting. Once a report has been made, a meeting of the creditors shall be summoned unless the court orders otherwise. If the creditors do not approve of the debtor's proposals, the court may discharge the interim order, and the protection enjoyed by the debtor since the order is discharged. If the proposal is approved, the composition or scheme binds every person who has notice of and was entitled to vote at the meeting, regardless of whether he in fact attended or was represented at it, and regardless of whether he voted for or against the proposal.

6. Implementation of approved composition or scheme. The person responsible for implementing an approved composition or scheme is known as the 'supervisor' who will either be the original nominee, or someone who was substituted for him, either by the court or the creditors.

7. Bankruptcy orders. Many aspects of the previous law and procedure regarding the commencement of bankruptcy proceedings have been completely eliminated. In particular, the whole concept of an 'act of bankruptcy' has been abolished, as has the preliminary species of order formerly known as the receiving order.

(*a*) *Creditor's petition.* This introduced, in place of the former requirements relating to acts of bankruptcy, the new single concept of the debtor's apparent inability to pay the debt on which the petition is founded (or, in the case of a petition founded on a debt which is not immediately payable, if the debtor appears to have no reasonable prospect of paying the debt). The bankruptcy level is £750. The court has a duty to satisfy itself that the petitioning creditor's debt is either one that has become due and has in no sense been satisfied, or one which though not presently due for payment is a debt which the debtor has no reasonable prospect of being able to pay when it does fall due. The Act also effectively requires the creditor whose petition is based on a debt payable at a future time to show that circumstances have materially altered since he allowed the debtor to incur the debt, and that there was at the time a reasonable prospect, which has subsequently ceased to be operative, that the debt would be paid on time. The principle is retained from the earlier law that a debtor should not be adjudicated bankrupt if he is able to pay all his debts. The novel requirement is that the debtor must also have made an offer to secure or compound for the petitioning creditor's debt under circumstances where acceptance of that offer would have required the dismissal of the petition, and that offer has been unreasonably refused.

(*b*) *Debtor's petition.* The court is now required to give active consideration to the circumstances of each debtor presenting his own petition in order to establish whether the possibility exists for the conclusion of a voluntary arrangement between the debtor and his creditors. Even if this alternative to the making of a bankruptcy order is not undertaken, the court must still have regard to the appropriateness of invoking the summary administration procedure through the issue of a summary administration certificate. The aggregate amount of the unsecured bankruptcy debts must not be less than the small bankruptcies level, which will be determined in the Insolvency Rules.

8. Duration of bankruptcy. Persons who are adjudicated bankrupt for the first time will obtain an automatic discharge after three years from the commencement of bankruptcy, and in the case where the summary administration procedure is employed, that period is shortened to two years. Where a person has been previously adjudicated bankrupt, and had the status of undischarged bankrupt at any time in the period of fifteen years prior to the date of commencement of his subsequent bankruptcy, it will be necessary for him to apply for discharge by order of the court, as it also will where a person is adjudged bankrupt on a petition based on a criminal bankruptcy order. A criminal bankruptcy order may be made under the Powers of Criminal Courts Act 1973. The procedure is designed to facilitate the recovery of the proceeds of criminal activity, or of compensation for the victims of such activities. Where an undischarged bankrupt who is eligible for automatic discharge after two or three years, as the case may be, is reported to the Official Receiver as failing or as having failed to comply with the obligations to which, as an undischarged bankrupt, he is subject for the time being, the court may make an order which suspends the running of the time up to automatic discharge.

9. Effect of discharge. The essential principle is that discharge releases the bankrupt from all those debts known as the 'bankruptcy debts'. These are any debt or liability to which the bankrupt is subject at the beginning of the bankruptcy or which, though the bankrupt did not become subject to them after the commencement of the bankruptcy (or even until after his discharge), arise from an obligation incurred before the commencement of the bankruptcy. The term 'bankruptcy debt' also includes any amount specified in a criminal bankruptcy order made against the debtor before the commencement of bankruptcy.

Discharge from bankruptcy does not release a bankrupt from any debt incurred by means of fraud or fraudulent breach of trust to which he was a party; from a fine, except with the consent of the Treasury; from other prescribed bankruptcy debts which are not debts provable in the bankruptcy; or from a bankruptcy debt which consists in a liability to pay damages for negligence, nuisance or breach of any duty, being damages in relation to personal injuries or from any order made in family or domestic proceedings, except to such extent as a court may order. Discharge from bankruptcy shall not affect the right of any secured creditor of the bankrupt to enforce his security for the payment of a debt from which the bankrupt is released.

10. Definition of bankrupt's estate. All property belonging to or vested in the bankrupt at the commencement of the bankruptcy is deemed to be part of his estate. This does not apply to such tools, books, vehicles and other items of equipment as are necessary to the bankrupt for use personally by him in his employment, business or vocation, or to such clothing, bedding, furniture, household equipment and provisions as are necessary for satisfying the basic domestic needs of the bankrupt and his family. A notable change in the rule regarding the vesting of the bankrupt's available estate in his trustee in bankruptcy is the abolition of the doctrine of 'relation back'. Another notable change in the law is the abolition of the doctrine of 'reputed ownership'.

11. Restrictions on dispositions of property. The making of a bankruptcy order has the effect of rendering void any disposition of property made by the bankrupt between the time of the presentation of the petition for the bankruptcy order which is subsequently made against him and the time when the estate vests in his trustee in bankruptcy, except to the extent that the disposition was made with the consent of the court or is or has been subsequently ratified by the court. A person is, however, protected from this particular provision if he either received the property in good faith before the day on which the order was made, for value, and without notice that the petition has already been presented, or if he is a person who derived his title from any such person. A special provision gives protection to bankers among others, who, after the commencement of the bankruptcy, honour a cheque drawn by the bankrupt before the commencement date in effecting a payment which is rendered void. The debt incurred by the bankrupt would, but for this particular provision, be provable in the bankruptcy because it was incurred after the commencement of the bankruptcy. However, provided that the banker did not have notice of the bankruptcy before the debt was incurred by, in this case, the banker's honouring the cheque, and provided also that it was not reasonably practicable for the amount of the payment to be recovered from the party by whom or on whose behalf payment was collected, the payment is deemed to have been made before the commencement of bankruptcy, with the effect that it will count as a provable debt in the bankruptcy.

12. Restrictions on proceedings and remedies. The Act provides for a moratorium under the control of the court in respect of all kinds of action and legal process against the person or property of a debtor or bankrupt, with effect from the moment of the presentation of a bankruptcy petition. The Act also provides that there is an exemption from the moratorium in respect of any creditors whose debts would not be provable in the bankruptcy; such creditors remain free to commence or continue any legal proceedings against the debtor pertaining to claims of that character. There is also a saving in respect of the right of a secured creditor to enforce his security notwithstanding the bankruptcy and the general terms of the moratorium imposed by the Act.

13. Interim receiver. The Act empowers the court, after presentation of a bankruptcy petition and before a bankruptcy order is made, to appoint the Official Receiver to be interim receiver of the debtor's estate where this is shown to be necessary for the protection of the debtor's property. This replaces the former provisions as to receiving orders. In most cases there will be an interval between the making of the bankruptcy order and the appointment of the trustee in bankruptcy in whom the bankrupt's estate will then automatically vest. During that period the Official Receiver is to be the receiver and manager of the bankrupt's estate, with the same powers as a receiver or manager appointed by the High Court. Immunity is granted to the Official Receiver when acting in the bona fide and reasonable belief that property which he is seizing or of which he is disposing is part of that which he is entitled to seize or of which he is entitled to dispose.

14. Statement of affairs. The period of time allowed for the preparation and submission by the bankrupt of his statement of affairs is 21 days from the date of the bankruptcy order, and can be extended by the Official Receiver at his discretion. The Official Receiver also has the power to release the bankrupt from the duty to submit such a statement. It is intended that the Official Receiver should exercise his discretion under this provision to release a bankrupt who is too ill to lodge a statement of affairs, but in such cases the rules will provide that the Official Receiver will be subject to a duty to send out a report to all creditors explaining why no statement has been obtained.

15. Investigatory duties of Official Receiver. The Official Receiver is placed under a duty to investigate the conduct and affairs of every bankrupt and to report to the court if he considers it appropriate. Where the bankrupt applies for discharge, the Official Receiver must report to the court.

16. Public examination of the bankrupt. The holding of a public examination will only take place if the Official Receiver makes an application to the court for this to be done, and the court agrees. This reverses the previous law. It is also made possible for the creditors, or at least as many of them as represent one half of the value of the bankrupt's debts, to serve notice on the Official Receiver requiring him to apply to the court for a direction that a public examination be held.

17. Summoning of meeting to appoint first trustee. The Official Receiver must decide within twelve weeks of the day on which the bankruptcy order is made whether to call a meeting of creditors for the purpose of appointing a trustee in bankruptcy. If he decides not to convene such a meeting, he is required to notify the court and all the creditors of the bankrupt and will be required at the same time to send the creditors a summary of the statement of affairs and a report thereon. Where no meeting of creditors has been summoned, or where the Official Receiver has decided not to summon a meeting, one quarter or more in value of the creditors may require the Official Receiver to call a meeting. Where a general meeting of creditors is convened, but no appointment of a trustee in bankruptcy results, the Official Receiver must decide whether or not to refer the matter to the Secretary of State. If this is done, the Secretary of State may at his discretion appoint a qualified person to be the trustee in bankruptcy. If the Official Receiver decides not to refer the matter to the Secretary of State, or if the latter declines to make an appointment, the Official Receiver shall be the trustee in bankruptcy with effect from the date of his giving the requisite notice. The Act also gives the Official Receiver the general permission to apply to the Secretary of State for the appointment of a person as trustee in bankruptcy in place of the Official Receiver himself. The general rule is that the trustee may be removed from office only by an order of the court or by a general meeting summoned specially for that purpose.

18. Control of trustee. The Act empowers the creditors at a general meeting to appoint a committee to function for the purposes of the Act. A general meeting for this purpose may be convened by the trustee of his own initiative. If he elects not to convene a committee for this purpose, he can be compelled to do so if at least one tenth in value of the creditors concur in formally requesting him to summon one. No meeting of creditors may establish a committee at any time when the Official Receiver is trustee, except where this happens in conjunction with the appointment by such a meeting of a person to replace him as trustee. However, the Act also provides for the functions which would otherwise be vested in a committee of creditors to be vested in the Secretary of State during any period when the Official Receiver is the trustee in bankruptcy, and to be likewise vested in the Secretary of State at any time when a person other than the Official Receiver is the trustee in bankruptcy but no committee of creditors has been established. The Act restates the former provisions of the Bankruptcy Act establishing a general principle that the trustee's actions are ultimately subject to control by the court at the instance of any properly interested party.

19. Liability of trustee. The Act establishes a summary procedure against the trustee in respect of loss to the estate caused by his misapplication or retention of property, or by his misfeasance or breach of duty.

20. Vesting of bankrupt's estate. The Act provides for the vesting of the bankrupt's estate in the trustee in bankruptcy immediately upon the latter's appointment taking effect. In the case where the Official Receiver becomes trustee, the vesting occurs simultaneously with his becoming trustee. All vesting of property by virtue of these provisions occurs automatically by operation of law, without the need for any conveyance, assignment or transfer.

21. After-acquired property. The Act establishes a procedure whereby any property acquired by the bankrupt after the date of the bankruptcy order may be vested in the trustee upon the latter's intervention to claim it. After-acquired property does not vest automatically in the trustee. Where notice has been served, and either before or afterwards a person acquires property in good faith for value and without notice of the bankruptcy, or a banker enters into a transaction in good faith and without such notice, the trustee shall not in respect of that property or transaction be entitled to any remedy against that person or banker, or any person whose title to any property derives from that person or banker.

22. Vesting in trustee of tools, clothes, etc. Under the procedure established by the Act, the trustee may claim by means of a notice in writing any item of the bankrupt's exempted property (*see* **10** *above*) which appears to have a higher intrinsic value than the cost of providing a reasonable replacement for the bankrupt or his family to use. The cost of providing a replacement is a first charge on the funds comprised in the bankrupt's estate.

23. Income payment orders. The court is enabled on the application of the trustee to make an income payment order whereby a proportion of the income of the bankrupt is claimed for his estate available for distribution to his creditors. The principle is laid down that any income of an undischarged bankrupt constitutes after-acquired property, so that the proper approach should be to ascertain by investigation what proportion of income can be regarded as 'necessary' for meeting the reasonable domestic needs of the bankrupt and his family.

24. Acquisition by trustee of control. The trustee is required to take control of the bankrupt's estate and of all his papers and records relating thereto. For this purpose, he is clothed with the power and rights enjoyed by a receiver of property appointed by the High Court, and may invoke any appropriate remedies for the purpose of invoking his rights of acquisition and retention. The bankrupt is required to surrender control of his property, papers and records to the trustee. Special provision is made with respect to the bankrupt's interest in a dwelling-house occupied by the bankrupt, his spouse or former spouse.

25. General powers of trustee. The Act gives extensive powers to the trustee and indicates which of them are exercisable on his own initiative without permission and which are exercisable with the permission of the creditors' committee if there is one. The former requirement that the trustee must obtain permission from the creditors' committee before employing a solicitor has been replaced by the requirement that where a trustee other than the Official Receiver employs a solicitor in the exercise of his powers, he must give notice of that fact to the creditors' committee if there is one in being at the time. Where the trustee disposes of the property of a bankrupt to an associate of the bankrupt, he must inform the creditors' committee if there is one. The onus then rests with the committee to determine whether the transaction was abusive or not. It is also possible for the trustee to be challenged retrospectively on account of any transaction not initially received to be abusive and detrimental to the creditors' interests. The trustee is empowered to disclaim onerous property which is comprised in the bankrupt's estate. The Act also allows for the court to make a vesting order on the application of any person who has an interest in, or is subject to, a continuing liability in respect of any property disclaimed by the trustee.

26. Proof of debts. The proof of all bankruptcy debts by all categories of creditor is to take place in accordance with provisions to be contained in the rules. Interest is provable as part of a debt for any period up to the date of the making of the bankruptcy order. Payments in respect of any interest due for the period since the commencement of the bankruptcy will only be made if any surplus remains after payment in full of the preferential and ordinary debts.

27. Mutual credit and set off. The provisions as to mutual credit and set off apply where, before the commencement of the bankruptcy, there have been mutual credits, mutual debts or other mutual dealings between the bankrupt and any creditor of the bankrupt

18. Bankruptcy 317

proving or claiming to prove a bankruptcy debt. An account is to be taken of what is due from each party to the other in respect of the mutual dealings and the sums due from one party shall be set off against the sums due from the other. Sums due from the bankrupt to another party shall not be included in the account taken if that other party had notice at the time they became due that a bankruptcy petition was pending. Only the balance, if any, of the account shall be provable as a bankrupt's debt or be paid to the trustee as part of the bankrupt's estate.

28. Manner of distribution of estate. When the trustee has sufficient funds for the purpose he is required, subject to the retention of such sums as may be necessary for the expenses of the bankruptcy, to declare and distribute dividends among the creditors in respect of the bankruptcy debts which they have respectively provided. The relevant provisions essentially re-enact the provisions of the Bankruptcy Act. However, there is no longer any provision requiring the trustee to distribute dividends at specified intervals of time. The following are the preferential debts: debts due to the Inland Revenue; debts due to Customs and Excise; social security contributions; contributions to occupational pension schemes, etc. and remuneration of employees. These debts shall be paid in full, unless there are insufficient funds available in which case they shall all be abated in equal proportions. Debts which are not preferential debts are subject to the same rules as to distribution. Bankruptcy debts owed in respect of credit provided by a person who was a bankrupt's spouse at the commencement of the bankruptcy rank after other non-preferential debts. The Act provides for the final distribution of dividend, or alternatively that no dividend, or no further dividend, will be declared. The Act also provides for the convening of a final meeting of creditors when the administration of the bankrupt's estate is complete. No such requirement is imposed in cases where the Official Receiver is acting as trustee, which is likely to be the case when the assets available for distribution are small. The purposes of the meeting are that the trustee should report on his administration of the estate and that the creditors should determine whether the trustee is to have his release. If the meeting resolves against release, he must apply to the Secretary of State to determine when his release becomes effective. If the final meeting does not resolve against his release, it is effective from the time he vacates office. There is no provision requiring the trustee to report on the outcome of the final meeting, but on his giving notice to the court that the final meeting has been held, together with a report of decisions there taken, the trustee is to vacate office.

29. Right of occupation, etc. of bankrupt's spouse. The Matrimonial Homes Act 1983 confers on a spouse without any beneficial interest in the matrimonial home rights of occupation as against the other spouse. Hitherto, where the spouse with a beneficial estate became bankrupt, the spouse without any such interest lost his or her rights of occupation against the trustee in bankruptcy. The Insolvency Act reverses that former position so that the spouse who has no beneficial interest in the property is placed in a similar position to a spouse with a beneficial interest. In the case of a spouse who already has a beneficial interest in the home, the trustee must make an application to the court before being able to sell the property concerned. The court's discretion is to make such orders as it thinks 'just and reasonable'.

30. Transactions at an undervalue and preferences. The general rule is that, where an individual is adjudged bankrupt and he has at any relevant time entered into a transaction with any person at an undervalue or given a preference to any person, the court may, on an application from the trustee, restore the position before the transaction or preference. A transaction is at an undervalue if: a gift is made to a person or the bankrupt otherwise enters into a transaction with that person which provides for him to receive no consideration; he enters into a transaction with that person in consideration of marriage; or he enters into a transaction with that person for a consideration the value of which, in money or money's worth, is significantly less than the value, in money or money's worth, of the consideration provided by the bankrupt. An individual gives a preference to a person if that person is one of his creditors or a surety or a guarantor for any of his debts or other liabilities, and the individual does anything or suffers anything to be done which has the effect of putting that person into a position which, in the event of the individual's bankruptcy, will be better than the position he would have been in if that thing had not been done.

18. Bankruptcy

31. Extortionate credit transactions. The court, on an application by the trustee, may vary or set aside any extortionate credit transaction between the bankrupt and the creditor. The Act provides that no application may be made by the trustee nor an undischarged bankrupt under the provisions of the Consumer Credit Act 1974 allowing for the reopening of extortionate credit agreements.

32. Contracts to which the bankrupt is a party. The court is empowered to discharge a contract between the bankrupt and another person, on the latter's application, on such terms as the court considers equitable.

33. Distress. The Act regulates the levying of distress by a landlord and by other persons on the property of the bankrupt. It generally restates the law formerly contained in the Bankruptcy Act.

34. Deeds of arrangement. A creditor who has not assented to a deed of composition is not bound by it, and can sometimes use it as grounds for filing a petition in bankruptcy against the debtor. The upheavals in bankruptcy law caused by the insolvency legislation have left the law on deeds of arrangement virtually untouched.

Progress test 6

Bankruptcy

1. In what way are insolvency practitioners now subject to statutory control? (18: **2**)
2. Explain what is meant by a creditor's petition and by a debtor's petition. (18: **7**)
3. What is the duration of bankruptcy and what is the effect of discharge? (18: **8,9**)
4. What are the powers of the trustee in bankruptcy? (18: **25**)
5. Explain how a bankrupt's estate is distributed. (18: **28**)

Specimen questions

1. Explain what are meant by bankruptcy petitions, bankruptcy orders and the commencement and duration of bankruptcy.

2. What is the effect of bankruptcy on rights of occupation of the family home?

3. Explain the position of a trustee in bankruptcy in connection with the following matters:

(*a*) a lease held by the bankrupt;

(*b*) a claim by a bankrupt for damages arising out of a collision between a Post Office van and the bankrupt's car while driven by him;

(*c*) securities held by the bankrupt under a settlement created by his uncle.

Appendix
Examination technique

Questions in Business Law are of two types: (*a*) text-book questions — asking the student to expound or discuss a topic, e.g. 'What is specific performance and in what conditions will it not be granted?'; (*b*) problems — in which the facts of a case are given and the student is asked to apply the various appropriate rules of law and discuss the situation (or advise one of the parties), e.g. 'P's agent, A, exceeds his authority in contracting with C, and does not tell C that he is acting merely as an agent. Discuss. (Or 'Advise C.')

These two types of question require slightly different approaches, but the following general points should always be borne in mind:

(*a*) First read the question carefully, to make sure you understand precisely what is involved. (If in doubt, underline *key-words*, or note the points you think are involved on a separate piece of paper.)

(*b*) Read the question a second time, noting down any points which may be involved but are not actually mentioned in the question. For instance in the problem on agency stated above: 'breach of warranty,' 'ratification,' 'agency by estoppel,' etc.

(*c*) Shuffle the points you have noted into a logical sequence. Thus in the agency problem above: (1) Agency; (2) Exceeding authority; (3) Breach of warranty of authority — damages; (4) Estoppel and Ostensible authority; (5) Undisclosed principal.

(Time spent on these preliminary stages is not wasted. It helps you to put your answer into logical order, saves you time in writing, and — most important — shows the examiner that you have taken the trouble to plan your answer instead of leaping into the question without preparation. It will also make your answer easier to mark, and go some way towards endearing you to the examiner.)

> NOTE: Citation of cases, etc. In studying law you should first learn the facts and names of leading cases; secondly, the facts of other cases; thirdly, the names of all. If in an examination you cannot remember the name of a case but can remember the facts, cite the facts on their own. If you cannot remember either name or facts it is permissible to invent facts of your own to illustrate an argument, providing you make it clear that they are your own invention (and do not pretend they come from some fictitious case). As to the method of incorporating cases in an answer, note the method used in the model answers below. (Remember always to underline case-names and references to statutes; this is a legal tradition, and it also helps attract the examiner's attention.)

Textbook questions. These test: (*a*) your memory of your textbook and notes; (*b*) your ability to organise your information. Therefore before answering you should assemble your information carefully, and then write it down in a logical sequence. Use short sentences; long sentences tend to confuse you if you are in a hurry (and are also harder for an examiner to read).

In Business Law text-book questions do not usually require a very detailed knowledge, but they do require that the information sought should be known precisely.

Example: 'Summarise (or 'state briefly' or 'state' or 'describe,' etc.) the conditions and warranties implied in contracts for the sale of goods, and explain how these terms may be excluded.'

Model answer: Under the Sale of Goods Act 1979, the following conditions and warranties are implied in every contract covered by the Act (unless excluded by express agreement):
 1. A condition that the seller has or will have the legal right to sell the goods at the time the property is to pass: s. 12(1).
 2. A condition, in sales by sample, that bulk shall correspond with sample and that the buyer shall have reasonable opportunity to examine and compare, and that the goods shall be free of any defect not likely to be apparent on reasonable examination: s. 15(2).
 3. A condition in sales by description (where the buyer merely

describes what he wants and leaves it to the seller to select the goods) that the goods shall correspond with the description: s. 13.

4. A condition or warranty as to quality or fitness is only implied in the following cases.

(*a*) Where the seller is a dealer in the goods sold, and the purchaser makes clear that he relies on the seller's skill and judgment, a condition is implied that the goods shall be reasonably fit for the purpose intended: s. 14(3).

(*b*) Where the seller is a dealer in the goods sold, there is an implied condition that they shall be of merchantable quality, i.e. of a quality generally acceptable: s. 14(2).

5. A warranty that the buyer shall enjoy quiet possession: s. 12(1).

Any condition (main term) or warranty (subordinate term) implied by the Act can be excluded by express agreement: s. 55(1). But exclusionary clauses are construed strictly against the party inserting them and certain clauses are in any case void against consumers: s. 55(3) and (4). The seller cannot avail himself of an exclusionary clause if he broke the contract in some other way: *Karsales Ltd* v. *Wallis* (1956). Thus where printed conditions of sale excluded liability for misdescriptions, it was held that the express and written exclusion was cancelled by an express oral representation: *Couchman* v. *Hill* (1947).

Problems: This type of question tests: (*a*) your understanding of the application of basic rules of law to an unfamiliar situation; (*b*) your ability to present a rational argument.

Conseqently you should (*i*) state the points of law involved in the problem, (*ii*) decide whether they are in fact applicable to the particular circumstances, and (*iii*) state your decision as to who is liable (if asked), etc. The most important parts of this answer are (*i*) and (*ii*). You can still get a good mark on a problem question, even if you fail to reach a decision on point (*iii*) or reach a wrong decision.

Example: 'A is P's agent for the purchase of certain goods, and is authorised to pay up to £100. In fact he buys the goods from X at a price of £120. Can X enforce the contract against A and/or P? Would it make any difference to your answer if A had concealed the fact that he was merely acting as agent for P?'

Model answer: This question appears to involve two main points, namely (*i*) excess of authority by an agent, and (*ii*) the doctrine of the undisclosed principal.

Where an agent exceeds his authority, his principal incurs no liability to the third party, but the agent is liable for damages for breach of his implied warranty of authority: *Collen* v. *Wright* (1857).

The principal may however incur liability where:

(*a*) He ratifies the agent's transaction, in which case the agent ceases to be liable. Ratification is only possible where:
   (*i*) the principal had capacity to make the particular contract at the time the agent contracted, and at the time of ratification;
   (*ii*) the agent contracted expressly as agent for the principal, naming him;
   (*iii*) the principal was in possession of all material information or agreed to dispense with it;

(*b*) he is estopped from denying the agent's authority to make the contract in question, e.g.:
   (*i*) where the principal has held out the agent as having authority to make the contract in question (for instance where the agent has in the past made such contracts with the principal's concurrence); or
   (*ii*) where the agent's ostensible authority covers the transaction in question, even though he has exceeded his actual authority (for instance where the agent occupies a position which normally carries with it authority to make such contracts, and the principal has imposed restrictions on that authority which are unknown to X).

Thus a factor has implied authority to sell goods in his possession, and can give a good title to a purchaser even though he was instructed not to sell the particular goods: Factors Act 1889, s. 2.

The doctrine of the undisclosed principal would be applicable to the problem stated if A had concealed the fact of his agency. The doctrine is that in such a case the third party (here X) can enforce the contract against the agent, and on discovering the identity and existence of the principal has an alternative right of action against the principal.

In the problem therefore it is submitted that:

(*a*) X has a right of action against A for breach of his warranty of authority, and is entitled to damages whether the breach was innocent or fraudulent;

(*b*) X has no right of action against P, unless P ratifies the transaction or is estopped from denying A's authority.

Index

acceptance,
  bills of exchange, 256–8
  contracts, 16–19
  sale of goods, 167
  subject to contract, 16
accident insurance, 209–10
accommodation party, 252
accord and satisfaction, 76
agency, 113–29
  authority of agent, 122–5
  definition, 113
  by estoppel, 115
  formation of, 113–16
  implied, 114–15
  kinds of, 113–14
  of necessity, 116
  Power of Attorney, 114
  ratification by, 115–16
  termination of, 116–18
  undisclosed principal, 124–5
  vicarious liability, 121–2
  warranty of authority, 123
agents, 118–29
  auctioneers, 175–6
  authority, 122–5
  bankers, 126–7
  brokers, 125–6
  del credere, 114
  duties of, 118–20
  estate agents, 127–9
  factors, 125
  wives, 115
air, carriage by, 194–5
aliens, contracts by, 41
American share certificates, 270–1
arbitration and awards, 224–30
  arbitration agreements, 225
  arbitrators, 226–7
  awards, 228–9
  conduct of proceedings, 227–8
  construction of agreements, 225–6
  consumer arbitration agreements, 230
  reference to arbitration, 224–5
  remission to arbitrator, 229
  stay of proceedings, 225
arrangement, deeds of, 319
assignment of contracts, 91–3
auction sales, 175–6
average loss, 197–8, 208

bailees, 216–19
  duties of, 216–17
  involuntary, 217–18
  power of sale, 219
bailment, 216–22
  definition, 216
  duties in, 216–18
  gratuitous, 37

innkeepers, 221–2
  right of sale in, 219
  types of, 220
bankers,
  cheques, 260–8
  collecting, 265–6
  drafts, 269–70
  liens, 291
  paying, 265
  position of, 126–7
  protection of, 265–6
bank notes, 269
bankruptcy, 307–19
  acts of, 307
  after-acquired property, 315
  contracts to which bankrupt is party, 319
  control by trustee, 315
  control of trustee, 314
  creditor's meetings, 309
  creditor's petition, 309
  debtor's petition, 309
  deeds of arrangement, 319
  definition of bankrupt's estate, 311
  discharge of bankrupt, 77, 310–11
  disposition of property, 311–12
  distress, 319
  distribution of estate, 317–19
  duration, 310
  extortionate credit transaction, 319
  guarantors, 300
  implementation of approved composition of scheme, 308
  income payment orders, 315
  insolvency practitioners, 307
  interim receiver, 312
  liability of trustee, 314

  Official Receiver, 312–14
  orders, 309
  partnerships, 134, 139, 145
  proceedings and remedies, 312
  proof of debts, 316
  public examination of bankrupt, 313
  report by nominee, 308
  spouse's rights, 318
  statement of affairs, 312
  transactions at undervalue and preferences, 318
  trustee in bankruptcy, 313–14, 316
  vesting of bankrupt's estate, 314–5
  voluntary settlements, 307–8
barter, 152
bidding rings, 176
bills of exchange, 239–45
  acceptance, 256–8
  accommodation party, 252
  alterations, 243–4
  banker's drafts, 269–70
  bearer bills, 242
  cheques, 260–8
  conditional indorsements, 250

Index 327

conditional orders, 245
consideration, 241
definition, 239
delivery, 248–9
discharge, 260
dishonour, 259–60
fictitious payees, 253
foreign bills, 243
forged signatures, 246–8
holders, 254–6
inchoate bills, 243
indorsements, 249–50
inland bills, 242–3
liability of parties, 250–6
lost bills, 245
negotiation, 245
non-existing payees, 253
order bills, 242
overdue, 244
payment, 257–8
presentment, 257–8
promissory notes, 268–9
qualified acceptance, 257
referee in case of need, 252
restrictive indorsements, 250
rights of holders, 256
sets, 243
signature, 245–50
sum payable, 241–2
bills of lading, 195, 198–200, 270
bills of sale, 286–7
breach of contract, 82–8
    actions for, 173–4
    damages, 83–6
    injunctions to restrain, 88
    remedies, 83
brokers, 125–6, 214
burglary insurance, 209
business names, 64
Business Names Act 1985, 64

carriage of goods, 188–201
    by air, 194–5
    average loss, 197–8
    bills of landing, 195, 198–200
    Carriage of Goods by Sea Act 1971, 198–200
    Carriers Act 1830, 192
    cesser and lien, 201
    charterparties, 195, 200–1
    common carriers, 188–91
    damages, 189–90
    dangerous goods, 91
    demurrage, 201
    freight, 197
    full and complete cargo, 201
    by land, 195, 198–200
    paramount clause, 200
    by rail, 192–4
    by road, 194
    by sea, 195–8
    Transport Acts, 191–4
Carriage of Goods by Sea Act 1971, 198–200
caveat emptor, 49, 54
champerty, 67

charterparties, 195, 200–1
cheques, 260–8
    alterations, 263–4
    banker's authority, 266–8
    collecting banker, 265–6
    crossings, 262–5
    dating, 261–2
    definition, 260–1
    duties of customer, 267–8
    indorsements, 244
    paying banker, 265
    payment by, 74–5, 262
    post-dated, 262
    stale and overdue, 261
    undated, 261–2
choses in action, 93
    assignments, 92
    mortgages, 286
choses in possession, 92
C.I.F. contracts, 168–9
common carriers, 188–91
    duties, 189
    liability, 189–90
condition,
    breach of, 174
    kinds of, 26
    Sale of Goods Act 1893, 153–4
conflict of laws, 29–30
consensus ad idem, 3
consideration,
    bills of exchange, 241
    contracts, 36–41
    doctrine of, 36
    guarantees, 293
    rules relating to, 37–41
    valuable, 36–7
construction of contracts, 28
consumer arbitration agreements, 230
consumer credit,
    agreements, 179
    hiring, 179
    licences, 179–80
Consumer Credit Act 1974, 64
consumer hire agreements, 220
Consumer Protection Advisory Committee, 96
continuing guarantees, 292
contracts, 3–103
    affreightment, 195–6
    by agents, 122–5
    assignment of, 91–3
    breach of, 82–8
    capacity of parties, 41–3
    certainty of terms, 23–4
    collateral, 29
    conflict of laws, 29–30
    consideration, 36–41
    construction of terms, 28
    corporations, 42–3
    damages for breach, 83–6
    deeds, 6–8
    disabilities, 63–6
    discharge by agreement, 75–6
    discharge by breach, 82–8
    discharge by frustration, 79–82

discharge by operation of law, 76–9
discharge by performance, 72–5
duress, 59
exemption clauses, 21–3
form of, 31–6
fraud, 57–9
freedom to contract, 94–5
frustration of, 79–82
guarantees, 23, 33–4
illegal at common law, 66–7
illegality, 61–3
indemnity clauses, 23
injunctions, 87–8
innocent misrepresentation, 55–7
limitation of actions, 77–8
minors, 43–6
misrepresentation, 54–9
mistake, 47–53
offer and acceptance, 12–16
part performance, 35–6
Privity, Doctrine of, 89–91
quantum meruit, 11, 86
quasi-contracts, 9–10
rectification, 53
rescission, 56
restraint of trade, 67–71
sale of goods, 151–3
signatures, 19–20
simple, 8
specialty, 6–7
specific performance, 87
standard form, 19–21
terms, 25–9
transfer of, 91–3
uberrimae fidei, 58–9
undue influence, 59–60
unenforceable, 8–9, 32–3, 76
void, 8, 31–2, 44–5
voidable, 8, 45–6
warranties, 26
contracts of record, 6
credit sale, 179
damages,
  breach of contract, 83–6
  carriage of goods, 189–90
  liquidated, 85–6
  misrepresentation, 56–8
  warranty of authority, 123
dangerous goods, 191
deeds, 6–8
deeds of arrangement, 317
del credere agency, 114
demurrage, 201
depositum, 220
description, sale by, 156–7
diplomatic immunity, 41–2
discharge, bills of exchange, 260
discharge of contracts, 72–88
  agreement, 75–6
  breach, 82–8
  frustration, 79–82
  operation of law, 76–9
  performance, 72–5
dishonour, of bills of exchange, 259–60
dissolution of partnership, 138–43

dock warrants, 270
duress, 59

employees, 69–71
equitable interests, 284–5
equitable mortgages, 285
escrow, 6–7
estate agents, 127–9
estoppel, 162, 251–2
  agency by, 115

factors, 125
fair trading, 94–103
Fair Trading Act 1973, 99, 102
Financial Services Act 1986, 64
fire insurance, 207–8
foreign bills, 243
forgery of bills, 246–8
fraud, 57–9
Frauds, Statute of, 1677, 27
freight, 197
frustration, doctrine of, 79–82
future goods, 152

gaming contracts, 64–6
goods, meaning of, 151–2
goodwill, 142–3
guarantees, 292–301
  bankruptcy of guarantor, 300
  capacity to contract, 294–5
  characteristics, 292–3
  continuing, 292
  death of guarantor, 300
  definition, 292
  discharge of guarantor, 298–301
  form of, 293
  joint guarantors, 295–6
  liability of guarantor, 296–7
  not *uberrimae fidei*, 293–4
  rights of guarantor, 297
  specific, 292
  written evidence, 32, 34
hire contracts, 178–9
hire-purchase, 178–84
  agreements, 180–1
  ancillary credit business, 184
  definition, 177
  extortionate credit bargains, 184
  form of contract, 177
  implied terms, 177
  information for customers, 183
  liability, 182–3
  licensing of businesses, 179–80
  powers of court, 184
  protected goods, 183–4
  regulated, 179
  statutory rights, 181–2
  unlicensed trading, 180
holders of bills, 254–6
holders in due course, 254–6
holders for value, 256

illegal contracts, 67–71
  at common law, 66–7

Index 329

restraint of trade, 67–71
impossibility of performance, 79
inchoate bills, 243
indemnities, 294
injunctions, 87–8
inland bills, 242–3
innkeepers, 220–2
innocent misrepresentation, 55–7
insolvency, *see* bankruptcy
insurance, 203–14
  accident, 209–10
  assignment of life policies, 206–7
  burglary, 209
  definition, 203
  double, 204–5
  fire, 207–8
  insurable interest, 203, 205, 207, 210
  life, 205–7
  marine, 210–13
  mortgages, 206–7
  policyholders' protection, 214
  state supervision, 213–14
  uberrimae fidei, 4
interests in property, 284
invitation to treat, 13
I.O.U.s, 271

lay days, 201
legal interests, 284–5
liens, 289–91
  bankers', 291
  common law, 289–90
  definition, 289
  equitable, 290
  innkeeper's, 221–2
  maritime, 290
  possessory, 289–90
  seller's, 171
life insurance, 205–7
Limitation Act 1980, 77, 300–1
limitation of actions, 7–8, 77–8, 300
limited partnerships, 143–5

maintenance, 67
marine insurance, 210–13
  assignment, 213
  definition, 210
  general average loss, 213
  insurable interest, 210
  loss, 212–13
  re-insurance, 210
  warranties, 211–12
maritime lien, 290
market overt, 164
marriage, 66, 67
married women,
  agency of, 115
  contracts by, 42
merger, 7, 76
mergers, 97, 98
minors' contracts, 43–6
misrepresentation, 54–9
  damages, 56–8
  definition, 54–5
  innocent, 55–7

  remedies, 57–8
mistake, in contract, 47–53
mock auctions, 176
money lenders, 63
monopolies, 96–9
Monopolies and Mergers
  Commission, 97–9
mortgages, 285–6

necessaries, 43
necessity, agency of, 116
negotiable instruments, 237–71
  banker's drafts, 269–70
  bills of exchange, 239–45
  characteristics, 237–8
  cheques, 260–8
  consumer credit, 271
  Consumer Credit Act 1974, 271
  dividends, 270
  examples, 238
  interest warrants, 270
  promissory notes, 268–9
  quasi-negotiable instruments, 270
  suing on, 238–9
novation, 134

offers, 12–16
Official Receiver, 312–14
options, 15–16

'parol' contracts, 3
partnership, 130–48
  agency of partners, 133
  articles of, 136
  assignment of shares, 138
  bankruptcy, 134, 139
  change of partners, 134–5
  definition, 130–1
  dissolution, 138–43
  distribution of assets, 138
  expulsion of partners, 137
  firm name, 132
  formation, 131–2
  goodwill, 142–3
  illegal associations, 132–3
  liability of partners, 134–5
  limited, 143–5
  property, 137–8
  retirement of partners, 134
  rights and duties in, 136–8
  tests for establishing, 131–2
pawn and pledge,
  definition, 283
  lien, distinguished from, 283
  mortgage, distinguished from, 283
  pawnbrokers, 288–9
  realisation, 289
  redemption, 288–9
payment,
  appropriation of, 75
  discharge of contracts, 74–5
penalties, 85–6
performance,
  complete, 72
  discharge of contracts, 72–5

330 Index

impossibility of, 79
  part, 72–3
  sale of goods, 165–9
  specific, 87, 174
  substantial, 73
pledges, 287–8
Policyholders' Protection Board, 214
possessory liens, 289–90
post, contracts by, 17
Power of Attorney, 100
principal and agent, 118–22
Privity, Doctrine of, 89–91
promissory notes, 268
public policy, 62
pyramid selling, 102

quantum meruit, 11, 86
quasi-contracts, 9–10
quasi-negotiable instruments, 270–1

rail, carriage by, 192–4
ratification, of agency, 115–16
rectification, 53
release, deed of, 76
representation, 154–5
resale price maintenance, 100
restraint of trade, 67–71
Restrictive Practices Court, 96, 100
restrictive trade practices, 99–100
revocation of offers, 15
road, carriage by, 188–92

sale of business, 71
sale of goods, 151–76
  acceptance by buyer, 167
  agreement for sale, 152
  ascertained goods, 160
  auction sales, 175–6
  breach of contract, 173–4
  C.I.F. contracts, 168–9
  consumer credit, 178–84
  delivery, 165–9
  by description, 156–7
  F.O.B. contracts, 168
  goods, meaning of, 151–2
  hire-purchase, 178–84
  implied conditions, 153–4
  market overt, 164
  nemo dat quod non habet, 162
  passing of ownership, 159–61
  passing of risk, 162
  by sample, 159
  seller's duties, 165–9
  seller's lien, 171
  specific goods, 160–1
  stoppage in transit, 171–3
  tests of intention, 160–1
  unascertained goods, 160–1
  under voidable title, 164
  unpaid sellers, 169–73
  warranties implied, 153–4
  work and materials, 152
  writs of execution, 163
Sale of Goods Act 1979, 163

Sale of Goods (Implied Terms) Act 1973, 154–9
  correspondence with description, 156–7
  exclusion clauses, 156–9
  fitness for particular purpose, 158
  merchantable quality, 157–8
sample, sale by, 159
sea, carriage by, 195–8
secret profit (agency), 119
securities, 281–91
  definition, 282
  formalities, 283–4
  liens, 283, 289–91
  mortgages, 282–6
  personal property, 281–2
  pledges or pawns, 283, 286
  real property, 282
severance, doctrine of, 61–2
sheriff, sale by, 163
shipowners, 196–7, 201
specific performance, 87, 174
stoppage in transit, 171–2
subrogation, 208
suicide clause, 205–6
supply of goods and services,
  contracts for, 177–8
sureties, *see* guarantees

tender, legal, 73
tender of payment, 73
tender of performance, 73
tenders, 18–19
third parties, 123–4
time for performance, 74
time policy, 211
Trade Descriptions Act 1968, 100–2
trustee in bankruptcy, 311–14

uberrimae fidei contracts,
  general, 58–9
  guarantees, 293–4
  insurance, 204
unascertained goods, 160–1
undue influence, 59–61
unenforceable contracts, 8–9
Unfair Contract Terms Act 1977,
  5–6, 158, 159

valuable consideration, 36–7
valued policy, 211
vicarious liability, 121–2
voidable contracts, 8, 45–6
void contracts, 8, 31–2, 44–5
voyage policy, 211
wagering contracts, 64–6
warranty,
  auctioneer's, 175
  of authority, 123
  breach of, 174
  definition, 21
  ex post facto, 26–7, 154
  implied, 153–4, 212
  marine insurance, 211–12
writs of execution, 163

- 8   Carte des itinéraires de visite
- 11 La Suisse, terre de vacances
- 12 Carte des lieux de séjour
- 14 La Confédération helvétique

15 Introduction au voyage

- 16 Physionomie du pays
- 22 Un peu d'histoire
- 25 Une économie créatrice
- 26 La démocratie en action
- 30 La Suisse pittoresque
- 35 La table

37 Villes et curiosités

273 Renseignements pratiques

- 274 Avant le départ
- 275 Vie pratique
- 277 Hébergement - Restauration
- 278 A la découverte de la Suisse
- 283 Livres, films, musique
- 284 Principales manifestations
- 287 Conditions de visite
- 312 Index

Dans une grande ville, dans un village de montagne ou sur les bords paisibles d'un lac... Pour trouver un toit, pour trouver une table, consultez le guide Rouge Michelin Suisse *(hôtels et restaurants).*
A la suite d'un chapitre explicatif en plusieurs langues, le guide vous présente un choix d'hôtels avec l'indication de leur équipement (piscines, tennis, plages aménagées au bord des lacs, jardins de repos...) ainsi que les périodes d'ouverture et de fermeture des établissements, les numéros de téléphone et de fax, les cartes de crédit acceptées.
Le guide Rouge Michelin Suisse *vous propose également un choix de restaurants allant du simple plat du jour généralement servi le midi en semaine, aux tables gastronomiques signalées à votre attention par les étoiles de bonne table.*
Des plans de villes localisant chaque établissement, des cartes et bien d'autres informations pratiques facilitent votre voyage.
Mis à jour chaque année, ce guide est le complément du guide Vert Michelin Suisse.

Lexique touristique commenté

Pour les termes d'hôtellerie, se reporter au chapitre : La table

Bahnhof	gare		**Pass**	col
Brücke	pont		**Rathaus**	hôtel de ville
Burg	château fort		**Schloss**	château
Denkmal	monument		**Schlucht**	gorge
Fähre	bac		**Schwimmbad**	piscine
Fall	chute, cascade		**See**	lac, mer
Garten	jardin		**Spielplatz**	parc de sports
Gasse	rue, ruelle		**Strandbad**	plage
Gletscher	glacier		**Strasse**	rue, route
Hafen	port		**Tal**	vallée
Haupt	(dans un mot composé) principal (Hauptpost : poste principale)		**Talsperre**	barrage
			Tobel	ravin escarpé
			Tor	portail, porte de ville
Kirche	église		**Unter**	inférieur, bas (Untertor : porte du bas)
Kleintaxi	petit taxi (taxi courant)			
Kloster	abbaye, couvent		**Verboten**	interdit
Kursaal	casino		**Wald**	forêt
Markt	marché		**Zytgloggeturm**	tour à horloge
Münster	église importante (cathédrale)		**Zeughaus**	arsenal
Ober	haut, supérieur (Obergasse : rue Haute)			

PETIT VOCABULAIRE DU SKIEUR

Allemand	**Français**	**Italien**
Skischule	École de ski	Scuola di sci
Skilehrer	Moniteur de ski	Maestro di sci
Abfahrt	Départ, piste	Partenza, pista
Schi, Ski (Bergski, Talski)	Ski (amont, aval)	Sci (a monte, a valle)
Kanten	Carres	Spigoli
Bindung	Fixation	Attacco
Skistock	Bâton	Bastone
Skiwachs	Fart	Sciolina
Schussfahrt	Descente directe (schuss)	Discesa in linea diretta
Querfahrt	Traversée	Diagonale
Schneepflug, Stemmen	Position de chasse-neige	Posizione di spazzaneve
Abrutschen	Dérapage	« Dérapage »
Kurvenschwung, Bogen	Virage	Curva
Wedeln	« Godille »	Serpentina, Scodinzolio
Spezialslalom	Slalom spécial	Slalom speciale
Riesenslalom	Slalom géant	Slalom gigante
Abfahrtslauf	Descente libre	Discesa libera
Kombination	Combiné	Combinato
Langstreckenlauf	Course de fond	Corsa di fondo
Sprungschanze	Tremplin de saut	Trampolino di salto
Skilift	Téléski, remonte-pente	Sciovia, ski-lift
Sessellift	Télésiège	Seggiovia
Kabinenbahn	Télécabine	Cabinovia, piccola funivia
Schwebebahn	Téléphérique	Funivia
Drahtseilbahn	Funiculaire	Funicolare
Lawine	Avalanche	Valanga
Schutzhütte	Refuge	Rifugio
Skiwerkstatt	Atelier de réparation de skis	Laboratorio di riparazione de glisci
Rodelbahn	Piste de luge	Pista per slitte
Eisbahn	Patinoire	Pista di pattinaggio

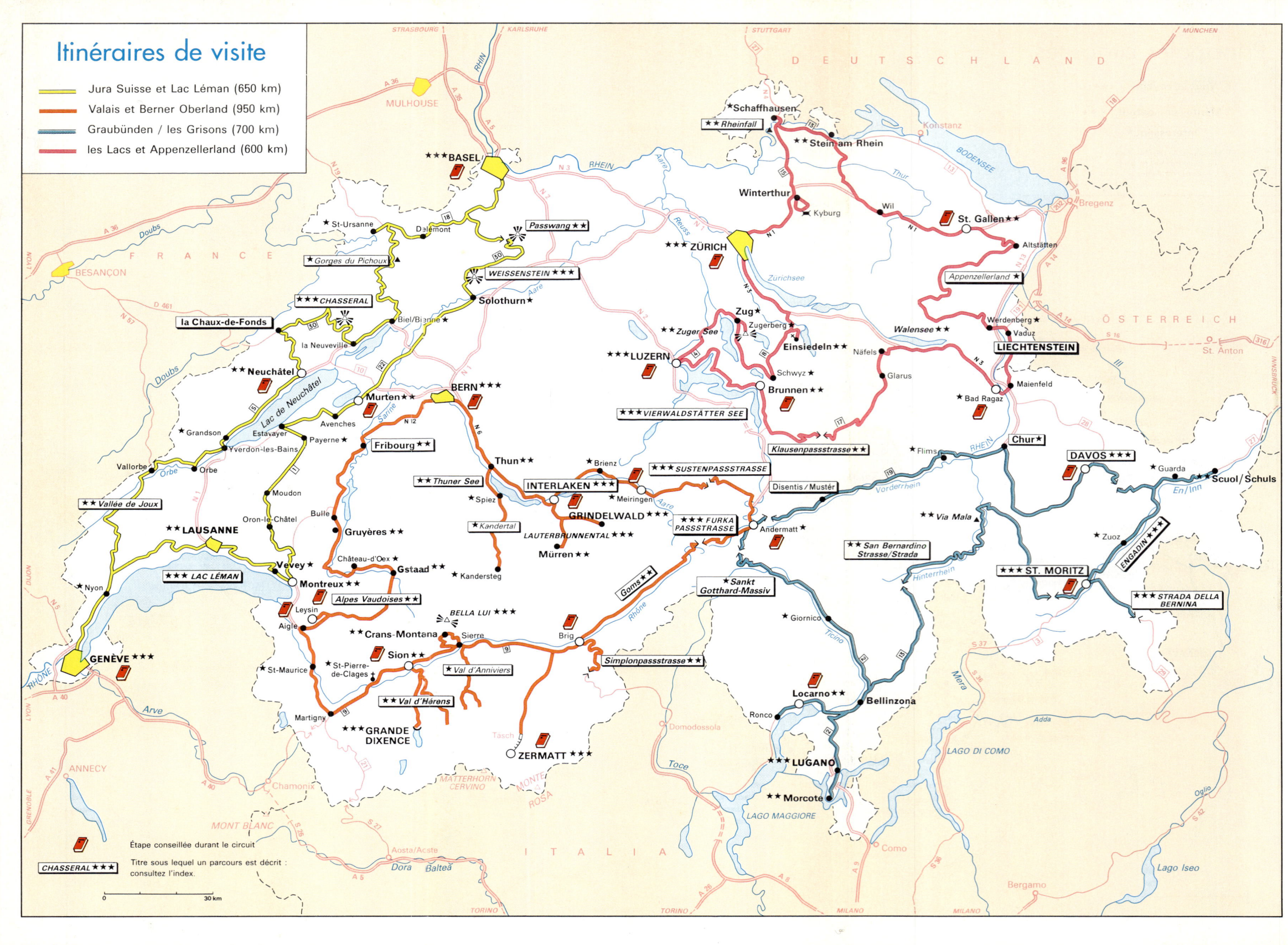

La Suisse, terre de vacances

Dès qu'il a posé le pied sur le sol helvétique, l'étranger se sent pris en charge par un pays essentiellement occupé à la mise en valeur de son patrimoine et au développement du tourisme. Spécialistes de l'hôtellerie et jaloux d'une réputation justement acquise, les Suisses ont su créer pour lui, quelles que soient la région et la saison, l'atmosphère correspondant à ses goûts : cadre pittoresque ou somptueux, confort, netteté irréprochable, accueil empressé. Une gamme étendue de distractions lui est également proposée : il peut choisir entre les fêtes folkloriques les plus colorées et les manifestations culturelles ou sportives les plus suivies.

Pourvue d'un réseau ferroviaire et routier très dense, reliée au TGV français (train à grande vitesse mettant Paris à quelque 3 h 1/2 de Genève ou Lausanne), escale importante des lignes aériennes internationales, véritable carrefour de l'Europe, la Confédération s'ouvre largement à l'invasion pacifique des touristes et des sportifs.

A QUELLE ÉPOQUE VISITER LA SUISSE ?

Pendant les saisons « sportives » — Le mois de juin qui permet à l'alpiniste de trouver, en haute montagne, le glacier en bonnes conditions, sera choisi aussi par le touriste qui ne peut concevoir l'alpe sans sa parure de fleurs fraîchement déployée.

Le plein été ne garantit pas toujours, en montagne, un beau temps stable, en dehors de l'Engadine, du Valais ou du Tessin. Il n'en reste pas moins l'époque vivante par excellence. Tandis que la vie des champs bat son plein, l'automobiliste trouve ouverts tous les itinéraires alpins, l'amateur de sites est comblé par le spectacle des torrents et des cascades (dans la plaine, c'est l'époque où il faut admirer l'Aare et le Rhin coulant à pleins bords), et le grimpeur peut s'attaquer à un rocher propre et sec.

Dès les premières chutes de neige, toute l'activité touristique s'oriente vers le même pôle d'intérêt : les sports d'hiver. Pour accueillir le flot de citadins avides d'oublier la grisaille des plaines et de s'élancer sur les pistes éblouissantes de soleil, chaque station fait appel à toutes les ressources d'un équipement hôtelier et sportif constamment perfectionné.

Pendant les saisons de détente — Au printemps et en automne, les bords des lacs suisses constituent de très agréables séjours. Sur le versant Sud des Alpes, les rivages des bassins de Lugano et du lac Majeur sont recherchés dès le début du printemps. Grâce à l'influence réchauffante du föhn (voir plus loin : Physionomie du pays), les lacs des Quatre-Cantons et de Thoune se frangent, eux aussi, dès le mois d'avril, de véritables petites Rivieras. A la saison des vendanges, début octobre, la région du Léman (Riviera vaudoise) présente ses charmes les plus prenants. Jusqu'à fin novembre, une belle arrière-saison peut être très favorable à un circuit d'art en Suisse.

QUE RAPPORTER DE SUISSE ?

La carte ci-dessous dresse une sélection de spécialités suisses paraissant les plus dignes de figurer parmi les souvenirs de voyage (spécialités gastronomiques, voir le chapitre : La table).

Les centres d'artisanat de Zurich et de Stein-am-Rhein organisent des expositions sur des thèmes différents pour la sauvegarde de l'art populaire suisse et de l'artisanat.

Lieux de séjour
LUZERN
Wengen
Morgins
Caractère dominant de la station :
Station thermale
Station de sports d'hiver
Altitude au dessus de 1000 m
0
50 km
MULHOUSE
RHIN
A 35
A 5
BASEL
Rheinfelden
Schinznach
Aarau
Olten
Porrentruy
Besançon
Doubs
FRANCE
Solothurn
Aare
N 1
N 2
Biel/Bienne
la Neuveville
Neuchâtel
Murten
BERN
Emme
Saane
Pontarlier
Ste-Croix-les-Rasses
N 5
N 9
Yverdon-les-Bains
N 12
Fribourg
N 6
Hasliberg
Spiez
INTERLAKEN
Grindelwald
le Pont
le Brassus
Bulle
Gruyères
Zweisimmen
Mürren
Wengen
LAUSANNE-OUCHY
Châtel-St-Denis
les Paccots
Saanen
Rougemont
Saanenmöser
Kandersteg
St-Cergue
Morges
les Avants
Gstaad
Adelboden
Nyon
LAC LÉMAN
Vevey
MONTREUX
Château-d'Oex
les Diablerets
Lenk
Leukerbad
Bellwald
Bettmeralp
Evian
Leysin
Crans-Montana
Riederalp
Brig
GENÈVE
RHÔNE
Villars-sur-Ollon
Gryon
Anzère
Sierre
Chandolin
Morgins
Sion
Grimentz
St-Luc
Champéry
Rhône
Zinal
Salvan-les-Marécottes
Grächen
Arve
FRANCE
Martigny
Verbier
Evolène
Saas-Fee
Champex
Arolla
ZERMATT
Chamonix
Annecy
ITALIA

BERNER OBERLAND ET VIERWALDSTÄTTERSEE
0
20 km
Küssnacht
N 4
LUZERN
Weggis
Rigi-Kaltbad
Gersau
Brunnen
Bürgenstock
Stoos
N 2
Seelisberg
Stans
Beckenried-Klewenalp
Bauen
Sarnen
Reuss
Altdorf
Emme
Engelberg
N 6
Aare
Lungern
Thun
Brienz
Hasliberg
Meiringen
Beatenberg
Ringgenberg
Spiez
Merligen
INTERLAKEN
Aare
Andermatt
Wengen
Grindelwald
Frutigen
Lauterbrunnen
Mürren
Kleine Scheidegg
Airolo
Adelboden
Kandersteg
Münster

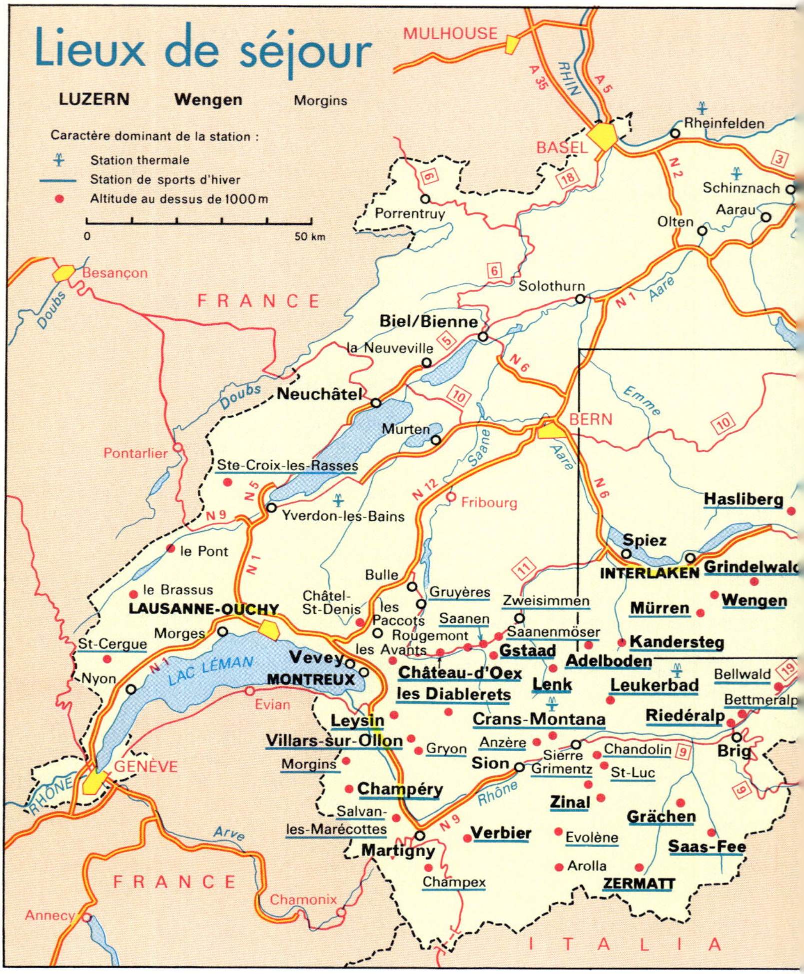

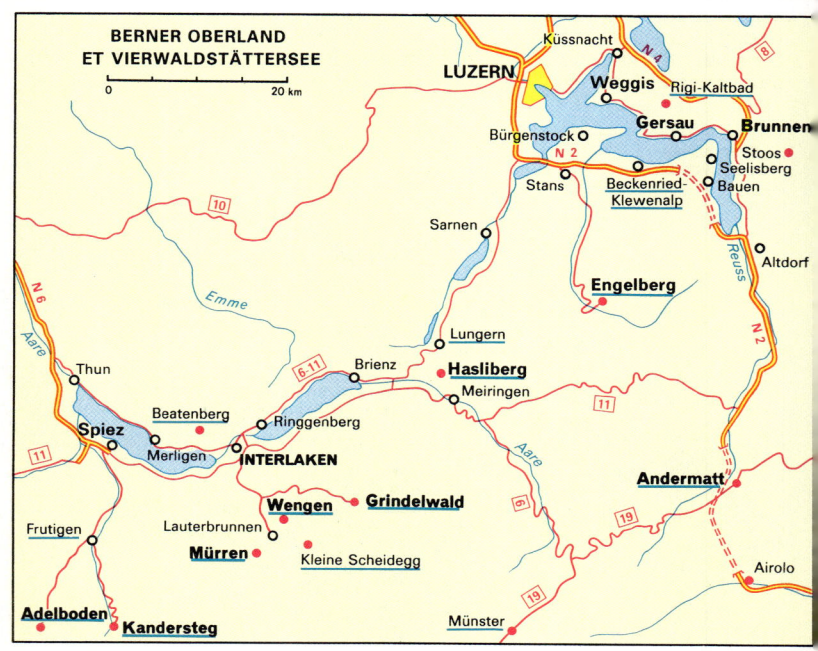

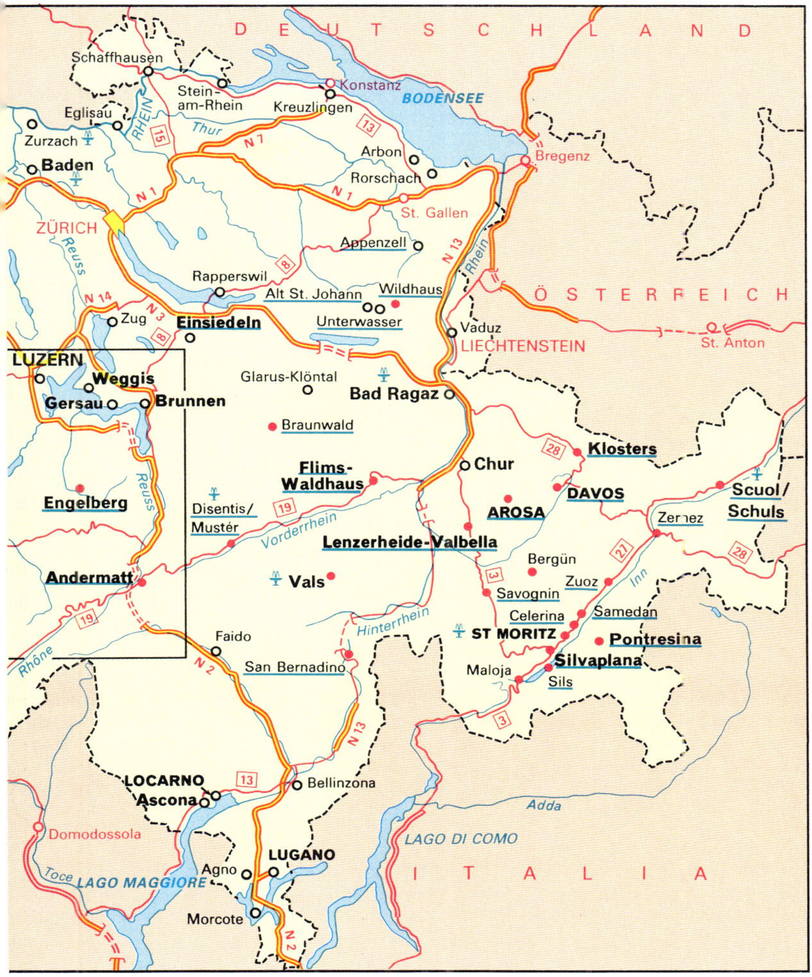

Lac Léman

LA CONFÉDÉRATION HELVÉTIQUE

La physionomie de la Confédération helvétique est empreinte d'une forte originalité. Pays divers, la Suisse rassemble, entre ses frontières étroites, des peuples de races, de langues et de religions différentes. Malgré la juxtaposition de régions naturelles des plus variées, elle offre cependant un caractère de réelle et profonde unité.

Aux foules de touristes qui, chaque année, le découvrent ou le retrouvent, le pays offre la sérénité et le charme de ses paysages : chaînes majestueuses aux sommets fameux, vallées riantes ou sauvages, immenses champs de neige, torrents fougueux et cascades bondissantes, plaines fertiles, villages fleuris dispersés dans la montagne, cités florissantes s'étalant au bord de lacs paisibles.

A l'amateur d'art, la Suisse dispense les richesses de son architecture et de ses musées, lui révélant, en cours de route, la silhouette massive d'un château fortifié, la haute stature d'un monastère baroque, la hardiesse de ses réalisations modernes. Elle l'invite encore à s'arrêter auprès d'une gracieuse fontaine ou à s'attarder dans un hameau aux chalets reluisants comme des jouets neufs.

QUELQUES CHIFFRES

Le territoire de la Confédération helvétique s'étend sur 41 300 km^2, soit le 1/13 de la superficie de la France et l'équivalent de 6 à 7 départements français. Il pourrait tenir dans un cercle de 115 km de rayon (distance Paris-Orléans). Si toute la Suisse était nivelée, elle se trouverait à 1 350 m au-dessus du niveau de la mer (altitude moyenne de la France : 342 m).

La population résidante comptait début 1994 environ 6 968 600 habitants, dont 1,3 million d'étrangers, ce qui représente une densité de 168,8 personnes au km^2 et peut être comparée à la population de l'agglomération parisienne. Le cinquième de cette population se groupe dans les cinq grandes villes du pays, soit, par ordre d'importance, Zurich, Bâle, Genève, Berne et Lausanne.

Les principaux sommets au-dessus de 4 000 mètres

Mont Rose (Valais)	4 634 m	Aletschhorn (Valais)	4 195 m
Dom (Mischabel ; Valais)	4 545 m	Breithorn (Valais)	4 164 m
Weisshorn (Valais)	4 505 m	Jungfrau (Berne-Valais)	4 158 m
Le Cervin (Valais)	4 478 m	Mönch (Berne-Valais)	4 099 m
Dent Blanche (Valais)	4 357 m	Schreckhorn (Berne)	4 078 m
Grand Combin (Valais)	4 314 m	Piz Bernina (Grisons)	4 049 m
Finsteraarhorn (Valais)	4 274 m	Lauteraarhorn (Berne)	4 042 m

Les plus grands lacs

Lac Léman	580 km^2	Lac des Quatre-Cantons	114 km^2
Bodensee (Lac de Constance)	540 km^2	Lac de Lugano	48 km^2
Lac de Neuchâtel	217 km^2	Lac de Thoune	48 km^2

GUIDES MICHELIN

Les guides Rouges (hôtels et restaurants) :
Benelux - Deutschland - España Portugal - Europe - France - Great Britain and Ireland - Ireland - Italia - London - Paris et environs - Portugal - Suisse

Les guides Verts (paysages, monuments, routes touristiques) :
Allemagne - Autriche - Belgique Grand-Duché de Luxembourg - Californie - Canada - Écosse - Espagne - Europe - France - Grande-Bretagne - Grèce - Hollande - Irlande - Italie - Maroc - Nouvelle Angleterre - Portugal - Le Québec - Suisse
Bruxelles - Florence et la Toscane - Londres - New York - Paris - Rome - Venise
...et la collection des guides régionaux sur la France.

Introduction au voyage

Le Cervin

Physionomie du pays

La Suisse se présente, dans son ensemble, comme une dépression (le Plateau ou Moyen-Pays) allongée entre les barrières montagneuses des Alpes et du Jura.

LES ALPES SUISSES

Les Alpes occupent les 3/5 du territoire helvétique, faisant de la Suisse le second des États alpins après l'Autriche où cette proportion est des 2/3. En mettant à part la portion des Grisons située à l'Est de la vallée du Rhin Postérieur – qui évoque déjà l'Europe centrale – les Alpes suisses sont à rattacher, comme les Alpes françaises, au groupe des Alpes occidentales, c'est-à-dire au secteur de la chaîne le plus arqué, le plus violemment plissé et, par voie de conséquence, le plus disséqué par l'érosion.

Le point culminant de ce monde de glaciers, de pics et de lacs est, pour la Confédération, le Mont Rose (Pointe Dufour – alt. 4 634 m), mais c'est le massif du St-Gothard (Pizzo Rotondo – alt. 3 192 m), ce château d'eau de l'Europe, qui représente ici la clé de voûte de tout l'édifice.

La dissymétrie de profil transversal est sans doute la caractéristique la plus frappante de la chaîne depuis l'effondrement de la plaine du Pô : le passage d'un col comme le St-Gothard rend sensible à l'automobiliste le contraste brutal qui oppose les pentes relativement douces du versant Nord à la subite dégringolade du versant Sud.

Dans le sens longitudinal, le très remarquable sillon qui se creuse en pleine montagne, de Martigny jusqu'à Coire et que drainent, suivant des directions opposées, le Rhône et le Rhin Antérieur, forme une grande rocade stratégique et touristique.

Les glaciers – Les Alpes suisses possèdent environ 2 000 km² de glaciers, soit cinq fois plus que les Alpes françaises. Le type le plus classique d'appareil glaciaire est le « glacier de vallée », dont le glacier d'Aletsch *(voir à ce nom)*, le plus vaste d'Europe (169 km²), offre un somptueux exemple. D'amont en aval, on relève la succession d'un **névé** (en allemand « Firn »), bassin d'accumulation où la neige se tasse et se transforme en glace, et d'une **langue glaciaire** (en allemand « Gletscher ») – zone d'écoulement et de fusion – fissurée d'un réseau serré de crevasses.

Les ruptures de pente qui, sur un torrent, se traduiraient par une cascade ou des rapides sont marquées par les amoncellements chaotiques et instables des **séracs**.

Les **moraines**, accumulations de débris rocheux entraînés par le glacier, souillent fréquemment la blancheur de la langue glaciaire, quand elles ne la masquent pas complètement, comme au Steingletscher. Une fois stabilisées, elles forment sur ses bords des remblais caractéristiques *(voir illustrations au paragraphe concernant le relief alpin)*.

L'héritage des glaciers quaternaires – Il y a une centaine de siècles, les glaciers, abondamment alimentés, comblaient complètement la dépression séparant le Jura des Alpes.

A l'intérieur du massif, ces fleuves solides atteignaient des proportions monstrueuses : le glacier du Rhône, dans le Valais, n'avait pas moins de 1 500 m d'épaisseur.

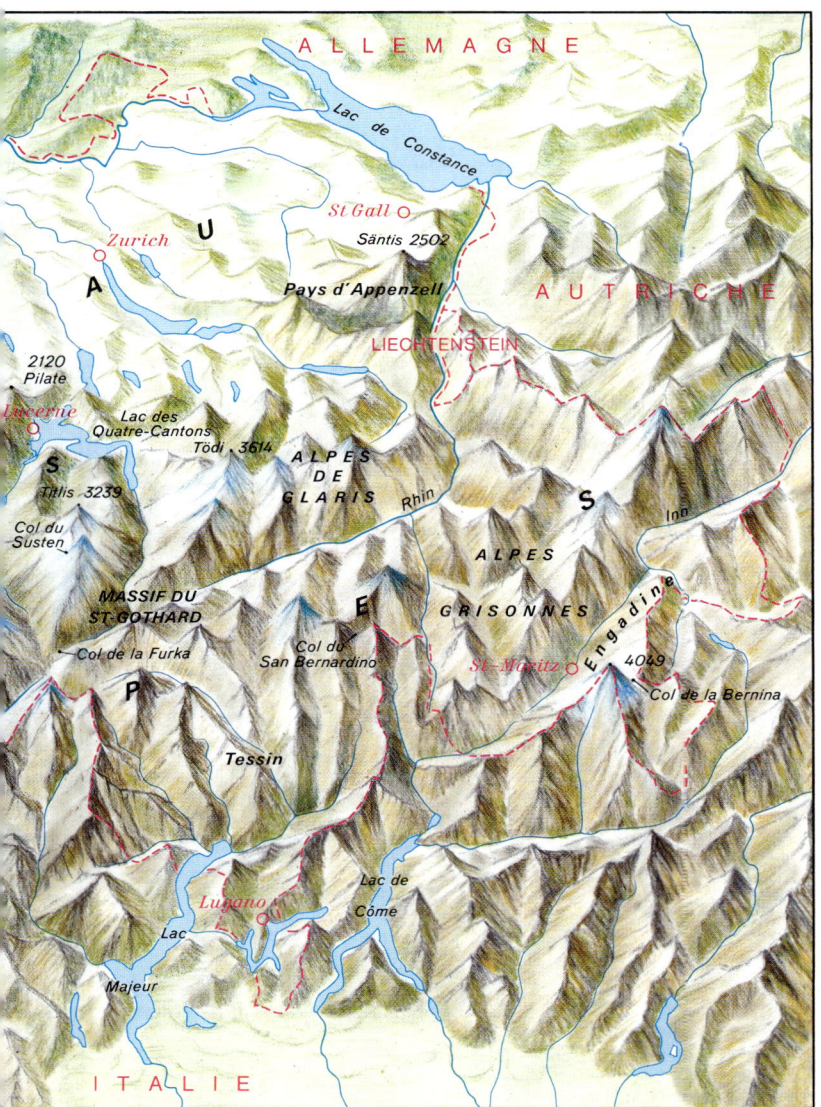

Le relief alpin

A l'intention des touristes peu familiarisés avec les formes particulières de relief en montagne, dues à l'action des torrents ou à celle des glaciers, nous donnons ci-dessous quelques indications sommaires permettant d'en reconnaître les traits caractéristiques ainsi que les termes géographiques qui les désignent.

| RELIEF TORRENTIEL | RELIEF GLACIAIRE |

Haute vallée : creusement

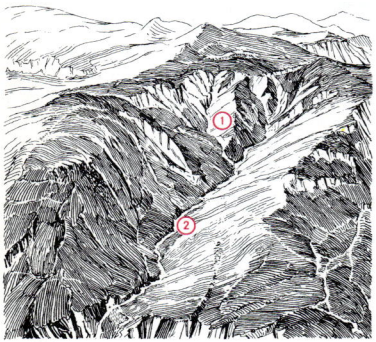 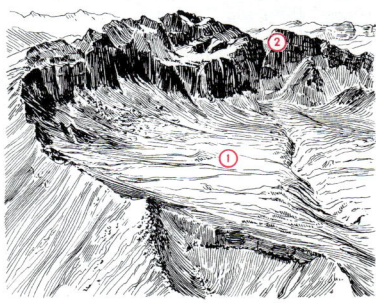

Cirque torrentiel.
1) Bassin de réception en demi-entonnoir et fortement raviné.
2) Chenal d'écoulement.

Cirque glaciaire abandonné.
1) Fond aplani.
2) Parois escarpées.

Moyenne vallée : transport

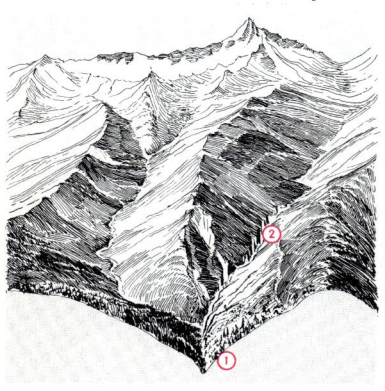 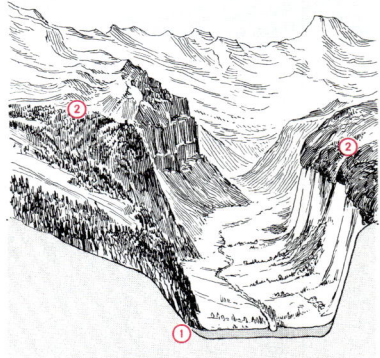

Vallée torrentielle.
1) Vallée en V.
2) Vallée très encaissée.

Vallée glaciaire abandonnée.
1) Auge en U, fond large souvent remblayé.
2) Épaulement.

Basse vallée : accumulation

 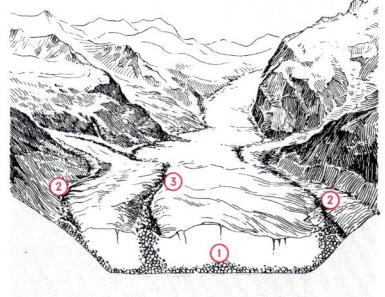

Cône de déjection.
Quand la pente devient trop faible pour permettre au torrent de charrier des matériaux, ceux-ci s'entassent en un « cône de déjection ».

Moraines.
1) Moraine de fond.
2) Moraine latérale.
3) Moraine médiane.

Ces géants ont laissé partout des traces frappantes : succession de rétrécissements et d'épanouissements, ruptures de pente brisant le profil longitudinal, bosses rocheuses des **verrous** encombrant certains fonds de vallées au point de les obturer presque complètement, vallées affluentes « **suspendues** » se raccordant par un ressaut très marqué avec la vallée principale, dite « **en auge** » à cause de la forme particulière de son profil transversal *(voir croquis au paragraphe concernant le relief alpin)*. Toutes ces formes de relief ont favorisé l'aménagement de hautes chutes pour la production d'énergie hydro-électrique.

Après la disparition des glaces, les eaux fluviales réapparues ont travaillé à atténuer ces contrastes.

Des **gorges de raccordement** ont alors approfondi leur trait de scie, échancrant les verrous, comme aux gorges de l'Aare, ou reliant le fond d'une vallée suspendue à celui de la vallée principale.

Mais les torrents alpins construisent aussi d'encombrants **cônes de déjection**, dont l'exemple le plus frappant est fourni, en Suisse, par le cône de l'Illgraben, tel qu'on le voit de Loèche.

La végétation alpine

Si la végétation est toujours étroitement tributaire du climat et des sols, elle l'est aussi, en montagne, de l'exposition des versants et de l'altitude qui détermine l'étagement des espèces. Cet étagement connaît des correctifs dus à l'action de l'homme, qui a souvent modifié les paysages originels, et à l'exposition. Le versant « endroit » (exposé au Sud), le plus propice aux cultures et à l'habitat, a été très défriché, alors que le versant « envers » (exposé au Nord), le plus souvent vide d'hommes, bénéficie d'une humidité favorisant le développement de vigoureux peuplements forestiers. Cette opposition est particulièrement marquée lorsque la vallée est orientée Ouest-Est.

Au-dessus des cultures qui s'élèvent jusqu'à 1 500 m environ, on trouve l'étage montagnard, domaine des forêts de conifères. A partir de 2 200 m, les arbres laissant la place aux alpages, c'est l'étage alpin où poussent les herbes vivaces, les myrtilles et la flore alpine. Après 3 000 m, on entre dans le domaine minéral : seuls quelques mousses et lichens s'accrochent aux rochers.

La forêt — Nous rappelons ci-dessous les caractères essentiels des spécimens les plus familiers de la tribu des conifères, si bien représentée dans les Alpes.

Épicéa — En allemand « Fichte », en italien « abete rosso ». Essence spécifiquement montagnarde, caractéristique des versants exposés au Nord (versants « envers »). Cime pointue en forme de fuseau. Aspect général hirsute, avec branches infléchies « en queue d'épagneul ». L'écorce, tirant sur le rouge, devient très crevassée avec l'âge. Aiguilles piquantes. Les cônes, pendants, tombent à maturité, tout d'une pièce, sur le sol.

Sapin — En allemand « Tanne », en italien « abete bianco ». Cime large, à pointe aplatie « en nid de cigogne » chez les arbres âgés. Écorce tirant sur le gris. Les cônes, dressés comme des chandelles, se désagrègent sur place, à maturité, en perdant leurs écailles. Les aiguilles, molles, disposées sur le même plan comme les dents d'un peigne (d'où le nom de « sapin pectiné ») présentent sur leur face interne une double ligne blanche (d'où le nom de « sapin argenté »).

Mélèze — En allemand « Lärche », en italien « larice ». C'est le seul conifère des Alpes suisses qui perde ses feuilles en hiver. Arbre caractéristique des versants ensoleillés de haute montagne, particulièrement dans le Valais et les Grisons. Cônes tout petits. L'ombre légère du feuillage, vert clair et ténu, n'interdit pas la pousse du gazon, aussi le charme des sous-bois de mélèzes est-il connu des touristes.

Pin arolle — En allemand « Arve », en italien « pino cembro ». Les nombreuses espèces de pins ont pour caractéristique commune la présentation de leurs aiguilles, réunies par une gaine écailleuse en bouquets de 2 à 5. Leurs cônes sont à écailles dures et coriaces. Le pin arolle se reconnaît à la disposition de ses ramures, profondément incurvées comme les branches d'un candélabre. Il est fréquemment mutilé par les vents.

Mélèze

La flore — On réserve le nom de plantes alpines aux végétaux qui poussent au-dessus de la limite supérieure des forêts. La floraison précoce de ces espèces, vivaces et de petite taille, est commandée par la brièveté de la période végétative (juin-août). Le développement disproportionné de la fleur par rapport au reste de la plante et sa belle coloration s'expliquent par la richesse de la lumière des hautes altitudes en rayons ultraviolets.

Des sites adéquats – En montagne, les plantes ne poussent pas n'importe où : aux unes il faut un sol calcaire, à d'autres un sol siliceux ; un éboulis, une fente rocheuse, une tourbière ont des hôtes bien différents, en fonction des conditions de vie qu'ils leur dispensent. A chaque emplacement type correspond ainsi une espèce végétale particulière, ou une association d'espèces – toujours les mêmes – également capables d'y subsister.

Ancolie des Alpes   Gentiane pourpre   Lis martagon   Lis orangé

Protection de la flore alpine – La cueillette de certaines fleurs des Alpes menacées de disparition (cyclamen, aster des alpes, primevère, edelweiss) est sévèrement réglementée en Suisse.

Le climat alpin

Comparé aux conditions climatiques régnant dans les plaines voisines, le climat alpin apparaît infiniment contrasté, suivant les différences d'altitude, les formes de relief, l'exposition.
Certains phénomènes météorologiques comme les brises et le föhn ne laisseront pas indifférents les touristes.

Les brises – Pendant la saison chaude, les décalages qui se produisent journellement entre le refroidissement et le réchauffement des différents paliers d'une vallée montagnarde engendrent des vents locaux, les brises, de mécanisme analogue à celui des brises de terre et de mer.
A la fin de la matinée, l'air chaud et dilaté des vallées remonte les couloirs naturels qui lui offrent un passage vers les hauteurs et vient provoquer la formation de nuages autour des sommets. Cette augmentation de la nébulosité, au cours de l'après-midi, est un gage de beau temps stable (elle doit cependant inciter les promeneurs à monter aux belvédères de très bon matin). Vers cinq heures de l'après-midi, cette « brise de vallée » cesse de souffler : c'est maintenant au tour de la « brise de montagne », froide et généralement plus violente, de balayer en sens inverse la vallée.

Le föhn – Ce vent marque, pendant la saison froide, un bouleversement complet de la situation climatique des Alpes, généralement très stable à cette époque de l'année. Il sévit sous sa forme la plus brutale au Nord de la chaîne, dans les hautes vallées de l'Aar et de la Reuss.
Le phénomène est déclenché par le passage d'une forte dépression barométrique le long du versant Nord des Alpes. S'étant dépouillé de son humidité sur le versant italien de la chaîne, où la pluie et les orages ne cessent alors de régner, l'air aspiré par cette dépression se précipite par-dessus la ligne de crête et, se réchauffant par compression en perdant de l'altitude, se transforme en un souffle sec et brûlant, tandis que l'atmosphère prend une transparence idéale.
En montagne, chacun est sur le qui-vive : les torrents se sont gonflés, les avalanches grondent, les eaux des grands lacs se soulèvent en tempête, les risques d'incendies catastrophiques se multiplient. Certaines communes mettent alors en application un plan de sécurité draconien (on le verra affiché dans les cafés de la haute vallée de la Reuss) allant jusqu'à l'interdiction absolue de fumer. Le föhn provoque, chez les humains, des malaises si caractérisés qu'un laboratoire bâlois a pu lancer sur le marché une médication spéciale « anti-föhn ».
En compensation, le föhn provoque la fonte des neiges et permet d'ouvrir très tôt aux troupeaux l'accès des « alpes » ; grâce à lui certaines vallées voient prospérer des espèces méditerranéennes (maïs, vigne, châtaignier) bien au-delà de leur aire normale d'extension : son apparition est un événement de premier plan dans la vie de toute la Suisse montagnarde.
En 1861, le föhn joua un rôle très actif dans l'incendie qui ravagea Glarus, chef-lieu du canton du même nom.

LE JURA SUISSE

Le Jura, qui culmine à 1 723 m au Crêt de la Neige, en France, se présente en territoire helvétique comme un faisceau de chaînons calcaires vigoureusement plissés, s'arquant sur une longueur de 200 km entre la Dôle (alt. 1 677 m) et le Lägern (alt. 859 m — au-dessus de Baden). Alors que le Jura s'abaisse du côté de la plaine de la Saône en un gigantesque escalier de plateaux, les dernières rides du massif forment au-dessus du Plateau *(voir ci-dessous)* un rempart continu, s'élevant d'un seul élan à plus de 1 000 m d'altitude, face à l'admirable décor des Alpes bernoises et du massif du Mont-Blanc.

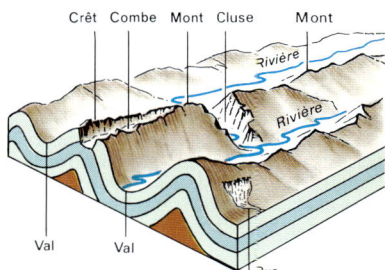

Coupe théorique d'un plissement jurassien

Comme en France, les frais paysages de la montagne jurassienne dévoilent une structure régulièrement plissée, héritée des mouvements de l'écorce terrestre qui ont fait surgir, à l'époque tertiaire, la chaîne des Alpes.

Mais à côté de cette « houle figée » de « vals » et de « monts », il y a encore place, de ce côté de la frontière, pour de hauts plateaux à peine moutonnés, comme celui des Franches Montagnes *(voir à ce nom)*. Les attaques de l'érosion ont développé dans ce socle

Les **vals** parallèles sont séparés par les **monts**. Les balafres de l'érosion au flanc des monts forment les **ruz** (terme tiré du nom du Val de Ruz — voir à ce nom).
La **cluse** entaille transversalement un mont et fait communiquer deux vals.
La **combe** se creuse longitudinalement au sommet d'un mont ; ses rebords escarpés sont appelés **crêts**.

rocheux tout un réseau de coupures, de bassins intérieurs et dégagent, à la grande satisfaction du touriste, des escarpements rocheux souvent inattendus.

LE PLATEAU OU MOYEN-PAYS

Le Plateau suisse s'allonge entre les Alpes et le Jura, du lac Léman au lac de Constance, formant un glacis en pente douce à la surface duquel s'est accumulée la masse de débris arrachés aux Alpes. La disposition du réseau hydrographique de l'Aare montre que tout le drainage se fait, ici, au profit du Rhin, par une gouttière creusée au pied de la dernière ride du Jura. Avant les glaciations quaternaires, le Rhône filait dans cette dépression que jalonnent aujourd'hui un chapelet de lacs (lacs de Bienne et de Neuchâtel) et de zones marécageuses.

En fait, le Plateau se présente comme une région de collines, accidentée : ravins, vallées à méandres encaissés. Le Plateau rassemble les centres vitaux de l'activité agricole suisse. Les cités les plus populeuses de la Confédération s'y concentrent.

Pour organiser vous-même vos itinéraires :
  – Tout d'abord consultez la carte des p. 5 à 7. Elle indique les parcours décrits, les régions touristiques, les principales villes et curiosités.
  – Reportez-vous ensuite aux descriptions, à partir de la p. 38.
    Au départ des principaux centres,
    des buts de promenades sont proposés sous le titre Excursion.
  – En outre les **cartes Michelin** n^{os} *216, 217, 218, 219* et *427* signalent les routes pittoresques, les sites et les monuments intéressants, les points de vue, les rivières, les forêts...

Un peu d'histoire

L'Helvétie primitive – Colonisé par les Romains dès le 1er s. avant J.-C., occupé plus tard par les Barbares – Burgondes et Alamans – dont les caractères ethniques et les tempéraments différents se retrouvent aujourd'hui chez les Suisses romands et les Suisses alémaniques, le territoire actuel de la Confédération fait partie, au Moyen Âge, du Saint Empire Romain Germanique. L'affaiblissement progressif de ce dernier permet à certaines dynasties féodales, telles que les familles de Zähringen, de Savoie, de Kybourg et de Habsbourg, d'apparaître, au début du 13e s., comme de véritables puissances territoriales. Cependant, comme en Allemagne, certaines cités (Zurich, Berne), objets de la sollicitude du lointain Empereur, bénéficient déjà du statut de villes libres, tandis que les petites cellules montagnardes isolées s'administrent de façon à peu près autonome.

Le Pacte fondamental – Dans les vallées alpestres proches du lac des Quatre-Cantons – les « Waldstätten » d'Uri, Schwytz et Unterwald –, la gestion des baillis nommés par les Habsbourg suscite un vif mécontentement. Le 1er août 1291, les représentants des trois communautés concluent un pacte d'assistance mutuelle. Ce pacte est le véritable acte de naissance de la Confédération helvétique. La version traditionnelle de ces événements est plus héroïque *(voir détails à Vierwaldstätter See)*.

La lutte contre les Habsbourg – Le 14e s. est marqué par une lutte permanente des « cantons primitifs » contre les Habsbourg-Autriche. Opposée aux lourds escadrons recrutés parmi la fleur de la noblesse de Haute-Allemagne et les féodaux locaux, la piétaille confédérée triomphe à Morgarten (1315), à Laupen (1339), à Sempach (1386) et à Näfels (1388). Entre-temps, plusieurs villes ou « Länder » (communautés paysannes) se sont agrégées au premier noyau : Lucerne en 1332, Zurich en 1351, Glaris et Zoug en 1352, Berne en 1353. Dans l'histoire de Suisse, cette formation est dite « des VIII cantons ».

L'expansion territoriale – Ces faits d'armes donnent aux cantons le goût de l'aventure, et le désir d'étendre leur influence politique à des régions plus lointaines. Le prestige militaire suisse trouve une consécration retentissante dans les victoires de Grandson et de Morat remportées sur le duc de Bourgogne, Charles le Téméraire, en 1476. Sur les théâtres d'opération d'Italie, les belligérants se disputent le concours des contingents helvétiques et les Confédérés ne se font pas faute de se faire payer en fructueuses compensations territoriales. Mais la politique antifrançaise trop ambitieuse inspirée par le cardinal Schiner *(voir à ce nom)* place ses compatriotes dans le camp des vaincus de Marignan. Une alliance perpétuelle est signée avec François Ier. La Suisse se retire désormais de la scène politique internationale, tout en continuant à fournir aux cours d'Europe leurs contingents d'élite.

Cependant, les derniers liens de dépendance avec l'Empire ont été rompus. Au début du 16e s., le puzzle fédéral apparaît augmenté de Fribourg, Soleure, Bâle, Schaffhouse et Appenzell. Dans les vides de cet assemblage des « XIII cantons » s'encastrent les territoires des « pays alliés » (Valais, ligues grisonnes) et ceux des « bailliages » (Thurgovie, Tessin) tenus en tutelle par un ou plusieurs cantons.

De la Réforme à l'invasion – Trouvant en Suisse, grâce aux travaux critiques d'humanistes comme Érasme, un terrain favorable à son expansion, la Réforme, prêchée par Zwingli *(voir à ce nom)* et Calvin, propagée par les armes bernoises dans toute la Suisse romande, pénètre profondément l'organisme encore mal soudé des XIII cantons. Soucieux d'éviter en leur sein des sécessions catastrophiques, les Confédérés se gardent de participer aux luttes religieuses qui ensanglantent les États voisins (guerres de Religion, guerre de Trente Ans). Ainsi prend corps la tradition de la neutralité suisse, que fortifie la reconnaissance en bonne et due forme de la souveraineté helvétique par les signataires du traité de Westphalie (1648).

Sous la Révolution française, la Suisse se voit dotée par le Directoire d'un statut de république centralisée et unitaire (la « République helvétique ») tout à fait inadapté à son tempérament ; elle devient un champ de bataille où se heurtent Français et Alliés (Autrichiens, Prussiens et Russes). Les désordres intérieurs et les factions sévissent dans le pays. Bonaparte laisse pourrir la situation et impose sa médiation (Acte de Médiation – 1803). La nature fédérative de l'État helvétique est reconnue, mais la triple égalité « des cantons entre eux, des habitants des villes entre eux, des habitants des villes et de ceux de la campagne » est proclamée. Six nouveaux cantons (Argovie, St-Gall, Grisons, république du Tessin, Thurgovie, Vaud) accèdent à la majorité politique. Cependant, avec l'hégémonie française, la Suisse se trouve amputée du Valais, du Jura. Les conscriptions, les effets économiques désastreux du blocus continental sont amèrement ressentis dans tout le pays.

Du Pacte de 1815 à la Constitution de 1848 – Après la chute de l'Empire, l'adhésion de trois nouveaux territoires – Valais, républiques de Genève et de Neuchâtel – porte à 22 le nombre des cantons. Au Congrès de Vienne, les grandes puissances proclament la neutralité perpétuelle de la Suisse. Mais des troubles intérieurs menacent les fondements de l'État : les profondes divisions religieuses, en

1846, aboutissent à la conclusion d'une Ligue séparatiste entre cantons catholiques, le Sonderbund. Réunie à Berne, la Diète, groupant tous les autres cantons, proclame la dissolution du **Sonderbund** et intervient par les armes. Le général Dufour, chef de l'armée fédérale, met fin aux hostilités dans les délais les plus brefs et ouvre les voies à une réconciliation générale. La Constitution de 1848, établie au lendemain de ces événements et révisée en 1874, puis en 1978, définit l'organisation politique encore en vigueur de nos jours (lire La démocratie en action, quelques pages plus loin).

La Suisse contemporaine – La Suisse n'a jamais cessé de maintenir sa neutralité. Mais elle a dû, pour cela, monter une garde vigilante à ses frontières lors des grands conflits internationaux. Cette neutralité, la Suisse l'a mise à profit pour développer un rôle humanitaire qui l'honore : en 1863 est créée, sous l'impulsion d'Henri Dunant, la Croix-Rouge Internationale ; depuis le début du siècle, Genève a été choisie comme siège de nombreux organismes internationaux.

LANGUES ET RELIGIONS

La coexistence de plusieurs groupes linguistiques et confessionnels au sein d'une même communauté nationale est une des réussites du régime fédéral helvétique. Depuis le 19e s., l'industrialisation du pays, en provoquant de nombreux mouvements de population, surtout dans les villes, a rendu impensable toute manifestation affichée d'intolérance.

Les races et les langues – *La majorité linguistique de chaque canton est donnée plus loin, dans le chapitre : Les cantons.* A la chute de l'empire romain, au 5e s., le territoire actuel de la Suisse romande est occupée par les Burgondes, chassés de la Gaule, qui assimilent progressivement les modes de vie de la civilisation latine et adoptent la religion chrétienne (plus exactement l'hérésie arienne).

Peu avant, d'autres Barbares, venus du Nord, les Alamans ou Alémanes, avaient déjà envahi le Plateau mais sont refoulés par les Burgondes jusqu'à la **Sarine** : ce dernier cours d'eau (« Saane » en allemand) est devenu, par le rôle frontière qu'il assume, le symbole même de la pluralité linguistique de la Suisse.

L'un des points les plus intéressants de la ligne de démarcation entre le français et l'allemand est la ville de Bienne, cité bilingue par excellence.

Les Suisses de langue allemande constituent 64 % de la population helvétique. Le « **Schwyzerdütsch** », patois suisse-allemand du groupe souabe comme l'alsacien, aux nombreuses variétés locales, est utilisé dans la conversation courante, l'emploi de l'allemand classique étant réservé aux relations officielles.

Le groupe de langue française (18 %) voit, par contre, ses dialectes tomber en désuétude. L'italien (11 %) est parlé dans la presque totalité du Tessin et dans une partie des Grisons. Le **romanche**, qui n'est pas un patois mais une langue de souche latine, n'est utilisé que par 7 % des Suisses, groupés dans le canton des Grisons (en Engadine et dans l'Oberland grison).

L'allemand, le français et l'italien sont considérés comme langues officielles de la Confédération et employés par les autorités et les administrations fédérales. Au moins deux de ces langues sont enseignées obligatoirement dès l'école primaire. Le romanche a été reconnu comme quatrième langue nationale en 1938, grâce aux efforts de la Ligue romanche pour développer cette langue par l'enseignement et la presse.

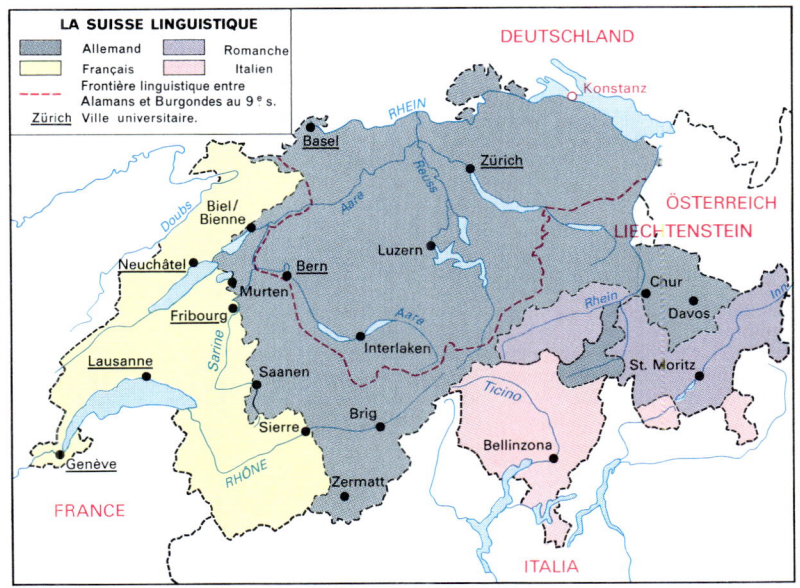

La question religieuse – *La majorité confessionnelle de chaque canton est donnée plus loin, dans le chapitre : Les cantons.* Jusqu'au milieu du 19e s., la question religieuse s'est posée avec acuité et a paru longtemps être un obstacle à l'unité de la Confédération. La guerre du Sonderbund *(voir le chapitre : Un peu d'histoire)* en fut la preuve. Mais depuis 1848 la tolérance la plus complète est de règle.

Actuellement, les protestants représentent 44,33 % de la population d'origine helvétique, les catholiques romains 47,60 %. La Suisse romande est en majorité protestante, à l'exception des cantons de Fribourg et du Valais. La Suisse centrale est catholique, celle du Nord et de l'Est protestante.

Le tempérament protestant, en Suisse, dans ce qu'il a de foncièrement démocratique et patriotique, doit beaucoup plus à la vigoureuse personnalité de Zwingli *(voir à ce nom)* qu'à la rigueur doctrinale de Calvin, celui-ci ayant fait école surtout à Genève. L'organisation des églises protestantes, assez lâche, reproduit la structure fédéraliste du pays et laisse subsister, à côté d'églises d'État subventionnées, des églises vivant des dons des fidèles.

Les catholiques romains dépendent de six diocèses : Bâle (évêché à Soleure), Lausanne-Genève-Fribourg (évêché à Fribourg), Sion, Coire, St-Gall, Lugano. Le clergé régulier se répartit entre un petit nombre de vastes abbayes, telles que St-Maurice, Einsiedeln ou Engelberg.

Enfin, de nombreuses églises dissidentes, catholiques ou protestantes, et sectes philosophiques ont trouvé en Suisse un terrain favorable.

LES SUISSES ILLUSTRES

Des héros de légende aux grands artistes... Des réformateurs religieux aux savants... Nombreux sont ces Suisses illustres. Il nous suffira d'en citer quelques-uns, parmi ceux ayant acquis un renom international.

14e s. : Guillaume **Tell** ; Arnold de **Winkelried**.
15e s. : Saint Nicolas de **Flüe**.
15e/16e s. : Mathieu **Schiner** ; Ulrich **Zwingli** ; Joachim von Watt, dit **Vadian** ; Theophrastus Bombastus von Hohenheim, dit **Paracelse**, médecin-alchimiste ; François de **Bonivard**.
16e/17e s. : Domenico **Fontana**, architecte, et son élève Carlo **Maderno**.
17e s. : Kaspar Jodok von **Stockalper**.
17e/18e s. : Jacques et Jean **Bernoulli**, mathématiciens.
18e s. : Daniel **Bernoulli**, mathématicien ; Jean-Étienne **Liotard**, peintre ; Leonhard **Euler**, mathématicien ; Jean-Jacques **Rousseau** ; Salomon **Gessner**, poète et peintre ; Horace Bénédict de **Saussure**, physicien.
18e/19e s. : Jacques **Necker**, financier et homme d'État ; Johann Caspar **Lavater**, philosophe ; Johann David **Wyss**, écrivain ; Johann Heinrich **Pestalozzi** ; Frédéric César de **Laharpe** ; Guillaume Henri **Dufour**, général ; Léopold **Robert**, peintre ; Albert Bitzius, dit Jeremias **Gotthelf**, écrivain ; Rodolphe **Toepffer**, dessinateur.
19e s. : Louis **Agassiz**, géologue ; Jacob **Burckhardt**, philosophe ; Gottfried **Keller**, poète ; Henri Frédéric **Amiel**, écrivain.
19e/20e s. : Arnold **Böcklin**, peintre ; Henri **Dunant**, fondateur de la Croix-Rouge ; César **Ritz**, homme d'affaires et hôtelier ; Carl **Spitteler**, poète ; Ferdinand **Hodler**, peintre ; Ferdinand de **Saussure**, linguiste ; Félix **Vallotton**, peintre ; Henri **Guisan**, général ; Carl Gustav **Jung**, psychanalyste ; Charles Ferdinand **Ramuz**, écrivain ; Adrien **Wettach**, plus connu sous le nom de **Grock**, clown de renommée internationale ; Ernest **Ansermet**, chef d'orchestre ; Frédéric Sauser, dit Blaise **Cendrars**, écrivain ; Édouard Jeanneret-Gris, dit **Le Corbusier**, architecte ; Frank **Martin** et Arthur **Honegger**, musiciens, Michel **Simon**, comédien.
20e s. : Alberto **Giacometti**, peintre et sculpteur ; Hans **Erni**, peintre ; Jean **Tinguely**, sculpteur..., Mario **Botta**, architecte.

A cette liste peuvent s'ajouter certains Suisses d'origine s'étant choisi une nouvelle patrie : tels les écrivains français (outre J.-J. Rousseau lui-même) Benjamin Constant et Mme de Staël... Ou, à l'inverse, des Suisses d'adoption : les peintres Conrad Witz, Holbein le Jeune, Paul Klee, le plasticien Daniel **Spoerri**, l'écrivain Hermann Hesse, le cinéaste Charlie Chaplin, l'écrivain Georges Simenon..., le négociant de cigares Zino Davidoff.

LA CONQUÊTE DES SOMMETS

Les multiples épisodes, dramatiques ou glorieux, de la lutte engagée entre l'homme et la montagne, n'ont cessé de passionner l'opinion. Si les victoires enregistrées au siècle dernier sur les sommets réputés les plus inaccessibles ont détruit peu à peu la crainte superstitieuse dont l'entourait l'imagination populaire *(voir le Pilate)*, l'alpinisme compte encore, à côté d'adeptes de plus en plus nombreux, bien des détracteurs.

La Suisse, qui peut s'enorgueillir de tant de « 4 000 », constitue un terrain de choix pour l'alpiniste. On raconte que, dès le 14e s., six ecclésiastiques de Lucerne entreprirent l'escalade du Pilate, non sans subir, à la suite de cet exploit, les foudres de leur supérieur. L'une des premières ascensions inscrite au palmarès de la Suisse est celle du Titlis effectuée en 1744 par quatre paysans d'Engelberg. En 1792, Spescha, moine de Disentis, triomphe de l'Oberalpstock. L'année 1811 est marquée par une remarquable expédition : les **frères Meyer**, riches négociants d'Aarau, gagnent le Valais par le Grimsel et, partant du Lötschental, escaladent la **Jungfrau** (4 158 m).

Parallèlement, la Savoie et l'Autriche s'attaquent à leurs points culminants. En 1786, le guide **Jacques Balmat**, de Chamonix, atteint le sommet du **Mont Blanc** et renouvelle son expédition en 1787, en compagnie du physicien suisse de Saussure *(voir guide Vert Michelin Alpes du Nord)*. Les Autrichiens, de leur côté, effectuent, en 1800, la première ascension du Grossglockner (3 797 m).
En 1813, le Breithorn (4 164 m) est vaincu à son tour, puis le Tödi en 1824 et le Piz Bernina (4 049 m) en 1850. Jusqu'alors, les Suisses s'étaient en quelque sorte réservé le monopole de ces performances. A partir de 1840, les Anglais vont inscrire à leur tour, dans la chronique de l'alpinisme, de célèbres « premières » : le **Stockhorn** en 1842 et le **Wasenhorn** en 1844, par **J.-D. Forbes**; la **Pointe Dufour** (4 634 m) en 1855, par les trois frères **Smyth**; l'**Eiger** en 1858, par **Ch. Barrington**; et surtout, en 1865, le **Cervin** (4 478 m) par **Edward Whymper**. Ces victoires, auxquelles s'ajouteront celles des Français et des Italiens, font du 19ᵉ s. la période classique de l'alpinisme.

La conquête des pentes — Introduit dans la Confédération à la fin du siècle dernier, le **ski alpin**, sport essentiellement populaire en Suisse, tirant parti d'un incomparable équipement en remontées mécaniques, permet aux citadins de retrouver les joies de l'effort physique, de la nature et du grand air.
Les champs de neige helvétiques ont amené les initiateurs (anglais) de ce ski de vitesse à codifier les formules de base des principales épreuves de compétition (course de descente, slalom) et à créer un «climat» britannique dans des stations comme Mürren ou Zermatt. Les cours de l'école officielle suisse de ski, quant à eux, reflètent le souci constant d'élever la moyenne de l'ensemble des élèves avant celui de former de brillants sujets. De même, le **ski de randonnée** est mis à la portée du plus grand nombre, grâce à de nombreux programmes de courses accompagnées. Au printemps, la « Haute Route » du Valais, la traversée des glaciers des Alpes bernoises, la descente de la Diavolezza (massif de la Bernina) rassemblent une foule de participants.

Une économie créatrice

Les progrès de la circulation et l'accroissement de la population ont orienté l'activité économique de la Suisse vers l'élevage spécialisé et l'industrie.
Les besoins croissants ont amené le pays à combler par l'importation l'insuffisance de sa production agricole qui représente seulement la moitié de la consommation totale.

Élevage — Dans ce pays montagneux, l'agriculture est défavorisée par la rudesse du climat et par la proportion des terrains improductifs (25,6 %) due à l'extension des lacs, des glaciers, des parois rocheuses stériles. Dans les régions plus hospitalières, les cultures fourragères, les pâturages et l'élevage ont pris l'avantage sur les labours qu'entravaient le climat humide et le terrain trop accidenté.
Deux races de bovins sont particulièrement connues : la race brune de Schwytz, et la race tachetée rouge du Simmental, la plus nombreuse.
Les efforts se sont concentrés sur la production laitière, et une industrie est née de cette spécialisation : fabrication du beurre, du fromage, des conserves de lait, du chocolat au lait (Lindt, Nestlé, Suchard, Tobler) et de la farine lactée, dont l'exportation a solidement établi la réputation à l'étranger.

Économie forestière — Les forêts couvrent un peu plus d'un million d'hectares (soit le quart de la superficie du pays), avec une proportion de 70 % de conifères *(voir Physionomie du pays : La végétation alpine)*, sapins en majorité. En plus de leur irremplaçable rôle écologique, elles fournissent à la Suisse l'une des rares matières premières locales pouvant suffire presque entièrement à ses besoins.

Industrie — État continental, isolée par de véritables barrières montagneuses, pauvre en ressources minières, la Confédération ne semblait pas appelée à un avenir industriel. Elle a suppléé à l'insuffisance des conditions naturelles grâce à l'ingéniosité et à l'activité de ses habitants. Pour vaincre l'obstacle de la montagne, ils ont foré de longs tunnels, construit des voies ferrées en rampes et en courbes, inventé le chemin de fer à crémaillère permettant de s'élever à plus de 3 000 m *(voir à Gornergrat)*; un réseau routier constamment amélioré complète cet équipement.
Placée au carrefour des grandes voies de commerce, la Suisse est devenue la « plaque tournante » de l'Europe. Elle s'est orientée vers les fabrications exigeant une main-d'œuvre qualifiée mais ne demandant qu'un minimum de matières premières, et elle s'est imposée sur le marché international par la qualité de ses produits.
L'activité industrielle est dirigée par des techniciens de valeur secondés par des équipes de chercheurs. Disposant d'importants capitaux, servie par un personnel compétent, elle se manifeste dans les domaines mécanique, chimique, électrique et textile.

Les machines — Les métaux sont transformés en machines-outils, destinées spécialement aux industries horlogère et textile, moteurs Diesel (Baden, Zurich), locomotives (Winterthur), machines agricoles, machines à imprimer, pièces détachées pour avions. Les appareils de précision (instruments d'optique, machines à calculer, appareils scientifiques et médicaux) et l'important matériel réclamé par l'essor de l'électricité industrielle satisfont aux exigences de la technique contemporaine.

Les véhicules à moteur — La Suisse n'a pas d'industrie automobile propre, sauf pour les poids lourds (camions et autocars N.A.W. – regroupement de Saurer, Berna et F.B.W. –, MOWAG).

L'industrie horlogère — C'est après le secteur des machines et avec celui des produits chimiques l'une des industries exportatrices les plus importantes du pays.

Les textiles — Le travail de la soie et la broderie sont pratiqués dans l'Est et le centre du pays. Les procédés chimiques de fabrication des tissus synthétiques (Lucerne) ont fait naître une nouvelle industrie qui tend à supplanter celle de la soie naturelle.

Les produits chimiques — Le travail des textiles, nécessitant des recherches dans le domaine des colorants, a donné l'essor à une industrie chimique dont Bâle est le centre. Produits pharmaceutiques, colorants, parfums sont exportés. En 1996, la fusion des deux sociétés Sandoz et Ciba crée un nouveau géant mondial, Novartis.

Énergie — En Suisse, la « houille blanche » représente actuellement la principale source d'énergie. Or, on prévoit que l'exploitation méthodique des disponibilités hydro-électriques, qui a déjà exigé des efforts titanesques *(voir à Barrage de la Grande-Dixence)*, aura épuisé intégralement ses possibilités avant l'an 2000. En septembre 1990 la Suisse s'est prononcée, par la voix des urnes, en faveur d'un moratoire interdisant pendant les dix années à venir toute construction de centrale nucléaire. Aussi afin de faire face à des besoins sans cesse accrus, le pays va-t-il poursuivre l'amélioration et le développement de son programme hydro-électrique.

Tourisme — Comme pourvoyeur de devises, le tourisme constitue une véritable industrie. Cependant, sensible aux crises aussi bien qu'aux conditions atmosphériques, l'importance de son apport peut varier d'une année à l'autre.

Banque — La prospérité économique de la Suisse, sa stabilité politique et monétaire, l'esprit d'épargne de la population ont favorisé l'accumulation des capitaux dans les banques. L'importance des fonds étrangers qui lui sont confiés profite d'abord à l'industrie et au commerce nationaux. D'autre part, ces capitaux permettent à la Confédération de financer les entreprises qu'elle a dû établir en dehors de son territoire afin d'échapper aux mesures protectionnistes de l'étranger (industries textiles et alimentaires) et, par leur placement dans des affaires et des titres étrangers, de rétablir en partie l'équilibre de sa balance commerciale compromis par l'excédent des importations sur les exportations.

Autre manifestation de l'esprit de prévoyance de la population, **l'assurance** joue un rôle de premier plan dans l'économie de la Suisse. Les compagnies privées d'assurance et de réassurance ont des bureaux presque partout dans le monde.

Un bref palmarès suisse — On doit à des Suisses : les vitamines, le DDT, la première locomotive à crémaillère d'Europe (celle du Rigi), la première turbine à gaz pratiquement utilisable, l'incorporation du lait au chocolat et à la farine, la formule moderne de l'Assurance-Vie, la montre automatique, le chronographe sportif, la cellophane, etc.

La démocratie en action

La Constitution de 1848, révisée en 1874, puis en 1978, a remplacé par un État fédératif moderne l'ancienne confédération de cantons qui pratiquaient une politique individualiste, chacun possédant sa monnaie propre, ses postes, ses douanes.

Les communes — Liberté individuelle, liberté de croyance et de conscience, liberté de presse et d'association sont reconnues par la Constitution qui fait de tout Suisse âgé de vingt ans révolus un citoyen actif, électeur et éligible. Si les femmes ont acquis le droit de vote sur le plan fédéral en 1971, leur participation n'est pas admise partout en matières cantonales et communales. Cependant, tout le régime repose sur le principe de la souveraineté des citoyens, qui, vivant dans quelque 3 000 communes, forment le fondement même de la volonté nationale.

Dans tous les domaines, la commune est habilitée à trancher en première instance, le canton n'intervenant qu'en appel. Particularité très révélatrice : l'acquisition de la nationalité helvétique par un étranger requiert l'admission préalable du postulant dans le corps des « bourgeois » d'une commune déterminée.

L'autorité cantonale — Les cantons ont conservé chacun leur souveraineté politique, avec leur constitution et leur législation propres. Dans chacun des 23 cantons *(voir ci-après : Les cantons)*, le pouvoir exécutif est détenu par le Conseil d'État, le pouvoir législatif par le **Grand Conseil**.

Les pratiques de la démocratie directe survivent encore dans quelques cantons de montagne (Appenzell, Glaris et Unterwald), où l'on peut voir se réunir chaque printemps, en plein air, l'ensemble des citoyens actifs, appelés à voter à main levée sur

Landsgemeinde à Glaris

toutes les questions intéressant la collectivité : ce sont les **«Landsgemeinden»** *(tableau des principales manifestations en fin de guide)* accompagnées d'un grand déploiement de cérémonies religieuses, de serments et de proclamations solennelles.

Les autorités fédérales — Le pouvoir législatif est exercé par deux assemblées, le **Conseil national** et le **Conseil des États** ; l'exécutif par un collège de sept membres, le **Conseil fédéral**. Les deux assemblées législatives réunies forment l'Assemblée fédérale. Le Conseil national représente le peuple : ses membres sont élus à raison d'un député pour un peu plus de 30 000 habitants (200 membres), chaque canton ou demi-canton obtenant au moins un siège. Le Conseil des États, mandataire des cantons, compte 46 députés, soit deux par canton quelle qu'en soit la population.
Ce système bicaméral, qui évoque les institutions parlementaires américaines, sauvegarde, dans toute la mesure du possible, les intérêts des petites communautés.
Le pouvoir exécutif est confié au Conseil fédéral : élus pour quatre ans (par l'Assemblée fédérale), ses sept membres administrent chacun un département, c'est-à-dire un ministère. L'élection annuelle du président, qui porte le titre de «président de la Confédération», et celle du vice-président, apparaît comme une simple formalité, le vice-président étant toujours appelé à devenir président et son successeur étant nommé selon un tour établi par convention. On peut déceler dans ces usages la méfiance de l'opinion suisse vis-à-vis des personnalités trop brillantes et de tout ce qui peut rappeler un régime présidentiel.

Le peuple souverain — Les décisions de l'Assemblée fédérale ne sont prises qu'après un vote favorable des deux chambres. Mais là encore intervient la souveraineté populaire : il suffit que dans les 90 jours qui suivent la décision de l'Assemblée soient réunies 50 000 signatures de citoyens actifs pour que le peuple entier soit appelé à décider de l'adoption ou du rejet définitif de la loi. C'est le **droit de référendum**, qui joue surtout dans un sens conservateur. «Le référendum c'est le droit que nous avons de dire non quand Berne a dit oui», fait-on dire au Vaudois moyen. Le peuple dispose encore du **droit d'initiative :** 100 000 citoyens peuvent demander la modification d'articles de la Constitution ou l'adoption d'articles nouveaux.
Ainsi la volonté populaire peut s'exprimer à tous les stades de la vie politique et exercer un contrôle permanent sur la bonne marche des institutions du pays.
Début décembre 1992, le peuple suisse, appelé aux urnes, répond par la négative au projet de rejoindre l'Espace économique européen (EEE), premier pas vers la Communauté puis, l'Union européenne.

LES CANTONS

Sous l'écusson : le nom français du canton et son abréviation officielle (utilisée pour l'immatriculation des automobiles).
Sur la carte : les limites des cantons et leur capitale.
Dans le répertoire : le nom français et, s'il y a lieu, le nom du canton dans la langue majoritaire, la superficie, la population, la majorité linguistique et la majorité confessionnelle.
Abréviations :
A. : *allemand,* **F.** : *français,* **I.** : *italien,* **P.** : *protestant,* **C.** : *catholique.*

Appenzell — Rhodes-Intérieures (AI) : 172 km^2 – 13 870 h. (**A.-C.**).
— Rhodes-Extérieures (AR) : 243 km^2 – 52 229 h. (**A.-P.**).
On retrouve, dans l'écusson d'Appenzell, l'ours, emblème de l'abbaye de St-Gall.

Argovie (Aargau) — 1 404 km^2 – 507 508 h. (**A.-P.**).
Ce nom signifie pays de l'Aar, rivière figurée par des lignes ondées. Les trois étoiles symbolisent les trois territoires dont le regroupement a formé le canton.

Bâle (Basel) – Bâle-Campagne (BL) : 428 km² – 233 488 h. (**A.-P.**).
– Bâle-Ville (BS) : 37 km² – 198 428 h. (**A.-P.**).
La ville fut le siège d'un prince-évêque. Aussi ses armoiries ont-elles gardé la crosse épiscopale (rouge pour Bâle-Campagne, noire pour Bâle-Ville).

Berne (Bern) – 6 050 km² – 958 192 h. (**A.-P.**). *Origine du blason : voir à Berne.*

Fribourg – 1 670 km² – 213 571 h. (**F.-C.**).
Fribourg (« Ville libre ») porte sur son blason le blanc et le noir, couleurs des ducs de Zähringen.

Genève – 282 km² – 379 590 h. (**F.-P.**). *Origine du blason : voir à Genève.*

Glaris (Glarus) – 684 km² – 38 508 h. (**A.-P.**).
Ses armoiries représentent saint Fridolin, patron du pays.

Grisons (Graubünden) – 7 106 km² – 173 890 h. (**A.-P.**).
L'histoire moderne des Grisons – l'ancienne Rhétie – commence avec l'alliance de trois « Ligues » constituées aux 14ᵉ et 15ᵉ s. sur les débris de la féodalité.
La ligue de la Maison-Dieu groupait sous l'écu chargé du « bouquetin saillant de sable » les sujets de l'évêque et du chapitre de Coire (Coire et ses environs, l'Engadine).
La ligue Grise (écu mi-parti de sable et d'argent) – d'où les Grisons tirent leur nom – avait pour domaine le bassin supérieur du Rhin.
La bannière « écartelée d'azur et d'or à la croix de l'un à l'autre » de la ligue des Dix-Juridictions flottait dans le Prättigau, région de Davos et d'Arosa.

Jura – 837 km² – 66 163 h. (**F.-C.**). *Origine du blason : voir à Delémont.*
Canton constitué le 24 septembre 1978 par une votation nationale approuvant un arrêté fédéral du 9 mars 1978. Ses trois districts, de Delémont (la capitale), Porrentruy et des Franches Montagnes, formaient auparavant l'extrémité Nord du canton de Berne.

Lucerne (Luzern) – 1 492 km² – 326 268 h. (**A.-C.**).

Neuchâtel – 797 km² – 163 985 h. (**F.-P.**).
Le blason actuel date de la proclamation, en 1848, de la République neuchâteloise ; la croix blanche sur fond rouge rappelle l'adhésion à la Confédération.

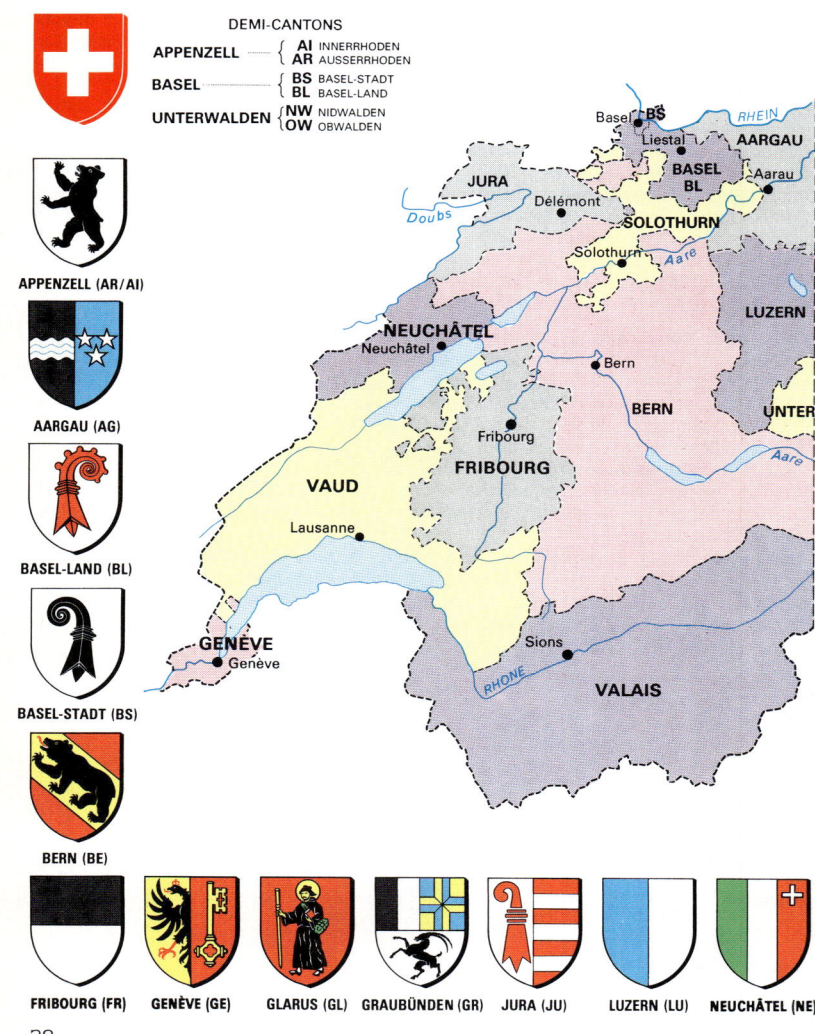

St-Gall (St-Gallen) – 2 014 km² – 427 501 h. (**A.-C.**).
Le faisceau qui orne l'écusson de St-Gall rappelle l'union des territoires qui, en 1803, constituèrent ce nouveau canton.

Schaffhouse (Schaffhausen) – 298 km² – 72 160 h. (**A.-P.**).
Schaffhouse signifierait « maison du mouton » (de Schaf : mouton).

Schwytz (Schwyz) – 908 km² – 111 964 h. (**A.-C.**).
A l'origine entièrement rouge, l'écusson de Schwytz fut timbré par la suite d'une croix blanche et adopté par la Confédération comme drapeau fédéral.

Soleure (Solothurn) – 791 km² – 231 746 h. (**A.-C.**).

Tessin (Ticino) – 2 811 km² – 282 181 h. (**I.-C.**).

Thurgovie (Thurgau) – 1 013 km² – 209 362 h. (**A.-P.**).
Les deux lions qui figurent dans les armoiries ont été empruntés au blason des comtes de Kybourg.

Unterwald (Unterwalden) – Nidwald (NW) : 276 km² – 33 044 h. (**A.-C.**).
– Obwald (OW) : 491 km² – 29 025 h. (**A.-C.**).
Les armoiries portent les clefs de saint Pierre : celles de Nidwald sont sur fond rouge, celles d'Obwald sur fond rouge et blanc.

Uri – 1 076 km² – 34 208 h. (**A.-C.**).

Valais – 5 226 km² – 249 817 h. (**F.-C.**).
Son écusson, dont le rouge et le blanc évoquent la bannière épiscopale de Sion, est constellé de treize étoiles représentant les treize dizains (districts) du canton.

Vaud – 3 219 km² – 601 816 h. (**F.-P.**).
En 1798, lors de la fondation de la République lémanique, fut adopté le drapeau vert. En 1803, à l'occasion de l'entrée de Vaud dans la Confédération, furent adoptés le blanc et la devise « Liberté et Patrie ».

Zoug (Zug) – 239 km² – 85 546 h. (**A.-C.**).

Zurich (Zürich) – 1 729 km² – 1 179 044 h. (**A.-P.**).

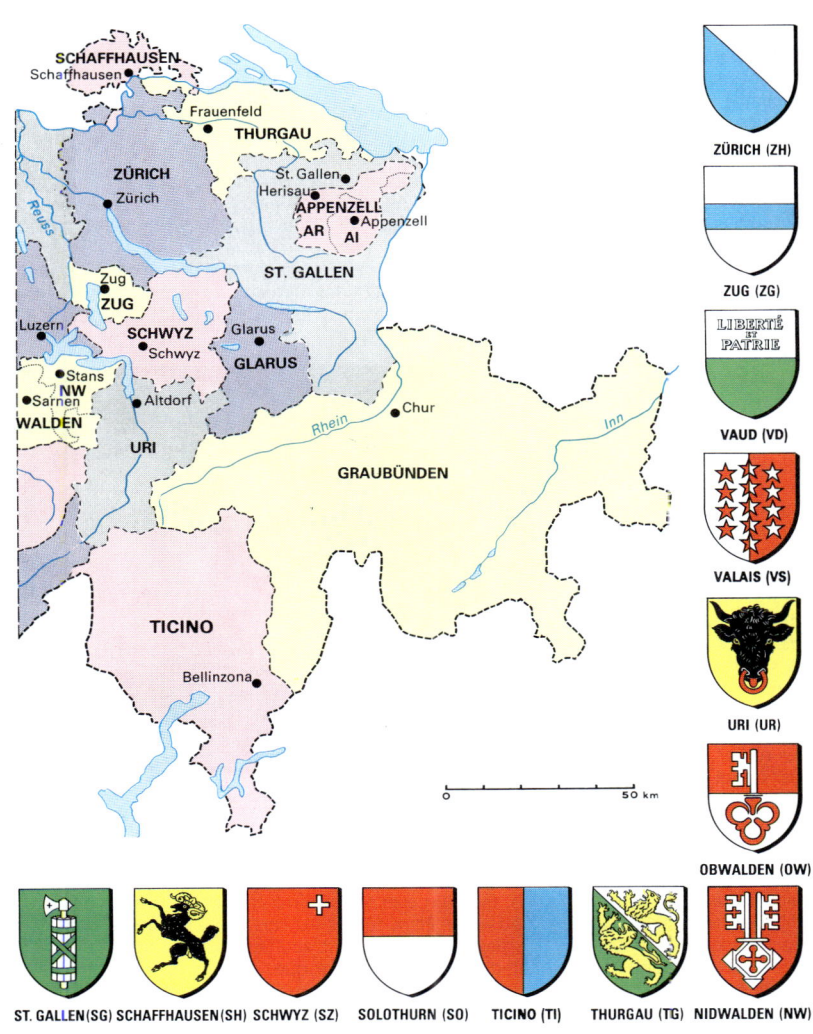

La Suisse pittoresque

TRADITIONS ET FOLKLORE

Le folklore suisse peut toujours se prévaloir d'une riche collection de costumes régionaux. Toutefois, c'est surtout en montagne que l'étranger rencontrera des populations quotidiennement fidèles à leur costume traditionnel. La Gruyère et le Valais sont, sous ce rapport, favorisés.

L'**armailli** (vacher) de la Gruyère continue à porter le « bredzon », courte veste de toile à manches ballon – héritage des modes de l'Empire – brodée de points d'épine et, aux revers, d'edelweiss. La toque de paille bordée de velours est dite « capette ». Dans toutes les régions pastorales de l'Oberland bernois se retrouvent, mais moins fréquemment, des tenues du même genre (la veste y est souvent en velours).

A Évolène, le costume de travail comporte une simple robe, un « mouchoir » rouge et blanc pour le cou, un chapeau de paille aux bords garnis de velours rabattus sur les oreilles et au fond cerclé de rubans brochés disposés en escaliers. Les jours de grandes fêtes, les Évolénardes revêtent le tablier de soie chatoyant, le « mandzon » (sorte de jaquette à manches longues) et coiffent sur un bonnet de dentelle blanche le feutre rond, extra-plat.

Anciens costumes d'Appenzell

Traditions pastorales – Elles sont encore bien vivantes dans les régions de montagne comme le Val d'Anniviers *(voir à ce nom)*, où les mouvements du bétail du village au « mayen » *(voir à ce nom)* et à « l'alpe », lorsque la neige a disparu, continuent à régler toute la vie de la population.

La montée à l'alpe (fin mai - début juin) est, sur tout le versant Nord de la chaîne, l'occasion de joyeuses et pittoresques parades : les bêtes aux cornes enrubannées et fleuries se succèdent le long des chemins, toutes cloches sonnantes, escortées des vachers, pliant sous l'attirail nécessaire à leur installation dans les chalets (les plus robustes portent sur un bâti de bois l'énorme chaudron à fromage). En Valais (Verbier, col de Balme – entre Trient et Argentière), l'arrivée au terme du voyage est marquée par des combats de vaches, à l'issue desquels la « reine » du troupeau pourra arborer la cloche géante qui lui est dévolue.

Le plein été, période de travail acharné, est peu propice aux distractions. Cependant une fête de la « Mi-Été », qui attire la foule des parents et amis, vient parfois rompre la solitude des armaillis.

La descente de l'alpe, la « désalpe », met aussi beaucoup d'animation sur les routes et dans les villages. C'est par un tel cortège que s'ouvrent les représentations en plein air de « Guillaume Tell » à Interlaken.

Montée à l'alpage

Traditions urbaines – Elles sont d'inspiration plus volontiers civique et patriotique, comme la fête de l'Escalade à Genève qui commémore l'échec savoyard de 1602 ou le « Knabenschiessen » de Zurich. Dans un esprit tout différent et plus proche des traditions rhénanes, le Carnaval de Bâle, mêlant toutes les classes de la société dans les bals masqués et autour des cortèges satiriques, fait souffler un vent de folie sur la cité d'Érasme. Sous l'anonymat d'une figurine grotesque, chacun peut donner libre cours à son humeur railleuse, en visant de préférence ses proches et ses amis, toutes conventions étant alors abolies.

Les sports nationaux – L'activité des sociétés de tir et de gymnastique, qui touche plus du tiers de la population masculine âgée de plus de 19 ans, se manifeste par des défilés martiaux de sportifs et par l'exposition des trophées de concours dans les salles d'auberge et de café.

Quant aux sports rustiques traditionnels, comme la lutte sur le pré, le lancer de la pierre, le hornuss (sport populaire qui consiste à renvoyer à l'aide d'une raquette une balle dure propulsée par l'équipe adverse au moyen d'une sorte d'arquebuse), le jeu du drapeau, ceux-ci survivent encore dans quelques fêtes villageoises de Suisse alémanique – en particulier dans l'Emmental – où l'on pourra entendre, en outre, les accents caverneux de l'immense trompe dite « cor des Alpes » et les vocalises des yodleurs.

LE PAYSAGE URBAIN

Fontaine de la justice à Berne

Certaines grandes villes suisses proposent d'admirables ensembles urbains et disposent de points d'observation bien choisis (mentionnés dans les textes ou sous les rubriques « Belvédères »). Lors de son voyage de 1779, Goethe déclarait déjà que Berne était la plus belle ville qu'il eût jamais vue.

De nombreuses cités du Moyen-Pays conservent des fragments de leur décor médiéval : les quartiers historiques, habités « bourgeoisement », n'ont pas connu, ici, la destinée du noyau ancien de tant de villes européennes, souvent détruit par la guerre ou abandonné à une dégradation regrettable.

Fontaines – Toujours fleuries, elles rendent accueillantes les places et les rues qui constituent le centre d'animation traditionnel de la cité. Leur fût central, repeint et redoré avec soin, supporte souvent un animal ou un sujet allégorique : guerrier, héros légendaire et, surtout, « banneret » (homme d'armes portant la bannière aux armes de la ville).

Arcades (en allemand « Lauben ») – D'origine transalpine, ce procédé de construction a été popularisé au Nord des Alpes, à partir du 14e s., par les « Messieurs de Berne » : les rues à arcades de nombreuses villes du Moyen-Pays témoignent d'une période d'hégémonie bernoise.

Peintures extérieures – Elles sont en très grande faveur, depuis la Renaissance, non seulement dans les régions au climat sec comme l'Engadine (1), mais encore dans nombre de cités de la Suisse alémanique, où les façades s'enluminent de vastes compositions allégoriques ou historiques, faisant appel à l'Olympe aussi bien qu'à la Bible.

Dans toute la Confédération, les monuments historiques et certains bâtiments publics arborent des volets peints de chevrons aux couleurs du canton (voir écussons dans le chapitre : Les cantons).

Ponts couverts – Ce type de construction, très populaire dans toute la Suisse alémanique, répondait surtout à une nécessité technique : la protection d'un toit réduit les dépenses d'entretien d'un ouvrage bâti entièrement en charpente. Le dernier pont couvert construit en Suisse date de 1943 (Hohe Brücke, sur la route de Flüeli à Kerns, voir à Sachseln). Quelques rares localités établies à flanc de pente (Lausanne, Erlenbach, Thoune) montrent des escaliers publics couverts, tout en bois.

Oriels (en allemand « Erker ») – Ces loggias en encorbellement, parfois à double étage, sont dans les villes du Nord-Est (St-Gall, Stein am Rhein, Rorschach) de

(1) Ne pas confondre peinture murale et « sgraffite » (lire « la maison engadinoise », à Engadin).

Oriel à Stein am Rhein

LA MAISON PAYSANNE

Entretenue et fleurie avec un soin jaloux, la maison paysanne suisse témoigne – surtout en Suisse alémanique – d'un souci remarquable de confort et de décorum, ainsi que d'un sens pratique très développé.

Maison de l'Oberland bernois
(région de la Jungfrau)

Toit aplati, largement débordant de tous côtés, encore pourvu, dans les hautes vallées, de sa couverture de bardeaux lestés de grosses pierres. Décoration très poussée : poutres taillées à facettes, consoles supportant le toit complètement ouvragées, etc.
C'est ce type d'habitation, localement appelé « Schali » (petit château, chalet), qui a popularisé, dans le monde entier, le « chalet suisse ».

Maison de la Suisse centrale
(région de Lucerne)

Construction d'une grande distinction caractérisée par un toit en très forte pente et des auvents individuels, abritant, du côté pignon, la rangée de fenêtres de chaque étage.
Le rez-de-chaussée, très surélevé, n'est accessible que latéralement, par un escalier extérieur.

Maison appenzelloise
(environs de Trogen)

Dans ce pays au climat pluvieux, le regroupement des bâtiments agricoles en un même bloc s'impose et les tavaillons, disposés en écailles de poisson, forment une cuirasse protectrice jusque sur les façades.
Le pignon du pavillon d'habitation fait toujours face à la vallée. Au niveau du sol s'ouvrent les fenêtres de la cave où les brodeuses trouvent l'atmosphère convenant à leurs délicats travaux. Les volets se rabattent verticalement et peuvent disparaître dans une fente en haut de la fenêtre.

Maison de la campagne bernoise
(Emmental)

Immense toit retombant, sur les côtés, jusqu'au 1er étage et abritant une grange très vaste.
Les paysans les plus cossus, imitant les gens de la ville, ont rogné souvent le pan de toiture triangulaire du pignon – se présentant, ici, de face – et dressé, de ce côté, une arche de charpente (pointillé rouge) entièrement lambrissée.

Maison tessinoise
(Foroglio, Val Bavona)

Construction de pierre aux dispositions primitives : les communications entre les différents étages se font uniquement par des escaliers et galeries de bois en plein air. Les murs doivent être construits très épais jusqu'à 0.90 m) étant donné l'irrégularité des moellons employés. Couverture en dalles de pierre. Le sommet du pignon est ouvert à tous les vents, ou clos par une claire-voie grossière de madriers superposés.

Maison valaisanne
(Évolène)

Dans le Valais de langue française, les maisons de bois poussent souvent en hauteur. Les étages habitables (partie bois sont reliés par des galeries latérales ouvertes au bloc des cuisines (partie maçonnerie – partiellement visible à droite).
Au premier plan, un « raccard » ou « mazot » *(voir illustration au Valais).*

véritables œuvres d'art décorées de sculptures ou de peintures. Avec des moyens plus modestes, le paysan de l'Engadine a fait saillir des murs gris de sa maison des oriels d'une fantaisie exquise.

Bâtiments officiels – Une impression de confort bourgeois se dégage des monuments publics suisses, tels que ces hôtels de ville dont s'enorgueillissent les moindres cités. Ces constructions constituent de précieux exemples de l'architecture civile aux époques gothique, Renaissance et classique. Leurs aménagements intérieurs – salles ornées de stucs, de boiseries, de vitraux de cabinet, de poêles de faïence – reflètent un art de vivre raffiné.

Rivalisant avec ces édifices, les anciennes maisons de corporation (Zunfthaus) proposent souvent, dans leur salle d'honneur embellie d'un plafond à caissons, un panorama complet des arts décoratifs ayant fleuri à leur époque : mobilier, vaisselle, orfèvrerie, etc. Transformées, de nombreuses maisons de corporation sont devenues des restaurants. Ainsi prend forme, par petites touches, le décor avenant des cités suisses. Il est révélateur que les monuments exceptionnels, comme les grandes cathédrales gothiques, soient, en Suisse, les témoins de styles étrangers. Le génie helvétique trouve son épanouissement moins dans le chef-d'œuvre isolé, la «curiosité», que dans la présentation d'ensemble d'un quartier, d'une rue, d'une simple église de campagne.

L'ART RELIGIEUX

La Suisse, pays-carrefour, a toujours accueilli les influences artistiques les plus diverses; ses cathédrales et ses abbatiales en témoignent. Les clochers dressant dans la campagne un toit en accent circonflexe (Käsebissendach : «toit en tranche de fromage» disent les paysans de façon imagée), une flèche très fine ou un bulbe rutilant, sont des éléments essentiels du paysage helvétique.

Il n'est pas question ci-dessous des églises de Suisse italienne dont l'évolution architecturale est semblable à celle de la Lombardie.

L'art roman – Les monuments romans, rares sur le versant Nord des Alpes et d'autant plus précieux, illustrent deux traditions architecturales différentes.
En Suisse alémanique, l'abbatiale de Tous-les-Saints à Schaffhouse rappelle les sanctuaires rhénans, élevés suivant le plan des antiques basiliques chrétiennes.
En Suisse romande, le grandiose vaisseau de Payerne, voûté en berceau, illustre la pénétration de l'art roman bourguignon, à la suite des moines de Cluny. L'harmonieuse abbatiale de Romainmôtier laisse apparaître une même filiation.

L'art gothique – La cathédrale de Lausanne (début du 13ᵉ s.), qui témoigne d'une assimilation tout originale des différents procédés des maîtres d'œuvre français, en est le chef-d'œuvre.
Les modes de la Renaissance ayant eu, en Suisse, peu de prise sur l'architecture religieuse, le gothique s'y attarde jusqu'en plein 16ᵉ s. Le dessin de plus en plus compliqué des voûtes («voûtes en étoile» des chœurs), et l'apparition de somptueux retables à décoration flamboyante (cathédrale de Coire), en caractérisent la dernière période qui, dite «gothique tardif», est très représentée dans toute la Suisse alémanique et les Grisons.

L'art baroque – A partir du 17ᵉ s., le mouvement de la Contre-Réforme, fruit des délibérations du concile de Trente, amène dans toutes les Alpes un grand nombre de missionnaires appartenant à des ordres plus soucieux d'action directe que de mysticisme.

Payerne – Intérieur de l'église abbatiale

A ce renouveau catholique, Franciscains, Capucins et Jésuites veulent associer un nouvel art religieux, savant et populaire à la fois, destiné à relayer le gothique, devenu synonyme de «barbare». Les recherches des grands architectes italiens et tessinois à la mode sont largement mises à profit.
Les stucs, les peintures murales, recouvrent toute la surface disponible.
Les retables géants, devenus souvent la pièce principale du mobilier, exaltent de tous leurs ors le dogme de l'Eucharistie et font une place importante à la Vierge et aux Saints. C'est alors que les grandes abbayes bénédictines suisses, comme Einsiedeln, St-Gall ou Disentis prennent l'aspect solennel qui les caractérise aujourd'hui.

Mais à côté de ces chefs-d'œuvre de l'« **École du Vorarlberg** », une sève plus paysanne survit dans maints sanctuaires du Valais et des Grisons : c'était l'époque où une cellule montagnarde comme le Val de Conches (haute vallée du Rhône) avait ses dynasties locales de fabricants d'autels (les Ritz) et de facteurs d'orgues (les Carlen).
De raffinement en raffinement, le baroque d'église jette ses derniers feux dans un sanctuaire-bonbonnière comme la collégiale d'Arlesheim, puis s'éteint aux environs de 1770. Désormais, pendant un siècle et demi, l'imitation de l'antique prévaudra.

Recherches contemporaines – Dans la recherche d'un nouvel art religieux, les pays de l'Europe Centrale et la Suisse alémanique en particulier occupent une place de premier plan.
Une unité se dégage des édifices construits par Karl Moser – qui a fait œuvre de précurseur à St-Antoine de Bâle (« exemple le plus rigoureux de ce que peut être l'église moderne » affirment ses admirateurs) – et par ses élèves Fritz Metzger (St-Charles de Lucerne), Hermann Baur (St-Nicolas-de-Flüe à Berne), Otto Dreyer (St-Joseph de Lucerne).
Ces vastes églises surprennent au premier abord. Le visiteur le plus prévenu contre l'art moderne ne peut cependant rester insensible à l'envolée de leur campanile, à leur éclairage magistralement distribué et nuancé – la décoration vitrée joue un rôle essentiel – et à la richesse de certaines pièces de leur mobilier (travaux d'orfèvrerie). Moins révolutionnaires, les églises construites à la même époque en Suisse française, par l'architecte Dumas, par exemple, doivent aux artistes du groupe romand de la « **Société St-Luc** », qu'animait le peintre Cingria, leur décoration fraîche et vigoureuse.

LA SUISSE AU QUOTIDIEN...

Certains aspects de la vie courante, évoqués ci-dessous, reflètent assez bien la personnalité suisse : l'observateur étranger, séduit, en percevra bien d'autres !

Service de presse – Les principaux quotidiens de la presse locale sont parfois encore laissés, au coin des rues, à la discrétion des passants ; et fixés à une hampe de bois, à la disposition de la clientèle des cafés ou restaurants.

Citoyens en armes – Le touriste parcourant la pacifique Helvétie ne peut manquer de faire, un jour ou l'autre, le genre de rencontres qui caractérise ailleurs un pays sur le pied de guerre : convois militaires sur la route, soldats casqués en tenue de campagne postés aux carrefours, exercices de tir à la cible dans le champ voisin... La « démobilisation » lui apparaîtra ensuite sous la forme de cyclistes en civil rentrant de leur période annuelle d'exercice *(voir ci-dessous)*, le fusil d'assaut posé en travers du guidon.

La tournée du facteur – Le même touriste sera peut-être intrigué de voir, dans les villes les plus modernes, le facteur du quartier, en uniforme, « attelé » à un lourd caisson sur roues ou le tirant par le timon pour aller distribuer courrier et colis postaux...

Attention aux enfants – En Suisse, « l'étalement » des vacances scolaires n'est pas un vain mot : elles varient selon les cantons, et l'étranger au volant peut voir déambuler, en plein mois de juillet ou d'août, écolières et écoliers, cartable au dos...

... ET SES CHOIX CIVIQUES

Obligations militaires – Les obligations militaires tiennent une place de premier plan dans la vie du citoyen suisse. L'armée, en opérant un brassage continu des classes de la société et des différents groupes ethniques suisses, constitue un agent essentiel d'« helvétisation ». Tout homme apte au service est appelé à devenir soldat de 20 à 50 ans, 55 ans pour les officiers. Les femmes peuvent être volontaires pour s'engager dans le service féminin de l'armée (SFA).
L'armée suisse est une armée de milices ne comportant pas d'« active » (le terme de service actif désigne la situation créée par la mobilisation). Elle n'a de « général » qu'en temps de guerre ou de mobilisation générale (général Guisan, de 1939 à 1945).
Le service proprement dit, appelé « école de recrues », à 20 ans, n'excède ordinairement pas 4 mois, mais, par la suite, les rappels pour « cours de répétition » se renouvellent en moyenne tous les ans. De 20 à 32 ans, le réserviste appartient à l'« élite » où il est astreint à 8 cours de répétition de 3 semaines. De 33 à 42 ans, il est versé ensuite dans la landwehr et tenu à 3 cours de complément de 2 semaines. De 43 à 50 ans, il est placé dans la landsturm et soumis à un cours de 2 semaines.
Le soldat suisse est dépositaire de tout son équipement : uniforme, fusil, munitions, masque à gaz... En dehors des périodes militaires, l'entraînement au tir à l'arme de guerre reste obligatoire : il faut réunir dans l'année un certain nombre de points, inscrits au livret militaire. Mais de nombreux Suisses renouvellent, par goût, cette épreuve : les pétarades résonnant dans les vallons les plus reculés caractérisent les premières heures du dimanche suisse.
Les années où le citoyen-soldat n'est pas convoqué à un cours, il doit se présenter aux inspections d'armes et d'équipement dans la commune de sa résidence.

Les votations — Bien que cumulées dans toute la mesure du possible sur tel ou tel dimanche, les « votations » populaires — communales, cantonales et fédérales — reviennent dans la vie du citoyen actif, à une cadence qui pourra étonner l'étranger. Dans des cantons comme Berne et Zurich, très férus d'un contrôle strict des différents budgets, on peut dire plaisamment que le vote revient aussi souvent que la partie de « jass » (la belote suisse).

On votera aussi bien sur l'opportunité de construire un abri pour arrêt d'autobus (votation communale) ou de corriger un torrent de montagne (votation cantonale) que sur le contrôle des prix (votation fédérale). *Voir chapitre : La démocratie en action.*

Le nombre de ces consultations explique le désintérêt que leur témoigne une fraction importante de l'électorat, dont le taux moyen de participation ne varie guère que de 50 à 35 %, voire à moins de 30 % dans le cas des votations cantonales !

On ne peut travailler toujours... — La Suisse reste l'une des nations du monde où la durée du travail est la plus élevée : de 2.000 à 2.300 heures par an. Une fois quittes du labeur quotidien, les Suisses prennent plaisir à la lecture de leur journal favori — ils sont, malgré radio et télévision, les plus grands « consommateurs » de journaux de la planète ! —, et en sortant éventuellement, après le dîner, pour quelque station au café ou à la brasserie, dans la fumée des cigares, devant un verre de vin, une chope de bière et même quelque assiette de charcuterie.

Assez rarement, car il n'en faut pas galvauder le cérémonial intime, une fondue *(voir chapitre : La table)* forme prétexte à de chaleureuses réunions amicales, se prolongeant parfois fort avant dans la nuit.

Mais, en général, le Suisse est à classer parmi les « couche-tôt », exception faite dans les grandes villes. Dans les cinémas, la séance de la soirée commerce à 20 h 30 (l'entracte a lieu au milieu du grand film) et il n'est pas question, dans les villes suisses, d'animation « by night » après minuit, sauf dans les grandes villes bien évidemment.

Les casinos ou « Kursaal » sont recherchés surtout pour leurs concerts, leurs orchestres de danse, leurs programmes de variétés, car les jeux de hasard, au-delà d'une mise modique *(5 F)*, sont interdits sur le territoire de la Confédération.

La marine suisse — Avec sa trentaine de cargos sillonnant les océans, elle se classe au 50ᵉ rang des 111 pays possédant une flotte commerciale... et au premier rang de ceux, parmi eux, qui sont privés d'accès à la mer.

La table

Dans un pays où se rencontrent les traditions culinaires germaniques, italiennes et françaises, la cuisine est riche en spécialités gastronomiques régionales, sinon raffinées, du moins saines et savoureuses, qui méritent d'être mises à l'épreuve.

Le repas au restaurant — Le menu présenté habituellement dans les restaurants suisses comprend un potage (à midi comme le soir), une entrée (poisson de lac ou de torrent, œufs, croûte au fromage, etc.) et un plat de viande garni. Le dessert est souvent un supplément. Les mets commandés « à la carte » sont très copieux.

La fondue — Les grands fromages à pâte dure, Gruyère et Emmental, qui portent le prestige de l'industrie laitière suisse à l'étranger, sont à la base de la fondue, véritable institution nationale pour les Suisses français. Chaque canton romand, Vaud, Neuchâtel et Fribourg, revendique le secret des dosages (entre le Gruyère, l'Emmental ou le Vacherin) et des additions qui font la meilleure fondue. La recette de base est, en tout cas, la suivante : faire bouillir du vin blanc dans un poêlon de terre cuite — le « caquelon » — au fond préalablement frotté d'ail. Y verser d'un coup le fromage coupé en lamelles ou en cubes et brasser jusqu'à ce que le mélange soit bien liquide. Ajouter alors les épices, le kirsch, etc. Servir bouillant sur un réchaud soigneusement réglé. La fondue est dégustée en trempant dans le caquelon des petits cubes de pain piqués au bout de longues fourchettes. Et gare au maladroit qui laisse choir son pain dans le caquelon : il devra payer une nouvelle bouteille de « Fendant ».

La **raclette** est une spécialité du Valais. Elle se prépare en présentant au feu une moitié de pièce de fromage du Valais (fromage à pâte douce de Bagnes ou de Conches). La tranche ainsi ramollie est « râclée » directement dans l'assiette avec un couteau ou une palette de bois. On la déguste avec des pommes de terre en robe des champs et des cornichons.

Viandes, cochonnailles et poissons — Au chapitre de la viande de boucherie, la **Bündnerfleisch** ou viande séchée des Grisons est la spécialité helvétique la plus originale : il s'agit de viande de bœuf crue, fumée et séchée, servie en minces copeaux. Cette curiosité mise à part, les menus suisses courants voient revenir surtout l'escalope de veau (Schnitzel), la côte de porc et le bifteck de cheval. Les Zurichois, réputés fins gourmets, ont popularisé des préparations telles que l'émincé de veau (ou de foie de veau) à la crème (geschnetzeltes Kalbsfleisch) et les Leberspiessli (brochettes de foie de veau entrelardé).

Contrastant avec cette gamme assez pauvre, les charcuteries présentent un extraordinaire échantillonnage de saucisses et saucissons (« Wurst »). Les Suisses alémaniques font une grande consommation de produits doux : Gnagi (jarret de porc, très apprécié à Berne pour la collation de quatre heures), Klöpfer (cervelas) de Bâle, Schüblig de St-Gall, Kalbsbratwurst (saucisse de veau) de Zurich, Salsiz (petit salami) de l'Engadine. Les Suisses romands donnent la préférence aux saucisses fumées, d'un goût plus relevé (boutefas de Payerne, longeole de Genève, etc.). Tirant parti de ces ressources, la monumentale **Berner Platte** (« Plat de Berne ») associe le lard, les saucisses, le jambon, le bœuf bouilli parfois, la choucroute et les pommes de terre ou les haricots verts. Mais le plat national de la Suisse allemande est l'amalgame doré des **Rösti** (pommes de terre bouillies, coupées en dés et passées à la poêle, puis au four).

Rivières et lacs fournissent une grande variété de poissons comme la perche (filets de perche des bords du Léman), la truite, le brochet, la bondelle, la tanche, la carpe, la féra qui, accommodés selon la région, séduiront les connaisseurs.

Entremets et desserts — La crème fraîche entre dans la composition de nombreux desserts et entremets : meringues, Schaffhauserzungen (biscuits fourrés).
La tourte au kirsch de Zoug, les Basler Leckerli — pain d'épice à base de miel et d'amandes — ont leurs fidèles partisans. Quant au chocolat, dont la renommée n'est plus à faire, il est utilisé dans la préparation de gâteaux et d'entremets exquis. A l'hôtel, on le trouve souvent sur la table de nuit ou l'oreiller.

Les vins — Le vignoble, qui compte moins de 14 000 ha, n'assure que 36 % de la consommation nationale de vin.
Les vins blancs vaudois ont un goût de pierre à fusil. Le Lavaux, le Dézaley, le Féchy, l'Aigle et l'Yvorne en sont les crus les plus renommés.
On trouve en Valais une très grande variété de vins blancs et de vins rouges : le Fendant est blanc, ainsi que le Johannisberg dont le bouquet, plus délicat, rappelle les vins du Rhin. La Dôle, le cru rouge le plus populaire de Suisse, est un vin bouqueté issu d'un mélange de pinot noir et de gamay, cépages constituant la majeure partie du vignoble bourguignon. Si le Cortaillod est un vin rouge corsé et vigoureux, la plupart des autres vins neuchâtellois — tels ceux d'Auvernier, de Boudry, de Colombier — sont des blancs frais et pétillants, provenant d'un plant noble, le chasselas, et issus d'un sol calcaire. Le vignoble tessinois donne des crus capiteux, riches en alcool, et constituant d'agréables vins de dessert, tels le Mezzana (vins rouges et vins blancs) et le Nostrano (rouge). Les vins rouges et blancs et les rosés (« Süssdruck ») de Suisse orientale et de la vallée alpestre du Rhin sont appréciés pour leur finesse et leur légèreté.

Le service des vins ; l'étoile — La diversité des plants et des terroirs offre une gamme assez étendue pour satisfaire aux exigences d'un menu bien ordonné. Les blancs vaudois (Dorin) et le Fendant valaisan, les crus blancs de Neuchâtel *(voir ci-dessus)* et de Bienne (Twanner) accompagnent hors-d'œuvre et poissons. Un Cortaillod ou une grande Dôle feront apprécier les rôtis et les venaisons. Le Johannisberg et la Malvoisie du Valais, certains vins tessinois ont toutes les qualités de vins de dessert. Kirsch de Zoug, marc du Valais et Williamine terminent agréablement le repas. Certains vins blancs se doivent de « faire l'étoile » : ceux de Neuchâtel, par exemple, mis en bouteilles très tôt, gardent en suspension du gaz carbonique et, une fois débouchés et versés de haut (remarquer le geste des serveuses), pétillent dans le verre en formant une sorte d'étoile.
Les vins de pays sont servis « ouverts », en carafe de 2, 3 ou 5 « décis » (décilitres).

Termes d'hôtellerie

Bündnerstube	« salle grisonne » : dans les hôtels des Grisons, c'est une pièce intime, meublée et décorée suivant les traditions du pays
Café	salon de thé (en Suisse alémanique)
Carnotzet	dans les hôtels du Pays de Vaud et du Valais, salle (ou caveau) typique où l'on vient déguster la fondue et les vins du pays
Garni	hôtel sans restaurant
Gasthaus	café (restaurant si cela est précisé)
Grotto	au Tessin : guinguette champêtre où l'on vient déguster le vin du pays
Kurhaus	établissement généralement isolé, de dimensions imposantes et d'un aménagement souvent rustique. Il existe des « Kurhaus » thermaux, de montagne, qui se présentent comme des lieux de villégiature.
Meublé	hôtel sans restaurant
Pension	petit établissement recevant une clientèle familiale
Restaurant	dans certaines villes de Suisse alémanique, en particulier à Lucerne, certains « Restaurants » ne servent que des consommations comme un café, à moins d'afficher « Speise-Restaurant »
Wirtschaft	buvette

Villes et curiosités

Berne – Tour de l'Horloge

AARAU

C Argovie – 16 481 habitants
Carte Michelin n° 427 pli 5 ou 216 plis 16, 17 – Alt. 383 m

Capitale du canton d'Argovie, Aarau occupe un site agréable au pied du Jura. Du pont sur l'Aare, se découvre la meilleure **vue d'ensemble** sur la ville ancienne, étagée en terrasse au-dessus du fleuve et dominée par les tours du beffroi, de l'église et du vieux château.

La ville ancienne – Au hasard des rues étroites, le touriste découvre de belles maisons, parfois ornées d'oriels *(voir Introduction : La Suisse pittoresque)*, d'enseignes de fer forgé, rappelant par leur style la longue domination bernoise : façades couvertes de fresques, toits bruns aux pignons en escaliers ou aux avant-toits décorés.

Église paroissiale (Stadtkirche) – Perchée sur l'extrême bord d'un éperon s'avançant vers l'Ouest, elle est surmontée d'un clocher de la fin du 17ᵉ s. Sur une petite place attenante, belle « fontaine de la Justice » de 1643 et vue agréable sur la campagne.

ENVIRONS

★ **Schönenwerd** – *4,5 km au Sud-Ouest par ⑤ du plan, route d'Olten.*
A l'écart du bourg ancien, que domine une église collégiale remontant au 12ᵉ s., s'est développé un quartier moderne qui doit son existence aux usines Bally.

★★ **Musée de la chaussure Bally** (Schuhmuseum) ⊙ – Installé dans la maison du « Felsgarten », que le fondateur de la firme habita et où il aménagea ses bureaux et ses premiers ateliers, il renferme des collections d'une valeur exceptionnelle, provenant de toutes les époques, suivant l'histoire de la chaussure au cours des siècles chez les peuples les plus différents. Des emblèmes corporatifs, des livres de maîtrise et de voyage, des ordonnances royales et impériales complètent cette exposition originale.

★ **Château de Hallwil** ⊙ – *18 km au Sud-Est par ③ du plan, route de Suhr. De Teufenthal, gagner Hallwil et Boniswil, puis la route de Seengen.*
Il s'agit en fait d'un double et ravissant château, à tours rondes pointues et enceinte crénelée, élevé et agrandi du 11ᵉ au 16ᵉ s. (puis restauré) sur deux îlots d'une rivière tributaire du Hallwiler See. Son entrée se fait par un pont-levis et une cour d'honneur par où l'on gagne la deuxième île pour visiter le corps de logis aménagé en musée d'arts et de traditions populaires (forge, imprimerie, intérieur paysan argovien reconstitué, mannequins de carnaval). Dans la tour du corps de logis de la première île, on voit au 1ᵉʳ étage, un appartement seigneurial meublé du 17ᵉ s., et au 2ᵉ étage, un appartement bourgeois du 19ᵉ s.

AARAU

Färbergasse .... **A** 4	Aumattweg .... **B** 3	Metzgergasse .... **A** 16
Kronengasse .... **A** 13	Frey-Herose-	Rain .... **A** 18
Laurenzentorgasse ... **A** 15	Strasse .... **B** 6	Rössligutstrasse .... **B** 21
Rathausgasse .... **A** 19	Güterstrasse .... **B** 7	Schachenallee .... **A** 22
Storchengasse .... **A** 27	Hintere	Schlossplatz .... **A** 24
Zwischen den Toren .. **A** 31	Vorstadt .... **A** 9	Sengelbachweg .... **B** 25
	Hunzikerstrasse .... **B** 10	Viehmarktplatz .... **A** 28
	Kirchgasse .... **A** 12	Vordere Vorstadt .... **A** 30

ADELBODEN★★

Berne — 3 347 habitants
Carte Michelin n° 427 pli 13 ou 217 pli 16 — Schéma : BERNER OBERLAND — Alt. 1 356 m

Dans l'ample **bassin**★ ensoleillé qui marque l'origine de la vallée de l'Engstligen, Adelboden compte parmi les villégiatures élégantes de l'Oberland bernois les plus élevées et les plus réputées, été comme hiver, pour la bienfaisance de leur climat.
Le village, bien groupé à mi-pente, s'allonge face à un majestueux horizon de montagnes calcaires. Le sommet tabulaire neigeux du Wildstrubel (alt. 3 243 m) fermant l'immense cirque d'alpages de l'Engstligenalp d'où s'échappent, sautant un gradin rocheux, les **chutes de l'Engstligen**★★★ (Engstligenfälle), constitue l'élément le plus frappant de cet ensemble.

AIGLE

Vaud — 7 825 habitants
Carte Michelin n° 427 pli 12 ou 217 pli 14 — Schéma : ALPES VAUDOISES — Alt. 417 m

Centre viticole et industriel, et dépôt militaire, au confluent de la vallée du Rhône et de celle des Ormonts, Aigle est une avenante petite ville de plaine, encadrée de hauteurs d'où dévale (jusqu'au cœur de l'agglomération) un vignoble estimé que cloisonnent des murets de pierres ou de ciment.
On flânera sur la promenade ombragée Gustave Doret (au bord du torrent de la Grande Eau) et, dans le centre, devant le curieux passage, couvert de galeries de bois fleuries, de la « Ruelle de Jérusalem ». A l'extrémité Est du pays, le château et l'église St-Maurice à flèche de pierre gothique forment un ensemble plaisant.

> **Château** — Encore dans son enceinte cantonnée de tourelles pointues et cernée de vignes, cet ancien petit fief savoyard du 13ᵉ s., pris et reconstruit par les Bernois au 15ᵉ s. et restauré de nos jours, abrite un musée du pays vaudois, ainsi que quelques meubles anciens. Le chemin de ronde, couvert, conserve des peintures murales polychromes (fleurs et fruits).
>
> **Musée de la Vigne et du Vin** ⊙ — Le musée vigneron occupe plusieurs salles du corps de logis et trois étages de la tour principale : verrerie, étains, tonnellerie, outils, étiquettes... du 17ᵉ s. à nos jours ; on remarque particulièrement deux énormes pressoirs (d'environ 1600 à levier ; de 1706, à vis), ainsi qu'une lumineuse tapisserie de Lurçat sur le thème de la vigne et du raisin (1943).

Les ALPES VAUDOISES★★

Carte Michelin n° 427 plis 12, 13 ou 217 plis 14, 15

Partagées entre le bassin du Rhône et le bassin de l'Aare (haute vallée de la Sarine), les Alpes vaudoises doivent leur individualité à leurs paysages d'amples vallées verdoyantes, d'escarpements calcaires et de sommets enneigés.
Leurs populations montagnardes parlent le français, pratiquent la religion réformée et construisent leurs chalets comme en Oberland bernois *(illustration en Introduction : La Suisse pittoresque)*.
Les vallées desservies par les routes décrites ci-après — vallée des Ormonts et Pays d'Enhaut — sont tout indiquées comme voies de passage entre la région du Léman et l'Oberland bernois. Au touriste, elles offrent le calme et la tranquillité de villégiatures telles que Château-d'Oex ou les Diablerets, tandis que sur les hauteurs, en terrasse à 1 000 m au-dessus de la vallée du Rhône, face aux Dents du Midi, Leysin et Villars-Chesières attirent une clientèle sportive et mondaine.
L'extraordinaire dispersion des chalets, sur le versant de la Grande Eau comme sur le versant de la Sarine, constitue un trait frappant du paysage régional.

★★ ① VALLÉE DES ORMONTS
D'Aigle à Saanen 45 km — environ 1 h 1/2

> *Le col du Pillon peut se trouver fermé entre novembre et avril, en période de fort enneigement.*

Aigle — *Voir à ce nom.*
On pénètre bientôt, à haute altitude, dans l'étroit sillon boisé des **gorges**★ creusées par la Grande Eau.

> **Leysin** — De la route d'itinéraire, 4 km par une route à gauche avant d'atteindre le Sépey. Son **site**★★ forme une splendide terrasse dominant la vallée du Rhône, face aux Dents du Midi. La station bénéficie d'un climat doux et d'un ensoleillement intense. On apprécie ensuite, surtout dans la descente qui précède l'arrivée à la station, le site du village des Diablerets, au pied des superbes escarpements du même nom.

★ **Les Diablerets** — Bourg principal de la vallée des Ormonts, la station se disperse dans un bassin de prairies très évasé, piqueté de frênes et d'érables. Le **site**★★ est à la fois gracieux et grandiose.

Les ALPES VAUDOISES

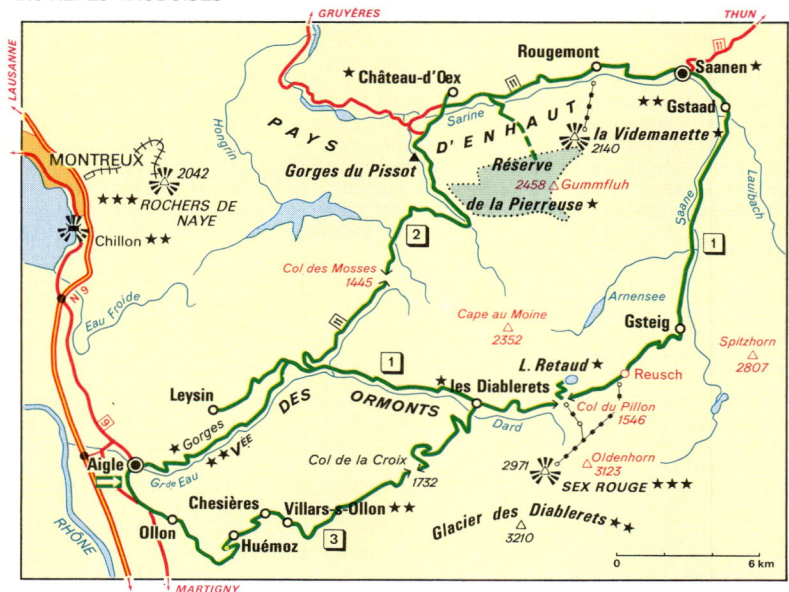

Les murailles des Diablerets apparaissent ici profondément incurvées en cirque (Creux de Champ), entre l'éperon du Sex Rouge et le Culan.

Entre les Diablerets et le col du Pillon, une boucle serrée dans le ravin du pont Bourquin fait apparaître, entre les arbres, de curieux monolithes blanchâtres, dus à un phénomène de dissolution du gypse. Sur le versant opposé, le torrent du Dard s'échappe, en cascades ténues, de deux **cirques**★ rocheux emboîtés.

★★★ **Sex Rouge** ⊙ — *Accès : 35 mn, par télécabine et téléphériques au départ du col du Pillon, ou par téléphériques au départ de Reusch.* Au cours de la montée, on pourra guetter marmottes et chamois, mais l'attention se partage surtout entre le bassin des Diablerets et la formidable paroi enneigée précédant l'arrivée à la station supérieure. De cette dernière, un escalier *(praticable seulement en plein été)* mène au sommet du Sex Rouge (alt. 2 971 m) d'où s'observe un merveilleux **panorama**★★★ : au Sud, sur la chaîne des Alpes suisses (Cervin, visible derrière un monolithe) et françaises (Mont Blanc) entre les autres sommets tout proches des Diablerets (tremplin neigeux du point culminant, d'un côté, Oldenhorn rocheux aux blanches « épaules », de l'autre), et sur l'éblouissant **glacier des Diablerets**★★ prolongement Nord du glacier de Tsanfleuron ; au Nord, sur les sommets plus modestes mais aigus (Tornette, Palette...) se dressant derrière la vallée des Ormonts.

★ **Lac Retaud** — *Du col du Pillon, 1,5 km par chemin de montagne étroit.* Cette jolie nappe aux eaux vertes noie un creux d'alpages, face au double cirque du Dard dominé à gauche par l'Oldenhorn à droite par le Sex Rouge.

Un troisième cirque se découvre, entre les contreforts Nord-Est de l'Oldenhorn (vallon de l'Oldenbach), lors de la descente du col du Pillon vers Gsteig ; celle-ci se termine en vue de la pyramide du Spitzhorn.

Gsteig — Une église, à la flèche de charpente aiguë, est inséparable du **site**★ de ce joli village, le plus élevé de la vallée de la Sarine. Le vallon rocheux « suspendu » (lire « l'héritage des glaciers quaternaires » dans le chapitre : Physionomie du pays) qui se dessine, plus en amont, entre les escarpements du Spitzhorn et du Mittaghorn et d'où dévale la gerbe d'une puissante cascade, conduit au col du Sanetsch, passage autrefois très fréquenté entre l'Oberland et le Valais. L'hôtel Bären est aménagé dans une vaste **construction**★ de style oberlandais, en pignon décoré de frises géométriques et d'inscriptions.

★★ **Gstaad** — *Voir à ce nom.*

★ **Saanen** — *Voir à ce nom.*

★★ 2 PAYS D'ENHAUT

De Saanen à Aigle *45 km — environ 1 h (visites non comprises)*

Entre Saanen et Château-d'Oex, le court **défilé des Allamans** marque à la fois la limite entre les cantons de Berne et de Vaud et la frontière linguistique entre le français et l'allemand, comme en témoigne le nom même de ce défilé et du hameau qui le borde. Le sommet rocheux élancé bien nommé Rubli (carotte) qui culmine à 2 284 m, fixe longtemps l'attention.

Les ALPES VAUDOISES

Rougemont – De son passé monastique, cette charmante localité aux chalets en bois, siège d'un prieuré clunisien entre le 11e s. et la Réforme, a gardé une église pittoresquement abritée sous un vaste toit retombant. A l'intérieur, le sévère vaisseau à trois nefs supportées par de lourds piliers carrés, est caractéristique des constructions romanes primitives, en territoire helvétique. Remarquer, aux vitraux du chœur, le motif de la grue, symbole de la Gruyère (voir à Gruyères).
Le prieuré a fait place au château (16e s.), lui-même entièrement reconstruit et restauré, suite à l'incendie de février 1973 ; les bâtiments contigus aux murailles s'harmonisent plaisamment avec la silhouette encapuchonnée du sanctuaire.

★ **La Videmanette** ⊙ – Alt. 2 140 m. *Accès par télécabine en 18 mn au départ de Rougemont.* La station supérieure coiffe une crête de la Videmanette qu'encadrent les sommets, voisins et dominants, du Rubli et du Rocher Plat. Monter sur le toit-terrasse du restaurant pour profiter de la **vue**★ embrassant entre autres, de droite à gauche, les trois cimes caractéristiques de la Tornette, celles, cornues, des Diablerets, les lacs Arnensee et de Retaud derrière la Gummfluh, la chaîne de l'Oldenhorn et, lointaines, les crêtes du massif de la Jungfrau avec, à l'extrême gauche, l'Eiger...

★ **Réserve de la Pierreuse** – *Visite à pied : compter 1/2 journée.* Aux Granges, tourner à gauche *(attention : à angle très aigu)* dans la route, en descente, de Gérignoz qui emprunte un tunnel *(voie unique)*, et le pont sur la Sarine.
Avant une importante scierie, prendre à droite pour remonter le versant opposé de la vallée.
Laisser la voiture avant le pont des Leyssalets.
La réserve naturelle de la Pierreuse couvre environ 1 000 ha au pied des parois rocheuses Nord de la Gummfluh, dans un **site**★ accidenté d'éboulis couverts de bois ou d'alpages. La flore et la faune, aux espèces d'origine ou réintroduites (épicéas, marmottes, bouquetins), y sont intégralement protégées.
Les cimes jumelles de la Gummfluh se présentent par l'échancrure du vallon affluent de Gérignoz.

★ **Château-d'Oex** – *Voir à ce nom.*

Gorges du Pissot – Un belvédère aménagé dans un virage permet d'apprécier l'encaissement et le cadre boisé de cette coupure rocheuse, parcourue par la Torneresse.
Après la traversée de ces gorges, la route fait une courbe au creux du vallon pastoral de l'Etivaz, donnant, en contrebas, un bref aperçu sur la petite dent de la Cape au Moine. On aboutit dans la très large dépression de prés-bois des Mosses. A la Lécherette, on atteint la haute vallée de l'Hongrin, qu'occupe un lac de barrage.
Le versant des Ormonts, en aval de la Comballaz, offre une vue dégagée sur les coupoles glaciaires des Diablerets, à gauche desquelles pointent le Sex Rouge et l'Oldenhorn. Dans l'enfilade du sillon de la Grande Eau, en aval, se situent les installations de cure et les grands hôtels de Leysin et, à l'horizon, les Dents du Midi. Entre le Sépey et Aigle, la route se maintient longtemps, en haute corniche, au-dessus des **gorges**★ boisées de la **Grande Eau**, puis, en quelques lacets, s'abaisse vers le fond de la vallée du Rhône. La cité d'Aigle, annoncée par son château, se présente alors dans son cadre de vignobles.

Aigle – *Voir à ce nom.*

★★ ③ ROUTE DU COL DE LA CROIX

D'Aigle aux Diablerets, par Villars 29 km – environ 1 h

Aigle – *Voir à ce nom.*
Au départ d'Aigle, la route, en palier, file entre les vignes, les arbres fruitiers, les prairies parsemées de ruches, en vue des crêtes enneigées du Grand Muveran et des Diablerets.

Ollon – Charmant village vigneron étagé autour de son église.
La route grimpe désormais, sinueuse mais excellente, tantôt en corniche, tantôt sous bois. 3 km après Ollon, une **vue**★★ superbe se dégage sur les deux massifs du Grand Muveran et les Diablerets, séparés par la dépression du Pas de Cheville derrière laquelle se profile le Mont Gond.

Huémoz – Village montagnard typique, vieux chalets.

Chesières ; Villars-sur-Ollon – *Voir à ce nom.*
Après Villars, la montée devient sévère (13 %), et le massif des Diablerets emplit l'horizon de ses cimes aux cornes neigeuses. A partir du **col de la Croix** (alt. 1 727 m), le parcours procure des vues magnifiques sur les architectures rocheuses du massif, avant la descente finale vers l'immense cuvette où s'étale la station des Diablerets.

★ **Les Diablerets** – *Voir plus haut.*

ALPI TICINESI★

Carte Michelin n° 427 pli 15 ou 218 plis 1, 2, 11 et 12
Schéma : SANKT GOTTHARD MASSIV

Le Tessin (Ticino) est le canton le plus méridional de la Confédération, « italien » par sa langue et sa personnalité mais politiquement suisse depuis le Moyen Âge. Il creuse sa vallée sur les pentes du versant Sud du St-Gothard, de la plaine lombarde au centre culminant du massif dont la barrière protectrice permet aux régions des lacs Majeur et de Lugano de jouir d'un climat exceptionnellement doux pour leur latitude.
Le caractère montagneux du pays, à cette extrémité Sud de la chaîne des Alpes, s'observe pleinement dans le parcours des routes du St-Gothard et du Lukmanier, comme aussi de la route du Nufenen *(voir à ce nom)*.

★ ROUTE DU ST-GOTHARD

Lire à Massif du St-Gothard les détails historiques concernant cette route.

Le tracé actuel date, dans son ensemble, de 1830, mais de grands travaux de rectification et d'élargissement de la chaussée — particulièrement nécessaires au passage du Val Tremola — en ont amélioré les caractéristiques. Sur le versant du Tessin, la chaussée est beaucoup plus roulante que le long de la Reuss. La route du Gothard connaît pendant toute sa période d'ouverture une animation intense.

Le col du St-Gothard est généralement obstrué par la neige de novembre à juin.

Le tunnel routier du St-Gothard entre Göschenen et Airolo, ouvert depuis fin 1980, détient le nouveau record mondial de longueur : 16,918 km.

D'Andermatt à Biasca

65 km — environ 2 h — itinéraire ② *de la visite du massif du St-Gothard*

★ Andermatt — *Voir à ce nom.*
C'est au pied de l'antique tour de garde d'Hospental que débute, sur le versant d'Andermatt, la dernière rampe du St-Gothard ; la route s'élève au-dessus du Val d'Urseren que ferme, à droite de la Furka, le cimier neigeux du Galenstock, puis elle s'engage dans l'ingrat vallon de Gams.

Col du St-Gothard (Passo del San Gottardo) — Alt. 2 108 m. Dans un cadre morne de roches moutonnées parsemées de lacs, le passage doit son nom à une chapelle érigée vers 1300 en l'honneur de saint Gothard, évêque d'Hildesheim (près de Hanovre).

Val Tremola — *Accessible en août seulement.* Il s'étend sur 13 km à partir du col du St-Gothard. La chaussée de 1830 n'est qu'une suite de lacets, à l'assaut de ce raide couloir au nom inquiétant (val du tremblement). Vue d'en bas (se placer sur le pont désaffecté, au fond du ravin), avec son accumulation de murs de soutènement, apparemment enchevêtrés, elle donne une haute idée de l'audace de ses constructeurs.
La chaussée moderne, d'une hardiesse exceptionnelle, évite le passage difficile du Val Tremola grâce à un tracé dévié à flanc de montagne comprenant 3 lacets seulement — l'un d'eux est édifié, en partie, sur un viaduc courbe : un autre est aménagé en **belvédère★** — et un tunnel de 700 m.
La descente se poursuit, très rapide, en vue de la Haute-Léventine, mollement ouverte entre ses versants forestiers et toute parsemée de villages mêlant, au pied de quelque campanile, les maisons de pierre tessinoises et les chalets alpestres à superstructures de bois.
D'Airolo au défilé de Piottino, s'épanouit le bassin d'Ambri-Piotta, encore encadré de sapins et de mélèzes, où l'on remarque les conduites forcées de la centrale de Ritom.
En aval du défilé de Piottino, la vallée se resserre progressivement au pied d'une succession d'éperons abrupts, délimitant des ravins sauvages dont les torrents se terminent en cascade.

★ Val Piora — Alt. 1 796 m. *De la grande centrale de Ritom, 12 mn de funiculaire.* Une très belle promenade le long de sentiers bien dessinés, où l'on découvre de petits lacs d'alpage ainsi qu'une flore et une faune variées.

Faido — Grâce à son équipement hôtelier, à ses environs riches en sous-bois et en eaux vives (cascades de la Piumogna), ce bourg, chef-lieu administratif de la Léventine, peut être conseillé comme villégiature estivale.
L'hémicycle de sa place principale compose, avec son couvert de tilleuls, sa statue dédiée à la gloire locale, ses vieilles maisons coiffées de curieux toits de pierre tronconiques, ses cafés poussant quelques chaises en plein air, un ensemble déjà latin. Dès la sortie de Faido, remarquer la jolie silhouette perchée de l'église de Calonico.

★ Giornico — *Voir à ce nom.*
Le palier inférieur de la Léventine voit prospérer la vigne. Obscurcie par les fumées de l'usine électrochimique de Bodio, cette section doit aux épaulements escarpés de la Cima Bianca, du Pizzo di Mezzodi et du Madone Grosso, un cadre encore farouche.

Biasca — *Description ci-dessous.*

ALPI TICINESI

★ROUTE DU LUKMANIER
De Biasca à Disentis/Mustér

66 km – environ 2 h 3/4 – itinéraire 1 *de la visite du massif du St-Gothard*

Le col du Lukmanier est généralement obstrué par la neige de novembre à mai.

Biasca – Petite ville-carrefour au confluent des vallées du Tessin et du Brenno, elle est dominée par son imposante **église Sts-Pierre-et-Paul** du 12ᵉ s., bâtie à même le roc et accessible par de longs escaliers. L'édifice, en granit du pays, présente un haut clocher à arcatures et une façade à double perron sous péristyle ornée d'une fresque murale (Christ bénissant) à demi effacée. A l'intérieur, vaste nef à plafond plat décoré, chapelle baroque (à droite), restes d'intéressantes **fresques** polychromes des 14ᵉ et 15ᵉ s. dans les bas-côtés (à gauche : *Noces de Cana*) et du 17ᵉ s. dans l'abside (autre Christ bénissant, dans une mandorle).

Malvaglia – Le **campanile★** roman de l'église, dont le nombre d'arcatures s'accroît, suivant la mode lombarde, à mesure que l'on se rapproche du couronnement, est le plus élégant du Val Blenio.
L'aridité du Val Blenio inférieur, aggravée naguère par l'activité dévastatrice des affluents du Brenno, s'atténue en amont de Dongio : c'est un bassin plus verdoyant qui s'épanouit maintenant, tandis qu'apparaît, en amont, la pyramide hardie du Sosto.

★ **Lottigna** – Ce village, étiré en balcon sur la vallée, a installé dans l'ancienne maison (15ᵉ s.) de ses baillis, décorée des écussons des premiers cantons suisses, le **musée du Blenio** ⊙ intéressant par ses collections d'ethnographie (outils, ustensiles et costumes régionaux traditionnels), d'art sacré (sculptures anciennes, ornements ecclésiastiques) et surtout d'armes (plus d'un millier, du 14ᵉ s. à nos jours, dont de rares spécimens de pistolets de duel et «à système» du 18ᵉ s.).

A Acquarossa, prendre à gauche la petite route sur le versant Ouest du val Blenio.

Prugiasco – L'intérieur de l'église San Ambrogio séduit par son décor baroque : dessus d'autel en bois sculpté doré, chapelle (à droite) ornée de stucs et de peintures en médaillons (Vie de la Vierge) au-dessus d'une statue de Madone à l'Enfant.

Prendre à gauche de l'église la rue montante continuée par une route étroite que l'on suit sur 2 km jusqu'au pied de la butte herbeuse portant le sanctuaire du Negrentino.

★ **Église San Carlo du Negrentino** ⊙ – *1/2 h à pied AR.* Dans une position aussi dominante que solitaire, cette vénérable petite église romane (11ᵉ s.) tourne vers la vallée son chevet à double abside flanqué d'un campanile ajouré de baies géminées. L'intérieur est peint d'une admirable série de **fresques★★** polychromes, dont la réalisation s'est poursuivie du 11ᵉ au 16ᵉ s. ; parmi les plus belles : Nativité, Jésus en croix, et gloire...
Après Castro, dont on remarque la petite église datée de 1730 (au clocher plus ancien) et Ponto-Valentino, on retrouve à Aquila la route directe du Lukmanier.
D'Olivone à Acquacalda, la route s'échappe latéralement du cul-de-sac d'Olivone, par deux séries de lacets séparées par le palier de Camperio, après lesquels s'offre une **vue★**, à l'Est, sur les cimes neigeuses du massif de l'Adula.

Col du Lukmanier (Passo del Lucomagno) – Alt. 1 916 m. Sur la ligne de partage des eaux et des langues (italien et romanche), le col sépare, aussi, deux types d'architecture régionale : au Sud, les bâtisses en maçonnerie groupées autour d'un campanile élancé, au Nord les chalets de bois et les églises coiffées d'un bulbe.
Le Lukmanier est le plus bas des passages transalpins de Suisse, mais le tracé trop détourné de ses voies d'accès, sur le versant Nord des Alpes, lui a fait préférer le St-Gothard, pour le grand trafic international. Sur le versant du Rhin, la haute dépression alpestre est noyée, en partie, par les eaux du barrage de Santa Maria. Entre le barrage de Santa Maria et Disentis, au-delà d'un val noyé d'éboulis, où la végétation arbustive se réduit à quelques plaques d'aulnes nains et de rhododendrons, la chaussée traverse le Rhin de Cristallina, aux eaux transparentes, et, tandis que les conifères réapparaissent, débouche dans le bassin central du Val de Medel. Avec ses pentes de prairies, coupées de ravins en zigzag, ses chalets sombres, le clocher à bulbe de Curaglia, cette petite cellule montagnarde forme un **ensemble★** des plus attachants. Remarquer les claies verticales où s'achève la maturation des céréales moissonnées prématurément en raison de la rigueur du climat à cette altitude voisine de 1 500 m.

Gorges de Medel (Medelserschlucht) – Les chutes du Rhin de Medel remplissent de vacarme cette faille rocheuse où la nouvelle route comporte de nombreux passages en tunnel. L'ancien tracé, que l'on ne peut plus suivre qu'à pied, à partir de la porte de sortie du 2ᵉ tunnel (long de plus de 500 m) est plus spectaculaire.
La trouée des gorges de Medel ouvre bientôt une perspective sur Disentis et la masse blanche de son abbaye et, par-delà, sur le massif du Tödi.

Disentis/Mustér – *Voir à ce nom.*

ALTDORF

C Uri — 8 282 habitants
Carte Michelin n° 427 pli 15 ou 217 pli 10
Schémas : VIERWALDSTÄTTER SEE et SANKT-GOTTHARD-MASSIV — Alt. 462 m

Placée entre le lac des Quatre-Cantons et les défilés de la haute vallée de la Reuss, Altdorf, clé du passage du St-Gothard sur le versant Nord des Alpes, a gardé sa dignité de petite capitale traditionnelle. Le passant attentif aux changements d'ambiance sera sensible aux influences méridionales qui se manifestent déjà dans la ville : l'assortiment des épiceries, les menus des restaurants, la rencontre de quelques habitants de type tessinois, quelques vestiges de **binario** *(voir à Andermatt ci-dessous)*, sont autant d'indices qui préparent à un plus complet dépaysement.

   Monument de Tell (Telldenkmal) — La statue du célèbre arbalétrier, sur la place centrale du bourg, contre une tour à dôme peinturluré, est intéressante surtout par le fait qu'elle a créé le type physique de Tell. Cette effigie (datant de 1895) est bien à sa place dans le canton qui, le premier, s'émancipa de la tutelle étrangère. Un petit **musée Tell** ⊙ est aménagé à Bürglen sur la route du col du Klausen *(voir à ce nom)*.

ENVIRONS

   ★**Bauen** — *10 km au Nord-Ouest.* Ravissant village blotti dans la verdure et les fleurs au pied des montagnes et sur la rive Ouest du lac d'Uri. Son **site★**, son élégante petite église (de 1812 ; intérieur néo-baroque), ses hôtels et chalets fleuris, sa végétation témoignant d'un micro-climat privilégié (pins, araucarias, palmiers, bananiers...) lui confèrent le cachet d'une minuscule Riviera.

ANDERMATT★

Uri — 1 319 habitants
Carte Michelin n° 427 pli 15 ou 217 Sud du pli 10
Schémas : BERNER OBERLAND et SANKT-GOTTHARD-MASSIV — Alt. 1 436 m

Au fond de la conque harmonieuse et austère du Val d'Urseren, cœur du massif du St-Gothard, Andermatt se trouve à la jonction des routes du Gothard, de la Furka et de l'Oberalp : c'est, par excellence, le carrefour des Alpes suisses. L'animation locale, marquée d'une pointe d'exubérance méridionale, se répartit le long d'une étroite rue de traversée dont certaines sections de chaussée montrent encore le « binario » typiquement italien (chemin de roulement en dalles de granit).
En hiver, alors que la neige ensevelit les versants voisins, tout striés d'ouvrages de protection contre les avalanches, Andermatt reçoit de nombreux skieurs attirés par ses commodités d'accès. Les principaux centres d'activité sportive sont la région de Nätschen (direction du col de l'Oberalp), desservie régulièrement par des navettes ferroviaires et par télésiège, ainsi que les pentes du Gemsstock équipées d'une télécabine.

Val d'ANNIVIERS★

Carte Michelin n° 427 plis 13, 22 ou 217 pli 16 et 219 pli 3 — Schéma : VALAIS

Bien connu des spécialistes de géographie humaine pour les déplacements saisonniers de sa population, perpétuellement en mouvement entre les vignobles de la vallée du Rhône, le village principal (Vissoie par exemple), les mayens *(voir à ce nom)* et les alpes — situant les différents niveaux d'activité de ses habitants — , **le Val d'Anniviers** est resté jusqu'à nos jours le fief de quelques « purs » de l'alpinisme, conquis par le charme d'une station comme **Zinal**.

DE SIERRE A ZINAL

49 km — environ 2 h 1/2 — itinéraire ③ *de la visite du Valais*

   Sierre — *Voir à ce nom.*
   Se détachant de la route de Brigue à l'orée de la forêt de Finges, la route s'élève rapidement au-dessus du bassin de Sierre, où se dressent les grosses usines d'aluminium de Chippis. Très haut sur le versant Nord de la vallée du Rhône, s'alignent les hôtels de Montana et de Crans. Niouc et sa chapelle marquent le début de la pénétration proprement dite dans le Val d'Anniviers. En contrebas, la Navisence reste très encaissée. La vue s'éclaircit, en amont, en direction du Zinalrothorn et de l'Ober Gabelhorn, de part et d'autre de la double pointe rocheuse du Besso.

   Chapelle des Pontis — Au bord de l'à-pic — le nouveau tracé de la route évite ce passage par un tunnel — ce petit sanctuaire permet à ces perpétuels voyageurs que sont les Anniviards de se mettre sous la protection de la Vierge et de saint Christophe. On remarque, sur le versant opposé, le long d'une croupe en forte pente, les chalets de Pinsec.

Val d'ANNIVIERS

Vissoie – Joli village-balcon que signalent sa tour carrée et son église rustique. Dans la montée en lacet qui mène à St-Luc, la vue s'attache encore au site étonnant de Pinsec. L'horizon montagneux s'élargit : la tête du Cervin surgit au dernier plan.

St-Luc – Bourg admirablement situé et aménagé en station de sports d'hiver. De la table d'orientation située à l'entrée du village, la vue ★★ est impressionnante sur la vallée et sur la chaîne de montagnes d'où se détachent à gauche le mont Marais (2 412 m) et à droite le mont Boivin (2 995 m). La route de St-Luc à Chandolin, tracée à flanc de montagne, pénètre bientôt sous bois, offrant, au cours du trajet, de superbes échappées sur le sillon du Val d'Anniviers, Sierre, les massifs du Wildhorn et du Wildstrubel.

★★ **Chandolin** – Alt. 1 936 m. L'arrivée se fait par le nouveau village, en fait station de sports d'hiver composée de chalets modernes et d'immeubles de hauteur modeste construits dans le style du pays. *Poursuivre à pied.*
Le vieux village, typique avec ses vieux chalets en bois, l'un des plus hauts d'Europe habités en permanence, lui fait suite. La petite agglomération s'agrippe à la pente, en vue d'un **panorama** ★★ splendide sur les Alpes valaisannes (de gauche à droite : Zinalrothorn, Besso, Ober Gabelhorn, pointe de Zinal, Dent Blanche). On peut choisir comme belvédère la croix érigée sur une bosse en arrière de l'église.

Revenir à Vissoie et prendre au Sud la route de Grimentz.

La route escalade d'abord le versant Ouest du Roc d'Orzival, parfois en corniche sur le ravin, aux allures de gouffre, au fond duquel coule la Navisence et qu'enserrent de magnifiques parois rocheuses.
Des crêtes neigeuses barrent l'horizon.

★ **Grimentz** – Cette ravissante station-village, disposée face à la Corne de Sorebois dont la proue sépare la vallée de Zinal de celle de Moiry, compte encore de nombreux mazots que ne déparent pas ses hôtels-chalets également « tout bois ».

★ **Val de Moiry** – *13 km au départ de Grimentz.* Autre prolongement du Val d'Anniviers, son parcours fait découvrir, au bout de 2 km, une belle cascade (à gauche), le site de Grimentz (à droite), puis la Dent Blanche, bien nommée, dans l'axe de la route. Au 4ᵉ km, ample **vue** ★ d'enfilade, à gauche, sur Grimentz et le Val d'Anniviers. 1 km plus loin s'aperçoit, devant la Dent Blanche, la concavité du **barrage de Moiry** qui, bientôt, semble barrer la route, laquelle le contourne et, après un tunnel, débouche sur sa gauche. Du milieu du barrage (alt. 2 249 m ; capacité : 77 millions de m³), **vue** ★ sur le lac, les sommets des Alpes Pennines et leurs glaciers. En suivant la route *(médiocre)* qui domine en palier le lac, où dévalent d'innombrables cascatelles, on jouit soudain, à l'extrémité de la retenue, d'une **vue** ★ saisissante sur le glacier de Moiry et celui de Zinal à sa gauche. La route s'achève au bassin de compensation du barrage, entre deux versants rocheux, face au glacier de Moiry.

Revenir à Grimentz et prendre la route de Zinal.

★★ **Vallée de Zinal** – Le parcours offre une double et saisissante **vue** ★★ d'enfilade : en avant, sur la vallée de Zinal et le bourg d'Ayer juché sur l'autre versant, en arrière sur tout le Val d'Anniviers que ferme au loin le massif neigeux du Wildstrubel. La vallée se rétrécit ensuite, bordée de sapins et de plus en plus « écrasée » par la silhouette acérée du Weisshorn. Après avoir franchi la Navisence et longé l'usine hydro-électrique de Pralong, la route traverse **Zinal**, centre d'alpinisme réputé, et se termine 2 km plus loin au lieu dit la Tsoudanaz, dans un petit cirque glaciaire, animé de cascatelles, au pied du glacier de Zinal.

APPENZELL

C Appenzell (Rhodes-Intérieures) – 4 781 habitants
Carte Michelin n° 427 pli 7 ou 216 pli 21 – Schéma : APPENZELLERLAND – Alt. 789 m

Au pied des contreforts verdoyants de l'Alpstein, dans un décor de pastorale, Appenzell est resté l'un des centres traditionnels de la « Suisse primitive de l'Est ». Ni ville ni village, Appenzell est un « **Flecken** » – ce terme désigne dans les pays germaniques une catégorie d'agglomérations, de caractère à la fois rustique et bourgeois.
Le nom même d'Appenzell (« Abbatis cella » : cellule de l'abbé) est un héritage de la colonisation primitive du pays par les moines de St-Gall.
On y parcourra à pied, avec agrément... et non sans quelques motifs de tentation (magasins de broderies, étalages de gâteaux fourrés d'Appenzell décorés du vacher à culotte jaune et gilet écarlate), la **rue principale** (Hauptgasse), entre l'église, au décor baroque exubérant, et la maison de la Löwendrogerie. L'élégant pignon en accolade de cette demeure abrite une série de peintures consacrées aux plantes médicinales, accompagnées de ce commentaire désabusé : « Beaucoup de plantes contre la maladie, aucune contre la mort. »

APPENZELL

Appenzell Museum ⓘ – Aménagé dans l'hôtel de ville et dans la maison mitoyenne, construits après un incendie en 1560, ce musée entraîne le visiteur à travers la culture du canton. Commencer la visite par l'étage supérieur. Outre des monnaies que les Rhodes-Intérieures n'ont pu frapper que durant cinq ans (1737-1742) et une cellule de prison datant de 1570, on remarque des costumes appenzellois (dont la coiffe en tulle noir est particulièrement raffinée), des bannières, un triptyque dû à Jacob Girtanner (16ᵉ s.), des planches de morts (aujourd'hui disparues, elles chassaient les démons). Le musée s'enorgueillit en outre de posséder un sarcophage égyptien (vers 1 000 av. J.-C.) provenant d'un temple thébain.

Blaues Haus ⓘ – Le charme de ce tout petit musée de folklore et d'artisanat local est personnifié par la propriétaire, qui a rassemblé et conservé tout ce qui concerne sa chère localité (dont l'atelier d'ébéniste de son défunt mari).

ENVIRONS

★★ **Hoher Kasten** ⓘ – Alt. 1 795 m. *7 km au Sud-Est par la route de Weissbad, puis celle de Brülisau. Téléphérique au départ de Brülisau.*

La montée en téléphérique, au-dessus des sapins et des pâturages (cabanes de bergers), procure de belles vues à droite sur le défilé boisé au fond duquel dort la nappe bleue du Sämtisersee et en avant sur le gros éperon calcaire du Hoher Kasten. Du sommet-belvédère *(panneaux d'orientation)*, rapidement accessible en contre-haut du restaurant de la station supérieure, ample **panorama**★★ : à l'Ouest et au Nord-Ouest, sur la ville d'Appenzell et les collines du « Pays » de ce nom ; à l'Est, en vue plongeante, sur le vaste sillon du Rheinthal où s'étirent les méandres du fleuve, du lac de Constance (au Nord) aux monts du Liechtenstein (au Sud), avec à l'arrière-plan le moutonnement des Alpes autrichiennes ; au Sud-Ouest, sur le massif de l'Alpstein où domine le Säntis.

★★ **Ebenalp** ⓘ – Alt. 1 640 m. *7 km – environ 1 h 1/2 – en suivant la route de Weissbad-Wasserauen jusqu'à son terminus, puis 8 mn de téléphérique.*

Le promontoire d'alpages d'Ebenalp, ceinturé de falaises, s'avance au-dessus du Pays d'Appenzell, dont les ondulations apparaissent toutes mouchetées de fermes. De l'Ebenalp, on peut redescendre à pied, en 1 h 1/2 environ, sur Wasserauen, par la **grotte-tunnel de Wildkirchli** (longue de 80 m et où des fouilles ont mis au jour les vestiges de l'établissement préhistorique le plus ancien de Suisse) et le **lac de Seealp**★, dont la nappe sombre s'étale au pied de l'éperon du Rossmad, détaché du Säntis.

APPENZELLERLAND★

Carte Michelin nº 427 plis 7, 8 ou 216 plis 21, 22

Le **Pays d'Appenzell** et la grande combe alpestre du Toggenbourg (haute vallée de la Thur), bien que séparés par une frontière administrative – Appenzell est un canton séparé depuis 1513 alors que le Toggenbourg vit toujours dans la dépendance de St-Gall, comme au temps de l'apogée de la célèbre abbaye – forment une seule région touristique : ils constituent en effet, géographiquement, les dépendances de la chaîne préalpine de l'Alpstein, dont les crêtes dentelées, culminant au Säntis (alt. 2 502 m), s'allongent au-dessus de la vallée du Rhin, face aux montagnes du Vorarlberg.

Les automobilistes appelés à passer la frontière autrichienne à St-Margrethen-Höchst profiteront de leur arrivée à St-Gall pour abandonner la route nº 7 et suivre les petits chemins sinueux desservant les communes de Trogen et de Heiden en vue du lac de Constance.

La vie en Appenzell – Le Pays d'Appenzell présente, au pied de la barrière Nord de l'Alpstein, un doux paysage de collines uniformément verdoyantes, toutes piquetées de fermes *(description de la maison rurale appenzelloise, voir Introduction au voyage)*.

Ses bourgs cossus, aux coquettes maisons à pignons en accolade, voient encore se réunir les traditionnelles « Landsgemeinden » *(voir Introduction : La Démocratie en action)* : ces assemblées de paysans portant l'épée –

Une coiffe

APPENZELLERLAND

attribut de leur dignité de citoyens actifs – ont lieu à Appenzell pour le demi-canton des Rhodes-Intérieures (catholique), et, pour le demi-canton des Rhodes-Extérieures (protestant), alternativement à Trogen (années paires) et à Hundwil (années impaires).
Voir tableau des principales manifestations touristiques, en fin de guide.
La survivance de l'élégant costume féminin de cérémonie, caractérisé par une coiffe aux immenses ailes de tulle, le maintien de spécialités gastronomiques telles que le fromage gras d'Appenzell, l'un des plus forts de la gamme helvétique, et la petite saucisse sèche de montagne dite « Alpenklübler », la persistance de la belle industrie traditionnelle de la broderie, subsistant encore sous sa forme familiale dans les Rhodes-Intérieures, confirment une originalité bien digne d'attirer l'étranger. Les amateurs de costumes régionaux choisiront, ici, l'époque de la Fête-Dieu ou de la descente de l'alpage.

★ 1 VALLÉE DE LA SITTER ET ROUTE DE STOSS

De St-Gall à Altstätten *34 km – environ 2 h*

Les routes empruntées sont longées, sur certaines sections, par des voies de tramway sur accotement. Attention aux passages à niveau non gardés.

★★ St-Gallen – *Visite : 2 h. Voir à ce nom.*
Au départ de St-Gall, l'itinéraire recommandé offre d'agréables coups d'œil tout le long de la vallée de la Sitter. D'abord profond ravin, celle-ci se transforme en une molle dépression mamelonnée où se disséminent des fermes du plus pur style appenzellois : le groupe situé à 1 km au Sud-Est de la bifurcation de Hundwil en constitue l'exemple le plus typique.

Stein – La traversée de ce village, posé sur un plateau dont l'altitude (823 m) dépasse celle de ses voisins, procure des vues étendues sur le pays environnant. L'**Appenzeller Volkskunde Museum** ⊙ – présente au rez-de-chaussée une reconstitution d'une fromagerie alpestre *(début de la production à 13 h 30)* entourée d'objets traditionnels (sellerie, cloches, tonnellerie). Au sous-sol, deux personnes font la démonstration d'un métier à tisser et d'un tambour à broder (très beaux tissus jacquards). Au 1er étage, ne pas manquer les trois parois en bois (16e s.), aux dessins délicieusement naïfs, provenant de la proche localité de Gais.

Peinture sur bois (16e s.)

Appenzell – *Voir à ce nom.*

Gais – Ce bourg attirait encore au siècle dernier les adeptes des cures de petit-lait. Sur la place centrale, une rangée de maisons à pignon en accolade constitue un bel exemple d'architecture baroque, avec ses boisages bien entretenus.

★ Stoss – Ce large seuil fut le théâtre, en 1405, de la bataille qui marqua, pour les Appenzellois, leur affranchissement du joug autrichien. Pour apprécier le **panorama★★**, très lointain, sur le Rheinthal et les Alpes du Vorarlberg, monter à la chapelle commémorative puis, à droite de celle-ci, à l'obélisque situé à 100 m de là et signalé par un bouquet d'arbres.

Altstätten – Au cœur du Rheinthal – vallée alpestre du Rhin, entre les Grisons et le lac de Constance – chaude plaine intérieure avec ses riches cultures de maïs, ses vergers, sa frange de vignobles. Altstätten présente un fort cachet médiéval, surtout dans la pittoresque Marktgasse, bordée de maisons aux pignons aigus, bâties sur un soubassement à piliers formant galeries, où le passant peut flâner à couvert. L'Engelplatz, avec sa fontaine fleurie et ses maisons dégingandées, offre un autre ensemble plaisant.

APPENZELLERLAND

★② LE TOGGENBOURG
D'Appenzell à Buchs 62 km – environ 2 h 1/2

Appenzell – *Voir à ce nom.*

Urnäsch – Le village est connu pour son petit **musée folklorique** (Museum für Appenzeller Brauchtum) ⊙, installé dans un chalet en bois du 19ᵉ s. dont l'intérieur amuse par ses pièces exiguës au plafond bas et au plancher de guingois... On y trouve : au rez-de-chaussée, une quinzaine de somptueux costumes de fête et des chapeaux extraordinaires ; au 1ᵉʳ étage (7 salles), des collections d'habits anciens, ceintures et bretelles, bijoux, pipes, tableaux, figurines peintes, clarines, cloches, plus un atelier de menuiserie ; au 2ᵉ étage (8 salles), un intérieur appenzellois aux meubles peints dont un lit-armoire, avec sa chambre réservée au vacher ; dans les combles (3 salles), une salle de musique, une laiterie, des poupées et jouets de bois anciens.
Entre Urnäsch et Schwägalp, la route quitte le fond du vallon, semé de frênes et de sapins, pour déboucher au pied des imposantes falaises Nord du Säntis.

★★★ **Le Säntis** – *Voir à ce nom.*

Le trajet Schwägalp-Nesslau, par le « col » à peine sensible de Kräzeren (alt. 1 300 m), fait longer la barrière Sud-Ouest de l'Alpstein (Silberplatten, Lütispitz). A un paysage de parc succèdent des alpages accidentés d'éboulis. Un fond de vallée tout boursouflé de pitons verdoyants d'origine morainique forme le cadre des bâtiments neufs abritant l'établissement thermal de Rietbad.
Entre Nesslau et Wildhaus, en amont de deux cluses boisées, s'ouvre, harmonieusement, la dépression du Haut-Toggenbourg ; celle-ci est parsemée d'habitations dont on remarquera les murs protégés des intempéries par un revêtement d'écailles de bois. La route qui s'élève entre Unterwasser (lieu de séjour) et Wildhaus permet d'admirer les escarpements vigoureusement plissés du Wildhuser-Schafberg et les surprenantes dentelures des Churfirsten. Les deux stations exploitent en hiver avec Alt St-Johann (lieu de séjour) un immense champ de neige.

★ **Wildhaus** – Cette agréable station est située sur un seuil, séparant le Toggenbourg du Rheinthal, en vue du Wildhuser-Schafberg, des Churfirsten et des Drei Schwestern. Wildhaus est la patrie du grand réformateur Zwingli *(voir à ce nom)* dont on voit encore la maisonnette familiale *(ne se visite pas)*.

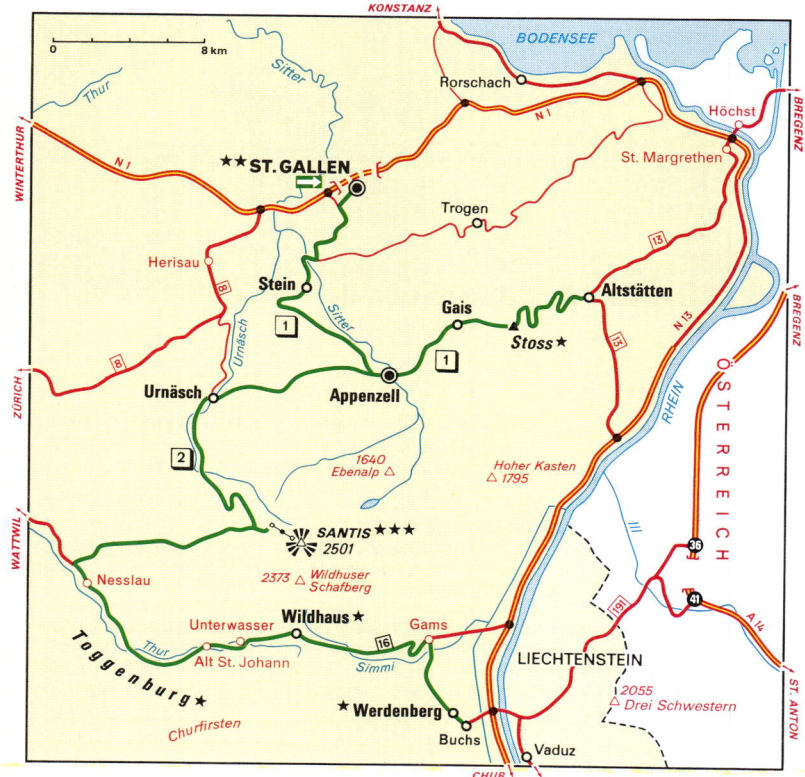

APPENZELLERLAND

De Wildhaus à Gams, la route plonge vers le Rheinthal dont l'apparition marque la fin de l'étape. Dans les lacets précédant Gams, on apprécie l'ampleur de cette dépression que dominent à l'Est les montagnes du Vorarlberg et du Liechtenstein ; celles-ci sont séparées par la trouée de Feldkirch, qu'empruntent la route et la voie ferrée de l'Arlberg.
Le territoire de la commune de Grabs est un immense verger. Remarquer les énormes poiriers.

★ **Werdenberg** – *Voir à ce nom.*

Dans le prolongement de ce village, Buchs constitue la dernière étape.

Schloss ARENENBERG

Thurgovie

Carte Michelin n° 427 pli 7 ou 216 pli 9 – 1,5 km à l'Ouest d'Ermatingen

Le petit château d'Arenenberg, entouré de jardins et d'un beau parc, se dresse sur une terrasse dominant le bassin occidental du lac de Constance (Untersee).

Une Malmaison suisse – Construit au 16ᵉ s. par un riche bourgeois de Constance, le château devint en 1817 propriété de la reine Hortense, fille de Joséphine de Beauharnais et épouse de l'ancien roi de Hollande, Louis Bonaparte. Hortense et son fils, le futur empereur Napoléon III, passèrent tous les étés à Arenenberg jusqu'en 1837 ; après la chute du Second Empire, l'impératrice Eugénie et le prince impérial y séjournèrent fréquemment.
En 1906, Eugénie fit don du château d'Arenenberg au canton de Thurgovie, qui le transforma en musée.

★ **Musée Napoléonien** ⊙ – Le château a conservé les objets d'art et le mobilier rassemblés par ses anciens propriétaires. On y voit le salon de la reine Hortense, magnifiquement meublé, dans le style de l'époque, la bibliothèque, les chambres et les boudoirs qui renferment des souvenirs de la famille impériale.
De la chambre de la reine Hortense, **vue** sur le lac de Constance et l'île de Reichenau. Une petite chapelle abrite une belle statue en marbre de la reine Hortense.

Gorges de l'AREUSE★

Cartes Michelin nᵒˢ 427 pli 12 et 216 pli 12 ou 217 pli 4 – Schéma : JURA SUISSE

La visite de ces gorges du Jura neuchâtelois s'inscrit dans l'itinéraire du Val de Travers *(voir à ce nom)*.

Visite – *Environ 1 h à pied au départ de la gare de Noiraigue.*
Après l'usine du Plan-de-l'Eau, le sentier, en palier ou en descente, longe l'Areuse, torrent domestiqué par les ingénieurs hydro-électriciens mais qui coule au fond de gorges en V, très boisées, aux sommets crêtés de falaises calcaires.
A mi-parcours, un belvédère domine un à-pic impressionnant à l'endroit le plus resserré des gorges, où l'Areuse se précipite en cascade : le **site★**, agrémenté par un vieux pont en dos d'âne, est romantique à souhait.

Champ-du-Moulin – *Accès par un chemin revêtu, sous bois.* Hameau disséminé dans le joli site boisé de l'issue des gorges et avant lequel on découvre, soitaire à 100 m du chemin, à gauche, la **maison de J.-J. Rousseau**, datée de 1722 (et dotée aujourd'hui de fenêtres Renaissance provenant d'une maison de Valangin), où séjourna l'illustre vagabond en septembre 1764.
Monter à la gare de Champ-du-Moulin, d'où se révèle une vue agréable sur la sortie des gorges de l'Areuse et d'où l'on reviendra par le train *(passages fréquents)* à Noiraigue.

Afin de donner à nos lecteurs l'information la plus récente possible, les Conditions de Visite des curiosités décrites dans ce guide ont été groupées en fin de volume.

Les curiosités soumises à des conditions de visite y sont énumérées soit sous le nom de la localité soit sous leur nom propre si elles sont isolées.

Dans la partie descriptive du guide, le signe ⊙ placé à la suite du nom de la curiosité les signale au visiteur.

AROSA ★★★

Grisons — 2 271 habitants
Carte Michelin n° 427 pli 17 ou 218 pli 5 — Schéma : GRAUBÜNDEN — Alt. 1 742 m

L'élégante station d'Arosa disperse ses hôtels dans la cuvette supérieure du Schanfigg, vallée de la Plessur. Elle séduit par son cadre de versants boisés doucement inclinés, où miroitent de petits lacs.

Située en dehors des grandes routes, Arosa ignore les arrivées massives de touristes, mais, favorisée par son climat de montagne, son atmosphère sans cesse renouvelée et son ensoleillement intense, elle se prête, été comme hiver, à la détente autant qu'aux activités sportives.

Accès — *De Coire à Arosa, 31 km — environ 1 h.* La **route d'Arosa ★** (ou **de la vallée du Schanfigg ★**), sinueuse et pittoresque, en corniche élevée sur le Schanfigg, traverse des villages-terrasses fleuris aux charmantes églises. Elle coupe en outre, dans le dernier tiers de son parcours, de curieuses arêtes calcaires, convexes et boisées côté Nord, concaves et stériles côté Sud.

Remarquer aussi, des abords du hameau de Langwies, très en contrebas à droite, le viaduc ferroviaire, lui-même jeté au-dessus d'un abîme.

La station — La route de Coire, après avoir desservi **Ausser-Arosa**, le principal centre d'animation (quartier de la gare et des lacs), sort de la forêt et se termine à **Inner-Arosa**, à l'origine du cirque supérieur de la Plessur (Aroser Alp).

Plus isolé, le centre annexe de **Maran** que les séjournants d'Arosa prennent comme but de promenade en suivant des sentiers sous bois, en pente douce (Eichhörnliweg : « sentier des Écureuils »), se disperse, à découvert, dans les alpages.

En hiver — la grande saison d'Arosa — les remontées mécaniques, dont la pièce maîtresse est le téléphérique de l'Aroser Weisshorn, offrent aux skieurs des parcours faciles, accidentés ou difficiles, dont certains dépassent 1 000 m de dénivellation.

★★ **Weisshorn** ⊙ — *Alt. 2 653 m. Accès en 20 mn par téléphérique.*

La montée jusqu'à la station intermédiaire, Law Mittel Station (alt. 2 013 m), procure des vues de plus en plus amples sur Arosa et ses lacs, son bassin verdoyant et son cirque de montagnes.

Au sommet (table d'orientation), très beau **panorama ★★** sur les hauteurs environnantes et les crêtes neigeuses des Alpes grisonnes que barrent au Sud le Piz Kesch, le Piz d'Ela, l'Erzhorn... Arosa reste visible, et Coire se découvre au Nord-Ouest, au pied du Calanda.

ASCONA ★

Tessin — 4 540 habitants
Carte Michelin n° 427 pli 24 ou 219 Nord des plis 7, 8 — Schéma : LOCARNO
Alt. 210 m — Plan dans le guide Rouge Michelin Suisse

Au bord du lac Majeur, Ascona occupe une position de choix identique à celle de Locarno, par rapport à l'embouchure de la Maggia, et bénéficie, comme sa grande voisine, des vastes dégagements qu'offrent, pour les installations sportives, les terres basses du delta formé par ce torrent.

Cette bourgade de pêcheurs, colorée, depuis longtemps goûtée par les artistes, est devenue une importante villégiature particulièrement appréciée (Semaines musicales d'Ascona en septembre).

Église N.-D.-de-la-Miséricorde — Formant un côté du cloître de l'établissement religieux (Collegio Papio) qui s'est bâti auprès d'elle, cette église a été fondée en 1399 et transformée au 15ᵉ s. - à l'exception du chœur, resté gothique. Elle est connue pour ses fresques polychromes des 15ᵉ-16ᵉ s. *(certaines très dégradées ou quasi effacées)* décorant les murs de la nef (St-Christophe, Père Éternel, Vierge au chêne, St Roch, St Sébastien...), les murs et les voûtes du chœur (Ancien Testament, Vierge au manteau, Nouveau Testament...), ainsi que pour son très beau **retable** de la vie de la Vierge (dû à Giovanni Antonio della Gaïa — 1519) surmontant le maître-autel. *Éclairage à droite de l'entrée.*

ENVIRONS

★★ **Circuit de Ronco** — *17 km — environ 1 h 1/2. Prendre la route de Losone. Description : voir à Locarno - Environs.*

Îles de Brissago ⊙ — Ces îles minuscules représentent le but de promenade classique des touristes séjournant à Ascona.

Ces îles bénéficient d'un climat privilégié. La plus grande, l'île de San Pancrazio, fut aménagée en jardin botanique au début du siècle par la propriétaire d'alors, la baronne de Saint-Léger. De nos jours les deux îles forment le jardin botanique cantonal planté de très belles essences.

Ruines romaines d'AUGST★★

AUGUSTA RAURICA-Bâle-Campagne
Carte Michelin n° 427 pli 4 ou 216 plis 4-5 – 11 km au Sud-Est de Bâle

C'est à un ami de Jules César, le général romain Munatius Plancus, que la Suisse doit la présence des vestiges de la plus ancienne colonie romaine établie sur le Rhin, la «colonia raurica», fondée en 44-43 avant J.-C. L'implantation de la colonie sur le site d'Augst lui-même semble remonter à l'an 10 avant J.-C.

Une ville antique importante – Au 2e s. après J.-C., la ville qui s'est considérablement étoffée compte 20 000 habitants, possède une activité commerciale florissante et un artisanat prospère. Bien située sur la frontière Nord de l'Empire romain, la cité est aussi un foyer de culture antique, auréolé de riches bâtiments publics.

Dans le contexte troublé de la fin du 3e s., il semble bien qu'Augst ait été à peu près détruite, peut-être dès 260, lors de la chute du Limes (frontière) de l'empire sous les assauts des Alamans. L'armée, pour tenir le très important passage sur le Rhin a construit dans les premières années du 4e s., légèrement au Nord d'Augst, le puissant castrum de **Kaiseraugst**. Une bonne partie de ces fortifications a dû survivre à la fin de l'empire romain et servir de protection aux populations locales durant tout le haut Moyen Âge.

Les fouilles – Au 16e s., période de rayonnement des grands humanistes bâlois, le célèbre juriste **Amerbach** *(voir à Bâle)* réalisa les premières investigations scientifiques en utilisant les travaux des fouilles entreprises quelques années plus tôt par le négociant bâlois Andreas Ryff. Périodiquement, d'autres fouilles eurent lieu çà et là.

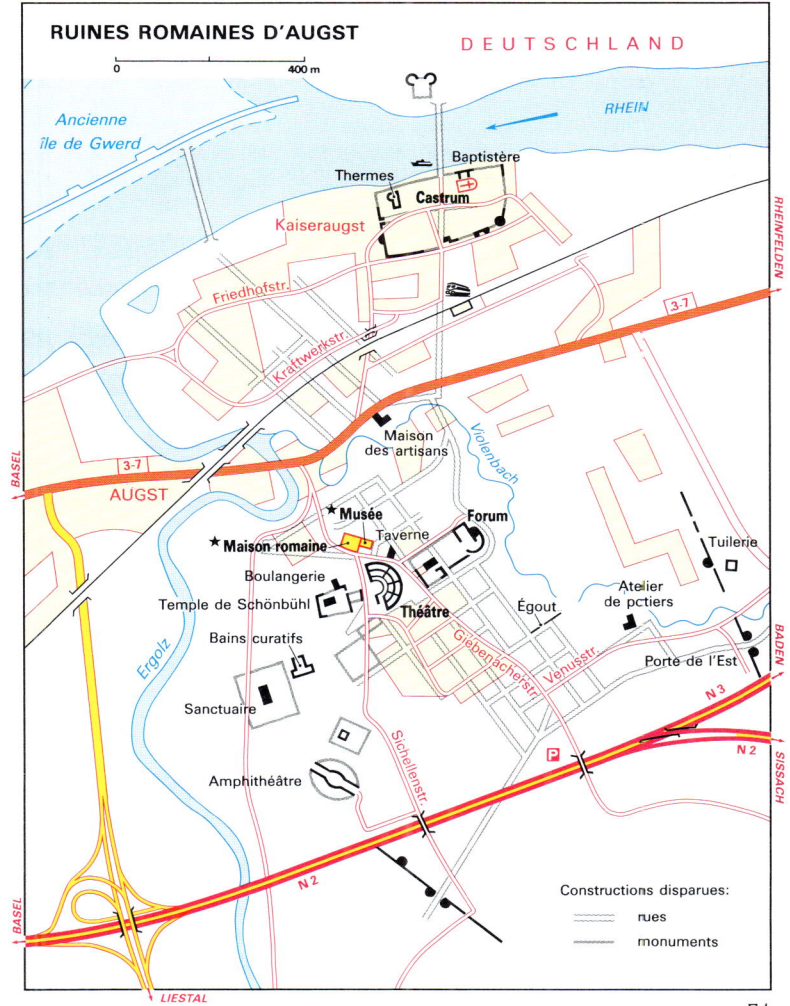

51

Ruines romaines d'AUGST

En 1839, la Société historique et archéologique de Bâle (Historische und Antiquarische Gesellschaft zu Basel) organisa des recherches sur la cité romaine puis, à partir de 1878, des fouilles systématiques et scientifiquement organisées. Ces recherches continuent à l'époque actuelle.

Les vestiges antiques ⊙ — *Visite : 1/2 h à une journée, selon le circuit choisi. Dépliant en français et plan des parcours proposés au musée. Balisage des ruines en français et allemand.* Une vingtaine de monuments ont pu être restaurés parmi lesquels le **théâtre**, la plus importante ruine romaine de Suisse, qui pouvait recevoir 8 000 spectateurs. Il se

Mosaïque romaine

prête aujourd'hui à des représentations et des concerts en plein air. Le centre administratif, politique et religieux de la ville était le **forum** avec basilique, curie (dans la cave : exposition de mosaïques) et temple de Jupiter. C'est au forum que se tenaient les marchés, mais aussi certaines festivités officielles.

★ **Maison romaine (Römisches Wohnhaus)** ⊙ — Cette maison d'habitation et de commerce est une reconstitution fidèle du type de demeure que l'on construisait à Augst à l'époque romaine. Ses pièces principales (cuisine, salle à manger, chambre à coucher, salle d'eau, atelier et magasin) sont garnies de copies ou d'authentiques objets ou ustensiles trouvés au cours des fouilles. Le sol de l'étuve montre en coupe l'astucieux système romain de chauffage par le sol, ou hypocauste.

★ **Musée romain (Römermuseum)** ⊙ — Attenant à la maison romaine, il présente une sélection représentative des quelque 700 000 objets glanés au cours des fouilles de la cité antique. Le **trésor d'argenterie** ★★ (Silberschatz), découvert en 1962 au pied des anciennes murailles de Kaiseraugst, recèle notamment 68 pièces d'un service de table fastueux : plats décorés de scènes mythologiques, gobelets, écuelles, cuillers, candélabre... Trois lingots d'argent appartenant au trésor ont pu être précisément datés de l'an 350, grâce au sceau qu'ils portent. L'ensemble du trésor pourrait bien avoir été enterré lors d'invasions des Germains en 352-353.

AVENCHES

Vaud — 2 505 habitants

Carte Michelin nº 427 pli 12 ou 217 pli 5 — 4 km au Sud du lac de Morat — Alt. 480 m

La petite ville d'Avenches est bâtie à l'emplacement de l'ancienne capitale des Helvètes, l'Aventicum romaine fondée par Auguste et développée par Vespasien. Aventicum, qui compta jusqu'à 20 000 habitants, connut une période florissante pendant tout le 2e s. avant d'être dévastée en 259. Au centre de la ville, le château à la façade Renaissance fut construit à la fin du 16e s. par les évêques de Lausanne, suzerains d'alors.
La ville actuelle, ancien Capitole, est beaucoup moins étendue que l'antique cité, dont les vestiges mis au jour permettent de mesurer l'importance.

Au temps des légions — Une enceinte de presque 6 km de tour, dont les murs hauts de 7 m étaient garnis de créneaux, défendait Aventicum.
Des tours semi-circulaires, adossées à l'intérieur de la muraille, étaient utilisées comme postes d'observation ; l'une d'elles subsiste, la « Tornallaz », mais elle a été maladroitement restaurée.
On peut visiter les ruines de l'amphithéâtre, du théâtre romain et d'un grand sanctuaire dit « du Cigognier », dont ne subsiste qu'une seule colonne. Des restes du podium du temple et d'un portique ont également été dégagés. La capacité de l'amphithéâtre était de 8 000 places.

★ **Musée romain** ⊙ — Installé dans une grosse tour carrée, construite au Moyen Âge au-dessus de l'entrée principale de l'amphithéâtre romain, le musée renferme les objets découverts au cours des fouilles.
Au rez-de-chaussée, sont exposées une très belle louve allaitant Romulus et Rémus et de nombreuses inscriptions, des peintures murales et des mosaïques ; un programme audiovisuel relate l'histoire d'Avenches.

AVENCHES

Au 1er étage, à la copie du buste en or de Marc-Aurèle (l'original se trouve au musée d'archéologie et d'histoire de Lausanne) s'ajoutent des bronzes (Bacchus, Silène, main votive, divinité gauloise), des marbres (Minerve, Mercure, art funéraire), ainsi qu'une présentation de monnaies frappées à Aventicum.

Au second étage, un beau bronze de danseuse, une intéressante vitrine titrée « jardin zoologique », des outils et poteries complètent cette collection qui donne une image vivante de la civilisation romaine en Suisse.

Musée A.M.V.A.N.A.S. ⊙ – Ce petit musée présente une exposition bien documentée sur le pionnier de l'aviation en Suisse, Ernest Failloubaz, natif d'Avenches. Le « gamin volant » s'arracha du sol le 10 mai 1910, à l'âge de 17 ans.

BADEN

Argovie – 15 718 habitants
Carte Michelin n° 427 pli 5 ou 216 plis 6, 7 – Alt. 385 m

Bâtie au pied des derniers contreforts du Jura, Baden occupe un **site ★** pittoresque sur les rives de la Limmat.

La ville thermale et les quartiers industriels s'étendent au pied de la ville ancienne, massée sur un éperon dominant le fleuve et portant les ruines du château de Stein. Cette imposante forteresse avait servi d'arsenal et de refuge aux Autrichiens lors des campagnes qui s'étaient soldées pour eux par les défaites de Morgarten et de Sempach.

En 1415, les Confédérés s'en emparent et la brûlent. Reconstruite au 17e s. par les habitants de Baden que soutenaient les cantons catholiques, elle fut de nouveau détruite en 1712 par les Bernois et les Zurichois.

Centre industriel mondialement connu pour ses fabrications de matériel électromécanique, Baden est l'une des villes les plus actives du canton d'Argovie.

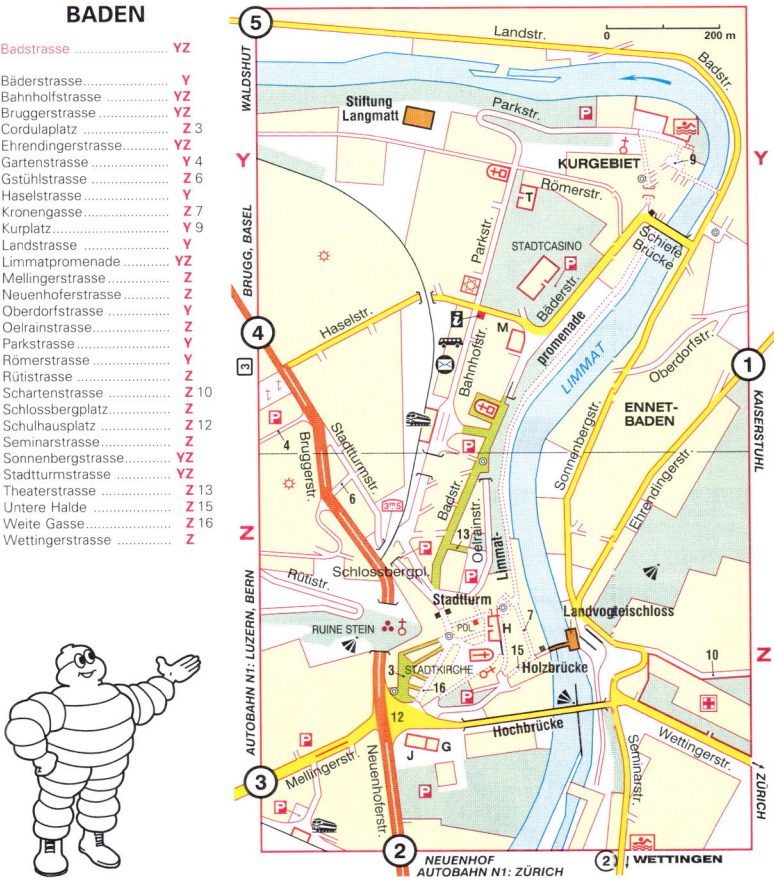

BADEN

Badstrasse	YZ
Bäderstrasse	Y
Bahnhofstrasse	YZ
Bruggerstrasse	YZ
Cordulaplatz	Z 3
Ehrendingerstrasse	YZ
Gartenstrasse	Y 4
Gstühlstrasse	Z 6
Haselstrasse	Y
Kronengasse	Z 7
Kurplatz	Y 9
Landstrasse	Y
Limmatpromenade	YZ
Mellingerstrasse	Z
Neuenhoferstrasse	Z
Oberdorfstrasse	Y
Oelrainstrasse	Z
Parkstrasse	Y
Römerstrasse	Y
Rütistrasse	Z
Schartenstrasse	Z 10
Schlossbergplatz	Z
Schulhausplatz	Z 12
Seminarstrasse	Z
Sonnenbergstrasse	YZ
Stadtturmstrasse	YZ
Theaterstrasse	Z 13
Untere Halde	Z 15
Weite Gasse	Z 16
Wettingerstrasse	Z

53

BADEN

CURIOSITÉS

★**Vieille ville** (Z) – Du pont-route moderne, on découvre une belle **vue**★ sur la ville ancienne. Ses maisons aux pignons en escaliers, aux beaux toits bruns percés de nombreuses lucarnes, descendent jusqu'à la Limmat que franchit un vieux pont de bois couvert (Holzbrücke).
L'église paroissiale (Stadtkirche) et la tour de ville (Stadtturm) ornée d'un clocheton, de tourelles d'angles et couverte d'un toit de tuiles vernissées, dominent l'ensemble.

Château des Baillis (Landvogteischloss) (Z) ⊙ – Il se dresse près du pont couvert (Holzbrücke), sur la rive droite de la Limmat.
Un **musée** est installé dans le donjon de ce vieux château qui servit de résidence aux baillis, de 1415 à 1798.
On remarque des collections d'armes, du mobilier ancien, des peintures et sculptures, des poteries, bronzes et monnaies d'origine romaine découverts dans la région et des costumes du canton d'Argovie. Des différents étages du donjon, on découvre de jolies vues sur le pont couvert et la ville ancienne avec ses pignons à redents et ses toits à lucarnes.

★**Stiftung «Langmatt» Sidney und Jenny Brown** (Y) ⊙ – *Römerstrasse 30. Expositions temporaires au premier étage.*
La maison de Sidney Brown, industriel dont le nom est perpétué par la firme ABB (Area Brown Boveri), abrite pour l'essentiel des toiles impressionnistes de petit format. Si la force de la collection repose sur deux séries d'œuvres signées P.-A. Renoir et P. Cézanne, son âme s'exprime pleinement à travers quelques tableaux de grande qualité réalisés par d'autres artistes de renom. L'*Étude de nu* de E. Degas, *Rentrée des bateaux de pêche à Trouville* de E. Boudin, *Châtaigniers à Louveciennes* de C. Pissarro, *La Débâcle de la Seine* de C. Monet, trois dessins à l'encre de Chine dus à H. Matisse et une marine de O. Redon retiennent particulièrement l'attention. Des toiles de C. Corot, G. Courbet, H. Fantin-Latour, P. Gauguin, A. Sisley et V. van Gogh, ainsi qu'un petit salon présentant des œuvres françaises du 18e s. (Fragonard, Greuze et Watteau) et des paysages du Zurichois S. Gessner complètent la visite.

La ville thermale – Connue sous le nom de «Aquae Helvetciae» à l'époque romaine, Baden était, vers la fin du Moyen Âge, l'une des plus importantes stations balnéaires de toute la Suisse.
Avec ses 19 sources chaudes sulfureuses chlorurées sodiques (48°), débitant environ 1 million de litres par jour, Baden est une station spécialisée dans le traitement des rhumatismes articulaires et des affections des troubles circulatoires.
La Limmat-Promenade, tracée au bord de la rivière entre le quartier des bains et le pont couvert, est agréable à parcourir à pied.

ENVIRONS

★**Abbaye de Wettingen (Ehem. Zisterzienserkloster Wettingen)** ⊙ – *3 km au Sud de Baden, entre la voie ferrée et la Limmat.*
Cette ancienne abbaye cistercienne fondée au 13e s., à la suite d'un vœu, par le comte Henri de Rapperswil, abrite actuellement une école cantonale.
Le **cloître** de style gothique montre des arcades cloisonnées et ornées de vitraux du 13e s. au 17e s. Tout autour des galeries ont été placées des statues de moines et d'abbés.
L'**église conventuelle** a été reconstruite en 1517 dans le style baroque, à la suite d'un incendie. L'**intérieur**★, malgré une décoration souvent surchargée, ne manque pas d'homogénéité : fresques, tableaux, statues, stucs et marbres, boiseries (**stalles**★★) sont distribués à profusion.

Cailler, Suchard, Kohler, Nestlé, Lindt, Tobler...

Des noms prestigieux qui évoquent de séduisantes présentations au contenu délicat.
En fait, ces noms sont ceux de pionniers de la fabrication du chocolat suisse qui, au cours du 19e s. et au début du 20e s., ont permis au pays d'accéder en ce domaine à une renommée internationale.
Comme un grand vin, un bon chocolat a du bouquet et se déguste. On le trouve sous trois types : noir, blanc ou au lait, et présenté sous la forme de tablettes, napolitains (tablettes en miniature), bonbons, figurines.

BASEL ★★★

C Bâle – 178 428 habitants
Carte Michelin n° 427 pli 4 ou 216 pli 4 – Schéma : JURA SUISSE
Plan d'agglomération dans le guide Rouge Michelin Suisse

Sise à l'extrême Nord-Ouest du territoire suisse, face au pays de Bade et à l'Alsace, baignée par le Rhin à l'endroit où il devient navigable et lui ouvre l'horizon du trafic maritime, Bâle est la deuxième ville de Suisse par sa population. Important centre commerçant et industriel grâce à cette situation géographique ouverte aux échanges, elle assoit aujourd'hui sa prospérité sur son port, ses banques, ses compagnies d'assurances, ses industries. Elle est le siège, au printemps, d'une **Foire** qui draine plus d'un million de visiteurs chaque année. Tous les ans en juin, le Salon International d'Art (Art Internationale Kunstmesse) compte parmi les grands rendez-vous de l'art moderne.

La ville tire son origine de la colonie romaine d'Augusta Raurica, fondée en 44 av. J.-C. Elle fait partie de l'Empire germanique dès 1032, mais passe sous la domination d'un prince-évêque, vassal de l'Empereur, ce que rappellent les armes de Bâle où figure une crosse épiscopale. La cité n'entrera que tardivement dans la Confédération, en 1501.

Une grave crise religieuse – De 1431 à 1448, le concile de Bâle s'attache à réformer le clergé et à ramener à l'Église les hérétiques. Des discordes graves entre le pape et les évêques troublent cette assemblée, si bien qu'Eugène IV tente de réunir un autre concile à Ferrare.
Le concile de Bâle offre alors la tiare à Amédée VIII, duc de Savoie, qui accepte et prend le nom de Félix V ; c'est l'époque du Grand Schisme qui ne prendra fin qu'avec la renonciation d'Amédée à la papauté en 1449.

Ville réformée – Accueillante à la Réforme, la ville adopta très vite (en 1529) la nouvelle confession (en 1529), telle que l'avait introduite Johannes Hussgen, connu sous le nom d'Œcolampade. Cet ancien moine et prêtre prêcha une réforme modérée respectueuse de l'attachement des fidèles aux pratiques catholiques, ce qui valut à la cité une réputation de tolérance qu'aujourd'hui encore on attache à son nom.
Sa situation géographique comme son ouverture lui valurent d'accueillir, après la révocation de l'Édit de Nantes, des huguenots français réfugiés qui introduisirent à Bâle le tissage de la soie, posant les prémices de l'essor industriel de la ville. Ainsi démarra la production de rubans de soie dont Bâle se fit une spécialité, fournissant toute l'Europe pour les chapeaux, crinolines… L'industrie corollaire de la teinture prit bientôt le pas sur cette activité et marqua le début de l'industrie chimique bâloise avec la création en **1785** de l'entreprise Geigy.
L'âge d'or de Bâle au 18e s. a marqué de son cachet la vieille ville aux nombreux hôtels classiques.

Le carnaval – Enraciné en terre alémanique, le carnaval bâlois tire son origine du Moyen Âge catholique, et son originalité de ce qu'il fut le seul à subsister en pays protestant après la Réforme. Parenthèse ouverte dans la vie quotidienne par l'irruption trois jours durant de cortèges et de mascarades régis par des rites précisément codés, il marque le début du Carême.

Bâle – Le carnaval

BASEL

Son déroulement actuel est le fruit d'une lente élaboration qui prit sa forme définitive en 1946 seulement, se greffant sur les traditions des cortèges de carnaval des corporations bâloises. Le «Morgestraich», tradition remontant au 18e s., marque l'ouverture des festivités, le premier lundi de Carême à 4 h du matin, lorsque toutes les lumières de la ville s'éteignent.

Les participants masqués et costumés, rangés en «cliques» de 20 à 200 personnes derrière un lampion coloré pouvant atteindre 3 m de haut, «la laterne», s'ébranlent en cortège au son des fifres et des tambours. La manifestation s'achève vers 6 h dans les restaurants de la ville par les traditionnelles soupe à la farine et tarte à l'oignon. Couleurs et musique des masques défilant en ordre ou déambulant individuellement selon les moments animeront la ville jusqu'au mercredi. Le mardi après midi, réservé aux enfants, voit défiler le cortège des petits garçons.

SORTIR A BÂLE

Pour tout renseignement concernant les manifestations ou les spectacles, s'adresser à l'Office du tourisme, Schifflände 5, ☏ (061) 261 50 50.

Théâtre et musique

Théâtre de Bâle, Theaterstrase 7, ☏ (061) 295 11 33.
Komödie, Steinenvorstadt 63, ☏ (061) 295 11 00.
Stadtcasino, Steinberg 14, ☏ (061) 272 66 58.
Musical Theater, Rheinring, ☏ (061) 686 20 01.

Cinémas

Plusieurs salles comme le **Plaza**, l'**Hollywood**, le **Rex**, l'**Eldorado** ou le **Kücklin** se trouvent dans Steinenvorstadt.

Vitrines et marchés

Pour faire des achats ou tout simplement faire du lèche-vitrines : **Aeschenvorstsdt**, **Freie Strasse**, **Gerbergasse**, **Steinenvorstadt**, **Schneudergasse**, **Spalenberg**, **Barfüsserplatz** (**marché** – *tous les jeudis de janvier à mi-octobre, de 7 h à 18 h 30* – articles divers). **Marktplatz** (**marché** – *tous les jours de 6 h à 13 h 30 - 18 h 30 les lundis, mercredis et vendredis* – fleurs, fruits et légumes).

Où prendre un verre dans un cadre agréable ?

Le bar de l'**hôtel des Trois Rois** (Mittlere Rheinbrucke) est très agréable en été avec sa terrasse couverte qui domine le Rhin. La couverture de la carte est originale, elle comporte les signatures et commentaires de personnalités ayant fréquenté l'établissement.
Dans la Clarastrasse, rue commerçante très animée, se trouvent quelques établissements très fréquentés : **Mr Pickwick Pub** (ambiance pub anglais), le **Plaza Club** qui présente des soirées à thèmes (karaoké, concerts, spectacles) et le **Grischuna Bar** de l'hôtel Alexander (concerts tous les soirs).
Comme dans de nombreuses villes, le quartier de la gare centrale fourmille de cafés et de restaurants, et reste très animé tard dans la nuit. Pour prendre un verre dans une ambiance feutrée on peut s'arrêter au bar de l'hôtel **Euler**. Dans un cadre raffiné le **Old City Bar** de l'hôtel Hilton s'adresse plus particulièrement aux amateurs de piano-bar. Pour les couche-tard, le même hôtel propose en fin de semaine sa boîte de nuit le **Bora-Bora**.
Le piano-bar du **Café des Arts** du Stadt-Casino (Barfüsserplatz) accueille des pianistes de tous les pays.
Le vin rend triste ou gai selon les tempéraments. Pour s'en assurer, le **Caveau** (Grünpfahlgasse 4) propose chaque semaine plusieurs variétés de vins suisses, français, californiens, italiens et autres.
Dans la vieille ville, les fans de musique jeune et rythmée iront écouter l'orchestre de l'**Atlantis** (9 Klosterberg), assis autour de la scène ou en mezzanine.

★ LA VIEILLE VILLE *visite : 3 h*

★★ **Cathédrale (Münster) (CY)** ⊙ – C'est un vaste édifice bâti au 12e s., reconstruit partiellement aux 14e et 15e s. et restauré au 19e s. En grès rouge, il est surmonté de deux tours gothiques, du sommet desquelles on a une belle vue sur la ville. Entre les tours s'élève un porche du milieu du 13e s. Les voussures du portail principal sont délicatement ornées de figurines de prophètes et d'anges et de cordons de feuillages et de fleurs. A droite, statues du Tentateur et d'une Vierge Folle.
En contournant l'édifice par la gauche, on atteint le portail roman de St-Gall : au tympan, le Christ Juge, les Vierges Sages et les Vierges Folles au linteau et une Résurrection des Morts au-dessus de l'archivolte ; une «roue de fortune»

BASEL

surmonte l'ensemble. L'intérieur compte cinq vaisseaux; la nef centrale possède des chapiteaux et un triforium romans. A l'extrémité du bas-côté gauche se trouve un bas-relief en grès rouge du 11e s. représentant le martyre de saint Vincent. Au bas-côté droit, autre bas-relief du 11e s. montrant, sous des arcades, des apôtres s'entretenant deux à deux.

A l'extérieur, le chevet, en partie roman, est décoré d'une frise et d'amusants modillons; il donne sur la terrasse du « Pfalz » — nom de l'ancien « palais » épiscopal —, d'où l'on découvre une jolie **vue**★ sur le Rhin, la ville, la Forêt-Noire et les Vosges.

On accède par un passage, étroit et sombre, à un cloître gothique du 15e s., que prolonge un autre cloître de la même époque contenant de nombreuses épitaphes.

Traverser la place et prendre à droite l'Augustinergasse.

Dans l'Augustinergasse s'alignent les maisons du 16e s.

Bâle — La cathédrale

★ **Musée d'Ethnographie** (Museum für Völkerkunde) (**BY** M¹) ⊙ — Il se double en outre d'une importante section de **sciences naturelles** et de préhistoire.

Sa partie ethnographique présente près de 140 000 pièces : masques, armes, sculptures, céramiques, étoffes du monde entier, œuvres d'art d'Océanie et de l'Amérique précolombienne. On remarque particulièrement, au rez-de-chaussée, les collections concernant la Mélanésie : case-temple papoue haute de 16 m, masques, totems, pirogues... D'autres collections intéressantes se rapportent à l'Indonésie, Bali notamment. Plusieurs salles exposent de précieux tissus, indonésiens pour la plupart; une autre salle, des objets de l'Égypte antique (momies, sarcophages).

Le reste des salles, aux étages, est consacré à la géologie, à une évocation didactique de la préhistoire, aux sciences naturelles (s'appliquant principalement à la Suisse).

Continuer tout droit par le Rheinsprung, ruelle en pente bordée de maisons des 15e et 16e s. qui offre une jolie vue sur le Rhin, la ville et le Mittlere Rheinbrücke avec sa chapelle aux tuiles vernissées. Le Rheinsprung débouche sur l'Eisengasse, rue aux nombreuses boutiques, que l'on prend à gauche vers la place du Marché.

Place du Marché (Marktplatz) (**BY**) — La place, entourée de maisons à encorbellement, est animée chaque matin par le marché; il se tient devant les arcades de l'hôtel de ville, près de la maison de la Corporation des Tonneliers (1578).

Hôtel de ville (Rathaus) (**BY** H) ⊙ — Construit entre 1504 et 1514, dans un style gothique tardif, il a été agrandi et restauré de 1898 à 1902. La façade, décorée de fresques, est flanquée d'un beffroi moderne orné de clochetons. Dans la cour intérieure, fresques du 17e s. très restaurées et statue du fondateur de la ville : Munatius Plancus. La salle du Conseil d'État a gardé ses boiseries richement décorées et ses vitraux héraldiques du 16e s.

A l'extrémité de la Marktplatz, prendre à gauche la Marktgasse (rue du Marché), qui rejoint la Fischmarktplatz.

La Fischmarktplatz (place du Marché aux Poissons), partie bruyante du quartier commercial de Bâle, est décorée par la fontaine du Marché aux Poissons.

★ **Fontaine du Marché aux Poissons** (Fischmarktbrunnen) (**BY**) — Colonne gothique surmontée d'une Vierge et de deux saints dont l'original, dû à Jacob Sarbach et datant de 1390, est exposé au musée historique.

★ **Vieilles rues** (BY) – Prendre à gauche la Stadthausgasse et suivre la Schneidergasse aboutissant au Spalenberg, petite rue en montée particulièrement pittoresque qui offre tout un choix de boutiques d'antiquités, de produits artisanaux.

Tourner à gauche dans le Gemsberg, jolie ruelle qui mène à une place entourée de maisons des 13e et 14e s. aux façades claires et colorées. La fontaine du Chamois ajoute au charme de la place.

Tourner à droite dans le Heuberg, où l'on remarque des maisons des 13e et 14e s.

Fontaine de Holbein (Holbeinbrunnen) (BY) – *Située à gauche du Spalenvorstadt.* Datant du 16e s., elle représente un joueur de cornemuse, inspiré d'une gravure de Dürer, et une danse de paysans, d'après un dessin de Holbein.

BASEL

Aeschenvorstadt	**CYZ**
Barfüsserplatz	**BY** 7
Centralbahnplatz	**BZ** 16
Claraplatz	**CX**
Eisengasse	**BY** 24
Falknerstrasse	**BY** 27
Freie Strasse	**BY**
Gerbergasse	**BY**
Greifengasse	**BCY** 33
Marktplatz	**BY**
Steinenvorstadt	**BYZ**
Alermannengasse	**DY** 3
Andreas Heusler-Strasse	**DZ** 4
Augustinergasse	**BY** 6
Bäumleingasse	**CY** 9
Bernoullistrasse	**ABY** 12
Brunngässlein	**CYZ** 15
Centralbahnstrasse	**BZ** 18
Drahtzugstrasse	**CX** 19
Dufourstrasse	**CY** 22
Erdbeergraben	**BZ** 25
Fischmarkt	**BY** 28
Gemsberg	**BY** 31
Innere Margarethen-Strasse	**BZ** 43
Isteinerstrasse	**DX** 45
Kannenfeldstrasse	**AX** 46
Klingentalstrasse	**CX** 48
Klosterberg	**BZ** 49
Kohlenberg	**BY** 51
Kohlenberggasse	**BY** 52
Leonhardsgraben	**BY** 55
Leonhardsstrasse	**BY** 57
Lindenhofstrasse	**CZ** 58
Luftgässlein	**CY** 60
Marktgasse	**BY** 61
Marschalkenstrasse	**AZ** 63
Messeplatz	**DX** 64
Mühlenberg	**CDY** 66
Münsterberg	**BY** 69
Münsterplatz	**BY** 70
Peter Merian-Strasse	**CZ** 73
Riehentorstrasse	**CY** 75
Rümelinsplatz	**BY** 76
St. Alban-Graben	**CY** 78
Schaffhauserrheinweg	**DY** 81
Schneidergasse	**BY** 82
Spalengraben	**BY** 84
Spalenvorstadt	**BY** 85
Stadthausgasse	**BY** 87
Steinentorstrasse	**BZ** 88
Streitgasse	**BY** 90
Wettsteinstrasse	**CY** 94

E	Mühlegraben
F	Fasnachtsbrunnen
H	Rathaus
M¹	Museum für Völkerkunde
M²	Pharmazie-historisches Museum
M³	Sammlung alter Musikinstruments
M⁴	Stadt- und Münster museum
M⁵	Skulpturhalle
M⁶	Basler Papiermühle
M⁷	Architekturmuseum

Porte de Spalen (Spalentor) (**ABY**) – Belle porte monumentale des 13ᵉ et 14ᵉ s., restaurée à la fin du 19ᵉ s. Deux tours rondes crénelées encadrent le corps de logis surmonté d'un haut toit pointu aux tuiles vernissées. Le sommet de la façade Ouest, au-dessus de la herse, est orné de statues en grès rose et des armoiries de Bâle.

Revenir sur ses pas par le Spalenvorstadt et, au carrefour, tourner à gauche.

Église St-Pierre (Peterskirche) (**BY**) – Édifice en grès rose qui date de la fin du gothique. A l'intérieur, des fresques (14ᵉ et 15ᵉ s.) sont visibles dans le bas-côté droit et dans la chapelle à gauche du chœur.

A gauche du chevet de l'église, prendre la Petersgasse, au charme tout médiéval.
Le Blumenrain conduit au Mittlere Rheinbrücke qui permet de gagner la rive droite du Rhin. A l'extrémité du pont, descendre quelques marches à droite.

BASEL

Oberer Rheinweg (**CY**) — Cette promenade tracée le long du Rhin offre une jolie **vue ★** — surtout depuis le pont **Wettsteinbrücke**, qui la limite à l'Est — sur les vieux quartiers de Bâle, les tours de la cathédrale et des églises, les palais et les étroites maisons d'artisans au bord de l'eau.

Traverser le Wettsteinbrücke.

★★★ **Musée des Beaux-Arts (Kunstmuseum)** (**CY**) ⊙ — La présentation des œuvres est renouvelée régulièrement, aussi n'est-il pas toujours possible de les voir toutes en même temps. L'accent porte sur les peintures et dessins du 15ᵉ et 16ᵉ s., ainsi que sur l'art du 19ᵉ et 20ᵉ s.

La plupart des œuvres anciennes exposées proviennent du fonds d'un collectionneur du 16ᵉ s., le Bâlois Basilius Amerbach dont le père était l'ami d'Érasme et de Holbein. Acquises par la ville en 1661, elles sont à l'origine de la création du musée.

Cour d'entrée — Sculptures de Rodin (monument des Bourgeois de Calais), de Alexandre Calder et de Edouardo Chillida.
Dans la galerie qui entoure la cour d'entrée, on remarque les œuvres de deux peintres suisses du 19ᵉ s., Arnold Böcklin et Ferdinand Hodler.

Rez-de-Chaussée — A droite se trouve le Cabinet des estampes exposant par roulement de riches collections de dessins et de gravures.

Premier étage — Les salles 1 à 15 sont consacrées à l'art pictural du Haut-Rhin de 1400 à 1600. Du Bâlois Konrad Witz (env. 1400-1445), une admirable série de panneaux du retable *Miroir de la Sainte-Salvation* est caractérisée par l'observation des volumes, le charme des paysages (panneau de saint Christophe), la recherche de la composition et du rapport des couleurs.
Martin Schongauer, peintre alsacien (env. 1445-1491), adapte les expériences de l'école de Konrad Witz à la description pleine de tendresse des scènes familiales, notamment dans *Marie et l'enfant dans leur chambre*.
De Grünewald (mort en 1528), remarquer le Christ en croix, d'un réalisme effrayant, puis de son contemporain le Strasbourgeois Hans Baldung Grien, *La Mort et la jeune fille*.
Niklaus Manuel Deutsch (env. 1484-1530), Bernois, a le goût de l'étrange et du narratif comme en témoignent *Le Jugement de Pâris* ou *Pyrame et Thisbé*.
Hans Holbein le Jeune marque l'apogée de la Renaissance. Une vingtaine de tableaux résume son œuvre. Son art, analytique et pessimiste, exprime le réel avec simplicité. Remarquer le *Christ au tombeau* aux membres raidis, l'admirable *Portrait de la femme de l'artiste et ses enfants*, exprimant une tristesse indicible, et le *Portrait du vieil Érasme*, au regard perspicace.
Les salles 16 à 21 sont réservées à la peinture néerlandaise du 17ᵉ s. Remarquable œuvre de jeunesse de Rembrandt : *David devant Saül*.
Les salles situées dans les ailes Est et Nord réunissent des œuvres importantes de Caspar Wolf et Yohann Heinrich Füssli, des œuvres romantiques (Delacroix, Géricault, Daumier), réalistes (Courbet, Manet), ainsi qu'une belle collection d'œuvres impressionnistes et post-impressionnistes : paysages de Monet *(Effet de neige)*, Pissarro *(Les Moissonneuses)* et Sisley *(Bords du Loing à Moret)* ; *Jeune fille couchée sur l'herbe* de Renoir ; *Montagne Ste-Victoire* de Cézanne ; *Ta Matete* de Gauguin, qui ordonne les couleurs en larges aplats ; paysages et portraits de Van Gogh.

Deuxième étage — Les différentes étapes de la peinture du 20ᵉ s. sont illustrées par une remarquable collection de tableaux provenant en partie de donations de grands collectionneurs. Le cubisme qui apparut vers 1908 est très bien représenté par les compositions de Braque *(Paysage, Broc et violon)*, Picasso *(Pains et compotier aux fruits sur une table, L'aficionado)*, Juan Gris *(Le violon)*, Fernand Léger *(La femme en bleu)*. Parmi les expressionnistes allemands, on remarque Franz Marc *(Tierschicksale)*, Emil Nolde *(Vorabend : Marschlandschaft)*. Parmi les surréalistes, on distingue des tableaux de Salvador Dalí. Quelques salles réunissent des exemples de l'art abstrait dus à Juan Miró, Max Ernst, Mondrian, van Doesburg, Vantongerloo, Kandinsky. Le Douanier Rousseau, Chagall, Paul Klee sont également représentés. Parmi les représentants les plus typiques du Pop Art, citons Jasper Johns, Andy Warhol, Claes Oldenburg.

Revenir à la Münsterplatz.

QUARTIER ST-ALBAN (ST. ALBAN-TAL) (DY)

Ce quartier doit son nom au couvent le plus ancien de la ville, fondé par l'évêque de Bâle en 1083. Il ne subsiste de l'édifice clunisien initial qu'une aile de cloître romane, intégrée dans une maison d'habitation et visible depuis l'ancien cimetière de l'église St-Alban (chœur et tour gothiques, nef 19ᵉ s.). C'est dans cette demeure que le peintre **Arnold Böcklin** a passé son enfance.
Quelques moulins témoignent d'une spécialisation du quartier remontant à la création d'un canal par les moines au 12ᵉ s. : point de vue sur le bief et plusieurs moulins au début de la rue St-Alban-Tal.

BASEL

★ **Musée du Papier** (Basler Papiermühle) (**M⁶**) ⊙ – C'est en 1980 qu'a été installé dans ce qui fut à l'origine le moulin à blé du couvent de Klingental, puis un moulin à papier à partir de 1453, ce moulin très complet. Il offre sur quatre niveaux une présentation vivante de l'histoire du papier et des activités qui s'y rapportent. Chaque thème fait l'objet de démonstrations dans les ateliers du musée : fabrication du papier, fonte de caractères, typographie, reliure.

Mühlegraben (**E**) – Vestiges très restaurés d'une portion du mur d'enceinte de Bâle, construit au 14ᵉ s., avec une reconstitution du chemin de ronde en bois. La majeure partie des fortifications médiévales de la ville fut détruite à partir de 1860, pour faire face à l'accroissement démographique entraîné par l'industrialisation du 19ᵉ s.

St. Alban-Berg – En traversant le canal, on pourra suivre le tracé de l'ancienne fortification de la ville, lisible par ses restes arasés, en empruntant le sentier qui grimpe sur la colline St-Alban. Un jardin couvre l'éminence où se dresse la porte St-Alban (St. Alban-Tor) dont l'origine remonte au 13ᵉ s.

Musée d'Art contemporain (Museum für Gegenwartskunst) ⊙ – Dépendance du musée des Beaux-Arts. Un ensemble original formé d'un bâtiment moderne éclairé par de grandes baies vitrées et accolé à une usine du 19ᵉ s., sert de cadre à des expositions temporaires illustrant les tendances les plus marquantes de l'art contemporain depuis 1960 : Art minimal, Art conceptuel, Arte povera, Figuration libre. Des noms comme Frank Stella, Bruce Nauman, Joseph Beuys y sont associés.

AUTRES CURIOSITÉS

★★★ **Jardin zoologique** (Zoologischer Garten) (**AZ**) ⊙ – Situé au cœur de la ville, ce zoo de réputation internationale, le plus grand de Suisse avec celui de Berne (13 ha chacun), a été fondé en 1874. Il compte actuellement plus de 5 600 animaux de tous les continents et se spécialise dans la reproduction et l'élevage des espèces menacées de disparition : rhinocéros d'Asie, gorilles, ours à lunettes…
Son parc de verdure, émaillé de pièces d'eau où s'ébattent cygnes, canards, flamants et autres oiseaux exotiques, est pourvu de restaurants, aires de pique-nique, jeux d'enfants, etc. Un « zoo des enfants » permet à ceux-ci d'approcher certains animaux jeunes ou nouveau-nés et d'effectuer des promenades à dos de poney ou d'éléphant. Les repas des fauves et des otaries, la présentation de celles-ci et des éléphants au public constituent des intermèdes très prisés.
En plus de nombreux enclos, divers bâtiments regroupent la plupart des familles animales exposées : on découvre ainsi le pavillon des singes abritant les chimpanzés, gorilles et orangs-outangs, celui des oiseaux, la « maison » des éléphants et celle des fauves.
La visite du zoo se termine par son prestigieux **vivarium** où sont représentées maintes espèces de poissons (de mer ou d'eau douce), de reptiles et d'amphibiens, dont certains spécimens rarissimes. Dernier bassin du parcours, la « vitrine » des manchots et pingouins (plusieurs dizaines d'individus) en est l'attraction principale.

★ **Musée du Kirschgarten** (Haus zum Kirschgarten) (**BZ**) ⊙ – Il est installé dans un hôtel du 18ᵉ s. Au rez-de-chaussée on admire une rare collection de montres du 16ᵉ au 19ᵉ s., des poêles de faïence, et une importante collection de figurines de porcelaine. Aux 1ᵉʳ et 2ᵉ étages : salons ornés de tapisseries d'Aubusson, de tableaux, de meubles français, boudoirs, costumes des 18ᵉ et 19ᵉ s., salle à manger, salle de musique, cuisine aux cuivres magnifiques ; dans une annexe, intérieurs Biedermeier et Art Déco.
Le troisième étage abrite une curieuse collection de jouets anciens : maisons de poupées, calèches miniatures, bateaux et premières automobiles.
La cave renferme des faïences et porcelaines de Suisse, d'Allemagne, de France et de Chine, des tonneaux sculptés datant de 1723, dont un d'une capacité de 10 000 litres.

★ **Musée historique** (Historisches Museum) (**BY**) ⊙ – Ancienne église des franciscains (14ᵉ s.). Au sous-sol sont exposées des céramiques gauloises et romaines, de l'orfèvrerie barbare du 5ᵉ au 7ᵉ s. provenant des cimetières de la région de Bâle, des sculptures romanes. Près de l'escalier qui y conduit, populaire « Roi Lälli » (Lällenkönig), petite figure joviale (17ᵉ s.) à yeux et langue mobiles.
Dans la nef, stalles de la cathédrale de Bâle et colonnes de fontaines du 14ᵉ au 17ᵉ s. Dans les bas-côtés ont été reconstituées plusieurs salles du 16ᵉ au 17ᵉ s. avec leur mobilier, des vitraux, tissus, portraits, monnaies et médailles. Le bas-côté Sud abrite en outre de magnifiques tapisseries gothiques, des coffres et produits d'artisanat du 15ᵉ s. ; le bas-côté Nord, des souvenirs des Corporations bâloises.
Dans le chœur, retable de Yvo Strigel de Memmingen (1512), sculptures religieuses et vitraux (15ᵉ-16ᵉ). Des objets du culte garnissent les petites sacristies Nord. Au sous-sol, la salle du Trésor contient le fonds original du musée (cabinets d'art Amerbach – 16ᵉ s. et Faesch – 17ᵉ s.) : orfèvrerie bâloise et trésors des Corporations. La partie inférieure de la tribune abrite des fragments de la Danse macabre de Conrad Witz (15ᵉ s.), des pierres tombales et inscriptions datant du Concile de Bâle (voir Bâle : « Une grave crise religieuse »).

BASEL

Descendre vers la petite sacristie Sud, pour découvrir le trésor (12ᵉ au 16ᵉ s.) de la cathédrale de Bâle avec son buste-reliquaire de sainte Ursule. Cette œuvre d'art en argent et or était commandée vers 1300 par les Bâlois pour recueillir les reliques de la martyre et de ses compagnes.

Remarquer en outre, au sous-sol, des objets d'art – non bâlois – des 13ᵉ et 14ᵉ s. ainsi que des souvenirs d'Érasme (mort à Bâle en 1536).

★ **Musée d'Art antique** (Antikenmuseum Basel und Sammlung Ludwig) (**CY**) ⊙ – Les objets exposés illustrent les périodes de l'Antiquité depuis les temps préhelléniques jusqu'à la fin de l'époque romaine. L'accent est mis sur l'art grec du premier millénaire av. J.-C. Au rez-de-chaussée sont rassemblées des sculptures de marbre et des statuettes de bronze des époques archaïque et classique (600-300 av. J.-C.). On y voit entre autres la stèle funéraire d'un médecin (480 av. J.-C.) appelée « relief du médecin de Bâle ». Le sous-sol renferme des œuvres hellénistiques et romaines : groupe d'Achille et Penthésilée, sarcophages romains d'où se détache le sarcophage de marbre représentant la légende de Médée, stèles funéraires de Phrygie, statuettes en terre cuite et petits bronzes. Le 1ᵉʳ étage contient une belle collection de vases attiques (520-350 av. J.-C.) : œuvres du peintre dit de Berlin parmi lesquelles une grande amphore avec couvercle montrant sur une face la déesse Athéna et sur l'autre Héraclès ; des monnaies (Italie du Sud et Sicile) et des bijoux. Le 2ᵉ étage rassemble des vases grecs des périodes géométrique (1100-700 av. J.-C.) et archaïque (620-500 av. J.-C.), les plus anciens se distinguant par des figures noires sur fond d'argile clair ; des armes grecques et italiques (Italie ancienne), des objets étrusques (statuettes votives et figurines en bronze).

Fontaine de Carnaval (Fasnachtsbrunnen) (**BY** F) – Au cœur du « quartier culturel » de la ville, elle anime de ses jeux d'eaux l'esplanade du théâtre municipal. Dans un vaste bassin, neuf créations métalliques articulées, par leurs seuls mouvements cocasses et répétitifs, représentent avec humour et fantaisie l'agitation inutile de l'homme. L'auteur, **Jean Tinguely** (1925-1991), étudia la peinture à l'École des Beaux-Arts de Bâle avant de s'établir à Paris comme sculpteur. Par ses constructions animées, utilisant des matériaux divers et inusités dans la création artistique, refusant les moyens d'expression traditionnels de l'art, il porte un regard amusé sur la civilisation contemporaine.

Musée des Moulages (Skulpturhalle) (**AY** M⁵) ⊙ – Il complète le musée précédent et expose de nombreux moulages consacrés aux sculptures grecques dont une importante collection des sculptures du Parthénon.

Musée de la Ville et de la Cathédrale (Stadt- und Münstermuseum) (**BX** M⁴) ⊙ – Dans la partie subsistante (« petit Klingental ») d'un monastère fondé au 13ᵉ s. et partiellement détruit en 1860, l'ancien réfectoire, salle voûtée en carène de bois renversée, réunit nombre d'originaux ou copies, en grès rouge ou bois, des sculptures médiévales de la cathédrale de Bâle, que l'on peut ainsi admirer de tout près : gargouilles, gisants, statues (plusieurs équestres), frises, bas-reliefs.

Dans les autres salles, on trouve des chapiteaux, des stalles, des modèles en plâtre de la porte dite de St-Gall et du portail principal, ainsi que des maquettes et dessins du vieux Bâle.

Musée historique de la pharmacie (Pharmazie-historisches Museum) (**BY** M²) ⊙ – Il renferme des instruments et médicaments utilisés autrefois ; reconstitution d'un laboratoire et d'une pharmacie avec boiseries des 18ᵉ-19ᵉ s. Remarquer aussi une curieuse pharmacie portative du 18ᵉ s. Belle collection de pots du 16ᵉ au 19ᵉ s.

Collection des instruments de musique anciens (Musikinstrumenten-Sammlung) (**BY** M³) ⊙ – Remarquable présentation d'instruments de musique à cordes, vent ou percussion (16ᵉ au 20ᵉ s.). Retransmission de leurs sons enregistrés.

Musée d'architecture (Architekturmuseum) (**BY** M⁷) ⊙ – Accueille des expositions temporaires consacrées à un architecte ou un courant d'architecture contemporaine.

Église St-Antoine (St-Antonius-Kirche) (**AX**) – Construction en béton armé, exécutée, à partir de 1925, d'après les plans de l'architecte Moser, et terminée en 1931.

La nef en berceau est voûtée en caissons, tandis que les bas-côtés sont couverts de plafonds à caissons. Des vitraux multicolores de Hans Stocker et Otto Staiger éclairent l'immense vaisseau.

LE PORT (HAFEN) par *Klybeckstrasse* (**BX**)

La ville participe depuis le Moyen Âge à l'échange de marchandises entre la mer du Nord et la Méditerranée, entre la Souabe et la Bourgogne.

La navigation fluviale disparut avec la construction des grandes routes alpines et des voies ferrées, et ce n'est qu'en 1904 que le trafic reprit jusqu'à Anvers et Rotterdam. Depuis, le port de Bâle permet à la Suisse de participer aux activités maritimes. Ses principaux bassins s'étendent en aval de la ville, au Petit-Huningue, où se trouvent l'obélisque et la table d'orientation marquant la jonction des frontières française, allemande et suisse.

BASEL

Cette proximité de la frontière est un obstacle à l'extension du port qui ne peut être envisagée que sur les territoires français et allemand, à l'exemple de l'aérodrome de Blotzheim utilisé en commun avec Mulhouse.
Les ports de Bâle-Ville et de Bâle-Campagne sont équipés pour recevoir les plus grands bâtiments et convois poussés. Hydrocarbures, houille, céréales, produits métallurgiques et matières premières de l'industrie alimentent la majeure partie du trafic, essentiellement d'importation.

Vue d'ensemble ⊙ – De la terrasse du silo de la Compagnie Suisse de Navigation, on découvre un vaste **panorama**★ sur la ville et les installations du port. Au-delà s'étend la plaine d'Alsace. Les Vosges, la Forêt-Noire et le Jura forment toile de fond.

★ **Exposition « De Bâle à la haute mer »** (Unser Weg zum Meer) ⊙ – Cette présentation fait état des différents aspects de la navigation suisse sur le Rhin et illustre le rôle de cette voie d'eau pour le commerce extérieur de la Confédération.

Visite en bateau ⊙ – L'été, des excursions sur le Rhin et le canal de Kembs, comportant la visite du port, sont organisées. *Embarcadère* (**BY**).

ENVIRONS

★★ **Ruines romaines d'Augst** – *Voir à ce nom.*

★ **Liestal** – *16 km au Sud-Est.* Cette jolie petite ville, appuyée à un versant boisé de la vallée de l'Ergolz, est le chef-lieu du demi-canton de Bâle-Campagne. On flânera dans sa rue principale (Rathausstrasse) aux maisons peintes du siècle dernier, entre sa porte médiévale et son hôtel de ville décoré de fresques d'époque Renaissance, restaurées en 1900. Sur les hauteurs du Schleirenberg, belvédère de l'Aussichtsturm : vue sur le Rhin et jusqu'aux Alpes. Nombreuses possibilités de promenades dans les forêts environnantes.
Un *petit train à vapeur* touristique (Waldenburger Dampfzug) relie, pendant la saison touristique, Liestal à Waldenburg, à 14 km au Sud.

★ **Rheinfelden** – *17 km à l'Est par la route n° 3.* Station terminale des **croisières sur le Rhin**, Rheinfelden passe pour être la plus ancienne cité d'Argovie. Elle conserve de nombreux vestiges de son passé : tours et remparts médiévaux, église gothique, baroquisée... Centre de cures thermales, la ville s'est parée de très beaux parcs. La **brasserie Feldschlösschen** (bâtiment en briques rouges et jaunes) ⊙, l'une des plus importantes du pays, fut fondée en 1876.

★ **Chapelle St-Chrischona** – *8 km – environ 1/4 h.* Quitter Bâle par la route de Riehen. A hauteur de la poste de Riehen, prendre à droite en direction de Bettingen. La route traverse les quartiers résidentiels de Bâle, puis Bettingen et s'élève jusqu'à la chapelle St-Chrischona. De la terrasse voisine : **panorama**★ allant du Säntis à l'Est, aux chaînons du Jura à l'Ouest ; on aperçoit Bâle dans la plaine du Rhin.

★ **Château d'eau (Wasserturm) du Bruderholz** ⊙ – *3,5 km au Sud.*
Un château d'eau se dresse sur la vaste esplanade de la Batterie, ainsi nommée en souvenir des redoutes élevées par les Confédérés en 1815, lors de la dernière campagne des Alliés contre Napoléon Ier. Du sommet de la tour (164 marches) on découvre un **panorama**★ circulaire sur Bâle, le Jura et la Forêt-Noire.

Muttenz – *5 km au Sud-Est.* Dans le centre-ville s'élève une église fortifiée, la « Pfaarrfkirche », romane à l'origine puis transformée aux 15e et 16e s., s'entourant d'une enceinte circulaire crénelée. Dans la petite nef unique, au plafond de bois sculpté, beaux fragments, restaurés, de fresques religieuses du début de la Renaissance.

Visitez au Nord de Bâle, les régions situées de part et d'autre du Rhin en territoire français ou allemand qui forment aujourd'hui la « Regio ».
Le guide Vert Michelin Pays Rhénans « Rhin Supérieur », premier guide Vert transfrontalier, couvre l'Alsace, le Palatinat du Sud, la Forêt-Noire ainsi que Bâle et sa région. Il met en valeur les attraits culturels, paysagers et monumentaux de ces régions qui ont su maintenir leurs caractères profonds tout en laissant apparaître leur unité historique.
Avec ce guide, utilisez la carte Michelin n° 278 « Pays Rhénans » à 1/200 000 qui vous invite à flâner le long de ses nombreuses routes pittoresques.

BEATENBERG ★

Berne — 1 373 habitants
Carte Michelin n° 427 pli 13 ou 217 pli 7 — Schéma : INTERLAKEN (Environs)
Alt. 1 150 m

Accès : d'Interlaken, 10 km jusqu'à l'extrémité du pays, également accessible par funiculaire à partir de la route de Thoune (voir à lac de Thoune). La route d'accès (s'embranchant sur la rue Scheidgasse, dans Unterseen), sinueuse mais excellente, procure de belles échappées sur le site d'Interlaken, puis sur la Jungfrau et le lac de Thoune.
Beatenberg, « station-terrasse » toute en longueur (plus de 7 km) faite d'hôtels et de chalets de villégiature noyés dans les arbres, offre des vues sur le lac de Thoune et plus loin à droite, sur le Niesen et à gauche, sur la Jungfrau et le Mönch. Mais il faut monter au Niederhorn pour compléter le panorama.

★★ **Niederhorn** ⊙ — Alt. 1 950 m. *Accès par télésiège.* Du sommet (tables d'orientation) de cette « montagne à vaches », très beau **panorama** ★★ au Sud, par-delà le lac de Thoune, sur les glaciers du massif de la Jungfrau ; au Sud-Ouest, sur le Niesen et au loin le Mont Blanc, visible de justesse ; à l'Ouest, sur la pointe du Stockhorn ; au Nord-Ouest, jusqu'aux lacs de Neuchâtel et de Morat ; au Nord, sur les montagnes précédent l'Emmental ; à l'Est, par-delà le lac de Brienz, sur les falaises du Brienzer Rothorn.

BELLINZONA

[C] Tessin — 16 849 habitants
Carte Michelin no 427 plis 24, 25 ou 218 Sud du pli 12
Schéma : GRAUBÜNDEN — Alt. 223 m

Point de passage inévitable pour le trafic transalpin empruntant les itinéraires du St-Gothard, du Lukmanier ou du San Bernardino, sur le versant italien des Alpes, Bellinzona a hérité de sa fonction millénaire de place forte verrouillant la vallée du Tessin le rôle de capitale administrative du canton auquel fut attribué, en 1803, le nom de ce cours d'eau.

★ **Châteaux** — Le dispositif fortifié de Bellinzona, construit entre le 13e et le 15e s., s'appuyait sur trois châteaux reliés par des murailles encore visibles.

Château d'Uri (Castello Grande) — Il est le plus ancien des trois. Bâti sur la bosse rocheuse qui obligeait la route du Gothard à se coller à la montagne, au fond d'une encoche facile à surveiller, il montre de loin ses deux tours quadrangulaires. D'importants vestiges de son enceinte, à « merlons gibelins », sont encore visibles, çà et là, dans la ville.

★ **Château de Schwytz** (Castello di Montebello) — *Accès par la rampe qui se détache de la rue de la Gare.* Cette citadelle formidable, au plan en losange, a été l'objet, en 1903, d'une restauration très poussée qui en a fait une reconstitution type de forteresse bâtie suivant les règles de l'architecture militaire lombarde. Elle abrite un musée d'histoire et d'archéologie.

Château d'Unterwald (Castello di Sasso Corbaro) — La route empruntée pour monter à Schwytz se poursuit jusqu'au troisième château.
Point d'appui supérieur de l'ensemble fortifié de Bellinzona, le château « Sasso Corbaro » d'Unterwald, émergeant des châtaigneraies, se signale surtout comme **belvédère** ★. De la terrasse de l'avant-cour, belle perspective de la basse vallée du Tessin jusqu'au lac Majeur.
Le musée des coutumes et traditions du Tessin est installé dans ce château.

VILLAGES PITTORESQUES

	Canton		Canton
Gandria	*Tessin*	**Morcote**	*Tessin*
Giornico	*Tessin*	**St-Ursanne**	*Jura*
Gruyères	*Fribourg*	**Soglio**	*Grisons*
Guarda	*Grisons*	**Stein am Rhein**	*Schaffhouse*
Kippel	*Valais*	**Zuoz**	*Grisons*

BERN★★★

C Berne — 136 338 habitants
Carte Michelin n° 427 pli 13 ou 217 pli 6 — Alt. 548 m
Plan d'agglomération dans le guide Rouge Michelin Suisse

Berne, siège des autorités fédérales helvétiques et de plusieurs organisations internationales, est située à l'intérieur d'un méandre encaissé de l'Aare, face aux Alpes. La ville, rebâtie en grès teinté d'un vert jaune après le terrible incendie de 1405, reste par son plan d'ensemble un modèle d'adaptation au site.
Centre universitaire depuis 1834, Berne est aussi un centre industriel et de recherche scientifique.
Du jardin des Roses (Rosengarten, **FY**), se révèle un joli **coup d'œil★** sur l'ensemble de la vieille ville, une des cités médiévales les mieux conservées d'Europe, s'inscrivant dans une boucle de la rivière.

UN PEU D'HISTOIRE

La fondation de Berne — Une chronique du 15ᵉ s. rapporte ainsi la fondation de la ville par le duc **Berchtold V de Zähringen**, en 1191. Désireux de créer une cité, le duc demanda conseil à ses chasseurs et à son grand veneur. L'un d'entre eux lui répondit : « Maître, dans la boucle, là où s'élève votre château de la Nydegg, se trouve un emplacement favorable. » Le gibier étant fort abondant, le duc convint avec ses conseillers de donner à la nouvelle ville le nom du premier animal qui serait capturé à la chasse. Le sort voulut que ce fût un ours (Bär). Le duc baptisa donc la cité « Berne » et lui donna comme armes un ours. C'est pourquoi aujourd'hui l'ours est resté l'emblème héraldique de la ville.

Les grandes heures de son histoire — Du 14ᵉ au 16ᵉ s., Berne a mené une adroite politique d'expansion et a joué un rôle prééminent au sein de la Confédération. De nombreuses annexions ont assuré son hégémonie sur les deux rives de l'Aare.
Au 15ᵉ s., la conquête de l'Argovie lui permet de s'étendre jusqu'à la limite de la Reuss inférieure et son attitude résolue au cours des guerres de Bourgogne la place au premier rang des cantons suisses.
Au 16ᵉ s., avec l'annexion de la Gruyère et du Pays de Vaud, Berne domine tout le pays s'étendant de la Reuss inférieure au Léman.

Berne dans la Confédération — Lorsqu'au lendemain de la défaite du Sonderbund (voir dans l'introduction au voyage, le chapitre : Un peu d'histoire) est élaborée la Constitution de 1848, Berne est, d'un commun accord, choisie comme siège des autorités fédérales. Un rôle politique de premier plan, renforcé par une position privilégiée au centre de la Confédération, point de jonction des cultures latine et germanique, justifiait ce choix. Mais si la ville est devenue le siège des chambres fédérales, des régies publiques, des P.T.T. et des Chemins de fer fédéraux, elle n'est pas pour autant la capitale de la Confédération, ni le centre administratif du pays au même titre que Paris ou Washington. Le système fédéraliste suisse s'est opposé en effet à ce qu'une seule ville détienne la prééminence politique.

Ferdinand Hodler — C'est à Berne que ce peintre voit le jour en 1853. Après une enfance difficile — la mort de ses parents et frères le marque profondément — Hodler entre en apprentissage chez Ferdinand Sommer, peintre de « vues suisses » à Thoune, puis passe quelque temps à Langenthal (Berne). A l'âge de 19 ans il part pour Genève afin d'y copier les paysages romantiques du peintre Calame. Grâce à son professeur Barthélemy Menn (1815-1893), élève d'Ingres et ami de Corot, Hodler s'éloigne de la peinture conventionnelle. Parmi les nombreuses toiles qu'il exécute se trouvent beaucoup de portraits dont certains annoncent les grandes œuvres décoratives. Un voyage en Espagne (1878-1879) permet à Hodler d'admirer la technique de Vélasquez et Titien, ainsi que les compositions de Raphaël. Par la suite il perfectionne sa technique et sa palette s'éclaircit. A cette époque Hodler réalise de nombreux paysages ; les Alpes et le lac de Thoune sont des sujets qu'il affectionne particulièrement.
Si l'on reconnaît dans l'œuvre de Hodler les courants de son époque (réalisme, symbolisme, Art nouveau), l'artiste se distingue dès 1885 par le parallélisme, système pictural caractérisé par la répétition de motifs semblables, la symétrie et une composition à axe vertical ou horizontal. Ce procédé, qui procure une forte expression d'unité aux tableaux, est considéré par Hodler comme « une loi qui dépasse l'art ». On retrouve le parallélisme aussi bien dans les sujets allégoriques (La Nuit, 1889/1890 ; Le Jour, 1899/1900) que dans les peintures d'histoire telles La Retraite de Marignan, qui vaut à Hodler le premier prix du concours de décoration du Musée National de Zurich (1897), et le vigoureux Guillaume Tell (illustration, voir à Vierwaldstätter See). Hodler simplifie de plus en plus les compositions de ses paysages et ne copie plus la nature. Les reflets dans les lacs accentuent la symétrie et la tendance à la monochromie — le bleu est sa couleur préférée — renforce encore l'unité des tableaux. A la fin de sa vie — Hodler meurt en 1918 à Genève —, l'artiste se consacre à ce qu'il appelle « des paysages planétaires » où il n'y a plus que lignes et espace et aucune trace de vie ou de mort.

BERNE PRATIQUE

Pour tout renseignement, s'adresser à l'Office du tourisme et des Congrès (Verkehrs- und Kongressbüro), Gare CCF (Bahnhof), ☏ (031) 311 66 11.

Shopping

Principales rues commerçantes : Spitalgasse, Marktgasse, Kramgasse, Gerechtigkeisgasse. Marchés de fruits, légumes, fleurs et marchandises diverses : Bundesplatz, Bärenplatz, Waisenhausplatz.

Théâtre et musique

Théâtre municipal, Kornhausplatz 20, ☏ (031) 311 07 77.
Berner Marionettentheater (Théâtre de Marionnettes), Gereichtigkeitsgasse 50.
Casino, Herrengasse 25, ☏ (031) 31 42 42.
Kursaal, Schänzlistrasse 71-77, ☏ (031) 333 10 10.

Un verre dans un endroit agréable

Le **Président Club Bar**, piano-bar de l'hôtel Métropole (Zeughausgasse 28) doit son nom aux portraits de chefs d'État du monde entier ou de personnalités bernoises ou suisses, qui ornent ses murs. Dans la même rue, le piano-bar de l'hôtel Bern possède un décor qui marie harmonieusement cuivre, marbre et miroirs.
Sur la Kornhausplatz se trouve la **Kornhauskeller**. Un profond escalier conduit à cette cave magnifique aux voûtes et piliers peints dont l'origine remonte au 18e s. Toutes les soirées sont animées par un pianiste et souvent les fins de semaine un orchestre folklorique s'y produit.
Dans le quartier de la mairie, le **Swiss Chalet** de l'hôtel Glocke (Rathausgasse 75) fera le bonheur des amateurs de fondues et de musique folklorique. Dans la même rue (au n° 62), **Klötzlikeller**, la plus ancienne taverne de la ville, propose du vin servi au verre, dans une cave aux murs faits de grosses pierres. Apéritif suisse typique : verre de vin blanc accompagné de rebibes (copeaux de fromage).
Le **Kursaal** propose un ensemble composé de salles de jeux, d'un bistrot, d'un piano-bar, d'un dancing et d'un cabaret (variétés de niveau international).
Jazz au **Marian's Jazzroom** au sous-sol de l'hôtel Innere Enge (Engerstrasse 54). Établissement fort prisé des connaisseurs.

★★ LE VIEUX BERNE visite : 2 h 1/2

La vieille ville, qu'il faut découvrir à pied, a conservé son caractère moyenâgeux très pittoresque. De vieilles tours, des rues abondamment pavoisées et bordées d'arcades constituent un immense centre commercial couvert, offrent des perspectives harmonieuses, agrémentées de nombreuses **fontaines** ornées de sculptures et fleuries. Tramways et trolleybus portant les emblèmes cantonaux et fédéraux sillonnent les différentes artères, qui résonnent en saison du martèlement des calèches.
Six kilomètres d'arcades et certaines rues sont réservés aux piétons. De Pâques à fin octobre, les monuments principaux sont illuminés tous les soirs jusqu'à minuit.

Église du St-Esprit (Heiliggeist-Kirche) (**DZ**) – Cette église baroque a été édifiée de 1726 à 1729. De nuit, ses abords sont fréquentés par de nombreux drogués.
Prendre la Spitalgasse, rue commerçante très animée et bordée d'arcades, ornée en son centre de la fontaine du Joueur de cornemuse.

Bärenplatz (**DZ**) – Jadis s'y trouvait la fosse aux ours. Aujourd'hui, c'est une vaste esplanade animée où se côtoient des terrasses de cafés.

Tour des Prisons (Käfigturm) (**DZ A**) – Cette porte marquait la limite Ouest de la ville de 1250 à 1350. Restaurée au 18e s., elle s'élève à l'entrée de la Marktgasse.

★ **Marktgasse** (**DZ**) – Élégante et animée, rue principale de la ville ancienne, avec ses magasins de luxe et ses nombreux éventaires de fleuristes, elle est le centre d'une intense activité. De belles maisons des 17e et 18e s. offrent une suite d'arcades, donnant à l'ensemble beaucoup d'unité.
Remarquer la fontaine d'Anna Seiler, qui en 1354 dota la ville de son premier hôpital. Plus loin, la fontaine du Tireur représente un porte-bannière avec entre les jambes un petit ours revêtu d'une armure et tirant un coup de fusil.
Sur la Kornhausplatz, la fontaine de l'Ogre (Kindlifresserbrunnen) représente un ogre dévorant un petit garçon et tenant de la main gauche d'autres marmots qui vont subir le même sort.

★ **Tour de l'Horloge** (Zytgloggeturm) (**EZ C**) ⊙ – Porte Ouest de la ville de 1191 à 1250. Son célèbre carillon se met en marche quatre minutes avant chaque heure. Avec son jaquemart du 16e s. (du côté de la Kramgasse) et ses nombreux personnages peints, en particulier les amusants oursons qui défilent au son des clochettes du Fou, elle représente l'image-souvenir la plus goûtée de Berne. La visite de l'intérieur permet d'admirer le mécanisme de l'horloge.

BERN

★ **Kramgasse** (**EZ**) – Prolongeant la Marktgasse, la Kramgasse, plus populaire, a également conservé son cachet ancien. Dans la première rue à droite après la tour de l'Horloge, on voit des maisons anciennes à oriel (p. 29) et à tourelles d'angle.

Kramgasse

Le long de la Kramgasse, on remarque : la fontaine de Zähringen avec un ours revêtu d'une armure, la bannière des Zähringen au poing ; celle de Samson surmontée d'une statue du colosse ouvrant la gueule d'un lion.

C'est au n° 49 de cette rue que se trouve la **maison d'Albert Einstein** ⊙. Il y écrivit en 1905 sa théorie de la relativité restreinte. Seize ans plus tard, il se vit décerner le prix Nobel de physique pour ses travaux sur les photons. Son cabinet de travail, sa chambre avec son pupitre pour écrire debout, divers documents font revivre les années qu'il passa à Berne de 1902 à 1909. Cette année-là, il fut nommé professeur de physique à l'université de Zurich.

A l'extrémité de la Kramgasse, tourner à gauche dans la Kreuzgasse.

La Rathausplatz est ornée de la fontaine du Banneret (Vennerbrunnen), œuvre de Hans Gieng (1542).

Hôtel du Gouvernement (**EY H**) – A la fois le siège du Conseil municipal (assemblée législative de la ville de Berne) et celui du Grand Conseil (assemblée législative cantonale), cet édifice, construit de 1406 à 1417 et maintes fois restauré, reste, avec son escalier à double volée et son perron couvert, l'un des monuments bernois les plus symboliques.

Reprendre la Kreuzgasse qui rejoint la Gerechtigkeitsgasse.

Là s'élève la fontaine de la Justice (Gerechtigkeitsbrunnem) (1543) dont le fût est couronné d'un chapiteau corinthien.

A gauche de la Nydeggasse qui prolonge la Gerechtigkeitsgasse, est située l'église de la Nydegg (Nydeggkirche), édifiée au 14ᵉ s. sur les fondements d'un château fort.

Pont de la Nydegg (**Nydeggbrücke**) (**FY**) – Il offre de jolies **vues**★ sur les quartiers qui se pressent dans la boucle de l'Aare et les versants boisés qui la dominent.

★ **Fosse aux ours** (**Bärengraben**) (**FZ**) ⊙ – Depuis la fin du 15ᵉ s., les ours de Berne ont les faveurs populaires. Ils sont l'objet de visites nombreuses, non seulement de la part des touristes mais aussi des Bernois, qui les affectionnent particulièrement et leur donnent à manger friandises et carottes. Une Bernoise fonda même à leur intention une rente perpétuelle !

Faire demi-tour. A l'entrée de la Gerechtigkeitsgasse prendre la Junkerngasse.

La Junkerngasse est bordée de maisons anciennes. Au n° 47, se trouve l'**Erlacher Hof**, bel hôtel du 18ᵉ s. dont le style classique s'inspire de l'architecture française. Abordant la cathédrale par le chevet, on a une jolie vue d'ensemble sur la tour, le vaisseau, les arcs-boutants et les pinacles qui surmontent les contreforts.

Contourner l'édifice par la gauche : de la belle terrasse plantée d'arbres et ornée de parterres fleuris, la **vue** plonge sur les écluses de l'Aare et à droite sur le Kirchenfeldbrücke qui enjambe de 40 m une courbe de l'Aare. Gagner le Münsterplatz (place de la cathédrale) ; à son extrémité : fontaine de Moïse.

★ **Cathédrale St-Vincent** (**Münster**) (**EZ**) ⊙ – La dernière en date des grandes églises gothiques de Suisse, couramment appelée cathédrale, est en réalité une collégiale. La construction commença en 1421 et se poursuivit jusqu'en 1573 ; la tour, la plus haute de Suisse (100 m), ne fut achevée qu'en 1893.

Le **tympan**★★ du portail principal, œuvre d'Erhard Küng, est remarquable. Il illustre le Jugement dernier en une multitude de personnages (234) dont certains sont encore peints, où les figures des élus et des damnés sont traitées avec beaucoup de réalisme. Aux voussures, statues de prophètes ; dans les ébrasements, Vierges Sages à gauche et Vierges Folles à droite ; de chaque côté du portail, fresques en grisaille, du début du 16ᵉ s.

Entrer par la porte latérale droite de cette façade. A gauche en entrant, un escalier à vis de 270 marches permet d'accéder à la plate-forme de la tour d'où l'on découvre un **panorama**★★, mettant en relief les quartiers de la ville aux beaux toits de tuiles rouge-brun, les nombreux clochers et clochetons, les ponts sur l'Aare et la chaîne des Alpes bernoises.

67

BERN

Bärenplatz	**DZ**	Amthausgasse	**DEZ** 3	Kochergasse	**DEZ** 13
Kramgasse	**EZ**	Brunngasse	**EY** 6	Kreuzgasse	**EZ** 15
Marktgasse	**DZ**	Bundesterrasse	**DZ** 7	Münstergasse	**EZ** 16
Spitalgasse	**DYZ**	Christoffelgasse	**DZ** 9	Münsterplatz	**EZ** 18
		Helvetiaplatz	**EZ** 10	Nägeligasse	**DY** 19
		Jubiläumsstrasse	**EZ** 12	Nydeggasse	**FY** 22

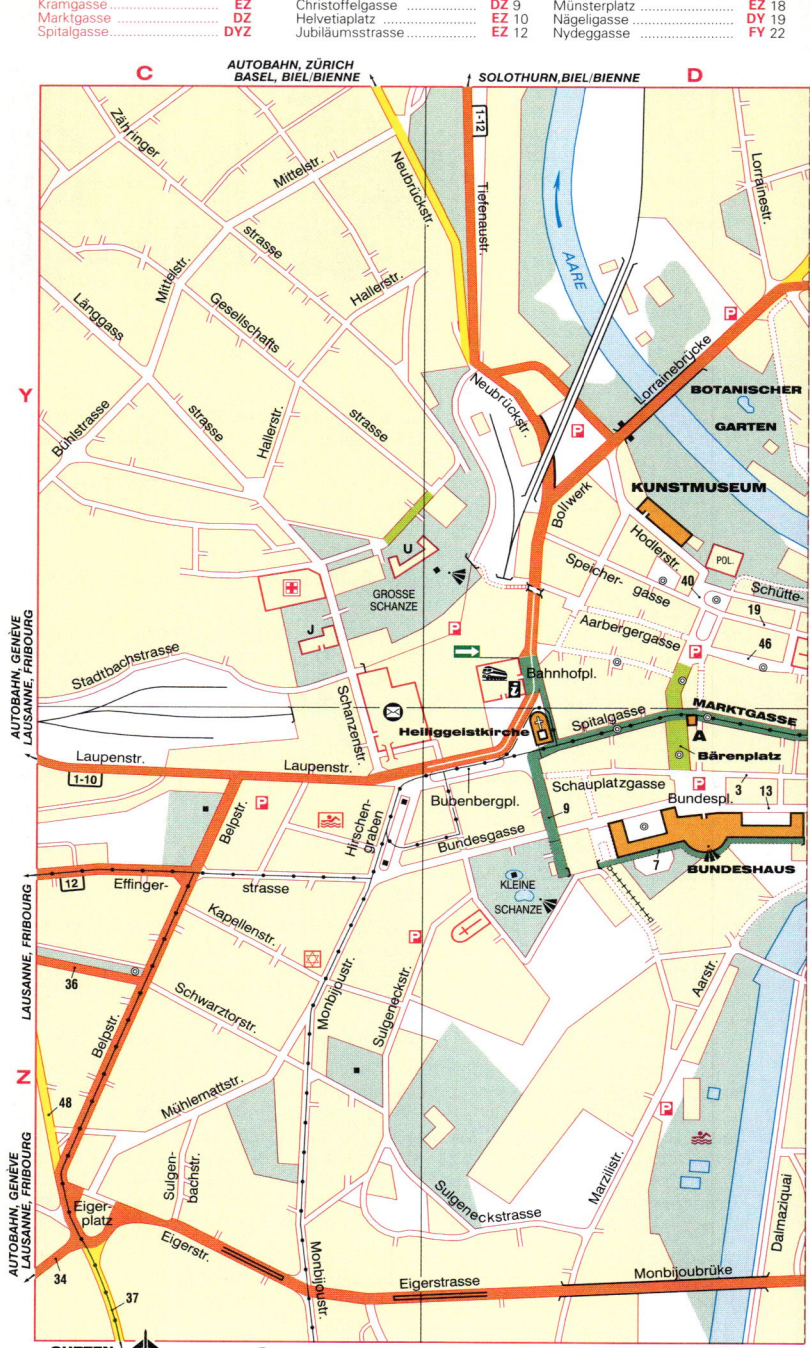

La nef est un vaste vaisseau à voûtes réticulées et aux clés de voûtes peintes et armoriées. Le chœur est orné de grandes verrières du 15ᵉ s. représentant : au centre la Passion avec la Crucifixion, œuvre de Hans Acker, la Victoire des 10 000 chevaliers ; à gauche les Rois Mages. Stalles de style Renaissance.

En sortant de la cathédrale, traverser la Münsterplatz et prendre à gauche la Münstergasse (plusieurs passages couverts et étroits rejoignent la Kramgasse) qui mène à la place du Casino.

Juste avant le pont (Kirchenfeldbrücke), prendre à droite la Bundesterrasse.

Rathausgasse	EY 28	Schwarztorstrasse	CZ 36	**A**	Käfigturm
Rathausplatz	EY 30	Seftigenstrasse	CZ 37	**C**	Zytgloggeturm
Schosshalden-strasse	FZ 33	Untertorbrücke	FY 39	**H**	Rathaus
Schwarzenburg-strasse	CZ 34	Waisenhausplatz	DY 40		
		Zeughausgasse	DY 46		
		Zieglerstrasse	CZ 48		

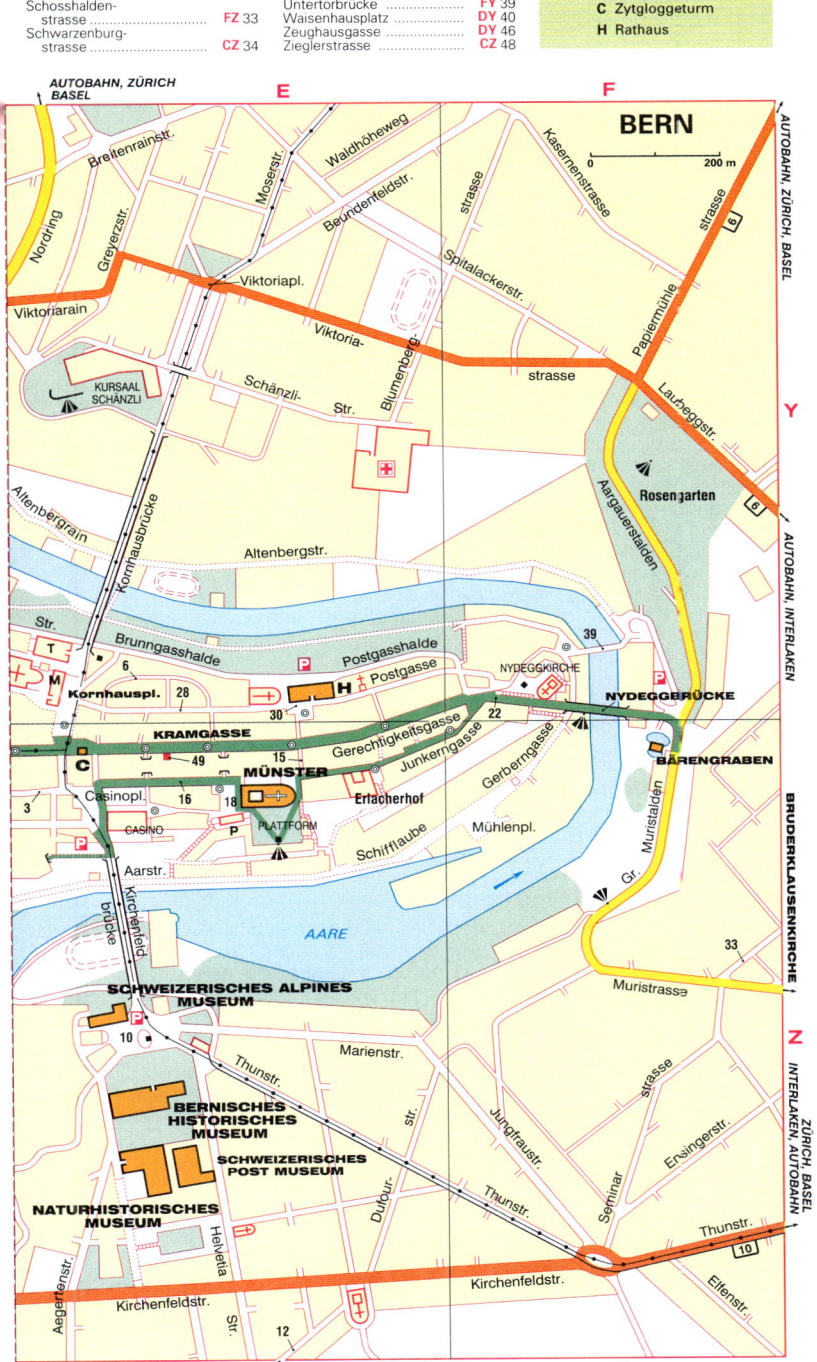

Cette promenade domine la vallée de l'Aare.

Palais fédéral (Bundeshaus) (DZ) ⊙ – Les assemblées fédérales sont logées dans ce lourd bâtiment à coupole, inspiré de la Renaissance florentine. En parcourant les différentes salles de séances (Conseil des États, Conseil national), le visiteur s'initiera aux différents rouages de la démocratie helvétique.

De la terrasse, située au Sud du palais fédéral, belle **vue** sur l'Aare, la ville et, à l'arrière-plan, les Alpes bernoises. Cette terrasse, comme le parc voisin Kleine Schanze, est fréquentée par de nombreux drogués.

BERN

AUTRES CURIOSITÉS

★★ Musée des Beaux-Arts (Kunstmuseum) (DY) ⊙ — Ce musée contient outre une très belle collection de peintures, illustrant diverses écoles du 13e au 20e s., un remarquable ensemble d'œuvres de **Paul Klee** (1879-1940), peintre ayant vécu de nombreuses années à Berne.

Au rez-de-chaussée, une salle est consacrée aux primitifs italiens du 13e au 15e s., parmi lesquels Duccio di Buoninsegna, dont la *Maestà* dénote la tradition byzantine propre à l'école siennoise et Fra Angelico (*Vierge à l'Enfant*). Les primitifs suisses des 15e et 16e s. — en particulier le *Maître à l'Œillet de Berne* et le *Maître de Berne* — frappent par leur minutie d'exécution, mais aussi par leur raideur et leur naïveté.

L'école du 16e s., fidèle à la représentation de scènes religieuses se distingue par le Bernois Niklaus Manuel Deutsch (env. 1484-1530) dont la facture et la recherche dans la composition s'apparentent à l'art de la Renaissance (*Saint Luc peignant la Madone, Martyre des 10 000 chevaliers du mont Ararat*) et par deux excellents portraits de Luther et de sa femme par l'atelier de l'Allemand Cranach.

Au rez-de-chaussée encore sont exposées des collections des peintres suisses et européens des 19e et 20e s. Albert Anker (1831-1910) s'attache à représenter des scènes populaires, des gens ou des enfants (*Vieille femme qui se chauffe, Fillette qui tricote*). L'école française est représentée par Delacroix, les principaux impressionnistes tels que Monet, Cézanne, Manet, Sisley, Pissarro, Renoir et Bonnard qui fit partie du groupe des Nabis et Utrillo le peintre des paysages de Montmartre. Ferdinand Hodler, l'enfant du pays, se voit naturellement attribuer une place de choix. Ses grandes compositions aux sujets allégoriques (*le Jour, la Nuit, les Âmes déçues*) traduisant sa préoccupation de la mort voisinent avec ses paysages qui reflètent souvent un état d'âme (*Le lac de Thoune et le Stockhorn*) et ses portraits (*Jeune fille à la fleur de pavot, l'Insensé* où il s'est représenté lui-même le regard menaçant).

Au premier étage on distingue des tableaux des expressionnistes Rouault, Soutine et Modigliani, de même que des œuvres de Picasso. Une salle est réservée à la peinture de la première moitié du 20e s. : œuvres de Cuno Amiet, qui utilise une palette aux tons violents et chauds. Important ensemble de toiles cubistes de Braque, Picasso, Juan Gris et Fernand Léger.

Enfin, cinq salles au sous-sol présentent une riche **collection de Paul Klee.** Le musée possède plus de 2 000 dessins ainsi que des tableaux, gouaches et aquarelles permettant de suivre l'évolution de l'artiste (*les œuvres sur papier sont exposées par roulement*). La recherche des effets de couleurs donne naissance aux tableaux carrés (« architecture picturale rouge, jaune, bleue »), aux œuvres « divisionnistes » des années 1930 à 1932 (*Ad Parnassum*), aux peintures où figures et signes se détachent sur un fond coloré (*Fleurs au rocher* 1940).

★ Jardin botanique (Botanischer Garten) (DY) — Ce vaste jardin, aménagé avec goût, descend en terrasses jusqu'aux rives de l'Aare. Des fontaines et des pièces d'eau ajoutent à l'agrément de la visite. Outre une grande variété de plantes alpines, on admire, dans les serres, une collection de plantes exotiques.

★★ Musée d'Histoire naturelle (Naturhistorisches Museum) (EZ) ⊙ — Au rez-de-chaussée, le hall révèle un fossile d'ichtyosaure, et la vaste salle de Wattenwyl est remarquable ; les animaux d'Afrique qu'elle contient sont présentés dans leur cadre de vie habituel. Au sous-sol, d'autres dioramas évoquent la faune asiatique.

Le premier étage abrite une belle collection de vertébrés de la faune locale, de mammifères de la zone arctique. Biologie de la baleine.

Le deuxième étage expose des oiseaux, reptiles et insectes.

Le troisième étage est consacré à la minéralogie, aux pierres précieuses, à la géologie du pétrole et à la paléontologie.

★★ Musée d'Histoire de Berne (Bernisches Historisches Museum) (EZ) ⊙ — Ce bâtiment, de style néo-gothique, renferme des collections très variées, historiques, préhistoriques, archéologiques et ethnographiques.

On remarque à l'entresol inférieur le salon Pourtalès et son mobilier du 18e s., à l'entresol supérieur la collection orientale Henri Moser Charlottenfels. Au 1er étage, outre une maquette de la ville, de précieuses collections dont le butin pris aux Bourguignons en 1476, à Grandson et à Morat : étendards, broderies, tapisseries ayant appartenu à Charles le Téméraire, dont l'une aux armes de Philippe le Bon, exécutée en 1466 par un atelier flamand.

D'autres tapisseries, provenant des ateliers flamands et de ceux de Tournai, retiennent l'attention, par la finesse du dessin et la richesse des coloris : ainsi celle dite « La Justice de Trajan et d'Herkenbald » exécutée au 15e s. d'après les tableaux de Roger van der Weyden ; celle « des Rois Mages » (1460), de la vie de saint Vincent (provenant de la cathédrale) ; d'autres enfin illustrant plusieurs épisodes de la vie de Jules César. Au 2e étage, on remarque la balance géante de 1752 qui, à l'arsenal de Berne, pouvait peser des canons de 2 tonnes. Une partie de l'étage est également consacré aux aspects de la vie quotidienne des 19e et 20e s.

BERN

Sur l'Helvetiaplatz, s'élève l'imposant monument symbolisant l'Union Télégraphique Internationale fondée à Paris en 1865 à l'initiative du gouvernement français. Ce groupe de bronze avec fontaines a été exécuté, en 1915, par le sculpteur tessinois Romagnoli.

★★ **Musée alpin suisse (Schweizerisches Alpines Museum) (EZ)** ⊙ – Totalement rénové entre 1990 et 1993, le Musée alpin suisse permet de visiter les Alpes (60 % de la superficie du pays) depuis le centre de la capitale. Après un montage audio-visuel intitulé «Pays de montagnes», plusieurs magnifiques plans-reliefs – les premiers furent créés à partir de 1750 – réunissent les sommets et vallées célèbres : Bietschhorn, Cervin, Dents-du-Midi, Jungfrau, Säntis, Bernina, etc. Le parcours muséographique est agrémenté de bornes interactives proposant d'approfondir chacun des thèmes de l'exposition (histoire, géologie, transport et industrie, tourisme, climat, flore et faune, etc.) ; tous les commentaires sont en allemand, français, italien et anglais.
A l'étage, «La Montagne à travers les cartes», du 16e au 18e s., précède des sections consacrées à l'art et aux traditions populaires, ainsi qu'à l'habitat. Une salle, décorée d'un diorama (1894) de Ferdinand Hodler, *L'Ascension et la chute*, évoque l'alpinisme, l'évolution de l'équipement alpin et du matériel de sauvetage afin d'illustrer les efforts entrepris par l'homme pour dompter ce monstre sauvage. Au centre se trouve un vaste plan-relief de l'Oberland bernois.
On gagne ensuite le dernier niveau où sont réunis des documents relatifs aux expéditions réalisées sur d'autres sommets du monde.

★ **Musée des PTT suisses (Schweizerisches Post-Museum) (EZ)** ⊙ – Moderne et accueillant, le Musée des PTT suisses relate l'histoire des postes (niveau 0), l'histoire des télécommunications (niveau 1) et la philatélie (niveaux -1 et -2). Il s'agit donc d'une rétrospective consacrée au premier employeur du pays.
Si les premières institutions postales et les postes cantonales et fédérales sont très bien illustrées (diligence de 1909, ambulant, fourgonnette Tatra de 1947, train postal souterrain de Zurich qui fonctionna de 1956 à 1980), le visiteur sera peut-être davantage captivé par l'expérimentation des techniques de télécommunication. En effet, on peut notamment essayer un appareil Morse de 1837, une liaison par téléscripteur, un central téléphonique ou encore comprendre la transmission par faisceaux hertziens. La section philatélique retiendra les collectionneurs (on pourra y poster une lettre qui recevra le sceau du musée).

★ **Jardin zoologique (Tierpark) du Dählhölzli** ⊙ – *Accès par la Jübilaumstrasse* **(EZ)**. Ce beau parc de 13 ha, dominant l'Aare, est peuplé d'un millier d'animaux, parqués dans de vastes enclos.
Vivarium – Cette installation abrite des centaines d'oiseaux exotiques au plumage bariolé, ainsi que des spécimens rares de la faune locale, des reptiles et des poissons.

★ **Église St-Nicolas (Bruder Klausenkirche)** – *Par la Muristrasse* **(FZ)**. Elle est dédiée à saint Nicolas de Flüe *(voir à ce nom)*, familièrement connu en Suisse sous le nom de «Bruder Klaus». Bâtie sur une vaste esplanade, cette église, dont la tour-clocher est isolée, est d'une grande sobriété de lignes. C'est l'un des édifices les plus représentatifs de l'art moderne en Suisse.

ENVIRONS

★★ **Le Gurten** ⊙ – Alt. 858 m. *2,5 km – environ 1/2 h, dont 10 mn de funiculaire. Quitter Berne par la Seftigenstrasse* **(CZ)**, *route de Belp-Thoune et, à l'entrée de Wabern, prendre à droite vers la station inférieure du funiculaire.*
Magnifique belvédère (**panorama**★★ sur Berne et les Alpes bernoises), le Gurten constitue un agréable lieu de promenade, pourvu de distractions pour les enfants.

Presqu'île d'Enge – *4 km au Nord, dans la première boucle de l'Aare. Quitter Berne par la route de Bienne*. Après la gare de Tiefenau, prendre à gauche puis, à un carrefour, à droite la Reichenbachstrasse jusqu'à hauteur d'une église protestante moderne (Matthäuskirche), où un panneau donne l'emplacement des différents vestiges archéologiques de la presqu'île : remparts de l'ancien oppidum helvète, constructions romaines postérieures (1er s.). Parmi ces dernières mises au jour, on peut voir, derrière l'église, les restes du plus petit amphithéâtre trouvé en Suisse, ovale, d'environ 3 000 places, et, moins d'un kilomètre plus loin, en forêt, ceux de thermes publics (sous abri).

Le lexique touristique commenté en début de guide, donne la traduction française des termes touristiques les plus couramment utilisés en suisse alémanique.

BERNER OBERLAND ★★★

Carte Michelin n° 427 plis 13 à 15 ou 217 plis 6 à 10 et 16 à 20

Délimité au Nord par le croissant des lacs de Thoune et de Brienz, à l'Est par les Grisons, au Sud par le Haut-Valais, à l'Ouest par les Alpes vaudoises et fribourgeoises, ce massif du cœur de la Suisse abonde en merveilles de renommée internationale : naturelles, comme les sommets de la Jungfrau et de l'Eiger, le glacier du Rhône, les chutes du Trümmelbach, le lac de Thoune... ; créées de main d'homme, telles les grandes stations d'Interlaken et de Grindelwald, ou le plus haut chemin de fer d'Europe (celui du Jungfraujoch)...

Au Sud et au Sud-Est s'alignent fièrement les montagnes formant la grandiose barrière naturelle qui sépare l'Oberland bernois du Haut-Valais. Certaines de leurs cimes, éclatantes de blancheur neigeuse, comptent parmi les plus célèbres des Alpes : outre l'Eiger et la Jungfrau, déjà cités, le Mönch, le Finsteraarhorn (point culminant du massif avec ses 4 274 m), le Wetterhorn, la Blümlisalp... Entre elles, et s'égrenant du col du Grimsel jusqu'à proximité du lac Léman, brillent aussi les principaux glaciers de la Suisse, dont ceux d'Aletsch (le plus grand d'Europe) et du Rhône ; c'est d'eux que naissent les torrents qui creusent ces larges vallées caractéristiques du paysage bernois : Haslital, Kandertal, Simmental, Lütschinental...

Tirant parti de la densité prodigieuse de curiosités naturelles et de « terrains de jeux » propres à l'exercice des sports alpins dans l'espace relativement restreint compris entre l'Aare et le Rhône, le génie touristique suisse a fait de l'Oberland bernois le plus extraordinaire parc naturel d'attractions de l'Europe.

La vue éblouissante de la Jungfrau, depuis la promenade du Höheweg, à Interlaken, constitue, traditionnellement, l'image-souvenir de cette zone supérieurement équipée. La région reste aussi un haut lieu de l'alpinisme international.

Victoire sur l'Eigerwand — L'un des épisodes les plus dramatiques qui suivit la conquête du Cervin *(voir à Zermatt)* fut celle de la face Nord de l'Eiger *(voir à Interlaken)*. Dès 1858, le sommet (3 970 m) avait été atteint par l'Anglais Ch. Barrington. Successivement, les arêtes Sud et Sud-Ouest avaient été vaincues en 1874 et 1876. L'ascension de la face Nord, rendue particulièrement difficile par le temps souvent instable de l'Oberland bernois et la structure complexe de la paroi, avait déjà tenté maints grimpeurs. Elle avait aussi été le théâtre de nombreux accidents. A partir de 1935, les essais se multiplient : cette année-là, deux Allemands y trouvent la mort ; l'année suivante, trois cordées allemandes et autrichiennes y périssent. Le récit de ces tragiques échecs soulève de telles protestations que les autorités cantonales de Berne interdisent toute nouvelle tentative. L'interdiction est cependant levée en 1937, année marquée par la défaite de l'Autrichien Rebitsch et de l'Allemand Wiggerl Vörg. En 1938, Vörg et son compagnon Anderl Heckmair préparent dans le plus grand secret une expédition qu'ils veulent décisive. Devancés au départ par deux

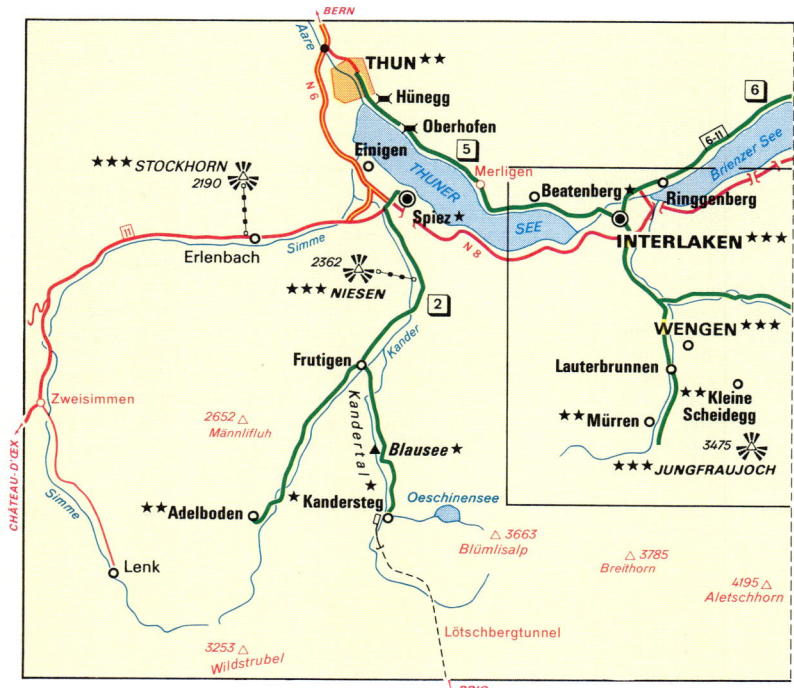

Autrichiens, Kasparek et Harrer, ils les rejoignent dès le second jour et décident d'unir leurs chances à celles de la cordée rivale. Leur lente et pénible progression, entravée par la menace constante des orages et des avalanches, est suivie anxieusement de la vallée. Alerté par la presse et la radio, le monde se passionne pour leur équipée. Lorsque, enfin, après des jours d'efforts, ils franchissent l'arête terminale, aveuglés par la fatigue et la tempête, ils ne se rendent pas immédiatement compte de leur victoire !

Leur difficile descente par la face Ouest, au milieu de la bourrasque, consacre le succès de leur expédition.

VISITE
Itinéraires recommandés

Par ordre décroissant de la durée du parcours.

Voir les noms à l'index.

★★★ **Région de la Jungfrau** — Visite en auto, téléphériques et train, au départ d'Interlaken — compter 2 journées.

★★★ **Circuit des Trois Cols (Grimsel, Furka, Susten)** — Au départ d'Interlaken — compter au moins 1 journée. Incluant les 4, 3 et 1 ci-dessous.

★★★ 1 **Sustenpassstrasse** — D'Andermatt à Meiringen — environ 2 h 1/2.

★ 2 **Kandertal** — Route de Spiez à Kandersteg — environ 2 h 1/2.

★★★ 3 **Furkapassstrasse** — De Gletsch à Andermatt — environ 2 h 1/4.

★ 4 **Grimselstrasse** — De Meiringen à Gletsch — environ 1 h 1/2.

★★ 5 **Thuner See** — Route de Thun à Interlaken — environ 1 h.

★ 6 **Lac de Brienz** — Route d'Interlaken à Meiringen — environ 3/4 h.

Chardon bleu

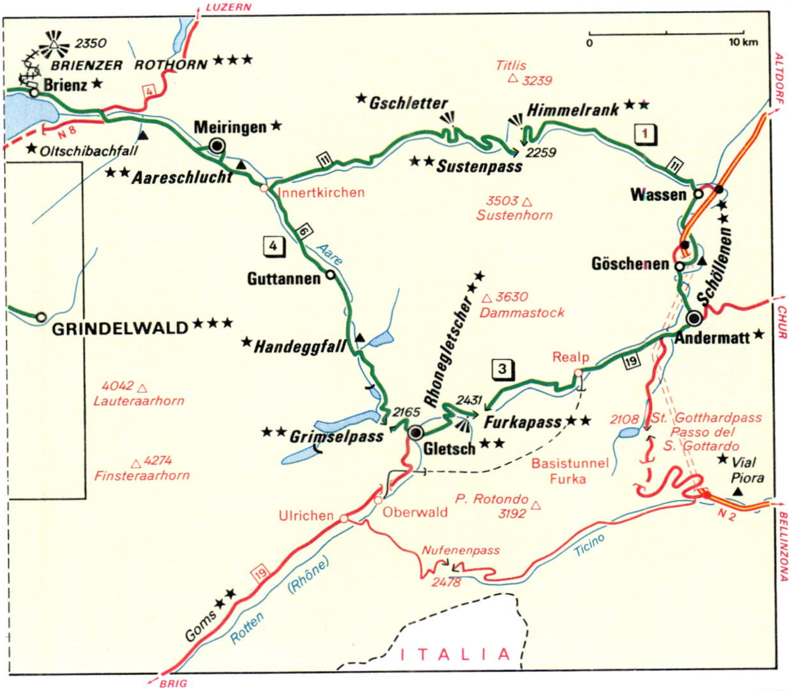

BERNINASTRASSE ★★★

Carte Michelin n° 427 plis 17, 26 ou 218 plis 15, 16 – Schéma : GRAUBÜNDEN

Ce magnifique parcours de haute montagne remonte le Val Bernina jusqu'au col au Sud duquel le Val Poschiavo plonge sur Tirano ; il relie ainsi l'Engadine en Suisse à la Valteline en Italie.

DE ST-MORITZ A TIRANO

56 km – environ 2 h – itinéraire 7 *de la visite des Grisons.*

Ne pas entreprendre trop tard dans l'après-midi le parcours du versant engadinois, afin de ne pas trouver dans l'ombre le cirque glaciaire de Morteratsch.
Le col de la Bernina risque d'être obstrué par la neige d'octobre à mai. La route du col n'est pas déneigée la nuit. Seule la voie ferrée – la plus haute d'Europe pour un parcours ne comportant pas de sections à crémaillère – assure le transit en toutes saisons. Contrôle douanier suisse à Campocologno ; contrôle douanier italien à Piattamala.

★★★ **St-Moritz** – *Visite : 1 h 1/2. Voir à ce nom.*

Quitter St-Moritz en direction de Pontresina.

★★ **Muottas Muragl** – *Voir à ce nom.*

★★ **Pontresina** – *Voir à ce nom.*

Entre Pontresina et la bifurcation du chemin de Chünetta, la vallée prend rapidement un caractère sauvage. A droite du Munt Pers, se détachent les trois sommets éblouissants du Piz Palü puis, plus à droite, les bosses neigeuses de Bellavista moins élevées.

★★★ **Belvédère de Chünetta** – Alt. 2 083 m. *De la route de la Bernina, 2 km AR, plus 1 h à pied AR.* Bifurquer dans le chemin du glacier de Morteratsch, et laisser la voiture avant le pont de bois donnant accès à la gare de Morteratsch. Traverser le pont, puis la voie ferrée, et, à l'extrémité d'un champ de cailloux roulés par le torrent, prendre le sentier de droite en montée sous les mélèzes. Au bout de 20 mn, à la 2ᵉ bifurcation rencontrée, offrant une vue dégagée, tourner à droite pour grimper en quelques instants au belvédère.

De là, se découvre le grandiose cirque glaciaire de **Morteratsch** dominé, de gauche à droite, par le Piz Palü, Bellavista, le Piz Bernina, pyramide à la pointe ébréchée (point culminant du massif – alt. 4 049 m), le Piz Morteratsch et sa lourde calotte de neige, le Piz Boval. Au premier plan meurt la langue terminale du glacier, encadrée d'énormes remblais morainiques et divisée, longitudinalement, par la traînée d'une moraine médiane.

Aussitôt après deux lacets suivis d'un passage à niveau, la **vue**★★ devient splendide. A droite de Bellavista se déploient les cimes les plus glorieuses du massif de la Bernina – Piz Bernina et Piz Morteratsch – d'où descend le magnifique glacier de Morteratsch. La route débouche ensuite dans la dépression supérieure de la Bernina, encore verdoyante.

Le glacier de Morteratsch

BERNINASTRASSE

★★★ **Diavolezza** ⊙ – Alt. 2 973 m. *De la route de la Bernina, 1 h AR environ dont 9 mn de téléphérique*. L'ancien refuge *(aujourd'hui restaurant)* de la Diavolezza a constitué déjà, pour des générations d'alpinistes et de skieurs, le point de départ d'une des courses de glacier les plus fameuses d'Europe. Grâce au téléphérique, les touristes peuvent aujourd'hui accéder à ce col de haute montagne et admirer son inoubliable panorama glaciaire.

A Curtinatsch, par l'échancrure supérieure du Val d'Arlas, réapparaissent, sur la droite, les trois cimes du Piz Palü.

★★ **Piz Lagalb** ⊙ – *Accès en 8 mn par téléphérique au départ de Curtinatsch*. On gagne à pied *(1/4 h AR)*, dans un paysage minéral, le sommet enneigé du Piz Lagalb (alt. 2 959 m) d'où le **panorama**★★ embrasse une quarantaine des principaux sommets grisons, avec au Sud-Ouest le massif de la Diavolezza et ses glaciers Nord, au Sud la belle retenue d'eau – verte, malgré son nom – du Lago Bianco, plus d'autres lacs, naturels, dont, à droite de la Diavolezza, le petit Lej de la Diavolezza scintillant au fond d'un gouffre. Plus loin, alors qu'on aborde les premiers lacs de la Bernina, le groupe du Piz Cambrena se profile à son tour.

★★ **Col de la Bernina** – Alt. 2 328 m. La route, quittant la dépression occupée par le lac Blanc et suivie de bout en bout par la voie ferrée, s'élève jusqu'à ce passage latéral, offrant des **vues**★★★ parfaitement dégagées sur le Piz Cambrena et son glacier.

★★★ **Alp Grüm** ⊙ – Alt. 2 091 m. *De la gare de «Ospizio Bernina» (accessible en voiture par un chemin en descente s'amorçant au col de la Bernina, 1 h environ AR dont 10 mn de chemin de fer*. Belvédère très réputé sur le glacier du Palü et le Val Poschiavo.

Du col de la Bernina au replat de la Rösa, la route, plongeant dans le **Val Agone**, encadré par les escarpements chaudement colorés du Piz Campasc et de la Cima du Cardan, adopte un tracé capricieux. Le groupe du Cambrena montre longtemps à l'arrière-plan quelques pans de glacier. La végétation forestière se réduit encore à quelques bouts de mélèzes chétifs. L'arrivée à la Rösa se fait face au beau cirque rocheux du Teo.

De la Rösa à Poschiavo, la parure forestière des versants s'assombrit, en raison de la multiplication des épicéas. 1 km après deux lacets rapprochés – secteur où la route virevolte au-dessus d'un frais vallon – un large virage en corniche fait découvrir en contrebas les villages de San Carlo et de Poschiavo, dominés par l'épaule glaciaire du Pizzo Scalino.

Poschiavo – La rue principale du bourg, resserrée entre de hauts bâtiments uniformes, aux fenêtres régulièrement distribuées, qui ne doivent plus rien au style architectural de l'Engadine, plonge le voyageur descendu de la Bernina dans une ambiance toute transalpine. Fermant la place communale, l'église St-Victor (début du 16ᵉ s.) témoigne par son architecture de la situation particulière des Grisons, terre de transit, non seulement pour les hommes et les biens, mais encore pour les influences artistiques. Si l'allure générale de l'édifice, avec son toit à faible pente, et surtout son campanile élancé à cinq étages d'arcatures, est bien lombarde, le réseau de voûtes en étoile, particulièrement remarquable dans le chœur, procède d'une mode germanique, propre à la dernière période du gothique *(voir p. 33)*.

Le **lac de Poschiavo** fait l'agrément du trajet Poschiavo-Miralago. Très haut sur le versant Est, escarpé et boisé, pointe le clocher de San Romerio.

Miralago – De ce hameau au nom évocateur («regarde le lac»), la **vue**★ se portant vers l'amont découvrira, pour la dernière fois, un horizon de haute montagne.

De Miralago à **Tirano**, la pente redevient rapide. Les vignes, les champs de tabac se multiplient. Remarquer à Brusio la boucle, entièrement à ciel ouvert, que décrit la voie ferrée. L'église de pèlerinage de Madonna di Tirano, de style Renaissance, marque l'arrivée en terre italienne.

Mine de sel de BEX★

Vaud
Carte Michelin n° 427 pli 12 ou 217 pli 14

L'existence de cette **mine** ⊙, toujours en exploitation et produisant 150 t de sel par jour, remonte à trois siècles. Elle se compose de quelque 40 km de galeries, boyaux, puits, escaliers creusés à l'origine à la massette et à la cisette. Le sel est obtenu selon un procédé classique : lessivage (injection d'eau douce sous pression dans la roche saline et dans la moindre entaille), remontée de l'eau salée à 30 %, évaporation par ébullition, recueil du dépôt de sel.

La visite d'une partie de la mine transformée en musée se fait en petit train et à pied. Dans l'ancien réservoir de saumure creusé en 1826, un diaporama et une exposition font revivre l'histoire de la mine. Plusieurs salles exposent ensuite les différents outils et matériels utilisés (troncs de mélèzes évidés pour faire couler l'eau, cacolets pour le transport des matériaux à dos d'homme, lampes à huile, soufflets pour envoyer de l'air aux mineurs, wagonnets, etc.), témoignant ainsi de l'œuvre accomplie au cours des siècles.

BIEL/BIENNE ★

Berne – 51 893 habitants
Carte Michelin n° 427 plis 12, 13 ou 216 pli 14 – Schéma : JURA SUISSE – Alt. 438 m

Bienne, au pied des derniers contreforts du Jura et au bord du lac portant son nom, est un bon centre d'excursions, et sa plage, située non loin de Nidau, est très appréciée. Elle marque la frontière linguistique franco-allemande *(voir carte « la Suisse linguistique » dans l'introduction)* : un tiers des habitants parle français.
La ville basse faite de constructions modernes contraste avec les vieux quartiers de la ville haute.

La vie à Bienne – Axée sur le progrès, Bienne connaît une activité intense. Le nombre de ses habitants a plus que décuplé en un siècle grâce à l'horlogerie, qui emploie encore près de 6 000 personnes. C'est à Bienne que fut fondée, en 1879, la première fabrique « Omega ».

BIEL	BIENNE		
Bahnhofstrasse	R. de la Gare	ABZ	4
Industriegasse	R. de l'Industrie	ABY	18
Marktgasse	R. du Marché	BY	28
Nidaugasse	R. de Nidau	BY	33
Unionsgasse	R. de l'Union	ABY	46
Zentralstrasse	R. Centrale	BZ	
Adam Göuffi-Strasse	R. Adam Göuffi	BY	3
Bözingenstrasse	Rte de Boujean	BY	6
Brühlstrasse	R. du Breuil	BY	7
Burggasse	R. du Bourg	BY	9
Florastrasse	R. de Flore	BY	10
Freiburgstrasse	R. de Fribourg	BZ	12
General Guisan-Platz	Pl. du Gén. Guisan	AZ	13
Gerbergasse	R. des Tanneurs	BY	15
Güterstrasse	R. des Marchandises	BZ	16
Jakob Rosius-Strasse	R. Jakob Rosius	ABY	19
Juravorstadt	Faubourg du Jura	BY	21
Kanalgasse	R. du Canal	BY	22
Karl Stauffer-Strasse	R. Karl Stauffer	BY	24
Kreuzplatz	Pl. de la Croix	BZ	25
Logengasse	R. de la Loge	BY	27
Murtenstrasse	R. de Morat	BZ	30
Neumarktplatz	Pl. du Marché-Neuf	BY	31
Obergasse	R. Haute	BY	34
Quellgasse	R. de la Source	ABY	36
Reuchenettestrasse	Rte de Reuchenette	BY	37
Rüschlistrasse	R. de Rüschli	ABY	39
Schüsspromenade	Promenade de la Suze	AYZ	
Silbergasse	R. de l'Argent	BZ	42
Spitalstrasse	R. de l'Hôpital	AYZ	43
Tschärisplatz	Pl. de la Charrière	AY	45
Unterer Quai	Quai du Bas	AZ	48
Untergasse	R. Basse	BY	49
Zentralplatz	Pl. Centrale	BY	51

BIEL/BIENNE

Des industries annexes se sont établies pour pallier les effets des crises : des fabriques de machines-outils de précision, des tréfileries, des ateliers d'arts graphiques.
Le bilinguisme est, à Bienne, très attachant : les deux langues allemande et française sont officielles et placées sur un plan d'égalité. Il n'est pas rare d'entendre deux Biennois converser, sans gêne, chacun dans sa langue. Dans les écoles, on enseigne le français et l'allemand et un gymnase (lycée) français s'est ouvert en 1956. Un inconvénient sérieux du bilinguisme est l'altération de la pureté de chacune des langues, par contamination réciproque.

CURIOSITÉS

★ **Musée Schwab** (**AY** M) ⊙ — Constitué par les collections provenant des découvertes faites par le colonel Schwab (1803-1869), « pionnier de la préhistoire en Suisse romande », ce musée réunit les échantillons les plus célèbres de l'époque lacustre de la Suisse. Aux collections provenant des lacs de Bienne, Neuchâtel et Morat, s'ajoutent les trouvailles de la station gallo-romaine de Petinesca et de celle de la Tène.
Cette dernière station, découverte par Schwab en 1857, a donné son nom à la période qui s'étend de 500 avant J.-C. jusqu'à notre ère, c'est-à-dire le second âge du Fer.

Du musée, emprunter le faubourg du lac (Seevorstadt), puis à gauche pénétrer dans la rue du Bourg (Burggasse).

★ **Ville ancienne** (**BY**) — Très pittoresque, elle offre au touriste une variété de fontaines et de façades décorées de nombreuses et remarquables enseignes de fer forgé.

Rue du Bourg (Burggasse) (**BY** 9) — Elle se signale par son hôtel de ville au pignon en escalier et à la façade ornée de fenêtres aux meneaux de grès, ainsi que par sa fontaine de Justice de 1744.

Ring — Cette charmante place fut, durant tout le temps que Bienne vécut sous la crosse des princes-évêques de Bâle (du 11e s. à la Révolution), le centre de la ville ancienne ; c'est là qu'était rendue la justice : l'accusé comparaissait devant les membres du Conseil assis en demi-cercle ; cette disposition des sièges a valu son nom à la place.
Au centre du Ring, la curieuse fontaine du Banneret (1546) symbolise la milice et la guerre. Les maisons à arcades et à tourelles forment un bel ensemble architectural tandis qu'à côté se dresse la puissante tour de l'église St-Benoît.

Rue Haute (Obergasse) (**BY** 34) — Elle est bordée de maisons à arcades bernoises

Le Ring

(voir Introduction : La Suisse pittoresque) et de maisons bourguignonnes. On y voit une très belle fontaine de 1564, appelée fontaine de l'Ange : un ange tient dans ses bras un agneau et le protège contre les menaces du Diable.

Prendre ensuite la rue Basse (Untergasse) qui rejoint le faubourg du lac.

ENVIRONS

★★ **Île St-Pierre** (St. Petersinsel) — *Voir à Bieler See.*

★ **Gorges du Taubenloch** (Taubenlochschlucht) — *2,5 km — environ 1 h 1/2. Quitter Bienne par ② du plan, route de Soleure-Zurich, et prendre le sentier qui s'amorce à Boujean (Bözingen), aussitôt avant le pont de la Suze près d'une tréfilerie.* Ces gorges, présentant des aspects sauvages, sont parcourues par un excellent sentier touristique.

★ **Macolin** — *8 km — environ 1/2 h. Quitter Bienne par ① du plan, route de Delémont.* 200 m après un passage inférieur entre virages, tourner à gauche dans la petite route d'Évilard. Poursuivre jusqu'à Macolin, d'où l'on découvre un **panorama** ★

77

BIEL/BIENNE

étendu sur le Plateau suisse, les lacs qui s'allongent au pied du Jura, et les Alpes. Macolin est également connu pour son École fédérale de gymnastique. *Le site est aussi accessible par funiculaire au départ de Bienne (Ouest du plan).*

Aarberg — *11 km au Sud route n° 22.* Prospère petite cité qu'un canal relie au lac de Bienne. La ville haute, accessible de la ville basse par un pont couvert en bois (16e s.) franchissant l'Aare, mérite une visite pour sa **grand-place**★ (Stadtplatz) oblongue, agrémentée de deux fontaines et bordée de nobles façades classiques, ainsi que d'une petite église du 15e s. (très restaurée).

Une pittoresque foire à la brocante s'y tient, chaque année, les derniers vendredis et samedis d'avril et d'août.

BIELER See★

Carte Michelin n° 427 plis 12, 13 ou 216 plis 13, 14 — Schéma : JURA SUISSE

D'origine glaciaire, le **lac de Bienne** s'allonge sur 15 km au pied de la dernière ride du Jura. Il était jadis plus étendu, mais le niveau des eaux fut abaissé de 2,20 m en 1878, ce qui permit de découvrir une vingtaine d'installations lacustres sur la rive Sud. A la même époque, une partie des eaux de l'Aare fut détournée dans le lac.

« Les rives du lac de Bienne sont plus sauvages et romantiques que celles du lac de Genève... mais elles ne sont pas moins riantes » a dit Jean-Jacques Rousseau. La rive Nord, avec ses villages blottis au milieu des vignes, est la plus pittoresque. On y remarque la délicieuse cité ancienne de la Neuveville.

En saison des promenades en bateau sont organisées sur le lac avec des escales dans de petites villes pittoresques et des visites possibles.

★★ **Île St-Pierre (St. Petersinsel)** ⊘ — *On y accède, de préférence, en bateau au départ de Bienne ou de la Neuveville. Compter une demi-journée.* A l'extrémité Sud-Ouest du lac, l'île St-Pierre, devenue presqu'île depuis l'abaissement du plan d'eau, a conservé son nom d'« Île » consacré par la tradition. **J.-J. Rousseau** évoque, dans les *Confessions* et *Les Rêveries du promeneur solitaire*, le délicieux séjour qu'il y fit en 1765 ; le Sénat de Berne l'obligea à se retirer d'abord à Bienne, puis à Soleure.

Le piéton fera facilement le tour de l'île par le Nord et bénéficiera de jolies échappées, particulièrement en direction du village de Glérésse (Ligerz) ; après avoir vu le petit embarcadère dont usa Rousseau, il parviendra à la maison habitée par l'Ami de la Nature, ancien prieuré clunisien du 12e s. transformé, après la Réforme, en auberge : on y montre la chambre de l'écrivain, émouvante dans sa simplicité. L'île St-Pierre et sa voisine, la petite **île des Lapins** (soudée, elle aussi, à la terre ferme par une langue de terrain marécageuse depuis la baisse du plan d'eau du lac) sont des réserves naturelles où vivent en paix oiseaux migrateurs, lièvres et chevreuils.

★ **Rive Nord** — Le cachet ancien de ses localités confère à cette partie romande du lac un charme supplémentaire.

Cressier — En retrait du lac, ce vieux village viticole garde quelques édifices anciens dont, rue de St-Martin, une maison à oriel datée de 1576 et à proximité le joli château de Vallier (1610) cantonné de tourelles pointues.

Le Landeron — Plus proche du lac, ceinturé de potagers et d'arbres fruitiers, le petit bourg séduit par sa longue place ombragée, ornée de deux fontaines à bannerets, défendue à chaque issue par une porte fortifiée (de 1659 côté Nord, 1596 côté Sud), bordée de vieilles maisons dont l'hôtel de ville (15e s.) accolé à la chapelle des Martyrs et, au n° 36, une demeure datée de 1550 (fenêtre à torsades au 2e étage).

La Neuveville — *Voir à ce nom.*

BREMGARTEN

Argovie — 5 280 habitants
Carte Michelin n° 427 pli 5 ou 216 plis 17, 18 — Alt. 386 m

Enserrée dans la vaste boucle d'un méandre de la Reuss, Bremgarten fut au temps des Habsbourg une forteresse et une tête de pont. Son site est comparable, quoique moins imposant, à ceux de Berne et de Fribourg.

De la route de Lucerne, ou de la Casinoplatz, on a une belle **vue panoramique** sur la ville ancienne et ses maisons aux toits étagés au-dessus de la rivière. Remarquer un pont couvert du 16e s., au milieu duquel s'élèvent deux petites chapelles.

D'anciennes portes ou tours de fortifications — Obertor (Porte d'En Haut), Hexenturm (tour des Sorcières) — des maisons à oriel, aux toits débordant en auvent, forment un ensemble intéressant.

BRIENZ★

Berne — 2 849 habitants
Carte Michelin n° 427 pli 14 ou 217 pli 8 – Schéma : BERNER OBERLAND – Alt. 570 m

Allongée au bord du lac de ce nom, face aux chutes du Giessbach, Brienz est une des stations estivales de l'Oberland bernois qui a le mieux conservé son cachet rural traditionnel. Grand centre de sculpture sur bois, le bourg possède une école professionnelle assurant la continuité de cette tradition, ainsi qu'une école de lutherie.
Les plantigrades de toutes tailles, aux postures variées, vendus comme souvenirs à Berne, Interlaken ou Lucerne sortent, en majeure partie, des ateliers de Brienz.

★★★ **Brienzer Rothorn** ⊙ – Alt. 2 350 m. *Environ 3 h AR dont 2 h 20 mn de chemin de fer à crémaillère.*
Le magnifique tour d'horizon dont on profite, au sommet, englobe les Alpes bernoises, le lac de Brienz et l'Hasli.

★★ **Cascades du Giessbach (Giessbachfälle)** – Impressionnant ensemble de chutes dans un cadre très boisé.

- **Au départ de Brienz** ⊙ – Embarcadère de Brienz-Bahnhof. *Environ 2 h AR, dont 3/4 h de bateau et de funiculaire.*

- **Au départ d'Interlaken** ⊙ – Embarcadères d'Interlaken-Brienzersee ou de Bönigen. *Environ 3 h AR, dont 2 h de bateau et de funiculaire.*

★★ **Ballenberg (Musée suisse de l'Habitat rural)** ⊙ – *2,5 km. Préférer l'entrée Ouest à l'entrée Est (route de Brünig) : quitter Brienz à l'Est par la route de Hofstetten se détachant, à gauche, de la rue principale (suivre la direction Freilichtmuseum). Laisser la voiture au très vaste parc de stationnement.*
Dans un immense et splendide site boisé réservé aux piétons, ce musée de plein air inauguré en 1978 dissémine sur environ 80 ha des bâtiments qui étaient condamnés à disparaître. Sa visite constitue une promenade instructive, et très agréable par beau temps ; si l'on a un peu traîné, un bus gratuit assure la navette entre les entrées Ouest et Est.
L'originalité de ce musée privé est de présenter des architectures authentiques provenant de presque tous les cantons du pays, d'y préserver un mobilier original et d'y entretenir des activités artisanales et rurales, à la manière d'autrefois (droguerie, fromagerie d'alpage, boulangerie, passementerie, récolte de résine, etc.), ce qui permet de comprendre les conditions parfois extrêmement difficiles dans lesquelles vivaient leurs occupants.
Réparties en treize groupes selon leur origine géographique, les maisons paysannes sont reliées par des sentiers agrémentés d'aires de pique-nique et de jeux ainsi que d'enclos enfermant des animaux domestiques. Parmi les bâtiments les plus remarquables reconstitués ici : la maison polyvalente (n° 111) de la Chaux-de-Fonds est une image typique du Haut-Jura ; celle d'Oberentfelden (n° 221) en Argovie date de 1609 et se cache sous un immense toit de chaume ; l'auberge dite du Vieil Ours (n° 311) a été transférée de Rapperswil ; la maison d'Ostermundigen (n° 331) présente des fenêtres en trompe l'œil sous le pignon ; celle de Lancy (n° 551), impressionnante, n'était à l'origine qu'un simple pressoir de vigneron ; la maison de Richterswil (n° 611) aux pittoresques colombages a été construite vers 1780 dans la région zurichoise ; celle d'Erstfeld (n° 721) est un chef-d'œuvre du 17e s. du type « Saint-Gothard » de la Renaissance tardive ; celle d'Adelboden (n° 1 011), du 17e s. également, est bâtie en madriers.
Le site comprend trois auberges où sont servis des plats traditionnels, et des magasins vendant de l'artisanat généralement fabriqué sur place.

★ LAC DE BRIENZ

Moins grandiose et légèrement plus petit que son jumeau le lac de Thoune auquel il est relié par l'Aare, le lac de Brienz est d'un aspect plus sauvage.

★ **Rive Nord** – *D'Interlaken à Meiringen, 30 km – environ 3/4 h.*
D'Interlaken *(voir à ce nom)* à Ringgenberg, la route, tracée sous bois, prend de la hauteur.

Ringgenberg – L'église *(pour y accéder, tourner dans le chemin du débarcadère)*, élevée au bord du ressaut escarpé où s'est fixé le village, occupe une situation charmante. De ses abords, jolies échappées sur le lac et sur les montagnes qui dominent immédiatement Interlaken. L'édifice a été bâti au 17e s. sur les ruines d'un « Burg », dont le donjon a été réutilisé lors de la construction du clocher.
Le parcours, de Ringgenberg à Brienz, mais surtout la section Oberried-Brienz, offre une ample vue sur le lac de Brienz, encadré par le chaînon du Brienzer Rothorn et par les contreforts du Faulhorn. A 600 m au Nord-Est d'Oberried, quand on rejoint la rive, commence à se dessiner, vers l'amont, la chaîne des Sustenhörner avec la coupole du Sustenhorn (alt. 3 503 m). Plus loin, Brienz apparaît au pied de son église.

BRIENZ

★ **Brienz** – *Description ci-dessus.*

★★★ **Brienzer Rothorn** – *De Brienz, excursion comprenant un parcours en chemin de fer à crémaillère – environ 3 h AR. Description du panorama ci-dessus.*

Peu après Brienz, la route suit le fond plat de la vallée de l'Aare. Parmi les chutes d'eau des alentours, la **cascade de l'Oltschibach**★ est la plus remarquable.

★ **Meiringen** – *Voir à ce nom.*

BRIG

Valais – 10 602 habitants

Carte Michelin n° 427 pli 14 ou 217 pli 18 – Schéma : VALAIS – Alt. 681 m

Plan dans le guide Rouge Michelin Suisse

A la bifurcation de la chaussée du Simplon et de la route menant à la Furka, Brig est une petite ville-relais très animée, dotée d'une importante gare frontière, à la tête Nord du tunnel du Simplon, le plus long du monde (19 823 m).

Le Roi du Simplon – Brig doit son attrait monumental aux ambitions de **Kaspar Jodok von Stockalper** (1609-1691). Commis à la garde du passage du Simplon, ce génial brasseur d'affaires, qui tire d'énormes profits du trafic transalpin qu'il a organisé et de ses privilèges commerciaux (monopole du sel), est aussi un mécène, qui contribue à la floraison de l'art religieux en Haut Valais. Mais sa puissance aiguise la jalousie de ses compatriotes. Stockalper doit s'exiler en Italie et ne reviendra à Brig qu'à la fin de sa vie pour y mourir dans son fier château.

Château de Stockalper (Stockalperschloss) ⊙ – Cet édifice qui fut, en son temps, la plus vaste résidence privée de Suisse, se signale de loin au voyageur par ses trois tours coiffées de bulbes rutilants, plantées au départ de la route du Simplon.
Le premier corps de bâtiment rencontré en venant du centre de Brig est la maison familiale des Stockalper (début du 16ᵉ s.) flanquée d'une jolie échauguette. Relié à celle-ci par une pittoresque galerie de passage à deux étages d'arcades, l'énorme bloc de l'habitation principale ne compte pas moins de huit étages, caves comprises. Pénétrer dans la grande cour par le portail qui s'ouvre dans l'aile en retour d'angle. Cette **cour**★ bordée de deux ou trois étages de galeries entièrement à jour a gardé très grande allure, cantonnée de tours qui tranchent, par la rudesse de leur appareil, sur cette élégante composition, étroitement inspirée de la Renaissance toscane.

BRUGG

Argovie – 9 482 habitants

Carte Michelin n° 427 pli 5 ou 216 pli 6

Fondée par les Habsbourg tôt dans le 12ᵉ s., la « ville des ponts » établie au confluent de l'Aar et de la Reuss, conserve de nombreux édifices de son passé.
Ce carrefour routier et ferroviaire est aussi un actif centre industriel.

Vieille ville – Vestiges des fortifications : tour des Archives, tour des Cigognes (Storchenturm) et imposante **tour Noire** (Schwarzer Turm) des 12ᵉ et 16ᵉ s., commandant le pont sur l'Aar. De là, vue intéressante sur les rives boisées où s'accrochent de vieilles maisons. Ancien hôtel de ville (16ᵉ s.), église protestante (gothique tardif, intérieur 18ᵉ s.).
Sur la jolie place Hofstatt, ancien arsenal (17ᵉ s.) et ancien cellier (18ᵉ s.).

Musée Vindonissa ⊙ – Il rassemble le produit des fouilles effectuées dans la Vindonissa romaine *(voir ci-dessous)* : bijoux, armes, monnaies, poteries, verreries, statuettes, objets en cuir et en bois... A noter : dans son sarcophage, le squelette d'une Romaine du 4ᵉ s. ; la maquette du camp militaire de Vindonissa ; à l'extérieur, le musée lapidaire.

Abbaye de Königsfelden – *Voir à ce nom.*

Amphithéâtre romain de Vindonissa – *A Windisch, 1 km par la route de Zurich puis, à droite de l'église de Konigsfelden, la Hauserstrasse.* Relique la plus importante de Vindonissa – camp militaire qui fut au 1ᵉʳ s. le quartier général romain pour toute l'Helvétie et occupait l'emplacement de l'actuelle ville de Windisch –, cet amphithéâtre ovale (de 112 m sur 98 m), d'une capacité d'au moins 10 000 spectateurs, a gardé sa double enceinte concentrique en bel appareil de moellons.

Pour les excursions à pied autour des lieux de séjour renseignez-vous auprès des Offices de Tourisme habilités à vous délivrer toute la documentation nécessaire.

BRUNNEN★★

Schwyz – 6 232 habitants

Carte Michelin n° 427 pli 15 ou 218 pli 1 – Schéma : VIERWALDSTÄTTER SEE – Alt. 439 m

Brunnen qui, jusqu'à l'ouverture de l'Axenstrasse, fut un port essentiel pour les relations entre les cantons de Schwyz et d'Uri, et une place de transit de première importance sur l'itinéraire du Gothard, doit aujourd'hui son animation intense à la rencontre des courants de circulation de cette grande voie transalpine (route N° 2, par Arth) et de la route côtière de Vitznau.

Par sa **situation**★★ à l'origine du sauvage lac d'Uri, cœur de la Suisse pittoresque et historique, Brunnen impose au moins une halte prolongée.

★★ **Les quais** – Du quai ombragé, que prolonge, à l'Est, en contrebas de l'Axenstrasse, la nouvelle promenade de l'Axenquai, le flâneur découvre toute la **perspective**★★ du lac d'Uri, enfoncé comme un fjord entre de farouches éperons montagneux. La silhouette maîtresse du panorama est l'Uri-Rotstock, présentant ses deux dents émoussées au-dessus d'un petit glacier.

Au premier plan, sur la rive opposée, la prairie historique du **Rütli** (**Grutli** pour les Suisses français) tranche en vert tendre sur les abrupts boisés du saillant de Seelisberg ; à l'extrême pointe de ce promontoire, on distingue l'obélisque naturel que les « cantons primitifs » ont dédié à la mémoire de Schiller « chantre de Tell », sous le nom de **Schillerstein**.

Un court périple en canot à moteur permettra d'approcher de ces lieux historiques.

BULLE

Fribourg – 9 062 habitants

Carte Michelin n° 427 pli 12 ou 217 Sud-Ouest du pli 5 – Alt. 769 m

Situé au centre de la « verte Gruyère », l'une des régions les plus attirantes de la Suisse pour l'harmonie apaisante de ses paysages et l'originalité de son folklore, le gros bourg-marché de Bulle se livre au commerce du bois, du bétail bovin (race tachetée blanc et noir de Fribourg) et du fromage.

★★ **Musée Gruérien** ⊙ – Fondé par l'écrivain bullois Victor Tissot (créateur à Paris de l'« Almanach Hachette ») et maintenant aménagé en sous-sol dans un bâtiment moderne au pied du château, cet important musée d'art populaire réparti sur un espace de 1 500 m², divisé en deux sections, rassemble une profusion impressionnante d'objets remarquablement présentés en surélévation et vitrines ou cages de plastique transparent.

La section la plus vaste compte 25 « îlots d'exposition » thématiques et plusieurs intérieurs paysans reconstitués (le plus curieux étant une chambre de 1673, peinte de scènes de la vie du prophète Élie), ainsi qu'une fromagerie d'alpage ; de nombreux **meubles anciens** : tables, lits, coffres, armoires, bahuts, sièges (« banc bourgeois » fribourgeois du 16e s.), berceaux… peints, sculptés ou décorés ; les costumes gruériens du 18e s., les crèches en papier de la même époque, les canivets (médaillons sur papier) vosgiens ou bavarois des 18e et 19e s., les statues religieuses Renaissance ou baroques, l'orfèvrerie religieuse (ostensoir de 1752 en or et brillants), les clarines et cors des Alpes, le diorama de la faune du pays, les mille et un objets de la vie courante d'autrefois composent une remarquable évocation du folklore de la Gruyère.

La section peintures abrite des gravures et tableaux des écoles italienne des 16e et 17e s., française avec Corot et Courbet (joli Portrait d'une petite Bulloise), suisse (Vallotton, Alexis Grimou), et aussi quelques meubles d'art anciens et modernes (armoire peinte par Netton Bosson).

Un montage audiovisuel présente les traditions de la Gruyère actuelle.

Château – C'est un imposant édifice flanqué de quatre tours rondes, construit au 13e s. par l'évêque Boniface de Lausanne, dans le style bourguignon-savoyard comme les châteaux de Rolle et d'Yverdon *(voir à ces noms)*. Sur la muraille sont peints deux écussons accolés sur lesquels figurent les deux chaudrons fribourgeois.

Quelques numéros de téléphone utiles

111	En cas d'accident
117	Police-secours
120	Hiver : enneigement
120	Été : informations touristiques
140	Secours routier : jour et nuit
162	Prévisions météorologiques
163	État des routes
164	Nouvelles en français
187	Bulletin des avalanches

BURGDORF

Berne — 15 373 habitants
Carte Michelin n° 427 pli 13 ou 216 pli 15 — Alt. 533 m — Schéma : EMMENTAL

A l'entrée de l'Emmental (vallée de l'Emme, réputée pour ses pâturages et son industrie fromagère — *voir à l'Emmental*), Burgdorf est une petite ville active du canton de Berne. La ville moderne, centre d'une importante industrie textile, est dominée par le vieux bourg que couronne un château.

Château — Cette massive construction en brique, élevée à la fin du 12e s. par les ducs de Zähringen et vendue aux Bernois en 1384, fut restaurée à plusieurs reprises.

Musée ⊙ — Le musée occupe trois étages de la tour. On y voit la salle des Chevaliers, au beau mobilier ancien, des costumes de l'Emmental, des faïences et une collection d'instruments de musique, des souvenirs de J. H. Pestalozzi *(voir à ce nom)* qui œuvra ici de 1799 à 1804. Du dernier étage, jolie **vue** sur Burgdorf et sur les Alpes bernoises.

Église — Édifiée à la fin du 15e s., elle a été fortement restaurée. Le chœur est voûté en étoile. Un beau jubé, du 16e s., sert de tribune d'orgues.

ENVIRONS

★**Belvédère de la Lueg** — Alt. 887 m. *8,5 km — environ 1/2 h. Quitter Burgdorf au Nord par la route de Wynigen.* A la sortie de la ville, on franchit deux ponts en béton armé sur l'Emme. A 1,5 km, prendre à droite une route sinueuse qui traverse Gutisberg. Garer la voiture après avoir laissé à gauche une petite route rejoignant Wynigen. Par un sentier en très forte montée au milieu des sapins, on gagne le sommet, où un monument a été élevé à la cavalerie bernoise (1914-1918). **Panorama**★ semi-circulaire : au-delà de prairies et de bois de sapins se détachent le Jura et les Alpes bernoises.

Sumiswald — *16 km à l'Est. Quitter Burgdorf au Sud par la route n° 23 et à Ramsei prendre à gauche.* Ce coquet village de la campagne bernoise a de belles maisons de bois d'aspect très caractéristique : grande façade offrant un ou deux étages de fenêtres très rapprochées les unes des autres, toit immense débordant largement et avant-toit souvent peint et décoré de motifs aux couleurs vives. La **Kramerhaus** et l'Auberge **«Zum Kreuz»** sont tout à fait remarquables.

CELERINA★

Grisons — 975 habitants
Carte Michelin n° 427 pli 17 ou 218 pli 15 — 6 km au Nord-Est de St-Moritz
Schéma : GRAUBÜNDEN

Au pied du ressaut boisé de mélèzes qui sépare le bassin de Samedan du gradin supérieur des lacs de la Haute-Engadine, Celerina (en romanche «Schlarigna») joue un peu le rôle d'une annexe de St-Moritz, surtout dans le domaine de l'équipement sportif. C'est d'ailleurs ici — plus précisément au quartier de Cresta, où se concentrent les grands hôtels de la station — que se terminent les fameuses pistes de bob et de skeleton de Cresta.
Près de l'Inn, le vieux Celerina conserve un bel ensemble de **maisons engadinoises**.

Église St-Jean (San Gian) ⊙ — Isolée sur une butte, elle se dresse à 500 m à l'Est de la localité.
Ce sanctuaire roman surmonté d'une tour décoronnée est une des silhouettes monumentales familières de la vallée de l'Inn. A l'intérieur, beau plafond peint de 1478 et vestiges de fresques de la même époque.

ENVIRONS

Les excursions proposées au départ de St-Moritz peuvent tout aussi bien s'accomplir en partant de Celerina.

Protection de la flore alpine
La cueillette de certaines fleurs des Alpes menacées de disparition :
    cyclamen,
    grand chardon bleu,
    lis martagon,
    edelweiss,
est sévèrement réglementée en Suisse.

Le CHASSERAL★★★

Berne
Carte Michelin n° 427 plis 3, 12 ou 216 pli 13 – 12 km au Sud-Est de St-Imier
Schéma : JURA SUISSE

Point culminant du Jura du Nord, le Chasseral (alt. 1 607 m) offre sur les Alpes suisses un beau panorama. Les automobilistes que ne rebutent pas quelques difficultés traverseront les chaînons du Jura suisse en empruntant l'itinéraire indiqué ci-dessous. Un télésiège permet, au départ de Nods, d'atteindre plus rapidement le sommet.

DE ST-IMIER A LA NEUVEVILLE

33 km – environ 1 h 1/2 – itinéraire 7 de la visite du Jura suisse

⊙ La route, étroite, est généralement obstruée par la neige de décembre à la mi-mai (un mois plus tôt, côté Sud).

St-Imier – Cette active cité horlogère, déployée sur le versant Sud du mont Soleil, ne conserve de son passé médiéval que sa tour St-Martin (ou de la Reine Berthe), clocher d'une église du 11ᵉ s. démolie en 1828, et son **ancienne collégiale** ⊙ (à présent temple réformé) du 12ᵉ s., dont l'intérieur offre un narthex à chapiteaux archaïques (têtes, à droite), une belle abside en cul-de-four, un chœur à voûtes d'ogives et peintures murales (Évangélistes, Christ en gloire dans une mandorle).

Au départ de St-Imier, suivre la route de Neuchâtel. 1 km après les Pontins, prendre à gauche la route du Chasseral.

La route, après s'être infléchie dans une combe typiquement jurassienne (voir le schéma d'un plissement jurassien en Introduction, au chapitre : Physionomie du pays), atteint la crête supérieure du Chasseral.

Tourner alors à gauche vers l'hôtel du Chasseral, où on laisse la voiture.

★★★ **Panorama** – A côté de l'hôtel du Chasseral – terminus de la route autorisée – situé un peu en contrebas du point culminant, une table d'orientation permet de repérer les silhouettes maîtresses des Alpes bernoises, des Alpes valaisannes et du massif du Mont-Blanc. Cette grandiose toile de fond s'allonge sur 250 km environ.

L'automobiliste qui dispose d'un peu de temps pourra gagner à pied le signal du Chasseral (1 h AR par un large chemin en pente douce), à proximité d'une station-relais des télécommunications postales suisses. On effectue alors un **tour d'horizon** ★★★ complet, des Alpes suisses au Jura du Nord, aux Vosges et à la Forêt-Noire.

Reprendre la voiture et descendre vers la bifurcation, puis tourner à gauche en direction de Nods, Lignières et la Neuveville.

Avant d'arriver à la Neuveville, la route, qui descend en lacet vers le bourg, offre de belles échappées sur les lacs de Bienne et de Neuchâtel.

La Neuveville – Voir à ce nom.

CHÂTEAU-D'OEX★

Vaud – 3 110 habitants
Carte Michelin n° 427 pli 12 ou 217 pli 15 – Schéma : ALPES VAUDOISES – Alt. 1 000 m

Chef-lieu du Pays d'Enhaut (secteur de la vallée de la Sarine compris entre le défilé de la Tine et la frontière bernoise), petite cellule montagnarde des Préalpes ayant longtemps mené une vie à part, Château-d'Oex (prononcer : Châteaudait) offre une succession de chalets et d'hôtels au pied des derniers contreforts boisés de la Gummfluh et des Vanils. C'est la villégiature familiale type des Alpes vaudoises, réputée également pour ses nombreuses activités nautiques...

D'abord partie intégrante du comté de Gruyère, conformément à la logique géographique, cette région passa à la cause bernoise et réformée au 16ᵉ s., pour être enfin rattachée au canton de Vaud, lors de la création de celui-ci.

Chaque année à la mi-janvier, a lieu à Château-d'Oex une compétition internationale de montgolfières (à l'angle des routes de Saanen et du col des Mosses).

★ **Musée d'Art populaire du Vieux Pays d'Enhaut** ⊙ – Aménagé de façon chaude et intime dans un bâtiment de 3 étages, il illustre le riche passé humain de la région, du 12ᵉ au 19ᵉ s., sous forme de documents, gravures, photographies, œuvres d'art religieux ou populaire, armes, outils, ustensiles et autres objets d'usage révolu, meubles peints ou sculptés, intérieurs reconstitués : cuisines paysanne (rez-de-chaussée) et bourgeoise (2ᵉ étage), chambres montagnarde et de tisserand (3ᵉ étage). Des verreries et vitraux de couleur, des papiers découpés du 19ᵉ s. (2ᵉ étage), des dentelles noires aux fuseaux (3ᵉ étage) sollicitent spécialement l'attention. Deux petits bâtiments annexes reconstituent, l'un le chalet d'alpage (à l'escalier 16ᵉ s.) avec sa fromagerie où le chaudron de cuivre géant (ici, de 800 l) tenait la place d'honneur, l'autre le « grenier » occupé par un atelier de menuiserie et les instruments de différents métiers.

CHÂTEAU-D'OEX

Papier découpé de SAUGY « Montée à l'alpage »

Dépendant du musée mais situé tout en haut du bourg, le **chalet de l'Etambeau**, pavillon du 18ᵉ s., à toiture et cheminée de tavaillons, aux étroites fenêtres, abrite des expositions d'architecture régionale. La grange abrite une exposition consacrée au transport en montagne.

La CHAUX-DE-FONDS

Neuchâtel – 36 894 habitants
Carte Michelin n° 427 pli 12 ou 216 pli 12 – Schéma : JURA SUISSE – Alt. 992 m
Plans de ville et d'agglomération dans le guide Rouge Michelin Suisse

La Chaux-de-Fonds est le plus grand centre horloger de la Suisse et l'un de ses plus grands centres agricoles. Capitale des Montagnes neuchâteloises (appelées plus simplement « Le Haut »), elle est située dans une haute vallée du Jura, à près de 1 000 m d'altitude. La ville a été presque entièrement détruite par un incendie en 1794 et reconstruite selon un plan géométrique. Berceau de l'industrie horlogère qui prit son essor au début du 18ᵉ s., la cité vit également de la microtechnique, de la mécanique, de l'électronique et du secteur tertiaire (services).
La Chaux-de-Fonds se signale encore par une production particulière : elle fournit en timbres-poste la Confédération et de nombreux pays étrangers.

Célébrités locales – La Chaux-de-Fonds est la patrie du constructeur d'automates Pierre Jaquet-Droz (1721-1790), du peintre Léopold Robert (1794-1835), du constructeur automobile Louis Chevrolet (1870-1941), de l'écrivain Frédéric Sauser plus connu sous le nom de **Blaise Cendrars** (1887-1961). Précurseur avec Guillaume Apollinaire du surréalisme, son œuvre se confond avec sa vie, remplie de voyages réels et imaginaires.

Le Corbusier – Le 6 octobre 1887 naît Charles Édouard Jeanneret. Il commence des études de peinture et d'architecture à l'École d'art de la ville avant d'entreprendre un voyage en Europe qui lui permettra de rencontrer d'éminents architectes. En 1918, il se fait connaître comme peintre en publiant avec Amédée Ozenfant le manifeste du purisme (« Après le cubisme »), dans lequel il prône le dépouillement, la simplicité des formes et l'ordre mathématique sans pour autant proscrire l'expression des sentiments et la poésie. Ces principes animeront toute son œuvre architecturale. En 1920 Charles Édouard Jeanneret adopte le pseudonyme de Le Corbusier. La même année, il crée avec Ozenfant et le poète Paul Dermé la revue « L'Esprit nouveau » qui sera publiée jusqu'en 1925. Novateur, Le Corbusier préconise une solution d'habitat vertical et invente « la machine à habiter », fruit de ses réflexions sur les rapports de l'homme et de la machine. Dans ses réalisations révolutionnaires d'habitat collectif, il oppose les masses entre elles, mêle des matériaux différents et crée des jeux de lumière sur un béton brut dont il tire toutes les possibilités plastiques. Son œuvre ne se limite pas seulement à l'Europe mais on trouve également son empreinte en ex-U.R.S.S., au Brésil, au Japon, en Inde. Controversé ou loué, Le Corbusier est incontestablement l'un des grands maîtres de l'urbanisme du 20ᵉ s. et son influence reste entière aujourd'hui.

Un itinéraire Le Corbusier permettant de découvrir ses réalisations locales peut être retiré auprès de l'office de tourisme.

La CHAUX-DE-FONDS

LE BERCEAU DE L'INDUSTRIE HORLOGÈRE

De Genève au Jura — C'est au 16e s. que cet artisanat, existant déjà depuis près d'un siècle, reçoit une impulsion nouvelle. Établi à Genève où il règne en maître, Calvin oblige les orfèvres à orienter leurs activités vers la fabrication des montres, leur interdisant de faire des «croix, callices ou autres instruments servant à la papauté et idolâtrie». Un peu plus tard, l'arrivée à Genève, vers 1587, de huguenots français pourchassés, permet à cette industrie naissante de se développer. De Genève, elle n'allait pas tarder à s'implanter dans le Jura neuchâtelois.

Daniel Jean Richard et le maquignon — En 1679, un marchand de chevaux rentrant au «Pays Haut» avait rapporté de Londres une montre qui fit l'admiration de tous, jusqu'au jour où le mouvement s'arrêta. Les gens de la Sagne, près de la Chaux-de-Fonds, conseillèrent au maquignon de faire examiner sa montre par le jeune Daniel Jean Richard, qui passait pour bricoleur consommé. L'apprenti parvint à remettre la montre en état, en comprit le mécanisme et décida d'en fabriquer une lui-même à l'aide d'outils qu'il inventa et exécuta après de longs tâtonnements. Établi au Locle, Daniel Jean Richard forma de nombreux ouvriers et l'industrie horlogère se propagea dans les montagnes neuchâteloises et, de là, à travers tout le Jura.

Une industrie de renommée mondiale — C'est en Suisse romande, et surtout au pied du Jura, que se concentre la majeure partie de l'industrie horlogère.
La Chaux-de-Fonds, le Locle, Bienne, Neuchâtel, Soleure, Granges, groupent la majorité des entreprises occupant environ 32 000 employés et ouvriers. Les ateliers disposent d'un outillage technique très poussé permettant une production de haute qualité, mais en même temps très importante en quantité.
Mais la recherche de la perfection a toujours été le souci majeur des horlogers suisses : les tolérances admises aujourd'hui dans la précision sont de l'ordre de 1/400e, voire de 1/1000e de mm. L'introduction de l'électronique a permis des progrès dans la précision.

En 1992 la production était d'environ 145 millions de montres et mouvements, ce qui correspond à 58 % de la production mondiale en valeur.
C'est, avec le secteur des produits chimiques et celui des machines, l'une des plus importantes industries exportatrices du pays.
L'industrie horlogère joue ainsi un rôle de premier plan dans l'économie de la Confédération et, malgré les contrecoups dus à la concurrence du marché extérieur, elle est l'un des éléments essentiels de la stabilité de la balance commerciale.

★★ MUSÉE INTERNATIONAL D'HORLOGERIE ⊘ visite : 1 h

Fondé en 1902 et installé dans des salles souterraines dont l'entrée se situe à l'intérieur d'un petit parc, le musée expose de façon chronologique l'histoire de la mesure du temps («l'Homme et le Temps») depuis l'Antiquité, illustrée par plus de 3 000 pièces de valeur, suisses et étrangères. Il possède en outre un centre de restauration d'horlogerie ancienne et un centre d'études interdisciplinaires du temps.
Par une passerelle surplombant des mécanismes d'horloges de clocher, on accède à la salle principale d'exposition que l'on parcourt entre les nombreuses vitrines contenant les premiers instruments antiques de mesure du temps, les pièces d'époque Renaissance et de marine, des 17e (magnifique ensemble de montres émaillées) et 18e s., de pendules neuchâteloises, françaises et d'autres pays, de curieuses horloges astronomiques ou à musique, d'amusants sujets à automates du 19e s., etc. ; avant de la quitter, observer à gauche la salle vitrée où travaillent des réparateurs ou restaurateurs en horlogerie ancienne. On passe ensuite devant le centre d'horlogerie scientifique (pendules astronomiques, horloges atomiques et à quartz) — par lequel on peut monter au «beffroi» procurant une vue agréable sur le parc du musée —, puis dans une salle surélevée initiant à l'horlogerie moderne.
A l'extérieur, s'impose à l'attention l'ensemble monumental du **Carillon**, dressé en 1980, structure tubulaire de 15 tonnes en acier et à lamelles colorées conçue par le sculpteur italien Onelio Vignando. Elle ponctue chaque quart d'heure de sons musicaux (les ritournelles changent selon les saisons) et, la nuit, de captivants jeux de lumière.

La CHAUX-DE-FONDS

AUTRES CURIOSITÉS

★ Musée des Beaux-Arts ⊙ — Complètement réaménagé et agrandi par l'adjonction d'un vaste bâtiment moderne bien éclairé et réservé à des expositions temporaires, le musée présente des collections permanentes donnant un bon aperçu d'œuvres réalisées par des artistes suisses, notamment originaires de la Chaux-de-Fonds. Au rez-de-chaussée (majestueux hall d'entrée au sol de mosaïque et escalier monumental décoré de balustres sculptées), une succession de salles rassemble les œuvres d'artistes comme Charles l'Eplattenier (paysages : *Printemps, Le Doubs*), Lucien Schwob *(Rue du Pont, Autoportrait)*, François Barraud (portraits : *Marie et Louise, Autoportrait*). Au 1er étage une salle est consacrée à Léopold Robert (1794-1835), né à la Chaux-de-Fonds. Peintre romantique, élève de l'atelier de Girodet et de David, Robert fit de fréquents voyages en Italie qui lui inspirèrent de nombreuses toiles : *Brigand au fusil, Brigand blessé, Danse à l'île de Capri*. Les compositions de grand format d'Édouard Kaiser (1855-1931), illustrent avec réalisme différents métiers : *Les Barons (fondeurs d'or), Atelier de graveurs, Atelier de boîtiers*. D'autres artistes marquants comme Hodler *(Guerrier de Marignan)*, Vallotton *(Coucher de soleil)*, Le Corbusier *(Femme au peignoir)*, complètent l'évocation de la peinture suisse.

Le musée s'est également enrichi de la **collection René et Madeleine Junod** qui comprend des œuvres d'artistes principalement de 1900 à 1950 : Renoir, *Les Colettes*; Derain, *L'Estaque*; Matisse, *Jeunes filles au jardin*; Soutine, *Vue de Cagnes*.

Des œuvres – peintures, sculptures, tapisseries – postérieures à 1950 représentent les différentes écoles contemporaines. On y trouve des artistes français et étrangers : Manessier *(la Passion de notre seigneur Jésus-Christ)*, Afro *(Souvenir d'enfance)*, Winter *(Taches rouges)*, Jacobsen (Sculpture mobile).

Musée d'Histoire naturelle ⊙ — *Au 2e étage (ascenseur) de la Grande Poste*. Intéressantes collections d'animaux naturalisés (mammifères, oiseaux, reptiles), suisses et exotiques (en majorité d'origine africaine, d'Angola notamment). Des dioramas présentent les différentes espèces dans leur milieu naturel. Une salle consacrée à la faune marine expose plusieurs centaines d'espèces de coquillages

Musée d'Histoire et médaillier ⊙ — Une ancienne maison patricienne, dans laquelle se réunit le conseil communal, abrite ce musée qui retrace plusieurs années d'histoire locale.

Au 1er étage des intérieurs neuchâtelois du 17e au 19e s. ont été reconstitués : chambre au plafond sculpté, cuisine avec ses ustensiles, etc. La salle des médailles renferme plusieurs collections de pièces de monnaie locale et étrangère ainsi que des médailles frappées à l'effigie de personnalités suisses (Calvin, le général Dufour, Le Corbusier) ou étrangères (Abraham Lincoln, Louis XVI, la reine Victoria).

Bois du Petit Château ⊙ — *Accès par la rue du Docteur-Coullery*. Dans ce parc d'acclimatation ombragé, de nombreux animaux ont été répartis en différents enclos (loups, daims, cerfs, palmipèdes, etc.).

Musée Paysan ⊙ — *Au faubourg (Sud-Ouest) des Éplatures « Grise », 5, rue Chevrolet*. La maison qui le constitue, ancienne ferme jurassienne restaurée, datée de 1612 mais réemployant quelques éléments «gothiques» (fenêtre à meneaux du rez-de-chaussée) de la construction originelle (1507), est de noble allure avec sa large assise, son vaste fronton triangulaire sous toit de bardeaux, sa discrète décoration sculptée.

L'intérieur, à ossature de sapin ordonnée autour de la grande cheminée dont la hotte pyramidale traverse étage et grenier, reconstitue le cadre de vie des paysans aisés de la région au 17e s., une chambre d'horloger, une fromagerie; meubles, ustensiles et outils d'époque, poêle de faïence... y font renaître le passé.

Le premier dimanche de chaque mois, des dentellières exécutent leurs travaux sous les yeux du public.

Chaque année, une exposition temporaire illustre la vie paysanne.

ENVIRONS

Le Locle — *8 km au Sud-Ouest. Voir à ce nom*.

La Sagne — *10 km au Sud, puis à 4 km une route à droite qui longe la voie ferrée*. Sur le trajet, de loin en loin, belles fermes jurassiennes des 16e-18e s. Ce village du Jura neuchâtelois a vu naître, au 17e s., Daniel Jean-Richard.

L'église, bien mise en valeur par le site, à flanc de coteau, fut construite aux 15e et 16e s. et restaurée en partie en 1891, puis surtout en 1952 et en 1983. La nef est voûtée d'ogives; les vitraux modernes sont de simples verrières aux tons très pâles : vert, jaune, gris, violet.

La CHAUX-DE-FONDS

★★ ROUTE DE LA VUE DES ALPES
De la Chaux-de-Fonds à Neuchâtel

22 km – environ 3/4 h – itinéraire 8 *de la visite du Jura suisse*

Les automobilistes venant de France ont intérêt à accéder à la Chaux-de-Fonds par Morteau et le Locle. Le choix de ces itinéraires leur permet d'admirer, au moment de passer la frontière, le Saut du Doubs décrit dans le guide Vert Michelin Jura.

Un peu après la Chaux-de-Fonds, au cours de la montée à la Vue des Alpes, s'offrent d'attrayantes échappées rapprochées sur le vallon des Ponts (versant Nord du col). Le fond plat de ce vallon, tranche en vert tendre sur les pentes boisées qui l'encadrent.

★ **Vue des Alpes** – Alt. 1 283 m. La table d'orientation permettra de détailler le **panorama ★** : Finsteraarhorn, Jungfrau, Weisshorn, Dent Blanche, Mont Blanc, etc. Le meilleur éclairage est celui d'une belle fin d'après-midi.

★★ **Tête de Ran** – Alt. 1 422 m. *De la Vue des Alpes, 2,5 km jusqu'à l'hôtel de Tête de Ran, plus 1/2 h à pied AR pour gagner le sommet en grimpant directement sur la croupe qui domine cet hôtel, à droite.*

Les amateurs de panoramas pourront préférer ce belvédère moins facilement accessible (sentier pierreux abrupt) à celui de la Vue des Alpes : Tête de Ran est mieux placé pour apprécier les premiers plans jurassiens du tour d'horizon (Val de Ruz, chaînons du Chasseral et de Chaumont), bien que les sapins masquent la vue au Nord-Ouest ; la majeure partie du lac de Neuchâtel est visible.

La descente, à travers les sapins du versant Sud, ménage des vues intéressantes sur la dépression du Val de Ruz.

Cet immense « fond de bateau » n'a pas manqué de frapper les géographes, par la régularité de ses traits ; aussi « ruz » est-il devenu un terme scientifique, caractérisant le premier stade des attaques de l'érosion sur le flanc d'un « mont » *(illustration en Introduction, chapitre : Physionomie du pays).*

Valangin – Bourg pittoresque, bien groupé au pied de son joli château (12e et 15e s.), que protège une imposante enceinte à tours rondes (arasées).

La belle collégiale gothique cruciforme, du 16e siècle (à l'intérieur, tombes et plaques funéraires intéressantes), la porte de ville ornée d'un clocheton à horloge, des maisons des 16e et 17e siècles font bonne figure dans cet ensemble au cachet ancien.

A partir de Valangin, la route suit les gorges boisées du Seyon jusqu'à Neuchâtel.

★★ **Neuchâtel** – *Visite : 2 h 1/2. Voir à ce nom.*

Château de CHILLON★★

Vaud

Carte Michelin n° 427 pli 12 ou 217 pli 14 (entre Territet et Villeneuve)
Schémas : Lac LÉMAN et MONTREUX

Bâti sur un îlot rocheux, ses tours se reflétant en silhouette, dans les eaux du Léman, le château de Chillon occupe un **site ★★** très pittoresque, dans le cadre admirable que constituent le lac, Montreux, la rive française et la chaîne des Alpes d'où se détachent les Dents du Midi.

C'est vers le 9e s. qu'une première forteresse fut édifiée en cet endroit, pour surveiller la grande route qui, venant d'Avenches, se dirigeait vers l'Italie par le Grand-St-Bernard, après avoir longé le Léman.

Propriété des évêques de Sion qui l'agrandirent, puis des comtes de Savoie (à partir de 1150), le château prit, au milieu du 13e s., l'aspect que nous lui connaissons encore aujourd'hui.

Le « prisonnier de Chillon » – Le château et ses souterrains ont servi plus d'une fois de prison d'État ; de tous les détenus, **Bonivard** est le plus célèbre.

Prieur de St-Victor de Genève, François de Bonivard voulait introduire la Réforme à Genève. Ses thèses ayant déplu au duc de Savoie qui avait des visées sur la ville et qui était un ardent défenseur du catholicisme, il fut arrêté et jeté dans les souterrains du château, qui portent son nom. Il resta quatre ans enchaîné à l'un des piliers.

On voit encore, dit-on, dans le roc, les traces de pas du captif délivré par les Bernois en 1536.

De passage à Chillon en 1816, alors qu'il effectuait un pèlerinage au pays de Jean-Jacques Rousseau (ce dernier, né à Genève, avait situé à Clarens le cadre romantique de la Nouvelle Héloïse), le poète anglais Byron a chanté la captivité de Bonivard dans une œuvre débordante de lyrisme qui a contribué à faire du château le monument le plus populaire de toute la Suisse.

Château de CHILLON

VISITE ⏱ environ 1 h

On franchit le fossé par un pont du 18ᵉ s. ayant remplacé le pont-levis. Les souterrains, qui servirent d'arsenal pour la flotte bernoise aux 17ᵉ et 18ᵉ s., ont de belles voûtes d'ogive et ont été aménagés à même le roc. Dans le souterrain Bonivard, Byron a gravé son nom sur le 3ᵉ pilier.

La Grande-Salle du bailli-châtelain qui portent les armoiries de Savoie, est pourvue d'un magnifique plafond et d'une imposante cheminée du 15ᵉ s. Des colonnes en chêne, un beau mobilier et une belle collection d'étains retiennent également l'attention. L'ancienne salle des Fêtes des châtelains ou « aula nova », décorée d'un plafond de bois en forme de carène renversée, abrite actuellement le musée (armes – mousquet orné de nacre et d'os –, armures, étains, mobilier). La « camera paramenti » servait de chambre d'hôtes à l'époque savoyarde. La vaste salle des Chevaliers ou salle des Armoiries, porte sur ses parois les armoiries des baillis bernois de Vevey (vaisselier contenant des pots en étain, trône en bois). La chambre du duc ou « camera domini » lui fait suite. La chapelle (peintures murales), la salle de Justice ou grande salle du comte qui était utilisée pour les fêtes et les réceptions (colonnes en marbre noir), la salle des clercs, le musée lapidaire (pierres trouvées dans le fossé, maquettes montrant les différentes étapes de la construction du château) se succèdent après la cour d'honneur. Du sommet du donjon (montée difficile par un escalier étroit), on découvre de très belles **vues**★★ sur Montreux, le lac et les Alpes. La visite s'achève par une partie du chemin de ronde et de deux tours de défense, transformées en prison au 17ᵉ s.

Château de Chillon

CHUR★

COIRE-Grisons – 32 868 habitants
Carte n° 427 pli 16 ou 218 pli 4 – Schéma : GRAUBÜNDEN – Alt. 585 m

Dans la vallée du Rhin, au point de rencontre des influences latines et germaniques, Coire est depuis le 16ᵉ s. la capitale historique, administrative et religieuse des Grisons. La ville a été construite, à l'écart du fleuve, sur un cône de déjection édifié par le torrent affluent de la Plessur.

★ **Le coup d'œil** – A l'Est de la ville, le premier lacet de la route d'Arosa (Arosastrasse) après la sortie de l'agglomération constitue un observatoire favorable pour examiner l'ensemble de celle-ci, hérissée de clochers, et son cadre d'âpres chaînons rocailleux longtemps enneigés (Calanda).

CURIOSITÉS

Ville ancienne – Elle se regroupe autour de l'église St-Martin, au pied de la cathédrale et du palais épiscopal. Des escaliers passant sous une vieille porte (Hoftor) y donnent accès. Les rues étroites aux belles maisons parfois flanquées de tourelles, les jolies places ornées de fontaines fleuries aux armes des Grisons, l'hôtel de ville (Rathaus) du 15ᵉ s. forment un ensemble curieux et pittoresque.

CHUR

Obere Gasse	Z
Poststrasse	YZ
Alexanderplatz	Y 2
Alexanderstrasse	Y
Arosastrasse	Z
Bahnhofstrasse	Y
Brandisstrasse	Y
Engadinstrasse	YZ
Fontanaplatz	Z
Fontanastrasse	Z 3
Gäuggelistrasse	Y
Goldgasse	Z 4
Grabenstrasse	YZ
Gürtelstrasse	YZ 6
Hartbertstrasse	Y 7
Herrengasse	Z 10
Hofstrasse	Z
Kirchgasse	Z
Komplatz	Z
Kupfergasse	Z 12
Majoranplatz	Z 13
Malixerstrasse	Z
Masanserstrasse	Y
Mühleplatz	Z 15
Nikolaigasse	Z 16
Obere Plessurstrasse	Z 18
Ottoplatz	Y 19
Ottostrasse	Z
Pfisterplatz	Z 21
Planaterrastrasse	YZ
Plessurquai	Z
Postplatz	Y
Quaderstrasse	Z
Reichsgasse	YZ
St. Luzistrasse	Z
Steinbruchstrasse	Y
Storchengasse	Y
Untere Gasse	Z 22
Vazerolgasse	YZ 24
Zeughausstrasse	Y 27

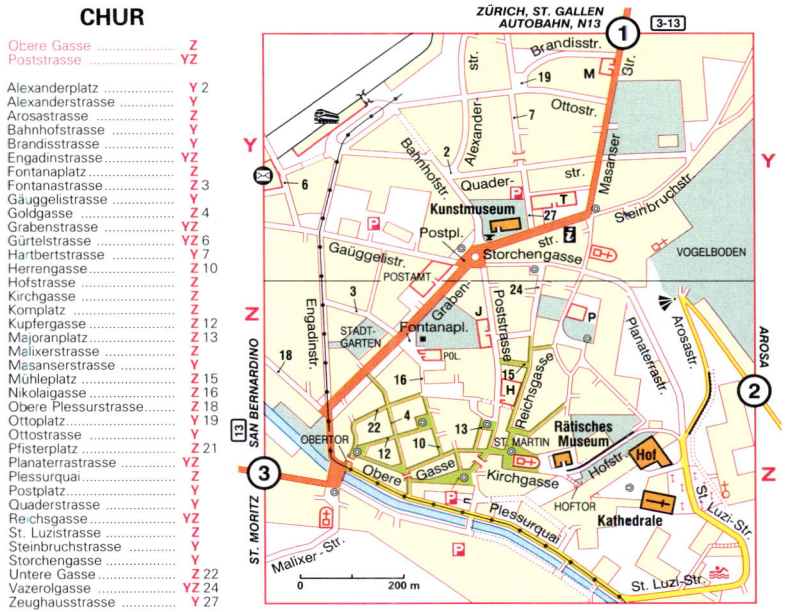

Cathédrale Notre-Dame (Kathedrale) (Z) – Édifiée aux 12ᵉ et 13ᵉ s., elle offre un mélange de style roman et de style gothique. L'extérieur a été remanié à la suite d'un incendie, en 1811. La tour se termine par un clocher à bulbe. Le porche est orné de voussures peintes.

L'édifice présente un plan étant décalé par rapport à celui du chœur. La nef principale, voûtée d'arêtes renforcées, est très sombre, éclairée de fenêtres hautes sur le côté droit seulement.

Le chœur, très surélevé, montre au maître-autel un très beau **triptyque** ★ du 15ᵉ s., en bois doré : consacré à Notre-Dame, c'est le plus grand triptyque gothique de Suisse. Quatre statues d'apôtres, du 13ᵉ s., encadrent l'autel placé en contrebas du chœur.

Trésor (Domschatz) ⊙ – Châsses d'époque carolingienne ou du Moyen Âge et bustes-reliquaires d'une grande valeur. Tout près de la cathédrale s'élèvent les bâtiments de l'**évêché** (Hof) (Z), élégant édifice du 18ᵉ s.

Musée rhétique (Rätisches Museum) (Z) ⊙ – Installé dans la maison Buol, construction de la fin du 17ᵉ s., ce musée cantonal renferme d'intéressantes collections préhistoriques, historiques et folkloriques.

Musée des Beaux-Arts (Kunstmuseum) (Y) ⊙ – Le musée présente surtout des œuvres de peintres et de sculpteurs grisons d'origine ou d'adoption, du 18ᵉ au 20ᵉ s. : Barthélemy Menn, Angelika Kauffmann, Giovanni Segantini – et contemporains : Giovanni, Augusto et Alberto Giacometti, E.-L. Kirchner, entre autres.

★ROUTE DE LENZERHEIDE – GORGES DU SCHIN
Circuit au départ de Coire

73 km – environ 3 h – itinéraire 5 *de la visite des Grisons*

Au départ de Coire par le Sud, la montée, très accentuée, offre une bonne vue d'ensemble de la cité avec, à l'arrière-plan, le chaînon du Calanda. Plus haut, à la sortie d'un premier passage sous bois, la rampe s'adoucit et le regard plonge sur le débouché du **Schanfigg** *(voir à Arosa)* et les bâtiments de l'établissement thermal de **Passugg** qui a donné son nom à l'une des eaux de table les plus répandues en Suisse. Remontant ensuite le vallon de la Rabiusa, on voit apparaître les ruines de la tour de Strassberg. Les petites stations de **Churwalden** – annoncée par son église construite à la lisière de la forêt – et **Parpan** jalonnent la fin de ce parcours conduisant, dans un cadre toujours très ouvert, au seuil de Lenzerheide, ligne de partage des eaux et limite linguistique entre l'allemand et le romanche.

★ **Lenzerheide-Valbella** – « Site de col » typique, l'agglomération de Lenzerheide-Valbella dispose ses immeubles modernes au fond de la dépression (agrémentée de deux lacs) qui constitue pourtant, à 1 500 m d'altitude, le sommet du premier dos d'âne franchi par la route depuis Coire. Le charmant **paysage de parc** ★ que l'automobiliste apprécie entre Valbella et Lenzerheide-centre, suffirait à assurer le succès de la station. En hiver, la régularité des versants favorise le ski de piste, particulièrement sur les pentes du Piz Scalottas et du Stätzerhorn, équipées d'une longue chaîne de remonte-pentes atteignant l'altitude de 2 861 m au Parpaner Rothorn.

CHUR

★★ Parpaner Rothorn ⊙ – *Accès en 1/4 h par téléphérique au départ de Lenzerheide-Valbella*. La montée, au-dessus des sapins jusqu'à Scharmoin (alt. 1 900 m), puis de pentes rases, aboutit au sommet rocheux du Parpaner Rothorn (alt. 2 861 m) d'où la **vue★★**, très belle à l'Ouest sur le bassin de Valbella, cette station et son lac transparent, est barrée à l'Est par les pics neigeux du Weisshorn, du Tschirpen et de l'Aroser Rothorn. Pour bénéficier d'une vue un peu plus dégagée, gagner à pied un sommet proche tel que l'Ostgipfel (alt. 2 899 m ; *1/4 h AR*).
De Lenzerheide à Lenz, la vue s'étend, aux abords de la chapelle San-Cassian, sur la dépression de l'Oberhalbstein dont les contreforts tout boisés du Piz Mitgel et les dernières pentes du Piz Curvèr, de caractère plus agreste, rétrécissent l'entrée. A **Lenz** apparaissent les premières maisons annonciatrices du style engadinois *(voir à l'Engadine)*.

Brienz – L'église abrite un **retable★** à décoration flamboyante (1519) représentant la Vierge entourée de saints. Saint Luzins, évangélisateur de la Rhétie, y figure avec les insignes de la royauté.
De Lenz à Tiefencastel, on descend dans la vallée de l'Albula qui, jusqu'au dernier moment, paraît inhabitée alors que, plus haut, les villages perchés de Mon et de Stierva égayent les replats que domine le Piz Curvèr. Le beau groupe montagneux du Piz Mitgel se détache de mieux en mieux. Enfin, après deux lacets, la claire église de Tiefencastel apparaît. Plus loin, le clocher de **Mistail** signale l'un des sanctuaires les plus vénérables des Grisons (époque carolingienne).

Tiefencastel – *Voir à ce nom.*
De Tiefencastel aux ponts de Solis, la vallée de l'Albula se resserre et le groupe montagneux du Piz Mitgel se dégage. L'Albula s'enfonce alors dans les gorges du Schin.

★ Ponts de Solis – Imposants ouvrages d'art. Du pont routier, vue sur le viaduc ferroviaire dont l'arche centrale, de 42 m de portée, est lancée à 89 m au-dessus de l'Albula.

Gorges du Schin – La végétation qui s'accroche à leurs escarpements schisteux ne permet pas d'en apprécier la profondeur. La traversée du ravin (Tobel) latéral de Mutten en compose le passage le plus impressionnant.
De Thusis à Coire, la route est décrite à Route du San Bernardino.

COLOMBIER

Neuchâtel – 4 636 habitants
Carte Michelin n° 427 pli 12 ou 216 pli 12 – 7 km à l'Ouest de Neuchâtel

Ce village, situé non loin du lac de Neuchâtel et réputé pour ses vins blancs, est dominé par la masse imposante de son château, reconstruit au 15ᵉ s. dans le style gothique et agrandi aux deux siècles suivants. Longtemps propriété des comtes de Neuchâtel, séjour occasionnel de J.-J. Rousseau (en 1762), l'édifice est aujourd'hui à la fois une caserne de l'armée suisse et un musée militaire.

Musée du château ⊙ – Aux 2 premiers étages, on parcourt les vastes salles communes réservées aux officiers, imposantes par leurs plafonds à solives et leurs immenses cheminées ; des fresques patriotiques animent les murs de la salle des Chevaliers au 1ᵉʳ étage (mobilisation suisse de 1914) et de la salle correspondante au 2ᵉ étage (grands épisodes de l'histoire suisse médiévale).
Des centaines d'armes, blanches ou à feu, du 14ᵉ au 20ᵉ s., en panoplies, râteliers ou vitrines, des armures, drapeaux et autres souvenirs régimentaires (portraits, uniformes, tambours, décorations...) décorent les autres salles et particulièrement, avec en plus des canons, la grande salle des combles du 3ᵉ étage. On voit en outre, au 2ᵉ étage, une petite salle de toiles peintes « indiennes » fabriquées dans la région aux 18ᵉ et 19ᵉ s.

Val de CONCHES

Voir à GOMS

Les röstis

Ce « plat national », qui accompagne bon nombre de viandes, se compose de pommes de terre émincées ou râpées, dorées à la poêle dans de la graisse chaude et servies avec des oignons frits et des lardons.

COPPET

Vaud — 1 827 habitants
Carte Michelin n° 427 pli 11 ou 217 bord Est du pli 11 (au bord du Léman)
Schéma : Lac LÉMAN — Alt. 380 m

Cette petite ville riveraine du Léman est traversée par une Grand'Rue bordée de maisons à arcades, construites au 16ᵉ s. après l'invasion des troupes bernoises (lire « le paysage urbain » dans l'introduction au voyage).

Château ⊙ — Reconstruit au 18ᵉ s. dans un style sobre et entouré d'un beau parc, il appartenait à Jacques Necker, banquier genevois et ministre de Louis XVI ; sa fille, Germaine de Staël, surnommée Corinne, du nom de l'héroïne d'un de ses romans, habita le château lorsqu'elle fut jugée indésirable par l'« ogre » Bonaparte. Elle y présida une sorte de principauté littéraire, que l'on surnomma « les États Généraux de l'Europe », dont Benjamin Constant, Mme Récamier, Schlegel et Sismondi furent les principaux sujets.

A l'**intérieur**★, élégamment meublé dans les styles Louis XVI et Directoire, on visite la bibliothèque, autrefois salle de réception, la chambre de Mme de Staël et celle de Mme Récamier décorée de « papier de la Chine ». Au 1ᵉʳ étage, salons ornés de tapisseries d'Aubusson, de deux bustes très expressifs de Buffon par Houdon et Pajou, ainsi que d'intéressants portraits par Duplessis, Gérard, Carmontelle, Girodet, etc.

CRANS-MONTANA★★

Valais
Carte Michelin n° 427 pli 13 ou 217 pli 16 — Schéma : VALAIS
Plan dans le guide Rouge Michelin Suisse

MONTANA

Sur un replat de prés-bois parsemé de petits lacs, et prolongée à l'Ouest par la station plus récente de Crans-sur-Sierre avec qui elle forme le complexe touristique de « Crans-Montana », l'agglomération de Montana (altitude 1 500 m) s'éparpille face au décor majestueux que tendent, dans le lointain, les Alpes valaisannes. Celles-ci, vues de Montana, donnent l'illusion de se dresser immédiatement à l'arrière-plan alors que, en réalité, le fossé du Rhône s'interpose entre leurs sommets et l'observateur.

L'exposition splendide de cette terrasse à 1 500-1 700 m, orientée plein midi, attire en été et en hiver les villégiateurs en grand nombre. C'est là qu'en 1921, Katherine Mansfield séjourna et écrivit quelques-unes de ses charmantes nouvelles (la Garden-Party, Maison de Poupée).

En hiver, les skieurs peuvent bénéficier de pistes ensoleillées fort bien équipées en remontées mécaniques.

Accès — De Sierre, 13 km. La route partant de Sierre s'élève en lacet à travers les vignobles puis les pâturages.
Une fois à Montana, l'automobiliste de passage qui désire regagner le fond de la vallée du Rhône par un autre chemin peut emprunter, à la descente, l'une des routes reliant Crans à la route n° 9 pour découvrir les Alpes pennines tout le long d'un parcours très varié.

★★ **Vermala** — Alt. 1 670 m. *1,5 km. Laisser la voiture en contrebas du café-restaurant du Cervin, pour gagner le belvédère aménagé, à droite, au bord d'un petit escarpement.*
Vue plongeante sur la vallée du Rhône ; panorama très dégagé sur les hauts sommets qui ferment le Val d'Anniviers (en particulier le Weisshorn, le Zinalrothorn et, de justesse, le Cervin).

★★ **Plans Mayens** — Alt. 1 622 m. *1,5 km. On peut s'arrêter au bord de la route, à côté de la terrasse du restaurant du Mont Blanc.*
Ample panorama sur les Alpes valaisannes, s'étendant jusqu'au massif du Mont-Blanc, dans le lointain.

CRANS-SUR-SIERRE

Créée en 1929 aux abords immédiats de Montana, face aux Alpes valaisannes, sur un plateau largement exposé au midi, la station de Crans (altitude 1 460 m) a connu une croissance rapide. Son golf aux parcours alpins réputés (18 et 9 trous), ses hôtels modernes, ses promenades ravissantes et faciles, en font une villégiature très recherchée. En hiver, les skieurs avides de pentes ensoleillées peuvent se lancer dans des descentes totalisant, en période de fort enneigement, 2 000 m de dénivellation. La longue chaîne de télécabines reliant Crans aux contreforts du Wildstrubel est la pièce maîtresse de l'équipement mécanique de l'agglomération.

★★★ **Bella Lui** ⊙ — Alt. 2 543 m. *Accès par téléphérique. Durée de l'excursion : 1 h 1/2 AR.* Immense panorama sur les Alpes valaisannes. Magnifique montée en téléphérique au-dessus de la vallée du Rhône. Étape à Croix (ou Cry) d'Er (alt. 2 258 m — panneaux d'orientation du T.C.S.).

DAVOS ★★★

Grisons – 10 957 habitants
Carte Michelin n° 427 pli 17 ou 218 pli 5 – Schéma : GRAUBÜNDEN – Alt. 1 560 m

La station de Davos, lancée successivement par la cure climatique et par les sports d'hiver, se présente comme une petite ville commerçante et animée. Le nom de Davos est couramment associé à celui de « Parsenn », désignant ses champs de ski les plus fameux.

Tous les ans, Davos devient pour quelques jours la capitale mondiale de l'économie et des finances. C'est en effet en février que se tient le **World Economic Forum** qui réunit politiques et économistes du monde entier.

La station – L'agglomération s'allonge sur près de 4 km, sans apparente continuité, entre Davos-Dorf et Davos-Platz, au fond de la vallée alpestre où coule la Landwasser avant de s'enfoncer dans le défilé des « Zügen ». Les torrents débouchant du Sud-Est dans ce bassin, en particulier le Flüelabach, le Dischmabach et le Sertigbach, ont entaillé largement les montagnes qui s'élevaient de ce côté et ont par là favorisé l'ensoleillement de la station. Au Nord-Est, au-delà du lac de Davos, aménagé pour les sports nautiques, le seuil boisé peu marqué de Wolfgang fait passer sans difficultés en Prättigau. **Davos-Platz**, principal centre administratif, rassemble autour de sa place centrale les bâtiments publics les plus importants et les plus représentatifs de l'ancien village (église St-Jean et hôtel de ville). L'animation qui se répartit tout au long de la grande voie de traversée, la « Promenade », atteint sa plus grande intensité au voisinage de l'Europe-Hôtel. Davos doit sa réputation mondiale à sa patinoire naturelle, la

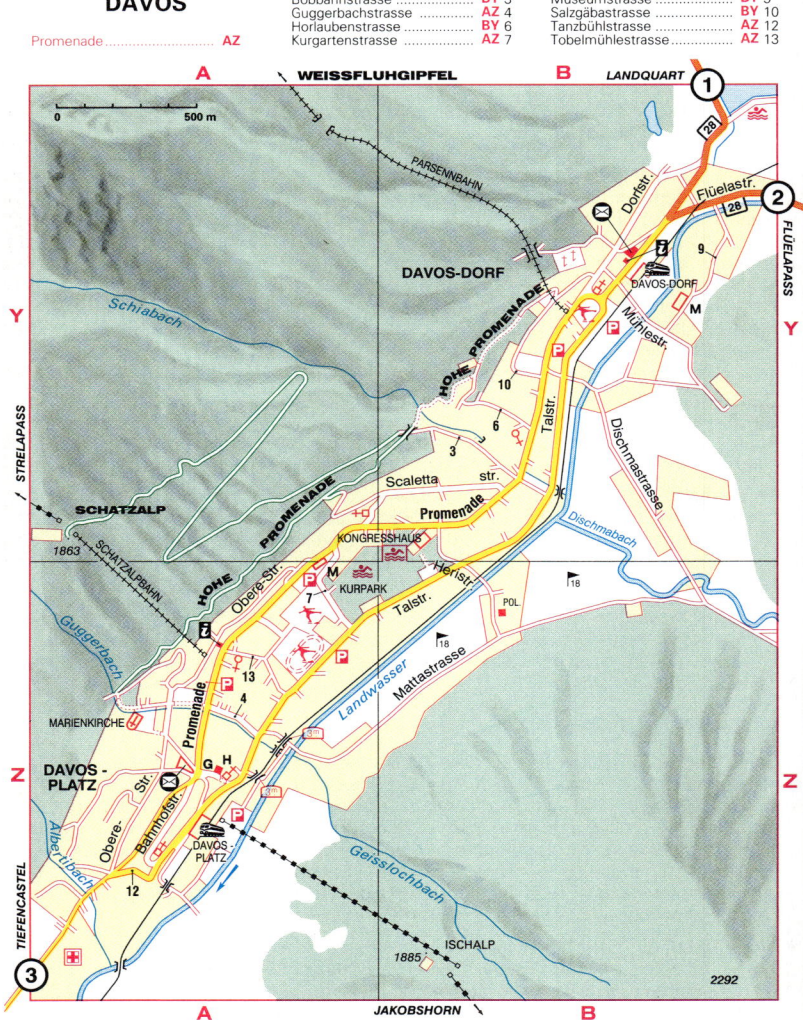

DAVOS	Bobbahnstrasse .... **BY** 3	Museumstrasse .... **BY** 9
	Guggerbachstrasse .... **AZ** 4	Salzgäbastrasse .... **BY** 10
Promenade .... **AZ**	Horlaubenstrasse .... **BY** 6	Tanzbühlstrasse .... **AZ** 12
	Kurgartenstrasse .... **AZ** 7	Tobelmühlestrasse .... **AZ** 13

plus vaste d'Europe, et pendant la saison du ski, au funiculaire de **Parsenn**, qui ouvre aux sportifs les terrains les plus remarquables accessibles en Suisse en plein hiver. Le terminus de ce funiculaire, le Weissfluhjoch (alt. 2 693 m), ou celui du téléphérique du Weissfluhgipfel (alt. 2 844 m) sont les points de départ de pistes balisées, constamment surveillées.

Cet ensemble, complété par le téléphérique Parsennhütte-Weissfluhjoch, et plusieurs téléskis, permet aux skieurs expérimentés d'effectuer en une journée les descentes les plus variées dans toutes les directions. La dénivellation de certaines pistes atteint parfois 2 000 m (parcours du « Parsenn Derby » aboutissant à Küblis, en Prättigau, à 813 m d'altitude). La station offre en outre aux débutants et aux skieurs moyens les pentes du Strela. Enfin, le versant opposé de la vallée, exposé au Nord et destiné aux skieurs de toutes catégories, est largement équipé lui aussi (Pischahorn, Jakobshorn, Rinerhorn).

CURIOSITÉS

- ★★ **Weissfluhgipfel** ⊙ – Alt. 2 844 m. *Environ 2 h 1/2 AR.*
  Magnifique panorama, s'étendant jusqu'aux Alpes bernoises et valaisannes.

- ★ **Schatzalp** ⊙ – Alt. 1 863 m. *3/4 h AR dont 5 mn de funiculaire (Schatzalpbahn) partant simultanément de Davos-Platz et de Schatzalp.*
  Des abords de l'hôtel Schatzalp, on découvre une belle vue sur la vallée principale de Davos et les vallées latérales. Un petit jardin alpin (alpinum) se trouve aussi à proximité *(10 mn AR)*. Au départ de Schatzalp, des télécabines permettent d'atteindre le col de Strela, à 2 350 m d'altitude.

- ★ **Hohe Promenade** – *1 h à pied AR.* Ce chemin horizontal, en partie sous bois, est parfaitement aménagé (déneigé en hiver). On accède à cette promenade : de Davos-Dorf, par le chemin montant derrière l'hôtel Seehof (à côté de la station du funiculaire de Parsenn) ; de Davos-Platz, par le sentier en forte montée prolongeant le chemin vers l'église catholique.

Davos – Vue générale

★★ LES ZÜGEN ET LA FLÜELA

Circuit au départ de Davos

135 km – compter une journée – itinéraire 1 *de la visite des Grisons*

Quitter Davos par ③ du plan.

Frauenkirch – La petite église est dotée d'une étrave brise-avalanches. Les habitations voisines, dont les superstructures de bois commencent à prendre de l'importance, annoncent, pour le touriste arrivant en sens inverse, les modes de construction germaniques du Prättigau.

- ★ **Défilé des « Zügen »** – *On le longe en gagnant Bärentritt.*
  Les eaux claires et bondissantes de la Landwasser bouillonnent superbement. « Zügen » désigne les couloirs d'avalanches voisins, qui connaissent des hivers souvent catastrophiques.

- ★★ **Bärentritt** – *2 h à pied AR par l'ancienne route des Zügen prise à la sortie Est du tunnel (côté Davos). Garer la voiture à Schmelzbaden.*

DAVOS

De ce point – où un saillant du parapet forme belvédère – qui marque l'entrée du défilé des «Zügen», la vue plonge de façon impressionnante, 80 m plus bas, sur le confluent de la Landwasser et du torrent formant, à droite, la cascade du Sägetobel.

A la sortie du profond ravin du Tieftobel, on découvre en contrebas, le grand **viaduc de Wiesen** ★ (longueur 210 m, portée centrale 55 m, hauteur 88 m), l'un des plus importants ouvrages d'art des chemins de fer rhétiques.

Après Schmitten la vue plonge à gauche sur le confluent de l'Albula et de la Landwasser, son affluent dont on descend la vallée depuis Davos.

Jusqu'à Tiefencastel les sous-bois de mélèzes succèdent aux profonds ravins (Tobel) ; le dernier de ceux-ci, à hauteur de Surava, sert de cadre aux ruines du repaire féodal de Belfort, juchées sur un escarpement.

Brienz – *Voir à ce nom.*

Tiefencastel – *Voir à ce nom.*

De Tiefencastel à la Punt, l'itinéraire (route de l'Albula) est décrit à St-Moritz et de la Punt à Susch, à l'Engadine.

Susch – Village dont les deux tours (clocher de l'église et tour coiffée d'un bulbe) se détachent devant les dernières pentes forestières du Piz Arpiglias.

Prenant le départ à Susch, la route de la Flüela domine bientôt ce village.

Une première série de lacets fait vite gagner de la hauteur au-dessus de l'âpre vallon de la Susasca. Au-delà et durant un parcours en corniche de 4 km, la **vue** ★ plonge sur le cirque glaciaire qui termine la combe désolée du Val Grialetsch, noyée sous des éboulis aux colorations verdâtres. On reconnaît ainsi, de part et d'autre d'un col neigeux bien marqué, le Piz Grialetsch (à droite) et le Piz Vadret (à gauche). Deux lacets mènent à l'entrée de la combe désertique de Chantsura dominée par la pyramide du Schwarzhorn.

Au-delà de Chantsura, aussitôt après deux lacets, une échappée lointaine, en aval, mérite un arrêt. Sur le fond des Dolomites de la Basse-Engadine, la silhouette perchée du château de Tarasp se détache en blanc ; plus proche, mais moins distincte, la tour grise de Steinsberg garde le bourg d'Ardez.

Col de la Flüela – Alt. 2 383 m. *Fermeture temporaire en cas de danger d'avalanche.*

Deux lacs, un hospice, les pentes d'éboulis descendus du Schwarzhorn et du Weisshorn caractérisent le paysage ingrat de ce col.

La descente sur Davos se déroule dans un long couloir monotone. Après le deuxième pont sur la Flüela – remarquer ici les premiers pins arolles, avant-garde de la zone forestière – se découvrent peu à peu les crêtes de la Weissfluh, bien connues des skieurs de Davos. En finale, à partir de Tschuggen, prairies fleuries, bols de mélèzes et de sapins agrémentent la vallée.

DELÉMONT

Jura – 11 548 habitants

Carte Michelin n° 427 pli 4 ou 216 pli 14 – Schéma : JURA SUISSE – Alt. 436 m

Delémont fut, jusqu'en 1792, la résidence d'été des princes-évêques de Bâle dont la crosse est reproduite dans les armes de la ville. Elle doit aujourd'hui son importance à sa gare et à ses fabriques d'horlogerie et de machines de précision. Elle est enfin, depuis 1978, la capitale du nouveau canton du Jura.

Vieille ville – La vieille ville ou ville haute, axée sur la rue du 23-Juin, a gardé ses portes monumentales, ses fontaines Renaissance (16ᵉ s.) et de nobles bâtiments du 18ᵉ s.

Le château des évêques, l'église St-Marcel et l'hôtel de ville sont les éléments les plus représentatifs de ce Delémont ancien.

Hôtel de ville – Construction remarquable par son escalier extérieur, sa porte d'entrée baroque et sa décoration intérieure.

Musée jurassien d'Art et d'Histoire ⊘ – Il rassemble des trouvailles archéologiques (de la préhistoire à l'époque mérovingienne) faites alentour, ainsi que des objets religieux anciens, des souvenirs révolutionnaires et napoléoniens – Delémont faisait partie, comme Porrentruy, du département français de «Mont Terrible» – des réalisations d'artisanat et folklore, des œuvres d'artistes jurassiens, le trésor paroissial avec la précieuse crosse (7ᵉ s.), en or, argent et émaux, de saint Germain, premier abbé de Moutier-Grandval.

Chapelle du Vorbourg – *2 km au Nord-Est.* Ce lieu de pèlerinage s'atteint par une route ombragée offrant de beaux points de vue sur Delémont et jalonnée d'un chemin de croix. La chapelle, aux autels baroques et aux murs garnis d'ex-voto des 18ᵉ et 19ᵉ s. s'élève dans un site sauvage et boisé, au-dessus d'une vallée profonde.

DENT DE VAULION★★★

Vaud
Carte Michelin n° 427 pli 11 ou 217 pli 2 – 15 km au Sud-Ouest de Vallorbe
Schéma : JURA SUISSE – Alt. 1 483 m

La Dent de Vaulion, l'un des sommets les plus escarpés du Jura suisse, constitue un belvédère de tout premier ordre, révélant un panorama immense sur les Alpes, de la Jungfrau à la Meije, et sur la vallée de Joux.

La montée – *De la route de Romainmôtier à l'Abbaye, 5 km – environ 3/4 h.* Le chemin d'accès, goudronné jusqu'au chalet de la Dent-de-Vaulion, se détache de la route au passage du seuil séparant le vallon de Vaulion de la vallée de Joux. Il devient rapidement très étroit *(croisement possible seulement en certains points)*. Du chalet, se diriger à vue vers le signal qui marque le point culminant (table d'orientation).

★★★ **Panorama** – L'apparition du massif du Mont-Blanc, derrière la nappe vaporeuse du lac Léman, en est l'attrait, mais la disposition des premiers plans jurassiens, en direction de la vallée de Joux et de ses lacs, est aussi très majestueuse.
Côté vallée de Joux, la montagne présente un à-pic vertigineux de 200 m.

DISENTIS/MUSTÉR

Grisons – 2 176 habitants
Carte Michelin n° 427 pli 15 ou 218 pli 2
Schémas : GRAUBÜNDEN et SANKT-GOTTHARD-MASSIV – Alt. 1 133 m

Dominant tout de sa large terrasse, au confluent du Rhin de Tavetsch – descendu du col de l'Oberalp, à l'Ouest – et du Rhin de Medel – descendu du col du Lukmanier, au Sud – Disentis, centre de la culture romanche (imprimerie) et station thermale, est la petite capitale des hautes vallées de l'Oberland grison colonisées, au Moyen Âge, par les moines de saint Benoît. Le séjournant trouvera ici toute une gamme de promenades (belvédères, chapelles peintes). En hiver, de nombreuses remontées mécaniques conduisent aux pistes neigeuses jusqu'à une altitude de 3 000 m.

Abbaye – C'est une des plus anciennes fondations bénédictines en Suisse (8ᵉ s.). Les bâtiments, utilisés par les Pères comme institut d'éducation, datent, pour une partie, du 17ᵉ, le reste des 19ᵉ et 20ᵉ s. L'abbaye, dont le bourg a emprunté le nom romanche de Mustér, a établi ses bâtiments au flanc d'un long versant d'alpages.

★ **Église abbatiale** (Klosterkirche) – Cet imposant sanctuaire baroque (1695-1712), flanqué de deux clochers à bulbe, présente intérieurement un vaisseau très clair dont les tribunes s'ordonnent de façon savante : la double rangée de fenêtres qui diffusent cette lumière reste invisible du bas de la nef, conformément aux règles baroques de l'éclairage indirect. Les stucs et les peintures de la voûte ont été restaurés au début de ce siècle, à la suite de l'incendie de l'abbaye par les troupes françaises en 1799.

★ ROUTE DE L'OBERALP
De Disentis/Mustér à Andermatt

31 km – environ 1 h – itinéraire 5 *de la visite du massif du St-Gotthard*

Le col de l'Oberalp ⊙ *est généralement obstrué par la neige de novembre à mai ; lorsque la route est fermée, un train effectue le transbordement des voitures.*

Il est possible d'apprécier de part et d'autre du couloir de l'Oberalp (point culminant : 2 044 m), noyé dans sa plus grande longueur par un lac, les passages les plus marquants de l'itinéraire ; ce sont principalement :
– **la sortie amont du bassin de Sedrun** : après Camischolas, la route se recourbe pour pénétrer dans un «étroit» boisé. Du virage à l'entrée de ce défilé, la vue est charmante sur le **Val Tavetsch**, où naît le Rhin Antérieur. Les villages sont disposés sur des terrasses verdoyantes entaillées de ravins et nivelées avec une régularité parfaite.
– **la descente de l'Oberalp à Andermatt** : la **vue**★★ prend bientôt en enfilade la conque d'alpages du Val d'Urseren jusqu'à la trouée de la Furka, et plonge sur Andermatt, agglomérée au pied des débris de la forêt d'Urseren, qu'ont ravagée les avalanches.

★ **Andermatt** – *Voir à ce nom.*

★ VALLÉE DU RHIN ANTÉRIEUR
De Disentis/Mustér à Reichenau

52 km – environ 1 h 3/4 – itinéraire 8 *de la visite du massif du St-Gotthard*

Peu après avoir quitté Disentis/Mustér au Nord-Est, en amont du viaduc ferroviaire et du pont routier moderne qui franchissent le ravin du Russeinbach, subsiste l'ancien pont couvert désaffecté. Remarquer, plus loin, l'élégant clocher à bulbe de Somvix.

DISENTIS/MUSTÉR

Trun – Le vaste bâtiment de la « **Cuort Ligia Grischa** » (volets blanc et noir) ⊙, ancienne résidence des abbés de Disentis, construite en 1674, était, en quelque sorte, le Parlement et le Tribunal de la Ligue. On visite la « chambre de l'abbé », décorée de boiseries (17ᵉ s.) et la salle du Tribunal, à l'ornementation baroque. L'érable dans l'enclos contigu à la chapelle Ste-Anne (18ᵉ s. – peintures commémoratives modernes) provient d'un rejet du célèbre érable de Trun, arbre sacré à l'ombre duquel avait été solennellement confirmé, en 1424, le Pacte de la Ligue Grise.

Ilanz – Ancienne capitale politique de la « Ligue Grise » *(voir les Cantons – article « Grisons »)* – Disentis/Mustér ayant plutôt été la capitale religieuse – fondée ici, en 1395. C'est la seule localité de l'Oberland grison honorée du titre de « ville ». Le quartier le plus pittoresque, que l'on atteint en passant le pont sur le Rhin et en suivant l'itinéraire de sortie en direction de Vals ou Vrin, possède encore des demeures seigneuriales du 17ᵉ s. à décoration baroque, dont la « Casa Gronda » (volets noir et jaune), avec sa tourelle d'angle, ses grilles de fenêtres, ses encadrements de porte finement ouvragés.

★ **Route de Versam** – *D'Ilanz à Bonaduz, 21 km.* Elle offre des échappées sur les gorges du Rhin et sur les crêtes du Bifertenstock (massif du Tôdi), à gauche des Vorab.
La clairière qui précède immédiatement le village de Versam invite à la halte. La **vue**★ se porte alors sur quelques sommets caractéristiques du versant opposé : le groupe des Vorab, avec son vaste glacier de plateau, à gauche, le Ringelspitz, à droite. Au premier plan, s'avance le promontoire du Flimserstein, aux imposantes falaises. La petite route, accrochée en corniche au flanc des ravinements blanchâtres (bizarres phénomènes d'érosion) qu'ont dégagés le Rhin et son affluent la Rabiusa, se fraie un passage dans la masse de matériaux hétéroclites amenés par l'éboulement de Flims.
De Laax à Trin, le paysage, très boisé et mouvementé, témoigne de la topographie d'origine, toute chaotique, de l'énorme coulée d'éboulis descendue de la chaîne de la Sardona dans la vallée du Rhin.
On remarque, en contrebas de la route, le petit lac de Cresta. L'éboulement de Flims contraint la route à franchir un très fort dos d'âne dont la station de Flims, 1 103 m d'altitude, marque le point culminant.

★ **Flims** – *Voir à ce nom.*
Les vues les mieux dégagées du trajet s'offrent de la descente de Trin (joli village perché) à Reichenau : c'est le moment favorable pour considérer le bassin de Reichenau où confluent le Rhin Antérieur, à peine libéré de ses gorges, et le Rhin Postérieur, débouchant de façon plus aisée près de Bonaduz, du bassin du Domleschg.

Reichenau – Avec ses trois ponts en triangle encadrant le confluent du Rhin Antérieur et du Rhin Postérieur, cette petite agglomération – qui se réduit, en fait, à un château et ses dépendances – doit son existence à un site éminemment favorable à la perception des péages. Elle reste un important nœud de communications, à la bifurcation des routes du Domleschg (Thusis) et de l'Oberland grison (Disentis/Mustér).
Pendant la période mouvementée de la Révolution française, un institut d'éducation occupait les bâtiments. Louis-Philippe d'Orléans, futur roi des Français, y passa son premier hiver d'émigration (1793-1794), enseignant les langues, l'histoire, la géographie, les mathématiques, sous le nom d'emprunt de Chabaud-Latour.

Bassins du DOUBS★★

Carte Michelin n° 427 pli 12 ou 216 pli 12

Sous ce titre, nous entendons la partie la plus épanouie des gorges du Doubs-frontière, dans ses élargissements du lac des Brenets (ou de Chaillexon) et de la retenue du Chatelot. Ce secteur de la grande rivière jurassienne (dont le tracé capricieux forme sur 43 km la frontière franco-suisse) est plus accessible à l'automobiliste et plus favorisé en belvédères du côté français *(consulter le guide Vert Michelin Jura).* Cependant, la rive suisse n'est pas dénuée d'intérêt, et la navigation sur le lac des Brenets offre le même pittoresque aux touristes partant de l'une et l'autre rives...

DES BRENETS AU SAUT DU DOUBS

A pied (par un chemin forestier longeant la rive Est), 2 h 1/4 AR, ou 1 h plus le retour effectué en bateau.
En bateau ⊙ *: 1 h AR, plus 20 mn à pied AR. Embarcadère à Pré-du-Lac (rive suisse).*

Les Brenets – Petite ville frontière agréablement étagée sur les pentes plongeant dans le lac de ce nom, face à la rive française.

★ **Lac des Brenets (ou de Chaillexon)** – Il s'agit en fait d'un méandre du Doubs que des éboulements ont converti en réservoir long de 3,5 km et large en moyenne de 200 m – dont le Saut du Doubs *(voir ci-dessous)* constitue le déversoir. En un point du lac, un resserrement des rives le divise en deux « bassins » : dans le premier il s'étale entre des pentes d'abord douces et riantes ; dans le second, il s'encaisse entre d'abruptes falaises calcaires couronnées de sapins, hêtres ou épicéas, et dont les arêtes offrent parfois des profils évocateurs (**Tête de Louis-Philippe Tête-à-Calvin** – ou Sphinx pour les Français...). La croix fédérale, peinte à même la roche (en 1853), et la grotte dite du Roi de Prusse se remarquent sur la paroi de la rive suisse.

★★★ **Saut du Doubs** – *Accès depuis le débarcadère marquant la fin du lac, par un chemin forestier.*
Cette célèbre chute de 27 m doit être vue du côté français pour en apprécier son côté spectaculaire *(description dans le guide Vert Michelin Jura).* Le site, en entonnoir, est très boisé.

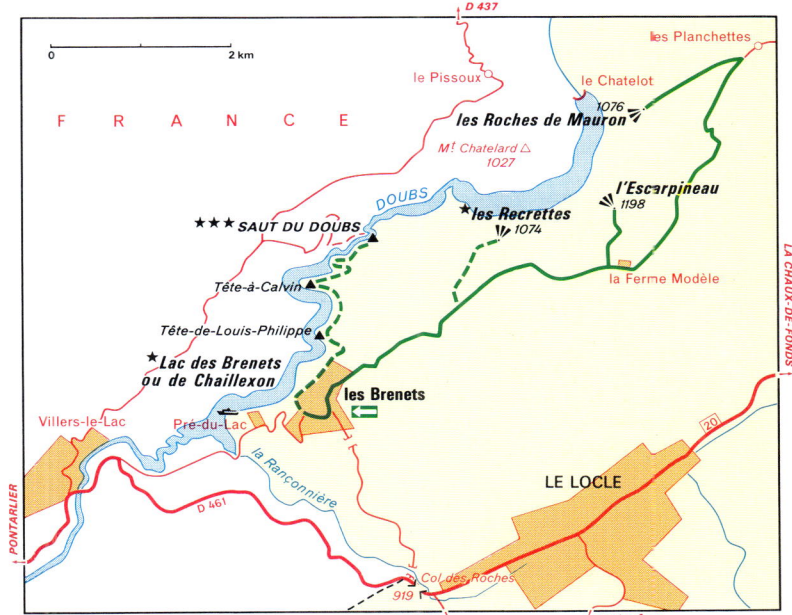

BELVÉDÈRES SUISSES DU DOUBS

Des Brenets aux Roches de Mauron 11 km – environ 1 h

Les Brenets – *Description ci-dessus.*
Au carrefour suivant la sortie des Brenets en direction du Locle, prendre à gauche la route forestière vers les Planchettes. Celle-ci, en partie sous bois, escalade le plateau sur lequel on émerge aux abords du hameau des Recrettes.

★ **Point de vue des Recrettes** – Alt. 1 074 m. *1/2 h à pied AR.* D'un belvédère aménagé, belle **vue**★ sur la boucle du Doubs engendrée par le môle impressionnant du mont Châtelard, côté français, et l'arrière-pays couvert de sapins ou de pâtures.
Peu avant la Ferme Modèle, prendre à gauche un chemin de terre privé *(refermer les barrières derrière soi)*, sur environ 700 m, jusqu'à proximité immédiate de la falaise.

Point de vue de l'Escarpineau – Alt. 1 198 m. D'un autre belvédère, parfaitement aménagé, **vue** belle et ample (malheureusement contrariée par des sapins en premier plan) sur le barrage et la retenue du Chatelot, les crêtes jurassiennes françaises.
Devant la Ferme Modèle, tourner à gauche. Avant le village des Planchettes, emprunter à gauche un chemin revêtu, sous bois.

Les Roches de Mauron – Alt. 1 076 m. Gagner à pied le belvédère proche du restaurant, d'où l'on a une **vue** plongeante sur le Doubs, limitée entre le promontoire du Châtelard et le barrage convexe du Chatelot.

L'EUROPE en une seule feuille : carte Michelin n° 970.

EINSIEDELN★★

Schwyz — 10 869 habitants
Carte Michelin n° 427 pli 15 ou 216 pli 19 — Alt. 881 m

Dans une région assez tourmentée de collines et de bois de pins coupés de torrents, qui rappelle par certains traits le Jura français et les Vosges, Einsiedeln, agréable villégiature été comme hiver, est le lieu de pèlerinage le plus célèbre de Suisse. Son rayonnement se fait sentir jusqu'en Alsace et en Allemagne méridionale.

C'est à l'emplacement d'un couvent, fondé en 934 par Othon Ier et la duchesse Reglinde de Souabe, et incendié plusieurs fois par la suite, que furent édifiés, au 18e s., l'église et les bâtiments conventuels qui forment l'ensemble fastueux actuel.

La grand-rue du bourg débouche à l'Est sur la vaste place de l'église abbatiale. Au centre du parvis en hémicycle, bordé d'arcades, se dresse la fontaine de la Vierge, dominée par l'imposante façade de l'abbaye bénédictine qui s'étend sur une longueur de 140 m. C'est dans ce décor qu'ont lieu la grande fête de la Dédicace *(voir tableau des principales manifestations en fin de guide)* et, tous les cinq ans seulement (la prochaine fois de juin à septembre 1997), les représentations : « Le Grand Théâtre du Monde » de Calderón de la Barca (600 figurants).

CURIOSITÉS

★★ **Église abbatiale** (Klosterkirche) — Elle a été construite de 1719 à 1735 dans le style baroque dit « du Vorarlberg » très répandu dans les régions proches du lac de Constance. C'est le plus remarquable édifice de ce style, en Suisse. Deux hautes tours encadrent la façade légèrement bombée et d'une grande élégance.

L'intérieur étonne par son ampleur — longueur de l'église y compris le chœur supérieur 113 m, largeur de la nef 41 m, hauteur sous la lanterne de la coupole de la Nativité 37 m — et surtout par l'extraordinaire richesse de sa décoration : les voûtes de l'immense vaisseau — coupoles et octogone de la nef — ainsi que les bas-côtés et le chœur sont couverts de fresques et ornés de stucs.

La décoration est due en grande partie aux frères Asam, originaires de Bavière et connus, l'un comme peintre, l'autre comme stucateur ; les statues des autels sont l'œuvre des frères Carlone de Sciara (près de Côme dans le Nord de l'Italie) et d'artistes milanais.

Construit de 1674 à 1680, le chœur a été transformé et orné de fresques par Kraus d'Augsbourg. Derrière le tableau de l'Assomption, on aperçoit le chœur supérieur où se réunissent chaque jour les moines pour la récitation de l'office. Les grilles du chœur, en fer forgé, sont remarquables.

La Sainte-Chapelle, édifiée à l'entrée de la nef à l'emplacement de la cellule où vécut saint Meinrad, martyrisé en 861, renferme la statue de Notre-Dame-des-Ermites qui fait l'objet d'une vénération toute spéciale de la part des pèlerins. Malgré la diversité et l'exubérance des éléments décoratifs, l'édifice conserve une grande unité.

Grande Salle de l'abbaye (Grosser Saal) ⊙ — Elle est située au 2e étage des bâtiments conventuels. On y accède en contournant l'église par la droite.

Construite au début du 18e s., elle est ornée de stucs et de fresques dus à Marsiglio Roncati, de Lugano, et à Jean Brandenberg, de Zoug. On y expose périodiquement des objets provenant des différentes collections d'art du monastère.

Einsiedeln — Église abbatiale

EMMENTAL★

Carte Michelin n° 427 plis 13, 14 ou 216 plis 15, 16 et 217 plis 6, 7

L'Emmental, petite région au nom évocateur d'un célèbre fromage, est une large vallée de l'Est du canton de Berne, comprise entre l'Aare et le canton de Lucerne, et que partage en son milieu, du Sud au Nord, l'Emme, affluent de l'Aare qu'elle rejoint à l'Est de Soleure. Née dans le massif du Hohgant, au Nord du lac de Brienz, l'Emme traverse d'abord cette zone montagneuse de caractère subalpin aux versants couverts de sapins et de pâturages, puis sillonne une riante contrée de faible relief au vert manteau de forêts et de prairies semé de pittoresques chalets fleuris composant de charmantes agglomérations. La richesse du pays – bois, cultures, élevage – est pour une bonne part à mettre au crédit de ses paysans.

> **Le fromage d'Emmental**
>
> Il est à la Suisse alémanique ce que le gruyère est à la Suisse romande. Il est en outre le fromage le plus exporté : ses meules énormes, sa pâte dure ajourée de grands trous irréguliers (alors que le gruyère, plus compact, n'est percé que de rares petits trous ronds), son goût de noisette, sont connus dans le monde.

VILLES ET CURIOSITÉS

Burgdorf ; Belvédère de la Lueg★ – *Voir à Burgdorf.*

Hasle – (Hasle-Rüegsau). Le village, sur la rive gauche de l'Emme, est relié au bourg de Rüegsauschachen (rive droite) par un remarquable **pont couvert**, en bois (1838), d'une seule portée. L'église protestante, ancienne chapelle reconstruite au 17ᵉ s., abrite des petits vitraux d'époque, armoriés ; des fresques naïves, de tons brun et vert, du 15ᵉ s., remontées sur le mur gauche de la nef (Jugement dernier, Montée au Golgotha, Crucifixion...).

Jegenstorf – Ce bourg pimpant et fleuri ordonne ses maisons autour d'une église de style gothique tardif au clocher en bâtière à tavaillons et dont l'intérieur, ceint de boiseries et coiffé d'un plafond de bois décoré d'entrelacs, conserve de nombreux vitraux (saints, blasons, etc.) du 16ᵉ au 18ᵉ s. Son «château» ⊙, riche demeure du 18ᵉ s. ajoutée à une tour féodale, s'élève dans un petit parc boisé et accueille des expositions temporaires et de belles suites de salons à décoration et mobilier du 18ᵉ s.

Kirchberg – L'église protestante (1506, restaurée), dans le cimetière surplombant la localité, présente à l'abside d'intéressants vitraux des 16ᵉ et 17ᵉ s. : sur les fenêtres latérales gauches, saint Georges tuant le dragon, blasons bernois ; sur celles de droite, Vierge en gloire et diverses figurations symboliques. Les vitraux des fenêtres centrales sont modernes.

★ **Langnau im Emmental** – *Voir à ce nom.*

Lützelflüh – Joli village sur l'Emme. L'église, datée de 1494 mais modernisée, détient six petits vitraux anciens et un beau buffet d'orgue de 1785. Tombe de Jeremias Gotthelf, pasteur-écrivain renommé du 19ᵉ s.

Marbach – *Voir à ce nom.*

Sumiswald – *Voir à ce nom.*

EMMENTAL

Trachselwald — Église réformée (17ᵉ s. ; clocher du 18ᵉ s.) avec dans la nef un curieux plafond peint et dans l'abside un mausolée baroque (1695). À l'écart du village, sur une butte boisée, gracieux **castel** (Schlösschen) ⊙ du 15ᵉ s., rénové mais ayant conservé une tour du 12ᵉ s., auquel on accède par un escalier couvert et coudé.

Utzenstorf — *Voir à ce nom.*

Worb — Ce bourg, carrefour routier et centre industriel très animé, est dominé par ses deux châteaux du 12ᵉ et du 18ᵉ s. et par son église de style gothique tardif dont le chœur conserve des stalles sculptées et l'abside de jolis vitraux des 16ᵉ et 17ᵉ s. aux motifs très variés.

Barrage d'EMOSSON★★

Carte Michelin n° 427 pli 21 ou 72 pli 9 — 24 km au Sud-Ouest de Martigny

Accès ⊙ — *Au départ du Châtelard Giétroz, par le funiculaire menant de la centrale électrique des C.F.F. au Château d'Eau, puis le petit train s'arrêtant au pied du barrage. Un petit funiculaire (le Minifunic) mène jusqu'au col de la Gueulaz (durée totale : environ 1 h). Inauguré en 1991 pour le 700ᵉ anniversaire de la Confédération, ce petit chef-d'œuvre de technicité parcourt 260 m de dénivellation en 2 mn.*

Le trajet en train procure des vues d'une belle ampleur sur le massif du Mont-Blanc. *Ou accès (en été seulement), à partir de la route de la Forclaz, par Finhaut (emprunter la boucle évitant la traversée difficile du village).* Dans les derniers kilomètres de la route, bordée de fleurs et de sapins, on découvre le massif du Mont-Blanc.

Le barrage ⊙ — Le barrage-voûte d'Emosson, haut de 180 m et situé juste en contrebas du col de la Gueulaz (alt. 1 970 m), retient une nappe d'eau de 225 millions de m³ sur une surface de 327 ha, bien intégrée au décor rocheux qui l'entoure. Réalisé en coopération avec la France, le barrage a été construit de 1967 à 1975 en remplacement de l'ancien barrage de la Barberine, submergé de 42 m quand le niveau d'eau atteint son maximum. La centrale hydro-électrique du palier supérieur, au Châtelard-Vallorcine, est située en territoire français. La centrale suisse de la Bâtiaz marque le palier inférieur, au fond de la vallée du Rhône. La production annuelle d'énergie est de l'ordre de 850 millions de kWh, que se partagent les deux partenaires, EDF côté français et ATEL côté suisse.

De la terrasse-parking du café-restaurant voisin, **vue**★★ magnifique sur le massif du Mont-Blanc : de droite à gauche, les Aiguilles Rouges, le Mont Blanc lui-même, le Mont Maudit, le Mont Blanc du Tacul, l'Aiguille du Midi, l'Aiguille du Dru, l'Aiguille Verte, les Aiguilles du Chardonnet et d'Argentière, l'Aiguille et le glacier du Tour, le glacier des Grands.

Gagner, en contre-haut, la chapelle N.-D.-des-Neiges, moderne mais d'allure traditionnelle, dont l'intérieur présente de jolis vitraux (fleurs et animaux des Alpes).

ENGADIN★★★

Carte Michelin n° 427 plis 17, 18 ou 218 plis 6, 7, 15, 16 — Schéma : GRAUBÜNDEN

L'**Engadine**, dont la « Route Supérieure » constitue l'accès millénaire, offre un paysage différent de celui des grandes vallées alpestres fortement encaissées où les bassins et les étranglements se succèdent de façon parfois fastidieuse. Son altitude moyenne étant voisine de 1 500 m (1 800 m pour la Haute-Engadine), l'automobiliste venant du Nord est surpris, après le passage des cols du Julier ou de l'Albula, de voir s'étaler devant lui une vallée profonde de quelques centaines de mètres seulement ; et celui qui arrive d'Italie par le « col » de la Maloja débouche de plain-pied dans le berceau du Haut Inn. Les montagnes de l'Engadine, malgré leurs sommets de plus de 4 000 m (Piz Bernina – alt. 4 049 m), apparaissent alors comme privées de leur soubassement. Elles sont surtout appréciées pour leurs splendeurs glaciaires. Mais plus encore que par l'originalité du coup d'œil, le touriste est attiré ici par un climat de montagne continental. La limpidité du ciel, la légèreté et la sécheresse de l'air caractérisent ce climat violemment contrasté, subissant au minimum les perturbations océaniques. La puissance de l'insolation est tout particulièrement frappante en hiver, avec les effets de réverbération sur la neige, et c'est à juste titre qu'une station comme St-Moritz a pu se placer sous le signe du soleil. Le fameux Marathon de l'Engadine qui se dispute sur une quarantaine de kilomètres réunit tous les ans les amateurs de ski de fond *(renseignements : Engadin Skimarathon, CH 7504 Pontresina).*

La maison engadinoise — Lourde construction cubique grisâtre, la maison engadinoise abrite facilement deux familles sous son vaste pignon dominant une façade dont un décrochement rompt parfois l'alignement. Sur la blancheur de ses murs ressortent des motifs floraux, géométriques ou héraldiques exécutés au pinceau – la sécheresse

ENGADIN

du climat favorise la conservation des peintures – ou suivant la technique du **sgraffito** : le maçon pose une première couche de crépi gris, puis recouvre celle-ci d'un lait de chaux : par simple grattage – mais avec quel coup de main ! – il fait ensuite réapparaître, en gris, la décoration désirée (rosettes, rinceaux, etc., dans la manière de la Renaissance).

Les fenêtres, petites et irrégulièrement distribuées, s'évasent de l'intérieur vers l'extérieur. De luxueuses grilles de fer forgé signalent les pièces d'apparat, tandis que de charmants oriels *(voir à ce nom)* forment saillie. Les « Bündnerstuben » *(voir*

Maison engadinoise

le lexique en début de guide) des hôtels pourront donner, lorsqu'elles ne sont pas trop fantaisistes, un premier aperçu du style du mobilier régional, apparenté à celui du Tyrol. Une visite au musée engadinois de St-Moritz reste cependant indispensable à qui désire se faire une idée d'ensemble des aménagements intérieurs. La pièce la plus typique est certainement le **sulèr**, sorte de cour couverte, commune à la grange et au local d'habitation, qui sert de salle de travail et de lieu de réunion. Un pavage impeccablement entretenu, une voûte surbaissée blanchie à la chaux et sobrement décorée de caissons caractérisent cette salle sombre et fraîche, qui ne reçoit le jour que par un large guichet pratiqué dans la porte cochère.

DE ST-MORITZ A SOGLIO

33 km – environ 1 h 1/2 – itinéraire 4 *de la visite des Grisons*

★★★ **St-Moritz** – *Visite : 1 h 1/2. Voir à ce nom.*
Au départ de St-Moritz, les crêtes neigeuses du Piz de la Margna ferment l'horizon.

★★★ **Piz Corvatsch** ⊙ – *Accès en 16 mn par téléphérique au départ de Surlej (à l'Est du lac de Silvaplana).*
La montée jusqu'à la station de Murtel (2 702 m) fait déjà découvrir en totalité les lacs de Silvaplana et de Sils. De la station supérieure (Corvatsch, 3 303 m), magnifique **panorama**★★★ au Sud-Ouest sur l'éblouissant tremplin que constitue le sommet (alt. 3 451 m) du Piz Corvatsch, les champs de neige avoisinants *(ski d'été)*, le massif de la Bernina et ses glaciers plus à l'Est ; au Nord et à l'Ouest sur la vallée et les lacs de la Haute-Engadine que dominent les Alpes grisonnes du Nord.

La route file au pied des versants de la haute vallée de l'Inn en longeant les **lacs**★★ **de Silvaplana et de Sils** égayés par une presqu'île boisée.

Lac de Sils et Piz de la Margna

★ **Sils** – Cette villégiature élégante et tranquille de la Haute-Engadine groupe, à l'origine de la vallée de l'Inn, les localités de Sils-Baselgia (Sils-Église) et de Sils-Maria, dans un cadre très boisé. Les lignes adoucies du paysage, tant dans la vallée principale que dans la vallée affluente de Fex, les lacs, participent à son charme. Entre les deux lacs on bénéficie vers le Sud d'une échappée sur le cirque glaciaire très évasé qui marque l'origine du Val Fex, au pied du massif de la Bernina.

Le souvenir de Frédéric Nietzsche, qui choisit ce séjour comme résidence estivale entre 1881 et 1888, revit dans sa maison aménagée en musée.

Maloja – *Voir à ce nom.*

Col de Maloja – Alt. 1 815 m. Ce col, le moins élevé entre la Suisse et l'Italie, marque la limite de l'Engadine proprement dite et la ligne de partage des eaux entre le versant « danubien » et le versant « italien » des Grisons.

S'il est à peine perçu du côté engadinois, il l'est bien davantage du côté opposé, le torrent de la Mera ayant creusé sa vallée (le Val Bregaglia) beaucoup plus profondément que l'Inn la sienne.

En aval du col le **Val Bregaglia** ★★ (Bergell) prolonge la percée alpine de l'Inn. Une série de lacets permet de gagner Casaccia qui marque la jonction avec l'antique chemin du Septimer. En avant du Piz Cacciabella, repérable à son petit névé arrondi, se creuse la vallée « suspendue » *(voir Introduction : La Physionomie du pays)* typique d'Albigna, coupée par un grand barrage.

En aval de Löbbia s'offre une **vue** ★ dégagée, en contrebas, sur le palier de Stampa Vicosoprano bordé, du côté Nord, de magnifiques sapinières et de quelques massifs de mélèzes.

Les villages entre Vicosoprano et Promontogno – et parmi eux Stampa où est né le peintre et sculpteur Alberto Giacometti – manifestent la régression de l'influence engadinoise : hautes maisons dégingandées, étroites rues pavées, groupes de petites granges alignant leurs pignons à claire-voie se font moins prédominants. La végétation alpestre laisse peu à peu sa place aux châtaigneraies, à la vigne et aux arbres fruitiers.

La Porta – Cet « étroit » de la vallée, fortifié dès l'époque romaine, marque la frontière naturelle entre le Bergell alpestre et le Bergell méridional. Le donjon de Castelmur apparaît sur un éperon, en contre-haut du campanile roman de Nossa Donna. La chaussée ancienne, surélevée et encore bien visible, coupait plus directement le promontoire en traversant la muraille d'enceinte, aux vestiges encore importants. Castelmur était la position clé de « l'Obere Strasse » sur le versant italien.

★★ **Soglio** – Accès par chemin étroit en très forte montée. Ce village, dont le **site** ★★ réunit les aspects les plus pittoresques du Bergell, s'élève vis-à-vis du cirque rocheux qui ferme le Val Bondasca. La paroi lisse du Pizzo Badile compte parmi les plus étonnantes des Alpes. Tranchant parmi les maisons qui se serrent auprès du campanile de l'église, les nobles façades de plusieurs « palais Salis » évoquent ici le souvenir d'une des familles grisonnes les plus connues en dehors de la Confédération, nombre de ses représentants ayant fait carrière dans la diplomatie.

DE ST-MORITZ A MARTINA

78 km – environ 3 h – itinéraire [4] *de la visite des Grisons*

★★★ **St-Moritz** – *Visite : 1 h 1/2. Voir à ce nom.*

Après le versant boisé séparant St-Moritz de Celerina, l'itinéraire se déroule sur le palier inférieur de la Haute-Engadine.

★ **Celerina** – *Voir à ce nom.*

★ **Samedan** – *Voir à ce nom.*

La vallée de l'Inn est d'abord très large et son fond plat alluvial doit être protégé contre les débordements du torrent.

★ **Zuoz** – *Voir à ce nom.*

La vallée se resserre et se vide d'habitations entre Punt Ota, frontière traditionnelle entre la Haute et la Basse-Engadine, et Zernez. Aux approches de Zernez apparaît le Piz Linard, veiné de neige.

Zernez.
De Zernez à Susch, la route, côtoyant l'Inn, s'enfonce dans le défilé boisé de la « Clüs ». Le Piz Linard laisse peu à peu apercevoir, dans l'axe de ce paysage, ses faces rocheuses toujours veinées de neige.

Susch – *Voir à ce nom.*
Au-delà de Susch, l'épanouissement de la vallée, que surveille, de sa terrasse, le village de Guarda, fait place à un nouvel « étroit » où la route domine par endroits d'environ 150 m les eaux troubles du torrent.

★ **Guarda** – *2,5 km au départ de Giarsun, plus 1/2 h de visite.* Avec ses maisons décorées de sgraffiti *(voir à ce nom)* et, au-dessus des portes, de blasons, ses rues pavées, tortueuses et escarpées, ses fontaines, Guarda est considéré comme le village typique de la Basse-Engadine.

Bientôt apparaît, en amont, la **tour de Steinsberg**, dressée sur le mamelon rocheux auquel s'adosse le blanc village d'Ardez.

Ardez – Toits groupés au pied de la tour de Steinsberg, ce village mérite un arrêt pour ses maisons peintes à charmants oriels fleuris. Le sujet de la faute originelle a permis au décorateur de la « maison d'Adam et d'Ève » de brosser un luxuriant décor végétal.

D'Ardez à Scuol, la route tracée en corniche au-dessus d'un troisième défilé boisé dans lequel elle s'enfonce, offre, dès le départ, un premier coup d'œil sur le fier château de Tarasp.

Au loin, se succèdent les plans montagneux des Dolomites de la Basse-Engadine (groupes du Piz Lischana et du Piz St-Chalambert) jusqu'aux crêtes marquant la frontière entre la Suisse, l'Italie et l'Autriche.

★★ **Scuol** – *Voir à ce nom.*

En aval de Scuol, la vallée se resserre entre les crêtes marquant la frontière italienne à droite et les versants striés de torrents descendus du massif de la Silvretta à gauche. À Martina, elle se creuse dans un défilé de direction Nord en contrebas du village autrichien de Nauders et du Reschenpass où s'ouvre un itinéraire vers les Dolomites.

ENGELBERG ★

Obwald – 2 958 habitants
Carte Michelin n° 427 plis 14, 15 ou 217 pli 9 – Alt. 1 002 m

Dans un site encaissé et cependant ensoleillé, Engelberg, la grande station d'altitude de la Suisse centrale, associe des activités touristiques et monastiques. Piscine, salons de thé, courts de tennis, patinoire voisinent ici avec l'une de ces vastes abbayes bénédictines que la Suisse recèle dans ses hautes vallées.

Alors que l'alpiniste n'a que l'embarras du choix entre les coupoles glaciaires du Titlis, les crêtes dentelées des Spannörter et de l'Uri Rotstock, le promeneur, grâce aux remontées mécaniques qui font la réputation de l'équipement local à la période du ski, accède aisément à des sites aussi connus que celui du Trübsee ou du Titlis.

Abbaye – Le couvent, fondé au 12ᵉ s., régenta toute la vallée jusqu'à l'invasion française de 1798. Le lourd quadrilatère de ses bâtiments est affecté en grande partie à un collège religieux.

L'**église**, qui sert également de sanctuaire paroissial, présente l'ordonnance et la décoration propres aux édifices de l'école baroque du 18ᵉ s. *(voir « l'art religieux en Suisse »).* Le grand orgue est un des plus importants de Suisse.

ENVIRONS

★★ **Titlis** ⊙ – Alt. 3 239 m. Table d'orientation. Au Sud d'Engelberg, une télécabine et deux téléphériques permettent l'accès à la terrasse supérieure (alt. 3 020 m) d'où s'offre un panorama s'étendant du Sustenhorn au Rigi.

Compter 3 h environ AR, dont 3/4 h de téléphérage. Promenades possibles par sentier pédestre en été.

★ **Schwand** – *4 km au Nord – environ 1 h.* L'accès se fait par une route de montagne très étroite, offrant des vues bien dégagées (demi-tour possible en contrebas de la chapelle). Beau site alpestre, en vue du Titlis.

ERLENBACH

Berne – 1 668 habitants
Carte Michelin n° 427 pli 13 ou 217 pli 6 – Schéma : BERNER OBERLAND

Plusieurs **maisons** ★ du type bernois le plus majestueux *(voir généralités sur la maison de la campagne bernoise dans l'introduction au voyage)* donnent beaucoup d'allure à l'entrée de ce village du côté de Spiez. Du carrefour central de la localité, un original escalier de bois couvert donne accès à la terrasse servant de support à l'église. Contourner l'édifice pour gagner la façade, en passant par l'enclos qui, avec ses tombes éparses dans le gazon et ses arbres touffus, compose, avec le sanctuaire, un **tableau** ★ romantique.

Intérieurement, la nef et le chœur sont presque complètement décorés de peintures naïves du début du 15ᵉ s. : entre autres motifs religieux, remarquer le cortège des Vierges Sages et des Vierges Folles (arc triomphal) et les symboles des Quatre Évangélistes (voûtes du chœur).

ERLENBACH

★★★ **Stockhorn** ⊙ – *Accès en 25 mn par téléphérique.* La «molaire» du Stockhorn, bien que d'altitude relativement modeste (2 190 m), offre un des plus beaux panoramas qu'il soit donné d'observer en Oberland... avec la vision éventuelle, en prime, des chamois hantant son massif ! D'Erlenbach à la station intermédiaire de Chrindi (1 637 m), le téléphérique «remonte» un profond vallon creusé par un torrent et bordé de sapins ou de chalets. Entre Chrindi et la station supérieure (2 139 m), on survole le joli lac de Stockensee (pêche), nappe émeraude à îlot boisé, dans sa cuvette glaciaire piquetée de sapins. De la station supérieure, gagner à pied *(1/4 h AR)* le sommet du Stockhorn (table d'orientation en contrebas, côté Sud), environné de versants ravinés herbeux ou boisés : **panorama**★★★ aérien, au Nord vers Thoune et une partie de son lac, à leur gauche les lacs d'Amsoldingen et d'Allmendingen, au Sud sur les lacs de Stockensee et le lac plus petit (à droite et plus haut) d'Oberstockensee, Erlenbach entre les sommets du Walpersbergfluh et du Mieschfluh ; de tous côtés, en toile de fond circulaire, les cimes blanches les plus prestigieuses des Alpes suisses et françaises, de la Jungfrau au Mont Blanc.

ESTAVAYER-LE-LAC

Fribourg – 3 808 habitants
Carte Michelin n° 427 pli 12 ou 217 pli 4 – Alt. 454 m

Bâtie sur la rive Sud du lac de Neuchâtel, la petite ville d'Estavayer a su conserver un aspect médiéval, avec ses restes de remparts, ses tours et ses rues à arcades, ses rues et ses maisons anciennes. Son port de plaisance en fait un centre nautique apprécié.

Église St-Laurent – De style gothique tardif, elle est coiffée d'une grosse tour carrée à la croisée du transept. A l'intérieur, le **chœur**★, fermé par une grille de fer forgé très ouvragée, est orné de belles stalles du 16e s. et d'un maître-autel, peint et doré, de style baroque.

Château de Chenaux – Cet édifice imposant, construit du 13e au 15e s., est flanqué de plusieurs tours rondes et possède encore son enceinte fortifiée.

Musée ⊙ – L'ancienne maison de la Dîme (1435), élégante demeure de grès jaune à la façade percée de baies triples, abrite un musée d'histoire locale : importante collection d'armes et gravures anciennes, reconstitution d'une vieille cuisine avec ses ustensiles, grenouilles naturalisées caricaturant des scènes humaines (banquet électoral, partie de cartes), salle consacrée au rail (lanternes des CFF, chemins de fer suisses).

FLIMS ★

Grisons – 2 258 habitants
Carte Michelin n° 427 pli 16 ou 218 Est du pli 3 – Schéma : GRAUBÜNDEN – Alt. 1 103 m

La station se répartit en deux agglomérations. **Flims-Dorf** regroupe ses maisons montagnardes en terrain découvert au pied des grandes falaises du Flimserstein (ou Crap de Flem) ; **Flims-Waldhaus** dissémine ses hôtels en pleine forêt de conifères, sur un léger seuil reliant le vallon de la Flem et la cuvette où s'étale le petit lac de Cauma (plage) tempéré par des sources chaudes souterraines.
La topographie confuse des versants tout boisés, qui, de là, ondulent vers le fond des gorges du Rhin Antérieur, témoigne encore de l'aspect chaotique que présenta la région, à l'époque préhistorique : un énorme éboulement, descendu dans l'axe du vallon actuel de la Flem, vint former bouchon dans la vallée du Rhin et contraignit le fleuve à reprendre son travail de creusement.
Son site en terrasse, son exposition plein midi, la proximité de sous-bois, font de Flims une villégiature familiale d'été très recherchée. En hiver on peut aussi bien se livrer à de magnifiques promenades à pied qu'aux descentes des pistes de ski équipées de remontées mécaniques.

★★ **Cassons Grat** ⊙ – *Au départ de Flims, montée en 1/2 h, d'abord par télésiège puis téléphérique.* Par beau temps, le parcours en télésiège, au moins jusqu'à la 1re station (Foppa, 1 424 m), est un enchantement : on survole de verts pâturages, de luxueux chalets décorés à la mode grisonne et cernés de fleurs, tandis qu'en arrière se déploient les deux agglomérations de Flims dans leur écrin montagneux.
Après Foppa, le décor devient plus sévère mais une **vue**★ prometteuse se développe, culminant à la 2e station (Naraus, 1 850 m), sur le replat de Flims et les crêtes neigeuses surgissant au lointain.
Le téléphérique pris ensuite aboutit à Cassons (2 637 m) après avoir longé les formidables falaises du Flimserstein, devant lesquelles tournoient des choucas. Gagner à pied *(1/4 h AR)* l'échine du Cassons Grat (2 700 m), où est planté le drapeau suisse : **vue**★★ superbe orientée au Sud vers la trouée du Rhin et les Alpes grisonnes, arrêtée au Nord par un hémicycle de crêtes ravinées.

FLIMS

★ **Crap Masegn** ⊙ – Au départ de Murschetg (3,5 km au Sud-Ouest, sur la route de l'Oberalppass), montée en 25 mn par téléphérique.

D'abord « montagne à vaches » parsemée de sapins et de chalets, ce contrefort du mont Vorab présente, à partir de la station intermédiaire de Crap Sogn Gion (2 213 m), un aspect plus austère. Mais, autour de la station supérieure (Crap Masegn, 2 472 m) qu'enveloppent aux deux tiers les farouches ravines des sommets voisins (Fil de Rueun, Vorab, Siala), la **vue**★ embrasse une désolation qui touche au grandiose, atténuée par la seule échappée qui s'offre, au Sud, vers Flims et la vallée du Rhin Antérieur.

Une télécabine poursuit jusqu'à la station de Vorab (2 570 m), aux abords du glacier de ce nom (ski d'été).

Route de la FORCLAZ★★

Carte Michelin n° 427 pli 21 ou 219 plis 1, 2

La route du col de la Forclaz, en permettant une liaison directe entre Chamonix et le carrefour valaisan de Martigny, tient une place de choix parmi les grands itinéraires internationaux des Alpes.

DE VALLORCINE A MARTIGNY

26 km – environ 3/4 h – visite du barrage d'Emosson et randonnée au glacier du Trient non comprises

Entre Vallorcine et la frontière suisse, la chaussée est étroite. Douane au Châtelard.

Depuis Vallorcine *(voir le guide Vert Michelin Alpes du Nord)*, la chaussée se fraie audacieusement un passage à travers le défilé de Tête Noire.

★ **Défilé de Tête Noire** – Le passage le plus impressionnant de cette gorge se localise entre le tunnel de la Roche-Percée et le hameau de Tête Noire. Remarquer alors le village de Finhaut, pittoresquement tapi au bord de l'abîme, sur le versant opposé.

★★ **Barrage d'Emosson** – *Voir à ce nom.*

Pour gagner le col, la route se noue ensuite dans la haute combe pastorale de Trient, évidée au pied des glaciers du Trient et des Grands, que sépare l'aiguille du Tour.

Col de la Forclaz – Alt. 1 527 m. Au Sud, la vue est barrée par les crêtes détachées de l'aiguille du Tour (visible à l'extrême gauche, au-dessus du glacier des Grands).

Au Nord, les sommets des Alpes bernoises sont rarement dégagés de la brume qui, par les belles journées d'été, monte du grand fossé du Valais. Le piton rocheux de Pierre-Avoi – entre la vallée du Rhône et la vallée de la Drance – est plus facile à repérer.

Du col de la Forclaz, de nombreuses **randonnées pédestres** ⊙ au cœur des montagnes valaisannes s'offrent aux touristes amoureux d'une nature sauvage. Parmi celles-ci, la randonnée au **glacier du Trient**★ *(compter environ 3 h AR ; inaccessible en hiver du fait de la neige)* s'effectue le long d'un bisse (canalisation naturelle qui amène l'eau des glaciers vers la vallée) creusé à flanc de montagne, traversant une forêt de mélèzes, d'arolles et d'épicéas. Du sentier, des vues dégagées sur le glacier des Grands et la vallée de la Dzornevettaz, ainsi que sur les alpages des Petoudes d'en Haut et les Herbagères, au-dessous du col de Balme.

L'arrivée sur le glacier du Trient est saisissante. Telle une gigantesque avalanche poudreuse dont l'avancée se serait durcie comme une coulée de lave, la « langue » du glacier se pare de reflets bleutés au fur et à mesure que l'on s'approche.

A mi-parcours, la « Buvette du Trient », ancien refuge du glacier, et où logeaient, dans la seconde moitié du 19ᵉ s., les ouvriers chargés de l'exploitation de la glace à des fins commerciales est une halte bien agréable pour les excursionnistes.

Du col à Martigny, une vue étendue ne s'offre vraiment, sur le bassin de Martigny et la trouée du Rhône valaisan, que 2,5 km en contrebas du seuil. Le chicot rocheux de Pierre-Avoi caractérise toujours les premiers plans ; on reconnaît bientôt, débouchant dans la plaine, l'étroit sillon de la Drance, voie de pénétration vers le Grand-St-Bernard. Le site de Martigny et de la tour de la Bâtiaz se précise enfin, tandis que la route court à travers les vignobles.

Martigny – *Visite : 1 h 1/2. Voir à ce nom.*

LA SUISSE, PATRIE DE L'HORLOGERIE

Découvrez les merveilles de cet art en visitant :
– le musée international d'Horlogerie à la Chaux-de-Fonds,
– le musée d'Horlogerie du château des Monts au Locle,
– le musée de l'Horlogerie et de l'Émaillerie à Genève.

Les FRANCHES MONTAGNES★

Carte Michelin n° 427 pli 3 ou 216 pli 13.

Le haut plateau des Franches Montagnes (1 000 m d'altitude moyenne) délimité par la vallée du Doubs et le chaînon du Mont Soleil est l'un des pays les plus originaux du Jura suisse. Ses maisons basses, ses prés-bois de sapins, parcs naturels où pâturent en liberté des chevaux bais ou des vaches laitières, composent des tableaux pastoraux d'un charme très pénétrant. Le tourisme hivernal est encouragé par le grand succès contemporain du ski de fond, qui trouve ici un terrain d'exercice idéal («traversée» de Moutier à la Chaux-de-Fonds).

La région et le district de ce nom ont pour chef-lieu le bourg de **Saignelégier** bien connu dans tout le pays jurassien pour son marché-concours hippique du mois d'août (voir tableau des Principales manifestations).

De belles excursions pourront être faites dans les régions avoisinantes, en particulier celle de la **corniche du Jura**★ ou, en France, celle de la **corniche de Goumois**★★ (voir le guide Vert Michelin Jura).

Cette dernière est une route très pittoresque offrant sur un parcours de 3 km des points de vue magnifiques dont les meilleurs marqués par des garde-fous. On domine ainsi le fond des gorges d'une centaine de mètres.

★**Corniche du Jura** – Itinéraire ⑨ (environ 1/2 h) du schéma Le Jura Suisse. Au pied de la Sentinelle des Rangiers, bifurquer dans la route de St-Brais tracée au sommet de la crête séparant la vallée du Doubs de la vallée de la Sorne (ou «Vallée de Delémont»), cette dernière toute parsemée de villages industriels prospères. Pour découvrir le fond de la vallée du Doubs, en direction de St-Ursanne, passer sous la ligne à haute tension et faire halte près du belvédère aménagé 100 m plus loin.

FRIBOURG★★

Ⓒ Fribourg – 36 355 habitants
Carte Michelin n° 427 pli 12 ou 217 pli 5 – Alt. 640 m
Plan d'agglomération dans le guide Rouge Michelin Suisse

Fribourg occupe un **site**★★ remarquable sur un promontoire rocheux cerné par une boucle de la Sarine. Le cours profondément encaissé de la rivière marque toujours la frontière entre les deux grandes régions ethniques et linguistiques de la Suisse : il est caractéristique de relever, en aval de la ville, des lieux-dits portant des noms français sur la rive gauche et des noms allemands sur la rive droite. Les quartiers anciens, qui s'étendent entre la Sarine et la ville haute, hérissés de clochers d'églises et de couvents, ont conservé leur aspect médiéval.

Fribourg s'enorgueillit de posséder un grand nombre de **fontaines** sculptées que l'on peut découvrir en parcourant la ville. Les différentes sources qui alimentaient la ville en eau avaient nécessité au Moyen Âge, dans les rues et sur les places, la construction de fontaines qui reçurent à partir du 15e s. bassins et colonnes de pierre. Chefs-d'œuvre de sculpture, on les doit au ciseau d'artistes comme Hans Geiler, Hans Gieng et Stephan Ammann.

C'est à Fribourg que se tient la Triennale internationale de la photographie.

UN PEU D'HISTOIRE

De la fondation à la Réforme – En 1157, Berchtold IV de Zähringen fonde Fribourg à hauteur d'un gué sur la Sarine et en fait une place forte destinée à contrôler cet important passage. Après l'extinction de la famille des Zähringen, la ville change plusieurs fois de maîtres, passe aux Kybourg, aux Habsbourg, puis préfère la domination savoyarde à celle de Berne. En 1481, Fribourg adhère à la Confédération, après avoir acquis d'importants territoires en Pays de Vaud. Le grand mouvement de la Réforme n'a pas d'influence décisive sur les esprits, et la restauration catholique, animée par le Père Canisius, ne fait qu'affirmer les convictions profondément catholiques de la ville, qui devient le siège de l'évêché de Lausanne-Genève-Fribourg.

Le bastion du catholicisme – Au 17e s., de nombreux ordres religieux viennent se joindre à ceux établis à Fribourg dès le 13e s. ; Franciscains, Jésuites et communautés diverses en font la métropole catholique de la Suisse. Parmi les établissements les plus célèbres, le collège St-Michel, fondé par les Jésuites, le couvent et l'église des Capucins, le couvent des Cordeliers et le couvent de la Maigrauge, bâti au 13e s. par les Cisterciens, ont brillé d'un vif éclat.

L'Université – La fondation, en 1889, d'une université d'État catholique et internationale a donné une impulsion nouvelle au rôle primordial joué par l'enseignement religieux. Cette université, foyer de haute culture, jouit toujours d'une renommée justifiée tant en Suisse qu'à l'étranger. Elle se compose de cinq facultés (théologie, droit, sciences économiques et sociales, lettres et sciences naturelles) et de quinze instituts autonomes (informatique, journalisme, etc.) accueillent des étudiants de toutes nations ; l'enseignement y est bilingue voire plurilingue.

SORTIR A FRIBOURG

Pour tout renseignement, s'adresser à l'Office du tourisme, 1, avenue de la Gare, ☏ (037) 81 31 75.

Shopping

Les principales artères commerçantes sont : le boulevard de Pérolles de la gare jusqu'au jardin des Pérolles, les rues de Romont, St-Pierre et de Lausanne.
Marchés : aux légumes et aux fleurs, chaque mercredi matin place Georges-Python et le samedi matin place de l'Hôtel-de-Ville.
Maison des produits régionaux : **La clef des champs**, rue Tilleul 1.

Théâtre et musique

Aula Uni, avenue Louis Weck-Reynold, ☏ (037) 21 91 11.
Église St-Michel : musique classique.
Centre Frison, route de la Fonderie : musique moderne.

Où prendre un verre ? Où passer la soirée ?

Grands-Places, juste devant l'Eurotel, le **Café des Grands-Places** possède un restaurant avec bar au rez-de-chaussée, et à l'étage une grande salle où viennent se produire différents orchestres (jazz, rock, blues, samba, boogie, etc.).
Boulevard de Pérolles le **Rock Café** est très fréquenté par les amateurs de rock. La décoration résolument moderne inclut des disques d'or, de platine et instruments de musique d'artistes connus (Johnny Hallyday, Elton John...).
Près du pont de Zaehringen, le **Rösti bar** présente un cadre agréable dans un bâtiment du 13ᵉ s. (murs de gros galets, poutres et piliers massifs en bois). Après dîner on peut terminer agréablement la soirée à l'auberge située au-dessus.
Plusieurs établissements se trouvent place Notre-Dame, le **Gothard** (fondue fribourgeoise), très fréquenté, ambiance conviviale ; **les Arcades**, restaurant et bar plus calme ; le bar de l'**hôtel de la Rose,** cave aux murs de pierre, qui ouvre ses portes à partir de 22 h.
Au n° 37, route de Villars, le piano-bar de l'hôtel **Au Parc**, est un endroit très chic, très bien décoré, animé par des groupes musicaux variés.

★★ LE COUP D'ŒIL *1/2 h en auto*

Partant de la place de l'Hôtel-de-Ville, passer le pont de Zaehringen. De cet important ouvrage de maçonnerie, qui a remplacé le « Grand pont » suspendu si familier aux illustrateurs du siècle dernier, la vue plonge sur le cours encaissé de la Sarine, en direction du petit pont couvert de Berne et du nouveau pont du Gottéron. A la sortie du pont, tourner à droite, dans la route de Bourguillon qui passe entre la tour Rouge et la tour des Chats, vestiges d'une ancienne enceinte fortifiée de la ville. Du pont du Gottéron *(laisser le véhicule au petit parking aménagé à la sortie du pont, à gauche),* très belle **vue★★** sur les vieux toits de Fribourg, comprimés entre les murailles d'enceinte et le ravin à gauche, et étagés au pied de la tour de la cathédrale.
600 m environ après le pont, tourner à droite à angle aigu dans la rue Beau Chemin et passer sous la porte de Bourguillon *(circulation interdite le dimanche).* Près de la chapelle de Lorette, petit édifice de style classique inspiré du célèbre sanctuaire de la Marche d'Ancône, s'offrent, entre les arbres, quelques **vues★** sur le site de Fribourg. Une forte descente conduit ensuite à la vieille ville ou basse ville.

★ LA VIEILLE VILLE *visite : 1/2 h à pied*

Pour garer son véhicule, tourner à gauche juste avant le pont de Berne dans le chemin de la Patinoire.

Pont de Berne (DY) – Pittoresque pont de bois couvert, aux éléments porteurs en chêne, enjambant la Sarine sur une longueur de 40 m.

Prendre la rue d'Or en montée.

A l'angle de cette rue se trouve l'auberge de la Cigogne, ancienne hostellerie du couvent des Augustins, dont la façade montre une peinture rococo représentant des cigognes.

A droite s'amorce la rue des Augustins.

Église des Augustins (DY) – Témoin de l'architecture des ordres mendiants, elle présente à l'intérieur une nef à quatre travées rythmées par des arcs brisés reposant sur des piliers ronds. Le mobilier constitue un bel exemple de la période baroque. Dominant le maître-autel, le retable en bois doré et peint en faux marbre, présentant trois étages, dont les deux premiers à niches encadrées de colonnes, est l'œuvre de Peter et Jacob Spring. On y voit principalement des épisodes de la vie de la Vierge. De chaque côté de l'entrée du chœur, les retables sont de l'atelier Reyff. Sur celui de droite se détache une gracieuse Vierge à l'Enfant polychrome.

FRIBOURG

Sur la place une galerie à six arcades surmontée d'un étage à colombage s'adosse à l'église, à côté les bâtiments conventuels abritent des services administratifs.

Tourner à gauche au bout de la rue de la Lenda.

Rue de la Samaritaine — Cette rue pavée, en descente, ramène à la place du Petit St-Jean. La fontaine de la Samaritaine (1551), due à Hans Gieng, représente Jésus et la Samaritaine au puits de Jacob. A sa hauteur, s'élève une intéressante maison de style gothique tardif dont la façade est percée de huit baies surmontées de remplages flamboyants.

Place du Petit St-Jean (DY) — En contrebas du quartier de l'Auge, elle s'étend jusqu'au pont de Berne et doit son nom à une ancienne chapelle des chevaliers de St-Jean de Jérusalem construite au 13e s. et démolie au 19e. La fontaine de Ste-Anne (1560), patronne des tanneurs fribourgeois, est l'œuvre de Hans Gieng ; remarquer la belle façade du n° 29.

Reprendre son véhicule et regagner la ville haute par le pont de Berne, la rue des Forgerons à gauche, la tour des Chats, la route de Stadtberg et le pont de Zaehringen.

★ LA VILLE HAUTE   visite : 2 h 1/2

★ **Hôtel de ville** (CY H) — Situé près de la place où l'on voit un tilleul planté, dit-on, le jour de la victoire remportée à Morat par les Confédérés sur Charles le Téméraire le 22 juin 1476, l'hôtel de ville, bel édifice du début du 16e s., se distingue avec son escalier à double rampe et à auvent (du 17e s.), son beffroi à jaquemart couronné de clochetons et son grand toit de tuiles brunes. Sur la place se dresse la fontaine de St-Georges (1525), groupe sculpté par Hans Geiler.

★ **Cathédrale St-Nicolas** (CDY) ⊙ — La cathédrale dresse au-dessus des toits de la ville ancienne sa belle tour gothique. En 1283 est posée la première pierre d'un édifice destiné à remplacer l'église dédiée à saint Nicolas et construite un siècle plus tôt par le fondateur de la ville, Berchtold IV de Zähringen. Les travaux commencent par le chœur, élevé vers 1280.
La partie postérieure de l'église a été modifiée au 17e s. par la construction d'une abside à trois pans et cinq baies remplaçant le chevet plat.

Extérieur — La belle tour de 76 m a été édifiée au 14e s. et l'octogone terminé vers 1490 par une couronne de clochetons, dans le goût de l'époque.
Le **tympan**★★ du porche principal, que surmonte une rosace, est consacré au Jugement dernier : le Paradis et l'Enfer encadrent le Pèsement des âmes, les archivoltes représentent des anges, des prophètes et des patriarches ; de chaque côté du portail, statues d'apôtres. Les sculptures du porche latéral Sud, figurant l'union du Christ et de l'Église, datent de la première moitié du 14e s.

Intérieur — Un vestibule carré, formé par la partie inférieure de la tour et dont les murs latéraux sont ornés de belles arcatures, précède la nef voûtée d'ogives. Des tableaux du 17e s. garnissent les écoinçons des grandes arcades — au-dessus et en dessous du triforium — que surmontent des fenêtres hautes à vitraux modernes (1983) d'A. Manessier. Les bas-côtés, également voûtés d'ogives, sont éclairés de fenêtres décorées de verrières exécutées au début du 20e s. par le peintre polonais Mehoffer. Les chapelles latérales des 16e et 17e s. ont été pourvues d'autels baroques au 18e s.
Le chœur, fermé par une grille gothique de fer forgé, est orné de **stalles**★ du 15e s. représentant les prophètes et les apôtres. Au-dessus de la grille, une poutre de gloire supporte un grand Calvaire de la première moitié du 15e s. A droite, en entrant, la chapelle du Saint-Sépulcre contient une **Mise au tombeau** de 1433 et d'autres statues de Manessier.
Les fonts baptismaux (fin du 15e s.), installés dans la 4e travée à droite du chœur, sont en pierre finement ciselée ; le couvercle, en bois, est du 17e s.
Les grandes orgues, l'une des gloires de Fribourg au siècle dernier, datent de 1834.

★ **Musée d'Art et d'Histoire** (CY) ⊙ — Les collections exposées dans l'hôtel Razé, élégant édifice de la Renaissance (16e s.), et dans un ancien abattoir, transformé en 1981, illustrent l'art et l'histoire de Fribourg des origines à nos jours.
Dans le premier bâtiment, le Moyen Âge, période florissante sur le plan artistique, est bien représenté par de nombreuses œuvres d'art, ainsi le gothique tardif doit-il à des artistes locaux comme Martin Gramp, Hans Geiler, Hans Gieng et Hans Fries des œuvres remarquables. Le dernier, peintre officiel de la cité de 1501 à 1510, marqua profondément son époque, on peut voir plusieurs panneaux de retable. Le 17e s. est illustré par des œuvres de Pierre Wuilleret et Jean-François Reyff, le 18e s. par des toiles de Gottfried Locher. Dans la salle des corporations, plusieurs gravures et aquarelles montrent Fribourg et son canton. La section consacrée à l'archéologie rassemble objets préhistoriques, romains et du haut Moyen Âge.
Dans l'ancien abattoir, le musée lapidaire inclut un étonnant groupe de **14 statues**★ en pierre du 15e s. figurant l'Annonciation et les Apôtres et provenant de la cathédrale St-Nicolas, ainsi qu'une belle Crucifixion du 11e s. de Villars-les-Moines et d'autres sculptures (dessus de fontaines) dues à Hans Gieng

FRIBOURG

(16e s.), contrastant avec des sculptures monumentales de Jean Tinguely. De remarquables bijoux burgondes (7e-8e s.), de précieux objets d'orfèvrerie du 14e au 18e s. et des œuvres de Marcello (pseudonyme de la duchesse Castiglione Colonna, née Adèle d'Affry, d'origine fribourgeoise) en vogue au 19e s., complètent la visite.

Dans les combles de l'ancien abattoir sont exposées des œuvres du 19e et 20e s. signées entre autres, Eugène Delacroix, Félix Vallotton et Ferdinand Hodler.

Église des Cordeliers (**CDY**) ⊙ – Une communauté de Cordeliers s'installe à Fribourg en 1256. La construction des bâtiments conventuels est achevée dès la fin du 13e s. Le couvent possède alors un célèbre atelier de reliure et la plus riche bibliothèque de la ville. Il reçoit les hôtes de marque de passage à Fribourg : papes, cardinaux, empereurs et princes. Au 18e s., les bâtiments conventuels sont transformés, la nef de l'église est même complètement reconstruite.

Tandis que la nef, à plafond plat, est voûtée de bois, le chœur a conservé ses voûtes d'ogives.

La première chapelle, à droite en entrant, renferme un beau **triptyque**★. Cette œuvre d'art en bois doré et sculpté dénote une influence alsacienne ; elle a été exécutée pour Jean de Furno vers 1513.

Le panneau central figure la Crucifixion, avec Madeleine au pied de la croix : le panneau de gauche, l'Adoration des Bergers ; celui de droite, l'Adoration des Mages. Les volets refermés présentent, à gauche, l'Annonciation, à droite, le Couronnement de la Vierge et sur la prédelle la Dormition de la Vierge.

Chœur – Avec ses quatre clefs de voûte figurant les symboles des Évangélistes, le chœur est un bon exemple de l'architecture franciscaine du 13e s. Il est orné de **stalles**★ en chêne datant de 1280 environ.

A gauche du chœur, on voit le retable de saint Antoine, représentant « la Mort de l'Usurier », exécuté en 1506 par le peintre fribourgeois Hans Fries. Ce tableau illustre la parole évangélique : « Là où est votre trésor, là est aussi votre cœur. »

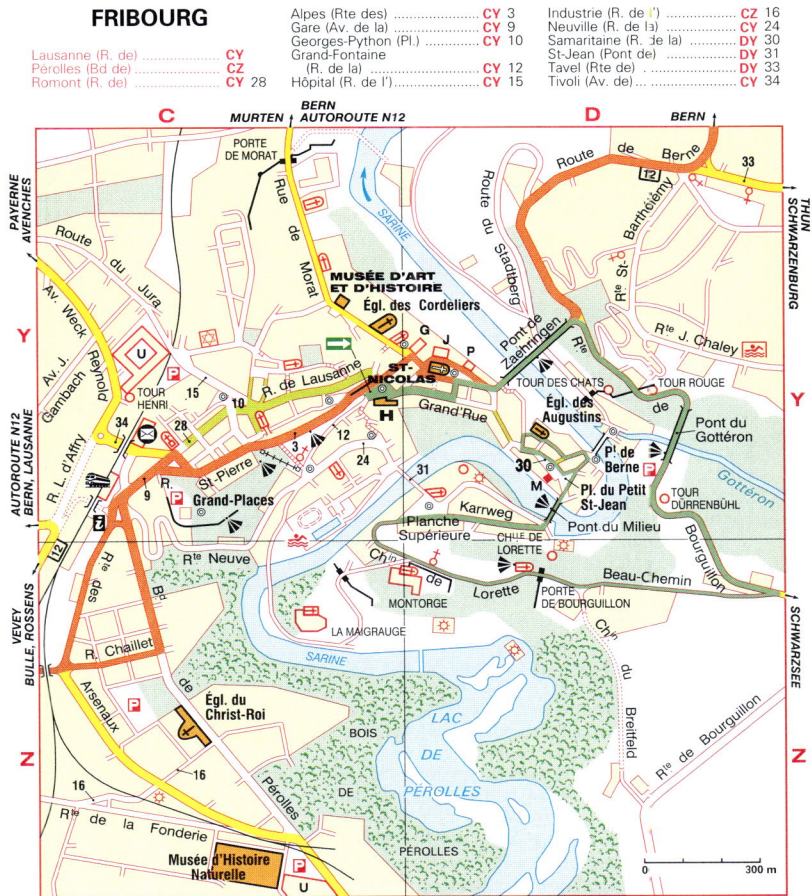

FRIBOURG

Lausanne (R. de)		CY
Pérolles (Bd de)		CZ
Romont (R. de)		CY 28

Alpes (Rte des)	CY	3
Gare (Av. de la)	CY	9
Georges-Python (Pl.)	CY	10
Grand-Fontaine (R. de la)	CY	12
Hôpital (R. de l')	CY	15

Industrie (R. de l')	CZ	16
Neuveville (R. de la)	CY	24
Samaritaine (R. de la)	DY	30
St-Jean (Pont de)	DY	31
Tavel (Rte de)	DY	33
Tivoli (Av. de)	CY	34

109

FRIBOURG

Au-dessus du maître-autel, est exposé le magnifique **retable**★★ des Maîtres à l'Œillet exécuté à Soleure et Bâle en 1480 par deux peintres qui signaient avec des œillets rouge et blanc. De très grandes dimensions (8,12 m × 2,70 m), il a été réinstallé dans le chœur lors de la restauration de 1936, remplaçant un retable baroque qu'on lui avait préféré en 1692.

La scène centrale représente une Crucifixion : elle est encadrée de quatre saints franciscains – saint Bernardin de Sienne, saint Antoine de Padoue, saint François d'Assise, saint Louis, évêque de Toulouse. L'Adoration des Bergers figure sur le volet de gauche, l'Adoration des Mages, sur celui de droite ; à l'arrière-plan, le paysage évoque les Alpes fribourgeoises.

Les volets refermés présentent au centre une Annonciation : à droite figure sainte Élisabeth de Hongrie, patronne du Tiers-Ordre franciscain et, à gauche, sainte Claire d'Assise.

Jean Tinguely

Né à Fribourg en 1925, il étudie d'abord la peinture à l'École des Beaux-Arts de Bâle. La jugeant trop statique, il l'abandonne très vite et s'installe à Paris en 1953. Tout au long de sa vie, sa conception de l'art, sa passion du jeu et du mouvement à l'image de ses «drôles de machines», en feront un personnage original à l'imagination débordante. Déjà ses premières œuvres, des reliefs mobiles constitués de figures géométriques, le singularisent. En 1959 ses Metamatics, machines sonores à dessiner et à peindre, peuvent apparaître comme une réaction contre l'abstraction appliquée. Aux constructions faites de cartons, fil de fer et tôle, succèdent des objets de récupération (pièces de moteurs, engrenages), qui assemblés à des bois et tissus créent d'inquiétantes machines qui vont s'autodétruire lors de spectacles-happenings. C'est ainsi qu'en 1960, il présente, dans les jardins du Musée d'Art moderne de New York, une machine délirante, Hommage à New York, dont la destruction entraîna le recours des pompiers. Puis il rejoint le groupe des Nouveaux Réalistes fondé par Pierre Restany. Influencé par l'esprit Dada, par Duchamp et Picabia, il bouscule l'ordre établi en créant avec insolence mais non sans humour, de grandes machines extravagantes.

En 1983, son côté ludique, joyeux, fantaisiste se manifeste par la Fontaine Stravinski, réalisée avec Niki de Saint-Phalle pour la ville de Paris (près du centre Georges-Pompidou).

Les années suivantes, l'œuvre de Tinguely devient plus sombre, représentant même des scènes macabres (expositions en 1987 à Venise et 1988 à Paris au centre Georges-Pompidou). «La mort m'a fréquenté, m'a caressé. De ses menaces, j'ai fait une fête, un dialogue burlesque», déclarait-il.

Il s'éteint à Berne le 30 août 1991, ayant fortement marqué son époque.

AUTRES CURIOSITÉS

Grand-Places (**CY**) – Par beau temps, ses pelouses y attirent bon nombre de gens. La fontaine est décorée d'une réalisation de **Jean Tinguely**.

Près du monument sur la gauche, la **vue** plonge sur les toits de la vieille ville, dominée par la tour de la cathédrale St-Nicolas.

Église du Christ-Roi (**CZ**) – *43, boulevard de Pérolles.*

Achevée en 1953, cette église, construite sur une vaste esplanade, présente une façade en forme d'hémicycle.

Triomphe du béton armé, l'architecture intérieure offre un plan très curieux avec sa nef oblongue que soutiennent de nombreuses colonnes.

Le chœur, entouré par un déambulatoire, est surmonté d'une coupole et éclairé par de nombreux vitraux.

Musée d'Histoire naturelle (**CZ**) ⊙ – *A la Faculté des Sciences, route de Marly (hors plan), par le boulevard de Pérolles.*

Il occupe sept salles au premier étage. Dans les premières sont exposés une maquette en relief du glacier d'Aletsch et des régions voisines, une riche collection minéralogique avec la reconstitution d'une «grotte à cristaux», des fossiles (salle de géologie et de paléontologie). Les salles restantes sont consacrées à la zoologie : animaux naturalisés du canton de Fribourg dans leur milieu naturel reconstitué, diorama montrant différentes espèces d'oiseaux (chants enregistrés), et à la faune des différents continents, la dernière exposant crustacés, invertébrés, poissons et reptiles.

Le visiteur découvre également le monde insolite des insectes pour lesquels une place particulière est donnée : morphologie, reproduction, évolution, espèces, enregistrement du chant de la sauterelle et du grillon. Des examens au microscope complètent la connaissance du milieu.

FRIBOURG

ENVIRONS

★ **Lac Noir (Schwarzsee)** – 27 km – environ 1 h. Quitter Fribourg par la route du Bourguillon (DZ) et la n° 74.
A Tafers, une route pittoresque, prise à droite, offre de jolies vues, à droite, en direction de la Berra, et à gauche, vers le Guggershorn. Après Plaffeien, coquet village aux chalets de bois verni, la route remonte la vallée de la Singine (en allemand «Sense»), avant de se terminer au lac Noir (pêche sportive), dans un joli **site ★** de montagne. Au bord du lac encadré de sapins s'est développée une agréable station de sports d'hiver, centre d'excursions estivales et hivernales.

★ **Barrage de Rossens** – Circuit de 55 km. Quitter Fribourg par la route n° 12. A 13 km prendre à gauche la route de Rossens.
En amont du village de Rossens a été aménagé, en 1948, un important barrage sur la Sarine. Long de 320 m et haut de 83 m, cet ouvrage est du type barrage-voûte. La retenue, longue de 14 km, forme un magnifique plan d'eau, dans un joli cadre encaissé : c'est le **lac de la Gruyère**. Pour en avoir une belle vue, prendre à droite la direction de Pont-la-Ville. A La Roche, emprunter la route n° 77 à droite, puis franchir le lac à Corbières. A Riaz, on rejoint la route n° 12, pour revenir à Fribourg.

Abbaye d'Hauterive ⊙ – 7 km au Sud-Ouest de Fribourg par la route de Bulle (CZ) A 4,5 km, à la sortie de Marly-le-Grand, tourner à droite.
Après Chesalles, un chemin à gauche conduit à l'abbaye, située dans une boucle de la Sarine, à l'écart de toute habitation. Fondée en 1138, l'abbaye cistercienne d'Hauterive, sécularisée en 1848, a repris depuis 1939 sa vie de prière et de travail. On y voit s'activer les moines en robe de bure et sandales, le crâne rasé.
Construite vers 1160 dans le plus pur style cistercien, l'église conventuelle a subi de nombreux remaniements, notamment aux 14e et 18e s. Elle a été pourvue de vitraux au 14e s. et, au 15e s., dans le chœur, de belles stalles aux panneaux sculptés de personnages et couronnés de baldaquins ajourés. Elle garde aussi des restes de peintures murales du 16e s. et, dans le collatéral gauche, le gisant d'un chevalier appuyant ses pieds sur un lion. Les bâtiments conventuels – hôtellerie, poterie, chapelle des étrangers – ont été reconstruits au 18e s. et présentent une façade de style baroque.
A l'intérieur, l'escalier d'honneur est orné d'élégantes rampes en fer forgé.
Entièrement remanié au 14e s., le **cloître**, de style gothique, est couvert de voûtes d'arêtes peintes, aux belles clefs de voûte sculptées.

FURKAPASSSTRASSE ★★★

Carte Michelin n° 427 plis 14, 15 ou 217 plis 10, 19 – Schéma : BERNER OBERLAND

La vision du glacier du Rhône et des plus hautes cimes de l'Oberland bernois suffit à rendre inoubliable ce parcours en altitude.

DE GLETSCH A ANDERMATT

32 km – environ 2 h 1/4 – itinéraire ③ de la visite de l'Oberland bernois

★★ **Gletsch** – Voir à l'index.
Au départ de Gletsch, le regard est captivé par le spectacle qu'offre le glacier du Rhône, depuis son plateau supérieur, visible par le rebord, jusqu'au terme de sa cataracte figée emprisonnée entre des roches moutonnées.

★★ **Glacier du Rhône** (Rhonegletscher) (**hôtel Belvédère**) – Voir à Goms
L'ascension du col révèle des vues très lointaines sur les Alpes bernoises et valaisannes. Pour contempler le **panorama ★★★** dans toute son ampleur, faire halte près de la bifurcation d'une petite route militaire (interdite), 1 500 m avant le col géographique, et s'avancer de quelques pas dans les prés. Dans l'alignement de la vallée de Conches (Haut-Valais), brillent les neiges du Weisshorn et des Mischabel ; plus proches, en direction du col du Grimsel, se dressent les parois farouches des grands «4 000» de l'Oberland bernois (Lauteraarhorn, Finsteraarhorn, Schreckhorn).

★★ **Col de la Furka** ⊙ – Alt. 2 431 m. Faire halte à l'hôtel Furkablick pour admirer le majestueux Galenstock. Le col de la Furka, seuil le plus élevé du grand sillon longitudinal qui coupe les Alpes suisses de Martigny à Coire, est un passage essentiel pour les communications touristiques entre la Suisse romande, le carrefour d'Andermatt et les Grisons. Depuis 1982, un tunnel ferroviaire passe sous le col, reliant Oberwald à Realp.
Du col à l'hôtel Galenstock, la route, longtemps tracée en pente douce au-dessus du vallon désert de Garschen, longe les soubassements du Galenstock, sommet le plus familier de l'itinéraire. Le **panorama ★★** permet bientôt de découvrir toute la perspective du sévère **Val d'Urseren**, avec les trois villages de Realp, d'Hospental – celui-ci signalé par une antique tour de garde et une église, toutes deux bien détachées – et d'Andermatt. Dans le même alignement, à l'arrière-plan, on distingue les zigzags de la route de l'Oberalp. L'arrivée à Andermatt est proche.

★ **Andermatt** – Voir à ce nom.

GENÈVE★★★

© Genève — 171 042 habitants
Carte Michelin n° 427 Sud du pli 11 ou 217 pli 11 – Schéma : Lac LÉMAN
Alt. 375 m – Plan d'agglomération dans le guide Rouge Michelin Suisse

De toutes les villes suisses, Genève est certainement la grande cité la plus favorisée par un site incomparable. Le soin avec lequel l'environnement y a été protégé pour contribuer à une qualité de vie exceptionnelle donne à l'arrivant l'impression d'une cité confortable.

La rade et son jet d'eau, les bords du lac et leurs incomparables perspectives d'eaux, de verdures et de montagnes, des édifices cossus ne laissent pas indifférent.

Genève est le second centre de l'O.N.U. après New York, ses nombreuses instances y travaillent dans les domaines économique et socio-humanitaire ainsi que sur le désarmement. De grandes organisations telles que le Comité international de la Croix-Rouge (C.I.C.R.), le Bureau International du Travail, le Centre Européen de la Recherche Nucléaire, l'Organisation Météorologique Mondiale y gardent leur siège permanent.

Mais Genève reste aussi la ville de Calvin, la citadelle de la Réforme, bâtie autour de sa cathédrale, une ville intellectuelle, pépinière de naturalistes et de pédagogues, et la métropole de la Suisse romande, aux artères commerçantes et animées (quartier de la place du Molard où se situe notamment, place Longemalle, un magasin des célèbres cigares Davidoff). Une empreinte tout helvétique de netteté et de discipline fait l'unité de ces trois Genève.

Plusieurs types d'excursions peuvent être entreprises à partir de la ville. Ainsi au départ de Genève-Eaux-Vives, le **train animé** Léman-Mont-Blanc permet-il de découvrir en saison de somptueux paysages de montagne ainsi que les rives accueillantes du lac Léman.

UN PEU D'HISTOIRE

Le jet d'eau

L'aigle et la clé – Les armes du canton (voir dans l'Introduction au voyage le chapitre consacré aux Cantons) illustrent le statut sous lequel vécut Genève avant la Réforme. Ville d'Empire (la « demi-aigle »), ville épiscopale (la « clé d'or en pal contournée »), Genève dut fréquemment être défendue par ses tuteurs contre les entreprises de ses voisins – en particulier contre celles de la Maison de Savoie.

En 1530, le duc de Savoie par la paix de Saint-Julien s'engage à respecter les droits de la ville.

Les franchises très libérales accordées, au 14e s., par le prince-évêque Adhémar Fabri ont fait date dans l'évolution politique et économique de la cité dont l'indépendance et le cosmopolitisme devaient s'affirmer avec le caractère de cité spirituelle que lui donna Calvin.

La ville de Calvin – A partir de 1532, la Réforme est prêchée avec succès à Genève par des humanistes français. Quelques années plus tard, Calvin s'installe dans la ville qui devient la « Rome du protestantisme ». Calvin agit en dictateur, promulgue des lois, construit de nouveaux remparts, accueille Clément Marot, Théodore de Bèze et le prédicateur écossais John Knox, envoie au bûcher le médecin espagnol Micael Serveto (dit Michel Servet) dont les opinions théologiques lui ont déplu.

Cependant, les ducs de Savoie ne peuvent se résigner à la perte définitive de la capitale naturelle de leurs États sur le versant du Rhône. Le 12 décembre 1602, Charles-Emmanuel fait attaquer par surprise, de nuit, en pleine paix, les remparts de Genève. C'est la fameuse tentative de **l'Escalade** qui s'est soldée pour l'assaillant par un échec que les Genevois commémorent chaque année.

GENÈVE

Genève, capitale de la pensée – Au 18ᵉ s., la vie intellectuelle est florissante : J.-J. Rousseau, Mme d'Épinay, le banquier Necker et sa fille Germaine, future Mme de Staël, le médecin Tronchin, le savant et alpiniste de Saussure, le peintre Liotard, Voltaire, sont genevois de naissance ou d'adoption.

Les troupes françaises entrent à Genève en 1798 et la ville devient pour seize ans le chef-lieu du département français du Léman. Après l'effondrement de l'empire napoléonien, elle entre dans la Confédération helvétique le 1ᵉʳ juin 1814.

SORTIR A GENÈVE

Pour tout renseignement, s'adresser à l'Office du tourisme, Gare Cornavin, ☎ (022) 738 52 00.

Shopping

Dans les rues suivantes on trouvera des commerces de toutes sortes : rue du Mont-Blanc, rue de Chantepoulet, rue Rousseau, rue de Pâquis, rue de la Confédération (« Confédération Centre », galerie marchande), rue du Marché, rue de la Croix d'Or, rue et cours de Rivel, cours de Rive, rue du Rhône, rue de la Cité, Grande-Rue.
Grand magasin : **Grand Passage** (Place du Molard).

Théâtre et musique

Comédie de Genève, boulevard des Philosophes 6, ☎ (022) 320 50 02. Théâtre classique et contemporain.
Théâtre de Carouge, rue Ancienne 39, ☎ (022) 343 43 443. Théâtre classique et contemporain.
Nouveau Théâtre de poche, rue du Cheval-Blanc, ☎ (022) 310 37 59. Théâtre contemporain.
Les marionnettes de Genève, rue Rodo 3, ☎ (022) 329 68 66. Spectacles de marionnettes.
Grand Théâtre, place Neuve, ☎ (022) 311 23 11. Opéras, ballets.
Grand Casino, Quai du Mont-Blanc, ☎ (022) 732 00 00. Galas, variétés, concerts.
Victoria Hall, Rue Hornung, ☎ (022) 328 35 73. Musique classique.

Où prendre un verre ? Où finir la soirée ?

Le soir, le quartier sétendant entre la gare Corvavin et les Pâquis est particulièrement animé en raison de ses nombreux cinémas, bars, brasseries et restaurants surtout exotiques.
Le **Casino de Genève** (quai du Mont-Blanc) et sa discothèque attirent beaucoup de monde. Ambiance intime, décor rétro au **Chaumette** (rue des Étuves) animé par des musiciens excellant dans le **Frenchstyle**. Au **Palais Mascotte** (rue de Berne), l'orchestre interprète valses, tangos ou cha-cha-chas.
Dans la vieille ville dont le pôle d'attraction est la place du Bourg-de-Four, le **Mortimer** est un endroit original avec sa collection d'affiches publicitaires, ses gadgets anciens et son très beau bar en zinc. En été, la terrasse du **Clémence** est très agréable (fontaine et jeu d'échecs géant).
Place du Molard et alentours, se trouvent plusieurs cinémas et établissements distingués très fréquentés à l'heure de l'apéritif ou en soirée. Citons le **Harry's New York Bar** (rue de la Confédération), piano-bar, et la **Brasserie Lipp**, antichambre du monde du commerce et de la finance.
Dans le quartier des Eaux-Vives, plusieurs établissements très chic sont fréquentés par de nombreux étrangers résidant à Genève. **La Coupole** (rue Pierre Fatio/boulevard Helvétique) offre plusieurs ambiances : **le café** pour les petits déjeuners, **le bistrot** pour le déjeuner, le **Meeting Point** pour déguster un des innombrables cocktails et le **Dancing Floor** pour ceux qui veulent danser sur des airs des années 60. Au-dessus du **Griffin's** (club privé de renommée internationale), le **Splash** (boulevard Helvétique) est un piano-bar offrant une élégante terrasse abritée. Sur le même boulevard le **Francis**, piano-bar de grand standing. **L'Opéra Bouffe** (rue de Frontenex) avec une musique d'opéra comme fond musical attire artistes, journalistes et intellectuels.
A l'extérieur de Genève à **St-julien-en-Genevois** (au Sud, autoroute A 40 puis N 201), le **Macumba**, gigantesque ensemble de divertissement nocturne offre 10 salles et 10 ambiances : musique des années 60-70, musette, reggae, zouk salsa, etc., chacun trouve selon ses goûts. Si la musique et la danse peuvent « creuser », deux restaurants, un grill et le **Spaghetti Bar**, sont là pour y remédier.

GENÈVE

Confédération (R. de la)	**FY**	42
Marché (R. du)	**FY**	81
Mont-Blanc (R. du)	**FY**	85
Rhône (R. du)	**FGY**	
Rive (R. de)	**FGZ**	
Bel-Air (Pl.)	**FY**	10
Bergues (Quai des)	**FY**	12
Candolle (R. de)	**FZ**	21
Chantepoulet (R. de)	**FY**	28
Cirque (R. du)	**FZ**	37
Cornavin (Pl. de)	**FY**	43
Corraterie (R. de la)	**FY**	45
Coulouvrenière (Pont de la)	**FY**	48
Croix-d'Or (R. de)	**FY**	49
Eaux-Vives (Pl. des)	**GZ**	52
Fort-Barreau (R. du)	**FX**	58
Frontenex (Av. du)	**GZ**	61
Italie (R. d')	**GZ**	72
Jeunes (Rte des)	**EZ**	75
Longemalle (Pl.)	**FY**	76
Malagnou (Rte de)	**GZ**	79
Molard (Pl. du)	**FY**	84
Monthoux (R. de)	**FXY**	87
Pépinière (R. de la)	**FY**	90
Pictet de Rochemont (Av.)	**GZ**	93
Pierre Fatio (R.)	**GYZ**	94
Rive (Rond-Point de)	**GZ**	105
St-Georges (Pont de)	**EZ**	114
St-Léger (R.)	**FZ**	118
Temple (R. du)	**FY**	120
Terrassière (R. de la)	**GZ**	121
Terreaux-du-Temple (R. des)	**FY**	123
Théatre (Bd du)	**FZ**	124
Tour (Bd de la)	**FZ**	126
Turrettini (Quai)	**FY**	127
Versonnex (R.)	**GY**	133
Villereuse (R. de)	**GZ**	139
22-cantons (Pl. des)	**FY**	142

B	Mausolée du duc de Brunswick
D	Monument de la Réformation
E	Porte de la Treille
H	Hôtel de ville
K	Église St-Germain
M²	Musée Barbier-Mueller
N	Église orthodoxe Ste-Croix

*Dans le
guide Rouge Michelin Suisse
de l'année
vous trouverez un choix
d'hôtels agréables,
tranquilles, bien situés
avec l'indication
de leur équipement :
piscines, tennis,
plages aménagées,
aires de repos...
ainsi que les périodes
d'ouverture et de fermeture
des établissements.
Vous y trouverez aussi
un choix de maisons
qui se signalent
par la qualité de leur cuisine :
étoiles de bonne table.*

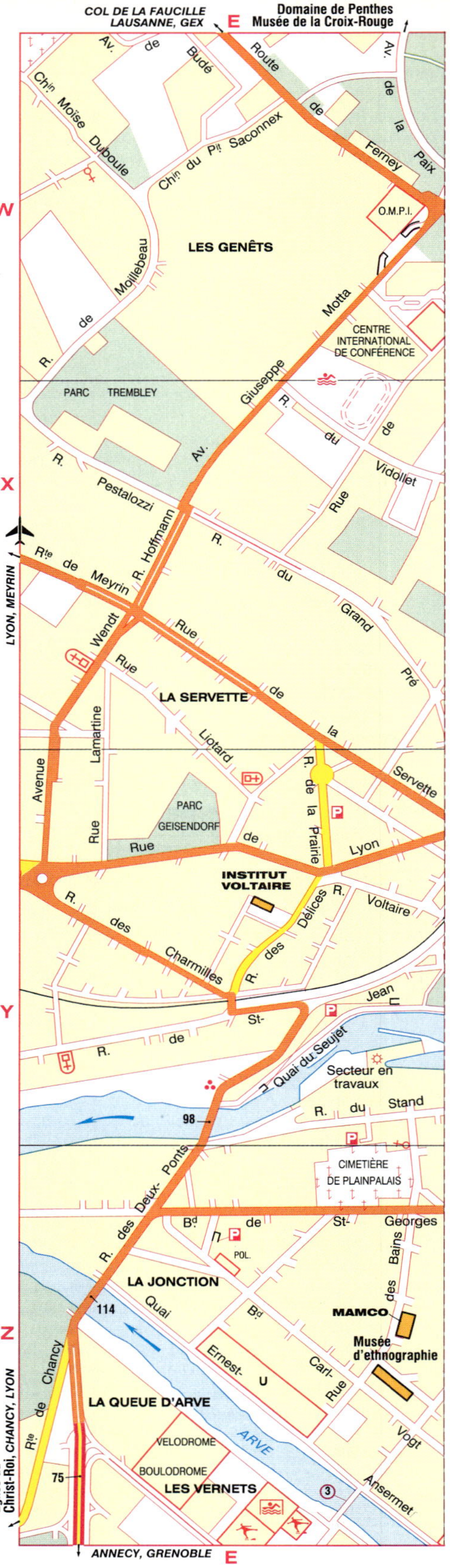

GENÈVE

★★ LA RADE ET LES BORDS DU LAC visite : 3 h

Qui vient à Genève va de toute évidence voir sa célèbre rade d'où fuse son majestueux **jet d'eau**, le plus haut du monde (145 m), et dont le panache blanc signale l'agglomération de très loin. Le lac, survolé par les mouettes et animé par les nombreuses embarcations et par le spectacle des bateaux à aubes, reste fixé dans les mémoires.

Rive droite

La promenade sur la rive droite du lac, le long du quai du Mont-Blanc bordé de cossus immeubles pavoisés, offre des **perspectives** ★★★ lointaines sur la chaîne de montagnes (Voirons, Môle, Salève, Mont Blanc, par temps clair).

Partir du carrefour formé par le pont, la rue et le quai du Mont-Blanc.
En aval du pont au-delà duquel le Rhône reprend son cours, s'avance la proue de l'île J.-J. Rousseau où se dresse la statue du célèbre écrivain.
Le quai du Mont-Blanc déborde d'animation, Genevois et touristes s'y promènent nombreux, s'arrêtant ici ou là devant les cafés ou les marchands de souvenirs.

Mausolée du duc de Brunswick (**FY B**) – Élevé en 1879 sur le modèle des tombeaux des Scaliger à Vérone, c'est le mausolée de Charles II de Brunswick (1804 - mort à Genève en 1873), bienfaiteur insigne de la ville.

Poursuivre par le quai Wilson, prolongeant le quai du Mont-Blanc, ou bien depuis le débarcadère des Pâquis, utiliser le service régulier des « Mouettes genevoises » qui desservent divers points de la rade.

★★ **Parcs Mon Repos, la Perle du Lac et Villa Barton** (**GWX**) – Ces trois parcs, communiquant entre eux, forment le plus bel ensemble paysager de Genève. A leurs portes, voire dans leurs enceintes, se dressent d'élégantes maisons patriciennes classiques. Un point de vue se révèle sur le « Petit lac », en direction de Lausanne.

Musée d'Histoire des Sciences (**GWX**) ⊙ – Dans le parc de la Perle du Lac, la noble villa Bartholoni (1825) abrite, dans ses salons richement décorés de peintures murales, ce musée d'instruments scientifiques anciens datant pour la plupart des 18e et 19e s. Au rez-de-chaussée, une salle est consacrée au physicien genevois Saussure (inventions, appareils et objets personnels), d'autres à l'astronomie (planétaires, cadrans solaires), aux instruments de marine (sextants, boussoles) ou d'arpentage (théodolites). A l'étage : instruments de physique (appareils de Colladon : cuillères acoustiques pour mesurer la vitesse du son dans l'eau), électricité et électromagnétisme, maquettes de machines à vapeur, météorologie (baromètres, thermomètres), médecine (stéthoscope de Laennec, pharmacies portatives).

★ **Conservatoire et jardin botaniques** (**FW**) ⊙ – S'étendant sur 17 ha, ce jardin a été aménagé pour l'agrément et afin de faire connaître au public la vie végétale. Il comprend un **jardin de rocaille** ★★ ou jardin alpin dans lequel les plantes ont été réparties en groupes géographiques ; des serres avec un jardin d'hiver abritant une luxuriante végétation tropicale et équatoriale, un parc aux biches, une volière. Des jalonnements indiquent les fleurs les plus intéressantes.

Rive gauche

Au-delà du pont du Mont-Blanc, les quais de la rive gauche sont bordés de longs espaces verts plantés d'arbres et ornés de massifs fleuris.

Jardin anglais (**GY**) – Une horloge fleurie décore sa bordure côté quai Général-Guisan. De sa terrasse la vue est intéressante sur la rade et sur la chaîne du Jura. Le quai Gustave-Ador permet d'avoir une vue rapprochée du jet d'eau qui jaillit au bout de la jetée des Eaux-Vives. Des bassins où sont amarrés de nombreux bateaux à voiles se succèdent, témoignant ainsi de l'importance de Genève comme port de plaisance.

★ **Parc de la Grange** (**GY**) – Il comporte la plus belle roseraie de Suisse (floraison mi-juin) ; au milieu s'élève une élégante maison du 18e s.
L'agréable **parc des Eaux-Vives** ★ lui fait suite.

Promenades en bateau

Elles sont multiples depuis la simple promenade dans la rade jusqu'aux croisières sur le lac *(voir à lac Léman).*

★ LA VIEILLE VILLE (H) visite : 1 h 1/2

Place Neuve – La statue équestre en bronze du général Dufour, héros suisse du 19e s., est au centre de cette grande place, entourée de plusieurs édifices majestueux : le Conservatoire de musique (19e s.), œuvre de Jean-François Bartholoni, le Grand Théâtre (19e s.) et le musée Rath.

Musée Rath ⊙ – Cette bâtisse qui s'ouvre par un portique, fut construite au 19e s. dans le style grec. Des expositions artistiques temporaires y sont organisées par le musée d'Art et d'Histoire.

GENÈVE

VIEILLE VILLE

Corraterie (R. de la)	H 2
Croix-Rouge (R. de la)	H 3
Fazy (R. Henri)	H 4
Grand-Mézel (Pl. du)	H 7
Hôtel de ville (R. de l')	H 8
Puits-St-Pierre (R. du)	H 9
St-Pierre (Cour)	H 12
Soleil-Levant (R. du)	H 13
Taconnerie (Pl. de la)	H 14

H Hôtel de ville
M² Musée Barbier-Mueller

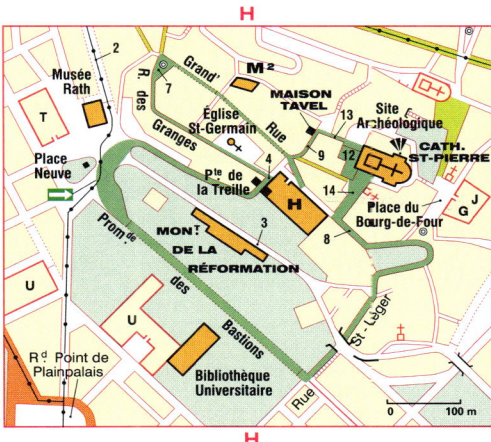

Promenade des Bastions – Ce jardin public, tracé au 18ᵉ s. au pied des anciens remparts, est bordé à droite, au-delà d'un platane géant, par les bâtiments de l'Université et de la Bibliothèque.

★ **Monument de la Réformation** – Adossé à un ancien rempart du 16ᵉ s., c'est une muraille de proportions monumentales (plus de 100 m de longueur) et d'une austérité voulue. Au centre, se détachent, immenses, sous la devise POST TENEBRAS LUX, les quatre statues des réformateurs Farel, Calvin, Bèze et Knox. Ce monument, érigé en 1917, évoque, par ses autres statues et ses bas-reliefs commentés, l'histoire de la Religion réformée et ses répercussions en Europe. En avant, sur le dallage, les armes de Genève – clé épiscopale et aigle impériale – figurent entre l'ours de Berne et le lion d'Écosse.

Bibliothèque universitaire ⊙ – La salle Ami-Lullin est réservée à une exposition permanente de manuscrits, livres et documents d'archives intéressant l'histoire de la Réforme et la vie littéraire genevoise. La **salle J.-J.-Rousseau** renferme des souvenirs de l'écrivain (manuscrits, estampes, buste par Houdon).

Quitter la promenade des Bastions, à l'opposé de la place Neuve, par la porte de la rue St-Léger, puis tourner à gauche et passer sous le pont.

Place du Bourg-de-Four – C'est sur cette place pittoresque située au cœur du vieux Genève, qu'avaient lieu les foires au Moyen Âge. Elle est bordée de vieilles demeures dont certaines ont conservé leurs enseignes d'auberges. Des boutiques d'antiquaires, des galeries d'art, des cafés s'ordonnent autour de sa fontaine fleurie.

Prendre à gauche la rue de l'Hôtel-de-Ville, puis à droite, traverser la place de la Taconnerie.

★ **Cathédrale St-Pierre** ⊙ – Église protestante depuis 1536, ce vaste édifice élevé aux 12ᵉ et 13ᵉ s., en partie reconstruit au 15ᵉ s., a été pourvu, au 18ᵉ s., d'une façade néo-grecque inattendue. L'intérieur est imposant et sobre. On y voit le siège de Calvin *(dans le bas-côté gauche, aussitôt avant la croisée du transept)*, des stalles du 15ᵉ s. *(dans le bas-côté droit)*, le tombeau du duc de Rohan, chef du parti réformé en France au temps de Henri IV et de Louis XIII *(première chapelle à droite du chœur)*. La chapelle St-Pierre, élégante construction de style gothique flamboyant, bâtie par le cardinal de Brogny au début du 15ᵉ s. et profondément restaurée au 19ᵉ s., s'ouvre à la première travée du bas-côté droit.

Tour Nord ⊙ – Superbe **panorama**★★ sur Genève, le lac, le Jura, la chaîne des Alpes.

Sortir de la cathédrale pour gagner la cour St-Pierre.

★ **Site archéologique** ⊙ – Devant la façade occidentale de la chapelle des Macchabées (au Sud-Ouest de la cathédrale), un escalier permet de descendre au site archéologique. Ce vaste ensemble présente les vestiges de plus de 2 000 ans d'histoire. Des passerelles mènent au sous-sol de la cathédrale où un montage audiovisuel aide le visiteur à mieux comprendre la christianisation de la région. Une première église et un baptistère ont été construits pendant la deuxième moitié du 4ᵉ siècle. Dès le début du siècle suivant, Isaac, évêque de Genève, dispose d'un palais, de deux cathédrales et d'un nouveau baptistère. Une salle de réception décorée d'un pavement de mosaïques polychromes, ajoutée au milieu du même siècle, a pu être remise en valeur. Vers l'an mille une grande cathédrale remplace trois églises épiscopales et un baptistère. Les murs de ce sanctuaire ont servi de fondations à l'édifice actuel, commencé vers 1160. Le petit musée aménagé au milieu de la visite contient des reconstitutions des principaux monuments ainsi que des objets trouvés lors des fouilles.

GENÈVE

Traverser la cour St-Pierre et prendre à droite la rue du Soleil-Levant.
A l'angle, statue en bronze du prophète Jérémie par Rodo.
La rue du Soleil-Levant conduit à la rue du Puits-St-Pierre.

★ **Maison Tavel** ⊙ – Plus ancienne demeure de la ville, elle fut reconstruite après l'incendie de 1334 qui détruisit une bonne moitié de la ville, puis remaniée au cours des siècles. Son élégante façade de pierre, percée par trois rangées de baies et flanquée d'une tourelle d'angle, est ornée d'amusants mascarons à têtes humaines et animales. Au-dessus d'une fenêtre du rez-de-chaussée, une niche est sculptée des armes de la famille Tavel, nobles genevois qui ont donné leur nom à cette maison. La visite de l'intérieur dont les salles et les caves ont été restaurées avec goût, apporte une bonne connaissance de l'histoire genevoise du 14e au 19e s. Les fortifications, la vie politique et religieuse, l'architecture urbaine, la vie quotidienne y sont retracées au moyen de collections incluant monnaies, vieilles photos, vantaux de portes, ornements de toiture, serrures et au 2e étage intérieurs reconstitués. Un beau mobilier, une riche vaisselle d'argent et d'étain (Genève fut un grand centre producteur) garnissent les pièces tendues de papiers peints ou d'indiennes d'origine. Dans les combles, étonnant plan-relief en métal (maisons et fortifications en zinc, toits en cuivre) représentant la ville en 1850, dû à un architecte genevois Auguste Magnin (1842-1903).
En face et à quelques pas de la maison Tavel, les arcades de l'**ancien arsenal** abritent quelques canons de la République helvétique. Au mur, mosaïques modernes de Cingria rappelant trois pages de l'histoire genevoise.

Hôtel de ville (H) – Édifice datant des 16e et 17e s., dont la partie la plus ancienne, la tour Baudet, fut construite en 1455. Entrer dans la cour pour voir la curieuse rampe, pavée de galets, qui permettait d'accéder en litière aux étages.
Au rez-de-chaussée, on visite la **salle de l'Alabama** ⊙ où fut signée, le 22 août 1864, la première convention de la Croix-Rouge, appelée la Convention de Genève.

Grand'Rue – Cette vieille rue pittoresque, une des mieux conservées du Vieux-Genève, offre au promeneur tout un choix de boutiques d'antiquaires, de libraires, de galeries d'art. Plusieurs maisons gardent le souvenir de personnes célèbres : au n° 40, maison natale de Jean-Jacques Rousseau ; au n° 27, maison natale du comédien Michel Simon (1895-1975).
Sur la place du Grand-Mézel, agrémentée d'une fontaine fleurie, prendre à gauche.

Rue des Granges – Cette rue est bordée d'une série d'hôtels patriciens de style français du 18e s. Au n° 2, l'hôtel de Sellon abrite la **collection Zoubov** ⊙, qui rassemble, dans les anciens appartements de la comtesse du même nom, de précieux objets ramenés lors de voyages. Certains proviennent de Chine (émaux cloisonnés de Pékin, émaux peints de Canton) ou de Russie (palais impériaux de Saint-Pétersbourg). Des meubles estampillés par de grands ébénistes français du 18e s., des portraits signés par des peintres de cour comme Vigée-Lebrun, le baron Gérard, Lampi le Vieux et Lampi le Jeune, de somptueux tapis et tapisseries, embellissent les différentes pièces qui se succèdent, de la salle à manger à l'entrée privée en passant par le grand salon, les chambres ou le cabinet Catherine II.
Au n° 7 se trouve la maison natale d'Albert Gallatin (1761-1849), devenu homme d'État américain et rédacteur de la Constitution des États-Unis d'Amérique.

Église St-Germain ⊙ – C'est une basilique des 4e et 5e s. agrandie aux 14e et 15e s. L'intérieur est éclairé par des vitraux modernes. Des fragments d'un autel primitif (fin du 4e s.) sont visibles. Au chevet est accolée une fontaine à auvent surmontée d'un cadran solaire.

On débouche sur la rue Henri-Fazy que l'on prend à droite.

Passer sous la porte de la Treille. À gauche, la tour Baudet (1455) abrite la Salle du Pouvoir Exécutif.

Descendre à droite la promenade de la Treille qui ramène à la place Neuve.

LE QUARTIER INTERNATIONAL

Place des Nations (FW) – Vaste place que bordent le parc de l'Ariana et les modernes buildings d'organismes bancaires ou internationaux. Remarquer, entre autres, la tour concave, en verre bleuté, de l'O.M.P.I. (Organisation Mondiale de la Propriété Intellectuelle), devant laquelle tombe une cascade en rideau qu'encadrent les copies, en bronze, des naïades de la fontaine de Neptune à Florence.

★★ **Musée Ariana** (FW) ⊙ – Fondé par un mécène genevois Gustave Revilliod (1817-1890), le musée reçut le nom d'Ariana en hommage à Ariane Revilliod-De la Rive, mère du fondateur. Le bâtiment, dont l'architecture s'inspire d'un palais italien, a été construit par Émile Grobety entre 1879 et 1884.
Au rez-de-chaussée, les collections illustrent magnifiquement près de dix siècles d'histoire de la céramique en Europe, Proche-Orient et Asie, depuis les origines de la faïence avec une coupe mésopotamienne du 9e s. (salle 1) aux premières porce-

GENÈVE

laines de Meissen au début du 18ᵉ s. (salle 6). Les vitrines renferment des majoliques de la Renaissance italienne, de la faïence de Delft et des pièces de nombreux ateliers européens, et présentent l'évolution de la porcelaine chinoise et japonaise importée en Europe du 16ᵉ s. à la fin du 18ᵉ s. Une zone didactique explique les techniques de l'art du feu ainsi que les fonctions de la céramique et du verre.

Au 1ᵉʳ étage, plusieurs salles sont consacrées aux manufactures suisses (faïences de Winterthur, porcelaines de Genève, Nyon et Zürich, terres cuites de la campagne bernoise). La salle 14 regroupe des collections d'étude présentées de manière systématique. La belle galerie aux colonnes torses est agrémentée d'un salon de thé et enrichie de verrerie suisse et européenne.

Au sous-sol, trois salles recevront bientôt des expositions temporaires et les tendances de la céramique contemporaine (le Musée Ariana est le siège de l'Académie internationale de céramique).

★★ **Palais des Nations** (FW) ⊙ — *Entrée, 14, avenue de la Paix, Portail de Pregny.* Le palais, situé dans le parc de l'Ariana et construit dans les années 1929-1936 pour la Société des Nations (S.D.N.), est depuis 1946 le second centre de l'Organisation des Nations Unies, le siège se trouvant à New York. Une nouvelle aile, très moderne, lui a été ajoutée en 1973. Il est l'un des centres de conférences internationales les plus actifs du monde. La **salle des Pas Perdus**, dont on remarque la variété des marbres donnés par les différents pays de l'O.N.U., dessert la grande **salle des Assemblées** (2 000 places), utilisée pour les séances plénières.

Après avoir longé une galerie sur laquelle s'ouvrent des salles de réunion, on arrive à la **salle du Conseil** où se déroulent les conférences les plus importantes. Cette salle est aussi appelée salle espagnole en l'honneur de Francisco de Vitoria, fondateur du droit international. L'artiste espagnol José Maria Sert a orné cette pièce de vastes fresques évoquant les progrès de l'humanité (progrès technique, social, scientifique). La visite s'achève par un film ayant trait à l'action de l'O.N.U.

Parc — Il s'étend sur quelque 25 ha plantés de cèdres, cyprès et autres belles essences. On y voit plusieurs œuvres d'art : sphère armillaire en bronze offerte par les États-Unis en mémoire du président Woodrow Wilson ; monument en forme de flèche, don de l'U.R.S.S. symbolisant le succès de l'homme dans la conquête de l'espace ; sculpture en bronze intitulée *Famille*, due à Edwina Sandys et offerte à l'occasion de l'année internationale de l'enfant (1979).

Du parc, la masse colossale du Palais des Nations, faite de travertin, de calcaire et de différents marbres, dégage une impression de puissance, de majesté.

De la partie supérieure de la terrasse, **vue** entrecoupée sur le lac Léman et la chaîne du Mont-Blanc.

Musée philatélique ⊙ — *Dans le hall, point de départ des visites du Palais des Nations.* Collection de timbres, enveloppes sur le thème de la Société des Nations et des Nations Unies complétée par une présentation audiovisuelle.

★ **Musée international de la Croix-Rouge et du Croissant-Rouge** ⊙ — *Par avenue de la Paix* (EW). Une étroite tranchée en béton mène au musée, enterré dans une colline en contrebas du C.I.C.R.

La bataille de Solferino (25 juin 1859), qui opposa les Français et Piémontais aux Autrichiens, donna à Henri Dunant, homme d'affaires genevois témoin du massacre, l'idée de créer un mouvement d'assistance aux blessés. C'est ainsi qu'il fonda la Croix-Rouge en 1863. Cette page de l'histoire est retracée par un diaporama qui s'achève par la présentation, lorsque l'écran se dérobe, d'une sculpture de George Segal montrant Henri Dunant à sa table de travail. Plusieurs espaces dans une harmonie de béton, de verre et de lumière illustrent ensuite, de façon chronologique, l'action de la Croix-Rouge et du Croissant-Rouge à travers le monde (lors de la guerre russo-ottomane de 1870 à 1875, les Turcs, musulmans, avaient obtenu l'autorisation de remplacer la croix par le croissant). Sur le mur du temps sont rassemblés les grands événements qui ont marqué la Croix-Rouge de 1863 à 1988 : aide humanitaire en temps de guerre ou lors de catastrophes naturelles, intervention en vue de la libération de prisonniers politiques ou otages. Un impressionnant fichier composé de quelque 7 millions de fiches, toutes authentiques, contient les noms des prisonniers secourus pendant la Première Guerre mondiale. Plus loin, une cellule de 4 m² dans laquelle 17 détenus ont passé de 6 à 90 jours, a été reconstituée. Des films, des terminaux à la disposition du visiteur contribuent à faire connaître l'immensité de l'œuvre entreprise.

Un voyage émouvant dans l'histoire de l'humanité, suscitant respect et réflexion.

LES MUSÉES DE LA RIVE GAUCHE

★★ **Musée d'Art et d'Histoire** (GZ) ⊙ — Ses collections offrent un aperçu général de l'histoire des civilisations, de la préhistoire au milieu du 20ᵉ s. Les sections d'archéologie *(au rez-de-chaussée inférieur)* et de peinture *(au 1ᵉʳ étage)* sont les plus importantes.

Le cabinet de numismatique renferme une vaste collection de poids monétaires antiques et de monnaies. Les collections d'art appliqué rassemblent des pièces du 12ᵉ au 19ᵉ s. : mobilier sculpté (15ᵉ-18ᵉ s.), vitraux du Moyen Âge, armes (pisto-

GENÈVE

lets avec crosses en ivoire sculptée, fusils) et armures du 12ᵉ au 18ᵉ s. Reconstitution de plusieurs salles d'un château avec mobilier du 17ᵉ s. et boiseries sculptées.

Archéologie – Plusieurs salles sont consacrées successivement à la préhistoire (objets d'origine locale), à l'Égypte, à la Mésopotamie, au Proche-Orient, à la Grèce, aux Étrusques et à Rome.

Peinture – Le célèbre retable de Konrad Witz (1444) représente la deuxième pêche miraculeuse ; cette œuvre marque la première représentation exacte d'un paysage dans la peinture européenne : on aperçoit Genève et le Salève à l'arrière-plan.

Aux salles affectées aux écoles italienne et hollandaise, font suite celles consacrées aux peintres du 17ᵉ s. et surtout du 18ᵉ s. Le grave François Duchatel et sa « Religieuse morte », Rigaud, Largillière et leurs portraits un peu apprêtés, aux couleurs brillantes, précèdent deux grands pastellistes du 18ᵉ s. Parmi plusieurs chefs-d'œuvre de Quentin de La Tour, se remarquent « le portrait de l'abbé Hubert », pittoresque et vrai, et le délicat, malicieux portrait de Belle de Zuylen ; le Genevois Liotard, dont la très longue barbe était connue de toute la société européenne, est le deuxième grand pastelliste représenté ici : son portrait de Mme d'Épinay se révèle d'une fraîcheur étonnante.

Du 19ᵉ s., on admire les paysages transparents de Corot, les œuvres du Genevois Toepffer et celles de Hodler (« Les Buveurs », « Les Régents du collège » au centre le recteur est peint sous les traits de Calvin) symboliste d'un art violent et robuste. Le mouvement impressionniste est bien illustré par des œuvres de Pissarro (« Le port de Rouen »), Monet (« Pivoines »), Cézanne (« La maison de Bellevue »), Renoir (« L'été »), Sisley (« L'écluse de Bourgogne à Moret-sur-Loing »).

★ **Collections Baur** (GZ) ⊙ – Ce musée, installé dans un hôtel particulier du 19ᵉ s., est consacré à l'art d'Extrême-Orient. Plusieurs salles sont réservées à des expositions temporaires. Au rez-de-chaussée et au premier étage : intéressantes collections de porcelaine, grès, céladons et jades réunissant la pureté des formes, la richesse des couleurs, la finesse des décors. Elles permettent de suivre l'évolution de l'art de la céramique en Chine, de la dynastie des T'ang (618-908) à celle des T'sing (1644-1911).

L'art du Japon est représenté au deuxième étage. La plupart des objets réunis (sabres et leurs ornements, porcelaine du 18ᵉ s., laques et netsukés – boutons de bois sculpté –, etc.) appartiennent à l'époque Tokugawa (1615-1868) ou Meiji (1868-1912).

★★ **Petit Palais – Musée d'Art Moderne** (GZ) ⊙ – Cet ancien hôtel particulier du 19ᵉ s. est devenu un « temple » de la peinture d'avant-garde française et européenne, de 1880 à 1930 (de l'impressionnisme au surréalisme), et de ses prolongements jusqu'à l'art abstrait. Fondé par Oscar Ghez de Castelnuovo, ancien industriel passionné de peinture, le musée expose des œuvres de grande qualité, certaines par roulement, provenant de son fonds propre. Des expositions temporaires sur un thème, une école ou un artiste viennent en complément.

Rez-de-chaussée – Le **mouvement impressionniste** qui débuta vers 1830-1840, naquit en réaction contre les conventions et s'efforça d'après une observation minutieuse de la nature, de traduire les sensations visuelles à grand renfort de couleurs et de lumière. Les impressionnistes et post-impressionnistes sont représentés par des peintures de Manet *(Berthe Morisot à la voilette)*, Puvis de Chavannes *(La Grande Sœur)*, Boudin *(Marine)*, Caillebotte *(Le Pont de l'Europe)*, Fantin-Latour *(La Toilette de Vénus)*, Renoir *(Portrait de la poétesse Alice Vallière)*, Cézanne *(Paysage au bord de l'Oise)*, Degas *(Femme nue à sa toilette)*.

Les **nabis** (mot hébreu signifiant prophète) dont le mouvement est né de la rencontre de Gauguin et de Sérusier à Pont-Aven en 1888, eut comme chef de file ce dernier. On compte parmi ses adeptes : Gauguin, sculptures et céramiques *(La Belle Angèle, La Tahitienne)*, Sérusier *(La Marchande d'étoffes, La Guirlande de roses)*, Émile Bernard *(La Plage de Cancale)*, Maurice Denis *(La Famille de l'artiste)*, Lacombe *(Les Âges de la vie)*, Vuillard *(Le Grand Teddy)*, Maxime Maufra *(Place St-André-des-Arts)*, Vallotton, O'Conor, etc.

La salle **Louis Valtat**, rassemble des œuvres de ce peintre du groupe des fauves : *Chez Maxim's, Baigneuses, Les Porteuses d'eau à Arcachon*.

1ᵉʳ étage – Le **mouvement néo-impressionniste**, appelé également divisionnisme ou pointillisme, reprend les petites touches rapides des impressionnistes et les divise en petits points de couleur pure afin d'obtenir le maximum de luminosité. Citons Signac, Cross *(Marine aux cyprès)*, Charles Angrand *(La Seine à l'aube)*, Henri Martin *(La Joie de vivre)*, Mengarini (superbe *Nu à la fenêtre*), Van Rysselberghe, Van de Velde *(La Faneuse)*.

Au Salon d'automne de Paris en 1905, de jeunes artistes firent sensation par la violence des couleurs employées dans leurs toiles. Ainsi naquit le mouvement des **fauves**, représenté ici par Van Dongen *(Le Vieux Clown, pathétique ; inquiétant*

GENÈVE

Portrait de Kazhnweiler), Chabaud *(Le Moulin Rouge, la nuit)*, Derain *(Déjeuner sur l'herbe)*, Dufy *(Marché à Marseille)*, Othon Friesz *(Les Demoiselles de Marseille)*, Manguin, Marquet *(Printemps à la Frette)*, Vlaminck *(Passage à niveau le 14 juillet)*.

Dans la salle **Moïse Kisling**, rétrospective de toiles de ce peintre d'origine polonaise, membre de l'École de Paris *(Nu d'Arletty, Portrait de Jean Cocteau assis dans son atelier)*.

2e étage (Orangerie) – Plusieurs salles sont dédiées à Nicolas Tarkhoff (1871-1930), peintre russe de l'École de Paris, dont on peut admirer ses paysages de jour et de nuit, ses peintures de rues, ses vues de Paris, ses maternités.

1er sous-sol – Dans la salle Ernest Ansermet, sont représentés les peintres **« montmartrois »** : Utrillo *(Notre-Dame)*, Suzanne Valadon, Steinlen *(La Rentrée du soir)* ; les **« montparnos »** : Picasso *(L'Aubade)*, Chagall *(Le Juif errant)*, Foujita *(La Dompteuse et le Lion)*, Soutine *(Le Bœuf écorché)* ; les **cubistes** : Lhote *(Dimanche avec Alain Fournier)*, Metzinger, Marie Laurencin, Survage.

2e sous-sol – La salle des Remparts abrite des expositions temporaires. A côté, une grande voûte (vestige du vieux Genève) sert de cadre à des sculptures de Zadkine, parmi lesquelles on remarque une œuvre en bois polychrome intitulée *Arlequin et Colombine*.

★★ **Muséum d'Histoire naturelle** (GZ) ⊘ – Dès l'époque de la Révolution française vint l'idée de créer un tel musée. Il vit le jour en 1872 dans le parc des Bastions et fut transféré à son emplacement actuel en 1975.
La présentation des diverses collections, aquariums et vivariums rend la visite très attrayante.
Le rez-de-chaussée abrite la faune régionale (oiseaux et mammifères dans leurs milieux naturels reconstitués) ; le premier étage des oiseaux et mammifères exotiques (dodo ou dronte : oiseau qui nichait dans la forêt et ne pouvait voler en raison de son poids élevé) ; le deuxième étage des poissons, amphibiens (crocodiles, tortues), reptiles exotiques, et des invertébrés (crabe géant du Japon dont l'envergure des pattes pouvait atteindre 4 m pour un corps de 45 cm de diamètre). Le troisième étage est consacré à la paléontologie, géologie, minéralogie (remarquer le cabinet des minéraux luminescents) de la Suisse et de la région de Genève. Ce niveau résume également l'histoire de la terre avec les planètes, les météorites, la dérive des continents, les volcans et tremblements de terre. Le quatrième étage est entièrement consacré à l'histoire géologique de la Suisse, la pièce maîtresse en est un relief animé construit selon la courbure terrestre à l'échelle du 1/100 000, sur lequel apparaissent distinctement les trois composantes du pays : le Jura, le plateau et les Alpes. Des minéraux et des fragments de sol complètent cette description.

Musée de l'Horlogerie et de l'Émaillerie (GZ) ⊘ – Installé dans une belle demeure du 19e s., il est consacré à l'histoire de la mesure du temps. En outre il illustre l'école de peinture genevoise sur émail, appliquée au décor de la montre, de la tabatière, du bijou et du portrait du 17e au 20e s.
La période allant du 15e au 18e s. est représentée au rez-de-chaussée par des sabliers, cadrans solaires, horloges (horloge en bois de 1700, horloge astronomique à automates de 1711), et principalement des montres genevoises (montres-bijoux en forme de coquillages, d'insectes, exécutées entre 1830 et 1870).
Au premier étage, montres genevoises émaillées des 19e et 20e s., souvent munies d'automates à musique, collection de réveille-matin. L'atelier d'un horloger-réparateur, Louis Cottier, a été reconstitué comme il se doit, sous les combles. En effet, c'est dans cet endroit de la maison que le « cabinotier », nom sous lequel on désignait l'artisan, possédait son cabinet. La salle des émaux explique les différentes techniques de l'émaillerie, art qui trouva son épanouissement à Genève dès la seconde moitié du 17e s. La finesse, la maîtrise du dessin, la richesse des couleurs et l'extrême dextérité que cet art requiert, trouvent leur application sur les pièces exposées (tabatières, émaux peints, montres, etc.).

La Fête de l'Escalade

Elle a lieu tous les ans en décembre. A cette occasion, les Genevois, revêtus de costumes d'époque, défilent à la lueur des torches dans les rues de la vieille ville et sur les rives du Rhône. Le cortège s'arrête en divers endroits pour permettre à un héraut de donner lecture, du haut de son cheval, de la proclamation de la victoire sur la Savoie. Le jour de cette fête, les confiseurs de la ville confectionnent des marmites en chocolat, symbolisant le geste de la « Mère Royaume » qui chassa un ennemi en lui déversant sur la tête le contenu bouillant d'une marmite. Service religieux dans la cathédrale St-Pierre, pétards et réjouissances accompagnent cette commémoration.

AUTRES CURIOSITÉS

Musée Barbier-Mueller (FZ M²) ⊙ – Il présente par roulement de très riches collections ayant trait aux civilisations dites primitives des cinq continents. Sculptures, céramiques, bijoux, tissus, ornements sont particulièrement bien mis en valeur dans des salles à l'éclairage adapté.

Église orthodoxe Ste-Croix (GZ N) ⊙ – Les bulbes d'or de ses coupoles se détachent dans ce quartier résidentiel de la fin du 19ᵉ s. L'édifice, conçu dans le style moscovite ancien, est en forme de croix grecque.
A l'intérieur, les murs, voûtes et piliers sont décorés de peintures inspirées de l'art byzantin. La nef est séparée du sanctuaire par l'iconostase formant un ensemble de cinq arcades en marbre de Carrare, finement sculpté et chargé d'icônes. Au centre, se détache la porte sainte, en bois de cyprès ajouré et doré.

Musée d'Ethnographie (EZ) ⊙ – Il contient divers objets, œuvres d'art ou humbles instruments de la vie quotidienne, des cinq continents. Parallèlement, des expositions temporaires se succèdent, ayant trait à un peuple ou sur un thème particulier.

M.A.M.C.O. (EZ) ⊙ – Puisant dans près de 40 collections publiques et privées suisses et étrangères, le Musée d'art moderne et contemporain n'a pas misé, à quelques exceptions près, sur des artistes renommés pour intéresser à l'art postérieur à 1960. La vocation du M.A.M.C.O. est de confronter le visiteur à un parcours inattendu qui ne surprendra pas uniquement le néophyte. Débuter la visite par le 4ᵉ étage (réservé aux expositions temporaires), et ne pas hésiter à consulter les fiches placées dans chaque salle, ou mieux, à interroger le personnel.

★ **Institut et musée Voltaire** (EY) ⊙ – « Les Délices » où Voltaire vécut de façon plus ou moins suivie de 1755 à 1765 sont devenues un centre de recherches consacré à l'œuvre de leur hôte illustre et à son époque. Cet institut, qui a publié la 1ʳᵉ édition de l'énorme correspondance de l'écrivain et abrite une riche bibliothèque, présente sur deux niveaux une sélection de ses richesses permettant de suivre les grandes étapes de la carrière de François-Marie Arouet.
Les vitrines contiennent des imprimés (dont une édition originale de *Candide*) et des manuscrits regroupant principalement des lettres de Voltaire et de ses correspondants (notamment l'une des dernières lettres que lui adressa le roi de Prusse Frédéric II). Le recueil de 199 cachets de correspondance aux armoiries de Voltaire constitue une curiosité étonnante. Parmi les portraits, remarquer celui réalisé par Largillière, représentant l'écrivain à 24 ans (rez-de-chaussée), ainsi qu'un exemplaire en terre cuite, exécuté en 1781 pour Beaumarchais, du *Voltaire assis* de Houdon (1ᵉʳ étage). Un programme audiovisuel relate la présence de Voltaire à Genève *(45 mn)*.

Église St-Paul – *Sortir par la rue de la Terrassière* (GZ).
Ce sanctuaire attire ceux qu'intéresse l'histoire de l'art sacré contemporain, pour la part importante que Maurice Denis prit, dès 1915, à sa décoration intérieure (toile marouflée de l'abside évoquant, sous forme de triptyque, la vie de saint Paul ; les 14 vitraux de la nef).

Église du Christ-Roi – *Au Petit-Lancy, par la route de Chancy* (EZ).
Le clocher-tour de cette église moderne de banlieue est relié au reste de l'édifice par un péristyle.
Intérieurement, le **vaisseau**★ présente une vaste nef couverte d'une voûte lambrissée, à poutres apparentes. Le mur de droite est orné d'une fresque de Beretta, celui de gauche est éclairé par une verrière d'Albert Chavaz. Dans le chœur à chevet plat, un grand triptyque est décoré par une magnifique tapisserie réalisée par Alice Basset.

Domaine de Penthes – *A Pregny-Chambésy, 18, chemin de l'Impératrice. Accès par l'avenue de la Paix, au Nord du plan, puis la route de Pregny.*
Il se présente sous la forme d'un parc de 12 ha, accidenté et planté de hêtres magnifiques.

★ **Musée des Suisses à l'Étranger** ⊙ – Le château de Penthes, qui abrita en 1852 la duchesse d'Orléans et ses fils (comte de Paris, duc de Chartres), a été affecté à ce musée qui évoque les relations de la Suisse avec le reste du monde, du Moyen Âge à nos jours, sur les plans diplomatique et militaire mais aussi postal, etc. L'accent est mis sur les alliances franco-suisses de 1444 à 1830, ainsi que sur les contingents de mercenaires et les personnalités suisses ayant servi les puissances européennes.
Dans la salle Le Fort, aux belles boiseries, on remarque de nombreux portraits et un plat ovale, en argent repoussé, célébrant, d'après une tapisserie de Le Brun, le serment d'alliance de 1663 échangé entre les cantons suisses et Louis XIV.
Au 1ᵉʳ étage, avec l'époque révolutionnaire funeste aux gardes suisses de Louis XVI sont rappelées celle de l'occupation française et la situation des régiments suisses sous l'Empire, ainsi que les traditions de la garde pontificale recrutée en Suisse

GENÈVE

depuis le 16ᵉ s. *(voir le Valais)*. Les postes helvétiques et leur premier «grand-maître», Béat de Fischer, sont à l'honneur dans la salle de ce nom, aménagée en salon 18ᵉ s. que décorent de délicates **boiseries ★**, en sept panneaux dorés et peints représentant les divinités de l'Olympe et provenant du château de Reichenbach, près de Berne. Les salles du 2ᵉ étage font état des Suisses qui se sont rendus célèbres à travers le monde : industriels (Nestlé, Suchard, Kohler pour le chocolat, Breguet pour l'horlogerie), banquiers (Necker), diplomates (Gallatin), écrivains (Blaise Cendrars).

Musée militaire genevois ⊙ — L'ancienne écurie du château, aujourd'hui pavillon général Dufour, abrite ce musée qui relate la participation de l'armée suisse pendant la Seconde Guerre mondiale (mannequins en uniformes, matériel, armement, tickets de rationnement, livrets d'instruction, journaux).

★ **Musée international de l'automobile** ⊙ — Palexpo, halle nº 7, le long de l'autoroute de contournement, par la route de Ferney (**EW**). Garer sa voiture au parking P26.

Occupant deux plateaux de 7 000 m² chacun, le musée compte près de 400 véhicules répartis par marque et nation, selon un ordre chronologique. Tous les modèles sont en parfait état. La Jeep du général Patton, la Fiat de Mussolini, la Buick du général Guisan, la Zis de Staline, une cadillac et une Ferrari ayant respectivement appartenus à Elvis Presley et Sophia Loren, sont assurément les stars de l'exposition. Ne pas manquer les véhicules suisses (dont Ajax, Tribelthorn, Felber et Monteverdi) et les belles séries italiennes telles que Ferrari, Lamborghini et autres Maserati. Quelques voitures d'exception laisseront rêveur même le plus blasé des visiteurs : Bugatti T35 (1924), Voisin C14 (1930), Auburn Speedster (1932), Hispano-Suiza (1934), Alfa Romeo 2500 (1939), Allard 81M (1945), Facel-Vega HK500 (1959), Austin Healy MKIII (1967)...

Un héros national, le général Dufour

Né à Constance (Allemagne) en 1787 de parents genevois exilés, Guillaume Henri Dufour fait ses études militaires à l'École polytechnique de Paris, avant d'être officier du génie dans la Grande Armée. Rentré en Suisse en 1817, il fonde l'école militaire de Thoune en 1819, réorganise l'armée fédérale, en prend le commandement et s'illustre dans la guerre du Sonderbund (1847). De 1832 à 1864, son œuvre scientifique aboutit à la réalisation de la carte topographique de la Suisse (carte Dufour au 1/100 000).
En 1875, il s'éteint dans sa propriété de Contamines. Il eut des funérailles nationales.
La plus haute aiguille du Mont Rose (Valais) porte son nom : pointe Dufour.

GIORNICO★

Tessin — 1 048 habitants
Carte Michelin nº 427 pli 15 ou 218 pli 12 — 9 km au Nord-Ouest de Biasca
Schéma : SANKT-GOTTHARD-MASSIV — Alt. 378 m

Dans un cadre encaissé mais égayé par l'apparition des premières vignes en hautins soutenus par des piles de granit, Giornico est la plus attachante étape monumentale de la route du St-Gothard sur le versant de la Léventine (haute vallée du Tessin).

Le site — Vus du pont qui relie la route du Gothard à la rive droite du Tessin, les toits de pierre des maisons enfermées dans une île boisée du torrent et les deux antiques ponts en dos d'âne qui donnent accès à celle-ci s'ordonnent en un pittoresque tableau. En avant se hausse parmi les pampres le mince campanile, rongé et noirci par le temps, de l'église Ste-Marie-du-Château.

★ **Église St-Nicolas (San Nicolao)** — Sur la rive droite du Tessin *(1ʳᵉ église en aval du pont)*.
Cet édifice roman (12ᵉ s.), au charme pur et rude, est précédé d'un portail dont les colonnes reposent, suivant la tradition lombarde, sur des fauves accroupis.
A l'intérieur, les deux chœurs superposés présentent la disposition très rare des «confessions», remontant aux origines de l'Église (crypte à moitié engagée dans le sol et servant de support au chœur supérieur où étaient déposées les reliques ou «corps saint»). Cette disposition permettait aux fidèles de se mettre littéralement «sous» la protection du saint patron du sanctuaire.
Les chapiteaux de la crypte (ou chœur inférieur, très élégant), la cuve baptismale, se remarquent spécialement pour leur fruste décor sculpté (animaux symboliques, motifs géométriques).

GLARUS

C Glarus – 5 728 habitants
Carte Michelin n° 427 pli 16 ou 218 Nord du pli 3 – Alt. 472 m

Au pied des falaises du Vorder Glärnisch, Glarus occupe un site★ encaissé. Elle se présente, depuis l'incendie de ses quartiers anciens, en 1861, comme une cité active, bâtie sur un plan régulier.
La vaste Zaunplatz paraît pourtant bien déserte, lorsque la grande consultation populaire de la **Landsgemeinde** *(voir « La Démocratie en action » dans l'introduction au voyage)* ne vient pas l'animer. Depuis 1387, cette véritable institution se déroule tous les ans le premier dimanche de mai.

Une ruche industrielle – Le chapelet d'usines aux longues façades blanches qui marque la vallée de la Linth, artère vitale du canton de Glarus, rappelle certains paysages vosgiens.
Au 18ᵉ s. le pasteur Andreas Heidegger introduisit la filature du coton dans le pays. L'âge d'or fut marqué, vers 1860, par la mise en route des impressions sur étoffe, technique dans laquelle les artisans glaronnais sont restés maîtres. Les indiennes du Glarus inondèrent alors le marché oriental.
Aujourd'hui encore, le Glarus est le seul canton industriel de la montagne suisse. Mais le Glarus est aussi une région de tourisme : une station comme **Braunwald** maintient les traditions d'hospitalité du canton qui fut un pionnier de l'alpinisme (construction de la première cabane du Club Alpin Suisse, en 1863, dans le massif du Tödi) et du ski (premier championnat suisse de ski à Glarus, en 1905) ; les Semaines musicales qui se tiennent à Braunwald attirent également chaque année de nombreux mélomanes.

ENVIRONS

★**Klöntal** – *13 km – environ 3/4 h. Quitter Glarus par la route de Zurich puis gagner Riedern.*
Dans ce village, prendre à gauche la route du Klöntal, remontant la vallée de la Löntsch, bientôt étroite et solitaire. Au sommet d'une montée rapide sous les hêtres, on débouche en vue du lac du Klöntal.
Un barrage a agrandi ce plan d'eau, dans lequel plongent, d'une hauteur de 2 000 m, les escarpements déchiquetés du Glärnisch, aux ravins inaccessibles. Reprenant la montée pour longer le lac, s'arrêter, 300 m après le 2ᵉ lacet, près d'un banc, face à la majestueuse **perspective**★★ du Klöntal.

> **Le schabzieger**
>
> Une spécialité du canton de Glarus est ce fromage de couleur verte, sans croûte ni trou, de forme conique, fait de lait maigre et d'herbes pulvérisées. Son goût épicé lui est donné par une plante, le « Ziegerklee » ou trèfle des chevriers.

GOMS★★

Val de CONCHES – Carte Michelin n° 427 pli 14 ou 217 plis 18, 19
Schéma : le VALAIS

Remontant la haute vallée du Rhône – Val de Conches (ou **Goms** en alémanique) à partir de Fiesch – la route prend un caractère de plus en plus montagnard, desservant au passage les accès des nombreuses stations et remontées mécaniques accrochées au flanc du massif de l'Aletschhorn.

DE BRIG A GLETSCH

54 km – environ 2 h – itinéraire ④ *de la visite du Valais*

La route, que suit, de loin, la voie ferrée de la « Furka-Oberalp », peut être fermée pour de courtes durées en cas de fort enneigement, entre Brig et Oberwald.
La haute vallée du Rhône est constituée de quatre paliers successifs qui font franchir au fleuve une dénivellation de près de 1 000 m.

Brig – *Visite : 3/4 h. Voir à ce nom.*

De Brig à la bifurcation de Grengiols, on suit de près le Rhône écumant, au fond d'un sillon étroit et sinueux. La route passe à côté de la grande chapelle baroque isolée d'**Hohen Flühen** et dessert les stations inférieures des téléphériques de Riederalp Greicheralp (départ de Mérel) et de Bettmeralp (départ de la gare de Betten). Ces différentes lignes desservent un haut plateau d'alpages (2 000 m d'altitude) merveilleusement situé en vue des Alpes valaisannes et à proximité immédiate du glacier d'Aletsch, le plus vaste des Alpes (169 km² avec ses affluents).

GOMS

★ **Riederalp, Moosfluh**★★ ⊙ — *Accès à Riederalp par téléphérique ou télécabine au départ de Mörel ; à Moosfluh par télésiège au départ de Riederalp.* Disposée dans un **site**★ en balcon, sur un beau replat du versant Nord de la vallée du Rhône, la station de **Riederalp**★ étage ses chalets ou hôtels à partir de 1 930 m d'altitude face aux crêtes séparant la Suisse de l'Italie. En contre-haut de son extrémité Ouest se trouve la « Villa Cassel », centre de la Réserve naturelle d'Aletschwald.

De la gare d'arrivée du téléphérique, rejoindre (en quelques minutes à pied) celle de départ du télésiège pour Moosfluh.

La montée en télésiège, passant par la station intermédiaire de Blausee, située entre deux petits lacs, aboutit à la station supérieure de **Moosfluh**★★ (alt. 2 335 m), dans un chaos de rochers verdâtres dominant la splendide coulée incurvée du **glacier d'Aletsch**★★★ immédiatement au Nord, au pied des pentes et des glaciers affluents du massif de l'Aletschhorn, et la vallée du Rhône.

Le second palier (Lax-Fiesch) est marqué par l'apparition — soulignant le gain d'altitude réalisé — des pins arolles et des « raccards » sur pilotis *(voir : Le Valais)* : c'est l'entrée de la vallée de Conches proprement dite.

En contrebas, dans une gorge, confluent le Rhône et la Binna. Plus haut, au moment où apparaît le village de Fiesch, la coupure du Fieschertal permet d'entrevoir, au dernier plan, au Nord, le sommet neigeux du Finsteraar-Rothorn.

★★★ **Eggishorn** ⊙ — Alt. 2 927 m. *Accès par téléphérique au départ de Fiesch.* La montée jusqu'à la station intermédiaire de Kühboden (alt. 2 214 m) se fait au-dessus des sapins, la suite au-dessus d'éboulis verdâtres.

De la station supérieure (alt. 2 869 m), se dégage un merveilleux **panorama**★★★, au premier plan sur tout le glacier d'Aletsch en contrebas, à sa droite sur celui, parallèle, de Fiesch près duquel tombe une cascade, et sur tous les hauts massifs environnants.

Les personnes ingambes pourront escalader l'un des trois cônes d'éboulis proches de la station — dont celui du sommet de l'Eggishorn, surmonté d'une croix — pour mieux détailler le panorama. Second ressaut au-dessus de Fiesch : la vue peut porter désormais, très loin en aval, jusqu'aux neiges du Weisshorn (alt. 4 505 m). Après quelques lacets, remarquer, sur le versant opposé, le village de **Mühlebach**, patrie du cardinal Mathieu Schiner *(voir à ce nom).*

★ **Bellwald** — Lieu de séjour. *Accès par route sinueuse de 8 km ou par téléphérique, à partir de Fürgangen.* Petite station-village d'hiver et d'été. Bellwald dispose à 1 600 m d'altitude ses vieux chalets en bois de mélèze et ses hôtels sur une terrasse en arc de cercle orientée Sud-Ouest, procurant une **vue**★ de belle ampleur sur le Val de Conches de Fiesch à Brigue (Brig), sur l'Eggishorn, au-dessus à droite sur le massif du Wannenhorn et ses glaciers, à gauche sur les Alpes de la frontière italienne. Son **télésiège du Richinen et du Steibenkreuz** ⊙ fournit l'occasion d'un trajet agréable au-dessus des herbages, avec une vue rapprochée sur les glaciers du Wannenhorn et au Sud avec une vue éloignée sur le Cervin. La vallée se rouvre harmonieusement. Ce troisième palier est le plus long du val.

La combe alpestre offre maintenant un paysage ample et dépouillé que l'absence totale de clôtures rend très frappant et dont le manque d'arbres et de chalets, même isolés accentue le dépeuplement. Les villages concentrent leurs maisons de bois noiraudes, fleuries de géraniums, autour de leur svelte clocher blanc.

En amont, à droite du casque du Galenstock, on décèle la trouée de la Furka.

Reckingen — L'église baroque de Reckingen est la plus agréablement proportionnée du Val de Conches. Elle fut bâtie, au 18ᵉ s., sur les plans du curé du lieu, **Jean-Georges Ritz**, représentant d'une dynastie d'artisans qui a fourni en autels sculptés maints sanctuaires de la région. Le nom de cette famille est devenu mondialement connu depuis que l'un de ses membres, **César Ritz** (né à Niederwald en 1850, mort en 1918) s'orienta vers la profession d'hôtelier.

Les **Seiler**, qui firent la fortune de Zermatt et construisirent les deux hôtels proches du glacier du Rhône (à Gletsch et au « Belvédère »), étaient d'ailleurs, eux aussi, originaires de la vallée de Conches.

Münster — Ce grand village se regroupe au pied d'un cône de déjection quadrillé de parcelles cultivées, disposées en éventail. L'église, au clocher coiffé d'une flèche en éteignoir, mérite d'être visitée pour son **retable**★ flamboyant, dédié à la Vierge, œuvre d'un artiste lucernois (1509).

Au-delà d'Ulrichen, la vallée devient plus sauvage ; les maisons d'**Obergestelen**, reconstruites en pierre au siècle dernier à la suite d'un incendie, laissent, pour la première fois, une impression de pauvreté.

Les Muttenhörner semblent toujours fermer complètement la vallée.

Au-dessus d'**Oberwald**, le dernier village du Val de Conches — dont on remarque, d'en haut, la petite église dotée d'une étrave brise-avalanche en maçonnerie — , la route, aux caractéristiques toutes montagnardes, se glisse dans un défilé de plus en plus déboisé où le Rhône, déchaîné, bondit de chute en chute.

GOMS

On débouche enfin sur le quatrième palier, c'est-à-dire dans le bassin de Gletsch, en vue du glacier du Rhône, source du grand fleuve.

★★ **Gletsch** – Alt. 1 759 m. Station estivale bien située, au carrefour des routes de la Furka, du Grimsel et de la vallée de Conches (Haut-Valais), au fond du bassin désolé que venait recouvrir autrefois la langue terminale du glacier du Rhône.
Au-dessus de Gletsch sur la route du col de la Furka *(voir à ce nom)*, les abords du lacet à l'intérieur duquel a été construit l'hôtel Belvédère attirent un grand nombre de touristes. En effet, cette étape fameuse propose non seulement l'attraction du **glacier du Rhône**★★, dans lequel est creusée une **« grotte de glace »**★ (Eisgrotte) ⊙, mais encore un immense **panorama**★★ sur les Alpes bernoises et valaisannes.

Barrage de la GRANDE DIXENCE★★★

Carte Michelin nº 427 pli 22 ou 219 pli 3 – Schéma : VALAIS

Le nom de Grande Dixence évoque le plus gigantesque ouvrage de génie civil que le peuple suisse ait jamais entrepris. *Visite du barrage : 2 h.*
Implanté à l'altitude de 2 365 m (crête du barrage), le barrage-poids de la Grande Dixence, porté, par étapes successives, à la hauteur de 284 m, actuel record du monde – il formerait encore écran devant les touristes circulant sur la troisième plate-forme de la tour Eiffel –, a nécessité 5 900 000 m³ de béton. La mise en eau complète eut lieu en septembre 1966.
Ces travaux n'ont pourtant constitué que l'un des chapitres d'un aménagement d'ensemble qui a entraîné la percée d'une centaine de kilomètres de galeries d'adduction, allant chercher les eaux de fonte glaciaire jusqu'au pied du Cervin. Les eaux ont été ensuite « basculées » non seulement sur la nouvelle centrale de Fionnay, mais aussi sur la centrale de Riddes-Nendaz et Chandoline, dans la vallée du Rhône.
Le calme revenu dans cette haute vallée valaisanne, la production hydro-électrique suisse peut bénéficier d'un appoint annuel estimé à 1 600 millions de kWh.

Col du GRAND ST-BERNARD★

Valais et Italie

Carte Michelin nº 427 pli 21 ou 219 pli 2 – Schéma : VALAIS – Alt. 2 469 m

Dans une échancrure rocheuse balayée presque continuellement par une bise glaciale, au bord d'un lac gelé en moyenne 265 jours par an et où l'hiver règne pendant pratiquement huit mois, les sévères bâtiments de l'hospice du Grand St-Bernard illustrent la persistance d'une admirable tradition chrétienne d'assistance et d'hospitalité. Depuis neuf siècles, les religieux, de l'ordre des chanoines réguliers de St-Augustin, installés ici par saint Bernard de Menthon – une statue honorant ce « héros des Alpes » a été élevée au col, en territoire italien – hébergent et réconfortent les voyageurs se risquant en hiver dans ces parages. C'est en hiver, alors que le col était obstrué par la neige, que Bonaparte fit traverser les Alpes à ses 40 000 soldats avant de surprendre les Autrichiens à Marengo (1800).

Voyageurs dans la tempête

Hospice – En toutes saisons l'hospitalité des chanoines s'exerce sur les voyageurs désireux de passer quelque temps dans ce havre de calme.
Dans le hall se trouve le tombeau en marbre élevé par Napoléon au général Desaix, tué à Marengo.
Église – Englobée dans l'hospice, elle a été construite au 17ᵉ s. dans le style baroque sur une église primitive du 13ᵉ s., aujourd'hui la crypte.
De chaque côté du maître-autel se dressent les statues de saint Bernard et de saint Augustin. Les stalles en noyer sculpté et les peintures de la voûte du chœur à décoration surchargée et aux vives couleurs illustrent parfaitement la période baroque. Autour d'une représentation de la Trinité, on peut reconnaître plusieurs scènes du Nouveau Testament : Adoration des mages, Annonciation, Nativité. A gauche avant le chœur, sur l'autel de saint Bernard, un coffret en noyer doré contient les reliques du saint.

Col du GRAND ST-BERNARD

Trésor — Il présente une belle collection d'objets religieux parmi lesquels on remarque : un buste-reliquaire de saint Bernard du 13ᵉ s. en bois polychrome recouvert d'argent repoussé et de pierres précieuses, une croix processionnelle en argent doré ornée de pierres précieuses (13ᵉ-14ᵉ s.), une Vierge à l'Enfant du 15ᵉ s., un bréviaire enluminé du 15ᵉ s.

Musée ⊙ — La visite commence par le **chenil** dans lequel on peut voir les célèbres chiens, jadis compagnons fidèles des religieux dans leurs expéditions de secours. Aujourd'hui, ces chiens n'interviennent plus dans de telles expéditions, on leur préfère les bergers allemands, plus souples. Cependant, ils servent ici à perpétuer la race.
Le **musée** est consacré à l'histoire du col : son passage de l'Antiquité à nos jours (que de gens l'empruntèrent : marchands, soldats, pèlerins, migrants, contrebandiers!), la flore, la faune, le climat, la vie au col, la vie à l'hospice. Les produits de fouilles incluent à côté de pièces de monnaie et d'ex-voto, une belle statue de Jupiter, en bronze, et une main votive ouvragée. L'histoire de l'hospice dont les statuts de la congrégation sont inscrits dans un livre de 1438, est relatée principalement au moyen de photographies et d'images.

Route du GRAND ST-BERNARD★

Carte Michelin n° 427 pli 21 ou 219 plis 1, 2 – Schéma : VALAIS

Le col du Grand St-Bernard, mettant en communication les vallées de la Dranse et de la Doire Baltée, livre passage à la voie transalpine la plus chargée d'histoire. La grande tradition hospitalière qui s'y perpétue depuis le 11ᵉ s., des souvenirs aussi populaires que ceux du passage de Bonaparte en 1800, ont attiré dans ces farouches solitudes, depuis l'avènement du tourisme, des foules sensibles au côté « pèlerinage » de cette excursion, désormais privilégié depuis l'ouverture du tunnel sous le col.

DE MARTIGNY AU COL DU GRAND ST-BERNARD

55 km – environ 3 h 1/2 – itinéraire 1 *de la visite du Valais*

Les contrôles douaniers suisse et italien ont lieu au col même, en été. Pour les utilisateurs du tunnel, ils ont lieu en toutes saisons en Suisse, à la Gare Nord et en Italie, à la Gare Sud du tunnel.

Martigny — *Visite : 1 h 1/2. Voir à ce nom.*
Peu après Martigny, la route vient épouser le contour de la vallée de la Dranse, fortement encaissée, jusqu'aux Valettes.
Les moindres bassins apparaissent encore plantés de vigne et d'arbres fruitiers *(lire « un premier essai de Provence » au chapitre consacré au Valais).*

Route de Mauvoisin — *75 km à partir des Valettes* — *environ 3 h 1/2*. La route n° 21, jusqu'à Sembrancher, se faufile entre la Dranse et la voie ferrée.

★**Circuit des cols** — *Au départ de Sembrancher*. Cette petite excursion, très agréable par beau temps, fait passer par Vollèges (élégant clocher), le Levron (village montagnard en balcon), les cols – ou « pas » – du Lein (cuvette semée de rocs et de mélèzes), du Tronc et de Planches *(restaurant)*, et par le hameau de Vens *(d'où l'on regagne la route de Mauvoisin)*. Elle emprunte des routes forestières *(non revêtues sur 5 km entre le Levron et le col des Planches)* tantôt en corniche, tantôt sous bois (sapins et mélèzes), procurant des **vues**★ magnifiques sur les vallées alentour, le mont Pierre Avoi au Nord-Est, les sommets neigeux des Alpes françaises (Mont Blanc) au Sud-Ouest et des Alpes Pennines (Grand Combin) au Sud-Est.

★**Verbier** — *Au départ de Bagnes. Voir à Verbier.*
Revenir dans la vallée de la Dranse de Bagnes.

★★★**Barrage de Mauvoisin** — Alt. 1961 m (crête du barrage). Obturant un défilé sauvage de la haute vallée de Bagnes, ce barrage est l'un des ouvrages du type « voûte » les plus élevés du monde (237 m). Le gigantesque mur a créé une retenue de 180 millions de m³ dont les eaux sont « turbinées » par les centrales de Fionnay et de Riddes. A Mauvoisin, garer la voiture dans le parc réservé aux visiteurs, à mi-chemin entre l'hôtel et le barrage, et suivre la route à pied jusqu'au couronnement du barrage.
La petite **route**★★ des Valettes à Champex, difficile, compte 22 lacets rapprochés et durs au-dessus du Durnant, encaissé dans 1 km de gorges impressionnantes *(aménagées pour la visite). Les automobilistes peu exercés à la conduite en montagne y accéderont à partir d'Orsières.*

★★**Champex** — Alt. 1 465 m. Suspendue au-dessus du bassin d'Orsières, à la naissance d'un profond repli boisé où s'étale un lac ravissant, Champex, villégiature élégante, offre, pour un séjour d'été, le double agrément de la plage et de la terrasse pano-

127

Route du GRAND ST-BERNARD

ramique. Son miroir d'eau reflète le majestueux déroulement des sommets neigeux du Combin (Combin de Corbassière à gauche. Grand Combin à droite). Les promeneurs peuvent les admirer tout à loisir en flânant sur le chemin du Signal, qui dessert les hôtels-belvédères de la station.

★★ **La Breya** ⊙ — Alt. 2 374 m. *1 h 1/2 AR dont 15 mn de télésiège.* Agréable montée en télésiège au-dessus du lac de Champex ; vaste panorama sur les Alpes valaisannes.

De Champex à Orsières, la route en lacet, goudronnée, bien tracée en vue du massif du Combin et des contreforts valaisans du Mont Blanc qui plongent dans le Val Ferret, traverse de vastes cultures maraîchères de fraisiers : coup d'œil étonnant dans ce décor de montagne.

Orsières — Ce bourg s'agglomère au fond du bassin où le Val Ferret, après avoir longé toute la façade valaisanne du massif du Mont-Blanc, rejoint le Val d'Entremont. L'église a gardé son clocher de style roman lombard.

On distingue, parmi les contreforts valaisans du Mont Blanc qui dominent le Val Ferret, à l'arrière-plan, le sommet taché de neige du Portalet et de l'autre côté, l'énorme pyramide du Catogne. En amont, se hausse le mont Vélan, précédé de la face triangulaire du Petit Vélan.

Après la chapelle N.-D.-de-Lorette, la route longe sur la droite le village de Bourg-St-Pierre, aux toits couleur de rouille, massés au débouché du vallon de Valsorey qu'embellit une cascade.

Après avoir enjambé le Valsorey et ses gorges, la route surplombe le barrage des Toules, au niveau duquel on découvre une vue magnifique *(l'ancienne route du col s'amorçant à Bourg-St-Pierre n'est pas revêtue sur une courte section peu avant le barrage).* Ensuite, le décor de roches moutonnées et striées, de bassins encombrés d'éboulis, se fait de plus en plus sévère.

Bourg-St-Bernard — L'installation de remontées mécaniques (télécabine du col de Menouve) au départ de cette station frontière, créée à l'entrée du tunnel, a facilité le lancement du centre de sports d'hiver de Super-St-Bernard. Les derniers kilomètres *(nombreux lacets)* se déroulent dans la sinistre combe des Morts, ravagée par les avalanches. A gauche du Vélan se détache le beau sommet glaciaire du Grand Combin.

Tunnel du Grand St-Bernard ⊙ — En raison de l'accroissement du trafic routier entre la vallée du Rhône et le Val d'Aoste et pour éviter l'interruption de la circulation à cause de la neige pendant plus de six mois chaque année, la Suisse et l'Italie ont réalisé en commun, de 1959 à 1964, le tunnel routier (long de près de 6 km) accessible en toutes saisons, qui met Bâle à 450 km de Turin.

Sur le versant italien, certaines sections de route restent à ciel ouvert. Tout le long du parcours, on admire la structure audacieuse de cette voie artificielle et de ses viaducs franchissant d'un seul jet les gorges de l'Artanavaz.

De chaque côté du tunnel, des routes d'accès, généralement couvertes, dont la pente n'excède jamais 6 %, viennent se greffer sur la route du col en aval de Bourg-St-Pierre pour le versant suisse et en amont de St-Oyen pour le versant italien.

Une fois la combe des Morts dépassée, l'arrivée au col du Grand St-Bernard est très rapide.

★ **Col du Grand St-Bernard** — *Voir à ce nom.*

GRANDSON ★

Vaud — 2 473 habitants

Carte Michelin n° 427 pli 12 ou 217 pli 3 — Schéma : JURA SUISSE — Alt. 440 m

Située près de l'extrémité Sud du lac de Neuchâtel, la petite ville de Grandson vit se dérouler le 2 mars 1476, sous les murs du château, un combat resté célèbre, au cours duquel les Confédérés infligèrent une sévère défaite au duc de Bourgogne, Charles le Téméraire. Celui-ci abandonna à ses vainqueurs son artillerie et un riche trésor.

CURIOSITÉS

★★ **Château** ⊙ — La première construction fut entreprise au début du 11ᵉ s. par les sires de Grandson, mais le château, tel que nous le connaissons aujourd'hui, date du 13ᵉ s. Il passa au 15ᵉ s. à la maison de Chalon-Orange qui le remania en grande partie. Après 1476 la seigneurie de Grandson devint propriété des villes de Berne et de Fribourg : le château, promu résidence des baillis, fut réaménagé. Très imposant avec ses hautes murailles et ses grosses tours rondes que relie un chemin de ronde couvert, il occupe un **site**★★ remarquable au bord du lac de Neuchâtel qu'il domine.

A l'intérieur, salles historiques et collections d'armes anciennes. On parcourt successivement le chemin de ronde, la salle des Chevaliers (belles stalles Renaissance), le musée des guerres de Bourgogne (dioramas) et de Charles le Téméraire, le musée des châteaux forts (maquettes de batailles), les prisons souterraines (une chambre de torture et des oubliettes), la chapelle, ainsi qu'un musée de a contrée de Grandson.

Dans les salles du sous-sol, un **musée de l'automobile** présente une intéressante collection de modèles anciens, depuis une Delahaye de 1898 jusqu'à une Rolls Phantom blanche de 1927 ayant appartenu à l'actrice Greta Garbo.

Église St-Jean-Baptiste — Cet intéressant édifice, mi-roman, mi-gothique, présente une nef couverte en plein cintre très sobre, flanquée de bas-côtés voûtés en demi-berceaux ; des chapiteaux primitifs — certains sont historiés — surmontent des colonnes monolithes.

Le contraste est frappant entre la nef très sombre et le chœur, voûté d'arêtes et éclairé de nombreux vitraux. Dans la chapelle à droite du chœur, belle fresque représentant la Mise au tombeau. Autre élément de curiosité : les pots de résonance.

A l'extérieur, devant le chevet, fontaine de 1637 à tuyaux de bronze. A droite de l'église, l'ancienne Maison du Bailli arbore un fronton sculpté d'un soleil à visage humain entre des sauvages en pagne et à massue.

Les panoramas des grands cols sont souvent saisissants aux heures extrêmes de la journée.

GRAUBÜNDEN★★★

Les GRISONS — Carte Michelin n° 427 plis 15 à 18 ou 218 plis 1 à 7 et 11 à 17

Trois langues, deux religions, une évolution politique vers la démocratie analogue à celle des « cantons primitifs », font du plus vaste canton helvétique, les Grisons, un véritable modèle réduit de la Confédération.

Pour le voyageur, c'est sans doute la région de la Suisse la plus favorable à un complet dépaysement.

L'Engadine, avec les séductions de son ciel, de son pays « désencombré », constitue le pôle touristique de ce petit État montagnard à cheval sur les Alpes.

Un peu de géographie — Les Grisons correspondent, pour l'essentiel de leur territoire, au pays des sources du Rhin et de l'Inn. Ces deux bassins supérieurs sont séparés, au Sud-Ouest de la Silvretta, par la grande chaîne jalonnée par les sommets des Piz Linard, Kesch, d'Err et de la Platta entre lesquels s'ouvrent les vals de la Flüela, de l'Albula et du Julier. Ce vaste ensemble alpestre s'inscrit dans un large arc de cercle, jalonné de même, d'Ouest en Est, par les grands cols de l'Oberalp, du St-Gothard, du San Bernardino, de la Maloja, de la Bernina et de l'Umbrail. Le Rhin Antérieur, né dans le cirque de l'Oberalp, file, à partir de Disentis/Mustér, au fond du large sillon rectiligne de l'Oberland grison ; le Rhin Postérieur descend des glaciers de l'Adula. Ils se rejoignent au pied du château de Reichenau. La vallée supérieure de l'Inn — qui se jette dans le Danube à Passau, aux confins de l'Allemagne et de l'Autriche — relève par l'Engadine des pays de l'ancienne Rhétie.

Un peu d'histoire — Le territoire du canton des Grisons correspond aux régions les plus montagneuses de cette ancienne **Rhétie**, dont les tribus « welches » peuplaient primitivement l'espace compris entre le lac de Constance et la Vénétie. Maintenues à l'écart de la germanisation, les hautes vallées du Rhin et de l'Inn sont restées des terres « romanches », dont la langue, de souche latine, reconnue officiellement comme quatrième langue nationale suisse en 1938, pique la curiosité de l'étranger par ses consonances insolites et ses procédés graphiques.

Une terre de transit — Sous la domination romaine et pendant tout le Moyen Âge, la Rhétie monopolisait la presque totalité du trafic transalpin intéressant le territoire actuel de la Confédération, avec les passages de la « Route Supérieure » (ou « **Obere Strasse** »), par les cols du Julier et surtout du Septimer, et de la « Route Inférieure » (ou « **Untere Strasse** »), par le col du Splügen. La rareté des défilés, ordinairement si fréquents le long des routes transalpines, favorisait nettement la « Route Supérieure ». Semblable activité ne se retrouvait, plus à l'Ouest, que le long de la route du Grand St-Bernard. Le canevas des routes transalpines passant par les Grisons a pris sa forme actuelle avec l'exécution, entre 1818 et 1823, d'un programme dont la Suisse, l'Autriche et le Piémont assumaient en commun les charges ; il comportait la réfection de la route du Splügen et la construction d'une nouvelle chaussée carrossable entre Splügen et Bellinzona, par le San Bernardino, l'itinéraire millénaire du Septimer étant complètement abandonné.

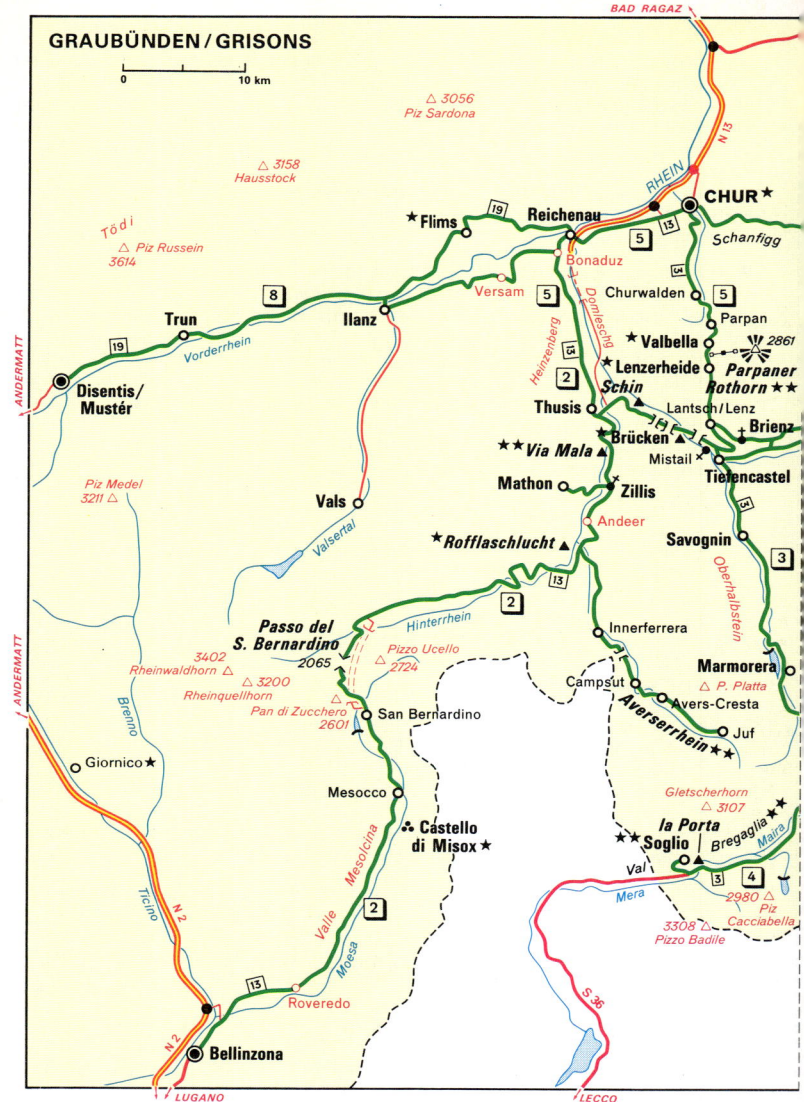

VISITE

Les itinéraires recommandés

Par ordre décroissant de la durée du parcours. *Voir les noms à l'index.*

- ★★ ① **Zügen, Flüela** – Circuit au départ de Davos – compter une journée.
- ★★ ② **San Bernardino** – Route de Bellinzona à Chur – compter une journée.
- ★ ③ **Julier, Albula** – Circuit au départ de St-Moritz – environ 5 h.
- ★★★ ④ **Engadin** – Haute-Engadine (Val Bregaglia) : route de St-Moritz à Soglio – environ 1 h 1/2. Basse-Engadine (vallée de l'Inn) : route de St-Moritz à Martina – environ 3 h.
- ★ ⑤ **Lenzerheide, gorges du Schin** – Circuit au départ de Chur – environ 3 h.
- ★ ⑥ **Ofen** (Parc national suisse et Val Müstair) – Route de Zernez au col de l'Umbrail – environ 2 h 1/2.
- ★★★ ⑦ **Berninastrasse** (Val Bernina et Val Poschiavo) – Route de St-Moritz à Tirano – environ 2 h.
- ★ ⑧ **Vallée du Rhin Antérieur** – Route de Disentis/Mustér à Reichenau – environ 1 h 3/4.
- ★ ⑨ **Schanfig** – Route de Chur à Arosa – environ 1 h.

GRIMSELSTRASSE★

Carte Michelin n° 427 pli 14 ou 217 plis 9, 19 – Schéma : BERNER OBERLAND

La **route du Grimsel**, qui remonte de la haute vallée de l'Aare (Haslital), introduit dans un décor de roches moutonnées, polies par les anciens glaciers. Mais, è chaque palier de la vallée, barrages et centrales électriques rappellent la civilisation.

DE MEIRINGEN A GLETSCH

37 km – environ 1 h 1/2 – itinéraire 4 *de la visite de l'Oberland bernois*

- ★ **Meiringen** – *Voir à ce nom.*
  A la sortie de Meiringen, la vallée est obstruée par la bosse rocheuse du Kirchet. Alors que le torrent a tranché ce «verrou» *(voir à ce nom)* – c'est la coupure bien connue des gorges de l'Aare, invisible de la route – celle-ci le contourne par les hauteurs, procurant d'agréables échappées sur le bassin parfaitement nivelé d'Innertkirchen, dominé par les grands escarpements du Burg et la pyramide du Bänzlauistock.

- ★★ **Gorges de l'Aare** (Aareschlucht) – *1 km au départ de la route du Grimsel plus 1/2 h de visite. Description à Meiringen.* La vallée prend alors son caractère pastoral, mais des plaques de végétation verdissent encore ses flancs rocheux. A la sortie du pont de Boden, en aval de Guttannen, on franchit le Spreitlauibach par une galerie d'avalanches en béton armé ; ce ravin, où des plaques de neige se maintiennent pendant toute la belle saison, collecte de terribles avalanches qui ont tout balayé à l'entour, à l'exception d'un pan de forêt.

Guttannen — C'est la seule agglomération de l'Oberhasli digne du nom de village. Son **musée des Cristaux** ⊙ présente une collection remarquable de quartz fumés et de cristaux de roche, et une grande variété de minéraux.

La montée se poursuit, par paliers, dans un **cadre**★★ de roches moutonnées verdâtres et de névés féconds en cascades : en certains endroits la route, taillée dans d'énormes bancs de granit clair, d'un poli extraordinaire, paraît avoir été ouverte la veille, par un gigantesque burin.

★ **Cascade de la Handegg (Handeggfall)** — L'Arlenbach et l'Aare confondent leurs eaux dans une chute disposée en Y, qui va s'écraser au fond d'une étroite gorge. A la nappe turquoise du lac-réservoir de **Räterichsboden** succède le grand lac artificiel du Grimsel dont deux barrages ancrés sur le rognon rocheux intermédiaire du Nollen – où un hôtel remplace l'hospice du Grimsel, submergé – retiennent les eaux troubles. La **vue**★ peut atteindre, dans l'axe de la vallée noyée, au dernier plan, les crêtes du Finsteraarhorn (alt. 4 274 m – point culminant des Alpes bernoises).

★★ **Col du Grimsel** — Alt. 2 165 m. Un « lac des Morts » rappelle les combats qui opposèrent ici Autrichiens et Français en 1799. De la butte qui s'élève derrière l'hôtel Grimselblick, la **vue**★★ embrasse la région désertique des sources du Rhône – l'hôtel Belvédère, près du glacier du Rhône, est le seul établissement humain visible – avec, de gauche à droite, le casque neigeux du Galenstock, le front du glacier du Rhône, la trouée de la Furka et les longues crêtes émoussées et monotones qui s'allongent entre le Haut-Valais et la vallée piémontaise du Toce. Vers le Nord-Ouest, on remarque, au dernier plan, la paroi du Lauteraarhorn (alt. 4 042 m).

La route s'abaisse ensuite vers le **Gletschboden**, fond de cuvette désolé. Le paysage redevient plus classiquement alpestre. La route développe ses lacets au flanc de la Meienwand et arrive à proximité de la cataracte terminale du glacier du Rhône, que domine la coupole neigeuse du Galenstock. Gletsch est alors en vue.

★★ **Gletsch** — Voir à ce nom.

GRINDELWALD★★★

Berne — 3 733 habitants
Carte Michelin n° 427 pli 14 ou 217 Sud du pli 8
Schéma : INTERLAKEN (Environs) — Alt. 1 034 m

Dans un site inoubliable, Grindelwald, le « village des glaciers », est la seule grande station d'altitude de la région de la Jungfrau accessible en auto et attire, à ce titre, non seulement des séjournants, mais encore une foule d'excursionnistes venus, pour la journée, de la région d'Interlaken. L'animation bigarrée qui règne dans la longue rue principale du bourg, plonge l'arrivant dans une ambiance de capitale alpine.

★★★ **Le site** — Grindelwald associe des premiers plans d'un charme tout agreste – prairies plantées d'arbres fruitiers ou d'érables et toutes semées de coquettes habitations – à une grandiose barrière rocheuse allongée entre l'épaule du Wetterhorn et la pyramide de l'Eiger. Devant un tel spectacle, il est facile de comprendre la fortune de la station : ici, la haute montagne, théâtre d'opérations de l'alpiniste ou de l'adepte du ski alpin ; là, se déployant entre les seuils de la Grande et de la Petite Scheidegg, en passant par le Faulhorn, un immense amphithéâtre d'alpages et de bois d'une topographie parfaitement adaptée à la pratique du ski de fond.

ENVIRONS

★★★ **Jungfraujoch** — Voir à ce nom. Consacrer au moins une demi-journée à cette « ascension » en partant de préférence par l'un des premiers trains du matin.

★★ **First** ⊙ — 1 h 1/2 AR environ dont 1 h de télécabine.
Excellent belvédère (table d'orientation) sur le bassin de Grindelwald et sur les cimes du Wetterhorn, du Schreckhorn, des Fiescherhörner et de l'Eiger.
De la station terminale, il est très recommandé de continuer à s'élever, sinon jusqu'au sommet du **Faulhorn**★★★ (panorama – 5 h à pied AR) du moins jusqu'au **Bachsee**★★ (2 h à pied AR) ; des rives de ce petit lac se découvre, encadrée par le Schreckhorn et les Fiescherhörner, la cime tranchante du Finsteraarhorn.

★ **Gorge du Glacier (Gletscherschlucht)** ⊙ — 2,5 km par un chemin s'amorçant à l'extrémité du village après l'église, à droite, plus 1/2 h de visite.
Fissure rocheuse, au fond de laquelle apparaît, réduit à une mince lame de glace, le mur terminal du glacier inférieur de Grindelwald (Unterer Grindelwaldgletscher).

GRUYÈRES★★

Fribourg — 1 460 habitants
Carte Michelin n° 427 pli 12 ou 217 Sud-Ouest du pli 5 — Altitude 830 m

Posée sur une colline, au centre d'un paysage tout empreint de mesure et de grâce, cette petite cité fortifiée, ville-musée à vocation touristique, ravit les visiteurs de la Suisse romande par son cachet aimable, évocateur de l'époque où la vallée de la Sarine tout entière vivait sous la suzeraineté bonhomme et gaillarde des comtes de Gruyères (12e-16e s.).

CURIOSITÉS

L'arrivée — *Parc de stationnement en dehors des murs de la ville.*
Le premier coup d'œil séduit l'arrivant qui se retrouve dans la rue principale. Celle-ci bordée de vieilles maisons à fenêtres géminées, abritées sous un large auvent, s'incline vers la fontaine communale avant de grimper à nouveau jusqu'au château.
Monter à pied au château en remarquant, au passage, à droite, creusées dans un massif de pierre, les anciennes mesures à grains de la ville. Juste avant d'atteindre le château on aperçoit à gauche une maison aux encadrements de fenêtres délicatement sculptés (16e s.) ; ce fut la demeure du bouffon Chalamala qui s'illustra à la cour des comtes de Gruyères.

★ **Château** ⊙ — L'ancien château des comtes de Gruyères, aujourd'hui propriété du canton de Fribourg, remonte, dans sa majeure partie, à la fin du 15e s. (façades sur cour du corps de logis principal).
Les aménagements intérieurs, très variés, évoquent aussi bien l'époque féodale (cuisine, salle des Gardes), que le 18e s. et ses raffinements. Leur décoration, plus ou moins bien venue, est, en grande partie, l'œuvre des Bovy, dynastie d'artistes qui, ayant sauvé le château de la destruction au siècle dernier, y accueillirent leurs nombreux amis peintres (dont Corot).

Rue principale

Le trésor des collections regroupées dans la salle de Bourgogne est constitué par les trois **chapes**★ de deuil de l'ordre de la Toison d'Or, qui devaient servir aux aumôniers de Charles le Téméraire, appelés à célébrer ces messes solennelles pour le repos des chevaliers défunts au cours de la campagne de 1476. Ces ornements somptueux devinrent, pour les Fribourgeois, le plus glorieux trophée de la bataille de Morat *(voir à ce nom)*. Quatre tapisseries des Flandres du 16e s. se trouvent dans une nouvelle salle.
Un peu partout, au-dessus des portes, sur les plaques de cheminée, sur les vitraux, se retrouve la grue figurant sur le blason des comtes de Gruyères.

Chapelle St-Jean — Du 15e s., elle se dresse sur une terrasse fort agréablement située en vue de la Basse-Gruyère (région de Bulle-Broc) — en partie noyée par le lac artificiel qu'a créé le barrage de Rossens — et des deux pitons de l'élégante Dent de Broc. Reprendre la rue principale qui, suivie en sens inverse, offre une perspective sur le Moléson, le sommet « gruérien » par excellence.

Devant la fontaine du village, tourner à droite.

Le Belluar — Ce pittoresque ouvrage de défense, restauré (dont le nom est de même origine que boulevard), gardait l'entrée principale du bourg au temps des palefrois et des haquenées.

Fromagerie de démonstration ⊙ — *1 km, à l'entrée de Pringy.*
Cette fromagerie modèle comprend, au rez-de-chaussée une cave-entrepôt, au 1er étage le local de salage, au 2e étage les galeries surplombant la salle de démonstration où s'effectue sous les yeux du public la fabrication moderne du gruyère, en meules de 35 kg.

GRUYÈRES

ENVIRONS

Moléson-sur-Gruyères – *6 km au Sud-Ouest.*
Cet accueillant village possède une **fromagerie d'alpage** ⊙ installée dans un chalet du 17ᵉ s., au toit recouvert de plus de 90 000 tavaillons. Un montage audiovisuel est consacré à la fabrication des différents produits du terroir exposés, puis vient la chambre de l'armailli (vacher) telle qu'elle se présente dans les alpages, rudimentaire. On voit ensuite un armailli fabriquer le fromage à l'ancienne dans une grande chaudière alimentée au feu de bois. La chambre à lait contient les produits du jour, les fromages affinés sont ensuite entreposés dans le saloir, petite maison carrée couverte de tavaillons située près de la ferme.
Un téléphérique conduit à l'**observatoire du Moléson** ⊙ (alt. 2 002 m). La vue panoramique s'étend sur le pays de Gruyères et le plateau suisse. Des soirées d'initiation à l'astronomie y sont organisées (télescopes).
En hiver 35 km de pistes balisées offrent de belles descentes à skis.
Installé à Moléson-Village dans les sous-sols du restaurant « La Locanda », un musée de cire, l'**Historial Suisse** ⊙, évoque en plusieurs tableaux des figures célèbres de l'histoire suisse de saint Maurice à Henri Dunant.

GSTAAD★★

Berne – 2 000 habitants
Carte Michelin n° 427 pli 13 ou 217 pli 15 – Schéma : ALPES VAUDOISES – Alt. 1 080 m

Aux confins des Alpes bernoises et des Alpes vaudoises, Gstaad, située à la convergence de quatre vallées mollement ouvertes – haute vallée de la Sarine, vallée de Lauenen, vallée du Turbach et dépression de Saanenmöser – plaît par son cadre reposant et par la variété de ses ressources sportives ou mondaines.
En hiver, saison la plus recherchée par le séjournant sensible à une ambiance élégante, Gstaad peut se prévaloir de la présence assurée de têtes couronnées, de vedettes et autres célébrités. Grâce aux trains bleus du M.O.B., la station exploite alors en commun avec **Saanenmöser** (alt. 1 272 m) (lieu de séjour) et même **Zweisimmen** (lieu de séjour) – doté d'une grande télécabine facilitant l'accès du Rinderberg –, un magnifique domaine skiable desservi par une soixantaine de remontées mécaniques permettant de varier les descentes au gré des préférences de chacun pour telle neige ou telle piste.
Un service d'hélicoptères permet aux touristes de survoler les massifs environnants (héliport de Gstaad-Grund).

*Créez vos propres itinéraires à l'aide
de la carte des principales curiosités en début de guide.*

Val d'HÉRENS★★

Carte Michelin n° 427 pli 22 ou 217 pli 16 et 219 pli 3 – Schéma : VALAIS

La visite du Val d'Hérens, l'une des vallées latérales les plus aisément pénétrables du Valais de langue française, est d'un grand intérêt. La région d'Évolène offre, dans un très beau décor de haute montagne (Dent Blanche), des spectacles de genre de vie traditionnelle qui combleront l'amateur de folklore.

Un musée vivant – Des tableaux comme ceux de la fenaison entre Évolène et les Haudères comptent parmi les spectacles les plus attachants de la Suisse pittoresque. Les habitants de cette haute vallée témoignent en effet d'une rare fidélité à leur costume traditionnel *(voir Introduction : La Suisse pittoresque)*, même au cours de leurs travaux journaliers. A voir ces femmes s'affairer dans les prés, en groupes colorés, caracoler à dos de mulet, ou conduire quelque troupeau de vaches à la robe uniformément brun sombre rappelant la patine des chalets, la tentation est souvent forte d'oublier l'âpreté des conditions de vie montagnardes. Les hommes sont pratiquement absents de ces scènes pastorales. Ils s'embauchent, pour la plupart, dans les grands chantiers ou les usines de la région.

DE SION AUX HAUDÈRES

29 km – environ 2 h – itinéraire ⑤ *de la visite du Valais*

★★**Sion** – *Visite : 3 h. Voir à ce nom.*
Dès le départ de Sion, la route, traversant le Rhône et laissant à droite la centrale de Chandoline, alimentée par le barrage de la Grande Dixence, s'élève en lacet, procurant de bonnes vues sur le site même de Sion, caractérisé par les deux pitons fortifiés de Valère et de Tourbillon.
A l'entrée de Vex, premier village du Val d'Hérens, commence à se dessiner, à l'extrémité de la vallée, la superbe pyramide rocheuse de la Dent Blanche, émergeant du cirque glaciaire de Ferpècle.

Val d'HÉRENS

★★★ **Barrage de la Grande Dixence** – *Voir à ce nom. De Vex, 16 km – environ 2 h par route étroite*. La route, tracée en corniche, à peu près horizontalement, se rapproche des ravinements qui dominent le confluent de la Borgne et de la Dixence. La vue s'attache à l'étonnante lame de terrain ébréchée d'où se sont dégagées les pyramides d'Euseigne.

★ **Pyramides d'Euseigne** – La route passe en tunnel sous ces « colonnes coiffées » dégagées par l'érosion dans des masses de conglomérats morainiques.
Ces conglomérats, peu résistants, sont préservés de la destruction par leur chapiteau rocheux en équilibre instable.
La vallée se rétrécit et la rampe s'accentue.
L'arrivée dans le bassin d'Évolène est marquée par la réapparition de la Dent Blanche. Au premier plan, à droite de celle-ci, se haussent les pyramides jumelles, aux arêtes vives, des Dents de Veisivi.

★ **Évolène** – Cette charmante villégiature, centre d'alpinisme (massifs du mont Collon et de la Dent Blanche) est très fréquentée par les touristes de langue française. Ses **maisons de bois**★★, bâties en hauteur, égayées de fleurs éclatantes, comptent parmi les plus belles du Valais.

Les Haudères – Ce village masse ses chalets dans un pittoresque désordre.
De là, deux routes conduisent, l'une à la station d'alpinisme d'Arolla (alt. 1 998 m – lieu de séjour) à 12 km au pied du mont Collon et l'autre à Ferpècle (alt. 1 770 m), à 9 km au pied de la Dent Blanche.
Elles offrent, lors de la montée aux hameaux de la Sage, de Villa et de la Forclaz, les vues les plus étendues de ce haut Val d'Hérens.

HÖLLOCHGROTTE★

Schwyz
Carte Michelin n° 427 pli 15 ou 218 Nord-Ouest du pli 2

Par l'étendue de ses galeries, le nombre de ses salles, la beauté et la variété de ses concrétions, la grotte du Hölloch est la plus vaste d'Europe et représente un phénomène géologique d'un très grand intérêt.

Accès – Au départ de Schwyz, prendre la route de Muotatal *(voir plan à Schwyz)*, étroite jusqu'à Hinterthal, puis, après avoir traversé la rivière, prendre sur la gauche un chemin qui monte assez fortement en direction de Stalden *(pancarte : Stalden-Hölloch)*.
Laisser la voiture à côté du « Gasthaus zur Höllgrotte », où habite le gardien, et gagner à pied l'entrée de la grotte.

Visite ⊙ – A peine connue au début du 20ᵉ s., la grotte du Hölloch fait l'objet, depuis 1949, d'une exploration continue. Elle est ouverte au public sur un parcours de 1 km, alors que plus de 147 km de galeries ont déjà fait l'objet d'un relevé cartographique.
Cette invraisemblable architecture souterraine est un spectacle fascinant : peu de stalactites ou de stalagmites, mais par contre des apparitions féeriques de concrétions délicates en forme de roses, de chandeliers, de coquillages, qui atténuent l'hostilité des gigantesques parois lisses des gouffres et des marmites d'érosion en pleine activité. Au long des galeries, on découvre en particulier l'« autel » et la « grande pagode ».

INTERLAKEN★★★

Berne – 4 852 habitants
Carte Michelin n° 427 pli 14 ou 217 plis 7, 8 – Alt. 564 m
Plan dans le guide Rouge Michelin Suisse

Foyer touristique de l'Oberland bernois, Interlaken connaît, pendant la saison d'été, une animation digne d'une capitale.

La station – Les consonances latines du nom évoquent les origines cléricales de la ville : celle-ci s'est développée en effet « entre les lacs » à partir du 12ᵉ s., autour d'un couvent d'Augustins dont certains vestiges (galerie du cloître) sont encore reconnaissables dans le bloc de constructions formé par le château et l'église réformée.
Encadrée par les chaînons boisés du Rugen et du Harder, l'agglomération se dispose aujourd'hui, en ordre lâche, sur la plaine basse du Bödeli formée par les atterrissements du Lombach, au Nord, et de la Lütschine, au Sud, qui ont fini par séparer en deux nappes – le lac de Thoune et le lac de Brienz – le bassin lacustre unique dans lequel l'Aare s'engloutissait primitivement entre Meiringen et Thoune.

INTERLAKEN

Interlaken – Vue générale

CURIOSITÉS

★★ Höheweg – Bordée d'un côté par les gazons et les massifs de fleurs de la Höhematte, de l'autre par une rangée de palaces, en retrait desquels se dresse le casino (Kursaal), cette promenade fameuse relie le noyau urbain d'Interlaken-Ouest à l'agglomération beaucoup plus dispersée d'Interlaken-Est. Elle offre des **vues ★★★** éblouissantes sur la cime de la Jungfrau qui s'encadre dans l'échancrure de la basse vallée de la Lütschine. Mais son animation n'est pas moins attachante. Il fait bon flâner sous les ombrages, en jetant un coup d'œil sur le pavillon des appareils météorologiques ou sur l'horloge florale, bien connue, des jardins du casino.
Sur la rive opposée de l'Aare, les installations de la piscine et du golf miniature forment un second centre d'attraction.

Église d'Unterseen – Avec son clocher rustique coiffé d'un toit en bâtière à forte pente, cet édifice compose, avec le Mönch (à gauche) et la Jungfrau (à droite), en arrière-plan, un **site ★★** très pittoresque.

Musée touristique ⊙ – *A Unterseen, Obere Gasse 26.*
Dans une maison du 17ᵉ s. rénovée, ce pimpant petit musée retrace l'essor touristique de la région de la Jungfrau, depuis le début du siècle dernier. Au rez-de-chaussée, un siècle de circulation routière dans l'Oberland est illustré (diligence de la poste de Habkern, maquettes de voitures postales, premier vélo ayant circulé à Interlaken). On découvre également plusieurs Stundensteine, pierres à l'usage des voyageurs qui se rendaient à pied à Berne et sur lesquelles était indiqué le nombre d'heures qui les séparaient de la ville.
Le premier étage évoque le développement des ressources hôtelières ainsi que le développement de la circulation ferroviaire (maquette de la première locomotive du Brünig). Les sports d'hiver (évolution du matériel : skis, luges), le développement des trains de montagne (trains du Giessbach, du Wetterhorn, de la Jungfrau) et l'alpinisme occupent le second étage.
Des expositions temporaires sont organisées sous les combles.

Les autoroutes suisses sont signalées par des panneaux à fond vert et non bleu contrairement à d'autres pays européens. La vitesse est limitée à 120 km/h.
Une vignette collée sur le pare-brise, est obligatoire pour circuler sur les autoroutes. Cette vignette est disponible – au prix de 40 FS – dans les bureaux de douane à la frontière ou dans les bureaux de poste. Tout contrevenant s'expose à une amende.

INTERLAKEN

ENVIRONS
Belvédères proches accessibles en funiculaire ou à pied

★★★ **Schynige Platte** ⊙ — Alt. 2 101 m. *Environ 4 h AR dont 2 h de chemin de fer à crémaillère, partant de la gare de Wilderswil.*
Cette «ascension» est indiquée surtout aux touristes qui n'auraient pas le loisir de pénétrer plus avant dans le massif de la Jungfrau.
Près de la station supérieure ont été aménagés un jardin alpin, une section botanique contenant des plantes alpestres et un hôtel doté d'une terrasse panoramique. Depuis là, il est facile de grimper jusqu'au sommet le plus proche (alt. 2 076 m — belvédère sur la Jungfrau, Interlaken et ses lacs).

★★ **Harderkulm** ⊙ — Alt. 1 323 m. *Environ 1 h AR dont 1/2 h de funiculaire.*
On découvre une vue bien dégagée sur les deux lacs d'Interlaken et sur le massif de la Jungfrau.

★ **Heimwehfluh** ⊙ — Alt. 670 m. *Environ 1/2 h AR, dont 5 mn de funiculaire.*
Cette colline aux frais ombrages forme belvédère sur les lacs de Thoune et de Brienz.

De nombreux sentiers de promenade ombragés sont ouverts aux amateurs de marche, en particulier sur les flancs du Rugen et du Harder.

Excursions en auto ou en téléphérique

★ **Beatenberg ; Niederhorn** ★★ — *Voir à Beatenberg.*

★★★ **Vallée de Lauterbrunnen** — *18 km — environ 3 h dont 2 h 3/4 de téléphérique et de visite. Quitter Interlaken au Sud, route de Grindelwald.*
La route, privant momentanément l'automobiliste de la vue sur la Jungfrau, s'enfonce dans le défilé boisé de la Lütschine.

A la bifurcation de Zweilütschinen, suivre tout droit la branche de Lauterbrunnen (Lütschine Blanche).

La vallée se rouvre bientôt, encadrée, en amont, par les immenses murailles qui font du fossé de Lauterbrunnen un exemple classique d'«auge» glaciaire *(voir le relief alpin dans l'introduction au voyage).*
En avant, de part et d'autre des sombres escarpements du Schwarzmönch, se détachent les sommets neigeux de la Jungfrau (à gauche) et du groupe Mittaghorn-Grosshorn (dans l'axe de la vallée).

Lauterbrunnen — Ce village connaît une intense activité de transit : les automobilistes désirant accéder à Wengen doivent en effet y laisser leur voiture *(parking).*
La **cascade du Staubbach** ★★, que Byron comparait à «la queue du cheval pâle que monte la Mort dans l'Apocalypse», s'abat ici, à 300 m de haut, de la terrasse de Mürren et se vaporise presque entièrement en fines gouttelettes.
Dans l'alignement de la vallée apparaît peu à peu, à droite du Grosshorn, le sommet bien détaché du Breithorn.

Laisser la voiture dans le parc des chutes du Trümmelbach.

★★★ **Chutes du Trümmelbach (Trümmelbachfälle)** ⊙ — *3/4 h à pied AR.* Un ascenseur installé dans le roc donne accès à l'entrée des galeries. Celles-ci, très bien aménagées au-dessus de la fissure tortueuse, sont si étroites parfois que l'éclairage électrique doit y être maintenu en permanence ; le Trümmelbach bondit et tourbillonne, se frayant un passage à travers une succession de gigantesques marmites d'érosion.
Le parcours se termine au fond du puits où la cascade supérieure écrase sa gerbe blafarde. Revenu à l'entrée inférieure du funiculaire, ne pas manquer d'aller voir de près, par le chemin montant à gauche, le formidable jet de l'avant-dernière chute du Trümmelbach.
Reprendre la voiture et remonter la vallée jusqu'à Stechelberg, gare du téléphérique de Mürren-Schilthorn d'où l'on aperçoit, au Sud *(1 km),* la belle et puissante chute quasi verticale de la **cascade de Sefinen** ★ (Sefinenfall).

★★ **Mürren** — *Accès en 10 mn par téléphérique. Voir à ce nom.*

★★★ **Schilthorn** ⊙ — *Environ 2 h AR, dont 1 h de téléphérique passant par Stechelberg. Description à Mürren.*

★★★ **Grindelwald** — *20 km au Sud-Est — environ 3/4 h. Voir à ce nom.* A Zweilütschinen tourner à gauche dans la vallée de la Lütschine Noire, plus mollement évidée que celle de la Lütschine Blanche.
Après avoir gravi par une suite de lacets le ressaut dressé par une ancienne moraine, on commence à découvrir le cadre montagneux de Grindelwald.
Apparaissent ainsi, successivement, de gauche à droite, le groupe du Wetterhorn avec le vaste névé du Grindelwald Firn (origine de l'Oberer Grindelwaldgletscher), le Mettenberg, le glacier inférieur de Grindelwald (Unterer Grindelwaldgletscher) ; enfin, à l'extrémité de longues falaises, la pyramide de l'Eiger.

INTERLAKEN

★★★ **Circuit des Trois Cols** (Grimsel, Furka, Susten) — *191 km — compter une grande journée (partir de bon matin). Quitter Interlaken au Sud-Ouest, route de Meiringen (décrite à Meiringen), puis suivre les routes des Trois Cols en commençant de préférence par le col du Grimsel* (voir à Grimselstrasse).

★ **Vallée de la Kander** — *43 km — environ 3 h. Quitter Interlaken au Sud-Est, route de Spiez. Voir à Kandertal.*

La route est tracée sur la rive Sud du lac de Thoune, face au promontoire boisé du « Nase » et à la terrasse de Beatenberg *(voir à ce nom).*

Après Därligen, un passage en corniche permet de découvrir le lac, dans son entier, et la ville de Thoune, dans le lointain.

A Leissigen, prendre la route d'Aeschi qui franchit le dos de terrain séparant le lac de la vallée de la Kander. Le **panorama**★ d'**Aeschi** — village marquant le sommet de la montée — est d'une belle ampleur. A la découverte du décor montagneux du lac de Thoune succède celle de la gigantesque pyramide du Niesen et — par la trouée du Kiental — des trois sommets neigeux de la Blümlisalp.

La suite de l'excursion, de Reichenbach à Kandersteg, est décrite sous le nom Kandertal.

Après être monté au lac d'Oeschinen, rentrer à Interlaken par Spiez *(voir à ce nom).*

D'autres belles excursions en auto sont possibles, au départ d'Interlaken, dans l'Oberland bernois (voir à ce nom, la liste des itinéraires recommandés).

★★★ **Circuit ferroviaire de la Jungfrau** ⊙

Compter pour ce circuit une journée entière. Le petit train rouge s'ébranle lentement et après plusieurs tunnels et arrêts atteint le « Top of Europe », terme d'un voyage constituant à lui seul une expérience inoubliable, un régal pour les yeux, des sensations fortes. La dénivellation peut atteindre 25 %.

Le touriste séjournant à Interlaken et tenant à monter au Jungfraujoch, choisira son jour de façon à profiter des meilleures conditions météorologiques possibles : un voile de nuages sur les sommets suffit à gâcher l'excursion. Se munir de vêtements chauds et, si l'on veut sortir en plein air au Jungfraujoch, de lunettes de soleil et de fortes chaussures.

Lauterbrunnen ; cascade du Staubbach★★ — *Voir plus haut.*

L'excursion très recommandée aux **chutes du Trümmelbach**★★★ *(Voir plus haut)* demande, à partir d'ici, 1 h 1/2 environ. *Emprunter l'autocar postal assurant la correspondance avec les trains d'Interlaken.*

INTERLAKEN

Wengwald – Alt. 1 182 m. Entre cet arrêt et la station de Wengen, le parcours offre une perspective★★★ splendide sur la fosse de Lauterbrunnen, tandis que, en avant, se dévoile la **Jungfrau**, flanquée à droite du Silberhorn, sommet conique, neigeux, d'une blancheur aveuglante.

★★★ **Wengen** – *Voir à ce nom.*

Wengernalp – Alt. 1 873 m. Site sauvage, au pied des gigantesques gradins rocheux et glaciaires de la Jungfrau. Le gouffre où coule le Trümmelbach, au premier plan, contribue à rendre plus impressionnante encore l'élévation de cette barrière, devant laquelle il est bien rare de passer, aux heures chaudes de la journée, sans voir dégringoler une avalanche. A gauche de la Jungfrau, on reconnaît la dépression neigeuse du Jungfraujoch – terminus de l'excursion (l'observatoire du Sphinx est visible) – puis le Mönch, l'Eigergletscher (glacier de l'Eiger) et l'Eiger.

★★ **Petite** (Kleine) **Scheidegg** – Alt. 2 061 m. Ce centre d'altitude, isolé sur le seuil qui fait communiquer les vallées de Lauterbrunnen et de Grindelwald, est très prisé des skieurs qui y trouvent, fort tard dans la saison, une neige encore abondante. Il reçoit en été les amateurs de calme. Les voyageurs qui ne montent pas au Jungfraujoch pourront admirer le cadre du bassin de Grindelwald et détailler le groupe Eiger-Mönch-Jungfrau dans d'excellentes conditions en montant au **belvédère**★★ aménagé sur les pentes Nord du col *(1/2 h à pied AR)*.

Eigergletscher – Alt. 2 320 m. Cet arrêt, à proximité du front du glacier de l'Eiger, tout craquelé et souillé de dépôts morainiques, marque le début du parcours souterrain de 7 km qui mène au Jungfraujoch. Au printemps, les skieurs friands de fortes dénivellations viennent, en grand nombre, « chausser » ici.

Eigerwand – Alt. 2 865 m. Station creusée dans le roc. Les baies d'aération, ouvertes en pleine face Nord de l'Eiger, permettent d'avoir une vue plongeante sur le bassin de Grindelwald et la région d'Interlaken. La paroi impressionnante donne une idée des dramatiques prouesses auxquelles ont dû se livrer les alpinistes pour la vaincre : la première réussite ne date que de 1938.

★★★ **Jungfraujoch** – *Voir à ce nom.*

Alpiglen – Alt. 1 616 m. A partir de cette station, la ligne, qui avait longé jusque-là le pied de l'Eiger, plonge vers l'ample et verdoyant bassin de Grindelwald, dont les prairies toutes parsemées d'habitations viennent buter contre les épaulements rocheux du Wetterhorn. En avant s'infléchit le seuil pastoral de la Grande Scheidegg.

★★★ **Grindelwald** – Alt. à la gare : 1 057 m. *Voir à ce nom. La station et les promenades les plus recommandées au départ de celle-ci (First et le Bachsee, gorge du Glacier) y sont décrites.*

Excursions en bateau

Les nombreux services de navigation organisés pendant la saison, sur le lac de Thoune (embarcadère dans la gare d'Interlaken-West) et sur le lac de Brienz (embarcadère derrière la gare d'Interlaken-Ost ou à Bönigen) permettent à chacun d'organiser des périples jalonnés d'escales attrayantes, comme celle des **cascades du Giessbach** ★★, principale curiosité des rives du lac de Brienz, ou de participer *(seulement en juillet et août)* à des croisières nocturnes.

Enfin les amateurs de sports nautiques trouveront à la base de Neuhaus, sur le lac de Thoune, des embarcations à louer, des écoles de yachting et de ski nautique.

STATIONS DE SPORTS D'HIVER

	Canton	Altitude
Arosa	Grisons	1 742 m
Crans-Montana	Valais	1 500 m
Davos	Grisons	1 563 m
Gstaad	Berne	1 080 m
Saas-Fee	Valais	1 790 m
St-Moritz	Grisons	1 856 m
Wengen	Berne	1 275 m
Zermatt	Valais	1 620 m

JAUNPASSSTRASSE

Carte Michelin n° 427 plis 12, 13 ou 217 plis 5, 6 et 7

Itinéraire le plus montagnard des Alpes fribourgeoises, la **route du col de Jaun** associe, pour le plaisir des yeux, les plans d'eau, les crêtes rocheuses et les vastes étendues pastorales.

DE SPIEZ A BULLE 63 km – environ 2 h 1/2

★**Spiez** – *Voir à ce nom.*

Une fois disparues les dernières maisons de Spiez, entre Wimmis et Reidenbach, la vallée de la Simme – dont le «Port», défilé rocheux semblable à une entaille dans le verrou de la Burgfluh marque l'entrée aval – se présente comme un couloir coudé aux frais paysages, caractérisé par une organisation agricole extrêmement poussée. De nombreux ponts couverts *(voir Introduction : La Suisse pittoresque)* empruntés par des routes affluentes se succèdent au-dessus du torrent. A l'Est, le grand cône régulier du Niesen s'affirme longtemps à l'arrière-plan.

Erlenbach ; Stockhorn ★★★ – *Voir à Erlenbach.*

De Reidenbach au col de Jaun, la route, plus étroite et multipliant les lacets en terrain découvert, procure des vues de plus en plus lointaines sur la vallée, parsemée de toits rouges, où coule la Simme endiguée. A l'horizon, plein Sud, brillent les neiges du Wildhorn.

Du col de Jaun (alt. 1 509 m ; sports d'hiver) à Jaun, le tracé, moins sinueux mais en plus forte pente que sur le versant bernois, compte de beaux passages en haute corniche, vis-à-vis des **Gastlosen**, escarpements profondément burinés, où les Fribourgeois viennent s'entraîner à la varappe.

Jaun – Ce bourg, tout voisin de la frontière linguistique entre la Suisse romande et la Suisse alémanique, montre encore quelques beaux chalets anciens et une église à toiture de bardeaux. Le site, encaissé, est égayé par le panache d'une abondante cascade.

Charmey – Village dont les environs constituent le principal attrait.

★**Pont du Javroz** – Quitter un instant la route du col de Jaun pour s'engager dans la route de Cerniat, à droite. Garer aussitôt la voiture au parc de stationnement aménagé à droite et descendre les quelques marches qui conduisent au belvédère. L'arche de béton armé, de 85 m de portée, franchit à 60 m de hauteur le profond vallon du Javroz à l'endroit où celui-ci commence à s'engloutir dans les eaux du lac artificiel de Montsalvens.

Jusqu'à la tour de Montsalvens, dont les pans de murs évoquent le passé féodal du comté de Gruyères, la **vallée de la Jogne** (Jauntal), devenue romande, s'épanouit et voit ses versants inférieurs disparaître peu à peu sous les eaux de la retenue ramifiée créée par le barrage de Montsalvens.

Comme en d'autres régions des Alpes, les agriculteurs utilisaient naguère ici pour rentrer les récoltes, de curieux véhicules, mi-traîneaux, mi-chars, bien adaptés au relief du pays. Une course de ces engins a lieu chaque année à Charmey *(voir tableau des Principales manifestations)*. Le trajet devient fortement accidenté entre la tour de Montsalvens et Bulle pour descendre vers le fond des ravins où coulent la Jogne et la Sarine et traverser ces torrents. Il offre alors des vues agréables sur le Pays de Gruyères, dominé par le Moléson.

Broc – Du jardin belvédère aménagé devant l'hôtel de ville, très jolie **vue**★ sur le site de Gruyères avec à l'arrière-plan les trois sommets familiers du pays : Vanil Blanc, Vudalla, Moléson.

Bulle – *Voir à ce nom.*

★★**Gruyères** – *Allongement de parcours de 7 km – compter en plus 1 h pour la visite de Gruyères (voir à ce nom).*

Vallée de JOUX ★★

Carte Michelin n° 427 pli 11 ou 217 plis 2, 12 – Schéma : JURA SUISSE

Fleuron du Jura vaudois, la vallée de Joux et son lac constituent un intermède aussi reposant qu'agréable sur l'itinéraire mouvementé qui conduit de la frontière française aux rivages du Léman.

DE VALLORBE A NYON

57 km – environ 3 h – itinéraire [2] *de la visite du Jura suisse*

La route du Marchairuz (le Brassus-St-George) est généralement obstruée par la neige de novembre à avril.

Vallorbe – *Voir à ce nom.*

Depuis Vallorbe, la route grimpe rapidement au flanc du raide versant boisé qui domine la «source» de l'Orbe *(voir à ce nom)* et passe au pied des escarpements de la Dent de Vaulion.

Vallée de JOUX

★★★ **Dent de Vaulion** – *De la station du Pont, 12 km – environ 1/2 h de route – par la route de Vaulion, puis le chemin de la Dent, à gauche, plus 1/2 h à pied AR. Description à ce nom.*

★★ **Vallée de Joux** – La route débouche ensuite dans la vallée de Joux mollement évidée entre les chaînons du mont Risoux et du mont Tendre. Au petit lac Brenet, autour duquel se disséminent les villas et les hôtels de la station du Pont (lieu de séjour), fait suite le lac de Joux, le plus vaste du Jura. Il étale ses eaux calmes que fige, pendant de longs mois, le rigoureux hiver des montagnes jurassiennes. Jusqu'aux années qui suivirent la guerre de 1914, sa glace découpée en blocs réguliers était entreposée au Pont dans des «glacières» souterraines avant d'être expédiée vers Paris par chemin de fer.

On longe la rive Sud du lac, bordée de collines boisées et d'amples prairies où s'échelonnent des villages accueillants qui sont à la fois d'agréables villégiatures et de petites cités animées par l'activité horlogère.

La montée s'amorçant au Brassus (lieu de séjour) pour finir au col du Marchairuz procure de plaisantes vues en enfilade sur le lac de Joux et sa vallée, que ferme l'éperon hardi de la Dent de Vaulion.

Combe des Amburnex – *De la route du col, 8,5 km.* Le chemin de la combe des Amburnex s'amorce un peu en contrebas du col du Marchairuz, sur le versant de la vallée de Joux. Sa chaussée est coupée de barrières qu'il faut refermer derrière soi. *Ne pas faire rouler la voiture sur les herbages. Zone militaire.* Les touristes recherchant un lieu de halte tranquille trouveront à cette combe, très retirée, un charme fait de paix profonde et d'isolement.

Sur le versant de Nyon, le trajet, qui réserve des vues admirables sur le Mont Blanc comporte deux passages d'allure différente :

- **entre le col et St-George**, la descente, sous bois, est coupée de larges replats de clairières, d'où se découvrent déjà, par échappées, le lac Léman et ses grandes cités riveraines (Lausanne, Thonon, Genève – facile à repérer en été, grâce au panache de son immense jet d'eau) ;

- **entre St-George et Nyon**, le Mont Blanc apparaît à peu près constamment.

Zoo de la Garenne ⊙ – Ce petit zoo présente dans ses enclos, cages, aquariums et vivariums un bon échantillonnage d'espèces surtout européennes (loup, chien viverrin, lynx, aigle...).

Le parcours en lacet qui sépare Burtigny de Begnins offre, en outre, des **vues**★★ très dégagées sur la rive savoyarde du Léman – remarquer la pointe d'Yvoire –, ses villes, ses montagnes (de gauche à droite : Dent d'Oche, Voirons, Salève) et sur les crêtes du Jura qui forment rempart au-dessus du Pays de Gex. L'arrivée à Nyon est imminente.

★ **Nyon** – *Visite : 1 h. Voir à ce nom.*

JUNGFRAUJOCH★★★

Berne

Carte Michelin n° 427 pli 14 ou 217 pli 18 – Schéma : INTERLAKEN – Alt. 3 475 m

Cette station de haute altitude – la plus haute desservie par un **chemin de fer à crémaillère** en Europe (sur le **circuit ferroviaire** ⊙ de la Jungfrau au départ d'Interlaken) – offre par beau temps au touriste, outre des points de vue uniques, un grand choix d'attractions (traîneaux à chiens, «Palais de la Glace»). Dans le domaine sportif, le Jungfraujoch est surtout un centre de ski alpin d'été.

Depuis la terrasse du plateau du Jungfraujoch et les belvédères du piton rocheux du «Sphinx», la vue s'étend au Sud jusqu'à l'immense coulée glaciaire d'Aletsch.

Au Nord se découvre la région d'Interlaken. Dans le lointain, s'estompent les crêtes du Jura, des Vosges et de la Forêt-Noire. *Ne pas s'aventurer sans un guide en dehors des pistes battues.*

Participez à notre effort permanent de mise à jour.

Adressez-nous vos remarques et vos suggestions.

Cartes et Guides Michelin
46 avenue de Breteuil
75341 Paris Cedex 07

141

Le JURA SUISSE ★★

Carte Michelin n° 427 plis 3, 4, 11, 12 ou 216 plis 2 à 5, 12 à 16
ou 217 plis 2 à 4, 11 et 12 et 70 plis 7 à 9, 16 et 17
Pour le Jura français, voir le guide Vert Michelin Jura

Le Jura suisse touristique, pour prestigieux que soient ses grands belvédères, n'est pas uniquement le spectateur des Alpes et mérite mieux qu'une rapide traversée. De « val » en « cluse », de pré-bois en forêt, l'automobiliste pourra trouver ici toute une gamme de sites rendant très harmonieuse la transition entre les terres burgondes de la plaine de la Saône et le « Moyen-Pays » suisse, de civilisation alémanique.

Le bouclier de la Suisse – Le Jura a représenté, au cours de l'histoire, pour la Confédération, beaucoup plus un glacis de protection qu'un foyer de démocratie. Sa majeure partie est restée découpée, politiquement, au profit des villes de la périphérie comme au temps où les princes de Neuchâtel et les évêques de Bâle détenaient les clés de ses principaux passages.

Ainsi peut-on encore parler de Jura vaudois, neuchâtelois, bernois, soleurois et bâlois, malgré la constitution, en 1978, d'un « canton du Jura » aux dépens de l'extrémité Nord du Jura bernois.

Cette dispersion politique n'a pas contrarié gravement le développement économique du Jura suisse, garanti depuis le début du 18e s. par l'industrie horlogère, née au Locle et à la Chaux-de-Fonds et qui s'est étendue à des villes comme Neuchâtel, Bienne ou Porrentruy.

La traversée du Jura – L'automobiliste venant de France suivra de préférence les routes du Pichoux, de la Vue des Alpes ou de Joux qui réservent, en fin de parcours, des vues dégagées sur le Plateau suisse (le « Moyen-Pays »), ses lacs et la chaîne des Alpes.

Parmi les passages transversaux du Jura, la route du Chasseral, entre St-Imier et le lac de Bienne, mérite d'être associée aux itinéraires décrits.

De nombreuses autres traversées du Jura offrent, sur de plus courtes sections, un intérêt panoramique soutenu, comme la route de la Cure à Nyon par St-Cergue (n° 90).

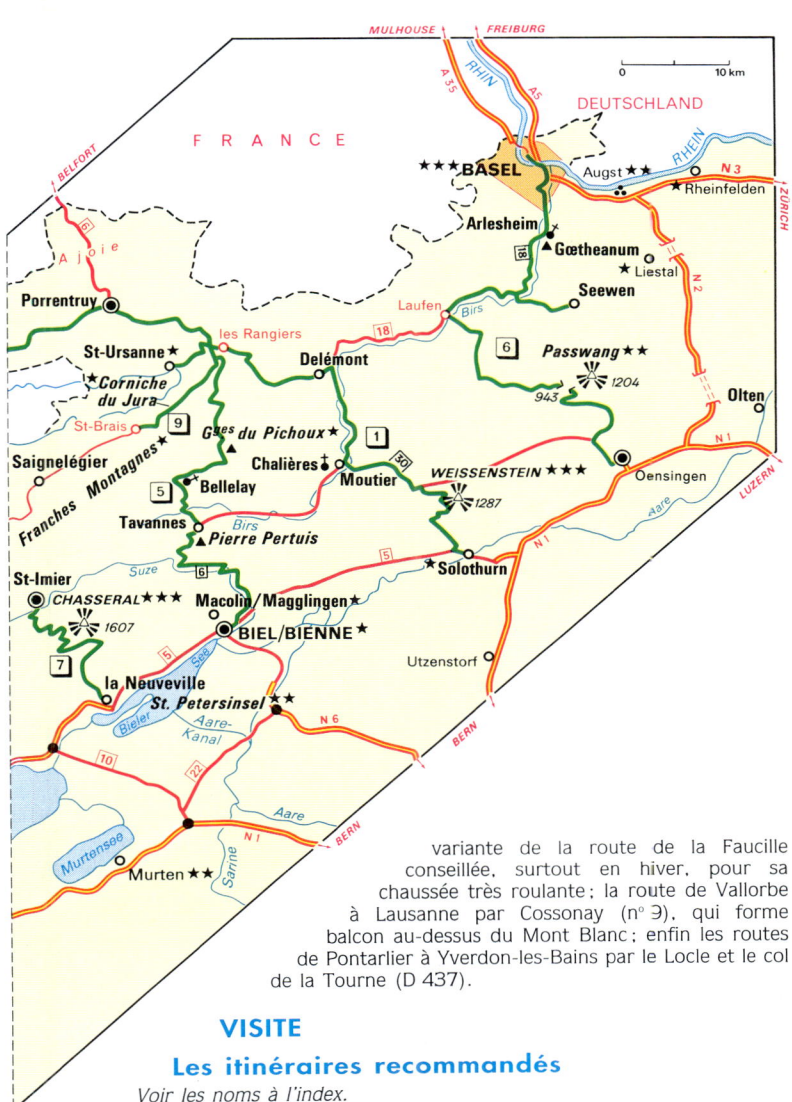

variante de la route de la Faucille conseillée, surtout en hiver, pour sa chaussée très roulante ; la route de Vallorbe à Lausanne par Cossonay (n° 9), qui forme balcon au-dessus du Mont Blanc ; enfin les routes de Pontarlier à Yverdon-les-Bains par le Locle et le col de la Tourne (D 437).

VISITE

Les itinéraires recommandés

Voir les noms à l'index.

★★ 1 **Weissensteinstrasse** – De Porrentruy à Soleure – environ 4 h 1/2.

★★ 2 **Vallée de Joux** – Route de Vallorbe à Nyon – environ 3 h.

3 **Val de Travers** – Route de Fleurier à Noiraigue – environ 3 h.

★★ 4 **Bassins du Doubs** – Visite en bateau, en auto et à pied – environ 2 h 1/2.

★ 5 **Gorges du Pichoux** – Route de Bienne à Porrentruy – environ 2 h 1/2.

6 **Passwangstrasse** – D'Oensingen à Bâle environ 2 h 1/4.

★★★ 7 **Le Chasseral** – Route de St-Imier à la Neuveville – environ 1 h 1/2.

★★ 8 **Route de la Vue des Alpes** – De la Chaux-de-Fonds à Neuchâtel – environ 3/4 h.

★ 9 **Franches Montagnes** – Corniche du Jura : route au départ des Rangiers – environ 1/2 h.

La Suisse sibérienne...

En hiver, dans le village de la Brévine et dans la région du même nom (canton de Neuchâtel), la température peut descendre jusqu'à - 40° (le record a été atteint le 12 janvier 1987 avec une température de - 41° 8).

KANDERSTEG★

Berne — 1 077 habitants
Carte Michelin n° 427 pli 13 ou 217 Nord-Ouest du pli 17
Schéma : BERNER OBERLAND – Alt. 1 176 m

Au pied d'escarpements déchiquetés encadrant, à l'Est, les sommets neigeux de la Blümlisalp et plongeant dans un frais bassin alpestre, Kandersteg est connue aujourd'hui, surtout, pour sa position à la tête Nord du **tunnel du Lötschberg**. Ce tunnel ferroviaire de 14 612 m (Kandersteg-Goppenstein) permet, depuis 1913, une liaison directe entre Berne et la vallée du Rhône. *Pour le transport des automobiles, se renseigner dans les bureaux de l'O.N.S.T. ou dans les gares.*

★★★ **Lac d'Oeschinen** ⊙ – *Environ 1 h 1/2 AR dont 7 mn de télésiège et 20 mn de marche.* La route menant à la station inférieure du télésiège se détache de la rue principale de Kandersteg aussitôt après le pont sur l'Oeschinenbach, à gauche. De la station supérieure, un chemin descend au bord du lac *(après 5 mn de marche, bifurquer à droite)* baignant un vaste amphithéâtre de falaises, couronnées par les neiges de la Blümlisalp. Arrivés au lac, les promeneurs un peu entraînés à la marche redescendront à pied à Kandersteg, par le chemin direct.

★★ **Klus** – *2,5 km, plus 1 h à pied AR.* Suivre la rue principale de Kandersteg en direction du fond de la vallée et laisser la voiture à la gare inférieure du téléphérique de Stock. Continuer alors à remonter, à pied, la petite route qui bientôt s'accroche à la paroi rocheuse et débouche, par un tunnel, au-dessus de la Klus, gorge sauvage où la Kander, descendue du Gasterntal, bondit impétueusement de chute en chute. Progresser jusqu'au pont jeté sur la Kander, après un second tunnel. A la descente, les touristes ingambes emprunteront, de préférence, le sentier escarpé, parfois aspergé d'écume, qui se détache de la route entre les deux tunnels.

Lac d'Oeschinen

KANDERTAL★

Carte Michelin n° 427 pli 13 ou 217 plis 7, 17 – Schéma : BERNER OBERLAND

Du lac de Thoune au lac d'Oeschinen, cette vallée se divise en deux parties : d'abord le Frutigtal, vers Frutigen ; puis le Kandertal, vers Kandersteg.

DE SPIEZ A KANDERSTEG

39 km – environ 2 h 1/2 – itinéraire ② *de la visite de l'Oberland bernois*

Cet itinéraire se termine en cul-de-sac à Kandersteg ; mais le chemin de fer est équipé pour transporter les autos par le tunnel du Lötschberg.

★ **Spiez** – *Voir à ce nom.*
Franchissant le dos de terrain qui sépare Spiez de la Kander, la route, tracée à mi-pente, s'abaisse vers le fond de la vallée pour contourner l'énorme pyramide du Niesen, d'une pureté de lignes quasi géométrique.

KANDERTAL

★★★ **Montée au Niesen** ⊙ – Alt. 2 362 m. *De la gare de Mülenen, 2 h AR environ dont 1 h de funiculaire.* Le funiculaire, s'élevant au-dessus du Frutigtal, puis l'accès final au sommet *(signal)* font découvrir un admirable **panorama**★★★, tant sur les Alpes bernoises et le lac de Thoune que sur le Plateau et le Jura.

En avant, par la trouée du Kiental, émergent les trois sommets de la Blümlisalp, que l'on admire surtout des abords de Reichenbach. Au-delà de Reichenbach, la vallée s'épanouit et s'infléchit vers le Sud. Parmi les habitations on remarque de nombreuses constructions neuves, absolument conformes à l'architecture traditionnelle de l'Oberland bernois. Précédant Frutigen, en avant et à gauche, au fond d'un nouvel alignement de la vallée de la Kander, brillent les glaces du Balmhorn et de l'Altels.

Frutigen – *1/4 h à pied AR pour monter à l'église (route d'Adelboden puis la première rampe à droite).* Ce gros bourg situé au confluent de la Kander et de l'Engstligen, torrent descendu d'Adelboden, est un des séjours de moyenne altitude les mieux équipés de la région du Lötschberg.

L'église, construite sur la hauteur, en vue du Balmhorn et de l'Altels, bénéficie d'une **présentation**★ ravissante au milieu des gazons et des arbres de son enclos.

★★ **Adelboden** – *Voir à ce nom.*

Passant la Kander au pied des ruines du Tellenburg on se rapproche du ressaut de Bühlstutz. Celui-ci, séparant le palier de Kandergrund du bassin de Kandersteg, force la voie ferrée du Lötschberg à adopter un tracé en lacet, autour des ruines du Felsenburg, bien découpées sur leur éperon.

★ **Lac Bleu (Blausee)** ⊙ – *3/4 h environ de marche et de promenade en bateau.* Ce site comporte un petit lac aux eaux bleues cristallines, arrondissant sa vasque en pleine forêt, en vue de la cime neigeuse du Doldenhorn, mais aussi un «chaos» rocheux et boisé, un élevage de truites, un restaurant.

La route attaque ensuite le ressaut de Bühlstutz, dans un décor plus sévère de prés-bois accidentés entrecoupés de rocs. On débouche enfin dans le bassin de Kandersteg, aux rudes escarpements tout rayés de cascades.

KIPPEL★

Valais – 370 habitants
Carte Michelin n° 427 pli 13 ou 217 pli 17 – Schéma : VALAIS

Le berceau alpestre du **Lötschental**★, parcouru par la Lonza, puissant affluent de la rive droite du Rhône, est resté une cellule à peu près complètement isolée du reste du monde jusqu'à l'ouverture, en 1913, du tunnel du Lötschberg entre Kandersteg et Goppenstein. Auparavant, en l'absence d'un chemin d'entretien facile dans les défilés inférieurs de la Lonza, balayés par les avalanches, les relations avec l'extérieur ne pouvaient guère se pratiquer que par des cols dépassant 2 500 m d'altitude.

La fidélité de la population du Lötschental à son mode de vie ancestral incitera l'automobiliste partant du Valais à entreprendre l'excursion à Kippel.

Accès – *De la bifurcation de Gampel à Kippel, 12 km – environ 3/4 h.* La route en forte rampe remonte les sauvages gorges de la Lonza inférieure, en contrebas des nombreux ouvrages d'art de la ligne du Lötschberg. Elle débouche, après Goppenstein, dans la vaste combe du Lötschental, doucement évasée.

★ **Le village** – C'est le village le plus typique de la vallée. Les rues du quartier de l'église présentent d'admirables ensembles de **maisons de bois**★★ noircies, finement décorées de frises en dents d'engrenage et de rosettes.

Les rassemblements de population que provoque la grand-messe font du dimanche et des jours de fêtes religieuses les jours les plus indiqués à l'amateur de folklore, mais c'est la procession de la Fête-Dieu *(voir tableau des Principales Manifestations)* qui, avec son défilé de «grenadiers du Bon Dieu» – les hommes du pays sortent, pour la circonstance, tout un arsenal anachronique de plumets, d'oursons, de buffleteries – tous drapeaux déployés, offre le spectacle le plus coloré.

Blatten – *4 km au départ de Kippel.* Ce petit parcours met en relief, dans un cadre de plus en plus sauvage, le charme et la rudesse de la vallée.

*Chaque année
le guide Rouge Michelin Suisse
rassemble, sous un format maniable, une multitude de renseignements à jour.
Emportez-le dans vos déplacements d'affaires,
　　　　lors de vos sorties de week-end,
　　　　　　en vacances.
Tout compte fait, le guide de l'année, c'est une économie.*

KLAUSENPASSSTRASSE ★★

Carte Michelin n° 427 pli 15 ou 218 plis 1, 2

Mettant en communication les vallées de la Reuss (canton d'Uri) et de la Linth (canton de Glarus), la route du Klausen est bien près de résumer tous les aspects physiques et économiques de la Suisse montagnarde. En moins de 50 km, le voyageur passe, ici, d'une haute combe alpestre, sauvage et primitive (Urner Boden) à une vallée comptant parmi les plus industrielles de la chaîne (vallée de la Linth).

D'ALTDORF A LINTHAL 48 km – environ 2 h

La route du Klausen est interdite aux véhicules tirant une remorque.
Le col du Klausen est généralement obstrué par la neige de novembre à mai.

Altdorf – *Voir à ce nom.*

Bürglen – Guillaume Tell serait né dans ce village où un **musée** ⊙ lui est consacré. Il réunit des chroniques, documents, sculptures, tableaux et objets divers créés sur le thème du héros national au cours de six siècles.
Entre Bürglen et Unterschächen, la route, jalonnée de chapelles, est d'abord tracée au fond de la coupure verdoyante où bouillonne le Schächen. Cette coupure va s'évasant vers l'amont et se couvre de frênes, d'érables et d'arbres fruitiers ; mais le versant Sud annonce déjà des passages plus sévères.
D'Unterschächen au col, deux grands lacets, aménagés face au débouché du Brunnital, vallon affluent se terminant en cirque au pied des parois du Ruchen et des Windgällen, font gagner Urigen, point d'origine d'un magnifique **parcours en corniche ★★** : désormais la vue plonge sur le sauvage cul-de-sac du Haut-Schächental fermé par les falaises gigantesques du Chammliberg. Le virage que signale un bloc rocheux isolé, du côté de l'escarpement (600 m en amont du 1er tunnel rencontré à la montée sur ce versant) forme **belvédère ★** sur la cascade du **Stäubi** (Stäubifall) et le hameau d'Aesch, à 400 m en contrebas. Les corniches neigeuses rebondies des Clarides se détachent derrière le Chammliberg.

★ Col du Klausen – Alt. 1 948 m. Les automobilistes font ordinairement halte en contrebas du col géographique, sur le versant du Schächental, à l'hôtel Klausenpasshöhe. Des abords de l'établissement sont visibles, de gauche à droite, les crêtes neigeuses des Clarides (Clariden), les falaises du Chammliberg, le double sommet du Schärhorn, les cornes rocheuses des Windgällen, enfin, dans l'axe de la trouée du Schächen, le massif de l'Uri-Rotstock, à l'horizon.
Après avoir dépassé les masures de Vorfrütt, on admire la face Nord des Clarides et la «Chlus», cirque rayé de deux cascades.

★ Urner Boden – Le passage au fond de cette gouttière, d'une régularité de traits schématique, se traduit, pour l'automobiliste, par un long palier, inattendu à pareille altitude (1 300 à 1 400 m). Le clocher du hameau principal, fiché au beau milieu de la dépression, est une des attractions de la descente du col du Klausen. Les lacets se multiplient à nouveau jusqu'à Linthal : c'est la vallée de la Linth, mi-agreste, mi-usinière *(lire « une ruche industrielle », à Glarus)*, qui se creuse maintenant en contrebas, butant, en amont, contre les murailles du Selbsanft (massif du Tödi).

KLOSTERS ★★

Grisons – 3 542 habitants
Carte Michelin n° 427 pli 17 ou 218 Est du pli 5 – Schéma : GRAUBÜNDEN – Alt. 1 194 m

Dans le cadre encore tout campagnard du Prättigau, Klosters constitue une villégiature d'été et d'hiver très complètement équipée : en été, les découpures de la Silvretta incitent les alpinistes à entreprendre de captivantes courses en montagne.
En hiver, les téléphériques de Gotschnagrat et de Madrisa ou les navettes ferroviaires Klosters-Davos, conduisent aux champs de neige fameux de la « Parsenn » *(voir à Davos)*.
Pendant les mois de mars et d'avril, des « semaines d'excursion de ski de printemps » sont organisées, sous la conduite de guides, dans les massifs de la Silvretta et de la Vereina.

Actualisée en permanence,
la carte Michelin au 200 000ᵉ bannit l'inconnu de votre route.
Elle permet de choisir d'un seul coup d'œil :
  – une route principale pour un grand itinéraire,
  – une route de liaison régionale ou de dégagement,
  – une petite route où il fait bon flâner.
Équipez votre voiture de cartes Michelin à jour.

Abbaye de KÖNIGSFELDEN

Argovie

Carte n° 427 pli 5 ou 216 pli 6 – à l'Ouest de Baden entre Brugg et Windisch

Cette abbaye franciscaine a été fondée en 1308 par la reine Élisabeth et la famille de Habsbourg à l'endroit où le roi Albert Ier fut assassiné par le duc Jean de Souabe. Les bâtiments conventuels servent actuellement d'asile psychiatrique.

Église (Klosterkirche) ⊘ – Situé dans un joli parc, ce sanctuaire désaffecté, de style gothique, a dû être restauré.

La nef, éclairée par des fenêtres hautes, est couverte d'un plafond plat, en bois. Les bas-côtés sont décorés de panneaux de bois peints : portraits de chevaliers, blasons. Dans la nef, un monument funéraire rappelle que Königsfelden fut le St-Denis des Habsbourg.

Le **chœur**★, profond, est éclairé par onze fenêtres dont les **vitraux**★, exécutés de 1325 à 1330, forment un ensemble intéressant. On reconnaît l'Enfance du Christ, la Passion, des scènes de la Vie des Saints, la Mort de la Vierge. Les tons, où domine le jaune d'argent, sont chatoyants, et le dessin, à la grisaille, d'une grande finesse d'exécution.

*Horaires de travail et jours fériés en Suisse,
lisez le chapitre « Renseignements pratiques ».*

KREUZLINGEN

Thurgovie – 17 239 habitants

Carte Michelin n° 427 pli 7 ou 216 plis 9, 10 – Alt. 407 m

Bâtie sur une ancienne moraine du glacier du Rhin, Kreuzlingen ne forme avec la ville allemande de Constance qu'une seule agglomération que divise la frontière. La ville doit son nom à une relique de la Vraie Croix (Kreuz) rapportée de Terre Sainte au 10e s. et conservée dans la basilique.

Basilique St-Ulrich – Ancienne église du couvent des Augustins, elle a été construite au 17e s. dans sa forme actuelle, et décorée intérieurement au 18e s. dans le style baroque. Ravagée par un incendie en 1963, elle est restaurée en 1967.

La chapelle du Mont des Oliviers renferme un extraordinaire groupe de 250 figurines en bois, disposées dans une curieuse rocaille et représentant les scènes de la Passion. Ces figurines, de 30 cm de haut environ, furent exécutées au début du 18e s. par un sculpteur tyrolien ; elles ne lui demandèrent pas moins de dix-huit années de travail. Le chœur est fermé par une belle grille de fer forgé.

ENVIRONS

Gottlieben – *4 km à l'Ouest par la route n° 13.*

A l'extrémité orientale de l'Untersee (lac inférieur), Gottlieben possède un château du 13e s., transformé au 19e s. L'édifice servit de prison, au 15e s., au pape déchu Jean III et au réformateur Jean Hus. Le prince Louis-Napoléon Bonaparte, futur Napoléon III, y résida en 1837 et 1838. Près du château, maintes maisons à colombage forment un ensemble pittoresque.

LANGNAU IM EMMENTAL★

Berne – 8 940 habitants

Carte Michelin n° 427 pli 13 ou 217 pli 7 – Schéma : EMMENTAL

Cette charmante cité, bordée par l'Ilfis, qu'enjambe un pont couvert, vit du commerce du bois et du fromage d'Emmental, dont elle est le principal centre exportateur.

Musée régional (Heimatmuseum) ⊘ – Installé dans un vaste chalet fleuri du 16e s., le «Chüechlihus», il expose des collections d'artisanat traditionnel (céramique, verrerie) et d'objets représentatifs des industries locales, avec leurs ateliers de fabrication (fromagerie de montagne), une chambre à mobilier de bois peint du 18e s., des ustensiles ménagers, horloges, instruments de musique et uniformes militaires anciens...

En face du musée, l'église réformée (17e s.) a gardé d'origine une chaire de pierre tarabiscotée et une douzaine de petits vitraux armoriés.

★ **Bois de Dürsrüti** – *3 km au Nord (à droite de la route de Burgdorf).*

Futaie de sapins géants, qui couronne une colline offrant des vues sur la vallée de Langnau.

LAUSANNE★★

C Vaud – 128 112 habitants
Carte Michelin n° 427 pli 11 ou 217 plis 3, 13 – Schéma : Lac LÉMAN – Alt. 455 m
Plan d'agglomération dans le guide Rouge Michelin Suisse

A Lausanne, cité avenante et cosmopolite, règne une douceur de vivre qu'apprécient les étudiants de son Université et la haute société, séduite par les perspectives sur le Léman et les Alpes.

La ville est bâtie sur un terrain mouvementé. Après avoir vécu, plusieurs siècles durant, sur le promontoire de la Cité actuelle, elle s'est épanouie vers le midi jusqu'aux délicieux rivages d'Ouchy, ancien hameau de pêcheurs. Ses quartiers neufs contrastent avec les vieilles rues étroites et déclives qui conduisent à la cathédrale.

L'animation se concentre surtout dans le quartier délimité par la place de la Riponne, la rue de Bourg, la place St-François, la rue du Grand-Chêne et la place Bel-Air reliée par le Grand Pont qui franchit le vallon où coulait autrefois le torrent du Flon.

Ville d'art et de spectacles, Lausanne bénéficie d'un renom international pour ses concerts de musique classique donnés par l'Orchestre de la Suisse Romande ou l'Orchestre de Chambre de Lausanne et pour sa troupe de ballet dirigée par Maurice Béjart (Béjart Ballet Lausanne). Le Palais de Beaulieu et le Théâtre Municipal accueillent maints spectacles de musique et de danse.

Ville olympique, Lausanne ou plus précisément Vidy, est le siège du Comité international olympique (C.I.O.) fondé en 1894 par le baron Pierre de Coubertin, et installé dans un immeuble moderne en verre fumé noir. Depuis juin 1993, le musée olympique, installé à Ouchy, fait de Lausanne la **capitale mondiale du Mouvement Olympique**.

UN PEU D'HISTOIRE

Lausanne primitive – Des fouilles ont montré que la Lausanne primitive se trouvait à l'emplacement de la Cité actuelle dressée sur son promontoire, où l'on a trouvé des squelettes néolithiques. Au Sud-Ouest, à **Vidy**, a été mis au jour un quartier de l'ancienne « Lousonna » avec, notamment, un tronçon de voie romaine, sur laquelle est construite précisément l'arrivée de l'autoroute Genève-Lausanne.

SORTIR A LAUSANNE

Pour tout renseignement, s'adresser à l'Office du tourisme, 2, avenue de Rhodanie, ☎ (021) 617 14 27.

Shopping

On trouvera, dans la vieille ville, l'essentiel des rues commerçantes. Parmi celles-ci : place St-François, rue des Terreaux, rue de l'Ale, rue Maubourget, rue Chaucrau, rue St-Laurent, rue du Bourg, rue St-Jean, rue St-François.
Grand magasin : Innovation (rue Centrale).

Théâtre et musique

La saison bat son plein de septembre à juin.
Théâtre Arsenic, 57, rue de Genève, ☎ (021) 625 11 22. Centre d'art scénique contemporain.
Théâtre Vidy-Lausanne, 5, avenue E. Jacques-Dalcroze, ☎ (021) 617 91 44. Créations théâtrales.
L'Octogone, 1, avenue de Lavaux-Pully, ☎ (021) 721 36 20. Théâtre, concerts, danse.
Le petit théâtre, 3, rue Curtat, ☎ (021) 323 62 13. Pièces également pour enfants.

Où prendre un verre ? Où finir la soirée ?

Le quartier d'Ouchy, dans son cadre magnifique en bordure du lac, est toujours très fréquenté de jour comme de nuit. Les nombreuses terrasses ne désemplissent pas en été quand le soleil est de la partie. Soirées avec disc-jockey au **Sherlock's Pub** (avenue de Rhodanie) dans un décor de pub anglais. On peut aller danser au **Château d'Ouchy** (place du Port) ou tout simplement regarder en dégustant un cocktail. Dans le cadre majestueux du **Beau Rivage**, le **James** (place du Général-Gruisan) est très prisé avec sa discothèque et son piano-bar.

Pour les amateurs de bière, le **Bavaria** (rue du Petit Chêne), l'un des plus vieux bistrots de la ville (1872) propose un choix de 22 bières à déguster comme il se doit.

A l'**Edelweiss** (rue de Genève), on peut dîner dans un cadre typique animé par un groupe folklorique et populaire suisse.

Le jazz est roi au **Pianissimo** (rue des Deux-Marchés) où le pianiste interprète brillamment des morceaux de choix. Au **V.O.** (place du Tunnel), des concerts jazz-soul et parfois rock sont organisés.

LAUSANNE

La cité épiscopale – A la fin du 6ᵉ s., le premier évêque, saint Maire, vient s'installer dans la cité. Au Moyen Âge, la prépondérance religieuse s'accompagne d'un développement économique et politique ; la ville s'accroît des quartiers de la place de la Palud, du Bourg, de St-Pierre, St-Laurent, St-François.
Au 13ᵉ s., de nombreux ordres religieux s'y établissent et le prince-évêque Guillaume de Champvent consacre la cathédrale au milieu de fêtes grandioses, tandis que le pape Grégoire X célèbre la dédicace en présence de l'empereur Rodolphe Iᵉʳ de Habsbourg. Le centre religieux et intellectuel est la Cité ou ville haute, alors que l'activité commerciale se manifeste surtout dans les bourgs adjacents.

De la Réforme à la domination bernoise – La Réforme remporte un succès total à Lausanne : elle y est prêchée en 1529 par l'un des plus célèbres humanistes français, le Dauphinois Guillaume Farel, disciple de Lefèvre d'Étaples. En 1536, les Bernois, déjà acquis à la Réforme, occupent militairement la ville ainsi que tout le Pays de Vaud. Les églises de Lausanne autres que la cathédrale et St-François disparaissent.
En 1723, les Bernois répriment durement une tentative des Vaudois pour retrouver leur indépendance : le major Davel, principal instigateur de la sédition, est décapité à Vidy. En 1803, le Pays de Vaud accède à l'autonomie politique.

Le siècle des lumières et son héritage – Au 18ᵉ s., Lausanne ressent l'influence des Encyclopédistes. Voltaire y fait jouer « Zaïre ». Les salons littéraires fleurissent. Benjamin Constant, l'auteur d'Adolphe, naît à Lausanne en 1767. L'Université, installée en partie dans l'« Académie » du 16ᵉ siècle, en perpétue brillamment les traditions. Des éditeurs très actifs secondent son rayonnement et les « témoins illustres » ne lui ont jamais manqué : Sainte-Beuve prononça à Lausanne son discours sur Port-Royal et Gide adapta « Les Caves du Vatican » au théâtre pour une Société d'étudiants.
Mais les gloires locales sont le docteur Tissot – vivant au 18ᵉ siècle – qui fut dénommé le « médecin de l'Europe malade », le docteur Jules Gonin, spécialiste de l'opération du décollement de la rétine, et Maurice Lugeon, mort en 1953, qui fut l'un des grands géologues de notre temps : ses études sur les Alpes font autorité.

★★ OUCHY

Devenue le « front du lac » de Lausanne, Ouchy constitue un centre hôtelier très réputé et un lieu de promenade très prisé par les Lausannois, le dimanche après-midi notamment. Les bateaux du Léman qui proposent plusieurs types de croisières sur le lac contribuent fortement à son animation. En effet, Ouchy est la base de navigation la plus animée du Léman, disposant d'un vaste port de plaisance à hauteur de la place de la Navigation. Réaménagée, celle-ci a été rendue aux piétons qui peuvent désormais profiter de ses fontaines et de ses 4 échiquiers géants.
Les quais ombragés, fleuris de plantes aux essences exotiques, s'allongent sur plus d'un kilomètre et se prolongent, à l'Est, par le sentier du Bord du Lac, offrant tout le long du parcours des **vues**★★ ravissantes sur le port, le Léman et les monts du Chablais.
Ouchy est reliée à Lausanne par le « métro », funiculaire à traction électrique qui autrefois fut familièrement appelé la ficelle (traction par câble) et plus tard le pneu (monté sur pneus).

★★ **Musée Olympique** (**DZ**) ⊙ – Un site unique en bordure du lac Léman annoncé par des jets d'eau et des pavillons multicolores, un environnement paysager aménagé en parc public et jardin de sculptures, servent de cadre à ce musée qui concrétise le rêve du baron Pierre de Coubertin et donne au mot « Olympisme » toute sa dimension.
Le **parc** planté de belles essences (cyprès d'Italie, genévriers, magnolias), de végétaux à feuilles persistantes, s'étage en pente douce offrant plusieurs points de vue sur le lac Léman et les Alpes savoyardes en arrière-plan. Le long du chemin de 420 m (longueur d'un stade olympique) qui serpente jusqu'à l'entrée du musée, des sculptures symbolisent le mariage du sport et de la culture.
Afin de protéger l'environnement naturel, une partie du musée a été enterrée. L'ensemble moderne inspiré d'un temple grec est l'œuvre de l'architecte mexicain Pedro Ramirez Vázquez (créateur du musée national d'Anthropologie de Mexico) et de l'architecte lausannois

Drapeau olympique

LAUSANNE
OUCHY

Acacias (Av. des)	DZ
Auguste Pidou (Ch.)	DZ 6
Beau-Rivage (Ch. de)	DZ
Beauregard (Av.)	DZ 9
Belgique (Quai de)	DZ
Bellerive (Ch. de)	DZ
Cour (Av. de)	DZ
Edouard Dapples (Av.)	DZ
Elysée (Av. de l')	DZ
Eugène Grasset (Ch.)	DZ
Floréal (Av.)	DZ
Fontenailles (R. des)	DZ
Grammont (Av. du)	DZ 34
Grancy (Bd. de)	DZ
Harpe (R. de la)	DZ
Jordils (Av. des)	DZ 40
Jurigoz (Quai de)	DZ
Mon Loisir (Av.)	DZ 58
Montchoisi (Av. de)	DZ
Mouettes (Ch. des)	DZ
Navigation (Pl. de la)	DZ
Ouchy (Av. d')	DZ
Port (Pl. du)	DZ
Rhodanie (Av. de)	DZ
Rod Edouard (Av.)	DZ
Servan (Av. du)	DZ
Voltaire (R.)	DZ 106
Warnery (Av.)	DZ 108

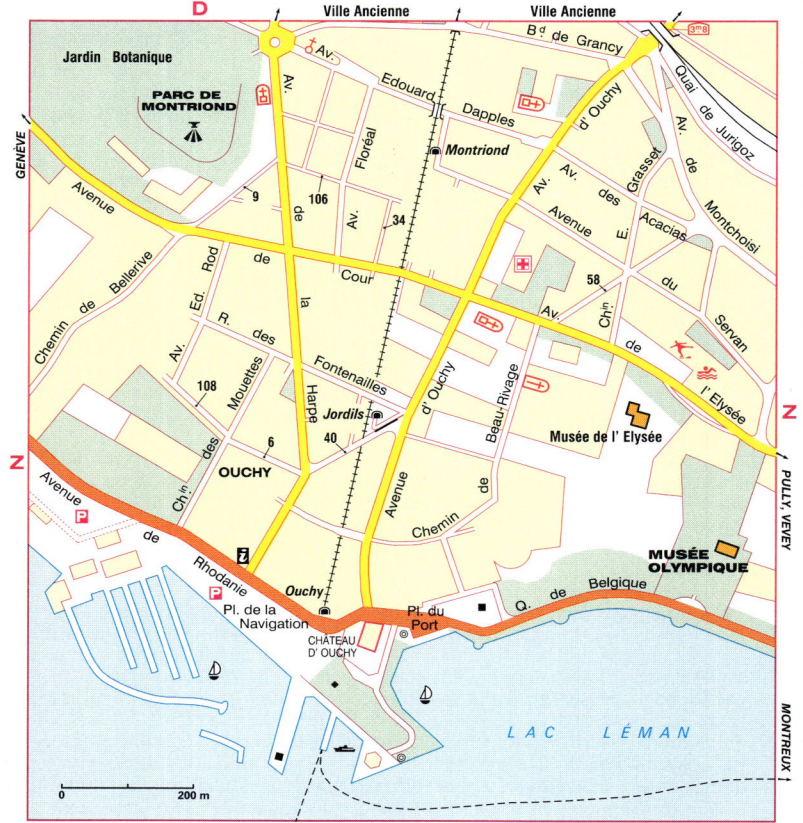

Jean-Pierre Cahen. Devant la façade en marbre blanc provenant de l'île de Thássos (Grèce), deux rangées de quatre colonnes portent les noms des villes olympiques et des présidents du C.I.O. Dans une vasque en granit décorée d'un motif allégorique évoquant le mythe de Prométhée, le feu olympique brûle à jamais.

Niveau 0 – Le rez-de-chaussée est consacré en grande partie à l'histoire des Jeux. La Grèce antique y détient une place de choix. Des œuvres d'art d'une très grande beauté, exposées par thèmes, rappellent l'origine des Jeux : figures en terre cuite ; sculptures en marbre et en bronze ; vases décorés de silhouettes d'athlètes ; strigiles — instruments avec lesquels les athlètes raclaient leur corps afin d'ôter la couche d'huile et de sable mélangée à la sueur dont ils étaient imprégnés ; couronnes de laurier en or. Sur le même niveau sont rassemblées les torches qui ont porté la flamme depuis 1936 (J.O. de Berlin). Viennent ensuite la vie et l'œuvre de Pierre de Coubertin (reconstitution de son bureau de Lausanne, meubles et objets personnels), les Comités nationaux olympiques, les présidents du C.I.O. qui se sont succédé (vidéo sur les événements internationaux qui ont marqué leur époque). Pour conclure, un espace présente les deux villes élues pour les prochains Jeux d'hiver et d'été. Remarquer également deux beaux bronzes, de Rodin, *L'Athlète américain*, de Bourdelle, *L'Archer*.

Niveau 1 – Consacré d'un côté aux Jeux olympiques d'été, de l'autre à ceux d'hiver. Dans les deux espaces, l'audiovisuel permet au visiteur de revivre de grands moments et de partager les efforts et les émotions de sportifs de haut rang. Des écrans géants diffusent cérémonies d'ouverture et de clôture, un réseau de bornes vidéo apporte des milliers de réponses à des milliers de questions sur les Jeux, les disciplines, les athlètes, les performances, etc.
Le département philatélie et numismatique rassemble une étonnante collection de timbres, pièces et médailles à l'effigie des Jeux.

LAUSANNE

Niveau 2 – Cafétéria et terrasse. **Vue** sur le parc, le lac et les montagnes. Sculptures de Botero, *Jeune fille à la balle*.

Niveau 1 – Bibliothèque et vidéothèque. La carte magnétique d'entrée permet de visionner trois films.

Musée de l'Élysée (DZ) ⊙ – Une grande villa de la fin du 18ᵉ s., à façade concave sculptée, entourée d'un agréable parc ombragé (marronniers, sapins, cèdre) descendant en gradins jusqu'aux quais du lac, abrite un musée de la photographie, présentant d'importantes expositions temporaires de photos des 19ᵉ et 20ᵉ s.

Lillehammer 1994, les Suisses sur le podium

Médailles d'or

Gustav Weder / Donat Acklin	Bobsleigh à deux
Andreas Schoenbaechler	Saut acrobatique
Vreni Schneider	Slalom : ski alpin dames

Médailles d'argent

Reto Goetschi / Guido Acklin	Bobsleigh à deux
Vreni Schneider	Combiné : ski alpin dames
Urs Kaelin	Slalom géant : ski alpin messieurs
Gustav Weder / Donat Acklin / Kurt Meier / Domenico Semerado	Bobsleigh à quatre

Médailles de bronze

Hippolyt Kempf / Jean-Yves Cuendet / Andreas Schaad	Combiné par équipes : ski nordique messieurs
Vreni Schneider	Slalom géant : ski alpin dames

LA VILLE ANCIENNE visite : 2 h

Place de la Palud (BX 70) – Bordée par des maisons anciennes et par la façade Renaissance de l'hôtel de ville dont le portail est surmonté des armes de la ville, elle est ornée de la charmante fontaine de la Justice (16ᵉ-18ᵉ s.). A proximité, au nº 23, une horloge animée se met en mouvement toutes les heures laissant apparaître un défilé de personnages historiques.
Derrière la fontaine, les pittoresques escaliers couverts en bois donnent accès à la place de la cathédrale. Jadis ces escaliers aboutissaient à la porte de la Cité dite du Marché.

Musée historique de Lausanne (BX M¹) ⊙ – Installé dans les salles joliment restaurées de l'ancien évêché, ses collections retracent l'histoire de la ville depuis les temps préhistoriques jusqu'au 20ᵉ s. Après une section consacrée à la géologie, à la préhistoire et au Moyen Âge, on découvre une vaste maquette représentant la ville en 1638 complétée par un montage audiovisuel. L'époque bernoise (17ᵉ-18ᵉ s.) lui fait suite, abondamment illustrée par des documents ou objets sur la vie politique, agricole, domestique. L'apparition du chemin de fer, les troubles politiques qu'il entraîna, le développement du tourisme, des affaires (banques, assurances) constituent d'autres pages exposées du riche passé lausannois. Dans la dernière salle plusieurs vitrines de boutiques du 19ᵉ s. ont été reconstituées : imprimerie, bazar vaudois, épicerie, photographe ; on remarque également le coffre-fort de la maison Kohler (1828), ingénieuse merveille de serrurerie.

★★ **Cathédrale** (CX) ⊙ – C'est le plus beau monument gothique de Suisse. Commencée sous l'épiscopat de saint Amédée (1145-1159), elle a été terminée dans son gros œuvre au milieu du 13ᵉ s. et consacrée en 1275 ; une complète restauration fut entreprise à la fin du 19ᵉ s. par Viollet-le-Duc.
Le chevet est la partie la plus ancienne ; accosté de deux pittoresques tours carrées et dominé par la tour-lanterne de la croisée du transept. Cette dernière tour avec le clocher marque une forte influence anglo-normande, transition entre le style roman et le style gothique.
Le **portail méridional**, ou portail peint ou porche des Apôtres, est orné d'un bel ensemble de sculptures du 13ᵉ s., peintes à l'origine et proches de la facture d'Ile-de-France (cinq des grandes statues sont des copies, les originaux se trouvant au musée de la cathédrale). Les piliers qui soutiennent la voûte du porche portent, à

151

gauche et au premier plan, les Prophètes (Isaïe, David et Jérémie) ; près de la porte, les Précurseurs (Moïse, Jean-Baptiste, Siméon) ; à droite et au premier plan, les Évangélistes (Jean, Matthieu, Luc et Marc) ; au fond, des Apôtres (Pierre, Paul, Jean). Le linteau est sculpté de deux bas-reliefs, Mort et Résurrection de la Vierge. Au tympan, le Couronnement de Marie présente le Christ en majesté prenant des mains d'un ange la couronne que la Vierge s'apprête à recevoir.

Le portail des Montfalcon du nom des évêques Aymon et Sébastien de Montfalcon, dont la construction remonte à 1517, a été entièrement refait au début du 20e s. ; il s'ouvre au milieu de la façade principale et donne accès au narthex flanqué de deux absides latérales arrondies. On remarque deux statues du 13e s. (malheureusement décapitées) représentant la Vierge, Salomon et la reine de Saba. Dans une chapelle, à droite, des peintures murales (1505) évoquent la vie de la Vierge.

L'intérieur, sobre et d'une rare unité, présente certains caractères bourguignons, tels que le plan général, le narthex, l'absence de chapelles rayonnantes ; d'autres dérivent du gothique anglais : le chemin de ronde passant devant les fenêtres hautes. Il faut noter une disposition originale avec l'alternance d'une pile forte et de deux piles faibles jumelées.

Retirées lors de la récente campagne de restauration, les très curieuses et très rares **stalles** du 13e s., dont les grandes figures des jouées sont d'une pureté de lignes exceptionnelle, n'ont pas encore retrouvé leur place dans le bas-côté droit.

D'autres stalles, celles-là flamboyantes (16e s.), placées dans une chapelle au bas du collatéral gauche, sont sculptées avec beaucoup de verve.

Dans le croisillon droit du transept, une rosace du 13e s., « Imago mundi » (éléments, saisons, mois, signes du Zodiaque), d'une harmonie décorative remarquable bien que quelque peu remaniée au 19e s., a été exécutée par Pierre d'Arras. Elle était déjà célèbre au 13e s., car Villard de Honnecourt la dessina dans son « Album », premier recueil consacré à l'architecture et à la décoration gothiques.

Dans le chœur est érigé le tombeau d'Othon Ier de Grandson, mort en 1328, qui fit une brillante carrière à la cour d'Angleterre et devint l'ami du roi Édouard Ier.

La cathédrale abrite un des derniers, sinon le dernier « guet » du monde, qui a pour tâche de clamer les heures nocturnes aux quatre vents de la ville (de 22 h à 2 h).

Tour ⊙ – *Entrée de l'escalier (232 marches) au bas du collatéral droit.* Du sommet de la tour, on a une belle **vue**★ sur la ville et le lac avec les Alpes en arrière-plan. Du parvis de la cathédrale, vue plongeante sur la ville et le lac.

Contourner la cathédrale et prendre, à gauche du chevet, la rue Cité-Derrière, petite rue médiévale décorée d'enseignes en fer forgé. Dans la rue de l'Académie qui lui est perpendiculaire, le sous-sol d'un magasin d'antiquités abrite le **musée de la pipe et objets du tabac** (**CX M²**) ⊙. Un collectionneur y a rassemblé plus de 2 500 pipes de tous pays, dont certains fourneaux sont sculptés de façon originale.

Château St-Maire (**CX B**) – Dans cet édifice du 15e s. en briques et pierres, résidèrent les évêques de Lausanne, puis les baillis bernois.

Le gouvernement cantonal y siège aujourd'hui.

De la terrasse, la **vue** plonge sur les toits de la ville et plus loin à gauche, sur le lac.

Poursuivre par la rue Cité-Derrière et à gauche par l'avenue de l'Université qui mène à la place de la Riponne au pied du promontoire de la Cité.

Palais de Rumine (**BX**) – Bâti au début du siècle dans le style de la Renaissance italienne, cet imposant édifice a été élevé grâce à un très important legs de Gabriel de Rumine. Il abrite la Bibliothèque et cinq musées.

Musée des Beaux-Arts ⊙ – *Chaque année, des expositions temporaires ayant trait à l'art contemporain sont organisées autour d'un thème ou d'un artiste. Un personnel très aimable répondra volontiers à vos questions.*

Le fonds permanent du musée cantonal occupe les trois premières salles et est surtout constitué d'œuvres d'artistes suisses, et en particulier vaudois. Aux toiles du 18e s. (voir les aquarelles de Ducros qui sont à l'origine de l'institution) succèdent des œuvres de Gleyre *(Le Coucher de Sapho)* qui vit passer dans son atelier parisien les principaux impressionnistes. Parmi les peintres qui ont célébré leur pays, on peut citer les paysagistes romands De La Rive, Diday, St-Ours, Calame, et plus spécialement les Vaudois Biéler, Bosshard et Bocion (nombreuses évocations de la région du lac Léman traitées avec une grande sensibilité). Plus proches de nous, on retient l'artiste alémanique Hodler *(Bleu Léman)* et le Lausannois Vallotton dont le musée possède le plus important **fonds**★ public. De prestigieux artistes français clôturent cette section : Largillière, Géricault, Courbet, Cézanne, Bonnard, Renoir, Degas, Matisse, Marquet, Vlaminck, Vuillard, Utrillo.

Les œuvres exposées dans les salles suivantes font l'objet d'un roulement. L'art désormais traditionnel de Rodin et Giacometti y est confronté aux acquisitions récentes de Nauman et Boltanski.

Musée de Géologie ⊙ – *Au 1er étage, à gauche.*

Il renferme des roches et fossiles provenant du Jura, des Alpes, de Lausanne et sa région : des reliefs du Jura, du Simplon, du Cervin complètent la collection. Un espace est consacré au quaternaire vaudois, dans lequel est exposé un squelette de mammouth trouvé en 1969 près de Brassus dans la vallée de Joux.

Musée de Paléontologie ⊘ — *A droite, face au musée de géologie.*
Collection de fossiles (plantes et animaux), surtout européens, mollusques et squelettes d'oiseaux et de mammifères.

Musée de Zoologie ⊘ — *Au 2ᵉ étage.*
Il présente la faune du monde entier, dans la salle centrale. A gauche, intéressante salle d'anatomie comparée dans laquelle l'homme voisine avec les animaux. A droite, dans la salle de collection régionale, sont exposés tous les vertébrés de la faune vaudoise : faune de la forêt, de la montagne ainsi que les poissons, oiseaux et insectes. On y voit également une impressionnante colonie de fourmis au travail, espèce en provenance du Mexique, s'affairant dans leur milieu tropical reconstitué. Au centre, une galerie est consacrée à la minéralogie.

Salle d'Archéologie et d'Histoire ⊘ — *Au 6ᵉ étage.*
Elle abrite des collections présentées de façon temporaire, provenant de fouilles effectuées dans le canton. Les nombreux objets trouvés dans la région des lacs Léman, de Neuchâtel et de Morat incluent céramiques et outils de l'âge du bronze, tombes celtiques, buste en or de Marc Aurèle, armes et bijoux du Haut Moyen Âge (5ᵉ-7ᵉ s.).

AUTRES CURIOSITÉS

★ **Collection de l'Art brut** (**AX**) ⊘ — Aménagée dans les dépendances du château de Beaulieu (18ᵉ s.), elle présente sur quatre niveaux une sélection d'objets (environ un millier, sur plus de 10 000) rassemblés depuis 1945 par le peintre Jean Dubuffet et reçus en donation par la ville de Lausanne.
Peintures, dessins, sculptures, modelages, broderies, réalisés à partir des matériaux les plus inattendus, ont en commun de provenir d'hommes ou de femmes en marge de la société : schizophrènes, détenus de prisons ou d'asiles, médiums spirites, sans aucun contact avec les milieux culturels. Leur production spontanée, dans sa singularité proprement individuelle, rappelle souvent celle, délibérée, des « vrais » artistes modernes (« naïfs », surréalistes, abstraits...).
Certaines de ces œuvres étranges ne sont pas sans posséder une réelle valeur esthétique : bois ciselés de Clément, étoffes peintes de Madge Gill, dessins (Les Aigles, notamment) de Guillaume Pujolle, de Wölfli, d'Aloïse, de Scottie Wilson, sculptures de Filippo Bentivegna, dessins géants de Jaki, livres enluminés de Metz, peintures de Walla...

Fondation de l'Hermitage (**CX**) ⊘ — *2, route du Signal.*
L'ancienne demeure de la famille vaudoise Bugnion, construite vers 1841 et entourée d'un beau parc aux arbres d'essences rares, accueille depuis 1984 d'importantes expositions temporaires d'art ou d'histoire.

★★ **Vue du Signal** (**CX**) — Alt. 643 m. Table d'orientation, longue-vue. De ce belvédère à proximité duquel s'élève une petite chapelle, la **vue** s'étend sur le Léman, les Alpes savoyardes, vaudoises et fribourgeoises, la vieille ville apparaît au premier plan.
A environ 1 km, le **lac de Sauvabelin**, avec son parc à biches et bouquetins, attire les promeneurs.

Parc Mon Repos (**CY**) — Dans cet agréable jardin paysager s'élève la villa de style Empire qu'habita Voltaire et où se visitait naguère un musée Olympique rappelant le souvenir du baron de Coubertin qui vécut longtemps à Lausanne et y est enterré. Au Nord du parc, le Tribunal Fédéral, juridiction suprême de Suisse, occupe un vaste édifice.

Musée des Arts Décoratifs (**CY**) ⊘ — Expositions temporaires d'art appliqué contemporain et de sculptures de verre.

Parc de Montriond (**AY**) — En cet endroit, où fut proclamée en 1037 la première trêve de Dieu de la région, se dresse une vaste esplanade à laquelle on accède par une rampe et des escaliers. De la table d'orientation, la **vue**★★ s'étend sur Ouchy, les rives du Léman, et au-delà sur les Alpes.
Dans une partie du parc s'étage le **jardin botanique** ⊘ qui inclut un alpinum rassemblant des plantes de montagne, un arboretum ainsi que plusieurs espèces de fleurs, plantes grasses, médicinales, aquatiques et carnivores.

PULLY *par l'avenue de l'Élysée (**DZ** plan d'Ouchy)*

L'ancien village de Pully est devenu un faubourg résidentiel de Lausanne, par son extension sur les pentes de sa colline jusqu'au lac. De la terrasse de l'église St-Germain (d'origine gothique, mais très remaniée), charmante **vue**★ sur le port de plaisance en contrebas, la partie Est du Léman, la rive française d'Évian à Meillerie en face.
Dans les parages de l'église se trouvent aussi un musée et les vestiges d'une « villa » romaine peu à peu exhumés depuis 1921.

LAUSANNE

Ale (R. de l')	ABX 4
Bourg (R. de)	BCX
Rue Centrale	BCX
St-François (R.)	BX 87
Acacias (Av. des)	BY 3
Alpes (Av. des)	CY
Avant-Poste (R. de l')	CY 7
Beau-Séjour (R.)	BCY
Beaulieu (Av. de)	AX
Beauregard (Av.)	AY 9
Bellefontaine (R.)	CY
Benjamin-Constant (Av.)	BCY 13
Bergières (Av. des)	AX
Bessières (Pont)	CX
Béthusy (Av. de)	CX
Borde (R. de la)	BX 16
Boston (Ch. de)	AX 19
Bugnon (R. du)	CX
Calvaire (Ch. du)	CX
Cèdres (Ch. des)	AX
César Roux (R. du Dr.)	CX
Charles Monnard (R.)	CY 22
Château (Pl.)	CX
Chauderon (Pl.)	AX
Chauderon (Pont)	AX
Cheneau de Bourg (R.)	CX 24
Cité Derrière (R.)	CX 27
Collonges (Av.)	AX 28
Cour (Av. de)	AY
Croix-Rouges (Ch. des)	AX 30
Davel (Av.)	BX
Echallens (Av. d')	AX
Edouard Dapples (Av.)	ABY
Fleurettes (Ch. des)	AY
Floréal (Av.)	AY
Florimont (Av. de)	CY
France (Av. de)	AX
Gare (Av. de la)	BCY
Gare (Pl. de la)	ABY
Genève (R. de)	ABX
Georgette (Av.)	CY 33
Grancy (Bd. de)	ABY
Grand Pont	BX
Grand-Chêne (R. du)	BXY 36
Haldimand (R.)	BX
Harpe (Av. de la)	AY
Jomini	AX 39
Jules Gonin (Av.)	ABX
Jura (R. du)	AX
Jurigoz (Av. de)	CY 42
Jurigoz (Quai de)	BY 43
Juste Olivier (Av.)	CY
Langallerie (R. de)	CX 45
Longeraie (Ch. de)	CY 48
Louis Ruchonnet (Av.)	AXY
Louve (R. de la)	BX 49
Lucinge (R. de)	CY
Madeleine (R.)	BX 51
Marc Dufour (Av.)	AX 52
Marterey (R.)	CX 55
Mauborget (R.)	BX 57
Maupas (R. du)	AX
Mercerie (R.)	BX
Messidor (Ch.)	CY
Midi (R. du)	BY
Milan (Av. de)	AY
Mon Repos (Av.)	CY
Mont d'Or (Av. du)	AY
Mont-Tendre (Ch. du)	AY 61
Montagibert (Av.)	CX
Montbenon (Pl. de)	AX
Montchoisi (Av. de)	BY
Morges (Av. de)	AX
Mornex (Ch. de)	ABY 66
Ouchy (Av. d')	BY
Ours (Pl. de l')	CX
Paix (R. de la)	CY 69
Palud (Pl. de la)	BX 70
Pépinet (Pl.)	BX 72
Petit-Chêne (R. du)	BY
Petit-Valentin (R. du)	BX 73
Pierre Decker (Av.)	CX 75
Pierre Viret (R.)	BX 76
Pont (R. du)	BX 78
Riant-Mont (R.)	BX 81
Riponne (Pl. de la)	BX
Rond-Point (Av. du)	AY 82
Rosiers (Ch. des)	AX 84

Rotillon (R. du)	BCX	Sainte-Beuve (R.)	CX 90
Rue Neuve	BX	Savoie (Av. de)	AX 93
Rumine (Av. de)	CY	Simplon (R. du)	ABY 94
St-François (Pl.)	BX 85	Terreaux (R. des)	AX
St-Laurent (R.)	BX 88	Théâtre (Av. du)	CY
St-Martin (R.)	CX	Tissot (R. du Dr.)	BCY
St-Roch (R.)	ABX	Tivoli (Av. de)	AX
Ste-Luce (Av.)	BY	Tour (R. de la)	ABX 97

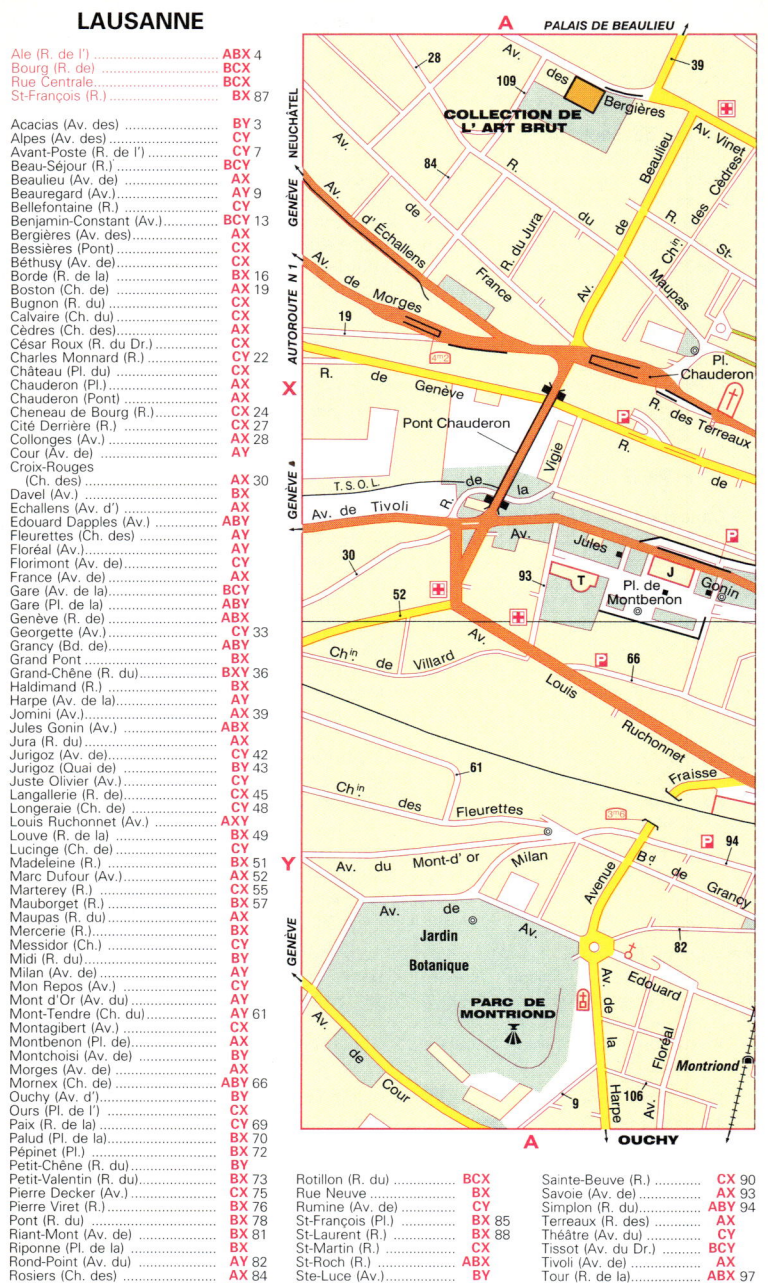

Musée ⓨ – Près de la maison où vécut jusqu'à 1947 Charles Ferdinand Ramuz, ce petit musée abrite des souvenirs de ce grand écrivain (photos, manuscrits, œuvres originales). On trouve également des peintures de R. Domenjoz, M. Borgeaud, V. Milliquet et des œuvres d'autres artistes pulliérans contemporains (J. Lecouttre, P. Besson, F. Simonin, M. Pellegrini), des sculptures en terre cuite de Derain et des objets précieux (écritoire, maquette de barque royale) ayant appartenu au roi de Siam qui habita Pully de 1925 à 1945.

Villa romaine ⓨ – Sous la terrasse de l'hôtel Le Prieuré (dont le pavement rose reproduit les contours des murs romains).
Ce qui a été dégagé du vaste et riche domaine qui s'élevait là au 2e s. représente un petit bâtiment où l'on séjournait l'été, comportant une abside faite d'un double mur semi-circulaire haut d'environ 3 m et que décore à nouveau, sur la paroi intérieure, la **fresque** polychrome de plus de 20 m², figurant des courses de chars, qui s'en était détachée.

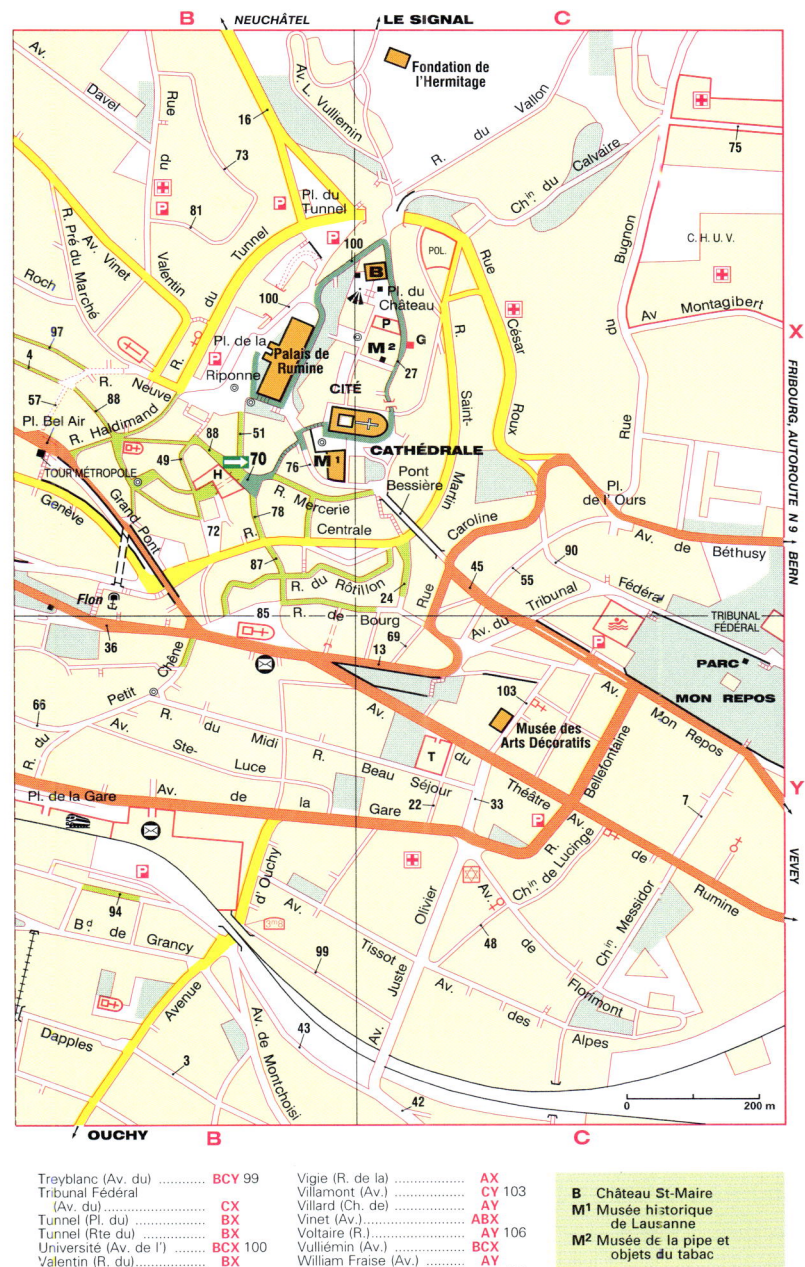

Treyblanc (Av. du)	BCY 99	Vigie (R. de la)	AX
Tribunal Fédéral (Av. du)	CX	Villamont (Av.)	CY 103
Tunnel (Pl. du)	BX	Villard (Ch. de)	AY
Tunnel (Rte du)	BX	Vinet (Av.)	ABX
Université (Av. de l')	BCX 100	Voltaire (R.)	AY 106
Valentin (R. du)	BX	Vulliémin (Av.)	BCX
Vallon (R. du)	CX	William Fraise (Av.)	AY
		24-Janvier (Av. du)	AX 109

B Château St-Maire
M¹ Musée historique de Lausanne
M² Musée de la pipe et objets du tabac

ENVIRONS

Lutry – *4 km par l'avenue de l'Élysée (DZ plan d'Ouchy), puis par la route n° 9.*
Agréablement situé au bord du lac Léman (petit port de plaisance, vue sur les Alpes), ce village aux rues étroites mérite une courte halte. Sur une placette décorée d'une fontaine, sa blanche église s'ouvre par un beau porche roman orné d'arabesques. A l'intérieur (stalles en bois sculpté), l'attention se porte sur la voûte peinte de motifs floraux.
A la sortie du village, sur les pentes couvertes de vignes se dresse un puissant château défensif (centre médico-social).

Échallens – *15 km par l'avenue d'Échallens (AX), puis par la route n° 5.*
Située dans une région riche de cultures céréalières, cette petite ville possède une intéressante **maison du Blé et du Pain** ⊙ installée dans une ancienne ferme restaurée du 18ᵉ s. Diaporama, instruments aratoires (herses, semoirs, charrues), chambres

à grains, types de moulins (à pierre, à main, mécaniques, à cylindre) et de fours font revivre le travail quotidien des paysans, meuniers et boulangers au cours des âges. En fin de visite, on peut assister à la fabrication de pains, petits pains et croissants.

Zoo de Servion ⊙ — *18 km par la route de Berne (***CX***).*
Sur un domaine de quelque 65 000 m² vivent des animaux de toutes provenances. Passé le bâtiment des singes (amusants ouistitis à pinceaux blancs ou noirs appelés ainsi à cause de la touffe de poils qui entoure leurs oreilles), le visiteur pénètre dans la serre tropicale où il côtoie des oiseaux exotiques en liberté (vanneaux armés d'Afrique, martins huppés d'Asie, etc.). Près du parc à autruches, grues couronnées d'Afrique, flamants du Chili, pélicans gris d'Afrique ont élu domicile. Cerfs rouges, bisons, loups, ours bruns jalonnent ensuite le parcours qui se termine par le puissant tigre de Sibérie et le bondissant wallaby. Aires de jeux et de pique-nique.

OIN-OIN

Le sympathique personnage de Oin-Oin à l'accent bien prononcé, à la voix nasillarde, racontant maintes histoires amusantes, fondées sur l'observation malicieuse de la Suisse romande et de ses habitants, a tenu la vedette sur les ondes de la radio romande de 1957 à 1978.
Oin-Oin aurait réellement existé. Né à Genève, il était employé comme ouvrier horloger à la Chaux-de-Fonds. Risée de ses camarades à cause d'un défaut de prononciation dû à un bec-de-lièvre, il laissait entendre — en réponse à une question — « oin-oin » au lieu de « ouais-ouais ». D'où ce sobriquet. Les aventures et mésaventures de Oin-Oin firent le tour des cafés et des campagnes, et passèrent même la frontière française. Selon le créateur de l'émission Émile Gardaz, il est un peu le Marius et Olive français, « le miroir quotidien de la vie en Suisse romande ».
Une maison de disques de Fribourg a réédité ses histoires en double CD.

Lac LÉMAN★★★

Carte Michelin n° 427 plis 11, 12 ou 217 plis 11 à 14

La rive helvétique du Léman *(1)* courbe harmonieusement son grand arc tout frangé de vignobles, longeant les derniers glacis du Jura, les coteaux du Plateau suisse, et les soubassements des Alpes vaudoises. Ce littoral, et surtout la région de Vevey-Montreux, devint, après J.-J. Rousseau, le sanctuaire des Romantiques, et les pèlerinages nombreux effectués par les « amants de la nature » donnèrent l'élan à un important mouvement touristique.

Visite — *Outre les itinéraires décrits ci-après, la section d'autoroute en corniche qui relie Vevey à Rennaz offre au voyageur des vues splendides sur le Haut lac.*

Le lac, en bateau — Les bateaux de la Compagnie Générale de Navigation sur le lac Léman, desservant régulièrement les rives suisse et française, offrent de multiples possibilités.
A retenir : les circuits d'un après-midi intitulés « Tour du Petit lac » au départ de Genève et « Tour du Haut lac » — le plus intéressant — au départ de Lausanne-Ouchy. Une excursion comportant le tour complet du lac dure entre onze et douze heures.

UN PEU D'HYDROGRAPHIE

Du jet d'eau de Genève au château de Chillon — Il n'y a pas dans toute la chaîne des Alpes de lac qui puisse rivaliser avec les 310 m de profondeur et les 58 000 ha du lac Léman (13 fois l'étendue du lac du Bourget, le plus vaste de la France intérieure). Sa forme est celle d'un croissant long de 72 km et large au maximum, entre Morges et Amphion, de 13 km. On sépare généralement le Petit lac — entre Genève et Yvoire — du Grand lac, secteur le plus épanoui, à l'intérieur duquel on distingue encore un « Haut lac », au large de Vevey-Montreux.
Le Léman est depuis des siècles un sujet d'études exceptionnel. La cote de référence de l'altimétrie suisse ayant été fixée à la Pierre du Niton (alt. 373,60 m au-dessus du niveau de la Méditerranée à Marseille), qui émerge du Léman dans le port de Genève, on considère que le lac constitue, en fait, le repère de base du nivellement de la Suisse à partir duquel sont mesurées les cotes d'altitudes du pays (en y ajoutant 373,60 m).
Les plissements alpins de l'ère tertiaire ont inversé la pente des vallées, faisant ainsi refluer les eaux en créant des lacs de bordure tels que le lac des Quatre-Cantons et le lac Léman.

---

(1) L'appellation « lac de Genève » n'est de mise que dans la cité de Calvin et de Saussure.

Lac LÉMAN

L'absorption, par le lac, des eaux troubles du Rhône valaisan ne va pas sans combat : c'est la **bataillère**, que l'on observe des terrasses ou des sommets qui dominent l'agglomération de Vevey-Montreux. Le puissant panache boueux semble se résorber entièrement : en réalité, le mélange ne s'effectue pas sur-le-champ et une tranche d'eaux fluviales troubles subsiste à une vingtaine de mètres de profondeur, jusqu'à l'automne, époque où le refroidissement provoque un brassage général des eaux et rétablit l'homogénéité. Le Rhône en sort ainsi purifié et régularisé.

Cependant, la profondeur du lac tend à diminuer progressivement en raison de l'accumulation des dépôts du Rhône et de l'approfondissement du lit du fleuve qui abaisse en même temps le niveau du lac.

Les échanges de valeur entre l'atmosphère et les eaux du lac se traduisent par un bilan climatique très favorable aux riverains, surtout en avant et en arrière-saison. L'automne, sur la Riviera vaudoise, jouit d'un prestige international : nous recommandons d'ailleurs de parcourir à la saison des vendanges les routes décrites sous la présente rubrique.

★ 1 LA ROUTE DU VIGNOBLE

Le trait dominant du paysage est en effet ici, avec le lac, le tapis de vignes quasi continu qui escalade les pentes du versant jurassien.

De Genève à Lausanne 70 km – environ 3 h

★★★ **Genève** – Visite : 2 h. Voir à ce nom.

Quitter Genève par ③ du plan et la route littorale de Lausanne, qui ne se dégage véritablement de l'agglomération genevoise qu'après Versoix.

Coppet – Visite : 1/2 h. Voir à ce nom.
La route côtière, que domine l'autoroute de Genève à Lausanne, procure des vues rapprochées sur le Petit lac et la rive française jusqu'à la pointe d'Yvoire.

Crans – Voir à Nyon.

★ **Nyon** – Visite : 1 h. Voir à ce nom.

Quitter Nyon par ⑤ du plan en direction d'Aubonne.

Après avoir laissé en arrière le charmant port de Nyon et dépassé Luins et le **site**★ ravissant de sa petite église, isolée parmi les vignes, dans un bouquet de cyprès, on gagne rapidement Bursins puis Mont-sur-Rolle ; l'horizon s'élargit : outre la rive savoyarde du lac – avec Thonon – et les sommets du Haut Chablais, le regard atteint alors la rive vaudoise, de la baie de Rolle aux Rochers de Naye en passant par Lausanne. En deçà d'une frange de villas et de maisons particulières, les collines qui descendent vers le lac, face au Midi, constituent l'un des grands vignobles de la Suisse.

Rolle – Cette agréable petite ville s'étale sur la rive Nord du Léman à mi-distance de Genève et de Lausanne. Tout au bord du lac, le long duquel a été aménagé un quai-promenade, se dresse le **château** construit à la fin du 13ᵉ s. par un prince de Savoie. De plan triangulaire, il est flanqué d'une grosse tour à chacun de ses angles.

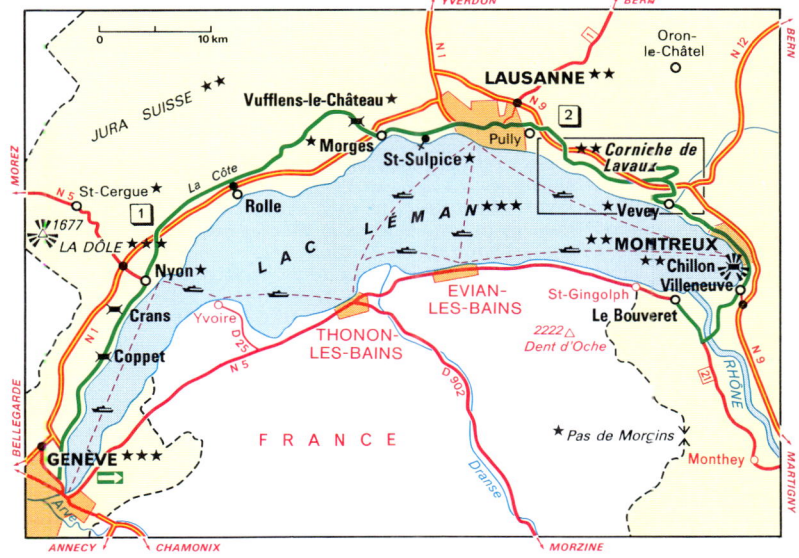

157

Au large, sur un petit îlot artificiel, un obélisque a été érigé à la mémoire du général **Frédéric de Laharpe** (1754-1838), qui fut précepteur du tsar Alexandre Ier et le gagna aux idées nouvelles. Également promoteur de l'indépendance vaudoise, Laharpe fut l'un des fondateurs de la République helvétique.

Entre Mont-sur-Rolle et Aubonne ce ne sont que villages typiques, reclus dans le vignoble, comme Féchy, tandis que les **vues**★★ se développent en direction du Petit lac, jusqu'à Genève (jet d'eau), et le Salève.

Dès la sortie d'Aubonne, en direction de Lavigny, la traversée du ravin de l'Aubonne permet une attrayante vue d'ensemble du bourg étagé au pied de son église et du château.

★ **Vufflens-le-Château** — Sur un plateau dominant le cours encaissé de la Morge et d'où l'on a une belle vue sur le Jura, le lac Léman et la chaîne des Alpes, le château de Vufflens *(on ne visite pas)* est l'un des plus fiers monuments civils de toute la Suisse.

Reconstruit totalement au début du 15e s. en faisant largement appel à la brique, suivant le goût piémontais de l'époque – Vufflens appartenait à une famille savoyarde – l'édifice a encore subi de très importantes restaurations au siècle dernier.

Le plan du château comporte deux parties. Le donjon, appelé « ancien château », dresse son énorme tour carrée coiffée d'un toit en lanterne à 60 m de hauteur : il est cantonné de quatre tours également carrées, moins élevées. Les couronnements en briques, avec mâchicoulis et frises décoratives, sont remarquables. Le logis d'habitation, flanqué de quatre tourelles effilées, est séparé du donjon par la cour d'entrée.

★ **Morges** — *Voir à ce nom.*

Entre Morges et Lausanne, on quitte un instant la route n° 1 pour faire un crochet par St-Sulpice.

★ **St-Sulpice** — La petite **église**★ de St-Sulpice, pur témoin de l'art roman en Pays de Vaud, et lieu de culte protestant depuis le 16e s., se dresse dans un **décor**★ rustique et paisible, en présence du Léman et des Alpes de Savoie.

De l'ancien édifice roman – qui fut à l'origine un prieuré bénédictin – ne subsistent actuellement que les absides en cul-de-four, le chœur, le transept voûté en berceau et la croisée sur laquelle s'élève un clocher rectangulaire. L'intérieur est d'une grande simplicité ; une décoration polychrome en atténue la sévérité. Les fresques de l'abside centrale représentent un Christ en majesté à l'intérieur d'une mandorle.

St-Sulpice – L'église

On retrouve la route n° 1 pour gagner Lausanne.

★★ 2 CORNICHE DE LAVAUX

De Lausanne à Villeneuve *39 km – environ 1 h 1/2*

La route décrite ci-dessous est celle qui, franchissant l'autoroute après le carrefour de la Croix, s'intercale jusqu'aux abords de Vevey entre cette autoroute et la route littorale (n° 9). On pourra éventuellement, si la circulation y est trop active, profiter plus commodément du paysage en empruntant plus haut les 5 km de la petite route qui s'y raccorde, à Chexbres, via Puidoux-gare, et qui longe ou surplombe l'autoroute. Enfin, l'autoroute elle-même procure des vues splendides, mais hachées par ses tunnels.

Partant d'Ouchy, il est possible de rejoindre l'itinéraire à hauteur de Grandvaux par la route littorale (n° 9) : à la sortie de Lutry, s'engager à gauche dans la route de la « Petite Corniche », puis suivre la direction de Riex.

★★ **Lausanne** — *Visite : 1 h. Voir à ce nom.*

Quitter Lausanne par l'avenue de Béthusy en direction de la Rosiaz, puis de Belmont.

Au-delà, se dégageant d'une banlieue résidentielle cossue, puis de ravins boisés, la route débouche sur un versant doucement vallonné, planté d'arbres fruitiers, en vue du Haut lac et de sa rive savoyarde, jalonnée, de gauche à droite, par les falaises de Meillerie, les ondulations verdoyantes du plateau Gavot (derrière Évian), le delta de la Dranse.

Lac LÉMAN

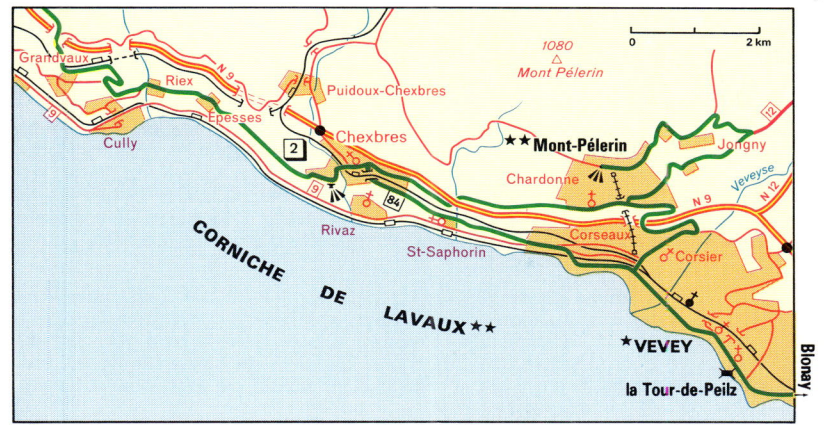

Plus loin, après le carrefour de la Croix, le Grand lac est à son tour visible en son entier : la courbe de sa rive vaudoise s'infléchit au pied du Jura en arrière de l'agglomération lausannoise. Sur la rive opposée s'avance la pointe d'Yvoire.
Il manque cependant au tableau la blancheur des grandes voiles latines qui le poétisaient naguère : les barques traditionnelles du Léman ont toutes disparu du lac, à l'exception de deux d'entre elles, l'une à Ouchy, l'autre à Genève.

Après une forte descente, on franchit l'autoroute, puis la voie ferrée.

On pénètre au cœur du splendide vignoble de Lavaux – chanté par le grand écrivain vaudois Ramuz – dont les pentes plongent dans la nappe du Haut lac, face aux abrupts de la rive savoyarde. Les villages vignerons typiques de Riex et d'Épesses apparaissent enserrés dans les vignes en terrasses.
Puis le versant se raidit : c'est le terroir du Dézaley.
A l'endroit où la route contourne une petite croupe escarpée, un **belvédère**★★ aménagé découvre la vallée du Rhône valaisan ; dans cette trouée se profile, au dernier plan, la cime neigeuse du Grand Combin.
Quelques centaines de mètres plus loin, l'agglomération de Vevey-Montreux, jusqu'alors cachée, apparaît, envahissant les moindres festons du rivage, au pied du piton caractéristique de la Dent de Jaman et des falaises des Rochers de Naye.
La dernière section de la Corniche, entre Chexbres, Chardonne et Vevey (d'autres belvédères dotés de bancs jalonnent ce parcours ; le premier est pourvu d'un panneau d'orientation) réserve la découverte des différents bastions rocheux des Dents du Midi.

★ **Vevey ; Mont-Pélerin** ★★ – *Visites : 1 h 1/2. Voir à Vevey.*

★★ **Montreux** – *Voir à ce nom.*

★★ **Château de Chillon** – *Visite : 1 h. Voir à ce nom.*

Villeneuve – Ce bourg de la plaine littorale occupe un site remarquable à l'extrémité Est du Léman et conserve quelques monuments d'un passé très ancien. Sur son agréable « front de lac » aux quais ombragés et fleuris (petit port de plaisance), s'érige une statue témoignant de la « reconnaissance des Alsaciens et Français » ayant trouvé asile en Suisse lors de la guerre de 1870.
La Grand-Rue, parée de drapeaux multicolores en été, a gardé ses étroites maisons anciennes à portail de bois. De pittoresques enseignes en fer forgé ornent les façades de plusieurs magasins. Près de la place du Temple qu'agrémente une jolie fontaine, se trouve l'église St-Paul du 12e s. (remarquer les vitraux). A proximité de la gare, inhabituelle Maison de ville (mairie) installée dans l'ancienne chapelle de l'hôpital. Bien des personnages illustres séduits par le charme de la ville l'adoptèrent. Des écrivains comme Lord Byron (un hôtel porte son nom), Victor Hugo, Romain Rolland (il y habita de 1922 à 1938, villa portant son nom dans le parc de l'hôtel Byron), les peintres comme Oskar Kokoschka (il s'y éteignit en 1980), restent liés au nom de Villeneuve.

A la sortie de Villeneuve, prendre à droite en direction de Noville, puis traverser le Rhône et de nouveau à droite (route n° 21) vers le Bouveret.

Le Bouveret – Dans ce village situé à quelques kilomètres de la frontière française, se trouve le **Swiss Vapeur Parc** ⊙. Sur un circuit aménagé au bord du lac, près du port de plaisance, des trains en modèle réduit circulent au milieu d'un décor ferroviaire reconstitué au milieu d'un parc verdoyant. Les voyageurs – les enfants y trouvent leur compte – peuvent prendre place à bord de petites voitures tirées par des locomotives à vapeur (Pacific 01, Waldenbourg 030...).
En été, le **Rive-Bleue Express**, train à vapeur de la Belle Époque, relie Évian.

LENK

Berne — 2 272 habitants
Carte n° 427 pli 13 ou 217 pli 16 — Schéma : BERNER OBERLAND — Alt. 1 068 m

Dans sa large cuvette entourée de verdoyantes « montagnes à vaches » et traversée par la Simme, ici canalisée, qui s'échappe du massif enneigé du Wildstrubel quelques kilomètres plus au Sud, la charmante station thermale et hivernale de Lenk propose aux curistes ses sources sulfureuses (soignant articulations et voies respiratoires) ; aux promeneurs l'été et aux skieurs l'hiver, ses remontées mécaniques desservant les proches pentes du Metschberg, du Betelberg et du Mülkerblatten (pour skieurs seuls) ; à tous, ses équipements sportifs, son agréable centre-ville aux rues plantées d'arbres et aux chalets aussi fleuris qu'opulents...

Chutes de la Simme (Simmenfälle) — *4 km, plus 10 mn à pied AR. Laisser la voiture au parc autos situé à gauche du restaurant, et suivre la signalisation* (indiquant « Barbarabrücke »). Puissantes et bruyantes, elles dévalent la paroi rocheuse du Wildstrubel pour s'écraser en fin de course aux pieds du spectateur, qui ne voit d'elles que leur partie terminale, le reste lui étant masqué par les sapins (et n'étant visible qu'avec un important recul, à partir du restaurant).

★ **Cascade d'Iffigen (Iffigenfall)** — *2,5 km, plus 3/4 h à pied AR.*
Quitter Lenk par la route d'Iffigen, au Sud : nous conseillons de laisser la voiture au terme de la section revêtue (en vue, déjà, de la cascade) et de gravir à pied, sur 2 km, le prolongement cailloutueux et raide *(15 % — circulation automobile autorisée seulement en convois et à heures fixes)* de la route. Un virage à gauche permet d'admirer au plus près cette impressionnante chute verticale de 80 m tombant entre les sapins et se scindant à mi-parcours.

LEUK

LOÈCHE — 3 253 habitants
Carte Michelin n° 427 pli 13 ou 217 plis 16, 17 — Schéma : VALAIS — Alt. 750 m

Leuk s'étage à mi-pente au-dessus de la vallée du Rhône, à la sortie des gorges de la Dala. La petite ville doit à son cadre de versants arides et de sommets lourdement modelés une âpreté de site bien caractéristique des aspects déjà méridionaux du Valais.
De l'esplanade des châteaux à l'entrée de la localité, le **coup d'œil ★** sur le fond de la vallée est étonnant : immédiatement en contrebas s'épanouit l'énorme cône de déjection de l'Illgraben recouvert d'une végétation mi-bocagère, mi-forestière (forêt de Finges ou Pfynwald), proposé à tous les écoliers suisses comme exemple de forme d'accumulation torrentielle. Ce bouchon continue à former frontière naturelle entre le Valais central de langue française et le Haut-Valais, de culture germanique.

Les châteaux — Leur nom évoque les titres des fonctionnaires de l'évêque de Sion qui y avaient élu résidence.
La première maison forte rencontrée en pénétrant dans l'agglomération est le **château des Vidommes** (les vidames de la France de l'Ancien Régime). Devenue hôtel de ville, cette construction du 16e s., toute en hauteur, aux pignons à redans flanqués d'échauguettes, rappelle, en beaucoup plus élégant et original, le monument de Sierre connu sous le même nom. Plus loin, le **château des Majors** (15e s.), assez délabré, se reconnaît à sa tour carrée crénelée.

ENVIRONS

Leukerbad — *15 km au Nord par la route directe — environ 1/2 h.* Cette station thermale d'altitude, dont les eaux sulfatées gypseuses et calcaires sont conseillées pour le traitement des rhumatismes, des troubles de la circulation, des affections gynécologiques et des maladies de peau, figurait obligatoirement, au 19e s., dans le programme de voyage du touriste à pied.
Leukerbad marque le terme de la fameuse traversée du col de la Gemmi (alt. 2 314 m) qui, prenant son origine en Oberland bernois, à Kandersteg *(voir à ce nom)*, se termine sur ce versant valaisan, par un chemin vertigineux, taillé en pleine paroi rocheuse. C'est dans ce site extraordinaire que Guy de Maupassant trouva l'inspiration d'un conte fantastique, l'Auberge.
Le spectacle grandiose qu'offre la tribune naturelle de la **Gemmi** (vues sur les Alpes valaisannes et bernoises) mérite qu'on aille l'apprécier.
Possibilité de monter au col de la Gemmi en téléphérique.

On peut également rejoindre Leukerbad par le pittoresque village d'**Albinen** dont les maisons de bois accrochées aux pentes semblent défier les lois de l'équilibre. La route étroite et sinueuse offre des vues vertigineuses en plusieurs points du parcours.

Le LIECHTENSTEIN

Carte Michelin n° 427 plis 7, 8, 16, 17 ou 216 Sud des plis 21, 22

Fragment de l'ancienne Confédération Germanique, la principauté du Liechtenstein, dont le territoire s'étend de la rive droite du Rhin aux monts du Vorarlberg, comprend 11 communes et attire de nombreux curieux.

Érigé en principauté souveraine par l'empereur Charles VI en 1719, en faveur du prince Jean Adam de Liechtenstein, le petit État doit, pour une grande part, le maintien de son statut à la sage politique menée par le prince Jean II « le Bon », dont le long règne (1858-1929) n'a guère été dépassé que par celui de Louis XIV. De 1939 à 1989, il a été gouverné par François Joseph II ; son fils, le prince Hans Adam, a depuis pris sa succession. Le Liechtenstein a desserré, depuis 1919, ses derniers liens avec l'Autriche et conclu avec la Confédération Helvétique des conventions monétaires, postales, douanières et diplomatiques : il fait aujourd'hui pratiquement partie de l'alliance économique suisse.

La frontière Sud marque nettement la séparation entre les civilisations germanique et rhétique : les grands villages disposés en désordre parmi les vergers, au pied de quelque « burg » ou autour d'églises à la flèche aiguë, contrastent avec les cités grisonnes étroitement agglomérées au milieu de leurs vignobles.

Quelques renseignements généraux :
160 km² – 29 386 habitants en 1990 ;
Abréviation officielle : FL (utilisée pour l'immatriculation des véhicules) ;
Langue officielle : l'allemand ;
Majorité confessionnelle catholique ;
Monarchie constitutionnelle ;
Parlement ou Diète, élu par le peuple pour 4 ans, composé de 25 membres ;
Gouvernement mandaté pour 4 ans, composé de 5 membres : le chef du gouvernement, son suppléant et trois conseillers.
Le passage de Suisse au Liechtenstein n'est soumis à aucune formalité.

VADUZ   visite : 1 h 1/2

Au pied de l'imposant **château** qui sert de résidence à la famille princière, le bourg-capitale où siège le gouvernement du Liechtenstein est devenu un attrayant foyer d'animation touristique à caractère international.

Bureau de Poste – Il offre aux philatélistes l'occasion unique du droit d'émission dont bénéficie ce petit État et n'attire pas moins de curieux que le musée postal.

Collections d'art de l'État du Liechtenstein (Liechtensteinische Staatliche Kunstsammlungen) 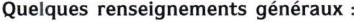 – Peinture et art graphique du 20e s. ainsi qu'une partie des célèbres **collections princières** ★ parmi lesquelles on peut voir, au 2e étage, le carrosse d'or, fabriqué à Paris par Nicolas Pineau, pour le prince Joseph Wenzel von Liechtenstein, ambassadeur d'Autriche à la cour de France en 1738.

Musée national (Liechtensteinisches Landesmuseum)  – Installé dans les bâtiments, restaurés, d'une ancienne auberge, il présente la géologie du pays (plan-relief ; minéralogie), des collections préhistoriques et de l'âge du bronze, des objets et monnaies de l'époque romaine, des bijoux et armes alémaniques de la même époque, des armes blanches et armures médiévales, des armes à feu du 16e au 18e s. (dont des canons-jouets), une collection d'ustensiles et objets d'art populaire anciens (plus une chambre paysanne), mais aussi différentes œuvres d'art : tableaux du 16e s., sculptures religieuses allemandes (Vierge à l'Enfant du 14e s. ; Pâmoison de la Vierge, haut-relief du 16e s. ; Nativité du 16e s. ; statues baroques des 17e et 18e s.), objets de culte...

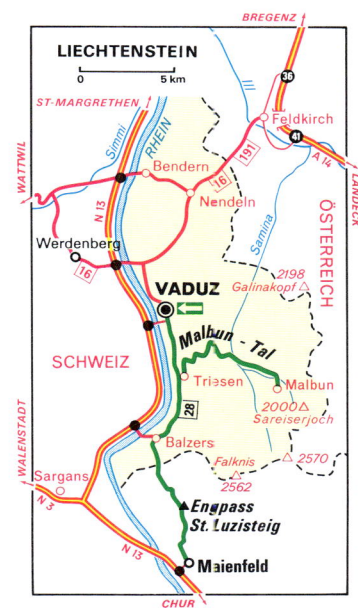

Le LIECHTENSTEIN

Musée postal (Briefmarkenmuseum) ⊙ – Occupant une petite salle du même bâtiment que le Musée d'art, il met fort bien en valeur l'art philatélique du Liechtenstein : timbres-poste en agrandissement, plaques de frappe, collections de timbres et médailles du pays.
Des expositions temporaires consacrées à de nouvelles émissions ou à des créateurs de timbres sont organisées périodiquement.

AU SUD DE VADUZ

De Vaduz à Maienfeld 16 km – environ 3/4 h

Quitter Vaduz au Sud par la route de Triesen.

Vallée de Malbun (Malbun Tal) – *15 km au départ de Triesen.* Cartes n°s 427 pli 16 ou 216 pli 22 et 218 pli 4. Au cœur du pays, pittoresque montée vers le cirque terminal du Sareiser Joch (alt. 2 000 m), relevant des premiers contreforts du Vorarlberg.

Défilé (Engpass) de St-Luzisteig – Ce défilé fortifié ne semble s'éloigner de la chaude et large vallée du Rhin que pour la retrouver aussitôt.
Étranglé entre la colline du Fläscherberg et les rudes escarpements du Falknis longtemps saupoudrés de neige, le défilé de St-Luzisteig présenta une importance stratégique tant que la route qui l'emprunte resta la seule voie carrossable entre l'Autriche et les Grisons.
Le passage est encore coupé aujourd'hui par une ligne de fortifications élevées certaines en 1703 et la plupart de 1831 à 1837.
Sur le revers grison du col de Luziensteig, la route en pente rapide est tracée à travers de frais sous-bois.
On peut choisir comme point de halte, à 1 km du village de Maienfeld, la clairière ombragée de chênes où une « fontaine d'Heidi » (Heidibrunnen) commémore le souvenir de Johanna Spyri (1827-1901), écrivain zurichois auteur de livres pour la jeunesse très populaire en Suisse, notamment pour son roman *Heidi*.

Maienfeld – Petite cité grisonne entourée de vignobles, d'une distinction déjà méridionale.

LOCARNO★★

Tessin – 13 796 habitants
Carte Michelin n° 427 pli 24 ou 219 plis 7 et 8 – Alt. 214 m
Plan dans le guide Rouge Michelin Suisse

Au creux d'une baie ensoleillée, dont la courbe se resserre à mesure que progresse, dans les eaux du **lac Majeur**★★★ *(description dans le guide Vert Michelin Italie)*, le delta formé par la Maggia, Locarno est favorisée par un climat privilégié et l'on y voit fleurir, dès le mois de mars, hortensias, magnolias, camélias.
Les jardins, les bords du lac, les versants plantés de vignes au flanc desquels se disséminent les villas d'Orselina, les hauteurs de Cardada sont, pour les hôtes de cette belle ville, autant d'incitations à la promenade.
Le monument historique de la ville est le **château des Visconti** (15e s.) où ont été installés un musée archéologique et un musée d'art contemporain.
Dans le palais de Justice (palazzo Pretorio) se déroula la conférence sur le désarmement qui mit, en 1925, la localité au premier plan de l'actualité internationale.

SORTIR A LOCARNO

Pour tout renseignement, s'adresser à l'Office du tourisme (Ente turistico), Largo Zorzi 1, ☎ (093) 751 03 33.

Shopping – Principales rues commerçantes : Via della Stazione, Via Sempione, Via Cattori, Via D. Recinto, Via F. Balli, Piazza Grande.

Théâtre – Teatro di Locarno.

Où prendre un verre ? – **Alle Grotto** (Via Sempione), l'apéritif dans un cadre typique de la région. A proximité, on peut finir la soirée au **Tarentella** bar-club-dancing. En fin de semaine, live-music à la **Cantina Canetti**, bar à vins très connu qui a conservé son cachet ancien. Le casino **Kursaal** (Largo Zorzi) attire les couche-tard pour ses machines à sous, mais aussi pour sa discothèque et son piano-bar. Dans le quatier du Muralto, le bar **Al Pozz** propose des soirées musicales où dominent l'accordéon, la mandoline et la guitare.

LOCARNO

★ **Madonna del Sasso** – Ce sanctuaire, très fréquenté par les touristes et les pèlerins, est perché au sommet (355 m) d'un éperon boisé que l'on atteint, soit en auto par les lacets de la Via ai Monti della Trinità, soit en 6 mn de funiculaire.

L'arrivée a lieu, invariablement, sur un palier plus élevé que celui de la basilique, vers laquelle on redescend (très bonne vue plongeante) par une rampe coupée d'escaliers.

Le couvent établi ici fut fondé en 1487 par Bartolomeo d'Ivrea et reconstruit en 1616. À l'intérieur de l'église se remarque une Fuite en Égypte, retable peint par Bramantino en 1522 (fond du bas-côté droit). D'une loggia, on jouit d'un beau **point de vue**★ sur Locarno et son lac.

Lac Majeur et Ascona

ENVIRONS

★★ **Cimetta** ⊙ – Le funiculaire de la Madonna del Sasso est prolongé par un téléphérique qui monte en 10 mn à l'Alpe de **Cardada** (alt. 1 350 m) : **vue**★★ très étendue.

De Cardada, un télésiège permet de gagner le sommet de la Cimetta (alt. 1 672 m) d'où l'on embrasse un beau **panorama**★★ qui s'étend du lac Majeur à la chaîne des Alpes.

★★ **Circuit de Ronco** – *17 km – environ 1 h 1/2 – par une route de corniche sur laquelle le croisement est difficile entre Ronco et Porto Ronco. Quitter Locarno au Sud-Ouest, route d'Ascona.*

Peu après le grand pont sur la Maggia, prendre à droite vers Losone. Dans ce village, après l'église, tourner à gauche (route d'Ascona et du Morte Verita) et à droite (route de Ronco) au croisement suivant. Après la traversée d'un vallon occupé par une scierie et une minoterie, laisser à droite la route d'Arcegno ; à la bifurcation suivante, prendre à droite.

La petite route de corniche, sortant de bois de châtaigniers, débouche au-dessus du lac Majeur et procure dès lors une série de **vues plongeantes**★★ de toute beauté sur le bassin helvétique du lac Majeur. En contrebas se succèdent Ascona, les deux îlots boisés de **Brissago** *(voir à Ascona)*, enfin Brissago. On découvre bientôt Ronco.

Ronco – Le village s'agrippe à flanc de pente, dans un **site**★★ tout méditerranéen. La terrasse de l'église se recommande comme belvédère, offrant une belle vue sur le lac Majeur et le Monte Gambarogno. Par un rude chemin en lacet, on rejoint la route côtière à Porto Ronco ; tourner à gauche. La chaussée comporte plusieurs passages taillés dans le rocher. La persévérance trouve sa récompense à l'entrée de la séduisante bourgade d'Ascona.

LOCARNO

★ **Ascona** – *Voir à ce nom.*

Le Val Verzasca, le Val Onsernone et les vallées affluentes de la Maggia (Val de Campo, Val de Bosco, Val Bavona), sont à signaler pour le cachet de leurs villages tessinois *(illustration en Introduction : La Suisse pittoresque).*

Des services de bateaux proposent de belles promenades, de la traversée menant aux pontons de la rive opposée du lac (Magadino) ou à Ascona et Brissago, au périple offrant, du printemps à l'automne, la possibilité de visiter Stresa et les îles Borromées.

Le LOCLE

Neuchâtel – 11 313 habitants
Carte Michelin nº 427 pli 12 ou 216 pli 12

Cette petite ville du Jura tapie au fond d'une vallée et reliée à la Franche-Comté toute proche par le Col-des-Roches doit sa prospérité à l'horlogerie qui apparut au 18ᵉ s. grâce à un jeune orfèvre Daniel Jean-Richard *(voir à ce nom)* venu s'établir dans la région.

CURIOSITÉS

★ **Musée d'Horlogerie** ⊙ – Sur les hauteurs du Locle, le **château des Monts,** élégante demeure classique du 18ᵉ s. entourée d'un beau parc, abrite un musée qui complète parfaitement celui de la Chaux-de-Fonds *(voir à ce nom)* exposant de très belles pièces de pays différents. Le rez-de-chaussée constitue un appartement témoin du style de l'époque : grand salon, antichambre, salle à manger lambrissée, bibliothèque, meublés et décorés avec goût, servent de cadre à la présentation d'une belle collection d'horloges et de pendules, chefs-d'œuvre d'orfèvrerie. La salle A.-L. Perrelet illustre l'évolution de la montre depuis la première montre à remontage automatique jusqu'à la plus petite montre électronique. Au 1ᵉʳ étage se trouve la salle Maurice-Yves Sandoz, qui renferme des sujets à automates miniaturisés dont la « fée Carabosse », objet en cuivre doré représentant une vieille femme marchant à grand-peine. Au second étage consacré en partie à la chronologie de la mesure du temps (instruments anciens, horloges, pendules, montres, chronomètres, outillage), l'atelier d'un horloger local a été reconstitué. Film et diaporama complètent la visite.

Musée des Beaux-Arts ⊙ – Outre une section consacrée à des peintures et des sculptures d'artistes suisses des 19ᵉ et 20ᵉ s. (Girardet, Koller, Kaiser, Mathey), le musée possède un intéressant cabinet des estampes réunissant des œuvres d'artistes suisses et étrangers, ainsi remarque-t-on : Richard Wagner par Vallotton, L'Atelier par Giacometti, Première neige par Lermite, la Ronde des étoiles par Dufy ; Portrait de Claude par Renoir.

Moulins souterrains du Col-des-Roches ⊙ – Ils furent installés au 16e s. afin d'utiliser la force des eaux de la vallée du Locle. Du milieu du 17e s. à la fin du 19e s. les moulins se développèrent et connurent une intense activité : battoirs, four à pain, scierie fonctionnèrent à plein grâce à d'imposantes roues entraînées par des eaux mugissantes. Transformés ensuite en abattoirs, puis désaffectés, les moulins furent sauvés de l'oubli et restaurés pour faire revivre une page de leur histoire.

Dans le hall d'entrée, une exposition sur les moulins, leur rôle, leur fonctionnement constitue une bonne introduction à la visite des installations.

La descente dans la grotte permet de découvrir galeries et puits creusés à la force du poignet, ainsi que d'impressionnantes roues superposées, engrenages, moulin à farine, scies.

LOÈCHE
Voir à LEUK

LUCERNE
Voir à LUZERN

LUGANO★★★
Tessin – 25 334 habitants
Carte Michelin n° 427 pli 24 ou 219 pli 8 – Alt. 273 m

La « reine du Ceresio » s'étend au fond d'une baie harmonieuse qu'encadrent le Monte Brè et le Monte San Salvatore, revêtus de bois. Exposée au midi, Lugano est une station climatique et touristique particulièrement appréciée aux saisons intermédiaires (printemps, automne). L'organisation des innombrables fêtes et distractions offertes au séjournant (plages, tennis, golf de 18 trous, équitation, bateaux, casino) fait honneur à la Suisse. Lugano est aussi un centre d'excursions bien placé pour visiter les trois lacs, Majeur, de Lugano et de Côme.

On flâne avec plaisir dans Lugano, sous les arcades de la via Nassa et surtout le long de la magnifique promenade ombragée aménagée en bordure du lac, depuis le parc municipal jusqu'à Paradiso, offrant des points de vue d'une variété infinie.

S'asseoir à la terrasse d'un café sur la Piazza della Riforma ne manque pas de charme.

★★ **Le lac de Lugano** – La plus grande partie de ce lac est en territoire suisse. Les Italiens, qui le nomment Ceresio, n'en possèdent que la branche Nord-Est (Porlezza), une partie de la rive Sud-Ouest (Porto Ceresio) et une enclave de la rive Est (Campione d'Italia).

D'un aspect plus sauvage que les lacs Majeur et de Côme, le lac de Lugano est enchâssé au milieu des pentes abruptes mais harmonieuses des Pré-Alpes, sur lesquelles ressortent, en taches claires, les feuillages argentés des oliviers. De forme irrégulière, l atteint 33 km dans sa plus grande longueur et une profondeur maximum de 288 m. Une chaussée, livrant passage à la route et à la voie ferrée du Gothard, le sépare, assez malheureusement, en deux bassins, entre lesquels le passage des bateaux est cependant assuré.

SORTIR A LUGANO

Pour tout renseignement, s'adresser à l'Office du tourisme (Ente turistico), riva Albertolli 5, ☎ (091) 921 46 64.

Shopping

Le centre-ville avec ses petites rues à majorité piétonnes rassemble quantité de magasins aux vitrines attirantes.

Théâtre et musique

La saison s'étale de mai à octobre, et de nombreux spectacles ont lieu au Palais des Congrès ou sur différentes places du centre-ville (Rifforma, Maghetti ou Chiesa S. ta Marta).

Un verre dans un endroit agréable

Le long de la Riva Paradisio, plusieurs établissements sont une invite pour finir la soirée dans un cadre chic ou sympathique. Ainsi le **Golfe**, le **Charlie Pub**, le **Karisma Pub**. Après 22 h le **Cecil**, cabaret-show-dancing.

Dans le centre-ville, on pourra déguster les vins du Tessin au **Bottegone del Vino** (v. Magatti) ou au **Trani** (Salira Mario et Antonion Chiattone).

Pour les noctambules, c'est après 23 h que le Corso Pestalozzi s'arime le plus, notamment après la sortie du cinéma le **Corso**. Après la séance on peut entrer au **Bar 90** ou a l'**Abbaino** où sont proposés spectacles et soirées à thèmes.

Canova (Via)	Y 12
Luvini (Via G.)	Y 31
Nassa (Via)	Z 43
Pessina (Via)	Y 48
Pestalozzi (Corso)	Y 49
Posta (Via della)	Y 51
Verla (Contrada di)	Y 66

Adamini (Via)	AX 3
Albonago (Via)	BV 4
Aldesago (Via)	BV 6
Bosia (Via)	AX 7
Calloni (Via S.)	AX 9
Camara (Via)	AV 10
Cantonale (Via)	Y 13
Capelli (Via P.)	BV 15
Cassarate (Viale)	BV 16
Casserinetta (Via)	AX 18
Castagnola (Viale)	BX 19
Cattaneo (Viale C.)	Y 21
Cattori (Via G.)	AX 22
Dante (Piazza)	Y 24
Franscini (Viale S.)	AV 25
Ginevra (Via)	AV 27
Indipendenza (Piazza)	Y 28
Laghetto (Via al)	AX 30
Maderno (Via C.)	AV 33
Madonna della Salute (V.)	AV 34
Madonnetta (Via)	BV 36
Manzoni (Piazza A.)	Y 37
Manzoni (Via R.)	AX 39
Maraini (Via C.)	AX 40
Monte Ceneri (Via)	AV 42
Paradiso (Riva)	AX 45
Peri (Via P.)	Y 46
Regazzoni (Via P.)	Y 52
Rezzonico (Piazza R.)	Z 54
Riforma (Piazza della)	YZ 55
Riva (Via A.)	AX 57
San Giorgio (Via)	BX 58
San Gottardo (Via)	Y 60
Scuole (Via delle)	AX 61
Sonvico (Via)	BV 63
Tesserete (Via)	AV 64
Vicari (Via G.)	BV 67

CURIOSITÉS

★★ **Parc municipal (Parco civico)** (BX) – Délicieux jardin public au bord du lac où de beaux arbres dispensent leur fraîcheur. On y donne parfois, en saison et par beau temps, des concerts en plein air. Des statues (Socrate, œuvre du sculpteur russe Antokolsky) et fontaines agrémentent le site.

« **Piccionaia** » (Y) – *A l'angle Nord-Est (en retrait) du carrefour Corso Pestalozzi-Via Pioda*. La jolie maison basse connue sous ce nom (« pigeonnier »), à la façade ornée de frises peintes, serait la plus ancienne de Lugano.

Cathédrale St-Laurent (San Lorenzo) (Y) – Elle possède une élégante façade avec trois portails aux fins motifs Renaissance. Au fond de la nef droite, tabernacle des frères Rodari, de Maroggia (début 16ᵉ s.). De l'esplanade, vue sur Lugano et le lac.

LUGANO

Église Ste-Marie-des-Anges (Santa Maria degli Angioli) (**Z**) – Cette ancienne église conventuelle, commencée en 1499, conserve trois des plus belles **fresques**★★ de Bernardo Luini (vers 1480-1532). La plus impressionnante, ornant la cloison séparant le chœur de la nef, expose une Passion où l'on remarque surtout une Crucifixion d'une ampleur et d'une expression extraordinaires ; au-dessous, figurent saint Sébastien et saint Roch. Dans la 1re chapelle de droite, sur le mur gauche, la fresque représentant une Vierge à l'Enfant et saint Jean « d'une beauté digne de Léonard » provient du cloître. Dans la nef est représentée la Cène.

★★★ **Monte San Salvatore** ⊙ – Alt. 912 m. *3/4 h AR environ dont 20 mn de funiculaire, partant du quartier de Paradiso* (**AX**). On découvre une vue admirable sur Lugano, le lac, les Alpes bernoises et valaisannes (belvédère avec balcons d'orientation).
Du sommet, il est possible de redescendre sur Lugano par des sentiers signalés.

★ **Villa Favorita** (**BX**) ⊙ – *A Castagnola. Bus n° 2 au départ de la Piazza Manzoni, descendre à Villa Favorita.*
On accède à cette construction de la fin du 17e s., à trois étages décalés surmontés par une gloriette, par un long et étroit parc-jardin en corniche sur le lac, planté de buis, cyprès, palmiers, araucarias... et peuplé de statues.
L'essentiel de la remarquable collection de peintures constituée de 1920 à nos jours par les barons Thyssen-Bornemisza, de la célèbre dynastie de sidérurgistes allemands, a été transférée à Madrid au musée Thyssen-Bornemisza *(voir guide Vert Michelin Espagne)*. La Villa Favorita organise périodiquement, à partir de la collection Thyssen-Bornemisza, des expositions temporaires de qualité ayant trait à un mouvement ou sur un thème donné. Ainsi l'exposition intitulée *L'Europe et l'Amérique : peintures et aquarelles des 19e et 20e s.* permit-elle d'apprécier les Écoles Luministe et de l'Hudson River, ainsi que les grands impressionnistes américains et les peintres de l'Ouest.

Villa Heleneum (**BX**) ⊙ – *De la Piazza Manzoni, bus n° 2. Descendre à San Domenico, puis 5 mn à pied le long de via Cortivo.*
Au bord du lac, une villa de style néo-classique abrite le **musée des Cultures non européennes** (Museo delle Culture Extraeuropee). Les collections rassemblent environ 600 objets, principalement des sculptures en bois océaniennes, asiatiques et africaines. Chacun des trois étages illustre sur un thème donné (environnement, vie sociale) les traits caractéristiques d'un groupe ethnique.

★★ **Monte Brè** ⊙ – Alt. 925 m. *1 h AR environ dont 30 mn de funiculaire, partant de Cassarate* (**BX**). *Possibilité de monter également en voiture.* Sommet extrêmement ensoleillé ; des terrasses, très belle vue sur le lac et les Alpes (nombreuses promenades à pied possibles dans ce secteur).

ENVIRONS

Excursions en auto ou en chemin de fer de montagne

★★★ **Monte Generoso** – Alt. 1 701 m. *L'excursion demande une grande demi-journée. 15 km par ③ du plan et la route de Côme, jusqu'à Capolago d'où l'on rejoint, à droite, Riva San Vitale.*

Riva San Vitale – Baptistère du 5e s. abritant des fresques des 14e et 15e s., restaurées ; élégante église Santa Croce (16e s.) surmontée d'une coupole octogonale et ornée de fresques.

Revenir à Capolago où l'on quitte la voiture pour emprunter le chemin de fer à crémaillère. Durée du trajet AR : 2 h.

★★★ **Monte Generoso** ⊙ – L'arrivée au sommet révèle la splendeur du **panorama**★★★ sur les Alpes, Lugano, les lacs, la plaine lombarde, s'étendant jusqu'aux Apennins par temps clair.

★ **Swissminiatur (Melide)** ⊙ – *7 km au Sud.* Pour l'enchantement des enfants, cette reconstitution à l'échelle 1/25 des principales curiosités de chaque canton suisse, occupant environ 1 ha de terrain verdoyant et fleuri en bordure du lac, présente en réduction monuments (reproduits en pierre), ponts, sites et nappes d'eau, mais évoque aussi les grandes activités économiques du pays. Trains (3 km de réseau), bateaux et téléphériques fonctionnent.

★★ **Morcote** ⊙ – *Circuit de 26 km – environ 2 h – faisant emprunter à l'aller une petite route de montagne assez accidentée. Accès par bateau.*
Quitter Lugano par Paradiso (③ du plan), puis prendre la route de Morcote.
Cette route par les hauteurs (via Pazzallo et Carona) offre de magnifiques **vues plongeantes**★★ sur le lac et des échappées lointaines pouvant atteindre le massif du Mont Rose.

LUGANO

★★ **Le village** – Les maisons à arcades lombardes de Morcote se mirent dans les eaux calmes du lac de Lugano, au pied des dernières pentes, couvertes de végétation méditerranéenne, du Monte Arbostora.

Par un escalier et des ruelles offrant des perspectives multiples, on arrive au sanctuaire Santa Maria del Sasso qui renferme de remarquables fresques du 16e s.; le lac, l'église, le baptistère, les cyprès et un romantique cimetière composent un **tableau ★★** remarquable.

Rentrer à Lugano en empruntant la route du bord du lac, qui est elle aussi très attrayante.

★ **Monte Lema** – 17 km au Nord-Ouest, par Bioggio. Quitter Lugano par ④ du plan. De Bioggio, la route, en montée sinueuse sous bois, mène d'abord à Cademario.

Cademario – De ce village-balcon, belle vue (surtout auprès de l'église paroissiale) sur la plaine en contrebas, une partie de la branche Ouest du lac de Lugano, les montagnes environnantes.

Isolée à une sortie du village (en direction de Lugano), la vieille **église S. Ambrogio** ⊙, au campanile lombard coiffé de lauzes et à la façade peinte de fresques (15e s.) semi-effacées, offre à l'intérieur d'intéressantes fresques polychromes du 13e s., notamment : dans la nef, à pilier unique (peint d'une Crucifixion), au mur de droite, une Crucifixion aux nombreux personnages, plus un martyre de saint Amboise ; à l'abside, un Christ bénissant de facture byzantine entouré d'anges et d'apôtres.

Miglieglia – Au pied de la masse boisée du Monte Lema, le village est dominé par son église S. Stefano (15e s.), à toits de lauzes, dont l'intérieur s'éclaire de fresques colorées des 16e et 17e s. : remarquer, dans la chapelle face à l'entrée latérale, Dieu le Père au-dessus de Marie en prière puis visitée par l'Esprit Saint ; dans le chœur, Évangélistes et leurs symboles, Nativité, Crucifixion sous un Christ bénissant (dans une mandorle, à la voûte).

★ **Monte Lema** ⊙ – Alt. 1 624 m. *Accès par télésiège depuis Miglieglia.* La montée, d'abord au-dessus des fougères, puis d'une herbe semée de rochers, offre une vue aérienne sur Miglieglia et l'église San Stefano. Du restaurant de la station supérieure, gagner le sommet *(20 mn AR, par sentier abrupt),* entre un relais de télévision et une grande croix de métal à plots lumineux, pour observer le **panorama ★** s'étendant à l'Ouest sur le lac Majeur et le mont Rose, à l'Est sur le lac de Lugano et le Monte Generoso. Les cimes de la Jungfrau et de l'Eiger sont visibles au Nord-Ouest.

LUGANO

★ **Monte Tamaro** – 15 km au Nord-Ouest. Quitter Lugano par ④ et prendre l'autoroute en direction de Bellinzona, sortie Rivera. Gagner Alpe Foppa en téléphérique (durée du trajet : 20 mn).
Alpe Foppa (alt. 1 530 m) est le point de départ de nombreuses excursions. On peut aussi y louer des VTT et y faire du parapente. Du sommet du Monte Tamaro (alt. 1 960 m), belle **vue**★ plongeante sur le lac de Lugano, le lac Majeur, le Monte Rosa et le Matterhorn. Possibilité d'atteindre le Monte Lema en 4 h de marche.

Promenades en bateau

Les services de navigation sur le lac de Lugano, qui permettent d'effectuer aussi bien de courtes promenades improvisées d'une heure qu'un périple complet d'une demi-journée, constituent l'un des agréments de la station.

En dehors des localités citées ci-dessous, les bateaux de la Société de Navigation sur le lac de Lugano desservent régulièrement Porlezza, Ponte Tresa, Campione, etc. Un tour du lac, dit « Grande Giro del Lago », est organisé au départ de Lugano.

★ **Gandria** – *1 h AR environ si l'on ne descend pas à terre.*
Village dont les terrasses fleuries de géraniums, les treilles, les berceaux de feuillage, le labyrinthe des ruelles en escalier, les maisons à arcades, la petite église baroque composent un ensemble charmant, très goûté des artistes.

Musée des Douanes ⓥ – *A Cantine di Gandria, sur la rive Sud du lac (accès en vedette : durée totale AR, visite comprise, 1 h 3/4).* Aménagé dans un poste de douane suisse sur le bord même du lac, il renseigne sur le rôle passé et présent des douaniers à l'aide de cartes, photos et mannequins en uniforme, ainsi que (au 2e étage) sur les diverses astuces (pièges, armes spécialisées, objets truqués) imaginées par les braconniers et contrebandiers. La curiosité principale du musée est sans doute un « Zodiac » submersible, saisi en 1946 et dont les boudins en tôle contenaient... du salami. Au 3e étage, sous les combles : expositions temporaires.

★★ **Morcote** – *Voir plus haut.*

LUZERN★★★

Ⓒ Lucerne – 61 034 habitants
Carte Michelin n° 427 pli 14 ou 216 pli 17 – Schéma : VIERWALDSTÄTTER SEE
Alt. 436 m – Plan d'agglomération dans le guide Rouge Michelin Suisse

Station touristique dont la renommée internationale est entretenue par un festival de musique fameux *(voir tableau des Principales manifestations)*, Lucerne occupe un **site**★★★ remarquable à l'extrémité Nord-Ouest du lac des Quatre-Cantons, à l'endroit où la Reuss retrouve son lit.
La ville ancienne, dont l'accès par l'eau était protégé par des ponts de bois couverts, s'adosse au flanc de la montagne où se profilent sept grosses tours carrées, reliées entre elles par des murailles – restes des fortifications –, tandis que les quartiers modernes escaladent les collines de la Musegg, du Gütsch et du Dietschiberg.
A l'origine simple village de pêcheurs, Lucerne acquiert un certain renom par la fondation, au 8e s., d'un petit couvent de Bénédictins dépendant de l'abbaye alsacienne de Murbach. Mais l'ouverture de la route du Gothard, au 13e s., fait de la cité une étape importante entre les Flandres et l'Italie. Située à proximité des « Waldstätten » *(voir à ce nom)*, Lucerne n'hésite pas à nouer avec ceux-ci des relations commerciales dont elle tire le plus grand profit. De là à conclure avec eux un traité d'alliance politique, il n'y avait qu'un pas, qui fut franchi en 1332.
Après l'offensive de la Réforme, Lucerne prend la tête de la résistance catholique. Les Jésuites y ouvrent, en 1574, leur premier collège de Suisse allemande.

LUCERNE PRATIQUE

Pour tout renseignement concernant les manifestations ou les spectacles, s'adresser à l'Office du tourisme (Verkehrsverein), Frankenstrasse 1, ☎ (041) 410 71 71. A l'Office du tourisme et dans les principaux hôtels, on peut également se procurer la brochure *Luzern City Guide* qui contient un plan de la ville ainsi que des adresses utiles, informations touristiques, etc.

Shopping

C'est notamment dans la vieille ville – si pittoresque avec ses rues piétonnes au cachet ancien – que bon nombre de boutiques sont installées et font le bonheur des touristes de passage.
Grands magasins : Jelmoli (Pilatusstrasse 4), Manor Warenhäuser (Weggisstrasse 5), Au Bon Marché (Kappellgasse 4).

LUZERN

Théâtre et musique

Stadttheater, Theaterstrasse 2, ☏ (041) 23 66 18.

Cinémas

Dans Pilatusstrasse : **ABC, Moderne, New Rex**.

Où prendre un verre ?

On peut passer un moment agréable dans le salon douillet du piano-bar du **Château Gütsch**, tout en bénéficiant d'une belle vue sur la ville.
Le **Penthouse** situé au 7e étage de l'hôtel Astoria (Pilatusstrasse 29) est le rendez-vous des jeunes. Musique d'ambiance. Dans la même rue, l'hôtel Schiller propose trois bars différents : le **Grand Café**, décor à l'antique, le **Casablanca** et la **Cucaracha**, bar au décor mexicain.
Sur les bords du lac, dans un cadre raffiné et reposant, piano-bar des hôtels **National** et **Palace**.
Pour ceux qui n'osent se risquer dans l'aventure des jeux, le **Casino** dispose également d'un agréable piano-bar et d'une grande salle où sont organisés des spectacles en fin de semaine.
Dans la vieille ville, on peut devant une fondue assister au spectacle folklorique au **Stadtkeller** (Sternenplatz 3). Ambiance décontractée au **Movie Bar** (Weinmarkt), grands choix de vins et de bières dans un décor ayant pour thème le cinéma. Au sous-sol, on peut commander un Al Capone, Jaws, Love Story ou d'autres plats portant le nom d'un film célèbre.
Pour les amateurs de danse et les noctambules, à Kriens à quelques kilomètres de Lucerne, le **Broadway Dancing** : live music.

★★ LA VILLE ANCIENNE ET LES BORDS DU LAC *visite : 3 h*

Partir de la Schwanenplatz (place du Cygne) et gagner la Kapellplatz sur laquelle s'élève la chapelle St-Pierre (St. Peter).

Au centre de la Kapellplatz, se dresse la fontaine du Fritschi (Fritschibrunnen) représentant le carnaval, le printemps et la joie (Fritschi est un personnage de légende qui fait l'objet d'un carnaval, chaque année depuis le 15e s.). La Kapellgasse, rue commerçante et animée, conduit au **Kornmarkt** (Marché aux grains).

★ **Ancien hôtel de ville (Altes Rathaus)** — Construit de 1602 à 1606 au bord de la Reuss, c'est un bel édifice de style Renaissance, flanqué d'une tour carrée, qui domine le Kornmarkt. A droite de l'hôtel de ville, la « Gasthaus zu Pfistern » présente une jolie façade peinte.

Collection Picasso (Picasso Sammlung) ⊙ — La maison Am Rhyn (Am Rhyn-Haus) à gauche de l'hôtel de ville et comme celui-ci de style Renaissance, abrite des tableaux, gouaches, lavis, dessins, gravures et un livre de Picasso. La plupart des œuvres, datant en majorité des vingt dernières années de la vie de l'artiste, font partie de donations de la famille Rosengart, marchands de tableaux à Lucerne.
Parmi les tableaux on remarque un portrait de 1956, représentant Jacqueline dans l'atelier du peintre à Cannes et un *Déjeuner sur l'Herbe*, version très libre du tableau de Manet ; on reconnaît Picasso, assis à droite. On voit également une importante collection de photographies illustrant différents moments de la vie de l'artiste, professionnelle ou privée.

Prendre à gauche la Kornmarktgasse, puis à droite une ruelle menant à la petite Hirschenplatz.

Hirschenplatz (Place du Cerf) — Entourée de jolies maisons restaurées, aux façades peintes et ornées d'enseignes en fer forgé, elle fut autrefois un lieu de rencontre. Goethe séjourna au « Goldener Adler » en 1779.

★ **Weinmarkt (Marché aux vins)** — Jolie place, située au cœur de la vieille ville, dont les anciennes maisons, couvertes de peintures et décorées de nombreuses enseignes et de drapeaux, abritaient les corporations ; remarquer au n° 7 l'hôtel des Balances, et la « pharmacie du Marché aux vins » (Weinmarktapotheke) construite en 1530. Au centre de la place, la fontaine gothique représente des guerriers et saint Maurice, patron des soldats ; l'original se trouve au palais du Gouvernement.
Par la Kramgasse, on arrive à la **Mühlenplatz** (place des Moulins) qui date du 16e s. ; les marchés y avaient lieu. Jolie vue sur le Spreuerbrücke, les anciennes maisons de l'autre rive de la Reuss, et plus loin, sur la colline du Gütsch.

Spreuerbrücke — Ce pont couvert, appelé « pont des Moulins », franchit un bras de la Reuss. Il a été construit en 1408 et restauré au siècle dernier. Il est décoré de panneaux de bois peints représentant la Danse macabre, exécutés au 17e s. par Kaspar Meglinger. De ce pont, au milieu duquel s'élève une petite chapelle édifiée en 1568, on a une jolie vue sur les quais de la ville ancienne et l'église des Jésuites.

LUZERN

VILLE ANCIENNE

Kapellgasse V	Pilatusstrasse V
Kornmarktgasse V	Rössligasse V
Gerbergasse V	Kramgasse V	Weggisgasse V

Au-delà du pont, emprunter un instant la Pfistergasse.

Le bâtiment au n° 24 a servi d'Arsenal depuis sa construction en 1567-1568 jusqu'en 1983. Il abrite actuellement le **musée historique** (Historisches Museum) ⊙ dont les collections ont trait au passé politique et militaire et aux anciennes activités économiques du canton de Lucerne (armures, uniformes, poids et mesures, costumes traditionnels, orfèvrerie).

Rejoindre le quai (Reuss-Steg)

Des maisons à « oriels » *(p. 29)* et façades peintes, des fontaines fleuries, composent un charmant décor ; à gauche se présentent les tours des anciennes fortifications.

Église des Jésuites (Jesuitenkirche) — De vastes dimensions, c'est la première église de « style jésuite » construite en Suisse (1667-1677). La façade, d'une grande sobriété, est encadrée par deux hautes tours surmontées d'un clocher à bulbe.
L'**intérieur**★ est de nobles proportions ; les voûtes de la nef sont couvertes de fresques, le maître-autel est décoré d'un gigantesque retable de stuc-marbre rose. Les stucs de la nef principale sont d'inspiration rococo. Ils datent de 1750 de même que la peinture du plafond, représentant l'apothéose de saint François Xavier, patron de l'église.

A droite de l'église, prendre la Bahnhofstrasse.

Palais du Gouvernement (Regierungsgebäude) — Typique du style de la Renaissance florentine avec ses bossages, cet édifice construit de 1557 à 1564 pour le bailli Ritter est, depuis 1804, le siège du gouvernement cantonal. La cour intérieure abrite l'original de la fontaine du Weinmarkt *(voir plus haut)* datant de 1481.

Église des Franciscains (Franziskanerkirche) — Édifiée au 13ᵉ s. et maintes fois remaniée, elle possède de belles stalles et une chaire en bois ouvragé du 17ᵉ s.

★ **Kapellbrücke** — Ce pont couvert en bois, reconstruit à l'identique en un temps record après l'incendie survenu dans la nuit du 17 au 18 août 1993, traverse la Reuss à l'endroit où elle sort du lac ; sa silhouette est devenue le symbole de Lucerne. Construit au début du 14ᵉ s. et long de plus de 200 m, l'ouvrage protégeait la ville du côté du lac. Il est flanqué d'une grosse tour octogonale, couverte de tuiles, appelée **Wasserturm** (château d'eau).
Le pont était décoré d'une centaine de peintures sur bois qui s'inscrivaient dans les triangles formés par les poutres de la toiture. Ces tableaux, exécutés au début du 17ᵉ s. par Hans Heinrich Wägmann et rénovés au début du 20ᵉ s., évoquaient l'histoire de Lucerne, de la Suisse, de saint Léger et saint Maurice, patrons de la ville. Des vers en allemand commentaient chacune de ces œuvres. Des copies des anciens panneaux remplacent désormais les originaux détruits par le feu.

Revenir à la Schwanenplatz.

Au-delà du pont moderne (Seebrücke) qui franchit la Reuss, s'étend un quartier aéré où abondent de nombreux commerces.

LUZERN

Kapellbrücke

AUTRES CURIOSITÉS

★**Collégiale St. Léger (Hofkirche) (DY)** – Consacrée à saint Léger (Leodegar), patron de la ville, cette église collégiale fondée en 735 fut détruite (sauf les tours gothiques) par un incendie en 1633 et rebâtie en style Renaissance. Un cloître à l'italienne l'entoure.

Un escalier monumental donne accès à un vaste **intérieur**★ de style Renaissance tardive. Le chœur, fermé par une grille de fer forgé, est orné de jolies stalles. Des retables dorés, à nombreux personnages, décorent les dix autels des bas-côtés (Pietà dans le bas-côté droit, Mort de la Vierge dans le bas-côté gauche). Les orgues (1650) comptent parmi les meilleures de Suisse.

Le rivage – Les quais (Schweizerhofquai, Nationalquai) plantés d'arbres et bordés de palais, offrent des **vues**★★ **(DY)** admirables sur le site de la ville, sur le lac des Quatre-Cantons, et au-delà, sur la chaîne des Alpes qui se développe du Rigi au Pilate *(tables d'orientation)*. En continuant la promenade le long du lac, on atteint le Carlspittelerquai ; à l'extrémité de celui-ci s'étendent d'agréables espaces verts ainsi que la plage du Lido.

★★★ **Musée Suisse des Transports (Verkehrshaus)** ⊙ – *Lidostrasse 15 (près du lac) par Haldenstrasse* **(DY)**. Créé en 1959, ce musée offre aux visiteurs de tous âges un attrayant voyage dans le passé et le présent, en même temps qu'une illustration du développement des transports en Suisse. Ses différentes sections se répartissent dans une douzaine de bâtiments que séparent des aires de jeux, de restauration ou de verdure.

Chemins de fer suisses – Deux hangars et une place couverte abritent une collection de véhicules ferroviaires, la plus importante en Suisse. La plus ancienne des locomotives à vapeur date de 1858, la plus récente de 1916. La collection est particulièrement riche en locomotives électriques de la période pionnière : première motrice de tramway de 1888, première locomotive électrique triphasée en Europe de 1899, première locomotive à courant monophasé à haute tension de 1904. D'autres modèles antérieurs à 1949 incluent le Crocodile et l'AE 8/14 (la plus puissante pour son époque). A signaler également des véhicules à crémaillère, dont un modèle de 1873 des chemins de fer à crémaillère « Vitznau-Rigi » (le premier en Europe). Plusieurs tramways et une riche collection de modèles réduits complètent la collection.

Une grande maquette animée de la rampe Nord de la ligne du St-Gothard reproduit le trajet de Wassen à Göschenen. Le poste de pilotage d'une locomotive moderne simule un voyage au St-Gothard. *Un train miniature à vapeur promène les jeunes enfants.*

Autos, motos, vélos... – Une collection d'environ 40 véhicules occupe le rez-de-chaussée : du plus ancien – voiture genevoise Thury-Nussberg de 1877 – à une Ford Concept Car de 1980, en passant par une voiture de course Dufaux (Genève) de 1905, un taxi zurichois de 1908, une Mercedes (« Flèche d'argent ») de 1933... A l'entresol sont exposés plusieurs traîneaux, diligences et calèches du 19e s., et à l'étage une cinquantaine de cycles (Grand cycle de 1875, quadricycle engadinois de 1880) et motocyclettes anciennes ou modernes, ainsi que des moteurs d'automobiles.

LUZERN

Postes et télécommunications – Le premier bâtiment montre l'évolution de la poste suisse ainsi que l'acheminement et les manipulations d'un envoi postal et la fabrication d'un timbre-poste ; un stand est consacré aux philatélistes. Dans un second local, sont retracées les phases historiques des télécommunications et présentées les réalisations modernes dans les domaines du télégraphe, du téléphone, de la radio et de la télévision. Certaines opérations peuvent être effectuées par les visiteurs.

Navigation, téléphériques, tourisme – Au rez-de-chaussée, machinerie du vapeur Pilatus (1895). La partie Navigation *(1er étage)* expose une intéressante collection de modèles réduits et d'instruments de bord traduisant les progrès de la marine au cours des siècles. Remarquer le comptoir d'un armateur, où a été rassemblée la belle collection de maquettes de bateaux, de livres et peintures sur la marine, léguée au musée par le commerçant Philipp Keller en 1980. La section Téléphériques *(2e étage)* montre aussi bien une cabine du tout premier téléphérique suisse (1908), qui transportait des passagers au Wetterhorn, que la cabine ultramoderne, construite en 1984 pour relier Spielboden à Längfluh, près de Saas-Fee. La partie Tourisme présente un échantillonnage des productions et activités suisses les plus typiques, et le Swissorama, un panorama filmé des sites réputés du pays.
L'authentique bateau Rigi de 1847, placé dans la cour intérieure du musée, sert aujourd'hui de restaurant self-service.

Des aérostats aux fusées – Maquettes de ballons libres ou dirigeables, nacelle de montgolfière... voisinent avec l'étalage de tout l'équipement nécessaire à un avion de ligne. Au-dessus sont suspendus les spécimens originaux de plus de 30 appareils suisses civils ou militaires, des premiers biplans aux « jets » supersoniques et hélicoptères. Les plus gros avions sont parqués au sol, et à l'extérieur. Aux étages supérieurs, la section astronautique conserve nombre d'objets des années 60 ayant servi à la conquête de l'espace et de la Lune par les Américains : matériaux de revêtement, éléments de fusées, satellites récupérés ; capsule spatiale Mercury, échantillons de roche lunaire et scaphandre lunaire, etc., plus divers accessoires et modèles réduits. A cette section correspondent les séances de projection commentées *(durée : 1/2 h)* du **« Cosmorama »** *(2e étage)* relatant les étapes de l'aventure spatiale sur un écran de 170 m², et du **Planétarium « Longines »** *(rez-de-chaussée)*, qui propose une captivante initiation à l'étude des phénomènes cosmiques.

Fondation Hans Erni – Destinée à l'interprétation artistique du monde technique moderne, elle s'est dotée, en 1979, d'un bâtiment qui abrite environ 300 tableaux (plus des céramiques) du grand peintre lucernois contemporain Hans Erni, des années 30 (toiles abstraites) aux décennies suivantes (toiles symbolistes ou figuratives), l'ensemble étant couronné par la double fresque (40 m) de l'auditorium où sont figurés les principaux savants ou penseurs de l'Occident, de l'Antiquité à nos jours.

Musée des Beaux-Arts (Kunstmuseum) (**DZ**) ⊙ – Ce musée, installé dans le Palais des Arts et des Congrès (Kunst-und Kongresshaus) où sont donnés les concerts du festival de Lucerne, ouvre ses portes à d'importantes expositions temporaires, notamment dans le cadre du festival de musique.
Les salles du 1er étage conservent, avec quelques sculptures religieuses, des peintures sur bois du 16e s. d'artistes suisses (Martin Moser : *Histoire de Lazare*) ou étrangers (Holbein le Jeune : *Suicide de Lucrèce*), des toiles du 17e s. (Kaspar Meglinger : *Danse macabre*) et du 18e s. (J. Melchior Wyrsch, Anton Graff : portraits).
Les salles suivantes (fin 19e s.-début 20e s.) exposent des œuvres suisses réalistes de Vallotton *(la Femme aux roses)*, Robert Zünd (paysages), Ferdinand Hodler (portraits, paysages, allégories), Max Buri, etc., mais aussi de petits tableaux de l'école française non conformiste signés par Dufy (*Bois de Boulogne*, en bleus et verts), Utrillo *(Moulin de la Galette)*, Foujita (paysage), Vlaminck (nature morte)...
Au 2e étage, d'autres compositions de peintres suisses du 19e s. et du 20e s. sont exposées.

Musée Richard Wagner ⊙ – *Accès en bateau depuis l'embarcadère situé près du Seebrück. En voiture, sortir par la Hirschmattstrasse (**CDZ**). A la Bundesplatz, prendre la Tribschenstrasse et suivre la signalisation vers Tribschen.*
La demeure où vécut Richard Wagner de 1866 à 1872, et dans laquelle il reçut Nietzsche, est agréablement située sur un promontoire, au milieu d'un vaste parc descendant en pente douce vers le lac. C'est là que le compositeur créa quelques-unes de ses œuvres maîtresses : *Les Maîtres-Chanteurs, Siegfried, Le Crépuscule des Dieux.*
Au rez-de-chaussée sont rassemblés des partitions originales et divers souvenirs dont le piano Erard qui l'accompagna lors de différents voyages.

Richard Wagner

LUZERN

Gerbergasse		DY 13
Kapellgasse		CDZ
Kornmarktgasse		CZ 21
Kramgasse		CZ 22
Pilatusstrasse		CDZ
Rössligasse		CZ 31
Theilinggasse		CY 36

Weggisgasse		CZ 39
Baselstrasse		CZ 3
Bundesstrasse		CDZ 7
Denkmalstrasse		DY 10
Europaplatz		DZ 12
Grendelstrasse		DY 15
Hirschenplatz		CZ 16
Kapellplatz		DZ 18
Kornmarkt		CZ 19

Löwengartenstrasse		DY 25
Morgartenstrasse		DZ 27
Mühlenplatz		CZ 28
Pfistergasse		CZ 30

D Franziskanerkirche
M¹ Natur-Museum
M² Historisches Museum
P Regierungsgebäude

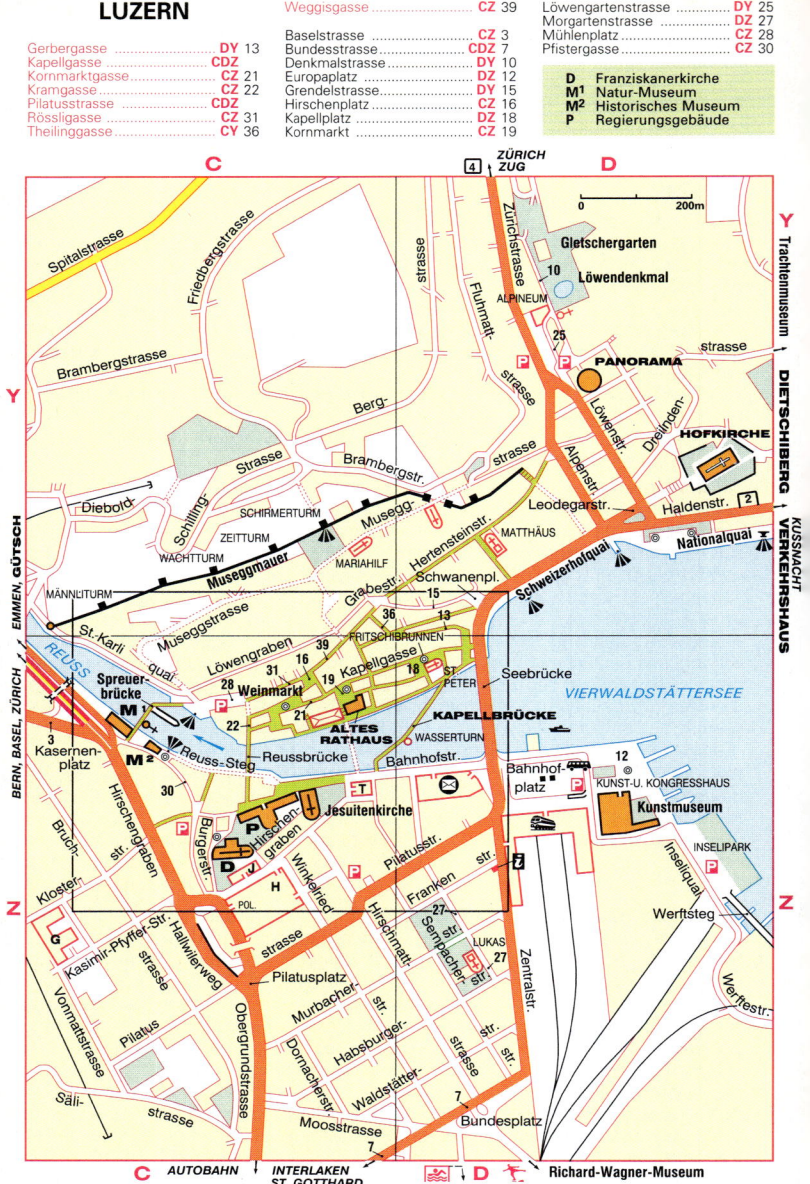

Le premier étage expose une collection d'instruments de musique anciens (dont quelques beaux spécimens de lutherie).

★ **Grand Panorama de Lucerne** (**DY**) ⊙ – Sur une toile circulaire de 1 100 m², le peintre genevois Castres a représenté l'un des épisodes de la guerre franco-allemande de 1870-71 : l'entrée en Suisse, le 1ᵉʳ février 1871, de l'armée française de Bourbaki.

Monument du lion (Löwendenkmal) (**DY**) – Sculpté dans un rocher de grès, ce lion expirant, une lance plantée dans le flanc gauche, rappelle l'héroïsme et la fidélité des gardes suisses de Louis XVI, tombés lors de la prise des Tuileries, le 10 août 1792. Monument pathétique que l'écrivain américain Mark Twain qualifia ainsi : « The saddest piece of stone in the world » (la sculpture la plus triste qui existe au monde).

Jardin des glaciers (Gletschergarten) (**DY**) ⊙ – Il transporte le visiteur à l'époque où toute la plaine jusqu'au Jura était recouverte par le glacier de la Reuss. On y voit 32 « marmites de géants », excavations mises au jour en 1872.
Ces marmites, dont l'une a une profondeur de plus de 9,5 m et un diamètre de 8 m, ont été creusées par l'eau descendue dans les crevasses du glacier et façonnées au moyen de pierres, ou « meules », tournées par l'eau (l'une d'elles atteint 6 t).

LUZERN

Un musée renferme, au rez-de-chaussée, des collections préhistoriques (fossiles de plantes et d'animaux), une reconstitution d'une grotte de chasseurs de rennes de la fin de l'époque glaciaire, le premier relief de la Suisse centrale établi au 18e s., des modèles réduits de maisons traditionnelles. Au premier étage, une chambre paysanne a été reconstituée, des documents retracent l'histoire du jardin des glaciers. Au deuxième étage, plans, gravures et maquettes font revivre le vieux Lucerne ; mobilier du 18e s.

Remparts de la Musegg (CY) ⊘ – Restes de l'enceinte fortifiée comptant neuf tours de garde et de défense, construite de 1350 à 1408, et qui jadis entourait toute la ville.
Du sommet de la tour Schirmer (91 marches) – reconstruite après l'incendie survenu au printemps 1994, **vue**★ sur Lucerne dont se détachent les flèches de la collégiale St-Léger, et le lac dans son cadre de montagnes.

Église St-Charles (St. Karlikirche) – *Sortir par Hirschengraben* (CZ) – Église moderne, bâtie en 1934 par l'architecte Metzger. Le porche est surmonté de statues figurant les évangélistes.
A l'intérieur, la nef, à plafond plat, est soutenue par de hautes colonnes. Elle est décorée de fresques et éclairée par des vitraux jaunes et violets. De la terrasse en bordure de la Reuss, on aperçoit les tours des remparts de la Musegg.

Musée d'Histoire naturelle et d'Archéologie (Naturmuseum) (V) ⊘ – Axé sur les particularités naturelles de la Suisse centrale, ce musée présente au 1er étage une abondante collection de minéralogie alpine et de fossiles, et surtout une remarquable **salle d'archéologie** rassemblant des objets (armes, poteries, etc.), néolithiques lacustres, de l'âge du bronze et celto-romains, trouvés dans la région, et évoquant d'attrayante façon (maquettes, dioramas) la vie dans les cités lacustres. Au 2e étage, collections zoologiques et botaniques, aquariums, terrariums, initiation à l'écologie.

★★ **Dietschiberg** – Alt. 629 m. *De la gare prendre le bus n° 14 et descendre à l'arrêt Konservatorium. De là 20 mn à pied, en suivant la signalisation Utenberg à Golfplatz.* Un magnifique **panorama**★★ se dégage sur le lac des Quatre-Cantons : à droite Lucerne et le Pilate, à gauche le Rigi, et sur les Alpes bernoises et glaronnaises (table d'orientation).

★ **Gütsch** ⊘ – Alt. 523 m. *1/2 h AR environ dont 6 mn de funiculaire (station sur la Baselstrasse. Sortir par Hirschengraben* (CZ). *De la terrasse de l'hôtel Château Gütsch, couronnant la colline boisée du Gütsch située sur la rive gauche de la Reuss,* **vue**★ sur la ville avec ses fortifications, le lac et les Alpes.

PROMENADES EN BATEAU ⊘

Les aspects sans cesse renouvelés du lac des Quatre-Cantons font d'un périple sur ses eaux, même par temps orageux, un enchantement continuel. Au départ de Lucerne, le tour complet du lac, à bord de confortables bateaux à vapeur pourvus de restaurants, demande 6 h environ. Des croisières conduisent aux hauts lieux historiques : chapelle de Guillaume Tell, Schillerstein... Il est également possible de combiner une promenade en bateau avec une excursion en train de montagne, ainsi l'express « Guillaume Tell » qui relie Lucerne au Tessin peut-il être inséré dans un programme de voyage.

ENVIRONS

★★★ **Le Pilate (Pilatus)** – *15 km – environ 3 h, dont 1 h de chemin de fer à crémaillère. Cartes Michelin n°s 427 pli 14 ou 216 pli 17 et 217 pli 9. Quitter Lucerne et prendre l'autoroute en direction d'Interlaken. 11 km plus loin, à la sortie d'un long tunnel, tourner à droite vers Alpnachstad. Dans cette localité, emprunter le chemin de fer du Pilate. La suite de l'excursion est décrite sous Pilatus.*

★★ **Bürgenstock** – *16 km au Sud par Obergrundstrasse* (CZ). *Cartes Michelin n°s 427 plis 14, 15 ou 216 pli 17 et 217 pli 9.*

On monte au Bürgenstock soit en auto depuis Stansstad (6 km par une petite route étroite et escarpée), soit en funiculaire depuis le débarcadère de Kehrsiten-Bürgenstock (services en correspondance avec les bateaux), en 7 mn.

Le nom de Bürgenstock, désignant une lourde échine rocheuse et forestière, s'applique aussi à un ensemble d'hôtels perchés 500 m au-dessus de la croisée centrale (Chrüztrichter) du lac et offrant à leurs hôtes, dans un cadre de parc naturel, tous les raffinements du confort. La promenade classique du Bürgenstock est le parcours du **Felsenweg**★★ *(1/2 h environ)*, sentier en corniche formant circuit panoramique autour de l'éperon de la Hammetschwand, dont un ascenseur, encagé dans une tour métallique, permet d'atteindre le point culminant (1 128 m).

★★★ **Le Rigi** – *24 km – environ 3/4 h de route – plus 3 h AR environ, dont 1 h de chemin de fer de montagne. Quitter Lucerne par Haldenstrasse* (DY)*, route n° 2. Laisser la voiture à la gare d'Arth-Goldau pour prendre le chemin de fer du Rigi, jusqu'à son terminus du Rigi-Kulm.*

La suite de l'excursion est décrite sous « Le Rigi ».

MALOJA

Grisons

Carte Michelin n° 427 pli 17 ou 218 pli 15 – Schéma : GRAUBÜNDEN – Alt. 1 815 m

Le passage de la Maloja, emprunté par un grand itinéraire international, met en communication les vallées de l'Inn et de la Mera.

Belvédère du col – Face à l'hôtel Maloja Kulm, un affleurement rocheux lisse, bordé d'une balustrade, permet d'avoir une **vue** plongeante, en contrebas, sur le palier du Bergell et les lacets de la route qui y descendent.

Château du Belvédère – *De Maloja-village, 1/2 h à pied AR par un chemin s'amorçant à hauteur de l'hôtel Schweizerhaus.*
Du sommet de la tour – vestige d'une grandiose entreprise du siècle dernier, restée inachevée – le **panorama**★ s'étend au Sud sur les montagnes du Bergell (Gletscherhorn, Piz Cacciabella) et, du côté de l'Engadine, au-delà du lac de Sils, sur le chaînon Rosatsch-Corvatsch.
L'ancien parc du château présente quelques belles marmites d'érosion glaciaire, visibles en contrebas de la tour, près des palissades de protection qui entourent ces cavités.

MARBACH

Lucerne – 1 220 habitants

Carte Michelin n° 427 pli 14 ou 217 plis 7, 8 – Schéma : EMMENTAL

Dans une vallée adjacente à l'Entlebuch, ce village se signale par sa grande église catholique au riche intérieur baroque, mais est surtout le point de départ d'intéressantes excursions.

ENVIRONS

★ **Marbachegg** ⊙ – Partie de Marbach, la télécabine, survolant prairies et bois d'épicéas, aboutit *(en 12 mn)* sur le mont Marbachegg où perche le village de Lochsitenberg (alt. 1 483 m).
De la terrasse du restaurant (table d'orientation), une belle **vue**★ se découvre sur la région. On détaille, de l'Est au Sud : les falaises crêtées du Schrattenflue, flanquées à droite de la curieuse dent verticale du Schibengütsch puis, à l'arrière-plan, des pics étincelants de blancheur du Fiescherhorn et de l'Eiger, enfin les ravines enneigées des sommets du Hohgant. Beau thalweg boisé béant en contrebas du Marbachegg.

★ **Route du Schallenberg** – *33 km de Marbach à Thun.*
Cette route pittoresque, sinuant au pied du Hohgant et entre les hauteurs qui marquent la limite Sud de l'Emmental, procure de belles échappées sur les montagnes du Schrattenflue puis du Hohgant et, après le col encaissé du Schallenberg (alt. 1 167 m) et la traversée d'un joli bois d'épicéas, sur les cimes du massif de la Jungfrau.
A partir de Süderen Oberei, les villages se succèdent, alternant avec des prairies et des bois de sapins ; puis la route longe la profonde vallée boisée de la Zulg (à gauche), en vue du sommet arrondi du Rüti, dans l'axe.
Après Kreuzweg, c'est la plongée vers Steffisburg, faubourg industriel de Thun : on découvre le caractéristique château de Thun, à gauche. De Steffisburg, gagner Thun.

★★ **Thun** – *Voir à ce nom.*

GUIDES MICHELIN

Les guides Rouges (hôtels et restaurants) :
Benelux - Deutschland - España Portugal - Europe - France - Great Britain and Ireland - Italia - London - Paris et ses environs - Portugal - Suisse

Les guides Verts (paysages, monuments, routes touristiques) :
Allemagne - Autriche - Belgique Grand-Duché de Luxembourg - Californie - Canada - Écosse - Espagne - Europe - France - Grande-Bretagne - Grèce - Hollande - Irlande - Italie - Maroc - Nouvelle Angleterre - Portugal - Le Québec - Suisse - Bruxelles - Florence et la Toscane - Londres - New York - Paris - Rome - Venise

...et la collection des guides régionaux sur la France.

MARTIGNY

Valais — 13 481 habitants
Carte Michelin n° 427 pli 21 ou 74 pli 9 — Schéma : VALAIS — Alt. 476 m
Plan dans le guide Rouge Michelin Suisse

L'agglomération de Martigny, dominée par la tour ronde de la Bâtiaz émergeant, au milieu des vignes, des ruines de son enceinte fortifiée, est un carrefour routier international et une étape touristique de choix.
Dans ce coude où le Rhône valaisan reçoit la Dranse, convergent en effet les courants de circulation qui proviennent à la fois des itinéraires du Simplon et du Grand St-Bernard, et de la route du col de la Forclaz.

CURIOSITÉS

Gagner d'abord le faubourg et la rue de la Bâtiaz que la Dranse sépare du centre-ville.

Tour de la Bâtiaz — *20 mn à pied AR, par la montée du Chemin du Château.* Du promontoire rocheux où s'élèvent cette tour ronde et sa « chemise » quadrangulaire, restes ruinés d'une forteresse du 13ᵉ s., jolie **vue**★ sur la cuvette de Martigny et le vignoble environnant.

Suivre, à droite du pont, la rive gauche de la rivière.

Chapelle N.-D.-de-Compassion — Ce sanctuaire du 17ᵉ s., à toit de lauzes, renferme un beau maître-autel baroque et une surprenante collection d'ex-voto sous forme de tableautins.
Passer le pont couvert (du 19ᵉ s., en bois) et descendre l'avenue Marc-Morand : au n° 7 (à droite) la **Grand'Maison** (16ᵉ s.), reconnaissable à sa belle toiture à flèche et tavaillons, fut une hôtellerie où logèrent nombre de célébrités européennes des 18ᵉ et 19ᵉ s. À droite, au début de l'avenue du Grand-St-Bernard, puissant bronze de Courbet, tête de femme symbolisant la Liberté.
Revenir Place Centrale et entrer dans l'Hôtel de ville (19ᵉ s.) pour y voir, décorant le grand escalier, une éclatante **verrière**★ de 55 m² (« le Rhône contemplant la Dranse ») et d'autres vitraux (Saisons, Zodiaque, Travaux des mois) dus au peintre valaisan Edmond Bille (1949).

Gagner l'église paroissiale N.-D.-des-Champs, qui se dresse derrière l'Hôtel de ville, place du Midi.

Église N.-D.-des-Champs — Reconstruite au 17ᵉ s. dans le style toscan et flanquée au 18ᵉ s. d'un clocher néo-gothique haut de 50 m, elle a noble allure, avec son portail monumental aux vantaux de bois finement ouvragés. On admire à l'intérieur un beau **mobilier** sculpté, de facture locale, des 17ᵉ s. (fonts baptismaux, chaire) et 18ᵉ s. (retable du maître-autel, statues d'apôtres, stalles du chœur), ainsi qu'un grand crucifix de 1495.
Pousser jusqu'au début de la rue des Alpes pour voir, à gauche, la **maison Supersaxo**, intéressant exemple de construction (restaurée) du 15ᵉ s. Suivre les rues de la Délèze, d'Octodure et du Forum, cette dernière passant devant le champ de fouilles archéologiques du site gallo-romain de Forum Claudii Vallensium *(entrée rue d'Oche)* : fondations du forum et des monuments alentour, vestiges (sous abri) d'hypocauste et de latrines.

Continuer la rue du Forum jusqu'au bâtiment moderne, en béton.

★★ **Fondation Pierre Gianadda** ⊙ — Pour honorer la mémoire de son frère décédé en 1976 des suites d'un accident d'avion, Léonard Gianadda a créé un centre culturel qui, à côté d'un fonds permanent, présente des expositions temporaires de qualité illustrant l'œuvre d'artistes prestigieux comme Goya, Renoir, Modigliani, Picasso, Klee, Braque, Botero, Degas, Manet.
Le **musée gallo-romain**, distribué en galeries surplombant les vestiges, dégagés en 1976, d'un temple romain du 1ᵉʳ s., expose des statuettes, monnaies, bijoux, ustensiles ménagers et fragments lapidaires du 1ᵉʳ au 4ᵉ s., et surtout les « bronzes d'Octodure », débris de statues, dont une tête de taureau tricorne, une jambe et un bras de taille gigantesque.
Le **musée de l'automobile** expose une très belle collection de véhicules anciens, en état de marche, datant de 1897 à 1939, dont certains sont des modèles uniques. Le plus ancien, une Benz de 1897 pouvait atteindre... 25 km/h. Des noms prestigieux comme Rolls-Royce (véhicule de 1923 en aluminium poli, ayant rejoint par la route en 1988 Mandelieu sur la Côte d'Azur), Bugatti, de Dion-Bouton, Delaunay-Belleville (torpédo de 1914-1917 commandé pour la chasse par le tsar Nicolas II, la révolution de 1917 empêcha sa livraison). On y trouve également des automobiles de fabrication suisse : Pic-Pic (double phaéton de 1906), Sigma (1910-1911), Martini (torpédo de 1912), Fischer (torpédo 6 places de 1913).

MARTIGNY

Martini 1903

Le **jardin** (vestiges archéologiques) constitue un musée de sculptures à ciel ouvert. Parmi les œuvres permanentes figurent des compositions de Joan Miró, Alicia Penalba, Jean Arp, Henry Moore, Dubuffet, Brancusi, Segal, Rodin.
Tourner à gauche dans le chemin de Surfrête, puis à gauche dans la route du Levant.

Amphithéâtre romain — Des années de fouilles, consolidation et restauration ont permis de mettre en valeur cet amphithéâtre (dimensions intérieures : 74 m sur 61,70 m), l'un des plus petits du monde romain, pouvant contenir environ 6 000 personnes (Nîmes : 133 m sur 101 m, 24 000 spectateurs). Un mur d'enceinte d'une hauteur de 1 à 2 m précédait le mur du podium qui bordait l'arène. Le podium lui-même était surmonté d'un parapet, afin de protéger les spectateurs des premiers rangs des bêtes sauvages. Six rampes d'accès menaient à la cavea, espace destiné au public qui prenait place sur des gradins en bois. Plusieurs carceres, sortes de petites pièces servant de cages à fauves ou à entreposer du matériel, s'ouvraient sur l'arène. Au-dessus de l'une d'elles se tenait la tribune des autorités ou pulvinar, accessible par un couloir voûté.
Faire demi-tour : la route du Levant mène à la place du Bourg.

Place et rue du Bourg — Agréable placette, avec un hôtel à tourelle daté de 1609 (très restauré), et rue pittoresque où l'on remarque, à gauche, l'ancienne Maison de Commune du quartier du Bourg, datée de 1645, aux arcades soutenues par sept colonnes de marbre.

ENVIRONS

De Martigny à Salvan — *7 km — environ 1/2 h. Quitter Martigny au Nord-Ouest, route de St-Maurice.*
Cette région de la **vallée du Trient** est un endroit rêvé pour les randonnées en montagne dans le cadre grandiose d'une nature sauvage. En hiver, les amateurs de ski de fond et de ski alpin y trouvent des pistes variées pour tous niveaux.
Après le pont couvert ou le nouveau pont, sur la Dranse, la route de Salvan prise à gauche s'élève, parfois taillée dans le rocher, au-dessus de la vallée du Rhône.

★★ **Pont du Gueuroz** — *Laisser la voiture à la sortie du pont.* De conception hardie, tout en béton armé monté sur une grêle ossature, il a été entrepris en 1934 ; il enjambe, à 187 m de haut, les gorges du Trient.
La traversée à pied de l'ouvrage réserve une vue plongeante impressionnante sur cette fissure, toute rocheuse en aval — où se situe la partie dont le fond a été aménagé pour la visite —, plus évasée et boisée en amont. La route, par la suite très sinueuse, offre à l'occasion quelques échappées sur cet ensemble.

Salvan — Cette jolie station d'altitude s'ordonne, comme une petite ville, autour d'une placette centrale.

Vallon de Van — La petite route tracée en balcon à plus de 800 m au-dessus de la vallée du Rhône procure un impressionnant parcours, jusqu'à Van d'en Haut où vient mourir la route dans un site particulièrement sauvage.
Le retour sur Salvan offre quelques vues saisissantes sur la vallée et sur Martigny.
Revenir à Salvan, et remonter la vallée du Trient jusqu'aux Marécottes.

Les Marécottes — Pittoresque village d'altitude aux chalets en bois. Par télécabine, on peut monter jusqu'à **la Creusaz** (alt. 1 777 m), et bénéficier ainsi d'un panorama sur le Mont Blanc et les Alpes valaisannes.
A proximité du village, à droite en redescendant, se tient le **zoo des Marécottes** ⊙. Dans un environnement naturel, plusieurs enclos regroupent différents spécimens de la faune alpine : chamois, castors, chevreuils, mouflons, bouquetins, chèvres du Valais.

MEIRINGEN ★

Berne — 4 346 habitants
Carte Michelin n° 427 pli 14 ou 217 plis 8, 9 — Schéma : BERNER OBERLAND — Alt. 595 m

Chef-lieu du Hasli (haute vallée de l'Aare, en amont du lac de Brienz), le bourg de Meiringen est devenu, dès l'avènement de l'automobile, un carrefour touristique de première importance.
C'est maintenant non seulement le point de départ des excursions classiques aux gorges de l'Aare et aux chutes de Reichenbach, mais encore une étape très bien placée sur les routes du Grimsel et du Susten.
Dans le square qui porte le nom du romancier écossais sir **Arthur Conan Doyle** (1859-1930), père de Sherlock Holmes, se trouve une statue en bronze du célèbre détective de fiction, œuvre du sculpteur anglais John Doubleday. Conan Doyle qui adorait la Suisse, était citoyen d'honneur de Meiringen.

Musée Sherlock Holmes ⊘ — Cette reconstitution de la salle de séjour londonienne du 221 B Baker Street rassemble les souvenirs du fin limier et de son fidèle compagnon le docteur Watson. Holmes disparut en 1891 dans les chutes de Reichenbach, poussé par le professeur Moriarty. Heureusement pour les lecteurs et sous leur pression, Conan Doyle fit ressusciter son héros quelques années plus tard.

Église — Elle se dresse dans la partie haute du village, où quelques maisons de bois rappellent le souvenir du vieux Meiringen, ravagé par l'incendie en 1879 et en 1891. Succédant à différentes constructions dévastées et remblayées par les débordements catastrophiques de l'Alpbach — torrent dont on remarque, en arrière, la cascade — l'église actuelle (1684) est le cinquième sanctuaire édifié à cet endroit. Son clocher roman isolé, d'allure imposante, se trouve ainsi compter aujourd'hui 7 m en sous-œuvre.
Au cours de travaux de restauration ont été dégagés les vestiges du sanctuaire primitif du 11ᵉ s. (crypte actuelle) et, dans l'église haute, une série de fresques romanes (scènes de l'Ancien Testament).

ENVIRONS

★★ **Gorges de l'Aare (Aareschlucht)** ⊘ — 2 km plus 1/2 h de visite. Le chemin donnant accès au parc de stationnement des gorges se détache de la route du Grimsel (n° 6) à la sortie de Meiringen — direction d'Innertkirchen — 200 m en amont du pont sur l'Aare. Les gorges sciées par l'Aare dans le « verrou » du Kirchet, entre Meiringen et Innertkirchen, sont l'une des curiosités naturelles les plus populaires de l'Oberland bernois.
Les galeries de circulation donnent immédiatement accès à la partie la plus étranglée des gorges, dont les parois, tantôt rigoureusement verticales, tantôt curieusement excavées et polies par le travail de l'érosion (on peut observer des roches moutonnées et de nombreux vestiges de « marmites d'érosion ») produisent une forte impression. Beaucoup plus étrange cependant est la lumière diffuse qui baigne le fond de cette fissure où file, d'un seul élan, presque silencieuse, la puissante coulée vert jade de l'Aare.
Au bout d'environ 1,5 km, en vue d'une cascade affluente, on atteint la sortie amont des gorges (au niveau du dernier lacet avant Innertkirchen).

★★ **Vallée de Rosenlaui** — 12 km — environ 1 h — par un chemin de montagne très étroit (croisement impossible en dehors des garages), caillouteux et parfois raviné, en très forte rampe au départ de Willigen. Le passage est interdit aux voitures de tourisme de 6 places et plus.

Quitter Meiringen par la route de Grimsel.

À Willigen, tourner à droite dans la route de Rosenlaui qui, durement sinueuse, pénètre dans la vallée solitaire du Reichenbach dominée, à gauche, par les extraordinaires découpures rocheuses des Engelhörner.
Bientôt apparaissent, en avant, de gauche à droite, le glacier de Rosenlaui, le Wellhorn et le Wetterhorn.
Un pont sur le lit corrigé du Reichenbach précède l'arrivée dans les prairies de Gschwandtenmad, d'où la **vue ★★★** est saisissante : au-delà d'un premier plan de sapins et à droite du glacier de Rosenlaui s'élève l'épaule rocheuse du Wellhorn, flanquant le cône glacé du Wetterhorn dressé au-dessus de la dépression de la Grande Scheidegg, large seuil qui permet aux piétons de passer de Rosenlaui à Grindelwald.

Rosenlaui — Cette station d'alpinisme se réduit en fait à un établissement hôtelier isolé et à ses dépendances.
Rosenlaui a cependant donné son nom à une célèbre école d'escalade (dont le siège est à Meiringen) au sein de laquelle ont été formés plusieurs animateurs, en vue de la conquête de l'Himalaya.
Les touristes de passage ici visitent des **gorges glaciaires ★** ⊘ (Gletscherschlucht) creusées par le torrent de fonte du glacier de Rosenlaui (3/4 h de marche assez pénible le long de galeries et d'escaliers sommairement aménagés).
Le décor devient complètement rocheux.

MEIRINGEN

En arrivant à Schwarzwaldalp, terminus de la route carrossable, c'est une surprise de découvrir, à une altitude où la seule rencontre plausible est celle des conifères, un versant entièrement planté d'érables.

★**Chutes de Reichenbach (Reichenbachfälle)** ⊙ — *1 km plus 1/2 h AR environ dont 10 mn de funiculaire. Quitter Meiringen par la route du Grimsel. Après le pont sur l'Aare, dans un croisement, tourner à droite et laisser la voiture à la station inférieure du funiculaire de Reichenbach.*

Après avoir franchi les chutes inférieures du torrent par un viaduc, le funiculaire aboutit bientôt à une terrasse-belvédère d'où l'on peut admirer la grande cascade de Reichenbach dont un ressaut rocheux pulvérise, à mi-hauteur, le jet puissant, formant un panache vaporeux.

Castello di MISOX★

Grisons

Carte Michelin n° 427 pli 16 ou 214 pli 13 — Ruine au Sud de Mesocco
Schéma : GRAUBÜNDEN

Coiffant un piton rocheux, les ruines féodales de Misox, gardiennes du Val Mesolcina et du passage du San Bernardino, sont les plus imposantes et les plus évocatrices des Grisons.

Ce massif ensemble fortifié, dont les lignes verticales d'un élégant campanile rompent la lourdeur, était aux mains des comtes de Sax-Mesocco.

Vendu en 1483 aux Trivulce de Milan, le château fut démantelé par les « Ligues » grisonnes *(lire en Introduction, au chapitre : La Démocratie en action, le commentaire du blason des Grisons)* en 1526. Une initiative des étudiants suisses l'a sauvé de la destruction complète en 1924-1925.

VISITE environ 1/2 h

Chapelle Ste-Marie-du-Château (Santa Maria del Castello) ⊙ — Au pied du château, ce sanctuaire au campanile roman très ajouré conserve un intéressant ensemble de **fresques**★ du 15ᵉ s. (mur gauche de la nef). Remarquer, au registre intermédiaire, plusieurs saints protecteurs des Grisons : saint Georges est représenté pourfendant le dragon, sous les traits d'un tout jeune chevalier ; saint Bernardin de Sienne, le patron de la vallée — dont le nom a été donné au passage du San Bernardino — sous l'habit du moine au visage émacié, tenant à la main le monogramme du Christ entouré de rayons.

Les allégories des mois de l'année qui se succèdent au registre inférieur mêlent des scènes d'amour courtois et des tableaux de la vie paysanne, conformes à ceux qu'occasionnent les travaux des champs sur le versant italien des Alpes (récolte des châtaignes).

Château — *Accès par le chemin herbeux s'élevant derrière la chapelle Ste-Marie jusqu'à la passerelle d'entrée.* Le vestige monumental le plus remarquable de cette forteresse est le campanile roman de sa chapelle, à cinq étages d'arcatures. Pour bénéficier d'une **vue**★ plongeante sur le Val Mesolcina et le village de Soazza, tourner à gauche dès que se présente une trouée à travers les corps de bâtiments en ruine et gagner, au bord de l'escarpement, un mur découronné dont on atteint le sommet par un escalier sans rampe.

MONTREUX★★

Vaud — 22 917 habitants

Carte Michelin n° 427 pli 12 ou 217 pli 14 — Schéma : Lac LÉMAN — Alt. 398 m
Plan d'agglomération dans le guide Rouge Michelin Suisse

Favorisée par la beauté de son **site**★★ et l'agrément de son séjour — consacrés par la littérature depuis que Rousseau choisit pour cadre de la Nouvelle Héloïse le village de Clarens, maintenant devenu faubourg —, Montreux, rajeunie par d'importants travaux d'urbanisme, est la station la plus animée du lac Léman, bénéficiant d'une réputation internationale.

Elle s'étale au bord d'une vaste baie, ouverte au Sud, et s'étage en amphithéâtre jusqu'aux hauteurs boisées ou couvertes de vignobles qui la protègent contre les vents du Nord et de l'Est. Ses palaces somptueux — multitude de stores jaunes, ses hôtels de la Belle Époque ne sont pas sans rappeler certaines stations de la Côte d'Azur. Ville artistique, elle connaît une intense activité lors de ses nombreux festivals et propose des festivités mondialement connues : Rencontres Chorales Internationales (semaine suivant Pâques), festival télévisé de la Rose d'Or (au printemps), festival de jazz (en juillet), concerts du festival de musique de Montreux-Vevey.

De la gare de Montreux partent plusieurs petits trains à destination de sommets qui offrent des vues étendues jusqu'à Genève, le Mont Blanc, le Cervin, etc.

Des **croisières** sur le Haut Lac sont organisées à bord de bateaux à vapeur.

MONTREUX PRATIQUE

Pour tout renseignement, s'adresser à l'Office du tourisme, Place du Débarcadère, ☏ (021) 963 12 12.

Shopping

On trouvera un grand nombre de boutiques dans les artères suivantes : avenue des Alpes, Grande-Rue, avenue du Casino, rue de la Paix.

Grand magasin : **Innovation** (avenue du Casino).

Théâtre et musique

Théâtre du Vieux-Quartier, rue du Pont, ☏ (021) 961 11 32.
Auditorium Stravinski, Grande-Rue, ☏ (021) 962 21 19.

Un verre dans un endroit agréable

La Grande Rue, secteur très animé de la ville, offre pour les amateurs de jazz le **Duke's jazz bar**, piano-bar de l'hôtel Royal Plazza. Non loin de l'Office du tourisme le **Carnotzet** bar du Palace Hôtel propose une grande variété de vins vaudois. L'animation nocturne bat son plein dans la rue du Théâtre grâce aux différents établissements qui composent le **Casino de Montreux**. Pour un cocktail dans un cadre intime : le **Montreusien**, piano-bar. Dépaysement et country music au **Western Saloon** ou bien pour se défouler sur des rythmes actuels, la discothèque **Le Platinum**.

★★ **Le coup d'œil** – Monter, à travers le vieux Montreux, jusqu'à la terrasse de l'église paroissiale pour contempler l'agglomération de Clarens-Montreux-Territet, le lac, dans lequel s'avance le château de Chillon, les monts du Chablais savoyard, les pointes étincelantes des Dents du Midi.

La Riviera vaudoise – La douceur de son climat (moyenne annuelle 10°) fait de Montreux une station climatique fréquentée toute l'année et vaut à son littoral le nom de Riviera vaudoise. Ce climat exceptionnel, le plus doux qui soit au Nord des Alpes, permet à une végétation luxuriante et variée de se développer : la vigne pousse jusqu'à 600 m d'altitude, le noyer jusqu'à 700 m et les arbres fruitiers jusqu'à 1 000 m.

Sur les rives du lac, on rencontre le figuier, l'amandier, le laurier, le mûrier et même les cyprès, les magnolias et les palmiers qui jouissent là d'une température toute méridionale. Au printemps, les prairies dominant la ville sont couvertes de narcisses, donnant aux coteaux un charme tout particulier.

Musée du Vieux-Montreux ⊘ – *40, rue de la Gare.*
Une ancienne maison forte du 14ᵉ s., plusieurs fois remaniée jusqu'au 18ᵉ s., abrite les collections de ce musée d'histoire locale ou musée historique de la Riviera suisse. Une série de photographies montre le développement de la ville au cours des siècles. La vie quotidienne y est évoquée par la reconstitution d'intérieurs (cuisines, chambre) et de vieux métiers (atelier de menuisier). L'activité économique de la région, fondée sur l'agriculture, est illustrée par une salle consacrée aux travaux de la vigne et la reconstitution d'un chalet d'alpage. Armes, étains, poids et mesures complètent ce panorama du passé.

Montreux

MONTREUX

ENVIRONS

★★★ **Rochers de Naye** ⊙ — Alt. 2 042 m. *Environ 3 h AR dont 2 h de chemin de fer à crémaillère.*

Le trajet permet d'apprécier le site de **Glion** (alt. 689 m), perché à moyenne altitude, et de **Caux** (alt. 1 050 m), autre station-balcon de vieille réputation aujourd'hui célèbre surtout par le mouvement du « Réarmement Moral ».

Du sommet, belle vue aérienne sur le Léman et splendide tour d'horizon sur les Alpes bernoises, valaisannes, savoyardes et le Jura.

★★ **Château de Chillon** — *3 km au Sud. Accès possible à pied en longeant le lac. Voir à ce nom.*

★★ **Circuit des Avants-Sonloup** — *25 km — environ 1 h. Suivre l'itinéraire fléché du schéma ci-dessus.*

Quitter Montreux par l'itinéraire signalé « Les Avants-Fribourg ».

La route surplombe, à gauche, la ville et le lac, tandis que se détache, au sommet d'une colline couverte de vignes, le château du Châtelard avec sa grosse tour rectangulaire à mâchicoulis du 15ᵉ s.

La route, qui s'élève rapidement, offre de jolies vues sur le lac et les Alpes.

A 4 km de Montreux, tourner à droite vers « Chernex-les-Avants » ; 200 m plus loin tourner à gauche avant Chamby (deux virages), passer la voie ferrée ; puis tourner à droite pour gagner les Avants.

★ **Les Avants** — Alt. 968 m. Cette petite station, dominée au Sud-Est par la Dent de Jaman et les Rochers de Naye, jouit d'une excellente exposition.

Col de Sonloup — Alt. 1 149 m. Belle **vue**★ sur les Rochers de Naye, les Dents du Midi et les Alpes de Savoie.

Le retour à Montreux s'effectue sur l'itinéraire Saumont-Chamby-Chernex.

Le long de la route, étroite au départ, nouvelles échappées sur le lac et la région de Vevey-Blonay.

★★ **Circuit des Pléiades** — *36 km — plus 1/2 h à pied AR.*

Suivre au départ l'itinéraire du circuit précédent, jusqu'à Saumont.

MONTREUX

A Saumont, prendre à droite vers les Bains de l'Alliaz et suivre ensuite la route qui s'élève à travers des prairies et des bois de sapins jusqu'à Lally où on laissera la voiture.
On peut également gagner Lally par train à crémaillère, à partir de Blonay.

★★ **Les Pléiades** – Alt. 1 360 m. *De Lally, 1/2 h à pied AR.* De ce sommet, se découvre un très beau **panorama**★★ sur le Léman, le Molard, la Dent de Jaman, les Rochers de Naye, les Alpes de Savoie et la chaîne du Mont Blanc.
Revenir sur la route de Blonay, qui procure de fréquentes échappées sur le lac et permet de découvrir à droite le **château de Blonay** (11ᵉ s.).

Peu après Brent on retrouve, pour rentrer à Montreux, la route empruntée au départ.

MORAT
Voir à MURTEN

MORGES ★
Vaud – 13 891 habitants
Carte Michelin n° 427 pli 11 ou 217 Nord-Ouest du pli 13 – Schéma : Lac LÉMAN
Alt. 378 m – Plan dans le guide Rouge Michelin Suisse

Important centre vigneron de la « Côte » vaudoise, la petite ville de Morges occupe un site agréable sur la rive du lac Léman, face aux Alpes de Savoie.
Construit de 1691 à 1696, d'après les plans du baron Duquesne d'Aubonne, fils du célèbre amiral, son port, aujourd'hui **port de plaisance**, a connu avant le développement des chemins de fer une grande activité commerciale, soutenue par les échanges entre le Pays de Vaud et Genève.
Du quai, près duquel se dresse le château – construit par Louis Iᵉʳ de Savoie, ancienne résidence des baillis bernois – on découvre une très belle **vue**★ sur le lac dont la nappe atteint, ici, son plein épanouissement et, au-delà, sur les Alpes, du Salève aux Alpes fribourgeoises, en passant par les Alpes de Savoie d'où se détachent la Dent d'Oche et le Mont Blanc.

★★ **Musée Alexis-Forel** ⊙ – *54, Grand'Rue.*
Ce musée d'objets précieux, rassemblés à l'origine par le graveur Alexis Forel et sa femme, est aménagé dans une moitié de l'ancienne maison Blanchenay, bel édifice composite des 15ᵉ, 17ᵉ et 18ᵉ s., construit en deux corps de bâtiment reliés à chaque étage par une galerie toscane et dont on remarquera, à l'intérieur, les plafonds des 15ᵉ et 16ᵉ s. à caissons, les portes bourguignonnes sculptées du 17ᵉ s. et les deux cheminées monumentales.
Chaque salle du musée fait revivre par la richesse de sa décoration la vie passée : mobilier français et suisse du 15ᵉ au 19ᵉ s., en partie rassemblé par Forel lui-même, bibelots (salons du 17ᵉ et du 18ᵉ s.), porcelaines de Nyon et de la Compagnie des Indes, verrerie du 16ᵉ au 19ᵉ s., argenterie des 18ᵉ et 19ᵉ s. Deux étages sont consacrés à une exposition de poupées du 18ᵉ au 20ᵉ s. avec leurs accessoires.

Château ⊙ – Érigée à un point stratégique à l'Ouest de la ville, cette massive forteresse du 13ᵉ s. flanquée de quatre tours d'angle cylindriques, délimitant quatre courtines qui s'ordonnent autour d'une cour centrale, abrite aujourd'hui les collections de trois musées.
Le **musée suisse de la figurine** (rez-de-chaussée) présente une succession de dioramas illustrant avec des soldats de plomb ou d'étain, des grands événements historiques de l'Antiquité au 19ᵉ s. (Babylone, Révolte aztèque contre les Espagnols, Camp du Drap d'or, Passage de la Bérézina...). Chaque figurine y est réalisée avec un remarquable souci du détail.
Le **musée militaire vaudois** (rez-de-chaussée et 1ᵉʳ étage) présente une rétrospective complète de l'armement, des uniformes et des coiffures militaires des régiments suisses (incluant la célèbre garde pontificale), de l'époque népoléonienne à nos jours. Plusieurs salles illustrant une époque se succèdent, parmi lesquelles la tour de la justice ou tour de la torture (roue de justice – 15ᵉ-18ᵉ s. sur laquelle le condamné était ligoté pour être supplicié) ; la salle Davel consacrée au major Jean-Daniel Abraham Davel, patriote vaudois exécuté en 1723 pour rébellion contre le pouvoir bernois ; la salle dédiée au général Guisan, commandant en chef de l'armée suisse de 1939 à 1945 (livret de service, objets personnels).
De belles caves voûtées en berceau servent de cadre au **musée de l'artillerie** qui expose une quarantaine de pièces réelles ainsi que des modèles réduits permettant de suivre l'évolution de cette arme (fauconneau ou pierrier du 16ᵉ s. ; artillerie de montagne tirée par des bêtes de somme ; inhabituel mortier de 12 en forme de boule – 1888 – pivotant à 360° et réglable en inclinaison, d'une portée de 3 km ; canon de campagne de 75 monté sur chevalets).

Val de MORGINS★

Carte Michelin n° 427 pli 12 ou 217 pli 14 – Schéma : VALAIS

Seule voie de transit internationale du massif préalpin du Chablais, la route du Pas de Morgins, reliant les vallées pastorales d'Abondance et de Morgins, toutes parsemées de grands chalets, se présente sur le versant du Valais comme une route moderne dont le tracé offre des vues multiples sur les crêtes des Dents du Midi.

DE MONTHEY A CHÂTEL

34 km – environ 2 h – itinéraire 8 *de la visite du Valais*

Contrôle douanier suisse aux abords du Pas ; contrôle douanier français à Vonne.

Au départ de Monthey, la route s'élève rapidement, en lacet, au-dessus de la vallée du Rhône que dominent, d'aval en amont, les sommets des Diablerets, du Grand Muveran et de la Dent de Morcles.

En avant, dans l'axe du Val d'Illiez, apparaissent, neigeuses, les Dents Blanches et les Dents du Midi.

Au fur et à mesure de la montée, les prairies plantées de noyers succèdent aux vignobles.

★ **Champéry** – A l'entrée du **Val d'Illiez** ★★, Champéry s'étire, à mi-pente, à l'ombre de la barrière des Dents du Midi.

Cette villégiature, restée familiale en dépit de son ambiance internationale, a surtout la faveur des amateurs de courses en montagne calcaire. Le **clocher** de l'église, coiffé d'une curieuse couronne de pierre ajourée, attire le regard.

En hiver, la cuvette de Planachaux, desservie par diverses remontées mécaniques, offre aux skieurs de belles pentes ensoleillées.

★★ **Croix de Culet** ⊙ – *De Champéry, 3/4 h environ, dont 1/4 h de téléphérique, plus 1 h de marche.* De la station supérieure du téléphérique de Planachaux, continuer à pied, le long de la crête, jusqu'à la croix (alt. 1 963 m). On profite alors d'une vue très étendue sur les différentes cimes des Dents du Midi, le Mont Ruan, les Dents Blanches et les Alpes Vaudoises.

La route continue à décrire des lacets, offrant des **vues**★ de plus en plus larges sur la vallée du Rhône et, vers le Sud, sur le Val d'Illiez, les falaises des Dents du Midi et, à droite de celles-ci, le Mont Ruan.

Par un passage en corniche au-dessus du ravin boisé de la Vièze, le parcours atteint ensuite le fond de la combe alpestre doucement modelée du Val de Morgins.

Les chalets s'abritent sous un toit débordant en éperon et couvert de tavaillons ; leurs balcons à double étage présentent à l'aplomb du faîte un double décrochement formant tribune.

Morgins – Le cadre apaisant de cette villégiature d'altitude faiblement encaissée est très propice à la détente estivale et hivernale.

★ **Pas de Morgins** – Alt. 1 369 m. La route, en pente insensible, se glisse dans cette encoche forestière parée d'un petit lac dans lequel se mirent les sapins. En direction du Sud-Est, au second plan, le couronnement des Dents du Midi est visible.

La descente, plus raide, dans la vallée savoyarde de la Dranse d'Abondance, fait découvrir le **site**★ majestueux de Châtel *(description dans le guide Vert Michelin Alpes du Nord)*.

En avant, les escarpements du Mont Chauffé (à gauche) et des Cornettes de Bise (à droite) barrent maintenant l'horizon.

Pour mieux connaître la végétation alpine, lisez le chapitre qui lui est consacré en introduction.

MOUDON

Vaud – 4 336 habitants

Carte Michelin n° 427 pli 12 ou 217 pli 4 – Alt. 522 m

Longtemps capitale du « Pays de Vaud savoyard », Moudon est joliment située dans la vallée de la Broye, au centre d'une riche région agricole. Important relais sur la route de Rome à Vindonissa (Windisch, près de Brugg) dès l'époque gallo-romaine, Moudon a connu une période de grande prospérité au temps des comtes de Savoie (14e s.). C'est de cette époque que datent la plupart des monuments qui donnent à l'actuelle cité son cachet médiéval.

Du pont par lequel la route de détournement (n° 1) franchit la Broye, on découvre au premier plan une jolie vue sur l'église St-Étienne et à l'arrière, la vieille ville ou ville haute avec ses maisons des 15e, 16e et 17e s. dont les grands toits débordants en auvent se regroupent au pied de la colline que couronnent les vieux châteaux de Rochefort et de Carrouge et l'antique tour de Broye.

MOUDON

CURIOSITÉS

Église St-Étienne – Construite dans la deuxième moitié du 13ᵉ s. et au début du 14ᵉ s., elle est flanquée d'un imposant clocher fortifié, ancienne tour d'enceinte de la ville. La nef gothique possède des voûtes armoriées, de jolis vitraux modernes, un bel orgue de 1764, de belles stalles du début du 16ᵉ s. ; d'autres stalles, du début du 17ᵉ s., sont visibles à gauche de l'entrée. Une restauration complète a mis en valeur des fresques originales du 16ᵉ s.

Rue du Château – *Au départ de la place de la Grenette.*
Voie principale du vieux quartier du Bourg : au bas, amusante fontaine de la Justice (statue polychrome abritant sous sa robe quatre magistrats nains) ; en montant, on remarque à droite la tour de Broye, ruine du 12ᵉ s., puis, des deux côtés de la rue, quelques maisons des 15ᵉ, 16ᵉ ou 17ᵉ s. ; à mi-parcours, vue dominante à gauche sur la rivière qu'enjambe un pont couvert ; en haut, on trouve les musées (à droite) et une deuxième fontaine, celle de Moïse, à bassin octogonal et fût sculpté, datée de 1557.

Musée du Vieux-Moudon ⊙ – Dans le château de Rochefort, ce musée présente des armes et uniformes anciens, des enseignes de fer forgé, des statuettes et poteries romaines ; deux salles des métiers évoquent l'activité ancienne de la région.

Musée Eugène-Burnand ⊙ – Dans le bâtiment du Grand'Air, œuvres d'E. Burnand (1850-1921), né à Moudon, peintre de la vie paysanne et illustrateur de l'écrivain provençal Frédéric Mistral.

MUOTTAS MURAGL★★

Grisons
Carte Michelin n° 427 pli 17 ou 218 pli 15 – Nord de Pontresina
Schéma : GRAUBÜNDEN

Les croupes gazonnées de Muottas Muragl, facilement accessibles par funiculaire depuis le fond du bassin de Samedan, constituent le belvédère classique de la Haute-Engadine.

★★ **Montée à Muottas Muragl** ⊙ – *De la gare inférieure de Punt Muragl, 1 h AR environ dont 1/2 h de funiculaire.*
La station supérieure (hôtel), à 2 453 m d'altitude, offre une **vue**★★ en enfilade, par la trouée de la Haute-Engadine, encadrée par les chaînons du Piz Rosatsch et du Piz Julier, avec son chapelet de lacs se succédant de St-Moritz à la Maloja. Plus à gauche, se déploient le cirque glaciaire de Roseg et les cimes éclatantes du massif de la Bernina : Piz Morteratsch, Piz Bernina, Piz Palü.
De nombreux touristes se plaisent à parcourir à pied cette haute région, réputée pour sa flore et sa faune (bouquetins, chamois, marmottes), le long de larges sentiers en pente douce, superbement tracés à flanc de montagne, tels que le « Hochweg » qui permet de redescendre en 3 h 1/2 à Pontresina.

MÜRREN★★

Berne
Carte Michelin n° 427 pli 14 ou 217 Nord-Est du pli 17
Schéma : INTERLAKEN (Environs) – Alt. 1 638 m

Perchée sur un replat d'alpages, formant balcon au-dessus de la formidable coupure de la vallée de Lauterbrunnen, Mürren est placée face au massif de la Jungfrau, visible depuis l'Eiger (à gauche) jusqu'au Breithorn (à droite) et au groupe du Gspaltenhorn (à l'extrême droite).
Le **site**★★ de ce village de chalets, à l'abri de toute incursion motorisée, et les caractéristiques sportives de ses parcours skiables, qui réunissent toutes les difficultés imaginables, expliquent le succès de la station auprès des Britanniques, qui ont recréé là leur ambiance familiale.
C'est à Mürren que fut fondé, en 1924, le Kandahar-Ski-Club, organisateur de la fameuse épreuve de l'« Arlberg-Kandahar » considérée de nos jours comme un championnat du monde officieux des pays alpins.

Accès – Les automobilistes pourront se rendre à Stechelberg, terminus de la route de Lauterbrunnen, puis prendre le téléphérique du Schilthorn jusqu'à Mürren.
Il est également possible d'aller jusqu'à Lauterbrunnen, de laisser son véhicule au parking et de prendre le funiculaire pour Grütschalp. De là un train conduit à Mürren.

ENVIRONS

★★★ **Schilthorn** ⊙ – *Alt. 2 970 m. 1 h 1/4 environ dont 35 mn de téléphérique.*
Du sommet, dans un site sauvage de ravines et d'éboulis, **vue panoramique**★★★ sur le massif de la Jungfrau, séparé seulement de l'observateur par le fossé de Lauterbrunnen. Le lac de Thoune est visible en partie.

MURTEN ★★

MORAT-Fribourg — 4 601 habitants
Carte Michelin n° 427 pli 12 ou 217 pli 5 – Alt. 458 m

Dominant la rive orientale du lac qui porte son nom, Morat est dotée d'un port de petite batellerie agréable aux plaisanciers. Elle reste célèbre dans l'histoire par la défaite que les Suisses y infligèrent à Charles le Téméraire. Cette ancienne cité, ayant conservé la majeure partie de ses remparts et de ses tours, est d'un charme très pittoresque.

La bataille de Morat — Impatient d'effacer l'échec que lui avaient infligé les Confédérés suisses à Grandson le 2 mars 1476, le duc de Bourgogne Charles le Téméraire rassemble en hâte une nouvelle armée. Quittant Lausanne le 27 mai, il se dirige sur la vallée de la Broye et arrive, le 9 juin, devant Morat qu'il assiège. L'arrivée de l'armée des Confédérés, le 22 juin, renverse la situation. Acculées au lac, n'ayant aucune possibilité de retraite en cas de défaite, les troupes du Téméraire ne peuvent échapper au massacre ou à la noyade ; le duc, lui, réussit à s'enfuir. Près de 8 000 Bourguignons y laissent la vie. Comme à Grandson, un riche butin — étoffes, fourrures, armes de prix — tombe aux mains des vainqueurs.

Le lac de Morat (Murtensee) — Cette paisible nappe d'eau rectangulaire de 23 km², parallèle à l'extrémité nord du lac de Neuchâtel, n'en est séparée que par une colline et moins de 4 km en ligne droite, mais communique avec lui par le canal de la Broye. Poissonneux, asile des oiseaux migrateurs sur sa rive nord, et des baigneurs sur la berge opposée *(plage aménagée)*, le lac est bordé à l'Est — seule rive alémanique — par la ville de Morat et ses villages adjacents.

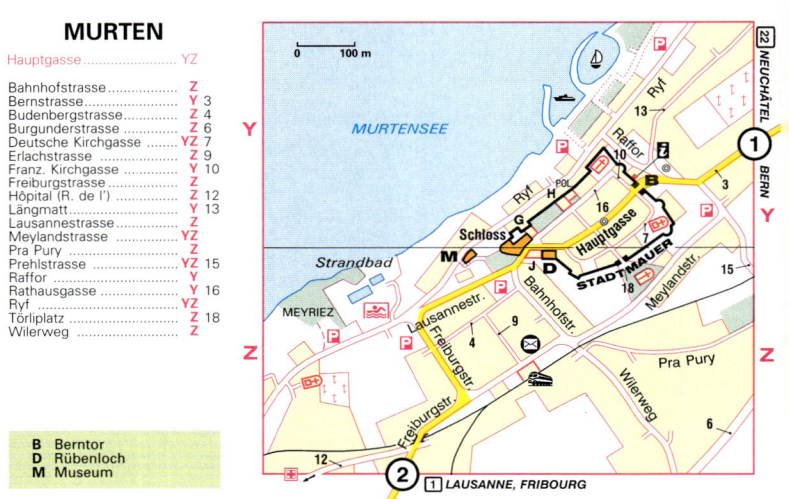

MURTEN

Hauptgasse	YZ
Bahnhofstrasse	Z
Bernstrasse	Y 3
Budenbergstrasse	Z 4
Burgunderstrasse	Z 6
Deutsche Kirchgasse	YZ 7
Erlachstrasse	Z 9
Franz. Kirchgasse	Y 10
Freiburgstrasse	Z
Hôpital (R. de l')	Z 12
Längmatt	Y 13
Lausannestrasse	Z
Meylandstrasse	YZ
Pra Pury	Z
Prehlstrasse	YZ 15
Raffor	Y
Rathausgasse	Y 16
Ryf	YZ
Törliplatz	Z 18
Wilerweg	Z

B Berntor
D Rübenloch
M Museum

CURIOSITÉS

Rue principale (Hauptgasse) — Tracée au cœur de la ville ancienne, elle présente une belle unité, avec ses maisons ornées d'arcades et aux toits en saillie couverts de tuiles brunes, ses fontaines et sa « porte de Berne » (Berntor-**B**) surmontée d'un élégant clocheton.

Prendre la rue qui s'amorce à droite, aussitôt avant la Porte de Berne et contourner l'église protestante allemande, derrière laquelle un escalier donne librement accès aux remparts.

★ **Remparts** (Stadtmauer) — Prendre à droite le chemin de ronde qui offre de jolies vues sur l'enchevêtrement des toits de la ville ancienne, le château et le lac, tandis qu'à l'horizon se dressent le mont Vully et les contreforts du Jura.

Emprunter le premier escalier de descente rencontré qui aboutit à une porte dans les remparts.

Cette porte donne accès à une petite place d'où l'on a une jolie vue extérieure de ceux-ci.

Repasser sous la porte et prendre à gauche vers le château.

On passe à l'extrémité de la rue principale, devant le Rübenloch (**D**), belle maison ancienne.

Château (Schloss) — Construit au 13ᵉ s., par le duc Pierre de Savoie, c'est un édifice imposant d'aspect sévère. De la cour intérieure, jolie vue sur le lac de Morat et le Jura.

Musée d'Histoire (Museum) (M) ⊘ – Très moderne, il occupe, au pied du château, l'ancien moulin à eau de la ville, aujourd'hui restauré dans son aspect du 18e s. On y voit, sur cinq niveaux *(ascenseur pour la sortie)*, de haut en bas : des vestiges préhistoriques et gallo-romains (poteries, armes, bijoux), des collections se rapportant à l'histoire locale du Moyen Âge au 18e s. (monnaies, étains, verreries, vitraux, ustensiles variés) ; des armes : épées, armures, canons... et un diaporama sur la bataille de Morat.

MÜSTAIR★

Grisons – 752 habitants
Carte Michelin n° 427 pli 18 ou 218 pli 17 – Schéma : GRAUBÜNDEN

Le chef-lieu du **Val Müstair**, est la seule portion du territoire helvétique faisant partie du bassin de l'Adige. A l'extrémité du village – côté frontière italienne – l'église, enclavée encore dans l'enceinte de l'abbaye St-Jean-Baptiste (moniales bénédictines), fondée, suivant la tradition, par Charlemagne, est un des monuments les plus archaïques du territoire helvétique.

★ **Église** – Sa triple abside est voûtée en cul-de-four. La nef, primitivement d'ordonnance basilicale, a été transformée au 15e s. en un vaisseau gothique, à deux bas-côtés, voûté d'ogives.
Les **fresques★★** qui décorent les parois offrent à l'amateur d'art le plus imposant ensemble de peintures murales de la Confédération ; certaines séries ont été transférées au musée national de Zurich. Cette décoration peinte, qui remonte à la période carolingienne (1er moitié du 9e s.), est recouverte, en partie, de fresques romanes (1150-1170) bien conservées. Parmi les autres œuvres d'art, on remarque une statue de Charlemagne (12e s.) et un bas-relief (le Baptême du Christ) du 11e s.

NÄFELS

Glarus – 3 882 habitants
Carte Michelin n° 427 pli 16 ou 216 pli 20 – Alt. 437 m

Näfels, seconde ville du canton, est située dans la plaine alluviale qui sépare les lacs de Zurich et de Walenstadt.

La bataille de Näfels – Le jeudi 9 avril 1388, les Glaronnais auxquels s'était jointe une petite troupe de Schwizois, remportèrent sur l'armée autrichienne une bataille déterminante restée célèbre dans l'histoire du pays. Les pertes furent très sévères pour les Autrichiens et les survivants ne durent leur salut qu'à la fuite.
Chaque année, le premier jeudi d'avril, cette victoire est commémorée par une marche patriotique de Glarus à Näfels et un office religieux.

★ **Palais Freuler (Freulerpalast)** ⊘ – L'architecture de ce monument, les souvenirs qu'il conserve, ramènent à l'époque où le service militaire dans les cours européennes représentait, pour les fils de certaines grandes familles suisses, la plus naturelle des vocations. Construit de 1642 à 1647 à l'initiative de Kaspar Freuler, un officier-mercenaire qui servit dans l'armée française, il se rattache, par sa décoration, à la Renaissance finissante (portail d'entrée, grand escalier, boiseries).
Remarquer, au rez-de-chaussée, une salle dallée de marbre, aux voûtes décorées de stucs suivant le goût italien, et surtout, au premier étage, les **chambres d'apparat★★**, où s'accumulent, du parquet au plafond à caissons, les chefs-d'œuvre de marqueterie. Les étages abritent les collections du musée régional du Pays de Glaris : la section de l'impression sur étoffes retient l'attention.

NEUCHÂTEL★★

C 33 579 habitants
Carte Michelin n° 427 pli 12 ou 216 pli 13 – Schéma : JURA SUISSE – Alt. 440 m

Neuchâtel jouit d'une situation charmante entre le lac, bordé de 4 km de quais, et la colline de Chaumont. Au centre du vignoble, la ville, aimable et souriante, étage ses quartiers aux maisons couleur d'ocre pâle, ce qui faisait dire à Alexandre Dumas qu'elle était taillée dans une motte de beurre. Les masses jumelées de la collégiale et du château dominent l'ensemble.

Le lac de Neuchâtel – Long de 38 km et large de 8, c'est le plus grand des lacs de stricte appartenance suisse. Il est très poissonneux. Des canaux (utilisés par des services de navigation de plaisance) le relient aux lacs de Bienne et de Morat. Ses eaux, aux couleurs changeantes, et ses rives, aux collines harmonieuses couvertes de vignes, en ont fait le sujet favori des peintres et des écrivains. Le lac a inspiré en particulier André Gide.

NEUCHÂTEL

UN PEU D'HISTOIRE

Le nom de Neuchâtel provient d'une construction érigée comme un château fort à l'époque du second royaume de Bourgogne (1011). La ville devient ensuite, par voie de succession, propriété de la famille française des Orléans-Longueville.
On rapporte que pour fêter son entrée dans la ville, en 1657, Henri II d'Orléans fit couler dans la fontaine du Griffon, qui existe toujours rue du Château, 6 000 litres de vin rouge du pays.
Toujours par succession, Neuchâtel est, à partir de 1707, possession personnelle du roi de Prusse. La vie intellectuelle et mondaine est très active et les idées des Encyclopédistes ont beaucoup de succès : Sébastien Mercier, Brissot et Mirabeau séjournent à Neuchâtel.

La lutte pour l'indépendance – Après avoir été attribuée de 1806 à 1814, en tant que principauté, au maréchal Berthier, chef d'état-major de Napoléon Ier, Neuchâtel, entrant en 1815 dans la Confédération Helvétique, est dans une curieuse situation politique. Son territoire est devenu canton suisse tout en reconnaissant son allégeance envers le royaume de Prusse, jusqu'en 1848. Il se forme dans l'intervalle un parti libéral qui tente de prendre le pouvoir en 1831, échoue, mais récidive en 1848 et, cette fois, réussit à proclamer la République.
En 1857, le roi de Prusse renonce formellement aux droits que lui conférait le titre de prince de Neuchâtel, qu'il conserve cependant symboliquement.
Aujourd'hui, Neuchâtel est un centre important de recherche horlogère dont l'observatoire donne l'heure à toute la Suisse. Marché du vin, elle voit se dérouler en septembre *(voir tableau des Principales manifestations)* un grand cortège des vendanges. Siège d'une Université, elle conserve sa réputation de foyer de culture française : c'est la ville d'Helvétie où l'on parle le français le plus pur.

NEUCHÂTEL PRATIQUE

Pour tout renseignement, s'adresser à l'Office du tourisme, 7, rue de la Place d'Armes, ☎ (038) 25 42 42.

Shopping

Principales artères commerçantes : la rue du Seyon et les rues voisines.

Théâtre et musique

Théâtre, rue de l'Hôtel-de-Ville, ☎ (038) 20 79 02.
Temple du Bas, rue du Temple, ☎ (038) 20 79 02.

Où prendre un verre ?

Au bord du lac, les pianos-bars des hôtels Beaulac et Beaufort sont des endroits très agréables. Le bar **Amiral** de l'hôtel Beaulac dispose lorsque le temps le permet, d'une terrasse avec vue sur le port de plaisance. Des soirées à thèmes sont organisées. Vinothèque à la disposition de la clientèle. Au **Siggi's Bar** de l'hôtel Beaufort, ambiance feutrée, très chic, clientèle internationale.
Pendant la saison estivale, en fin de semaine des croisières musicales sont organisées sur le lac. Dans le port, ambiance agréable au pub du **Vieux Vapeur**.
Rue de l'Hôtel-de-Ville, style début du siècle au **Café brasserie du théâtre** qui a vu passer maints acteurs et amateurs de théâtre.

CURIOSITÉS

★ **Ville ancienne (BZ)** – Entre l'hôtel de ville (1788), édifice classique dû à l'architecte bisontin Pâris, et l'ensemble de la collégiale et du château s'étend un quartier pittoresque (rue du Château, rue du Trésor, rue du Pommier, rue des Moulins) avec ses maisons anciennes, ses fontaines des 16e et 17e s., ses tours d'enceinte. Sur l'oblongue place des Halles, se dressent des maisons du 17e s. et celle Renaissance dite « des Halles » cantonnée de tourelles et marquée de l'écusson fleurdelisé des Orléans-Longueville.

★ **Collégiale, château** – Tous deux forment un même ensemble monumental.
La **collégiale**, bel édifice des 12e et 13e s., au toit couvert de tuiles vernissées, a connu d'importantes transformations en 1530 à cause de la Réforme, puis au 19e s., où elle fut considérablement restaurée. Le chevet est roman, comme en témoignent les trois absides coiffées d'arcatures ornées de têtes humaines ou animales. En contournant le chevet par la droite, on parvient au cloître du 15e s., dont subsiste une rangée d'arcades romanes contre le mur de l'église.

NEUCHÂTEL

Face à l'entrée principale de la collégiale, statue du Réformateur Guillaume Farel (1489-1565) dont les prédications entraînèrent les Neuchâtelois à adopter le culte réformé. La nef, voûtée d'ogives est de style gothique. A la croisée du transept s'élève une tour lanterne. Dans le chœur (chapiteaux romans historiés) sous une arcade, le cénotaphe des comtes de Neuchâtel (14e s.) constitue une œuvre marquante pour la sculpture du Moyen Âge. Ce bel ensemble en pierre se compose de quatorze rigides et imposantes statues polychromes, représentant chevaliers et dames dans les attitudes de prière.

Le portail Sud, roman, orné de voussures et de chapiteaux sculptés, est encadré des statues de saint Pierre et saint Paul.

Le **château** (15e et 16e s. – restauré) ⊙, autrefois demeure des seigneurs de Neuchâtel, aujourd'hui siège du gouvernement cantonal, comporte encore quelques vestiges du 12e s. (galerie romane à sept baies aveugles de la façade Sud-Ouest). D'allure fortifiée, le portail d'entrée est flanqué de deux tours couronnées de mâchicoulis et orné d'arcs brisés. Sous le passage des armes de Philippe de Hochberg, seigneur de Neuchâtel, sont visibles à la croisée d'ogives. Dans l'aile Nord, la plus ancienne, on visite l'ancienne cuisine (cheminée avec une hotte en bois) ; l'antichambre (horloge de Jaquet-Droz, toile de Robert Ferrier *Bénédiction de la charrue en Franche-Comté*) ; la salle du Grand Conseil en forme d'hémicycle, où siège le parlement cantonal composé de 115 députés élus pour 4 ans (vitraux de Georges Froidevaux représentant les armoiries des chefs-lieux de district) ; la grotte ou gloriette, petite pièce voûtée en berceau, où l'on gardait les archives du pays ; la salle des Chevaliers, la plus grande salle du château, utilisée pour des réceptions (beau plafond, armes de chaque côté de la cheminée, portraits des conseillers d'État qui se sont succédé). Dans l'aile Sud plusieurs salles se suivent parmi lesquelles la salle Marie de Savoie, nièce de Louis XI et épouse du comte Philippe de Hochberg en 1478 (au-dessus de la cheminée en pierre, armes du comte) ; la galerie Philippe de Hochberg, dans laquelle se réunissent les conseillers d'État ; la salle des États ou salle de tribunal, qui résume sur ses murs toute l'histoire du pays de Neuchâtel (écus armoriés).

Il est possible d'accéder au chemin de ronde offrant de jolies vues sur la ville.

Tour des Prisons ⊙ – Au pied de la colline du château, dans la rue Jehanne-de-Hochberg, se dresse une haute tour crénelée dite tour des Prisons. Édifice le plus ancien de la ville dans sa partie inférieure, elle conserve, à l'intérieur, deux cachots en bois utilisés jusqu'en 1848, et deux maquettes représentant Neuchâtel, fin 15e s. et fin 18e s. De la plate-forme, **panorama** sur la collégiale, la ville et le lac.

★★ Musée d'Art et d'Histoire (CZ) ⊙ – *Commencer par la section d'Art.*

Beaux-Arts – *A l'étage.* Un escalier monumental, décoré de fresques allégoriques de Paul Robert et de vitraux de Clément Heaton, mène à cette section. Ce panorama de la peinture helvétique – spécialement neuchâteloise – réserve huit de ses neuf salles à des expositions temporaires d'œuvres du 19e et 20e s., exposées par roulement sauf pour les salles consacrées à Léopold Robert *(Femme éplorée au bord de la mer)*, Ferdinand Hodler *(Soir d'automne)* et Albert Anker *(Paysan bernois lisant son journal).*

Histoire et Arts décoratifs – *Rez-de-chaussée et entresol, à droite.* Une dizaine de salles, dont quatre en entresol, abritent cette section du musée. La plus vaste, en deux parties, présente une multitude d'objets, remarquablement mis en valeur, évoquant l'artisanat et le cadre de vie local d'antan : meubles, bibelots, costumes, dentelles, tapisseries, jouets, ustensiles quotidiens...

D'autres salles retracent l'histoire du canton, exposent des collections d'orfèvrerie (coupes des corporations), de numismatique, de porcelaines, de céramiques paysannes...

La salle 4 renferme des pendules neuchâteloises et surtout les trois **automates** ★★ androïdes (la musicienne, l'écrivain et le dessinateur), merveilles d'ingéniosité, fabriqués au 18e s. par les Jaquet-Droz père et fils, et par Jean-Frédéric Leschot.

A l'entresol (dans l'escalier, enseignes d'auberges neuchâteloises), on admire de la verrerie ancienne, des armes, des vitraux des 16e et 17e s. aux armes des villes, et la **collection Strübin** ★, belle présentation d'armes, cuirasses, casques et uniformes français de la Révolution, du Premier Empire, de la Restauration et du Second Empire.

Automate « La Musicienne »

★ **Musée d'Ethnographie** (**AZ**) – Il est installé dans une villa du début du siècle entourée d'un parc. L'annexe moderne, dite Musée Dynamique est réservée à des expositions thématiques temporaires ; elle est décorée sur toute sa façade Nord par la fresque géante *Les Conquêtes de l'Homme*, du peintre suisse Hans Erni.
Au rez-de-chaussée de la villa, les riches collections exposées en permanence illustrent principalement l'ethnographie africaine : Égypte pharaonique (statuettes, barques funéraires), art nègre (masques, figures d'esprits tutélaires, bijoux, plats royaux, siège de chef) et océanienne (Nouvelle-Guinée, Polynésie). Le 1er étage, outre le cabinet du général Charles-Daniel de Meuron (1738-1806), grand voyageur et collectionneur : objets exotiques (éventail de Madagascar, carquois et flèches, vaisselle chinoise...), renferme une intéressante exposition consacrée au Bhoutan. Les collections, ayant trait à ce petit pays d'Asie voisin de la Chine et de l'Inde, ont été léguées par le feu roi, ainsi que par des membres de la famille royale : tapis, costumes traditionnels, instruments de musique, objets de la vie domestique, étonnant autel portatif en forme de pagode à trois étages, etc.

Quai Osterwald (**BZ**) – Table d'orientation. Très belle **vue**★★ sur le lac et les Alpes.

Musée d'Histoire naturelle (**BZ**) – Installé dans l'ancienne École de commerce, imposant bâtiment du 19e s. en pierre jaune, le musée compte outre ses collections de mammifères, de nombreuses espèces d'oiseaux aquatiques et des forêts exposés dans des dioramas reconstituant leur milieu naturel ; plusieurs chants et cris ont été enregistrés.

Musée cantonal d'Archéologie (**CY**) – Les objets les plus anciens proviennent de la grotte de Cotencher (Rochefort) et de celle du Bichon (La Chaux-de-Fonds) : parmi ceux-ci, le crâne d'un adulte de race Cro-Magnon, datant du paléolithique supérieur. Les fouilles effectuées en bordure du lac (Auvernier, Bevaix) ont permis la découverte de pièces très variées : faucille en bois avec lame de silex (vers 3000 avant J.-C.), peignes en bois ou en vannerie,

coupe avec louche en bois de la fin du néolithique, des poteries datant de la fin de l'âge du bronze ainsi qu'une pirogue de la même époque. Découvert en 1857, le site de **La Tène** (au Nord-Est de Neuchâtel) a donné son nom au 2e âge du fer; il a livré de nombreuses armes (fourreaux d'épée décorés), outils et bijoux celtiques. De l'époque gallo-romaine on admire le buste en marbre de Julia, fille de Drusus et Livilla.

Hôtel DuPeyrou (CZ) – Cet élégant édifice a été bâti au 18e s. par le financier DuPeyrou, ami de Jean-Jacques Rousseau. Une belle grille d'entrée laisse voir la façade, de lignes très pures et d'une grande unité de style, et donne accès à un jardin d'agrément. Au centre de la pièce d'eau, statue « La Baigneuse » de A. Ramseyer.

ENVIRONS

★★ **Chaumont** – 8 km. Prendre la rue des Acacias à droite (Nord-Ouest du plan - AY). Laisser la voiture à la station supérieure du funiculaire ⊙ Neuchâtel-Chaumont (alt. 1 087 m).
Accès également par le funiculaire qui part de la Coudre, à 3 km du centre de Neuchâtel. Durée du trajet : 12 mn.
A gauche, en retrait, la **tour-observatoire** ⊙ offre un immense **panorama** (table d'orientation) sur les Alpes bernoises, le massif du Mont-Blanc et les trois lacs jurassiens.

Auvernier – 4,5 km par la rue de l'Évole (AZ du plan) que prolonge une petite route typique du vignoble neuchâtelois.
C'est un charmant village viticole et, aussi, résidentiel. Il offre, autour de la Grand-Rue, des fontaines, une église des 15e-18e s. et un joli château des 16e-17e s.

Colombier – 7 km par ② du plan, route d'Yverdon. Voir à ce nom.

191

NEUCHÂTEL

Boudry — *10 km par ② du plan, route d'Yverdon.*
Cette petite ville d'aspect médiéval a vu naître **Jean-Paul Marat**, rédacteur de *l'Ami du peuple*, assassiné dans sa baignoire en 1793 par Charlotte Corday. A proximité de sa maison natale, une sculpture intitulée *Marat-L'œil* a été érigée en son hommage. Cette œuvre en acier peint de 14 m de hauteur tourne imperceptiblement, créant des effets de lumière. Au n° 7 de la rue Louis-Favre, Philippe Suchard, chocolatier de renom, vit le jour en 1797. Il passa plusieurs années de son enfance dans la maison située au n° 37 de la même rue, aujourd'hui l'hôtel de ville.

Le château (13ᵉ-16ᵉ s.) tour à tour résidence des comtes et prison, abrite le **musée de la Vigne et du Vin** ⊙, créé par la Compagnie des Vignolants. Les vins de Neuchâtel héritiers d'une longue tradition, sont produits à partir d'un vignoble s'étageant entre le lac et le Jura. La visite qui débute par «l'histoire de la bouteille» de l'amphore au vino-box, donne un bon aperçu de l'histoire vigneronne de la région depuis le 18ᵉ s. Le travail de la vigne, réglé selon les saisons, les outils utilisés, les maladies, les vendanges, la fabrication du vin jusqu'à sa mise en bouteille sont clairement expliqués grâce à une exposition incluant photographies, outils et matériel, tableaux, etc. Dans une tour ronde, de vieux documents évoquent l'activité viticole au 19ᵉ s.

La NEUVEVILLE

Berne — 3 324 habitants
Carte Michelin n° 427 pli 12 ou 216 pli 13 – Schéma : JURA SUISSE

Délicieuse petite cité, la Neuveville vit de ses vins, de la mécanique de précision et de sa situation touristique au bord du lac, face à l'île St-Pierre qui, d'ici, paraît être située sur la rive opposée. La ville, avec ses rues pavées, ses lanternes et les cinq tours subsistantes de ses fortifications, a gardé un séduisant cachet ancien.

Rue du Marché — Faisant office de place principale, elle est pittoresque par sa rigole médiane d'écoulement, ses jolies fontaines Renaissance (à bannerets) et maisons (dont deux datées de 1647 et 1697) fleuries, les anciennes portes (tours Rouge et de Rive) qui la ferment à ses deux extrémités.

«Blanche Église» ⊙ — *Sortie Est vers Bienne, à gauche.*
Construction d'origine carolingienne mais remaniée à l'époque gothique, puis restaurée en 1915, ceinte de dalles funéraires levées des 17ᵉ et 18ᵉ s. L'intérieur conserve d'autres pierres tombales sculptées, une belle chaire de 1536 peinte en bois, et d'intéressants vestiges de fresques du 14ᵉ s. aux tons bruns, à droite du chœur : Tentation de Jésus, Christ aux outrages, Entrée à Jérusalem. Adam et Ève.

NUFENENPASSSTRASSE★★

Carte Michelin n° 427 plis 14, 15 ou 217 plis 19, 20
Schéma : SANKT-GOTTHARD-MASSIV

Cette route spectaculaire, qui relie le Tessin au Valais, est la plus récemment construite du massif du St-Gothard.

D'AIROLO A ULRICHEN

40 km — environ 1 h 1/2 — itinéraire ③ de la visite du massif du St-Gothard

Le col du Nufenen est généralement obstrué par la neige de novembre à mai.

D'**Airolo** (alt. 1 142 m) jusqu'à 8 km du Nufen, la remontée du val Bedretto (et de la rivière Tessin vers sa source) s'effectue entre des versants couverts de sapins. D'Airolo à Fontana, l'œil est d'abord sollicité, en haut à droite, par les audacieux ouvrages de la route du St-Gothard, puis, après Ossasco, par une série de villages, dont Bedretto, alignés à mi-pente sur un replat. Au passage on aura parfois l'occasion d'assister à la traite manuelle, sur le bord même de la route, de tout un lot des majestueuses vaches brunes de la région...

A partir du hameau d'All'Acqua *(à gauche : télécabine)*, la végétation se raréfie, la montée s'accentue. Les lacets de la route procurent une belle vue d'enfilade, en arrière, sur les versants, qui paraissent se chevaucher, de la vallée. On escalade désormais le flanc droit dénudé du val Bedretto, aux parois de roche verdâtre ou d'éboulis striées de rares cascades. L'ascension s'achève, avec la section tessinoise du parcours, au col du Nufenen.

★★ **Col du Nufenen (Passo della Novena-Nufenenpass)** — Alt. 2 478 m. Bienvenu pour l'automobiliste qui vient d'endurer plus de 1 300 m de dénivellation depuis Airolo, ce col lui offre au surplus le spectacle, d'une désolation grandiose, de crêtes déchiquetées et d'abîmes où tournoient des choucas, avec la vision en contre-haut *(à gauche* *du restaurant*) du glacier et du lac-réservoir de Gries. La **vue**★★ s'étend par ailleurs, du Nord-Ouest au Sud-Ouest, sur les massifs du Haut-Valais et de l'Oberland bernois (cime du Finsteraarhorn), avec en premier plan la face noire du Faulhorn toute griffée de rainures verticales.

La descente côté Valais, après une vue rapprochée sur le glacier grisâtre de Gries et le barrage de son lac artificiel, fait plonger dans un paysage minéral seulement égayé de plaques d'herbe rase et de chardons, encore en vue du glacier et du Faulhorn, suivis d'une vallée suspendue d'où s'échappe une cascade. Quelque 5 km après le col, une intéressante vue d'enfilade se révèle sur la vallée du Rhône supérieur. La route accompagne ensuite le cours diminué de l'Agere, devenu le trop-plein du barrage de Gries, et à peine visible dans son lit de cailloux trop large, au pied de l'immense paroi rocheuse du Blashorn, à droite. La vallée devient plus aimable et se couvre de mélèzes à l'approche du village « walser » d'**Ulrichen** que l'on découvre, bien groupé autour de son église, dans l'épanouissement de sa propre vallée (rhodanienne).

NYON★

Vaud — 14 747 habitants
Carte Michelin nᵒ 427 pli 11 ou 217 pli 12 — Schéma : Lac LÉMAN — Alt. 410 m

Agréable petite ville étagée au-dessus du Léman, Nyon cultive jalousement le souvenir de son passé latin, ayant été fondée par Jules César sous le nom de Colonia Julia Equestris (succédant au bourg helvète de Noviodunum). L'occupation bernoise, au 16ᵉ s., y est rappelée par le château et les maisons à arcades de la place du Marché.

CURIOSITÉS

★ **Promenade des Vieilles Murailles** — Aménagée au 19ᵉ s., à l'abri des vents du Nord, en surplomb du quartier de Rive, elle longe des murs tapissés de vigne vierge et s'élargit sur l'Esplanade des Marronniers, d'où se découvre une belle **vue** sur la ville, le Petit lac jusqu'à Genève, le Salève et le Mont Blanc. L'érection, à cet endroit, de colonnes romaines (trouvées à proximité) avec leurs chapiteaux et leur entablement à frise corinthienne, ajoute une note romantique au tableau.

Château — Profondément remaniée au 16ᵉ s., cette construction d'origine féodale porte cinq tours dissemblables mais toutes coiffées en poivrière. De la terrasse, jolie **vue** sur le quartier de Rive et le Petit lac (table d'orientation).

Musée historique et des porcelaines ⊙ — C'est en 1781 que s'ouvrit la manufacture de porcelaine de Nyon. Le musée rassemble d'importantes collections de porcelaines et de faïences produites jusqu'au 20ᵉ s. En 1813, la faïence pour des raisons économiques remplaça la porcelaine. Parmi les pièces exposées : services à café (décor à l'or, monochrome, avec bleuets), services à thé, bols à bouillon, service ayant appartenu à Joachim Murat, maréchal de France et roi de Naples en 1808. Une salle est décorée avec du mobilier régional : armoire en noyer, commode au dessus en marbre noir. La collection Burkhard Reber du nom d'un pharmacien de l'hôpital de Genève, réunit des pots de pharmacie en faïence et majolique du 16ᵉ au 18ᵉ s. ainsi que des instruments de mesure.

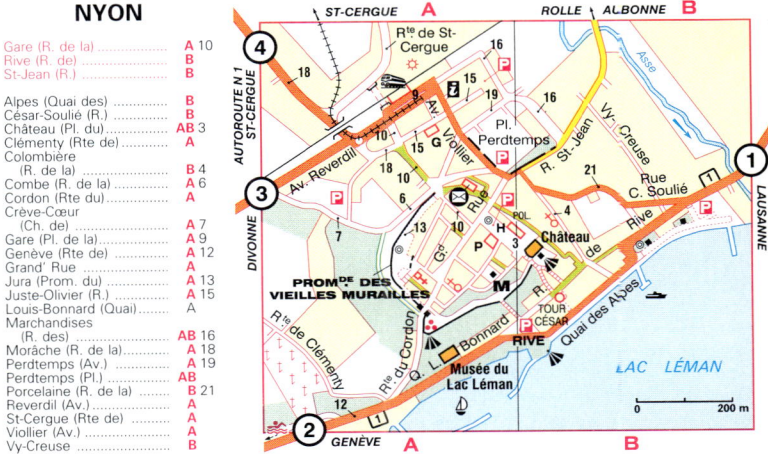

NYON

Gare (R. de la)	A 10
Rive (R. de)	B
St-Jean (R.)	B
Alpes (Quai des)	B
César-Soulié (R.)	B
Château (Pl. du)	AB 3
Clémenty (Rte de)	A
Colombière (R. de la)	B 4
Combe (R. de la)	A 6
Cordon (R. du)	A
Crève-Cœur (Ch. de)	A 7
Gare (Pl. de la)	A 9
Genève (Rte de)	A 12
Grand' Rue	A
Jura (Prom. du)	A 13
Juste-Olivier (R.)	A 15
Louis-Bonnard (Quai)	A
Marchandises (R. des)	AB 16
Morâche (R. de la)	A 18
Perdtemps (Av.)	A 19
Perdtemps (Pl.)	AB
Porcelaine (R. de la)	B 21
Reverdil (Av.)	A
St-Cergue (Rte de)	A
Viollier (Av.)	A
Vy-Creuse	B

NYON

Musée romain (M) – Souterrain, il est annoncé, en surface, par une statue de Jules César et l'emplacement, matérialisé au sol, de l'ancienne basilique du Forum dont l'architecture supposée est suggérée sur la façade aveugle d'une maison voisine. Cette « basilique civile », vaste édifice public du 1er s., constitue par la partie dégagée (un peu plus du tiers de ses fondations – en murs de moellons solidement maçonnés) l'élément principal du musée. Sur son pourtour, collections d'objets provenant des fouilles effectuées sur place et alentour : fragments de mosaïques à décor géométrique simple ou aux rinceaux (dont celle dite d'Artémis), vestiges lapidaires (bornes milliaires, chapiteaux), objets de la vie quotidienne (vaisselle, lampes, monnaies, céramiques), et surtout abondante série d'**amphores**, d'origines diverses.

Quartier de Rive – Un petit port de plaisance bien abrité, un parc et des quais fleuris d'où l'on a vue sur la rive française en face (à 4 km) font le charme de cette partie de Nyon qui touche au lac. Quai des Alpes, au sommet de la tour César (11e s.), on remarque le masque romain du dieu Attis, amant de Cybèle et symbole de la fécondité.

Musée du lac Léman – Il est situé dans un ancien hôpital du 18e s., près du port de plaisance. L'origine du lac, sa flore, sa faune (aquariums contenant les principales espèces de poissons), la végétation de ses rives servent d'introduction à la visite, qui évoque ensuite les activités humaines passées et présentes. La pêche, le transport du bois dans ces grandes barques qui ont sillonné le lac jusqu'à l'avènement du rail, les bateaux à vapeur, la navigation de plaisance sont illustrés grâce à de nombreux documents ou objets (éléments de barques, filets de pêche, machinerie du vapeur Helvétie II, maquettes).
Le 1er étage est consacré en partie aux peintres du Léman, suisses ou étrangers, séduits par le charme du site. Une salle dédiée à la Compagnie générale de navigation, réunit des maquettes de bateaux dont celle du premier vapeur de 1823.

ENVIRONS

Crans – *6 km par ② du plan.*
Le château, de proportions harmonieuses, traduit l'architecture de l'époque Louis XV. Près de la petite église, se dégage une vue intéressante sur le vignoble, le lac et au fond la chaîne de montagnes située en territoire français.

Gingins – *7 km par ④ du plan.*
Inauguré en 1994 au centre du village, la **Fondation Neumann** rassemble une belle collection de verrerie Art Nouveau riche de quelque 150 pièces des plus grandes signatures du début du siècle (Argy-Rousseau, Daum, Gallé, Tiffany, etc.), ainsi que le Suisse Eugène Grasset). Trois expositions temporaires annuelles sont consacrées aux domaines de l'art appliqué.

Abbaye de Bonmont – *10 km par ③ du plan et la Rippe.*
Au pied du Jura vaudois subsistent quelques bâtiments de l'ancienne abbaye de Bonmont, devenue cistercienne en 1131 pendant sa construction. Les vicissitudes qu'elle connut à partir du 16e s. (elle servit entre autres de fromagerie et même de garage) l'ont cependant préservée d'altérations trop importantes.
Bâtie sur le modèle de l'abbaye bourguignonne de Clairvaux : plan en croix latine, nef tripartite et chevet plat flanqué de chapelles rectangulaires, l'église, austère mais de proportions harmonieuses, a été récemment restaurée et présente un beau porche orné de chapiteaux à décoration florale.

L'OBERLAND BERNOIS

Voir à BERNER OBERLAND

LES GUIDES VERTS MICHELIN
Paysages
Monuments
Routes touristiques
Géographie
Histoire, Art
Itinéraires de visite régionaux
Plans de villes et de monuments

Un choix de guides pour vos vacances en France et à l'étranger.

OLTEN

Soleure — 17 805 habitants
Carte Michelin n° 427 pli 5 ou 216 pli 16 — Alt. 388 m
Plan dans le guide Rouge Michelin Suisse

Située à la lisière du Jura, Olten est agréablement disposée au bord de l'Aare. Un pont de bois couvert (Alte Brücke) réservé aux piétons mène à la ville ancienne.
Une grande activité industrielle — savonneries, cimenteries, ateliers des Chemins de fer fédéraux, alimentation — a modifié depuis le début du siècle l'aspect de la ville qui s'étend désormais de part et d'autre de l'Aare.

CURIOSITÉS

Musée des Beaux-Arts (Kunstmuseum) ⊙ — Le musée possède une bonne collection de peintures et sculptures du 19ᵉ s. et du 20ᵉ s.; les plus intéressantes se trouvent au 2ᵉ étage, et parmi elles, se distinguent les caricatures, études et dessins de **Martin Disteli** (1802-1844). Les scènes de l'histoire militaire suisse, de la vie politique, ainsi que les fables, ont été interprétées par cet artiste avec une grande vérité du mouvement, une précision du détail et une finesse d'exécution remarquables.

Musée historique (Historisches Museum) ⊙ — Il renferme diverses collections ayant trait à l'art local, aux coutumes, au mobilier, aux costumes de la région, ainsi qu'une section préhistorique bien connue.

ENVIRONS

★ **Panorama du Säli-Schlössli** — *5 km au Sud-Est. Sortir par la Aarburgerstrasse et prendre à gauche la Sälistrasse.*
La rue devient rapidement une route escaladant en lacet une colline boisée au sommet de laquelle (alt. 667 m) s'érige, sur les vestiges de l'ancien château féodal de Wartburg, un petit château néo-gothique *(aménagé en café-restaurant)*.
De sa tour carrée à créneaux, agréable **panorama** ★ ⊙ sur Olten et Aarburg, la vallée de l'Aare et tout un horizon circulaire de collines verdoyantes.

Zofingue (Zofingen) — *9 km au Sud-Est.*
La partie ancienne du bourg, contenue dans le quadrilatère que délimitent les allées remplaçant ses remparts — dont il ne reste que la Pulverturm, solide tour carrée du 12ᵉ s. —, est intéressante par sa grand'place (Thut-Platz), avec fontaine à banneret, et ses nombreuses maisons des 17ᵉ s. et 18ᵉ s.
L'église St-Maurice, rénovée, a gardé son clocher du 17ᵉ s. (d'allure Renaissance).
Du passé romain de Zofingue subsistent deux grandes mosaïques provenant d'une ancienne villa, conservées sous abris et visibles à la sortie Sud de la ville *(derrière l'hôtel Römerbad)*.

En vous rendant en Suisse romande,
si vous désirez effectuer une traversée intéressante
du Jura français ou de la Savoie, munissez-vous
des guides Verts Michelin Jura ou Alpes du Nord.

ORBE

Vaud — 5 084 habitants
Carte Michelin n° 427 pli 11 ou 217 pli 3 — Schéma : JURA SUISSE — Alt. 483 m

Orbe, étagée sur une colline qu'entoure un méandre de la rivière du même nom (dérivé du latin « Urba »), est une petite ville attachante, au cachet ancien.
De la place du Marché où s'élève une fontaine à banneret datée de 1753, on accède par une ruelle à l'église réformée, des 15ᵉ et 16ᵉ s. (à l'intérieur : bas-côtés aux curieuses clefs de voûtes), puis à la terrasse de l'ancien château d'où se révèlent des perspectives sur les bas quartiers et la vallée de l'Orbe.
Au bas de la rue fleurie des Moulinets, tableau pittoresque formé par le pont romain et le pont couvert usinier enjambant la rivière avec, entre eux, l'avancée d'une maison à tourelle.

Mosaïques d'Urba ⊙ — *2 km au Nord d'Orbe, sur la route d'Yverdon.*
Quatre pavillons isolés au bord de la route abritent des mosaïques romaines du début du 3ᵉ s. Dans l'ordre de leur proximité par rapport à la ferme voisine : Calendrier aux Divinités, la plus belle, constituée de médaillons polychromes ; Scène champêtre au chariot, la plus évocatrice ; Labyrinthe au lion et aux oiseaux ; mosaïque à décor géométrique noir et blanc.

ORON-LE-CHÂTEL

Vaud – 169 habitants

Carte Michelin n° 427 pli 12 ou 217 Sud du pli 4 (Nord d'Oron-la-Ville) – Alt. 720 m

Ce petit village situé dans la Haute-Broye, sur la rive gauche du Flon, est dominé par la masse imposante de son château fort.

Château ⊙ – Solidement assis sur un éperon rocheux, il fut construit à la fin du 12ᵉ s. et au début du 13ᵉ s. Les nombreuses transformations qu'il a subies ensuite n'ont pas altéré son allure défensive. Plusieurs familles s'y sont succédé, comme en témoignent les armoiries du grand vestibule. Pendant 241 ans, le château servit de résidence aux baillis bernois. Les appartements du 1ᵉʳ étage reflètent le cadre dans lequel vivait une famille bourgeoise. Dans la salle à manger, on remarque une belle collection de porcelaines de Sèvres et de Limoges ainsi que des faïences de Wedgwood. La bibliothèque (beau plafond à caissons du 15ᵉ s.) renferme environ 18 000 volumes du 16ᵉ au 19ᵉ s. D'autres pièces agréablement meublées se font suite : salon de musique (piano qui aurait appartenu à Chopin), fumoir aux papiers peints décorés de scènes de chasse, salle de jeux et d'études pour les enfants, salon de thé (commode Louis XV en bois de rose), chambre du prieur.

PASSWANGSTRASSE★

Carte Michelin n° 427 pli 4 ou 216 plis 4, 15 – Schéma : JURA SUISSE

La rugueuse vallée de la Lüssel, puis celle, riante, de la Birse composent la majeure partie de cet itinéraire sinueux, entre l'Aare et le Rhin, à l'extrémité Est du Jura.

D'OENSINGEN A BÂLE

73 km – environ 2 h 1/4 – itinéraire ⑥ *de la visite du Jura suisse*

Entre Oensingen et Balsthal, la route suit le fond de la « Klus » (cluse) tranchant perpendiculairement le chaînon du Weissenstein. Enfumant ce couloir, dont le château d'**Alt-Falkenstein**, malheureusement restauré à l'excès, surveille la sortie amont, les importantes fonderies de Roll maintiennent la tradition métallurgique du Jura.

Entre Balsthal et le col du Passwang, le tracé décrit un coude au pied des ruines altières du « Burg » de **Neu-Falkenstein**, dominées par un donjon cylindrique, pour pénétrer dans l'agreste **Guldental** par une nouvelle – mais fort courte – porte rocheuse. Les dernières sinuosités de la route précédant le tunnel de faîte du Passwang permettent des vues plongeantes sur cette vallée retirée, tandis que, dans le lointain, apparaissent les Alpes bernoises. Du col du Passwang, l'excursion au sommet du Passwang est recommandée.

★★**Sommet du Passwang** – Alt. 1 204 m. *De la sortie Nord du tunnel du Passwang, 2 km par un chemin étroit, coupé de raidillons (refermer les barrières derrière soi), plus 3/4 h à pied AR.* Laisser la voiture au café-restaurant « Wirtschaft Ober-Passwang » et continuer à suivre le chemin en montée. A la sortie d'un bois, après avoir passé une barrière, quitter ce chemin pour atteindre, sur la droite, le point culminant de la crête. De là, **panorama**★★ très varié, s'étendant au Nord sur les dernières ondulations du Jura bâlois, la plaine d'Alsace (remarquer le double ruban du Rhin et du bief de Kembs appartenant au grand canal d'Alsace) encadrée par les Vosges et la Forêt-Noire, et au Sud sur le Jura soleurois et sur une partie des Alpes bernoises.

Du col à Laufen, la solitaire vallée de la Lüssel se réduit rapidement à une étroite tranchée boisée. Entre Erschwil et Büsserach se postent, en sentinelle, les ruines de Thierstein, tour massive flanquée d'une tourelle. On débouche dans le bassin de Laufen dont les ondulations couvertes de cultures se déploient devant les croupes forestières des « Blauen ».

Entre **Laufen**, petite ville qui a gardé ses deux portes fortifiées, et Aesch, la **vallée de la Birse**, fraîche et verdoyante, garde encore de l'agrément, malgré son industrialisation de plus en plus marquée. L'énorme donjon cubique du château d'Angenstein, ancienne résidence des évêques de Bâle, donne au touriste l'impression furtive d'en obstruer le dernier « étroit ».

A Grellingen prendre la route à l'Est.

Seewen – A l'écart de ce joli village groupé dans une cuvette boisée au pied de sa blanche église, se visite un intéressant **musée d'automates musiciens** (Musikautomaten-Museum) ⊙ dont les salles abritent environ 800 modèles, du 18ᵉ s. au début du 20ᵉ s., de pianos mécaniques, orgues de foire, de Barbarie, orchestrions (orgues imitant des instruments d'orchestre), boîtes à musique, et d'amusants automates (musiciens, oiseaux, peintre, magicien...) présentés en fonctionnement.

Goetheanum ⊙ – *Les accès sont signalés au départ de Dornachbrugg ou d'Arlesheim.* Érigée sur les pentes qui dominent Dornach et Arlesheim, la construction du Goetheanum produit un effet déconcertant. C'est le siège international de la « Société Anthroposophique Universelle » ainsi que d'une « Université libre de science spirituelle », au sein de laquelle sont organisées, dans le cadre d'activités diverses, des représentations publiques de pièces d'auteurs classiques et modernes, notamment le Faust intégral de Goethe et les quatre drames-mystères de Rudolf Steiner. Le bâtiment et ses dépendances, même les plus utilitaires, sont construits, dans les moindres détails, conformément à la philosophie du fondateur de l'anthroposophie, Rudolf Steiner (1861-1925), qui, influencé par les idées de Goethe, créa son œuvre selon le principe de la métamorphose.

Arlesheim – L'**église collégiale** ★ (Domkirche) ⊙ est une des plus charmantes réussites de l'art baroque en Suisse. L'édifice, construit en 1680 pour le chapitre de la principauté épiscopale de Bâle, fut transformé dans le goût rococo (1769-1771). Il se dresse sur une calme placette ombragée, bordée par les anciennes maisons des chanoines. Intérieurement, le vaisseau, dont aucun détail décoratif discordant ne vient rompre l'harmonie, s'orne des stucs discrètement rehaussés de rose ou de jaune pâle, tandis que les voûtes surbaissées présentent de vastes compositions picturales vaporeuses, aux tons lavés, œuvres de Joseph Appiani (1760).

On pénètre alors dans la grande banlieue de Bâle.

★★★ **Basel** – *Visite : 3 h. Voir à ce nom.*

PAYERNE★

Vaud – 7 393 habitants
Carte Michelin n° 427 pli 12 ou 217 pli 4 – Schéma : JURA SUISSE – Alt. 450 m

Située dans la riche vallée de la Broye, Payerne possède une remarquable abbatiale, dépendant autrefois d'une abbaye de bénédictins : cette abbaye fut fondée au 10e s. par l'impératrice Adélaïde, épouse d'Othon le Grand, premier empereur germanique, fille de la légendaire reine Berthe (surnommée « la Reine filandière »), veuve de Rodolphe II, roi de Bourgogne transjurane.

★ **Église abbatiale** ⊙ – Principal vestige de cette importante abbaye, l'église du 11e s. a été désaffectée au milieu du 16e s., lorsque les Bernois introduisirent la Réforme dans le Pays de Vaud ; transformée en caserne et grenier, elle subit alors de multiples dégradations.
D'importants travaux de restauration ont rendu peu à peu à ce monument roman son aspect primitif.

★★ **Intérieur** – *Illustration, voir : La Suisse pittoresque, L'art religieux.* La nef, d'une grande sobriété, est couverte d'un berceau semi-circulaire, éclairé par des fenêtres hautes, tandis que les bas-côtés sont voûtés d'arêtes. L'abside est en cul-de-four. La pureté des lignes et l'harmonie des proportions donnent au visiteur une impression de grandeur, mais aussi d'austérité qu'accentue le manque de décoration (hormis la belle alternance du calcaire jaune et du grès gris). Une remarquable série de chapiteaux orne les fenêtres hautes du chœur et les piliers du transept. Leur dessin, fruste mais expressif, les fait dater de l'époque de fondation de l'abbaye. Des vestiges de fresques ornent les croisillons du transept.
La salle haute du narthex, ou chapelle St-Michel (fresques du 13e s.), est réservée au musée de l'Abbatiale.
Attenante à l'église, la belle **salle capitulaire**, à voûte d'arêtes, mérite un coup d'œil. Des expositions temporaires y sont organisées.
Face à l'abbatiale, l'église protestante conserve des vestiges de fresques et des pierres tombales anciennes.

Gorges du PICHOUX★

Carte Michelin n° 427 plis 3, 4 ou 216 plis 2, 14 – Schéma : JURA SUISSE

Du lac de Bienne à l'Ajoie (région de Porrentruy), des gorges profondes, pâturages, forêts de sapins ou de feuillus jalonnent une route qui, dans la vallée de la Sorne, vient se faufiler entre les Franches Montagnes et le pays de Delémont.

DE BIENNE A PORRENTRUY

61 km – environ 2 h 1/2 – itinéraire 5 *de la visite du Jura suisse*

★ **Biel/Bienne** – *Visite : 1 h. Voir à ce nom.*
De Bienne à Sonceboz, la route s'élevant rapidement au-dessus des faubourgs de Bienne, se glisse, à mi-hauteur, dans les gorges du Taubenloch (Taubenlochschlucht – *les amateurs de sites encaissés peuvent visiter ces gorges à pied, suivant l'itinéraire de promenade décrit aux environs de Bienne*). La route continue ensuite à remonter la vallée industrielle de la Suze (importante cimenterie de Reuchenette) étranglée de courtes portes rocheuses qui marquent la traversée des plis successifs du Jura.

Gorges du PICHOUX

Pierre-Pertuis – Le passage de Pierre-Pertuis peut évoquer la traversée d'un petit col alpestre. Utilisé dès le début du 3ᵉ s. par la voie romaine reliant Aventicum (Avenches) à Augusta Raurica (Augst), il tire son nom de l'arche artificielle alors créée sous laquelle passe l'ancien chemin, sur le versant de Tavannes. Le **site** est très connu dans toute la région.

A la hauteur du col, une clairière plantée de sapins et dotée de bancs invite à la halte.

Tavannes – Le nom de cette petite cité laborieuse et prospère, située dans la vallée supérieure de la Birse, au pied du rocher de Pierre-Pertuis, évoque immédiatement son activité horlogère. L'église catholique moderne a été décorée par les artistes de la « Société St-Luc », école d'art sacré bien connue en Suisse romande : la mosaïque de la façade, représentant l'Ascension, est due à Gino Severini.

Les paysages prennent un caractère très « haut-jurassien ». La route se transforme par endroits en une véritable avenue bordée de sapins.

Abbaye de Bellelay ⊙ – Les bâtiments du 18ᵉ s. de cette ancienne abbaye, occupée par les Prémontrés de 1136 à 1797, ont gardé, extérieurement, leur distinction monastique. L'**église abbatiale**, bâtie entre 1710 et 1714, présente intérieurement un ensemble d'architecture baroque qui se rapproche de ceux de St-Urban *(voir à ce nom)* et de Rheinau *(voir à ce nom)*. Malgré la disparition de son mobilier, ce **vaisseau** ★ garde une surprenante solennité. On attribue aux Pères de Bellelay la recette de fabrication de la **Tête de moine**, fromage à pâte demi-dure, servi en copeaux onctueux et parfumés détachés au couteau.

Après avoir sinué dans les pâturages boisés où paissent les chevaux bais des Franches Montagnes, la route se glisse au plus profond des gorges creusées par la Sorne.

★ **Gorges du Pichoux** – Cette coupure, au fond de laquelle la route, bâtie sur murs de soutènement, dispute la place au torrent, est la plus encaissée des cluses que la Sorne se soit percées entre le Pichoux et Berlincourt. Les gorges présentent de très hautes falaises calcaires auxquelles s'agrippent des forêts de sapins.

La **montée** ★ de Boécourt au col des Rangiers se déroule tout d'abord au flanc d'un versant découvert, planté de frênes et de beaux chênes tortus. On apprécie alors l'ampleur de la « Vallée de Delémont », harmonieusement incurvée et parsemée de gros villages industriels prospères. Le versant du Doubs est atteint au moment où la route rejoint l'itinéraire dit de la « Corniche du Jura », mais on ne peut que deviner la trouée de la grande rivière jurassienne.

La suite de l'itinéraire est décrite en sens inverse, au départ de Porrentruy (voir à ce nom).

Pour circuler en ville, utilisez les plans du guide Rouge Michelin Suisse *:*
  – axes de pénétration ou de contournement, rues nouvelles
  – parcs de stationnement, sens interdits...
Une abondante documentation, mise à jour chaque année.

PILATUS ★★★

Unterwald

Carte Michelin n° 427 pli 14 ou 217 Nord du pli 9 – Schéma : VIERWALDSTÄTTER SEE

Dominant de ses arêtes bien découpées et longtemps enneigées les bassins occidentaux du lac des Quatre-Cantons, le **Pilate** (point culminant : 2 129 m au Tomlishorn) est, à la fois, un repère indispensable au voyageur visitant la Suisse centrale et un baromètre fort populaire dans toute la région de Lucerne, si l'on en croit le dicton :

  « Quand le Pilate a son chapeau *(de nuages)*,
  Dans le pays il fait beau ;
  Mais quand il ceint son épée *(la cime émergeant d'un anneau nuageux)*
  Gare l'ondée. »

Après avoir inspiré longtemps une terreur superstitieuse – la légende prétendait que l'esprit de Ponce Pilate hantait un petit lac voisin de ses cimes et que l'approche de ce lieu maudit par quelque audacieux suffisait à déchaîner de terribles orages – le massif du Pilate est devenu l'une des attractions des Alpes suisses.

MONTÉE AU PILATE

D'Alpnachstad, 2 h AR environ dont 1 h de chemin de fer à crémaillère ⊙ *.*

La ligne, en rampe maximum de 48 % – c'est l'une des plus escarpées du monde pour ce mode de traction –, est spécialement impressionnante dans la traversée des escarpements de l'Esel.

PILATUS

Le Pilate

★★★ **Pilatus-Kulm** — De la station supérieure, dotée de deux hôtels de montagne, on grimpe en quelques minutes au sommet de l'Esel (alt. 2 121 m), belvédère d'où le regard, ébloui par la chaîne des Alpes, plonge sur le plan d'eau tortueux du lac des Quatre-Cantons, rétréci en son milieu par les promontoires du Rigi et du Bürgenstock. Le parcours de la galerie ajourée taillée en pleine paroi rocheuse de l'Oberhaupt est également recommandé.

On peut encore atteindre le Pilatus-Kulm en téléphérique au départ de Kriens, dans la banlieue de Lucerne, et effectuer une excursion circulaire (voir à Luzern).

PONTRESINA★★

Grisons — 1 604 habitants
Carte Michelin n° 427 pli 17 ou 218 pli 15 — Schéma : GRAUBÜNDEN — Alt. 1 777 m

A l'entrée du Val Bernina, en vue du cirque glaciaire de Roseg et des ressauts neigeux du Piz Palü, Pontresina est la station d'alpinisme de l'Engadine. Remontant le Val Roseg ou la vallée de Morteratsch, les amateurs de haute montagne entreprennent, à partir de là, de magnifiques courses de glacier dans le massif de la Bernina, en particulier le fameux « Tour de la Diavolezza ».

De leur côté, les promeneurs se dispersent dans les sous-bois de la forêt de Tais ou atteignent à Alp Languard, sur un chemin en corniche, les derniers contreforts du Piz Languard en s'y rendant depuis Muottas Muragl *(à 7 km).*

Pontresina, dont la « saison » d'hiver se prolonge fort avant dans le printemps, offre aux skieurs d'innombrables excursions de longue haleine et des pistes ensoleillées desservies par les téléskis d'Alp Languard et le funiculaire de Muottas Muragl.

Chapelle Ste-Marie (Santa Maria) ⊙ — Ce petit sanctuaire roman, voisin de la tour Spaniola (12ᵉ s.), conserve un ensemble de peintures murales, restaurées, exécutées dans leur plus grande partie par un artiste du Quattrocento (15ᵉ s.). La série consacrée à sainte Marie-Madeleine intéresse les touristes familiers de la Légende Dorée et des grandes traditions provençales.

★★ **Muottas Muragl** — *3 km par la route de Samedan, jusqu'à Punt Muragl, plus 1 h AR environ dont 1/2 h de funiculaire. Voir à ce nom.*

*Pour choisir un lieu de séjour à votre convenance,
consultez la carte des Lieux de séjour en début de guide.*

PORRENTRUY

Jura – 6 857 habitants

Carte Michelin n° 427 pli 3 ou 216 Sud du pli 2 – Schéma : JURA SUISSE – Alt. 445 m

Jadis fortifiée et d'aspect assez sévère, Porrentruy est bâtie au centre du pays de l'Ajoie. En annexant au territoire français cette petite région aux traits de paysage tout comtois, la Révolution avait fait de Porrentruy le chef-lieu du département de Mont-Terrible englobant les actuels canton du Jura et Jura bernois jusqu'à Bienne : l'honneur était bien grand pour le modeste piton boisé, appelé en réalité Mont Terri (alt. 804 m – au Sud du village de Cornol).

La ville ancienne – La ville ancienne est située sur un éperon dominant la vallée de l'Allaine et possède bon nombre de monuments intéressants : le château des princes-évêques de Bâle, dont l'altière tour Refousse atteint 45 m de haut (belle vue), caractérisé en outre par des bâtiments d'époques diverses depuis le 11ᵉ s. ; au bas du château, la porte de France, l'un des vestiges de l'ancienne enceinte. Dans la rue Pierre-Péquignat et la Grand'Rue, en forte pente, se situent l'hôtel des Halles (1769), l'Hôtel de Ville, également du 18ᵉ s., et l'hôpital désaffecté (1765) qui possède de belles grilles de fer forgé (le **Musée de l'ancien Hôtel-Dieu** ⊙ doit ouvrir en 1997).

Le centre de la localité compte trois belles fontaines monumentales dues à Laurent Perroud : celle du Banneret (1558), dite du «Suisse», et celles de la Samaritaine (1564) et de la Boule dorée (1568), démontée à la fin du 19ᵉ s. et rétablie en 1991. Enfin, la cour de l'ancien Séminaire (rue Thurmann) est équipée d'un pendule de Foucault, non loin d'un agréable jardin botanique.

ENVIRONS

Grottes de Réclère ⊙ – *A 15 km de Porrentruy par la route de Besançon.*
Un guide vous accompagne jusqu'à 100 m sous terre dans cette grotte découverte en 1886. Bel ensemble de stalactites et de stalagmites, dont la plus grande de Suisse, appelée «la grand dôme» (13 m de hauteur pour plus de 250 000 ans). La visite peut être jumelée avec celle d'un parc où sont disséminés quelques reproductions d'animaux préhistoriques.

Lac des QUATRE-CANTONS

Voir à VIERWALDSTÄTTERSEE

Bad RAGAZ★

St-Gall – 4 325 habitants

Carte Michelin n° 427 pli 16 ou 218 pli 4 – Alt. 502 m

Dans un des beaux sites de la vallée du Rhin alpestre, face aux crêtes vigoureusement découpées du Falknis, Ragaz vit au rythme de la cure thermale. La station exploite, depuis le 11ᵉ s., les eaux faiblement minéralisées jaillissant à une température de 37° dans les gorges de la Tamina, en contrebas du village de Pfäfers. Les maladies de la circulation, les rhumatismes, les paralysies et les séquelles d'accidents y sont soignés efficacement.

En plein hiver, Ragaz se présente comme une base de ski, depuis qu'une télécabine et des téléskis relient la ville aux immenses champs de neige de la région du Pizol.

ENVIRONS

★★ **Gorges de la Tamina (Taminaschlucht)** ⊙ – *2 h à pied AR par le chemin prenant à gauche de la route de Valens, au Sud-Ouest.*
Formidable fissure, au fond de laquelle les curistes de l'époque héroïque devaient se faire descendre par des cordes pour prendre les eaux, alors non captées.

Protection de la flore alpine
La cueillette de certaines fleurs des Alpes menacées de disparition :
  cyclamen,
  grand chardon bleu,
  lis martagon,
  edelweiss,
est sévèrement réglementée en Suisse.

RAPPERSWIL★

St-Gall – 7 463 habitants

Carte Michelin n° 427 pli 6 ou 216 pli 19 – Schéma : ZÜRICH (Environs) – Alt. 409 m

La petite ville de Rapperswil occupe un joli site sur une courte presqu'île de la rive Nord du lac de Zurich. La ville haute a conservé un caractère moyenâgeux, que souligne encore la masse imposante de son château.

Le « front de lac » de Rapperswil est très animé en été. De nombreuses excursions en bateau sont possibles vers les petites îles voisines.

CURIOSITÉS

Château – Élevé au 13ᵉ s. par les comtes de l'endroit, c'est une massive construction flanquée de trois tours d'aspect sévère mais aussi de parterres de roses. De la terrasse extérieure surplombant la ville, on découvre une belle vue sur ses maisons, le lac de Zurich et, au-delà, sur les Alpes de Glaris et de St-Gall. Du côté opposé, en contre-haut des anciens remparts et dominant le lac : parc aux daims.

Musée polonais (Polenmuseum) ⊙ – *Au 1ᵉʳ étage.* Sur les six salles *(plus une galerie d'expositions temporaires)* de ce petit musée fondé par des immigrés polonais, une est consacrée à Chopin et Adam Mickiewicz, une à la 2ᵉ Division polonaise qui combattit en France en 1940, une aux costumes des provinces, les trois autres à l'histoire générale du pays : documents, armes, tableaux, drapeaux, souvenirs de l'époque napoléonienne et du grand pianiste-président Paderewski.

Musée local (Heimatmuseum) ⊙ – Ce musée, installé dans une maison du 15ᵉ s., contient de nombreuses trouvailles de l'époque romaine, des collections d'armes et des œuvres d'art présentées dans des salles aux plafonds peints et au beau mobilier ancien.

Zoo des Enfants (Kinderzoo) ⊙ – *Derrière la gare – Accès par la Schönbodenstrasse puis, à droite, l'Obersee Strasse.*
Dépendance du Cirque Knie, il présente au milieu d'attractions amusantes (« Arche de Noé » et baleine-aquarium en ciment, petit train...) un échantillonnage limité d'animaux exotiques : zèbres, chameaux, zébus, rhinocéros, buffles, kangourous, girafes, lamas, singes, émeus, cigognes, perruches... Mais son attrait principal est constitué par un delphinarium où évoluent quatre cétacés adultes.

ENVIRONS

De Rapperswil à Pfäffikon – *22 km au Nord. Quitter Rapperswil par la route de Zurich puis, à droite, celle de Winterthur ; à Rüti, prendre à gauche vers l'autoroute : après le passage sous celle-ci, tourner à droite ; 300 m avant Bubikon, emprunter à droite le chemin signalé « Ritterhaus ».*

Commanderie de Bubikon (Ritterhaus) ⊙ – Fondée en 1192, reconstruite aux 15ᵉ et 16ᵉ s., cette maison des moines-chevaliers de l'Ordre de St-Jean de Jérusalem, dont les dépendances ont été converties en ferme, en est aujourd'hui le musée. On y voit retracée, sur trois niveaux, l'histoire de l'Ordre, des origines à nos jours, à l'aide de documents, armes, armures, tableaux, costumes, photos... Le cadre est évocateur, particulièrement l'ossuaire, la chapelle (vestiges de fresques), la belle cuisine 16ᵉ s., la bibliothèque et les grandes salles communes avec leurs plafonds et boiseries en trompe-l'œil, leurs cheminées, poêles et meubles de style gothico-Renaissance.

Le Cirque national Knie

En 1803, Friedrich Knie, fils du médecin particulier de l'impératrice Marie-Thérèse d'Autriche, est étudiant en médecine à Innsbruck. Il fait la connaissance d'une écuyère, membre d'une troupe d'artistes. C'en est fini de la médecine, il rejoint l'équipe et apprend le métier de saltimbanque. Puis il fonde sa propre troupe, et épouse en 1807 Antonia Stauffer, fille d'un barbier. A travers l'Allemagne, l'Autriche, la Suisse et la France, Friedrich, talentueux funambule, connaît vite le succès. Ses enfants et petits-enfants perpétuent la tradition, se produisant sur les places publiques devant des spectateurs ravis. En 1900, les Knie deviennent citoyens suisses (naturalisation en la commune de Gerlikon, canton de Thurgovie). De génération en génération, les métiers du cirque se maintiennent fermement et en 1919 à Berne, un rêve se réalise, le premier chapiteau voit le jour, le cirque Knie est né. Bien que cirque national, l'entreprise est toujours dans les mains de la famille (6ᵉ génération), vivant de ses propres deniers. De mi-mars à fin novembre, la longue caravane accompagnée de son zoo parcourt les routes et les voies ferrées, donnant 375 spectacles dans quelque 60 villes sous un chapiteau pouvant accueillir 3 000 personnes. C'est à Rapperswil que le cirque a établi ses quartiers d'hiver. En 1994, il célèbre son 75ᵉ anniversaire.

RAPPERSWIL

Regagner la route de Winterthur.

Après avoir longé, d'assez loin, le Pfäffikersee, lac aux rives frangées de roseaux et peu accessibles, on parvient à l'entrée de Pfäffikon où s'aperçoit, à gauche, le tumulus de l'ancien camp romain d'Irgenhausen.

Forteresse d'Irgenhausen (Römisches Kastell) — *Depuis le parking de l'usine 1/4 h AR en passant sous la voie ferrée.*

Cette petite citadelle, érigée de 285 à 305 après J.-C., faisait partie d'une chaîne de forts destinés à prévenir un retour offensif des Alamans; elle pouvait abriter 200 légionnaires au maximum. Ce qu'il en reste est un quadrilatère de murs en bel appareillage de galets en couches de sens alternés, érigé sur un tertre et dominant encore le lac et Pfäffikon : trois tours carrées, arasées, le renforcent côté lac.

RHEINAU★

Zurich — 1769 habitants

Carte Michelin n° 427 pli 6 ou 216 plis 7, 8 (sur le Rhin) — Alt. 372 m

Cette localité, joliment située dans un méandre du Rhin, en aval des célèbres chutes, fut le siège d'une abbaye bénédictine (aujourd'hui transformée en clinique psychiatrique) installée dans une île du fleuve. Son église abbatiale constitue une incontestable réussite de l'art baroque.

En 1956 a été achevée la construction, en amont de la petite ville, d'un important barrage hydro-électrique dont la retenue s'allonge sur 6,5 km, jusqu'aux chutes du Rhin.

Église abbatiale (Klosterkirche) ⊙ — L'édifice, reconstruit au début du 18ᵉ s., à l'exception de la tour Sud (16ᵉ s.), présente une façade assez sévère.

L'**intérieur★** n'en frappe que davantage par la richesse de sa décoration, du plus pur baroque. La nef, dont la voûte est couverte de fresques, est flanquée, de chaque côté, de quatre chapelles orientées, ornées comme le maître-autel d'une profusion de marbres et de dorures, tandis qu'une balustrade court sous les fenêtres hautes. Le chœur, fermé par une grille très ouvragée, renferme de jolies stalles. L'orgue date de 1715. Dans la petite salle située à gauche du chœur et abritant le trésor, très beaux meubles en marqueterie.

Le RHIN

RHEIN

Carte Michelin n° 427 ou 216 et 218

Le Rhin n'est suisse que pour le quart à peine de son cours, puisqu'il atteint Bâle après 388 km. Dans ce trajet relativement court, il perd de l'altitude, passant de 2 200 à 250 m, et offre l'aspect d'un fleuve impétueux et indompté.

UN PEU DE GÉOGRAPHIE

Un fleuve alpin — De tous les bassins fluviaux se partageant le territoire de la Suisse, le bassin du Rhin est de loin le plus important : il s'étend en effet sur tous les cantons suisses, sauf ceux de Genève, du Valais et du Tessin.

Le Rhin est le type même du fleuve alpin, avec ses basses eaux d'hiver et ses hautes eaux d'été, correspondant à la fonte des neiges. Il prend sa source dans les Grisons : les deux bras principaux, Rhin Postérieur (Hinterrhein) et Rhin Antérieur (Vorderrhein) se rejoignent à Reichenau, en amont de Coire, et font l'objet d'importants travaux d'aménagement hydro-électrique. Ils sont suivis, respectivement, par les routes du San Bernardino et de l'Oberalp. Grossi, à Coire, de la Plessur et, peu après, de la Landquart et de la Tamina, le fleuve suit le sillon du **Rheinthal** qui évoque déjà l'Alsace, par son orientation Nord-Sud, son ampleur, sa gamme de cultures (maïs, vigne, etc.) : il débouche dans le **lac de Constance** (Bodensee) qui joue un rôle régulateur analogue à celui du Léman pour le Rhône.

Une mer intérieure : le Bodensee — Long de 64 km, d'une largeur atteignant 12 km, le Bodensee (lac de Constance), un peu moins étendu (54 000 ha) que le Léman, donne cependant une impression d'immensité. A Constance, le Rhin quitte le bassin principal pour le lac Inférieur (Untersee), dont il s'échappe à Stein am Rhein.

La traversée du Jura — De Schaffhouse à Bâle, le Rhin change de caractère : resserré entre les versants de la Forêt-Noire et les contreforts du Jura, il doit s'ouvrir un passage dans les bancs de roches dures. C'est le cas en aval de Schaffhouse : la vallée se rétrécit, la violence du courant augmente et le fleuve se précipite au milieu des rochers, formant des chutes imposantes. Plus loin, la présence d'autres bancs calcaires se traduit par des rapides (Laufen).

Tous ces obstacles à la navigation ont permis, en contrepartie, l'équipement hydro-électrique du fleuve, grâce à la construction de centrales «au fil de l'eau», dont le type le plus récent est offert par le barrage-usine de Rheinau.

Le RHIN

Le confluent avec l'Aare – L'Aare est le plus grand cours d'eau entièrement suisse et son bassin couvre les 2/5 de la superficie du pays. Il traverse successivement les lacs de Brienz et de Thoune, arrose Berne et Soleure et reçoit de nombreux affluents dont les plus importants sont la Reuss et la Limmat.
Le confluent se situe près de Koblenz, en amont de Waldshut, après un cours plus long pour l'Aare que pour le Rhin (280 km contre 274). Ce confluent est spectaculaire, l'Aare roulant alors plus d'eau que le Rhin dans lequel il se jette. Désormais le Rhin fait figure de grand fleuve et peut se prêter, en aval de Bâle, à la grande batellerie internationale. *La visite, très instructive, du port de Bâle est décrite à Basel.*

LE RHIN PITTORESQUE

Entre le lac de Constance et Bâle, le tourisme automobile le long de la vallée du Rhin est gêné par le tracé capricieux des frontières du canton de Schaffhouse et il n'est pas conseillé de chercher à suivre, au plus près, le fleuve, en territoire helvétique. Il est préférable de prendre pour but d'excursion quelques points d'observation précis choisis parmi les vues les plus caractéristiques
- **le château de Hohenklingen**, près de Stein am Rhein *(voir à ce nom).*
- **la terrasse du Munot**, à Schaffhausen *(voir à ce nom).*
- **le château de Laufen**, aux chutes du Rhin *(voir à Schaffhausen).*
- **à Laufenburg (rive suisse)**, la promenade ombragée à gauche du pont-frontière.

Services de navigation – Le bassin principal du lac de Constance et le lac d'Überlingen (en territoire allemand) sont sillonnés par toute une flotte basée à Constance, Romanshorn, Arbon, Rorschach. Des bateaux de promenade assurent aussi le service Schaffhouse-Kreuzlingen, par le Rhin et l'Untersee, offrant d'incomparables aperçus sur les rives romantiques du fleuve, surveillées de loin en loin par quelque «Burg» en ruine, et sur les charmantes petites villes de Diessenhofen, Stein am Rhein, etc.

RIGGISBERG

Berne – 2 467 habitants
Carte Michelin n° 427 pli 13 ou 217 pli 6

A l'entrée Nord de la localité *(route de Berne),* emprunter à droite la route montant à la Fondation Abegg, dont les modernes bâtiments occupent un site verdoyant.

★★ **Fondation Abegg (Abegg-Stiftung)** ⊙ – L'institut fondé en 1961 par Werner Abegg a pour objectif la recherche scientifique concernant les arts appliqués, surtout les tissus, ainsi que leur conservation. Installées dans des salles fréquemment réaménagées, les collections présentent des œuvres européennes et moyen-orientales, depuis l'Antiquité jusqu'à la Renaissance. Outre une bibliothèque riche de quelque 160 000 publications, la fondation propose une exposition temporaire annuelle.

Tentures aux chevaux ailés (Égypte, 7e-9e s.)

RIGGISBERG

Parmi les œuvres des premières civilisations, on remarque des poteries néolithiques, des objets en marbre provenant des Cyclades, de la céramique et de l'orfèvrerie iraniennes (gobelets en or de Marlik), des bronzes du Luristan, des pièces égyptiennes (tête de Pabasa), des appliques de meuble en ivoire de la période préachéménide, un superbe bracelet à têtes de lion, plusieurs récipients zoomorphes dont un gracieux rhyton (vase à boire) en lapis-lazuli et or ayant la forme d'un bouquetin, deux épées sassanides ainsi que de la céramique byzantine.

La salle des tentures abrite des fragments représentant la déesse Artémis (4e s.), des scènes de la Genèse et de l'Exode (5e s.), Dionysos (Égypte, 4e s.), ainsi qu'un fragment d'une tapisserie, *Atalante et Méléagre* (Égypte, 3e-4e s.).

L'art roman met à l'honneur l'Italie du Sud, la France (chapiteaux, émaux de Limoges) et l'Espagne. L'une des pièces maîtresses est la chasuble de saint Vital, provenant de l'abbaye St. Pierre de Salzbourg. L'art gothique est représenté par des fenêtres géminées provenant d'Italie du Nord, de l'art français (Christ en Croix), des coffrets ou de l'orfèvrerie. Parmi les nombreuses et admirables pièces suivantes, ne pas manquer le cabinet de peintures qui réunit notamment une *Adoration des Rois Mages* de Fra Angelico, un triptyque attribué à Van der Weyden, *Saint Thomas d'Aquin* de Botticelli, *Saint Léonard* de Lorenzetti et une *Vierge à l'Enfant* de Multscher. Des œuvres Renaissance (velours, soieries, tapisseries de Bruxelles, bijoux, verrerie, argenterie) de premier ordre, dont de somptueux vases italiens en cristal de roche et or, clôturent la visite.

Le RIGI★★★

Carte Michelin n° 427 pli 15 ou 216 Sud du pli 18 – Schéma : VIERWALDSTÄTTER SEE

Isolé de tous côtés par la dépression que noient, dans sa plus grande partie, les eaux des lacs des Quatre-Cantons, de Zoug et de Lauerz, le Rigi dresse à 1 797 m d'altitude ses lourdes bosses boisées accidentées, coupées d'escarpements rougeâtres. Ce type de relief est désigné sous le nom de « montagne-île » par les géographes allemands.

Célèbre depuis un siècle pour son point culminant, le Rigi-Kulm, au sommet duquel la tradition exigeait qu'on passât la nuit pour attendre le lever du soleil sur les Alpes, le massif continue à attirer la foule des excursionnistes. Les amateurs de promenades faciles à travers les alpages et les bois, le long de chemins de crête d'un intérêt panoramique constamment soutenu, se retrouvent dans l'un des hôtels d'altitude. **Rigi-Kaltbad** est, à cet égard, un des centres les mieux situés (lieu de séjour).

Un grand spectacle – Le lever du soleil, vu du **Rigi-Kulm**, a été pour des générations d'« âmes sensibles » l'apothéose d'un voyage en Suisse. La splendeur du spectacle faisait oublier ses préliminaires austères, et la foule frissonnante, aux yeux lourds de sommeil, accédait à l'exaltation collective lorsque les premiers rayons de l'astre du jour illuminaient cet « horizon invraisemblable », ce « chaos d'exagérations absurdes et d'amoindrissements effrayants » (Victor Hugo).

MONTÉE AU RIGI-KULM ⊙

D'Arth-Goldau ou de Vitznau au Rigi-Kulm, la montée en chemin de fer à crémaillère demande 35 mn. Autre accès : de Weggis, par un téléphérique aboutissant à Rigi-Kaltbad (et de là, correspondance par chemin de fer à crémaillère pour Rigi-Kulm).

★★★ **Panorama** – Alt. 1 797 m. *De la station terminale, 1/4 h à pied AR jusqu'au signal et à la croix élevés au point culminant.*

Le regard erre d'un bord à l'autre de la prodigieuse toile de fond des Alpes, déployée entre le Säntis et les Alpes bernoises (Jungfrau) en passant par les Alpes de Glarus, d'Uri et le massif du Titlis. Moins éblouissante, mais plus attachante, apparaît la moitié opposée du tour d'horizon : de ce côté, au-delà des lacs de Lauerz, de Zoug et des Quatre-Cantons moutonnent les collines du pays zurichois, jusqu'à la ligne floue du Jura, des Vosges et de la Forêt-Noire.

Dans le guide Rouge Michelin Suisse de l'année
vous trouverez un choix d'hôtels agréables, tranquilles, bien situés
avec l'indication de leur équipement :
piscines, tennis, plages aménagées, aires de repos...
ainsi que les périodes d'ouverture et de fermeture des établissements.
Vous y trouverez aussi un choix de maisons qui se signalent
par la qualité de leur cuisine :
étoiles de bonne table.

ROMAINMÔTIER★

Vaud — 428 habitants
Carte Michelin n° 427 pli 11 ou 217 plis 2, 3
Schéma : JURA SUISSE - Alt. 676 m

Ce village ancien entoure une sobre et harmonieuse église romane appartenant à une abbaye (moûtier) fondée au 5ᵉ s. par saint Romain et passée aux moines de Cluny au 10ᵉ s. L'abbaye commandait à sept prieurés, vingt églises paroissiales, trente villages et cinquante fiefs.

★ **Église** — C'est dans cette église que Marguerite d'Autriche, fille de l'empereur Maximilien et petite-fille de Charles le Téméraire, épousa en 1501 Philibert le Beau en souvenir de qui elle fera plus tard élever l'église de Brou *(voir le guide Vert Michelin Bourgogne).*

On y accède en passant sous la porte fortifiée de l'ancienne enceinte monacale. Succédant à deux chapelles du 5ᵉ et du 7ᵉ s. (dont le plan est dessiné sur le sol de la nef), l'édifice a été construit en calcaire du Jura, au 11ᵉ s., mais modifié aux siècles suivants. La construction a été inspirée directement de l'ancienne abbatiale de Cluny, St-Pierre-le-Vieux, qui précéda l'immense édifice bâti au 12ᵉ s. : aussi le plan, l'élévation, la décoration, à base de bandes et arcatures lombardes, sont-ils typiquement bourguignons. Le transept dominé par une tour de croisée et la nef sont du 11ᵉ s. Un vaste narthex (début 12ᵉ s.) est précédé d'un porche gothique (13ᵉ s.).

A l'intérieur, le narthex, voûté d'arêtes et à deux étages, garde des peintures murales du 13ᵉ s. Dans la nef, des ogives du 13ᵉ s. ont remplacé la voûte primitive, tandis que les bas-côtés ont encore leurs voûtes en plein cintre ; la croisée du transept est couverte d'une coupole sur trompes. Le chœur et les absidioles ont été reconstruits aux 14ᵉ et 16ᵉ s. ; le chœur conserve des tombes de prieurs et un ambon (sorte de chaire) du 7ᵉ s. Depuis 1536, l'église est affectée au culte protestant.

Derrière le chevet se dresse un magnifique tilleul.

A 50 m à droite de la façade s'élève l'ancienne maison du Prieur, datée de 1605 — mais remontant au 13ᵉ s. —, à tourelle en poivrière et portail à bossages.

Noms en - ens
En Suisse romande, la terminaison « ens » de certains noms de lieux
se prononce « an ».
Exemple : Sottan (Sottens).

ROMONT

Fribourg — 4 098 habitants
Carte Michelin n° 427 pli 12 ou 217 pli 4 — Alt. 760 m

Construite au 13ᵉ s. par Pierre II de Savoie, la petite ville de Romont, encore entourée d'une partie de ses remparts, occupe un **site★** pittoresque sur une crête, au-dessus des vallées de la Glâne et du Glâney.

Collégiale N.-D.-de-l'Assomption — C'est un des beaux sanctuaires gothiques du pays romand. Édifié au 13ᵉ s., détruit aux deux tiers en 1434, et immédiatement reconstruit, il représente deux aspects du style gothique (13ᵉ et 15ᵉ s.). Le **chœur★**, du 15ᵉ s., est fermé d'une grille et orné de stalles et de boiseries sculptées, de la même époque. L'église est éclairée de beaux vitraux du 14ᵉ s. et du 15ᵉ s. dont une Annonciation et une Assomption d'origine bourguignonne. Un groupe de l'Assomption en bronze, de 1955, domine le maître-autel moderne. Une série de vitraux modernes du peintre Al. Cingria représente les douze apôtres, une autre, du peintre-verrier français Sergio de Castro, des personnages de l'Ancien Testament.

Avant de sortir, on peut voir dans une chapelle à gauche, une Vierge à l'Enfant romane décorant l'autel.

Château — Il date du 13ᵉ s., comme en témoigne le donjon de Pierre II de Savoie, mais a été remanié à plusieurs reprises.

Le portail principal (16ᵉ s.) est surmonté de plusieurs écussons de Fribourg et de Romont.

Depuis 1981 le château abrite le **musée suisse du Vitrail** ⊘. Les collections comprennent des vitraux médiévaux, des vitraux « suisses » héraldiques ou figurés et des œuvres de verriers suisses et étrangers datant du début du 20ᵉ siècle, marquant le renouveau du vitrail, jusqu'à nos jours. Une présentation audiovisuelle est consacrée à la création du vitrail et son histoire à travers les siècles. Lors des expositions temporaires sont présentées des œuvres anciennes ou contemporaines provenant de Suisse ou d'étranger.

RORSCHACH

St-Gall — 9 535 habitants
Carte Michelin n° 427 pli 7 ou 216 plis 10, 11 — Alt. 398 m

Située sur la rive suisse du lac de Constance, Rorschach, importante place de commerce et de transit, a connu une constante animation en tant que débouché «maritime» de la région saint-galloise.

Aujourd'hui, le port est une bonne base de navigation de plaisance pour les périples sur le lac.

Dans la rue principale (Hauptstrasse) quelques maisons à oriels peints et sculptés apportent une note pittoresque.

Musée local (Heimatmuseum) ⊙ — Aménagé près du lac, dans l'ancien grenier à blé (Kornhaus). La modestie de ses collections préhistoriques, d'histoire naturelle et d'art populaire est rachetée par une présentation évocatrice : habitats lacustres reconstitués, dioramas d'animaux naturalisés, maquettes diverses (dont une de Rorschach en 1797). La salle des dentelles, avec son métier à tisser, illustre l'activité principale de la région.

Le RÜTLI

Uri
Carte n° 218 pli 1 — Schéma : VIERWALDSTÄTTER SEE
Accès en bateau au départ de Brunnen

La prairie du Rütli ou Grütli qui domine le lac d'Uri et sur laquelle flotte le drapeau suisse, symbolise la fondation de la Confédération helvétique. C'est en effet sur cette terre que Walter Fürst, Werner Stauffacher et Arnold von Melchtal représentants des trois vallées d'Uri, de Schwyz et d'Unterwald — selon la tradition en présence de Guillaume Tell — y scellèrent le 1er août 1291 le pacte d'alliance qu'ils avaient conclu auparavant. Avant de devenir un haut lieu de pèlerinage pour les patriotes, cet endroit historique servit de lieu de rassemblement pour les chefs militaires en cas de crise grave. En juillet 1940 devant la menace allemande, le général Guisan, commandant en chef de l'armée suisse y réunit plusieurs centaines d'officiers.

> **La voie suisse**
>
> Pour célébrer le 700e anniversaire de la Confédération, un chemin pédestre d'environ 35 km a été créé à partir du Rütli et tracé autour du lac d'Uri. Dénommé **la Voie suisse**, ce parcours se divise en autant de tronçons (séparés par une borne) que de cantons ou demi-cantons existants, soit un total de 26. La longueur de chaque tronçon a été établie en fonction du nombre d'habitants du canton qu'il représente. La Voie suisse s'achève à Brunnen sur la place des Suisses de l'Étranger, au bord du lac. Tout au long du chemin, se succèdent lieux commémoratifs et sites naturels d'une très grande beauté.

Pour mieux connaître la végétation alpine, lisez le chapitre qui lui est consacré en introduction.

SAANEN★

Berne — 6 090 habitants
Carte Michelin n° 427 pli 13 ou 217 pli 15 — Schéma : ALPES VAUDOISES — Alt. 1 010 m

A l'endroit où la route de Lausanne à Interlaken (par Bulle ou par le col des Mosses) abandonne la vallée de la Sarine (Saane en allemand) pour gagner le seuil de Saanenmöser et, par là, la vallée de la Simme, Saanen bénéficie de conditions très favorables à la mise en vedette de son cachet traditionnel : le contraste est en effet piquant entre ce bourg paisible et pittoresque et sa brillante mais impersonnelle voisine, Gstaad. Il conserve toutefois une certaine autonomie à la saison d'hiver, grâce à un équipement sportif complet (télésiège Kalberhöni-Vorder Eggli).

★**Maisons de bois** — Elles alignent, le long de la rue de traversée, une série de pignons brunis, coiffés suivant la mode de l'Oberland bernois *(voir Introduction : La Suisse pittoresque)* de toits immenses dont l'auvent s'orne souvent de plantes grimpantes. Les constructions les plus anciennes remontent au 16e s. *(lire les inscriptions).*

Église — Son robuste clocher dressé comme un épieu la signale de loin au voyageur. A l'intérieur, le chœur est décoré d'un ensemble de **peintures murales**★ du 15e s. représentant des scènes bibliques, des épisodes de la vie de la Vierge et du martyre de saint Maurice, le patron du sanctuaire. *Sous la chaire, commutateur d'éclairage et tablette explicative.*

SAAS-FEE ★★

Valais – 1 242 habitants
Carte Michelin n° 427 pli 23 ou 219 plis 4, 5 – Schéma : VALAIS – Alt. 1 809 m

Saas-Fee, surnommée la « perle des Alpes », jadis rude village valaisan de haute montagne, aujourd'hui coquette station à la mode, jouit d'un **cadre**★★★ somptueux. Il n'est guère de station, dans toute la chaîne des Alpes, qui puisse offrir à l'arrivant un contact aussi brutal et éblouissant avec le monde des « 4 000 ». Ici, les moteurs à explosion sont bannis (des parcs de stationnement périphériques – *accès à péage* – accueillent les voitures), la desserte de l'agglomération s'effectue par véhicules électriques... C'est au 19ᵉ s. que la station fut lancée. L'abbé Johann Josef (1806-1869), dont la statue se dresse sur la place de l'église, en fut l'un des principaux initiateurs.

Errant du dôme glacé de l'Allalinhorn au groupe rocheux des Mischabel (point culminant : le Dom – alt. 4 545 m – reconnaissable à son sommet fourchu) en passant par le sommet neigeux aplati de l'Alphubel, le regard accompagne, en contrebas, dans sa chute, l'immense glacier de Fee (Feegletscher), séparé en deux langues terminales distinctes par le promontoire rocheux de la Längfluh.

Centre d'alpinisme réputé, Saas-Fee est devenu, pour les adeptes du ski de randonnée, le point d'aboutissement de la fameuse **Haute Route** (Chamonix-Saas-Fee ou, plus couramment, Verbier-Saas-Fee). Le ski de descente d'hiver bénéficie des télécabines et téléphériques du Plattjen et du Längfluh, celui d'été du téléphérique du Felskinn et, depuis 1984, du « Métro Alpin », funiculaire creusé dans la montagne et aboutissant à Mittelallalin (3 500 m).

Saas-Fee – Vue générale

Musée de Saas (Saaser Museum) ⊙ – L'ancienne cure de 1732 abrite un musée du Folklore consacré à la vallée de Saas. Intérieurs reconstitués, outils agricoles, coiffes et costumes, art sacré retracent plusieurs années de vie domestique et montagnarde. Une place particulière est donnée au développement de la station : pionniers du tourisme, sports d'hiver et évolution du matériel (comparer un ski de 1906 et un ski du champion suisse Pirmin Zurbriggen), escalade, hébergement. Une salle rassemblant divers objets authentiques évoque le cabinet de travail de l'écrivain Carl Zuckmayer, tel qu'il se présentait dans sa maison de Saas-Fee.

Les guides Verts Michelin sont périodiquement révisés.
L'édition la plus récente assure la réussite de vos vacances.

SACHSELN

Obwald — 3 819 habitants
Carte Michelin n° 427 pli 14 ou 217 pli 9 — 3 km au Sud de Sarnen — Alt. 472 m

Joliment situé au bord du lac de Sarnen, le bourg de Sachseln forme, avec la terre sacrée du Ranft, un émouvant foyer de pèlerinage.

En venant prier ici saint Nicolas de Flüe *(voir à ce nom)*, les catholiques suisses témoignent de leur foi et de leur patriotisme.

Église — Le grand vaisseau baroque, soutenu par des colonnes en marbre noir du Melchtal, conserve sur un autel spécial, à l'entrée du chœur, les reliques de saint Nicolas de Flüe. Les restes de « Frère Nicolas » sont enfermés dans un grand gisant en argent repoussé qui constitue un beau travail d'orfèvrerie moderne (1934).

Contourner ensuite l'édifice pour gagner, au pied du clocher isolé, de structure romane, la chapelle funéraire où les fidèles viennent se recueillir devant la pierre tombale sculptée à l'effigie du bienheureux en 1518. Au-dessous de celle-ci, la dalle de la première sépulture a été usée par les pèlerins.

ENVIRONS

De Sachseln à Ranft — *3 km plus 1 h 1/2 de marche et de visite.* Quitter Sachseln à l'Est par la route de Flüeli (route en montée derrière l'église). Laisser la voiture au parc aménagé sur l'esplanade centrale de Flüeli.

Flüeli — Le caractère rustique de ce hameau où frère Nicolas de Flüe mena la vie patriarcale de montagnard, entouré de sa nombreuse famille, a été sauvegardé. La chapelle (1618), visible de loin, sur sa butte, est dédiée à saint Charles Borromée ; elle est accessible par des escaliers et une esplanade offrant d'agréables perspectives, d'un côté sur la vallée de Sarnen, son lac, le Pilate, de l'autre sur l'entrée encaissée du Melchtal.

Outre ce sanctuaire, les pèlerins visitent encore la maison natale — qui serait la plus ancienne, en bois, de Suisse (14e s.) — et la maison familiale de Nicolas, beaux chalets soigneusement entretenus et fleuris.

★ **Ranft** — *Accès signalés au départ de Flüeli.* Par une rapide descente (rampe ou escaliers), en direction du fond de la vallée de la Melchaa, on parvient, tout d'abord, à la chapelle-ermitage. Le sanctuaire, qui ne remonte qu'au 17e s., est décoré de panneaux peints *(suivre les numéros d'ordre)* évoquant la vie de l'ascète ; mais il faut surtout y remarquer un beau **Christ★** gothique, provenant de l'ancienne église de Sachseln. La cellule attenante — où l'ermite ne pouvait se tenir que courbé — fut construite en 1468 par ses concitoyens d'Obwald.

En contrebas, une autre chapelle a été édifiée, au 16e s., à l'emplacement où la Vierge apparut à Nicolas.

Si, de Flüeli, on regagne Lucerne, bifurquer à droite vers Kerns : on franchit alors la Melchaa sur le **Hohe Brücke★**. Ce pont couvert, conçu en 1943 pour franchir le torrent à 100 m de haut, est l'œuvre des troupes suisses du Génie.

SACHSELNER STRASSE

Carte Michelin n° 427 pli 14 ou 216 pli 17 et 217 plis 8, 9

Cette agréable promenade, jalonnée de beaux lacs, offre aussi l'occasion d'un parcours accidenté (au **col du Brünig**) et d'une excursion au célèbre mont Pilate.

DE LUCERNE A BRIENZ *98 km — environ 2 h 1/2*

★★★ **Lucerne** — *Visite : 3 h. Voir à Luzern.*

Pour sortir de Lucerne, emprunter tout d'abord l'autoroute de Stans, première chaussée de cette catégorie construite en Suisse. Quitter celle-ci à la sortie « Hergiswil ». A partir de là, jusqu'à Alpnachstad, suivre le bord des lacs.

Le tracé de la route permet d'apprécier sous des angles très différents le massif du Rigi, les éperons boisés du Bürgenstock, le sommet bien détaché du Stanserhorn.

D'Alpnachstad, la montée en chemin de fer à crémaillère au Pilate est recommandée.

★★★ **Pilatus** — *D'Alpnachstad, environ 2 h AR dont 1 h 1/4 de chemin de fer à crémaillère. Voir à ce nom.*

La route traverse **Sarnen** et vient longer le lac de ce nom.

Sachseln — *Voir à ce nom.*

A Giswil, prendre à droite.

Sörenberg — La montée en lacet jusqu'au **col de Glaubenbüelen** procure de belles vues sur le lac de Sarnen et la dépression où il s'étale.

Au col se découvre la cuvette neigeuse du **Brienzer Rothorn**, au pied duquel on passe ensuite en descente *(à gauche : départ de téléphérique pour ce sommet)* parmi les sapins pour gagner Sörenberg, station de ski établie dans un cirque montagneux aux crêtes rocheuses.

Revenir à Giswil.

Entre Giswil et Kaiserstuhl, on découvre, avec un bon recul, les arêtes du Pilate dressées au-dessus de la molle dépression, toute parsemée de bosquets et de fermes, que submerge en partie le lac de Sarnen. En amont et au dernier plan, par la trouée du Brünig, surgissent les trois sommets neigeux du groupe du Wetterhorn.

De **Lungern** au col du Brünig, de jolies échappées s'offrent encore, à travers les sapins et les érables, sur le petit lac de Lungern aux rives sinueuses.

Sur le versant bernois du col, la pente devient très rapide, mais l'excellent tracé de la route permet de jouir à loisir d'un large **panorama**★ sur le fossé de l'Aare, creusé par les anciens glaciers entre les terrasses du **Hasliberg** (lieu de séjour) et les contreforts du Schwarzhorn, d'où s'abattent les cascades du Wandelbach et de l'Oltschibach.

Faire halte à l'endroit où la route est taillée dans le rocher, avant d'accomplir la dernière étape qui prend fin à Brienz.

★ **Brienz** – *Voir à ce nom.*

SAILLON

Valais – 1 169 habitants

Carte Michelin n° 427 pli 21 ou 217 Sud du pli 15 – Schéma : VALAIS – Alt. 522 m

Ancienne tête de pont et position stratégique de première importance avant que le Rhône n'ait changé de cours, dans ce secteur du Valais central, le vieux bourg fortifié de Saillon conserve les vestiges de ses anciens remparts sur un piton rocheux, dans un **site** pittoresque.

Le château, aux ruines imposantes, le vieux bourg, dont les toits gris se pressent au pied des remparts, l'église, bâtie sur une terrasse et dont le clocher roman est surmonté d'une pyramide de pierre, forment un ensemble très attachant.

★ **Point de vue** – Du village, une route en forte montée conduit au pied de la grosse tour du château – ancien donjon – d'où l'on domine le village et l'église, les vignes étagées sur les coteaux, la plaine alluviale où s'étendent les cultures d'arbres fruitiers. En fond de tableau, les Alpes Pennines dressent leur gigantesque muraille.

SAINT-CERGUE★

Vaud – 1 332 habitants

Carte Michelin n° 427 pli 11 ou 217 Nord-Est du pli 11
Schéma : JURA SUISSE – Alt. 1 044 m

Villégiature jurassienne d'altitude, réputée de longue date, tant auprès des Genevois que des Français, pour son climat de montagne reconstituant, St-Cergue se regroupe à l'endroit où le couloir du col de la Givrine débouche en vue du massif du Mont-Blanc et du lac Léman. Les proches environs de la station abondent en belvédères : les premiers plans forestiers dont ils bénéficient mettent en valeur l'apparition du « géant des Alpes » et de son cortège. Les amateurs de curiosités botaniques pourront se rendre au pâturage de la Borsattaz, hérissé de sapins géants, les « geçants », espèce unique dans le Jura. On y accède par la route de Lausanne ; à 1,5 km, prendre à gauche un chemin revêtu (« route de la Prangine et du Plumet ») ; 1,5 km plus loin, au « carrefour des Fruitières », prendre à droite.

St-Cergue offre plus de 50 km de pistes de ski de fond, et, aux amateurs de ski alpin, des terrains d'entraînement variés ainsi que des pistes de difficulté moyenne.

★★ **Belvédère du Vieux Château** – *1/2 h à pied AR par un chemin signalé « Le Vieux Château ».* Point de vue fort apprécié sur le Léman et le Mont Blanc.

ENVIRONS

★★★ **La Dôle** – Alt. 1 677 m. *21 km – environ 2 h 1/2. Quitter St-Cergue par la route de Nyon, puis tourner à droite jusqu'à Gingins. Prendre alors la route de la Dôle, la Barillette. Au pied de la Dôle, laisser la voiture et suivre un sentier, à gauche, signalé par des points jaunes.* Le sentier conduit au sommet où se trouvent un signal et un radar pour le guidage des avions. L'immense **panorama**★★★ s'étend des Alpes jusqu'aux cimes du Valais (Cervin) et de l'Oisans (Meije) entre lesquelles trône le Mont Blanc, avec le lac Léman au premier plan. Un tour d'horizon complet met en relief le Jura : mont Tendre et Chasseron d'un côté, et, de l'autre, la Valserine jusqu'au Reculet.

Massif du SAINT-GOTHARD

Voir SANKT-GOTTHARD-MASSIV

SAINT-MAURICE★

Valais – 3 731 habitants
Carte Michelin n° 427 plis 12, 21 ou 217 pli 14 – Alt. 422 m

La petite ville de St-Maurice, dominée à l'Ouest par les Dents du Midi et à l'Est par la Dent de Morcles, occupe un **site**★ pittoresque au débouché d'un défilé du Rhône. Principale bourgade de la tribu des Nantuates, Agaune (du nom celtique « acauno » signifiant rocher) devient, sous le règne de l'empereur Auguste, le chef-lieu de l'actuel Valais.

Le champ des martyrs – A la fin du 3ᵉ s., une légion recrutée en Afrique – la légion Thébaine – que commande le primicier **Maurice**, est massacrée à proximité de la ville pour avoir refusé d'adorer les dieux de Rome. Cet événement a dans toute la chrétienté un immense retentissement. Dès le siècle suivant, une communauté assume la garde du tombeau des martyrs.

La fondation par le roi de Bourgogne Sigismond, en 515, de l'abbaye de St-Maurice, répond au désir de perpétuer le souvenir de Maurice et de ses compagnons. Richement dotée dès son origine, l'abbaye attire de nombreux fidèles durant tout le Moyen Âge. Désormais le destin de la ville est lié à celui de son monastère.

Au 9ᵉ s., elle prend le nom de son illustre patron, accueille en 1125 des chanoines réguliers de l'ordre de St-Augustin et célèbre chaque année avec ferveur, le 22 septembre, anniversaire de leur mort, le souvenir de ses martyrs.

Au cours des siècles, l'abbaye se transforme et s'agrandit ; un riche trésor, constitué par les dons des pèlerins et des princes chrétiens, est peu à peu rassemblé. St-Maurice devient l'un des hauts lieux de la chrétienté.

CURIOSITÉS

Église abbatiale – Si le beau **clocher**★ à flèche de pierre est du 11ᵉ s. (13ᵉ s. pour la flèche), l'église actuelle, restaurée depuis 1949, date du début du 17ᵉ s. La nef, très sobre, est voûtée d'arêtes et éclairée de fenêtres hautes. Dans l'avant-chœur aménagé lors des derniers travaux, a été replacé un ambon (chaire) carolingien. Le chœur lui-même, assez vaste, est orné de belles stalles baroques. Sur l'autel, mosaïque de Maurice Denis.

★★ **Trésor de l'abbaye** ⊙ – Le trésor est l'un des plus importants trésors ecclésiastiques de la chrétienté. Une excellente présentation met en valeur les pièces d'orfèvrerie exceptionnelles.

Parmi les objets les plus anciens, signalons tout particulièrement un vase de sardonyx décoré de plusieurs scènes empruntées à la mythologie grecque, le coffret mérovingien de Teudéric, fait d'or, de perles et d'intailles, l'aiguière d'or du 9ᵉ s., dite de Charlemagne, dont les émaux semblent relever de la plus pure technique orientale, la châsse de saint Maurice, dont divers éléments de décoration – Christ en majesté, Vierge, anges et apôtres – appartenaient sans doute à un retable du 12ᵉ s. en argent repoussé et doré (les médaillons du toit de la châsse évoquent en six scènes l'histoire du péché originel).

Deux autres châsses, des 12ᵉ et 13ᵉ s., le buste-reliquaire de saint Candide, au noble regard (sur le socle, son martyre par décapitation) et le reliquaire-ostensoir donné par Saint Louis, complètent cet ensemble d'une valeur inestimable.

Fouilles du Martolet ⊙ – Près du clocher, au pied même du rocher qui domine l'abbaye, des fouilles ont permis de dégager les soubassements des édifices qui, dès le 4ᵉ s., ont précédé l'église actuelle et dont le plan apparaît très nettement. On montre également les vestiges d'un baptistère et un gracieux cloître moderne de style roman (quelques chapiteaux anciens réemployés).

Il est possible de visiter les « catacombes », étroites galeries souterraines conduisant aux cryptes et au tombeau de saint Maurice.

Château ⊙ – Bâti à partir du 16ᵉ s. sur un rocher dominant le Rhône et contre la falaise boisée du versant Est des Dents du Midi, ce compact petit château à « donjon » carré et ceinture de bastions ajoutés au 18ᵉ s. fait office de **musée cantonal d'histoire militaire** : drapeaux, médailles, trophées de tir, armes, nombreux mannequins costumés de miliciens et officiers de la garde cantonale, de 1815 à 1945. S'y ajoutent, au 2ᵉ étage, des plans-reliefs et maquettes de systèmes fortifiés participant de la « garde aux frontières » effectuée lors des deux conflits mondiaux. Dans les anciens cachots en sous-sol, armes lourdes de la période 1939-1945 ; dans les cours des bastions, canons antiaériens... Au rez-de-chaussée, un élégant salon d'apparat de style 18ᵉ s. fournit un contraste réconfortant...

Grotte aux Fées ⊙ – *Accès par le sentier en forte montée se détachant à hauteur du château et du pont sur le Rhône, à l'entrée Nord de la ville.*

Cette grotte est constituée par une galerie naturelle d'environ 900 m qui conduit à une cascade et à un lac souterrain.

De la terrasse du restaurant tout proche, on découvre une belle **vue**★ sur le site de St-Maurice et sur la Dent de Morcles.

SAINT-PIERRE-DE-CLAGES★

Valais

Carte Michelin n° 427 pli 21 ou 217 pli 15 – entre Ardon et Riddes – Alt. 526 m

Ce village possède une intéressante **église**★ romane ayant appartenu à un prieuré bénédictin.
L'édifice (11e-12e s.), de petites dimensions, présente une belle unité de style. Il faut se placer derrière le chevet pour voir le monument sous sa présentation la plus flatteuse, avec ses absidioles décorées d'une bande lombarde et sa tour octogonale à deux étages surmontant la croisée du transept.
La nef, très sombre, est voûtée d'arêtes et soutenue par des piliers massifs ; le transept, non saillant, est seulement marqué par un élargissement de la travée qui précède le chœur.

SAINT-URSANNE★

Jura — 918 habitants

Carte Michelin n° 427 pli 3 ou 216 plis 13, 14 – Schéma : JURA SUISSE – Alt. 494 m

A l'écart des grandes routes, au fond de la vallée du Doubs, la petite ville ancienne de St-Ursanne, demeurée inchangée depuis le début du 19e s., constitue une charmante étape dans la traversée du Jura Suisse *(voir à ce nom)*. Son origine est l'ermitage d'Ursanne, disciple de Colomban *(voir à Sankt Gallen)*.
On pénètre en ville par une des portes fortifiées, timbrées de l'ours portant la crosse symbolique des princes-évêques de Bâle : fontaines, maisons flanquées de tourelles, coiffées de vastes toits aigus et bruns, ornées d'enseignes en fer forgé, forment un ensemble séduisant.

★ **Vue du pont** — De cet ouvrage pittoresque protégé par un saint Jean Népomucène, patron des ponts, se dessine un tableau comprenant la porte fortifiée qu'encadrent les façades aux balcons de bois en encorbellement des maisons riveraines, les toits de la ville dominés par la tour de la collégiale, les pentes de la vallée et, sur la crête, les maigres ruines d'un château du 14e s.

Collégiale — Le chevet et l'abside de ce sobre édifice (restauré) sont romans et comprennent un joli **portail**★ en plein cintre orné des statues de la Vierge et de saint Ursanne ; jolis tympan et chapiteaux. A l'intérieur, le chœur roman abrite un autel à baldaquin baroque. La crypte est également romane, mais la nef est d'un style gothique primitif (13e s.).
L'église abrite, sur son flanc Nord, un vaste cloître gothique et un musée lapidaire où se trouvent des sarcophages du 7e au 9e s.

SAINTE-CROIX-LES-RASSES★

Vaud — 4321 habitants

Carte Michelin n° 427 pli 11 ou 217 pli 3 – Schéma : JURA SUISSE – Alt. 1 069 m

Situées sur un épaulement ensoleillé du Chasseron, face à la chaîne des Alpes, les localités jumelles de Ste-Croix et des Rasses méritent une place à part, parmi les villégiatures du Jura suisse, pour leur disposition en balcon et pour leur organisation touristique très soignée. En hiver, la station se recommande au skieur débutant ou moyen plus désireux de détente qu'amateur de performances. Dans le domaine du ski de fond — spécialité traditionnelle du Jura — la station offre plus de 80 km de pistes balisées.

Le village du son — L'histoire de Ste-Croix, depuis le milieu du siècle dernier, offre un bon exemple de la sensibilité de l'industrie suisse aux fluctuations économiques internationales. Vers 1850, comme la plupart des petites cités du Jura, le village fabriquait des montres. L'établissement aux États-Unis de grandes fabriques d'horlogerie, dotées de machines-outils perfectionnées, provoqua une crise grave à Ste-Croix, qui s'orienta vers l'industrie de la boîte à musique. Mais Edison ayant mis au point le phonographe, le public se désintéressa des musiquettes aux notes limpides et grêles, jugées puériles. Ste-Croix dut s'adapter à la fabrication des machines parlantes ; la popularisation de la radio nécessita une nouvelle reconversion des ateliers ; cependant, de nos jours, l'industrie de la boîte à musique a repris une place importante dans l'industrie locale et Ste-Croix reste toujours, par excellence, le « village du son ».

Centre international de la mécanique d'art ⊙ — Dans une ancienne fabrique de boîtes à musique (exposition de vieilles machines), le visiteur est transporté dans un monde magique et merveilleux, où il découvre et entend de véritables chefs-d'œuvre artisanaux, tant par leur ébénisterie que par leur mécanique. Boîtes à musique (à cylindre, à disques) dont le premier modèle remonte à 1815, automates (le clown, l'acrobate, Pierrot écrivant à Colombine), phonographes, postes de radio, instruments de salon (piano, orgue), de foires, de rues (orgues de Barbarie, serinette pour faire chanter les oiseaux) reprennent vie comme par enchantement.

SAINTE-CROIX-LES-RASSES

Les stations — **Ste-Croix** s'étale dans un bassin de pâturages, bien abrité des vents, à l'entrée de la brèche boisée des gorges de Covatannaz, par où se dévoile un large plan des Alpes bernoises.

Les Rasses ★, annexe touristique de Ste-Croix, se réduit à plusieurs hôtels et à quelques chalets épars, bénéficiant d'un magnifique **site ★★** en terrasse, en vue des Alpes. Les promeneurs trouveront dans la région plus de 200 km de chemins pédestres.

ENVIRONS

★★★ Le Chasseron — Alt. 1 607 m. Des Rasses, 3 km — environ 1 h 1/4 par une petite route revêtue mais sinueuse (il existe également un télésiège, aboutissant aux Avattes, à 1 h de marche environ du sommet). Suivre la route de Ste-Croix aux Rasses.
500 m après le Grand-Hôtel des Rasses, tourner à gauche dans le chemin du Chasseron. Au carrefour des Avattes, prendre à droite vers l'hôtel du Chasseron. A la sortie des bois, laisser la voiture au parking de l'hôtel. Gagner alors à vue l'hôtel du Chasseron, puis le point culminant (signal) qui offre un immense **panorama** sur les Alpes, le Jura, le lac de Neuchâtel.

L'Auberson — De Ste-Croix, 4 km à l'Ouest (route de Pontarlier). Tourner à gauche au Col des Étroits.

Musée Baud ⊙ — Ce petit musée de plain-pied, en deux salles, expose et maintient en état de marche une exceptionnelle **collection ★** de dizaines de pièces à musique anciennes : orchestrions, limonaires, orgues de Barbarie, pianos mécaniques... depuis une serinette vosgienne du début du 18e s. jusqu'à des phonographes de 1912 (à alcool...) et 1920, la plus rare étant un appareil Allard fabriqué à Genève vers 1900. On y montre et fait fonctionner aussi des automates ou tableaux animés français et allemands du 19e s. Des boîtes à musique, bonbonnières, mécanismes et rouages, etc., sont exposés en vitrines.

★★ Mont de Baulmes — Alt. 1 285 m. De Ste-Croix, 4,5 km — environ 1/2 h — par route de montagne étroite, escarpée dans sa dernière section, mais entièrement goudronnée, plus 1/4 h à pied AR.
Sortir de Ste-Croix par le passage à niveau de la gare et poursuivre par les hameaux de la Sagne et de Culliairy. Laisser la voiture au Chalet-Restaurant du mont de Baulmes et gagner, par une allée plantée d'arbres, l'esplanade où se dresse la table d'orientation, au bord de l'à-pic. Ce rebord d'escarpement réserve une **vue** aérienne sur le plateau suisse, ses lacs, en particulier le lac de Neuchâtel, et les Alpes.

SAMEDAN ★

Grisons — 2 875 habitants
Carte Michelin n° 427 pli 17 ou 218 pli 15
Schéma : GRAUBÜNDEN — Alt. 1 709 m

A l'entrée d'une petite plaine intérieure triangulaire où les grandes stations de la Haute-Engadine ont pu trouver les espaces nécessaires à l'aménagement d'un golf, d'un terrain d'aviation et de vol à voile, Samedan a pour horizon les hauts sommets du massif de la Bernina, visibles au Sud : Piz Morteratsch — cône glaciaire bien détaché — et Piz Palü — arête neigeuse accidentée de trois ressauts.
Le bourg constitue une villégiature convenant aux touristes épris de couleur locale. Ses **maisons engadinoises** (voir à Engadin) offrent l'ensemble le plus typique des environs immédiats de St-Moritz. On remarquera ainsi, au cœur du village, face à la Maison communale l'imposant bloc formé par la double « maison Planta » (chesa Planta — du nom d'une des plus anciennes familles des Grisons) où est installée la Bibliothèque romanche, institution très liée au maintien de la langue et des traditions du pays.

SAN BERNARDINO-STRASSE ★★

Carte Michelin n° 427 plis 15, 16, 25 ou 218 plis 4, 12, 13, 14
Schéma : GRAUBÜNDEN

Le col du San Bernardino livre passage au grand itinéraire transalpin qui relie Bellinzona dans la basse vallée ensoleillée du Tessin, aux portes du lac Majeur, à Coire, la capitale historique des Grisons installée peu en aval du confluent du Rhin Antérieur et du Rhin Postérieur.

Le col du San Bernardino est impraticable de novembre à mai.
Nous décrivons ci-dessous l'itinéraire qu'emprunte la vieille route (panneaux de signalisation bleus). L'autoroute qui la double et qui passe le col en tunnel n'est pas représentée sur notre schéma.

SAN BERNARDINO-STRASSE

Avers-Cresta

DE BELLINZONA A CHUR

194 km – compter une journée – itinéraire 2 *de la visite des Grisons*

Bellinzona – *Voir à ce nom.*
Au départ de Bellinzona la route remonte le Val Mesolcina qu'arrose la Moesa. A partir de Roveredo, la vallée se resserre en s'orientant au Nord. On peut profiter jusqu'à Soazza, à 628 m d'altitude, des dernières apparitions d'essences ou de cultures typiquement méditerranéennes : platanes, maïs, figuiers, vigne (jusqu'à Cama).
Après avoir admiré au passage la double **cascade de Buffalora**, suivre l'ancienne route qui, traversant le bourg de Soazza, passe devant sa grande église isolée.
L'ascension du col commence par des lacets bordés de châtaigniers vigoureux.

★ **Castello di Misox** – *Voir à ce nom.*
On traverse le bourg de **Mesocco** tassé sur un replat au pied des ruines de son château, puis la montée reprend, toujours plaisante, à travers des alpages mamelonnés (remarquer le tracé de l'autoroute et ses nombreux ouvrages d'art) jusqu'au replat de **San Bernardino**, station la plus élevée et la plus fréquentée du Val Mesolcina, qui possède en outre une curieuse église-rotonde.
Du village de San Bernardino au col, la route, qui longe le joli lac de Moesola, adopte un tracé capricieux qui, de palier en palier, fait passer de la zone de l'épicéa à celle du pin arolle.
A l'Est, les grands escarpements colorés du Pizzo Uccello se présentent de chant comme un éperon déchiqueté auquel fait pendant le Pan di Zucchero (Pain de Sucre).

Col du San Bernardino – Alt. 2 065 m. Ce seuil apparaît encombré de roches moutonnées, héritées de l'activité des glaciers quaternaires. Ouvert entre le Zapporthorn et le Pizzo Uccello, il marque la ligne de partage des eaux entre la Moesa au Sud, tributaire du Tessin, et par là, du Pô et le Rhin Postérieur, au Nord. Le parcours de l'ancienne chaussée, très montagnard, demeure difficile aux abords du col.
Sur le versant Nord, la haute vallée du Rhin Postérieur (Rheinwald) présente jusqu'à Splügen un paysage ouvert et pastoral, mais cependant sévère.
Des abords d'Hinterrhein, la **vue**★ s'étend en amont sur le massif des sources du Rhin, remarquable par l'ampleur de ses glaciers : le vaste Zapportgletscher, dominé par le cône écrasé du Rheinquellhorn, retient surtout l'attention.

SAN BERNARDINO-STRASSE

Entre Splügen et Andeer, le parcours se déroule à travers de profonds sous-bois d'épicéas, longe le vaste lac de retenue de Sufers et franchit la section la plus encaissée du Rheinwald, le défilé de Roffla, qui correspond à l'infléchissement de la vallée vers le Nord.

★ **Gorge de Roffla (Rofflaschlucht)** ⊘ — Les galeries, aménagées sur 300 m de longueur, entre 1907 et 1914, dans cette gorge où bouillonne le Rhin, se terminent sous une impressionnante chute, que l'observateur voit s'abattre à quelques centimètres au-dessus de sa tête.

A la sortie de cette gorge, on remarque, complétant les travaux d'aménagement du Rhin Postérieur, le lac du barrage de Bärenburg.

De Roffla, prendre la route au Sud-Est en direction de Innerferrera.

★★ **Vallée de l'Averserrhein (val Ferrera, val d'Avers)** — L'Averserrhein, affluent du Rhin Postérieur qu'il rejoint dans les gorges de Roffla, creuse une pittoresque vallée, tantôt épanouie, tantôt resserrée en gorge, dans les massifs du Piz Grisch et du Piz Platta.

La route remontant la vallée jusqu'à Innerferrera, dans sa partie orientée plein Sud (val Ferrera) suit le torrent parmi les sapins, en vue du rocheux Piz Miez barrant l'horizon, et traverse le gros village d'Ausserferrera installé dans un joli site boisé (cascades).

Après **Innerferrera**, qui domine une importante retenue du torrent, elle s'infléchit au Sud-Est, dans un parcours accidenté coupé de longs tunnels (entre ceux-ci, belle cascade visible à gauche, en arrière), pour déboucher dans le val d'Avers dont le premier hameau, **Campsut**, occupe un riant bassin aux versants ravinés couverts de sapins et de cascatelles.

A partir de Cröt, une soudaine montée permet de contempler les champs de neige et de glace du Piz Platta puis ramène au-dessus du torrent dont on franchit par deux ponts les gorges impressionnantes.

Après **Avers-Cresta** et sa charmante église blanche coiffée de lauzes, l'herbe rase remplace les sapins ; à droite s'ouvre une vallée glaciaire fermée par les névés du Tscheischhorn.

La route se termine à **Juf** (alt. 2 126 m), hameau — le plus élevé d'Europe — dans un site désolé cerné de hautes montagnes (glaciers).

En aval d'Andeer, la route traverse l'agreste bassin du Schons, dont le versant Ouest se couvre de villages.

Zillis — *Pour se rendre à l'église, quitter la rue de traversée et suivre l'itinéraire signalé « zur Kirche ».* Le plafond★★ de l'église de Zillis est l'un des plus précieux ensembles peints qu'aient légués à la Suisse les artistes de l'époque romane. L'œuvre qui, par sa facture, révèle le « coup de main » de l'enlumineur de manuscrits, remonterait au 12e s. Les 153 panneaux carrés s'ordonnent en deux cycles. Ceux du périmètre symbolisent l'Océan Primitif et la Mer de l'Apocalypse aux eaux peuplées de monstres fabuleux, avec, aux quatre angles, les anges du Jugement Dernier, représentés avec les attributs des quatre vents. Les caissons intérieurs (suivre les scènes de gauche à droite en regardant le chœur et à reculons) se rapportent à la vie du Christ et à quelques scènes de la vie de saint Martin.

Mathon — Ce rude village montagnard (alt. 1 521 m) occupe un site★ privilégié sur les pentes verdoyantes du Piz Beverin, au-dessus du bassin du Schons et en vue des sommets neigeux du versant Est du bassin. En contrebas de l'église, et en surplomb de l'abîme, ruines de l'ancienne église de 1528, avec des éléments remontant au 9e s.

★★ **Via Mala** — *Visite 1/4 h, non compris le parcours des galeries.* Ce passage fameux qui a constitué, au cours des siècles, le principal obstacle au développement du trafic sur l'« Untere Strasse » (Route Inférieure — *p. 112*), se subdivise en deux gorges, séparées par le petit bassin verdoyant de Rongellen.

Le défilé amont★★ — la Via Mala proprement dite — est encaissé dans de formidables escarpements schisteux entre lesquels quatre ponts sont jetés. Après avoir laissé la voiture à côté du pavillon d'entrée des galeries, se rendre au « Deuxième pont » (ouvrage amont) et se placer de préférence sur le vieux pont de 1739, restauré, lancé au-dessus du trait de scie au fond duquel coule, 68 m plus bas, le Rhin. Pour jouir du coup d'œil classique sur le site des ponts et pour approcher de plus près le lit du Rhin, on descend aux galeries★ ⊘ *(341 marches — 1/2 h AR).*

La route évite le fond du défilé aval et le passage connu sous le nom de « Verlorenes Loch » (trou perdu), réputé inaccessible jusqu'à l'ouverture en 1822 d'une chaussée carrossable dans les profondeurs.

On aperçoit, au sommet de l'escarpement opposé, les ruines féodales de Hohenrätien, site digne d'une gravure de Gustave Doré.

Thusis — Thusis est une active cité, située au pied des ruines de Hohenrätien (« château-refuge » avec église, détruits au 15e s.) perchées 200 m au-dessus de la Via Mala, à l'endroit où cette gorge débouche dans le bassin du Domleschg.

SAN BERNARDINO-STRASSE

Le trajet séparant Thusis du pont de Rothenbrunnen se déroule au fond de la dépression du Domleschg où court le Rhin Postérieur endigué. Au versant Est – **le Domleschg** proprement dit, couvert de villages noyés au milieu des vergers et de forteresses féodales en ruine – font face les pentes plus rapides et boisées de l'Heinzenberg.

Deux «sentinelles» surveillent la porte d'entrée du Domleschg : en amont, la citadelle d'Ortenstein et, en aval, le château de Rhäzüns solidement accroché au-dessus du cours encaissé du Rhin.

Reichenau – *Voir à ce nom.*
Dès la sortie, la route file dans la vallée du Rhin face aux pentes rocailleuses du Calanda, au Nord, d'où a dévalé, à l'époque préhistorique, l'éboulement responsable des boursouflures de terrain que l'on observe au voisinage de Domat.

★ **Chur** – *Voir à ce nom.*

SANKT GALLEN★★

C St-Gall – 75 327 habitants
Carte Michelin n° 427 pli 7 ou 216 pli 21 – Schéma : APPENZELLERLAND
Alt. 668 m – Plan d'agglomération dans le guide Rouge Michelin Suisse

Une abbaye fondée en 720 à l'endroit où mourut **Gallus** (compagnon du saint moine irlandais Colomban) est à l'origine de la fortune de St-Gall. La ville, à ses débuts, était blottie dans une étroite vallée du plateau suisse ; elle a débordé ses limites et gravi les collines toutes proches, où sont établis çà et là de grands ensembles tels que l'École des Hautes Études économiques et sociales (Hochschule für Wirtschafts-und Sozialwissenschaften), décorée par une pléiade d'artistes des années 60.

L'âge d'or de l'abbaye – Devenu dès le 8ᵉ s. un important monastère bénédictin grâce à saint Otmar, le couvent parvient, au 10ᵉ s., à un extraordinaire rayonnement intellectuel dont la renommée s'étend à travers l'Europe occidentale.
Les bâtiments conventuels sont devenus avec le temps trop exigus. Dès le 9ᵉ s., s'impose le projet d'un ensemble plus important : le plan carolingien du monastère (aujourd'hui dans la bibliothèque abbatiale) en témoigne.

Vadian et la Réforme – En 1524, Joachim von Watt – connu sous le nom savant de Vadian – médecin, humaniste et bourgmestre de la ville, introduit la Réforme à St-Gall, portant ainsi un coup fatal à l'abbaye.
A partir de cette date, à la suite de la scission qu'entraîne la Réforme, l'abbaye connaît un destin mouvementé. Il faut attendre le milieu du 18ᵉ s., pour qu'elle reprenne son essor, avec la création de l'abbatiale et de la bibliothèque. En 1805 s'effectue la sécularisation de l'abbaye, qui devient en 1846 le siège d'un évêché.

Le berceau de l'industrie textile suisse – Dès le Moyen Âge, les ateliers du couvent et de la ville tissent le lin ; les toiles jouissent d'une grande réputation et passent même les frontières d'Espagne et de Pologne. Plus tard, la fabrication des fins tissus de coton et des charmantes broderies prédomine, alimentant une très importante industrie qui s'étend à tout le canton.
Grâce à son esprit créateur, et à un matériel moderne bien adapté, St-Gall est aujourd'hui le centre de l'industrie suisse du coton et de la broderie.

CURIOSITÉS

Ancienne abbaye – Du Klosterhof (cour du couvent - C) on a une belle vue d'ensemble sur les bâtiments de l'ancienne abbaye bénédictine.
Attenants à la cathédrale, les bâtiments abbatiaux abritent l'évêché, la célèbre bibliothèque abbatiale, le gouvernement cantonal et des écoles. C'est, avec Einsiedeln *(voir à ce nom)*, le plus important ensemble monumental baroque de toute la Suisse.

★★ **Cathédrale (Kathedrale)** – Elle a été élevée de 1755 à 1768 sur l'emplacement d'un édifice gothique du 14ᵉ s. ; deux élégantes tours à bulbe encadrent la façade Est, qui porte au fronton un relief représentant le Couronnement de la Vierge, reproduction en 1933 d'une œuvre originale de J. A. Feuchtmayer.
L'extérieur, d'une grande sobriété, forme un contraste étonnant avec l'intérieur, triomphe du style baroque à son dernier stade d'évolution. L'harmonie de l'édifice, chef-d'œuvre de l'«école du Vorarlberg», est axée sur la coupole centrale, surmontant une rotonde au centre même de l'immense vaisseau. C'est de cette rotonde que s'étendent, vers l'Est et vers l'Ouest, le chœur et la nef. La décoration est d'une richesse somptueuse mais équilibrée. Les peintures à la caséine sur fond bleu ornant la coupole centrale (les huit Béatitudes), sont dues au peintre Josef Wannenmacher. D'autres peintures murales décorent la nef et le chœur. C'est à Christian Wenzinger que l'on doit les très beaux stucs.

SANKT GALLEN

Le chœur de la cathédrale

Le **chœur**★★★ est en tout point remarquable. Fermé par d'admirables grilles, il est orné d'un maître-autel exécuté en 1810 dans le style Empire. Les grandes stalles composent, avec les confessionnaux, un ensemble en bois sculpté d'une élégance rare.

★★★ **Bibliothèque abbatiale (Stiftsbibliothek)** ⊙ – Lorsqu'en 1805 l'abbaye fut sécularisée, la bibliothèque conserva heureusement son ancienne destination.
Exposées dans un cadre admirable, ses précieuses collections comptent environ 100 000 volumes, dont les pièces les plus rares sont constituées par 2 000 manuscrits saint-gallois, datant pour la plupart du haut et du bas Moyen Âge (8e-12e s.), et 1 650 incunables.
En dehors de ces ouvrages, on voit aussi nombre de manuscrits calligraphiés et enluminés des 15e et 16e s., témoins de l'art coloré de la Renaissance.
La salle de la bibliothèque, en dépit de ses proportions modestes, passe pour la plus belle salle suisse de style rococo. Construite à la même époque que la cathédrale (1758-1767), elle est l'œuvre des mêmes artistes. Ses lignes sont d'une harmonie et d'une élégance sans pareilles.
Ébloui par tant de magnificence, le visiteur ne sait ce qu'il doit admirer le plus, du parquet à la marqueterie étoilée où alternent le bois clair et le bois foncé, des riches boiseries, ornées de colonnes aux chapiteaux dorés, des peintures du plafond aux multiples personnages, ou des grisailles placées au-dessus des huit étagères de la galerie.

★ **Ville ancienne** – Tout près de la cathédrale, s'étend un quartier pittoresque dont le plan correspond à la partie de la ville qui fut autrefois entourée de remparts. Là sont groupées de nombreuses maisons des 16e et 18e s., aux façades parfois peintes, souvent ornées d'enseignes de fer forgé et d'oriels de bois sculpté et peint. Parmi les rues les plus caractéristiques, voir la **Spisergasse** ★, la **Gallusstrasse** (maison « zum Greif » ★), la **Schmiedgasse** (maison « zum Pelikan » ★), la **Marktgasse**.

Musée du Textile (Textilmuseum) ⊙ – Ce musée renferme en particulier la **collection Iklé et Jacoby** ★★, la plus complète des collections de travaux d'aiguille faits dans différents pays à différentes époques : dentelles, broderies, tissus.

★ **Musée historique (Historisches Museum)** (C) ⊙ – Ce musée rassemble d'importantes collections consacrées à l'histoire et aux monuments de St-Gall ; reconstitution de l'abbaye au 9e s., de la ville en 1642 ; vitraux, tapisseries, costumes régionaux, pièces de monnaie, porcelaines.
Il présente en outre des collections ethnologiques (Asie, Afrique, Amérique du Sud) réunies par des marchands saint-gallois.

Jardin botanique (Botanischer Garten) ⊙ – Au faubourg de Neudorf, par la Rorschacherstrasse (C) puis la Stephanshornstrasse à gauche.
Ce lieu d'observations scientifiques a aussi de quoi intéresser les touristes par la variété de ses aspects et l'étrangeté des plantes qu'il abrite. Distribué sur 1,5 ha autour d'un bâtiment principal, il permet de flâner au long d'allées bordées de plantes exotiques ou alpines de tous les continents (telle la Rhubarbe du Chili, aux feuilles démesurées), comme sous une pergola située devant une pièce d'eau où croissent joncs et roseaux, et de visiter deux serres tropicales peuplées de cactées, palmiers, euphorbes, orchidées, nénuphars géants...

ST. GALLEN

Marktgasse .... BC
Neugasse .... B

Bahnhofplatz .... B 3
Bankgasse .... B 4
Dierauerstrasse .... B 8
Engelgasse .... B 9
Frongartenstrasse .... B 12
Gallusplatz .... B 13
Harfenbergstrasse .... C 18
Rotachstrasse .... C 24
Sonnenstrasse .... C 25
Untere,
  Büschenstrasse .... C 31
Webergasse .... B 36

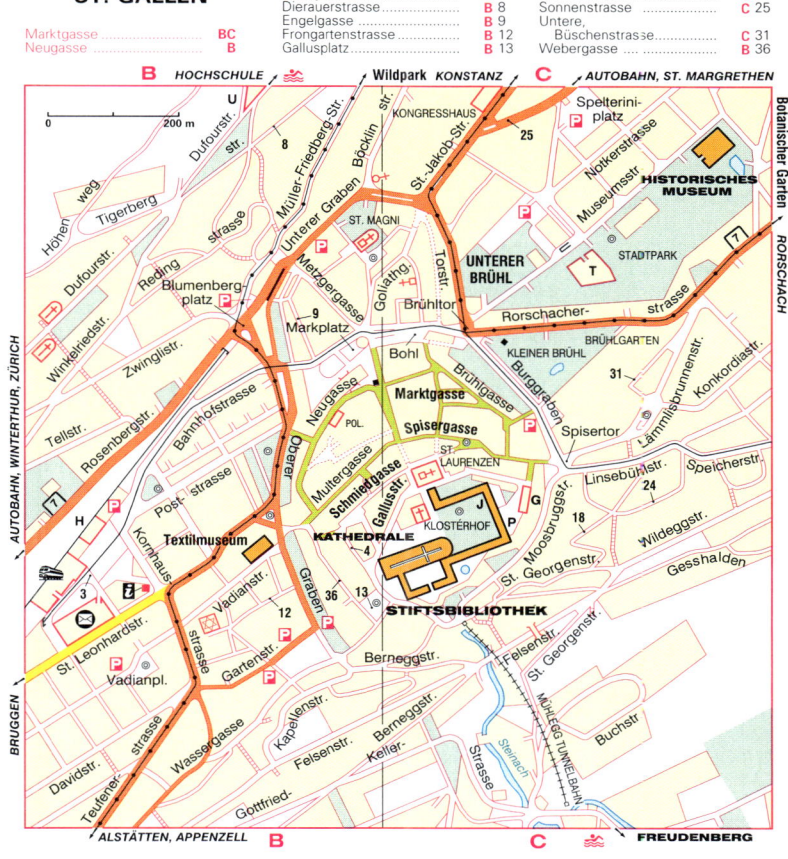

ST-GALL PRATIQUE

Pour tout renseignement, s'adresser à l'Office du tourisme, Bahnhofplatz, ☏ (071) 22 62 62. Une brochure est à la disposition des touristes contenant un plan, des adresses utiles, des informations touristiques.

Shopping

Les rues piétonnes de la vieille ville, si pittoresques avec leurs maisons à oriels, se prêtent volontiers à la flânerie et aux emplettes. On y trouve tous les commerces possibles. Citons notamment les rues suivantes : Multergasse, Spisergasse, Neugasse, Marktgasse.

Théâtre et musique

Stadttheater, Museum strasse 24, ☏ (071) 26 06 66.
Kellerbühle, St. Georgenstrasse 3, ☏ (071) 23 39 59.
Puppentheater (Théâtre de marionnettes), Lämmlisbrunnenstrasse 34, ☏ (071) 22 60 60.
Tonhalle, Museumstrasse 25, ☏ (071) 26 07 07.

Un petit verre pour finir la soirée ?

Confortablement installé dans des fauteuils en cuir, dans une ambiance feutrée le **Pub Bar**, piano-bar de l'hôtel Einstein (Berneggstrasse) permet de savourer quelques cocktails ou tout simplement une bière locale.
Les amateurs de billard pourront exercer leurs talents au **Sherlock's City Bistro** (Spisermarkt) décoré des souvenirs du fin limier. Au 46 Neugasse, le **Colony Cafe Bar** (1er étage) présente une décoration sur le thème des journaux, le **Colony Bar** (2e étage) offre une ambiance musicale avec disc-jockey.
Grand choix de vins et de plats italiens au **Vinoteca II** (Engelgasse).
Dans le quartier de la gare, ambiance pub anglais au **Mr. Pickwick Pub** (Poststrasse), Guiness et autres bières à la pression et jeu de fléchettes.

SANKT GALLEN

ENVIRONS

★ **Freudenberg** – Alt. 884 m. *2,5 km. Quitter St-Gall par la Gottfried-Keller-Strasse (C), puis prendre à gauche la Bitzistrasse.*

Un agréable chemin, tracé au milieu des pins, mène ensuite au point culminant du Freudenberg. Ce belvédère réserve un panorama presque circulaire sur St-Gall, les collines environnantes, en direction du lac de Constance et du massif de l'Alpstein (Säntis).

Parc d'acclimatation (Wildpark) « Peter und Paul » – *3,5 km. Quitter St-Gall par la Müller-Friedbergstrasse (B).*
Agréable parc zoologique (cerfs, daims, chamois, bouquetins) ouvrant sur de vastes espaces.
A l'entrée du parc, faire quelques pas, à droite, dans un petit sentier longeant la clôture grillagée, pour la beauté du **coup d'œil**★ sur le site de St-Gall et, au-delà, sur la chaîne de l'Alpstein.

SANKT-GOTTHARD-MASSIV ★

Carte Michelin n° 427 pli 15 ou 217 plis 9, 10, 19, 20 et 218 plis 1, 2, 11, 12

Nœud orographique principal des Alpes suisses, château d'eau alimentant les deux fleuves les plus puissants de l'Europe occidentale, le massif du St-Gothard voit converger, vers la croisée d'Andermatt, les deux plus grandes vallées longitudinales (Rhône et Rhin) et les deux plus grandes vallées transversales (Reuss et Tessin) du territoire de la Confédération. En fait pour le passant, le nom de St-Gothard évoque beaucoup plus une route et une succession de sites encaissés qu'un décor montagneux grandiose : les sommets, culminant à des altitudes étonnamment uniformes – environ 3 000 m – sont, ici, très lourdement taillés.

La route du St-Gothard – En dépit de sa réputation, cet itinéraire n'est pas, tant s'en faut, le plus anciennement pratiqué des Alpes – le trafic ne put s'y développer, à partir du 13ᵉ s., que lorsque furent forcées les terribles gorges des Schöllenen –, mais c'est de seul à présenter pour la Suisse un caractère d'artère vitale.
Sans la route du Gothard, les cantons forestiers (Waldstätten, *p. 251*), et particulièrement le canton d'Uri qui détenait les clés d'un passage si convoité, auraient arraché plus difficilement leur émancipation à l'Empereur et aux Habsbourg.

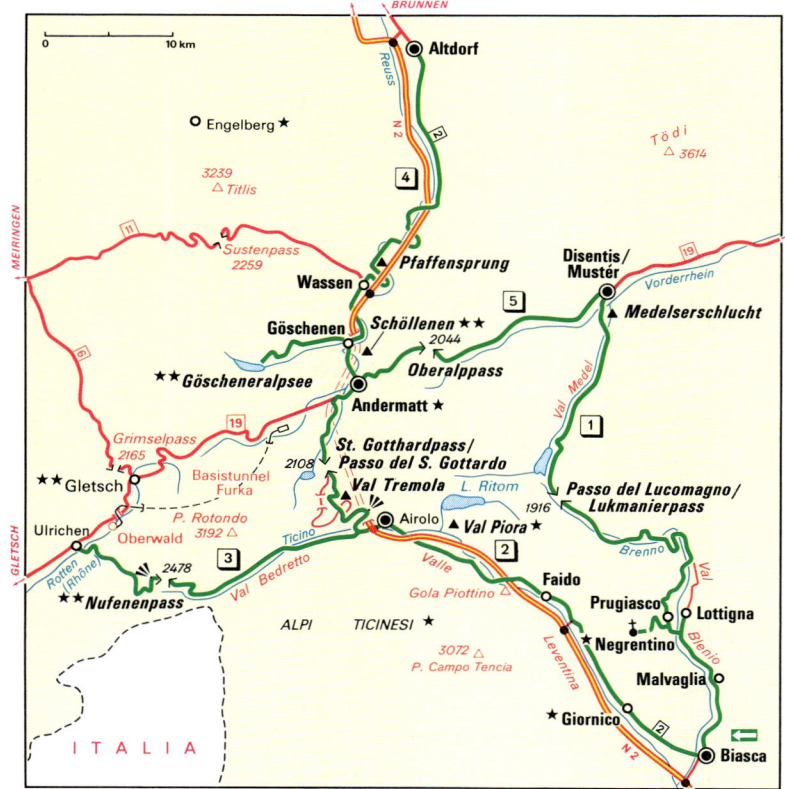

SANKT-GOTTHARD-MASSIV

Aujourd'hui encore, le Gothard – ferroviaire ou routier – est une voie de transit intérieur primordiale pour les relations entre la Suisse centrale alémanique et la Suisse italienne, autant qu'un itinéraire international.

Autres routes du massif – Les routes de l'Oberalp, du Lukmanier et de la Furka, complètent le réseau touristique régional et permettent de boucler de magnifiques circuits au départ d'Andermatt.

VISITE

Les itinéraires recommandés – Par ordre décroissant de la durée du parcours. *Voir les noms à l'index.*

★ ① **Route du Lukmanier** – De Biasca à Disentis/Mustér – environ 2 h 1/2.

★ ② **Route du St-Gothard** – D'Andermatt à Biasca – environ 2 h.

★★ ③ **Nufenenpassstrasse** – D'Airolo à Ulrichen – environ 1 h 1/2.

★ ④ **Schöllenenstrasse** – D'Altdorf à Andermatt – environ 1 h 1/2.

★ ⑤ **Route de l'Oberalp** – De Disentis/Mustér à Andermatt – environ 1 h.

*Le code de la conduite en montagne requiert,
sur les routes difficiles de laisser la priorité à la voiture montante.*

*De plus, sur les routes classées « postales »,
il est prescrit de se conformer aux indications
qui peuvent être éventuellement données par les conducteurs de cars postaux.*

SANKT MORITZ★★★

Grisons – 5 426 habitants
Carte Michelin n° 427 pli 17 ou 218 pli 15 – Schéma : GRAUBÜNDEN – Alt. 1 856 m
Plan dans le guide Rouge Michelin Suisse

Sous l'emblème du soleil, St. Moritz (en romanche San Murezzan), la plus fameuse métropole helvétique de haute montagne, rassemble deux stations jumelles, qui attirent, été comme hiver, la clientèle internationale, conquise autant par son site et la pureté de son ciel que par ses distractions mondaines et sportives de grande classe (compétitions de bob, de skeleton, courses de chevaux sur le lac gelé).
St. Moritz-Dorf, qui possède l'école de ski la plus ancienne du monde (1927), se regroupe à mi-pente au pied du campanile curieusement penché (Schiefer Turm) d'une église disparue, seul témoin monumental remarquable du village primitif.
Sur le fond plat de la vallée de l'Inn, sont dispersés les vastes aménagements du quartier thermal de St. Moritz-Bad dont les sources ferrugineuses sont appréciées pour leurs vertus curatives (en rhumatologie, neurologie, gynécologie, cardiologie, etc.) depuis la fin de l'Âge du Bronze.

CURIOSITÉS

★ **Musée Engadinois (Engadiner Museum)** ⊙ – Cette visite préludera très fructueusement à une randonnée à travers les villages de l'Engadine. Avec sa galerie à arcades, ses fenêtres à ébrasements extérieurs, son oriel, ses sgraffiti *(voir à l'index)*, le bâtiment lui-même est une reconstitution conforme aux dispositions originales du style local. Un « sulèr » *(voir à l'index)* introduit aux différentes salles, dotées d'ensembles mobiliers ramenés pour la plupart d'anciennes demeures patriciennes ou paysannes et décorées de boiseries de pin arolle plus ou moins fouillées. Les poêles intéressent l'amateur de céramique. La **salle engadinoise** n° II (maison de Zuoz) possède un plafond à poutres.
La **salle de parade** n° IX (maison Visconti-Venosta à Grosio) est la plus luxueuse. La **chambre de parade** n° VII (maison noble à Marca de Mesocco), rustique et cossue, conserve plus de cachet.

Musée Segantini ⊙ – Cette rotonde conserve quelques œuvres du peintre Giovanni Segantini (1858-1899), très populaire en Suisse, et en particulier la **trilogie**★ symbolique « Être – Passer – Devenir », où l'on peut reconnaître certains décors de haute montagne de l'Engadine et du Bergell.

★★ **Piz Nair** ⊙ – Alt. 3 057 m – *environ 3/4 h dont 1/2 h de funiculaire (jusqu'à Corviglia), puis de téléphérique, et 1/4 h à pied AR.*
De la terrasse de la station supérieure du téléphérique, la vue plonge sur la Haute-Engadine et ses lacs. Gagner ensuite, à pied, le point culminant pour jouir du **panorama**★★ circulaire englobant les sommets de la Bernina.

SANKT MORITZ

St. Moritz – Vue générale

★ROUTES DU JULIER ET DE L'ALBULA
Circuit au départ de St. Moritz
96 km – environ 5 h – itinéraire ③ *de la visite des Grisons*

Quitter St. Moritz au Sud.

Dans les virages de la montée qui suit Silvaplana s'allongent, étonnamment proches, les lacs de Champfèr et de Silvaplana.
Au cours de la montée vers le col, à l'entrée d'un virage à droite se révèle un **panorama**★★ sur la Haute-Engadine, depuis les montagnes qui dominent Zernez, à gauche, jusqu'au Piz de la Margna, à droite, en passant (de gauche à droite) par le groupe Piz Vadret-Piz Muragl (sommets dominant Pontresina), le Piz Rosatsch et le Piz Corvatsch entre lesquels la dépression très marquée de la Fuorcla Surlej laisse apparaître la cime neigeuse du Piz Bernina (alt. 4 049 m).

Col du Julier – Alt. 2 284 m. Les consonances latines et césariennes de ce nom suffiraient déjà à éveiller l'attention de l'archéologue. Les deux piles plantées de part et d'autre de la route comme des bornes constituent, en fait, les tronçons d'une même colonne qui, appartenant à un « sanctuaire de col » édifié par les Romains, pourrait avoir servi de socle à une statue (comme la colonne Joux du col du Petit-St-Bernard).
Dans la descente du col – la route perd 500 m d'altitude en 9 km – le paysage est d'une grande désolation; pourtant, près des masures de Mot, un vigoureux pin arolle au fût bien droit se dresse encore, parfaitement solitaire.
Étymologiquement, le nom de **Bivio** signifie « bifurcation » : le passage du Septimer, abandonné de nos jours, se sépare de la route du Julier à l'entrée du village, sous la forme d'un sentier qui s'éloigne vers le Sud, franchit le Septimerpass à 2 310 m d'altitude et rejoint le val Bregaglia au village de Casaccia.

Barrage (Talsperre) de Marmorera ⊙ – Cet ouvrage, qui a noyé sous ses eaux les hameaux de Cresta et de Marmorera, présente la particularité d'avoir été construit en terre. 2 700 000 m³ de matériaux ont créé une digue longue de 400 m, haute de 90 m et épaisse de 400 m à la base. La retenue (60 millions de m³) a pour fonction essentielle de régulariser, lors des basses eaux d'hiver, tous les aménagements hydro-électriques de la Julia et de l'Albula, entrepris pour le compte de la ville de Zurich. Le nouveau lac est bien intégré dans un paysage sévère.
Dans la descente tortueuse qui suit le barrage, trois torrents d'une abondance impressionnante à la fonte des neiges – en particulier l'Ava da Faller – sont franchis sur une distance de 1 km.

Savognin – Les amateurs d'art religieux pourront se rendre en voiture à l'église St-Martin située à la lisière de la forêt, sur les dernières pentes du Piz Arlos. Quitter la route du Julier près du bureau de poste pour descendre vers le fond de la vallée et, une fois la Julia franchie sur un pont en dos d'âne, prendre le 2ᵉ chemin à droite. Ce petit sanctuaire isolé, le plus élevé parmi les trois du village, doit son cachet à son fronton classique et à l'éclatante blancheur de ses murs. La coupole qui le coiffe a été décorée intérieurement par le peintre milanais Carlo Nuvolone (1681) : les différentes milices célestes ordonnées en cercles concentriques, comme à des tribunes, autour de la Sainte-Trinité et de la Vierge offrent un surprenant effet de perspective.

SANKT MORITZ

En contrebas du village de Riom, sur l'autre versant de la vallée, la construction démantelée de l'ancien château épiscopal de Raetia Ampla dresse ses murailles sur une motte encore bien visible. La sortie de l'Oberhalbstein, où la route se taille un passage en haute corniche sous roc, s'effectue par le court défilé du Crap Ses.

Tiefencastel — Ce bourg se tasse au fond de la vallée de l'Albula, à l'endroit où la grand'route de Coire en Engadine par le Julier franchit cette coupure. La claire silhouette — toute méridionale — de son église s'inscrit dans le souvenir du voyageur descendu de Lenzerheide, comme un premier témoignage de la civilisation romanche. Entre Tiefencastel et Bergün, la vallée de l'Albula, de plus en plus boisée (sapins, mélèzes, pins arolles) et déserte, laisse à gauche les bains sulfureux d'Alvaneu, puis se rétrécit et s'encaisse progressivement jusqu'à forcer la route à se tailler un passage dans le roc, au défilé du **Bergüner Stein** ★.

Bergün — Ce village, dominé par la face triangulaire du Piz Rugnux contrefort du Piz d'Ela visible par échappées, possède quelques maisons de style engadinois avec oriel et grilles de fenêtres, plus rustiques que celles que l'on rencontre dans la vallée de l'Inn.
De Bergün à Preda, alors que la chaussée grimpe rudement à travers des prés-bois moussus, les contorsions de la voie ferrée que lui imposent les lacets et tunnels hélicoïdaux pour gagner de l'altitude accaparent l'attention.
L'arrivée au palier de Preda est marquée par la découverte des découpures rocheuses bien nommées Igls Dschimels (« les Jumeaux ») et du Piz da las Blais qui ont très grande allure. Entre Preda et le col, les alpages restent accueillants jusqu'au petit lac vert de **Palpuogna**. Plus haut, au-delà de Crap Alv, la route s'élève au travers de bancs de rocailles, tout en contournant le « plan » marécageux où un écheveau de cascatelles signale l'une des sources de l'Albula. On débouche enfin dans l'immense combe gazonnée du col.

Col de l'Albula — Alt. 2 312 m. *Le col peut être obstrué par la neige de novembre à juin (trains-auto de Tiefencastel à Samedan).* Le col sépare le bassin de l'Albula au Nord, tributaire du Rhin, et le Val d'Alvra au Sud, tributaire de l'Inn.
Entre le col et la Punt, on voit rapidement apparaître, au fond de la vallée de l'Inn, déjà toute proche, les villages de la Punt et de Chamues-ch, surveillés par les ruines de Guardaval.
De la Punt à Samedan, on suit le fond plat de la vallée de l'Inn, jusqu'au moment où les sommets du massif de la Bernina se découvrent, par la trouée de Pontresina.

★ **Samedan** — *Voir à ce nom.*

★ **Celerina** — *Voir à ce nom.*

De Celerina, la route ramène à St. Moritz.

SANKT URBAN★

Lucerne

Carte Michelin n° 427 pli 5 ou 216 pli 16 – 5 km au Nord-Est de Langenthal

Le touriste ne découvre pas sans surprise la masse imposante de l'ancienne abbaye cistercienne de St. Urban. Ces bâtiments sont actuellement occupés par une clinique psychiatrique.

★ **Église (Klosterkirche)** ⊙ — Construite au début du 18ᵉ s., c'est un très bel exemple baroque. La façade, très sobre et d'une largeur inusitée, est encadrée par deux hautes tours symétriques qui se détachent du corps de l'église.
La nef, de belles proportions, est éclairée par des fenêtres au-dessous desquelles court une galerie à balustres. La décoration, faite de stucs et de quelques dorures, n'est pas trop surchargée ; les chapiteaux sont garnis de feuilles d'acanthe.
Le chœur, que ferme une belle **grille** ★, est orné de magnifiques **stalles** ★★ en bois sculpté du 18ᵉ s., dont les scènes représentent les différents épisodes de la vie du Christ.

*Actualisée en permanence,
la carte Michelin au 200 000ᵉ bannit l'inconnu de votre route.
    Golf, stades, hippodromes, plages, piscines, altiports,
    sentiers de grande randonnée, panoramas, routes pittoresques,
    forêts domaniales, monuments intéressants...
Pour vos loisirs, elle est le complément naturel des guides Verts Michelin.
Équipez votre voiture de cartes Michelin à jour.*

Le SÄNTIS ★★★

Carte Michelin n° 427 pli 7 ou 216 centre du pli 21 – Schéma : APPENZELLERLAND

Point culminant du massif de l'Alpstein (alt. 2 502 m), le Säntis doit à sa situation de bastion avancé des Préalpes, entre le Toggenbourg, la vallée du Rhin et le lac de Constance, de constituer le belvédère par excellence de la Suisse orientale.
Le sommet lui-même, avec ses épaulements calcaires aux stratifications tantôt calmement festonnées (face Nord), tantôt violemment plissées (Wildhuser Schafberg), est l'un des mieux dessinés de toute la chaîne.

Montée au Säntis ⊙ – De Schwägalp, terminus des routes venues d'Urnäsch ou de Neu-St-Johann, 1 h AR environ dont 20 mn de téléphérique.
De la station supérieure, on gagne facilement le sommet coiffé depuis 1956 d'une station de télécommunications dont la silhouette sera bientôt modifiée.
Le **panorama**★★★ sur les montagnes du Vorarlberg, les Alpes grisonnes, glaronnaises et bernoises, les lacs de Zurich et de Constance, est d'une indicible majesté ; son immensité est cependant souvent difficile à apprécier en plein été – et surtout au milieu de la journée –, lorsque la brume de beau temps estompe les lointains.
Pour bénéficier de vues plongeantes plus rapprochées, descendre, par des escaliers, à l'auberge du Säntis, bâtie au-dessus du sauvage vallon du lac de Seealp (voir à Appenzell).

Château de la SARRAZ

Vaud

Carte Michelin n° 427 pli 11 ou 217 pli 3

Entouré d'un petit parc-jardin, à l'écart du village qu'il domine, ce château du 11ᵉ s., remanié aux 15ᵉ et 16ᵉ s., présente un corps de logis à tourelles d'angle rondes, précédé de deux grandes tours carrées à mâchicoulis.

Visite ⊙ – Elle permet de découvrir plusieurs salles garnies de beaux meubles anciens, d'argenterie, de vaisselle, de pendules du 17ᵉ au 19ᵉ s., de tableaux et d'objets précieux.
Dans une ancienne chapelle à proximité du château, étonnant **cénotaphe** sculpté (14ᵉ s.) de François Iᵉʳ de la Sarra, dont le gisant, couvert de serpents et de crapauds, est veillé par son épouse, sa fille et ses deux fils.
Dans les dépendances du château a été installé un **musée du cheval** : collection de véhicules hippomobiles, remarquable présentation des différents modes d'utilisation et harnachements du cheval pour la guerre, le cirque, la chasse à courre...

SCHAFFHAUSEN ★

SCHAFFHOUSE – C – 34 225 habitants

Carte Michelin n° 427 pli 6 ou 216 pli 8 – Alt. 403 m

Étagée sur la rive droite du Rhin, au pied du donjon du Munot, la vieille cité de Schaffhouse est l'une des plus attachantes de Suisse grâce au cachet Renaissance ou classique de ses édifices.
C'est le point de départ de la promenade aux chutes du Rhin (Rheinfall), attraction traditionnelle de l'Helvétie romantique.

Un important entrepôt – Les chutes du Rhin contraignant les bateliers à décharger leurs cargaisons en cet endroit, des marchands s'y établirent et créèrent là un entrepôt qui ne tarda pas à prendre une grande importance. Dès la fin du 12ᵉ s., Schaffhouse était devenue une ville impériale libre et entrait, en 1501, dans la Confédération helvétique.
De nos jours, Schaffhouse tire parti, surtout, de son rôle de carrefour et de tête de pont. Elle est devenue un centre industriel tirant son énergie électrique du fleuve même. Des usines de constructions mécaniques, d'appareils électriques, des filatures, des aciéries se sont installées, en dehors de la cité ancienne qui a ainsi conservé intact son aspect médiéval.

CURIOSITÉS

★**Ville ancienne** – Elle est dominée par des restes de remparts que couronne le **Munot**, lourd donjon du 16ᵉ s., qui constitue un **belvédère**★ ⊙ de choix sur la ville et la vallée du Rhin (par des escaliers et une passerelle jetée sur les fossés, aménagés en parc aux daims, on accède à la plate-forme de l'ouvrage).
La ville basse renferme de belles maisons à façades peintes, souvent ornées d'oriels. La **Vordergasse**★ est l'une des rues les plus caractéristiques, avec ces maisons décorées de stucs et de sculptures, couronnées de beaux toits bruns percés de nombreuses lucarnes. La maison « zum Ritter » (**AB A**) mérite une mention toute

SCHAFFHAUSEN

Vorstadt	A
Vordergasse	AB

Bahnhofstrasse	A 3
Fischerhäuserstrasse	B 4
Freierplatz	B 7
Fronwagplatz	A 9
Goldsteinstrasse	B 10

Herrenacker	A 12
Kirchhofplatz	B 13
Klosterstrasse	B 15
Krummgasse	A 16
Münsterplatz	B 18
Pfarrhofgasse	B 19
Pfrundhausgasse	B 21
Promenadenstrasse	A 22
Rheinuferstrasse	B 23
Rosengasse	A 24
Safrangasse	B 25

Schutzengraben	B 27
Sporrengasse	A 28
Tanne	A 30
Unterstadt	B 31
Webergasse	B 33

A	Haus „zum Ritter"
M¹	Museum zu Allerheiligen
M²	Hallen für neue Kunst
P	Regierungsgebäude

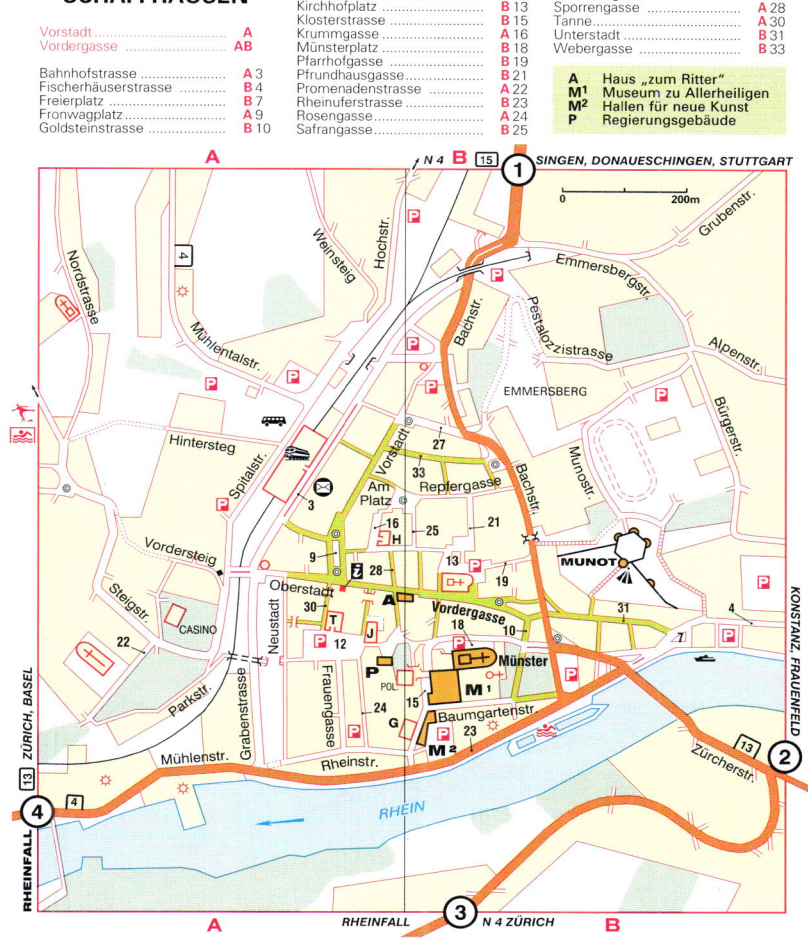

particulière : les peintures qui ornent sa façade ont été refaites en 1938 et 1939 par Carl Roesch, dans le même esprit que les célèbres fresques dues au maître schaffhousois Tobias Stimmer. Ces fresques réalisées vers 1570 sont en partie visibles au musée de Tous-les-Saints. Les sujets choisis ont été empruntés à la mythologie et à l'histoire de Rome.

Il faut voir aussi les jolies fontaines de la Fronwagplatz, le Palais du Gouvernement (Regierungsgebäude – **A**P), édifice du 17ᵉ s. à la belle façade sculptée et au pignon en escalier.

★ **Musée de Tous-les-Saints (Museum zu Allerheiligen)** (**B**M¹) ⊙ – Installé dans les bâtiments de l'ancienne abbaye de Tous-les-Saints, il renferme des collections préhistoriques provenant des fouilles effectuées dans la région, des manuscrits et incunables, la plupart du 15ᵉ s., ayant appartenu à la bibliothèque du couvent, des œuvres d'artistes suisses du 15ᵉ au 20ᵉ s. La pièce la plus remarquable est un onyx (début 13ᵉ s.), monté sur or et incrusté de pierres précieuses. Une section historique retrace l'histoire de la ville, une autre section est consacrée à l'histoire naturelle.

Plusieurs salles sont consacrées aux industries de Schaffhouse : des maquettes et une excellente documentation contribuent à rendre cette exposition des plus intéressantes.

Église de Tous-les-Saints (Münster) (**B**) – L'intérieur de cette abbatiale romane du 11ᵉ s. construite encore selon l'antique plan basilical et bâtie en belle pierre ocre, a subi une importante restauration. De hautes colonnes soutiennent un plafond de bois. Le chœur se termine par un chevet plat.

Adossé au bas-côté droit de l'église, le cloître, dont l'une des galeries est à baies gothiques, renferme de nombreuses pierres tombales.

Dans une petite cour voisine est conservée une cloche, dite « cloche de Schiller », qui inspira au poète sa « Ballade de la Cloche ». A proximité, le jardin des simples offre une grande variété d'herbes et d'épices.

SCHAFFHAUSEN

★ **Halles d'Art contemporain** (Hallen für neue Kunst) (**B** M²) ⊙ – En bordure du Rhin, une ancienne usine textile du début du siècle abrite sur 5 500 m² des œuvres représentatives de l'art conceptuel et minimaliste des décennies 1960 et 1970.
Ce véritable temple de l'art contemporain, vaste et lumineux, s'étage sur quatre niveaux, dont le premier est réservé aux expositions temporaires. Les œuvres présentées en permanence sont signées Mario Merz, Dan Flavin, Joseph Beuys (*Das Kapital Raum*), Richard Long (*Lightning Wood Circle*), Lawrence Weiner, Bruce Nauman (*Floating Room*), Jannis Kounellis, qui illustre l'Arte povera, Carl Andre (*37th Pieces of Work*), Sol LeWitt et Robert Ryman.

★★ CHUTES DU RHIN (RHEINFALL)

Les chutes du Rhin sont les plus puissantes d'Europe.
Le fleuve, large de 150 m en cet endroit, s'abat d'une hauteur de 21 m. Son débit peut atteindre 1 070 m³ par seconde (débit moyen : 700 m³/seconde). Le spectacle, à propos duquel Goethe pouvait évoquer les « sources de l'Océan », mérite d'être vu surtout en juillet à l'époque des hautes eaux.

Vue d'ensemble, de la rive droite (Rheinfallquai) – 4 km par ④ du plan et Neuhausen, où l'on quitte la route de Bâle, pour suivre la Rheinfallstrasse.

Vues rapprochées, de la rive gauche – 5 km plus 1/2 h à pied AR. Quitter Schaffhouse par ④ du plan, route de Zurich, puis cette route pour tourner ensuite à droite vers Laufen. Laisser la voiture à l'entrée du château de Laufen, transformé en restaurant.

Les belvédères ⊙ – Pénétrer dans la cour du château. Par un escalier, on descend jusqu'à hauteur des chutes. Dès l'amorce de l'escalier, on découvre, depuis un petit kiosque aux vitres de couleur, l'énorme masse d'eau que l'on domine. Plus bas, différentes plates-formes et passerelles s'avancent très près des chutes et permettent d'en découvrir les aspects les plus divers.

Promenades en bateau ⊙ – Des promenades en bateau sont organisées jusqu'au rocher qui se trouve au milieu des chutes. On peut également faire la traversée d'une rive à l'autre.

Les SCHÖLLENEN★★

Uri
Carte Michelin n° 427 pli 15 ou 217 pli 10 – 3 km au Nord d'Andermatt
Schéma : BERNER OBERLAND

Entre Göschenen et Andermatt, la vallée de la Reuss resserre en étau ses abrupts granitiques d'une continuité et d'un poli impressionnants. C'est le légendaire défilé des Schöllenen, principal obstacle au développement du trafic sur l'itinéraire du St-Gothard jusqu'aux environs du 13ᵉ s., époque où un chemin fut audacieusement établi dans ces profondeurs. L'aménagement routier de ce secteur a détruit l'aspect sauvage du passage, mais le parcours de l'ancienne chaussée, à pied, permettra aux amateurs de sensations fortes d'apprécier le caractère « infernal » du défilé.

Pont du Diable (Teufelsbrücke) – Ce pont, aujourd'hui désaffecté, avait remplacé, en 1830, l'ouvrage construit, selon la légende, grâce à l'intervention du diable, payé en monnaie de... bouc par les malicieux Uranais, alors que le marché exigeait en tribut l'âme du premier passant. L'ouvrage constitue un belvédère tout indiqué pour admirer les **chutes** écumantes de la **Reuss** (*mises en valeur par le soleil, vers midi*). Légèrement en aval, une croix monumentale taillée à même la paroi de la rive droite et accompagnée d'une inscription en caractères cyrilliques, commémore l'équipée hasardeuse du corps russe du général Souvarov qui, ayant forcé le passage, le 24 septembre 1799, à la poursuite de l'armée française, déboucha trop tard dans le plat pays pour empêcher Masséna de battre les coalisés à Zurich.

SCHÖLLENENSTRASSE

Carte Michelin n° 427 pli 15 ou 217 pli 10 – Schéma : SANKT-GOTTHARD-MASSIV

La vallée de la Reuss, qu'emprunte l'itinéraire et dont la curiosité la plus remarquable est le défilé des Schöllenen, constitue une commode voie de pénétration au cœur du massif du St-Gothard, depuis la région des Quatre-Cantons.

D'ALTDORF A ANDERMATT

56 km – environ 1 h 1/2 – itinéraire 4 *de la visite du massif du St-Gothard*

Altdorf – *Voir à ce nom.*

D'Altdorf à Amsteg, tandis que la vallée se resserre, le majestueux sommet conique du Bristen, s'élevant, d'un seul jet, à 3 072 m d'altitude, retient le regard. L'agglomération d'Erstfeld marque, pour la voie ferrée, le début de la rampe qui mène le rail 600 m plus haut à l'entrée Nord du tunnel du St-Gothard. Entre Amsteg et Wassen, le fond du sillon de la Reuss, où la route inaugure son parcours montagnard, garde de jolis recoins de fraîcheur. Les sinuosités du tracé – et surtout celles qui précèdent l'arrivée à Wassen, dont l'église est visible dès la sortie de Gurtnellen – permettent de découvrir, en aval, la pyramide bien dessinée des Kleine Windgällen.

Pfaffensprung – Du parc à voitures aménagé immédiatement en aval du pont sur la Reuss, gagner, en traversant la route, le belvédère protégé par des grilles. Le trop-plein du barrage construit dans ce « pas » crée parfois une cataracte spectaculaire qui se brise en écumant sur de gros rochers.

Wassen – Wassen a connu la célébrité lorsque les constructeurs du chemin de fer du St-Gothard ont fait décrire à la voie deux boucles successives, en partie souterraines, de part et d'autre de la localité. L'étonnement du voyageur non initié, découvrant successivement, sous trois aspects différents, une église que son voisin de compartiment, imperturbable, lui affirme être celle de Wassen, n'a cessé, depuis, de constituer un sujet de plaisanterie.
La construction de la route du Susten qui, sur le versant de la Reuss, prend ici son départ, a de nos jours considérablement stimulé l'activité touristique locale.
De Wassen à Göschenen, les éboulis, parmi lesquels on remarque un énorme bloc dit « pierre du Diable » (Teufelsstein), envahissent le fond du couloir. D'impressionnants travaux routiers ont été réalisés sur cette portion d'itinéraire.

Göschenen – Connue surtout pour sa gare située à la tête Nord du tunnel ferroviaire du Gothard (longueur : 15 003 m), ouvert en 1882, Göschenen fournit au touriste l'occasion d'une halte : il est agréable de se placer aux abords du petit pont central pour admirer le paysage glaciaire de la haute région du Dammastock se dévoilant par la trouée du Göschenertal.

★★ Lac de Göscheneralp – L'accès à ce lac-réservoir permet de contempler de près les glaciers du Dammastock, qui l'alimentent – au revers Est du glacier du Rhône. La route remonte l'étroite et farouche vallée de Göschenen, avec, en fin de parcours, des passages en corniche au flanc de superbes parois rocheuses.
Laisser la voiture au parking voisin du restaurant (alt. 1 783 m) et gagner le milieu de la crête gazonnée, toute proche, du barrage. Ce dernier, du type barrage-poids (volume : 9,3 millions de m³ ; largeur à la base : 700 m ; hauteur : 155 m ; longueur de crête : 540 m), retient une masse d'eau pouvant atteindre 75 millions de m³. Devant lui, magnifique **paysage★★** composé par la retenue, les cascades qui s'y déversent à droite et à gauche et, séparés par un cône rocheux, les glaciers étincelant sous les crêtes acérées du Winterberg. Se retourner pour admirer aussi, à l'opposé, le cirque rocheux, ponctué de sapins, d'où l'on est venu.

★★ Les Schöllenen – *Voir à ce nom.*

★ Andermatt – *Voir à ce nom.*

SCHWYZ★

C – 12 872 habitants

Carte Michelin n° 427 pli 15 ou 216 Sud des plis 18, 19 – Alt. 517 m

Cette petite ville quiète, qui s'honore d'avoir donné à la Confédération helvétique son nom et son drapeau, occupe un **site★** majestueux, au pied des pitons jumeaux des Mythen, entre le lac des Quatre-Cantons et le lac de Lauerz *(voir Vierwaldstätter See et sur l'histoire des cantons primitifs, lire « le sanctuaire national suisse »).*
La station de Stoos (alt. 1 295 m) installée sur une terrasse ensoleillée constitue son annexe en haute altitude.

Une pépinière de soldats – Lorsque, à partir du 16ᵉ s., les princes étrangers recrutent des mercenaires pour leur service, de nombreux habitants de Schwyz s'engagent dans leurs armées et en particulier dans les régiments français. Leur bravoure, leurs qualités militaires permettent à beaucoup d'entre eux de rentrer au pays fortune faite, chargés d'honneurs et de gloire. Ils construisent alors ces somptueuses demeures que possèdent encore leurs descendants dans la ville ancienne.

SCHWYZ

Bahnhofstrasse	A
Grundstrasse	B
Hauptplatz	B 3
Herrengasse	A
Hirzengasse	B 4
Maria Hilfstrasse	A 6
Postplatz	B 7
Reichsgasse	B 9
Rickenbachstrasse	B
Riedstrasse	A
St. Martinsstrasse	A
Schmiedgasse	A
Schützenstrasse	B 10
Sedierengasse	B 12
Sonnenplätzli	B
Strehlgasse	B 13

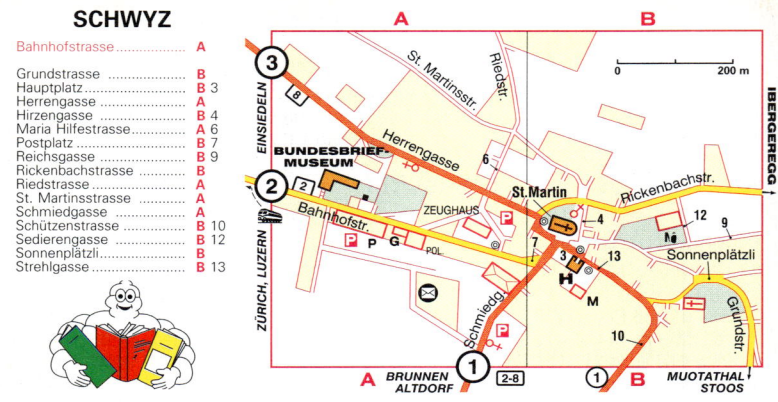

CURIOSITÉS

★ **Musée des Chartes fédérales (Bundesbriefmuseum)** ⊙ – Un édifice moderne, à la façade ornée d'une fresque de H. Danioth, a été construit pour abriter les documents originaux les plus précieux de la Confédération. Dans la grande salle que décorent une fresque de W. Clénin « Le Serment » ainsi que des bannières du canton de Schwyz, sont exposés le Pacte original de 1291 (Bundesbrief), le Pacte de Brunnen de 1315 (Morgartenbrief), des chartes de franchise et des pactes d'alliance concernant les « XIII cantons ».

Église St-Martin – Elle offre, à l'intérieur, une luxueuse décoration baroque du 18e s. : la nef est ornée de stucs et de fresques ; le maître-autel et les autels orientés des chapelles latérales, ainsi que la **chaire**★ en marbre (sur atlantes, et ornée d'une frise sculptée en haut relief) et le baptistère sont aussi très ouvragés. Le transept abrite les châsses de saint Polycarpe (à gauche) et saint Lazare (à droite).

Hôtel de ville (H) ⊙ – Incendié puis rebâti au 17e s., il est décoré, à l'extérieur, de peintures murales (1891) rappelant divers épisodes de l'histoire suisse. On peut visiter, à l'intérieur, des salles ornées de boiseries et de vitraux.

ENVIRONS

De Schwyz à Rigi-Scheidegg – *12 km. Quitter Schwyz par ② du plan et, à Seewen, prendre la route n° 2 vers Lucerne.*

Lac de Lauerz (Lauerzer See) – Cette jolie nappe d'eau, bordée de roseaux et de nénuphars, et qu'agrémentent deux îlots boisés, est malheureusement déparée par la proximité d'une carrière à son extrémité Est.

★★ **Rigi-Scheidegg** ⊙ – De la sortie Sud de Goldau, une route étroite et sinueuse de 3 km conduit à «Station Kräbel» *(arrêt intermédiaire du train à crémaillère du Rigi-Kulm)* d'où part le téléphérique du Scheidegg.
Au sommet de la longue crête du Rigi-Scheidegg (alt. 1 665 m) qu'occupe la petite station du même nom, grimper sur le monticule situé derrière la chapelle : immense **panorama**★★, analogue à celui du Rigi-Kulm *(voir Le Rigi)*, mais barré au Nord-Ouest par le promontoire de ce dernier.

★ **Route de l'Ibergeregg** – *Carte Michelin n° 218 pli 1 – 11 km. Quitter Schwyz à l'Est par la Rickenbachstrasse.*
Dès la côte qui succède à la traversée de Rickenbach, des vues se découvrent à gauche sur le Mythen, à droite, partiellement, sur les lacs des Quatre-Cantons de Lauerz et Lauerzersee que sépare le Hochflue. Après un passage sous bois, magnifique parcours en corniche au-dessus de la profonde vallée du Muotatal et, dans une boucle de la route, très belle **vue**★ en arrière, sur cette vallée et la région des Quatre-Cantons. Dans la rude montée qui suit, s'aperçoivent les sommets neigeux des Alpes glarines. Au **col de l'Ibergeregg** (alt. 1 406 m), remarquables **vues**★ d'enfilade sur les vallées adjacentes.

★ **Grotte du Hölloch** (Höllochgrotte) – *Carte Michelin n° 218 pli 1 – 15 km par la route du Muotatal (Sud-Est du plan), puis 1 h de visite. Voir à ce nom.* On peut combiner cette excursion avec la montée en funiculaire à Stoos, puis, de là, au **Fronalpstock** (alt. 1 922 m), magnifique belvédère.

Dans ce guide
les plans de villes indiquent essentiellement les rues principales
et les accès aux curiosités,
les schémas mettent en évidence les grandes routes et l'itinéraire de visite.

SCUOL/SCHULS ★★

Grisons – 1 889 habitants
Carte Michelin n° 427 pli 18 ou 218 pli 7 – Schéma : GRAUBÜNDEN – Alt. 1 244 m

Ce centre de cure hydrominérale et climatique, dont les installations se disséminent sur les versants du bassin le plus épanoui de la Basse-Engadine, est très apprécié pour son cadre de forêts, de sommets rocheux – les « Dolomites de la Basse-Engadine » se découpent ici sur le ciel – et pour son climat de montagne sec et abrité ; la région est en effet favorisée par un ensoleillement plus doux que celui de la haute vallée de l'Inn. Dans les établissements de bains de Scuol et de Tarasp, on traite plus particulièrement les affections gastro-intestinales, les troubles du métabolisme, de la circulation, des reins et de la vessie.

SCUOL/SCHULS

Bagnera	3
Bahnhofstrasse	4
Bogns (Via dals)	6
Gurlaina	8
Punt	9
S.-charl (Via da)	10
Stradun	12

M "Chagronda"
F Schweizerhof

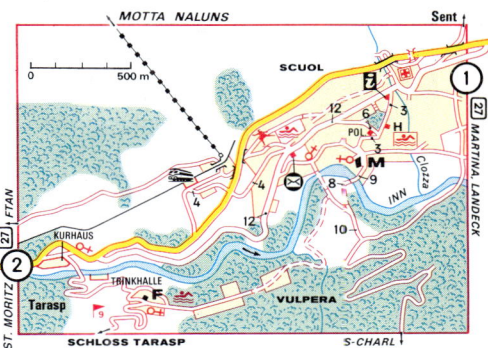

LES STATIONS

Des chemins de promenade relient les trois stations de Scuol, Tarasp et Vulpera et permettent au piéton d'éviter les routes.

★ **Scuol/Schuls** – Sur le versant cultivé de la vallée, ce village paysan s'est transformé en un centre touristique et commerçant, animé par le trafic qui emprunte l'itinéraire international Engadine-Autriche (St-Moritz-Landeck). Cependant, en contrebas de la route de traversée, le Bas-Scuol, noyau ancien de la localité, s'ordonne toujours autour de deux places pavées qui offrent des ensembles de constructions au cachet purement engadinois.

La **« Chagronda »** (Chasa Gronda) (**M**) ⊙, reconnaissable à ses deux galeries superposées est le bâtiment le plus imposant. Il date des 16e et 18e s. et abrite actuellement un « musée de la Basse-Engadine ».

Tarasp – Dans une situation encaissée, au fond de la vallée de l'Inn, le centre balnéaire de Tarasp se réduit aux vastes installations hôtelières et thermales du « Kurhaus Tarasp ».

★★ **Vulpera** – Quatre hôtels construits sur une terrasse du versant boisé de la vallée, au milieu de superbes parterres fleuris, composent la station. Les touristes venus rechercher le délassement dans une ambiance élégante trouvent sur place toute la gamme des distractions sportives désirables.

ENVIRONS

★ **Route d'Ardez** – *12 km à l'Ouest par une petite route sinueuse.*
La montée à **Ftan** fait apprécier le site du château de Tarasp. Dans la descente sur Ardez *(voir à ce nom)*, le virage qui marque la sortie du Val Tasna et le retour dans la vallée principale forme un excellent **belvédère**★★ au-dessus du bassin de Scuol, le château de Tarasp et leur cadre de montagnes.

De Tarasp au Kreuzberg – *Du Kurhaus Tarasp, 4 km, environ 1/2 h – par chemin étroit et sinueux, en forte montée, plus 1/2 h à pied AR pour monter au Kreuzberg.*
Traverser l'Inn et s'engager dans la montée de Vulpera ; aussitôt après l'hôtel Schweizerhof (**F**), tourner à droite (lacet).
Quitter la voiture à l'entrée de Tarasp-Fontana et prendre le chemin grimpant à Tarasp-Sparsels, au pied du château. A l'extrémité de Sparsels, prendre à droite le chemin débouchant dans les prés, en vue de la croix qui surmonte le tertre gazonné du Kreuzberg.

★ **Kreuzberg** – Alt. 1 474 m. De ce belvédère, on peut apprécier le **site**★★ du château et un **panorama**★ englobant toute la Basse-Engadine avec ses « Dolomites » (Piz Lischana et Piz Pisoc) et ses villages-balcons (Ftan, Sent).

SCUOL/SCHULS

Château de Tarasp

Château de Tarasp (Schloss Tarasp) ⊙ – Il resta une enclave autrichienne en terre grisonne jusqu'en 1803. Après maintes vicissitudes préjudiciables à ses aménagements intérieurs, aujourd'hui disparates, la forteresse a été restaurée (1907-1916) et est habitée, saisonnièrement, par la famille de Hesse-Darmstadt.

Sent – *4 km au Nord-Est*. On accède à la station de Sent par une petite route bordée d'érables, joliment tracée à flanc de coteau, en vue des « Dolomites » et du château de Tarasp.
C'est un beau village aux maisons impeccablement entretenues par des émigrés grisons revenant en villégiature dans leur petite patrie ; remarquer en particulier des pignons baroques dits « de Sent » curieusement festonnés.

SEELISBERG★

Uri – 569 habitants
Carte Michelin n° 427 pli 15 ou 218 pli 1 – au Sud-Ouest de Brunnen
Schéma : VIERWALDSTÄTTER SEE – Alt. 839 m

Étagée sur une croupe boisée plongeant dans le lac des Quatre-Cantons, en vue de la baie de Brunnen et du bassin de Schwyz, que surveillent les deux pitons des Mythen, Seelisberg se range parmi les stations estivales réputées de la Suisse centrale pour son isolement en fin de route, la majesté du panorama, l'équipement touristique.

Accès – On monte à Seelisberg :
– en voiture depuis Stans *(22 km par route décrite à Stans)*,
– en funiculaire, du débarcadère de Treib ⊙ *(services en correspondance avec les bateaux du lac des Quatre-Cantons – durée de la montée : 8 mn)*.

★★**Point de vue de Seelisberg** – De la promenade-belvédère publique, panorama sur le Fronalpstock et le lac d'Uri.

SEMPACH

Lucerne – 3 096 habitants
Carte Michelin n° 427 pli 14 ou 216 pli 17 – au bord du lac de Sempach – Alt. 518 m

Bâtie près du lac auquel elle a donné son nom, Sempach fut fondée par les Habsbourg pour contrôler la route du Gothard (Bâle-Lucerne-Milan). La route moderne est aujourd'hui tracée sur la rive opposée.
La rue principale présente un cachet ancien avec sa tour des Sorcières, son hôtel de ville (Rathaus) dont la façade est égayée d'un clayonnage blanc et rouge, sa fontaine fleurie et ses maisons aux larges toits de tuiles brunes.

Un héros national – Le 9 juillet 1386, se déroule près de Sempach un combat décisif entre les Confédérés suisses et les troupes autrichiennes commandées par le duc Léopold. Pour ouvrir une brèche au milieu du carré autrichien hérissé de piques, **Arnold de Winkelried** se précipite en avant, se saisit du plus grand nombre de fers qu'il peut embrasser et, par son sacrifice héroïque, décide de la victoire des Confédérés, dans laquelle le duc Léopold lui-même trouve la mort.
Un monument commémoratif perpétue le souvenir de cette journée historique.

SEMPACH

Station ornithologique suisse (Schweizerische Vogelwarte) ⊙ – Institut de recherches sur les oiseaux de la région, la survivance des espèces et les itinéraires des migrateurs. On peut en voir dans les volières, les jardins et, empaillés, dans le musée.

Kirchbühl – *2 km au Nord-Ouest.* Le but de la promenade est la vieille église de Kirchbühl, aux abords de laquelle on découvre une belle **vue★** sur le lac de Sempach et les Alpes (se placer dans l'ancien cimetière).
Un porche bas, couvert de tuiles, donne accès à la nef du 13ᵉ s., décorée de peintures fort endommagées : on reconnaît cependant le *Jugement Dernier*, la *Passion* et la *Résurrection du Christ*. Un retable du 16ᵉ s. orne le chœur.

SIERRE

Valais – 14 143 habitants
Carte n° 427 pli 13 ou 217 pli 16 – Schéma : VALAIS – Alt. 534 m

Enfoncée dans la vallée du Rhône, au pied des vignobles de la « Noble Contrée » et au débouché du Val d'Anniviers, Sierre est une des cités les plus ensoleillées de Suisse. Un éboulement survenu à l'époque préhistorique explique l'étrangeté du **site★** de la ville, au paysage de « gravière creusée et remuée à coup de pelle ».
Sierre (Siders) marque la limite linguistique entre le français et l'allemand *(carte dans le chapitre : Langues et religions)*. Plusieurs maisons fortes comme le château des Vidomnes ou la tour de Goubin, perchée sur son rocher, rappellent le temps du Valais épiscopal et féodal. L'écrivain autrichien **Rainer Maria Rilke** séjourna avant sa mort (1926) dans l'ancien château de la Cour, aujourd'hui l'hôtel de ville.

CURIOSITÉS

Hôtel de ville – Ancien manoir, puis hôtel, des 17ᵉ et 19ᵉ s. L'**intérieur★** surprend par le caractère à la fois riche et intime que lui confèrent ses beaux plafonds peints, fresques murales, tableaux et vitraux de couleur. Il renferme dans une cave, un **musée d'étains** ⊙ exposant, en vitrines, environ 180 pièces de collection (vaisselle, ustensiles) du 17ᵉ au 19ᵉ s.

Rue du Bourg – Petite rue pittoresque par ses vieilles maisons, dont la curieuse bâtisse à échauguettes, semblant surgie d'un dessin animé, dite « château des Vidomnes », et sa noble église catholique Ste-Catherine (17ᵉ au 19ᵉ s. ; à l'intérieur : chœur baroque, chaire sculptée, joli buffet d'orgues).
Au n° 30, la maison Pancrace de Courten (18ᵉ s.) abrite, au rez-de-chaussée, la **fondation Rainer Maria Rilke** ⊙ consacrée à l'écrivain autrichien qui séjourna avant sa mort (1926) dans l'ancien château de la Cour, aujourd'hui l'hôtel de ville.

Château Mercier – Ce manoir privé du 19ᵉ s. est entouré par le frais **parc de Pradec** qui domine la ville (vues sur celle-ci par échappées entre les arbres).

Château de Villa ⊙ – Dans les dépendances du château, le **musée valaisan de la Vigne et du Vin** est installé. La visite commence par un film vidéo sur le pressurage du raisin à l'ancienne, et se poursuit par quelques salles. La première est consacrée aux pressoirs (vieux pressoirs à levier à vis centrale, de taille impressionnante). Le travail du caviste est illustré dans la suivante. Puis la visite s'achève par les différents types de contenants (bouteilles et étiquettes, pots en étain, tonneaux), qui évoquent le commerce du vin et son rôle dans la société.

ENVIRONS

Salgesch – Un **sentier viticole** de 6 km reliant Sierre à Salgesch – **Salquenen** en français – permet de découvrir une partie du vignoble. Des panneaux explicatifs jalonnent le parcours, décrivant les cépages (Chasselas, Pinot, Sylvaner, Malvoisie), la qualité du sol, les différentes tailles, le traditionnel vignolage (journée de corvée printanière, pendant laquelle le travail de la vigne se fait au son des fifres et tambours).
Dans ce petit village paisible *(en voiture 3 km)*, la **maison Zumofen** (16ᵉ s.) ⊙, reconnaissable à son double pignon en bois, constitue le complément du musée du château de Villa. Plusieurs salles sont consacrées à la viticulture : la terre, les cépages, le travail de la vigne, les outils employés, les vendanges sous la protection de saint Théodule, patron des vignerons.

Avant de prendre la route,
consultez 3615 MICHELIN sur votre Minitel :
votre meilleur itinéraire,
le choix de votre hôtel, restaurant,
des propositions de visites touristiques.

SIMPLONPASSSTRASSE★★

Carte Michelin n° 427 plis 14, 23 ou 217 plis 18, 19 et 219 pli 6 – Schéma : VALAIS

La route du Simplon n'est pas la plus audacieuse des Alpes — les passages du Splügen ou même du St-Gothard sont des réalisations plus « héroïques » ; elle en reste cependant la plus noble et la plus majestueuse. Il est impossible de rester insensible à la beauté d'un **tracé**★★★ comme celui qui se développe entre le col (alt. 2 005 m) et Brigue, sur le versant du Rhône : ce lent cheminement à flanc de montagne, fait de calmes reploiements, excluant tout empilement de lacets serrés, reste un modèle d'adaptation à la topographie.

L'intérêt proprement pittoresque du parcours réside dans la succession des gorges et défilés encaissés de la vallée de la Diveria ou Val Divedro (versant Sud) et des balcons panoramiques du versant Nord.

Pour faire passer le canon — Dès le 17e s., le « Grand Stockalper », tirant le meilleur parti de la situation de Brigue, adapte au trafic commercial le chemin du Simplon, jusqu'alors fréquenté surtout par les contrebandiers et les mercenaires. Il y organise un service de courrier régulier et fait construire à Gondo et au col deux hospices encore debout. Mais il s'agit encore de portage à dos de mulet et non de roulage. Le Simplon moderne est fils du génie napoléonien.

Comprenant qu'une expédition comme celle du Grand-St-Bernard est appelée à rester une prouesse isolée — un détachement envoyé en même temps en Italie par le Simplon n'avait forcé le passage qu'au prix d'acrobaties encore plus risquées — le Premier Consul décide en septembre 1800, trois mois après Marengo, que « le chemin depuis Brig jusqu'à Domo d'Ossola sera rendu praticable pour les canons ». La faible altitude du col, son enneigement relativement réduit, ont motivé ce choix. Priorité absolue est donnée au projet, qui finit par l'emporter sur celui du Mont Cenis. La haute direction des travaux est confiée au Champenois Nicolas Céart, ingénieur en chef des Ponts et Chaussées pour le département du Léman, qui établit les plans d'une route large de 7 à 8 m, en rampe maximum de 10 %. Celle-ci est ouverte aux voitures le 9 octobre 1805 ; mais Napoléon n'aura jamais l'occasion de la parcourir.

DE DOMODOSSOLA A BRIG

65 km — environ 3 h — itinéraire ② *de la visite du Valais*

Malgré les galeries de protection destinées à le rendre praticable toute l'année, le col du Simplon peut exceptionnellement être obstrué par la neige à la suite de tempêtes entre décembre et mai.

En Italie, le parcours proprement alpestre commence à **Crévoladossola**, où l'on quitte la chaude plaine intérieure de l'Ossola, d'un caractère méridional plutôt ingrat.

De Crévoladossola à la frontière, la vallée resserrée de la Diveria ne propose guère de tableaux divertissants : quelques campaniles, la verdure fraîche de fourrés de noisetiers, de noyers ou de frênes ne suffisent pas à l'égayer.

A quelques kilomètres de Crévoladossola, sur la gauche, les ruines du petit village de San Giovanni, rasé par un éboulement en 1958, accroissent l'austérité de la vallée.

Les contrôles douaniers italien et suisse ont lieu respectivement à Paglino et à Gondo.

★ **Gorges de Gondo (Gondoschlucht)** — Le passage le plus sauvage de ce long défilé encadré de parois granitiques est le confluent de l'Alpienbach et de la Diveria, unissant leurs chutes au pied d'un éperon que la route traverse en tunnel.

Entre Gstein (Gabi) et le col, la route, laissant au Sud-Ouest le Laggintal s'enfoncer vers les hautes régions du Weissmies (4 023 m), s'élève progressivement dans les alpages de la combe inférieure du Simplon.

En amont du village de Simplon, l'aspect mouvementé du terrain témoigne encore des effets d'une formidable avalanche déclenchée, en 1901, par l'écroulement de tout un pan du Rossbodengletscher, dont on aperçoit la cataracte de séracs. Dominant ce glacier, le Fletschhorn va devenir la silhouette montagneuse la plus captivante du décor. Les mélèzes se dispersent et l'on pénètre dans la dépression supérieure du col.

★★ **Col du Simplon** — Alt. 2 005 m. La route se maintient à mi-pente au-dessus de cette longue dépression coudée, au fond bosselé, que dominent, au Sud, le Böshorn — et surtout, au second plan, le Fletschhorn neigeux — à l'Est, les dalles verdâtres du Hübschhorn et le Chaltwassergletscher, descendu du Monte Leone.

Des trois monuments qui caractérisent le site, celui qui a le plus de cachet est l'Alter Spittel (Ancien hospice, fondé par Stockalper), édifice tout en hauteur, flanqué d'une tourelle à clocheton du 17e s. L'hospice actuel (Hospiz), contemporain de la construction de la route, est également l'œuvre de Napoléon Ier ; resté inachevé, il a été repris plus tard par les religieux du Grand-St-Bernard. Enfin un aigle en maçonnerie commémore la « garde aux frontières » pendant la dernière guerre mondiale.

SIMPLONPASSSTRASSE

Le **belvédère**★★ du col se localise au point culminant, c'est-à-dire à l'origine de la dépression, côté Valais. Près de l'hôtel Simplon-Kulm, il est possible de repérer les sommets des Alpes bernoises, visibles entre le Schinhorn et le Finsteraarhorn (point culminant des Alpes bernoises – alt. 4 274 m). Une mince portion du glacier géant d'Aletsch peut être aussi remarquée.

Sur le versant du Rhône, le tracé, entre le col et le tunnel dit « Kapfloch », prime tous les autres passages pour la hardiesse de sa construction : la route, protégée par une série de galeries et de couvertures en béton, est accrochée ici aux abrupts supérieurs d'un amphithéâtre rocheux, que sillonnent les eaux de fonte du Chaltwasserglescher visible lui-même en contre-haut.

Aux abords du Kapfloch, on apprécie encore l'apparition, par la trouée du col, du Fletschhorn, flanqué à droite du Böshom.

Du Kapfloch à Rothwald, un long alignement, en corniche, sous les mélèzes, fait découvrir, 1 000 m plus bas, la cité de Brigue, s'encadrant dans l'échancrure des gorges de la Saltine. A l'horizon se déploient maintenant les montagnes séparant la vallée du Rhône du Lötschental, soit, de gauche à droite, le Bietschhorn, le Breithorn, le Nesthorn et le Schinhorn.

Entre Rothwald et Schallberg, la route fait un détour dans le Gantertal : au flanc du versant Nord de ce beau vallon se multiplient les pins arolles *(voir le chapitre : La Végétation alpine)* aux formes tourmentées.

Après avoir franchi le moderne et imposant pont du Ganter, en quittant le **Gantertal**, on distingue, très haut maintenant, le tracé de la route au voisinage du col.

Entre Schallberg et Brigue, la route, après avoir dominé les gorges de la Saltine (Saltinaschlucht) dont le fond est invisible, s'échappe de la forêt et se rabat enfin sur les versants bien cultivés du Brigerberg.

Les tours imposantes du château de Stockalper, les clochers des églises de Brigue se précisent, tandis que, en aval, le ruban scintillant du Rhône va se perdre dans les fumées des usines de Viège.

Brig – *Voir à ce nom.*

SION★★

|C| Valais – 25 336 habitants

Carte Michelin n° 427 plis 13, 22 ou 217 plis 15, 16 – Schéma : VALAIS – Alt. 512 m

Sion occupe dans la plaine du Valais central un **site**★★ que l'on apprécie dans de bonnes conditions en arrivant de Martigny ou en montant à Savièse. L'apparition des deux pitons rocailleux de Valère (côté Rhône) et de Tourbillon (côté montagne), coiffés de forteresses épiscopales, peut permettre d'évoquer le Puy et ses « aiguilles ».

L'évêché de Sion – Fondé au 4e s., l'évêché de Sion a joué un rôle politique et religieux considérable au Moyen Âge.

La donation du comté du Valais à l'église de Sion, à l'aube du 11e s., par le dernier roi de Bourgogne transjurane Rodolphe III, fait de l'évêque un seigneur temporel et un véritable prince souverain, jouissant de tous les droits régaliens : droit de justice, perception de nombreuses amendes, frappe de la monnaie, présidence des diètes ou assemblées générales. Lors de l'émancipation des communes, ces privilèges disparaissent les uns après les autres. Le choix des évêques, qui dépendait d'une part des chanoines de la cathédrale, d'autre part des députés de la Diète valaisanne jusqu'en 1848, puis des députés du Grand Conseil jusqu'en 1918, devient à cette date le privilège exclusif du Saint-Siège.

★**VALÈRE** *visite : 2 h 1/2*

Sur la colline de Valère, qui domine la vallée de 120 m, se situe une église-forteresse, ancienne résidence du chapitre de Sion.

Laisser la voiture sur une petite place, au parc de stationnement situé entre Valère et Tourbillon, à l'extrémité de la rue des Châteaux, qui monte à travers la ville ancienne. Gagner d'abord, au pied de l'enceinte, une esplanade herbeuse d'où l'on jouit de la **perspective**★ sur la vallée du Rhône, vers l'amont.

Pénétrer ensuite dans l'enceinte fortifiée ; au terme de la rampe, une terrasse *(panneau d'orientation)* permet de découvrir une belle **vue**★ sur les toits de Sion et sur le Bas-Valais, en aval.

★**Église N.-D.-de-Valère** ⊘ – Bâtie au sommet du piton, elle présente toutes les caractéristiques d'une église fortifiée, avec son enceinte, les créneaux de sa tour et de son collatéral Nord, sa passerelle de garde à l'intérieur. Commencée au début du 12e s., sa construction s'est poursuivie jusqu'au milieu du 13e s.

La nef, voûtée d'ogives, est séparée du chœur par un jubé qui rompt l'harmonie du vaisseau. Elle suit, par paliers successifs, la déclivité du sol, surélevé en deux fois jusqu'au chœur. De magnifiques **stalles**★★ du 17e s., dont les panneaux figurent diverses scènes de la Passion, ornent le chœur qui possède encore des chapiteaux historiés d'époque romane et des fresques du 16e s. Le buffet avec le jeu original des orgues date du début du 15e s.

231

SION

Sion – Colline de Valère

★ **Musée cantonal d'Histoire et d'Ethnographie** (Y M³) ⊙ – Ancienne résidence des chanoines, le château (12ᵉ s.), dont les salles ont été rénovées, abrite des expositions présentées par roulement ayant trait à l'histoire du Valais. L'art sacré, l'art populaire religieux (sculptures, orfèvrerie, imagerie) alternent avec la vie quotidienne (mobilier) ou militaire (armes, armures). Dans la grande salle embellie par ses poutres en bois et sa cheminée sculptée, on remarque face à la cheminée, plusieurs peintures murales représentant les Neuf Preux, trois héros païens (Hector, Alexandre et Jules César), trois héros judaïques (Josué, David et Judas Macchabée), trois héros chrétiens (Arthur, Charlemagne et Godefroy de Bouillon) modèles de l'idéal chevaleresque.

TOURBILLON (Y) visite : 1 h

Du parking, un sentier s'élève jusqu'aux ruines imposantes d'une ancienne forteresse dont les murailles crénelées couronnent la colline. Lors de la montée (assez pénible), la **vue**★ offerte sur Valère et son église-forteresse ainsi que sur les coteaux environnants couverts de vignes est superbe.
L'édifice et la chapelle furent construits à la fin du 13ᵉ s. par l'évêque Boniface de Challant. A l'origine ouvrage défensif, le château servit en temps de paix de résidence d'été aux évêques. Maintes fois assiégé, reconstruit au 15ᵉ s., il fut ravagé par un terrible incendie en 1788.
Après avoir franchi une première porte percée dans une ceinture de remparts, on pénètre dans l'enceinte du château dominée par son donjon. Dans la chapelle voûtée d'ogives reposant sur des colonnes aux chapiteaux sculptés, on remarque quelques fragments de peintures murales.

AUTRES CURIOSITÉS

Cathédrale N.-D.-du-Glarier (Y) – Le **clocher**★ roman, des 11ᵉ et 13ᵉ s., est décoré d'arcatures lombardes et se termine par une élégante flèche octogonale.
A l'intérieur, la nef, voûtée d'ogives, a été achevée au début du 16ᵉ s. Le chœur, orné de stalles du 17ᵉ s., est décoré, derrière le maître-autel, par un **triptyque**★ en bois doré (Arbre de Jessé).

Hôtel de ville (Y H) ⊙ – Édifice du 17ᵉ s. avec, dès l'entrée, une **porte**★ de bois sculpté, très ouvragée. Dans le vestibule, inscriptions romaines dont une, chrétienne, de 377. La **salle du Conseil bourgeoisial**★, au 1ᵉʳ étage, est enrichie de travaux de boiserie splendides et d'un mobilier fastueux.

SION

Maison Supersaxo (Y B) ⊙ – Édifiée en 1505 par Georges Supersaxo, qui voulut éblouir par son luxe son rival le cardinal Mathieu Schiner, cette somptueuse demeure a conservé une **salle**★ très haute et très vaste, au plafond en boiserie découpé en bandes rayonnantes avec, au centre, un énorme pendentif formant rosace et représentant la nativité du Christ et, tout autour, douze niches d'où émergent les bustes des rois mages et des prophètes.

Musée cantonal des Beaux-Arts (Y M¹) ⊙ – La Majorie et le Vidomat, anciennes résidences des officiers épiscopaux, abritent le musée des Beaux-Arts du Valais : estampes anciennes, toiles d'artistes valaisans anciens ou actuels.
Des différents étages de la Majorie (du 3ᵉ surtout), on a une très belle **vue**★ d'ensemble sur l'église-forteresse de Valère et les ruines du château de Tourbillon.

Musée cantonal d'Archéologie (Y M²) ⊙ – De présentation très moderne, ce petit musée expose plusieurs stèles préhistoriques gravées, les copies des bronzes d'Octodure conservés à Martigny *(voir à ce nom)*, des verreries romaines et islamiques anciennes. En sous-sol, des amphores et statuettes gallo-romaines, des céramiques grecques et étrusques, des vestiges néolithiques : armes, bijoux, fibules, poteries.

SION

Rue	Zone
Gare (Av. de la)	YZ
Lausanne (R. de)	YZ
Mayennets (Av. des)	Z
Midi (Av. du)	Z
Aubépines (R. des)	Z
Cèdres (R. des)	Z 3
Chanoine-Berchtold (R. du)	Z
Château (R. des)	Y 6
Condémines (R. des)	Z 7
Creusets (R. des)	Z
Dent-Blanche (R. de la)	Z 9
Dixence (R. de la)	Z
France (Av. de)	Z
Grand-Pont (R. du)	Y 10
Gravelone (R. de)	Y
Industrie (R. de l')	Z
Loèche (R. de)	Y 15
Midi (Pl. du)	Z
Planta (Pl. de la)	YZ 16
Porte-Neuve (R. de la)	YZ 18
Pratifori (Av. de)	Z 19
Rawyl (R.)	Y
Remparts (R. des)	Z 21
Rhône (R. du)	Z 22
Ritz (Av.)	Y
St-François (Av.)	Y
Savièse (R. de)	Y 24
Scex (R. du)	YZ
Tourbillon (Av. de)	Z
Tour (R. de la)	Y 25
Tunnel (R. du)	Y
Vergers (R. des)	Z 27

B	Maison Supersaxo
H	Hôtel de ville
M¹	Musée cantonal des Beaux-Arts
M²	Musée cantonal d'Archéologie
M³	Musée cantonal d'Histoire et d'Ethnographie

SION

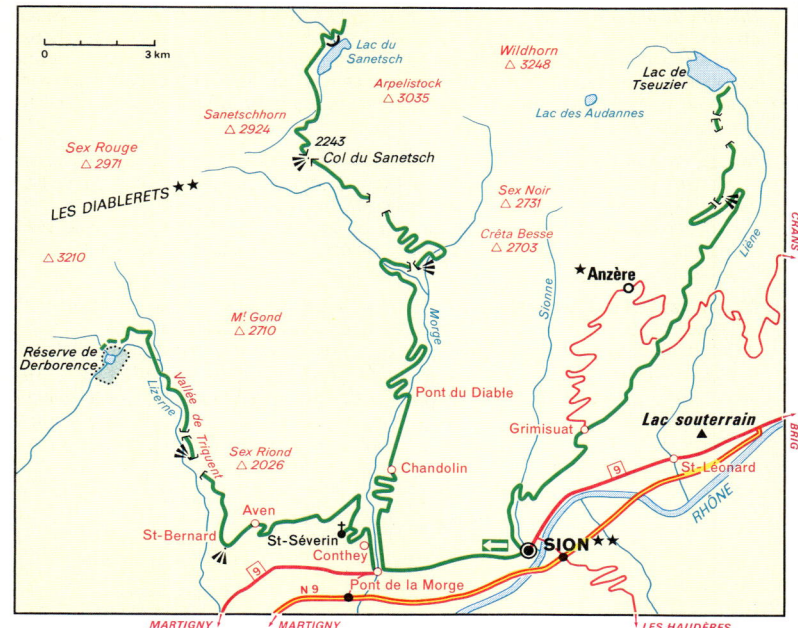

ENVIRONS

Lac souterrain de St-Léonard ⊙ – *6 km par* ① *du plan, route de Brig et à gauche. Du parc autos, 10 mn à pied AR. Visite en barque.*
Ce lac et la caverne qu'il occupe ont été formés par des eaux s'infiltrant à travers un banc gypseux et dissolvant peu à peu celui-ci. Ils ont été explorés à partir de 1943 puis aménagés pour la visite, la nappe d'eau étant maintenue par pompage à des dimensions moyennes d'environ 300 m de long, 20 m de large et 15 m de profondeur.
L'éclairage électrique met en valeur le relief tourmenté et les teintes contrastées (gypse blanchâtre, schiste charbonneux, marbre gris) des voûtes et parois rocheuses reflétées à la surface du lac. La seule touche de vie décelable a été introduite, sous forme de quelques dizaines de grosses truites restant cantonnées à proximité de l'embarcadère, d'où elles sont nourries.

★ **Anzère** – *16 km, par la rue de Loèche (Y 15).*
Cette moderne et avenante station de sports d'hiver et d'été, fort bien équipée, a été implantée à 1 549 m d'altitude dans un **site**★ admirablement choisi : au flanc du massif du Wildhorn et dominant la vallée de la Liène, avec pour horizon les Alpes valaisannes par-delà Crans-Montana.

★ **Route de Derborence** – *24 km. Quitter Sion par* ② *du plan, et suivre la route nº 9 jusqu'à Pont de la Morge.*
La route monte dans le vignoble et à travers les villages de Conthey, Sensine puis **St-Séverin** (belle église à clocher de pierre) où l'on prend à gauche. Après Erde, la vigne fait place aux arbustes et, dans le virage précédant les chalets d'Aven, se révèle une belle vue sur la vallée du Rhône. Après l'église de St-Bernard (dernière belle vue sur la vallée), la route oblique au Nord et longe la sauvage vallée de Triquent où coule la Lizerne. Au sortir d'un 1er tunnel, vue sur les cimes neigeuses des Diablerets barrant la combe au Nord, le paysage gagne en pittoresque : coulées de rocs coiffées de névés, pins, torrent (de la Lizerne, que la route coupe à trois reprises) entouré de blocs erratiques, cascades... pour s'épanouir enfin en un grandiose **amphithéâtre**★★ de chaos rocheux semé de pins et de mélèzes.
Prendre à gauche le chemin caillouteux aboutissant à la Réserve de Derborence « *réserve absolue* », dans un **cirque**★ rocheux (causé au 18e s. par un éboulement des Diablerets) où s'abritent un limpide petit lac vert et quelques chalets.

★★ **Route du Sanetsch** – *33 km. Quitter Sion par* ② *du plan et suivre la route nº 9 jusqu'à Pont de la Morge.*
Après avoir franchi la Morge, la route du vignoble, étroite, monte sur Chandolin, procurant d'agréables vues sur les pentes avoisinantes couvertes de vignes et sur la plaine rhodanienne. Au pont du Diable, une descente en corniche, coupée d'un tunnel, rejoint le torrent dans son ravin. La route remonte ensuite dans un paysage

plus riant, avec des sapins et, sur le versant opposé, une jolie cascade. A hauteur de l'embranchement pour Conthey (à gauche), on aperçoit en avant le beau sommet rocheux du Crêta Besse. Une rude montée (15 % sous bois) culmine aux chalets de Plan-Cernay. 2 km plus loin, devant l'auberge de Zenfleuron, la route franchit la Morge et passe en corniche sur le versant Est, offrant, après un tunnel, une **vue**★ sur la vallée et à l'opposé sur les hauteurs (d'où dévalent trois torrents de fonte glaciaire), suivie d'une montée à flanc de pente débouchant, avant un 2ᵉ tunnel, au pied des sombres parois rocheuses du Sex Noir face à la barrière neigeuse des Diablerets. Après un dernier et long tunnel, le parcours se maintient en montée presque rectiligne jusqu'au **col du Sanetsch** (2 243 m ; belle **vue**★★ sur les Diablerets précédés du glacier de Tsanfleuron), puis descend au lac de barrage du même nom, où se termine la route, dans un impressionnant décor de haute montagne.

★**Route de Tseuzier** – *23 km. Quitter Sion par la route de Crans-Montana, au Nord* (Y).

3 km après Grimisuat, prendre à gauche la route d'Ayent et, à St-Romain, la route fléchée « Barrage de Zeuzier », étroite mais facile, qui s'élève parmi les sapins au-dessus de la vallée de la Liène et procure bientôt quelques belles échappées sur celle-ci et les stations étagées de Crans et Montana par-delà (ample **vue**★, notamment, aux abords du premier tunnel). Au terme de la route, on découvre le petit lac de barrage de Tseuzier dans sa cuvette rocheuse semi-boisée.

SOLOTHURN★

SOLEURE – C 15 748 habitants

Carte n° 427 pli 4 ou 216 pli 15 – Schéma : JURA SUISSE – Alt. 436 m

Au pied du dernier rempart du Jura (Weissenstein), Soleure s'étend aujourd'hui de part et d'autre de l'Aare. Sur la rive gauche de la rivière, le noyau ancien de la ville, encore comprimé dans ses murailles du 17ᵉ s., conserve de beaux édifices Renaissance et baroques. La « Krummturn » (tour Tordue) (Z) est la silhouette la plus frappante de cet ensemble fortifié.

De 1530 à 1792, Soleure, restée catholique, obtint d'être choisie comme résidence des ambassadeurs du roi de France auprès de la Diète helvétique. Cette situation fut d'une grande importance pour la ville qui multiplia avec la France les relations intellectuelles et artistiques : les styles à la mode à la cour des Bourbons y fleurirent et les fortifications élevées à partir de 1667 le furent à l'école de Vauban.

CURIOSITÉS

★**Ville ancienne** – Les portes de Bâle (Baseltor) et de Bienne (Bieltor) y donnent accès. Nombreuses sont les rues présentant un aspect plein de charme et de pittoresque avec leurs maisons aux volets peints de couleurs vives, aux enseignes de fer forgé et aux toits débordants. La Hauptgasse, la St-Urbangasse et la Schmiedengasse sont caractéristiques.

La Marktplatz, centre de la vieille ville, est ornée d'une fontaine à personnages peints du 16ᵉ s. (St. Ursen-Brunnen) : elle est dominée par la tour de l'Horloge (Zeitglockenturm) (Y) du 12ᵉ s., dont l'horloge astronomique est surmontée de trois personnages (Le Roi entre la Mort et saint Urs, patron de la ville).

★**Cathédrale St-Urs (St. Ursenkathedrale)** (Y) – Cet imposant édifice de style baroque a été construit au 18ᵉ s. par deux architectes tessinois, dans le goût italien, et a remplacé la cathédrale primitive consacrée aux saints Urs et Victor, martyrs de la légion Thébaine qui, ayant échappé au massacre d'Agaune (*voir à St-Maurice*), furent décapités à Soleure. La vaste nef est soutenue par des colonnes à l'antique terminées par des pilastres à décoration florale. Cette décoration se retrouve tout le long de la fausse galerie qui court sous les fenêtres hautes. Une coupole surmonte la croisée du transept.

La chaire sculptée de marbre rose, les peintures du chœur et de la croisée du transept constituent les éléments essentiels de décoration de cet édifice d'une belle unité.

D'agréables jardins ont été aménagés derrière le chevet de la cathédrale.

Église des Jésuites (Jesuitenkirche) (Y) – Construite à la fin du 17ᵉ s., elle présente une **nef**★ de trois travées décorée de fresques et de stucs.

Une galerie court le long des deux premières travées si bien que la troisième semble former transept.

Le maître-autel, gigantesque, est orné d'une très vaste peinture figurant l'Assomption, encadrée de deux gros piliers de marbre vert. La double tribune d'orgue est d'un bel effet par l'élégance de ses proportions et la finesse de sa décoration.

SOLOTHURN

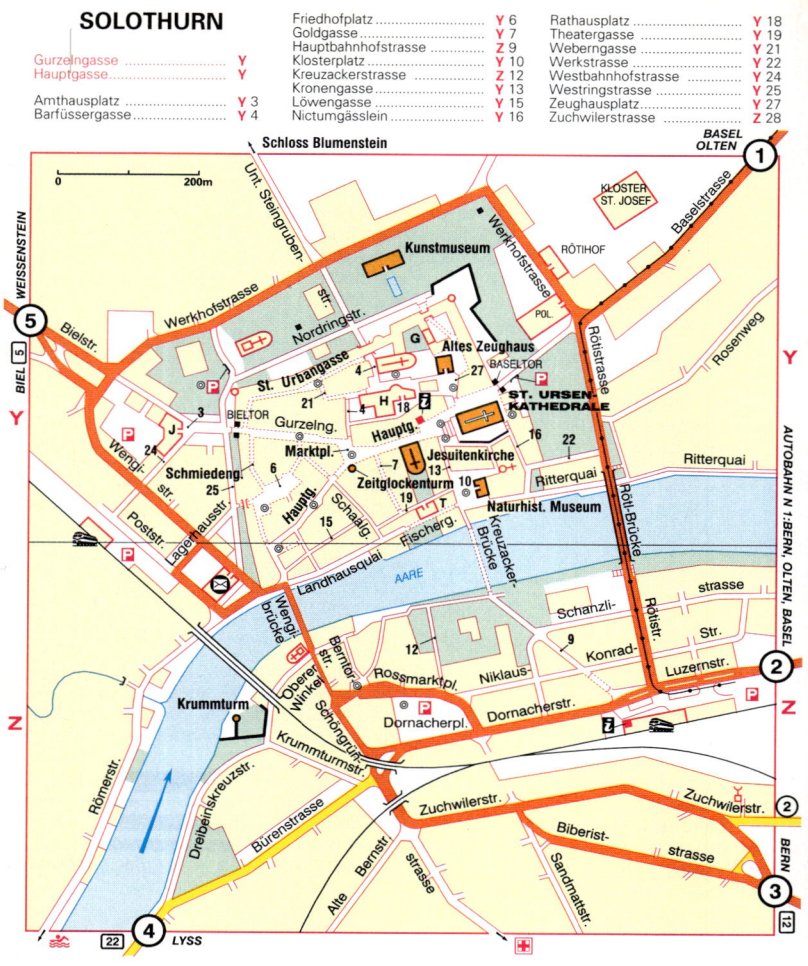

Ancien arsenal (Altes Zeughaus) (Y) ⊙ — Transformé en musée, il renferme une très importante collection d'armes et d'uniformes, du Moyen Âge au 17ᵉ s. et, au second étage, environ 400 armures ou cuirasses. Au rez-de-chaussée, canons anciens et modernes, plus un tank léger.

Musée des Beaux-Arts de Soleure (Kunstmuseum Solothurn) (Y) ⊙ — Ce musée est consacré principalement à l'art suisse à partir de 1850.
C'est au 1ᵉʳ étage que sont exposées les collections les plus intéressantes. A côté des grandes toiles de Ferdinand Hodler, Maurice Barraud, Cuno Amiet, tous peintres contemporains, on retient deux belles œuvres de maîtres anciens : une **Vierge aux Fraises** ★, peinture sur bois de l'école rhénane réalisée vers 1425, remarquable par l'éclat des tons bleu, vert, grenat, rouge, or, et la douceur des attitudes, et la **Madone de Soleure** ★, tableau de Hans Holbein le Jeune, plein de majesté, d'une grande rigueur d'exécution et où dominent les ors, les rouges et les bleus.

Musée d'Histoire naturelle (Naturhistorischesmuseum) (Y) ⊙ — Il renseigne essentiellement sur l'homme, la faune européenne, actuelle et fossile : au rez-de-chaussée, l'homme et les mammifères ; au 1ᵉʳ étage, les oiseaux, poissons et reptiles.
Le 2ᵉ étage est consacré à la géologie de la Suisse et à la minéralogie.
Le sous-sol abrite des expositions temporaires.

Château-musée Blumenstein ⊙ — Accès au Nord-Ouest par la Untere Steingrubenstrasse (Y), le Herrenweg à droite, puis le Blumensteinweg à gauche.
Cette grande demeure du 18ᵉ s., entourée d'un petit parc, expose des collections variées, d'époques diverses : meubles, tapisseries, tableaux, bibelots, sculptures religieuses et objets de culte, instruments de musique, costumes, céramiques... A remarquer particulièrement, dans la véranda du rez-de-chaussée, de beaux vitraux du 16ᵉ s. et une maquette de la ville.

SPIEZ ★

Berne — 11 182 habitants
Carte n° 427 pli 13 ou 217 pli 7 — Schéma : BERNER OBERLAND — Alt. 628 m

Sur la rive Sud du lac de Thoune, au pied du Niesen, cette charmante petite ville occupe un **site★** harmonieux, que l'on apprécie d'une terrasse aménagée à la sortie de l'agglomération, au bord de la route d'Interlaken.
Spiez est une agréable station d'été et un bon centre d'excursions.

Spiez

CURIOSITÉS

Château — Sur un contrefort du Spiezberg, dominant le lac et la baie, se dresse le château médiéval que couronnent de puissantes tours. Construit aux 12e et 13e s., il a été agrandi et restauré à plusieurs reprises.
Du jardin public aménagé sur l'esplanade précédant l'entrée du château, on domine la rade qui abrite de nombreux voiliers et bateaux de plaisance, et l'on découvre, en face, de multiples chalets nichés dans la verdure.

Musée ⊙ — Les diverses salles contiennent de nombreux souvenirs des anciens propriétaires du château, les d'Erlach et les Bubenberg, de très beaux meubles en marqueterie gothique, Renaissance et baroque ; elles sont ornées de riches boiseries et de vitraux.
Du sommet de la grosse tour, on découvre une très belle **vue panoramique★★** sur le site de Spiez, le lac de Thoune, le Niesen au Sud et la terrasse de Beatenberg à l'Est.

Vieille église (Alte Kirche) ⊙ — Proche du château, c'est une église romane (fin du 10e s. — actuellement désaffectée) de plan basilical, à trois nefs et trois absides semi-circulaires, ornée de belles fresques.
A gauche du chœur se trouvent les tombeaux de Jeanne de Bubenberg et de Sigismond d'Erlach.

Attention, il y a étoile et étoile !
Sachez donc ne pas confondre les étoiles
— des régions touristiques les plus riches
et celles de contrées moins favorisées,
— des villes d'art et celles des bourgs pittoresques ou bien situés,
— des grandes villes et celles des stations élégantes,
— des grands monuments (architecture) et celles des musées (collections),
— des ensembles et celles qui valorisent un détail...

STANS

C Nidwald – 6 217 habitants

Carte Michelin n° 427 pli 14 ou 217 pli 9 – Schéma : VIERWALDSTÄTTER SEE – Alt. 451 m

Stans est restée une aimable cité, d'animation purement locale, qui constitue une bonne base d'excursions – en particulier pour la montée en funiculaire, puis en téléphérique donnant accès au magnifique belvédère du Stanserhorn – ou encore une commode étape de dépannage, en période de très forte affluence dans les hôtels de la région de Lucerne.

C'est à l'occasion de la Diète de Stans (1481) que, par son intervention conciliatrice, Nicolas de Flüe *(voir à ce nom)* sauva l'édifice encore fragile de la jeune Confédération. Le centre-ville, incendié en 1713, a été reconstruit.

CURIOSITÉS

Église – Elle dresse au-dessus de la place centrale son imposant **clocher**★ roman à quatre étages d'arcatures (la flèche fut ajoutée au 16e s.). Intérieurement, l'ample vaisseau, de la première période baroque, laisse une forte impression monumentale. Les statues qui décorent le vaisseau sont éclatantes de blancheur. Le chœur et les bas-côtés sont dotés de retables taillés dans le marbre noir du pays.

A proximité, la chapelle de l'Ossuaire, en gothique tardif, contient des fresques du 16e s. au mur gauche de sa nef (Déposition de croix, Mise au tombeau) et un ossuaire dans sa crypte.

En contrebas de l'église, on remarque le monument (du 19e s.) très connu commémorant le sacrifice d'Arnold de Winkelried à la bataille de Sempach.

Museum für Geschichte ⊙ – Ce petit musée d'histoire locale situé au centre de la ville contient notamment une charmante petite chapelle embellie d'un retable daté de 1604. Une salle évoque le « Jour d'horreur » qui ensanglanta le Nidwald le 9 septembre 1798 lors de l'attaque portée par les Français contre la résistance des montagnards *(le programme audiovisuel est uniquement en allemand)*.

ENVIRONS

★★**Stanserhorn** ⊙ – Alt. 1 898 m. Une agréable montée en funiculaire *(10 mn)*, puis en téléphérique *(12 mn)* aboutit à la terrasse de la station supérieure, où sont visibles les grandes roues crantées du treuil qui hissait le funiculaire primitif, et d'où se révèle (table d'orientation) une partie du ravissant **panorama**★★ que l'on découvre au sommet *(accessible en 20 mn AR)* : les lacs des Quatre-Cantons au Nord dans leur écrin de montagnes, les sommets des Alpes suisses au Sud (dont le tremplin glacé du Titlias) et au Sud-Ouest les sommets des Alpes bernoises (dont le massif de la Jungfrau).

★**Route de Seelisberg** – 22 km – environ 1 h – itinéraire ② du tour du lac des Quatre Cantons.

De Stans gagner, en passant sous l'autoroute, le gros bourg de **Buochs**, bien situé sur la rive Sud du lac des Quatre-Cantons, et suivre le bord du lac par Niederdorf et le riant village de **Beckenried** (lieu de séjour), aux plages fréquentées. Après St-Anna, une forte montée fait découvrir, en arrière, le Pilate ; à la sortie d'un passage sous bois, à Emmetten, belle vue à gauche sur le lac. On pénètre ensuite dans un joli paysage de collines boisées ou semées de chalets. Vue à droite en contrebas sur le petit lac vert de Seeli, au pied des falaises du Niederbauen Chulm, avant l'arrivée à **Seelisberg**★ *(voir à ce nom)*.

STEIN AM RHEIN★★

Schaffhouse – 2 793 habitants

Carte Michelin n° 427 pli 6 ou 216 pli 8 – Alt. 413 m

Bâtie sur la rive droite du Rhin, tout près du déversoir de l'Untersee – bassin occidental du lac de Constance –, cette charmante petite ville a conservé intact son aspect médiéval et demeure l'une des localités les plus pittoresques de la Suisse.

★★LA VILLE ANCIENNE visite : 3/4 h

Son caractère apparaît dès qu'on aborde le pont sur le Rhin. Sur la rive droite se présentent de belles maisons à colombage dont les soubassements baignent dans le fleuve. Mais la place de l'Hôtel-de-Ville et la rue principale constituent un ensemble hors de pair avec leurs fontaines fleuries et leurs maisons à oriels, dont les façades entièrement peintes développent le motif choisi pour enseigne : maison du Pélican, auberge du Soleil, maison du Bœuf rouge, maison de l'Aigle blanc.

Musée historique (Historische Sammlung) ⊙ – Installé au 2e étage de l'hôtel de ville (Rathaus). Armes, porcelaines de Delft, un surtout en argent doré du 16e s., vitraux historiés des 16e et 17e s. évoquent ici le passé de la ville.

STEIN AM RHEIN

Maisons peintes

Couvent de St-Georges (Kloster St. Georgen) — Cet ancien couvent de Bénédictins, installé à Stein au 11ᵉ s. par l'empereur d'Allemagne Henri II, a conservé son caractère moyenâgeux, mais a été transformé en **musée ★** (histoire, art populaire). Les diverses salles sont ornées de plafonds sculptés, de boiseries, de meubles en marqueterie et parfois décorée de grisailles du 16ᵉ s. On visite les cellules des religieux, au beau pavement carrelé, la salle du bailli, le cloître, la salle du chapitre. L'église romane, basilique à plafond plat, sans transept, du 12ᵉ s., a été restaurée.

ENVIRONS

★ **Château de Hohenklingen** — *2,5 km au Nord.* Accès par un chemin en forte montée, partie au milieu des vignes, partie en sous-bois. Du sommet de la tour, on découvre un **panorama ★** semi-circulaire sur Stein et son site, le Rhin, les collines environnantes et, au-delà, sur la chaîne des Alpes d'où émerge le Säntis.

SURSEE

Lucerne — 8 143 habitants
Carte Michelin n° 427 plis 5, 14 ou 216 pli 17 — Alt. 504 m

Bâtie près du lac de Sempach, la petite ville ancienne de Sursee a gardé une partie de son cachet médiéval, en dépit des incendies qui la ravagèrent entre le 14ᵉ et le 17ᵉ s. En 1415, la ville passa aux mains des Lucernois lors d'une expédition en Argovie.

CURIOSITÉS

★ **Hôtel de ville (Rathaus)** — Ce très bel édifice de la dernière période gothique, construit au milieu du 16ᵉ s., est flanqué de deux tours : l'une se termine par un curieux clocheton ; l'autre, hexagonale, est coiffée d'un bulbe.
La façade, au pignon en escalier, est percée de nombreuses fenêtres à meneaux.

Maison Beck — Bâtie en 1631, elle présente une façade à trois étages, de style Renaissance ; les encadrements de ses fenêtres à meneaux sont richement décorés.

Porte de Bâle (Baseltor ou Untertor) — Cette porte de ville, vestige des anciens remparts, est flanquée d'une maison à colombage, dont la façade blanche est striée de poutres rouges.

L'hôtel de ville

SURSEE

Chapelle de Mariazell – *A la sortie de la ville, près de la route de Beromünster.* Construite au 17e s., cette chapelle de pèlerinage est ornée d'un plafond décoré de peintures naïves, représentant l'arche de Noé, la tour de Babel et d'autres scènes de l'Ancien Testament.

Du terre-plein près du portail, on découvre une belle **vue**★ sur le lac, les Alpes et le Jura.

ENVIRONS

Beromünster – *7,5 km au Nord-Est.* Ce petit bourg, près duquel se dressent les installations de l'émetteur national suisse de langue alémanique, tire son nom du couvent (Münster) fondé en 980 par le comte Bero de Lenzbourg et transformé au 13e s. en prieuré de chanoines séculiers.

Église collégiale (Stiftskirche) ⊙ – Construite aux 11e-12e s., elle fut profondément remaniée à la mode baroque. Le porche est décoré de nombreux écussons figurant les armoiries des anciens chanoines. Le chœur, surélevé, est clos pour une très belle grille de fer forgé et orné de **stalles**★ remarquables, exécutées en 1609, dont les panneaux sculptés représentent divers épisodes de la vie du Christ. Le Trésor conserve le reliquaire de Warnebert (7e s.).

Musée du château (Schloss-Museum) ⊙ – Situé dans la tour médiévale du château, il présente, dans 8 salles, une sélection de meubles, tableaux, vêtements folkloriques, outils et objets anciens de Beromünster et ses environs, et offre en outre la reconstitution de l'imprimerie Helyas Helye, où a été imprimé, en 1470, le 1er livre de la Suisse.

SUSTENPASSSTRASSE★★★

Carte Michelin n° 427 plis 14, 15 ou 217 plis 8, 9, 10 – Schéma : BERNER OBERLAND

Construite de 1938 à 1945, la route du Susten (Wassen-Innertkirchen), la première des grandes chaussées alpestres de Suisse qui ait été étudiée pour la circulation automobile est un chef-d'œuvre de génie civil, qu'il faut apprécier par beau temps.

D'ANDERMATT A MEIRINGEN

62 km – environ 2 h 1/2 – itinéraire 1 *de la visite de l'Oberland bernois*

★**Andermatt** – *Voir à ce nom.*

Le parcours Andermatt-Wassen fait emprunter la route du St-Gothard, tracée au fond de la vallée de la Reuss.

★★**Les Schöllenen** – *Voir à ce nom.*

Göschenen – *Voir à ce nom.*

Wassen – *Voir à ce nom.*

Jusqu'à Meiendörfli, le tracé de la route du Susten (du français « souste » : entrepôt de marchandises), taillée dans le rocher, s'enchevêtre d'abord curieusement avec celui de la voie ferrée, pour franchir le ressaut séparant la vallée principale de la Reuss de la vallée « suspendue » de la Meienreuss (Meiental). Remarquer, dans l'axe de la vallée de la Reuss, en aval, la pyramide bien détachée du Bristen. Le trajet de Meiendörfli au col, en rampe continue, se déroule en corniche de plus en plus élevée au-dessus du Meiental qui paraît longtemps fermé, en amont, par les crêtes dentelées des Fünffingerstöck (Cinq Doigts). Aux approches des lacets supérieurs et du tunnel de faîte, le cirque terminal de la vallée apparaît à son tour, avec les faces triangulaires, de la Sustenspitz et du Klein Sustenshorn, qui dominent le col, au Sud.

Un panneau d'orientation, placé à 700 m de l'entrée Est du tunnel de faîte, permet de repérer les principaux sommets rocheux du groupe des Spannörter et le Bristen.

★★**Col du Susten** – *Grand parc de stationnement à l'entrée Ouest du tunnel (versant bernois).* La route atteint son point culminant (2 224 m) dans le tunnel de faîte, long de 325 m, percé sous le col géographique (alt. 2 259 m).

La montée se fait facilement à pied conduisant aux plus beaux **sites**★★★ qui s'offrent désormais, sur ce versant bernois.

Les 4 km qui séparent l'entrée Ouest du tunnel de faîte du « Himmelrank » sont un émerveillement continuel et doivent être parcourus à l'allure la plus réduite possible. Au premier plan, l'énorme coulée du **Steingletscher** vient mourir sous une masse de dépôts moraniques rougeâtres ; la tranche du glacier réapparaît cependant sur les rives d'un petit lac, où flottent souvent quelques icebergs miniatures. Pour repérer les sommets du groupe des Sustenhörner, aux étincelants névés, faire halte au panneau d'orientation du T.C.S., installé 2 km en contrebas du col.

★★**Himmelrank** – Les constructeurs de la route ont baptisé « virage du Paradis » ce lacet aménagé sur un versant rocailleux appelé autrefois l'« Enfer d'en-haut » par la population du Gadmental, plus soucieuse de l'aspect scabreux du passage que du **point de vue**★★ sur la combe verdoyante de Gadmen, en aval, et sur les sommets glacés des Sustenhörner (Sustenhorn, Gwächtenhorn), en amont. C'est dans le secteur compris entre l'hôtel Steingletscher et Gadmen que les ingénieurs ont fait preuve de la plus grande hardiesse : les lacets et les ponts construits au flanc de la paroi escarpée de Gschletter sont particulièrement audacieux.

★ **Lacet de Gschletter** — Ce lacet aménagé en terrain très escarpé forme **belvédère**★ au-dessus du Bas-Gadmental et des escarpements ruiniformes grandioses de la Gadmerflue et des Wendenstöcke.

Très haut, les formidables murailles crénelées de la Gadmerflue et des Wendenstöcke, détachées du Titlis, se profilent dans le ciel. Aux abords de Gadmen, le fond de la vallée commence à présenter des aspects alpestres plus riants, avec ses prairies piquetées d'érables. De Gadmen à Innertkirchen, on descend encore de deux gradins : le palier de Nessental se singularise par la multiplication des noyers et des arbres fruitiers, mais la vallée reste toujours étroite et peu peuplée. Au passage de l'ultime ressaut qui précède l'arrivée dans le bassin d'Innertkirchen, la vue se développe en direction des sommets très enneigés qui encadrent l'Urbachtal, à gauche des crêtes sombres et capricieusement découpées des Engelhörner.

Entre Innertkirchen et Meiringen, on suit la route du Grimsel (voir à ce nom).

★★ **Gorges de l'Aare (Aareschlucht)** — De la route de Meiringen, 1 km.

★ **Meiringen** — Voir à ce nom.

THUN★★

THOUNE-Berne — 38 211 habitants
Carte Michelin n° 427 pli 13 ou 217 plis 6, 7 — Schéma : BERNER OBERLAND
Alt. 560 m — Plan d'agglomération dans le guide Rouge Michelin Suisse

Thoune, l'une des villes les plus originales de la Suisse, occupe un **site**★★ admirable, en vue des neiges des Alpes bernoises. Établie à l'origine sur un îlot de l'Aare, à l'endroit où la rivière sort du lac de Thoune, la cité s'est développée peu à peu sur les rives voisines, au pied du Schlossberg, tout en passant des mains des Zähringen (voir à Bern) à celles des Kybourg. Cette seconde dynastie s'étant éteinte à son tour, Thoune passa sous le contrôle des « Messieurs de Berne ».

Tandis que les quartiers anciens sont groupés sur la rive droite de l'Aare, la ville moderne, avec ses usines métallurgiques, s'est étendue sur la rive gauche.

LA VILLE ANCIENNE

★ **Obere Hauptgasse** (28) — Centre d'une grande animation, cette rue présente une amusante particularité : les terrasses fleuries des maisons servent de trottoir, de sorte que l'on marche sur les toits des boutiques installées dans les arcades du rez-de-chaussée. De sa partie haute aux larges toits débordants, part un curieux escalier couvert (Kirchtreppe) qui conduit à l'église et au château de Kybourg.

THUN

Bälliz
Hauptgasse

Allmendstrasse	4
Bahnhofbrücke	6
Bahnhofplatz	7
Berntorplatz	10
Grabenstrasse	13
Guisanplatz	15
Kirchtreppe	19
Kuhbrücke	21
Marktgasse	24
Maulbeerplatz	25
Obere Hauptgasse	28
Rathausplatz	30
Waisenhausstrasse	40

B Stadtkirche

THUN

- ★ **Rathausplatz** (30) — Entourée de maisons à arcades et ornée d'une fontaine fleurie, cette place constitue avec le château qui la domine un ensemble pittoresque. Deux ponts de bois couverts (Obere Schleuse et Untere Schleuse), forment une retenue sur l'Aare.

- ★ **Château** (Schloss) — Accès par l'escalier couvert (Kirchtreppe) mentionné ci-dessus. Il dresse, à l'extrémité Nord du Schlossberg, son puissant donjon roman flanqué de quatre tourelles d'angle, qui abrite aujourd'hui le musée historique.

- ★ **Musée** (Schlossmuseum) ⊙ — Au centre du dispositif, la magnifique salle des Chevaliers renferme de très belles tapisseries – dont l'une provenant de la tente de Charles le Téméraire et tombée aux mains des Confédérés après la bataille de Grandson en 1476 –, des étendards, des cuirasses, des bahuts et des coffres sculptés.
  Au-dessous, trois étages abritent des céramiques (belle collection de vieux « Heimberg »), des restes archéologiques et des pièces folkloriques, ainsi que des instruments, du mobilier et de l'art populaire évoquant la Thoune du 18ᵉ s.
  Au-dessus est évoquée l'armée suisse (armes à feu, uniformes).
  Du dernier étage de la tour, il est possible d'accéder aux quatre tourelles d'angle. De là, on découvre un **panorama**★★ sur la ville et sur l'Aare, sur le lac de Thoune et, au-delà, sur les Alpes bernoises, du Stockhorn à l'Ouest au Niesen au Sud en passant par le groupe de la Jungfrau, l'Eiger et le Mönch.

- **Église** (Stadtkirche) (**B**) — A l'extrémité opposée du Schlossberg se dresse l'église paroissiale, dont la grosse tour octogonale, au clocher couvert de petites tuiles rondes, domine un porche décoré de fresques.
  De la terrasse de l'église, on a une très belle **vue**★★ sur la ville, le lac et les Alpes.

LES BORDS DU LAC

★★ **Jakobshübeli** — De cette colline aménagée en belvédère (table d'orientation), on découvre un **panorama**★★ semi-circulaire en direction du Stockhorn et de la Jungfrau.

Parc de Schadau — De ce parc agréable, situé au bord du lac et entourant un château, la **vue**★★ (table d'orientation) embrasse les sommets des Alpes bernoises, en particulier le Finsteraarhorn (alt. 4 274 m), point culminant de ce massif.

Panorama Wocher ⊙ — Installé dans le parc du château, ce tableau circulaire représente la ville de Thoune vers 1810.

ENVIRONS

Einigen — 11 km au Sud par la Frutigenstrasse.
A mi-chemin entre Thoune et Spiez, le charmant village d'Einigen est situé sur la rive Sud du lac de Thoune, face à un joli paysage de montagnes. L'église, petit édifice roman au crépi éclatant, est surmontée d'un clocheton effilé, couvert de tavaillons. Elle forme, avec le minuscule cimetière qui l'entoure et descend en gradins jusqu'au lac, un **ensemble**★ pittoresque.
L'intérieur de l'église est décoré de vitraux des 15ᵉ et 16ᵉ s.

THUNER SEE★★

Carte Michelin n° 427 pli 13 ou 217 pli 7 – Schéma : BERNER OBERLAND

Long de plus de 18 km, large de près de 4 km, et d'une profondeur atteignant 217 m, le lac de Thoune (ou Thuner See) est l'une des plus belles grandes nappes d'eau de Suisse et l'une des plus appréciées des touristes. Des services fréquents de vedettes relient les localités de ses rives. Mais son cadre admirable de montagnes vertes et de pics neigeux (parmi lesquels la Jungfrau) demeure son principal attrait.

DE THUN A INTERLAKEN

23 km – environ 1 h – itinéraire 5 *de la visite de l'Oberland bernois*

★★ **Thun** — Visite : 1 h 1/2. Voir à ce nom.
De Thoune à Oberhofen, la route, laissant en arrière la coquette banlieue résidentielle de Thoune, ne perd pas de vue les cimes des Alpes bernoises (Eiger-Mönch-Jungfrau et, plus à droite, la Blümlisalp). Au premier plan, sur la rive opposée, la pyramide du Niesen, la corne rocheuse du Stockhorn, sont particulièrement en valeur.

Château de Hünegg ⊙ — Invisible de la route, dans son parc boisé s'étageant face au lac de Thoune, cette grande demeure de 1863 est surtout intéressante par ses appartements 1900 constitués en musée d'« Art nouveau » allemand (Jugendstil), style néo-rococo parent du « Modern style » français. S'y ajoute, au 2ᵉ étage, une exposition d'œuvres du peintre bernois Martin Lauterburg, mort en 1960.

THUNER SEE

Oberhofen — Un **château** ⊙ s'avançant dans les eaux du lac et constituant un **tableau★** enchanteur *(illuminé la nuit)*, face aux cimes des Alpes bernoises, fait aussi d'Oberhofen un centre d'intérêt artistique. Tour d'habitation à l'origine (12ᵉ s.), le château a été agrandi et restauré aux 17ᵉ, 18ᵉ et 19ᵉ s. Il constitue maintenant une dépendance du Musée d'histoire de Berne, spécialement affectée aux présentations de mobiliers de style (Louis XIV, Louis XV, Empire) et aux collections d'art populaire intéressant la vie dans l'Oberland bernois. Le parc paysager aménagé au bord du lac n'est pas l'un des moindres agréments de la visite.

Entre Oberhofen et Merligen, se déroule un superbe **parcours en quai★★**, sur la rive la plus ensoleillée et la plus fleurie du lac, face à Spiez et au débouché de la vallée de la Kander. Le massif de la Blümlisalp, bien visible par cette trouée, se rapproche.

A Merligen l'itinéraire change de physionomie : la chaussée est taillée en corniche dans les abrupts du promontoire du Nase (Nez), au-dessus du bassin oriental du lac, dont les rives solitaires et escarpées contrastent avec la petite Riviera précédente.

Au cours de la descente, qui commence 1 km après Beatenbucht (point de départ du funiculaire de Beatenberg), s'offre une large vue sur la plaine du Bödeli enserrée par les chaînons boisés du Harder (à gauche) et du Rugen (à droite), et dominée à l'arrière-plan par les chicots rocheux de la Schynige Platte : c'est le site d'Interlaken. Avant Unterseen, on passe au pied des grottes de St-Béat (Beatushöhlen) cachées dans une impressionnante falaise d'où s'échappe une cascade.

★★★ Interlaken — Visite : 1 h. Voir à ce nom.

Val de TRAVERS

Carte Michelin n° 427 plis 11, 12 ou 217 pli 3 et 216 pli 12 — Schéma : JURA SUISSE

Cette vallée épanouie où coule l'Areuse et qui étale ses cultures autour de riantes agglomérations, entre des versants couverts de sapinières, est une des grandes voies de passage reliant la France à la Suisse (la route de Pontarlier à Neuchâtel l'emprunte). Elle permet surtout au touriste d'y adjoindre, à son extrémité Est, deux belles promenades pédestres : celle des gorges de l'Areuse et celle de la réserve du Creux du Van.

DE FLEURIER A NOIRAIGUE 28 km — environ 3 h

Môtiers — Ce village avenant conserve quelques maisons des 17ᵉ et 18ᵉ s. et une église, ancienne abbatiale gothique, refaite en 1679. Un ensemble de deux petits **musées** ⊙ contigus peut y justifier une halte : musée J.-J.-Rousseau (évocation de l'écrivain : documents, bustes, portraits) dans la partie préservée de la maison que Rousseau habita de 1762 à 1765 ; musée régional (ethnographie et histoire, artisanat : ateliers reconstitués de « pendulier », dentellier, tapissier ; fromagerie, distillerie…) dans une demeure du 18ᵉ s. à linteau sculpté et façade ornée de gros mascarons de pierre, appelée Maison des Mascarons.

Mines d'asphalte de Travers ⊙ — Le premier gisement fut découvert en 1711 par Eirini d'Eyrinys, un médecin grec qui publia plus tard un ouvrage intitulé *Dissertation sur l'asphalte ou ciment naturel*. Le précieux minerai, mélange étanche de calcaire et de bitume, fut exporté aux quatre coins du monde de 1830 à 1986, terme de son exploitation. Plus de 2 millions de tonnes de roches ont pu être extraites pendant cette période à travers quelque 100 km de galeries creusées par l'homme. La visite commence par le musée des Mines (coupe géologique, schéma sur l'extraction et l'exploitation de l'asphalte, photos sur le travail dans la mine, vieilles machines utilisées, pains d'asphalte, etc.), et se poursuit à pied dans plusieurs galeries (casque et lampe électrique fournis). Toutes les opérations sont alors commentées au cours de différentes haltes (abattage par tirs d'explosifs, ventilation, soutènement, chargement, acheminement) qui permettent de faire revivre une page de l'histoire industrielle et humaine du Val de Travers.

La Brévine — Cette petite région de plateau a reçu le surnom de « Sibérie suisse » en raison des températures extrêmes *(pouvant atteindre $-40°$)*, les plus basses de Suisse, qui y règnent en hiver. La route qui y monte procure de belles vues sur le Val de Travers. Le plateau, cerné de sapins vert sombre, quadrillé de murets délimitant cultures et pâturages (bovins, chevaux), parsemé de chalets, a pour centre le village de **La Brévine** (alt. 1 043 m) à l'orée d'une immense combe d'alpages.

★★ Creux du Van — Depuis la ferme Robert, compter en plus 2 h 1/2 AR de marche pour la montée au Soliat par un sentier aboutissant au Dos d'Âne, sur la crête même de la falaise, à 1 km à l'Est du Soliat. Une réserve naturelle (flore et faune protégées ; chamois, bouquetins) de 11 km², englobe cette typique « reculée » jurassienne que couronne un superbe cirque de falaises, ouvert en U vers les gorges de l'Areuse, au-dessus d'éboulis couverts de sapins. De son point culminant, le Soliat (alt. 1 463 m), très belle **vue★★** au Sud sur le lac de Neuchâtel en contrebas et les cimes des Alpes au-delà. Des sentiers longeant le sommet des falaises, jolies vues également sur l'intérieur verdoyant et mamelonné de la réserve, ainsi que sur les hauteurs du Jura, au Nord.

★ Gorges de l'Areuse — Visite : 1 h 1/2. Voir à ce nom.

TROGEN

Appenzell (Rhodes-Extérieures) — 2 042 habitants
Carte Michelin n° 427 pli 7 ou 216 Nord-Est du pli 21 — 10 km au Sud-Est de St-Gall
Schéma : APPENZELLERLAND — Alt. 903 m

Bâtie sur une colline du pittoresque Pays d'Appenzell, en vue du lac de Constance, Trogen possède de nombreuses maisons bourgeoises dont certaines sont de véritables palais, construits autrefois par de riches commerçants comme la famille Zellweger (17e-19e s.).

Landsgemeindeplatz — Cette place voit, toutes les années paires, se dérouler la traditionnelle réunion *(voir Introduction : La Démocratie en action)* des citoyens du demi-canton d'Appenzell — Rhodes-Extérieures, tandis que cette cérémonie a lieu à Hundwil les années impaires. Parmi les belles maisons qui l'entourent, on remarque l'Auberge « zur Krone », au toit en avancée et aux deux auvents superposés. La façade, percée d'une multitude de fenêtres, est ornée de motifs répétés où dominent les tons gris-bleu, vert et marron.

Hôtel de Ville (Rathaus) — D'un aspect sévère, c'est l'ancien hôtel Zellweger.

Village d'enfants Pestalozzi — *1 km au Sud par la route de Bühler.*
Ses maisons d'enfants sont affectées à des orphelins de guerre de différentes nations. Le Zurichois Pestalozzi (1746-1827) est honoré dans toute la Suisse pour son rôle d'éducateur et ses méthodes d'enseignement laissant une large part de responsabilité aux enfants.

Une vache couleur lilas

La vache Milka, sympathique emblème publicitaire vivant du chocolat Suchard, doit sa couleur – qui rappelle celle des emballages – à un spray inoffensif qui disparaît au premier coup de brosse. Plusieurs vaches de la race du Simmental ont ainsi joué les stars en décor naturel. « Schwalbe » a tourné six spots publicitaires dont le dernier en septembre 1991. Depuis, « Lori » et « Perle » ont repris le rôle.

UTZENSTORF

Berne — 3 356 habitants
Carte Michelin n° 427 pli 13 ou 216 pli 15 — Schéma : EMMENTAL

Beau village ombragé et fleuri. Sa petite église garde encore, dans l'abside, huit vitraux du 16e s. aux thèmes symboliques.

★ **Château de Landshut** ⊙ — A la sortie Nord d'Utzenstorf, dans un ravissant parc à l'anglaise magnifiquement ombragé et entouré d'eau (cygnes, canards, truites), s'élève ce riche manoir blanc des 17e et 18e s. à tourelles pointues, résidence des baillis de Berne jusqu'en 1798.
A l'intérieur des deux corps de logis accolés, les salles ont gardé leur lourd mobilier sculpté d'époque et leurs poêles de faïence monumentaux. Certaines abritent un **musée suisse de la chasse**, avec dioramas d'animaux naturalisés, trophées, procédés d'identification du gibier, leurres figuratifs ou silhouettes (2e étage), et surtout (au 2e étage, salle René La Roche) une remarquable collection d'armes de chasse seigneuriales (couteaux, piques, arbalètes, pistolets, fusils, et leurs accessoires) du 16e s. au 20e s. Dans les combles, musée d'histoire de l'agriculture suisse (outils, ustensiles, machines).

Le VALAIS★★

Carte Michelin n° 427 plis 12 à 14 et 21 à 23 ou 217 plis 14 à 19 et 219 plis 1 à 5

Dans la mosaïque des cantons helvétiques, le Valais représente une « marche » correspondant à l'un des compartiments les plus fermés des Alpes : la vallée du Rhône supérieur, de la Furka au Léman. Ce large sillon, presque complètement isolé des foyers économiques de Suisse alémanique, est animé en contrepartie, depuis deux millénaires, par un intense trafic international (passages du Grand-St-Bernard et du Simplon). Il doit sa très forte individualité régionale à la luminosité toute méditerranéenne de son ciel, aux convictions foncièrement catholiques de sa population et à son impressionnant développement industriel, qui n'exclut pas la survivance, dans les hautes vallées, des genres de vie les plus archaïques.

Il ne faut pas venir chercher ici des décors de pastorale, mais bien plutôt des évocations héroïques, comme à St-Maurice et Sion ou, à l'entrée des **vallées latérales**★★★, parsemées de chalets *(voir Introduction : La Suisse pittoresque)*, de « raccards » ou de « mazots » (petites constructions dressées sur pilotis et servant de grenier ou de resserre), les inoubliables tableaux de haute montagne qu'offre le Valais, pays du Cervin et du Mont Rose. Dans ces régions où la nature peut paraître hostile, il est fréquent de

Le VALAIS

rencontrer des croix de la Passion (croix en bois portant les instruments de la Passion), érigées jadis pour protéger habitants et voyageurs des dangers de la terrifiante montagne.

LE RHÔNE VALAISAN

De glacier en vignoble — Issu de la fameuse cataracte terminale du glacier du Rhône, le grand fleuve naît à 2 200 m d'altitude, traverse le bassin du Gletschboden, puis pénètre dans la vallée de Conches (Goms). Son débit doublé à Brigue par les eaux de la Massaki, descendue du glacier d'Aletsch, le Rhône cesse de jouer au torrent de montagne et file au fond de la plaine alluviale, encadrée de rudes versants rocailleux, qu'enfument les usines de Viège et de Gampel.
Le double obstacle que constitue le cône de déjection de l'Illgraben, recouvert par la forêt de Finges (Rynwald), et l'éboulement de Sierre se traduit par une importante brisure du profil longitudinal de la vallée. C'est là que s'est fixée la limite traditionnelle entre le Haut-Valais de langue allemande et le Valais « romand » *(carte dans le chapitre : Un peu d'histoire, Langues et religions).*

Raccard (ou mazot).
Les disques de pierre interdisent l'approche des rongeurs

Un premier essai de Provence — Abrité des vents océaniques par des barrières montagneuses géantes, le Valais central, compris entre Sierre et Martigny, constitue la région la plus sèche de Suisse. Sierre connaît des étés brûlants et ne reçoit pas plus d'eau, en moyenne, que Marseille. Favorisé par ces conditions climatiques méditerranéennes, le vignoble local maintient son emprise sur les coteaux rugueux, tout grillés de soleil, du versant exposé au Midi, face aux pentes forestières et pastorales des **mayens** (pâturages où les troupeaux font étape au mois de mai en attendant que les « alpes » supérieures soient libérées des neiges). *Une route du vignoble valaisan a été balisée entre Martigny et Sierre.*
Dès que les débordements du fleuve ont pu être contenus, la basse plaine alluviale du Rhône s'est couverte de vergers (abricotiers, pêchers), de plantations d'asperges, de carrés de maïs. Les fraisiers, autre spécialité valaisanne, sont même cultivés en grand dans certaines vallées latérales (vallées de Bagnes et d'Entremont), en vue des neiges éternelles.

De verger en lac — A Martigny, le Rhône reçoit la Drance et se replie brusquement vers le Nord, adoptant l'orientation de ce puissant affluent. Repoussé contre les derniers contreforts des Alpes bernoises par le cône de déjection du torrent de St-Barthélemy, le fleuve franchit la porte rocheuse de St-Maurice, et débouche dans le Bas-Valais. Cette plaine marécageuse, qui va s'évasant jusqu'aux rives du Léman n'est, politiquement, valaisanne que sur sa rive gauche. Le tumultueux phénomène naturel de la bataillère *(voir : Lac Léman)* est la dernière manifestation de ce Rhône montagnard, long de 170 km.

Les combats de reines

Ces manifestations, héritières d'une longue tradition, connaissent un grand succès dans le canton du Valais, au printemps et en automne. Elles rassemblent plus d'une centaine de vaches de la race d'Hérens, réparties en plusieurs catégories selon leur âge et leur poids. Ces animaux trapus, au corps large et musclé, à la forte encornure, vifs et belliqueux, bons producteurs de lait et de viande, s'affrontent lors de la mise à l'herbe, de la montée à l'alpage ou lors de la réunion de deux troupeaux. A l'issue de plusieurs combats par catégorie, dans lesquels la perdante s'enfuit, refusant l'affrontement, la vache qui a vaincu les autres est élue « reine » par le jury. Des prix sont accordés aux six premières. Les reines vont ensuite se rencontrer pour l'élection de la « reine des reines » qui recevra le titre de « reine cantonale ».

Le VALAIS

LA VIE EN VALAIS

Valaisans et Walser – Tout au long de la vallée du Rhône, devant les manifestations d'unité religieuse que lui offre le pays – le premier vestige daté (377) témoignant de la christianisation de l'Helvétie a été découvert à Sion – , le voyageur de langue française peut se croire en présence d'une civilisation purement latine. Mais, aux approches de Brig, les sonorités gutturales d'un dialecte germanique commencent à frapper l'oreille, tandis que le nom de Valais fait place à celui de « Wallis » – rappelant que le Haut-Valais a été envahi, à partir du 6e s., par des peuplades alémaniques qui, descendues probablement du Grimsel, ont poussé leurs établissements jusqu'à Sierre. Ces « Walser » essaimèrent souvent par la suite dans d'autres vallées méridionales des Alpes, constituant d'irréductibles foyers de germanisation en terre romane, à Davos par exemple.

Au cours de l'évolution politique du pays, ces rudes montagnards – en particulier les habitants du Val de Conches *(voir à Goms)* – ont représenté l'élément le plus farouchement démocratique. Grands démolisseurs de châteaux (Raron, Saillon), rognant sans trêve sur les droits temporels des princes-évêques de Sion et sur les prétentions des féodaux locaux, au besoin par la violence, ils ne trouvaient pas inconciliables leur idéal d'indépendance et la mise en tutelle des populations romandes du Bas-Valais.

Le « cardinal de Sion » – La personnalité du Valaisan **Mathieu Schiner** appartient à la Suisse tout entière. Ses grands desseins – coiffer la tiare et former autour du Gothard un puissant État englobant, outre les cantons primitifs, la Souabe, la Bourgogne, le Milanais – aboutirent à placer les Suisses dans le camp des vaincus de Marignan ; mais ce prélat fut l'un des grands précurseurs de la formation confédérale actuelle. De cette époque de relations très cordiales avec le Saint-Siège date (1506) le privilège de recrutement, toujours en vigueur, par lequel Jules II réserva aux seuls Suisses, et spécialement aux Valaisans de la vallée de Conches, le droit de revêtir le chatoyant uniforme de la garde pontificale, dessiné par Michel-Ange. La réunion du Valais à la Confédération ne date que de 1815 *(voir le chapitre : Un peu d'histoire)*. Auparavant, le pays traitait, en allié, avec les « XIII cantons » puis, Bonaparte régnant, connaissait les statuts éphémères de république protégée et de département français, sous le nom de Simplon.

Les bisses – La mise en valeur des replats dominant la vallée du Rhône a posé, dans le Valais central (de Martigny à Brig), de redoutables problèmes d'irrigation. La rareté des précipitations, l'encaissement des torrents au fond de gorges inaccessibles, ont

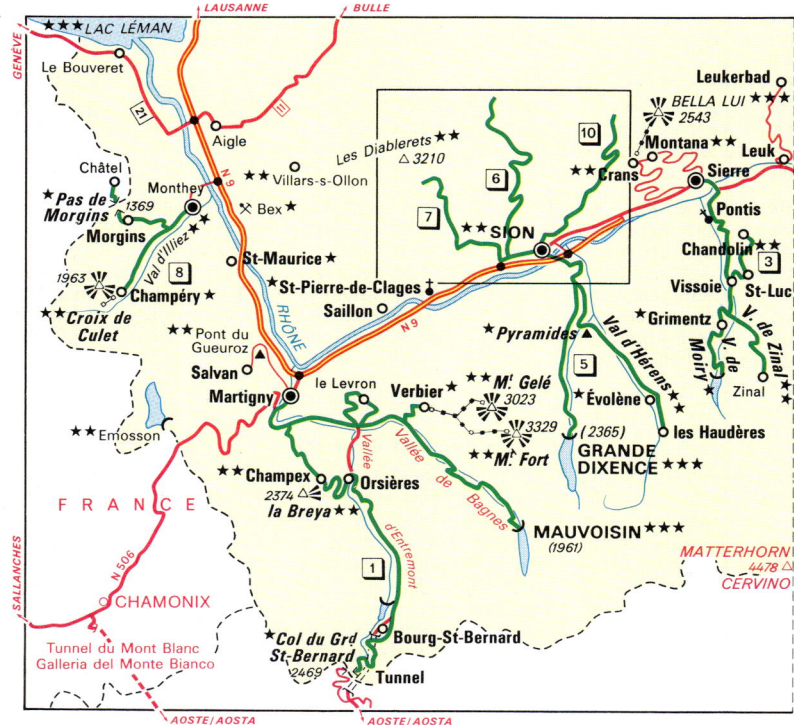

Le VALAIS

conduit à l'aménagement des bisses. Ces étroits canaux vont chercher presque à leur source les eaux de fonte glaciaire des affluents du Rhône, puis, malgré une pente insensible, cheminent à flanc de montagne. Lorsqu'une paroi rocheuse leur barrait le passage, on les a transformés en chéneaux de bois vertigineusement suspendus, dont l'entretien nécessite de dangereuses acrobaties.

La surveillance du bisse nourricier, la répartition minutieuse de ses eaux entre les différents ayants droit, tenaient une place très importante dans la vie des collectivités montagnardes.

Les progrès techniques réalisés dans le domaine des adductions d'eau ont fait abandonner bon nombre de ces aqueducs rustiques, dont certaines sections — celles établies sous bois par exemple — continuent cependant à offrir de charmants itinéraires de promenades.

On trouve dans le Valais (par exemple au-dessus de Verbier) une méthode originale de transport du lait par conduites : ces «lactoducs», reliant les alpages aux laiteries, totalisent 220 km environ.

EN REMONTANT LE RHÔNE

De Martigny à Gletsch *129 km — environ 1 h 1/2*

Entre Martigny et Sion, les longues sections rectilignes de la route, jadis bordée de peupliers par les ingénieurs des Ponts et Chaussées de Napoléon, ne prédisposent certes pas à la flânerie. Il faut pourtant savoir s'arrêter à bon escient : une cité aussi chargée d'histoire que Sion le mérite, de plus elle bénéficie d'un site remarquable.

Entre Sion et Brigue, nous recommandons, entre autres, l'excursion vers la haute terrasse de Montana.

De Brig à Gletsch, nous décrivons le Val de Conches *(voir à Goms)*, haute vallée du Rhône souvent parcourue trop rapidement par les automobilistes pressés de franchir le col de la Furka.

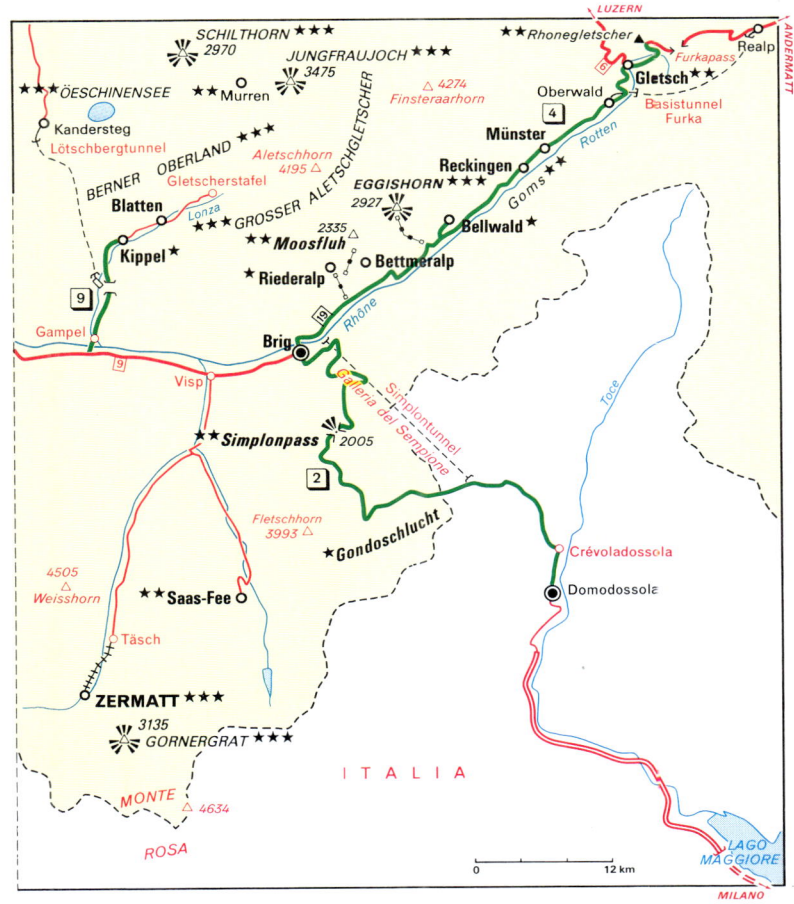

Le VALAIS

VISITE

Les itinéraires recommandés – Par ordre décroissant de la durée du parcours.
Voir les noms à l'index.

★ ① **Route du Grand-St-Bernard** – De Martigny au col du Grand-St-Bernard – environ 3 h 1/2.
★★ ② **Simplonpassstrasse** – De Domodossola à Brig – environ 3 h.
★ ③ **Val d'Anniviers** – Route de Sierre à Zinal – environ 2 h 1/2.
★★ ④ **Goms** – Route de Brig à Gletsch – environ 2 h.
★★ ⑤ **Val d'Hérens** – Route de Sion aux Haudères – environ 2 h.
★★ ⑥ **Route de Sanetsch** – Au départ de Sion – environ 1 h 1/2.
★ ⑦ **Route de Derborence** – Au départ de Sion – environ 1 h.
★ ⑧ **Val de Morgins** – Route de Monthey à Châtel – environ 1 h.
★ ⑨ **Lötschatel** – Route de la bifurcation de Gampel à Kippel – environ 3/4 h.
★ ⑩ **Route de Tseuzier** – Au départ de Sion – environ 1/2 h.

VALLORBE

Vaud – 3 271 habitants
Carte Michelin n° 427 pli 11 ou 217 pli 2 – Schéma : JURA SUISSE – Alt. 769 m

Sur le revers Sud du chaînon jurassien du Mont d'Or, le bourg de Vallorbe doit son animation à ses activités industrielles (petite métallurgie, industrie du plastique) et, surtout, à sa gare-frontière bien connue des habitués de la ligne du Simplon.
Pour l'automobiliste arrivant de France, Vallorbe est une base de charmants circuits d'une journée en Jura vaudois (Romainmôtier, Vallée de Joux, Dent de Vaulion, etc.).

Musée du Fer et du Chemin de fer ⊙ – *Accès par l'Office du tourisme.*

Musée du Fer – Aménagé au bord de l'Orbe sur le site des anciennes Grandes Forges, il rappelle la vocation métallurgique de la région et montre l'évolution du travail du fer : objets de l'âge du fer ; meules, enclumes et outils fabriqués par les Grandes Forges ; deux forges anciennes : l'une telle qu'elle était avant la fin de son activité et l'autre avec un forgeron travaillant comme autrefois ; expositions de réalisations actuelles en mécanique de précision et techniques de pointe. A l'extérieur, trois roues à aubes fournissent l'énergie motrice.

Musée du Chemin de fer – Les grandes heures de Vallorbe sur la ligne du Simplon sont présentées de façon très vivante à partir d'une maquette montrant la gare en 1908 et d'un diaporama. Matériel ferroviaire, outils de cheminots, billets, anciennes affiches, costume de contrôleur complètent l'évocation du développement du chemin de fer dans la région. Au second étage, le visiteur peut faire fonctionner le train de son choix sur un réseau miniature.

Fort de Vallorbe ⊙ – Construit juste avant la Seconde Guerre mondiale dans le roc et face à la frontière, cet ouvrage de défense se compose de trois fortins, six casemates et points d'observations puissamment armés, reliés par des galeries souterraines. A 30 m sous terre, salle des machines (filtrage de l'air, production de courant), dépôt de munitions, central téléphonique, casernement, dortoirs, cuisine, réfectoire, mess, salle d'opération, infirmerie, cabinet dentaire) s'offrent à la vue et à l'étonnement du visiteur. Mannequins, armes, documents, effets sonores complètent l'évocation de la vie du fort, dans lequel pouvait loger une centaine d'hommes.

ENVIRONS

Source de l'Orbe – *3 km, plus 1/2 h à pied AR. Quitter Vallorbe par la route de la Vallée de Joux ; prendre à gauche la route signalée « Source-Grottes », en légère descente. Laisser la voiture près de la centrale électrique.*
Un chemin ombragé de beaux hêtres ou sapins mène au petit cirque rocheux d'où sourd l'Orbe : il s'agit, en réalité, d'une résurgence des eaux des lacs de Joux et Brenet.

Grottes ⊙ – A l'issue d'un tunnel d'accès de 80 m, une galerie artificielle a été aménagée, mettant en valeur, le long du parcours, une succession de colonnes, draperies, stalactites (« tournées », ou fistuleuses : on remarque un « macaroni » de 4 m) et stalagmites dessinant de belles arabesques, jusqu'à la salle Noire offrant le spectacle des eaux tumultueuses de l'Orbe, mal contenues par les étonnantes parois rocheuses.
Le **trésor des Fées** ⊙ rassemble une riche collection de minéraux provenant de la résurgence de l'Orbe.

VERBIER★

Valais — 1 800 habitants

Carte Michelin n° 427 pli 21 ou 219 Nord du pli 2 — Schéma : VALAIS
Alt. 1 500 m (Verbier-station) — Plan dans le guide Rouge Michelin Suisse

Précédée de **Verbier-Village** aux deux églises (rurale et moderne), la jeune station valaisanne de Verbier, disséminée sur le versant ensoleillé de la vallée de Bagnes, en vue des massifs du Grand Combin et du Mont-Blanc, poursuit l'extension de ses luxueux hôtels et chalets dans ce **site**★★ privilégié.
L'amphithéâtre de versants régulièrement inclinés convergeant vers la nouvelle agglomération réunit en effet les conditions de topographie et d'exposition idéales pour les skieurs, qui trouvent là un cadre très ample et reposant, et un équipement mécanique très développé, adapté à leur goût pour la piste.
Verbier est aussi, pour l'adepte du ski de randonnée, un point de départ de la course de la « Haute Route », dont Zermatt ou Saas-Fee marquent le terminus.

★★ **Mont Fort** ⊙ — Alt. 3 329 m. *Accès (environ 3/4 h) : par télécabine de Verbier jusqu'aux Ruinettes ; par une navette (5 mn) ou à pied (1/2 h) jusqu'à la Chaux ; par le téléphérique Jumbo jusqu'aux Gentianes, puis par un autre téléphérique jusqu'au sommet.*
Domaine des skieurs et des amateurs de snowboard même en été tant la neige et la glace y sont persistantes, le Mont Fort offre, par temps clair, un très vaste **tour d'horizon**★★ (tables d'orientation) embrassant les Alpes bernoises (Eiger), italiennes (Cervin), valaisannes (Mont Fort, Grand Combin) et françaises (Mont Blanc).

★★ **Mont Gelé** ⊙ — Alt. 3 023 m. *Accès (environ 3/4 h) : par télécabine de Verbier aux Ruinettes ; par téléphérique jusqu'à Attelas I ; par un 2ᵉ téléphérique jusqu'à Attelas II (près du sommet).*
De la croix marquant le sommet rocailleux du Mont Gelé, vaste **tour d'horizon**★★ embrassant au Sud le massif du Grand Combin et ses glaciers, à l'Est le Mont Fort et ses glaciers, au Nord les cimes des Diablerets, à l'Ouest le Mont de Pierre Avoi (surmonté d'un chicot rocheux), Verbier et la vallée d'Entremont.

VEVEY★

Vaud — 15 968 habitants

Carte Michelin n° 427 pli 12 ou 217 pli 19 — Schéma : Lac LÉMAN — Alt. 400 m
Plan dans le guide Rouge Michelin Suisse

Vevey occupe, au débouché de la vallée de la Veveyse et au pied du Mont Pèlerin, un fort beau **site**★ face aux Alpes de Savoie qui constituent, avec la nappe bleue du Léman, un magnifique arrière-plan.
Déjà capitale du vignoble de Lavaux, Vevey est devenue, au 19ᵉ s., le berceau de l'industrie suisse des produits lactés, chocolatés et diététiques : le puissant groupe Nestlé y garde son siège et son laboratoire central, doublé d'une usine-pilote.
Elle est en outre l'une des plus agréables villégiatures de la Riviera vaudoise.
Tous les 25 ans environ — la dernière fois, en août 1977 — la ville connaît les fastes inouïs de la **fête des Vignerons**, manifestation folklorique d'une ampleur unique en Europe, qui se termine en apothéose par une farandole générale célébrant Bacchus.
Les marchés folkloriques (le samedi matin en juillet et août) et le festival international du film de comédie qui a lieu tous les ans en août, font également partie des traditions.
Vevey est également la ville d'adoption du sympathique Charlot alias Charlie Chaplin, dont on peut voir la statue au bord du lac.

CURIOSITÉS

Église St-Martin — Bâti sur une terrasse dominant la ville, l'édifice actuel qui date de 1530 est surmonté d'une grosse tour carrée flanquée de quatre clochetons d'angle. À l'origine, se trouvait une église du 11ᵉ s. dont les murs ont été découverts lors de travaux de fouilles. De la terrasse (table d'orientation), on découvre une **vue**★ étendue sur la ville, le lac Léman et les Alpes.

Musée Jenisch ⊙ — Installé dans un grand bâtiment du siècle dernier, il comprend deux sections.
Au rez-de-chaussée, le **cabinet des estampes** qui rassemble de nombreuses gravures des grands maîtres du passé (Dürer, Rembrandt, Le Lorrain, Belletto, Corot) et d'artistes suisses contemporains.
Au 1ᵉʳ étage, le **musée des Beaux-Arts** expose surtout des tableaux ou aquarelles d'artistes suisses contemporains (Robert, Bocion, Steinlen, Hodler, Poncet, Gimmi), mais aussi des œuvres de Courbet (dont un Coucher de soleil sur le Léman et le curieux bronze de La Mouette), Bissier, Tal-Coat, Music, Valenti et Kokoschka.

VEVEY

Musée historique du Vieux-Vevey ⊙ – Aménagé dans le château, ancienne demeure des baillis bernois, il est consacré à l'histoire de la région et renferme un très beau mobilier, de l'époque gothique au 18ᵉ s., une collection de petite ferronnerie et de coffrets, des costumes et des souvenirs régionaux. Au 1ᵉʳ étage, le **musée de la Confrérie des Vignerons** conserve les maquettes des costumes ayant figuré aux précédentes fêtes des Vignerons (depuis 1819), ainsi que des estampes, des documents et des bannières ayant trait à ces festivités grandioses.

Musée suisse de l'appareil photographique ⊙ – Ce musée présente sur cinq étages de nombreux appareils ou instruments photographiques suisses et étrangers, de la fin du 19ᵉ s. à nos jours, et la reconstitution d'un laboratoire de 1930. On y appréciera des raretés telles qu'une « camera obscura » ancêtre de l'appareil photographique, l'objectif Chevalier utilisé par Niepce et Daguerre, des « foldings » de 1885-1890, une « photosphère » de 1888, un « physiographe » de 1895. On pourra également manipuler plusieurs modèles et s'exercer à des jeux sur ordinateurs.

Alimentarium ⊙ – *Rue du Léman.*
Depuis 1985 un bâtiment néo-classique abrite le musée de l'Alimentation, créé par Nestlé. Les trois sections actuellement ouvertes au public informent sur les différents aspects de l'alimentation (production, transformation, conservation, préparation, consommation). L'exposition, conçue de façon didactique et moderne, montre que les problèmes liés à l'alimentation varient selon l'époque, le lieu géographique et la catégorie ethnique et sociale. Des présentations audiovisuelles ainsi que des jeux électroniques complètent la visite.

ENVIRONS

★★ **Mont-Pèlerin (Station)** – *Alt. 810 m. Circuit de 25 km – environ 1/2 h. Schéma p. 134.* Quitter Vevey par la route de Châtel-St-Denis-Fribourg. 2,5 km après avoir laissé à gauche la route de Chardonne, tourner à gauche vers Attalens, puis encore une fois à gauche, à angle aigu, en direction du Pèlerin.
Sur plusieurs sections, les routes forment « corniche » à travers les vignes.
Des abords de la gare d'arrivée du funiculaire, s'offre une large **vue**★★ sur le Léman et les crêtes des Alpes vaudoises (Dent de Jaman, Rochers de Naye, Tour d'Aï).
Le retour, par Chardonne et Chexbres, s'effectue le long de routes magnifiquement tracées en vue des Dents du Midi et des sommets du Haut-Chablais savoyard.

La Tour-de-Peilz – *2 km par la route nᵒ 9 vers Montreux.*
Le château construit au 13ᵉ s. par les comtes de Savoie a subi plusieurs modifications au 18ᵉ s. De son rôle défensif subsistent les remparts, deux tours d'angle et les fossés.
L'intérieur sert de cadre au **musée suisse du Jeu** ⊙ qui présente des jeux de toutes les époques et de tous les pays, classés selon cinq thèmes : jeux de l'éducation, de stratégie, de simulation, d'adresse et de hasard. Chaque thème met l'accent sur les différentes qualités requises et est illustré par plusieurs exemples. Dans chaque salle le visiteur a la possibilité de mettre en pratique son habilité en se livrant à un jeu. Plusieurs pièces exposées laissent apparaître une recherche artistique dans leur réalisation, ainsi des figurines d'échec en ivoire ou en os sculpté.
En contournant le château par la gauche, on arrive au port de plaisance ; on peut ensuite longer le bord du lac. En face, côté suisse, se dresse le Grammont (alt. 2 172 m).

Blonay – *4 km à l'Est.*
Le **chemin de fer-musée Blonay-Chamby** ⊙ fait revivre avec panache une ligne ferroviaire ouverte en 1902 et fermée en 1966. Tramways électriques ou vieux trains à vapeur transportent les voyageurs sur un parcours sinueux en montée de 2,950 km. A mi-parcours, l'ancien dépôt, aménagé en musée, rassemble de vieilles machines : fourgon postal (1914), locomotive de la ligne les Brenets-le Locle (1890), tramway de Fribourg (1904), etc.

VIERWALDSTÄTTER SEE★★★

Lac des QUATRE CANTONS – Carte Michelin nᵒ 427 plis 14, 15
ou 216 plis 17, 18 et 217 plis 9, 10

La région du lac des Quatre-Cantons offre au touriste son diorama de collines et de montagnes, ses petites cités d'atmosphère traditionnelle, ses innombrables sommets-belvédères. Le cachet d'une ville comme Lucerne symbolise, pour bien des passants, le charme de cette « Suisse centrale » que la route du col du Brünig (ou de Sachseln ; voir *Sachselner Strasse*) met commodément en relation avec l'Oberland bernois.
Quant au lac lui-même, premier responsable du pittoresque de la région grâce à son tracé capricieux, et qu'entourent du surplus d'importantes nappes d'eau « satellites » (lacs de Sempach et de Zoug, Agerisee, lac de Lauerz, Alpnachersee, Sarnersee) tandis que le cours de la Reuss s'y engage au Sud pour en ressortir au Nord (à Lucerne), il comporte trois bassins distincts, d'Ouest en Est : « lacs » de Vitznau, de Gersau-Beckenried et d'Uri, qu'engendrent deux étranglements de ses rives. Sa superficie totale

VIERWALDSTÄTTER SEE

(114 km²) fait du lac des Quatre-Cantons le deuxième – après celui de Neuchâtel – des grands lacs entièrement suisses.
Ses belvédères principaux sont le Pilate et le Rigi-Kulm.

UN PEU D'HISTOIRE

Le sanctuaire national suisse – Le moindre coin de terre a ici son héros, son champ de bataille, sa chapelle commémorative, ses ruines féodales dont les pans de murs croulants rappellent quelque brutale

Lac des Quatre-Cantons

flambée de fureur émancipatrice. C'est ici que la démocratie helvétique a trouvé son berceau.
Bien avant les débuts de la Confédération, les **Waldstätten** (cantons forestiers) riverains du lac menaient déjà, à l'exemple des populations de maintes vallées isolées des Alpes, une vie toute remplie d'obligations communautaires. L'exploitation des forêts, la mise en valeur des alpages, la répartition du « fruit » du troupeau ne cessaient d'exiger des réunions, des discussions et des élections. Rompus à de tels usages, les Waldstätten s'accommodaient sans trop de peine d'une allégeance symbolique à l'Empereur, toute l'Helvétie relevant alors du Saint-Empire Romain Germanique. Le Pays d'Uri, auquel sa situation sur l'itinéraire du St-Gothard valait des ménagements particuliers, s'était même vu garantir, dès 1231, son rattachement direct à l'empire.
Cette relative autonomie apparaît menacée lorsque la maison de Habsbourg-Autriche, soucieuse d'administrer efficacement son patrimoine dans la région, met en place, sans tenir compte des susceptibilités locales, un corps de fonctionnaires intéressés au revenu de leur charge. Ces baillis se font vite détester : se voir imposer, du dehors, un juge qui ne soit ni un concitoyen ni un pair, est la suprême offense pour un homme de condition libre.
La situation devient critique lorsque les Habsbourg accèdent au trône impérial (1273). Aussi, à la mort de Rodolphe, qui laisse présager une élection très controversée et une situation politique difficile, les représentants de Schwyz, Uri et Unterwald se réunissent-ils pour conclure une alliance perpétuelle. Ce pacte d'entraide qui, sans préconiser la désobéissance vis-à-vis des seigneurs, rejette tout système administratif et judiciaire imposé de l'extérieur, est considéré par les Suisses comme l'acte de naissance de la Confédération. Ses textes originaux sont conservés à Schwyz et son anniversaire (1er août 1291) est célébré comme fête nationale.
La victoire de Morgarten (1315), remportée sur les troupes de Léopold d'Autriche, marqua l'affranchissement définitif des trois cantons « primitifs ».

L'aurore de la liberté – Une telle évolution, surprenante dans la société féodale de l'époque, doit son retentissement à l'interprétation légendaire qu'on en fit dès le 15e s. et au drame de **Guillaume Tell** que Schiller (1804) a versé au trésor de la littérature germanique. Il ne s'agit plus d'une lutte tenace faisant alterner les négociations avec les coups de main, mais d'une conjuration organisée par les trois communautés, de Schwyz, Uri et Unterwald, présentées comme victimes du despotisme qu'incarne le Bailli Gessler, et solennellement nouée sur la prairie du Rütli, en face de Brunnen, par 33 représentants de ces communautés. Après avoir été condamné par Gessler à la fameuse épreuve de la pomme, l'archer Guillaume Tell devient le bras justicier de la conspiration : il exécute Gessler dans le chemin creux (Hohle Gasse) de Küssnacht, ouvrant la voie à une ère de liberté. Depuis lors, l'épisode du Rütli n'a pas cessé d'être la source vive de la tradition nationale suisse.

Le « protecteur de la Patrie » – Le Pays d'Unterwald, et plus précisément le demi-canton d'Obwald, que traverse la route du Brünig, s'honore de compter parmi ses enfants l'ermite **Nicolas de Flüe** (canonisé en 1947), dont l'intervention conciliatrice a marqué le tempérament patriotique suisse. Né en 1417 d'une famille de paysans aisés, « Frère Nicolas » (Bruder Klaus) – ainsi l'appellent ses concitoyens –, tout en montrant un goût très vif pour l'oraison et la vie contemplative, assume d'abord toutes les charges familiales et civiques auxquelles un homme de sa valeur peut prétendre. Mais, à cinquante ans, ce père de dix enfants, obéissant à un appel irrésistible, se sépare des siens pour mener la vie d'ascète à laquelle il aspire, dans la solitude du Ranft *(voir à ce nom)*, à l'entrée du Melchtal.
Cependant, les confédérés des « VIII cantons » de l'époque sont aux prises avec de graves difficultés intérieures. Deux politiques s'opposent, celle des « Villes » gouvernées par des oligarchies bourgeoises prudentes et celle des « Pays » (Länder) montagnards restés fidèles aux pratiques de la démocratie directe et donc plus sensibles aux poussées d'opinion.

VIERWALDSTÄTTER SEE

En 1477, les riverains du lac des Quatre-Cantons entrent en effervescence en apprenant que Lucerne, de concert avec Zurich et Berne, a conclu séparément une alliance avec Fribourg et Soleure. Lucerne ayant maintenu sa position, malgré toutes les objurgations de ses voisins d'Uri, Schwyz et Unterwald, le conflit devient aigu. En désespoir de cause, le curé de Stans se rend au Ranft consulter Frère Nicolas. Il en rapporte un admirable appel à la concorde, grâce auquel l'accord peut se faire en quelques instants sur la base d'un compromis (1481).

LE LAC EN BATEAU

Pour agrémenter un séjour, un périple en bateau sur le lac, complété par l'ascension de l'un des sommets qui l'encadrent, est indispensable : certains sites côtiers – et en premier lieu la prairie historique du Rütli – ne sont d'ailleurs accessibles, de façon pratique, que par voie d'eau.

★★★ 1 LES RIVES NORD

De Lucerne à Altdorf 54 km – environ 2 h 1/2

★★★ **Luzern** – *Visite : 3 h. Voir à ce nom.*

Entre Lucerne, Küssnacht et Weggis, la route, tracée dans une opulente campagne plantée de noyers et d'arbres fruitiers, contourne les ramifications du «lac de Lucerne» et du «lac de Küssnacht», se rapprochant des croupes accidentées du Rigi, aux affleurements rocheux rougeâtres. Au Sud, les arrière-plans montagneux du Nidwald (région de Stans-Engelberg) se distinguent assez mal, contrairement au Pilate reconnaissable à ses arêtes découpées.

Merlischachen – De belles maisons de bois à combles aigus offrent ici quelques excellents exemples du type de construction de la Suisse centrale *(voir illustration dans le chapitre : La Maison paysanne).*

Chapelle de la Reine Astrid (Astridkapelle) – La route longe ce petit sanctuaire, élevé à la suite du tragique accident du 29 août 1935, dans le verger où fut précipitée la voiture royale. Une simple croix marque l'endroit où fut retrouvée la reine Astrid de Belgique, après le choc fatal contre l'arbre aujourd'hui entouré d'une grille de protection.

Hohle Gasse – *De Küssnacht* (lieu de séjour), *3 km AR par la route d'Arth (N° 2), plus 1/4 h à pied AR.* Laissant la voiture à l'hôtel Hohle Gasse, prendre le chemin creux (en allemand «hohle Gasse») en montée, irrégulièrement pavé, où, suivant la tradition, Tell s'embusqua pour faire justice à Gessler. Le chemin, en sous-bois, aboutit à la chapelle commémorative qui représente pour tous les Suisses un pèlerinage patriotique indispensable.

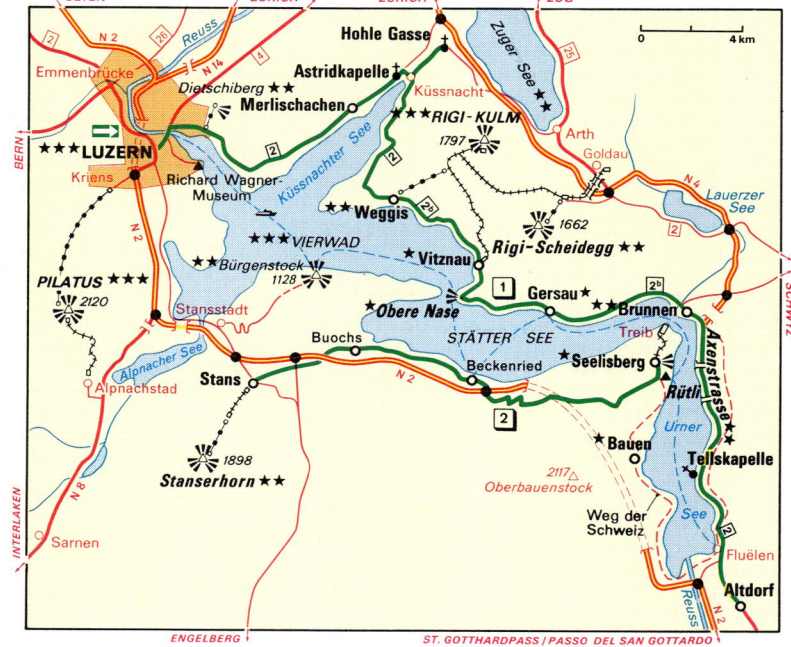

VIERWALDSTÄTTER SEE

★★ **Weggis** – Reine des stations situées sur les rives alpestres du lac des Quatre-Cantons, Weggis s'allonge en vue du Pilate et des montagnes d'Unterwald, le long d'un quai-promenade menant au promontoire d'Hertenstein : l'agglomération touristique se trouve ainsi à l'abri du trafic automobile qui suit la côte de Küssnacht à Brunnen.
Les plaisirs de l'eau, les promenades sur les dernières pentes du Rigi plantées de vergers et même de quelques espèces méridionales – l'influence du fœhn allant de pair avec une exposition plein midi –, les distractions mondaines, y sont autant de programmes de choix.
A partir de Weggis, le parcours des rives du lac révèle des paysages sans cesse renouvelés.

★ **Vitznau** – Les touristes peuvent abandonner leur voiture quelques heures dans cette élégante station, située entre le Rigi et le lac, pour monter au Rigi-Kulm en chemin de fer à crémaillère, le premier chemin de fer de montagne construit en Europe (1871).

★★★ **Rigi-Kulm** – De Vitznau, environ 3 h AR dont 1 h 1/4 de chemin de fer à crémaillère. Voir Le Rigi.

★ **Obere Nase** – Le coude très prononcé que décrit la chaussée au passage de ce cap est aménagé en **belvédère**★. Ce « Nez », projeté par un contrefort du Rigi, et l'Untere Nase, extrême avancée du Bürgenstock, qui lui fait face délimitent un détroit large de 825 m seulement, mettant en communication deux bassins d'allure bien différente : en quelques centaines de mètres, on passe d'un « lac de Vitznau », borné, au Sud, par l'éperon boisé du Bürgenstock, à un « lac de Gersau-Beckenried » étalé dans un cadre beaucoup plus ouvert et distrayant Le Pilate reste le seul repère familier.

★ **Gersau** – Dans l'un des **sites**★★ les plus ouverts des rivages alpestres du lac, la minuscule « République de Gersau » – tel fut le statut du bourg entre 1390 et 1817 –, rattachée aujourd'hui au canton de Schwyz, est devenue une station familiale, connue des gourmets pour ses spécialités de poisson.
Aux approches de Brunnen se dessine peu à peu le bassin bocager de Schwyz dominé par les pitons jumeaux des Mythen. Plus à droite, sous les falaises arquées du Fronalpstock, s'allonge la terrasse de Morschach. Le moment est alors venu de contourner la baie de Brunnen, à laquelle répond le saillant de Seelisberg.

★★ **Brunnen** – *Voir à ce nom.*
De Brunnen à Flüelen en partie au-dessus du romantique **lac d'Uri** (Urnersee), véritable fjord aux eaux d'un bleu profond, dont les rives sont jalonnées de pèlerinages patriotiques évoquant la naissance de la Confédération (Rütli, chapelle de Tell), se situe la corniche de l'Axenstrasse.

★★ **Axenstrasse** – Cette section de route, l'une des plus fameuses de l'itinéraire du St-Gothard et l'une des plus encombrées de toute la Suisse – on y a compté près de 10 000 voitures par jour, en plein été –, a été ouverte au siècle dernier dans les falaises qui plongent dans le lac d'Uri. Auparavant, le recours au bateau était indispensable pour le trajet de Brunnen à Flüelen. Le passage comporte deux tronçons d'allure différente :
– Entre Brunnen et Sisikon, la route est tracée en corniche face au promontoire de Seelisberg – dont la tache vert clair de la prairie du Rütli interrompt les pentes forestières – en vue des deux pointes jumelles de l'Uri-Rotstock. A la faveur d'un virage au-dessus de la voie ferrée, on se trouve exactement face au Rütli.
– Entre Sisikon et Flüelen, le trajet a changé de caractère depuis la construction d'un tunnel unique remplaçant la fameuse galerie ajourée *(désaffectée et interdite aux autos)* dont la photographie a été diffusée à des millions d'exemplaires.

Guillaume Tell par F. Hodler

VIERWALDSTÄTTER SEE

Chapelle de Tell (Tellskapelle) – *De l'hôtel Tellsplatte, 1/2 h à pied AR par un sentier en forte descente.* Édifiée dans un **site ★** solitaire, au bord du lac d'Uri, cette chapelle commémore l'un des épisodes les plus dramatiques de l'histoire de Tell : prisonnier de Gessler à l'issue de l'épreuve de la pomme, le vaillant arbalétrier est jeté dans une barque, qu'une subite tempête assaille ; le bailli et ses sbires doivent faire appel au concours de leur captif. Celui-ci en profite pour diriger l'esquif vers le rivage, bondit sur une plate-forme rocheuse et repousse aussitôt d'un violent coup de pied l'embarcation dans les flots déchaînés.
Les premières maisons d'Altdorf annoncent la fin de la randonnée.

Altdorf – *Voir à ce nom.*

★ ② **ROUTE DE SEELISBERG** *22 km – environ 1 h – description à Stans*

AUTRES CURIOSITÉS

★★★ **Pilatus** – *Voir à ce nom.*

★★ **Rigi-Scheidegg** – *Accès au départ de Schwyz. Voir à ce nom.*

Stans – *Voir à ce nom.*

★★ **Stanserhorn** – *Accès au départ de Stans. Voir à ce nom.*

★ **Bauen** – *Accès au départ d'Altdorf. Voir à ce nom.*

VILLARS-SUR-OLLON ★★
Vaud
Carte Michelin n° 427 pli 12 ou 217 Est du pli 14
Schéma : ALPES VAUDOISES – Alt. 1 253 m

Villars, Chesières et Arveyes ne constituent qu'une seule et même station, suspendue à 800 m au-dessus du Bas-Valais. C'est la station d'altitude la mieux développée de la Suisse française en même temps que l'une des plus facilement accessibles, face aux lointains horizons, en demi-cercle, des Alpes françaises, des Dents du Midi et de la chaîne des Muverans, où se situent tour à tour le Mont Blanc, le glacier du Trient et les sommets des Diablerets.

LES STATIONS

Villars – L'agglomération principale bénéficie d'une bonne exposition, sur une esplanade de prés-bois favorisée d'un ensoleillement intense, en vue des Dents du Midi, se présentant de chant. Elle dispose d'hôtels de toutes catégories. Un équipement varié, comprenant golf et piscine, y permet les activités estivales les plus détendues, aussi bien que les plus sportives. En hiver, après s'être entraînés sur les pentes voisines des hôtels, les skieurs ont la possibilité d'emprunter un chemin de fer à crémaillère ou deux télécabines pour atteindre le Roc d'Orsay, les Chaux ou Bretaye nouveau point de départ d'un réseau de remontées mécaniques en éventail, leur permettant de gagner les croupes de Chaux Ronde et de Chamossaire (point culminant : 2 113 m). La patinoire artificielle attire de nombreux amateurs ainsi que des curieux, venus de très loin pour assister aux spectacles qui y sont présentés.

Chesières et Arveyes – Ces stations se recommandent aux séjournants plus sensibles au calme qu'à la proximité du centre mondain.
Le panorama d'Arveyes permet d'apercevoir le massif du Mont-Blanc, à la droite du glacier du Trient et de l'Aiguille Verte.

ENVIRONS

De Villars à Pont de Nant – *22 km. Quitter Villars au Sud, direction Bex.*
La route, en descente, procure bientôt une **vue** plongeante sur la vallée boisée de la Gryonne qu'un hardi pont courbe en béton fait peu après enjamber. La Croix de Javerne et la Dent de Morcles se dressent en avant.

La Barboleusaz – Alt. 1 211 m. Station de sports d'hiver dans un joli site en vue des Diablerets. On peut de là se rendre au majestueux domaine skiable des **Chaux ★** *(5 km par route étroite et sinueuse ; en hiver, accès par télécabine),* ou, par une pittoresque petite route *(6 km)* remontant le joli torrent de l'Avançon, au **refuge de Solalex ★** (alt. 1 466 m) dans un cirque d'alpages aux murailles couronnées de névés ou éboulées, au pied des Diablerets.

Gryon – Vieux village en balcon sur la vallée de l'Avançon.
La route sinue entre sapins et mélèzes. 2 km avant Bex, tourner à gauche vers les Plans. A Frenières, remarquer à gauche le site perché de Gryon que l'on vient de quitter. Après les Plans on monte, en sous-bois, parallèlement à un torrent tumultueux.

★ **Pont de Nant** – Beau cirque rocheux égayé de sapins et d'épicéas, au pied des glaciers du Grand Muveran. Un jardin alpin de rocaille présente, outre un bassin à nénuphars, plus de 2 000 espèces de plantes montagnardes ou médicinales.

WALENSEE★★

Carte Michelin n° 427 pli 16 ou 216 plis 20, 21

Célébré par Liszt, le Walensee, ou **lac de Walenstadt**, allonge son miroir terni au pied des gigantesques bastions rocheux des Churfirsten.
Entre Näfels et Murg, le nouveau tracé de la route longeant le lac, parallèlement à la voie ferrée, a nécessité d'importants travaux de génie civil, en particulier 6 tunnels et 9 galeries taillés dans les contreforts à pic de la montagne. Il reste possible d'emprunter l'ancienne voie accidentée qui offre, par la terrasse boisée du Kerenzerberg, des **vues plongeantes**★★ multiples, à l'Ouest, sur la vallée glaronnaise de la Linth et la basse plaine alluviale dans laquelle débouche ce torrent, à l'Est, sur le lac et les Churfirsten.

Le WEISSENSTEIN★★★

Soleure

Carte Michelin n° 427 pli 4 ou 216 pli 15 – au Nord de Soleure – Schéma : JURA SUISSE

Les crêtes du Weissenstein, dressées comme un rempart au-dessus du bas-pays soleurois, réservent l'un des panoramas les plus impressionnants du Jura.

Accès ⊙ – *Au départ de Solothurn – 10 km – environ 2 h – par ⑤ du plan, Oberdorf, puis un tronçon de route de montagne dont on peut éviter le parcours pénible en empruntant le télésiège reliant la gare d'Oberdorf au Kurhaus Weissenstein (16 mn).
Au départ de Delémont – 24 km, par la route n° 6 jusqu'à Moutier, puis la route n° 30 jusqu'à Gänsbrunnen, où s'amorce la petite route de montagne (non revêtue dans sa majeure partie) menant au sommet.*

★★★ **Panorama** – Quelle que soit la route empruntée pour le trajet en auto, l'arrivée s'effectue toujours, après la montée, dans une combe de pâturages. Tourner alors dans le chemin du « Kurhaus » situé sur la crête, à 1 287 m d'altitude.

De là descend un « chemin planétaire » jalonnant sur plus de 7 km la route de Gänsbrunnen.

Laisser la voiture devant cet établissement et gagner la terrasse (par le passage à gauche du bâtiment si l'on n'y consomme pas), d'où se découvre l'immense barrière des Alpes, du Säntis, à gauche, au Mont Blanc à droite. La **vue aérienne**★★★ sur les campagnes du Moyen Pays *(voir Introduction : Physionomie du pays)* est sans égale dans le Jura du Nord. Berne, les lacs de Neuchâtel, ce Morat et de Bienne peuvent être repérés par temps clair.

WEISSENSTEINSTRASSE★★

Carte Michelin n° 427 plis 3, 4 ou 216 plis 2, 14, 15 – Schéma : JURA SUISSE

Cet itinéraire jurassien, riche de passages sous bois ou en gorge, réserve dans sa phase finale l'occasion de découvrir, au mont Weissenstein, un grandiose panorama.

DE PORRENTRUY A SOLOTHURN

102 km – environ 4 h 1/2 – itinéraire ① *de la visite du Jura suisse*

Entre Gänsbrunnen et Oberdorf, la petite route du Weissenstein, généralement obstruée par la neige de décembre à mai, se présente comme un chemin étroit, en mauvais état sur le versant Nord de la montagne et au profil très dur sur le versant de Soleure (pentes atteignant 22 % – aborder les lacets, aux dévers souvent accentués, avec une extrême prudence).

Porrentruy – *Voir à ce nom.*
Après Porrentruy, la route doit adopter un profil en fort dos d'âne pour franchir, au col des Rangiers, le chaînon du mont Terri.
En contrebas des Malettes, précédant de peu ce seuil, une rapide descente sous bois mène au plateau doucement ondulé de l'**Ajoie** – qui n'est autre qu'une portion de Franche-Comté rattachée à la Suisse – où pointent çà et là des clochers déjà casqués à la mode franc-comtoise.

★**St-Ursanne** – *Voir à ce nom.*
Ce parcours accidenté, presque continuellement sous bois, n'en reste pas moins roulant et agréable, mais les échappées lointaines sont rares.
La populaire « **Sentinelle des Rangiers** » (monument commémorant la mobilisation de l'armée suisse durant la guerre de 1914-1918) signale à peu près l'arrivée au col.

Prendre la direction de St-Brais.

★**Corniche du Jura** – *Voir à ce nom.*
A partir de là, jusqu'à Delémont, la route n° 6 présente les mêmes caractéristiques.

WEISSENSTEINSTRASSE

Delémont – *Voir à ce nom.*
De Delémont à Moutier, la Birse dont on suit maintenant le cours impétueux s'est taillé deux cluses que sépare le village de Roches. La cluse aval présente un aspect nettement industriel (usine métallurgique de Choindez). La cluse amont, beaucoup plus étranglée, tranche le chaînon du Raimeux, dont elle a pris le nom, et s'encaisse entre de grandes lames rocheuses que la voie ferrée perce en une succession de courts tunnels.

Chapelle de Chalières – *Au cimetière de Moutier, à la sortie Ouest du pays (route de Perrefitte).* Cette chapelle romane, très restaurée, abrite à l'intérieur de son abside (éclairer) des fresques du début du 11ᵉ s. dont, à la voûte, un Christ en gloire dans une mandorle, entouré d'anges, d'une licorne et d'un griffon.

★★★ **Weissenstein** – *Accès et description ci-dessus.*
Au rude passage du chaînon boisé du Weissenstein – le versant de Soleure présentant l'aspect le plus fourni – font finalement suite les grasses campagnes du Moyen Pays (Mittelland), toutes couvertes de vergers annonçant l'arrivée à Soleure.

★ **Solothurn** – *Visite : 1 h. Voir à ce nom.*

WENGEN★★★
Berne
Carte Michelin n° 427 pli 14 ou 217 pli 8 – Schéma : INTERLAKEN (Environs) – Alt. 1 275 m

Wengen est la station d'altitude la mieux équipée de l'Oberland bernois et l'une des plus mondaines. Le **site**★★★ de cet épaulement d'alpages et de forêts, d'où le regard, ébloui par la Jungfrau, capte en enfilade la perspective unique du fossé de Lauterbrunnen est un enchantement que les promenades le long de sentiers parfaitement aménagés – leur déneigement est même assuré en hiver – renouvellent sans cesse. La saison du ski se déroule au rythme des navettes du chemin de fer desservant la Petite Scheidegg (la station d'Eigergletscher au printemps) et des bennes du téléphérique du Männlichen. La compétition de classe internationale la plus connue est alors la **course du Lauberhorn**, organisée tous les ans début janvier.

WERDENBERG (BUCHS)★
St-Gall
Carte Michelin n° 427 pli 16 ou 216 pli 21 – Schéma : APPENZELLERLAND – Alt. 451 m.

A l'extrémité Nord de la populeuse agglomération de Buchs, le vieux village de Werdenberg, encadré de verdures profondes et d'eaux dormantes, compose un petit **tableau**★ particulièrement bien venu dans le large couloir du Rheinthal *(voir à ce nom)*, généralement plus frappant par sa prospérité agricole que par ses sites pittoresques.
Laisser la voiture soit juste avant la promenade longeant l'étang, soit juste après à droite. On pénètre dans le bourg minuscule par une ruelle que borde une série de maisons de bois sur arcades, remarquablement restaurées. Le flâneur y retrouve l'atmosphère des petites cités de la vallée du Rhin, aux 17ᵉ et 18ᵉ s., grâce aux inscriptions, millésimes et motifs décoratifs polychromes. Un passage (entre les nᵒˢ 8 et 9) mène à une promenade autour de l'étang. On se retrouve alors face aux maisons de Werdenberg étroitement emboîtées, au pied du château de ses comtes ; remarquer sur la gauche la belle façade peinte de la maison «Schlange» (le serpent, voir sous la toiture). Revenu à la ruelle, on s'engage dans la rampe du château auquel on accède par un long escalier.

Château ⊘ – Construit et modifié du 13ᵉ au 18ᵉ s., il a été aménagé au 19ᵉ s. en appartement de maître. Sous les combles, une section est consacrée au Rhin (trouvailles, cartographie, géologie, maquettes de ponts). Du sommet de la tour, on bénéficie d'une très belle **vue** sur le Rheinthal. Avant de sortir, ne pas manquer la collection d'armes (sabres, fusils, revolvers, coiffures).

WIL
St-Gall – 16 108 habitants
Carte Michelin n° 427 pli 7 ou 216 plis 9, 20 – Alt. 571 m

Ancienne résidence des princes-abbés de St-Gall, Wil est bâtie sur un mamelon à l'entrée de la dépression du Toggenbourg. La ville ancienne, avec sa Hofplatz et sa Marktgasse, dont les maisons à toits débordants et à arcades sont ornées d'encorbellements, forme un ensemble pittoresque. De la terrasse de l'église St-Nicolas (Stadtkirche), belle **vue**★ sur le massif de l'Alpstein (Säntis) et la chaîne des Churfirsten.

Musée municipal (Stadtmuseum im Hof zu Wil) ⊘ – Le «Hof», bâtiment massif du 15ᵉ s. occupant le faîte de la colline, était jadis la résidence des abbés de St-Gall. Aménagé au 3ᵉ étage, le musée renferme, avec une maquette de la ville, des documents retraçant le passé de Wil.

Schloss WILDEGG★

Argovie
Carte Michelin n° 427 pli 5 ou 216 Nord du pli 17 – 5 km au Nord de Lenzburg

Le **château** ⊙ de Wildegg dresse sa masse imposante au-dessus de la vallée de l'Aare. Construit au 12ᵉ s. par un comte de Habsbourg, il a été agrandi et transformé à plusieurs reprises, en particulier par la famille Effinger qui en fut propriétaire durant quatre siècles. Le château renferme un bel ameublement du 17ᵉ au 19ᵉ s. Le « cabinet Bleu », la « salle des Armures », la bibliothèque, retiennent particulièrement l'attention par la beauté de leur plafond et de leur mobilier. Des étages supérieurs, la vue embrasse un paysage doucement mamelonné de prairies et de forêts.

WILLISAU STADT

Lucerne — 2 866 habitants
Carte Michelin n° 427 pli 14 ou 216 pli 16 – Alt. 555 m

Fondée au 13ᵉ s., Willisau possède encore une bonne partie de son enceinte fortifiée. Menant à l'Obertor, ancienne porte de ville, la rue principale de cette petite ville présente un aspect pittoresque avec ses trois fontaines (aux statues religieuses modernes en fonte, dues à Meyer-Kistler) et ses maisons aux façades peintes, ornées d'enseignes de fer forgé et coiffées de toits aux auvents souvent décorés.

Chapelle du Précieux-Sang (Heiligblutkapelle) – *Devant l'Obertor, du côté opposé à l'église paroissiale.* Elle conserve un plafond à caissons peints. Cette chapelle (fin 17ᵉ s.) aurait succédé à une chapelle située à l'emplacement d'un cabaret : au moment où l'un des joueurs brandissait son épée dans la direction du ciel, des gouttes de sang tombèrent, dit-on, sur la table de jeu. Pour obtenir le pardon de ce sacrilège, la communauté de Willisau fit édifier une chapelle sur le lieu de la faute.

ENVIRONS

Wolhusen – *10 km au Sud-Est.* Dans le cimetière dominant l'église et la ville se dresse la **chapelle des Morts** (Totenkapelle). Cette minuscule chapelle est décorée à l'intérieur d'une étonnante fresque de 1661, aux tons bruns, représentant une **Danse macabre** (sous-titrée de quatrains en vers allemands exprimant les propos prêtés à chaque personnage) ; remarquer les squelettes dont les crânes font saillie sur le mur.

WINTERTHUR

Zurich — 86 959 habitants
Carte n° 427 pli 6 ou 216 pli 8 – Alt. 439 m – Plan dans le guide Rouge Michelin Suisse

Une bourgade, sous le nom de Vitudurum, existait déjà ici à l'époque romaine. Dès la fin du Moyen Âge, Winterthur fabriquait ces poêles de faïence monumentaux que l'on peut encore admirer dans certains intérieurs suisses. L'essor industriel de la cité, lié, de nos jours, au développement de l'industrie textile et de la construction mécanique (matériel ferroviaire, moteurs Diesel), n'a nullement entravé son rayonnement artistique, encouragé par des mécènes au goût très sûr : c'est une véritable rétrospective de la peinture européenne au 19ᵉ s. que les diverses collections publiques de Winterthur peuvent présenter à l'amateur.

Les concerts donnés par le Collegium Musicum, fondé en 1629, sont très suivis.

La crèche des enfants par A. Anker

WINTERTHUR

CURIOSITÉS

Collection Oskar Reinhart – Ce mécène, décédé en 1965, légua sa célèbre collection à la Confédération suisse, à la condition qu'elle reste dans sa ville natale. **Musée Oskar Reinhart «am Stadtgarten»** ⊙ – *Stadthausstrasse 6*. Œuvres d'artistes suisses, allemands et autrichiens, des 18e, 19e et 20e s. Les excellents dessins de Rudolf Wasmann, les portraits d'enfants d'Anker, des œuvres de Böcklin et de Koller, des tableaux de Romantiques allemands et de peintres de l'école de Munich, ainsi que les études d'animaux de Jacques Laurent Agasse retiennent particulièrement l'attention, tandis que de nombreuses toiles de Ferdinand Hodler attestent l'importance accordée à celui qui fut le chef de file de la peinture suisse avant 1914.

★★ **Collection Oskar Reinhart «Am Römerholz»** ⊙ – *Haldenstrasse 95*. La maison du collectionneur, située dans un vaste parc, abrite un fort bel ensemble représentant cinq siècles de peinture. Figurent côte à côte; l'Allemand Cranach dit l'Ancien, l'école flamande avec Brueghel, un tableau du Greco, des dessins de Rembrandt, des œuvres françaises de la fin du 17e au 19e s. avec Poussin, Le Lorrain, Watteau, Chardin, Fragonard et quelques dessins de Daumier; pour le 19e s., des maîtres dont les œuvres reflètent les tendances principales de l'époque en matière d'art pictural, tels que Corot, Delacroix, Courbet, Manet, Renoir et Cézanne auxquels se rattachent le Néerlandais Van Gogh et plus près de nous Picasso avec des dessins de la période bleue.

★ **Musée des Beaux-Arts (Kunstmuseum)** ⊙ – Les collections de la ville présentent des œuvres du 16e s. (Cranach), des peintres de l'école locale des 17e et 18e s. (Graff, Meyer, Füssli) et, pour les 19e et 20e s., des peintres suisses et allemands (Hodler, Vallotton, G. Giacometti, Auberjonois, Corinth, Hofer). La peinture française impressionniste est représentée par Renoir; les coloristes par Bonnard, Vuillard et Van Gogh. Une partie du bâtiment est réservée aux sculptures de Rodin, Maillol, Haller, Marini et Alberto Giacometti.

★★ **Villa Flora** ⊙ – *Tösstalstrasse 44. Accrochage renouvelé annuellement; le jardin (deux sculptures d'Aristide Maillol) n'est pas accessible.*

La collection d'œuvres post-impressionnistes qu'Arthur et Hedy Hahnloser-Bühler ont rassemblée ici entre 1907 et 1932 a pour originalité d'avoir été constituée grâce aux contacts personnels qu'ils entretenaient avec les artistes. On reste étonné par la cohérence et le caractère prophétique de leurs acquisitions, que le visiteur a la chance d'admirer dans la maison même de ces amateurs d'art éclairés.

Le groupe des Nabis, formé par des peintres nés entre 1860 et 1870 et en réaction contre l'impressionnisme, représente le noyau de la collection. Le Suisse F. Vallotton est à l'honneur (*La Charrette*, belle série de xylographies révélant son talent de caricaturiste) à côté d'œuvres remarquables de E. Vuillard (*La Partie de dames* à l'étonnante perspective plongeante) et de P. Bonnard (*La Carafe provençale* où sont représentés Marthe Bonnard et son chien Ubu, et *Effet de glace*, où se combinent différents angles de vue). Le Fauvisme, né d'une appellation du critique Louis Vauxcelles à l'occasion du Salon d'Automne de 1905, est représenté par son maître incontesté, H. Matisse (l'*Odalisque debout* illustre à merveille son séjour à Nice entre 1919 et 1930, période riche en nus féminins), ainsi que par H. Manguin, grand ami des Hahnloser-Bühler, et A. Marquet, dont les sujets évoquent souvent ses nombreux voyages. Les tons obscurs de la peinture de G. Rouault contrastent avec les couleurs pures et intenses des Fauves, auxquels il est trop souvent associé. Le grand intérêt des œuvres présentées ici est qu'elles forment un témoignage exceptionnel de sa première période (voir notamment *Les Trois Clowns* réalisé en 1912). Parallèlement aux Nabis et aux Fauves, l'un des points forts de la visite est le rare ensemble de 9 toiles du peintre de l'irrationnel, O. Redon (*Andromède*) à propos duquel Hedy Hahnloser-Bühler disait en 1919 : « Tous les éléments essentiels propres à la volonté artistique contemporaine se trouvent déjà dans son œuvre. » Enfin, la collection possède quelques œuvres de premier ordre telles que le *Portrait du peintre* de P. Cézanne, *Le Semeur* et *Le Café de nuit* de V. van Gogh, ainsi que des lithographies de H. de Toulouse-Lautrec et de nombreuses sculptures (bronzes de P. Bonnard, C. Despiau, A. Maillol, H. Matisse, M. Marini, P.-A. Renoir, A. Rodin et F. Vallotton).

Technorama ⊙ – *Technoramastrasse 1. Quitter l'autoroute à la sortie Oberwinterthur*. Sa présentation ludique et attrayante fait de ce musée une bonne introduction pour les jeunes au développement de la science et de la technique *(indications en allemand, souvent en français; écouteurs en langues étrangères dans certains secteurs)*. L'exposition permanente se divise en huit secteurs. Au rez-de-chaussée : physique (présentations didactiques); trains et jouets (collection de trains miniatures); énergie (machines thermiques). Au 1er étage : eau, nature, chaos (expérience des phénomènes naturels); musique mécanique (instruments et enregistrement du son); matériaux (transformation). Au second : textile (filage et tissage); automatisme (analogique et numérique). Le principe de la visite est de manipuler les appareillages et d'assister à des démonstrations; la plus impressionnante est certainement celle concernant la haute tension. Le « laboratoire » permet, sous la direction de moniteurs, d'apprendre tout en se divertissant.

A l'extérieur, un parc permet aux jeunes d'expérimenter des engins volants *(seulement le samedi et le dimanche).*

WINTERTHUR

ENVIRONS

Château de Kybourg ⊘ – 6 km au Sud. Quitter Winterthur par la route de Seen. A Sennhof prendre à droite une petite route le long de la Töss ; à 1 km, tourner à gauche. Érigé aux 10e et 11e s., ce château féodal passa, par héritages successifs, de la lignée des comtes de Kybourg à celle des Habsbourg pour devenir baillage de la ville de Zurich en 1424, jusqu'en 1798. Il appartient depuis 1917 au canton de Zurich et à la ville de Winterthur. Il contient de remarquables collections de meubles et d'armes, et offre une belle vue sur la campagne environnante.

YVERDON-LES-BAINS

Vaud – 22 758 habitants

Carte Michelin n° 427 pli 12 ou 217 pli 3 – Schéma : JURA SUISSE – Alt. 439 m
Plan sur le guide Rouge Michelin Suisse

Bâtie à la pointe Sud du lac de Neuchâtel, Yverdon bénéficie de la réputation due aux vertus de ses eaux sulfureuses et magnésiennes.
Plusieurs menhirs, que l'on peut voir à la sortie de la ville sur la route d'Estavayer-le-Lac, témoignent d'une présence humaine ancienne. Importante bourgade celtique (Eburodunum), puis gallo-romaine, la ville conserve de l'époque romaine les vestiges d'un castrum situés à proximité du cimetière.
L'hôtel de ville, avec sa façade de style Louis XV, et surtout le château, méritent l'un et l'autre de retenir l'attention.

Château – Il date du 13e s. C'est en effet sur l'emplacement d'une première forteresse entreprise quelques années avant lui et restée inachevée que Pierre II de Savoie, qui s'était emparé d'Yverdon en 1259, fit construire cet imposant château fort, flanqué de quatre tours rondes. Des transformations, apportées en particulier au siècle dernier, lui ont fait perdre son caractère féodal : les fossés qui l'entouraient ont été en grande partie comblés.

Musée ⊘ – Ses collections retracent l'histoire locale depuis la préhistoire. La faune régionale est également représentée. Dans la tour Nord-Est, une salle est consacrée à l'éminent éducateur Pestalozzi (voir à Tragen).

ZERMATT★★★

Valais – 4 225 habitants

Carte Michelin n° 427 pli 22 ou 219 pli 4 – Schéma : VALAIS – Alt. 1 616 m
Plan dans le guide Rouge Michelin Suisse

Les touristes ne peuvent accéder à Zermatt qu'en chemin de fer, soit à partir de Brigue ou Viège (Visp) où la plupart laissent leur voiture, soit à partir de Täsch, où un vaste parking a été aménagé. La station, ainsi protégée d'une circulation automobile excessive, procure à l'arrivant une ambiance de détente exceptionnelle. L'agglomération présente deux visages distincts : de la gare à l'église paroissiale, c'est une **rue** d'hôtels et de magasins dont le style permet d'évoquer le souvenir des Seiler, dynastie d'hôteliers à qui est dû le lancement de la station, en 1855 (année où fut ouvert l'hôtel du Mont Rose, sur la façade duquel a été scellé un médaillon dédié à Whymper). Au-delà de l'église, le **Vieux Zermatt** masse ses chalets valaisans et ses mazots couleur de pain brûlé. Zermatt, découverte il y a un siècle par les Anglais, reste, pour les alpinistes, un sanctuaire. Le Cervin (**Matterhorn** – alt. 4 478 m), dont la pyramide déversée et crochue apparaît, du centre de la station, sous son aspect le plus hardi, fait ici l'objet d'un véritable culte.

LA CONQUÊTE DU CERVIN

Depuis 1860, **Edward Whymper**, jeune illustrateur anglais conquis par les silhouettes montagneuses que son éditeur l'avait chargé de « croquer », sillonne, pour son plaisir, les Alpes du Valais, de Savoie et du Dauphiné, à la recherche d'ascensions inédites. Il a déjà inscrit à son tableau les « premières » de la Barre des Écrins, de l'Aiguille Verte, des Grandes Jorasses : mais il revient toujours à Zermatt ou en Valtournanche, fasciné par le Cervin qu'il n'a pas réussi à vaincre au cours de huit tentatives menées au départ de Breuil, avec la collaboration du fameux guide valdôtain Jean-Antoine Carrel.
En 1865, changeant son plan de campagne, Whymper décide d'attaquer la pyramide par son arête Nord-Est – celle qui regarde Zermatt. Et le 13 juillet de cette année, les habitants de Zermatt voient s'ébranler une caravane : trois grimpeurs anglais – Douglas, Hudson, Hadow – et le guide chamoniard Michel Croz sont venus se joindre, en dernière minute, à la cordée formée par Whymper et ses deux guides de Zermatt, les Taugwalder père et fils.

ZERMATT

Par un temps idéal et sans chutes de pierres, les alpinistes posent le pied sur la cime du Cervin le 14 juillet en début d'après-midi ; ils éprouvent la satisfaction de pouvoir narguer une cordée partie de Breuil, à leur insu, sous la conduite de Carrel, pour une offensive décisive sur la paroi italienne. S'arrachant à la contemplation du panorama, les vainqueurs reprennent le chemin du retour. Soudain le jeune Hadow, l'élément le moins entraîné du groupe, « dévisse », entraînant dans sa chute ses voisins de cordée, Croz, Hudson et Douglas. La corde d'assurance se rompt net entre Douglas et Taugwalder père. Whymper et ses guides assistent à l'effrayante chute de leurs quatre compagnons, 1 200 m plus bas.

Ils se ressaisissent enfin ; mais un phénomène céleste impressionnant, l'apparition de deux croix inscrites dans un immense arc de nuées, vient mettre encore leur sang-froid à rude épreuve, avant qu'ils ne retrouvent la vallée.

De son côté, Carrel trouvera, le 17 juillet, la récompense de ses efforts. Ce premier grand drame de l'« Alpe homicide » contribue à entretenir autour du Cervin une atmosphère de légende.

LA STATION

D'abord simple village de montagne au fond de la vallée du Nikolaital, Zermatt a désormais orienté toutes ses activités vers le sport.

L'attrait qu'exerce la douzaine de « 4 000 » dont Zermatt commande les accès se manifeste, en été, par l'afflux d'alpinistes de toutes les nationalités.

En hiver, alors que les crissements et les sonnailles des traîneaux ont remplacé le sifflement des chariots électriques, l'animation touristique se concentre, pendant la période utile de la journée, sur les croupes inondées de soleil du Riffelberg où les skieurs, amenés par le chemin de fer du Gornergrat, connaissent les griseries de la neige, en évoluant face au Cervin.

Les téléphériques du Stockhorn, du Klein Matterhorn, du Trockener Steg, de l'Unter Rothorn et des services d'hélicoptères facilitent l'accès aux plus hauts champs de neige tels que ceux du plateau Rosa et du col du Théodule, permettant la pratique aisée du ski d'été.

Musée alpin (Alpines Museum) ⊙ — Il conserve les reliques de la conquête du Cervin et perpétue le souvenir des premiers guides ou des hôtes illustres de Zermatt.

Un relief du Cervin intéressera tous ceux qui veulent se familiariser avec les différentes faces du célèbre pic. Une section importante est consacrée au Vieux Zermatt (reconstitution d'intérieurs montagnards).

ENVIRONS

★★★ **Gornergrat** ⊙ — Alt. 3 135 m. *2 h AR*. Cette excursion en chemin de fer à crémaillère – la plus haute voie ferrée d'Europe à ciel ouvert – réserve, après la halte à Riffelberg où l'on peut admirer le Cervin, l'inoubliable découverte du Mont Rose (point culminant : pointe Dufour, alt. 4 634 m) et de ses glaciers. Il faut consacrer une demi-journée à cette excursion que l'on peut prolonger par la montée en téléphérique au Stockhorn (alt. 3 407 m). *3/4 h AR*.

★★★ **Montée au Petit Cervin (Klein Matterhorn)** ⊙ — Alt. 3 886 m. *Accès par 4 téléphériques successifs (durée totale du trajet aller : 50 mn, dont 1/4 h à pied de Zermatt à la gare de départ)*. La 1re section se parcourt au-dessus d'un raide couloir d'éboulis dont on a une vue d'enfilade, jusqu'à Zermatt inclus, depuis la 1re station intermédiaire de **Furi** (alt. 1 865 m). De Furi à **Furgg** (alt. 2 434 m), d'abord au-dessus d'éboulis rocheux, puis de pentes herbues où paissent des moutons, on voit apparaître le Cervin, à droite ; vues splendides en avant sur le glacier de Théodule, en arrière sur les Alpes Pennines.

★ **Lac Noir (Schwarzsee)** ⊙ — De Furgg, un téléphérique mène en 3 mn les amateurs de sites solitaires jusqu'à la cuvette rocheuse et gazonnée où repose, au pied du Cervin qui s'y reflète, la vasque limpide de ce petit lac, dont un sentier fait le tour. Sur ses bords s'érige une petite chapelle (restaurée, comme ses peintures murales à l'intérieur) à toit de schistes.

Regagner Furgg pour reprendre la montée au Petit Cervin.

La 3e section, dans un décor minéral entre les deux branches en tenaille du glacier de Théodule, aboutit à **Trockener Steg** (alt. 2 929 m) où se dévoile le **glacier de Théodule**★★ bordant la station, avec ses séracs, dans son cirque de pentes rougeâtres striées de cascades et couronnées de pics neigeux.

Le 4e téléphérique, survolant le glacier, dépose à la station actuellement la plus haute d'Europe (alt. 3 820 m), juchée sur un petit replat au flanc du Petit Cervin, à 66 m du sommet *(non encore accessible aux promeneurs)* ; on débouche de cette station, par un long tunnel, juste au-dessus des champs de neige *(ski d'été)*, mais où l'horizon se limite à la masse toute proche du Breithorn et au Petit Cervin lui-même.

ZERMATT

★★ Rothorn — Alt. 3 103 m. *Montée, de Zermatt, par funiculaire (long couloir d'accès) jusqu'à Sunnegga, puis par télécabine jusqu'à Blauherd, enfin par téléphérique. Durée totale du trajet aller : environ 20 mn, dont 5 mn de funiculaire.*

La 1re partie, par funiculaire, se déroule en tunnel ; à **Sunnegga** (alt. 2 285 m), sur le rebord d'un plateau d'alpages agrémenté d'un petit lac, première vue sur le Cervin, au Sud-Ouest ; de la 2e station intermédiaire, **Blauherd** (alt. 2 577 m), en vue d'une belle sapinière à droite, le téléphérique parvient au sommet rocheux, arasé, du Rothorn d'où le **panorama★★**, barré à l'Est par l'Ober Rothorn, s'étend jusqu'au Cervin (visible de profil) au Sud-Ouest, sur le glacier de Findel au Sud, sur Zermatt à l'Ouest et la vallée du Nikolaital au Nord.

Gorges du Gorner ⊙ — *2 h à pied AR. A la sortie Sud de Zermatt, tourner à gauche (pont), puis suivre la signalisation.*

Superbes gorges, que surplombe le sentier, tracé dans les parois abruptes ; au fond de l'échancrure bouillonne le torrent. La traversée de bois de pins arolles et de mélèzes précède l'arrivée à Blatten, pittoresque hameau, avec sa chapelle, ses mazots *(illustration au texte du Valais)* et ses blocs erratiques.

Prendre, après Zumsee, le chemin regagnant Zermatt.

ZERNEZ

Grisons

Carte Michelin n° 427 pli 17 ou 218 pli 6 – Schéma : GRAUBÜNDEN – Alt. 1 474 m

Ce gros bourg pittoresque domine le confluent du Spöl et de l'Inn. La proximité du Parc national suisse et son équipement en font un site de villégiature recherché en particulier par les fervents de la nature.

★ROUTE DE L'OFEN

De Zernez au col de l'Umbrail

57 km – environ 2 h 1/2 – itinéraire ⑥ de la visite des Grisons

La route du col de l'Ofen relie l'Engadine au Val de Venosta en Italie.

Parc national suisse ⊙ — *Il est interdit à l'automobiliste de quitter la route et au piéton de s'écarter des sentiers autorisés.* Le Parc est traversé par le Val dal Spöl. Ses vallons sauvages, dont le manteau forestier abandonné à lui-même est interrompu seulement par le lit des torrents, laissent une impression de solitude parfois accablante et ses arbres morts laissés sur place offrent un spectacle étonnant pour la Suisse.

Fondé en 1909, à l'initiative de la Ligue pour la Protection de la Nature, il forme une réserve naturelle de 16 000 ha préservée de toute intervention humaine (interdiction de camper, de faire du feu, de quitter les routes et les sentiers autorisés, etc.) où la flore et la faune (cerfs, bouquetins, chamois, marmottes) sont intégralement protégées.

Du point de vue touristique, le parc frappe surtout par ses immenses solitudes boisées. Le fervent de nature sauvage ne sera pas moins profondément impressionné par les découvertes faites au cours des excursions pédestres guidées, régulièrement organisées pendant la saison.

Col de l'Ofen — Alt. 2 149 m. Il sépare le Val dal Spöl au Nord du Val Müstair au Sud dont le torrent, le Rom, est tributaire de l'Adige.

Du col à Tschierv plusieurs passages en corniche offrent de jolies échappées vers l'aval et surtout sur la coupole neigeuse de l'Ortles.

Après Tschierv, le trajet associant les espaces gazonnés et les bois de mélèzes offre un certain cachet tyrolien en particulier par les clochers à bulbe des églises de Fuldera et de Valchava.

Santa Maria — Beau village dont les maisons au crépi blanc évoquent l'Engadine.

★Müstair — *Voir à ce nom.*

Revenir à Santa Maria.

De Santa Maria au col de l'Umbrail, la route monte dans le sillon du Val Muraunza dont les aspects désolés et les horizons limités contrastent avec le **tableau★** frais et harmonieux qui se révèle à proximité du restaurant Alpenrösli. De la terrasse de cet établissement, la vue plonge dans le Val Müstair, conque de prairies allant se resserrant vers l'amont entre les versants boisés qui se ferment au col de l'Ofen.

---

*Certains hôtels possèdent leur court de tennis, leur piscine,
leur plage aménagée, leur jardin de repos,
consultez le* guide Rouge Michelin Suisse *de l'année.*

ZUG★

[C] Zoug – 21 705 habitants
Carte Michelin n° 427 Nord du pli 15 ou 216 pli 18 – Alt. 425 m

Bâtie à l'extrémité Nord-Est du lac qui porte son nom, cette charmante petite ville s'étend parmi les jardins et les vergers de la rive du lac, au pied des premiers contreforts boisés du Zugerberg.
Selon les résultats des fouilles archéologiques, le site de Zug aurait été occupé sans interruption par l'homme depuis l'époque néolithique. Au Moyen Âge, la ville appartint successivement aux familles de Lenzbourg, de Kybourg et de Habsbourg, avant d'entrer dans la Confédération en 1352. Son château du 13ᵉ s. a été entièrement restauré.

★★ **Lac de Zoug** (Zuger See) – Sixième lac proprement suisse avec plus de 38 km² de superficie et une profondeur de près de 200 m, il s'allonge, du Nord au Sud, sur environ 14 km, divisé en deux bassins par la presqu'île du Kiemen. Ses eaux bleutées, son site de collines riantes que domine le Rigi, au Sud, ses aménagements le font particulièrement apprécier des estivants.

CURIOSITÉS

★ **Les quais** – De la Seestrasse à l'Alpenquai, ils offrent de belles **vues**★ sur les sommets de la Suisse centrale (Rigi, Pilate, Bürgenstock, Stanserhorn) et, au dernier plan, sur les Alpes bernoises (Finsteraarhorn, Jungfrau, Blümlisalp).

★ **Ville ancienne** (Z) – Un certain nombre de vestiges fortifiés – tour de la Poudre (Pulverturm), tour des Capucins (Kapuzinerturm) – délimitent encore le noyau ancien de la ville.
Le quartier traversé par l'Unter-Altstadt et l'Ober-Altstadt présente, avec ses vieilles demeures à pignons à redans, un cachet médiéval plein de saveur.
Le Fischmarkt (marché aux poissons) montre des maisons à auvents peints et balcons en avancée.
La **tour de l'Horloge** (Zytturm), au toit de tuiles peintes aux couleurs de Zug (blanc et bleu), se termine par un clocheton effilé. Sous le cadran sont figurés les blasons des huit premiers cantons de la Confédération – Zug étant le 7ᵉ canton entré dans l'alliance.
La **Kolinplatz**, entourée de maisons anciennes dont la Maison de Ville (Stadthaus-POL. du plan), édifice du 16ᵉ s., est ornée d'une belle fontaine fleurie.

ZUG

Bahnhofstrasse	YZ
Bundesstrasse	Y
Aabachstrasse	Y
Aegeristrasse	Z
Alpenquai	Y
Alpenstrasse	Z
Artherstrasse	Z
Baarerstrasse	Y
Bundesplatz	Y
Chamerstrasse	Y
Dammstrasse	Y
Fischmarkt	Z 3
Gartenstrasse	Z 4
Gotthardstrasse	Y
Grabenstrasse	Z
Guggiweg	YZ
Hirschenplatz	Z
Hofstrasse	Z 6
Industriestrasse	Y 7
Kirchenstrasse	Z 9
Kolinplatz	Z
Landsgemeindeplatz	Z 10
Metallstrasse	Y
Neugasse	Z
Ober-Altstadt	Z 12
Postplatz	Z
Poststrasse	YZ
Registrasse	Y 13
St. Oswalds-Gasse	Z 15
Schmidgasse	Y 16
Seestrasse	Z
Unter-Altstadt	Z 18
Vorstadt	YZ
Vorstadtquai	YZ
Zeughausgasse	Z 19
Zugerbergstrasse	Z

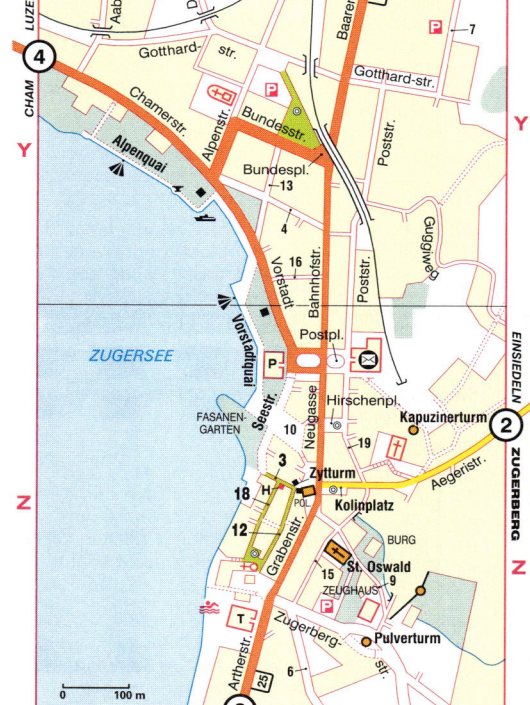

Cette fontaine porte la statue du banneret Wolfgang Kolin, représentant d'une famille locale qui s'illustra particulièrement à la bataille d'Arbedo – où les forces confédérées défendant la Léventine furent écrasées par les troupes du duc de Milan (1422); un membre de cette famille se fit tuer pour sauver sa bannière, tandis que son fils, à qui il l'avait tendue, succombait à son tour.

Église St-Oswald – De style gothique tardif, elle a été bâtie aux 15e et 16e s. L'intérieur, voûté d'ogives, est assombri par des piliers massifs. La nef est séparée du chœur par une cloison ornée de fresques.

De nombreuses statues de saints, dans le chœur et de chaque côté de la nef, des triptyques de bois peint et doré, dans chacune des chapelles latérales, ainsi que des fresques sur la voûte de la nef et dans les bas-côtés, forment la décoration.

ENVIRONS

★ **Zugerberg** ⊙ – Alt. 988 m. *7,5 km – environ 1/2 h de route – par chemin très étroit et en forte montée, plus 1/4 h à pied AR. Quitter Zug par ② du plan, route de Schwyz par Aegeri.* A 1 km, le petit chemin d'accès du Zugerberg pris à droite offre déjà de belles vues sur la ville et le lac.

Laisser la voiture près du carrefour qui se trouve un peu avant le village de Schönfels et gagner alors à travers prés le sommet du Zugerberg.

Du terre-plein, on découvre une **vue**★ presque circulaire, au Nord-Ouest sur Zug et le lac, au Sud-Ouest sur le Pilate, au Sud sur l'Uri-Rotstock et les Alpes d'Uri, à l'Est – par une trouée entre les sapins – sur le village d'Unter-Ägeri et son lac. Au Nord moutonnent les ondulations du « Moyen Pays », en direction de Zurich.

★ **Ancienne abbaye de Kappel** – *8 km par ① du plan.* Écrasant de sa masse le village blotti contre elle et près duquel fut tué le réformateur Zwingli *(voir à ce nom)*, la grande église abbatiale se signale de loin par sa haute silhouette à contreforts, toits aigus et fin clocher. Bâtie aux 13e s. (chœur) et 14e s. (nef), elle illustre l'art gothique à ses débuts par des lignes pures et la simplicité toute cistercienne de façades seulement ornées d'élégantes baies à lancettes.

A l'intérieur s'offrent maints sujets d'intérêt : l'architecture de la vaste nef et de ses collatéraux surbaissés, à voûtes ogivales et clefs peintes bellement ciselées, le chevet plat (à verrière moderne), le chœur fermé par d'amusantes boiseries reliées aux **stalles** (14e s.) sculptées de têtes humaines ou animales (remarquer le groupe de la chienne avec ses chiots), les vestiges de fresques (14e s.) décorant le pourtour du chœur (saint Martin, Christ et saints en médaillons). Des pierres tombales anciennes jonchent le sol de l'édifice. Remarquer surtout les admirables **vitraux**★ (14e s.) haut placés sur 6 fenêtres du mur de droite de la nef et retraçant des scènes de la vie de Jésus (le dernier, près de l'entrée, la Crucifixion). Deux des anciens bâtiments conventuels subsistent derrière l'abbatiale.

ZUOZ★★

Grisons – 1 199 habitants
Carte Michelin n° 427 pli 17 ou 218 Nord-Ouest du pli 16
Schéma : GRAUBÜNDEN – Alt. 1 716 m

Zuoz, station d'altitude bien équipée pour les séjours d'été, réserve à l'amateur de couleur locale la découverte d'un ensemble de **demeures engadinoises**★★ construites, pour la plupart, par des membres de la famille Planta, célèbre dans les annales des Grisons.

CURIOSITÉS

★★ **Place centrale** – Sa fontaine est surmontée de l'ours héraldique des Planta (le blason de la famille porte plus exactement une patte d'ours coupée, la plante – « planta » – tournée vers le haut). La place est bornée au Nord par la « maison Planta », composée de deux habitations distinctes abritées sous le même toit.

Cet ensemble reste soumis aux canons du style engadinois *(voir à l'Engadine)*, mais ses dimensions inaccoutumées, son escalier extérieur à rampe de style rococo lui donnent un cachet seigneurial.

Le long de la rue principale, l'Auberge Crusch Alva (1570) est décorée, au pignon, d'une série de blasons. On reconnaît, à droite de saint Luzius, l'évangélisateur de la Haute-Rhétie, les armes des trois « Ligues » *(voir dans le chapitre : La Démocratie en action, Les Cantons)*, des « XIII cantons » helvétiques de l'époque, enfin celles des trois familles Salis (un saule – « salix » en latin), Planta et Juvalta.

Faire le tour de la maison Planta pour passer sous les arcades qui relient ce bâtiment à la « Tuor » (tour Planta, du 13e s.) et descendre à l'église.

Église – Dominée par un clocher grêle, elle conserve un vaisseau couvert de voûtes en étoile.

Le motif de la patte d'ours revient souvent dans sa décoration intérieure. Trois fenêtres sont pourvues de vitraux modernes : ceux de l'abside (l'Espérance et la Charité), dus au talent vigoureux d'Augusto Giacometti, et celui des « Trois Rois » par Gian Casty.

ZÜRICH ★★★

C – 365 043 habitants
Carte Michelin n° 427 pli 6 ou 216 pli 18 – Alt. 408 m
Plan d'agglomération et plan général dans le guide Rouge Michelin Suisse

Bâtie entre les versants boisés de l'Uetliberg et du Zurichberg, à l'endroit où la Limmat, sortant du lac de Zurich, reçoit la Sihl, Zurich est actuellement le plus important centre financier, industriel et commercial, ainsi que la ville la plus peuplée de Suisse et la plus influencée par les mouvements contemporains liés à la jeunesse.

Zwingli et la réforme religieuse – Nommé curé de Glaris en 1506, à l'âge de 22 ans, Zwingli n'hésite pas à dénoncer, en chaire, le service mercenaire à l'étranger, qui affaiblit les forces vives de la nation, et la vénalité des magistrats. Après deux ans passés à Einsiedeln, il se voit confier la cure du Grossmünster de Zurich. C'est alors qu'il cherche à réaliser ses projets religieux : il s'élève violemment contre le trafic des indulgences et proclame que la Bible est la seule autorité, en matière de foi.

En janvier 1523, une « dispute » publique ayant opposé au Rathaus de Zurich partisans et adversaires de Zwingli, ce dernier triomphe, le Conseil s'étant déclaré favorable aux idées nouvelles. En trois ans, la Réforme s'implante complètement à Zurich. Zwingli obtient la suppression des pèlerinages, des processions et de certains sacrements, se montre favorable au mariage des prêtres – donnant lui-même l'exemple en 1524 et fait fermer les couvents dans le canton de Zurich, devenu la terre d'élection de la Réforme en Suisse allemande. L'autorité de Zwingli inquiète les cantons catholiques. Lucerne, Uri, Schwyz, Unterwald et Zoug s'entendent contre Zurich et l'écartent de la direction des affaires fédérales. Une nouvelle grande « dispute » religieuse ayant eu lieu à Berne en 1528, Zwingli en sort encore à son avantage, mais en 1531 la guerre ne peut être évitée : le 11 octobre, Zwingli trouve la mort à Kappel, au cours d'un violent engagement qui voit la déroute des siens. Mais sa disparition ne marque pas pour autant la faillite de ses thèses religieuses qui se propagent peu à peu à travers toute la Suisse allemande.

Un prodigieux essor – Zurich, qui compte 17 000 habitants en 1800, connaît à partir du 19ᵉ s. un développement prodigieux. Si elle doit, en 1848, abandonner à Berne le rang de ville fédérale, elle devient, six ans plus tard, le siège de l'École polytechnique fédérale – le fameux « Polytechnicum ». La constitution démocratique qu'elle s'est donnée en 1869 a servi de modèle à d'autres constitutions cantonales et même, en partie, à la Constitution fédérale de 1874. Au début du 19ᵉ s., la ville s'étend au-delà de ses fortifications et des constructions neuves s'élèvent dans les campagnes environnantes. Les banlieues industrielles se développent le long des voies de communication. Zurich est en fait, aujourd'hui, la capitale économique de la Confédération.

Naissance du mouvement Dada

Le 5 février 1916 est inauguré le **Cabaret Voltaire** (1, Spiegelgasse, plaque commémorative) par Hugo Ball, poète et metteur en scène, avec sa femme Emmy Hennings, auxquels se sont joints des amis et artistes de tous horizons : Tristan Tzara, Marcel Janco, Jean Arp, Richard Huelsenbeck, Sophie Taeuber. Tous sont animés par le désir de créer un art nouveau, original, d'avant-garde, en réaction à l'art existant. Bousculant l'ordre établi, ils donnent des spectacles de danse, récitent des poèmes, exposent des peintures, du jamais vu qui fait venir le succès. C'est en cherchant un nom pour la chanteuse du cabaret, qu'Hugo Ball et Richard Huelsenbeck découvrent par hasard le mot Dada. Vite ils l'adoptent pour désigner le groupe. En 1916, le mot apparaît dans le premier numéro du Cabaret Voltaire, publication éditée en allemand, français et anglais, reflet du premier sursaut d'une révolte morale et intellectuelle envers une société trop sûre d'elle-même. Six mois après son ouverture, le Cabaret Voltaire ferme ses portes, par contre la revue Dada lui survit.

CURIOSITÉS

Bahnhofstrasse (EYZ) – Construite sur l'emplacement du « Fröschengraben » (fossé aux grenouilles), la Bahnhofstrasse, qui conduit de la gare centrale (Hauptbahnhof) aux rives du lac, est l'artère la plus animée de la ville et constitue sans doute le centre d'affaires le plus important de toute la confédération helvétique. Tout le long de cette belle avenue plantée de tilleuls se succèdent les commerces de luxe, les grands magasins, les grandes banques et les immeubles modernes.

★★ **Les quais** (FZ) – Sur les rives de la Limmat et du lac de Zurich (Zürichsee), ils déroulent leurs verdures magnifiquement peignées – bouquets d'arbres d'essences variées, pelouses, parterres fleuris –, tandis que les nombreux voiliers et canots à moteur, qui se pressent près des embarcadères, constituent une invite à l'évasion. En poursuivant jusqu'au **Mythenquai** dans le prolongement du Général-Guisan-Quai, (EZ), on découvrira des **vues** ★ de plus en plus étendues sur le lac de Zurich et les Alpes (au loin l'Oberland).

ZÜRICH

ZURICH PRATIQUE

Pour tout renseignement concernant les manifestations ou les spectacles, s'adresser à l'Office du tourisme, Bahnhofplatz 15, ☎ (01) 211 40 00.
On trouve également dans les hôtels ou à l'Office du tourisme des brochures comme *Zürich little big city News* ou *Zürich little big city What's on* donnant de nombreuses informations sur les spectacles, hôtels, restaurants, cinémas, adresses utiles, etc.

Shopping

La **Bahnhofstrasse** est la rue commerçante par excellence. Bordée d'élégantes boutiques aux vitrines séduisantes, on y trouve aussi les grands magasins Globus, Vilan, Jelmoli, St. Annahof.
La **vieille ville**, rive gauche dans les ruelles qui avoisinent la Weinplatz, et rive droite le long de la Niederdorfstrasse, de la Münstergasse et des petites rues avoisinantes, se prête volontiers à la découverte de boutiques originales.

Théâtre et musique

Opernhaus, Falkenstrasse 1, ☎ (01) 262 09 09.
Bernhard-Theater, Theaterplatz, ☎ (01) 252 65 55.
Tonhalle, Gotthardstrasse 5 et Claridenstrasse 7, ☎ (01) 221 22 83.
Theater Stock, Hirschengraben 42, ☎ (01) 251 22 80.

Où prendre un verre et où finir la soirée ?

De mai à septembre, le tramway coloré **Chuchichäschtli** est un moyen original d'apprécier le centre-ville devant une boisson, une glace ou un en-cas.
Le **Bar Jules Vernes** de la Brasserie Lipp (Uraniastrasse) propose de succulents cocktails et offre une belle vue panoramique sur la ville. A proximité les amateurs d'informatique se retrouvent devant les ordinateurs de l'**Internet Café**.
Près du Bahnofbrücke, ambiance feutrée au piano-bar de l'**hôtel Central Plaza**.
La vieille ville rive droite, outre le charme de ses petites rues débordantes d'animation en été, offre bon nombre de cafés et de restaurants bondés et dont les terrasses ne désemplissent pas.
Un «déci» ou quelques «décis» de vin suisse ou étranger dans le cadre agréable de **la Barrique** avant de finir la soirée en écoutant de bons morceaux de jazz interprétés par l'orchestre du **Casa Bar** (Münstergasse).
Sympathique piano-bar (jazz, succès des Beattles et autres, repris souvent par les consommateurs réunis autour du piano) au **Splendid Bar** (Rosengasse).
Au **Kronenhalle** (Rämistrasse), dans un cadre très chic, confortablement calé dans un profond fauteuil on peut consommer devant des toiles de Chagall, Giacometti, Picasso, Kandinsky, Klee, Miró.
Café célèbre au cachet 1900, le **Café Odéon** (Limmatquai) fut jadis le rendez-vous des artistes et écrivains. Sur le même quai le **Café Select** s'adressera plus particulièrement aux amateurs de billard. Dans une ruelle voisine (Schifflände), au **Rene's Hard Rock Cafe**, clientèle jeune et musique enregistrée généreuse en décibels.
Grande variété de bières et atmosphère de pub anglais au **Lion's Pub** (Oetenbachgasse, rive gauche).

Les quais

Jardins du Zürichhorn — *Par l'Utoquai* (**FZ**).
Annoncés par les bâtiments du « Centre Le Corbusier », ils réservent une excellente **perspective**★ sur la ville. Mobile de Jean Tinguely, *Heureka*.

Weinplatz (**EZ**) — Au Sud de cette place que décore une jolie fontaine surmontée d'un vigneron portant sa hotte, on découvre, sur la rive opposée, quelques belles maisons anciennes aux toits « à la flamande », l'hôtel de ville (Rathaus) (**FZ H**) élégant édifice dans le goût de la Renaissance italienne – et la Wasserkirche (**FZ**), chapelle du 15e s. ; la cathédrale (Grossmünster) domine l'ensemble de ses deux hautes tours.

Lindenhof (**EZ**) — Cette esplanade, ombragée de platanes et ornée d'une fontaine, coiffe la colline qui, bien placée pour surveiller le passage de la Limmat, fut le site des établissements celte et romain autour desquels s'est développée la ville.
De la terrasse, on découvre la ville ancienne, étagée sur la rive droite : en face se dresse la Predigerkirche, à droite le Grossmünster.

Panorama Bar Jules Verne (**EY E**) ⊙ — On y bénéficie d'une belle vue sur le centre de la ville.

★**Cathédrale (Grossmünster)** (**FHZ**) ⊙ — Cet édifice imposant, bâti aux 11e et 13e s., a remplacé une collégiale fondée, dit-on, par Charlemagne. La cathédrale est le symbole de la Réforme en Suisse alémanique. Zwingli y a prêché de 1519 à sa mort. Sa façade est encadrée de hautes tours à trois étages, surmontées de deux coupoles de bois revêtues de plaques de métal. La tour Sud est ornée d'une gigantesque statue (l'original est dans la crypte) représentant Charlemagne assis tenant un glaive sur les genoux.
Entrer par le portail latéral gauche en bronze sculpté, dont les piédroits sont ornés de sculptures et de chapiteaux. La nef est voûtée d'ogives ; le chœur, surélevé, se termine par un chevet plat tandis qu'une galerie court au-dessus des collatéraux. On peut voir quelques vestiges de fresques dans le chœur et dans la crypte, vaste halle à trois nefs. Les vitraux modernes sont d'Augusto Giacometti (1932).
Le **cloître** roman voûté d'arêtes s'ouvre sur la cour par des groupes de trois arcades dont les arcs en plein cintre reposent sur des chapiteaux finement sculptés.

Fraumünster (**EZ**) ⊙ — Bâtie aux 12e et 15e s., cette église a succédé à un ancien couvent de femmes fondé en 853 par Louis le Germanique. A l'intérieur (nef voûtée d'ogives), on remarque de beaux **vitraux**★ de Marc Chagall dans le chœur et le croisillon Sud, d'Augusto Giacometti dans le croisillon Nord. Deux tribunes à arcades se font face.
Au côté Sud de l'église, les vestiges du **cloître**★ (Kreuzgang) roman sont ornés de fresques de Paul Bodmer (1921-1941) traitant la légende de la fondation de l'abbaye.

★★**Musée national suisse (Schweizerisches Landesmuseum)** (**EY**) ⊙ — D'une richesse considérable, les collections scrupuleusement sélectionnées intéressent toutes les manifestations de la civilisation helvétique. Son réaménagement n'est toujours pas achevé, d'où de nombreuses salles fermées ou temporairement inaccessibles *(le texte ci-dessous sélectionne les principales curiosités visibles actuellement)*.
Au rez-de-chaussée, outre une chambre en style gothique tardif (18) provenant de l'abbaye de Fraumünster, voir la salle consacrée à l'héraldique (7) et la fresque profane peinte vers 1300 (4).
Au 1er étage, la collection préhistorique (salles 69 à 73) compte parmi les plus riches par ses très beaux objets et bijoux en or. Voûtée d'ogives et décorée par F. Hodler de fresques représentant *La Retraite de Marignan*, la grande salle des Armes et Armures (50) présente une rétrospective très complète de la vie militaire du 13e au 18e s. Le trésor est formé de pièces d'orfèvrerie, profanes ou religieuses, certaines appartenant aux corporations zurichoises. De nombreuses salles des 16e et 17e s. ont été reconstituées, dont une salle de réception (43) aux boiseries embellies de portraits d'hommes illustres. Les « vitraux de cabinet », vitraux héraldiques de petit format, firent fureur en Suisse alémanique durant le 16e s. (30) ; voir également la collection d'horlogerie et d'instruments scientifiques du 16e au 19e s. (23), dont le globe terrestre réalisé vers 1750 d'après la carte du monde de Mercator et le beau globe céleste de Bürgi exécuté en 1594 pour l'empereur Rodolphe II.
Au second étage, une importante collection de costumes des différents cantons (18e et 19e s.) permet de suivre l'évolution du costume en Suisse.

Musée d'Arts appliqués de Zurich (Museum für Gestaltung Zürich) ⊙ — Accès par la Sihlquai (**EY**).
Des expositions temporaires y sont organisées, se rapportant aux arts appliqués, à l'architecture, à l'art graphique, à l'esthétique industrielle. Collection de graphismes et d'affiches.

★**Église Sts-Félix-et-Regula** — *Accès par Talacker, Ouest du Plan* (**EZ**). Cette église moderne est dédiée aux saints Félix et Regula, frère et sœur, qui, d'après la tradition, auraient subi le martyre à Zurich, décapités sur l'ordre de Décius. La haute tour-clocher est séparée du reste de l'édifice.

ZÜRICH

Bahnhofstrasse	EYZ
Bellevueplatz	FZ
Limmatquai	FYZ
Löwenstrasse	EY
Paradeplatz	EZ
Poststrasse	EZ 58
Rennweg	EYZ 63
Storchengasse	EZ 85
Strehlgasse	EZ 87
Uraniastrasse	EYZ
Augustinergasse	EZ 9
Bärengasse	EZ 10
Beethovenstrasse	EZ 12
Claridenstrasse	EZ 18
Clausiusstrasse	FY 19
Culmannstrasse	FY 21
Fraumünsterstrasse	EZ 28
Hafnerstrasse	EY 36
Kantonsschulstrasse	FZ 39
Konradstrasse	EY 40
Marktgasse	FZ 46
Münsterhof	EZ 48
Museumstrasse	EY 49
Nelkenstrasse	FY 52
Neumarkt	FZ 54
Rathausbrücke	FZ 60
Rindermarkt	FZ 64
Stadelhoferstrasse	FZ 78
Stampfenbachplatz	FY 79
Stampfenbachstrasse	EFY 81
Sumatrastrasse	FY 88
Talacker	EZ 90
Tannenstrasse	FY 91
Theaterstrasse	FZ 93
Usteristrasse	EY 100
Weinbergfussweg	FY 103

E	Panorama Bar Jules Verne
H	Rathaus
M¹	Haus "zur Meisen"

Dans une grande ville, dans un village de montagne ou sur les bords paisibles d'un lac...
Pour trouver un toit, pour trouver une table,
consultez le guide Rouge Michelin Suisse (hôtels et restaurants).

ZÜRICH

L'intérieur est fort curieux : le vaisseau, en forme d'amande, est surmonté d'une voûte à peine incurvée soutenue par des piliers obliques. Des vitraux modernes sont disposés à hauteur de la voûte.

Église de Zürich-Altstetten – *Accès par Talacker, Ouest du plan* (**EZ**). Dominée par une haute tour carrée ajourée, d'une grande élégance, cette église moderne offre une nef dissymétrique, éclairée d'un seul côté par de grandes baies.

Musée de l'Habitat (Wohnmuseum) (**EZ**) ⊙ – Ce musée du vieux Zurich occupe deux maisons contiguës de la fin du 17e s., très restaurées. Il présente sur trois étages d'abondants exemples de meubles, poêles et objets d'usage ou d'ornement, datant du milieu du 17e s. au milieu du 19e s. et mis en valeur dans leur cadre d'époque. Au sous-sol, exposition d'une collection de poupées créées dans les années 20 par une artiste locale.

★★ **Musée Rietberg** ⊙ – *Gablerstrasse 15. Accès par Bleicherweg* (**EZ**).
Ce musée est installé dans l'ancienne villa Wesendonck, au milieu d'un parc et en vue du lac.

Il renferme de précieuses collections réunies par le baron von der Heydt : sculptures des Indes, du Cambodge, de Java, et de Chine ; sculptures africaines et océaniennes. Des estampes japonaises, des œuvres d'art du Proche-Orient, du Tibet, et de l'Amérique précolombienne, des peintures d'Extrême-Orient, des masques suisses et des tapis flamands et arméniens complètent cette exposition.

Hôtel « Zur Meisen » (**EZ M¹**) – *Entre le Münsterhof et la Limmat.*
Cet hôtel de corporation (Zunfthaus) érigé en 1757, abrite les collections de céramique (faïences et porcelaines) suisse du 18e s. appartenant au Musée national suisse.

★★ **Musée des Beaux-Arts (Kunsthaus)** (**FZ**) ⊙ – Ce musée, dans le cadre duquel sont organisées de grandes expositions temporaires, réserve une place prééminente à la peinture moderne. Mais les sculptures du Haut Moyen Âge français et allemand, les primitifs suisses et allemands du 15e s. n'y méritent pas moins de retenir l'attention.

Au 1er étage, on peut admirer les toiles les plus représentatives de Ferdinand Hodler, considéré comme le chef de file de l'école suisse au début du siècle, ainsi que celles de Vallotton, Böcklin, Anker, Auberjonois, Barraud.

L'école française figure avec des œuvres de Toulouse-Lautrec, Cézanne, Renoir, Degas, Matisse, Utrillo, Léger, Braque et Picasso. L'une des salles est réservée à quatorze œuvres de Marc Chagall.

Le musée possède la plus importante collection – hors de Scandinavie – d'œuvres du peintre norvégien Edvard Munch (1863-1944).

La Fondation Alberto Giacometti fait une place importante à cet artiste (1901-1966).

★ **Jardin zoologique (Zoo Dolder)** ⊙ – *Accès par la Gloriastrasse* (**FY**).
Bien aménagé au Zurichberg, dans un très joli cadre de verdure, ce zoo compte plus de 2 000 animaux. Outre les tortues géantes, la loutre et le castor dont on peut observer les activités dans l'eau et sur la terre ferme, il ne faut pas manquer de voir les singes et surtout le bain des éléphants *(vers 10 h)*. Un tableau à l'entrée indique les naissances récentes.

★★ **Fondation Collection E.G. Bührle (Sammlung Bührle)** ⊙ – *Zollikerstrasse 172. Accès par la Zeltweg, Est du plan* (**FZ**).
Une villa, située dans la belle banlieue Sud-Est, abrite des tableaux et sculptures collectionnés par l'industriel Emil Bührle entre 1934 et 1956. Cet industriel allemand qui vint habiter Zurich en 1924, grand admirateur de Claude Monet, a formé en à peine vingt ans une collection superbe autour de toiles de maîtres de l'impressionnisme et du post-impressionnisme.

Rez-de-chaussée – Quatre pièces sont consacrées à des œuvres du 16e au 19e s. : le palier et le salon hollandais avec entre autres F. Hals *(Portrait d'homme)*, Rembrandt, S. van Ruysdael *(Vue de Rhenen)* et D. Teniers ; le salon Louis XVI avec notamment F. Boucher, E. Degas *(Portrait de Mme Camus* flanqué de deux études*)*, J.-H. Fragonard et J.-A.-D. Ingres *(Portrait de M. Devillers)* ; le salon vénitien avec Canaletto (deux représentations du Grand Canal appartenant à une série de six vues), F. Goya *(Procession à Valence)*, Le Greco et G. Tiepolo *(Le Bain de Diane)*.

Le salon rose et la salle de musique concentrent l'extraordinaire noyau de la collection. On verra *Tournesols sur un fauteuil* de P. Gauguin, *La Route de Versailles à Louveciennes* de C. Pissarro ou *Les Hirondelles* de E. Manet, exécuté en 1873 à Berck-sur-Mer. Le ravissant portrait de la *Petite Irène* de P.-A. Renoir a été réalisé peu avant que le peintre ne se détache de l'impressionnisme. De C. Monet on admire *Les Coquelicots près de Vétheuil* où les personnages, évoqués par des touches rapides, se fondent dans le paysage. *Messaline* de H. de Toulouse-Lautrec a influencé les Fauves par ses lumineuses plages de couleur.

ZÜRICH

Une belle série de trois portraits de P. Cézanne attire le regard, et notamment son fameux *Garçon au gilet rouge* à la pose mélancolique. Enfin, le magnifique *Branches de marronniers en fleur*, qui dénote l'influence de l'art japonais, fut réalisé par V. van Gogh lors d'une de ses rares périodes d'espoir.

Le jardin d'hiver présente quelques pièces antiques, dont un buste en marbre de César.

Escalier – Aux sept E. Delacroix *(Autoportrait)* et toiles de G. Courbet et de R. Dufy de la première volée s'ajoutent plus haut des tableaux de M. Chagall, P. Picasso, G. Rouault et un *Nu couché* de A. Modigliani.

Premier étage – Le palier est consacré au 20e s. avec des œuvres cubistes de G. Braque *(Le Violoniste)*, P. Picasso et J. Gris, mais surtout plusieurs toiles fauves de A. Derain, A. Marquet, H. Matisse (remarquer le changement de palette

L'Italienne par Pablo Picasso

entre le *Pont Saint-Michel à Paris* et la *Nature morte* réalisée cinq ans plus tard) et M. de Vlaminck *(Chalands sur la Seine près du Pecq)*. La salle Courbet réunit des tableaux réalistes dont le *spectacle gratuit* de H. Daumier et le *Portrait de A. Sisley* par Renoir, auquel est consacrée une salle adjacente où l'on verra les splendides *Jardin à Giverny* de C. Monet, et *Barques à voiles* de E. Boudin qui l'orienta vers ce qu'il est convenu d'appeler la peinture de plein air. Dans la salle Manet *(La Sultane, à l'érotisme subtil)*, ne pas manquer *Étang aux nénuphars* et *Waterloo Bridge* de C. Monet, ainsi que l'un des vingt-deux bronzes originaux de la *Danseuse* de E. Degas. Les trois dernières salles sont consacrées à V. van Gogh *(Autoportrait et Le Semeur)*, à A. Sisley *(Été à Bougival)* et à P. Bonnard *(Portrait d'Ambroise Vollard* où l'on distingue un hommage à P. Cézanne) ; salles enrichies notamment de *L'Offrande* de P. Gauguin (peint aux îles Marquises peu avant son décès), des *Modistes* de P. Signac, et du *Salon Natanson* (lieu de rencontre des Nabis) de E. Vuillard.

La salle gothique (voir les deux paysages de J. Patenier) et le deuxième étage contiennent de belles sculptures religieuses (12e-16e s.).

PROMENADES EN BATEAU ⊙

Très nombreuses possibilités au départ de Zurich, depuis le « Petit tour » de 1 h 30 (limité à Erlenbach et Thalwil) jusqu'au « Grand tour » d'une demi-journée, permettant de visiter Rapperswil *(voir à ce nom)*.

Embarcadère principal à la Bürkliplatz (**EZ**).

ENVIRONS

★★ **Uetliberg** ⊙ – *Alt. 874 m. 2 h AR environ dont 50 mn de chemin de fer.*

Le trajet s'effectue en grande partie à travers bois. De la gare d'arrivée, d'où l'on a déjà une belle vue sur les sommets neigeux, on gagne, par un sentier en forte montée, la terrasse proche de l'hôtel-restaurant (table d'orientation).

On peut encore monter au sommet de la tour-belvédère (167 marches) d'où l'on découvre un immense **panorama**★★ sur l'ensemble de l'agglomération zurichoise, la vallée de la Limmat, le lac de Zurich et la chaîne des Alpes – du Säntis, à l'Est, à la Jungfrau et aux Diablerets, au Sud-Ouest –, tandis qu'à l'Ouest et au Nord-Ouest s'estompent les croupes du Jura et des Vosges.

★ **Route du col d'Albis** – *53 km. Quitter Zurich au Sud-Ouest par la Gessnerallee* (**EY**) *puis la route n° 4.*

La route suit d'abord la vallée de la Sihl, entre les pentes de l'Uetliberg à droite et le lac de Zurich à gauche – devant lequel s'interposent l'autoroute et un chapelet d'agglomérations. A hauteur du bourg d'Adliswil, quitter la route n° 4 pour celle d'Albis, à droite, qui s'engage dans la forêt de Sihl.

ZÜRICH

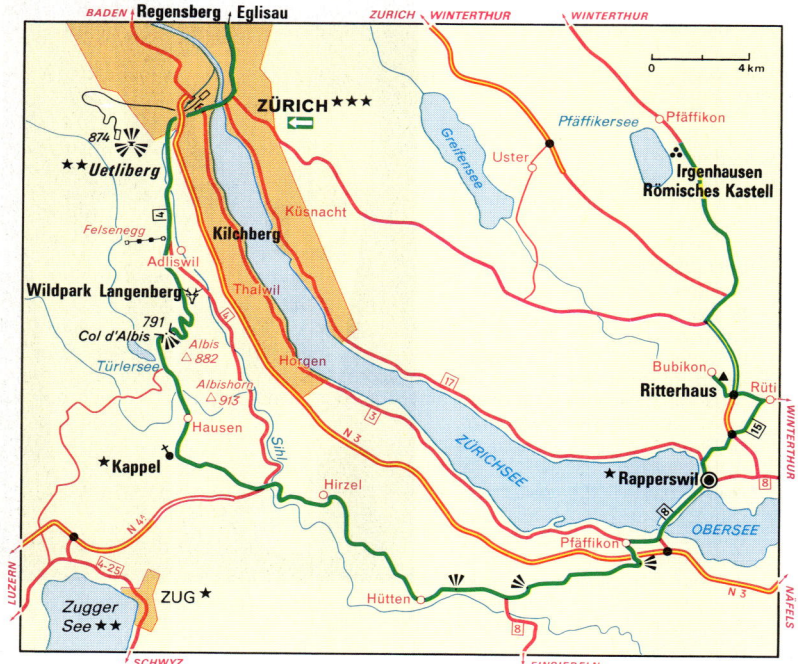

Wildpark Langenberg — Ce parc d'animaux sauvages (européens) s'étend de part et d'autre de la route (principalement à gauche), au Nord de Langnau am Albis, sur plusieurs hectares de forêt et de monticules rocheux : cerfs, daims, chevreuils, chamois, bouquetins, ours, lynx, sangliers, marmottes... s'y ébattent dans de grands enclos.

La route s'élève jusqu'au col d'Albis (alt. 791 m), d'où se dégagent des vues étendues sur le relief boisé de la région, puis descend entre le lac de Türler et le mont Albis avant d'obliquer à gauche vers Hausen que l'on traverse au pied de l'Albishorn.

★ **Ancienne abbaye de Kappel** — Voir à ce nom.

De Kappel, descendre à gauche jusqu'à retrouver la route n° 4 que l'on emprunte à gauche pour prendre, à Hirzel, celle de Schönenberg à droite.

Peu après Hütten, la route, en corniche sur 2 km, fait découvrir la partie la plus large du lac de Zurich. Elle s'élève ensuite, jusqu'à Feusisberg, dans une campagne riante agrémentée d'échappées sur le lac ; dans la descente qui suit se découvrent les deux îlots boisés de celui-ci.

Après un sinueux passage sous bois, c'est, dans la descente finale sur Pfäffikon, une **vue**★ plongeante qui se révèle sur les deux parties du lac (l'Obersee à droite, le Zürichsee à gauche) que sépare la chaussée de Rapperswil, sur cette ville même et son château.

★ **Rapperswil** — Voir à ce nom.

Regensberg — Alt. 617 m. *17 km. Quitter Zurich par l'Universitätstrasse (FY), et prendre immédiatement à gauche la route de Dielsdorf, puis, encore à gauche, une petite route.*

Ce petit village de vignerons, admirablement préservé avec ses vieilles maisons à colombage serrées autour de sa place unique, est un charmant but de promenade. De la tour de garde romane, la **vue** s'étend sur les vignobles et la campagne alentour.

De Zurich à Eglisau — *23 km. Quitter Zurich par l'Universitätstrasse (FY) et la route n° 4.*

5 km après Kloten, à la sortie Nord de Seeb-Winkel, prendre à gauche une petite route qui conduit, à 500 m, aux ruines romaines.

Ferme romaine de Seeb (Römischer Gutshof Seeb) — Dans un site riant offrant des vues étendues (tables d'orientation) sur la plaine et les hauteurs environnantes, se disséminent les vestiges d'une importante exploitation agricole du 1er s., agrandie jusqu'au 3e s. puis détruite ou abandonnée. Les fondations de l'aile Ouest de la villa d'habitation sont conservées sous abri : on y voit les piles en briques de l'hypo-

causte et une partie des thermes, une belle mosaïque en noir et blanc, la maquette et les relevés topographiques du domaine, une vitrine de poteries récupérées sur place.
A l'extérieur, on remarque ce qui reste du château d'eau qui servait à alimenter la ferme, d'un four de potier, d'une piscine avec puits central (profond de 6 m), etc.

Eglisau – Ce vieux bourg pimpant, proche de la frontière allemande, occupe un site ★ charmant sur la rive Nord du Rhin où il s'étage, au milieu d'arbres et de vignes. En contre-haut de l'église du clocher à bulbe (transformée au 18e s.) une terrasse-belvédère ombragée, et ornée de la statue en bronze d'une jeune femme contemplant le Rhin, offre un joli coup d'œil sur le fleuve, en amont des deux ponts qui l'enjambent.

Kilchberg – *7 km. Quitter Zurich par Gal Guisan-Quai* (**EZ**).
La route n° 3 longe la rive Ouest du lac, bordée de somptueuses propriétés particulières, jusqu'à Kilchberg, le faubourg résidentiel de Zurich. Le poète et romancier suisse Conrad Ferdinand Meyer (1825-1898) et l'écrivain allemand Thomas Mann (1875-1955) y ont fini leurs jours et reposent dans le petit cimetière. En bordure du lac s'élevait l'ancienne manufacture de porcelaine de Zurich, connue pour la finesse de ses décors paysagers.

ZURZACH

Argovie – 3 594 habitants
Carte Michelin n° 427 pli 5 ou 216 pli 6 – Alt. 339 m

C'est l'ancienne Tenedo romaine et une petite ville thermale (on y soigne les rhumatismes) près du Rhin, avec quelques monuments ou maisons des 17e et 18e s. dans sa rue principale et, au bord du fleuve, un château élevé au 19e s.

Musée August Deusser ⊙ – Le château abrite ce musée constitué par les collections personnelles et des œuvres du peintre allemand August Deusser (1870-1942). Au 1er étage on remarque, entre autres, le mobilier (en partie Louis XVI), plusieurs tableaux, un bas-relief chinois du 18e s., et un lit sculpté, à dorures et angelots, fabriqué pour le roi Louis II de Bavière. Le 2e étage abrite des toiles léguées par Deusser, dont bon nombre évoquant la guerre de 1870 et dont le style, pour certaines, s'apparente à celui des impressionnistes.
Dans le parc du château, agrémenté de beaux arbres et d'un étang artificiel, nombreuses sculptures modernes de Johann Ulrich Steiger.

INFOTELEFON

Renseignements touristiques par téléphone (uniquement en Suisse)

157 120 111	**Suisse Tourisme : informations générales**
157 120 101	**Suisse Tourisme : manifestations importantes**
157 120 109	**Sports d'hiver (pistes : ski alpin, ski de fond, luge)**
157 120 180	**Région des Grisons**
157 120 170	**Suisse orientale et principauté du Liechtenstein**
157 120 210	**Région de Zurich**
157 120 140	**Suisse centrale**
157 120 160	**Région de Bâle**
157 120 230	**Oberland bernois**
157 120 130	**Mittelland bernois**
157 120 120	**Région du Léman**
157 120 220	**Région de Genève**
157 120 150	**Valais**
157 120 190	**Tessin**
157 120 260	**Société suisse des hôteliers**
157 120 200	**Hôtels E&G (chaîne hôtelière)**

Renseignements pratiques

Horloge en fer (16e s.)

Musée International d'Horlogerie, La Chaux-de-Fonds

Avant le départ

Pour organiser son voyage, rassembler la documentation nécessaire, vérifier certaines informations, s'adresser en premier lieu à **Suisse tourisme (ST)** : – 11 bis, rue Scribe 75009 Paris ☎ 44 51 65 51 Fax 47 42 43 88 Minitel 3615 code Suisse
– Avenue Brugmann 24 1060 Bruxelles ☎ (02) 345 54 45 Fax 218 30 29.

Comment se rendre en Suisse

En voiture – La **carte Michelin n° 911** France indique les grands itinéraires, les kilométrages, les temps de parcours, les itinéraires de dégagement, les prévisions de circulation entre les grandes villes françaises et de pays limitrophes avec des grandes villes suisses. La **carte Michelin n° 970** Europe indique les autoroutes, routes nationales, régionales, etc. entre les différents pays d'Europe.
Sur Minitel le **3615 code Michelin** permet d'établir plusieurs itinéraires entre un point de départ en France et un point de destination en Suisse. Le kilométrage total et le temps de parcours sont alors indiqués (ainsi que les sites touristiques et la sélection Michelin des hôtels, restaurants et terrains de camping). Pour les itinéraires avec autoroutes, le coût des péages sur le parcours français est également indiqué.
Vous pouvez choisir plusieurs types d'itinéraires : celui conseillé par Michelin (le meilleur compromis), le plus rapide en temps, le plus court en kilomètres, l'itinéraire favorisant les autoroutes ou évitant les péages. Le **3617 Michelin** permet d'obtenir toutes ces informations immédiatement par fax.

En train – Le TGV relie Paris à Genève, Lausanne et Berne. Par ailleurs, des trains internationaux relient la plupart des grandes villes européennes à de grandes villes suisses. Pour les horaires, prix et réductions, se renseigner dans les gares, agences de voyages, bureaux des chemins de fer nationaux (SNCF en France, SNCB en Belgique) ou aux bureaux de Suisse Tourisme. L'indicateur des Chemins de fer suisses (CFF) est en vente aux bureaux de Suisse Tourisme de Paris et de Bruxelles.

En avion – Paris et Bruxelles sont reliées aux aéroports de Bâle, Berne, Genève, Lugano et Zurich. La ville de Luxembourg est reliée à Genève et Zurich.
D'autres liaisons directes sont assurées à partir de villes françaises, ainsi :
– Biarritz-Genève ; Bordeaux-Genève ; Lyon-Zurich ; Marseille-Genève et Zurich ; Montpellier-Genève ; Nantes-Clermont-Ferrand-Genève ; Nice-Genève, Lugano et Zurich ; Strasbourg-Zurich ; Toulouse-Genève.
Les compagnies aériennes assurant ces liaisons sont Swissair, Crossair, Air France, Sabena, Luxair, Air Inter, Air Littoral, Air Vendée, TWA, TAT, United Airlines.
Il existe des tarifs réduits Apex et Week-end/Vols Vacances. Se renseigner auprès des compagnies aériennes ou agences de voyages.

INFORMATIONS GÉNÉRALES

Papiers d'identité – Pour un séjour touristique de 3 mois maximum, les ressortissants français, belges et luxembourgeois doivent être en possession de la carte nationale d'identité ou d'un passeport, ces deux documents en cours de validité. Un passeport périmé depuis moins de 5 ans peut toutefois suffire.
Les **enfants mineurs de nationalité française** doivent être en possession d'une carte nationale d'identité ou figurer sur le passeport de la personne qui les accompagne. Un enfant mineur voyageant seul muni d'une carte nationale d'identité doit de plus posséder une attestation d'autorisation de sortie du territoire donnée par un représentant légal (père, mère ou tuteur). Les **enfants de nationalité belge** âgés de moins de 12 ans doivent être en possession de la carte blanche sans photo, à condition de voyager avec les parents. Sinon se procurer un certificat d'identité à la commune du domicile.

Documents pour la circulation – **Voitures** : permis international ou permis national à 3 volets pour le conducteur, carte grise et carte verte internationale d'assurance automobile dite « carte verte » pour le véhicule. Ce dernier doit également porter la plaque réglementaire de nationalité. Pour les possesseurs de **caravane**, celle-ci ne doit être attelée qu'au véhicule tracteur indiqué sur le permis de circulation.
Les **motocyclistes et cyclomotoristes** sont soumis au même régime que les automobilistes, sauf pour des engins inférieurs à 125 cm³. Le port du casque est obligatoire.

Animaux familiers – Les chiens et les chats doivent avoir été vaccinés contre la rage au moins 30 jours et au plus un an avant le passage de la frontière, un certificat vétérinaire est obligatoire.

Réglementations douanières – La Suisse n'étant pas un pays membre de l'Union européenne, il convient de se renseigner auprès de Suisse Tourisme sur les prescriptions en vigueur au moment du départ ou au passage de la frontière.

Santé – Les frais médicaux engagés doivent être réglés sur place. Conserver les factures pour les envoyer à la Sécurité sociale au retour.
Aussi peut-il être prudent de contracter une assurance maladie-accidents avant le voyage (Europ-Assistance, Mondial assistance, Elvia).

Vie pratique

Ambassades et consulats

Berne
Ambassade de France Schosshaldenstrasse 46, 3006 Berne ☏ (031) 359 21 11
Ambassade de Belgique Weststrasse 6, 3005 Berne ☏ (031) 351 04 62
Ambassade du Luxembourg Kramgasse 45, 3000 Berne ☏ (031) 311 47 32

Bâle
Consulat général de France Elisabethenstrasse 33, 4051 Bâle ☏ (061) 272 63 18

Genève
Consulat général de France 11, rue J.-Imbert-Galloix, 1205 Genève ☏ (022) 311 34 11
Consulat général de Belgique Rue Moillebeau 56-58, 1209 Genève ☏ (022) 733 81 50

Lausanne
Bureau consulaire de France 26, avenue de Cour, 1007 Lausanne ☏ (021) 617 60 54

Zurich
Consulat général de France Mühlebachstrasse 7, 8008 Zurich ☏ (01) 251 85 44
Consulat honoraire de Belgique Basteiplatz 5, 8001 Zurich ☏ (01) 212 11 55

Ouverture des magasins et banques – Magasins : du lundi au vendredi généralement de 8 h à 18 h 30, le samedi 16 h ou 17 h ; banques de 8 h à 16 h, fermées le samedi.

Heure – La Suisse adopte l'heure d'été et l'heure d'hiver comme la France et la Belgique.

Monnaie – Le franc suisse.
Billets de banque : 10, 20, 50, 100, 500, 1 000 F.
Pièces : 5, 10, 20 et 50 centimes ; 1, 2 et 5 F.

Change – Dans les banques, certains grands magasins, les aéroports, certaines grandes gares, certains hôtels.

Cartes de crédit – Les principales cartes de crédit American Express, Diners Club, Eurocard/Mastercard, Visa, Japan Card Bank sont acceptées.
Le **guide Rouge Michelin Suisse** (hôtels et restaurants) signale les établissements qui acceptent le paiement par carte de crédit.

Jours fériés – Le calendrier des jours fériés varie d'un canton à un autre, compte tenu de sa religion officielle et de son passé historique. Les fêtes « générales » sont généralement les 1er et 2 janvier, Vendredi saint, Lundi de Pâques, Ascension, Lundi de Pentecôte, 25 et 26 décembre. Le 1er août, jour de la fête nationale, est généralement chômé. Le Jeûne fédéral (Fête fédérale d'action de grâce ; Bettag en allemand) se fête dans tous les cantons sauf Genève le 3e dimanche de septembre. Le canton de Genève fête le Jeûne genevois le 2e jeudi de septembre.

Poste – Les timbres sont en vente dans les bureaux de poste (fermés le samedi à partir de 11 h).

Téléphone – En Suisse, l'indicatif se compose d'un premier groupe de trois chiffres (indicatif régional) commençant par 0, suivi d'un groupe de cinq, six ou sept chiffres. On ne compose pas le premier groupe pour téléphoner à un abonné de la même ville ou d'une ville ayant le même indicatif.

Pour appeler la Suisse :
– de France 19 41 + indicatif régional sans le 0 + numéro de l'abonné,
– de Belgique et du Luxembourg 00 41 + indicatif régional sans le 0 + numéro de l'abonné.
Pour appeler de Suisse :
– la France : Paris et région parisienne 00 33 + 1 + numéro de l'abonné,
– la province 00 33 + numéro de l'abonné,
– la Belgique : 00 32 + indicatif de la zone sans le 0 + numéro de l'abonné,
– le Luxembourg : 00352 + indicatif de la zone sans le 0 + numéro de l'abonné.
Une télécarte, la **taxcard**, est en vente dans les bureaux de poste. Prix variable selon le nombre d'unités.
La nuit ou pendant le week-end, le tarif des communications est réduit d'environ 20 %.

Quelques numéros utiles

111	En cas d'accident
114	Renseignements téléphoniques internationaux
117	Police-secours
120	Hiver : enneigement
120	Été : informations touristiques
140	Secours routier : jour et nuit
162	Prévisions météorologiques
163	État des routes
168	Nouvelles en français
187	Bulletin des avalanches

Sur la route et en ville

Cartes routières – Pour circuler dans l'ensemble du pays, utiliser la carte Michelin n° 427 Suisse (couverture orange) à 1/400 000, avec répertoire des localités et agrandissements de Bâle, Berne, Genève, Lausanne et Zürich.
Les cartes Michelin détaillées, à 1/200 000 (couverture jaune) couvrent le pays entier :
– n° 216 Neuchâtel-Basel-St-Gallen
– n° 217 Genève-Bern-Andermatt
– n° 218 Andermatt-St-Moritz-Bolzano/Bozen
– n° 219 Aosta/Aoste-Zermatt-Milan
Les cartes à 1/400 000 et 1/200 000 signalent les grandes routes périodiquement enneigées, avec la date probable de leur fermeture, ainsi que les routes équipées en téléphones de secours.
Les cartes à 1/200 000 signalent les voies très étroites (croisement difficile ou impossible), les montées et descentes accentuées, les parcours difficiles ou dangereux, les tunnels, l'altitude des principaux cols.

Carburant – Si le super et l'essence sont meilleur marché qu'en France, le gazole moins répandu est plus cher. Le super sans plomb (indice d'octane 95) est le plus avantageux.
La plupart des stations-service sont fermées la nuit. Cependant, des pompes automatiques fonctionnent avec des billets de 10 et 20 F.

Quelques règles impératives – Le port de la **ceinture de sécurité** est obligatoire à l'avant et à l'arrière du véhicule.
Les enfants de moins de 12 ans doivent être assis à l'arrière du véhicule.

Vitesse – Dans les villages et agglomérations, sauf indication spéciale, la vitesse est limitée à 50 km/h. A certains carrefours, lorsque l'attente au feu rouge est relativement longue, un panneau **« coupez votre moteur »** invite l'automobiliste à lutter ainsi contre la pollution.
Sur route la vitesse est limitée à 80 km/h, sur autoroute à 120 km/h.

Phares – Les feux de croisement (codes) sont obligatoires dans les tunnels et la nuit dans les agglomérations.

Triangle de panne – Obligatoire en plus des feux de détresse.

En montagne – La voiture descendante doit la priorité à celle qui monte ainsi qu'aux poids lourds. Les cars postaux, reconnaissables à leur couleur jaune, ont priorité absolue.

Pneus cloutés – En principe autorisés du 1er novembre au 30 avril (vitesse autorisée 80 km/h). Ils sont **strictement interdits** sur les autoroutes.

Caravanes et remorques – Le code de la route suisse limite la largeur des caravanes et remorques à 2,50 m et leur longueur à 12 m, timon compris. Pour les caravanes immatriculées à l'étranger qui dépassent légèrement les dimensions requises, des autorisations peuvent être accordées en s'adressant au Bureau des Douanes et en acquittant une taxe de 20 FS.
Les véhicules 4 × 4 peuvent tracter des caravanes ou remorques d'une largeur de 2,50 m au plus.
Vitesse maximum autorisée sur tout le réseau routier et autoroutier :
– jusqu'à 1 t : 80 km/h
– au-dessus de 1 t : 60 km/h.
Routes interdites : cols du Klausen, du Nufenen, du Schelten et du Weissenstein. Accès au Bürgenstock, Diemtigtal.

Tramways – Plusieurs villes disposent d'un réseau de tramways, attention aux piétons qui montent ou descendent, ils sont prioritaires.

Autoroutes – Une **vignette autoroutière** (valable 14 mois à compter du 1er décembre) est obligatoire pour les véhicules à moteur (et les remorques) jusqu'à 3,5 t. Cette vignette, de **40 francs suisses**, est en vente aux bureaux de douane suisses et doit être collée sur le pare-brise. En Belgique, elle peut être achetée à Suisse Tourisme ou dans les automobiles clubs ; au Luxembourg, dans les automobiles clubs. Elle n'est pas vendue en France. Les Français doivent l'acheter au passage de la frontière.
Contrairement à la plupart des pays européens, le fléchage des **autoroutes** est signalé sur un **fond vert** et non bleu. Le fond bleu étant réservé aux routes à priorité.

Secours routier – Des bornes téléphoniques SOS, utilisables en cas de panne, sont à la disposition des automobilistes sur les autoroutes, ainsi que sur quelques routes à grande circulation et en montagne.
De plus, il est possible d'obtenir des secours routiers de jour comme de nuit en composant le 140 de n'importe quel téléphone.

État des routes – En Suisse en composant le 163. Hors de Suisse : indicatif international + 41 21 163.

Automobiles Clubs – Touring Club Suisse (TCS) 9, rue Pierre-Fatio 1211 Genève 3 ☏ (022) 737 12 01 Fax (022) 737 13 10.
Automobile Club de Suisse (ACS) Theaterplatz 13 3000 Bern 7 ☏ (031) 311 26 37 Fax (031) 311 38 13.

Hébergement

Hôtels – Le **guide Rouge Michelin Suisse**, mis à jour chaque année, recommande un large choix d'établissements avec indication de leur classe et de leur confort, de leur situation, de leur agrément, de leur prix. Ce choix a été établi après visites et enquêtes sur place. Les établissements qui se distinguent par leur agrément et leur tranquillité (décor original, site, vue exceptionnelle ou intéressante) sont indiqués par des symboles rouges. Les localités qui disposent de tels hôtels sont repérées sur plusieurs cartes dans les pages d'introduction du guide. Les hôtels où les chambres sont facilement accessibles aux handicapés physiques sont signalés par le symbole &.

Locations – Les Offices du tourisme locaux disposent de listes de propriétaires ou d'agences immobilières louant chalets ou appartements de vacances.
Suisse Tourisme à Paris et Bruxelles distribue un catalogue donnant des adresses d'organismes locatifs.

Logement chez l'habitant – Signalé sur place par le panneau Zimmer frei/Chambres. Se renseigner auprès des Offices du tourisme locaux pour obtenir les adresses.

Vacances à la ferme – Suisse Tourisme distribue une brochure consacrée au tourisme rural.

Auberges de jeunesse – Réservées aux personnes âgées de moins de 25 ans et aux personnes en possession d'une carte de membre des auberges de jeunesse.
La carte de membre est en vente aux adresses suivantes :
– Fédération Unie des Auberges de Jeunesse
  27, rue Pajol
  75018 Paris ☎ 44 89 87 27
– Auberges de Jeunesse (ASBL)
  Rue Van Oost 52
  1030 Bruxelles ☎ 215 31 00
S'adresser à Suisse Tourisme pour se procurer la liste des auberges de jeunesse.

Camping, caravaning – Le camping sauvage n'est pas autorisé. De plus il est interdit de passer la nuit dans un camping-car ou une caravane sur les parkings et les aires de repos.

Cabanes du club alpin suisse (CAS) – Les randonneurs en montagne peuvent être hébergés dans les cabanes du CAS. Pour obtenir un répertoire de ces cabanes, s'adresser à Suisse Tourisme ou au Club alpin suisse, Helvetiaplatz 4, CH-3005 Berne ☎ (031) 351 36 11.

Restauration

Le **guide Rouge Michelin Suisse** propose un grand choix de restaurants qui permettront de découvrir et savourer les meilleures spécialités de Suisse. Les établissements remarquables, pour la qualité de leur cuisine, sont signalés par des étoiles de bonne table (une à trois étoiles). Les localités possédant de tels établissements sont repérées sur plusieurs cartes dans les pages d'introduction du guide.
Au restaurant, il n'est pas rare de payer le pain qui accompagne le repas.
Les buffets de gare proposent des repas de bonne qualité à des prix modérés.
Voir dans l'introduction de ce guide Vert le chapitre consacré à La Table, ainsi que dans le guide Rouge Michelin Suisse, le chapitre consacré aux Principaux Vins et spécialités régionales.

Quelques spécialités

Le filet de perche du lac Léman consommé au bord du lac à la terrasse d'un sympathique établissement et devant quelques « décis » de Fendant ou de Perlan, la fondue au vacherin (ou au gruyère) ou aux deux fromages accompagnée d'un blanc sec, la raclette, les tripes à la Neuchâteloise avec un œil de perdrix rosé, le gibier du Valais avec un cornalin robuste, la viande de bœuf fumée et séchée des Grisons avec un pinot noir velouté, l'émincé de veau (Geschnetzeltes Kalbfleisch) à la zurichoise avec un pinot noir, l'assiette bernoise, le polpettone (viandes hachées aromatisées) du Tessin avec un merlot corsé, les Rösti (savoureuses pommes de terre coupées en dés, passées à la poêle puis au four), et la saucisse de veau que l'on trouve partout. Sans oublier de consistantes pâtisseries à la crème, des sucreries en Suisse alémanique, et bien sûr le chocolat si renommé.

Les boissons

Le vin — Parmi les vins les plus connus :
- les blancs : le Fendant (Valais), le Perlan (Genève), le Chasselas (Neuchâtel, Vaud), le Johannisberg (Valais)
- les rouges : le Gamay (Genève), le Pinot noir (Grisons, Neuchâtel), le Dôle (mélange de Pinot noir et de Gamay, Valais), le Merlot (Tessin)
- les rosés : l'Œil de Perdrix (Neuchâtel), le Merlot rosato (Tessin)

1989, 1990, 1992 sont les meilleurs millésimes récents.
Les vins « ouverts » c'est-à-dire en carafe sont servis en décilitres (de 2 à 5). On commande par exemple 2 décis de Fendant.
En Suisse alémanique, le **Weinstub** permet, dans un cadre agréable et une atmosphère chaleureuse, de déguster les meilleurs vins au verre.

La bière — Dans les différents cantons, les amateurs apprécieront un grand choix de bières savoureuses, à la pression ou en bouteille (Adler, Cardinal, Egger, Eichhof, Feldschlösschen...).
En Suisse alémanique, le **Bierstub** est pour la bière ce que le Weinstub est pour le vin.

L'eau minérale — L'eau ordinaire ou « du robinet » comme on dit en France ne fait pas tellement partie des coutumes. Au restaurant, il est de bon usage de commander une bouteille d'eau minérale gazeuse ou non (les plus courantes sont Henniez, San Pellegrino, Passuger).

Le café — Il est souvent servi avec un petit pot de crème (Kaffesahne). L'après-midi, on peut faire une pause dans un « café » (salon de thé) qui propose un large choix de pâtisseries.

A la découverte de la Suisse

EN TRAIN, BUS ET BATEAU

Des forfaits sont offerts par le Swiss Travel System :
- le **Swiss Pass** permet de voyager librement sur tout le réseau : 16 000 km du réseau des trains, des bateaux et des cars postaux, ainsi que les tramways et autobus de 25 villes du territoire helvétique. De plus, une réduction de 25 % est accordée sur les excursions sur la plupart des sommets. Validité : 4, 8, 15 jours ou 1 mois.
- le **Swiss Flexi Pass** permet de voyager trois jours sur tout le réseau. Validité : 15 jours.
- la **Swiss Card** donne droit à un voyage aller et retour d'une gare frontière ou d'un aéroport au lieu de séjour choisi. De plus, elle permet d'obtenir une réduction de 50 % sur les parcours en train, bateau, car postal, chemins de fer de montagne.
Validité : 1 mois.
- le **Regional Pass** donne droit – entre le 1er mai et le 31 octobre – à plusieurs jours de libre circulation au choix dans une région donnée. En vente en Suisse.
Valable 7 jours et autorisant 3 jours de circulation dans la région. Les autres jours 50 % de réduction sur les trains, bateaux et cars postaux.
Valable 7 jours et autorisant 2 jours de circulation dans la région. Les autres jours 50 % de réduction sur les trains, bateaux et cars postaux.
Valable 15 jours et autorisant 5 jours de circulation dans la région. Les autres jours 50 % de réduction sur les trains, bateaux et cars postaux.
Valable 7 jours de circulation.

Cars postaux — Les célèbres autocars, reconnaissables à leur couleur jaune vif ou à un disque frappé du cor postal, sont familiers du paysage suisse. Ils partent généralement de la gare ferroviaire ou de la poste, et peuvent conduire le voyageur jusqu'au village le plus isolé.

Circuits touristiques en train

- Le **Guillaume-Tell-Express** relie la Suisse centrale au Tessin. En bateau à aubes de Lucerne à Flüelen-Lugano/Locarno et continuation en train.
- Le **Glacier-Express** de Zermatt à St-Moritz ou Davos (été seulement). Un voyage inoubliable dans les Alpes majestueuses.
- Le **Bernina-Express** de Coire à Tirano (Italie) par le col de la Bernina. Un parcours impressionnant.
- Le **Golden-Pass-Express** en train panoramique de Montreux à Zweisimmen.
- Le **Palm-Express** en car postal de St-Moritz à Lugano-Locarno/Ascona, et en train pour Domodossola-Brig et Zermatt.
- Le **MOB** (Montreux-Oberland bernois), avec son Panoramic Express ou son Superpanoramic Express, traverse des paysages enchanteurs.
- Le **Train du Vignoble** assure la liaison Vevey-Chexbres-Puidoux dans le Lavaux au bord du lac Léman. Il traverse vignes et villages pittoresques, et permet d'admirer le lac ainsi que les Alpes suisses et savoyardes. Plusieurs arrêts sont prévus à partir desquels des visites sont possibles (caveaux de vignerons, musées, etc.).

Petits trains à vapeur – Ils font partie du paysage suisse crachant avec une petite note nostalgique leur panache de fumée.
En saison touristique, souvent en fin de semaine, ils reprennent du service, remis à neuf par des associations de bénévoles passionnés. En voiture!
– Canton de Vaud : **Blonay-Chamby** ☎ (021) 943 21 21, **le Pont-le-Brassus** ☎ (021) 845 56 15, **Lausanne-Echallens-Berger** surnommé « la Brouette » ☎ (021) 881 11 15, **Montreux-Caux-Rochers-de-Naye** ☎ (021) 964 55 11.
– Canton du Valais : le **Rive-Bleue Express** du Bouveret à Évian (France) ☎ (025) 81 43 12.
– Canton de Neuchâtel : **St-Sulpice-Travers** ☎ (038) 61 36 78.
– Oberland bernois : **Interlaken-Brienz** ou **Grindelwald** ☎ (036) 51 32 42.
– Mittelland bernois : **Berne Weissenbühl-Interlaken Ost-Brienz** ☎ (031) 327 28 23, **Flamatt-Laupen-Gümmenen** ☎ (031) 740 62 62, **Huttwil-Ramsei-Huttwil** ☎ (034) 22 31 51, **Worblaufen-Worb Dorf/Soleure** ☎ (031) 925 55 55.
– Canton de Soleure : **Soleure-Burgdorf-Thoune-Soleure** ☎ (034) 22 31 51.
– Canton du Tessin : **Capolago-Generoso Velta** ☎ (091) 648 11 05.

Bateaux à vapeur sur les lacs – Une autre silhouette familière du paysage suisse est le bateau à aubes qui arbore fièrement à sa poupe le pavillon rouge à croix blanche. En saison touristique, des croisières sont organisées. Un service de restauration dans des salles à manger luxueuses est offert sur plusieurs bateaux. En avant toutes!
– Sur le **lac Léman**,
– Sur le **lac des Quatre-Cantons**,
– Sur le **lac de Zurich**,
– Sur le **lac de Brienz**,
– Sur le **lac de Constance**,
– Sur le **lac de Thoune**,
– Sur le **lac Majeur**,
– Sur le **Greifensee**.
Par ailleurs, des bateaux à vapeur ou plus classiques sillonnent les lacs, en service régulier. Le **Swiss Boat Pass** (abonnement 1/2 tarif) donne droit à un nombre illimité de voyages pendant une ou deux semaines. En vente dans les bureaux de Suisse Tourisme, aux guichets des ports, sur les bateaux.

LE PARC NATIONAL SUISSE *voir également à Zernez*

La visite du parc dont la vocation est la sauvegarde de la flore et de la faune est soumise à un règlement strict. Les automobilistes doivent laisser leur voiture à l'un des parkings. Les chemins autorisés sont balisés d'une marque blanche sur fond rouge, il est proscrit de les quitter. Les amis de la nature ont à leur disposition 80 km de sentiers, plusieurs points d'observation pour admirer les paysages extraordinaires, observer marmottes, cerfs, bouquetins ou rapaces et une végétation variée. Des panneaux explicatifs jalonnent le territoire du parc.
Pour tout renseignement, s'adresser à Suisse Tourisme ou à la **Maison du Parc** à Zernez. Cette dernière dispose d'un nombre de livres ou de cartes pouvant faciliter la visite. Les offices du tourisme locaux proposent des excursions accompagnées et des itinéraires. La brochure éditée par la Commission fédérale du Parc national, intitulée *Le Parc national suisse*, renferme de multiples informations sur le parc et propose un choix d'excursions avec schémas correspondants.

Chemins vers la Suisse – Sous cette appellation, Suisse Tourisme propose un choix d'itinéraires permettant de découvrir la beauté des paysages, mais aussi de revivre des grands événements du passé. Ces itinéraires sont au nombre de dix :
– les **voies romaines**,
– **sur les traces des pèlerins de St-Jacques**,
– le **grand chemin Walser**,
– **sentiers muletiers et routes de commerce**,
– **sur les traces des machines à vapeur**,
– la **Voie Suisse**.
Brochure gratuite à Suisse Tourisme et vente de guides spécifiques.

LES LOISIRS

Pêche – Les fervents de ce sport ou de ce passe-temps ont l'embarras du choix pour lancer leur ligne dans les quelque 32 000 km de cours d'eau et 135 000 ha de lacs poissonneux. Pour tout renseignement (permis, etc.), s'adresser à la Fédération suisse de pêche, Postfach 8218, CH-3001 Bern, ☎ (031) 381 32 52, ou à Suisse Tourisme ou aux Offices du tourisme locaux.

Cyclotourisme – Les Chemins de fer fédéraux suisses (CFF) ainsi que des compagnies privées peuvent se charger du transport des vélos comme bagages accompagnés.
Dans de nombreuses gares CFF ou privées, il est possible de louer des vélos et les restituer dans une autre gare. La formule train + vélo permet d'allier transport et location. Pour tout renseignement, s'adresser dans les gares ou les Offices du tourisme locaux. Suisse Tourisme fournit brochures (Vacances à vélo) ou cartes sur les différents itinéraires régionaux.

Tourisme pédestre – La meilleure façon de découvrir la nature en profondeur est sans aucun doute la marche. Suisse Tourisme fournit gratuitement un certain nombre de brochures proposant des itinéraires pédestres de difficultés variables, conduisant à des lacs de montagne situés dans le Jura, les Préalpes et les Alpes, le long des lacs et des rivières, à travers les cols, sur des chemins panoramiques ou de ville en ville. L'Association suisse de tourisme pédestre (ASTP) a établi les normes de balisage des chemins. Les panneaux sont sur fond jaune. Pour tout renseignement : ASTP Im Hirshalm 49, 4125 Riehen ☎ (061) 601 15 35.

Voile et planche à voile – Des écoles de voile existent sur tous les grands lacs.

Ski nautique – Des écoles existent sur tous les grands lacs.

Aviron, canoë, rafting – Le grand nombre de lacs et de rivières se prête à la pratique de ces activités. Près de Lucerne, le Rotsee est un lieu privilégié pour les amateurs d'aviron.

Alpinisme et varappe – Les grandes stations disposent d'écoles. Des ascensions sont organisées sous la conduite de guides expérimentés.

Balades en roulotte – Le charme désuet d'une roulotte pour découvrir à pas lents les beautés de la nature.

Le couteau suisse

Faisant partie de la panoplie des scouts, le véritable couteau suisse, reconnaissable à sa couleur rouge et à sa croix blanche inscrite dans un carré aux côtés légèrement arrondis, comporte plus de deux cents modèles, du plus petit au plus complet. Les gauchers n'ont pas été laissés pour compte puisqu'une gamme particulière a été réalisée à leur intention.

Ce petit bijou de la coutellerie de poche est né il y a plus d'un siècle pour équiper l'armée suisse. Très vite le Schweizer Offiziersmesser ou Swiss Army knife ou simplement couteau suisse a connu la célébrité à travers le monde, pour devenir le fidèle compagnon des débrouillards, des férus d'aventure.

Ses fonctions sont multiples : il peut être utilisé pour couper, trancher, limer, tailler, ouvrir (des boîtes de conserve par exemple), déboucher, décapsuler, serrer, desserrer, visser, dévisser, s'orienter, écailler, mesurer, démonter, aiguiser, percer... ne mérite-t-il pas l'appellation « la plus petite boîte à outils du monde » ?

SPORTS D'HIVER

Ils sont rois en Suisse, où ils constituent une activité commune à la plupart des régions, alpines ou jurassiennes.

Le **ski alpin** ou de descente, le plus ancien et réservé aux amateurs de vitesse et de sensations fortes, est pratiqué dans toutes les stations. Location de skis, bâtons et chaussures sur place.

Le **ski de fond** connaît la vogue depuis plusieurs années, et bon nombre de stations ont créé des parcours réservés à la pratique de ce sport considéré – à tort ou à raison – comme moins dynamique. A coup sûr il permet d'apprécier la beauté et le calme de la montagne (l'Engadine en est la terre d'élection). Les skis sont plus longs que pour le ski alpin, les chaussures plus légères, ne sont pas fixées au talon.

Le **ski de randonnée** est une sorte de compromis entre le ski alpin et le ski de fond. Le talon est laissé libre pour les montées et fixé pour les descentes.

Le **skijöring** dans lequel le skieur est tiré par un cheval au galop, nécessite une très bonne forme.

Le **monoski**, le **snowboard** (surf sur neige) et le **ski acrobatique** sont enseignés dans plusieurs stations.

Les **sports de glace** comme le patinage, le curling ou le hockey peuvent se pratiquer dans les nombreuses patinoires naturelles et artificielles, couvertes ou en plein air.

Les amateurs de **luge** peuvent s'exercer sur un simple chemin ou sur des pistes balisées. Quant au **bobsleigh** (descente possible avec pilote, notamment à St-Moritz), il procure des sensations à couper le souffle.

Ski de fond

Le **deltaplane** et le **parapente**, qui transforment l'homme en oiseau, lui permettent de survoler les grands espaces blancs.

Les **promenades en traîneaux**, les **marches en raquettes**, activités plus reposantes, sont proposées aux abords de nombreuses stations. Les **promenades en traîneaux à chiens** peuvent atteindre des pointes de 40 km/h.

Si le touriste peut pratiquer toutes ces activités, il peut aussi les revivre comme spectateur et assister à des compétitions ou championnats organisés durant la saison d'hiver.

Principales stations de sports d'hiver – La carte des lieux de séjour en début de guide localise un certain nombre de stations figurant dans cette liste. Consultez également, dans le guide Rouge Michelin Suisse, la carte des stations de sports d'hiver. Suisse Tourisme fournit gratuitement un tableau des stations avec leurs équipements.

STATIONS	Altitude de la station	Altitude au sommet	Remontées mécaniques	École de ski	Ski de fond	Patinoire	Curling	Piscine couverte
Adelboden BE	1 356	2 350	24	●	●	●	●	●
Alt. St. Johann SG	894	1 620	5	●	●			
Andermatt UR	1 436	2 963	9	●	●	●	●	
Anzère VS	1 500	2 462	12	●	●	●	●	●
Appenzell AI	785	922	1	●	●			●
Arosa GR	1 742	2 653	16	●	●	●	●	
Bettmeralp VS	1 950	2 709	14	●	●	●		●
Bever GR	1 710				●			
Blatten/Belalp VS	1 322	3 100	9	●	●			●
Breil/Brigels GR	1 289	2 400	7	●	●	●		●
Bruson VS	820	2 200	6	●	●			●
Celerina/Schlarigna GR	1 720	3 030	9	●	●		●	
Cernier et Val-de-Ruz NE	822	1 435	18		●	●		
Champéry VS	1 049	2 300	6	●	●	●		●
Charmey FR	981	1 630	8	●	●			●
Château-d'Oex VD	968	1 700	11	●	●	●	●	
La Chaux-de-Fonds NE	994	1 234	2	●	●	●		●
Churwalden GR	1 230	2 865	11	●	●	●		
Crans-Montana VS	1 484	2 927	40	●	●	●	●	●
Davos GR	1 560	2 844	35	●	●	●	●	●
Les Diablerets VD	1 155	3 000	25	●	●	●	●	●
Diemtigtal BE	820	1 850	17	●	●			
Disentis/Muster GR	1 150	3 000	9	●	●	●		
Einsiedeln SZ	900	1 113	8	●	●	●		
Engelberg OW	1 002	3 020	23	●	●	●	●	●
Falera GR	1 218	3 018	32	●	●	●		
Fiesch VS	1 062	2 869	10	●	●	●		●
Fleurier et Val-de-Travers NE	742	1 450	6		●	●		
Flims-Waldhaus GR	1 103	3 018	12	●	●	●	●	●
Flond-Surcuolm GR	1 081	2 280	18	●	●			
Flumserberg SG	1 390	2 222	18	●	●			
Grächen VS	1 617	2 920	11	●	●	●	●	●
Grimentz VS	1 570	3 000	12	●	●	●	●	●
Grindelwald BE	1 034	2 468	17	●	●	●	●	●
Gstaad BE	1 080	3 000	17	●	●	●	●	●
Hasliberg BE	1 230	2 433	15	●	●	●		●
Haute-Nendaz VS	1 255	3 330	39	●	●	●	●	●
Hoch-Ybrig SZ	1 048	1 850	9	●	●			●
Kandersteg BE	1 176	2 000	6	●	●	●	●	
Klosters GR	1 191	2 844	29	●	●	●	●	●
Laax GR	1 023	2 976	19	●	●	●		●
Lenk BE	1 068	2 098	21	●	●	●		●
Lenzerheide/Lai GR	1 476	2 865	37	●	●	●	●	●
Leukerbad/Loèche-les-Bains VS	1 411	2 700	18	●	●	●	●	●
Leyzin VD	1 268	2 300	19	●	●	●		●
Maloja GR	1 815	2 159	1		●			
Marbach LU	874	1 500	4		●	●		
Meiringen BE	595	2 245	15	●	●	●		●
Les Marécottes/Salvan VL	1 100	2 300	5	●	●	●		●
Les Mosses VD	1 448	1 900	12	●	●	●		
Morgins VS	1 320	2 277	18	●	●	●		
Münster MS	1 359	2 180	1	●	●			
Mürren BE	1 650	2 970	9	●	●	●	●	●

STATIONS	Altitude de la station	Altitude au sommet	Remontées mécaniques	École de ski	Ski de fond	Patinoire	Curling	Piscine couverte
Oberiberg SZ	1 126	1 856	12	✓	✓			
Obersaxen GR	1 281	2 310	8	✓	✓	✓		
Parpan GR	1 511	2 865	38	✓	✓			✓
Pontresina GR	1 800	2 978	11	✓	✓		✓	✓
Riederalp VS	1 930	2 335	10	✓	✓			
Rougemont VD	992	2 156	6	✓	✓			
Saas-Fee VS	1 809	3 600	25	✓	✓	✓	✓	✓
Saas-Grund VS	1 560	3 100	5	✓	✓	✓		✓
Saignelegier/Franches-Montagnes JU	978	1 260			✓	✓		✓
St-Cergue VD	1 047	1 680	3	✓	✓			
St-Imier-et-Vallon BE	793	1 460	7	✓	✓	✓		✓
St-Luc VS	1 650	2 580	8	✓	✓			
Samedan GR	1 720	2 276	5	✓	✓		✓	
Samnaun GR	1 846	2 872	12	✓	✓	✓	✓	✓
St-Moritz GR	1 856	3 030	23	✓	✓	✓	✓	✓
St-Stephan BE	993	1 989	3	✓	✓			
Savognin GR	1 210	2 700	17	✓	✓	✓	✓	✓
Schwarzenburg BE	792				✓			
Schwarzsee FR	1 050	1 750	10	✓	✓			✓
Scuol/Schuls GR	1 244	2 800	17	✓	✓	✓	✓	✓
Sedrun GR	1 441	3 000	13	✓	✓	✓	✓	✓
Le Sentier VD	1 024	1 476	14	✓	✓	✓	✓	
Sils-Maria GR	1 815	3 303	8	✓	✓	✓		
Silvaplana GR	1 816	3 303	7	✓	✓	✓		
Sörenberg LU	1 166	2 350	19	✓	✓	✓		✓
Splügen GR	1 450	2 215	8	✓	✓	✓	✓	
Tarasp-Vulpera GR	1 268	2 800	16	✓	✓	✓	✓	✓
Ulrichen/Oberwald VS	1 347	2 080	5	✓	✓			✓
Unteriberg SZ	931	1 856			✓			✓
Unterwasser SG	910	2 262	5	✓	✓			✓
Val D'Illiez VS	946	2 300	16	✓				✓
Val Müstair GR	1 248	2 519		✓	✓	✓		✓
Verbier VS	1 406	3 330	49	✓	✓	✓	✓	✓
Veysonnax VS	1 235	3 300	10	✓	✓			✓
Villars-sur-Ollon VD	1 253	2 217	25	✓	✓	✓		✓
Wengen BE	1 275	2 440	18	✓	✓	✓	✓	
Wildhaus SG	1 098	2 076	11	✓	✓	✓	✓	✓
Zermatt VS	1 620	3 820	34	✓	✓	✓	✓	✓
Zernez GR	1 471				✓	✓		✓
Zuoz GR	1 750	2 500	4	✓	✓	✓	✓	
Zweisimmen BE	1 000	2 000	5	✓	✓	✓		

Une enseigne

Livres, films, musique

Ouvrages généraux – Tourisme – Géographie

La Suisse et le Liechtenstein, par M. Chamson (Ed. J. A., Paris)
Suisse, par Jean-Robert Probst (Guides Olizane, Genève)
Découvrir la Suisse (Reka, ONST)
Le Grand Atlas Suisse des Promenades (Kümmerly + Frey, Berne)
Alpes valaisannes, 5 volumes par Maurice Brandt (Club Alpin Suisse, Berne)
Alpes bernoises, par Maurice Brandt (Club Alpin Suisse, Berne)
Préalpes fribourgeoises, par Maurice Brandt (Club Alpin Suisse, Berne)
Alpes et préalpes vaudoises, par Maurice Brandt (Club Alpin Suisse, Berne)
Préalpes franco-suisses, par Pierre Bossus (Club Alpin Suisse, Berne)
Notre Flore Alpine, par Landoldt-Corbar (Club Alpin Suisse, Berne)
Des villes en Suisse (Autrement, Paris)

Histoire – Civilisation – Art

Histoire de la Suisse, par Ch. Gilliard (Que sais-je?)
Les Suisses (Payot, Lausanne)
La Suisse, démocratie-témoin, par A. Siegfried et P. Béguin (la Baconnière, Boudry)
Suisse préhistorique, par M.-R. Sauter (la Baconnière, Boudry)
Guide des musées suisses, par Schärer-Lapaire (Paul Haupt Verlag, Berne)
De nombreuses monographies de qualité sont publiées par les éditions du Griffon à Neuchâtel (collection Trésors de mon Pays) et par la Société d'Histoire de l'Art en Suisse à Berne (Guides des Monuments Suisses)

La Suisse à travers la littérature

La Nouvelle Héloïse, par Jean-Jacques Rousseau (Gallimard, Paris)
La Montagne magique, par Thomas Mann (Le Livre de Poche, Paris)
La Grande Peur dans la montagne, par Charles Ferdinand Ramuz (Grasset, Paris)
Matterhorn, par Joseph Peyré (Grasset, Paris)
Justice, par Friedrich Dürrenmatt (Julliard/L'Age d'homme, Paris)
Helvétie, par Maurice Denuzière (J'ai lu, Paris)
Rive-Reine, par Maurice Denuzière (Denoël, Paris)

La Suisse à travers la bande dessinée

Astérix chez les Helvètes, par Goscinny et Uderzo

La Suisse sur le grand écran

Charles mort ou vif d'Alain Tanner (1969)
La Salamandre d'Alain Tanner (1971)
L'Invitation de Claude Goretta (1972)
Le cœur glacé de Xavier Koller (1980)
Voyage vers l'espoir de Xavier Koller (1991)

La chanson de variétés

Originaire de Suisse allemande (canton de Berne), mais chantant le plus souvent en français, **Stephan Eicher** représente la jeune génération qui a vite conquis le public hors des frontières.

Principales manifestations

La fête nationale : le 1ᵉʳ août — Toute la Suisse célèbre chaque année l'anniversaire de l'alliance perpétuelle jurée le 1ᵉʳ août 1291 par les représentants des trois communautés d'Uri, Schwyz et Unterwald. La soirée du 1ᵉʳ août est consacrée à des manifestations patriotiques : les sites historiques du lac d'Uri, en particulier la plaine du Rütli, l'Axenstrasse, sont embrasés et, dans tout le reste du pays, les jeunes des villages allument de grands feux sur les hauteurs, spectacle captivant pour qui peut observer du haut du sommet du Jura ou des Alpes. Nombreux feux d'artifice.

Janvier
Solothurn .... Journées cinématographiques de Solothurn, consacrées au cinéma suisse

1ᵉʳ lundi de Carême
Basel .... Carnaval (3 jours)

Début mars
Genève .... Salon international de l'automobile

Février ou début mars
Tessin .... Carnaval itinérant, avec risotto en plein air

1ʳᵉ semaine début mars
Fribourg .... Festival international de films

Mi-mars
Basel .... Foire suisse d'échantillons

3ᵉ lundi d'avril
Zürich .... Sechseläuten : fête symbolisant la fin de l'hiver ; défilé des corporations ; autodafé du « Böögg (Bonhomme Hiver)

Une semaine en avril
Basel .... Foire européenne de l'horlogerie et de la bijouterie

Derniers vendredi et samedi d'avril
Aarberg .... Foire à la brocante

Dernier dimanche d'avril
Appenzell .... Landsgemeinde
Hunswill .... 216 pli 21 *(1)* Landsgemeinde (années impaires)
Trogen .... (années paires) Landsgemeinde

Mi-avril à mi-mai
Morges .... Fête de la Tulipe

Fin avril ou fin avril-début mai
Montreux .... Festival du Rire
« Rose d'or de Montreux » : concours international d'émissions de variétés à la télévision

1ᵉʳ dimanche de mai
Glarus .... Landsgemeinde

Une semaine en mai
Bern .... Kursaal : festival international de jazz

Ascension
Beromünster .... Chevauchée de l'Ascension. Plus de cent cavaliers portant croix, ostensoires, oriflammes se mettent en route au lever du jour, accompagnés par musique et cantiques. Retour l'après-midi pour la bénédiction

Jeudi de la Fête-Dieu
Appenzell, Fribourg, Saas-Fee .... Messe solennelle et procession de la Fête-Dieu

Fête-Dieu et jeudi précédent
Kippel .... Procession avec défilé des « grenadiers du Bon Dieu »

Juin
Basel .... Salon international d'art (art moderne et contemporain)

Fin juin-début septembre
Interlaken .... Représentation en plein air et en allemand du *Guillaume Tell* de Schiller

Juillet

Fribourg	Festival international de jazz
(années paires)	Festival de musique sacrée
Lausanne	« Athlétissima » : rencontre internationale d'athlétisme
Lugano	Estival jazz
Montreux	Festival international de jazz
Nyon	« Paléo » : festival international en plein air de rock et de folk
Vevey	Festival international du film de comédie

Fin juillet-début septembre

Gstaad/Saanen — Festival de musique classique sous l'égide de Yehudi Menuhin

Fin juillet-fin septembre

Altdorf — Représentation en allemand du *Guillaume Tell* de Schiller

1re quinzaine d'août

Genève — « Fêtes de Genève », corso fleuri, feux d'artifice
Locarno — Festival international du film

2e samedi et dimanche d'août

Saignelégier — Marché-concours national de chevaux : courses campagnardes, cortège folklorique

De mi-août à début septembre

Luzern — Semaines internationales de musique : concerts, cours d'interprétation, représentations théâtrales

Dernière semaine d'août

Fribourg — Rencontres folkloriques internationales

Derniers vendredi et samedi d'août

Aarberg — Foire à la brocante

Fin août

Willisau — Festival international de jazz

De fin août à mi-octobre

Ascona — Semaines internationales de musique classique
Montreux, Vevey — Festival de musique classique Montreux-Vevey

8 septembre

Saas-Fee — Pèlerinage à la chapelle de Hohen Stiege (costumes locaux)

2e dimanche de septembre

Zürich — (à l'Albisgütli) Knabenschiessen (« tir des jeunes ») : grande compétition réservée aux écoliers zurichois, clôturée par l'élection du « roi du tir » et une distribution de prix

14 septembre

Einsiedeln — Grande fête de la Dédicace miraculeuse : procession aux flambeaux

2e quinzaine de septembre

Lausanne — Comptoir suisse, foire nationale

Derniers vendredi, samedi et dimanche de septembre

Neuchâtel — Fête des vendanges : parade des fanfares, grand cortège, Corso fleuri

Dernier samedi de septembre

Charmey — Fête de la Désalpe

En octobre

St-Gallen — OLMA, foire nationale de l'économie agricole et laitière

1ers vendredi, samedi et dimanche d'octobre

Lugano — Fête des vendanges

1er dimanche d'octobre

Martigny — Combats de reines dans le cadre de la foire du Valais

2ᵉˢ samedi et dimanche d'octobre
Charmey................... Bénichon de la montagne (course de charrettes à foin)

3ᵉ dimanche d'octobre
Châtel-St-Denis .... 217 pli 14 *(1)* La Bénichon (bénédiction) : fête marquant la fin des gros travaux d'été ; défilé folklorique, menus traditionnels « de Bénichon »

4ᵉ lundi de novembre
Bern................... Zibelemärit : traditionnel marché aux oignons symbolisant l'arrivée de l'hiver ; bataille de confettis

En décembre (date variable)
Genève .... Fête de l'Escalade

1ᵉʳ samedi de décembre
Fribourg.................. Marché et foire St-Nicolas

Deux semaines avant Noël
Bern................... Marché de Noël

La Jungfrau

---

(1) Pour les localités non décrites dans le guide, nous indiquons le n° de la carte Michelin au 200 000ᵉ et le n° du pli.

Conditions de visite

Les renseignements énoncés ci-dessous s'appliquent à des touristes voyageant isolément et ne bénéficiant pas de réduction. Pour les groupes constitués, il est généralement possible d'obtenir des conditions particulières concernant les horaires ou les tarifs. Ces données ne peuvent être fournies qu'à titre indicatif en raison de l'évolution du coût de la vie et de modifications fréquentes dans les horaires d'ouverture de nombreuses curiosités. Lorsqu'il nous a été impossible d'obtenir des informations à jour, les éléments figurant dans l'édition précédente ont été reconduits. Dans ce cas ils apparaissent en italique.

Les **édifices religieux** ne se visitent pas pendant les offices. Certaines églises et la plupart des chapelles sont souvent fermées. Les conditions de visite en sont précisées si l'intérieur présente un intérêt particulier ; dans le cas où la visite ne peut se faire qu'accompagnée par la personne qui détient la clé, une rétribution ou une offrande est à prévoir.

Lorsque les curiosités décrites bénéficient de facilités concernant l'accès pour les handicapés, le symbole figure à la suite de leur nom.

Les numéros de téléphone sont précédés de l'indicatif interurbain (3 chiffres dont le premier est 0). Ne pas composer le 0 à partir de l'étranger. Voir dans les pages précédentes, le paragraphe intitulé Téléphone (rubrique Vie pratique).

Les prix sont donnés en francs suisses.

A

Gorges de l'AARE
Visite tous les jours de 8 h à 18 h en juillet et août ; de début avril (si le temps le permet) à fin juin et en septembre et octobre de 9 h à 17 h. 5 F. ☏ (036) 71 40 48.

AIGLE
🛈 rue de la Gare 4 — 1860 — ☏ (025) 26 12 12

Musée de la Vigne et du Vin — Visite tous les jours de 10 h à 18 h en juillet et août ; tous les jours (sauf le lundi), de 10 h à 12 h 30 et de 14 h à 18 h d'avril à juin, en septembre et en octobre. Fermé du 1ᵉʳ novembre au 31 mars. 6 F ou 8 F billet combiné incluant la visite du musée de l'Étiquette. ☏ (024) 466 21 30.

ALP GRÜM
Chemin de fer au départ d'Osizio Bernina — *4,40 F.*

APPENZELL
🛈 Hauptgasse 4 — 9050 — ☏ (071) 788 96 41

Appenzell Museum — Visite de 10 h à 12 h et de 14 h à 17 h. Fermé le dimanche de Pâques. 5 F. ☏ (071) 788 36 31.

Blaues Haus — Visite de 9 h à 18 h, le samedi de 10 h à 18 h, les dimanches et jours fériés de 10 h à 17 h. Fermé à Pâques et le 25 décembre. ☏ (071) 787 12 84.

Château d'ARENENBERG
Napoleonmuseum — Visite tous les jours de 10 h à 17 h. Fermé le lundi, et du 24 décembre au 1ᵉʳ janvier. 5 F. ☏ (071) 664 18 66.

ARLESHEIM
Domkirche — *Fermée de 14 h à 16 h.*

AROSA
🛈 7050 — ☏ (081) 31 16 21

Téléphérique du Weisshorn — Départs du téléphérique toutes les 20 mn ou 10 mn selon l'affluence, de 8 h 20 à 16 h 20. Le parcours se fait en deux sections. 24 F aller simple, 30 F AR. ☏ (081) 378 84 50.

L'AUBERSON
Musée Baud — ♿ Visite accompagnée (1 h) tous les jours de juillet à mi-septembre, en semaine de 14 h à 17 h, les dimanches et jours fériés de 10 h à 12 h et de 14 h à 18 h ; le reste de l'année, le samedi de 14 h à 16 h, les dimanches et jours fériés de 10 h à 12 h et de 14 h à 18 h. 7 F. ☏ (024) 61 24 84.

AUGST

Vestiges antiques – Visite tous les jours de 10 h (13 h le lundi) à 17 h (18 h le dimanche) de mars à octobre; de 10 h (13 h le lundi) à 12 h et de 13 h à 16 h (17 h le dimanche) le reste de l'année. Fermé le 1ᵉʳ janvier, le Vendredi saint, les 24, 25 et 31 décembre. 5 F. ☎ (061) 816 22 22.

Römerhaus – Mêmes conditions de visite que pour les vestiges antiques.

Römermuseum – ♿ Mêmes conditions de visite que pour les vestiges antiques.

AVENCHES
🛈 3, place de l'Église – 1580 – ☎ (037) 75 33 93

Musée romain – Visite tous les jours (sauf le mardi), de 10 h à 12 h et de 13 h à 17 h du 1ᵉʳ avril au 30 septembre; de 14 h à 17 h le reste de l'année. Fermé les 1ᵉʳ et 2 janvier ainsi que les 25, 26 et 31 décembre. 2 F. ☎ (037) 75 17 27.

Musée A.M.V.A.N.A.S. – Visite du mercredi au dimanche de 14 h à 16 h du 1ᵉʳ mai au 30 septembre. 1 F. ☎ Office du tourisme (037) 75 33 93.

B

BADEN
🛈 Bahnhofstrasse 50 – 5400 – ☎ (056) 222 53 18

Landvogteischloss – Visite de 13 h à 17 h du mardi au vendredi, de 10 h à 17 h les samedis, dimanches et jours fériés. Fermé le lundi, les 1ᵉʳ et 2 janvier, à Pâques, à la Pentecôte, les 24, 25, 26 et 31 décembre. 5 F. ☎ (056) 222 75 74.

Stiftung «Langmatt» Sidney und Jenny Brown – Visite du 1ᵉʳ avril au 31 octobre, de 14 h à 18 h (également de 10 h à 12 h les dimanches et jours fériés). Fermé le lundi, le 1ᵉʳ août et du 1ᵉʳ novembre au 31 mars. 5,10 F. ☎ (056) 222 58 42.

BALLENBERG

Musée de l'Habitat rural suisse – Visite tous les jours de 10 h à 17 h du 15 avril au 31 octobre. 12 F. ☎ (036) 51 11 23.

BASEL
🛈 Schiffände 5 – 4001 – ☎ (061) 261 50 50

Peterskirche – Fermée le lundi. Ouverture le samedi de 11 h 30 à 17 h, de 9 h à 17 h les autres jours. ☎ (061) 261 87 24.

Visite guidée de la ville – S'adresser à l'Office du tourisme.

Münster – Visite de Pâques au 15 octobre, du lundi au vendredi de 10 h à 17 h, le samedi de 10 h à 12 h et de 14 h à 16 h, le dimanche de 13 h à 17 h; du 16 octobre au dimanche de Pâques, du lundi au samedi de 11 h à 16 h, le dimanche de 14 h à 16 h. Fermée les 1ᵉʳ janvier, Vendredi saint, 1ᵉʳ mai, 1ᵉʳ août, 24 et 25 décembre. Montée à la tour – 2 F.

Museum für Völkerkunde – Visite du mardi au dimanche ainsi que les lundis de Pâques et de Pentecôte, de 10 h à 17 h du 2 mai au 31 octobre; de 10 h à 12 h et de 14 h à 17 h du mardi au samedi, de 10 h à 17 h le dimanche le reste de l'année. Fermé le lundi, 1ᵉʳ janvier (matin), le mercredi des Cendres, les 1ᵉʳ mai, 1ᵉʳ août, 24, 25 et 31 décembre. 6 F, gratuit le 1ᵉʳ dimanche du mois. ☎ (061) 266 55 00.

Rathaus – Visite accompagnée. S'adresser à l'Office du tourisme. ☎ (061) 261 50 50.

Kunstmuseum – ♿ Visite tous les jours sauf le lundi, de 10 h à 17 h. Fermé les 1er janvier, Vendredi saint, 1er mai, 1er août, 24, 25 et 31 décembre. 7 F (gratuit le 1er dimanche du mois). ☎ (061) 271 08 28.

Basler Papiermühle – Visite du mardi au dimanche de 14 h à 17 h. Fermé le lundi, sauf les lundis de Pâques et de Pentecôte, ainsi que pendant le carnaval de Bâle et la plupart des jours fériés. 8 F. ☎ (061) 272 96 52.

Museum für Gegenwartskunst – ♿ Visite tous les jours (sauf le lundi), de 11 h à 17 h. Fermé les 26 et 28 février, 1ᵉʳ mai, 1ᵉʳ août, 24, 25 et 31 décembre. 7 F, gratuit le 1ᵉʳ dimanche du mois. ☎ (061) 272 81 83.

Zoologischer Garten – ♿ Visite de 8 h à 18 h 30 de mai à août; de 8 h à 18 h en mars, avril, septembre et octobre; de 8 h à 17 h 30 de novembre à février. 10 F (enfants 4 F). ☎ (061) 295 35 35.

Haus zum Kirschgarten – Visite tous les jours (sauf le lundi) de 10 h à 17 h. Fermé la plupart des jours fériés. 5 F, gratuit le 1ᵉʳ dimanche du mois. ☎ (061) 271 05 05.

BASEL

Historisches Museum – Visite tous les jours (sauf le mardi) de 10 h à 17 h. Fermé la plupart des jours fériés. 5 F. gratuit le 1er dimanche du mois. ☎ (061) 271 05 05.

Antikenmuseum Basel und Sammlung Ludwig – ⚹ Visite tous les jours (sauf le lundi) de 10 h à 17 h. Fermé la plupart des jours fériés. 5 F. gratuit le 1er dimanche du mois. ☎ (061) 271 22 02.

Skulpturhalle – Visite tous les jours (sauf le lundi) de 10 h à 12 h et de 14 h à 17 h. Pour les visites accompagnées, s'annoncer trois semaines à l'avance. Fermé la plupart des jours fériés. Entrée gratuite sauf pour les visites guidées. ☎ (061) 261 52 45.

Carnaval de Bâle

Stadt- und Münstermuseum – Musée en cours de réaménagement : réouverture prévue en 1998. ☎ (061) 267 66 25.

Pharmazie-historisches Museum – Visite du lundi au vendredi, de 9 h à 12 h et de 14 h à 17 h. Entrée gratuite. ☎ (061) 261 79 40.

Musikinstrumenten-Sammlung – Visite les mercredis et vendredis de 14 h à 17 h ; en outre le dimanche de 10 h à 12 h. Fermé la plupart des jours fériés. Entrée gratuite. ☎ (061) 271 05 05.

Architekturmuseum – Visite du mardi au vendredi de 13 h à 18 h, le samedi de 10 h à 16 h, le dimanche et les jours fériés de 10 h à 13 h. Fermé le lundi et les Vendredi saint, lundi de Pâques ainsi que la semaine du Carnaval. 5 F. ☎ (061) 261 14 13.

Überblick – Accès à la terrasse : de mars à octobre, tous les jours de 10 h à 12 h et de 14 h à 17 h ; le reste de l'année, les mercredis, samedis et dimanches aux mêmes heures. Pas d'accès le 1er janvier, jour des Cendres, Jeudi saint, 24, 25 et 31 décembre. 4 F. ☎ (061) 66 33 49.

Ausstellung – Visite du chaque samedi et chaque dimanche ainsi que du 1er mars au 30 novembre, sauf le lundi, de 10 h à 17 h ; le reste de l'année, chaque mardi aux mêmes heures. Fermée les 1er janvier, 1er août, 24, 25 et 31 décembre. 6 F. ☎ (061) 631 42 65.

Visite en bateau – Des visites de la ville, du port ainsi que des passages d'écluses sont proposés de début mai à début octobre. S'adresser à la Basler Personenschiffahrt-Gesellschaft AG, Postfach 4019. ☎ (061) 639 95 00.

BEATENBERG
🛈 3803 – ☎ (036) 41 12 86

Accès au Niederhorn par télésiège – Service interrompu de mi-avril à fin mai et de fin octobre à mi-décembre. Le reste de l'année, fonctionne généralement de 8 h 30 à 17 h 30 en été et de 8 h 30 à 16 h 30 en hiver. AR : 22 F. ☎ (036) 41 11 96.

BELLELAY

Abbaye – Visite de mi-juin à mi-septembre, de 10 h à 12 h et de 14 h à 18 h., sur demande le reste de l'année. Fermé durant la première quinzaine de juin. 5 F ou 3 F (de mi-juin à mi-septembre). ☎ (032) 917 237.

BELLWALD

Télésiège du Richinen et du Steibenkreuz – Fonctionne de 9 h 15 à 16 h 15. Fermé mi-avril. 8 F. ☎ (028) 71 19 26.

BERN
🛈 Bahnhof – 3000 – ☎ (031) 311 66 11

Visite guidée de la ville – S'adresser à l'Office du tourisme.

Zytgloggeturm – Visite.

Einsteinhaus – Visite tous les jours (sauf le lundi, les dimanches et jours fériés) de 10 h à 17 h (16 h le samedi). Fermée en janvier et décembre. 2 F. ☎ (031) 312 00 91.

BERN

Bärengraben – Visite de 8 h à 18 h d'avril à septembre ; le reste de l'année, de 9 h à 16 h. ☎ (031) 311 66 11.

Münster St. Vincenz – Visite tous les jours (sauf le lundi) de 10 h (11 h le dimanche) à 17 h de Pâques au 31 octobre ; tous les jours (sauf le lundi) de 10 h à 12 h et de 14 h à 16 h (17 h le samedi) en semaine, de 11 h à 14 h le dimanche le reste de l'année.

Montée à la tour – Fermeture 1/2 h avant l'heure de fermeture de la cathédrale. 3 F.

Bundeshaus – Visite accompagnée (3/4 h - pour les groupes) du lundi au samedi à 9 h, 10 h, 11 h, 14 h, 15 h et 16 h, le dimanche à 9 h, 10 h, 11 h, 14 h et 15 h. Fermé les jours fériés ainsi que pendant les sessions du Parlement (pendant cette période accès aux tribunes seulement). ☎ (031) 322 85 22.

Kunstmuseum – Visite le mardi de 10 h à 21 h, du mercredi au dimanche de 10 h à 17 h.
Fermé le lundi et la plupart des jours fériés. 6 F. ☎ (031) 311 09 44.

Naturhistorisches Museum – Visite le lundi de 14 h à 17 h, du mardi au samedi de 9 h à 17 h, le dimanche de 10 h à 17 h. Fermé la plupart des jours fériés. 3 F. ☎ (031) 350 72 00.

Bernisches Historisches Museum – ♿ Visite tous les jours (sauf le lundi) de 10 h à 17 h. Fermé les 1er janvier, Vendredi saint, le dimanche de Pâques, le jeudi de l'Ascension, le dimanche de Pentecôte et le 25 décembre. 5 F. ☎ (031) 350 77 11.

Schweizerisches Alpines Museum – Visite le lundi toute l'année de 14 h à 17 h ; les autres jours, du 2 mai au 16 octobre, de 10 h à 17 h, du 17 octobre au 1er mai de 10 h à 12 h et de 14 h à 17 h. 5 F. ☎ (031) 351 04 34.

Schweizerisches PTT-Museum – ♿ Visite tous les jours (sauf le lundi) de 10 h à 17 h. Fermé les 1er janvier, Vendredi saint, dimanches de Pâques et de Pentecôte, Ascension. 2 F. ☎ (031) 338 77 77.

Tierpark im Dählhölzli – ♿ Visite en été de 8 h à 18 h 30, en hiver de 9 h à 17 h. 6 F (enfants : 3 F). ☎ (031) 351 06 16.

BEROMÜNSTER

Stiftskirche – Visite accompagnée sur demande préalable, en semaine de 10 h à 12 h et de 14 h à 17 h, les dimanches et jours fériés de 11 h à 12 h. 5 F. ☎ (041) 930 38 68.

Schloss-Museum – Visite accompagnée (1 h) de mai à octobre, les dimanches et jours fériés de 15 h à 17 h. 3 F. ☎ (041) 930 29 34.

Mine de sel de BEX   🛈 1880 – ☎ (025) 63 30 80

Visite accompagnée (2 h 15) de 9 h à 16 h du 1er avril au 15 novembre. Réservation indispensable au bureau d'accueil. ☎ (025) 63 24 62. 15 F. Température moyenne à l'intérieur de la mine : 17°.

BIEL/BIENNE   🛈 Bahnhofplatz – 2500 – ☎ (032) 22 75 75

Museum Schwab – Visite tous les jours (sauf le lundi) de 10 h à 12 h et de 14 h à 17 h, les dimanches et jours fériés de 11 h à 17 h. 5 F. ☎ (032) 22 76 03.

BLAUSEE

Site ouvert de mai à octobre. 4,30 F comprenant la promenade en bateau.

BLONAY   🛈 1800 – ☎ (021) 943 10 15

Chemin de fer Blonay-Chamby – Fonctionne de début mai à fin octobre, le samedi après-midi et le dimanche toute la journée. AR : 11 F incluant la visite du musée. ☎ (021) 943 21 21.

BONMONT

Abbaye – Visite de fin mars à fin juin et en septembre et octobre les lundis, samedis et dimanches de 13 h à 17 h, en juillet et août tous les jours de 13 h à 17 h. Fermé le plupart des jours fériés. 5 F. ☎ (077) 26 72 50.

BOUDRY

Musée de la Vigne et du Vin – Visite du jeudi au dimanche de 14 h à 17 h. Fermé du 24 décembre à début janvier. 5 F. ☎ (038) 25 42 44.

Le BOUVERET
🛈 route cantonale 42 – 1897 – ☏ (025) 81 11 01

Swiss Vapeur Parc – Fonctionne du 20 mai au 30 septembre de 10 h à 18 h ; du 1er avril au 19 mai les week-ends de 10 h à 18 h, les mercredis après-midi de 13 h 30 à 18 h. Ne fonctionne pas de novembre à mars. 8,50 F, enfants : 7,50 F. ☏ (025) 481 44 10.

Lac des BRENETS

Promenade en vedette au Saut du Doubs – Service d'été de mai à septembre, départs toutes les 45 mn à partir de 10 h. AR : 11 F. ☏ (032) 932 14 14.

La BREYA

Télésiège – Fonctionne de mi-juin à mi-septembre de 8 h 30 à 17 h. AR : 12 F. ☏ (026) 83 13 44.

BRIENZER ROTHORN
🛈 Brienz – 3855 – ☏ (036) 51 32 42

Chemin de fer à crémaillère à vapeur au départ de Brienz – Fonctionne de juin à octobre. Départ toutes les heures. AR : 62 F. ☏ (036) 951 12 32.

BRIG
🛈 Banhnofplatz – 3900 – ☏ (028) 23 19 01

Stockalperschloss – Visite accompagnée (1 h) tous les jours (sauf le lundi), à 9 h, 10 h, 11 h, 12 h, 14 h, 15 h, 16 h et 17 h de mai à octobre. Pas de visites à 9 h et 17 h en mai et octobre. 4 F. ☏ (028) 23 19 01.

Îles de BRISSAGO

Accès à l'île principale – Un service de bateau est assuré de 9 h à 18 h d'avril à octobre. Se renseigner à l'Office du tourisme d'Ascona ou de Losone ou au bureau de la Navigazione Lago Maggiore d'Ascona, au port d'Ascona. Parc exotique, exposition d'art. 6 F. ☏ (091) 791 43 61.

BRUDERHOLZ

Wasserturm Bruderholz – Visite du 1er avril au 15 septembre de 8 h à 20 h ; de 8 h à 16 h le reste de l'année. 0,50 F. ☏ (061) 275 51 11.

BRUGG

Vindonissa-Museum – Visite tous les jours (sauf le lundi), de 10 h à 12 h et de 14 h à 17 h du 2 janvier au 24 décembre. Fermé les jours fériés sauf les lundis de Pâques et de la Pentecôte et le jeudi de l'Ascension. 4 F. ☏ (056) 441 21 84.

BUBIKON

Ritterhaus – *Visite de début avril à fin octobre, du jeudi au dimanche, de 9 h à 11 h et de 14 h à 18 h. Fermé à Pâques et Pentecôte. 4 F. ☏ (055) 38 12 60.*

BULLE
🛈 4, avenue de la Gare – ☏ (029) 2 80 22
🛈 ☏ (029) 2 80 22

Musée Gruérien – ♿ Visite du mardi au samedi de 10 h à 12 h et de 14 h à 17 h ; les dimanches et jours fériés de 14 h à 17 h. Fermé le 25 décembre. 4 F. ☏ (026) 912 72 60.

BURGDORF
🛈 Poststrasse 10 – 3400 – ☏ (034) 22 24 45

Museum im Schloss – Visite du lundi au samedi de 14 h à 17 h de début avril à fin octobre, les dimanches et jours fériés de 11 h à 17 h. 5 F. ☏ (034) 23 02 14.

BÜRGLEN

Tell-Museum – Visite en juillet et août de 9 h 30 à 17 h 30 ; de fin avril à fin juin et de début septembre à début octobre de 10 h à 11 h 30 et de 13 h 30 à 17 h. Fermé les 1er janvier, Vendredi saint et 25 décembre. 4 F. ☏ (044) 2 41 55.

Participez à notre effort permanent de mise à jour.

Adressez-nous vos remarques et vos suggestions.

Cartes et Guides Michelin
46 avenue de Breteuil
75341 Paris Cedex 07

C

CADEMARIO
San Ambrogio – Travaux de restauration en prévision. 👁 (044) 605 47 35.

CANTINE DI GANDRIA
Musée des Douanes – Accessible seulement par bateau. Visite du dimanche des Rameaux au dernier dimanche d'octobre, de 13 h 30 à 17 h 30. Entrée gratuite. 👁 (091) 923 98 43 (Musée) ou (091) 51 52 23 (Società Navigazione Lago di Lugano).

CELERINA
🛈 7500 – 👁 (081) 3 39 66

S. Gian – *Ouverte le mardi de 14 h à 16 h, le mercredi de 16 h à 17 h, le vendredi de 10 h 30 à 12 h.*

Le CHASSERAL
Route à péage – 4 F.

CHÂTEAU-D'OEX
🛈 1837 – 👁 (029) 4 77 88

Musée d'Art populaire du Vieux Pays d'Enhaut – Visite les mardis, jeudis et vendredis de 10 h à 12 h et de 14 h à 16 h 30; les samedis, dimanches et jours fériés, de 14 h à 16 h 30. Fermé les trois dernières semaines d'octobre et les 1er janvier, dimanche de Pâques et 25 décembre. 4 F. 👁 (029) 4 65 20.

CHAUMONT
Tour-observatoire – Tourniquet : 1 F. 👁 (038) 25 42 42.

Funiculaire – Départs environ toutes les heures, aller simple : 5,80 F ; AR : 9,20 F. 👁 (038) 25 42 42.

La CHAUX-DE-FONDS
🛈 1 Espacité – 2300 – 👁 (039) 24 20 10

Musée international d'Horlogerie – ♿ Visite de juin à septembre, de 10 h à 17 h ; le reste de l'année, de 10 h à 12 h et de 14 h à 17 h. Fermé le lundi (sauf si férié), les 1er janvier et 24, 25 et 31 décembre. 8 F. 👁 (32) 967 68 61.

Musée des Beaux-Arts – ♿ Visite tous les jours (sauf le lundi) de 10 h à 12 h et de 14 h à 17 h (20 h le mercredi). Fermé les 1er janvier, Vendredi saint et 25 décembre. 8 F gratuit le mercredi. 👁 (039) 23 04 44.

Musée d'Histoire naturelle – Visite tous les jours (sauf le lundi) de 14 h à 17 h et en outre de 10 h à 12 h les dimanches et jours fériés. Fermé les 1er janvier et 25 décembre. 👁 (039) 23 39 76.

Musée d'Histoire et médaillier – Visite tous les jours (sauf le lundi) de 14 h à 17 h (18 h le samedi), en outre de 10 h à 12 h les dimanches et jours fériés. Fermé les 1er janvier, 1er mai et 25 décembre. 3 F. 👁 (039) 913 50 10.

Bois du Petit Château – ♿ Vivarium ouvert de 10 h à 12 h (sauf le mercredi) et de 14 h à 17 h. 👁 (039) 285 262.

Musée Paysan – Visite tous les jours (sauf le vendredi) de 14 h à 17 h de mai à octobre ; les mercredis, samedis et dimanches de 14 h à 17 h le reste de l'année. Fermé les 1er janvier et 25 décembre. 3 F. 👁 (039) 926 71 89.

Château de CHILLON
Visite en juillet et août de 9 h à 18 h 15 ; en avril, mai, juin et septembre de 9 h à 17 h 45 ; en octobre de 10 h à 16 h 45 ; de novembre à février, de 10 h à 12 h et de 13 h 30 à 16 h ; en mars de 10 h à 12 h et de 13 h 30 à 16 h 45. 6,50 F. 👁 (021) 963 39 12.

CHUR
🛈 Grabenstrasse, 5 – 7000 – 👁 (081) 22 18 18

Domschatz – Visite en semaine de 10 h à 12 h et de 14 h à 16 h. Fermé le dimanche matin, pendant la Semaine sainte et à la Fête Dieu. 👁 (081) 22 92 50.

Rätisches Museum – Visite tous les jours (sauf le lundi) de 10 h à 12 h et de 14 h à 17 h. Fermé la plupart des jours fériés. 5 F. 👁 (081) 257 28 88.

Kunstmuseum – Visite tous les jours (sauf le lundi) de 10 h à 12 h et de 14 h à 17 h. Tarif variable suivant les expositions. Fermé la plupart des jours fériés. 👁 (081) 257 28 68.

CIMETTA
Télésiège au départ de Cardada – Le télésiège fonctionne au départ de Cardada, sauf de mi-novembre à début septembre, de 8 h 30 à 12 h et de 13 h 30 à 17 h 30 de juin à septembre et de 9 h à 12 h et de 13 h à 17 h le reste de l'année. AR : 8 F. 👁 (091) 756 92 91.

COLOMBIER

Musée du château – Visite accompagnée (1 h 15) les mercredis, jeudis, vendredis à 15 h ainsi que le premier dimanche du mois à 14 h et 15 h 30 de mars à octobre. Entrée gratuite. ☎ (038) 43 96 25.

COPPET

Château – Visite accompagnée (30 mn) de 10 h à 12 h (12 h 30 en juillet et août) et de 14 h à 18 h. Fermé le lundi sauf en juillet et août. 7 F. ☎ (022) 776 10 28.

CRANS-MONTANA   🛈 ☎ (027) 41 21 32

Bella lui – Téléphérique au départ de Crans et de Montana. Service jusqu'à Cry d'Err de 8 h 30 à 12 h 30 et de 13 h 45 à 17 h, en continu de juillet à septembre. Service toutes les 20 mn en été depuis Cry d'Err, en continu en hiver. *22 F AR, 15 F aller simple*. ☎ (027) 41 16.

Croix de CULET

Téléphérique au départ de Champéry – En juillet et août, départ en moyenne toutes les 1/2 h de 9 h à 18 h ; de début juin à début juillet et du 2 septembre au 3 novembre, départs variables de 9 h à 17 h. Fermé du 15 avril au 2 juin et du 4 novembre au 7 décembre. AR : 15 F. ☎ (025) 79 12 28.

D

DAVOS   🛈 Promenade 67 – 7270 – ☎ (081) 415 21 21

Funiculaire et téléphérique du Weissfluhgipfel – Service toutes les 1/2 h de 8 h à 12 h et de 13 h 30 à 16 h de mi-juin à mi-octobre. AR : 28 F. ☎ (081) 415 21 21.

Funiculaire du Schatzalp – Service durant l'année toutes les 1/2 h. AR : 12 F. ☎ (081) 415 21 21.

DELÉMONT   🛈 12, place de la Gare – 2800 – ☎ (066) 22 97 78

Musée jurassien d'Art et d'Histoire – Visite tous les jours (sauf le lundi) de 14 h à 17 h du 15 mai au 15 octobre ; le reste de l'année, seulement le dimanche de 14 h à 17 h. Fermé du 24 décembre au 2 janvier. 6 F. Musée en cours de rénovation, réouverture prévue : fin 1996. ☎ (032) 422 80 77.

Glacier des DIABLERETS

Télécabine et téléphérique au départ du col du Pillon ou de Reusch – *L'accès au glacier est assuré en alternance depuis l'un ou l'autre de ces points de départ, tous les jours de juillet à mai et les week-ends au mois de juin. Se renseigner par* ☎ *au col du Pillon : (025) 53 13 77 ou à Reusch : (030) 5 10 70. AR : 37 F.*

DIAVOLEZZA

Téléphérique – Fonctionne de mi-juin à mi-octobre et de début décembre à fin avril. Départ toutes les 1/2 h. 25 F AR. ☎ (081) 842 64 19.

E

EBENALP

Téléphérique – Départs toutes les 1/2 h, de 8 h 30 à 19 h en juillet et août, de 7 h 40 à 16 h du 28 mai à fin juin et en septembre, de 8 h à 17 h 30 en mai et octobre, de 8 h 30 à 17 h le reste de l'année. Service interrompu du mardi de Pâques à début mai et du 1er novembre à mi-décembre. 21 F AR. ☎ (071) 88 12 12.

ÉCHALLENS

Maison du Blé et du Pain – Visite du 15 janvier au 20 décembre, tous les jours (sauf le lundi) de 9 h à 18 h. Fermée de mi-décembre à mi-janvier. 7 F. ☎ (021) 881 50 71.

EGGISHORN

Téléphérique au départ de Fiesch – Départ toutes les 1/2 h ou 20 mn. Service interrompu en mai et novembre. 38,80 F. ☎ (028) 71 27 00.

EINSIEDELN
☎ Hauptstrasse 85 – 8840 – 📞 (055) 418 44 88

Grosser Saal – Visite de 13 h 30 à 18 h. Les dimanches et jours fériés, en cas de concert, fermée de 16 h 45 à 18 h. 3 F. 📞 (055) 526 240.

Barrage d'EMOSSON

Funiculaire de Barberine, chemin de fer d'Emosson, minifuniculaire du barrage – En service de début juin à mi-octobre. Aller simple : 19 F ; AR : 33 F. 📞 (027) 769 11 11. en saison.

Visite du barrage – S'adresser au préalable à la centrale de la Bâtiaz à Martigny. 📞 (026) 210 210.

ERLENBACH
☎ 📞 (033) 81 14 37

Téléphérique du Stockhorn – Fonctionne de juin à début novembre de 8 h 10 à 17 h 40 ; du 15 décembre à mars de 9 h 40 (8 h 40 les samedis et dimanches) à 17 h 10. AR : 36 F. 📞 (033) 681 21 81.

ESTAVAYER-LE-LAC
☎ place du Midi – 1470 – 📞 (037) 63 12 37

Musée – Visite en juillet et août, de 9 h à 11 h et de 14 h à 17 h ; de mars à juin et en septembre et octobre, du mardi au vendredi de 9 h à 11 h et de 14 h à 17 h et les samedis, dimanches et jours fériés de 14 h à 17 h ; de novembre à février, de 14 h à 17 h. Fermé le lundi. 4 F. 📞 (037) 63 24 48.

F

FIRST

Accès en télécabine au départ de Grindelwald – Fonctionne de mi-mai à fin octobre, puis de mi-décembre à début avril. AR : 43 F. 📞 (036) 53 36 38.

FLIMS
☎ 7018 – 📞 (081) 920 92 00

Télésiège et téléphérique du Cassons Grat – Fonctionnent de mi-décembre à fin mai et de début juin jusqu'à fin octobre. AR : 39 F. 📞 (081) 911 58 18.

Téléphériques du Crap Sogn Gion et du Crap Masegn – Services toutes les 1/2 h. De Laax-Murschteg à Crap Sogn Gion, AR : 23 F. De Laax-Murschteg à Crap Masegn, AR : 30 F. Service interrompu de fin avril à mi-octobre.

Col de la FORCLAZ

Randonnées pédestres – S'adresser à Tourisme et Transport aux Marécottes qui fournit tous renseignements. 📞 (026) 61 15 89.

FRIBOURG
☎ 1, avenue de la Gare – 1700 – 📞 (037) 81 31 75

Visite guidée de la ville – S'adresser à l'Office du tourisme.

Cathédrale St-Nicolas – Ouverte en semaine de 9 h à 18 h, le dimanche de 13 h à 20 h.

Musée d'Art et d'Histoire – Visite tous les jours de 10 h à 17 h. Fermé le lundi, les 1er janvier, Vendredi saint et 25 décembre. 5 F 📞 (037) 22 18 71.

Église des Cordeliers – Visite tous les jours (sauf le lundi matin) de 9 h 30 à 18 h 30 (17 h d'octobre à mars) en semaine, de 13 h à 18 h les dimanches et jours fériés. 📞 (026) 322 47 87.

Musée d'Histoire naturelle – ♿ Visite de 14 h à 18 h. Fermé les 1er janvier, Vendredi saint et 25 décembre. 📞 (037) 29 90 40.

FURKAPASSSTRASSE

Pendant la période d'enneigement, généralement de novembre à mai, le passage des voitures peut se faire par voie ferrée, aux gares d'Oberwald ou de Realp. Départs des trains toutes les heures de 6 h à 21 h. Forfait de 28 F incluant voiture et passager(s).

LA SUISSE, TERRE DE FOLKLORE
Le chapitre Traditions et folklore en début de guide
ainsi que le tableau des manifestations touristiques en fin de guide,
vous invitent à découvrir la Suisse pittoresque.

G

Zoo de la GARENNE

Visite de 9 h à 18 h (17 h en hiver). 8 F. enfants de 6 à 15 ans : 4 F. ☎ (022) 366 11 14. ☎ (022) 366 11 14.

GENÈVE
🛈 Gare Cornavin – 1200 – ☎ (022) 738 52 00

Visite guidée de la ville – S'adresser à l'Office du tourisme. Tours en bus : Keytours SA, ☎ (022) 731 41 40. Tours à pied : Genève Tourisme, ☎ (022) 738 52 00.

Musée d'Histoire des Sciences – Visite tous les jours sauf le mardi, de 13 h à 17 h. Fermé les 25 décembre et 1er janvier. ☎ (022) 731 69 85.

Conservatoire et jardin botaniques – ♿ Visite de 8 h à 19 h 30 du 1er avril au 30 septembre ; de 9 h 30 à 17 h le reste de l'année. Serres ouvertes (sauf le vendredi) de 9 h 30 à 11 h et de 14 h à 16 h 30. Visite guidée gratuite le mardi à 12 h 30, de mai à octobre sur rendez-vous uniquement. ☎ (022) 732 69 69.

Musée Rath – Visite tous les jours (sauf le lundi) de 10 h à 17 h (le mercredi de 12 h à 21 h). 10 F. ☎ (022) 310 52 70.

Genève – Feux d'artifice

Bibliothèque universitaire – Visite de 9 h à 12 h et de 14 h à 17 h. Fermée le samedi après-midi, les dimanches et jours fériés ainsi que du jeudi saint au mercredi suivant Pâques ainsi que du 24 décembre au 2 janvier. ☎ (022) 418 28 00.

Cathédrale St-Pierre – *De juin à septembre, ouverte de 9 h à 12 h ; de novembre à février de 9 h à 12 h et de 14 h à 17 h ; de mars à mai et en octobre, de 9 h à 12 h et de 14 h à 18 h.* ☎ (022) 738 56 50.

Montée à la Tour Nord – *Mêmes heures d'ouverture que pour la cathédrale.* 2,50 F.

Site archéologique – Visite de 10 h à 13 h et de 14 h à 18 h. 5 F.

Maison Tavel – ♿ Visite tous les jours (sauf le lundi) de 10 h à 17 h. Fermé les 1er janvier et 25 décembre. ☎ (022) 310 29 00.

Hôtel de Ville : salle de l'Alabama – Visite accompagnée (1/4 h) du 3 janvier au 20 décembre, de 9 h à 11 h et de 14 h à 17 h, fermé les samedis, dimanches et jours fériés. S'adresser à l'Office du tourisme de Genève ou auprès des huissiers de la Chancellerie d'État, Hôtel de ville. ☎ Office du Tourisme : (022) 738 52 00.

Collection Zoubov – Visite accompagnée (50 mn) du 15 juin au 30 septembre, du lundi au vendredi à 15 h 45 ; visite également comprise dans le tour à pied de la vieille ville ; le reste de l'année, visite le jeudi à 18 h, le samedi à 14 h 30 et 15 h 30. 5 F : ☎ (022) 311 92 55.

Église St-Germain – Visite de mi-avril à fin septembre de 14 h à 17 h du lundi au vendredi.

Musée Ariana – ♿ Visite tous les jours (sauf le mardi) de 10 h à 17 h. Fermé certains jours fériés. Entrée gratuite. ☎ (022) 418 54 50.

Palais des Nations – ♿ Visite accompagnée (1 h) de 9 h à 18 h en juillet et août ; le reste de l'année de 10 h à 12 h et 14 h à 16 h. Fermé les samedis et dimanches de novembre à mars ainsi que tous les jours de la deuxième quinzaine de décembre. 8,50 F. ☎ (022) 907 48 96.

Musée philatélique – Visite de 9 h à 12 h et de 14 h à 16 h 30 du 2 janvier au 15 décembre. Fermé les samedis et dimanches ainsi que certains jours fériés et de mi-décembre à début janvier. ☎ (022) 907 48 82.

GENÈVE

Musée international de la Croix-Rouge et du Croissant-Rouge – ♿ Visite tous les jours (sauf le mardi) de 10 h à 17 h. Fermé les 1er et 2 janvier ainsi que les 25 et 26 décembre. 8 F. ☏ (022) 734 52 48.

Musée d'Art et d'Histoire – Visite tous les jours (sauf le lundi) de 10 h à 17 h. Fermé les 1er janvier et 25 décembre. Certaines expositions temporaires peuvent être payantes. ☏ (022) 418 26 00.

Collections Baur – Provisoirement fermé pour cause de travaux; réouverture prévue : printemps 1997. ☏ (022) 346 17 29.

Petit Palais - Musée d'Art moderne – Visite tous les jours, de 10 h à 12 h et de 14 h à 18 h en semaine, de 10 h à 13 h et de 14 h à 17 h les samedis et dimanches. 10 F.

Musée d'Histoire naturelle – ♿ Visite tous les jours (sauf le lundi) de 9 h 30 à 17 h. Fermé les 1er janvier et 25 décembre. ☏ (022) 735 91 30.

Musée de l'Horlogerie et de l'Émaillerie – Visite tous les jours (sauf le mardi) de 10 h à 17 h. Fermé les 1er janvier et les 24, 25 et 31 décembre. ☏ (022) 418 64 70.

Musée Barbier-Mueller – Visite tous les jours de 11 h à 17 h. 5 F. ☏ (022) 312 02 70.

Église orthodoxe Ste-Croix – Visite tous les jours (sauf le lundi) de 9 h à 12 h et de 14 h à 17 h de juin à septembre; de 9 h à 12 h le reste de l'année.

Musée d'Ethnographie – Visite tous les jours (sauf le lundi) de 10 h à 17 h. Fermé 1er janvier et 25 décembre. 5 F. ☏ (022) 328 12 18.

M.A.M.C.O. – Visite tous les jours (sauf le lundi) de 12 h à 18 h (21 h le mardi). Fermé les Vendredi saint, 1er août, le jour du Jeûne genevois (un jeudi en septembre), du 24 décembre au 2 janvier. 9 F. ☏ (022) 320 61 22.

Institut et musée Voltaire – Visite de 14 h à 17 h du lundi au vendredi, ainsi que le Vendredi saint, Ascension, lundi de Pentecôte, jour de Jeûne genevois. Fermé le lundi de Pâques, du 24 au 26 décembre et du 31 décembre au 2 janvier. ☏ (022) 344 71 33.

Musée des Suisses à l'étranger – Visite tous les jours (sauf le mardi) de 10 h à 12 h et de 14 h à 18 h. Fermé du 22 décembre au 6 janvier. 5 F. ☏ (022) 734 90 21.

Musée militaire genevois – Visite tous les jours (sauf le lundi et le mardi) de 10 h à 12 h et de 14 h à 18 h. Fermé du 24 décembre à début janvier. ☏ (022) 734 90 21.

Musée international de l'Automobile – Visite de 10 h à 19 h. Fermé les 1er janvier et 25 décembre. 10 F ou 6 F (enfants de 6 à 16 ans). ☏ (022) 788 84 84.

Cascades de GIESSBACH

7 services quotidiens pendant la saison d'été. Depuis Brienz, AR : 10 F en 2e classe. Depuis Interlaken, AR : 20 F en 2e classe (incluant le funiculaire).

GINGINS

Fondation Neumann – Visite les jeudis et vendredis de 14 h à 17 h, les samedis et dimanches de 10 h 30 à 17 h. Fermé les 1er janvier, Vendredi saint et 25 décembre. 8 F. ☏ (022) 369 36 53.

GLETSCH

Eisgrotte – Visite de 8 h à 18 h de mi-juin à mi-octobre. 5 F. ☏ (028) 73 11 29.

GOETHEANUM

Visite libre de 8 h 30 (9 h les samedis et dimanches) à 12 h 30 et de 14 h à 18 h (20 h 15 et sans interruption à midi lors des sessions importantes. Visites guidées à 10 h et 14 h 30 : 9 F. ☏ (061) 706 42 69.

GORNERGRAT

Chemin de fer à crémaillère au départ de Zermatt – AR : 58 F.

Téléphérique du Gornergrat au Stockhorn – Fonctionne de début juin à fin octobre de 7 h 05 à 18 h. Départs toutes les 24 mn. AR : 63 F. ☏ (027) 967 27 44.

Gorges du GORNER

Entrée : 3 F.

Col du GRAND ST-BERNARD

Musée – Visite de 8 h à 19 h du 1er juillet au 14 septembre; de 9 h à 12 h et de 13 h à 18 h la 2e quinzaine de juin et de mi-septembre à mi-octobre. 6 F. ☏ (026) 87 12 36.

Route du GRAND ST-BERNARD

Tunnel – Entrée à Bourg-St-Bernard. Voitures : aller simple 27 F, AR 38 F ; motos : aller simple 27 F, AR : 30 F.

GRANDSON

Château – Visite tous les jours de 8 h 30 à 18 h de mars à novembre ; le reste de l'année, le samedi de 9 h à 17 h. 8 F. ☏ (024) 24 29 26.

GRINDELWALD

Gletscherschlucht – Accès du 1er juin au 31 octobre. 4 F. ☏ (036) 54 12 12.

GRUYÈRES 1663 – ☏ (029) 6 10 30

Château – Visite de juin à septembre, de 9 h à 18 h ; de mars à mai et en octobre, de 9 h à 12 h et de 13 h à 17 h ; en janvier, février, novembre et décembre, de 9 h à 12 h et de 13 h à 16 h 30. Dernière entrée 1/2 avant l'heure de fermeture. Fermé à Noël. 5 F. ☏ (029) 921 21 02.

Fromagerie de démonstration – Visite de 8 h à 18 h. Fabrication du fromage de 10 h à 11 h et de 14 h à 15 h. ☏ (029) 921 14 10.

GURTEN

Funiculaire – Il fonctionne toute l'année. Aller simple : 3 F ; 5 F AR. ☏ (031) 961 23 23.

GUTTANNEN

Kristallmuseum – Visite de juin à septembre du lundi au vendredi, de 8 h à 17 h. 3 F. ☏ (036) 73 12 47.

H

Château de HALLWIL

Visite de début avril à fin octobre, tous les jours de 9 h 30 à 11 h 30 et de 13 h 30 à 17 h 30, sans interruption le dimanche. Fermé le lundi, le jour de Pâques ainsi que du 2 novembre au 31 mars. 5 F. ☏ (062) 777 11 21.

HARDERKULM

Funiculaire – Fonctionne de mai à octobre. Départ toutes les 1/2 h. 20 F. ☏ (033) 828 71 11.

Abbaye d'HAUTERIVE

Visite accompagnée (3/4 h) de fin mars à fin septembre, en semaine de 14 h à 17 h, les dimanches et jours fériés de 10 h 45 à 11 h 30 et de 14 h 45 à 16 h 45 ; le reste de l'année, en semaine de 14 h à 16 h 30, les dimanches et jours fériés de 10 h 45 à 11 h 30 et de 14 h à 16 h. ☏ (037) 42 17 83.

HEIMWEHFLUH

Funiculaire – Fonctionne de fin mars à fin octobre de 9 h 30 à 17 h 30. Départ tous les 1/4 h ou 1/2 h. 8 F. ☏ (033) 822 89 33.

HOHER KASTEN

Téléphérique au départ de Brülisau – Le téléphérique au départ de Brülisau fonctionne toutes les 1/2 h. Se renseigner sur les périodes d'ouverture. AR : 23 F. ☏ (071) 799 13 22.

HÖLLOCHGROTTE

Visite accompagnée (1 h 1/2) du mercredi au vendredi à 10 h 30, 13 h 30 et 16 h, les samedis et dimanches à 10 h, 13 h, 15 h et 17 h de juin à septembre. 8,80 F. On peut entreprendre toute l'année de courtes expéditions sur réservation, 70 F par adulte ou 35 F par enfant. Se renseigner sur les autres types d'excursions. ☏ (01) 950 33 88.

Château de HÜNEGG

Visite de mi-mai à mi-octobre, en semaine de 14 h à 17 h, le dimanche de 10 h à 12 h et de 14 h à 17 h. 5 F. ☏ (033) 43 19 82.

I – J

INTERLAKEN
🛈 Höheweg 37 – 3800 – ☎ (036) 26 53 00

Touristikmuseum – Visite tous les jours (sauf le lundi) de 14 h à 17 h de début mai à mi-octobre. 3 F. ☎ (036) 22 64 64.

JEGENSTORF

Schloss – Visite tous les jours (sauf le lundi) de 10 h à 12 h et de 14 h à 17 h de mi-mai à mi-octobre. 5 F. ☎ (031) 761 01 59.

JUNGFRAUJOCH

Circuit ferroviaire – Billet circulaire Interlaken-Jungfraujoch-Interlaken : 153,20 F ; en utilisant l'un des deux premiers trains du matin et les trains en correspondance immédiate : 115,20 F. Billet circulaire Interlaken-Petite Scheidegg-Interlaken (sans monter au Jungfraujoch) : 59.20 F. Billet depuis Lauterbrunnen : 136,80 F ; en utilisant les deux premiers trains : 98,80 F. Billet depuis Grindelwald Grund : 132 F ; en utilisant les deux premiers trains : 94 F.

K

Abbaye de KÖNIGSFELDEN

Klosterkirche – Visite tous les jours (sauf le lundi) d'avril à octobre, de 9 h à 12 h et de 14 h à 17 h ; le reste de l'année, de 10 h à 12 h et de 14 h à 16 h. Fermé les 1er et 2 janvier, du Vendredi saint au dimanche de Pâques, 24, 25 et 26 décembre. 3 F. ☎ (056) 441 88 33.

Château de KYBURG

Visite tous les jours (sauf le lundi) de mars à octobre de 10 h à 12 h et de 13 h à 17 h ; de novembre à février de 10 h à 12 h et de 13 h à 16 h. Fermé les jours fériés. 4 F ☎ (052) 232 46 64.

L

LANGNAU IM EMMENTAL
🛈 3550 – ☎ (035) 234 34

Heimatmuseum – Visite tous les jours (sauf le lundi) de 13 h 30 à 18 h de février à novembre. Fermé le Vendredi saint. ☎ (034) 402 18 19.

LAUSANNE
🛈 2, avenue de Rhodanie – 1000 – ☎ (021) 617 14 27

Visite guidée de la ville – S'adresser à l'Office du tourisme.

Musée Olympique – Visite de 10 h à 19 h (21 h 30 le jeudi) de mai à septembre ; tous les jours (sauf le lundi) de 10 h à 18 h (21 h 30 le jeudi) le reste de l'année. Fermé les 1er janvier et 25 décembre. 14 F. ☎ (021) 621 65 11.

Musée de l'Élysée – Visite tous les jours (sauf le lundi) de 10 h à 18 h (21 h le jeudi). Fermé les 1er et 2 janvier ainsi que le 25 décembre. 5 F. ☎ (021) 617 48 21.

Musée historique de Lausanne – Visite accompagnée possible (durée : 1 h) ou libre tous les jours (sauf le lundi) de 11 h à 18 h (20 h le jeudi). Fermé les 1er janvier et 25 décembre. 4 F ☎ (021) 312 13 68.

Tour de la cathédrale – Montée de mars à septembre de 8 h 30 à 11 h 30 et de 13 h 30 à 17 h 30, le dimanche de 14 h à 17 h 30 ; le reste de l'année de 8 h 30 à 11 h 30 et de 13 h 30 à 16 h 30, le dimanche de 14 h à 16 h 30. 2 F. ☎ (021) 316 71 61.

Musée de la pipe et objets du tabac – Visite le lundi de 10 h à 12 h et de 14 h à 17 h (15 h à 18 h d'avril à septembre), du mardi au samedi sur rendez-vous. Fermé les dimanches, 1er et 2 janvier, Vendredi saint et 25 décembre. ☎ (021) 323 43 23.

Musée des Beaux-Arts – Visite de 11 h à 18 h les mardi et mercredi, 20 h le jeudi, 17 h les autres jours. Fermé le lundi, ainsi que les 25 décembre et 1er janvier. Visite guidée : 12 F. ☎ (021) 312 83 32.

Musée de Géologie, de Paléontologie, de Zoologie, salle d'Archéologie et d'Histoire – Visite de 10 h à 12 h et de 14 h à 17 h. Fermé les 1er janvier, dimanche de Pâques et 25 décembre. ☎ (021) 692 44 70.

Collection de l'Art brut – Visite tous les jours (sauf le lundi) de 11 h à 13 h et de 14 h à 18 h. Fermé les 1er janvier et 25 décembre. 6 F. ☎ (021) 647 54 36.

LAUSANNE

Fondation de l'Hermitage – Jours d'ouverture, horaires et tarifs d'entrée en fonction des expositions, en général visite tous les jours (sauf le lundi) de 10 h à 18 h (22 h le jeudi). ☎ (021) 312 50 13.

Musée des Arts Décoratifs – Visite tous les jours (sauf le lundi) de 11 h à 18 h (21 h le mardi sauf en été). Fermé les 1er janvier et 25 décembre. 4 F. ☎ (021) 323 07 56.

Jardin botanique – & *Visite de mars à avril et en octobre, de 10 h à 12 h et de 13 h 30 à 17 h 30 (18 h 30 de mai à septembre).* ☎ *(021) 26 24 09.*

Musée de Pully – & Visite de 14 h à 18 h. Fermé le lundi, le lundi de Pâques ainsi que du 23 décembre au 3 janvier. 3 F. ☎ (021) 729 55 81.

Villa romaine de Pully – Visite du 1er avril à fin octobre, tous les jours sauf le lundi, de 14 h à 17 h ; le reste de l'année, les samedis et dimanches seulement aux mêmes heures. ☎ (021) 728 33 04 ou 729 55 81.

Le LOCLE 🛈 31, rue Daniel-Jean-Richard – 2400 – ☎ (039) 31 43 30

Musée d'Horlogerie – Visite tous les jours (sauf le lundi) de mai à octobre de 10 h à 12 h et de 14 h à 17 h ; le reste de l'année de 14 h à 17 h seulement. Fermé les lundis sauf fériés, les 1er janvier et 25 décembre. 6 F. ☎ (039) 31 16 80.

Musée des Beaux-Arts – *Visite tous les jours, sauf le lundi, de 14 h à 17 h. Fermé les 1er et 2 janvier, les 24, 25 et 26 décembre. 6 F.* ☎ *(039) 31 13 13.*

Moulins souterrains du Col-des-Roches – Visite accompagnée (1 h) de 10 h à 12 h et de 13 h 30 à 17 h 30 (dernière visite à 17 h) du 1er mai au 15 juin ainsi que du 16 septembre au 31 octobre, de 10 h à 17 h 30 (dernière visite à 17 h) du 16 juin au 15 septembre. 7 F. ☎ (039) 931 89 89. Se munir de vêtements chauds, température : 7°.

LOTTIGNA

Musée du Blenio – Visite tous les jours de Pâques au 31 octobre, de 14 h à 17 h et en outre de 10 h à 12 h les samedis, dimanches et jours fériés. Fermé le lundi et du 1er novembre à Pâques. 4 F. ☎ (091) 871 17 65.

LUGANO 🛈 Palazzo Civico – 6900 – ☎ (091) 921 46 64

Visite guidée de la ville – S'adresser à l'Office du tourisme ou à l'Agence de voyages Danzas, Via Gen. Guisan 2, Paradiso.

Monte San Salvatore – Accès par funiculaire. Fonctionne de mi-mars à novembre. Départ toutes les 1/2 h. AR : 17 F.

Villa Favorita – Visite les vendredis, samedis et dimanches de début avril à début novembre de 10 h à 17 h. 10 F, 12 F lors d'expositions temporaires, 5 F (visite du jardin seul). ☎ (091) 971 61 52.

Villa Heleneum – Visite du mardi au dimanche de 10 h à 17 h. 5 F. ☎ (091) 971 73 53.

Monte Brè – Accès par funiculaire au départ de Cassarate. Service interrompu en janvier. Départ toutes les 1/2 h. AR : 18 F. ☎ (091) 971 31 71.

LUZERN 🛈 Haldenstrasse 6 – 6000 – ☎ (041) 410 71 71

Visite guidée de la ville – S'adresser à l'Office du tourisme.

Picasso-Sammlung – Visite de 10 h à 18 h d'avril à octobre, de 11 h à 13 h et de 14 h à 16 h le reste de l'année. 6 F. ☎ (041) 410 35 33.

Historisches Museum – & Visite du lundi au vendredi, de 10 h à 12 h et de 14 h à 17 h, les samedis, dimanches et jours fériés de 10 h à 17 h. 4 F. ☎ (041) 228 54 24.

Verkehrshaus der Schweiz – & Visite de 9 h à 18 h d'avril à octobre, de 10 h à 17 h le reste de l'année. Fermé les 24 et 25 décembre. 16 F. ☎ (041) 370 44 44.

Kunstmuseum – *Visite de juillet à septembre, tous les jours de 10 h à 17 h (21 h le mercredi) ; le reste de l'année, tous les jours sauf le lundi, de 10 h à 12 h et de 14 h à 17 h (21 h le mercredi, le dimanche sans interruption le midi). 6 F.* ☎ *(041) 23 10 24.*

Richard-Wagner-Museum – Visite du 1er février au 31 octobre (en été tous les jours sauf le lundi) de 10 h à 12 h et de 14 h à 17 h, en dehors de cette période les mardis, jeudis, samedis et dimanches aux mêmes heures. 5 F. ☎ (041) 44 23 70.

Grand panorama de Lucerne – *De mars à novembre de 9 h à 17 h. 3 F.* ☎ *(041) 52 99 42.*

Gletschergarten – Visite de 8 h à 18 h de mai à mi-octobre, de 9 h à 17 h en mars et avril et de mi-octobre à mi-novembre ; tous les jours (sauf le lundi) de 10 h 30 à 16 h 30 de mi-novembre à février. 7 F. ☎ (041) 410 43 40.

Museggmauer – Visite de Pâques à la Toussaint, de 8 h à 19 h. ☎ (041) 208 81 11.

LUZERN

Naturmuseum und Saal zur Archäologie – ♿ Visite tous les jours (sauf le lundi) de 10 h à 12 h et de 14 h à 17 h (le dimanche sans interruption à midi). Fermé les 24 et 25 décembre. 4 F. ☏ (041) 228 54 11.

Gütsch – Le funiculaire fonctionne de 7 h à 24 h 30. Départ toutes les 10 mn. 2 F. ☏ (041) 249 41 00.

Promenades en bateau – Avec sa flotte de bateaux à vapeur et de confortables bateaux-salons, la Compagnie de Navigation sur le lac des Quatre-Cantons relie toute l'année Lucerne aux célèbres lieux de villégiature bordant le lac et offre des croisières commentées sur les sites chargés d'histoire, des croisières nocturnes avec musique l'été, des correspondances ou combinaisons avec tous les téléphériques et funiculaires de la région ainsi qu'avec l'express «Guillaume Tell» pour un voyage en voitures panoramiques de 1ʳᵉ classe ou dans des bateaux de 2ᵉ classe sur la ligne du St-Gothard. En saison, les bateaux de Lucerne à Flüelen et de Lucerne à Alpnachstad partent environ toutes les heures. ☏ (041) 40 45 40.

M

MARBACHEGG

Télécabine au départ de Marbach – Fonctionne en été de 8 h à 12 h et de 13 h à 17 h 30 ; en hiver de 8 h à 17 h. AR : 14 F. ☏ (035) 6 37 95.

Les MARÉCOTTES

Zoo – Visite de 9 h à la tombée de la nuit. 7,50 F, enfants de 6 à 15 ans : 4,50 F. ☏ (027) 761 15 62.

Barrage de MARMORERA

Visite accompagnée de mai à octobre de 9 h à 12 h et de 14 h à 16 h. ☏ (081) 74 12 31.

MARTIGNY   🛈 9, place Centrale – 1920 – ☏ (026) 21 22 20

Fondation Pierre Gianadda – ♿ Visite de juin à octobre, de 9 h à 19 h ; de novembre à janvier, de 10 h à 12 h et de 13 h 30 à 18 h ; de février à mai, de 10 h à 18 h. 12 F. ☏ (026) 22 39 78.

MEIRINGEN   🛈 3860 – ☏ (036) 71 43 22

Sherlock-Holmes-Museum – Visite de mai à septembre tous les jours de 10 h à 18 h ; d'octobre à avril de 15 h à 18 h sauf les lundis et mardis. 3,80 F. ☏ (036) 71 41 41.

MELIDE   🛈 via Pocobelli – 6815 – ☏ (091) 649 63 83

Swissminiatur – ♿ Visite de mi-mars à fin octobre de 9 h à 18 h. 10,50 F, enfants : 6 F. ☏ (091) 649 79 51.

Castello di MISOX

Santa Maria del Castello – Visite de 9 h à 11 h et de 15 h à 18 h. S'adresser à la «cancelleria comunale» de Mesocco. Fermé en mai et tous les jours fériés. ☏ (092) 831 17 17.

MOLÉSON-SUR-GRUYÈRES   🛈 1662 – ☏ (029) 6 24 34

Fromagerie d'alpage – ♿ Visite du 15 mai au 15 octobre de 9 h 30 à 18 h 30. Fabrication du fromage à 10 h et 15 h. 3 F. ☏ (021) 921 24 34.

Observatoire du Moléson – Téléphérique au départ de Moléson-Village : service interrompu de mi-avril à mi-juin et de mi-octobre à mi-décembre. L'observatoire est ouvert de Noël à Pâques et de mi-juin à mi-octobre : il propose des soirées d'initiation à l'astronomie sur réservation de 16 h 30 à 10 h le lendemain suivant ou des journées d'observation. 65 F ou 50 F (enfants jusqu'à 13 ans). ☏ (026) 921 24 34.

Historial suisse – Visite tous les jours (sauf le mardi) de 9 h à 22 h. Fermé en octobre. 3 F. ☏ (026) 921 24 34.

MONTE GENEROSO

Chemin de fer à crémaillère au départ de Capolago – Départ chaque heure de début avril à fin octobre. AR : 42 F. ☏ (091) 648 17 05.

MONTE LEMA
Télésiège au départ de Miglieglia – Réouverture prévue en septembre 1996. Fonctionne toutes les 18 mn. ☎ (091) 606 29 86.

MONTREUX
🛈 5, rue du Théâtre – 1820 – ☎ (021) 963 12 12

Musée du Vieux-Montreux – Visite d'avril à octobre tous les jours de 10 h à 12 h et de 14 h à 17 h. 6 F. ☎ (021) 963 13 53.

MORCOTE
Accès par bateau au départ de Lugano – Durée : 1 h environ. Renseignements sur les promenades (avec ou sans déjeûner à bord) et croisières auprès de la Società Navigazione del Lago di Lugano. ☎ (091) 971 52 23.

MORGES
🛈 1, place du Casino – 1110 – ☎ (021) 801 32 33

Musée Alexis-Forel – Visite de 14 h à 17 h 30. Fermé le lundi, les 1ᵉʳ janvier, les 25, 26 et 31 décembre. 5 F. ☎ (021) 801 26 47.

Château – Visite de 10 h à 17 h en juillet et août, de 10 h à 12 h et de 13 h 30 à 17 h le reste de l'année. Fermé du 16 décembre au 31 janvier. 5 F. ☎ (021) 801 26 16.

MÔTIERS
Musées – Visite accompagnée (1 h) du 2 mai au 15 octobre, de 14 h à 17 h. Fermés les lundis, mercredis et vendredis. 5 F. ☎ (038) 61 35 51.

MOUDON
Musée du Vieux-Moudon – Fermé pour travaux.

Musée Eugène-Burnand – Visite du 20 mars au 15 décembre, les mercredis, samedis et dimanches de 14 h à 17 h 30. 5 F. ☎ (021) 905 33 18.

MUOTTAS MURAGL
Funiculaire – Départ toutes les 1/2 h.

MURTEN
🛈 Franz Kirchgasse 6 – 3280 – ☎ (037) 71 51 12

Musée d'Histoire – Visite de mai à septembre de 10 h à 12 h et de 14 h à 17 h ; le reste de l'année, tous les jours de 14 h à 17 h. Fermé le lundi toute l'année ainsi qu'en janvier et février les samedis et dimanches. 4 F. ☎ (037) 71 31 00.

N

NÄFELS
🛈 8752 – ☎ (055) 612 23 73

Freulerpalast – Visite tous les jours (sauf le lundi) de 10 h à 12 h et de 14 h à 17 h 30 de début avril à fin novembre. Fermé Vendredi saint et les dimanches de Pâques et de Pentecôte. 3 F. ☎ (055) 612 13 78.

Rochers de NAYE
Chemin de fer à crémaillère – *8 services par jour en été, départ toutes les heures, à l'heure pile, sauf à midi. En été train à vapeur les samedis et dimanches. En hiver, dernier départ à 15 h. AR : 45 F.*

NEGRENTINO
Église San Carlo – Pour visiter, s'adresser au restaurant de Leontica ou d'Acquarossa ou auprès de l'Office du tourisme du Blenio. Caution pour la clé : 15 F. ☎ (091) 871 17 65.

NEUCHÂTEL
🛈 7, rue de la Place d'Armes – 2000 – ☎ (038) 25 42 42

Visite guidée de la ville – S'adresser à l'Office du tourisme.

Château – Visite accompagnée du château et de la collégiale (3/4 h) de début avril à fin septembre, du lundi au vendredi à 10 h, 11 h, 12 h, 14 h, 15 h, 16 h ; le samedi à 10 h, 11 h, 14 h, 15 h, 16 h ; les dimanches et jours fériés à 14 h, 15 h, 16 h. ☎ (038) 39 60 11.

Tour des Prisons – Visite d'avril à fin septembre de 8 h à 18 h. Tourniquet : 0, 50 F. ☎ (038) 25 42 42.

Musée d'Art et d'Histoire – Visite tous les jours (sauf le lundi) de 10 h à 17 h. Fermé les 1ᵉʳ janvier, 24, 25, 26 et 31 décembre. 7 F, entrée gratuite le jeudi. ☎ (038) 20 79 25. Les automates fonctionnent le 1ᵉʳ dimanche de chaque mois à 14 h, 15 h et 16 h.

NEUCHÂTEL

Musée d'Ethnographie – Visite tous les jours (sauf le lundi) de 10 h à 17 h. Fermé les 1er janvier et 25 décembre. 7 F. ☎ (038) 24 41 20.

Musée d'Histoire naturelle – Visite tous les jours (sauf le lundi) de 10 h à 17 h. Fermé les 1er janvier et 25 décembre. 4 F ou 6 F lors des expositions. ☎ (038) 20 79 60.

Musée cantonal d'Archéologie – Visite tous les jours (sauf le lundi) de 14 h à 17 h. Fermé les 1er janvier, les 24, 25 et 31 décembre. ☎ (038) 36 69 10.

La NEUVEVILLE 4, rue du Marché – 2520 – ☎ (038) 51 49 49

« **Blanche Église** » – Pour visiter, s'adresser à l'Office du tourisme. ☎ (038) 51 49 49.

NIESEN

Funiculaire au départ de Mülenen – Fonctionne de début mai à fin octobre. AR : 38 F. ☎ (033) 676 11 12.

NYON 7, avenue Viollier – 1260 – ☎ (022) 361 62 61

Musée historique et des porcelaines – *Visite d'avril à octobre tous les jours de 9 h à 12 h et de 14 h à 18 h. 5 F (billet valable pour les autres musées).* ☎ *(022) 363 82 82.*

Musée romain – ♿ *Visite d'avril à octobre, tous les jours de 9 h à 12 h et de 14 h à 18 h ; de novembre à mars, du mardi au dimanche de 14 h à 17 h. Fermé les 24, 25 et 31 décembre ainsi que le 1er janvier. 5 F (billet valable pour les autres musées).* ☎ *(022) 363 82 82.*

Musée du lac Léman – ♿ *Mêmes conditions de visite que pour le musée romain. 5 F (billet valable pour les autres musées).* ☎ *(022) 363 82 82.*

O

OBERALPPASS

Rail-route – *En hiver entre Andermatt et Sedrun. Pour connaître les horaires du train et pour réserver (obligatoire),* ☎ *(044) 672 20 ou* ☎ *(081) 949 11 37.*

OBERHOFEN

Schloss – *Visite de mai à mi-octobre de 10 h à 12 h (sauf le lundi matin) et de 14 h à 17 h ; 4 F.* ☎ *(033) 43 14 19.*

Lac d'OESCHINEN

Télésiège – Fonctionne de mi-mai à fin octobre et de fin décembre à mi-avril. AR : 16 F. ☎ (033) 75 11 18.

OLTEN Klosterplatz 21 – 4600 – ☎ (062) 212 38 88

Historisches Museum – Visite tous les jours (sauf le lundi) de 14 h à 17 h ; les dimanches et jours fériés de 10 h à 12 h et de 14 h à 17 h. Fermé les 1er janvier, Vendredi saint, dimanche de Pâques et 25 décembre. ☎ (062) 212 89 89.

Kunstmuseum – Visite tous les jours (sauf le lundi) de 14 h à 17 h ; les samedis et dimanches, de 10 h à 12 h et de 14 h à 17 h. Fermé la plupart des jours fériés. 2 F. ☎ (062) 212 86 76.

ORBE

Mosaïques d'Urba – Visite de 9 h à 12 h et de 13 h 30 à 17 h 30, les samedis, dimanches et jours fériés uniquement de 13 h 30 à 17 h 30 de Pâques à fin octobre. 3 F. ☎ (024) 441 31 15.

Source de l'ORBE

Grottes – Visite en juillet et août de 9 h à 18 h ; d'avril à fin juin et de septembre à octobre de 9 h 30 à 16 h 30. Fermé le lundi hors saison (sauf les jours fériés). 12 F. ☎ (021) 843 25 83.

Trésor des Fées – ♿ Mêmes horaires de visite que les grottes. 6 F en cas de visite seule des grottes.

ORON-LE-CHÂTEL

Château – Visite accompagnée (1/2 h) de mars à novembre, les samedis et dimanches de 10 h à 12 h et de 14 h à 18 h. Visite possible en semaine sur rendez-vous seulement. 5 F. ☎ (021) 907 90 51.

P

PARPANER ROTHORN

Téléphérique – Fonctionne 8 h 15 à 17 h 15 (17 h 10, 16 h 50, 16 h 45 ou 16 h 40 suivant la saison). Fermé de mi-octobre à mi-décembre et de mi-avril à mi-juin. 32 F AR ☎ (081) 385 03 85.

PAYERNE
🛈 Hôtel de Ville – 1530 – ☎ (037) 61 61 61

Église abbatiale – Visite d'avril à octobre, en semaine de 9 h à 12 h et de 14 h à 18 h, les dimanches et jours fériés de 10 h 30 à 12 h et de 14 h à 18 h ; le reste de l'année de 10 h à 12 h et de 14 h à 17 h, les dimanches et jours fériés de 10 h 30 à 12 h et de 14 h à 17 h. 3 F. ☎ (037) 61 61 61.

PETIT CERVIN

Montée – Téléphérique au départ de Zermatt toutes les 20 mn. AR : 56 F. ☎ (028) 67 11 73.

Schwarzsee – Téléphérique au départ de Zermatt. AR : 29,50 F.

PILATUS

Montée en chemin de fer à crémaillère au départ d'Alpnachstad – Service interrompu de fin novembre à mi-mai. AR : 58 F.

PIZ CORVATSCH

Téléphérique – Départs toutes les 20 mn de 8 h 10 (8 h 20 en hiver) à 17 h de juillet à mi-octobre et de décembre à avril. AR : 30 F. ☎ (081) 828 82 42.

PIZ LAGALB

Téléphérique au départ de Curtinatsch – *Fonctionne.*

PONTRESINA
🛈 7504 – ☎ (081) 842 64 88

Santa Marie – *Ouverte de juillet à mi-octobre.*

PORRENTRUY
🛈 5, Grand-Rue – 2900 – ☎ (066) 66 18 53

Musée de l'ancien Hôtel-Dieu – ♿ Le musée permanent est fermé jusqu'en 1997 pour cause de réaménagement. Seules les expositions temporaires sont visibles les vendredis, samedis et dimanches de 14 h à 17 h. Fermé à Pâques, les 23 juin et 25 décembre. ☎ (066) 66 72 72.

R

RAPPERSWIL
🛈 Seequai – 8640 – ☎ (055) 210 70 00

Polenmuseum – Visite de 13 h à 17 h d'avril à octobre ; en mars, novembre et décembre les samedis et dimanches seulement aux mêmes heures. Fermé en janvier, février. 4 F. ☎ (055) 210 18 62.

Heimatmuseum – Visite le samedi de 14 h à 17 h, le dimanche de 10 h à 12 h et de 14 h à 17 h du lundi de Pâques à fin octobre. 3 F. ☎ (055) 210 71 64.

Kinderzoo – ♿ Visite du 15 mars au 1er novembre tous les jours de 9 h à 18 h (19 h les dimanches et jours fériés). 7 F, enfants : 3,50 F. ☎ (055) 220 67 67.

Grottes de RÉCLÈRE

Visite accompagnée (1 h) de 10 h à 12 h et de 13 h 30 à 17 h 30 de fin mars à début décembre ; le reste de l'année, le dimanche seulement. 8 F. ☎ (066) 76 61 55.

Chutes de REICHENBACH

Funiculaire – Fonctionne de la Pentecôte au Jeûne fédéral, tous les jours de 8 h à 11 h 50 et de 13 h 15 à 18 h. 4,40 F ou 6,50 F AR. ☎ (036) 71 33 22.

RHEINAU

Klosterkirche – Visite du mardi au samedi de 14 h à 16 h, les dimanches et jours fériés de 13 h 30 à 17 h 30 en avril, mai et octobre ; du mardi au vendredi et les dimanches et jours fériés de 10 h à 12 h et de 13 h 30 à 16 h, le samedi de 10 h à 11 h 30 de juin à septembre. Fermée le lundi et de novembre à mars. ☎ (052) 319 31 00.

RHEINFELDEN
🛈 Marktgasse – 4310 – ☎ (061) 831 55 20

Bierbrauerei Feldschlösschen – Pour visiter prendre rendez-vous par téléphone. ☎ (061) 835 01 11.

Chutes du RHIN
Château de Laufen (belvédères) – 1 F.

Promenades en bateau – Jusqu'au rocher, AR : 5,50 F.

RIEDERALP
🛈 3987 – ☎ (028) 27 29 32

Téléphérique ou télécabine au départ de Mörel – Départ toutes les 1/2 h. AR : 14,40 F. ☎ (028) 27 22 27.

Télésiège de Moosfluh au départ de Riederalp – Fonctionne de mi-juin à fin octobre et de mi-décembre à Pâques : de 8 h à 17 h en été et de 9 h à 16 h 30 en hiver. AR : 13 F. ☎ (028) 27 22 67.

RIGGISBERG

Abegg-Stiftung – ♿ Visite de début mai à début novembre de 14 h à 17 h 30. 5 F. ☎ (031) 808 12 01.

RIGI

Montée au Rigi-Kulm par chemin de fer à crémaillère – Depuis Arth-Goldau, Vitznau ou Weggis : AR 52 F, 52 F ou 32 F. ☎ (041) 390 18 44.

RIGI-SCHEIDEGG

Téléphérique au départ de Kräbel – Fonctionne de mi-mai à fin avril. Départs toutes les 1/2 h. AR : 27 F. ☎ (041) 828 18 38.

ROFFLASCHLUCHT

Visite de 8 h 30 (9 h les samedis, dimanches et jours fériés à la tombée de la nuit) de mai à octobre. Fermé de novembre à mi-décembre, les mardis et mercredis de décembre à avril. 2,50 F. ☎ (081) 61 11 97.

ROMONT
🛈 87, rue de l'Église – 1680 – ☎ (037) 52 31 52

Musée suisse du Vitrail – Visite tous les jours (sauf le lundi) de 10 h à 12 h et de 14 h à 18 h de début avril à début novembre ; le reste de l'année, seulement les samedis, dimanches et jours fériés aux mêmes heures. Fermé le lundi sauf lundis de Pâques et de Pentecôte. 6 F. ☎ (037) 52 31 52.

RORSCHACH
🛈 Hauptstrasse 63 – 9400 – ☎ (071) 841 70 34

Heimatmuseum – Visite du mardi au samedi de 14 h à 17 h, le dimanche de 10 h à 12 h et de 14 h à 17 h. Fermé généralement de mi-octobre à fin avril. 4 F. ☎ (071) 841 40 62.

ROSENLAUI

Gletscherschlucht – *Visite de fin mai à fin octobre de 9 h à 17 h (8 h à 18 h de fin juin à fin septembre). 5 F. ☎ (036) 71 43 22.*

S

SAAS-FEE
🛈 3906 – ☎ (028) 57 14 57

Saaser Museum – Visite de juin au 20 octobre, tous les jours (sauf le lundi) de 10 h à 12 h et de 14 h à 18 h ; de décembre à avril, du lundi au vendredi, de 14 h à 18 h. 3 F. ☎ (028) 957 14 75.

SAINT-IMIER

Ancienne collégiale – Visite de mai à octobre de 8 h à 18 h 30 ; en dehors de cette période, s'adresser à la cure.

SAINT-LEONARD

Lac souterrain – Visite en barque (1/2 h) en juillet et août de 9 h à 18 h 30 ; en juin et septembre de 9 h à 18 h ; du 15 mars au 1er novembre de 9 h à 17 h (17 h 30 les week-ends et jours fériés). 6 F. ☎ (027) 31 22 66.

SAINT-MAURICE
🛈 48, Grand-Rue – 1890 – 👁 (025) 65 27 77

Trésor de l'abbaye – Visite accompagnée (1/2 h) en juillet et août à 9 h 30, 10 h 30, 14 h 30, 15 h 30 et 16 h 30 ; en mai et juin, en septembre et octobre, à 10 h 30, 15 h et 16 h 30 ; de novembre à avril, à 15 h et 16 h 30. Pas de visite le dimanche matin, le lundi et les jours fériés. Offrande libre. 👁 (025) 65 11 81/ 6 72.

Fouilles du Martolet – Mêmes conditions de visite que pour le trésor de l'abbaye.

Château (Musée cantonal d'Histoire militaire) – *Visite sauf le lundi, de 10 h à 12 h et de 14 h à 18 h. Fermé les 1ᵉʳ janvier et 25 décembre. 4 F.* 👁 (025) 65 24 58.

Grotte aux Fées – Visite tous les jours, en juillet et août de 9 h à 21 h ; du 15 mars du 30 juin et du 1ᵉʳ septembre au 15 novembre de 10 h à 18 h. Fermée le reste de l'année. 6 F. 👁 (025) 65 10 45.

Île de SAINT-PIERRE

Accès en bateau au départ de Bienne – *D'avril à mi-octobre. AR : 15,60 F.*

Accès en bateau au départ de Neuveville – *D'avril à mi-octobre. AR : 8,60 F.*

SAINTE-CROIX-LES-RASSES
🛈 1450 – 👁 (024) 61 27 02

Centre international de la mécanique d'art – Visite accompagnée (1 h) de 13 h 30 à 18 h (dernière entrée à 17 h). Fermé le lundi sauf de juin à août et le 25 décembre. 9 F. 👁 (024) 61 44 77.

SALGESCH

Maison Zumofen – Visite de mars à octobre du mardi au dimanche de 14 h à 17 h ; le reste de l'année les vendredis, samedis et dimanches de 14 h à 17 h. Fermé en janvier. 5 F. 👁 (027) 456 35 25.

SÄLI-SCHLÖSSLI

Panorama – *Accès par le château-restaurant. Fermé le lundi, le Vendredi saint, les 24 et 25 décembre ainsi que de janvier à mi-février.*

SANKT GALLEN
🛈 Bahnhofplatz – 9000 – 👁 (071) 22 62 62

Stiftsbibliothek – Visite de mai à octobre, en semaine de 9 h à 12 h et de 13 h 30 à 17 h, les dimanches et jours fériés de 10 h 30 à 12 h (en outre de juin à août de 14 h à 16 h) ; de décembre à mars tous les jours (sauf le dimanche) de 9 h à 12 h et de 13 h 30 à 16 h ; en avril tous les jours (sauf le dimanche) de 9 h à 12 h et de 13 h 30 à 17 h. Fermée la plupart des jours fériés ainsi que les 3 dernières semaines de novembre. 5 F. 👁 (071) 227 34 15.

Textilmuseum – Visite du 1ᵉʳ avril au 31 octobre du lundi au samedi de 10 h à 12 h et de 14 h à 17 h ; du 1ᵉʳ novembre au 31 mars du lundi au vendredi aux mêmes heures ; le reste de l'année, tous les 1ᵉʳ mercredis de 10 h à 17 h. Fermé les jours fériés. 5 F. 👁 (071) 222 17 44.

Historisches Museum – Visite tous les jours (sauf le lundi) de 10 h à 12 h et de 14 h à 17 h (le dimanche sans interruption le midi). Fermé la plupart des jours fériés. 6 F. 👁 (071) 244 78 32.

Botanischer Garten – ♿ Visite de 8 h à 12 h et de 13 h 30 à 17 h. Serres : de 9 h 30 à 12 h et de 14 h à 17 h. 👁 (071) 35 15 30.

SANKT MORITZ
🛈 via Maistra 12 – 7500 – 👁 (082) 837 33

Engadiner Museum – Visite tous les jours (sauf le samedi) de 9 h 30 à 12 h et de 14 h à 17 h, le dimanche de 10 h à 12 h de juin à octobre ; tous les jours (sauf le samedi) de 10 h à 12 h et de 14 h à 17 h, le dimanche de 10 h à 12 h le reste de l'année. Fermé en mai et novembre. 5 F. 👁 (081) 833 43 33.

Segantini-Museum – Visite de début juin au 20 octobre, du mardi au samedi de 9 h à 12 h 30 et de 14 h 30 à 17 h, le dimanche de 10 h 30 à 12 h 30 et de 14 h 30 à 16 h 30 ; de décembre à avril, du mardi au samedi de 10 h à 12 h 30 et de 15 h à 17 h, le dimanche de 15 h à 17 h. Fermé le 25 décembre. 7 F. 👁 (082) 344 54.

Piz Nair – Téléphérique : départ toutes les 20 mn de fin juin à mi-octobre et de fin novembre à mi-avril. AR : 32 F. 👁 (082) 3 32 06.

SANKT URBAN

Klosterkirche – *Ouverte de 10 h (11 h le dimanche) à 17 h (19 h en été).* 👁 *(063) 48 50 01.*

Le SÄNTIS

Téléphérique au départ de Schwägalp – Départs toutes les 1/2 h. Ne fonctionne pas la 2ᵉ quinzaine de janvier. 27 F.

Château de la SARRAZ

Visite accompagnée (3/4 h) de juin à août, de 11 h à 17 h (dernière visite à 16 h 30) ; en avril, mai, septembre et octobre, les samedis, dimanches et jours fériés aux mêmes heures ; 6 F. Visite libre du musée du Cheval ; 6 F. Billet combiné : 10 F. ☏ (021) 866 64 23. Pour voir le cénotaphe, en faire la demande au château.

SCHAFFHAUSEN   ℹ Fronwagtum – 8200 – ☏ (052) 625 51 41

Belvédère du Munot – De mai à septembre de 8 h à 20 h, le reste de l'année de 9 h à 17 h.

Museum zu Allerheiligen – *Visite du mardi au samedi de 10 h à 12 h et de 14 h à 17 h. Fermé les 1ᵉʳ janvier, Pâques, 1ᵉʳ mai, 1ᵉʳ juin, 1ᵉʳ août, 3ᵉ samedi de septembre, 25 décembre.* 3 F. ☏ (053) 25 43 77.

Hallen für neue Kunst – Visite du 1ᵉʳ mai au 31 octobre le jeudi de 17 h à 19 h, les samedis et dimanches de 11 h à 17 h. ☏ (052) 625 25 15.

SCHILTHORN

Téléphérique au départ de Stechelberg – Fonctionne en été de 7 h 25 à 16 h 25, en hiver de 7 h 55 à 15 h 55. AR : 83 F. Fermé 3 jours en mai et trois semaines en octobre et novembre. ☏ (036) 23 14 44.

SCHÖNENWERD

Bally Schuhmuseum – Visite accompagnée (1 h 1/2) de 8 h 30 à 17 h. Fermé le samedi et le dimanche, les jours fériés ainsi que de mi-juillet à mi-août et de mi-décembre à fin décembre. Prévenir environ 2 semaines à l'avance pour être intégré à un groupe. ☏ (062) 858 26 41.

SCHWYZ   ℹ 6430 – ☏ (043) 22 19 91

Bundesbriefmuseum – Visite de 9 h 30 à 11 h 30 et de 14 h à 17 h. Fermé les 24 et 25 décembre et Vendredi saint. ☏ (041) 819 20 64.

Rathaus – Visite accompagnée (1/2 h) du lundi au vendredi, à 10 h et 15 h. Fermé les jours fériés. ☏ (041) 811 42 66.

SCHYNIGE PLATTE

Chemin de fer à crémaillère au départ de Wilderswil – Fonctionne de mai à octobre. Départ toutes les 40 mn. AR : 45 F. ☏ (033) 828 71 11.

SCUOL/SCHULS   ℹ 7550 – ☏ (081) 864 94 94

Maison de la « Chagronda » et musée – Visite de juillet à septembre les lundis, mardis, jeudis et vendredis de 15 h à 18 h, visite guidée le mercredi à 17 h ; en mai, juin et octobre, les mardis et jeudis de 16 h à 18 h ; de novembre à avril, visite guidée les mardis et jeudis à 17 h. 4 F. ☏ (081) 864 10 36.

SEELISBERG   ℹ 6377 – ☏ (043) 31 15 63

Funiculaire au départ du débarcadère de Treib – Fonctionne toute l'année. 4,20 F. ☏ (041) 820 15 63.

SEEWEN

Musikautomaten Museum – Visite accompagnée (1 h) tous les jours (sauf les lundis et dimanches) de 14 h à 17 h. 8 F. Fermé de décembre à février, les Vendredi saint et 1ᵉʳ novembre. 8 F. ☏ (061) 911 02 08.

SEMPACH

Station ornithologique suisse – Visite accompagnée (1 h 1/2) de début avril à fin septembre tous les jours (sauf le samedi matin) de 8 h (10 h le dimanche) à 12 h et de 14 h à 17 h. 2 F. ☏ (041) 462 97 00.

SERVION

Zoo – ♿ Visite de 9 h à 19 h (18 h de novembre à mars). Dernière entrée 1 h avant la fermeture. 9 F. enfants : 4,50 F. ☏ (021) 903 16 71.

SEX ROUGE

Voir Glacier des Diablerets.

SIERRE   ℹ 10, place de la Gare – 3960 – ☏ (027) 55 85 35

Musée d'étains – Visite du lundi au vendredi de 8 h à 11 h 30 et de 14 h à 17 h. Entrée gratuite. ☏ (027) 57 01 11.

Fondation Rainer Maria Rilke – Visite tous les jours sauf le lundi de 15 h à 19 h. Fermé du 15 novembre à fin février. 5,30 F. ☏ (027) 56 26 46.

SIERRE

Château de Villa – Visite de mars à octobre du mardi au dimanche de 14 h à 17 h; le reste de l'année les vendredis, samedis et dimanches de 14 h à 17 h. 5 F. ☎ (027) 55 85 35.

SION
🛈 place de la Planta – 1950 – ☎ (027) 322 85 86

Visite guidée de la ville – S'adresser à l'Office du tourisme.

Église N.-D.-de-Valère – Visite tous les jours (sauf le lundi) de 10 h à 12 h et de 14 h à 18 h (17 h d'octobre à mars), les dimanches et jours fériés de 14 h à 18 h (17 h d'octobre à mars). Fermée les 1er janvier et 25 décembre. 3 F. ☎ (027) 60 46 70.

Musée cantonal d'Histoire et d'Ethnographie – Visite tous les jours (sauf le lundi) de 10 h à 12 h et de 14 h à 18 h. Fermé les 1er janvier et 25 décembre. 5 F. ☎ (027) 60 46 70.

Hôtel de Ville – Visite du lundi au vendredi de 8 h à 12 h et de 14 h à 18 h. Fermé les jours fériés. En juillet et août, visite accompagnée de l'hôtel de ville incluse dans la visite de la ville : les mardis et jeudis de 14 h à 18 h. ☎ (027) 322 85 86.

Maison Supersaxo – *Visite du lundi au vendredi de 8 h à 12 h et de 14 h à 18 h.*

Musée cantonal des Beaux-Arts – Visite tous les jours (sauf le lundi) de 10 h à 12 h et de 14 h à 18 h. Fermé les 1er janvier et 25 décembre. 5 F. ☎ (027) 60 46 70.

Musée cantonal d'Archéologie – Visite tous les jours (sauf le lundi) de 10 h à 12 h et de 14 h à 18 h. Fermé les 1er janvier et 25 décembre. 4 F. ☎ (027) 60 46 70.

SOLOTHURN
🛈 Hauptgasse 69 – 4500 – ☎ (065) 22 19 24

Altes Zeughaus – Visite de mai à octobre, tous les jours (sauf le lundi) de 10 h à 12 h et de 14 h à 17 h; le reste de l'année, de 14 h à 17 h, en outre les samedis et dimanches de 10 h à 12 h. Fermé les 1er janvier, Vendredi saint, à Pâques et à la Pentecôte et le 25 décembre. 6 F. ☎ (032) 623 35 28.

Kunstmuseum Solothurn – Visite tous les jours (sauf le lundi) de 10 h à 12 h et de 14 h à 17 h (21 h le jeudi), les dimanches et jours fériés de 10 h à 17 h. Fermé à Pâques, à la Pentecôte et le jour de Noël. ☎ (032) 622 23 07.

Naturhistorisches Museum – ♿ Visite en semaine sauf le lundi de 14 h à 17 h (21 h le jeudi), le dimanche de 10 h à 12 h et de 14 h à 17 h. Fermé les 1er janvier, Vendredi saint, dimanches de Pâques et de Pentecôte, 25 décembre. ☎ (032) 622 70 21.

Museum Schloss Blumenstein – Musée fermé. Réouverture prévue : mars 1998. ☎ (065) 22 54 70.

SPIEZ
🛈 Bahnhofstrasse 12 – 3700 – ☎ (033) 54 21 38

Museum im Schloss – Visite du Vendredi saint à mi-octobre, le lundi de 14 h à 17 h (18 h en juillet et août), du mardi au dimanche de 10 h à 17 h (18 h en juillet et août). Fermé le lundi matin et du 15 octobre au 31 mars. 4 F. ☎ (033) 54 15 06.

Alte Kirche – Visite du Vendredi saint à mi-octobre, le lundi de 14 h à 17 h, du mardi au dimanche de 10 h à 17 h. ☎ (033) 54 15 06.

STANS
🛈 Engelbergstr. 34 – 6370 – ☎ (041) 610 88 33

Museum für Geschichte – Visite du 1er avril au 31 octobre, du mardi au samedi de 14 h à 17 h, du 1er novembre au 31 mars, le mercredi et le samedi de 14 h à 17 h, toute l'année les dimanches et jours fériés de 10 h à 12 h et de 14 h à 17 h. 5 F. ☎ (041) 618 75 22.

STANSERHORN

Funiculaire puis téléphérique au départ de Stans – Fonctionnent d'avril à octobre. Départs toutes les 1/2 h. AR : 40 F. ☎ (041) 610 14 41.

STEIN

Appenzeller Volkskunde Museum – Visite d'avril à octobre en semaine de 10 h à 12 h et de 13 h 30 à 15 h, le dimanche de 10 h à 18 h. Fermé le lundi matin. 7 F. ☎ (071) 368 50 56.

STEIN AM RHEIN
🛈 Oberstadt 10 – 8260 – ☎ (052) 741 28 35

Historische Sammlung – Visite tous les jours (sauf le mardi) de 10 h à 17 h de mars à octobre. ☎ (052) 741 25 12.

Kloster St. Georgen – Visite de mars à octobre, tous les jours (sauf le lundi) de 10 h à 12 h et de 13 h 30 à 17 h. Fermé la plupart des jours fériés. 3 F. ☎ (052) 741 21 42.

SURSEE
🛈 6210 – ☎ (045) 21 19 77

Visite guidée de la ville – De mai à septembre, tous les samedis à 14 h. ☎ (041) 926 31 11.

T

Gorges de la TAMINA

♿ Visite du premier samedi de mai au dernier dimanche d'octobre, de 10 h à 17 h 30. 3 F. ☏ (081) 302 10 61.

Château de TARASP

Visite accompagnée (1 h), de juin à début juillet à 14 h 30 ; de début juillet au 20 août, à 11 h, 14 h 30, 15 h 30 et 16 h 30 ; du 21 août à mi-octobre, à 14 h 30 et 15 h 30 ; le reste de l'année les mardis et jeudis à 16 h 30. 6 F. ☏ (081) 864 93 68.

THUN
🛈 Bahnhofplatz – 3600 – ☏ (033) 22 23 40

Schlossmuseum – Visite de juin à septembre de 9 h à 18 h ; de début avril à fin mai et en octobre de 10 h à 17 h. 5 F. ☏ (033) 23 20 01.

Panorama Wocher – Accès sauf le lundi, en juillet et août de 10 h à 18 h ; les Vendredi saint, lundi de Pâques, jeudi de l'Ascension, dimanche et lundi de Pentecôte ainsi qu'en mai, juin, septembre et octobre, de 10 h à 17 h. 4 F. ☏ (033) 222 23 40.

TITLIS

Télécabine et téléphériques – Fonctionnent de 8 h 30 (9 h suivant la saison) à 16 h 45 (17 h, 17 h 30 ou 18 h suivant la saison) de mi-décembre à fin octobre. 73 F. ☏ (041) 639 50 50. Sur la section supérieure entre Strand et Titlis, un téléphérique pivotant le « Rotair » est en service. Le trajet se fait en 5 mn. La rotation de la cabine autour de son axe offre aux passagers un panorama spectaculaire.

La TOUR-DE-PEILZ

Musée suisse du Jeu – ♿ Visite libre ou accompagnée sur demande (1 h 30) de 14 h à 18 h. Fermé le lundi (sauf les lundis de Pâques et de Pentecôte), les 1er janvier et 25 décembre. 6 F. ☏ (021) 944 40 50.

TRACHSELWALD

Schlösschen – *Visite les 1er et 3e dimanches de chaque mois, de 13 h à 18 h, ou sur rendez-vous préalable.* ☏ (034) 402 42 52.

TRAVERS

Mines d'asphalte – Visite accompagnée (durée : 1 h) du 1er mai au 20 octobre à 10 h et 14 h (en juillet et août, visites supplémentaires) ; du 21 octobre au 30 avril, les samedis, dimanches et jours fériés à 14 h et 16 h. 11 F. Température environ 8°, se munir de vêtements chauds. ☏ (038) 63 30 10.

TRÜMMELBACHFÄLLE

Visite de juin à août, de 8 h à 18 h ; en avril, mai et octobre, de 9 h à 17 h. 10 F. Prévoir des vêtements de pluie.

TRUN

« **Cuort Ligia Grischa** » – Visite accompagnée (1 h) les lundis, mercredis, samedis et dimanches (2e et derniers du mois) à 14 h, 15 h et 16 h. Fermé du 15 novembre au 15 avril et la plupart des jours fériés. 5 F. ☏ (081) 943 23 09.

U

UETLIBERG

Chemin de fer au départ de la gare centrale de Zürich – Départ toutes les 1/2 h. Aller simple : 7,20 F ; AR : 14,40 F. ☏ (01) 202 88 84.

URNÄSCH

Museum für Appenzeller Brauchtum – Visite du musée folklorique de 14 h 30 à 17 h. 4 F. ☏ (071) 364 23 22.

UTZENSTORF

Schloss Landshut – Visite de mi-mai à fin octobre tous les jours (sauf le lundi) de 14 h à 17 h ; les samedis, dimanches et jours fériés de 10 h à 17 h. Fermé le 1er août et au moment du Jeûne fédéral. 5 F. ☏ (065) 45 40 27.

V

VADUZ
📧 P. O. Box 139 – 9490 – ☎ (075) 392 11 11

Liechtensteinische staatliche Kunstsammlungen – Visite tous les jours de 10 h à 12 h et de 13 h 30 à 17 h 30 (17 h du 1ᵉʳ novembre au 31 mars). Fermé le 25 décembre. 5 F. ☎ (075) 232 23 41.

Liechtensteinisches Landesmuseum – Fermé pour une durée indéterminée. ☎ (075) 232 23 10.

Briefmarkenmuseum – Visite tous les jours de 10 h à 12 h et de 13 h 30 à 17 h 30. Fermé les 1ᵉʳ janvier et les 24, 25 et 31 décembre. ☎ (075) 236 61 01.

VALLORBE
📧 Grandes-Forges 11 – 1337 – ☎ (021) 843 25 83

La Carte Trèfle (24 F, enfants : 14 F) est un billet valable des Rameaux à la Toussaint, permet de visiter les grottes, le «trésor des Fées», le musée du Fer et du Chemin de Fer ainsi que le Fort de Vallorbe ; gratuité pour le 3ᵉ enfant et les suivants. S'adresser à l'Office du tourisme.

Musée du Fer et du Chemin de fer – Visite des Rameaux à la Toussaint de 9 h 30 à 12 h et de 13 h 30 à 18 h. 9 F. ☎ (021) 843 25 83.

Fort de Vallorbe – *Visite accompagnée (1 h 1/2) en juillet et août, tous les jours de 12 h à 17 h 30 ; d'avril à juin et de septembre à novembre, les samedis, dimanches et jours fériés aux mêmes heures. 8 F. ☎ (021) 843 25 83.*

VERBIER
📧 1936 – ☎ (026) 31 62 22

Télécabine et téléphériques du Mont Gelé et du Mont Fort – Mont Gelé : fonctionne de décembre à avril uniquement. Mont Fort : fonctionne de décembre à avril et de fin juin à fin août. 38 F. ☎ (026) 35 25 11.

VEVEY
📧 29, Grande-Place – 1800 – ☎ (021) 922 20 20

Musée Jenisch – ♿ Les collections du fonds sont montrées en alternance avec les expositions temporaires, toujours visibles sur demande. Visite de mars à octobre, de 10 h 30 à 12 h et de 14 h à 17 h ; le reste de l'année, de 14 h à 17 h 30. Fermé le lundi (sauf les lundis de Pâques et de Pentecôte) et jour de Jeûne fédéral. 8 à 12 F selon les expositions temporaires. ☎ (021) 921 29 50.

Musée historique du Vieux-Vevey – Visite de mars à octobre, de 10 h 30 à 12 h et de 14 h à 17 h 30 ; de novembre à février, de 14 h à 17 h 30. Fermé le lundi, les 1ᵉʳ janvier et 25 décembre. 4 F. ☎ (021) 921 07 22.

Musée suisse de l'appareil photographique – ♿ Visite tous les jours sauf le lundi, d'avril à octobre, de 11 h à 17 h 30 ; le reste de l'année de 14 h à 17 h 30 uniquement. 5 F. ☎ (021) 921 94 60.

Alimentarium – Visite tous les jours (sauf le lundi excepté lundis de Pâques et de Pentecôte) de 10 h à 17 h de fin mars à début novembre ; le reste de l'année de 10 h à 12 h et de 14 h à 17 h. Fermé les 1ᵉʳ janvier, 24, 25 et 31 décembre. 5 F. ☎ (021) 924 41 11.

VIA MALA

Galeries – Visite tous les jours d'avril à octobre de 9 h à 17 h. 3 F. ☎ (081) 651 11 34.

La VIDEMANETTE

Télécabine – Fonctionne de juillet à septembre et de mi-décembre à fin mars, de 9 h à 16 h 45. 18 F. ☎ (029) 481 61.

W

WEISSENSTEIN

Télésiège au départ d' Oberdorf – Fonctionne de 8 h 30 (8 h le samedi) à 18 h d'avril à octobre, de 9 h (8 h le samedi) à 17 h le reste de l'année. AR : 16,80 F.

WERDENBERG

Château – Visite du 1ᵉʳ avril au 31 octobre tous les jours (sauf le lundi) de 9 h 30 à 17 h. 3 F. ☎ (081) 771 29 50.

WETTINGEN
🅿 Alberich Zwysigstr. 81 – 5430 – ☎ (056) 426 22 90

Ehem. Zisterzienserkloster – Église conventuelle et cloître : visite accompagnée d'avril à octobre de 14 h à 17 h (dernière visite à 16 h 15). 5 F. Église : ouverte de mars à octobre de 10 h (12 h les dimanches et jours fériés) à 17 h. ☎ (056) 437 24 10.

WIL
🅿 Tonhallerstrasse 29 – 9500 – ☎ (073) 22 58 02

Musée municipal – Des travaux de rénovation sont en cours. Visite accompagnée (1 h) sur demande effectuée au moins 10 jours à l'avance auprès de M. Rudolf Gruber, Toggenburgerstr. 30, 9500 Wil. 3 F. ☎ (071) 911 04 57.

Château de WILDEGG
Visite de mi-mars à fin octobre, du mardi au dimanche de 10 h à 12 h et de 14 h à 17 h. 5 F. ☎ (062) 893 10 33.

WINTERTHUR
🅿 Bahnhofplatz 12 – 8400 – ☎ (052) 212 00 88

Museum Oskar Reinhart am Stadtgarten – Visite tous les jours (sauf le lundi) de 10 h à 17 h (20 h le mardi). Fermé la plupart des jours fériés. 6 F. ☎ (052) 267 51 72.

Sammlung Oskar Reinhart « Am Römerholz » – Visite tous les jours (sauf le lundi) de 10 h à 17 h. Fermé certains jours fériés. 6 F. ☎ (052) 213 41 21.

Kunstmuseum – Visite tous les jours (sauf le lundi) de 10 h à 17 h (20 h le mardi). Fermé les 1er janvier, dimanches de Pâques et de Pentecôte, 25 décembre. 10 F. ☎ (052) 267 51 62.

Villa Flora – Visite tous les jours (sauf le lundi) de 15 h à 17 h en semaine, de 11 h à 15 h le dimanche. Fermé la plupart des jours fériés. 6 F. ☎ (052) 212 99 65.

Technorama – Visite tous les jours (sauf le lundi) de 10 h à 17 h. Fermé à Noël. 14 F, enfants de 6 à 16 ans : 8 F. ☎ (052) 243 05 05.

Y

YVERDON-LES-BAINS
🅿 Place Pestalozzi – 1400 – ☎ (024) 23 62 90

Musée du château – Visite de juin à septembre, de 10 h à 12 h et de 14 h à 17 h ; le reste de l'année, de 14 h à 17 h. Fermé le lundi, les 1er janvier et 25 décembre. 4 F. ☎ (024) 21 93 10.

Z

ZERMATT
🅿 Bahnhofplatz – 3920 – ☎ (028) 66 11 81

Alpines Museum – Visite tous les jours de juin à octobre de 10 h à 12 h et de 16 h à 18 h ; le reste de l'année tous les jours (sauf le samedi) de 16 h à 18 h 30. Fermé du 1er novembre au 20 décembre. 3 F. ☎ (028) 67 41 00.

ZERNEZ
🅿 Chasa Fuschina – 7530 – ☎ (081) 856 13 00

Schweizerischer Nationalpark – Visite de juin à octobre de 8 h 30 à 18 h (22 h le mardi). 4 F. ☎ (081) 856 13 78.

Excursions pédestres – S'adresser à l'Office du tourisme de Zernez, ☎ (081) 856 13 00 ou à la Maison du Parc à Zernez, ☎ (081) 856 13 78.

ZUG
🅿 Bahnhofstrasse 23 – 6300 – ☎ (042) 21 00 78

Visite guidée de la ville – S'adresser à l'Office du tourisme.

ZUGERBERG
Accès par télésiège – Fonctionne toute l'année. Départs toutes les 1/2 h. AR : 3,20 F.

ZÜRICH
🅿 Bahnhofplatz 15 – 8000 – ☎ (01) 211 40 00

Visite guidée de la ville – S'adresser à l'Office du tourisme.

Panorama Bar Jules Verne – Accès par la Brasserie Lipp, Uraniastrasse 9, du lundi au jeudi de 9 h à 24 h, le vendredi et le samedi de 9 h à 1 h, le dimanche de 11 h 45 à 23 h.

ZÜRICH

Grossmünster – Visite de mi-mars à octobre de 9 h à 18 h ; le reste de l'année de 10 h à 16 h (17 h les lundis et jeudis). ☎ (01) 252 61 44.

Fraumünster – Ouverte en semaine de mai à septembre de 9 h à 12 h et de 14 h à 18 h ; en mars, avril et octobre de 10 h à 12 h et de 14 h à 17 h ; de novembre à février de 10 h à 12 h et de 14 h à 16 h ; le dimanche ouverte en juin, juillet, août et septembre de 14 h à 18 h. ☎ (01) 211 41 00.

Schweizerisches Landesmuseum – Visite tous les jours (sauf le lundi) de 10 h à 17 h. ☎ (01) 218 65 11/65 65.

Museum für Gestaltung Zürich – Visite les mardis, jeudis et vendredis de 10 h à 18 h ; le mercredi de 10 h à 21 h ; les samedis et dimanches de 10 h à 17 h. Fermé en août. 4 F et 6 F ou 8 F, billet combiné. ☎ (01) 446 22 11.

Wohnmuseum – Musée fermé pour réaménagement : réouverture prévue au printemps 97. ☎ (01) 218 65 11.

Museum Rietberg – ♿ Visite du mardi au dimanche de 10 h à 17 h (21 h du mardi au jeudi du avril au 14 juillet). Fermé la plupart des jours fériés. 12 F. ☎ (01) 202 45 28.

Kunsthaus – Visite du mardi au jeudi de 10 h à 21 h ; du vendredi au dimanche de 10 h à 17 h. Fermé les jours fériés. ☎ (01) 251 67 55.

Zoo Dolder – Visite en été de 8 h à 18 h (17 h en hiver). 12 F, enfants de 6 à 16 ans : 6 F. ☎ (01) 251 54 11.

Stiftung Sammlung E. G. Bührle – Visite les mardis et vendredis de 14 h à 17 h, le mercredi de 17 h à 20 h. Fermé les jours fériés. 9 F. ☎ (01) 422 00 86.

Promenades en bateau – Elles durent de 1 h à 5 h ; on peut prendre des repas à bord d'avril à octobre. Réservations : (01) 482 68 30.

ZURZACH
🛈 Quellenstrasse 1 – 8437 – ☎ (056) 249 24 00

August-Deusser-Museum – ♿ Visite de 13 h à 18 h. Fermé en février et juillet, les 1ᵉʳ janvier, Jeudi saint, Vendredi saint, 25 et 31 décembre. 6 F. ☎ (055) 249 20 50.

Index

Aare (Gorges) .... Villes, curiosités et régions touristiques.
5000 Argovie .... Code postal de la localité et canton.
Bonivard (François de) ...... Noms historiques et termes faisant l'objet d'une explication.

Les curiosités isolées (châteaux, abbayes, barrages, cols, cascades...) sont répertoriées à leur nom propre.

A

Aarau *5000 Argovie*	38
Aarberg *3270 Berne*..................	78
Aare (Gorges)	131
L'Aare	179
Aareschlucht	179
Adelboden *3715 Berne*...............	39
Aeschi *3703 Berne*....................	138
Agno *6982 Tessin*	13
Agone (Val)	75
Aigle *1860 Vaud*.......................	39
Airolo *6780 Tessin*	192
Ajoie (Plateau)	255
Albinen *3941 Valais*..................	160
Albis (Route, col)	269
Albula (Col, Route)	221
Aletsch (Glacier).......................	125
Allamans (Défilé)	40
Les Alpes tessinoises : voir à Alpi Ticinesi	
Les Alpes vaudoises	39
Alp Grüm *7749 Grisons*.............	75
Alpiglen *3818 Berne*.................	139
Alpi Ticinesi.............................	42
Altorf *6460 Uri*........................	44
Alt-Falkenstein (Château)	196
Altstätten *9450 St-Gall*	47
Alt St-Johann *9656 St-Gall*	13
Amburnex (Combe)	141
Andermatt *6490 Uri*..................	44
Anniviers (Val)	44
Anzère *1972 Valais*...................	134
Appenzell *9050*........................	45
Appenzell (Pays d') : voir à Appenzellerland	
Appenzellerland........................	46
Arbon *9320 Thurgovie*	13
Arcades	32
Ardez *7549 Grisons*..................	103
Ardez (Route)	227
Arenenberg (Château)	49
Areuse (Gorges)	49
Arlesheim *4144 Bâle-Campagne*........................	197
Armailli	30
Arolla *1961 Valais*	12
Arosa *7050 Grisons*..................	50
Arosa (Route)	50
Arveyes *1883 Vaud*	254
Ascona *6612 Tessin*	50
Astrid (Chapelle de la Reine)	251
Astridkapelle...........................	251
L'Auberson *1451 Vaud*..............	212
Augst (Ruines romaines).............	51
Augusta Raurica	51
Auvernier *2012 Neuchâtel*..........	191
Les Avants *1833 Vaud*...............	182
Avants-Sonloup (Circuit)	182
Avenches *1580 Vaud*................	52
Avers (Val)	214
Avers-Cresta *7431 Grisons*.........	214
Averserrhein (Vallée).................	214
L'Axenstrasse	253

B

Bachsee	132
Baden *5400 Argovie*..................	53
Bâle *4000* : voir à Basel	
Ballenberg (Musée)	79
La Barboleusaz *Vaud*................	254
Bärentritt	93
Basel *4000*	55
Bataillère...............................	157
Bauen *(6499) Uri*......................	44
Baulmes (Mont)	212
Beatenberg *3803 Berne*.............	64
Beckenried *6375 Nidwald*..........	238
Bella Lui	91
Bellelay (Abbaye)	198
Bellinzona *6500 Tessin*	64
Bellwald *3981 Valais*	125
Berchtold V de Zähringen	58
Bergün *7482 Grisons*	221
Bergüner Stein (Défilé)	221
Bern *3000*	65
Berne *3000*	65
Berner Oberland	72
Berner Platte...........................	36
Bernina (Col)	75
Berninastrasse..........................	74
Beromünster *6215 Lucerne*........	240
Berthoud *3400 Berne* : voir à Burgdorf	
Bettmeralp *3981 Valais*	12
Bex (Mine de sel)	75
Biasca *6710 Tessin*	43
Biel *2500 Berne*	76
Bielersee	78
Bienne *2500 Berne*...................	76
Bienne (Lac)	78
Binario...................................	44
Birse (Vallée)	196
Bisses....................................	246
Blatten *3901 Valais*	145
Blauherd.................................	261

Blausee	145
Bleu (Lac)	145
Blonay *1807 Vaud*	250
Blonay (Château)	183
Bodensee	202
Bonivard (François de)	87
Bonmont (Abbaye)	194
Boudry *2017 Neuchâtel*	192
Bourg-St-Bernard *1931 Valais*	128
Le Bouveret *1897 Vaud*	159
Le Brassus *1348 Vaud*	12
Braunwald *8784 Glaris*	124
Bré (Monte)	167
Bregaglia *(Val)*	102
Bremgarten *5620 Argovie*	78
Les Brenets *2416 Neuchâtel*	96
Brenets (Lac)	97
La Brévine	243
La Brévine *2125 Neuchâtel*	243
La Breya	128
Brienz *3855 Berne*	79
Brienz *7099 Grisons*	90
Brienz (Lac)	79
Brienzer Rothorn	79
Brig *3900 Valais*	80
Brigue *3900 Valais*	80
Brises	20
Brissago *6614* (Îles)	50
Broc *1636 Fribourg*	140
Bruderholz (Château d'eau)	63
Brugg *5200 Argovie*	80
Brünig (Col)	208
Brunnen *6440 Schwytz*	81
Bubikon (Commanderie)	201
Buchs *9470 St-Gall*	256
Buffalora (Cascade)	213
Bulle *1630 Fribourg*	81
Bündnerfleisch	35
Buochs *6374 Nidwald*	238
Burgdorf *3400 Berne*	82
Bürgenstock *6366 Nidwald*	175
Bürglen *6463 Uri*	146

C

Cademario *6936 Tessin*	168
Calvin	112
Campsut *7431 Grisons*	214
Cantons suisses	27-28
Cardada *6611 Tessin*	163
Cassons Grat	104
Caux *1824 Vaud*	182
Celerina *7505 Grisons*	82
Cendrars (Blaise)	84
Le Cervin	259
Chalières (Chapelle)	256
Champ-du-Moulin *2149 Neuchâtel*	49
Champéry *1874 Valais*	184
Champex *1938 Valais*	127
Chandolin *3961 Valais*	45
Charmey *1637 Fribourg*	140
Le Chasseral	83
Le Chasseron	212
Château-d'Œx *1837 Vaud*	83
Châtel-St-Denis *1618 Fribourg*	12
Chaumont	191
Les Chaux	254
La Chaux-de-Fonds *2300*	84
Chesières *1885 Vaud*	254

Chillon (Château)	87
Chünetta (Belvédère)	74
Chur *7000 Grisons*	88
Churwalden *7075 Grisons*	89
Cimetta	163
Cluse	21
Coire *7000 Grisons* : voir à Chur	
Colombier *2013 Neuchâtel*	90
Combats de reines	245
Combes	21
Communes	26
Conches (Val) : voir à Goms	
Cônes de déjection	19
Conseil d'État	27
Conseil des États	27
Conseil fédéral	27
Conseil national	27
Constance (Lac) : voir à Bodensee	
Coppet *1296 Vaud*	91
Couteau suisse	280
Crans *1299 Vaud*	194
Crans-Montana *Valais*	91
Crans-sur-Sierre *3963 Valais*	91
Crap Masegn	105
Cressier *Neuchâtel*	78
Crêts	21
Crévoladossola	230
La Creusaz	178
Creux du Van	243
Croix (Route, col)	41
Culet (Croix de)	184

D

Davos *7270 Grisons*	92
Delémont *2800 Jura*	94
Delémont (Vallée)	94
Dent de Vaulion	95
Derborence (Route)	234
Diable (Pont)	224
Les Diablerets *1865 Vaud*	39
Diablerets (Glacier)	39
Diavolezza	75
Disentis/Mustér *7180 Grisons*	95
La Dôle	209
Le Domleschg	215
Doubs (Bassins)	96
Doyle (Conan)	179
Dufour (Général)	123
Dunant (Henri)	24
Dürsrüti (Bois)	127

E

Ebenalp	46
Échallens *1040 Vaud*	155
Eggishorn	125
Eglisau *8193 Zurich*	271
Eicher (Stephan)	283
Eigergfetscher *3801*	139
Eigerwand	72-139
Einigen *3646 Berne*	242
Einsiedeln *8840 Schwytz*	98
L'Emmental	99
Emmental (Fromage)	99

313

Emosson (Barrage)	100
Engadin	100
Enge (Presqu'île)	71
Engelberg *6390 Obwald*	103
Engstligen (Chutes)	39
Engstligenfälle	39
Enhaut (Pays d')	40
Épicéa	19
Erker	31
Erlenbach *3762 Berne*	103
Escarpineau (Point de vue)	97
Estavayer-le-Lac *1470 Fribourg*	104
Étoile (L')	36
Euseigne (Pyramides)	135
Evolène *1968 (Valais)*	135

F

Faido *6760 Tessin*	42
Faulhorn	132
Felsenweg	175
Ferrera (Val)	214
Fête de l'Escalade	121
Firn	17
First	132
Flecken	45
Flims *7018 Grisons*	104
Flüela (Col, route)	94
Flüeli *6073 Obwald*	208
Föhn	20
Fondue (La)	35
Fontaines	31
Forclaz (Col, route)	105
Fort *(Mont)*	249
Les Franches Montagnes	106
Frauenkirch *7275 Grisons*	93
Freudenberg	218
Fribourg *1700*	106
Fronalpstock	226
Frutigen *3714 Berne*	145
Ftan *7551 Grisons*	227
Furgg	260
Furi	260
Furka (Col, route)	111
Furkapassstrasse	111

G

Gais *9056 Appenzell*	47
Gallus	215
Gandria *6978 Tessin*	169
Gantertal (Vallon)	231
La Garenne (Zoo)	141
Les Gastlosen	140
Gelé (Mont)	249
Gemmi (Col)	160
Generoso (Monte)	167
Genève *1200*	112
Gersau *6442 Schwytz*	253
Giessbach (Cascades)	79-139
Giessbachfälle	79
Gingins *1276 Vaud*	194
Giornico *6745 Tessin*	123
Glacier (Gorge)	132
Glaris *8750*	124

Glarus *8750*	124
Glaubenbüelen (Col)	208
Gletsch *3981 Valais*	126
Le Gletschboden	132
Gletscherschlucht	132
Glion *1823 Vaud*	182
Gœtheanum	196
Goms	124
Gondo (Gorges)	230
Gondoschlucht	230
Gorges de raccordement	19
Gorner (Gorges)	261
Gornergrat	260
Göschenen *6487 Uri*	225
Göscheneralp (Lac)	225
Gottlieben *8274 Thurgovie*	147
Goumois (Corniche)	106
Grächen *3925 Valais*	12
Grand Conseil	26
Grande Dixence (Barrage)	126
Grande Eau (Gorges)	41
Grand St-Bernard (Col)	126
Grand St-Bernard (Route)	127
Grand St-Bernard (Tunnel)	128
Grandson *1422 Vaud*	128
Graubünden	129
Grimentz *3961 Valais*	45
Grimsel (Col, lac, route)	131
Grimselstrasse	131
Grindelwald *3818 Berne*	132
Les Grisons : voir à Graubünden	
Le Grutli	81
Gruyère (Lac)	111
Gruyères *1663 Fribourg*	133
Gryon *1882 Vaud*	254
Gschletter (Lacet)	241
Gstaad *3780 Berne*	134
Gsteig *3781 Berne*	40
Guarda *7549 Grisons*	103
Gueuroz (Pont)	178
Guillaume Tell	251
Guldental (Vallée)	196
Le Gurten	71
Guttannen *3861 Berne*	132

H

Hallwil (Château)	38
Handegg (Cascade)	132
Handeggfall	132
Harderkulm	137
Hasle *3415 Berne*	99
Hasliberg *6083 Berne*	209
Les Haudères *1961 Valais*	135
Hauterive (Abbaye)	111
Haute Route	207
Heimwehfluh	137
Hérens (Val)	134
Himmelrank	240
Hodler (Ferdinand)	65
Hohe Brücke	208
Hohen Flühen (Chapelle)	124
Höhenklingen (Château)	239
Hoher Kasten	46
Hohle Gasse	251
Hölloch (Grotte)	226
Huémoz *1861 Vaud*	41
Hünegg (Château)	242

I

Ibergeregg (Route, col)	226
Iffingen (Cascade)	160
Ilanz *7130 Grisons*	96
Illiez *(Val)*	184
Initiative (Le droit d')	27
Innerferrera *7431 Grisons*	214
Interlaken *3800 Berne*	135
Irgenhausen (Forteresse)	202

J

Jaun *1631 Fribourg*	140
Jaunpassstrasse	140
Javroz *(Pont)*	140
Jean-Richard (Daniel)	85
Jegenstorf *3303 Berne*	99
Jogne (Vallée)	140
Joux (Vallée)	140-141
Juf *7931 Grisons*	214
Julier (Route, col)	220
Jungfrau (Circuit ferroviaire)	141
Jungfraujoch *3801 Valais*	141
Jura (Corniche)	106
Le Jura suisse	142

K

Kander (Vallée)	144
Kandertal	144
Kandersteg *3718 Berne*	144
Kappel (Abbaye)	263
Kilchberg *8802 Zurich*	271
Kippel *3903 Valais*	145
Kirchberg *Berne*	99
Kirchbühl *6204 Lucerne*	229
Klausen (Col, route)	146
Klausenpassstrasse	146
Klee (Paul)	70
Klein Matterhorn	260
Kleine Scheidegg *3801 Berne*	139
Klewenalp *6375 Nidwald*	12
Klöntal *8750 Glaris*	124
Klosters *7250 Grisons*	146
Klus	144
Knie (Cirque national)	201
Konigsfelden (Abbaye)	147
Kreuzberg	227
Kreuzlingen *8280 Thurgovie*	147
Küssnacht *6403 Schwytz*	12
Kybourg (Château)	259

L

Laharpe (Général de)	158
Le Landeron *2525 Neuchâtel*	78
Landsgemeinden	27
Langnau im Emmental *3550 Berne*	147
Lapins (Iles des)	78
Lauben	31
Lauberhorn (Course du)	256
Lauerz (Lac)	226
Laufen *4242 Berne*	196
Laufenburg *4335 Argovie*	203
Lausanne *1000 Vaud*	148
Lauterbrunnen *3822 Berne*	137
Lauterbrunnen (Vallée)	137
Lavaux (Corniche)	158
Le Corbusier	84
Léman (Lac)	156
Lenk *3775 Berne*	160
Lenz *7099 Grisons*	90
Lenzerheide (Col, route)	89
Lenzerheide-Valbella *7078-7077 Grisons*	89
Leuk *3953 Valais*	160
Leukerbad *3954 Valais*	160
Le Levron *1931 Valais*	127
Leysin *1854 Vaud*	39
Le Liechtenstein	161
Liestal *4410 Bâle-Campagne*	63
Ligue de la Maison-Dieu	28
Ligue des Dix-Juridictions	28
Ligue Grise	28
Linth (Vallée)	146
Linthal *8783 Glaris*	146
Locarno *6600 Tessin*	162
Le Locle *2412 Neuchâtel*	164
Lötschberg (Tunnel)	144
Lötschental	145
Lottigna *6711 Tessin*	43
Lucerne *6000* : voir à Luzern	
Lucomagno (Passo del)	43
Lueg (Belvédère)	82
Lugano *6900 Tessin*	165
Lugano (Lac)	165
Lukmanier (Col, route)	43
Lungern *6078 Obwald*	209
Lutry *1905 Vaud*	155
Lützelflüh *3432 Berne*	99
Luzern *6000*	169

M

Macolin *2532 Berne*	77
Maienfeld *7304 Grisons*	162
Maison paysanne suisse	32
Malbun (Vallée)	162
Maloja *7516 Grisons*	176
Maloja (Col)	102
Malvaglia *6713 Tessin*	43
Marat (Jean-Paul)	192
Marbach *6196 Lucerne*	176
Marbachegg	176
Les Marécottes *1922 Valais*	178
Les Marécottes (Zoo)	178
Marmorera (Barrage)	220
Martigny *1920 Valais*	177
Mathon *7431 Grisons*	214
Matterhorn	260
Maurice (Saint)	210
Mauvoisin (Barrage)	127
Mauvoisin (Route)	127
Mayens	245
Mazots	245
Medel (Gorges)	43
Medelserschlucht	43
Meiringen *3860 Berne*	179
Mélèze	19
Melide *6815 Tessin*	167
Merligen *3658 Berne*	12

Merlischachen 6402
  Schwytz 252
Mesocco 6563 Grisons 213
Miglieglia 6981 Tessin 167
Miralago 7749 Grisons 75
Misox (Castello) 180
Mistail Grisons 90
Moiry (Val, barrage) 45
Le Moléson 134
Moléson-sur-Gruyères 1662
  Vaud 134
Montana 3962 Valais 91
Monte Lema 168
Monthey 1870 Valais 154
Mont-Pélerin Vaud 250
Montreux 1820 Vaud 180
Monts 21
Moosfluh Valais 125
Moraines 18
Morat 3280 Fribourg : voir à Murten
Morat (Lac) 186
Morcote 6922 Tessin 167
Morges 1110 Vaud 183
Morgins 1875 Valais 184
Morgins (Pas) 184
Morgins (Val) 184
Morteratsch (Cirque et glacier) ... 74
Môtiers 2112 Neuchâtel 243
Moudon 1510 Vaud 184
Mühlebach 3981 Valais 125
Münster 3985 Valais 125
Muottas Muragl 185
Mürren 3825 Berne 185
Murten 3280 Fribourg 186
Murtensee 186
Müstair 7531 Grisons 187
Müstair (Val) 187
Muttenz 4132 Bâle 63

N

Näfels 8752 Glaris 187
Naissance du mouvement Dada 265
Nationalpark 260-279
Naye (Rochers) 183
Negrentino (Eglise) 43
Neuchâtel 2000 187
Neuchâtel (Lac) 187
Neu-Falkenstein (Burg de) 196
La Neuveville 2520 Berne 192
Névé 17
Nicolas de Flüe (Saint) 251
Niederhorn 64
Le Niesen 145
Noir (Lac) 111-260
Nufenen (Route, col) 192
Nufenenpassstrasse 192
Nyon 1260 (Vaud) 193

O

Oberalp (Route) 95
Obere Nase 253
Obere Strasse 129
Obergestelen 3981 Valais 125
Oberhofen 3653 Berne 243
L'Oberland bernois :
  voir à Berner Oberland

Oberwald 3982 Valais 125
Œschinen (Lac) 144
Ofen (Col, route) 261
Ollon 1867 Vaud 41
Olten 4600 Soleure 195
Oltschibach (Cascade) 80
Orbe 1350 Vaud 195
Orbe (Source) 248
Oriel 31
Ormonts (Vallée) 39
Oron-le-Châtel 1699 Vaud 196
Orsières 1937 Valais 128
Oin-Oin 156

P

Palpuogna (Lac) 221
Parc national suisse 260-273
Parpan 7076 Grisons 89
Parpaner Rothorn 90
Parsenn 7260 Grisons 93
Pas de Morgins 184
Passugg 7062 Grisons 89
Passwang (Route) :
  voir à Passwangstrasse
Passwang (Sommet) 196
Passwangstrasse 196
Payerne 1530 Vaud 197
Pestalozzi 244
Peter und Paul (Park) 218
Petit Cervin 260
Petite Scheidegg 139
Pfaffensprung 225
Pichoux (Gorges, route) 197
Pierre Pertuis 198
Pierreuse (Réserve) 41
Le Pilate : voir à Pilatus
Pilatus 198
Pilatus Kulm 6099 Obwald 199
Pin arolle 19
Piora (Val) 42
Pissot (Gorges) 41
Piz Corvatsch 101
Piz Lagalb 75
Piz Nair 219
Plans Mayens 3963 Valais 91
Les Pléiades 1807 Vaud 183
Pléiades (Circuit) 182
Pont de Nant 254
Pontis (Chapelle) 44
Pontresina 7504 Grisons 199
Ponts couverts 31
Porrentruy 2900 Jura 200
La Porta 102
Poschiavo 7742 Grisons 75
Poschiavo (Lac) 75
Prugiasco 6711 Tessin 43

Q - R

Quatre-Cantons (Lac) :
  voir à Vierwaldstätter See
Raccard 245
Râclette 35
Ragaz (Bad) 7310 St-Gall 200
Ranft 6073 Obwald 208
Rapperswil 8640 St-Gall 201

Räterichsboden (Lac)	132
Reckingen *3981 Valais*	125
Réclère (Gorges)	200
Recrettes (Point de vue)	97
Référendum	27
Regensberg *8158 Zurich*	273
Reichenau *7015 Grisons*	96
Reichenbach (Chutes)	180
Reichenbachfälle	180
Reine Astrid (Chapelle)	251
Retaud (Lac)	40
Reuss (Chutes)	224
Rhein	202
Rheinau *8462 Zurich*	202
Rheinfall	224
Rheinfelden *4310 Argovie*	63
Rheinthal	202
Rhétie	129
Le Rhin	202
Rhin (Chutes)	224
Rhin Antérieur (Vallée, route)	95
Rhône (Glacier)	111
Riederalp *3981 Valais*	125
Riggisberg *3132 Berne*	203
Le Rigi	204
Rigi-Kaltbad *6356 Lucerne*	204
Rigi-Kulm *6411 Schwytz*	204
Rigi-Scheidegg *6410 Schwytz*	226
Ringgenberg *3852 Berne*	79
Ritz (Les)	125
Riva San Vitale *6826 Tessin*	167
Les Roches de Mauron	97
Roffla (Gorge)	214
Rofflaschlucht	214
Rolle *1180 Vaud*	157
Romainmôtier *1349 Vaud*	205
Romanche	23
Römische Gutshof Seeb	270
Romont *1680 Fribourg*	205
Ronco *6622 Tessin*	163
Ronco (Circuit)	163
Rorschach *9400 St-Gall*	206
Rosenlaui *3860 Berne*	179
Rosenlaui (Vallée)	179
Rossens (Barrage)	111
Les Röstis	36-90
Rothorn	261
Rougemont *1838 Vaud*	41
Rousseau (Jean-Jacques)	78
Le Rütli	206
Ruz (Les)	21

S

Saanen *3792 Berne*	206
Saanenmöser *3777 Berne*	134
Saas-Fee *3906 Valais*	207
Sachseln *6072 Obwald*	208
Sachseln (Route) : voir Sachselner Strasse	
Sachselner Strasse	208
La Sagne *2314 Neuchâtel*	86
Saignelégier *6757 Jura*	106
Saillon *1913 Valais*	209
St-Cergue *1264 Vaud*	209
St-Chrischona (Chapelle)	63
St-Gall *9000*	215
St.Gallen *9000*	215
St-Gothard (Col, route)	42
St-Gothard (Massif) : voir à Sankt-Gotthard-Massiv	
St-Imier *2610 Berne*	83
St-Léonard (Lac souterrain)	234
St-Luc *3961 Valais*	45
St-Luc (Société)	34
St-Luzisteig (Défilé)	162
St-Maurice *1890 Valais*	210
St.Moritz *7500 Grisons*	219
St-Petersinsel	78
St-Pierre (Ile)	78
St-Pierre-de-Clages *1916 Valais*	211
St-Séverin *1961*	234
St-Sulpice *1025 Vaud*	158
St-Urban : voir à Sankt Urban	
St-Ursanne *2882 Jura*	211
Ste-Croix-les-Rasses *1450 Vaud*	211
Salgesch *3970 Valais*	229
Sali-Schlössli (Panorama)	195
Salquenen *3970 Valais*	229
Salvan *1922 Valais*	178
Salvan-les-Marécottes *1923 Valais*	12
Samedan *7503 Grisons*	206
San Bernardino *6549 Grisons*	213
San Bernardino (Col)	213
San Bernardino-Strasse	212
Sanetsch (Route, col, barrage)	234-235
San Gottardo (Passo del)	42
Sankt-Gotthard-Massiv	218
Sankt Urban *4915 Lucerne*	221
Santa Maria *Grisons*	261
Le Säntis	222
Sapin	19
La Sarine	23
Sarnen *6060 Obwald*	12
La Sarraz (Château)	222
Saut du Doubs	97
Savognin *7451 Grisons*	220
Schabzieger	124
Schaffhausen *8200*	222
Schaffhouse *8200*	222
Schallenberg (Route)	176
Schanfigg (Route)	50
Schatzalp *7270 Grisons*	93
Scheidegg (Petite)	139
Schillerstein	81
Schilthorn	185
Schin (Gorges)	90
Schiner (Mathieu)	246
Schinznach *5116 Argovie*	12
Schloss Tarasp	228
Les Schöllenen	224
Schöllenen (Route)	225
Schöllenenstrasse	225
Schönenwerd *5012 Soleure*	38
Schuls *7550 Grisons*	227
Schwand *6055 Obwald*	103
Schwarzee	111
Schwytz *6430*	225
Schwyz *6430*	225
Schwyzerdütsch	23
Schynige Platte *3801*	137
Scuol *7550 Grisons*	227
Sedrun (Bassin)	95
Seealp (Lac)	46
Seeb (Ferme romaine)	270
Seelisberg *6446 Uri*	228
Seelisberg (Route)	238
Seewen *4206 Soleure*	196
Sefinen (Cascade)	137
Seiler (Les)	125
Sempach *6204 Lucerne*	228
Sent *7551 Grisons*	228
La Sentinelle des Rangiers	255

Séracs	17
Servion (Zoo)	156
Sex Rouge	40
Sgraffito	101
Sierre *3960 Valais*	229
Silos (Lac)	101
Sils (Engadine) *7515 Grisons*	102
Sils (Lac)	101
Silvaplana *7513 Grisons*	13
Simme (Chutes)	160
Simme (Vallée)	160
Simplon (Col)	230
Simplon (Route)	230
Simplonpassstrasse	230
Sion *1950 Valais*	231
Sitter (Vallée)	47
Soglio *7649 Grisons*	102
Solalex (Refuge)	254
Soleure *4500* : voir à Solothurn	
Solis (Ponts)	90
Solothurn *4500*	235
Sonderbund	23
Sonloup (Col)	182
Sörenberg (Station, route)	208
Spiez *3700 Berne*	237
Stans *6370 Nidwald*	238
Stanserhorn	238
Staubbach (Cascade)	137
Stäubi (Cascade)	146
Stäubifall	146
Stein *9463 St-Gall*	47
Stein am Rhein *8260 Schaffhouse*	238
Steingletscher	240
Steinsberg (Tour)	103
Stockalper (Kaspar Jodok von)	80
Stockhorn	104
Stoos *9056 Appenzell*	195
Stoss *6433 Schwytz*	47
Stoss (Route)	47
Sulèr	101
Sumiswald *3454 Berne*	82
Sunnegga	261
Sursee *6210 Lucerne*	239
Susch *7549 Grisons*	94
Susten (Col, route)	240
Sustenpassstrasse	240
Swissminiatur	167

T

Tamina (Gorges)	200
Taminaschlucht	200
Tarasp (Château)	228
Tarasp *7553 Grisons*	227
Taubenloch (Gorges)	77
Taubenlochschlucht	77
Tavannes *2710 Berne*	198
Tavetsch (Val)	95
Tell (Chapelle)	254
Tell (Guillaume)	254
Tellskapelle	254
Tête de moine	198
Tête de Ran	87
Tête Noire (Défilé)	105
Théodule (Glacier)	260
Thoune *3600* : voir à Thun	
Thoune (Lac)	242
Thun *3600 Berne*	241
Thuner See	242

Thusis *7450 Grisons*	214
Tiefencastel *7450 Grisons*	221
Tinguely (Jean)	110
Tirano *Grisons*	75
Titlis	103
Le Toggenbourg	48
La Tour-de-Peilz *1814 Vaud*	250
Trachselwald *3456 Berne*	100
Travers (Mines d'asphalte)	243
Travers (Val)	243
Tremola (Val)	42
Trient (Glacier)	105
Trient (Vallée)	178
Trockener Steg	260
Trogen *9043 Appenzell*	244
Trümmelbach (Chutes)	137
Trümmelbachfälle	137
Trun *7166 Grisons*	96
Tseuzier (Route, barrage)	235

U

Uetliberg *8138 Zurich*	269
Ulrichen *Valais*	193
Untere Strasse	129
Unterwasser *9657 St-Gall*	13
Urba (Mosaïques)	195
Uri (Lac)	253
Urnäsch *9107 Argovie*	48
Urner Boden *8751*	146
Urnersee	253
Urseren (Val)	111
Utzenstorf *3427 Berne*	244

V

Vadian	215
Vaduz *Principauté du Liechtenstein*	161
Le Valais	244
Valaisans	246
Valangin *2042 Neuchâtel*	87
Vallée en auge	19
Vallées latérales	244
Vallée suspendue	19
Vallorbe *1337 Vaud*	248
Vals *7132 Grisons*	13
Vals	21
Van (Vallon)	178
Vaulion (Dent de)	141
Verbier *1936 Valais*	249
Verbier-Village *1935 Valais*	249
Vermala (Belvédère)	91
Verrou	19
Versam (Route)	96
Vevey *1800 Vaud*	247
Via Mala	214
La Videmanette	41
Vierwaldstättersee	250
Villars-sur-Ollon *1884 Vaud*	254
Villeneuve *1844 Vaud*	159
Vindonissa (Amphithéâtre romain)	80
Vins de Suisse	36
Vissoie *3961 Valais*	45
Vitznau *6354 Lucerne*	253
Voie suisse	206

Vorarlberg (École du)	34	Willisau Stadt 6130 Lucerne	257
Vorbourg (Chapelle)	94	Winkelried (Arnold de)	228
Vue des Alpes (et route)	87	Winterthour 8400 Zurich	257
Vufflens-le-Château 1141 Vaud	158	Winterthur 8400 Zurich	257
		Wolhusen (Chapelle des Morts)	257
Vulpera 7552 Grisons	227	Worb 3076 Berne	100

W

Y - Z

Waldstätten	251	Yverdon-les-Bains 1400 Vaud	259
Walensee	255	Zähringen (Berthold de)	
Walenstadt (Lac)	255	Zermatt 3920 Valais	259
Walser	246	Zernez 7530 Grisons	261
Wassen 6484 Uri	225	Zillis 7431 Grisons	214
Weggis 6353 Lucerne	253	Zinal 3961 Valais	45
Le Weissenstein	255	Zinal (Vallée)	45
Weissensteinstrasse	255	Zofingen 4800 Argovie	195
Weissfluhgipfel	93	Zofingue 4800 Argovie	195
Weisshorn Grisons	50	Zoug 6300	262
Wengen 3823 Berne	256	Zoug (Lac)	262
Wengernalp	139	Zug 6300	262
Wengwald	139	Zügen (Défilé, route)	93
Werdenberg 9470 St-Gall	256	Zugerberg 6316 Zoug	263
Wettingen (Abbaye)	54	Zuger See	262
Whymper (Edward)	259	Zuoz 7524 Grisons	263
Wiesen (Viaduc)	94	Zurich 8000	264
Wil 9500 St-Gall	256	Zürich 8000	264
Wildegg (Schloss)	257	Zurzach 8437 Argovie	271
Wildhaus 9658 St-Gall	48	Zweisimmen 3770 Berne	134
Wildkirchli (Grotte)	46	Zwingli	264
Wildpark Langenberg	270		

MANUFACTURE FRANÇAISE DES PNEUMATIQUES MICHELIN
Société en commandite par actions au capital de 2 000 000 000 de francs
Place des Carmes-Déchaux - 63 Clermont-Ferrand (France)
R.C.S. Clermont-Fd B 855 200 507

Michelin et Cie, Propriétaires-Éditeurs 1996
Dépôt légal septembre 1996 – ISBN 2-06-056003-9 – ISSN 0293-9436

Toute reproduction, même partielle et quel qu'en soit le support
est interdite sans autorisation préalable de l'éditeur.

Plans reproduits avec l'autorisation de la Direction Fédérale des
Mensurations Cadastrales, en date du 4 octobre 1995.
Les cartes régionales de ce guide ont été établies d'après les publications du Service
Topographique Fédéral avec autorisation en date du 2 novembre 1955.

Printed in the EU 09 - 96
Photocomposition : M.C.P., Saran – Impression et brochage : AUBIN Imprimeur, Ligugé

Illustration de la couverture par Didier WIBROTTE/Pascal VITRY